THE ENGLISH POETS

GENERAL EDITOR: CHRISTOPHER RICKS

Also available in this series

Robert Browning: The Poems, volume two
Robert Browning: The Ring and the Book
Edmund Spenser: The Faerie Queene
Henry Vaughan: The Complete Poems
William Wordsworth: The Poems, volume one
William Wordsworth: The Poems, volume two
William Wordsworth: The Prelude
Sir Thomas Wyatt: The Complete Poems

Robert Browning:
The Poems

VOLUME ONE

EDITED BY JOHN PETTIGREW

Supplemented and Completed by
THOMAS J. COLLINS

NEW HAVEN AND LONDON
YALE UNIVERSITY PRESS

First published 1981 in the United Kingdom in a paperback
edition by Penguin Books Limited in the series Penguin
English Poets. First published 1981 in the United States of
America by Yale University Press.

Printed in the United States of America.

Library of Congress Cataloging in Publication Data

Browning, Robert, 1812–1889.
  Robert Browning, The poems.

  (The English poets ; 1–2)
  Includes bibliographical references and indexes.
  I. Pettigrew, John. II. Series: English poets ; 1–2.
PR4202.P44 1981   821'.8   80–53976
ISBN 0–300–02675–7 (v. 1)
ISBN 0–300–02683–8 (pbk. : v. 1)
ISBN 0–300–02676–5 (v. 2)
ISBN 0–300–02684–6 (pbk. : v. 2)

10 9 8 7 6 5 4 3 2 1

To Pat and Sara

Contents

Preface *xiii*
Acknowledgements *xxii*
Table of Dates *xxiv*
Further Reading *xxvii*

The Poems *1*

Pauline; A Fragment of a Confession *5*

Paracelsus *35*
  I Paracelsus Aspires *37*
  II Paracelsus Attains *57*
  III Paracelsus *74*
  IV Paracelsus Aspires *101*
  V Paracelsus Attains *118*

Sordello *149*

Pippa Passes: A Drama *297*

Dramatic Lyrics *345*
Cavalier Tunes *347*
  I Marching Along *347*
  II Give a Rouse *348*
  III Boot and Saddle *348*
My Last Duchess *349*
Count Gismond *351*
Incident of the French Camp *355*

Soliloquy of the Spanish Cloister 356
In a Gondola 358
Artemis Prologizes 365
Waring 368
Rudel to the Lady of Tripoli 375
Cristina 376
Johannes Agricola in Meditation 378
Porphyria's Lover 380
Through the Metidja to Abd-el-Kadr 381
The Pied Piper of Hamelin; A Child's Story 383

Dramatic Romances and Lyrics 393
'How They Brought the Good News from Ghent to Aix' 395
Pictor Ignotus 397
The Italian in England 399
The Englishman in Italy 403
The Lost Leader 410
The Lost Mistress 411
Home-Thoughts, from Abroad 412
Home-Thoughts, from the Sea 412
The Bishop Orders His Tomb at Saint Praxed's Church 413
Garden Fancies 416
  I The Flower's Name 416
  II Sibrandus Schafnaburgensis 417
The Laboratory 420
The Confessional 422
The Flight of the Duchess 424
Earth's Immortalities 447
Song ('Nay but you, who do not love her') 448
The Boy and the Angel 448
Meeting at Night 451
Parting at Morning 452
Nationality in Drinks 452
Time's Revenges 453
The Glove 455

Christmas-Eve and Easter-Day *461*
Christmas-Eve *463*
Easter-Day *496*

Men and Women *525*
Love Among the Ruins *527*
A Lovers' Quarrel *529*
Evelyn Hope *534*
Up at a Villa – Down in the City *536*
A Woman's Last Word *539*
Fra Lippo Lippi *540*
A Toccata of Galuppi's *550*
By the Fire-Side *552*
Any Wife to Any Husband *561*
An Epistle Containing the Strange Medical Experience of Karshish,
    the Arab Physician *565*
Mesmerism *573*
A Serenade at the Villa *578*
My Star *580*
Instans Tyrannus *580*
A Pretty Woman *582*
'Childe Roland to the Dark Tower Came' *585*
Respectability *592*
A Light Woman *593*
The Statue and the Bust *595*
Love in a Life *603*
Life in a Love *604*
How It Strikes a Contemporary *605*
The Last Ride Together *608*
The Patriot *611*
Master Hugues of Saxe-Gotha *612*
Bishop Blougram's Apology *617*
Memorabilia *643*
Andrea del Sarto *643*
Before *650*

After *651*
In Three Days *652*
In a Year *653*
Old Pictures in Florence *656*
In a Balcony *665*
Saul *689*
'De Gustibus –' *701*
Women and Roses *702*
Protus *704*
Holy-Cross Day *705*
The Guardian-Angel *710*
Cleon *712*
The Twins *721*
Popularity *722*
The Heretic's Tragedy *724*
Two in the Campagna *728*
A Grammarian's Funeral, Shortly after the Revival of Learning in Europe *730*
One Way of Love *734*
Another Way of Love *734*
'Transcendentalism: A Poem in Twelve Books' *735*
Misconceptions *737*
One Word More *737*

Dramatis Personae *745*
James Lee's Wife *747*
Gold Hair: A Story of Pornic *759*
The Worst of It *764*
Dîs Aliter Visum; or, Le Byron de Nos Jours *768*
Too Late *773*
Abt Vogler *777*
Rabbi Ben Ezra *781*
A Death in the Desert *787*
Caliban upon Setebos *805*
Confessions *812*

May and Death *814*
Deaf and Dumb *814*
Prospice *815*
Eurydice to Orpheus *816*
Youth and Art *816*
A Face *819*
A Likeness *819*
Mr Sludge, 'The Medium' *821*
Apparent Failure *860*
Epilogue *862*

Balaustion's Adventure; including a Transcript from Euripides *867*

Prince Hohenstiel-Schwangau, Saviour of Society *943*

Appendix 1: Browning's 'Introductory Essay' ['Essay on
    Shelley'] *999*
Appendix 2: Browning's Rearrangement of the Poems Originally
    Published in 1842, 1845 and 1855 *1015*
Notes *1019*
Index of Titles *1185*
Index of First Lines *1188*

Preface

This edition, complementing Professor Altick's of *The Ring and the Book* in the Penguin English Poets series, includes the poems that Robert Browning himself collected, those he printed but did not collect, some first published after his death, and some poems and fragments previously unpublished; the important prose essay on Shelley is here in an Appendix. Except for *Pippa Passes*, the plays that appeared between 1837 and 1846 are excluded, as is the 'transcript' of the *Agamemnon* of Aeschylus. Otherwise completeness has been aimed at. It has not, however, been achieved: among verses still to be added to the canon are some in private hands, some recorded in sales catalogues that seem temporarily to have disappeared, and some verses in letters as yet unpublished (some letters of Browning's sister in the University of Texas are, for example, reported to include recollected snatches of Browning verses, but I was not permitted to see them). Missing also are some unpublished verses in the great Armstrong Browning Library for which permission to print has been refused: an eight-line lyric called 'Magari'; ten comic lines called 'On Andrea del Sarto's "Jupiter and Leda"'; and a translation of *Iliad* xviii, 202–31, the exclusion of which is the more regretted since the lines are a rendering of the same passage translated by Tennyson as 'Achilles Over the Trench'.

The Penguin edition is the first aiming at completeness and newly edited since Browning revised his works for the sixteen-volume collection of 1888–9 (in 1894 a seventeenth volume incorporated the poems in *Asolando*, which appeared on the day Browning died). Three earlier collections lack textual apparatus, and are more reprints than editions: the pioneering 'Florentine' edition (1898) of Charlotte Porter and Helen A. Clarke with extensive introductions and annotation, the 'Centenary' edition (1912) of F. G. Kenyon with brief introductions and no annotation, and the 'Macmillan' edition (1915) with negligible annotation. In progress is the 'Ohio' edition in a projected thirteen volumes, of which four have so far appeared. Edited by a large team, it aims at definitiveness, and has full textual apparatus and limited annotation. Some of the edition's principles and procedures have been challenged, and it is unfortunate that, in the volumes so far published, important manuscript materials have been ignored, and that the text, textual apparatus and annotation are not reliable.

Like these editions, the present one uses as its basic copy-text the collected edition of 1888-9. The first edition of *Asolando* has been used for the poems first published in that volume. Other poems are printed from manuscripts or first printings: for one poem the copy-text is – surely delightfully – a gravestone in the additional burying-ground of Saint Mary's Church, Barnsley, Yorkshire. There is much to be said for printing some of Browning's poems from the first edition, as Professor Altick did with *The Ring and the Book* – the 1833 *Pauline*, for instance, is more interesting, though less satisfactory, than the 1888 *Pauline*. For a collected edition aiming at consistency, however, the 1888-9 edition is as obviously the right basic copy-text as is, say, the Eversley for Tennyson. Browning revised his poems for it, and took pains over what was conceived of as the final text. Carefully planned by a great publisher who wished the edition to honour his friend, it was seen through the press with Browning's usual meticulous attention. 'Authorship has the alteration-itch,' and it is true that Browning's revisions seem often to testify more to a sense of insecurity within the poet than to anything else, and that, in Professor Altick's words, 'concentration on minutiae frequently drifted into a profitless concern with trivia'. Nevertheless, the 1888-9 text is almost invariably better than that of earlier editions. Moreover, Browning gave further attention to the text after the first impression appeared: sales were good, and the poet set about correcting typographical errors and making minor revisions for the second impression that was soon needed. When he left for Italy in 1889, he had revised the first ten volumes (the poems up to, and including, *The Ring and the Book*). He left a record of the over 200 planned alterations, only a few of them verbal ones, in a copy of the first impression of *1888-9* which is now in the British Library; some of the changes are recorded also on papers now in the Brown University Library (full details are given by Philip Kelley and William S. Peterson, 'Browning's Final Revisions', *Browning Institute Studies* I, 1973, 87-118). My collation of the British Museum and Brown University records shows that the poet's instructions were scrupulously followed. The present edition therefore incorporates the wanted changes (they affect the poems up to, and including, those in *Dramatis Personae*; in the few insignificant cases where the two records differ the present text is eclectic).

The texts have been collated with those of textually significant editions, the most important of which are the first editions, the collected editions of 1849, 1863 and 1868, and the second edition of *Dramatis*

Personae. They have been collated also with available manuscripts, the most important of which are those of *Paracelsus* and *Christmas-Eve and Easter-Day* in the Victoria and Albert Museum, *Dramatis Personae* and *Asolando* in the Pierpont Morgan Library in New York, and the volumes published between 1871 and 1887 in the Library of Balliol College, Oxford. Also consulted have been proofsheets (the most interesting of which are the sets of *Red Cotton Night-Cap Country* in the Berg Collection of the New York Public Library), and copies of poems with holograph alterations, like those of the first edition of *Paracelsus* that Browning used in preparing the *Poems* of 1849, which are now in the Berg Collection and the Beinecke Library of Yale University. Between manuscript and first edition, changes are often extensive; it was the poet's general practice to use his proof to make many alterations, especially in punctuation. The present edition also makes use of such fascinating volumes as J. S. Mill's review copy of *Pauline*, which with Mill's detailed comments was returned to Browning, who in turn wrote remarks and notes in it; the copy of *Ferishtah's Fancies* which Browning annotated for Mrs Orr; and the copy of *Sordello* owned by the poet's friend, Alfred Domett, and written in by both Domett and Browning.

Among the notes in the present edition is a generous selection of manuscript and textual variants of a kind not previously available except in the Ohio edition now in progress. As a general rule (to which such works as *Paracelsus*, *Pippa Passes* and 'Gold Hair' are exceptions), Browning's changes are not extensive from one printing to another, but they often can be most illuminating in any number of ways. Browning, incidentally, usually revised his work for the various collected editions using the immediately preceding collected edition for poems previously gathered, and the first or more recent edition otherwise.

The poet's reach for perfect texts inevitably exceeded his grasp as a proofreader, a capacity in which he was no match for, say, Tennyson. His final text is nevertheless a very good one indeed, and it is seldom necessary or desirable to depart from it. The odd spelling mistake ('villany', 'obsidion') and a few typographical errors have been silently corrected. Otherwise the text here – the same principles have been applied in the Notes – differs from copy-text in the following respects only:

(a) Spelling has been generally standardized (both 'gray' and 'grey', 'balk' and 'baulk', 'thro'' and 'through', English and American spellings of words ending in -or and -our, appear in Browning's text, for instance); also standardized is the use of the hyphen in adjectival combinations. Not standardized, however, is the spelling of the preterite or past participle, because sometimes one form seems clearly preferable to the other: in 'The Pied Piper', 'stept' and 'pressed' seem in context superior to 'stepped' and 'prest' in lines 98 and 221. Spellings preferred in Penguin style have normally been used ('gypsy' for 'gipsy', 'tonight' for 'to-night', 'judgement' for 'judgment'), but no change of this kind has been made if it would affect pronunciation ('sty' is substituted for 'stye', but not 'burden' for 'burthen'). Browning felt strongly about his Greek spellings; these have been kept, and inconsistencies in them from one poem to another remain. Not modified, capricious though it often is, is capitalization. The young poet threw capitals around with gay abandon, but after *Dramatis Personae* the older poet reduced their number considerably, and I have judged it best to leave well enough alone. I do not understand, for instance, the 'Man' of 'An Epistle' (line 69), but the use of the capital for 'He' in the last line of that masterpiece may be the most exciting in all literature.

(b) Among extant printers' manuscripts, that of *Paracelsus* gives the only example of a work in which Browning's punctuation was subjected to extensive (and there very much needed!) editorial work by the printer; Browning himself remarked, perhaps accurately, that the printers were responsible for the errors and inadequacies in punctuation in the first edition of *Sordello*. In later years, we know too, others made minor changes in Browning's texts; in a letter of 1889 for instance, the poet thanked his printer's reader for his care, and for his corrections and changes, in preparing *1888–9*. There is, however, a host of evidence to show that the poet had final control over punctuation and that he was deeply concerned about it. In the present edition, then, Browning's punctuation has been only very slightly modified, even, in many cases, when by today's rules it is technically incorrect: Browning often uses, for instance, double punctuation (a parenthesis and a comma, or a colon and a dash) where a modern writer would use single. As Dr Honan has indicated in his *Browning's Characters* (284–91), Browning's punctuation is very much his own, developed during a period when theories of punctuation were coming to be founded on syntactical rather than elocutionary bases. The implication of Dr Honan's penetrating discussion is clear: to interfere much with Browning's punctuation is often to meddle with effects deliberately sought, and to substitute mere technical correctness for demonstrable substantive significance. Penguin style has been followed in the handling of quotation marks: the inverted commas which, especially in the earlier volumes of *1888–9*, in many cases introduced each line of quoted matter, have been deleted. Again, single quotation marks replace Browning's double ones, and double ones consequently replace

Browning's single ones within quotations. In texts printed here from published texts not supervised by Browning and from manuscripts, of which some are very rough drafts, I have tried to use pointing that accords with Browning's practice elsewhere. The odd comma has been supplied in places where Browning, for no apparent reason, departed from his normal rules, and such definite errors as the omission of necessary periods or quotation marks have been corrected. In twelve instances where question marks are incorrectly placed within quotations in the copy-text, silent transpositions have been made: *Pippa Passes*, i, 171; *Christmas-Eve*, 1054, 1056; 'Blougram', 197; 'In a Balcony', 120; 'Rabbi Ben Ezra', 54; *Red Cotton*, 3277; 'Of Pacchiarotto', 559; 'Doctor ——', 78; 'Cherries', 74; 'Mihrab Shah' ('So, the head aches'), 20; 'Parleying with Dodington', 146. Otherwise Browning's own punctuation is reproduced.

(c) Paragraphing in the present edition often silently departs from that of the copy-text to follow that of the manuscript or first edition, and this for two reasons. Browning generally, though not invariably, preferred not to indent his verse paragraphs, but simply to use a space in the text to mark a new paragraph; consequently both printer and Browning, using an earlier printing for copy, often failed to note the desirable paragraph division when, in the earlier edition, a paragraph had ended at the foot of a page. The second reason is that the spaces between paragraphs in the proofs of first editions often presented the thrifty Browning with irresistible temptation; in would go a new line to fill the gap, and – since Browning worked with page proofs, not galleys – the printer could not without unreasonable expense make a new space. Thus desirable divisions disappeared from first editions and were usually not restored in later printings. No changes in paragraph structure have, however, been made in this edition without manuscript or textual authority.

(d) Browning sometimes used accents to assist readers with pronunciation. These have been retained, and others have been added in accordance with series policy: the *e* of the participial ending has been given a grave accent if the syllable containing it is, for metrical reasons, to be pronounced where in modern usage it would normally be silent; an acute accent is used to indicate a difference in stress from normal stress today (in 'Mílan' and 'illústrate', for example).

(e) Very occasionally a compositor's error led to a reading less satisfactory than that of the copy, a reading that escaped attention. In line 608 of 'Bishop Blougram's Apology', for instance, the 'soil' of first edition and *1863* became the less good 'soul' of *1868*, and the error was perpetuated in *1888–9*; in line 1736 of *Balaustion's Adventure*, all editions have read 'stud', but the manuscript reading is the superior 'steeds'; in line 951 of *Aristophanes' Apology*, all editions have 'Let', but the manuscript reading, 'Set', is better. In this edition 'soil', 'steeds' and 'Set' are printed. Sometimes one cannot be sure whether misprint or authorial revision is involved. In *Prince Hohenstiel-Schwangau*, line 539 has 'leaving' in the first edition and *1888-9*, 'having' in the manuscript: both are acceptable readings, but the latter seems more likely and, if anything, superior, and is printed in this edition. In line 91 of *Pauline* the 'wide' of 1833 became 'wild' in *1868*, a reading retained in *1888-9*; this edition prints 'wide', judging 'wild' an unnoted error and not a revision. In *Sordello* V, 483, both the 'crown' of *1840* and *1863* and the 'crowd' of *1868* and *1888-9* are acceptable, and since Browning made similar revisions elsewhere, a decision is called for: the present edition departs from copy-text to print 'crown'. The present text is generally extremely conservative, and, corrected spelling errors and misprints apart, there is only a handful of readings representing departures from all manuscripts and all editions supervised by Browning: 'grate' is emended to 'gate' in 'Donald', line 234, and 'captive' to 'capture' in 'Flute-Music', line 93, while lines 87–103 of the 'Parleying with Christopher Smart' print revisions, recorded in a late letter to J. T. Nettleship, that Browning proposed to incorporate in his next printing. Except for obvious misprints, the annotation records the few verbal differences between Browning's final text and that of the present edition.

There is no clearly right order in which to print Browning's poems. One does not slavishly follow the order of the final collected edition, especially since it was sometimes determined by a wish to have the volumes approximately equal in size (which is why *Sordello* there precedes *Paracelsus*). Many of Browning's poems cannot be accurately dated, and to attempt to print the poems in the order of composition would involve much bluffing and be misleading. In arranging his own works, Browning reclassified the poems originally printed in *Dramatic Lyrics* (1842), *Dramatic Romances and Lyrics* (1845), and *Men and Women* (1855), but his regroupings, details of which are given in an Appendix to this volume, have generally been thought as unprofitable as, say, those of Wordsworth and Arnold. Everything considered, I have judged it best to print poems gathered by the poet in the order in which they first appeared, and in the chronological order of Browning's volumes. Verses that Browning left ungathered or unpublished appear in this edition in a group at the end of the text of Volume II in an order approximating that of composition.

'There is a crying need for a really good popular edition of Browning's works.' Thus Dr Isobel Armstrong (*Browning Society Notes* II, No. 1, 1972, 20), noting what is certainly true: that 'the twentieth century has created gratuitous difficulty for readers of Browning because editions of his work have been, for the most part, simply appalling'. Comments like Dr Armstrong's are frequent, and so are complaints that Browning scholarship is not yet mature: Browning has been in all probability the worst served of major English poets. The present edition comes reasonably close, I believe, to being textually definitive; annotation is far from being so.

The ideal Browning annotator needs – besides sympathy – to be thoroughly at home with music, art, and seven or eight languages and literatures, to know the Bible and the plays of Euripides and Aristophanes (and Victorian scholarship on them) by heart, to be intimately familiar – for a start – with Keats and Shelley and Donne and Milton and Homer and Anacreon and Alciphron and Herodotus and Thucydides and Horace and Shakespeare and Wanley and Quarles and the *Illustrated London News* and Johnson's *Dictionary* and the fifty-odd – very odd – volumes of the *Biographie Universelle*. He needs to possess an outstanding knowledge of Italian topography and art and the more obscure recesses of Italian history, and to have read all those strange books which, one comes to believe, have had in their long history only one reader – Robert Browning. It would be helpful to have a photographic memory, to have lived an eon or two with faculties unimpaired, and to possess the kind of diligence that would have brought sweat into the brow of Browning's grammarian. Being therefore disqualified hopelessly in every essential respect from annotating Browning, one falls back on others' work and is able to steal much and verify it (the process often involving discrimination between quite irreconcilable scholarly 'facts'). Unfortunately one also finds, especially with the later poems, deserts of vast vacuity in which the planting of the odd signpost, let alone the creation of oases, is far from easy. At any rate, I have not consciously ducked difficulties, with the result that where I have failed, I have reminded myself – and doubtless will others – of Lounsbury's foghorn which proclaims the existence of fog without doing anything to disperse it.

The notes attempt to be concise without being cryptic, to provide important facts (dates, sources, textual details, biographical relevance, etc.) about each poem, and to give the usual kind of help with terms, allusions, words and phrases that may create difficulties for readers. The notes deliberately avoid paraphrase and criticism, but references to much of the best scholarship and criticism are there for readers who want them. While Browning's own notes are in the text itself as he wished them to be, the annotation includes important remarks by the poet in letters or in others' records. The annotation is thin on cross-references between one Browning poem and another simply because with a writer as prolific and repetitious as Browning such annotation can easily swamp other and more important kinds. And of these kinds the most helpful for Browning is unquestionably that which the Penguin English Poets series generally stresses: the linguistic.

The present edition aims to be fully glossed, for Browning is, as Mary Wilson remarked many years ago, a poet who had 'the curiosities of all dictionaries at his fingers' ends' (*Primer on Browning*, 37), and also because Dr Philip Drew is, I believe, right when he declares that 'a fully glossed edition of Browning would encourage many people to read him who are at present deterred by not knowing the meaning of all the words he uses' (*The Poetry of Browning*, 76). Browning is not only among the most prolific of English poets, but the employer of one of the most voluminous of poetic vocabularies: roughly 40,000 words, or about double that of Tennyson or of Shakespeare. With Browning as much as with any poet it would seem true that the *critical* relevance of the *Oxford English Dictionary* is prodigious, and the work indispensable to full understanding. I have stolen liberally from it.

Browning's vast poetic vocabulary, his delight in language of all kinds, familiar and remote, literary and technical and colloquial, his struggle to subdue language to his will – these things create both barriers to understanding, and huge rewards for those who read him in the right spirit. The same is true of the wealth of literary and historical reference, often to people, places, works and events that were scarcely of importance in their own day, let alone part of the stock in trade of literate readers of Browning's time or ours. To have the slightest chance of arriving at anything like understanding of that superb disaster of a poem, *Sordello*, for instance, one must have help (of a kind that this edition seeks to provide) with references to lore that is indeed quaint and curious. The same kind of thing is even more true of a later poem like *Aristophanes' Apology*, which has daunted even leading Browning scholars and which has been called by one of them, Philip Drew, 'the most erudite of Browning's poems and probably the most truly difficult' (*The Poetry of Browning*, 99). In fact *Aristophanes' Apology* is no such thing, and it is very different from *Sordello* and very much easier in every way because the sole real source of difficulty is the apparent erudition. It is otherwise one of the most straightforward of Browning's poems. It will not appeal to readers who are not prepared to be fascinated by such things as the proper method of cooking Copaic eels, the lost plays of Euripides, the curious position adopted by Euripides in writing his plays and the mysterious place in which he is buried, the rival claims of comic and tragic art, the astonishingly fertile mind of the father of comic drama and the grandeur of the old Sophocles. The annotation in this edition strives to help readers willing to give themselves to such interests to overcome – and to feel the joy of overcoming – the surface obstacles to the appreciation of what may well be (as it is for me) the masterpiece of Browning's later years.

For many of Browning's poems the present edition provides the first full glosses; this is perhaps a manifestation of the strange belief generally held until fairly recently that somehow or other the Victorians were close enough to us not to need editing. Inevitably, since some of Browning's later poems have received almost no attention and have, for practical purposes, never been annotated before, there is much that is new in the notes to the present edition. There is also much that is new in the notes to poems that have been treated in detail: in the notes to *Sordello*, for instance, which correct many traditional errors and which attempt to deal with some of the problems about which scholars and critics have been discreetly silent. It is, however, more important to point out that the notes would be even less adequate than they are were it not for the labours of many students of Browning over the years. I have stolen a great deal from many scholars, but I am especially conscious of debts to Paul Turner's recent edition of *Men and Women*, to T. L. Hood's work on Browning's classical sources and that of Elvan Kintner and E. C. McAleer on the letters, to S. W. Holmes on the sources of *Sordello*, to C. N. Jackson and F. M. Tisdel on *Aristophanes' Apology*, to A. B. Crowder and C. C. Watkins on *The Inn Album*, and to W. C. DeVane on the *Parleyings*. And all students of Browning know that while it is easy and true to say that the late Dean DeVane's *Handbook* is out of date on many matters, often wrong on textual matters particularly, and given to confusing conjecture with fact, it remains a work without which the reader of Browning can scarcely function.

Catharine Parr Traill College, Peterborough, Ontario   1976

John Pettigrew was a man of wit, intelligence and humanity. The quality of his work on Browning, represented by this edition, is proof of the loss created by his death. It has been my privilege to see *Browning: The Poems* through the press. My thanks to Pat Pettigrew for allowing me to fulfil his brother's wish.

University of Western Ontario   Thomas J. Collins   1981

Acknowledgements

I am deeply grateful to many institutions and individuals:

to the Canada Council for a research grant;

to the authorities and staffs of the Library of Wellesley College, the Houghton and Widener Libraries of Harvard University, the Boston Public Library, the Beinecke Rare Book and Manuscript Library of Yale University, the Henry W. and Albert A. Berg Collection of the New York Public Library, the New York Public Library, the Pierpont Morgan Library, the Carl H. Pforzheimer Library, the Library of Congress, the Folger Shakespeare Library, the Armstrong Browning Library of Baylor University, the Miriam Lutcher Stark Library of the University of Texas, the Henry E. Huntington Library, the Library of Scripps College, the Mills Library of McMaster University, the Robarts Library of the University of Toronto, the Bata Library of Trent University, the Tennyson Research Centre in the City Library of Lincoln, the Cambridge University Library, the Library of King's College, Cambridge, the University of London Library, the British Library, the Library of the Victoria and Albert Museum, the Bodleian Library of Oxford University, the Balliol College Library, the Keats-Shelley House in Rome, the Biblioteca Nazionale in Florence, the Library of the Casa Goldoni in Venice;

to the following for permission to print materials owned by them: the Houghton Library; the Trustees of the Boston Public Library; the Library Board of Cornell University; the Beinecke Rare Book and Manuscript Library; the Pierpont Morgan Library; the Henry W. and Albert A. Berg Collection, the New York Public Library, Astor, Lenox and Tilden Foundations; the Carl and Lily Pforzheimer Foundation, Inc.; the Armstrong Browning Library; the Huntington Library, San Marino, California; the Library of the Victoria and Albert Museum; the British Library; the Master and Fellows of Balliol College, Oxford; the Tennyson Research Centre;

to John Murray for permission to publish materials on which the firm holds the copyright;

and to individuals for help of various kinds: my parents and my brother and sister, Professor F. E. L. Priestley, Professor T. J. Collins, Principal Nancy Sherouse, Professor Robert Chambers, Professor David Glassco, Professor and Mrs James Neufeld, Professor Ian Storey, Professor W. Whitla, and many other friends and former colleagues. My greatest debt is to the General Editor of the series for his encouragement, patience and careful criticism.

Table of Dates

1812	*7 May* Born at Camberwell, suburb of London. Son of Robert Browning, eccentric bibliophile, amateur scholar and bank-clerk, and Sarah Anna Browning (née Wiedemann).
1814	Birth of Sarah Anna (Sarianna), Browning's sister.
c. 1820–26	At the school of Rev. Thomas Ready at Peckham. Most of Browning's education was informal, at his home, where he had professional tutors, his father, and a huge library to guide him.
1826	Discovers Shelley and becomes atheist and vegetarian.
1828	Enters London University, where he remains for almost the entire academic year.
1833	*March Pauline* published anonymously; unsold and little noticed.
1834	*March and April* Visits St Petersburg.
1835	*October Paracelsus* published.
1836	*May* John Forster's *Life of Strafford* in which Browning had some share, perhaps a large one.
1837	*May Strafford* published, and performed five times.
1838	*April–July* First visit to Italy (Venice and surrounding area).
1840	*March Sordello* published; becomes notorious for obscurity.
1841	*April Bells and Pomegranates I : Pippa Passes.*
1842	*March Bells and Pomegranates II : King Victor and King Charles.* *July* 'Essay on Chatterton' published anonymously in *Foreign Quarterly Review.* *November Bells and Pomegranates III : Dramatic Lyrics.*
1843	*January Bells and Pomegranates IV : The Return of the Druses.* *February Bells and Pomegranates V : A Blot in the 'Scutcheon*; performed three times.

1844   *April   Bells and Pomegranates VI: Colombe's Birthday.*
Browning's last play for the stage, it was presented
successfully in London and Manchester in 1853.
Autumn   Second visit to Italy (Naples, Rome, Florence;
return along the Rhine).

1845   *10 January*   First letter to Elizabeth Barrett.
20 May   First visit to Wimpole Street.
*November   Bells and Pomegranates VII: Dramatic
Romances and Lyrics.*

1846   *April   Bells and Pomegranates VIII: Luria* and *A Soul's
Tragedy.*
12 September   Marriage to Elizabeth Barrett.
19 September   The Brownings leave England for Pisa.

1847   *April*   Move to Florence, where Casa Guidi shortly
becomes their home for the rest of the marriage.

1849   *January   Poems* (2 volumes).
March   Son, Robert Wiedemann Barrett Browning
('Penini', 'Pen'), born. Browning's mother dies.

1850   *April   Christmas-Eve and Easter-Day* published.

1852   'Essay on Shelley' published.

1855   *November   Men and Women.*

1856   John Kenyon's legacy of £11,000 solves the Brownings'
financial problems.

1860   *June*   Buys the 'Old Yellow Book'.

1861   *29 June*   Death of Elizabeth Barrett Browning.
August   Browning leaves Florence, and never returns.
October   Browning settles in London after a holiday in
France.

1863   *The Poetical Works* (3 volumes).

1864   *May   Dramatis Personae* published.
Autumn   Begins writing *The Ring and the Book.*

1866   Death of Browning's father.

1867   Honorary M.A. from Oxford; Honorary Fellow of Balliol
College, Oxford.

1868   *The Poetical Works* (6 volumes).

1868–9   *November–February   The Ring and the Book.*

1869   *September*   Proposal of marriage (by ?, to ?) Lady
Ashburton?

1871   *August   Balaustion's Adventure.*
December   Prince Hohenstiel-Schwangau.

1872   *June   Fifine at the Fair.*

1873   *May   Red Cotton Night-Cap Country.*
1875   *April   Aristophanes' Apology.*
        November   The Inn Album.
1876   *July   Pacchiarotto and How He Worked in Distemper.*
1877   *October   The Agamemnon of Aeschylus.*
1878   *May   La Saisiaz: Two Poets of Croisic.*
        Revisits Italy, as in most years for the rest of his life.
1879   *April   Dramatic Idyls.*
        LL.D. from Cambridge.
1880   *June   Dramatic Idyls: Second Series.*
1881   *October*   Founding of the Browning Society.
1882   D.C.L. from Oxford.
1883   *March   Jocoseria.*
1884   LL.D. from Edinburgh.
        November   Ferishtah's Fancies.
1886   *September*   Death of Browning's friend Joseph Milsand.
1887   *January   Parleyings with Certain People of Importance in
        Their Day.*
        October   Marriage of Pen Browning and Fannie
        Coddington.
1888-9 *The Poetical Works* (16 volumes).
1889   *12 December   Asolando*; Browning dies at Venice later in
        the day.
        31 December   Buried in Poets' Corner, Westminster
        Abbey.
1903   Death of Sarianna.
1912   Death of Pen at Asolo.
1913   Dispersal of the Browning estates at auction.

Further Reading

Works concerned with a single volume and with a single poem or a handful of poems are listed in the appropriate places in the 'Notes'.

EDITIONS

The sixteen-volume *Poetical Works of Robert Browning*, Smith, Elder, 1888–9, is copy-text for most subsequent editions (a second impression in which all volumes are dated 1889 followed); in 1894 a seventeenth volume appeared, edited by Edward Berdoe, and including *Asolando* and notes. In 1898 Charlotte Porter and Helen A. Clarke published their twelve-volume edition (Crowell). Called the 'Florentine Edition' in one of its forms, it subsequently appeared in various formats with a variety of names. The best edition to date, it includes extensive introductions tending to often useful summary, and annotation of varying bulk, accuracy and usefulness. The ten-volume 'Centenary Edition' of 1912, edited by F. G. Kenyon (Smith, Elder) has brief introductions but no annotation; it is often regarded as the standard edition. In 1914 Smith, Elder published Kenyon's *New Poems by Robert Browning and Elizabeth Barrett Browning*; the new poems were included in the *Complete Poetical Works*, published in 1915 in New York by Macmillan. What are virtual reprints of that edition, one that includes the occasional note, have been published by John Murray since 1929. In progress – four volumes appeared between 1969 and 1973 – is the projected fourteen-volume *The Complete Works of Robert Browning* (the 'Ohio Browning'), published by the Ohio University Press under the general editorship of Roma A. King, Jr. In 1977 Baylor University joined Ohio as joint publisher, and the original editorial board was much altered. The edition is the first to include full textual apparatus, is annotated, and aims at definitiveness. Regrettably, however, the volumes so far published are not definitive: the editorial principles have been challenged, important manuscript materials have been neglected, and the inaccuracy of text, textual apparatus and annotation has been demonstrated (see, for instance, Thomas J. Collins in *Victorian Studies* XIII, 1970, 441–4; John Pettigrew in *Essays in Criticism*

XXII 1972, 436–41 – the same journal printed Roma A. King's reply: XXIV, 1974, 317–19, and Pettigrew's rejoinder: XXV, 1975, 480–83; and Donald H. Reiman in *Victorian Poetry* XII, 1974, 86–96). Extensive problems in the Ohio notes to *Sordello* are detailed in John Pettigrew's posthumously published essay in *The Library* XXXIII, 1978, 162–9. An edition in the Longman Annotated English Poets series, edited by John Woolford, is announced for the future. The unannotated Oxford Standard Authors edition by Ian Jack (1970) includes only the poems published of selections before *The Ring and the Book*.

Among usefully annotated volumes of selections are: Kenneth Allott (ed.), *Browning: Selected Poems*, Oxford University Press, 1967; Joseph E. Baker (ed.), '*Pippa Passes' and Shorter Poems*, Odyssey, 1947; E. K. Brown and J. O. Bailey (eds.), in *Victorian Poetry*, 2nd edn, Ronald, 1962; William Clyde DeVane (ed.), *The Shorter Poems of Robert Browning*, Appleton-Century-Crofts, 1934; Walter E. Houghton and G. Robert Stange (eds.), *Victorian Poetry and Poetics*, 2nd edn, Houghton-Mifflin, 1968; Jacob Korg (ed.), *The Poetry of Robert Browning*, Bobbs-Merrill, 1971; Donald Smalley (ed.), *Poems of Robert Browning*, Houghton-Mifflin, 1956. Browning's so-called *Essay on Shelley* (included in the Appendix to this volume) was edited by L. Winstanley in 1911, and by H. F. B. Brett-Smith in 1921. Donald Smalley edited Browning's *Essay on Chatterton*, Harvard University Press, 1948.

BIBLIOGRAPHIES AND REFERENCE WORKS

The standard bibliography is Leslie Nathan Broughton, Clark Sutherland Northup and Robert Brainard Pearsall, *Robert Browning: A Bibliography, 1830–1950*, Cornell University Press, 1953. It is continued by William S. Peterson, *Robert and Elizabeth Barrett Browning: An Annotated Bibliography, 1951–1970*, Browning Institute, 1974, and in the annual bibliographies published in *Browning Institute Studies*, 1973–.

Still of value despite the inclusion of his own forgeries are Thomas J. Wise's *Bibliography* (1897) and *A Browning Library* (1929). Valuable too is the Sotheby, Wilkinson and Hodge sales catalogue, *The Browning Collections* (1913). Expert guidance is available from Park Honan in *The Victorian Poets: A Guide to Research*, ed. Frederic E. Faverty, Harvard University Press, 1968; from Ian Jack in *English Poetry: Select Bibliographical Guides*, ed. A. E. Dyson, Oxford University Press, 1971; and from P. J. Keating in *Robert Browning*, ed. Isobel

Armstrong, Bell, 1974. Also useful are the annual bibliographies in the June issues of *Victorian Studies*, the check lists in *The Browning News-letter* and *Studies in Browning and His Circle*, and the annual guides in summer issues of *Victorian Poetry*. Warner Barnes compiled the *Catalogue of the Browning Collection at the University of Texas*, 1966. The standard *Concordance* is that of Leslie N. Broughton and Benjamin F. Stelter, 2 volumes, Steckert, 1924–5.

Journals: Victorian Poetry and *Victorian Studies* include much Browning material. Three journals are devoted to the Brownings: *Studies in Browning and His Circle* (formerly called *The Browning Newsletter*) appears twice a year from the Armstrong Browning Library of Baylor University, *Browning Institute Studies* is published annually by the Browning Institute of New York, and *Browning Society Notes* is published three times a year by the Browning Society of London.

Handbooks: Still indispensable, despite being dated and often erroneous, is William Clyde DeVane, *A Browning Handbook*, 2nd edn, Appleton-Century-Crofts, 1955. Also important, since it was written by a close friend of Browning, who in a sense gave his blessing to it despite its frequent errors, is Mrs Sutherland Orr's *A Handbook to the Works of Robert Browning*, 6th edn, Bell, 1892. Norton B. Crowell, *A Reader's Guide to Robert Browning*, University of New Mexico Press, 1972, has a misleading title: it focuses on twenty-three better-known poems.

Collections of Critical Essays: Criticism from 1833 to 1891 is collected in Boyd Litzinger and Donald Smalley (eds.), *Browning: The Critical Heritage*, Routledge & Kegan Paul, 1970. Other standard collections are: Boyd Litzinger and K. L. Knickerbocker (eds.), *The Browning Critics*, University of Kentucky Press, 1965; Philip Drew (ed.), *Robert Browning: A Collection of Critical Essays*, Methuen, 1966; Clarence Tracy (ed.), *Browning's Mind and Art*, Oliver & Boyd, 1968; and Isobel Armstrong (ed.), *Robert Browning*, Bell, 1974.

LETTERS

Most of Browning's letters remain unpublished, and Philip Kelley and Ronald Hudson project an edition of the complete letters of Browning and his wife in about forty volumes. Their *Checklist* of Browning correspondence, published in 1978 (Browning Institute and Wedgestone Press) contains 9,789 entries. Many letters have appeared singly or in small gatherings in periodicals, biographies, etc. The most important collections so far are:

W. R. Benét (ed.), *Twenty-Two Unpublished Letters of Elizabeth Barrett Browning and Robert Browning*, United Feature Syndicate, 1935.

Thomas J. Collins (ed.), *The Brownings to the Tennysons*, Baylor Browning Interests, 1971.

Richard Curle (ed.), *Robert Browning and Julia Wedgwood : A Broken Friendship as Revealed in Their Letters*, John Murray and Jonathan Cape, 1937.

David J. De Laura (ed.), 'Ruskin and the Brownings: Twenty-five Unpublished Letters', *Bulletin of John Rylands Library* LIV, 1972, 314–56.

William Clyde DeVane and Kenneth Leslie Knickerbocker (eds.), *New Letters of Robert Browning*, Yale University Press, 1950.

Thurman L. Hood (ed.), *Letters of Robert Browning Collected by Thomas J. Wise*, Yale University Press, 1933.

Gertrude Reese Hudson (ed.), *Browning to His American Friends : Letters Between the Brownings, the Storys, and James Russell Lowell, 1841–1890*, Bowes & Bowes, 1965.

F. G. Kenyon (ed.), *Robert Browning and Alfred Domett*, Smith, Elder, 1906.

Elvan Kintner (ed.), *The Letters of Robert Browning and Elizabeth Barrett, 1845–1846*, 2 volumes, Belknap Press of Harvard University Press, 1969.

Paul Landis (ed.), *Letters of the Brownings to George Barrett*, University of Illinois Press, 1958.

Edward C. McAleer (ed.), *Dearest Isa : Robert Browning's Letters to Isa Blagden*, University of Texas Press, 1951.

Edward C. McAleer (ed.), *Learned Lady : Letters from Robert Browning to Mrs. Thomas FitzGerald 1876–1889*, Carl H. Pforzheimer Library, 1966.

BIOGRAPHIES

W. Hall Griffin and Harry Christopher Minchin, *The Life of Robert Browning*, Methuen, 1910. (A standard Life. The photographs in *1910* make it more useful than the very slightly revised version of 1938.)

William Irvine and Park Honan, *The Book, the Ring, and the Poet : A Biography of Robert Browning*, McGraw-Hill, 1974. (Probably the best biography, it includes valuable criticism.)

John Maynard, *Browning's Youth*, Harvard University Press, 1977. (An invaluable source of information on the early years, containing much new material.)

Betty Miller, *Robert Browning: A Portrait*, John Murray, 1952. (The most widely read Life, it is readable, challenging, often cavalier with facts and Freud.)

Mrs Sutherland Orr, *Life and Letters of Robert Browning*, revised and in part rewritten by F. G. Kenyon, Smith, Elder, 1908. (First published in 1891, the Life is important as the product of a close friend, and for its letters.)

Maisie Ward, *Robert Browning and His World*, 2 volumes, Cassell, 1967, 1969.

Lilian Whiting, *The Brownings: Their Life and Art*, Little, Brown, 1911.

Among other useful biographical sources are the short story of Henry James, 'The Private Life' (1892), with its central character modelled on Browning and James; James's *William Wetmore Story and His Friends*, 2 volumes, 1903; Katherine C. de K. Bronson, 'Browning in Asolo', *Century Magazine* LIX, 1900, 920–31, and 'Browning in Venice', *Cornhill Magazine* LXXXV, 1902, 145–71; Fannie B. Browning, *Some Memories of Robert Browning by His Daughter-in-Law*, Marshall Jones, 1928; E. A. Horsman (ed.), *The Diary of Alfred Domett, 1872–1885*, Oxford University Press, 1953; B. R. Jerman, 'The Death of Robert Browning', *University of Toronto Quarterly* XXXV, 1965, 47–74; William Whitla, 'Browning and the Ashburton Affair', *Browning Society Notes* II, No. 2, 1972, 12–41. Richard D. Altick's contentious 'The Private Life of Robert Browning' and Kenneth L. Knickerbocker's reply in 'A Tentative Apology for Robert Browning' are both included in Litzinger and Knickerbocker, *The Browning Critics*.

GENERAL SCHOLARSHIP AND CRITICISM

Isobel Armstrong, 'Browning and the Grotesque Style', in Isobel Armstrong (ed.), *The Major Victorian Poets: Reconsiderations*, Routledge & Kegan Paul, 1969, 93–123.

Kingsbury Badger, '"See the Christ Stand!": Browning's Religion', *Boston University Studies in English* I, 1955, 53–73. (In Drew, *Robert Browning*, 72–95.)

G. K. Chesterton, *Robert Browning*, Macmillan, 1903.

J. M. Cohen, *Robert Browning*, Longmans, Green, 1952.

Thomas J. Collins, *Robert Browning's Moral-Aesthetic Theory 1833–1855*, University of Nebraska Press, 1967.

Eleanor Cook, *Browning's Lyrics: An Exploration*, University of Toronto Press, 1974.

Norton B. Crowell, *The Convex Glass: The Mind of Robert Browning*, University of New Mexico Press, 1968.

Norton B. Crowell, *The Triple Soul: Browning's Theory of Knowledge*, University of New Mexico Press, 1963.

A. Dwight Culler, 'Monodrama and the Dramatic Monologue', *PMLA* XC, 1975, 366–85.

William Clyde DeVane, 'Browning and the Spirit of Greece', in *Nineteenth-Century Studies*, ed. H. Davis, W. C. DeVane and R. C. Bald, Cornell University Press, 1940, 179–98.

William Clyde DeVane, 'The Virgin and the Dragon', *Yale Review*, new series XXXVII, 1947, 33–46. (In Drew, *Robert Browning*, 96–109, and Litzinger and Knickerbocker, *The Browning Critics*, 181–96.)

Edward Dowden, *Robert Browning*, Dent, 1904.

Philip Drew, *The Poetry of Browning: A Critical Introduction*, Methuen, 1970.

F. R. G. Duckworth, *Browning: Background and Conflict*, Benn, 1931.

Henry Charles Duffin, *Amphibian: A Reconsideration of Browning*, Bowes & Bowes, 1956.

F. J. Furnivall (ed.), *The Browning Society's Papers*, 3 volumes, Browning Society, 1881–91.

Donald S. Hair, *Browning's Experiments with Genre*, University of Toronto Press, 1972.

Park Honan, *Browning's Characters*, Yale University Press, 1961.

Thurman L. Hood, 'Browning's Ancient Classical Sources', *Harvard Studies in Classical Philology* XXXIII, 1922, 79–180.

Ian Jack, *Browning's Major Poetry*, Clarendon Press, 1973.

Henry James, 'Browning in Westminster Abbey' (1890). (In Drew, *Robert Browning*, 11–16.)

E. D. H. Johnson, 'Browning', in his *The Alien Vision of Victorian Poetry*, Princeton University Press, 1952, 71–143.

Henry Jones, *Browning as a Philosophical and Religious Teacher*, Maclehose, 1891.

Roma A. King, Jr, *The Bow and the Lyre: The Art of Robert Browning*, University of Michigan Press, 1957.

Robert Langbaum, *The Poetry of Experience*, Random House, 1957.

Barbara Melchiori, *Browning's Poetry of Reticence*, Oliver & Boyd, 1968.

J. Hillis Miller, 'Robert Browning', in his *The Disappearance of God*, Belknap Press of Harvard University Press, 1963, 81–156.

William S. Peterson, *Interrogating the Oracle: A History of the London Browning Society*, Ohio University Press, 1970.

F. A. Pottle, *Shelley and Browning, A Myth and Some Facts* Pembroke Press, 1923.

Robert O. Preyer, 'Robert Browning: A Reading of the Early Narratives', *ELH* XXVI, 1959, 531–48. (In Drew, *Robert Browning*, 157–75; and Litzinger and Knickerbocker, *The Browning Critics*, 343–63.)

Robert O. Preyer, 'Two Styles in the Verse of Robert Browning', *ELH* XXXII, 1965, 62–84.

Ralph W. Rader, 'The Dramatic Monologue and Related Lyric Forms', *Critical Inquiry* III, 1976, 131–51.

William O. Raymond, *The Infinite Moment and Other Essays in Robert Browning*, 2nd edn, University of Toronto Press, 1965.

Clyde de L. Ryals, *Browning's Later Poetry: 1871–1889*, Cornell University Press, 1975.

W. David Shaw, *The Dialectical Temper: The Rhetorical Art of Robert Browning*, Cornell University Press, 1968.

C. Willard Smith, *Browning's Star-Imagery: The Study of a Detail in Poetic Design*, Princeton University Press, 1941.

Lionel Stevenson, 'The Pertinacious Victorian Poets', *University of Toronto Quarterly* XXI, 1952, 232–45.

Lionel Stevenson, 'Tennyson, Browning, and a Romantic Fallacy', *University of Toronto Quarterly* XIII, 1944, 175–95.

Arthur Symons, *An Introduction to the Study of Browning*, rev. edn, Dent, 1906.

Michael Timko, 'Ah, Did You Once See Browning Plain?', *Studies in English Literature* VI, 1966, 731–42.

C. R. Tracy, 'Browning's Heresies', *Studies in Philology* XXXIII, 1936, 610–25.

William Whitla, *The Central Truth: The Incarnation in Browning's Poetry*, University of Toronto Press, 1963.

The Poems

I DEDICATE THESE VOLUMES TO MY OLD
FRIEND JOHN FORSTER, GLAD AND GRATEFUL
THAT HE WHO, FROM THE FIRST
PUBLICATION OF THE VARIOUS POEMS THEY
INCLUDE, HAS BEEN THEIR PROMPTEST AND
STAUNCHEST HELPER, SHOULD SEEM EVEN
NEARER TO ME NOW THAN ALMOST THIRTY
YEARS AGO.

R.B.

London: 21 April 1863

The poems that follow are printed in the order of their publication. The first piece in the series I acknowledge and retain with extreme repugnance, indeed purely of necessity; for not long ago I inspected one, and am certified of the existence of other transcripts, intended sooner or later to be published abroad: by forestalling these, I can at least correct some misprints (no syllable is changed) and introduce a boyish work by an exculpatory word. The thing was my earliest attempt at 'poetry always dramatic in principle, and so many utterances of so many imaginary persons, not mine,' which I have since written according to a scheme less extravagant and scale less impracticable than were ventured upon in this crude preliminary sketch – a sketch that, on reviewal, appears not altogether wide of some hint of the characteristic features of that particular *dramatis persona* it would fain have reproduced: good draughtsmanship, however, and right handling were far beyond the artist at that time.

R. B.

London: 25 December 1867

I preserve, in order to supplement it, the foregoing preface. I had thought, when compelled to include in my collected works the poem to which it refers, that the honest course would be to reprint, and leave mere literary errors unaltered. Twenty years' endurance of an eyesore seems more than sufficient: my faults remain duly recorded against me, and I claim permission to somewhat diminish these, so far as style is concerned, in the present and final edition where 'Pauline' must needs, first of my performances, confront the reader. I have simply removed solecisms, mended the metre a little, and endeavoured to strengthen the phraseology – experience helping, in some degree, the helplessness of juvenile haste and heat in their untried adventure long ago.

The poems that follow are again, as before, printed in chronological order; but only so far as proves compatible with the prescribed size of each volume, which necessitates an occasional change in the distribution of its contents. Every date is subjoined as before.

R. B.

London : 27 February 1888

Pauline;

A Fragment of a Confession

1833

Plus ne suis ce que j'ai été,
Et ne le sçaurois jamais être. – Marot

Non dubito, quin titulus libri nostri raritate sua quamplurimos alliciat ad legendum: inter quos nonnulli obliquae opinionis, mente languidi, multi etiam maligni, et in ingenium nostrum ingrati accedent, qui temeraria sua ignorantia, vix conspecto titulo clamabunt: Nos vetita docere, haeresium semina jacere: piis auribus offendiculo, praeclaris ingeniis scandalo esse: ... adeo conscientiae suae consulentes, ut nec Apollo, nec Musae omnes, neque Angelus de coelo me ab illorum execratione vindicare queant: quibus et ego nunc consulo, ne scripta nostra legant, nec intelligant, nec meminerint: nam noxia sunt, venenosa sunt: Acherontis ostium est in hoc libro, lapides loquitur, caveant, ne cerebrum illis excutiat. Vos autem, qui aequa mente ad legendum venitis, si tantam prudentiae discretionem adhibueritis, quantam in melle legendo apes, jam securi legite. Puto namque vos et utilitatis haud parum et voluptatis plurimum accepturos. Quod si qua repereritis, quae vobis non placeant, mittite illa, nec utimini. NAM ET EGO VOBIS ILLA NON PROBO, SED NARRO. Caetera tamen propterea non respuite ... Ideo, si quid liberius dictum sit, ignoscite adolescentiae nostrae, qui minor quam adolescens hoc opus composui. – *Hen. Corn. Agrippa, De Occult. Philosoph. in Praefat.*

London : January 1833
V.A. XX.

[This introduction would appear less absurdly pretentious did it apply, as was intended, to a completed structure of which the poem was meant for only a beginning and remains a fragment.]

Pauline

Pauline, mine own, bend o'er me – thy soft breast
Shall pant to mine – bend o'er me – thy sweet eyes,
And loosened hair and breathing lips, and arms
Drawing me to thee – these build up a screen
To shut me in with thee, and from all fear;
So that I might unlock the sleepless brood
Of fancies from my soul, their lurking-place,
Nor doubt that each would pass, ne'er to return
To one so watched, so loved and so secured.
10 But what can guard thee but thy naked love?
Ah dearest, whoso sucks a poisoned wound
Envenoms his own veins! Thou art so good,
So calm – if thou shouldst wear a brow less light
For some wild thought which, but for me, were kept
From out thy soul as from a sacred star!
Yet till I have unlocked them it were vain
To hope to sing; some woe would light on me;
Nature would point at one whose quivering lip
Was bathed in her enchantments, whose brow burned
20 Beneath the crown to which her secrets knelt,
Who learned the spell which can call up the dead,
And then departed smiling like a fiend
Who has deceived God, – if such one should seek
Again her altars and stand robed and crowned
Amid the faithful! Sad confession first,
Remorse and pardon and old claims renewed,
Ere I can be – as I shall be no more.

I had been spared this shame if I had sat
By thee for ever from the first, in place
30 Of my wild dreams of beauty and of good,
Or with them, as an earnest of their truth:
No thought nor hope having been shut from thee,
No vague wish unexplained, no wandering aim
Sent back to bind on fancy's wings and seek
Some strange fair world where it might be a law;
But, doubting nothing, had been led by thee,
Through youth, and saved, as one at length awaked
Who has slept through a peril. Ah vain, vain!

Thou lovest me; the past is in its grave
40 Though its ghost haunts us; still this much is ours,
To cast away restraint, lest a worse thing
Wait for us in the dark. Thou lovest me;
And thou art to receive not love but faith,
For which thou wilt be mine, and smile and take
All shapes and shames, and veil without a fear
That form which music follows like a slave:
And I look to thee and I trust in thee,
As in a Northern night one looks alway
Unto the East for morn and spring and joy.

50 Thou seest then my aimless, hopeless state,
And, resting on some few old feelings won
Back by thy beauty, wouldst that I essay
The task which was to me what now thou art:
And why should I conceal one weakness more?

Thou wilt remember one warm morn when winter
Crept agèd from the earth, and spring's first breath
Blew soft from the moist hills; the black-thorn boughs,
So dark in the bare wood, when glistening
In the sunshine were white with coming buds,
60 Like the bright side of a sorrow, and the banks
Had violets opening from sleep like eyes.
I walked with thee who knew'st not a deep shame
Lurked beneath smiles and careless words which sought
To hide it till they wandered and were mute,
As we stood listening on a sunny mound
To the wind murmuring in the damp copse,
Like heavy breathings of some hidden thing
Betrayed by sleep; until the feeling rushed
That I was low indeed, yet not so low
70 As to endure the calmness of thine eyes.
And so I told thee all, while the cool breast
I leaned on altered not its quiet beating:
And long ere words like a hurt bird's complaint
Bade me look up and be what I had been,
I felt despair could never live by thee:
Thou wilt remember. Thou art not more dear
Than song was once to me; and I ne'er sung
But as one entering bright halls where all
Will rise and shout for him: sure I must own

80   That I am fallen, having chosen gifts
Distinct from theirs – that I am sad and fain
Would give up all to be but where I was,
Not high as I had been if faithful found,
But low and weak yet full of hope, and sure
Of goodness as of life – that I would lose
All this gay mastery of mind, to sit
Once more with them, trusting in truth and love
And with an aim – not being what I am.

Oh Pauline, I am ruined who believed
90   That though my soul had floated from its sphere
Of wide dominion into the dim orb
Of self – that it was strong and free as ever!
It has conformed itself to that dim orb,
Reflecting all its shades and shapes, and now
Must stay where it alone can be adored.
I have felt this in dreams – in dreams in which
I seemed the fate from which I fled; I felt
A strange delight in causing my decay.
I was a fiend in darkness chained for ever
100   Within some ocean-cave; and ages rolled,
Till through the cleft rock, like a moonbeam, came
A white swan to remain with me; and ages
Rolled, yet I tired not of my first free joy
In gazing on the peace of its pure wings:
And then I said 'It is most fair to me,
Yet its soft wings must sure have suffered change
From the thick darkness, sure its eyes are dim,
Its silver pinions must be cramped and numbed
With sleeping ages here; it cannot leave me,
110   For it would seem, in light beside its kind,
Withered, though here to me most beautiful.'
And then I was a young witch whose blue eyes,
As she stood naked by the river springs,
Drew down a god: I watched his radiant form
Growing less radiant, and it gladdened me;
Till one morn, as he sat in the sunshine
Upon my knees, singing to me of heaven,
He turned to look at me, ere I could lose
The grin with which I viewed his perishing:
120   And he shrieked and departed and sat long

By his deserted throne, but sunk at last
Murmuring, as I kissed his lips and curled
Around him, 'I am still a god – to thee.'

Still I can lay my soul bare in its fall,
Since all the wandering and all the weakness
Will be a saddest comment on the song:
And if, that done, I can be young again,
I will give up all gained, as willingly
As one gives up a charm which shuts him out
130   From hope or part or care in human kind.
As life wanes, all its care and strife and toil
Seem strangely valueless, while the old trees
Which grew by our youth's home, the waving mass
Of climbing plants heavy with bloom and dew,
The morning swallows with their songs like words,
All these seem clear and only worth our thoughts:
So, aught connected with my early life,
My rude songs or my wild imaginings,
How I look on them – most distinct amid
140   The fever and the stir of after years!

I ne'er had ventured e'en to hope for this,
Had not the glow I felt at HIS award,
Assured me all was not extinct within:
HIS whom all honour, whose renown springs up
Like sunlight which will visit all the world,
So that e'en they who sneered at him at first,
Come out to it, as some dark spider crawls
From his foul nets which some lit torch invades,
Yet spinning still new films for his retreat.
150   Thou didst smile, poet, but can we forgive?

Sun-treader, life and light be thine for ever!
Thou art gone from us; years go by and spring
Gladdens and the young earth is beautiful,
Yet thy songs come not, other bards arise,
But none like thee: they stand, thy majesties,
Like mighty works which tell some spirit there
Hath sat regardless of neglect and scorn,
Till, its long task completed, it hath risen
And left us, never to return, and all

160 Rush in to peer and praise when all in vain.
    The air seems bright with thy past presence yet,
    But thou art still for me as thou hast been
    When I have stood with thee as on a throne
    With all thy dim creations gathered round
    Like mountains, and I felt of mould like them,
    And with them creatures of my own were mixed,
    Like things half-lived, catching and giving life.
    But thou art still for me who have adored
    Though single, panting but to hear thy name
170 Which I believed a spell to me alone,
    Scarce deeming thou wast as a star to men!
    As one should worship long a sacred spring
    Scarce worth a moth's flitting, which long grasses cross,
    And one small tree embowers droopingly –
    Joying to see some wandering insect won
    To live in its few rushes, or some locust
    To pasture on its boughs, or some wild bird
    Stoop for its freshness from the trackless air:
    And then should find it but the fountain-head,
180 Long lost, of some great river washing towns
    And towers, and seeing old woods which will live
    But by its banks untrod of human foot,
    Which, when the great sun sinks, lie quivering
    In light as some thing lieth half of life
    Before God's foot, waiting a wondrous change;
    Then girt with rocks which seek to turn or stay
    Its course in vain, for it does ever spread
    Like a sea's arm as it goes rolling on,
    Being the pulse of some great country – so
190 Wast thou to me, and art thou to the world!
    And I, perchance, half feel a strange regret
    That I am not what I have been to thee:
    Like a girl one has silently loved long
    In her first loneliness in some retreat,
    When, late emerged, all gaze and glow to view
    Her fresh eyes and soft hair and lips which bloom
    Like a mountain berry: doubtless it is sweet
    To see her thus adored, but there have been
    Moments when all the world was in our praise,
200 Sweeter than any pride of after hours.
    Yet, sun-treader, all hail! From my heart's heart

I bid thee hail! E'en in my wildest dreams,
I proudly feel I would have thrown to dust
The wreaths of fame which seemed o'erhanging me,
To see thee for a moment as thou art.

And if thou livest, if thou lovest, spirit!
Remember me who set this final seal
To wandering thought – that one so pure as thou
Could never die. Remember me who flung
210   All honour from my soul, yet paused and said,
'There is one spark of love remaining yet,
For I have naught in common with him, shapes
Which followed him avoid me, and foul forms
Seek me, which ne'er could fasten on his mind;
And though I feel how low I am to him,
Yet I aim not even to catch a tone
Of harmonies he called profusely up;
So, one gleam still remains, although the last.'
Remember me who praise thee e'en with tears,
220   For never more shall I walk calm with thee;
Thy sweet imaginings are as an air,
A melody some wondrous singer sings,
Which, though it haunt men oft in the still eve,
They dream not to essay; yet it no less
But more is honoured. I was thine in shame,
And now when all thy proud renown is out,
I am a watcher whose eyes have grown dim
With looking for some star which breaks on him
Altered and worn and weak and full of tears.

230   Autumn has come like spring returned to us,
Won from her girlishness; like one returned
A friend that was a lover, nor forgets
The first warm love, but full of sober thoughts
Of fading years; whose soft mouth quivers yet
With the old smile, but yet so changed and still!
And here am I the scoffer, who have probed
Life's vanity, won by a word again
Into my own life – by one little word
Of this sweet friend who lives in loving me,
240   Lives strangely on my thoughts and looks and words,
As fathoms down some nameless ocean thing

Its silent course of quietness and joy.
O dearest, if indeed I tell the past,
Mayst thou forget it as a sad sick dream!
Or if it linger – my lost soul too soon
Sinks to itself and whispers we shall be
But closer linked, two creatures whom the earth
Bears singly, with strange feelings unrevealed
Save to each other; or two lonely things
250 Created by some power whose reign is done,
Having no part in God or his bright world.
I am to sing whilst ebbing day dies soft,
As a lean scholar dies worn o'er his book,
And in the heaven stars steal out one by one
As hunted men steal to their mountain watch.
I must not think, lest this new impulse die
In which I trust; I have no confidence:
So, I will sing on fast as fancies come;
Rudely, the verse being as the mood it paints.

260 I strip my mind bare, whose first elements
I shall unveil – not as they struggled forth
In infancy, nor as they now exist,
When I am grown above them and can rule –
But in that middle stage when they were full
Yet ere I had disposed them to my will;
And then I shall show how these elements
Produced my present state, and what it is.

I am made up of an intensest life,
Of a most clear idea of consciousness
270 Of self, distinct from all its qualities,
From all affections, passions, feelings, powers;
And thus far it exists, if tracked, in all:
But linked, in me, to self-supremacy,
Existing as a centre to all things,
Most potent to create and rule and call
Upon all things to minister to it;
And to a principle of restlessness
Which would be all, have, see, know, taste, feel, all –
This is myself; and I should thus have been
280 Though gifted lower than the meanest soul.

And of my powers, one springs up to save
From utter death a soul with such desire
Confined to clay – of powers the only one
Which marks me – an imagination which
Has been a very angel, coming not
In fitful visions but beside me ever
And never failing me; so, though my mind
Forgets not, not a shred of life forgets,
Yet I can take a secret pride in calling
290   The dark past up to quell it regally.

A mind like this must dissipate itself,
But I have always had one lode-star; now,
As I look back, I see that I have halted
Or hastened as I looked towards that star –
A need, a trust, a yearning after God:
A feeling I have analysed but late,
But it existed, and was reconciled
With a neglect of all I deemed his laws,
Which yet, when seen in others, I abhorred.
300   I felt as one beloved, and so shut in
From fear: and thence I date my trust in signs
And omens, for I saw God everywhere;
And I can only lay it to the fruit
Of a sad after-time that I could doubt
Even his being – e'en the while I felt
His presence, never acted from myself,
Still trusted in a hand to lead me through
All danger; and this feeling ever fought
Against my weakest reason and resolve.

310   And I can love nothing – and this dull truth
Has come the last: but sense supplies a love
Encircling me and mingling with my life.

These make myself: I have long sought in vain
To trace how they were formed by circumstance,
Yet ever found them mould my wildest youth
Where they alone displayed themselves, converted
All objects to their use: now see their course!

They came to me in my first dawn of life
Which passed alone with wisest ancient books
320 All halo-girt with fancies of my own;
And I myself went with the tale – a god
Wandering after beauty, or a giant
Standing vast in the sunset – an old hunter
Talking with gods, or a high-crested chief
Sailing with troops of friends to Tenedos.
I tell you, naught has ever been so clear
As the place, the time, the fashion of those lives:
I had not seen a work of lofty art,
Nor woman's beauty nor sweet nature's face,
330 Yet, I say, never morn broke clear as those
On the dim clustered isles in the blue sea,
The deep groves and white temples and wet caves,
And nothing ever will surprise me now –
Who stood beside the naked Swift-footed,
Who bound my forehead with Proserpine's hair.

And strange it is that I who could so dream
Should e'er have stooped to aim at aught beneath –
Aught low or painful; but I never doubted:
So, as I grew, I rudely shaped my life
340 To my immediate wants; yet strong beneath
Was a vague sense of power though folded up –
A sense that, though those shades and times were past,
Their spirit dwelt in me, with them should rule.

Then came a pause, and long restraint chained down
My soul till it was changed. I lost myself,
And were it not that I so loathe that loss,
I could recall how first I learned to turn
My mind against itself; and the effects
In deeds for which remorse were vain as for
350 The wanderings of delirious dream; yet thence
Came cunning, envy, falsehood, all world's wrong
That spotted me: at length I cleansed my soul.
Yet long world's influence remained; and naught
But the still life I led, apart once more,
Which left me free to seek soul's old delights,
Could e'er have brought me thus far back to peace.

As peace returned, I sought out some pursuit;
And song rose, no new impulse but the one
With which all others best could be combined.
360 My life has not been that of those whose heaven
Was lampless save where poesy shone out;
But as a clime where glittering mountain-tops
And glancing sea and forests steeped in light
Give back reflected the far-flashing sun;
For music (which is earnest of a heaven,
Seeing we know emotions strange by it,
Not else to be revealed,) is like a voice,
A low voice calling fancy, as a friend,
To the green woods in the gay summer time:
370 And she fills all the way with dancing shapes
Which have made painters pale, and they go on
Till stars look at them and winds call to them
As they leave life's path for the twilight world
Where the dead gather. This was not at first,
For I scarce knew what I would do. I had
An impulse but no yearning – only sang.

And first I sang as I in dream have seen
Music wait on a lyrist for some thought,
Yet singing to herself until it came.
380 I turned to those old times and scenes where all
That's beautiful had birth for me, and made
Rude verses on them all; and then I paused –
I had done nothing, so I sought to know
What other minds achieved. No fear outbroke
As on the works of mighty bards I gazed,
In the first joy at finding my own thoughts
Recorded, my own fancies justified,
And their aspirings but my very own.
With them I first explored passion and mind, –
390 All to begin afresh! I rather sought
To rival what I wondered at than form
Creations of my own; if much was light
Lent by the others, much was yet my own.

I paused again: a change was coming – came:
I was no more a boy, the past was breaking
Before the future and like fever worked.

I thought on my new self, and all my powers
Burst out. I dreamed not of restraint, but gazed
On all things: schemes and systems went and came,
400 And I was proud (being vainest of the weak)
In wandering o'er thought's world to seek some one
To be my prize, as if you wandered o'er
The White Way for a star.

                          And my choice fell
Not so much on a system as a man –
On one, whom praise of mine shall not offend,
Who was as calm as beauty, being such
Unto mankind as thou to me, Pauline, –
Believing in them and devoting all
His soul's strength to their winning back to peace;
410 Who sent forth hopes and longings for their sake,
Clothed in all passion's melodies: such first
Caught me and set me, slave of a sweet task,
To disentangle, gather sense from song:
Since, song-inwoven, lurked there words which seemed
A key to a new world, the muttering
Of angels, something yet unguessed by man.
How my heart leapt as still I sought and found
Much there, I felt my own soul had conceived,
But there living and burning! Soon the orb
420 Of his conceptions dawned on me; its praise
Lives in the tongues of men, men's brows are high
When his name means a triumph and a pride,
So, my weak voice may well forbear to shame
What seemed decreed my fate: I threw myself
To meet it, I was vowed to liberty,
Men were to be as gods and earth as heaven,
And I – ah, what a life was mine to prove!
My whole soul rose to meet it. Now, Pauline,
I shall go mad, if I recall that time!

430 Oh let me look back ere I leave for ever
The time which was an hour one fondly waits
For a fair girl that comes a withered hag!
And I was lonely, far from woods and fields,
And amid dullest sights, who should be loose
As a stag; yet I was full of bliss, who lived

With Plato and who had the key to life;
And I had dimly shaped my first attempt,
And many a thought did I build up on thought,
As the wild bee hangs cell to cell; in vain,
440 For I must still advance, no rest for mind.

'Twas in my plan to look on real life,
The life all new to me; my theories
Were firm, so them I left, to look and learn
Mankind, its cares, hopes, fears, its woes and joys;
And, as I pondered on their ways, I sought
How best life's end might be attained – an end
Comprising every joy. I deeply mused.

And suddenly without heart-wreck I awoke
As from a dream: I said ''Twas beautiful,
450 Yet but a dream, and so adieu to it!'
As some world-wanderer sees in a far meadow
Strange towers and high-walled gardens thick with trees,
Where song takes shelter and delicious mirth
From laughing fairy creatures peeping over,
And on the morrow when he comes to lie
For ever 'neath those garden-trees fruit-flushed
Sung round by fairies, all his search is vain.
First went my hopes of perfecting mankind,
Next – faith in them, and then in freedom's self
460 And virtue's self, then my own motives, ends
And aims and loves, and human love went last.
I felt this no decay, because new powers
Rose as old feelings left – wit, mockery,
Light-heartedness; for I had oft been sad,
Mistrusting my resolves, but now I cast
Hope joyously away: I laughed and said
'No more of this!' I must not think: at length
I looked again to see if all went well.

My powers were greater: as some temple seemed
470 My soul, where naught is changed and incense rolls
Around the altar, only God is gone
And some dark spirit sitteth in his seat.
So, I passed through the temple and to me
Knelt troops of shadows, and they cried 'Hail, king!

We serve thee now and thou shalt serve no more!
Call on us, prove us, let us worship thee!'
And I said 'Are ye strong? Let fancy bear me
Far from the past!' And I was borne away,
As Arab birds float sleeping in the wind,
480 O'er deserts, towers and forests, I being calm.
And I said 'I have nursed up energies,
They will prey on me.' And a band knelt low
And cried 'Lord, we are here and we will make
Safe way for thee in thine appointed life!
But look on us!' And I said 'Ye will worship
Me; should my heart not worship too?' They shouted
'Thyself, thou art our king!' So, I stood there
Smiling – oh, vanity of vanities!
For buoyant and rejoicing was the spirit
490 With which I looked out how to end my course;
I felt once more myself, my powers – all mine;
I knew while youth and health so lifted me
That, spite of all life's nothingness, no grief
Came nigh me, I must ever be light-hearted;
And that this knowledge was the only veil
Betwixt joy and despair: so, if age came,
I should be left – a wreck linked to a soul
Yet fluttering, or mind-broken and aware
Of my decay. So a long summer morn
500 Found me; and ere noon came, I had resolved
No age should come on me ere youth was spent,
For I would wear myself out, like that morn
Which wasted not a sunbeam; every hour
I would make mine, and die.

                              And thus I sought
To chain my spirit down which erst I freed
For flights to fame: I said 'The troubled life
Of genius, seen so gay when working forth
Some trusted end, grows sad when all proves vain –
How sad when men have parted with truth's peace
510 For falsest fancy's sake, which waited first
As an obedient spirit when delight
Came without fancy's call: but alters soon,
Comes darkened, seldom, hastens to depart,
Leaving a heavy darkness and warm tears.

But I shall never lose her; she will live
Dearer for such seclusion. I but catch
A hue, a glance of what I sing: so, pain
Is linked with pleasure, for I ne'er may tell
Half the bright sights which dazzle me; but now
520 Mine shall be all the radiance: let them fade
Untold – others shall rise as fair, as fast!
And when all's done, the few dim gleams transferred,' –
(For a new thought sprang up how well it were,
Discarding shadowy hope, to weave such lays
As straight encircle men with praise and love,
So, I should not die utterly, – should bring
One branch from the gold forest, like the knight
Of old tales, witnessing I had been there) –
'And when all's done, how vain seems e'en success –
530 The vaunted influence poets have o'er men!
'Tis a fine thing that one weak as myself
Should sit in his lone room, knowing the words
He utters in his solitude shall move
Men like a swift wind – that though dead and gone,
New eyes shall glisten when his beauteous dreams
Of love come true in happier frames than his.
Ay, the still night brings thoughts like these, but morn
Comes and the mockery again laughs out
At hollow praises, smiles allied to sneers;
540 And my soul's idol ever whispers me
To dwell with him and his unhonoured song:
And I foreknow my spirit, that would press
First in the struggle, fail again to make
All bow enslaved, and I again should sink.

'And then know that this curse will come on us,
To see our idols perish; we may wither,
No marvel, we are clay, but our low fate
Should not extend to those whom trustingly
We sent before into time's yawning gulf
550 To face what dread may lurk in darkness there.
To find the painter's glory pass, and feel
Music can move us not as once, or, worst,
To weep decaying wits ere the frail body
Decays! Naught makes me trust some love is true,
But the delight of the contented lowness

With which I gaze on him I keep for ever
Above me; I to rise and rival him?
Feed his fame rather from my heart's best blood,
Wither unseen that he may flourish still.'

560 Pauline, my soul's friend, thou dost pity yet
How this mood swayed me when that soul found thine,
When I had set myself to live this life,
Defying all past glory. Ere thou camest
I seemed defiant, sweet, for old delights
Had flocked like birds again; music, my life,
Nourished me more than ever; then the lore
Loved for itself and all it shows – that king
Treading the purple calmly to his death,
While round him, like the clouds of eve, all dusk,
570 The giant shades of fate, silently flitting,
Pile the dim outline of the coming doom;
And him sitting alone in blood while friends
Are hunting far in the sunshine; and the boy
With his white breast and brow and clustering curls
Streaked with his mother's blood, but striving hard
To tell his story ere his reason goes.
And when I loved thee as love seemed so oft,
Thou lovedst me indeed: I wondering searched
My heart to find some feeling like such love,
580 Believing I was still much I had been.
Too soon I found all faith had gone from me,
And the late glow of life, like change on clouds,
Proved not the morn-blush widening into day,
But eve faint-coloured by the dying sun
While darkness hastens quickly. I will tell
My state as though 'twere none of mine – despair
Cannot come near us – this it is, my state.

Souls alter not, and mine must still advance;
Strange that I knew not, when I flung away
590 My youth's chief aims, their loss might lead to loss
Of what few I retained, and no resource
Be left me: for behold how changed is all!
I cannot chain my soul: it will not rest
In its clay prison, this most narrow sphere:
It has strange impulse, tendency, desire,

Which nowise I account for nor explain,
But cannot stifle, being bound to trust
All feelings equally, to hear all sides:
How can my life indulge them? yet they live,
600 Referring to some state of life unknown.

My selfishness is satiated not,
It wears me like a flame; my hunger for
All pleasure, howsoe'er minute, grows pain;
I envy – how I envy him whose soul
Turns its whole energies to some one end,
To elevate an aim, pursue success
However mean! So, my still baffled hope
Seeks out abstractions; I would have one joy,
But one in life, so it were wholly mine,
610 One rapture all my soul could fill: and this
Wild feeling places me in dream afar
In some vast country where the eye can see
No end to the far hills and dales bestrewn
With shining towers and towns, till I grow mad
Well-nigh, to know not one abode but holds
Some pleasure, while my soul could grasp the world,
But must remain this vile form's slave. I look
With hope to age at last, which quenching much,
May let me concentrate what sparks it spares.

620 This restlessness of passion meets in me
A craving after knowledge: the sole proof
Of yet commanding will is in that power
Repressed; for I beheld it in its dawn,
The sleepless harpy with just-budding wings,
And I considered whether to forego
All happy ignorant hopes and fears, to live,
Finding a recompense in its wild eyes.
And when I found that I should perish so,
I bade its wild eyes close from me for ever,
630 And I am left alone with old delights;
See! it lies in me a chained thing, still prompt
To serve me if I loose its slightest bond:
I cannot but be proud of my bright slave.

How should this earth's life prove my only sphere?
Can I so narrow sense but that in life
Soul still exceeds it? In their elements
My love outsoars my reason; but since love
Perforce receives its object from this earth
While reason wanders chainless, the few truths
640   Caught from its wanderings have sufficed to quell
Love chained below; then what were love, set free,
Which, with the object it demands, would pass
Reason companioning the seraphim?
No, what I feel may pass all human love
Yet fall far short of what my love should be.
And yet I seem more warped in this than aught,
Myself stands out more hideously: of old
I could forget myself in friendship, fame,
Liberty, nay, in love of mightier souls;
650   But I begin to know what thing hate is –
To sicken and to quiver and grow white –
And I myself have furnished its first prey.
Hate of the weak and ever-wavering will,
The selfishness, the still-decaying frame . . .
But I must never grieve whom wing can waft
Far from such thoughts – as now. Andromeda!
And she is with me: years roll, I shall change,
But change can touch her not – so beautiful
With her fixed eyes, earnest and still, and hair
660   Lifted and spread by the salt-sweeping breeze,
And one red beam, all the storm leaves in heaven,
Resting upon her eyes and hair, such hair,
As she awaits the snake on the wet beach
By the dark rock and the white wave just breaking
At her feet; quite naked and alone; a thing
I doubt not, nor fear for, secure some god
To save will come in thunder from the stars.
Let it pass! Soul requires another change.
I will be gifted with a wondrous mind,
670   Yet sunk by error to men's sympathy,
And in the wane of life, yet only so
As to call up their fears; and there shall come
A time requiring youth's best energies;
And lo, I fling age, sorrow, sickness off,
And rise triumphant, triumph through decay.

And thus it is that I supply the chasm
'Twixt what I am and all I fain would be:
But then to know nothing, to hope for nothing,
To seize on life's dull joys from a strange fear
680 Lest, losing them, all's lost and naught remains!

There's some vile juggle with my reason here;
I feel I but explain to my own loss
These impulses: they live no less the same.
Liberty! what though I despair? my blood
Rose never at a slave's name proud as now.
Oh sympathies, obscured by sophistries! –
Why else have I sought refuge in myself,
But from the woes I saw and could not stay?
Love! is not this to love thee, my Pauline?
690 I cherish prejudice, lest I be left
Utterly loveless? witness my belief
In poets, though sad change has come there too;
No more I leave myself to follow them –
Unconsciously I measure me by them –
Let me forget it: and I cherish most
My love of England – how her name, a word
Of hers in a strange tongue makes my heart beat!

Pauline, could I but break the spell! Not now –
All's fever – but when calm shall come again,
700 I am prepared: I have made life my own.
I would not be content with all the change
One frame should feel, but I have gone in thought
Through all conjuncture, I have lived all life
When it is most alive, where strangest fate
New-shapes it past surmise – the throes of men
Bit by some curse or in the grasps of doom
Half-visible and still-increasing round,
Or crowning their wide being's general aim.

These are wild fancies, but I feel, sweet friend,
710 As one breathing his weakness to the ear
Of pitying angel – dear as a winter flower,
A slight flower growing alone, and offering
Its frail cup of three leaves to the cold sun,
Yet joyous and confiding like the triumph

Of a child: and why am I not worthy thee?
I can live all the life of plants, and gaze
Drowsily on the bees that flit and play,
Or bare my breast for sunbeams which will kill,
Or open in the night of sounds, to look
720 For the dim stars; I can mount with the bird
Leaping airily his pyramid of leaves
And twisted boughs of some tall mountain tree,
Or rise cheerfully springing to the heavens;
Or like a fish breathe deep the morning air
In the misty sun-warm water; or with flower
And tree can smile in light at the sinking sun
Just as the storm comes, as a girl would look
On a departing lover – most serene.

Pauline, come with me, see how I could build
730 A home for us, out of the world, in thought!
I am uplifted: fly with me, Pauline!

Night, and one single ridge of narrow path
Between the sullen river and the woods
Waving and muttering, for the moonless night
Has shaped them into images of life,
Like the uprising of the giant-ghosts,
Looking on earth to know how their sons fare:
Thou art so close by me, the roughest swell
Of wind in the tree-tops hides not the panting
740 Of thy soft breasts. No, we will pass to morning –
Morning, the rocks and valleys and old woods.
How the sun brightens in the mist, and here,
Half in the air, like creatures of the place,
Trusting the element, living on high boughs
That swing in the wind – look at the silver spray
Flung from the foam-sheet of the cataract
Amid the broken rocks! Shall we stay here
With the wild hawks? No, ere the hot noon come,
Dive we down – safe! See this our new retreat
750 Walled in with a sloped mound of matted shrubs,
Dark, tangled, old and green, still sloping down
To a small pool whose waters lie asleep
Amid the trailing boughs turned water-plants:
And tall trees overarch to keep us in,

Breaking the sunbeams into emerald shafts,
And in the dreamy water one small group
Of two or three strange trees are got together
Wondering at all around, as strange beasts herd
Together far from their own land: all wildness,
760 No turf nor moss, for boughs and plants pave all,
And tongues of bank go shelving in the lymph,
Where the pale-throated snake reclines his head,
And old grey stones lie making eddies there,
The wild-mice cross them dry-shod. Deeper in!
Shut thy soft eyes – now look – still deeper in!
This is the very heart of the woods all round
Mountain-like heaped above us; yet even here
One pond of water gleams; far off the river
Sweeps like a sea, barred out from land; but one –
770 One thin clear sheet has overleaped and wound
Into this silent depth, which gained, it lies
Still, as but let by sufferance; the trees bend
O'er it as wild men watch a sleeping girl,
And through their roots long creeping plants out-stretch
Their twined hair, steeped and sparkling; farther on,
Tall rushes and thick flag-knots have combined
To narrow it; so, at length, a silver thread,
It winds, all noiselessly through the deep wood
Till through a cleft-way, through the moss and stone,
780 It joins its parent-river with a shout.

Up for the glowing day, leave the old woods!
See, they part, like a ruined arch: the sky!
Nothing but sky appears, so close the roots
And grass of the hill-top level with the air –
Blue sunny air, where a great cloud floats laden
With light, like a dead whale that white birds pick,
Floating away in the sun in some north sea.
Air, air, fresh life-blood, thin and searching air,
The clear, dear breath of God that loveth us,
790 Where small birds reel and winds take their delight!
Water is beautiful, but not like air:
See, where the solid azure waters lie
Made as of thickened air, and down below,
The fern-ranks like a forest spread themselves
As though each pore could feel the element;

Where the quick glancing serpent winds his way,
Float with me there, Pauline! – but not like air.

Down the hill! Stop – a clump of trees, see, set
On a heap of rock, which look o'er the far plain:
800　So, envious climbing shrubs would mount to rest
And peer from their spread boughs; wide they wave, looking
At the muleteers who whistle on their way,
To the merry chime of morning bells, past all
The little smoking cots, 'mid fields and banks
And copses bright in the sun. My spirit wanders:
Hedgerows for me – those living hedgerows where
The bushes close and clasp above and keep
Thought in – I am concentrated – I feel;
But my soul saddens when it looks beyond:
810　I cannot be immortal, taste all joy.

O God, where do they tend – these struggling aims?*
What would I have? What is this 'sleep' which seems
To bound all? can there be a 'waking' point
Of crowning life? The soul would never rule;
It would be first in all things, it would have
Its utmost pleasure filled, but, that complete,
Commanding, for commanding, sickens it.
The last point I can trace is – rest beneath
Some better essence than itself, in weakness;
820　This is 'myself,' not what I think should be:
And what is that I hunger for but God?

*Je crains bien que mon pauvre ami ne soit pas toujours parfaitement compris dans ce qui reste à lire de cet étrange fragment, mais il est moins propre que tout autre à éclaircir ce qui de sa nature ne peut jamais être que songe et confusion. D'ailleurs je ne sais trop si en cherchant à mieux coordonner certaines parties l'on ne courrait pas le risque de nuire au seul mérite auquel une production si singulière peut prétendre, celui de donner une idée assez précise du genre qu'elle n'a fait qu'ébaucher. Ce début sans prétention, ce remuement des passions qui va d'abord en accroissant et puis s'apaise par degrés, ces élans de l'âme, ce retour soudain sur soi-même, et par-dessus tout, la tournure d'esprit tout particulière de mon ami, rendent les changemens presque impossibles. Les raisons qu'il fait valoir ailleurs, et d'autres encore plus puissantes, ont fait trouver grâce à mes yeux pour cet écrit qu'autrement je lui eusse conseillé de jeter au feu. Je n'en crois pas moins au grand principe de toute composition – à ce principe de Shakespeare, de Rafaelle, de Beethoven, d'où il suit que la concentration des idées est due bien plus à leur conception qu'à leur mise en exécution: j'ai tout lieu de

My God, my God, let me for once look on thee
As though naught else existed, we alone!
And as creation crumbles, my soul's spark
Expands till I can say, – Even from myself
I need thee and I feel thee and I love thee.
I do not plead my rapture in thy works
For love of thee, nor that I feel as one
Who cannot die: but there is that in me
830 Which turns to thee, which loves or which should love.

Why have I girt myself with this hell-dress?
Why have I laboured to put out my life?
Is it not in my nature to adore,
And e'en for all my reason do I not
Feel him, and thank him, and pray to him – now?
Can I forego the trust that he loves me?
Do I not feel a love which only ONE . . .
O thou pale form, so dimly seen, deep-eyed!
I have denied thee calmly – do I not
840 Pant when I read of thy consummate power,
And burn to see thy calm pure truths out-flash
The brightest gleams of earth's philosophy?
Do I not shake to hear aught question thee?
If I am erring save me, madden me,
Take from me powers and pleasures, let me die
Ages, so I see thee! I am knit round
As with a charm by sin and lust and pride,
Yet though my wandering dreams have seen all shapes
Of strange delight, oft have I stood by thee –
850 Have I been keeping lonely watch with thee
In the damp night by weeping Olivet,

---

craindre que la première de ces qualités ne soit encore étrangère à mon ami, et je doute fort qu'un redoublement de travail lui fasse acquérir la seconde. Le mieux serait de brûler ceci; mais que faire?

Je crois que dans ce qui suit il fait allusion à un certain examen qu'il fit autrefois de l'âme, ou plutôt de son âme, pour découvrir la suite des objets auxquels il lui serait possible d'atteindre, et dont chacun une fois obtenu devait former une espèce de plateau d'où l'on pouvait apercevoir d'autres buts, d'autres projets, d'autres jouissances qui, à leur tour, devaient être surmontés. Il en résultait que l'oubli et le sommeil devaient tout terminer. Cette idée, que je ne saisis pas parfaitement, lui est peut-être aussi inintelligible qu'à moi.

Or leaning on thy bosom, proudly less,
Or dying with thee on the lonely cross,
Or witnessing thine outburst from the tomb.

A mortal, sin's familiar friend, doth here
Avow that he will give all earth's reward,
But to believe and humbly teach the faith,
In suffering and poverty and shame,
Only believing he is not unloved.

860 And now, my Pauline, I am thine for ever!
I feel the spirit which has buoyed me up
Desert me, and old shades are gathering fast;
Yet while the last light waits, I would say much,
This chiefly, it is gain that I have said
Somewhat of love I ever felt for thee
But seldom told; our hearts so beat together
That speech seemed mockery; but when dark hours come,
And joy departs, and thou, sweet, deem'st it strange
A sorrow moves me, thou canst not remove,
870 Look on this lay I dedicate to thee,
Which through thee I began, which thus I end,
Collecting the last gleams to strive to tell
How I am thine, and more than ever now
That I sink fast: yet though I deeplier sink,
No less song proves one word has brought me bliss,
Another still may win bliss surely back.
Thou knowest, dear, I could not think all calm,
For fancies followed thought and bore me off,
And left all indistinct; ere one was caught
880 Another glanced; so, dazzled by my wealth,
I knew not which to leave nor which to choose,
For all so floated, naught was fixed and firm.
And then thou said'st a perfect bard was one
Who chronicled the stages of all life,
And so thou bad'st me shadow this first stage.
'Tis done, and even now I recognize
The shift, the change from last to past – discern
Faintly how life is truth and truth is good.
And why thou must be mine is, that e'en now
890 In the dim hush of night, that I have done,
Despite the sad forebodings, love looks through –

Whispers, – E'en at the last I have her still,
With her delicious eyes as clear as heaven
When rain in a quick shower has beat down mist,
And clouds float white above like broods of swans.
How the blood lies upon her cheek, outspread
As thinned by kisses! only in her lips
It wells and pulses like a living thing,
And her neck looks like marble misted o'er
900   With love-breath, – a Pauline from heights above,
Stooping beneath me, looking up – one look
As I might kill her and be loved the more.

So, love me – me, Pauline, and naught but me,
Never leave loving! Words are wild and weak,
Believe them not, Pauline! I stained myself
But to behold thee purer by my side,
To show thou art my breath, my life, a last
Resource, an éxtreme want: never believe
Aught better could so look on thee; nor seek
910   Again the world of good thoughts left for mine!
There were bright troops of undiscovered suns,
Each equal in their radiant course; there were
Clusters of far fair isles which ocean kept
For his own joy, and his waves broke on them
Without a choice; and there was a dim crowd
Of visions, each a part of some grand whole:
And one star left his peers and came with peace
Upon a storm, and all eyes pined for him;
And one isle harboured a sea-beaten ship,
920   And the crew wandered in its bowers and plucked
Its fruits and gave up all their hopes of home;
And one dream came to a pale poet's sleep,
And he said, 'I am singled out by God,
No sin must touch me.' Words are wild and weak,
But what they would express is, – Leave me not,
Still sit by me with beating breast and hair
Loosened, be watching earnest by my side,
Turning my books or kissing me when I
Look up – like summer wind! Be still to me
930   A help to music's mystery which mind fails
To fathom, its solution, no mere clue!
O reason's pedantry, life's rule prescribed!

I hopeless, I the loveless, hope and love.
Wiser and better, know me now, not when
You loved me as I was. Smile not! I have
Much yet to dawn on you, to gladden you.

No more of the past! I'll look within no more.
I have too trusted my own lawless wants,
Too trusted my vain self, vague intuition –
940   Draining soul's wine alone in the still night,
And seeing how, as gathering films arose,
As by an inspiration life seemed bare
And grinning in its vanity, while ends
Foul to be dreamed of, smiled at me as fixed
And fair, while others changed from fair to foul
As a young witch turns an old hag at night.
No more of this! We will go hand in hand,
I with thee, even as a child – love's slave,
Looking no farther than his liege commands.

950   And thou hast chosen where this life shall be:
The land which gave me thee shall be our home,
Where nature lies all wild amid her lakes
And snow-swathed mountains and vast pines begirt
With ropes of snow – where nature lies all bare,
Suffering none to view her but a race
Or stinted or deformed, like the mute dwarfs
Which wait upon a naked Indian queen.
And there (the time being when the heavens are thick
With storm) I'll sit with thee while thou dost sing
960   Thy native songs, gay as a desert bird
Which crieth as it flies for perfect joy,
Or telling me old stories of dead knights;
Or I will read great lays to thee – how she,
The fair pale sister, went to her chill grave
With power to love and to be loved and live:
Or we will go together, like twin gods
Of the infernal world, with scented lamp
Over the dead, to call and to awake,
Over the unshaped images which lie
970   Within my mind's cave: only leaving all,
That tells of the past doubt. So, when spring comes
With sunshine back again like an old smile,

And the fresh waters and awakened birds
And budding woods await us, I shall be
Prepared, and we will question life once more,
Till its old sense shall come renewed by change,
Like some clear thought which harsh words veiled before;
Feeling God loves us, and that all which errs
Is but a dream which death will dissipate.
980   And then what need of longer exile? Seek
My England, and, again there, calm approach
All I once fled from, calmly look on those
The works of my past weakness, as one views
Some scene where danger met him long before.
Ah that such pleasant life should be but dreamed!

But whate'er come of it, and though it fade,
And though ere the cold morning all be gone,
As it may be; – though music wait to wile,
And strange eyes and bright wine lure, laugh like sin
990   Which steals back softly on a soul half saved,
And I the first deny, decry, despise,
With this avowal, these intents so fair, –
Still be it all my own, this moment's pride!
No less I make an end in perfect joy.
E'en in my brightest time, a lurking fear
Possessed me: I well knew my weak resolves,
I felt the witchery that makes mind sleep
Over its treasure, as one half afraid
To make his riches definite: but now
1000   These feelings shall not utterly be lost,
I shall not know again that nameless care
Lest, leaving all undone in youth, some new
And undreamed end reveal itself too late:
For this song shall remain to tell for ever
That when I lost all hope of such a change,
Suddenly beauty rose on me again.
No less I make an end in perfect joy,
For I, who thus again was visited,
Shall doubt not many another bliss awaits,
1010   And, though this weak soul sink and darkness whelm,
Some little word shall light it, raise aloft,
To where I clearlier see and better love,
As I again go o'er the tracts of thought

Like one who has a right, and I shall live
With poets, calmer, purer still each time,
And beauteous shapes will come for me to seize,
And unknown secrets will be trusted me
Which were denied the waverer once; but now
I shall be priest and prophet as of old.

1020 Sun-treader, I believe in God and truth
And love; and as one just escaped from death
Would bind himself in bands of friends to feel
He lives indeed, so, I would lean on thee!
Thou must be ever with me, most in gloom
If such must come, but chiefly when I die,
For I seem, dying, as one going in the dark
To fight a giant: but live thou for ever,
And be to all what thou hast been to me!
All in whom this wakes pleasant thoughts of me
1030 Know my last state is happy, free from doubt
Or touch of fear. Love me and wish me well.

Richmond : 22 October 1832

Paracelsus

1835

Inscribed to
AMÉDÉE DE RIPERT-MONCLAR
by his affectionate friend

R.B.

London : 15 March 1835

PERSONS

Aureolus Paracelsus, a student
Festus and *Michal*, his friends
Aprile, an Italian poet

Paracelsus

PART I
PARACELSUS ASPIRES

Scene: Würzburg; a garden in the environs. 1512.

FESTUS, PARACELSUS, MICHAL

PARACELSUS: Come close to me, dear friends; still closer; thus!
  Close to the heart which, though long time roll by
  Ere it again beat quicker, pressed to yours,
  As now it beats – perchance a long, long time –
  At least henceforth your memories shall make
  Quiet and fragrant as befits their home.
  Nor shall my memory want a home in yours –
  Alas, that it requires too well such free
  Forgiving love as shall embalm it there!
10 For if you would remember me aright,
  As I was born to be, you must forget
  All fitful strange and moody waywardness
  Which e'er confused my better spirit, to dwell
  Only on moments such as these, dear friends!
  – My heart no truer, but my words and ways
  More true to it: as Michal, some months hence,
  Will say, 'this autumn was a pleasant time,'
  For some few sunny days; and overlook
  Its bleak wind, hankering after pining leaves.
20 Autumn would fain be sunny; I would look
  Liker my nature's truth: and both are frail,
  And both beloved, for all our frailty.
MICHAL: Aureole!
PARACELSUS: Drop by drop! she is weeping like a child!
  Not so! I am content – more than content;
  Nay, autumn wins you best by this its mute
  Appeal to sympathy for its decay:
  Look up, sweet Michal, nor esteem the less
  Your stained and drooping vines their grapes bow down,
  Nor blame those creaking trees bent with their fruit,
30 That apple-tree with a rare after-birth
  Of peeping blooms sprinkled its wealth among!
  Then for the winds – what wind that ever raved

Shall vex that ash which overlooks you both,
So proud it wears its berries? Ah, at length,
The old smile meet for her, the lady of this
Sequestered nest! – this kingdom, limited
Alone by one old populous green wall
Tenanted by the ever-busy flies,
Grey crickets and shy lizards and quick spiders,
40 Each family of the silver-threaded moss –
Which, look through near, this way, and it appears
A stubble-field or a cane-brake, a marsh
Of bulrush whitening in the sun: laugh now!
Fancy the crickets, each one in his house,
Looking out, wondering at the world – or best,
Yon painted snail with his gay shell of dew,
Travelling to see the glossy balls high up
Hung by the caterpillar, like gold lamps.
MICHAL: In truth we have lived carelessly and well.
50 PARACELSUS: And shall, my perfect pair! – each, trust me, born
For the other; nay, your very hair, when mixed,
Is of one hue. For where save in this nook
Shall you two walk, when I am far away,
And wish me prosperous fortune? Stay: that plant
Shall never wave its tangles lightly and softly,
As a queen's languid and imperial arm
Which scatters crowns among her lovers, but you
Shall be reminded to predict to me
Some great success! Ah see, the sun sinks broad
60 Behind Saint Saviour's: wholly gone, at last!
FESTUS: Now, Aureole, stay those wandering eyes awhile!
You are ours tonight, at least; and while you spoke
Of Michal and her tears, I thought that none
Could willing leave what he so seemed to love:
But that last look destroys my dream – that look
As if, where'er you gazed, there stood a star!
How far was Würzburg with its church and spire
And garden-walls and all things they contain,
From that look's far alighting?
PARACELSUS: I but spoke
70 And looked alike from simple joy to see
The beings I love best, shut in so well
From all rude chances like to be my lot,
That, when afar, my weary spirit, – disposed

To lose awhile its care in soothing thoughts
Of them, their pleasant features, looks and words, –
Needs never hesitate, nor apprehend
Encroaching trouble may have reached them too,
Nor have recourse to fancy's busy aid
And fashion even a wish in their behalf
80 Beyond what they possess already here;
But, unobstructed, may at once forget
Itself in them, assured how well they fare.
Beside, this Festus knows he holds me one
Whom quiet and its charms arrest in vain,
One scarce aware of all the joys I quit,
Too filled with airy hopes to make account
Of soft delights his own heart garners up:
Whereas behold how much our sense of all
That's beauteous proves alike! When Festus learns
90 That every common pleasure of the world
Affects me as himself; that I have just
As varied appetite for joy derived
From common things; a stake in life, in short,
Like his; a stake which rash pursuit of aims
That life affords not, would as soon destroy; –
He may convince himself that, this in view,
I shall act well advised. And last, because,
Though heaven and earth and all things were at stake,
Sweet Michal must not weep, our parting eve.
100 FESTUS: True: and the eve is deepening, and we sit
As little anxious to begin our talk
As though tomorrow I could hint of it
As we paced arm-in-arm the cheerful town
At sun-dawn; or could whisper it by fits
(Trithemius busied with his class the while)
In that dim chamber where the noon-streaks peer
Half-frightened by the awful tomes around;
Or in some grassy lane unbosom all
From even-blush to midnight: but, tomorrow!
110 Have I full leave to tell my inmost mind?
We have been brothers, and henceforth the world
Will rise between us: – all my freest mind?
'Tis the last night, dear Aureole!
PARACELSUS: Oh, say on!
Devise some test of love, some arduous feat

To be performed for you: say on! If night
Be spent the while, the better! Recall how oft
My wondrous plans and dreams and hopes and fears
Have – never wearied you, oh no! – as I
Recall, and never vividly as now,
120   Your true affection, born when Einsiedeln
And its green hills were all the world to us;
And still increasing to this night which ends
My further stay at Würzburg. Oh, one day
You shall be very proud! Say on, dear friends!
   FESTUS: In truth? 'Tis for my proper peace, indeed,
Rather than yours; for vain all projects seem
To stay your course: I said my latest hope
Is fading even now. A story tells
Of some far embassy dispatched to win
130   The favour of an eastern king, and how
The gifts they offered proved but dazzling dust
Shed from the ore-beds native to his clime.
Just so, the value of repose and love,
I meant should tempt you, better far than I
You seem to comprehend; and yet desist
No whit from projects where repose nor love
Has part.
   PARACELSUS: Once more? Alas! As I foretold.
   FESTUS: A solitary briar the bank puts forth
To save our swan's nest floating out to sea.
140   PARACELSUS: Dear Festus, hear me. What is it you wish?
That I should lay aside my heart's pursuit,
Abandon the sole ends for which I live,
Reject God's great commission, and so die!
You bid me listen for your true love's sake:
Yet how has grown that love? Even in a long
And patient cherishing of the self-same spirit
It now would quell; as though a mother hoped
To stay the lusty manhood of the child
Once weak upon her knees. I was not born
150   Informed and fearless from the first, but shrank
From aught which marked me out apart from men:
I would have lived their life, and died their death,
Lost in their ranks, eluding destiny:
But you first guided me through doubt and fear,
Taught me to know mankind and know myself;

And now that I am strong and full of hope,
That, from my soul, I can reject all aims
Save those your earnest words made plain to me,
Now that I touch the brink of my design,
160   When I would have a triumph in their eyes,
A glad cheer in their voices – Michal weeps,
And Festus ponders gravely!

FESTUS: When you deign
To hear my purpose . . .

PARACELSUS: Hear it? I can say
Beforehand all this evening's conference!
'Tis this way, Michal, that he uses: first,
Or he declares, or I, the leading points
Of our best scheme of life, what is man's end
And what God's will; no two faiths e'er agreed
As his with mine. Next, each of us allows
170   Faith should be acted on as best we may;
Accordingly, I venture to submit
My plan, in lack of better, for pursuing
The path which God's will seems to authorize.
Well, he discerns much good in it, avows
This motive worthy, that hope plausible,
A danger here to be avoided, there
An oversight to be repaired: in fine
Our two minds go together – all the good
Approved by him, I gladly recognize,
180   All he counts bad, I thankfully discard,
And naught forbids my looking up at last
For some stray comfort in his cautious brow.
When, lo! I learn that, spite of all, there lurks
Some innate and inexplicable germ
Of failure in my scheme; so that at last
It all amounts to this – the sovereign proof
That we devote ourselves to God, is seen
In living just as though no God there were;
A life which, prompted by the sad and blind
190   Folly of man, Festus abhors the most;
But which these tenets sanctify at once,
Though to less subtle wits it seems the same,
Consider it how they may.

MICHAL: Is it so, Festus?
He speaks so calmly and kindly: is it so?

PARACELSUS: Reject those glorious visions of God's love
And man's design; laugh loud that God should send
Vast longings to direct us; say how soon
Power satiates these, or lust, or gold; I know
The world's cry well, and how to answer it.
200   But this ambiguous warfare ...
FESTUS: ... Wearies so
That you will grant no last leave to your friend
To urge it? – for his sake, not yours? I wish
To send my soul in good hopes after you;
Never to sorrow that uncertain words
Erringly apprehended, a new creed
Ill understood, begot rash trust in you,
Had share in your undoing.
PARACELSUS: Choose your side,
Hold or renounce: but meanwhile blame me not
Because I dare to act on your own views,
210   Nor shrink when they point onward, nor espy
A peril where they most ensure success.
FESTUS: Prove that to me – but that! Prove you abide
Within their warrant, nor presumptuous boast
God's labour laid on you; prove, all you covet
A mortal may expect; and, most of all,
Prove the strange course you now affect, will lead
To its attainment – and I bid you speed,
Nay, count the minutes till you venture forth!
You smile; but I had gathered from slow thought –
220   Much musing on the fortunes of my friend –
Matter I deemed could not be urged in vain;
But it all leaves me at my need: in shreds
And fragments I must venture what remains.
MICHAL: Ask at once, Festus, wherefore he should scorn ...
FESTUS: Stay, Michal: Aureole, I speak guardedly
And gravely, knowing well, whate'er your error,
This is no ill-considered choice of yours,
No sudden fancy of an ardent boy.
Not from your own confiding words alone
230   Am I aware your passionate heart long since
Gave birth to, nourished and at length matures
This scheme. I will not speak of Einsiedeln,
Where I was born your elder by some years
Only to watch you fully from the first:

In all beside, our mutual tasks were fixed
Even then – 'twas mine to have you in my view
As you had your own soul and those intents
Which filled it when, to crown your dearest wish,
With a tumultuous heart, you left with me
240   Our childhood's home to join the favoured few
Whom, here, Trithemius condescends to teach
A portion of his lore: and not one youth
Of those so favoured, whom you now despise,
Came earnest as you came, resolved, like you,
To grasp all, and retain all, and deserve
By patient toil a wide renown like his.
Now, this new ardour which supplants the old
I watched, too; 'twas significant and strange,
In one matched to his soul's content at length
250   With rivals in the search for wisdom's prize,
To see the sudden pause, the total change;
From contest, the transition to repose –
From pressing onward as his fellows pressed,
To a blank idleness, yet most unlike
The dull stagnation of a soul, content,
Once foiled, to leave betimes a thriveless quest.
That careless bearing, free from all pretence
Even of contempt for what it ceased to seek –
Smiling humility, praising much, yet waiving
260   What it professed to praise – though not so well
Maintained but that rare outbreaks, fierce and brief,
Revealed the hidden scorn, as quickly curbed.
That ostentatious show of past defeat,
That ready acquiescence in contempt,
I deemed no other than the letting go
His shivered sword, of one about to spring
Upon his foe's throat; but it was not thus:
Not that way looked your brooding purpose then.
For after-signs disclosed, what you confirmed,
270   That you prepared to task to the uttermost
Your strength, in furtherance of a certain aim
Which – while it bore the name your rivals gave
Their own most puny efforts – was so vast
In scope that it included their best flights,
Combined them, and desired to gain one prize
In place of many, – the secret of the world,

Of man, and man's true purpose, path and fate.
– That you, not nursing as a mere vague dream
This purpose, with the sages of the past,
280 Have struck upon a way to this, if all
You trust be true, which following, heart and soul,
You, if a man may, dare aspire to KNOW:
And that this aim shall differ from a host
Of aims alike in character and kind,
Mostly in this, – that in itself alone
Shall its reward be, not an alien end
Blending therewith; no hope nor fear nor joy
Nor woe, to elsewhere move you, but this pure
Devotion to sustain you or betray:
290 Thus you aspire.

PARACELSUS: You shall not state it thus:
I should not differ from the dreamy crew
You speak of. I profess no other share
In the selection of my lot, than this
My ready answer to the will of God
Who summons me to be his organ. All
Whose innate strength supports them shall succeed
No better than the sages.

FESTUS: Such the aim, then,
God sets before you; and 'tis doubtless need
That he appoint no less the way of praise
300 Than the desire to praise; for, though I hold
With you, the setting forth such praise to be
The natural end and service of a man,
And hold such praise is best attained when man
Attains the general welfare of his kind –
Yet this, the end, is not the instrument.
Presume not to serve God apart from such
Appointed channel as he wills shall gather
Imperfect tributes, for that sole obedience
Valued perchance! He seeks not that his altars
310 Blaze, careless how, so that they do but blaze.
Suppose this, then; that God selected you
To KNOW (heed well your answers, for my faith
Shall meet implicitly what they affirm)
I cannot think you dare annex to such
Selection aught beyond a steadfast will,
An intense hope; nor let your gifts create

Scorn or neglect of ordinary means
Conducive to success, make destiny
Dispense with man's endeavour. Now, dare you search
320   Your inmost heart, and candidly avow
Whether you have not rather wild desire
For this distinction than security
Of its existence? whether you discern
The path to the fulfilment of your purpose
Clear as that purpose – and again, that purpose
Clear as your yearning to be singled out
For its pursuer. Dare you answer this?
    PARACELSUS [*after a pause*]: No, I have naught to fear! Who
        will may know
The secret'st workings of my soul. What though
330   It be so? – if indeed the strong desire
Eclipse the aim in me? – if splendour break
Upon the outset of my path alone,
And duskest shade succeed? What fairer seal
Shall I require to my authentic mission
Than this fierce energy? – this instinct striving
Because its nature is to strive? – enticed
By the security of no broad course,
Without success forever in its eyes!
How know I else such glorious fate my own,
340   But in the restless irresistible force
That works within me? Is it for human will
To institute such impulses? – still less,
To disregard their promptings! What should I
Do, kept among you all; your loves, your cares,
Your life – all to be mine? Be sure that God
Ne'er dooms to waste the strength he deigns impart!
Ask the geier-eagle why she stoops at once
Into the vast and unexplored abyss,
What full-grown power informs her from the first,
350   Why she not marvels, strenuously beating
The silent boundless regions of the sky!
Be sure they sleep not whom God needs! Nor fear
Their holding light his charge, when every hour
That finds that charge delayed, is a new death.
This for the faith in which I trust; and hence
I can abjure so well the idle arts
These pedants strive to learn and teach; Black Arts,

Great Works, the Secret and Sublime, forsooth –
Let others prize: too intimate a tie
360   Connects me with our God! A sullen fiend
To do my bidding, fallen and hateful sprites
To help me – what are these, at best, beside
God helping, God directing everywhere,
So that the earth shall yield her secrets up,
And every object there be charged to strike,
Teach, gratify her master God appoints?
And I am young, my Festus, happy and free!
I can devote myself; I have a life
To give; I, singled out for this, the One!
370   Think, think! the wide East, where all Wisdom sprung;
The bright South, where she dwelt; the hopeful North,
All are passed o'er – it lights on me! 'Tis time
New hopes should animate the world, new light
Should dawn from new revealings to a race
Weighed down so long, forgotten so long; thus shall
The heaven reserved for us at last receive
Creatures whom no unwonted splendours blind,
But ardent to confront the unclouded blaze
Whose beams not seldom blessed their pilgrimage,
380   Not seldom glorified their life below.
FESTUS: My words have their old fate and make faint stand
Against your glowing periods. Call this, truth –
Why not pursue it in a fast retreat,
Some one of Learning's many palaces,
After approved example? – seeking there
Calm converse with the great dead, soul to soul,
Who laid up treasure with the like intent
– So lift yourself into their airy place,
And fill out full their unfulfilled careers,
390   Unravelling the knots their baffled skill
Pronounced inextricable, true! – but left
Far less confused. A fresh eye, a fresh hand,
Might do much at their vigour's waning-point;
Succeeding with new-breathed new-hearted force,
As at old games the runner snatched the torch
From runner still: this way success might be.
But you have coupled with your enterprise,
An arbitrary self-repugnant scheme
Of seeking it in strange and untried paths.

400 What books are in the desert? Writes the sea
The secret of her yearning in vast caves
Where yours will fall the first of human feet?
Has wisdom sat there and recorded aught
You press to read? Why turn aside from her
To visit, where her vesture never glanced,
Now – solitudes consigned to barrenness
By God's decree, which who shall dare impugn?
Now – ruins where she paused but would not stay,
Old ravaged cities that, renouncing her,
410 She called an endless curse on, so it came:
Or worst of all, now – men you visit, men,
Ignoblest troops who never heard her voice
Or hate it, men without one gift from Rome
Or Athens, – these shall Aureole's teachers be!
Rejecting past example, practice, precept,
Aidless 'mid these he thinks to stand alone:
Thick like a glory round the Stagirite
Your rivals throng, the sages: here stand you!
Whatever you may protest, knowledge is not
420 Paramount in your love; or for her sake
You would collect all help from every source –
Rival, assistant, friend, foe, all would merge
In the broad class of those who showed her haunts,
And those who showed them not.

PARACELSUS: What shall I say?
Festus, from childhood I have been possessed
By a fire – by a true fire, or faint or fierce,
As from without some master, so it seemed,
Repressed or urged its current: this but ill
Expresses what I would convey: but rather
430 I will believe an angel ruled me thus,
Than that my soul's own workings, own high nature,
So became manifest. I knew not then
What whispered in the evening, and spoke out
At midnight. If some mortal, born too soon,
Were laid away in some great trance – the ages
Coming and going all the while – till dawned
His true time's advent; and could then record
The words they spoke who kept watch by his bed, –
Then I might tell more of the breath so light
440 Upon my eyelids, and the fingers light

Among my hair. Youth is confused; yet never
So dull was I but, when that spirit passed,
I turned to him, scarce consciously, as turns
A water-snake when fairies cross his sleep.
And having this within me and about me
While Einsiedeln, its mountains, lakes and woods
Confined me – what oppressive joy was mine
When life grew plain, and I first viewed the thronged,
The everlasting concourse of mankind!
450   Believe that ere I joined them, ere I knew
The purpose of the pageant, or the place
Consigned me in its ranks – while, just awake,
Wonder was freshest and delight most pure –
'Twas then that least supportable appeared
A station with the brightest of the crowd,
A portion with the proudest of them all.
And from the tumult in my breast, this only
Could I collect, that I must thenceforth die
Or elevate myself far, far above
460   The gorgeous spectacle. I seemed to long
At once to trample on, yet save mankind,
To make some unexampled sacrifice
In their behalf, to wring some wondrous good
From heaven or earth for them, to perish, winning
Eternal weal in the act: as who should dare
Pluck out the angry thunder from its cloud,
That, all its gathered flame discharged on him,
No storm might threaten summer's azure sleep:
Yet never to be mixed with men so much
470   As to have part even in my own work, share
In my own largess. Once the feat achieved,
I would withdraw from their officious praise,
Would gently put aside their prófuse thanks.
Like some knight traversing a wilderness,
Who, on his way, may chance to free a tribe
Of desert-people from their dragon-foe;
When all the swarthy race press round to kiss
His feet, and choose him for their king, and yield
Their poor tents, pitched among the sand-hills, for
480   His realm: and he points, smiling, to his scarf
Heavy with riveled gold, his burgonet
Gay set with twinkling stones – and to the East,

Where these must be displayed!
FESTUS: Good: let us hear
No more about your nature, 'which first shrank
From all that marked you out apart from men!'
PARACELSUS: I touch on that; these words but analyse
The first mad impulse: 'twas as brief as fond,
For as I gazed again upon the show,
I soon distinguished here and there a shape
490   Palm-wreathed and radiant, forehead and full eye.
Well pleased was I their state should thus at once
Interpret my own thoughts: – 'Behold the clue
To all,' I rashly said, 'and what I pine
To do, these have accomplished: we are peers.
They know and therefore rule: I, too, will know!'
You were beside me, Festus, as you say;
You saw me plunge in their pursuits whom fame
Is lavish to attest the lords of mind,
Not pausing to make sure the prize in view
500   Would satiate my cravings when obtained,
But since they strove I strove. Then came a slow
And strangling failure. We aspired alike,
Yet not the meanest plodder, Tritheim counts
A marvel, but was all-sufficient, strong,
Or staggered only at his own vast wits;
While I was restless, nothing satisfied,
Distrustful, most perplexed. I would slur over
That struggle; suffice it, that I loathed myself
As weak compared with them, yet felt somehow
510   A mighty power was brooding, taking shape
Within me; and this lasted till one night
When, as I sat revolving it and more,
A still voice from without said – 'Seest thou not,
Desponding child, whence spring defeat and loss?
Even from thy strength. Consider: hast thou gazed
Presumptuously on wisdom's countenance,
No veil between; and can thy faltering hands,
Unguided by the brain the sight absorbs,
Pursue their task as earnest blinkers do
520   Whom radiance ne'er distracted? Live their life
If thou wouldst share their fortune, choose their eyes
Unfed by splendour. Let each task present
Its petty good to thee. Waste not thy gifts

In profitless waiting for the gods' descent,
But have some idol of thine own to dress
With their array. Know, not for knowing's sake,
But to become a star to men for ever;
Know, for the gain it gets, the praise it brings,
The wonder it inspires, the love it breeds:
530 Look one step onward, and secure that step!'
And I smiled as one never smiles but once,
Then first discovering my own aim's extent,
Which sought to comprehend the works of God,
And God himself, and all God's intercourse
With the human mind; I understood, no less,
My fellows' studies, whose true worth I saw,
But smiled not, well aware who stood by me.
And softer came the voice – 'There is a way:
'Tis hard for flesh to tread therein, imbued
540 With frailty – hopeless, if indulgence first
Have ripened inborn germs of sin to strength:
Wilt thou adventure for my sake and man's,
Apart from all reward?' And last it breathed –
'Be happy, my good soldier; I am by thee,
Be sure, even to the end!' – I answered not,
Knowing him. As he spoke, I was endued
With comprehension and a steadfast will;
And when he ceased, my brow was sealed his own.
If there took place no special change in me,
550 How comes it all things wore a different hue
Thenceforward? – pregnant with vast consequence,
Teeming with grand result, loaded with fate?
So that when, quailing at the mighty range
Of secret truths which yearn for birth, I haste
To contemplate undazzled some one truth,
Its bearings and effects alone – at once
What was a speck expands into a star,
Asking a life to pass exploring thus,
Till I near craze. I go to prove my soul!
560 I see my way as birds their trackless way.
I shall arrive! what time, what circuit first,
I ask not: but unless God send his hail
Or blinding fireballs, sleet or stifling snow,
In some time, his good time, I shall arrive:
He guides me and the bird. In his good time!

MICHAL: Vex him no further, Festus; it is so!
FESTUS: Just thus you help me ever. This would hold
 Were it the trackless air, and not a path
 Inviting you, distinct with footprints yet
570 Of many a mighty marcher gone that way.
 You may have purer views than theirs, perhaps,
 But they were famous in their day – the proofs
 Remain. At least accept the light they lend.
PARACELSUS: Their light! the sum of all is briefly this:
 They laboured and grew famous, and the fruits
 Are best seen in a dark and groaning earth
 Given over to a blind and endless strife
 With evils, what of all their lore abates?
 No; I reject and spurn them utterly
580 And all they teach. Shall I still sit beside
 Their dry wells, with a white lip and filmed eye,
 While in the distance heaven is blue above
 Mountains where sleep the unsunned tarns?
FESTUS: And yet
 As strong delusions have prevailed ere now.
 Men have set out as gallantly to seek
 Their ruin. I have heard of such: yourself
 Avow all hitherto have failed and fallen.
MICHAL: Nay, Festus, when but as the pilgrims faint
 Through the drear way, do you expect to see
590 Their city dawn amid the clouds afar?
PARACELSUS: Ay, sounds it not like some old well-known tale?
 For me, I estimate their works and them
 So rightly, that at times I almost dream
 I too have spent a life the sages' way,
 And tread once more familiar paths. Perchance
 I perished in an arrogant self-reliance
 Ages ago; and in that act, a prayer
 For one more chance went up so earnest, so
 Instinct with better light let in by death,
600 That life was blotted out – not so completely
 But scattered wrecks enough of it remain,
 Dim memories, as now, when once more seems
 The goal in sight again. All which, indeed,
 Is foolish, and only means – the flesh I wear,
 The earth I tread, are not more clear to me
 Than my belief, explained to you or no.

FESTUS: And who am I, to challenge and dispute
    That clear belief? I will divest all fear.
MICHAL: Then Aureole is God's commissary! he shall
610   Be great and grand – and all for us!
PARACELSUS: No, sweet!
    Not great and grand. If I can serve mankind
    'Tis well; but there our intercourse must end:
    I never will be served by those I serve.
FESTUS: Look well to this; here is a plague-spot, here,
    Disguise it how you may! 'Tis true, you utter
    This scorn while by our side and loving us;
    'Tis but a spot as yet: but it will break
    Into a hideous blotch if overlooked.
    How can that course be safe which from the first
620   Produces carelessness to human love?
    It seems you have abjured the helps which men
    Who overpass their kind, as you would do,
    Have humbly sought; I dare not thoroughly probe
    This matter, lest I learn too much. Let be
    That popular praise would little instigate
    Your efforts, nor particular approval
    Reward you; put reward aside; alone
    You shall go forth upon your arduous task,
    None shall assist you, none partake your toil,
630   None share your triumph: still you must retain
    Some one to cast your glory on, to share
    Your rapture with. Were I elect like you,
    I would encircle me with love, and raise
    A rampart of my fellows; it should seem
    Impossible for me to fail, so watched
    By gentle friends who made my cause their own.
    They should ward off fate's envy – the great gift,
    Extravagant when claimed by me alone,
    Being so a gift to them as well as me.
640   If danger daunted me or ease seduced,
    How calmly their sad eyes should gaze reproach!
MICHAL: O Aureole, can I sing when all alone,
    Without first calling, in my fancy, both
    To listen by my side – even I! And you?
    Do you not feel this? Say that you feel this!
PARACELSUS: I feel 'tis pleasant that my aims, at length
    Allowed their weight, should be supposed to need

A further strengthening in these goodly helps!
My course allures for its own sake, its sole
650 Intrinsic worth; and ne'er shall boat of mine
Adventure forth for gold and apes at once.
Your sages say, 'if human, therefore weak':
If weak, more need to give myself entire
To my pursuit; and by its side, all else . . .
No matter! I deny myself but little
In waiving all assistance save its own.
Would there were some real sacrifice to make!
Your friends the sages threw their joys away,
While I must be content with keeping mine.
660 FESTUS: But do not cut yourself from human weal!
You cannot thrive – a man that dares affect
To spend his life in service to his kind
For no reward of theirs, unbound to them
By any tie; nor do so, Aureole! No –
There are strange punishments for such. Give up
(Although no visible good flow thence) some part
Of the glory to another; hiding thus,
Even from yourself, that all is for yourself.
Say, say almost to God – 'I have done all
670 For her, not for myself!'
PARACELSUS: And who but lately
Was to rejoice in my success like you?
Whom should I love but both of you?
FESTUS: I know not:
But know this, you, that 'tis no will of mine
You should abjure the lofty claims you make;
And this the cause – I can no longer seek
To overlook the truth, that there would be
A monstrous spectacle upon the earth,
Beneath the pleasant sun, among the trees:
– A being knowing not what love is. Hear me!
680 You are endowed with faculties which bear
Annexed to them as 'twere a dispensation
To summon meaner spirits to do their will
And gather round them at their need; inspiring
Such with a love themselves can never feel,
Passionless 'mid their passionate votaries.
I know not if you joy in this or no,
Or ever dream that common men can live

On objects you prize lightly, but which make
Their heart's sole treasure: the affections seem
690 Beauteous at most to you, which we must taste
Or die: and this strange quality accords,
I know not how, with you; sits well upon
That luminous brow, though in another it scowls
An eating brand, a shame. I dare not judge you.
The rules of right and wrong thus set aside,
There's no alternative – I own you one
Of higher order, under other laws
Than bind us; therefore, curb not one bold glance!
'Tis best aspire. Once mingled with us all . . .
700 MICHAL: Stay with us, Aureole! cast those hopes away,
And stay with us! An angel warns me, too,
Man should be humble; you are very proud:
And God, dethroned, has doleful plagues for such!
– Warns me to have in dread no quick repulse,
No slow defeat, but a complete success:
You will find all you seek, and perish so!
PARACELSUS [*after a pause*]: Are these the barren
          first-fruits of my quest?
Is love like this the natural lot of all?
How many years of pain might one such hour
710 O'erbalance? Dearest Michal, dearest Festus,
What shall I say, if not that I desire
To justify your love; and will, dear friends,
In swerving nothing from my first resolves.
See, the great moon! and ere the mottled owls
Were wide awake, I was to go. It seems
You acquiesce at last in all save this –
If I am like to compass what I seek
By the untried career I choose; and then,
If that career, making but small account
720 Of much of life's delight, will yet retain
Sufficient to sustain my soul: for thus
I understand these fond fears just expressed.
And first; the lore you praise and I neglect,
The labours and the precepts of old time,
I have not lightly disesteemed. But, friends,
Truth is within ourselves; it takes no rise
From outward things, whate'er you may believe.
There is an inmost centre in us all,

Where truth abides in fulness; and around,
730   Wall upon wall, the gross flesh hems it in,
This perfect, clear perception – which is truth.
A baffling and perverting carnal mesh
Binds it, and makes all error: and to KNOW
Rather consists in opening out a way
Whence the imprisoned splendour may escape,
Than in effecting entry for a light
Supposed to be without. Watch narrowly
The demonstration of a truth, its birth,
And you trace back the effluence to its spring
740   And source within us; where broods radiance vast,
To be elicited ray by ray, as chance
Shall favour: chance – for hitherto, your sage
Even as he knows not how those beams are born,
As little knows he what unlocks their fount:
And men have oft grown old among their books
To die case-hardened in their ignorance,
Whose careless youth had promised what long years
Of unremitted labour ne'er performed:
While, contrary, it has chanced some idle day,
750   To autumn loiterers just as fancy-free
As the midges in the sun, gives birth at last
To truth – produced mysteriously as cape
Of cloud grown out of the invisible air.
Hence, may not truth be lodged alike in all,
The lowest as the highest? some slight film
The interposing bar which binds a soul
And makes the idiot, just as makes the sage
Some film removed, the happy outlet whence
Truth issues proudly? See this soul of ours!
760   How it strives weakly in the child, is loosed
In manhood, clogged by sickness, back compelled
By age and waste, set free at last by death:
Why is it, flesh enthrals it or enthrones?
What is this flesh we have to penetrate?
Oh, not alone when life flows still, do truth
And power emerge, but also when strange chance
Ruffles its current; in unused conjuncture,
When sickness breaks the body – hunger, watching,
Excess or languor – oftenest death's approach,
770   Peril, deep joy or woe. One man shall crawl

Through life surrounded with all stirring things,
Unmoved; and he goes mad: and from the wreck
Of what he was, by his wild talk alone,
You first collect how great a spirit he hid.
Therefore, set free the soul alike in all,
Discovering the true laws by which the flesh
Accloys the spirit! We may not be doomed
To cope with seraphs, but at least the rest
Shall cope with us. Make no more giants, God,
780   But elevate the race at once! We ask
To put forth just our strength, our human strength,
All starting fairly, all equipped alike,
Gifted alike, all eagle-eyed, true-hearted –
See if we cannot beat thine angels yet!
Such is my task. I go to gather this
The sacred knowledge, here and there dispersed
About the world, long lost or never found.
And why should I be sad or lorn of hope?
Why ever make man's good distinct from God's,
790   Or, finding they are one, why dare mistrust?
Who shall succeed if not one pledged like me?
Mine is no mad attempt to build a world
Apart from his, like those who set themselves
To find the nature of the spirit they bore,
And, taught betimes that all their gorgeous dreams
Were only born to vanish in this life,
Refused to fit them to its narrow sphere,
But chose to figure forth another world
And other frames meet for their vast desires, –
800   And all a dream! Thus was life scorned; but life
Shall yet be crowned: twine amaranth! I am priest!
And all for yielding with a lively spirit
A poor existence, parting with a youth
Like those who squander every energy
Convertible to good, on painted toys,
Breath-bubbles, gilded dust! And though I spurn
All adventitious aims, from empty praise
To love's award, yet whoso deems such helps
Important, and concerns himself for me,
810   May know even these will follow with the rest –
As in the steady rolling Mayne, asleep
Yonder. is mixed its mass of schistous ore.

My own affections laid to rest awhile,
Will waken purified, subdued alone
By all I have achieved. Till then – till then . . .
Ah, the time-wiling loitering of a page
Through bower and over lawn, till eve shall bring
The stately lady's presence whom he loves –
The broken sleep of the fisher whose rough coat
820   Enwraps the queenly pearl – these are faint types!
  See, see, they look on me: I triumph now!
  But one thing, Festus, Michal! I have told
  All I shall e'er disclose to mortal: say –
  Do you believe I shall accomplish this?
FESTUS: I do believe!
MICHAL: I ever did believe!
PARACELSUS: Those words shall never fade from out my brain!
  This earnest of the end shall never fade!
  Are there not, Festus, are there not, dear Michal,
  Two points in the adventure of the diver,
830   One – when, a beggar, he prepares to plunge,
  One – when, a prince, he rises with his pearl?
  Festus, I plunge!
FESTUS: We wait you when you rise!

PART II
PARACELSUS ATTAINS

Scene : Constantinople ; the house of a Greek Conjurer. 1521.

PARACELSUS

Over the waters in the vaporous West
The sun goes down as in a sphere of gold
Behind the arm of the city, which between,
With all that length of domes and minarets,
Athwart the splendour, black and crooked runs
Like a Turk verse along a scimitar.
There lie, sullen memorial, and no more
Possess my aching sight! 'Tis done at last.
Strange – and the juggles of a sallow cheat
10   Have won me to this act! 'Tis as yon cloud
Should voyage unwrecked o'er many a mountain-top

And break upon a molehill. I have dared
Come to a pause with knowledge; scan for once
The heights already reached, without regard
To the extent above; fairly compute
All I have clearly gained; for once excluding
A brilliant future to supply and perfect
All half-gains and conjectures and crude hopes:
And all because a fortune-teller wills
20 His credulous seekers should inscribe thus much
Their previous life's attainment, in his roll,
Before his promised secret, as he vaunts,
Make up the sum: and here amid the scrawled
Uncouth recordings of the dupes of this
Old arch-genethliac, lie my life's results!

A few blurred characters suffice to note
A stranger wandered long through many lands
And reaped the fruit he coveted in a few
Discoveries, as appended here and there,
30 The fragmentary produce of much toil,
In a dim heap, fact and surmise together
Confusedly massed as when acquired; he was
Intent on gain to come too much to stay
And scrutinize the little gained: the whole
Slipt in the blank space 'twixt an idiot's gibber
And a mad lover's ditty – there it lies.

And yet those blottings chronicle a life –
A whole life, and my life! Nothing to do,
No problem for the fancy, but a life
40 Spent and decided, wasted past retrieve
Or worthy beyond peer. Stay, what does this
Remembrancer set down concerning 'life'?
'"Time fleets, youth fades, life is an empty dream,"
It is the echo of time; and he whose heart
Beat first beneath a human heart, whose speech
Was copied from a human tongue, can never
Recall when he was living yet knew not this.
Nevertheless long seasons pass o'er him
Till some one hour's experience shows what nothing,
50 It seemed, could clearer show; and ever after,
An altered brow and eye and gait and speech

Attest that now he knows the adage true
"Time fleets, youth fades, life is an empty dream."'

Ay, my brave chronicler, and this same hour
As well as any: now, let my time be!

Now! I can go no farther; well or ill,
'Tis done. I must desist and take my chance.
I cannot keep on the stretch: 'tis no back-shrinking –
For let but some assurance beam, some close
60   To my toil grow visible, and I proceed
At any price, though closing it, I die.
Else, here I pause. The old Greek's prophecy
Is like to turn out true: 'I shall not quit
His chamber till I know what I desire!'
Was it the light wind sang it o'er the sea?

An end, a rest! strange how the notion, once
Encountered, gathers strength by moments! Rest!
Where has it kept so long? this throbbing brow
To cease, this beating heart to cease, all cruel
70   And gnawing thoughts to cease! To dare let down
My strung, so high-strung brain, to dare unnerve
My harassed o'ertasked frame, to know my place,
My portion, my reward, even my failure,
Assigned, made sure for ever! To lose myself
Among the common creatures of the world,
To draw some gain from having been a man,
Neither to hope nor fear, to live at length!
Even in failure, rest! But rest in truth
And power and recompense . . . I hoped that once!

80   What, sunk insensibly so deep? Has all
Been undergone for this? This the request
My labour qualified me to present
With no fear of refusal? Had I gone
Slightingly through my task, and so judged fit
To moderate my hopes; nay, were it now
My sole concern to exculpate myself,
End things or mend them, – why, I could not choose
A humbler mood to wait for the event!
No, no, there needs not this; no, after all,

90   At worst I have performed my share of the task:
The rest is God's concern; mine, merely this,
To know that I have obstinately held
By my own work. The mortal whose brave foot
Has trod, unscathed, the temple-court so far
That he descries at length the shrine of shrines,
Must let no sneering of the demons' eyes,
Whom he could pass unquailing, fasten now
Upon him, fairly past their power; no, no –
He must not stagger, faint, fall down at last,
100   Having a charm to baffle them; behold,
He bares his front: a mortal ventures thus
Serene amid the echoes, beams and glooms!
If he be priest henceforth, if he wake up
The god of the place to ban and blast him there,
Both well! What's failure or success to me?
I have subdued my life to the one purpose
Whereto I ordained it; there alone I spy,
No doubt, that way I may be satisfied.

Yes, well have I subdued my life! beyond
110   The obligation of my strictest vow,
The contemplation of my wildest bond,
Which gave my nature freely up, in truth,
But in its actual state, consenting fully
All passionate impulses its soil was formed
To rear, should wither; but foreseeing not
The tract, doomed to perpetual barrenness,
Would seem one day, remembered as it was,
Beside the parched sand-waste which now it is,
Already strewn with faint blooms, viewless then.
120   I ne'er engaged to root up loves so frail
I felt them not; yet now, 'tis very plain
Some soft spots had their birth in me at first,
If not love, say, like love: there was a time
When yet this wolfish hunger after knowledge
Set not remorselessly love's claims aside.
This heart was human once, or why recall
Einsiedeln, now, and Würzburg which the Mayne
Forsakes her course to fold as with an arm?

And Festus – my poor Festus, with his praise
130 And counsel and grave fears – where is he now
With the sweet maiden, long ago his bride?
I surely loved them – that last night, at least,
When we ... gone! gone! the better. I am saved
The sad review of an ambitious youth
Choked by vile lusts, unnoticed in their birth,
But let grow up and wind around a will
Till action was destroyed. No, I have gone
Purging my path successively of aught
Wearing the distant likeness of such lusts.
140 I have made life consist of one idea:
Ere that was master, up till that was born,
I bear a memory of a pleasant life
Whose small events I treasure; till one morn
I ran o'er the seven little grassy fields,
Startling the flocks of nameless birds, to tell
Poor Festus, leaping all the while for joy,
To leave all trouble for my future plans,
Since I had just determined to become
The greatest and most glorious man on earth.
150 And since that morn all life has been forgotten;
All is one day, one only step between
The outset and the end: one tyrant all-
Absorbing aim fills up the interspace,
One vast unbroken chain of thought, kept up
Through a career apparently adverse
To its existence: life, death, light and shadow,
The shows of the world, were bare receptacles
Or indices of truth to be wrung thence,
Not ministers of sorrow or delight:
160 A wondrous natural robe in which she went.
For some one truth would dimly beacon me
From mountains rough with pines, and flit and wink
O'er dazzling wastes of frozen snow, and tremble
Into assured light in some branching mine
Where ripens, swathed in fire, the liquid gold –
And all the beauty, all the wonder fell
On either side the truth, as its mere robe;
I see the robe now – then I saw the form.
So far, then, I have voyaged with success,
170 So much is good, then, in this working sea

Which parts me from that happy strip of land:
But o'er that happy strip a sun shone, too!
And fainter gleams it as the waves grow rough,
And still more faint as the sea widens; last
I sicken on a dead gulf streaked with light
From its own putrefying depths alone.
Then, God was pledged to take me by the hand;
Now, any miserable juggle can bid
My pride depart. All is alike at length:
180 God may take pleasure in confounding pride
By hiding secrets with the scorned and base –
I am here, in short: so little have I paused
Throughout! I never glanced behind to know
If I had kept my primal light from wane,
And thus insensibly am – what I am!

Oh, bitter; very bitter!
                          And more bitter,
To fear a deeper curse, an inner ruin,
Plague beneath plague, the last turning the first
To light beside its darkness. Let me weep
190 My youth and its brave hopes, all dead and gone,
In tears which burn! Would I were sure to win
Some startling secret in their stead, a tincture
Of force to flush old age with youth, or breed
Gold, or imprison moonbeams till they change
To opal shafts! – only that, hurling it
Indignant back, I might convince myself
My aims remained supreme and pure as ever!
Even now, why not desire, for mankind's sake,
That if I fail, some fault may be the cause,
200 That, though I sink, another may succeed?
O God, the despicable heart of us!
Shut out this hideous mockery from my heart!

'Twas politic in you, Aureole, to reject
Single rewards, and ask them in the lump;
At all events, once launched, to hold straight on:
For now 'tis all or nothing. Mighty profit
Your gains will bring if they stop short of such
Full consummation! As a man, you had
A certain share of strength; and that is gone

210 Already in the getting these you boast.
Do not they seem to laugh, as who should say –
'Great master, we are here indeed, dragged forth
To light; this hast thou done: be glad! Now, seek
The strength to use which thou hast spent in getting!'

And yet 'tis much, surely 'tis very much,
Thus to have emptied youth of all its gifts,
To feed a fire meant to hold out till morn
Arrived with inexhaustible light; and lo,
I have heaped up my last, and day dawns not!
220 And I am left with grey hair, faded hands,
And furrowed brow. Ha, have I, after all,
Mistaken the wild nursling of my breast?
Knowledge it seemed, and power, and recompense!
Was she who glided through my room of nights,
Who laid my head on her soft knees and smoothed
The damp locks, – whose sly soothings just began
When my sick spirit craved repose awhile –
God! was I fighting sleep off for death's sake?

God! Thou art mind! Unto the master-mind
230 Mind should be precious. Spare my mind alone!
All else I will endure; if, as I stand
Here, with my gains, thy thunder smite me down,
I bow me; 'tis thy will, thy righteous will;
I o'erpass life's restrictions, and I die;
And if no trace of my career remain
Save a thin corpse at pleasure of the wind
In these bright chambers level with the air,
See thou to it! But if my spirit fail,
My once proud spirit forsake me at the last,
240 Hast thou done well by me? So do not thou!
Crush not my mind, dear God, though I be crushed!
Hold me before the frequence of thy seraphs
And say – 'I crushed him, lest he should disturb
My law. Men must not know their strength: behold
Weak and alone, how he had raised himself!'

But if delusions trouble me, and thou,
Not seldom felt with rapture in thy help
Throughout my toils and wanderings, dost intend

To work man's welfare through my weak endeavour,
250 To crown my mortal forehead with a beam
From thine own blinding crown, to smile, and guide
This puny hand and let the work so wrought
Be styled my work, – hear me! I covet not
An influx of new power, an angel's soul:
It were no marvel then – but I have reached
Thus far, a man; let me conclude, a man!
Give but one hour of my first energy,
Of that invincible faith, but only one!
That I may cover with an eagle-glance
260 The truths I have, and spy some certain way
To mould them, and completing them, possess!

Yet God is good: I started sure of that,
And why dispute it now? I'll not believe
But some undoubted warning long ere this
Had reached me: a fire-labarum was not deemed
Too much for the old founder of these walls.
Then, if my life has not been natural,
It has been monstrous: yet, till late, my course
So ardently engrossed me, that delight,
270 A pausing and reflecting joy, 'tis plain,
Could find no place in it. True, I am worn;
But who clothes summer, who is life itself?
God, that created all things, can renew!
And then, though after-life to please me now
Must have no likeness to the past, what hinders
Reward from springing out of toil, as changed
As bursts the flower from earth and root and stalk?
What use were punishment, unless some sin
Be first detected? let me know that first!
280 No man could ever offend as I have done . . .

[*A voice from within*]

I hear a voice, perchance I heard
Long ago, but all too low,
So that scarce a care it stirred
If the voice were real or no:
I heard it in my youth when first
The waters of my life outburst:

But, now their stream ebbs faint, I hear
That voice, still low, but fatal-clear –
As if all poets, God ever meant
Should save the world, and therefore lent
Great gifts to, but who, proud, refused
To do his work, or lightly used
Those gifts, or failed through weak endeavour,
So, mourn cast off by him for ever, –
As if these leaned in airy ring
To take me; this the song they sing.

'Lost, lost! yet come,
With our wan troop make thy home.
Come, come! for we
Will not breathe, so much as breathe
Reproach to thee,
Knowing what thou sink'st beneath.
So sank we in those old years,
We who bid thee, come! thou last
Who, living yet, hast life o'erpast.
And altogether we, thy peers,
Will pardon crave for thee, the last
Whose trial is done, whose lot is cast
With those who watch but work no more,
Who gaze on life but live no more.
Yet we trusted thou shouldst speak
The message which our lips, too weak,
Refused to utter, – shouldst redeem
Our fault: such trust, and all a dream!
Yet we chose thee a birthplace
Where the richness ran to flowers:
Couldst not sing one song for grace?
Not make one blossom man's and ours?
Must one more recreant to his race
Die with unexerted powers,
And join us, leaving as he found
The world, he was to loosen, bound?
Anguish! ever and for ever;
Still beginning, ending never.
Yet, lost and last one, come!
How couldst understand, alas,
What our pale ghosts strove to say,

290

300

310

320

As their shades did glance and pass
Before thee night and day?
330   Thou wast blind as we were dumb:
Once more, therefore, come, O come!
How should we clothe, how arm the spirit
Shall next thy post of life inherit –
How guard him from thy speedy ruin?
Tell us of thy sad undoing
Here, where we sit, ever pursuing
Our weary task, ever renewing
Sharp sorrow, far from God who gave
Our powers, and man they could not save!'

[APRILE *enters*]
340   Ha, ha! our king that wouldst be, here at last?
Art thou the poet who shall save the world?
Thy hand to mine! Stay, fix thine eyes on mine!
Thou wouldst be king? Still fix thine eyes on mine!
PARACELSUS: Ha, ha! why crouchest not? Am I not king?
So torture is not wholly unavailing!
Have my fierce spasms compelled thee from thy lair?
Art thou the sage I only seemed to be,
Myself of after-time, my very self
With sight a little clearer, strength more firm,
350   Who robes him in my robe and grasps my crown
For just a fault, a weakness, a neglect?
I scarcely trusted God with the surmise
That such might come, and thou didst hear the while!
APRILE: Thine eyes are lustreless to mine; my hair
Is soft, nay silken soft: to talk with thee
Flushes my cheek, and thou art ashy-pale.
Truly, thou hast laboured, hast withstood her lips,
The siren's! Yes, 'tis like thou hast attained!
Tell me, dear master, wherefore now thou comest?
360   I thought thy solemn songs would have their meed
In after-time; that I should hear the earth
Exult in thee and echo with thy praise,
While I was laid forgotten in my grave.
PARACELSUS: Ah fiend, I know thee, I am not thy dupe!
Thou art ordained to follow in my track,
Reaping my sowing, as I scorned to reap
The harvest sown by sages passed away.

Thou art the sober searcher, cautious striver,
As if, except through me, thou hast searched or striven!
370   Ay, tell the world! Degrade me after all,
To an aspirant after fame, not truth –
To all but envy of thy fate, be sure!
APRILE: Nay, sing them to me; I shall envy not:
Thou shalt be king! Sing thou, and I will sit
Beside, and call deep silence for thy songs,
And worship thee, as I had ne'er been meant
To fill thy throne: but none shall ever know!
Sing to me; for already thy wild eyes
Unlock my heart-strings, as some crystal-shaft
380   Reveals by some chance blaze its parent fount
After long time: so thou reveal'st my soul.
All will flash forth at last, with thee to hear!
PARACELSUS: (His secret! I shall get his secret – fool!)
I am he that aspired to KNOW: and thou?
APRILE: I would LOVE infinitely, and be loved!
PARACELSUS: Poor slave! I am thy king indeed.
APRILE: Thou deem'st
That – born a spirit, dowered even as thou,
Born for thy fate – because I could not curb
My yearnings to possess at once the full
390   Enjoyment, but neglected all the means
Of realizing even the frailest joy,
Gathering no fragments to appease my want,
Yet nursing up that want till thus I die –
Thou deem'st I cannot trace thy safe sure march
O'er perils that o'erwhelm me, triumphing,
Neglecting naught below for aught above,
Despising nothing and ensuring all –
Nor that I could (my time to come again)
Lead thus my spirit securely as thine own.
400   Listen, and thou shalt see I know thee well.
I would love infinitely . . . Ah, lost! lost!

Oh ye who armed me at such cost,
How shall I look on all of ye
With your gifts even yet on me?

PARACELSUS: (Ah, 'tis some moonstruck creature after all!
Such fond fools as are like to haunt this den:
They spread contagion, doubtless: yet he seemed

To echo one foreboding of my heart
So truly, that . . . no matter! How he stands
410 With eve's last sunbeam staying on his hair
Which turns to it as if they were akin:
And those clear smiling eyes of saddest blue
Nearly set free, so far they rise above
The painful fruitless striving of the brow
And enforced knowledge of the lips, firm-set
In slow despondency's eternal sigh!
Has he, too, missed life's end, and learned the cause?)
I charge thee, by thy fealty, be calm!
Tell me what thou wouldst be, and what I am.

420 APRILE: I would love infinitely, and be loved.
First: I would carve in stone, or cast in brass,
The forms of earth. No ancient hunter lifted
Up to the gods by his renown, no nymph
Supposed the sweet soul of a woodland tree
Or sapphirine spirit of a twilight star,
Should be too hard for me; no shepherd-king
Regal for his white locks; no youth who stands
Silent and very calm amid the throng,
His right hand ever hid beneath his robe
430 Until the tyrant pass; no lawgiver,
No swan-soft woman rubbed with lucid oils
Given by a god for love of her – too hard!
Every passion sprung from man, conceived by man,
Would I express and clothe in its right form,
Or blend with others struggling in one form,
Or show repressed by an ungainly form.
Oh, if you marvelled at some mighty spirit
With a fit frame to execute its will –
Even unconsciously to work its will –
440 You should be moved no less beside some strong
Rare spirit, fettered to a stubborn body,
Endeavouring to subdue it and inform it
With its own splendour! All this I would do:
And I would say, this done, 'His sprites created,
God grants to each a sphere to be its world,
Appointed with the various objects needed
To satisfy its own peculiar want;
So, I create a world for these my shapes
Fit to sustain their beauty and their strength!'

450 And, at the word, I would contrive and paint
Woods, valleys, rocks and plains, dells, sands and wastes,
Lakes which, when morn breaks on their quivering bed,
Blaze like a wyvern flying round the sun,
And ocean isles so small, the dog-fish tracking
A dead whale, who should find them, would swim thrice
Around them, and fare onward – all to hold
The offspring of my brain. Nor these alone:
Bronze labyrinth, palace, pyramid and crypt,
Baths, galleries, courts, temples and terraces,
460 Marts, theatres and wharfs – all filled with men,
Men everywhere! And this performed in turn,
When those who looked on, pined to hear the hopes
And fears and hates and loves which moved the crowd,
I would throw down the pencil as the chisel,
And I would speak; no thought which ever stirred
A human breast should be untold; all passions,
All soft emotions, from the turbulent stir
Within a heart fed with desires like mine,
To the last comfort shutting the tired lids
470 Of him who sleeps the sultry noon away
Beneath the tent-tree by the wayside well:
And this in language as the need should be,
Now poured at once forth in a burning flow,
Now piled up in a grand array of words.
This done, to pérfect and consúmmate all,
Even as a luminous haze links star to star,
I would supply all chasms with music, breathing
Mysterious motions of the soul, no way
To be defined save in strange melodies.
480 Last, having thus revealed all I could love,
Having received all love bestowed on it,
I would die: preserving so throughout my course
God full on me, as I was full on men:
He would approve my prayer, 'I have gone through
The loveliness of life; create for me
If not for men, or take me to thyself,
Eternal, infinite love!'
                If thou hast ne'er
Conceived this mighty aim, this full desire,
Thou hast not passed my trial, and thou art
490 No king of mine.

PARACELSUS: Ah me!

APRILE: But thou art here!
Thou didst not gaze like me upon that end
Till thine own powers for compassing the bliss
Were blind with glory; nor grow mad to grasp
At once the prize long patient toil should claim,
Nor spurn all granted short of that. And I
Would do as thou, a second time: nay, listen!
Knowing ourselves, our world, our task so great,
Our time so brief, 'tis clear if we refuse
The means so limited, the tools so rude
500   To execute our purpose, life will fleet,
And we shall fade, and leave our task undone.
We will be wise in time: what though our work
Be fashioned in despite of their ill-service,
Be crippled every way? 'Twere little praise
Did full resources wait on our goodwill
At every turn. Let all be as it is.
Some say the earth is even so contrived
That tree and flower, a vesture gay, conceal
A bare and skeleton framework. Had we means
510   Answering to our mind! But now I seem
Wrecked on a savage isle: how rear thereon
My palace? Branching palms the props shall be,
Fruit glossy mingling; gems are for the East;
Who heeds them? I can pass them. Serpents' scales,
And painted birds' down, furs and fishes' skins
Must help me; and a little here and there
Is all I can aspire to: still my art
Shall show its birth was in a gentler clime.
'Had I green jars of malachite, this way
520   I'd range them: where those sea-shells glisten above,
Cressets should hang, by right: this way we set
The purple carpets, as these mats are laid,
Woven of fern and rush and blossoming flag.'
Or if, by fortune, some completer grace
Be spared to me, some fragment, some slight sample
Of the prouder workmanship my own home boasts,
Some trifle little heeded there, but here
The place's one perfection – with what joy
Would I enshrine the relic, cheerfully
530   Foregoing all the marvels out of reach!

Could I retain one strain of all the psalm
Of the angels, one word of the fiat of God,
To let my followers know what such things are!
I would adventure nobly for their sakes:
When nights were still, and still the moaning sea,
And far away I could descry the land
Whence I departed, whither I return,
I would dispart the waves, and stand once more
At home, and load my bark, and hasten back,
540 And fling my gains to them, worthless or true.
'Friends,' I would say, 'I went far, far for them,
Past the high rocks, the haunt of doves, the mounds
Of red earth from whose sides strange trees grow out,
Past tracts of milk-white minute blinding sand,
Till, by a mighty moon, I tremblingly
Gathered these magic herbs, berry and bud,
In haste, not pausing to reject the weeds,
But happy plucking them at any price.
To me, who have seen them bloom in their own soil,
550 They are scarce lovely: plait and wear them, you!
And guess, from what they are, the springs that fed them,
The stars that sparkled o'er them, night by night,
The snakes that travelled far to sip their dew!'
Thus for my higher loves; and thus even weakness
Would win me honour. But not these alone
Should claim my care; for common life, its wants
And ways, would I set forth in beauteous hues:
The lowest hind should not possess a hope,
A fear, but I'd be by him, saying better
560 Than he his own heart's language. I would live
For ever in the thoughts I thus explored,
As a discoverer's memory is attached
To all he finds; they should be mine henceforth,
Imbued with me, though free to all before:
For clay, once cast into my soul's rich mine,
Should come up crusted o'er with gems. Nor this
Would need a meaner spirit, than the first;
Nay, 'twould be but the selfsame spirit, clothed
In humbler guise, but still the selfsame spirit:
570 As one spring wind unbinds the mountain snow
And comforts violets in their hermitage.

But, master, poet, who hast done all this,
How didst thou 'scape the ruin whelming me?
Didst thou, when nerving thee to this attempt,
Ne'er range thy mind's extent, as some wide hall,
Dazzled by shapes that filled its length with light,
Shapes clustered there to rule thee, not obey,
That will not wait thy summons, will not rise
Singly, nor when thy practised eye and hand
580 Can well transfer their loveliness, but crowd
By thee for ever, bright to thy despair?
Didst thou ne'er gaze on each by turns, and ne'er
Resolve to single out one, though the rest
Should vanish, and to give that one, entire
In beauty, to the world; forgetting, so,
Its peers, whose number baffles mortal power?
And, this determined, wast thou ne'er seduced
By memories and regrets and passionate love,
To glance once more farewell? and did their eyes
590 Fasten thee, brighter and more bright, until
Thou couldst but stagger back unto their feet,
And laugh that man's applause or welfare ever
Could tempt thee to forsake them? Or when years
Had passed and still their love possessed thee wholly,
When from without some murmur startled thee
Of darkling mortals famished for one ray
Of thy so-hoarded luxury of light,
Didst thou ne'er strive even yet to break those spells
And prove thou couldst recover and fulfil
600 Thy early mission, long ago renounced,
And to that end, select some shape once more?
And did not mist-like influences, thick films,
Faint memories of the rest that charmed so long
Thine eyes, float fast, confuse thee, bear thee off,
As whirling snow-drifts blind a man who treads
A mountain ridge, with guiding spear, through storm?
Say, though I fell, I had excuse to fall;
Say, I was tempted sorely: say but this,
Dear lord, Aprile's lord!
PARACELSUS: Clasp me not thus,
610 Aprile! That the truth should reach me thus!
We are weak dust. Nay, clasp not or I faint!
APRILE: My king! and envious thoughts could outrage thee?

Lo, I forget my ruin, and rejoice
In thy success, as thou! Let our God's praise
Go bravely through the world at last! What care
Through me or thee? I feel thy breath. Why, tears?
Tears in the darkness, and from thee to me?
PARACELSUS: Love me henceforth, Aprile, while I learn
To love; and, merciful God, forgive us both!
620 We wake at length from weary dreams; but both
Have slept in fairy-land: though dark and drear
Appears the world before us, we no less
Wake with our wrists and ankles jewelled still.
I too have sought to KNOW as thou to LOVE —
Excluding love as thou refusedst knowledge.
Still thou hast beauty and I, power. We wake:
What penance canst devise for both of us?
APRILE: I hear thee faintly. The thick darkness! Even
Thine eyes are hid. 'Tis as I knew: I speak,
630 And now I die. But I have seen thy face!
O poet, think of me, and sing of me!
But to have seen thee and to die so soon!
PARACELSUS: Die not, Aprile! We must never part.
Are we not halves of one dissevered world,
Whom this strange chance unites once more? Part? never!
Till thou the lover, know; and I, the knower,
Love — until both are saved. Aprile, hear!
We will accept our gains, and use them — now!
God, he will die upon my breast! Aprile!
640 APRILE: To speak but once, and die! yet by his side.
Hush! hush!
　　　　　　Ha! go you ever girt about
With phantoms, powers? I have created such,
But these seem real as I.
PARACELSUS:　　　　　Whom can you see
Through the accursèd darkness?
APRILE:　　　　　　　　Stay; I know,
I know them: who should know them well as I?
White brows, lit up with glory; poets all!
PARACELSUS: Let him but live, and I have my reward!
APRILE: Yes; I see now. God is the perfect poet,
Who in his person acts his own creations.
650 Had you but told me this at first! Hush! hush!
PARACELSUS: Live! for my sake, because of my great sin,

To help my brain, oppressed by these wild words
And their deep import. Live! 'tis not too late.
I have a quiet home for us, and friends.
Michal shall smile on you. Hear you? Lean thus,
And breathe my breath. I shall not lose one word
Of all your speech, one little word, Aprile!
APRILE: No, no. Crown me? I am not one of you!
'Tis he, the king, you seek. I am not one.
660 PARACELSUS: Thy spirit, at least, Aprile! Let me love!

I have attained, and now I may depart.

PART III
PARACELSUS

Scene : Basil; a chamber in the house of PARACELSUS. *1526.*

PARACELSUS, FESTUS

PARACELSUS: Heap logs and let the blaze laugh out!
FESTUS: True, true!
'Tis very fit all, time and chance and change
Have wrought since last we sat thus, face to face
And soul to soul – all cares, far-looking fears,
Vague apprehensions, all vain fancies bred
By your long absence, should be cast away,
Forgotten in this glad unhoped renewal
Of our affections.
PARACELSUS: Oh, omit not aught
Which witnesses your own and Michal's own
10   Affection: spare not that! Only forget
The honours and the glories and what not,
It pleases you to tell profusely out.
FESTUS: Nay, even your honours, in a sense, I waive:
The wondrous Paracelsus, life's dispenser,
Fate's commissary, idol of the schools
And courts, shall be no more than Aureole still,
Still Aureole and my friend as when we parted
Some twenty years ago, and I restrained
As best I could the promptings of my spirit
20   Which secretly advanced you, from the first,

To the pre-eminent rank which, since, your own
Adventurous ardour, nobly triumphing,
Has won for you.
PARACELSUS: Yes, yes. And Michal's face
Still wears that quiet and peculiar light
Like the dim circlet floating round a pearl?
FESTUS: Just so.
PARACELSUS: And yet her calm sweet countenance,
Though saintly, was not sad; for she would sing
Alone. Does she still sing alone, bird-like,
Not dreaming you are near? Her carols dropt
30   In flakes through that old leafy bower built under
The sunny wall at Würzburg, from her lattice
Among the trees above, while I, unseen,
Sat conning some rare scroll from Tritheim's shelves
Much wondering notes so simple could divert
My mind from study. Those were happy days.
Respect all such as sing when all alone!
FESTUS: Scarcely alone: her children, you may guess,
Are wild beside her.
PARACELSUS: Ah, those children quite
Unsettle the pure picture in my mind:
40   A girl, she was so perfect, so distinct:
No change, no change! Not but this added grace
May blend and harmonize with its compeers,
And Michal may become her motherhood;
But 'tis a change, and I detest all change,
And most a change in aught I loved long since.
So, Michal – you have said she thinks of me?
FESTUS: O very proud will Michal be of you!
Imagine how we sat, long winter-nights,
Scheming and wondering, shaping your presumed
50   Adventure, or devising its reward;
Shutting out fear with all the strength of hope.
For it was strange how, even when most secure
In our domestic peace, a certain dim
And flitting shade could sadden all; it seemed
A restlessness of heart, a silent yearning,
A sense of something wanting, incomplete –
Not to be put in words, perhaps avoided
By mute consent – but, said or unsaid, felt
To point to one so loved and so long lost.

60 And then the hopes rose and shut out the fears –
How you would laugh should I recount them now!
I still predicted your return at last
With gifts beyond the greatest of them all,
All Tritheim's wondrous troop; did one of which
Attain renown by any chance, I smiled,
As well aware of who would prove his peer.
Michal was sure some woman, long ere this,
As beautiful as you were sage, had loved ...

PARACELSUS: Far-seeing, truly, to discern so much
70 In the fantastic projects and day-dreams
Of a raw restless boy!

FESTUS: Oh, no: the sunrise
Well warranted our faith in this full noon!
Can I forget the anxious voice which said
'Festus, have thoughts like these ere shaped themselves
In other brains than mine? have their possessors
Existed in like circumstance? were they weak
As I, or ever constant from the first,
Despising youth's allurements and rejecting
As spider-films the shackles I endure?
80 Is there hope for me?' – and I answered gravely
As an acknowledged elder, calmer, wiser,
More gifted mortal. O you must remember,
For all your glorious ...

PARACELSUS: Glorious? ay, this hair,
These hands – nay, touch them, they are mine! Recall
With all the said recallings, times when thus
To lay them by your own ne'er turned you pale
As now. Most glorious, are they not?

FESTUS: Why – why –
Something must be subtracted from success
So wide, no doubt. He would be scrupulous, truly,
90 Who should object such drawbacks. Still, still, Aureole,
You are changed, very changed! 'Twere losing nothing
To look well to it: you must not be stolen
From the enjoyment of your well-won meed.

PARACELSUS: My friend! you seek my pleasure, past a doubt:
You will best gain your point, by talking, not
Of me, but of yourself.

FESTUS: Have I not said
All touching Michal and my children? Sure

You know, by this, full well how Aennchen looks
Gravely, while one disparts her thick brown hair;
100 And Aureole's glee when some stray gannet builds
Amid the birch-trees by the lake. Small hope
Have I that he will honour (the wild imp)
His namesake. Sigh not! 'tis too much to ask
That all we love should reach the same proud fate.
But you are very kind to humour me
By showing interest in my quiet life;
You, who of old could never tame yourself
To tranquil pleasures, must at heart despise ...
PARACELSUS: Festus, strange secrets are let out by death
110 Who blabs so oft the follies of this world:
And I am death's familiar, as you know.
I helped a man to die, some few weeks since,
Warped even from his go-cart to one end –
The living on princes' smiles, reflected from
A mighty herd of favourites. No mean trick
He left untried, and truly well-nigh wormed
All traces of God's finger out of him:
Then died, grown old. And just an hour before,
Having lain long with blank and soulless eyes,
120 He sat up suddenly, and with natural voice
Said that in spite of thick air and closed doors
God told him it was June; and he knew well,
Without such telling, harebells grew in June;
And all that kings could ever give or take
Would not be precious as those blooms to him.
Just so, allowing I am passing sage,
It seems to me much worthier argument
Why pansies,* eyes that laugh, bear beauty's prize
From violets, eyes that dream – (your Michal's choice) –
130 Than all fools find to wonder at in me
Or in my fortunes. And be very sure
I say this from no prurient restlessness,
No self-complacency, itching to turn,
Vary and view its pleasure from all points,
And, in this instance, willing other men
May be at pains, demónstrate to itself
The realness of the very joy it tastes.
What should delight me like the news of friends

*Citrinula (flammula) herba Paracelso multum familiaris.—DORN.

Whose memories were a solace to me oft,
140   As mountain-baths to wild fowls in their flight?
Ofter than you had wasted thought on me
Had you been wise, and rightly valued bliss.
But there's no taming nor repressing hearts:
God knows I need such! – So, you heard me speak?
FESTUS: Speak? when?
PARACELSUS: When but this morning at my class?
There was noise and crowd enough. I saw you not.
Surely you know I am engaged to fill
The chair here? – that 'tis part of my proud fate
To lecture to as many thick-skulled youths
150   As please, each day, to throng the theatre,
To my great reputation, and no small
Danger of Basil's benches long unused
To crack beneath such honour?
FESTUS: I was there;
I mingled with the throng: shall I avow
Small care was mine to listen? – too intent
On gathering from the murmurs of the crowd
A full corroboration of my hopes!
What can I learn about your powers? but they
Know, care for naught beyond your actual state,
160   Your actual value; yet they worship you,
Those various natures whom you sway as one!
But ere I go, be sure I shall attend ...
PARACELSUS: Stop, o' God's name: the thing's by no means yet
Past remedy! Shall I read this morning's labour
– At least in substance? Naught so worth the gaining
As an apt scholar! Thus then, with all due
Precision and emphasis – you, beside, are clearly
Guiltless of understanding more, a whit,
The subject than your stool – allowed to be
170   A notable advantage.
FESTUS: Surely, Aureole,
You laugh at me!
PARACELSUS: I laugh? Ha, ha! thank heaven,
I charge you, if't be so! for I forget
Much, and what laughter should be like. No less,
However, I forego that luxury
Since it alarms the friend who brings it back.
True, laughter like my own must echo strangely

To thinking men; a smile were better far;
So, make me smile! If the exulting look
You wore but now be smiling, 'tis so long
180 Since I have smiled! Alas, such smiles are born
Alone of hearts like yours, or herdsmen's souls
Of ancient time, whose eyes, calm as their flocks,
Saw in the stars mere garnishry of heaven,
And in the earth a stage for altars only.
Never change, Festus: I say, never change!
FESTUS: My God, if he be wretched after all!
PARACELSUS: When last we parted, Festus, you declared,
— Or Michal, yes, her soft lips whispered words
I have preserved. She told me she believed
190 I should succeed (meaning, that in the search
I then engaged in, I should meet success)
And yet be wretched: now, she augured false.
FESTUS: Thank heaven! but you spoke strangely: could I
venture
To think bare apprehension lest your friend,
Dazzled by your resplendent course, might find
Henceforth less sweetness in his own, could move
Such earnest mood in you? Fear not, dear friend,
That I shall leave you, inwardly repining
Your lot was not my own!
PARACELSUS: And this for ever!
200 For ever! gull who may, they will be gulled!
They will not look nor think; 'tis nothing new
In them: but surely he is not of them!
My Festus, do you know, I reckoned, you —
Though all beside were sand-blind — you, my friend,
Would look at me, once close, with piercing eye
Untroubled by the false glare that confounds
A weaker vision: would remain serene,
Though singular amid a gaping throng.
I feared you, or I had come, sure, long ere this,
210 To Einsiedeln. Well, error has no end,
And Rhasis is a sage, and Basil boasts
A tribe of wits, and I am wise and blest
Past all dispute! 'Tis vain to fret at it.
I have vowed long ago my worshippers
Shall owe to their own deep sagacity
All further information, good or bad.

Small risk indeed my reputation runs,
Unless perchance the glance now searching me
Be fixed much longer; for it seems to spell
220   Dimly the characters a simpler man
Might read distinct enough. Old Eastern books
Say, the fallen prince of morning some short space
Remained unchanged in semblance; nay, his brow
Was hued with triumph: every spirit then
Praising, *his* heart on flame the while: – a tale!
Well, Festus, what discover you, I pray?
FESTUS: Some foul deed sullies then a life which else
Were raised supreme?
PARACELSUS: Good: I do well, most well!
Why strive to make men hear, feel, fret themselves
230   With what is past their power to comprehend?
I should not strive now: only, having nursed
The faint surmise that one yet walked the earth,
One, at least, not the utter fool of show,
Not absolutely formed to be the dupe
Of shallow plausibilities alone:
One who, in youth, found wise enough to choose
The happiness his riper years approve,
Was yet so anxious for another's sake,
That, ere his friend could rush upon a mad
240   And ruinous course, the converse of his own,
His gentle spirit essayed, prejudged for him
The perilous path, foresaw its destiny,
And warned the weak one in such tender words,
Such accents – his whole heart in every tone –
That oft their memory comforted that friend
When it by right should have increased despair:
– Having believed, I say, that this one man
Could never lose the light thus from the first
His portion – how should I refuse to grieve
250   At even my gain if it disturb our old
Relation, if it make me out more wise?
Therefore, once more reminding him how well
He prophesied, I note the single flaw
That spoils his prophet's title. In plain words,
You were deceived, and thus were you deceived –
I have not been successful, and yet am
Most miserable; 'tis said at last; nor you

Give credit, lest you force me to concede
That common sense yet lives upon the world!
260　FESTUS: You surely do not mean to banter me?
PARACELSUS: You know, or – if you have been wise enough
To cleanse your memory of such matters – knew,
As far as words of mine could make it clear,
That 'twas my purpose to find joy or grief
Solely in the fulfilment of my plan
Or plot or whatsoe'er it was; rejoicing
Alone as it proceeded prosperously,
Sorrowing then only when mischance retarded
Its progress. That was in those Würzburg days!
270　Not to prolong a theme I thoroughly hate,
I have pursued this plan with all my strength;
And having failed therein most signally,
Cannot object to ruin utter and drear
As all-excelling would have been the prize
Had fortune favoured me. I scarce have right
To vex your frank good spirit late so glad
In my supposed prosperity, I know,
And, were I lucky in a glut of friends,
Would well agree to let your error live,
280　Nay, strengthen it with fables of success.
But mine is no condition to refuse
The transient solace of so rare a godsend,
My solitary luxury, my one friend:
Accordingly I venture to put off
The wearisome vest of falsehood galling me,
Secure when he is by. I lay me bare,
Prone at his mercy – but he is my friend!
Not that he needs retain his aspect grave;
That answers not my purpose; for 'tis like,
290　Some sunny morning – Basil being drained
Of its wise population, every corner
Of the amphitheatre crammed with learned clerks,
Here Oecolampadius, looking worlds of wit,
Here Castellanus, as profound as he,
Munsterus here, Frobenius there, all squeezed
And staring, – that the zany of the show,
Even Paracelsus, shall put off before them
His trappings with a grace but seldom judged
Expedient in such cases: – the grim smile

300   That will go round! Is it not therefore best
    To venture a rehearsal like the present
    In a small way? Where are the signs I seek,
    The first-fruits and fair sample of the scorn
    Due to all quacks? Why, this will never do!
  FESTUS: These are foul vapours, Aureole; naught beside!
    The effect of watching, study, weariness.
    Were there a spark of truth in the confusion
    Of these wild words, you would not outrage thus
    Your youth's companion. I shall ne'er regard

310   These wanderings, bred of faintness and much study.
    'Tis not thus you would trust a trouble to me,
    To Michal's friend.
  PARACELSUS: I have said it, dearest Festus!
    For the manner, 'tis ungracious probably;
    You may have it told in broken sobs, one day,
    And scalding tears, ere long: but I thought best
    To keep that off as long as possible.
    Do you wonder still?
  FESTUS: No; it must oft fall out
    That one whose labour perfects any work,
    Shall rise from it with eye so worn that he

320   Of all men least can measure the extent
    Of what he has accomplished. He alone
    Who, nothing tasked, is nothing weary too,
    May clearly scan the little he effects:
    But we, the bystanders, untouched by toil,
    Estimate each aright.
  PARACELSUS: This worthy Festus
    Is one of them, at last! 'Tis so with all!
    First, they set down all progress as a dream;
    And next, when he whose quick discomfiture
    Was counted on, accomplishes some few

330   And doubtful steps in his career, – behold,
    They look for every inch of ground to vanish
    Beneath his tread, so sure they spy success!
  FESTUS: Few doubtful steps? when death retires before
    Your presence – when the noblest of mankind,
    Broken in body or subdued in soul,
    May through your skill renew their vigour, raise
    The shattered frame to pristine stateliness?
    When men in racking pain may purchase dreams

Of what delights them most, swooning at once
340   Into a sea of bliss or rapt along
As in a flying sphere of turbulent light?
When we may look to you as one ordained
To free the flesh from fell disease, as frees
Our Luther's burning tongue the fettered soul?
When . . .

PARACELSUS: When and where, the devil, did you get
This notable news?

FESTUS: Even from the common voice;
From those whose envy, daring not dispute
The wonders it decries, attributes them
To magic and such folly.

PARACELSUS: Folly? Why not
350   To magic, pray? You find a comfort doubtless
In holding, God ne'er troubles him about
Us or our doings: once we were judged worth
The devil's tempting . . . I offend: forgive me,
And rest content. Your prophecy on the whole
Was fair enough as prophesyings go;
At fault a little in detail, but quite
Precise enough in the main; and hereupon
I pay due homage: you guessed long ago
(The prophet!) I should fail – and I have failed.

360 FESTUS: You mean to tell me, then, the hopes which fed
Your youth have not been realized as yet?
Some obstacle has barred them hitherto?
Or that their innate . . .

PARACELSUS: As I said but now,
You have a very decent prophet's fame,
So you but shun details here. Little matter
Whether those hopes were mad, – the aims they sought,
Safe and secure from all ambitious fools;
Or whether my weak wits are overcome
By what a better spirit would scorn: I fail.

370   And now methinks 'twere best to change a theme
I am a sad fool to have stumbled on.
I say confusedly what comes uppermost;
But there are times when patience proves at fault,
As now: this morning's strange encounter – you
Beside me once again! you, whom I guessed
Alive, since hitherto (with Luther's leave)

No friend have I among the saints at peace,
To judge by any good their prayers effect.
I knew you would have helped me – why not he,
380   My strange competitor in enterprise,
Bound for the same end by another path,
Arrived, or ill or well, before the time,
At our disastrous journey's doubtful close?
How goes it with Aprile? Ah, they miss
Your lone sad sunny idleness of heaven,
Our martyrs for the world's sake; heaven shuts fast:
The poor mad poet is howling by this time!
Since you are my sole friend then, here or there,
I could not quite repress the varied feelings
390   This meeting wakens; they have had their vent,
And now forget them. Do the rear-mice still
Hang like a fretwork on the gate (or what
In my time was a gate) fronting the road
From Einsiedeln to Lachen?

FESTUS: Trifle not:
Answer me, for my sake alone! You smiled
Just now, when I supposed some deed, unworthy
Yourself, might blot the else so bright result;
Yet if your motives have continued pure,
Your will unfaltering, and in spite of this,
400   You have experienced a defeat, why then
I say not you would cheerfully withdraw
From contest – mortal hearts are not so fashioned –
But surely you would ne'ertheless withdraw.
You sought not fame nor gain nor even love,
No end distinct from knowledge, – I repeat
Your very words: once satisfied that knowledge
Is a mere dream, you would announce as much,
Yourself the first. But how is the event?
You are defeated – and I find you here!

410 PARACELSUS: As though 'here' did not signify defeat!
I spoke not of my little labours here,
But of the break-down of my general aims:
For you, aware of their extent and scope,
To look on these sage lecturings, approved
By beardless boys, and bearded dotards worse,
As a fit consummation of such aims,
Is worthy notice. A professorship

At Basil! Since you see so much in it,
And think my life was reasonably drained
420   Of life's delights to render me a match
For duties arduous as such post demands, –
Be it far from me to deny my power
To fill the petty circle lotted out
Of infinite space, or justify the host
Of honours thence accruing. So, take notice,
This jewel dangling from my neck preserves
The features of a prince, my skill restored
To plague his people some few years to come:
And all through a pure whim. He had eased the earth
430   For me, but that the droll despair which seized
The vermin of his household, tickled me.
I came to see. Here, drivelled the physician,
Whose most infallible nostrum was at fault;
There quaked the astrologer, whose horoscope
Had promised him interminable years;
Here a monk fumbled at the sick man's mouth
With some undoubted relic – a sudary
Of the Virgin; while another piebald knave
Of the same brotherhood (he loved them ever)
440   Was actively preparing 'neath his nose
Such a suffumigation as, once fired,
Had stunk the patient dead ere he could groan.
I cursed the doctor and upset the brother,
Brushed past the conjurer, vowed that the first gust
Of stench from the ingredients just alight
Would raise a cross-grained devil in my sword,
Not easily laid: and ere an hour the prince
Slept as he never slept since prince he was.
A day – and I was posting for my life,
450   Placarded through the town as one whose spite
Had near availed to stop the blessed effects
Of the doctor's nostrum which, well seconded
By the sudary, and most by the costly smoke –
Not leaving out the strenuous prayers sent up
Hard by in the abbey – raised the prince to life:
To the great reputation of the seer
Who, confident, expected all along
The glad event – the doctor's recompense –
Much largess from his highness to the monks –

460　And the vast solace of his loving people,
　　　Whose general satisfaction to increase,
　　　The prince was pleased no longer to defer
　　　The burning of some dozen heretics
　　　Remanded till God's mercy should be shown
　　　Touching his sickness: last of all were joined
　　　Ample directions to all loyal folk
　　　To swell the complement by seizing me
　　　Who – doubtless some rank sorcerer – endeavoured
　　　To thwart these pious offices, obstruct
470　The prince's cure, and frustrate heaven by help
　　　Of certain devils dwelling in his sword.
　　　By luck, the prince in his first fit of thanks
　　　Had forced this bauble on me as an earnest
　　　Of further favours. This one case may serve
　　　To give sufficient taste of many such,
　　　So, let them pass. Those shelves support a pile
　　　Of patents, licences, diplomas, titles
　　　From Germany, France, Spain, and Italy;
　　　They authorize some honour; ne'ertheless,
480　I set more store by this Erasmus sent;
　　　He trusts me; our Frobenius is his friend,
　　　And him 'I raised' (nay, read it) 'from the dead.'
　　　I weary you, I see. I merely sought
　　　To show, there's no great wonder after all
　　　That, while I fill the class-room and attract
　　　A crowd to Basil, I get leave to stay,
　　　And therefore need not scruple to accept
　　　The utmost they can offer, if I please:
　　　For 'tis but right the world should be prepared
490　To treat with favour e'en fantastic wants
　　　Of one like me, used up in serving her.
　　　Just as the mortal, whom the gods in part
　　　Devoured, received in place of his lost limb
　　　Some virtue or other – cured disease, I think;
　　　You mind the fables we have read together.
FESTUS: You do not think I comprehend a word.
　　　The time was, Aureole, you were apt enough
　　　To clothe the airiest thoughts in specious breath;
　　　But surely you must feel how vague and strange
500　These speeches sound.
PARACELSUS:　　　　　Well, then: you know my hopes;

I am assured, at length, those hopes were vain;
That truth is just as far from me as ever;
That I have thrown my life away; that sorrow
On that account is idle, and further effort
To mend and patch what's marred beyond repairing,
As useless: and all this was taught your friend
By the convincing good old-fashioned method
Of force – by sheer compulsion. Is that plain?
FESTUS: Dear Aureole, can it be my fears were just?
510   God wills not . . .
PARACELSUS: Now, 'tis this I most admire –
The constant talk men of your stamp keep up
Of God's will, as they style it; one would swear
Man had but merely to uplift his eye,
And see the will in question charactered
On the heaven's vault. 'Tis hardly wise to moot
Such topics: doubts are many and faith is weak.
I know as much of any will of God
As knows some dumb and tortured brute what Man,
His stern lord, wills from the perplexing blows
520   That plague him every way; but there, of course,
Where least he suffers, longest he remains –
My case; and for such reasons I plod on,
Subdued but not convinced. I know as little
Why I deserve to fail, as why I hoped
Better things in my youth. I simply know
I am no master here, but trained and beaten
Into the path I tread; and here I stay,
Until some further intimation reach me,
Like an obedient drudge. Though I prefer
530   To view the whole thing as a task imposed
Which, whether dull or pleasant, must be done –
Yet, I deny not, there is made provision
Of joys which tastes less jaded might affect;
Nay, some which please me too, for all my pride –
Pleasures that once were pains: the iron ring
Festering about a slave's neck grows at length
Into the flesh it eats. I hate no longer
A host of petty vile delights, undreamed of
Or spurned before; such now supply the place
540   Of my dead aims: as in the autumn woods
Where tall trees used to flourish, from their roots

Springs up a fungous brood sickly and pale,
Chill mushrooms coloured like a corpse's cheek.
FESTUS: If I interpret well your words, I own
It troubles me but little that your aims,
Vast in their dawning and most likely grown
Extravagantly since, have baffled you.
Perchance I am glad; you merit greater praise;
Because they are too glorious to be gained,
550   You do not blindly cling to them and die;
You fell, but have not sullenly refused
To rise, because an angel worsted you
In wrestling, though the world holds not your peer;
And though too harsh and sudden is the change
To yield content as yet, still you pursue
The ungracious path as though 'twere rosy-strewn.
'Tis well: and your reward, or soon or late,
Will come from him whom no man serves in vain.
PARACELSUS: Ah, very fine! For my part, I conceive
560   The very pausing from all further toil,
Which you find heinous, would become a seal
To the sincerity of all my deeds.
To be consistent I should die at once;
I calculated on no after-life;
Yet (how crept in, how fostered, I know not)
Here am I with as passionate regret
For youth and health and love so vainly lavished,
As if their preservation had been first
And foremost in my thoughts; and this strange fact
570   Humbled me wondrously, and had due force
In rendering me the less averse to follow
A certain counsel, a mysterious warning –
You will not understand – but 'twas a man
With aims not mine and yet pursued like mine,
With the same fervour and no more success,
Perishing in my sight; who summoned me
As I would shun the ghastly fate I saw,
To serve my race at once; to wait no longer
That God should interfere in my behalf,
580   But to distrust myself, put pride away,
And give my gains, imperfect as they were,
To men. I have not leisure to explain
How, since, a singular series of events

Has raised me to the station you behold,
Wherein I seem to turn to most account
The mere wreck of the past, – perhaps receive
Some feeble glimmering token that God views
And may approve my penance: therefore here
You find me, doing most good or least harm.
590   And if folks wonder much and profit little
'Tis not my fault; only, I shall rejoice
When my part in the farce is shuffled through,
And the curtain falls: I must hold out till then.
FESTUS: Till when, dear Aureole?
PARACELSUS: Till I'm fairly thrust
From my proud eminence. Fortune is fickle
And even professors fall: should that arrive,
I see no sin in ceding to my bent.
You little fancy what rude shocks apprise us
We sin; God's intimations rather fail
600   In clearness than in energy: 'twere well
Did they but indicate the course to take
Like that to be forsaken. I would fain
Be spared a further sample. Here I stand,
And here I stay, be sure, till forced to flit.
FESTUS: Be you but firm on that head! long ere then
All I expect will come to pass, I trust:
The cloud that wraps you will have disappeared.
Meantime, I see small chance of such event:
They praise you here as one whose lore, already
610   Divulged, eclipses all the past can show,
But whose achievements, marvellous as they be,
Are faint anticipations of a glory
About to be revealed. When Basil's crowds
Dismiss their teacher, I shall be content
That he depart.
PARACELSUS: This favour at their hands
I look for earlier than your view of things
Would warrant. Of the crowd you saw today,
Remove the full half sheer amazement draws,
Mere novelty, naught else; and next, the tribe
620   Whose innate blockish dullness just perceives
That unless miracles (as seem my works)
Be wrought in their behalf, their chance is slight
To puzzle the devil; next, the numerous set

Who bitterly hate established schools, and help
The teacher that oppugns them, till he once
Have planted his own doctrine, when the teacher
May reckon on their rancour in his turn;
Take, too, the sprinkling of sagacious knaves
Whose cunning runs not counter to the vogue
630 But seeks, by flattery and crafty nursing,
To force my system to a premature
Short-lived development. Why swell the list?
Each has his end to serve, and his best way
Of serving it: remove all these, remains
A scantling, a poor dozen at the best,
Worthy to look for sympathy and service,
And likely to draw profit from my pains.
FESTUS: 'Tis no encouraging picture: still these few
Redeem their fellows. Once the germ implanted,
640 Its growth, if slow, is sure.
PARACELSUS: God grant it so!
I would make some amends: but if I fail,
The luckless rogues have this excuse to urge,
That much is in my method and my manner,
My uncouth habits, my impatient spirit,
Which hinders of reception and result
My doctrine: much to say, small skill to speak!
These old aims suffered not a looking-off
Though for an instant; therefore, only when
I thus renounced them and resolved to reap
650 Some present fruit – to teach mankind some truth
So dearly purchased – only then I found
Such teaching was an art requiring cares
And qualities peculiar to itself:
That to possess was one thing – to display
Another. With renown first in my thoughts,
Or popular praise, I had soon discovered it:
One grows but little apt to learn these things.
FESTUS: If it be so, which nowise I believe,
There needs no waiting fuller dispensation
660 To leave a labour of so little use.
Why not throw up the irksome charge at once?
PARACELSUS: A task, a task!
                    But wherefore hide the whole
Extent of degradation, once engaged

In the confessing vein? Despite of all
My fine talk of obedience and repugnance,
Docility and what not, 'tis yet to learn
If when the task shall really be performed,
My inclination free to choose once more,
I shall do aught but slightly modify
670 The nature of the hated task I quit.
In plain words, I am spoiled; my life still tends
As first it tended; I am broken and trained
To my old habits: they are part of me.
I know, and none so well, my darling ends
Are proved impossible: no less, no less,
Even now what humours me, fond fool, as when
Their faint ghosts sit with me and flatter me
And send me back content to my dull round?
How can I change this soul? – this apparatus
680 Constructed solely for their purposes,
So well adapted to their every want,
To search out and discover, prove and perfect;
This intricate machine whose most minute
And meanest motions have their charm to me
Though to none else – an aptitude I seize,
An object I perceive, a use, a meaning,
A property, a fitness, I explain
And I alone: – how can I change my soul?
And this wronged body, worthless save when tasked
690 Under that soul's dominion – used to care
For its bright master's cares and quite subdue
Its proper cravings – not to ail nor pine
So he but prosper – whither drag this poor
Tried patient body? God! how I essayed
To live like that mad poet, for a while,
To love alone; and how I felt too warped
And twisted and deformed! What should I do,
Even though released from drudgery, but return
Faint, as you see, and halting, blind and sore,
700 To my old life and die as I began?
I cannot feed on beauty for the sake
Of beauty only, nor can drink in balm
From lovely objects for their loveliness;
My nature cannot lose her first imprint;
I still must hoard and heap and class all truths

With one ulterior purpose: I must know!
Would God translate me to his throne, believe
That I should only listen to his word
To further my own aim! For other men,
710   Beauty is prodigally strewn around,
And I were happy could I quench as they
This mad and thriveless longing, and content me
With beauty for itself alone: alas,
I have addressed a frock of heavy mail
Yet may not join the troop of sacred knights;
And now the forest-creatures fly from me,
The grass-banks cool, the sunbeams warm no more.
Best follow, dreaming that ere night arrive,
I shall o'ertake the company and ride
720   Glittering as they!

FESTUS: I think I apprehend
What you would say: if you, in truth, design
To enter once more on the life thus left,
Seek not to hide that all this consciousness
Of failure is assumed!

PARACELSUS: My friend, my friend,
I toil, you listen; I explain, perhaps
You understand: there our communion ends.
Have you learnt nothing from today's discourse?
When we would thoroughly know the sick man's state
We feel awhile the fluttering pulse, press soft
730   The hot brow, look upon the languid eye,
And thence divine the rest. Must I lay bare
My heart, hideous and beating, or tear up
My vitals for your gaze, ere you will deem
Enough made known? You! who are you, forsooth?
That is the crowning operation claimed
By the arch-demonstrator – heaven the hall,
And earth the audience. Let Aprile and you
Secure good places: 'twill be worth the while.

FESTUS: Are you mad, Aureole? What can I have said
740   To call for this? I judged from your own words.

PARACELSUS: Oh, doubtless! A sick wretch describes the ape
That mocks him from the bed-foot, and all gravely
You thither turn at once: or he recounts
The perilous journey he has late performed,
And you are puzzled much how that could be!

You find me here, half stupid and half mad;
It makes no part of my delight to search
Into these matters, much less undergo
Another's scrutiny; but so it chances
750 That I am led to trust my state to you:
And the event is, you combine, contrast
And ponder on my foolish words as though
They thoroughly conveyed all hidden here –
Here, loathsome with despair and hate and rage!
Is there no fear, no shrinking and no shame?
Will you guess nothing? will you spare me nothing?
Must I go deeper? Ay or no?
FESTUS: Dear friend ...
PARACELSUS: True: I am brutal – 'tis a part of it;
The plague's sign – you are not a lazar-haunter,
760 How should you know? Well then, you think it strange
I should profess to have failed utterly,
And yet propose an ultimate return
To courses void of hope: and this, because
You know not what temptation is, nor how
'Tis like to ply men in the sickliest part.
You are to understand that we who make
Sport for the gods, are hunted to the end:
There is not one sharp volley shot at us,
Which 'scaped with life, though hurt, we slacken pace
770 And gather by the wayside herbs and roots
To staunch our wounds, secure from further harm:
We are assailed to life's extremest verge.
It will be well indeed if I return,
A harmless busy fool, to my old ways!
I would forget hints of another fate,
Significant enough, which silent hours
Have lately scared me with.
FESTUS: Another! and what?
PARACELSUS: After all, Festus, you say well: I am
A man yet: I need never humble me.
780 I would have been – something, I know not what;
But though I cannot soar, I do not crawl.
There are worse portions than this one of mine.
You say well!
FESTUS: Ah!
PARACELSUS: And deeper degradation!

If the mean stimulants of vulgar praise,
If vanity should become the chosen food
Of a sunk mind, should stifle even the wish
To find its early aspirations true,
Should teach it to breathe falsehood like life-breath –
An atmosphere of craft and trick and lies;
790 Should make it proud to emulate, surpass
Base natures in the practices which woke
Its most indignant loathing once . . . No, no!
Utter damnation is reserved for hell!
I had immortal feelings; such shall never
Be wholly quenched: no, no!
                                        My friend, you wear
A melancholy face, and certain 'tis
There's little cheer in all this dismal work.
But was it my desire to set abroach
Such memories and forebodings? I foresaw
800 Where they would drive. 'Twere better we discuss
News from Lucerne or Zurich; ask and tell
Of Egypt's flaring sky or Spain's cork-groves.
    FESTUS: I have thought: trust me, this mood will pass away!
I know you and the lofty spirit you bear,
And easily ravel out a clue to all.
These are the trials meet for such as you,
Nor must you hope exemption: to be mortal
Is to be plied with trials manifold.
Look round! The obstacles which kept the rest
810 From your ambition, have been spurned by you;
Their fears, their doubts, the chains that bind them all,
Were flax before your resolute soul, which naught
Avails to awe save these delusions bred
From its own strength, its selfsame strength disguised,
Mocking itself. Be brave, dear Aureole! Since
The rabbit has his shade to frighten him,
The fawn a rustling bough, mortals their cares,
And higher natures yet would slight and laugh
At these entangling fantasies, as you
820 At trammels of a weaker intellect, –
Measure your mind's height by the shade it casts!
I know you.
    PARACELSUS: And I know you, dearest Festus!
And how you love unworthily; and how

All admiration renders blind.

FESTUS: You hold
That admiration blinds?

PARACELSUS: Ay and alas!

FESTUS: Naught blinds you less than admiration, friend!
Whether it be that all love renders wise
In its degree; from love which blends with love –
Heart answering heart – to love which spends itself
830   In silent mad idolatry of some
Pre-eminent mortal, some great soul of souls,
Which ne'er will know how well it is adored.
I say, such love is never blind; but rather
Alive to every the minutest spot
Which mars its object, and which hate (supposed
So vigilant and searching) dreams not of.
Love broods on such: what then? When first perceived
Is there no sweet strife to forget, to change,
To overflush those blemishes with all
840   The glow of general goodness they disturb?
– To make those very defects an endless source
Of new affection grown from hopes and fears?
And, when all fails, is there no gallant stand
Made even for much proved weak? no shrinking-back
Lest, since all love assimilates the soul
To what it loves, it should at length become
Almost a rival of its idol? Trust me,
If there be fiends who seek to work our hurt,
To ruin and drag down earth's mightiest spirits
850   Even at God's foot, 'twill be from such as love,
Their zeal will gather most to serve their cause;
And least from those who hate, who most essay
By contumely and scorn to blot the light
Which forces entrance even to their hearts:
For thence will our defender tear the veil
And show within each heart, as in a shrine,
The giant image of perfection, grown
In hate's despite, whose calumnies were spawned
In the untroubled presence of its eyes.
860   True admiration blinds not; nor am I
So blind. I call your sin exceptional;
It springs from one whose life has passed the bounds
Prescribed to life. Compound that fault with God!

I speak of men; to common men like me
The weakness you reveal endears you more,
Like the far traces of decay in suns.
I bid you have good cheer!
PARACELSUS: *Praeclare! Optime!*
Think of a quiet mountain-cloistered priest
Instructing Paracelsus! yet 'tis so.
870 Come, I will show you where my merit lies.
'Tis in the advance of individual minds
That the slow crowd should ground their expectation
Eventually to follow; as the sea
Waits ages in its bed till some one wave
Out of the multitudinous mass, extends
The empire of the whole, some feet perhaps,
Over the strip of sand which could confine
Its fellows so long time: thenceforth the rest,
Even to the meanest, hurry in at once,
880 And so much is clear gained. I shall be glad
If all my labours, failing of aught else,
Suffice to make such inroad and procure
A wider range for thought: nay, they do this;
For, whatsoe'er my notions of true knowledge
And a legitimate success, may be,
I am not blind to my undoubted rank
When classed with others: I precede my age:
And whoso wills is very free to mount
These labours as a platform whence his own
890 May have a prosperous outset. But, alas!
My followers – they are noisy as you heard;
But, for intelligence, the best of them
So clumsily wield the weapons I supply
And they extol, that I begin to doubt
Whether their own rude clubs and pebble-stones
Would not do better service than my arms
Thus vilely swayed – if error will not fall
Sooner before the old awkward batterings
Than my more subtle warfare, not half learned.
900 FESTUS: I would supply that art, then, or withhold
New arms until you teach their mystery.
PARACELSUS: Content you, 'tis my wish; I have recourse
To the simplest training. Day by day I seek
To wake the mood, the spirit which alone

Can make those arms of any use to men.
Of course they are for swaggering forth at once
Graced with Ulysses' bow, Achilles' shield –
Flash on us, all in armour, thou Achilles!
Make our hearts dance to thy resounding step!
910 A proper sight to scare the crows away!
FESTUS: Pity you choose not then some other method
Of coming at your point. The marvellous art
At length established in the world bids fair
To remedy all hindrances like these:
Trust to Frobenius' press the precious lore
Obscured by uncouth manner, or unfit
For raw beginners; let his types secure
A deathless monument to after-time;
Meanwhile wait confidently and enjoy
920 The ultimate effect: sooner or later
You shall be all-revealed.
PARACELSUS: The old dull question
In a new form; no more. Thus: I possess
Two sorts of knowledge; one, – vast, shadowy,
Hints of the unbounded aim I once pursued:
The other consists of many secrets, caught
While bent on nobler prize, – perhaps a few
Prime principles which may conduct to much:
These last I offer to my followers here.
Now, bid me chronicle the first of these,
930 My ancient study, and in effect you bid
Revert to the wild courses just abjured:
I must go find them scattered through the world.
Then, for the principles, they are so simple
(Being chiefly of the overturning sort),
That one time is as proper to propound them
As any other – tomorrow at my class,
Or half a century hence embalmed in print.
For if mankind intend to learn at all,
They must begin by giving faith to them
940 And acting on them: and I do not see
But that my lectures serve indifferent well:
No doubt these dogmas fall not to the earth,
For all their novelty and rugged setting.
I think my class will not forget the day
I let them know the gods of Israel,

Aëtius, Oribasius, Galen, Rhasis,
Serapion, Avicenna, Averröes,
Were blocks!
FESTUS: And that reminds me, I heard something
About your waywardness: you burned their books,
950   It seems, instead of answering those sages.
PARACELSUS: And who said that?
FESTUS: Some I met yesternight
With Oecolampadius. As you know, the purpose
Of this short stay at Basil was to learn
His pleasure touching certain missives sent
For our Zuinglius and himself. 'Twas he
Apprised me that the famous teacher here
Was my old friend.
PARACELSUS: Ah, I forgot: you went . . .
FESTUS: From Zurich with advices for the ear
Of Luther, now at Wittenberg – (you know,
960   I make no doubt, the differences of late
With Carolostadius) – and returning sought
Basil and . . .
PARACELSUS: I remember. Here's a case, now,
Will teach you why I answer not, but burn
The books you mention. Pray, does Luther dream
His arguments convince by their own force
The crowds that own his doctrine? No, indeed!
His plain denial of established points
Ages had sanctified and men supposed
Could never be oppugned while earth was under
970   And heaven above them – points which chance or time
Affected not – did more than the array
Of argument which followed. Boldly deny!
There is much breath-stopping, hair-stiffening
Awhile; then, amazed glances, mute awaiting
The thunderbolt which does not come: and next,
Reproachful wonder and inquiry: those
Who else had never stirred, are able now
To find the rest out for themselves, perhaps
To outstrip him who set the whole at work,
980   – As never will my wise class its instructor.
And you saw Luther?
FESTUS: 'Tis a wondrous soul!
PARACELSUS: True: the so-heavy chain which galled mankind

Is shattered, and the noblest of us all
Must bow to the deliverer – nay, the worker
Of our own project – we who long before
Had burst our trammels, but forgot the crowd,
We should have taught, still groaned beneath their load:
This he has done and nobly. Speed that may!
Whatever be my chance or my mischance,
990   What benefits mankind must glad me too;
And men seem made, though not as I believed,
For something better than the times produce.
Witness these gangs of peasants your new lights
From Suabia have possessed, whom Münzer leads,
And whom the duke, the landgrave and the elector
Will calm in blood! Well, well; 'tis not my world!
FESTUS: Hark!
PARACELSUS: 'Tis the melancholy wind astir
Within the trees; the embers too are grey:
Morn must be near.
FESTUS: Best ope the casement: see,
1000   The night, late strewn with clouds and flying stars,
Is blank and motionless: how peaceful sleep
The tree-tops altogether! Like an asp,
The wind slips whispering from bough to bough.
PARACELSUS: Ay; you would gaze on a wind-shaken tree
By the hour, nor count time lost.
FESTUS: So you shall gaze:
Those happy times will come again.
PARACELSUS: Gone, gone,
Those pleasant times! Does not the moaning wind
Seem to bewail that we have gained such gains
And bartered sleep for them?
FESTUS: It is our trust
1010   That there is yet another world to mend
All error and mischance.
PARACELSUS: Another world!
And why this world, this common world, to be
A make-shift, a mere foil, how fair soever,
To some fine life to come? Man must be fed
With angels' food, forsooth; and some few traces
Of a diviner nature which look out
Through his corporeal baseness, warrant him
In a supreme contempt of all provision

For his inferior tastes – some straggling marks
1020 Which constitute his essence, just as truly
As here and there a gem would constitute
The rock, their barren bed, one diamond.
But were it so – were man all mind – he gains
A station little enviable. From God
Down to the lowest spirit ministrant,
Intelligence exists which casts our mind
Into immeasurable shade. No, no:
Love, hope, fear, faith – these make humanity;
These are its sign and note and character,
1030 And these I have lost! – gone, shut from me for ever,
Like a dead friend safe from unkindness more!
See, morn at length. The heavy darkness seems
Diluted, grey and clear without the stars;
The shrubs bestir and rouse themselves as if
Some snake, that weighed them down all night, let go
His hold; and from the East, fuller and fuller,
Day, like a mighty river, flowing in;
But clouded, wintry, desolate and cold.
Yet see how that broad prickly star-shaped plant,
1040 Half-down in the crevice, spreads its woolly leaves
All thick and glistering with diamond dew.
And you depart for Einsiedeln this day,
And we have spent all night in talk like this!
If you would have me better for your love,
Revert no more to these sad themes.

FESTUS: One favour,
And I have done. I leave you, deeply moved;
Unwilling to have fared so well, the while
My friend has changed so sorely. If this mood
Shall pass away, if light once more arise
1050 Where all is darkness now, if you see fit
To hope and trust again, and strive again,
You will remember – not our love alone –
But that my faith in God's desire that man
Should trust on his support, (as I must think
You trusted) is obscured and dim through you:
For you are thus, and this is no reward.
Will you not call me to your side, dear Aureole?

PART IV
PARACELSUS ASPIRES

Scene: Colmar in Alsatia: an Inn. 1528.

PARACELSUS, FESTUS

    PARACELSUS [*to* JOHANNES OPORINUS, *his Secretary*]:
      Sic itur ad astra! Dear Von Visenburg
      Is scandalized, and poor Torinus paralysed,
      And every honest soul that Basil holds
      Aghast; and yet we live, as one may say,
      Just as though Liechtenfels had never set
      So true a value on his sorry carcass,
      And learned Pütter had not frowned us dumb.
      We live; and shall as surely start tomorrow
      For Nuremberg, as we drink speedy scathe
10   To Basil in this mantling wine, suffused
      A delicate blush, no fainter tinge is born
      I' the shut heart of a bud. Pledge me, good John –
      'Basil; a hot plague ravage it, and Pütter
      Oppose the plague!' Even so? Do you too share
      Their panic, the reptiles? Ha, ha; faint through these,
      Desist for these! They manage matters so
      At Basil, 'tis like: but others may find means
      To bring the stoutest braggart of the tribe
      Once more to crouch in silence – means to breed
20   A stupid wonder in each fool again,
      Now big with admiration at the skill
      Which stript a vain pretender of his plumes:
      And, that done, – means to brand each slavish brow
      So deeply, surely, ineffaceably,
      That henceforth flattery shall not pucker it
      Out of the furrow; there that stamp shall stay
      To show the next they fawn on, what they are,
      This Basil with its magnates, – fill my cup, –
      Whom I curse soul and limb. And now dispatch,
30   Dispatch, my trusty John; and what remains
      To do, whate'er arrangements for our trip
      Are yet to be completed, see you hasten
      This night; we'll weather the storm at least: tomorrow
      For Nuremberg! Now leave us; this grave clerk

Has divers weighty matters for my ear:

[OPORINUS *goes out*]

And spare my lungs. At last, my gallant Festus,
I am rid of this arch-knave that dogs my heels
As a gaunt crow a gasping sheep; at last
May give a loose to my delight. How kind,
40   How very kind, my first best only friend!
Why, this looks like fidelity. Embrace me!
Not a hair silvered yet? Right! you shall live
Till I am worth your love; you shall be proud,
And I – but let time show! Did you not wonder?
I sent to you because our compact weighed
Upon my conscience – (you recall the night
At Basil, which the gods confound!) – because
Once more I aspire. I call you to my side:
You come. You thought my message strange?

FESTUS: So strange

50   That I must hope, indeed, your messenger
Has mingled his own fancies with the words
Purporting to be yours.

PARACELSUS: He said no more,
'Tis probable, than the precious folk I leave
Said fiftyfold more roughly. Well-a-day,
'Tis true! poor Paracelsus is exposed
At last; a most egregious quack he proves:
And those he overreached must spit their hate
On one who, utterly beneath contempt,
Could yet deceive their topping wits. You heard
60   Bare truth; and at my bidding you come here
To speed me on my enterprise, as once
Your lavish wishes sped me, my own friend!

FESTUS: What is your purpose, Aureole?

PARACELSUS: Oh, for purpose,
There is no lack of precedents in a case
Like mine; at least, if not precisely mine,
The case of men cast off by those they sought
To benefit.

FESTUS: They really cast you off?
I only heard a vague tale of some priest,
Cured by your skill, who wrangled at your claim,
70   Knowing his life's worth best; and how the judge
The matter was referred to saw no cause

To interfere, nor you to hide your full
Contempt of him; nor he, again, to smother
His wrath thereat, which raised so fierce a flame
That Basil soon was made no place for you.
PARACELSUS: The affair of Liechtenfels? the shallowest fable,
   The last and silliest outrage – mere pretence!
   I knew it, I foretold it from the first,
   How soon the stupid wonder you mistook
80 For genuine loyalty – a cheering promise
   Of better things to come – would pall and pass;
   And every word comes true. Saul is among
   The prophets! Just so long as I was pleased
   To play off the mere antics of my art,
   Fantastic gambols leading to no end,
   I got huge praise: but one can ne'er keep down
   Our foolish nature's weakness. There they flocked,
   Poor devils, jostling, swearing and perspiring,
   Till the walls rang again; and all for me!
90 I had a kindness for them, which was right;
   But then I stopped not till I tacked to that
   A trust in them and a respect – a sort
   Of sympathy for them; I must needs begin
   To teach them, not amaze them, 'to impart
   The spirit which should instigate the search
   Of truth,' just what you bade me! I spoke out.
   Forthwith a mighty squadron, in disgust,
   Filed off – 'the sifted chaff of the sack,' I said,
   Redoubling my endeavours to secure
100 The rest. When lo! one man had tarried so long
   Only to ascertain if I supported
   This tenet of his, or that; another loved
   To hear impartially before he judged,
   And having heard, now judged; this bland disciple
   Passed for my dupe, but all along, it seems,
   Spied error where his neighbours marvelled most;
   That fiery doctor who had hailed me friend,
   Did it because my by-paths, once proved wrong
   And beaconed properly, would commend again
110 The good old ways our sires jogged safely o'er,
   Though not their squeamish sons; the other worthy
   Discovered divers verses of Saint John,
   Which, read successively, refreshed the soul,

But, muttered backwards, cured the gout, the stone,
The colic and what not. *Quid multa?* The end
Was a clear class-room, and a quiet leer
From grave folk, and a sour reproachful glance
From those in chief who, cap in hand, installed
The new professor scarce a year before;
120   And a vast flourish about patient merit
Obscured awhile by flashy tricks, but sure
Sooner or later to emerge in splendour –
Of which the example was some luckless wight
Whom my arrival had discomfited,
But now, it seems, the general voice recalled
To fill my chair and so efface the stain
Basil had long incurred. I sought no better,
Only a quiet dismissal from my post,
And from my heart I wished them better suited
130   And better served. Good night to Basil, then!
But fast as I proposed to rid the tribe
Of my obnoxious back, I could not spare them
The pleasure of a parting kick.

FESTUS: You smile:
  Despise them as they merit!

PARACELSUS: If I smile,
   'Tis with as very contempt as ever turned
Flesh into stone. This courteous recompense,
This grateful . . . Festus, were your nature fit
To be defiled, your eyes the eyes to ache
At gangrene-blotches, eating poison-blains,
140   The ulcerous barky scurf of leprosy
Which finds – a man, and leaves – a hideous thing
That cannot but be mended by hell fire,
– I would lay bare to you the human heart
Which God cursed long ago, and devils make since
Their pet nest and their never-tiring home.
Oh, sages have discovered we are born
For various ends – to love, to know: has ever
One stumbled, in his search, on any signs
Of a nature in us formed to hate? To hate?
150   If that be our true object which evokes
Our powers in fullest strength, be sure 'tis hate!
Yet men have doubted if the best and bravest
Of spirits can nourish him with hate alone.

I had not the monopoly of fools,
It seems, at Basil.
FESTUS: But your plans, your plans!
I have yet to learn your purpose, Aureole!
PARACELSUS: Whether to sink beneath such ponderous shame,
   To shrink up like a crushed snail, undergo
   In silence and desist from further toil,
160   And so subside into a monument
   Of one their censure blasted? or to bow
   Cheerfully as submissively, to lower
   My old pretensions even as Basil dictates,
   To drop into the rank her wits assign me
   And live as they prescribe, and make that use
   Of my poor knowledge which their rules allow,
   Proud to be patted now and then, and careful
   To practise the true posture for receiving
   The amplest benefit from their hoofs' appliance
170   When they shall condescend to tutor me?
   Then, one may feel resentment like a flame
   Within, and deck false systems in truth's garb,
   And tangle and entwine mankind with error,
   And give them darkness for a dower and falsehood
   For a possession, ages: or one may mope
   Into a shade through thinking, or else drowse
   Into a dreamless sleep and so die off.
   But I, – now Festus shall divine! – but I
   Am merely setting out once more, embracing
180   My earliest aims again! What thinks he now?
FESTUS: Your aims? the aims? – to Know? and where is found
   The early trust...
PARACELSUS: Nay, not so fast; I say,
   The aims – not the old means. You know they made me
   A laughing-stock; I was a fool; you know
   The when and the how: hardly those means again!
   Not but they had their beauty; who should know
   Their passing beauty, if not I? Still, dreams
   They were, so let them vanish, yet in beauty
   If that may be. Stay: thus they pass in song!
       [*He sings*]
190   Heap cassia, sandal-buds and stripes
            Of labdanum, and aloe-balls,
          Smeared with dull nard an Indian wipes

From out her hair: such balsam falls
Down sea-side mountain pedestals,
From tree-tops where tired winds are fain,
Spent with the vast and howling main,
To treasure half their island-gain.

And strew faint sweetness from some old
Egyptian's fine worm-eaten shroud
200 Which breaks to dust when once unrolled;
Or shredded perfume, like a cloud
From closet long to quiet vowed,
With mothed and dropping arras hung,
Mouldering her lute and books among,
As when a queen, long dead, was young.

Mine, every word! And on such pile shall die
My lovely fancies, with fair perished things,
Themselves fair and forgotten; yes, forgotten,
Or why abjure them? So, I made this rhyme
210 That fitting dignity might be preserved;
No little proud was I; though the list of drugs
Smacks of my old vocation, and the verse
Halts like the best of Luther's psalms.
FESTUS: But, Aureole,
Talk not thus wildly and madly. I am here –
Did you know all! I have travelled far, indeed,
To learn your wishes. Be yourself again!
For in this mood I recognize you less
Than in the horrible despondency
I witnessed last. You may account this, joy;
220 But rather let me gaze on that despair
Than hear these incoherent words and see
This flushed cheek and intensely-sparkling eye.
PARACELSUS: Why, man, I was light-hearted in my prime,
I am light-hearted now; what would you have?
Aprile was a poet, I make songs –
'Tis the very augury of success I want!
Why should I not be joyous now as then?
FESTUS: Joyous! and how? and what remains for joy?
You have declared the ends (which I am sick
230 Of naming) are impracticable.
PARACELSUS: Ay,

Pursued as I pursued them – the arch-fool!
Listen: my plan will please you not, 'tis like,
But you are little versed in the world's ways.
This is my plan – (first drinking its good luck) –
I will accept all helps; all I despised
So rashly at the outset, equally
With early impulses, late years have quenched:
I have tried each way singly: now for both!
All helps! no one sort shall exclude the rest.
240 I seek to know and to enjoy at once,
Not one without the other as before.
Suppose my labour should seem God's own cause
Once more, as first I dreamed, – it shall not balk me
Of the meanest earthliest sensualest delight
That may be snatched; for every joy is gain,
And gain is gain, however small. My soul
Can die then, nor be taunted – 'what was gained?'
Nor, on the other hand, should pleasure follow
As though I had not spurned her hitherto,
250 Shall she o'ercloud my spirit's rapt communion
With the tumultuous past, the teeming future,
Glorious with visions of a full success.
FESTUS: Success!
PARACELSUS: And wherefore not? Why not prefer
Results obtained in my best state of being,
To those derived alone from seasons dark
As the thoughts they bred? When I was best, my youth
Unwasted, seemed success not surest too?
It is the nature of darkness to obscure.
I am a wanderer: I remember well
260 One journey, how I feared the track was missed,
So long the city I desired to reach
Lay hid; when suddenly its spires afar
Flashed through the circling clouds; you may conceive
My transport. Soon the vapours closed again,
But I had seen the city, and one such glance
No darkness could obscure: nor shall the present –
A few dull hours, a passing shame or two,
Destroy the vivid memories of the past.
I will fight the battle out; a little spent
270 Perhaps, but still an able combatant.
You look at my grey hair and furrowed brow?

But I can turn even weakness to account:
Of many tricks I know, 'tis not the least
To push the ruins of my frame, whereon
The fire of vigour trembles scarce alive,
Into a heap, and send the flame aloft.
What should I do with age? So, sickness lends
An aid; it being, I fear, the source of all
We boast of: mind is nothing but disease,
280   And natural health is ignorance.

FESTUS: I see
But one good symptom in this notable scheme.
I feared your sudden journey had in view
To wreak immediate vengeance on your foes;
'Tis not so: I am glad.

PARACELSUS: And if I please
To spit on them, to trample them, what then?
'Tis sorry warfare truly, but the fools
Provoke it. I would spare their self-conceit,
But if they must provoke me, cannot suffer
Forbearance on my part, if I may keep
290   No quality in the shade, must needs put forth
Power to match power, my strength against their strength,
And teach them their own game with their own arms –
Why, be it so and let them take their chance!
I am above them like a god, there's no
Hiding the fact: what idle scruples, then,
Were those that ever bade me soften it,
Communicate it gently to the world,
Instead of proving my supremacy,
Taking my natural station o'er their head,
300   Then owning all the glory was a man's!
– And in my elevation man's would be.
But live and learn, though life's short, learning, hard!
And therefore, though the wreck of my past self,
I fear, dear Pütter, that your lecture-room
Must wait awhile for its best ornament,
The penitent empiric, who set up
For somebody, but soon was taught his place;
Now, but too happy to be let confess
His error, snuff the candles, and illustrate
310   (*Fiat experientia corpore vili*)
Your medicine's soundness in his person. Wait,

Good Pütter!

FESTUS: He who sneers thus, is a god!

PARACELSUS: Ay, ay, laugh at me! I am very glad
    You are not gulled by all this swaggering; you
    Can see the root of the matter! – how I strive
    To put a good face on the overthrow
    I have experienced, and to bury and hide
    My degradation in its length and breadth;
    How the mean motives I would make you think
320   Just mingle as is due with nobler aims,
    The appetites I modestly allow
    May influence me as being mortal still –
    Do goad me, drive me on, and fast supplant
    My youth's desires. You are no stupid dupe:
    You find me out! Yes, I had sent for you
    To palm these childish lies upon you, Festus!
    Laugh – you shall laugh at me!

FESTUS: The past, then, Aureole,
    Proves nothing? Is our interchange of love
    Yet to begin? Have I to swear I mean
330   No flattery in this speech or that? For you,
    Whate'er you say, there is no degradation;
    These low thoughts are no inmates of your mind,
    Or wherefore this disorder? You are vexed
    As much by the intrusion of base views,
    Familiar to your adversaries, as they
    Were troubled should your qualities alight
    Amid their murky souls; not otherwise,
    A stray wolf which the winter forces down
    From our bleak hills, suffices to affright
340   A village in the vales – while foresters
    Sleep calm, though all night long the famished troop
    Snuff round and scratch against their crazy huts.
    These evil thoughts are monsters, and will flee.

PARACELSUS: May you be happy, Festus, my own friend!

FESTUS: Nay, further; the delights you fain would think
    The superseders of your nobler aims,
    Though ordinary and harmless stimulants,
    Will ne'er content you. . . .

PARACELSUS: Hush! I once despised them,
    But that soon passes. We are high at first
350   In our demand, nor will abate a jot

Of toil's strict value; but time passes o'er,
And humbler spirits accept what we refuse:
In short, when some such comfort is doled out
As these delights, we cannot long retain
Bitter contempt which urges us at first
To hurl it back, but hug it to our breast
And thankfully retire. This life of mine
Must be lived out and a grave thoroughly earned:
I am just fit for that and naught beside.
360 I told you once, I cannot now enjoy,
Unless I deem my knowledge gains through joy;
Nor can I know, but straight warm tears reveal
My need of linking also joy to knowledge:
So, on I drive, enjoying all I can,
And knowing all I can. I speak, of course,
Confusedly; this will better explain – feel here!
Quick beating, is it not? – a fire of the heart
To work off some way, this as well as any.
So, Festus sees me fairly launched; his calm
370 Compassionate look might have disturbed me once,
But now, far from rejecting, I invite
What bids me press the closer, lay myself
Open before him, and be soothed with pity;
I hope, if he command hope, and believe
As he directs me – satiating myself
With his enduring love. And Festus quits me
To give place to some credulous disciple
Who holds that God is wise, but Paracelsus
Has his peculiar merits: I suck in
380 That homage, chuckle o'er that admiration,
And then dismiss the fool; for night is come,
And I betake myself to study again,
Till patient searchings after hidden lore
Half wring some bright truth from its prison; my frame
Trembles, my forehead's veins swell out, my hair
Tingles for triumph. Slow and sure the morn
Shall break on my pent room and dwindling lamp
And furnace dead, and scattered earths and ores;
When, with a failing heart and throbbing brow,
390 I must review my captured truth, sum up
Its value, trace what ends to what begins,
Its present power with its eventual bearings,

Latent affinities, the views it opens,
And its full length in perfecting my scheme.
I view it sternly circumscribed, cast down
From the high place my fond hopes yielded it,
Proved worthless – which, in getting, yet had cost
Another wrench to this fast-falling frame.
Then, quick, the cup to quaff, that chases sorrow!
400   I lapse back into youth, and take again
My fluttering pulse for evidence that God
Means good to me, will make my cause his own.
See! I have cast off this remorseless care
Which clogged a spirit born to soar so free,
And my dim chamber has become a tent,
Festus is sitting by me, and his Michal . . .
Why do you start? I say, she listening here,
(For yonder – Würzburg through the orchard-bough!)
Motions as though such ardent words should find
410   No echo in a maiden's quiet soul,
But her pure bosom heaves, her eyes fill fast
With tears, her sweet lips tremble all the while!
Ha, ha!

FESTUS: It seems, then, you expect to reap
No unreal joy from this your present course,
But rather . . .

PARACELSUS: Death! To die! I owe that much
To what, at least, I was. I should be sad
To live contented after such a fall,
To thrive and fatten after such reverse!
The whole plan is a makeshift, but will last
420   My time.

FESTUS: And you have never mused and said,
'I had a noble purpose, and the strength
To compass it; but I have stopped half-way,
And wrongly given the first-fruits of my toil
To objects little worthy of the gift.
Why linger round them still? why clench my fault?
Why seek for consolation in defeat,
In vain endeavours to derive a beauty
From ugliness? why seek to make the most
Of what no power can change, nor strive instead
430   With mighty effort to redeem the past
And, gathering up the treasures thus cast down,

To hold a steadfast course till I arrive
At their fit destination and my own?'
You have never pondered thus?

PARACELSUS: Have I, you ask?
Often at midnight, when most fancies come,
Would some such airy project visit me:
But ever at the end . . . or will you hear
The same thing in a tale, a parable?
You and I, wandering over the world wide,
440   Chance to set foot upon a desert coast.
Just as we cry, 'No human voice before
Broke the inveterate silence of these rocks!'
– Their querulous echo startles us; we turn:
What ravaged structure still looks o'er the sea?
Some characters remain, too! While we read,
The sharp salt wind, impatient for the last
Of even this record, wistfully comes and goes,
Or sings what we recover, mocking it.
This is the record; and my voice, the wind's.
    [*He sings*]
450   Over the sea our galleys went,
              With cleaving prows in order brave
              To a speeding wind and a bounding wave,
                  A gallant armament:
              Each bark built out of a forest-tree
                Left leafy and rough as first it grew,
              And nailed all over the gaping sides,
              Within and without, with black bull-hides,
              Seethed in fat and suppled in flame,
              To bear the playful billows' game:
460   So, each good ship was rude to see,
              Rude and bare to the outward view,
                But each upbore a stately tent
              Where cedar pales in scented row
              Kept out the flakes of the dancing brine,
              And an awning drooped the mast below,
              In fold on fold of the purple fine,
              That neither noontide nor starshine
              Nor moonlight cold which maketh mad,
                Might pierce the regal tenement.
470   When the sun dawned, oh, gay and glad
              We set the sail and plied the oar;

But when the night-wind blew like breath,
For joy of one day's voyage more,
We sang together on the wide sea,
Like men at peace on a peaceful shore;
Each sail was loosed to the wind so free,
Each helm made sure by the twilight star,
And in a sleep as calm as death,
We, the voyagers from afar,
480   Lay stretched along, each weary crew
In a circle round its wondrous tent
Whence gleamed soft light and curled rich scent,
    And with light and perfume, music too:
So the stars wheeled round, and the darkness past,
And at morn we started beside the mast,
And still each ship was sailing fast.

Now, one morn, land appeared – a speck
Dim trembling betwixt sea and sky:
'Avoid it,' cried our pilot, 'check
490   The shout, restrain the eager eye!'
But the heaving sea was black behind
For many a night and many a day,
And land, though but a rock, drew nigh;
So, we broke the cedar pales away,
Let the purple awning flap in the wind,
    And a statue bright was on every deck!
We shouted, every man of us,
And steered right into the harbour thus,
With pomp and paean glorious.

500 A hundred shapes of lucid stone!
    All day we built its shrine for each,
A shrine of rock for every one,
Nor paused till in the westering sun
    We sat together on the beach
To sing because our task was done.
When lo! what shouts and merry songs!
What laughter all the distance stirs!
A loaded raft with happy throngs
Of gentle islanders!
510 'Our isles are just at hand,' they cried,
    'Like cloudlets faint in even sleeping;

Our temple-gates are opened wide,
 Our olive-groves thick shade are keeping
For these majestic forms' – they cried.
Oh, then we awoke with sudden start
From our deep dream, and knew, too late,
How bare the rock, how desolate,
Which had received our precious freight:
 Yet we called out – 'Depart!
520 Our gifts, once given, must here abide.
  Our work is done; we have no heart
To mar our work,' – we cried.

FESTUS: In truth?

PARACELSUS: Nay, wait: all this in tracings faint
On rugged stones strewn here and there, but piled
In order once: then follows – mark what follows!
'The sad rhyme of the men who proudly clung
To their first fault, and withered in their pride.'

FESTUS: Come back then, Aureole; as you fear God, come!
This is foul sin; come back! Renounce the past,
530 Forswear the future; look for joy no more,
But wait death's summons amid holy sights,
And trust me for the event – peace, if not joy.
Return with me to Einsiedeln, dear Aureole!

PARACELSUS: No way, no way! it would not turn to good.
A spotless child sleeps on the flowering moss –
'Tis well for him; but when a sinful man,
Envying such slumber, may desire to put
His guilt away, shall he return at once
To rest by lying there? Our sires knew well
540 (Spite of the grave discoveries of their sons)
The fitting course for such: dark cells, dim lamps,
A stone floor one may writhe on like a worm:
No mossy pillow blue with violets!

FESTUS: I see no symptom of these absolute
And tyrannous passions. You are calmer now.
This verse-making can purge you well enough
Without the terrible penance you describe.
You love me still: the lusts you fear will never
Outrage your friend. To Einsiedeln, once more!
550 Say but the word!

PARACELSUS: No, no; those lusts forbid:
They crouch, I know, cowering with half-shut eye

Beside you; 'tis their nature. Thrust yourself
Between them and their prey; let some fool style me
Or king or quack, it matters not – then try
Your wisdom, urge them to forego their treat!
No, no; learn better and look deeper, Festus!
If you knew how a devil sneers within me
While you are talking now of this, now that,
As though we differed scarcely save in trifles!

560 FESTUS: Do we so differ? True, change must proceed,
Whether for good or ill; keep from me, which!
Do not confide all secrets: I was born
To hope, and you ...

PARACELSUS: To trust: you know the fruits!

FESTUS: Listen: I do believe, what you call trust
Was self-delusion at the best: for, see!
So long as God would kindly pioneer
A path for you, and screen you from the world,
Procure you full exemption from man's lot,
Man's common hopes and fears, on the mere pretext
570 Of your engagement in his service – yield you
A limitless licence, make you God, in fact,
And turn your slave – you were content to say
Most courtly praises! What is it, at last,
But selfishness without example? None
Could trace God's will so plain as you, while yours
Remained implied in it; but now you fail,
And we, who prate about that will, are fools!
In short, God's service is established here
As he determines fit, and not your way,
580 And this you cannot brook. Such discontent
Is weak. Renounce all creatureship at once!
Affirm an absolute right to have and use
Your energies; as though the rivers should say –
'We rush to the ocean; what have we to do
With feeding streamlets, lingering in the vales,
Sleeping in lazy pools?' Set up that plea,
That will be bold at least!

PARACELSUS: 'Tis like enough.
The serviceable spirits are those, no doubt,
The East produces: lo, the master bids, –
590 They wake, raise terraces and garden-grounds
In one night's space; and, this done, straight begin

Another century's sleep, to the great praise
Of him that framed them wise and beautiful,
Till a lamp's rubbing, or some chance akin,
Wake them again. I am of different mould.
I would have soothed my lord, and slaved for him
And done him service past my narrow bond,
And thus I get rewarded for my pains!
Beside, 'tis vain to talk of forwarding
600   God's glory otherwise; this is alone
The sphere of its increase, as far as men
Increase it; why, then, look beyond this sphere?
We are his glory; and if we be glorious,
Is not the thing achieved?

FESTUS: Shall one like me
Judge hearts like yours? Though years have changed you
    much,
And you have left your first love, and retain
Its empty shade to veil your crooked ways,
Yet I still hold that you have honoured God.
And who shall call your course without reward?
610   For, wherefore this repining at defeat
Had triumph ne'er inured you to high hopes?
I urge you to forsake the life you curse,
And what success attends me? – simply talk
Of passion, weakness and remorse; in short,
Anything but the naked truth – you choose
This so-despised career, and cheaply hold
My happiness, or rather other men's.
Once more, return!

PARACELSUS: And quickly. John the thief
Has pilfered half my secrets by this time:
620   And we depart by daybreak. I am weary,
I know not how; not even the wine-cup soothes
My brain tonight . . .
Do you not thoroughly despise me, Festus?
No flattery! One like you needs not be told
We live and breathe deceiving and deceived.
Do you not scorn me from your heart of hearts,
Me and my cant, each petty subterfuge,
My rhymes and all this frothy shower of words,
My glozing self-deceit, my outward crust
630   Of lies which wrap, as tetter, morphew, furfair

Wrapt the sound flesh? – so, see you flatter not!
Even God flatters: but my friend, at least,
Is true. I would depart, secure henceforth
Against all further insult, hate and wrong
From puny foes; my one friend's scorn shall brand me:
No fear of sinking deeper!

FESTUS: No, dear Aureole!
No, no; I came to counsel faithfully.
There are old rules, made long ere we were born,
By which I judge you. I, so fallible,
640   So infinitely low beside your mighty
Majestic spirit! – even I can see
You own some higher law than ours which call
Sin, what is no sin – weakness, what is strength.
But I have only these, such as they are,
To guide me; and I blame you where they bid,
Only so long as blaming promises
To win peace for your soul: the more, that sorrow
Has fallen on me of late, and they have helped me
So that I faint not under my distress.
650   But wherefore should I scruple to avow
In spite of all, as brother judging brother,
Your fate is most inexplicable to me?
And should you perish without recompense
And satisfaction yet – too hastily
I have relied on love: you may have sinned,
But you have loved. As a mere human matter –
As I would have God deal with fragile men
In the end – I say that you will triumph yet!

PARACELSUS: Have you felt sorrow, Festus? – 'tis because
660   You love me. Sorrow, and sweet Michal yours!
Well thought on: never let her know this last
Dull winding-up of all: these miscreants dared
Insult me – me she loved: – so, grieve her not!

FESTUS: Your ill success can little grieve her now.

PARACELSUS: Michal is dead! pray Christ we do not craze!

FESTUS: Aureole, dear Aureole, look not on me thus!
Fool, fool! this is the heart grown sorrow-proof –
I cannot bear those eyes.

PARACELSUS: Nay, really dead?

FESTUS: 'Tis scarce a month.

PARACELSUS: Stone dead! – then you have laid her

670 Among the flowers ere this. Now, do you know,
I can reveal a secret which shall comfort
Even you. I have no julep, as men think,
To cheat the grave; but a far better secret.
Know, then, you did not ill to trust your love
To the cold earth: I have thought much of it:
For I believe we do not wholly die.

FESTUS: Aureole!

PARACELSUS: Nay, do not laugh; there is a reason
For what I say: I think the soul can never
Taste death. I am, just now, as you may see,
680 Very unfit to put so strange a thought
In an intelligible dress of words;
But take it as my trust, she is not dead.

FESTUS: But not on this account alone? you surely,
– Aureole, you have believed this all along?

PARACELSUS: And Michal sleeps among the roots and dews,
While I am moved at Basil, and full of schemes
For Nuremberg, and hoping and despairing,
As though it mattered how the farce plays out,
So it be quickly played. Away, away!
690 Have your will, rabble! while we fight the prize,
Troop you in safety to the snug back-seats
And leave a clear arena for the brave
About to perish for your sport! – Behold!

PART V
PARACELSUS ATTAINS

Scene: Salzburg; a cell in the Hospital of Saint Sebastian. 1541.

FESTUS, PARACELSUS

FESTUS: No change! The weary night is well-nigh spent,
The lamp burns low, and through the casement-bars
Grey morning glimmers feebly: yet no change!
Another night, and still no sigh has stirred
That fallen discoloured mouth, no pang relit
Those fixed eyes, quenched by the decaying body,
Like torch-flame choked in dust. While all beside
Was breaking, to the last they held out bright,

As a stronghold where life intrenched itself;
10   But they are dead now – very blind and dead:
He will drowse into death without a groan.

My Aureole – my forgotten, ruined Aureole!
The days are gone, are gone! How grand thou wast!
And now not one of those who struck thee down –
Poor glorious spirit – concerns him even to stay
And satisfy himself his little hand
Could turn God's image to a livid thing.

Another night, and yet no change! 'Tis much
That I should sit by him, and bathe his brow,
20   And chafe his hands; 'tis much: but he will sure
Know me, and look on me, and speak to me
Once more – but only once! His hollow cheek
Looked all night long as though a creeping laugh
At his own state were just about to break
From the dying man: my brain swam, my throat swelled,
And yet I could not turn away. In truth,
They told me how, when first brought here, he seemed
Resolved to live, to lose no faculty;
Thus striving to keep up his shattered strength,
30   Until they bore him to this stifling cell:
When straight his features fell, an hour made white
The flushed face, and relaxed the quivering limb,
Only the eye remained intense awhile
As though it recognized the tomb-like place,
And then he lay as here he lies.
                    Ay, here!
Here is earth's noblest, nobly garlanded –
Her bravest champion with his well-won prize –
Her best achievement, her sublime amends
For countless generations fleeting fast
40   And followed by no trace; – the creature-god
She instances when angels would dispute
The title of her brood to rank with them.
Angels, this is our angel! Those bright forms
We clothe with purple, crown and call to thrones,
Are human, but not his; those are but men
Whom other men press round and kneel before;
Those palaces are dwelt in by mankind;

Higher provision is for him you seek
Amid our pomps and glories: see it here!
50   Behold earth's paragon! Now, raise thee, clay!

God! Thou art love! I build my faith on that.
Even as I watch beside thy tortured child
Unconscious whose hot tears fall fast by him,
So doth thy right hand guide us through the world
Wherein we stumble. God! what shall we say?
How has he sinned? How else should he have done?
Surely he sought thy praise – thy praise, for all
He might be busied by the task so much
As half forget awhile its proper end.
60   Dost thou well, Lord? Thou canst not but prefer
That I should range myself upon his side –
How could he stop at every step to set
Thy glory forth? Hadst thou but granted him
Success, thy honour would have crowned success,
A halo round a star. Or, say he erred, –
Save him, dear God; it will be like thee: bathe him
In light and life! Thou art not made like us;
We should be wroth in such a case; but thou
Forgivest – so, forgive these passionate thoughts
70   Which come unsought and will not pass away!
I know thee, who hast kept my path, and made
Light for me in the darkness, tempering sorrow
So that it reached me like a solemn joy;
It were too strange that I should doubt thy love.
But what am I? Thou madest him and knowest
How he was fashioned. I could never err
That way: the quiet place beside thy feet,
Reserved for me, was ever in my thoughts:
But he – thou shouldst have favoured him as well!

80   Ah! he wakens! Aureole, I am here! 'tis Festus!
I cast away all wishes save one wish –
Let him but know me, only speak to me!
He mutters; louder and louder; any other
Than I, with brain less laden, could collect
What he pours forth. Dear Aureole, do but look!
Is it talking or singing, this he utters fast?
Misery that he should fix me with his eye,

Quick talking to some other all the while!
If he would husband this wild vehemence
90   Which frustrates its intent! – I heard, I know
I heard my name amid those rapid words.
Oh, he will know me yet! Could I divert
This current, lead it somehow gently back
Into the channels of the past! – His eye
Brighter than ever! It must recognize me!

I am Erasmus: I am here to pray
That Paracelsus use his skill for me.
The schools of Paris and of Padua send
These questions for your learning to resolve.
100   We are your students, noble master: leave
This wretched cell, what business have you here?
Our class awaits you; come to us once more!
(O agony! the utmost I can do
Touches him not; how else arrest his ear?)
I am commissioned . . . I shall craze like him.
Better be mute and see what God shall send.
PARACELSUS: Stay, stay with me!
FESTUS: I will; I am come here
To stay with you – Festus, you loved of old;
Festus, you know, you must know!
PARACELSUS: Festus! Where's
110   Aprile, then? Has he not chanted softly
The melodies I heard all night? I could not
Get to him for a cold hand on my breast,
But I made out his music well enough,
O well enough! If they have filled him full
With magical music, as they freight a star
With light, and have remitted all his sin,
They will forgive me too, I too shall know!
FESTUS: Festus, your Festus!
PARACELSUS: Ask him if Aprile
Knows as he Loves – if I shall Love and Know?
120   I try; but that cold hand, like lead – so cold!
FESTUS: My hand, see!
PARACELSUS: Ah, the curse, Aprile, Aprile!
We get so near – so very, very near!
'Tis an old tale: Jove strikes the Titans down,
Not when they set about their mountain-piling

But when another rock would crown the work.
And Phaeton – doubtless his first radiant plunge
Astonished mortals, though the gods were calm,
And Jove prepared his thunder: all old tales!
FESTUS: And what are these to you?
PARACELSUS: Ay, fiends must laugh

130 So cruelly, so well! most like I never
Could tread a single pleasure underfoot,
But they were grinning by my side, were chuckling
To see me toil and drop away by flakes!
Hell-spawn! I am glad, most glad, that thus I fail!
Your cunning has o'ershot its aim. One year,
One month, perhaps, and I had served your turn!
You should have curbed your spite awhile. But now,
Who will believe 'twas you that held me back?
Listen: there's shame and hissing and contempt,

140 And none but laughs who names me, none but spits
Measureless scorn upon me, me alone,
The quack, the cheat, the liar, – all on me!
And thus your famous plan to sink mankind
In silence and despair, by teaching them
One of their race had probed the inmost truth,
Had done all man could do, yet failed no less –
Your wise plan proves abortive. Men despair?
Ha, ha! why, they are hooting the empiric,
The ignorant and incapable fool who rushed

150 Madly upon a work beyond his wits;
Nor doubt they but the simplest of themselves
Could bring the matter to triumphant issue.
So, pick and choose among them all, accursed!
Try now, persuade some other to slave for you,
To ruin body and soul to work your ends!
No, no; I am the first and last, I think.
FESTUS: Dear friend, who are accursed? who has done ...
PARACELSUS: What have I done? Fiends dare ask that? or you,
Brave men? Oh, you can chime in boldly, backed

160 By the others! What had you to do, sage peers?
Here stand my rivals; Latin, Arab, Jew,
Greek, join dead hands against me: all I ask
Is, that the world enrol my name with theirs,
And even this poor privilege, it seems,
They range themselves, prepared to disallow.

Only observe! why, fiends may learn from them!
How they talk calmly of my throes, my fierce
Aspirings, terrible watchings, each one claiming
Its price of blood and brain; how they dissect
170   And sneeringly disparage the few truths
Got at a life's cost; they too hanging the while
About my neck, their lies misleading me
And their dead names browbeating me! Grey crew,
Yet steeped in fresh malevolence from hell,
Is there a reason for your hate? My truths
Have shaken a little the palm about each prince?
Just think, Aprile, all these leering dotards
Were bent on nothing less than to be crowned
As we! That yellow blear-eyed wretch in chief
180   To whom the rest cringe low with feigned respect,
Galen of Pergamos and hell – nay speak
The tale, old man! We met there face to face:
I said the crown should fall from thee. Once more
We meet as in that ghastly vestibule:
Look to my brow! Have I redeemed my pledge?
FESTUS: Peace, peace; ah, see!
PARACELSUS: Oh, emptiness of fame!
Oh Persic Zoroaster, lord of stars!
– Who said these old renowns, dead long ago,
Could make me overlook the living world
190   To gaze through gloom at where they stood, indeed,
But stand no longer? What a warm light life
After the shade! In truth, my delicate witch,
My serpent-queen, you did but well to hide
The juggles I had else detected. Fire
May well run harmless o'er a breast like yours!
The cave was not so darkened by the smoke
But that your white limbs dazzled me: oh, white,
And panting as they twinkled, wildly dancing!
I cared not for your passionate gestures then,
200   But now I have forgotten the charm of charms,
The foolish knowledge which I came to seek,
While I remember that quaint dance; and thus
I am come back, not for those mummeries,
But to love you, and to kiss your little feet
Soft as an ermine's winter coat!
FESTUS: A light

Will struggle through these thronging words at last.
As in the angry and tumultuous West
A soft star trembles through the drifting clouds.
These are the strivings of a spirit which hates
210 So sad a vault should coop it, and calls up
The past to stand between it and its fate.
Were he at Einsiedeln – or Michal here!
PARACELSUS: Cruel! I seek her now – I kneel – I shriek –
I clasp her vesture – but she fades, still fades;
And she is gone; sweet human love is gone!
'Tis only when they spring to heaven that angels
Reveal themselves to you; they sit all day
Beside you, and lie down at night by you
Who care not for their presence, muse or sleep,
220 And all at once they leave you, and you know them!
We are so fooled, so cheated! Why, even now
I am not too secure against foul play;
The shadows deepen and the walls contract:
No doubt some treachery is going on.
'Tis very dusk. Where are we put, Aprile?
Have they left us in the lurch? This murky loathsome
Death-trap, this slaughter-house, is not the hall
In the golden city! Keep by me, Aprile!
There is a hand groping amid the blackness
230 To catch us. Have the spider-fingers got you,
Poet? Hold on me for your life! If once
They pull you! – Hold!
                              'Tis but a dream – no more!
I have you still; the sun comes out again;
Let us be happy: all will yet go well!
Let us confer: is it not like, Aprile,
That spite of trouble, this ordeal passed,
The value of my labours ascertained,
Just as some stream foams long among the rocks
But after glideth glassy to the sea,
240 So, full content shall henceforth be my lot?
What think you, poet? Louder! Your clear voice
Vibrates too like a harp-string. Do you ask
How could I still remain on earth, should God
Grant me the great approval which I seek?
I, you, and God can comprehend each other,
But men would murmur, and with cause enough;

For when they saw me, stainless of all sin,
Preserved and sanctified by inward light,
They would complain that comfort, shut from them,
250   I drank thus unespied; that they live on,
Nor taste the quiet of a constant joy,
For ache and care and doubt and weariness,
While I am calm; help being vouchsafed to me,
And hid from them. – 'Twere best consider that!
You reason well, Aprile; but at least
Let me know this, and die! Is this too much?
I will learn this, if God so please, and die!

If thou shalt please, dear God, if thou shalt please!
We are so weak, we know our motives least
260   In their confused beginning. If at first
I sought . . . but wherefore bare my heart to thee?
I know thy mercy; and already thoughts
Flock fast about my soul to comfort it,
And intimate I cannot wholly fail,
For love and praise would clasp me willingly
Could I resolve to seek them. Thou art good,
And I should be content. Yet – yet first show
I have done wrong in daring! Rather give
The supernatural consciousness of strength
270   Which fed my youth! Only one hour of that
With thee to help – O what should bar me then!

Lost, lost! Thus things are ordered here! God's creatures,
And yet he takes no pride in us! – none, none!
Truly there needs another life to come!
If this be all – (I must tell Festus that)
And other life await us not – for one,
I say 'tis a poor cheat, a stupid bungle,
A wretched failure. I, for one, protest
Against it, and I hurl it back with scorn.

280   Well, onward though alone! Small time remains,
And much to do: I must have fruit, must reap
Some profit from my toils. I doubt my body
Will hardly serve me through; while I have laboured
It has decayed; and now that I demand
Its best assistance, it will crumble fast:

A sad thought, a sad fate! How very full
Of wormwood 'tis, that just at altar-service,
The rapt hymn rising with the rolling smoke,
When glory dawns and all is at the best,
290   The sacred fire may flicker and grow faint
And die for want of a wood-piler's help!
Thus fades the flagging body, and the soul
Is pulled down in the overthrow. Well, well –
Let men catch every word, let them lose naught
Of what I say; something may yet be done.

They are ruins! Trust me who am one of you!
All ruins, glorious once, but lonely now.
It makes my heart sick to behold you crouch
Beside your desolate fane: the arches dim,
300   The crumbling columns grand against the moon,
Could I but rear them up once more – but that
May never be, so leave them! Trust me, friends,
Why should you linger here when I have built
A far resplendent temple, all your own?
Trust me, they are but ruins! See, Aprile,
Men will not heed! Yet were I not prepared
With better refuge for them, tongue of mine
Should ne'er reveal how blank their dwelling is:
I would sit down in silence with the rest.

310   Ha, what? you spit at me, you grin and shriek
Contempt into my ear – my ear which drank
God's accents once? you curse me? Why men, men,
I am not formed for it! Those hideous eyes
Will be before me sleeping, waking, praying,
They will not let me even die. Spare, spare me,
Sinning or no, forget that, only spare me
The horrible scorn! You thought I could support it.
But now you see what silly fragile creature
Cowers thus. I am not good nor bad enough,
320   Not Christ nor Cain, yet even Cain was saved
From Hate like this. Let me but totter back!
Perhaps I shall elude those jeers which creep
Into my very brain, and shut these scorched
Eyelids and keep those mocking faces out.

Listen, Aprile! I am very calm:
Be not deceived, there is no passion here
Where the blood leaps like an imprisoned thing:
I am calm: I will exterminate the race!
Enough of that: 'tis said and it shall be.
330   And now be merry: safe and sound am I
Who broke through their best ranks to get at you.
And such a havoc, such a rout, Aprile!

FESTUS: Have you no thought, no memory for me,
Aureole? I am so wretched – my pure Michal
Is gone, and you alone are left me now,
And even you forget me. Take my hand –
Lean on me thus. Do you not know me, Aureole?

PARACELSUS: Festus, my own friend, you are come at last?
As you say, 'tis an awful enterprise;
340   But you believe I shall go through with it:
'Tis like you, and I thank you. Thank him for me,
Dear Michal! See how bright Saint Saviour's spire
Flames in the sunset; all its figures quaint
Gay in the glancing light: you might conceive them
A troop of yellow-vested white-haired Jews
Bound for their own land where redemption dawns.

FESTUS: Not that blest time – not our youth's time, dear God!

PARACELSUS: Ha – stay! true, I forget – all is done since,
And he is come to judge me. How he speaks,
350   How calm, how well! yes, it is true, all true;
All quackery; all deceit; myself can laugh
The first at it, if you desire: but still
You know the obstacles which taught me tricks
So foreign to my nature – envy and hate,
Blind opposition, brutal prejudice,
Bald ignorance – what wonder if I sunk
To humour men the way they most approved?
My cheats were never palmed on such as you,
Dear Festus! I will kneel if you require me,
360   Impart the meagre knowledge I possess,
Explain its bounded nature, and avow
My insufficiency – whate'er you will:
I give the fight up: let there be an end,
A privacy, an obscure nook for me.
I want to be forgotten even by God.
But if that cannot be, dear Festus, lay me,

When I shall die, within some narrow grave,
Not by itself – for that would be too proud –
But where such graves are thickest; let it look
370   Nowise distinguished from the hillocks round,
So that the peasant at his brother's bed
May tread upon my own and know it not;
And we shall all be equal at the last,
Or classed according to life's natural ranks,
Fathers, sons, brothers, friends – not rich, nor wise,
Nor gifted: lay me thus, then say, 'He lived
Too much advanced before his brother men;
They kept him still in front: 'twas for their good
But yet a dangerous station. It were strange
380   That he should tell God he had never ranked
With men: so, here at least he is a man.'
FESTUS: That God shall take thee to his breast, dear spirit,
Unto his breast, be sure! and here on earth
Shall splendour sit upon thy name for ever.
Sun! all the heaven is glad for thee: what care
If lower mountains light their snowy phares
At thine effulgence, yet acknowledge not
The source of day? Their theft shall be their bale:
For after-ages shall retrack thy beams,
390   And put aside the crowd of busy ones
And worship thee alone – the master-mind,
The thinker, the explorer, the creator!
Then, who should sneer at the convulsive throes
With which thy deeds were born, would scorn as well
The sheet of winding subterraneous fire
Which, pent and writhing, sends no less at last
Huge islands up amid the simmering sea.
Behold thy might in me! thou hast infused
Thy soul in mine; and I am grand as thou,
400   Seeing I comprehend thee – I so simple,
Thou so august. I recognize thee first;
I saw thee rise, I watched thee early and late,
And though no glance reveal thou dost accept
My homage – thus no less I proffer it,
And bid thee enter gloriously thy rest.
PARACELSUS: Festus!
FESTUS: I am for noble Aureole, God!
I am upon his side, come weal or woe.

His portion shall be mine. He has done well.
I would have sinned, had I been strong enough,
410   As he has sinned. Reward him or I waive
Reward! If thou canst find no place for him,
He shall be king elsewhere, and I will be
His slave for ever. There are two of us.
PARACELSUS: Dear Festus!
FESTUS: Here, dear Aureole! ever by you!
PARACELSUS: Nay, speak on, or I dream again. Speak on!
   Some story, anything – only your voice.
   I shall dream else. Speak on! ay, leaning so!
FESTUS: Thus the Mayne glideth
                  Where my Love abideth.
420   Sleep's no softer: it proceeds
               On through lawns, on through meads,
               On and on, whate'er befall,
               Meandering and musical,
               Though the niggard pasturage
               Bears not on its shaven ledge
               Aught but weeds and waving grasses
               To view the river as it passes,
               Save here and there a scanty patch
               Of primroses too faint to catch
430   A weary bee.
PARACELSUS: More, more; say on!
FESTUS: And scarce it pushes
               Its gentle way through strangling rushes
               Where the glossy kingfisher
               Flutters when noon-heats are near,
               Glad the shelving banks to shun,
               Red and steaming in the sun,
               Where the shrew-mouse with pale throat
               Burrows, and the speckled stoat;
               Where the quick sandpipers flit
440   In and out the marl and grit
               That seems to breed them, brown as they:
               Naught disturbs its quiet way,
               Save some lazy stork that springs,
               Trailing it with legs and wings,
               Whom the shy fox from the hill
               Rouses, 'creep he ne'er so still.

PARACELSUS: My heart! they loose my heart, those simple
        words;
    Its darkness passes, which naught else could touch:
    Like some dark snake that force may not expel,
450   Which glideth out to music sweet and low.
    What were you doing when your voice broke through
    A chaos of ugly images? You, indeed!
    Are you alone here?
FESTUS: All alone: you know me?
    This cell?
PARACELSUS: An unexceptionable vault:
    Good brick and stone: the bats kept out, the rats
    Kept in: a snug nook: how should I mistake it?
FESTUS: But wherefore am I here?
PARACELSUS: Ah, well remembered!
    Why, for a purpose – for a purpose, Festus!
    'Tis like me: here I trifle while time fleets,
460   And this occasion, lost, will ne'er return.
    You are here to be instructed. I will tell
    God's message; but I have so much to say,
    I fear to leave half out. All is confused
    No doubt; but doubtless you will learn in time.
    He would not else have brought you here: no doubt
    I shall see clearer soon.
FESTUS: Tell me but this –
    You are not in despair?
PARACELSUS: I? and for what?
FESTUS: Alas, alas! he knows not, as I feared!
PARACELSUS: What is it you would ask me with that earnest
470   Dear searching face?
FESTUS: How feel you, Aureole?
PARACELSUS: Well:
    Well. 'Tis a strange thing: I am dying, Festus,
    And now that fast the storm of life subsides,
    I first perceive how great the whirl has been.
    I was calm then, who am so dizzy now –
    Calm in the thick of the tempest, but no less
    A partner of its motion and mixed up
    With its career. The hurricane is spent,
    And the good boat speeds through the brightening weather;
    But is it earth or sea that heaves below?
480   The gulf rolls like a meadow-swell, o'erstrewn

With ravaged boughs and remnants of the shore;
And now some islet, loosened from the land,
Swims past with all its trees, sailing to ocean;
And now the air is full of uptorn canes,
Light strippings from the fan-trees, tamarisks
Unrooted, with their birds still clinging to them,
All high in the wind. Even so my varied life
Drifts by me; I am young, old, happy, sad,
Hoping, desponding, acting, taking rest,
490   And all at once: that is, those past conditions
Float back at once on me. If I select
Some special epoch from the crowd, 'tis but
To will, and straight the rest dissolve away,
And only that particular state is present
With all its long-forgotten circumstance
Distinct and vivid as at first – myself
A careless looker-on and nothing more,
Indifferent and amused, but nothing more.
And this is death: I understand it all.
500   New being waits me; new perceptions must
Be born in me before I plunge therein;
Which last is Death's affair; and while I speak,
Minute by minute he is filling me
With power; and while my foot is on the threshold
Of boundless life – the doors unopened yet,
All preparations not complete within –
I turn new knowledge upon old events,
And the effect is . . . but I must not tell;
It is not lawful. Your own turn will come
510   One day. Wait, Festus! You will die like me.
FESTUS: 'Tis of that past life that I burn to hear.
PARACELSUS: You wonder it engages me just now?
In truth, I wonder too. What's life to me?
Where'er I look is fire, where'er I listen
Music, and where I tend bliss evermore.
Yet how can I refrain? 'Tis a refined
Delight to view those chances, – one last view.
I am so near the perils I escape,
That I must play with them and turn them over,
520   To feel how fully they are past and gone.
Still, it is like, some further cause exists
For this peculiar mood – some hidden purpose;

Did I not tell you something of it, Festus?
I had it fast, but it has somehow slipt
Away from me; it will return anon.

FESTUS: (Indeed his cheek seems young again, his voice
Complete with its old tones: that little laugh
Concluding every phrase, with upturned eye,
As though one stooped above his head to whom
530   He looked for confirmation and approval,
Where was it gone so long, so well preserved?
Then, the fore-finger pointing as he speaks,
Like one who traces in an open book
The matter he declares; 'tis many a year
Since I remarked it last: and this in him,
But now a ghastly wreck!)
                  And can it be,
Dear Aureole, you have then found out at last
That worldly things are utter vanity?
That man is made for weakness, and should wait
540   In patient ignorance, till God appoint . . .

PARACELSUS: Ha, the purpose: the true purpose: that is it!
How could I fail to apprehend! You here,
I thus! But no more trifling: I see all,
I know all: my last mission shall be done
If strength suffice. No trifling! Stay; this posture
Hardly befits one thus about to speak:
I will arise.

FESTUS: Nay, Aureole, are you wild?
You cannot leave your couch.

PARACELSUS: No help; no help;
Not even your hand. So! there, I stand once more!
550   Speak from a couch? I never lectured thus.
My gown – the scarlet lined with fur; now put
The chain about my neck; my signet-ring
Is still upon my hand, I think – even so;
Last, my good sword; ah, trusty Azoth, leapest
Beneath thy master's grasp for the last time?
This couch shall be my throne: I bid these walls
Be consecrate, this wretched cell become
A shrine, for here God speaks to men through me.
Now, Festus, I am ready to begin.

560 FESTUS: I am dumb with wonder.

PARACELSUS: Listen, therefore, Festus!

There will be time enough, but none to spare.
I must content myself with telling only
The most important points. You doubtless feel
That I am happy, Festus; very happy.
FESTUS: 'Tis no delusion which uplifts him thus!
Then you are pardoned, Aureole, all your sin?
PARACELSUS: Ay, pardoned: yet why pardoned?
FESTUS: 'Tis God's praise
That man is bound to seek, and you ...
PARACELSUS: Have lived!
We have to live alone to set forth well
570   God's praise. 'Tis true, I sinned much, as I thought,
And in effect need mercy, for I strove
To do that very thing; but, do your best
Or worst, praise rises, and will rise for ever.
Pardon from him, because of praise denied –
Who calls me to himself to exalt himself?
He might laugh as I laugh!
FESTUS: But all comes
To the same thing. 'Tis fruitless for mankind
To fret themselves with what concerns them not;
They are no use that way: they should lie down
580   Content as God has made them, nor go mad
In thriveless cares to better what is ill.
PARACELSUS: No, no; mistake me not; let me not work
More harm than I have worked! This is my case:
If I go joyous back to God, yet bring
No offering, if I render up my soul
Without the fruits it was ordained to bear,
If I appear the better to love God
For sin, as one who has no claim on him, –
Be not deceived! It may be surely thus
590   With me, while higher prizes still await
The mortal persevering to the end.
Beside I am not all so valueless:
I have been something, though too soon I left
Following the instincts of that happy time.
FESTUS: What happy time? For God's sake, for man's sake,
What time was happy? All I hope to know
That answer will decide. What happy time?
PARACELSUS: When but the time I vowed myself to man?
FESTUS: Great God, thy judgements are inscrutable!

600 PARACELSUS: Yes, it was in me; I was born for it –
I, Paracelsus: it was mine by right.
Doubtless a searching and impetuous soul
Might learn from its own motions that some task
Like this awaited it about the world;
Might seek somewhere in this blank life of ours
For fit delights to stay its longings vast;
And, grappling Nature, so prevail on her
To fill the creature full she dared thus frame
Hungry for joy; and, bravely tyrannous,
610 Grow in demand, still craving more and more,
And make each joy conceded prove a pledge
Of other joy to follow – bating naught
Of its desires, still seizing fresh pretence
To turn the knowledge and the rapture wrung
As an extreme, last boon, from destiny,
Into occasion for new covetings,
New strifes, new triumphs: – doubtless a strong soul,
Alone, unaided might attain to this,
So glorious is our nature, so august
620 Man's inborn uninstructed impulses,
His naked spirit so majestical!
But this was born in me; I was made so;
Thus much time saved: the feverish appetites,
The tumult of unproved desire, the unaimed
Uncertain yearnings, aspirations blind,
Distrust, mistake, and all that ends in tears
Were saved me; thus I entered on my course.
You may be sure I was not all exempt
From human trouble; just so much of doubt
630 As bade me plant a surer foot upon
The sun-road, kept my eye unruined 'mid
The fierce and flashing splendour, set my heart
Trembling so much as warned me I stood there
On sufferance – not to idly gaze, but cast
Light on a darkling race; save for that doubt,
I stood at first where all aspire at last
To stand: the secret of the world was mine.
I knew, I felt, (perception unexpressed,
Uncomprehended by our narrow thought,
640 But somehow felt and known in every shift
And change in the spirit, – nay, in every pore

Of the body, even,) – what God is, what we are,
What life is – how God tastes an infinite joy
In infinite ways – one everlasting bliss,
From whom all being emanates, all power
Proceeds; in whom is life for evermore,
Yet whom existence in its lowest form
Includes; where dwells enjoyment there is he:
With still a flying point of bliss remote,
650   A happiness in store afar, a sphere
Of distant glory in full view; thus climbs
Pleasure its heights for ever and for ever.
The centre-fire heaves underneath the earth,
And the earth changes like a human face;
The molten ore bursts up among the rocks,
Winds into the stone's heart, outbranches bright
In hidden mines, spots barren river-beds,
Crumbles into fine sand where sunbeams bask –
God joys therein. The wroth sea's waves are edged
660   With foam, white as the bitten lip of hate,
When, in the solitary waste, strange groups
Of young volcanos come up, cyclops-like,
Staring together with their eyes on flame –
God tastes a pleasure in their uncouth pride.
Then all is still; earth is a wintry clod:
But spring-wind, like a dancing psaltress, passes
Over its breast to waken it, rare verdure
Buds tenderly upon rough banks, between
The withered tree-roots and the cracks of frost,
670   Like a smile striving with a wrinkled face;
The grass grows bright, the boughs are swoln with blooms
Like chrysalids impatient for the air,
The shining dorrs are busy, beetles run
Along the furrows, ants make their ado;
Above, birds fly in merry flocks, the lark
Soars up and up, shivering for very joy;
Afar the ocean sleeps; white fishing-gulls
Flit where the strand is purple with its tribe
Of nested limpets; savage creatures seek
680   Their loves in wood and plain – and God renews
His ancient rapture. Thus he dwells in all,
From life's minute beginnings, up at last
To man – the consummation of this scheme

Of being, the completion of this sphere
Of life: whose attributes had here and there
Been scattered o'er the visible world before,
Asking to be combined, dim fragments meant
To be united in some wondrous whole,
Imperfect qualities throughout creation,
690 Suggesting some one creature yet to make,
Some point where all those scattered rays should meet
Convergent in the faculties of man.
Power – neither put forth blindly, nor controlled
Calmly by perfect knowledge; to be used
At risk, inspired or checked by hope and fear:
Knowledge – not intuition, but the slow
Uncertain fruit of an enhancing toil,
Strengthened by love: love – not serenely pure,
But strong from weakness, like a chance-sown plant
700 Which, cast on stubborn soil, puts forth changed buds
And softer stains, unknown in happier climes;
Love which endures and doubts and is oppressed
And cherished, suffering much and much sustained,
And blind, oft-failing, yet believing love,
A half-enlightened, often-chequered trust: –
Hints and previsions of which faculties,
Are strewn confusedly everywhere about
The inferior natures, and all lead up higher,
All shape out dimly the superior race,
710 The heir of hopes too fair to turn out false,
And man appears at last. So far the seal
Is put on life; one stage of being complete,
One scheme wound up: and from the grand result
A supplementary reflux of light,
Illustrates all the inferior grades, explains
Each back step in the circle. Not alone
For their possessor dawn those qualities,
But the new glory mixes with the heaven
And earth; man, once descried, imprints for ever
720 His presence on all lifeless things: the winds
Are henceforth voices, wailing or a shout,
A querulous mutter or a quick gay laugh,
Never a senseless gust now man is born.
The herded pines commune and have deep thoughts,
A secret they assemble to discuss

When the sun drops behind their trunks which glare
Like grates of hell: the peerless cup afloat
Of the lake-lily is an urn, some nymph
Swims bearing high above her head: no bird
730 Whistles unseen, but through the gaps above
That let light in upon the gloomy woods,
A shape peeps from the breezy forest-top,
Arch with small puckered mouth and mocking eye.
The morn has enterprise, deep quiet droops
With evening, triumph takes the sunset hour,
Voluptuous transport ripens with the corn
Beneath a warm moon like a happy face:
– And this to fill us with regard for man,
With apprehension of his passing worth,
740 Desire to work his proper nature out,
And ascertain his rank and final place,
For these things tend still upward, progress is
The law of life, man is not Man as yet.
Nor shall I deem his object served, his end
Attained, his genuine strength put fairly forth,
While only here and there a star dispels
The darkness, here and there a towering mind
O'erlooks its prostrate fellows: when the host
Is out at once to the despair of night,
750 When all mankind alike is perfected,
Equal in full-blown powers– then, not till then,
I say, begins man's general infancy.
For wherefore make account of feverish starts
Of restless members of a dormant whole,
Impatient nerves which quiver while the body
Slumbers as in a grave? Oh long ago
The brow was twitched, the tremulous lids astir,
The peaceful mouth disturbed; half-uttered speech
Ruffled the lip, and then the teeth were set,
760 The breath drawn sharp, the strong right-hand clenched
      stronger,
As it would pluck a lion by the jaw;
The glorious creature laughed out even in sleep!
But when full roused, each giant-limb awake,
Each sinew strung, the great heart pulsing fast,
He shall start up and stand on his own earth,
Then shall his long triumphant march begin,

Thence shall his being date, – thus wholly roused,
What he achieves shall be set down to him.
When all the race is perfected alike
770 As man, that is; all tended to mankind,
And, man produced, all has its end thus far:
But in completed man begins anew
A tendency to God. Prognostics told
Man's near approach; so in man's self arise
August anticipations, symbols, types
Of a dim splendour ever on before
In that eternal circle life pursues.
For men begin to pass their nature's bound,
And find new hopes and cares which fast supplant
780 Their proper joys and griefs; they grow too great
For narrow creeds of right and wrong, which fade
Before the unmeasured thirst for good: while peace
Rises within them ever more and more.
Such men are even now upon the earth,
Serene amid the half-formed creatures round
Who should be saved by them and joined with them.
Such was my task, and I was born to it –
Free, as I said but now, from much that chains
Spirits, high-dowered but limited and vexed
790 By a divided and delusive aim,
A shadow mocking a reality
Whose truth avails not wholly to disperse
The flitting mimic called up by itself,
And so remains perplexed and nigh put out
By its fantastic fellow's wavering gleam.
I, from the first, was never cheated thus;
I never fashioned out a fancied good
Distinct from man's; a service to be done,
A glory to be ministered unto
800 With powers put forth at man's expense, withdrawn
From labouring in his behalf; a strength
Denied that might avail him. I cared not
Lest his success ran counter to success
Elsewhere: for God is glorified in man,
And to man's glory vowed I soul and limb.
Yet, constituted thus, and thus endowed,
I failed: I gazed on power till I grew blind.
Power; I could not take my eyes from that:

That only, I thought, should be preserved, increased
810   At any risk, displayed, struck out at once –
The sign and note and character of man.
I saw no use in the past: only a scene
Of degradation, ugliness and tears,
The record of disgraces best forgotten,
A sullen page in human chronicles
Fit to erase. I saw no cause why man
Should not stand all-sufficient even now,
Or why his annals should be forced to tell
That once the tide of light, about to break
820   Upon the world, was sealed within its spring:
I would have had one day, one moment's space,
Change man's condition, push each slumbering claim
Of mastery o'er the elemental world
At once to full maturity, then roll
Oblivion o'er the work, and hide from man
What night had ushered morn. Not so, dear child
Of after-days, wilt thou reject the past
Big with deep warnings of the proper tenure
By which thou hast the earth: for thee the present
830   Shall have distinct and trembling beauty, seen
Beside that past's own shade when, in relief,
Its brightness shall stand out: nor yet on thee
Shall burst the future, as successive zones
Of several wonder open on some spirit
Flying secure and glad from heaven to heaven:
But thou shalt painfully attain to joy,
While hope and fear and love shall keep thee man!
All this was hid from me: as one by one
My dreams grew dim, my wide aims circumscribed,
840   As actual good within my reach decreased,
While obstacles sprung up this way and that
To keep me from effecting half the sum,
Small as it proved; as objects, mean within
The primal aggregate, seemed, even the least,
Itself a match for my concentred strength –
What wonder if I saw no way to shun
Despair? The power I sought for man, seemed God's.
In this conjuncture, as I prayed to die,
A strange adventure made me know, one sin
850   Had spotted my career from its uprise;

I saw Aprile – my Aprile there!
And as the poor melodious wretch disburthened
His heart, and moaned his weakness in my ear,
I learned my own deep error; love's undoing
Taught me the worth of love in man's estate,
And what proportion love should hold with power
In his right constitution; love preceding
Power, and with much power, always much more love;
Love still too straitened in his present means,
860 And earnest for new power to set love free.
I learned this, and supposed the whole was learned:
And thus, when men received with stupid wonder
My first revealings, would have worshipped me,
And I despised and loathed their proffered praise –
When, with awakened eyes, they took revenge
For past credulity in casting shame
On my real knowledge, and I hated them –
It was not strange I saw no good in man,
To overbalance all the wear and waste
870 Of faculties, displayed in vain, but born
To prosper in some better sphere: and why?
In my own heart love had not been made wise
To trace love's faint beginnings in mankind,
To know even hate is but a mask of love's,
To see a good in evil, and a hope
In ill-success; to sympathize, be proud
Of their half-reasons, faint aspirings, dim
Struggles for truth, their poorest fallacies,
Their prejudice and fears and cares and doubts;
880 All with a touch of nobleness, despite
Their error, upward tending all though weak,
Like plants in mines which never saw the sun,
But dream of him, and guess where he may be,
And do their best to climb and get to him.
All this I knew not, and I failed. Let men
Regard me, and the poet dead long ago
Who loved too rashly; and shape forth a third
And better-tempered spirit, warned by both:
As from the over-radiant star too mad
890 To drink the life-springs, beamless thence itself –
And the dark orb which borders the abyss,
Ingulfed in icy night, – might have its course

A temperate and equidistant world.
Meanwhile, I have done well, though not all well.
As yet men cannot do without contempt;
'Tis for their good, and therefore fit awhile
That they reject the weak, and scorn the false,
Rather than praise the strong and true, in me:
But after, they will know me. If I stoop
900   Into a dark tremendous sea of cloud,
It is but for a time; I press God's lamp
Close to my breast; its splendour, soon or late,
Will pierce the gloom: I shall emerge one day.
You understand me? I have said enough?
FESTUS: Now die, dear Aureole!
PARACELSUS: Festus, let my hand –
This hand, lie in your own, my own true friend!
Aprile! Hand in hand with you, Aprile!

FESTUS: And this was Paracelsus!

NOTE

The liberties I have taken with my subject are very trifling; and the reader may slip the foregoing scenes between the leaves of any memoir of Paracelsus he pleases, by way of commentary. To prove this, I subjoin a popular account, translated from the 'Biographie Universelle, Paris,' 1822, which I select, not as the best, certainly, but as being at hand, and sufficiently concise for my purpose. I also append a few notes, in order to correct those parts which do not bear out my own view of the character of Paracelsus; and have incorporated with them a notice or two, illustrative of the poem itself.

'Paracelsus (Philippus Aureolus Theophrastus Bombastus ab Hohenheim) was born in 1493 at Einsiedeln,[1] a little town in the canton of Schwyz, some leagues distant from Zurich. His father, who exercised the profession of medicine at Villach in Carinthia, was nearly related to George Bombast de Hohenheim, who became afterward Grand Prior of the Order of Malta: consequently Paracelsus could not spring from the dregs of the people, as Thomas Erastus, his sworn enemy, pretends.* It appears that his elementary education was much neglected, and that he spent part of his

* I shall disguise M. Renauldin's next sentence a little. 'Hic (Erastus sc.) Paracelsum trimum a milite quodam, alii a sue exectum ferunt: constat imberbem illum, mulierumque osorem fuisse.' A standing High-Dutch joke in those days at the expense of a number of learned men, as may be seen by referring to such rubbish as

youth in pursuing the life common to the travelling *literati* of the age; that is to say, in wandering from country to country, predicting the future by astrology and cheiromancy, evoking apparitions, and practising the different operations of magic and alchemy, in which he had been initiated whether by his father or by various ecclesiastics, among the number of whom he particularizes the Abbot Tritheim,[2] and many German bishops.

'As Paracelsus displays everywhere an ignorance of the rudiments of the most ordinary knowledge, it is not probable that he ever studied seriously in the schools: he contented himself with visiting the Universities of Germany, France and Italy; and in spite of his boasting himself to have been the ornament of those institutions, there is no proof of his having legally acquired the title of Doctor, which he assumes. It is only known that he applied himself long, under the direction of the wealthy Sigismond Fugger of Schwatz, to the discovery of the Magnum Opus.

'Paracelsus travelled among the mountains of Bohemia, in the East, and in Sweden, in order to inspect the labours of the miners, to be initiated in the mysteries of the oriental adepts, and to observe the secrets of nature and the famous mountain of loadstone.[3] He professes also to have visited Spain, Portugal, Prussia, Poland, and Transylvania; everywhere communicating freely, not merely with the physicians, but the old women, charlatans and conjurers of these several lands. It is even believed that he extended his journeyings as far as Egypt and Tartary, and that he accompanied the son of the Khan of the Tartars to Constantinople, for the purpose of obtaining the secret of the tincture of Trismegistus from a Greek who inhabited that capital.

'The period of his return to Germany is unknown: it is only certain that, at about the age of thirty-three, many astonishing cures which he wrought on eminent personages procured him such a celebrity, that he was called in 1526, on the recommendation of Oecolampadius,[4] to fill a chair of physics and surgery at the University of Basil. There Paracelsus began by burning publicly in the amphitheatre the works of Avicenna and Galen, assuring his auditors that the latchets of his shoes were more instructed than those two physicians; that all Universities, all writers put together, were less gifted than the hairs of his beard and of the crown of his head; and that, in a word, he was to be regarded as the legitimate monarch of medicine. "You shall follow me," cried he, "you, Avicenna, Galen, Rhasis, Montagnana, Mesues, you, gentlemen of Paris, Montpellier, Germany, Cologne, Vienna,* and whomsoever the Rhine and Danube nourish; you who inhabit the isles of the sea; you,

---

Melander's 'Jocoseria,' etc. In the prints from his portrait by Tintoretto, painted a year before his death, Paracelsus is *barbatulus*, at all events. But Erastus was never without a good reason for his faith – *e.g.* 'Helvetium fuisse (Paracelsum) vix credo, vix enim ea regio tale monstrum ediderit.' (De Medicina Nova.)

*Erastus, who relates this, here oddly remarks, 'mirum quod non et Garamantos, Indos et *Anglos* adjunxit.' Not so wonderful neither, if we believe what another adversary 'had heard somewhere,' – that all Paracelsus' system came of his pillaging 'Anglum quendam, Rogerium Bacchonem.'

likewise, Dalmatians, Athenians; thou, Arab; thou, Greek; thou, Jew: all shall follow me, and the monarchy shall be mine."*

'But at Basil it was speedily perceived that the new Professor was no better than an egregious quack. Scarcely a year elapsed before his lectures had fairly driven away an audience incapable of comprehending their emphatic jargon. That which above all contributed to sully his reputation was the debauched life he led. According to the testimony of Oporinus, who lived two years in his intimacy, Paracelsus scarcely ever ascended the lecture-desk unless half drunk, and only dictated to his secretaries when in a state of intoxication: if summoned to attend the sick, he rarely proceeded thither without previously drenching himself with wine. He was accustomed to retire to bed without changing his clothes; sometimes he spent the night in pot-houses with peasants, and in the morning knew no longer what he was about; and, nevertheless, up to the age of twenty-five his only drink had been water.[5]

'At length, fearful of being punished for a serious outrage on a magistrate,[6] he fled from Basil towards the end of the year 1527, and took refuge in Alsatia, whither he caused Oporinus to follow with his chemical apparatus.

'He then entered once more upon the career of ambulatory theosophist.†Accordingly we find him at Colmar in 1528; at Nuremberg in 1529; at St Gall in 1531; at Pfeffers in 1535; and at Augsburg in 1536: he next made some stay in Moravia, where he still further compromised his reputation by the loss of many distinguished patients, which compelled him to betake himself to Vienna; from thence he passed into Hungary; and in 1538 was at Villach, where he dedicated his "Chronicle" to the States of Carinthia, in gratitude for the many kindnesses with which they had honoured his father. Finally, from Mindelheim, which he visited in 1540, Paracelsus proceeded to Salzburg, where he died in the Hospital of St Stephen (*Sebastian* is meant), Sept. 24, 1541.' – (Here follows a criticism on his writings, which I omit.)

1. *Paracelsus* would seem to be a fantastic version of *Von Hohenheim*; Einsiedeln is the Latinized Eremus, whence Paracelsus is sometimes called, as in the correspondence of Erasmus, Eremita; Bombast, his proper name,

---

*See his works *passim*. I must give one specimen: – Somebody had been styling him 'Luther alter.' 'And why not?' (he asks, as he well might). 'Luther is abundantly learned, therefore you hate him and me; but we are at least a match for you. – Nam et contra vos et vestros universos principes Avicennam, Galenum, Aristotelem, etc. me satis superque munitum esse novi. Et vertex iste meus calvus ac depilis multo plura et sublimiora novit quam vester vel Avicenna vel universae academiae. Prodite, et signum date, qui viri sitis, quid roboris habeatis? quid autem sitis? Doctores et magistri, pediculos pectentes et fricantes podicem.' (Frag. Med.)

†'So migratory a life could afford Paracelsus but little leisure for application to books, and accordingly he informs us that for the space of ten years he never opened a single volume, and that his whole medical library was not composed of six sheets: in effect, the inventory drawn up after his death states that the only books which he left were the Bible, the New Testament, the Commentaries of St Jerome on the Gospels, a printed volume on Medicine, and seven manuscripts.'

probably acquired, from the characteristic phraseology of his lectures, that unlucky signification which it has ever since retained.

2. Then Bishop of Spanheim, and residing at Würzburg in Franconia; a town situated in a grassy fertile country, whence its name, Herbipolis. He was much visited there by learned men, as may be seen by his 'Epistolae Familiares,' Hag. 1536: among others, by his staunch friend Cornelius Agrippa, to whom he dates thence, in 1510, a letter in answer to the dedicatory epistle prefixed to the treatise De Occult. Philosoph., which last contains the following ominous allusion to Agrippa's sojourn: 'Quum nuper tecum, R.P. in coenobio tuo apud Herbipolim aliquamdiu conversatus, multa de chymicis, multa de magicis, multa de cabalisticis, caeterisque quae adhuc in occulto delitescunt, arcanis scientiis atque artibus una contulissemus,' etc.

3. 'Inexplebilis illa aviditas naturae perscrutandi secreta et reconditarum supellectile scientiarum animum locupletandi, uno eodemque loco diu persistere non patiebatur, sed Mercurii instar, omnes terras, nationes et urbes perlustrandi igniculos supponebat, ut cum viris naturae scrutatoribus, chymicis praesertim, ore tenus conferret, et quae diuturnis laboribus nocturnisque vigiliis invenerant una vel altera communicatione obtineret.' (Bitiskius in Praefat.) 'Patris auxilio primum, deinde propria industria doctissimos viros in Germania, Italia, Gallia, Hispania, aliisque Europae regionibus, nactus est praeceptores; quorum liberali doctrina, et potissimum propria inquisitione ut qui esset ingenio acutissimo ac fere divino, tantum profecit, ut multi testati sint, in universa philosophia, tam ardua, tam arcana et abdita eruisse mortalium neminem.' (Melch. Adam. in Vit. Germ. Medic.) 'Paracelsus qui in intima naturae viscera sic penitus introierit, metallorum stirpiumque vires et facultates tam incredibili ingenii acumine exploraverit ac perviderit, ad morbos omnes vel desperatos et opinione hominum insanabiles percurandum; ut cum Theophrasto nata primum medicina perfectaque videtur.' (Petri Rami Orat. de Basilea.) His passion for wandering is best described in his own words: 'Ecce amatorem adolescentem difficillimi itineris haud piget, ut venustam saltem puellam vel foeminam aspiciat: quanto minus nobilissimarum artium amore laboris ac cujuslibet taedii pigebit?' etc. ('Defensiones Septem adversus aemulos suos.' 1573. Def. 4ta. 'De peregrinationibus et exilio.')

4. The reader may remember that it was in conjunction with Oecolampadius, then Divinity Professor at Basil, that Zuinglius published in 1528 an answer to Luther's Confession of Faith; and that both proceeded in company to the subsequent conference with Luther and Melanchthon at Marpurg. Their letters fill a large volume. – 'D.D. Johannis Oecolampadii et Huldrichi Zuinglii Epistolarum lib. quatuor.' Bas. 1536. It must be also observed that Zuinglius began to preach in 1516, and at Zurich in 1519, and that in 1525 the Mass was abolished in the cantons. The tenets of Oecolampadius were supposed to be more evangelical than those up to that period maintained by

the glorious German, and our brave Bishop Fisher attacked them as the fouler heresy: – 'About this time arose out of Luther's school one Oecolampadius, like a mighty and fierce giant; who, as his master had gone beyond the Church, went beyond his master (or else it had been impossible he could have been reputed the better scholar), who denied the real presence; him, this worthy champion (the Bishop) sets upon, and with five books (like so many smooth stones taken out of the river that doth always run with living water) slays the Philistine; which five books were written in the year of our Lord 1526, at which time he had governed the see of Rochester twenty years.' (Life of Bishop Fisher, 1655.) Now, there is no doubt of the Protestantism of Paracelsus, Erasmus, Agrippa, etc., but the nonconformity of Paracelsus was always scandalous. L. Crasso ('Elogj d'Huomini Letterati,' Ven. 1666) informs us that his books were excommunicated by the Church. Quenstedt (de Patr. Doct.) affirms 'nec tantum novae medicinae, verum etiam novae theologiae autor est.' Delrio, in his Disquisit. Magicar., classes him among those 'partim atheos, partim haereticos' (lib. i. cap. 3). 'Omnino tamen multa theologica in ejusdem scriptis plane atheismum olent, ac duriuscule sonant in auribus vere Christiani.' (D. Gabrielis Clauderi Schediasma de Tinct. Univ. Norimb. 1736.) I shall only add one more authority: – 'Oporinus dicit se (Paracelsum) aliquando Lutherum et Papam, non minus quam nunc Galenum et Hippocratem redacturum in ordinem minabatur, neque enim eorum qui hactenus in scripturani sacram scripsissent, sive veteres, sive recentiores, quenquam scripturae nucleum recte eruisse, sed circa corticem et quasi membranam tantum haerere.' (Th. Erastus, Disputat. de Med. Nova.) These and similar notions had their due effect on Oporinus, who, says Zuingerus, in his 'Theatrum,' 'longum vale dixit ei (Paracelso), ne ob praeceptoris, alioqui amicissimi, horrendas blasphemias ipse quoque aliquando poenas Deo Opt. Max. lueret.'

5. His defenders allow the drunkenness. Take a sample of their excuses: 'Gentis hoc, non viri vitiolum est, a Taciti seculo ad nostrum usque non interrupto filo devolutum, sinceritati forte Germanae coaevum, et nescio an aliquo consanguinitatis vinculo junctum.' (Bitiskius.) The other charges were chiefly trumped up by Oporinus: 'Domi, quod Oporinus amanuensis ejus saepe narravit, nunquam nisi potus ad explicanda sua accessit, atque in medio conclavi ad columnam τετυφωμένος adsistens, apprehenso manibus capulo ensis, cujus κοίλωμα hospitium praebuit, ut aiunt, spiritui familiari, imaginationes aut concepta sua protulit: – alii illud quod in capulo habuit, ab ipso Azoth appellatum, medicinam fuisse praestantissimam aut lapidem Philosophicum putant.' (Melch. Adam.) This famous sword was no laughing-matter in those days, and it is now a material feature in the popular idea of Paracelsus. I recollect a couple of allusions to it in our own literature, at the moment.

> Ne had been known the Danish Gonswart,
> Or Paracelsus with his long sword.
>
> 'Volpone,' act ii. scene 2.

> Bumbastus kept a devil's bird
> Shut in the pummel of his sword,
> That taught him all the cunning pranks
> Of past and future mountebanks.
>
> 'Hudibras,' part ii. cant. 3.

This Azoth was simply '*laudanum suum*.' But in his time he was commonly believed to possess the double tincture – the power of curing diseases and transmuting metals. Oporinus often witnessed, as he declares, both these effects, as did also Franciscus, the servant of Paracelsus, who describes, in a letter to Neander, a successful projection at which he was present, and the results of which, good golden ingots, were confided to his keeping. For the other quality, let the following notice vouch among many others: – 'Degebat Theophrastus Norimbergae procitus a medentibus illius urbis, et vaniloquus deceptorque proclamatus, qui, ut laboranti famae subveniat, viros quosdam authoritatis summae in Republica illa adit, et infamiae amoliendae, artique suae asserendae, specimen ejus pollicetur editurum, nullo stipendio vel accepto pretio, horum faciles praebentium aures jussu elephantiacos aliquot, a communione hominum caeterorum segregatos, et in valetudinarium detrusos, alieno arbitrio eliguntur, quos virtute singulari remediorum suorum Theophrastus a foeda Graecorum lepra mundat, pristinaeque sanitati restituit; conservat illustre harum curationum urbs in archivis suis testimonium.' (Bitiskius.)* It is to be remarked that Oporinus afterwards repented of his treachery: 'Sed resipuit tandem, et quem vivum convitiis insectatus fuerat defunctum veneratione prosequutus, infames famae praeceptoris morsus in remorsus conscientiae conversi poenitentia, heu nimis tarda, vulnera clausere exanimi quae spiranti inflixerant.' For these 'bites' of Oporinus, see Disputat. Erasti, and Andreae Jocisci 'Oratio de Vit. ob. Opor[i];' for the 'remorse,' Mic. Toxita in pref. Testamenti, and Conringius (otherwise an enemy of Paracelsus), who says it was contained in a letter from Oporinus to Doctor Vegerus.†

Whatever the moderns may think of these marvellous attributes, the title of Paracelsus to be considered the father of modern chemistry is indisputable. Gerardus Vossius, 'De Philos[a] et Philos[um] sectis,' thus prefaces the ninth section of cap. 9, 'De Chymia' – 'Nobilem hanc medicinae partem, diu

---

*The premature death of Paracelsus casts no manner of doubt on the fact of his having possessed the Elixir Vitae: the alchemists have abundant reasons to adduce, from which I select the following, as explanatory of a property of the Tincture not calculated on by its votaries:—'Objectionem illam, quod Paracelsus non fuerit longaevus, nonnulli quoque solvunt per rationes physicas: vitae nimirum abbreviationem fortasse talibus accidere posse, ob Tincturam frequentiore ac largiore dosi sumtam, dum a summe efficaci et penetrabili hujus virtute calor innatus quasi suffocatur.' (Gabrielis Clauderi Schediasma.)

† For a good defence of Paracelsus I refer the reader to Olaus Borrichius' treatise – 'Hermetis etc. Sapientia vindicata,' 1674. Or, if he is no more learned than myself in such matters, I mention simply that Paracelsus introduced the use of Mercury and Laudanum.

sepultam avorum aetate, quasi ab orco revocavit Th. Paracelsus.' I suppose many hints lie scattered in his neglected books, which clever appropriators have since developed with applause. Thus, it appears from his treatise 'De Phlebotomia,' and elsewhere, that he had discovered the circulation of the blood and the sanguification of the heart; as did after him Realdo Colombo, and still more perfectly Andrea Cesalpino of Arezzo, as Bayle and Bartoli observe. Even Lavater quotes a passage from his work 'De Natura Rerum,' on practical Physiognomy, in which the definitions and axioms are precise enough: he adds, 'though an astrological enthusiast, a man of prodigious genius.' See Holcroft's translation, vol. iii. p. 179 – 'The Eyes.' While on the subject of the writings of Paracelsus, I may explain a passage in the third part of the Poem. He was, as I have said, unwilling to publish his works, but in effect did publish a vast number. Valentius (in Praefat. in Paramyr.) declares 'quod ad librorum Paracelsi copiam attinet, audio, a Germanis prope trecentos recenseri.' 'O foecunditas ingenii!' adds he, appositely. Many of these, were, however, spurious; and Fred. Bitiskius gives his good edition (3 vols. fol. Gen. 1658) 'rejectis suppositis solo ipsius nomine superbientibus quorum ingens circumfertur numerus.' The rest were 'charissimum et pretiosissimum authoris pignus, extorsum potius ab illo quam obtentum.' 'Jam minime eo volente atque jubente haec ipsius scripta in lucem prodisse videntur; quippe quae muro inclusa ipso absente, servi cujusdam indicio, furto surrepta atque sublata sunt,' says Valentius. These have been the study of a host of commentators, amongst whose labours are most notable, Petri Severini, 'Idea Medicinae Philosophiae. Bas. 1571;' Mic. Toxetis, 'Onomastica. Arg. 1574;' Dornei, 'Dict. Parac. Franc. 1584;' and 'P^i Philos^{ae} Compendium cum scholiis auctore Leone Suavio. Paris.' (This last, a good book.)

6. A disgraceful affair. One Liechtenfels, a canon, having been rescued *in extremis* by the '*laudanum*' of Paracelsus, refused the stipulated fee, and was supported in his meanness by the authorities, whose interference Paracelsus would not brook. His own liberality was allowed by his bitterest foes, who found a ready solution of his indifference to profit in the aforesaid swordhandle and its guest. His freedom from the besetting sin of a profession he abhorred – (as he curiously says somewhere, 'Quis quaeso deinceps honorem deferat professione tali, quae a tam facinorosis nebulonibus obitur et administratur?') – is recorded in his epitaph, which affirms – 'Bona sua in pauperes distribuenda collocandaque erogavit,' *honoravit*, or *ordinavit* – for accounts differ.

Sordello

1840

Dear Friend, – Let the next poem be introduced by your name, therefore remembered along with one of the deepest of my affections, and so repay all trouble it ever cost me. I wrote it twenty-five years ago for only a few, counting even in these on somewhat more care about its subject than they really had. My own faults of expression were many; but with care for a man or book such would be surmounted, and without it what avails the faultlessness of either? I blame nobody, least of all myself, who did my best then and since; for I lately gave time and pains to turn my work into what the many might, – instead of what the few must, – like: but after all, I imagined another thing at first, and therefore leave as I find it. The historical decoration was purposely of no more importance than a background requires; and my stress lay on the incidents in the development of a soul: little else is worth study. I, at least, always thought so – you, with many known and unknown to me, think so – others may one day think so; and whether my attempt remain for them or not, I trust, though away and past it, to continue ever yours,

R.B.

London : 9 June 1863

Sordello

BOOK THE FIRST

Who will, may hear Sordello's story told:
His story? Who believes me shall behold
The man, pursue his fortunes to the end,
Like me: for as the friendless-people's friend
Spied from his hill-top once, despite the din
And dust of multitudes, Pentapolin
Named o' the Naked Arm, I single out
Sordello, compassed murkily about
With ravage of six long sad hundred years.
10 Only believe me. Ye believe?
                          Appears
Verona . . . Never, – I should warn you first, –
Of my own choice had this, if not the worst
Yet not the best expedient, served to tell
A story I could body forth so well
By making speak, myself kept out of view,
The very man as he was wont to do,
And leaving you to say the rest for him.
Since, though I might be proud to see the dim
Abysmal past divide its hateful surge,
20 Letting of all men this one man emerge
Because it pleased me, yet, that moment past,
I should delight in watching first to last
His progress as you watch it, not a whit
More in the secret than yourselves who sit
Fresh-chapleted to listen. But it seems
Your setters-forth of unexampled themes,
Makers of quite new men, producing them,
Would best chalk broadly on each vesture's hem
The wearer's quality; or take their stand,
30 Motley on back and pointing-pole in hand,
Beside him. So, for once I face ye, friends,
Summoned together from the world's four ends,
Dropped down from heaven or cast up from hell,
To hear the story I propose to tell.
Confess now, poets know the dragnet's trick,
Catching the dead, if fate denies the quick,

And shaming her; 'tis not for fate to choose
Silence or song because she can refuse
Real eyes to glisten more, real hearts to ache
40 Less oft, real brows turn smoother for our sake:
I have experienced something of her spite;
But there's a realm wherein she has no right
And I have many lovers. Say, but few
Friends fate accords me? Here they are: now view
The host I muster! Many a lighted face
Foul with no vestige of the grave's disgrace;
What else should tempt them back to taste our air
Except to see how their successors fare?
My audience! and they sit, each ghostly man
50 Striving to look as living as he can,
Brother by breathing brother; thou art set,
Clear-witted critic, by . . . but I'll not fret
A wondrous soul of them, nor move death's spleen
Who loves not to unlock them. Friends! I mean
The living in good earnest – ye elect
Chiefly for love – suppose not I reject
Judicious praise, who contrary shall peep,
Some fit occasion, forth, for fear ye sleep,
To glean your bland approvals. Then, appear,
60 Verona! stay – thou, spirit, come not near
Now – not this time desert thy cloudy place
To scare me, thus employed, with that pure face!
I need not fear this audience, I make free
With them, but then this is no place for thee!
The thunder-phrase of the Athenian, grown
Up out of memories of Marathon,
Would echo like his own sword's griding screech
Braying a Persian shield, – the silver speech
Of Sidney's self, the starry paladin,
70 Turn intense as a trumpet sounding in
The knights to tilt, – wert thou to hear! What heart
Have I to play my puppets, bear my part
Before these worthies?
                          Lo, the past is hurled
In twain: up-thrust, out-staggering on the world,
Subsiding into shape, a darkness rears
Its outline, kindles at the core, appears
Verona. 'Tis six hundred years and more

Since an event. The Second Friedrich wore
The purple, and the Third Honorius filled
80 The holy chair. That autumn eve was stilled:
A last remains of sunset dimly burned
O'er the far forests, like a torch-flame turned
By the wind back upon its bearer's hand
In one long flare of crimson; as a brand,
The woods beneath lay black. A single eye
From all Verona cared for the soft sky.
But, gathering in its ancient market-place,
Talked group with restless group; and not a face
But wrath made livid, for among them were
90 Death's staunch purveyors, such as have in care
To feast him. Fear had long since taken root
In every breast, and now these crushed its fruit,
The ripe hate, like a wine: to note the way
It worked while each grew drunk! Men grave and grey
Stood, with shut eyelids, rocking to and fro,
Letting the silent luxury trickle slow
About the hollows where a heart should be;
But the young gulped with a delirious glee
Some foretaste of their first debauch in blood
100 At the fierce news: for, be it understood,
Envoys apprised Verona that her prince
Count Richard of Saint Boniface, joined since
A year with Azzo, Este's Lord, to thrust
Taurello Salinguerra, prime in trust
With Ecelin Romano, from his seat
Ferrara, – over-zealous in the feat
And stumbling on a peril unaware,
Was captive, trammelled in his proper snare,
They phrase it, taken by his own intrigue.
110 Immediate succour from the Lombard League
Of fifteen cities that affect the Pope,
For Azzo, therefore, and his fellow-hope
Of the Guelf cause, a glory overcast!
Men's faces, late agape, are now aghast.
'Prone is the purple pavis; Este makes
Mirth for the devil when he undertakes
To play the Ecelin; as if it cost
Merely your pushing-by to gain a post
Like his! The patron tells ye, once for all,

120   There be sound reasons that preferment fall
     On our beloved'...
                  'Duke o' the Rood, why not?'
     Shouted an Estian, 'grudge ye such a lot?
     The hill-cat boasts some cunning of her own,
     Some stealthy trick to better beasts unknown,
     That quick with prey enough her hunger blunts,
     And feeds her fat while gaunt the lion hunts.'
     'Taurello,' quoth an envoy, 'as in wane
     Dwelt at Ferrara. Like an osprey fain
     To fly but forced the earth his couch to make
130   Far inland, till his friend the tempest wake,
     Waits he the Kaiser's coming; and as yet
     That fast friend sleeps, and he too sleeps: but let
     Only the billow freshen, and he snuffs
     The aroused hurricane ere it enroughs
     The sea it means to cross because of him.
     Sinketh the breeze? His hope-sick eye grows dim;
     Creep closer on the creature! Every day
     Strengthens the Pontiff; Ecelin, they say,
     Dozes now at Oliero, with dry lips
140   Telling upon his perished finger-tips
     How many ancestors are to depose
     Ere he be Satan's Viceroy when the doze
     Deposits him in hell. So, Guelfs rebuilt
     Their houses; not a drop of blood was spilt
     When Cino Bocchimpane chanced to meet
     Buccio Virtù – God's wafer, and the street
     Is narrow! Tutti Santi, think, a-swarm
     With Ghibellins, and yet he took no harm!
     This could not last. Off Salinguerra went
150   To Padua, Podestà, "with pure intent,"
     Said he, "my presence, judged the single bar
     To permanent tranquillity, may jar
     No longer" – so! his back is fairly turned?
     The pair of goodly palaces are burned,
     The gardens ravaged, and our Guelfs laugh, drunk
     A week with joy. The next, their laughter sunk
     In sobs of blood, for they found, some strange way,
     Old Salinguerra back again – I say,
     Old Salinguerra in the town once more
160   Uprooting, overturning, flame before,

Blood fetlock-high beneath him. Azzo fled;
Who 'scaped the carnage followed; then the dead
Were pushed aside from Salinguerra's throne,
He ruled once more Ferrara, all alone,
Till Azzo, stunned awhile, revived, would pounce
Coupled with Boniface, like lynx and ounce,
On the gorged bird. The burghers ground their teeth
To see troop after troop encamp beneath
I' the standing corn thick o'er the scanty patch
170 It took so many patient months to snatch
Out of the marsh; while just within their walls
Men fed on men. At length Taurello calls
A parley: "let the Count wind up the war!"
Richard, light-hearted as a plunging star,
Agrees to enter for the kindest ends
Ferrara, flanked with fifty chosen friends,
No horse-boy more, for fear your timid sort
Should fly Ferrara at the bare report.
Quietly through the town they rode, jog-jog;
180 "Ten, twenty, thirty, – curse the catalogue
Of burnt Guelf houses! Strange, Taurello shows
Not the least sign of life" – whereat arose
A general growl: "How? With his victors by?
I and my Veronese? My troops and I?
Receive us, was your word?" So jogged they on,
Nor laughed their host too openly: once gone
Into the trap! –'
                    Six hundred years ago!
Such the time's aspect and peculiar woe
(Yourselves may spell it yet in chronicles,
190 Albeit the worm, our busy brother, drills
His sprawling path through letters anciently
Made fine and large to suit some abbot's eye)
When the new Hohenstaufen dropped the mask,
Flung John of Brienne's favour from his casque,
Forswore crusading, had no mind to leave
Saint Peter's proxy leisure to retrieve
Losses to Otho and to Barbaross,
Or make the Alps less easy to recross;
And, thus confirming Pope Honorius' fear,
200 Was excommunicate that very year.
'The triple-bearded Teuton come to life!'

Groaned the Great League; and, arming for the strife,
Wide Lombardy, on tiptoe to begin,
Took up, as it was Guelf or Ghibellin,
Its cry: what cry?
            'The Emperor to come!'
His crowd of feudatories, all and some,
That leapt down with a crash of swords, spears, shields,
One fighter on his fellow, to our fields,
Scattered anon, took station here and there,
210 And carried it, till now, with little care –
Cannot but cry for him; how else rebut
Us longer? – cliffs, an earthquake suffered jut
In the mid-sea, each domineering crest
Which naught save such another throe can wrest
From out (conceive) a certain chokeweed grown
Since o'er the waters, twine and tangle thrown
Too thick, too fast accumulating round,
Too sure to over-riot and confound
Ere long each brilliant islet with itself,
220 Unless a second shock save shoal and shelf,
Whirling the sea-drift wide: alas, the bruised
And sullen wreck! Sunlight to be diffused
For that! – sunlight, 'neath which, a scum at first,
The million fibres of our chokeweed nurst
Dispread themselves, mantling the troubled main,
And, shattered by those rocks, took hold again,
So kindly blazed it – that same blaze to brood
O'er every cluster of the multitude
Still hazarding new clasps, ties, filaments,
230 An emulous exchange of pulses, vents
Of nature into nature; till some growth
Unfancied yet, exuberantly clothe
A surface solid now, continuous, one:
'The Pope, for us the People, who begun
The People, carries on the People thus,
To keep that Kaiser off and dwell with us!'
See you?
        Or say, Two Principles that live
Each fitly by its Representative.
'Hill-cat' – who called him so? – the gracefullest
240 Adventurer, the ambiguous stranger-guest
Of Lombardy (sleek but that ruffling fur,

Those talons to their sheath!) whose velvet purr
Soothes jealous neighbours when a Saxon scout
– Arpo or Yoland, is it? – one without
A country or a name, presumes to couch
Beside their noblest; until men avouch
That, of all Houses in the Trevisan,
Conrad descries no fitter, rear or van,
Than Ecelo! They laughed as they enrolled
250 That name at Mílan on the page of gold,
Godego's lord, – Ramon, Marostica,
Cartiglion, Bassano, Loria,
And every sheep-cote on the Suabian's fief!
No laughter when his son, 'the Lombard Chief'
Forsooth, as Barbarossa's path was bent
To Italy along the Vale of Trent,
Welcomed him at Roncaglia! Sadness now –
The hamlets nested on the Tyrol's brow,
The Asolan and Euganean hills,
260 The Rhetian and the Julian, sadness fills
Them all, for Ecelin vouchsafes to stay
Among and care about them; day by day
Choosing this pinnacle, the other spot,
A castle building to defend a cot,
A cot built for a castle to defend,
Nothing but castles, castles, nor an end
To boasts how mountain ridge may join with ridge
By sunken gallery and soaring bridge.
He takes, in brief, a figure that beseems
270 The griesliest nightmare of the Church's dreams,
– A Signory firm-rooted, unestranged
From its old interests, and nowise changed
By its new neighbourhood: perchance the vaunt
Of Otho, 'my own Este shall supplant
Your Este,' come to pass. The sire led in
A son as cruel; and this Ecelin
Had sons, in turn, and daughters sly and tall
And curling and compliant; but for all
Romano (so they styled him) throve, that neck
280 Of his so pinched and white, that hungry cheek
Proved 'twas some fiend, not him, the man's-flesh went
To feed: whereas Romano's instrument,
Famous Taurello Salinguerra, sole

I' the world, a tree whose boughs were slipt the bole
Successively, why should not he shed blood
To further a design? Men understood
Living was pleasant to him as he wore
His careless surcoat, glanced some missive o'er,
Propped on his truncheon in the public way,
290 While his lord lifted writhen hands to pray,
Lost at Oliero's convent.
      Hill-cats, face
Our Azzo, our Guelf Lion! Why disgrace
A worthiness conspicuous near and far
(Atii at Rome while free and consular,
Este at Padua who repulsed the Hun)
By trumpeting the Church's princely son?
– Styled Patron of Rovigo's Polesine,
Ancona's march, Ferrara's . . . ask, in fine,
Our chronicles, commenced when some old monk
300 Found it intolerable to be sunk
(Vexed to the quick by his revolting cell)
Quite out of summer while alive and well:
Ended when by his mat the Prior stood,
'Mid busy promptings of the brotherhood,
Striving to coax from his decrepit brains
The reason Father Porphyry took pains
To blot those ten lines out which used to stand
First on their charter drawn by Hildebrand.
  The same night wears. Verona's rule of yore
310 Was vested in a certain Twenty-four;
And while within his palace these debate
Concerning Richard and Ferrara's fate,
Glide we by clapping doors, with sudden glare
Of cressets vented on the dark, nor care
For aught that's seen or heard until we shut
The smother in, the lights, all noises but
The carroch's booming: safe at last! Why strange
Such a recess should lurk behind a range
Of banquet-rooms? Your finger – thus – you push
320 A spring, and the wall opens, would you rush
Upon the banqueters, select your prey,
Waiting (the slaughter-weapons in the way
Strewing this very bench) with sharpened ear
A preconcerted signal to appear;

Or if you simply crouch with beating heart,
Bearing in some voluptuous pageant part
To startle them. Nor mutes nor masquers now;
Nor any . . . does that one man sleep whose brow
The dying lamp-flame sinks and rises o'er?
330 What woman stood beside him? not the more
Is he unfastened from the earnest eyes
Because that arras fell between! Her wise
And lulling words are yet about the room,
Her presence wholly poured upon the gloom
Down even to her vesture's creeping stir.
And so reclines he, saturate with her,
Until an outcry from the square beneath
Pierces the charm: he springs up, glad to breathe,
Above the cunning element, and shakes
340 The stupor off as (look you) morning breaks
On the gay dress, and, near concealed by it,
The lean frame like a half-burnt taper, lit
Erst at some marriage-feast, then laid away
Till the Armenian bridegroom's dying day,
In his wool wedding-robe.
                              For he – for he,
Gate-vein of this hearts' blood of Lombardy,
(If I should falter now) – for he is thine!
Sordello, thy forerunner, Florentine!
A herald-star I know thou didst absorb
350 Relentless into the consummate orb
That scared it from its right to roll along
A sempiternal path with dance and song
Fulfilling its allotted period,
Serenest of the progeny of God –
Who yet resigns it not! His darling stoops
With no quenched lights, desponds with no blank troops
Of disenfranchised brilliances, for, blent
Utterly with thee, its shy element
Like thine upburneth prosperous and clear.
360 Still, what if I approach the august sphere
Named now with only one name, disentwine
That under-current soft and argentine
From its fierce mate in the majestic mass
Leavened as the sea whose fire was mixt with glass
In John's transcendent vision, – launch once more

That lustre? Dante, pacer of the shore
Where glutted hell disgorgeth filthiest gloom,
Unbitten by its whirring sulphur-spume –
Or whence the grieved and óbscure waters slope
370 Into a darkness quieted by hope;
Plucker of amaranths grown beneath God's eye
In gracious twilights where his chosen lie, –
I would do this! If I should falter now!
    In Mantua territory half is slough,
Half pine-tree forest; maples, scarlet oaks
Breed o'er the river-beds; even Mincio chokes
With sand the summer through: but 'tis morass
In winter up to Mantua walls. There was,
Some thirty years before this evening's coil,
380 One spot reclaimed from the surrounding spoil,
Goito; just a castle built amid
A few low mountains; firs and larches hid
Their main defiles, and rings of vineyard bound
The rest. Some captured creature in a pound,
Whose artless wonder quite precludes distress,
Secure beside in its own loveliness,
So peered with airy head, below, above,
The castle at its toils, the lapwings love
To glean among at grape-time. Pass within.
390 A maze of corridors contrived for sin,
Dusk winding-stairs, dim galleries got past,
You gain the inmost chambers, gain at last
A maple-panelled room: that haze which seems
Floating about the panel, if there gleams
A sunbeam over it, will turn to gold
And in light-graven characters unfold
The Arab's wisdom everywhere; what shade
Marred them a moment, those slim pillars made,
Cut like a company of palms to prop
400 The roof, each kissing top entwined with top,
Leaning together; in the carver's mind
Some knot of bacchanals, flushed cheek combined
With straining forehead, shoulders purpled, hair
Diffused between, who in a goat-skin bear
A vintage; graceful sister-palms! But quick
To the main wonder, now. A vault, see; thick
Black shade about the ceiling, though fine slits

Across the buttress suffer light by fits
Upon a marvel in the midst. Nay, stoop –
410   A dullish grey-streaked cumbrous font, a group
Round it, – each side of it, where'er one sees, –
Upholds it; shrinking Caryatides
Of just-tinged marble like Eve's lilied flesh
Beneath her maker's finger when the fresh
First pulse of life shot brightening the snow.
The font's edge burthens every shoulder, so
They muse upon the ground, eyelids half closed;
Some, with meek arms behind their backs disposed,
Some, crossed above their bosoms, some, to veil
420   Their eyes, some, propping chin and cheek so pale,
Some, hanging slack an utter helpless length
Dead as a buried vestal whose whole strength
Goes when the grate above shuts heavily.
So dwell these noiseless girls, patient to see,
Like priestesses because of sin impure
Penanced for ever, who resigned endure,
Having that once drunk sweetness to the dregs.
And every eve, Sordello's visit begs
Pardon for them: constant as eve he came
430   To sit beside each in her turn, the same
As one of them, a certain space: and awe
Made a great indistinctness till he saw
Sunset slant cheerful through the buttress-chinks,
Gold seven times globed; surely our maiden shrinks
And a smile stirs her as if one faint grain
Her load were lightened, one shade less the stain
Obscured her forehead, yet one more bead slipt
From off the rosary whereby the crypt
Keeps count of the contritions of its charge?
440   Then with a step more light, a heart more large,
He may depart, leave her and every one
To linger out the penance in mute stone.
Ah, but Sordello? 'Tis the tale I mean
To tell you.
              In this castle may be seen,
On the hill tops, or underneath the vines,
Or eastward by the mound of firs and pines
That shuts out Mantua, still in loneliness,
A slender boy in a loose page's dress,

Sordello: do but look on him awhile
450 Watching ('tis autumn) with an earnest smile
The noisy flock of thievish birds at work
Among the yellowing vineyards; see him lurk
('Tis winter with its sullenest of storms)
Beside that arras-length of broidered forms,
On tiptoe, lifting in both hands a light
Which makes yon warrior's visage flutter bright
– Ecelo, dismal father of the brood,
And Ecelin, close to the girl he wooed,
Auria, and their Child, with all his wives
460 From Agnes to the Tuscan that survives,
Lady of the castle, Adelaide. His face
– Look, now he turns away! Yourselves shall trace
(The delicate nostril swerving wide and fine,
A sharp and restless lip, so well combine
With that calm brow) a soul fit to receive
Delight at every sense; you can believe
Sordello foremost in the regal class
Nature has broadly severed from her mass
Of men, and framed for pleasure, as she frames
470 Some happy lands, that have luxurious names,
For loose fertility; a footfall there
Suffices to upturn to the warm air
Half-germinating spices; mere decay
Produces richer life; and day by day
New pollen on the lily-petal grows,
And still more labyrinthine buds the rose.
You recognize at once the finer dress
Of flesh that amply lets in loveliness
At eye and ear, while round the rest is furled
480 (As though she would not trust them with her world)
A veil that shows a sky not near so blue,
And lets but half the sun look fervid through.
How can such love? – like souls on each full-fraught
Discovery brooding, blind at first to aught
Beyond its beauty, till exceeding love
Becomes an aching weight; and, to remove
A curse that haunts such natures – to preclude
Their finding out themselves can work no good
To what they love nor make it very blest
490 By their endeavour, – they are fain invest

The lifeless thing with life from their own soul,
Availing it to purpose, to control,
To dwell distinct and have peculiar joy
And separate interests that may employ
That beauty fitly, for its proper sake.
Nor rest they here; fresh births of beauty wake
Fresh homage, every grade of love is past,
With every mode of loveliness: then cast
Inferior idols off their borrowed crown
500 Before a coming glory. Up and down
Runs arrowy fire, while earthly forms combine
To throb the secret forth; a touch divine –
And the scaled eyeball owns the mystic rod;
Visibly through his garden walketh God.
  So fare they. Now revert. One character
Denotes them through the progress and the stir, –
A need to blend with each external charm,
Bury themselves, the whole heart wide and warm, –
In something not themselves; they would belong
510 To what they worship – stronger and more strong
Thus prodigally fed – which gathers shape
And feature, soon imprisons past escape
The votary framed to love and to submit
Nor ask, as passionate he kneels to it,
Whence grew the idol's empery. So runs
A legend; light had birth ere moons and suns,
Flowing through space a river and alone,
Till chaos burst and blank the spheres were strown
Hither and thither, foundering and blind:
520 When into each of them rushed light – to find
Itself no place, foiled of its radiant chance.
Let such forego their just inheritance!
For there's a class that eagerly looks, too,
On beauty, but, unlike the gentler crew,
Proclaims each new revealment born a twin
With a distinctest consciousness within,
Referring still the quality, now first
Revealed, to their own soul – its instinct nursed
In silence, now remembered better, shown
530 More thoroughly, but not the less their own;
A dream come true; the special exercise
Of any special function that implies

The being fair, or good, or wise, or strong,
Dormant within their nature all along –
Whose fault? So, homage, other souls direct
Without, turns inward. 'How should this deject
Thee, soul?' they murmur; 'wherefore strength be quelled
Because, its trivial accidents withheld,
Organs are missed that clog the world, inert,
540 Wanting a will, to quicken and exert,
Like thine – existence cannot satiate,
Cannot surprise? Laugh thou at envious fate,
Who, from earth's simplest combination stampt
With individuality – uncrampt
By living its faint elemental life,
Dost soar to heaven's complexest essence, rife
With grandeurs, unaffronted to the last,
Equal to being all!'
                In truth? Thou hast
Life, then – wilt challenge life for us: our race
550 Is vindicated so, obtains its place
In thy ascent, the first of us; whom we
May follow, to the meanest, finally,
With our more bounded wills?
                    Ah, but to find
A certain mood enervate such a mind,
Counsel it slumber in the solitude
Thus reached nor, stooping, task for mankind's good
Its nature just as life and time accord
' – Too narrow an arena to reward
Emprise – the world's occasion worthless since
560 Not absolutely fitted to evince
Its mastery!' Or if yet worse befall,
And a desire possess it to put all
That nature forth, forcing our straitened sphere
Contain it, – to display completely here
The mastery another life should learn,
Thrusting in time eternity's concern, –
So that Sordello....
               Fool, who spied the mark
Of leprosy upon him, violet-dark
Already as he loiters? Born just now,
570 With the new century, beside the glow
And efflorescence out of barbarism;

Witness a Greek or two from the abysm
That stray through Florence-town with studious air,
Calming the chisel of that Pisan pair:
If Nicolo should carve a Christus yet!
While at Siena is Guidone set,
Forehead on hand; a painful birth must be
Matured ere Saint Eufemia's sacristy
Or transept gather fruits of one great gaze
580 At the moon: look you! The same orange haze, –
The same blue stripe round that – and, in the midst,
Thy spectral whiteness, Mother-maid, who didst
Pursue the dizzy painter!
                Woe, then, worth
Any officious babble letting forth
The leprosy confirmed and ruinous
To spirit lodged in a contracted house!
Go back to the beginning, rather; blend
It gently with Sordello's life; the end
Is piteous, you may see, but much between
590 Pleasant enough. Meantime, some pyx to screen
The full-grown pest, some lid to shut upon
The goblin! So they found at Babylon,
(Colleagues, mad Lucius and sage Antonine)
Sacking the city, by Apollo's shrine,
In rummaging among the rarities,
A certain coffer; he who made the prize
Opened it greedily; and out there curled
Just such another plague, for half the world
Was stung. Crawl in then, hag, and couch asquat,
600 Keeping that blotchy bosom thick in spot
Until your time is ripe! The coffer-lid
Is fastened, and the coffer safely hid
Under the Loxian's choicest gifts of gold.
   Who will may hear Sordello's story told,
And how he never could remember when
He dwelt not at Goito. Calmly, then,
About this secret lodge of Adelaide's
Glided his youth away; beyond the glades
On the fir-forest border, and the rim
610 Of the low range of mountain, was for him
No other world: but this appeared his own
To wander through at pleasure and alone.

The castle too seemed empty; far and wide
Might he disport; only the northern side
Lay under a mysterious interdict –
Slight, just enough remembered to restrict
His roaming to the corridors, the vault
Where those font-bearers expiate their fault,
The maple-chamber, and the little nooks
620 And nests, and breezy parapet that looks
Over the woods to Mantua: there he strolled.
Some foreign women-servants, very old,
Tended and crept about him – all his clue
To the world's business and embroiled ado
Distant a dozen hill-tops at the most.
And first a simple sense of life engrossed
Sordello in his drowsy Paradise;
The day's adventures for the day suffice –
Its constant tribute of perceptions strange,
630 With sleep and stir in healthy interchange,
Suffice, and leave him for the next at ease
Like the great palmer-worm that strips the trees,
Eats the life out of every luscious plant,
And, when September finds them sere or scant,
Puts forth two wondrous winglets, alters quite,
And hies him after unforeseen delight.
So fed Sordello, not a shard dissheathed;
As ever, round each new discovery, wreathed
Luxuriantly the fancies infantine
640 His admiration, bent on making fine
Its novel friend at any risk, would fling
In gay profusion forth: a ficklest king,
Confessed those minions! – eager to dispense
So much from his own stock of thought and sense
As might enable each to stand alone
And serve him for a fellow; with his own,
Joining the qualities that just before
Had graced some older favourite. Thus they wore
A fluctuating halo, yesterday
650 Set flicker and tomorrow filched away, –
Those upland objects each of separate name,
Each with an aspect never twice the same,
Waxing and waning as the new-born host
Of fancies, like a single night's hoar-frost,

Gave to familiar things a face grotesque;
Only, preserving through the mad burlesque
A grave regard. Conceive! the orpine patch
Blossoming earliest on the log-house thatch
The day those archers wound along the vines –
660   Related to the Chief that left their lines
To climb with clinking step the northern stair
Up to the solitary chambers where
Sordello never came. Thus thrall reached thrall;
He o'er-festooning every interval,
As the adventurous spider, making light
Of distance, shoots her threads from depth to height,
From barbican to battlement: so flung
Fantasies forth and in their centre swung
Our architect, – the breezy morning fresh
670   Above, and merry, – all his waving mesh
Laughing with lucid dew-drops rainbow-edged.
     This world of ours by tacit pact is pledged
To laying such a spangled fabric low
Whether by gradual brush or gallant blow.
But its abundant will was balked here: doubt
Rose tardily in one so fenced about
From most that nurtures judgement, – care and pain:
Judgement, that dull expedient we are fain,
Less favoured, to adopt betimes and force
680   Stead us, diverted from our natural course
Of joys – contrive some yet amid the dearth,
Vary and render them, it may be, worth
Most we forego. Suppose Sordello hence
Selfish enough, without a moral sense
However feeble; what informed the boy
Others desired a portion in his joy?
Or say a ruthful chance broke woof and warp –
A heron's nest beat down by March winds sharp,
A fawn breathless beneath the precipice,
690   A bird with unsoiled breast and unfilmed eyes
Warm in the brake – could these undo the trance
Lapping Sordello? Not a circumstance
That makes for you, friend Naddo! Eat fern-seed
And peer beside us and report indeed
If (your word) 'genius' dawned with throes and stings
And the whole fiery catalogue, while springs,

Summers, and winters quietly came and went.
Time put at length that period to content,
By right the world should have imposed: bereft
700 Of its good offices, Sordello, left
To study his companions, managed rip
Their fringe off, learn the true relationship,
Core with its crust, their nature with his own:
Amid his wild-wood sights he lived alone.
As if the poppy felt with him! Though he
Partook the poppy's red effrontery
Till Autumn spoiled their fleering quite with rain,
And, turbanless, a coarse brown rattling crane
Lay bare. That's gone: yet why renounce, for that,
710 His disenchanted tributaries – flat
Perhaps, but scarce so utterly forlorn,
Their simple presence might not well be borne
Whose parley was a transport once: recall
The poppy's gifts, it flaunts you, after all,
A poppy: – why distrust the evidence
Of each soon satisfied and healthy sense?
The new-born judgement answered, 'little boots
Beholding other creatures' attributes
And having none!' or, say that it sufficed,
720 'Yet, could one but possess, oneself,' (enticed
Judgement) 'some special office!' Naught beside
Serves you? 'Well then, be somehow justified
For this ignoble wish to circumscribe
And concentrate, rather than swell, the tribe
Of actual pleasures: what, now, from without
Effects it? – proves, despite a lurking doubt,
Mere sympathy sufficient, trouble spared?
That, tasting joys by proxy thus, you fared
The better for them?' Thus much craved his soul.
730 Alas, from the beginning love is whole
And true; if sure of naught beside, most sure
Of its own truth at least; nor may endure
A crowd to see its face, that cannot know
How hot the pulses throb its heart below:
While its own helplessness and utter want
Of means to worthily be ministrant
To what it worships, do but fan the more
Its flame, exalt the idol far before

Itself as it would have it ever be.
740 Souls like Sordello, on the contrary,
Coerced and put to shame, retaining will,
Care little, take mysterious comfort still,
But look forth tremblingly to ascertain
If others judge their claims not urged in vain,
And say for them their stifled thoughts aloud.
So, they must ever live before a crowd:
– 'Vanity,' Naddo tells you.
                   Whence contrive
A crowd, now? From these women just alive,
That archer-troop? Forth glided – not alone
750 Each painted warrior, every girl of stone,
Nor Adelaide (bent double o'er a scroll,
One maiden at her knees, that eve, his soul
Shook as he stumbled through the arrassed glooms
On them, for, 'mid quaint robes and weird perfumes,
Started the meagre Tuscan up, – her eyes,
The maiden's, also, bluer with surprise)
– But the entire out-world: whatever, scraps
And snatches, song and story, dreams perhaps,
Conceited the world's offices, and he
760 Had hitherto transferred to flower or tree,
Not counted a befitting heritage
Each, of its own right, singly to engage
Some man, no other, – such now dared to stand
Alone. Strength, wisdom, grace on every hand
Soon disengaged themselves, and he discerned
A sort of human life: at least, was turned
A stream of lifelike figures through his brain.
Lord, liegeman, valvassor and suzerain,
Ere he could choose, surrounded him; a stuff
770 To work his pleasure on; there, sure enough:
But as for gazing, what shall fix that gaze?
Are they to simply testify the ways
He who convoked them sends his soul along
With the cloud's thunder or a dove's brood-song?
– While they live each his life, boast each his own
Peculiar dower of bliss, stand each alone
In some one point where something dearest loved
Is easiest gained – far worthier to be proved
Than aught he envies in the forest-wights!

780 No simple and self-evident delights,
But mixed desires of unimagined range,
Contrasts or combinations, new and strange,
Irksome perhaps, yet plainly recognized
By this, the sudden company – loves prized
By those who are to prize his own amount
Of loves. Once care because such make account,
Allow that foreign recognitions stamp
The current value, and his crowd shall vamp
Him counterfeits enough; and so their print

790 Be on the piece, 'tis gold, attests the mint,
And 'good,' pronounce they whom his new appeal
Is made to: if their casual print conceal –
This arbitrary good of theirs o'ergloss
What he has lived without, nor felt the loss –
Qualities strange, ungainly, wearisome,
– What matter? So must speech expand the dumb
Part-sigh, part-smile with which Sordello, late
Whom no poor woodland-sights could satiate,
Betakes himself to study hungrily

800 Just what the puppets his crude phantasy
Supposes notablest, – popes, kings, priests, knights, –
May please to promulgate for appetites;
Accepting all their artificial joys
Not as he views them, but as he employs
Each shape to estimate the other's stock
Of attributes, whereon – a marshalled flock
Of authorized enjoyments – he may spend
Himself, be men, now, as he used to blend
With tree and flower – nay more entirely, else

810 'Twere mockery: for instance, 'How excels
My life that chieftain's?' (who apprised the youth
Ecelin, here, becomes this month, in truth,
Imperial Vicar?) 'Turns he in his tent
Remissly? Be it so – my head is bent
Deliciously amid my girls to sleep.
What if he stalks the Trentine-pass? Yon steep
I climbed an hour ago with little toil:
We are alike there. But can I, too, foil
The Guelf's paid stabber, carelessly afford

820 Saint Mark's a spectacle, the sleight o' the sword
Baffling the treason in a moment?' Here

No rescue! Poppy he is none, but peer
To Ecelin, assuredly: his hand,
Fashioned no otherwise, should wield a brand
With Ecelin's success – try, now! He soon
Was satisfied, returned as to the moon
From earth; left each abortive boy's-attempt
For feats, from failure happily exempt,
In fancy at his beck. 'One day I will
830 Accomplish it! Are they not older still
– Not grown-up men and women? 'Tis beside
Only a dream; and though I must abide
With dreams now, I may find a thorough vent
For all myself, acquire an instrument
For acting what these people act; my soul
Hunting a body out may gain its whole
Desire some day!' How else express chagrin
And resignation, show the hope steal in
With which he let sink from an aching wrist
840 The rough-hewn ash-bow? Straight, a gold shaft hissed
Into the Syrian air, struck Malek down
Superbly! 'Crosses to the breach! God's Town
Is gained him back!' Why bend rough ash-bows more?
    Thus lives he: if not careless as before,
Comforted: for one may anticipate,
Rehearse the future, be prepared when fate
Shall have prepared in turn real men whose names
Startle, real places of enormous fames,
Este abroad and Ecelin at home
850 To worship him, – Mantua, Verona, Rome
To witness it. Who grudges time so spent?
Rather test qualities to heart's content –
Summon them, thrice selected, near and far –
Compress the starriest into one star,
And grasp the whole at once!
                      The pageant thinned
Accordingly; from rank to rank, like wind
His spirit passed to winnow and divide;
Back fell the simpler phantasms; every side
The strong clave to the wise; with either classed
860 The beauteous; so, till two or three amassed
Mankind's beseemingnesses, and reduced
Themselves eventually, – graces loosed,

Strengths lavished, – all to heighten up One Shape
Whose potency no creature should escape.
Can it be Friedrich of the bowmen's talk?
Surely that grape-juice, bubbling at the stalk,
Is some grey scorching Saracenic wine
The Kaiser quaffs with the Miramoline –
Those swarthy hazel-clusters, seamed and chapped,
870 Or filberts russet-sheathed and velvet-capped,
Are dates plucked from the bough John Brienne sent
To keep in mind his sluggish armament
Of Canaan: – Friedrich's, all the pomp and fierce
Demeanour! But harsh sounds and sights transpierce
So rarely the serene cloud where he dwells
Whose looks enjoin, whose lightest words are spells
On the obdurate! That right arm indeed
Has thunder for its slave; but where's the need
Of thunder if the stricken multitude
880 Hearkens, arrested in its angriest mood,
While songs go up exulting, then dispread,
Dispart, disperse, lingering overhead
Like an escape of angels? 'Tis the tune,
Nor much unlike the words his women croon
Smilingly, colourless and faint-designed
Each, as a worn-out queen's face some remind
Of her extreme youth's love-tales. 'Eglamor
Made that!' Half minstrel and half emperor,
What but ill objects vexed him? Such he slew.
890 The kinder sort were easy to subdue
By those ambrosial glances, dulcet tones;
And these a gracious hand advanced to thrones
Beneath him. Wherefore twist and torture this,
Striving to name afresh the antique bliss,
Instead of saying, neither less nor more,
He had discovered, as our world before,
Apollo? That shall be the name; nor bid
Me rag by rag expose how patchwork hid
The youth – what thefts of every clime and day
900 Contributed to purfle the array
He climbed with (June at deep) some close ravine
'Mid clatter of its million pebbles sheen,
Over which, singing soft, the runnel slipped
Elate with rains: into whose streamlet dipped

He foot, yet trod, you thought, with unwet sock –
Though really on the stubs of living rock
Ages ago it crenelled; vines for roof,
Lindens for wall; before him, aye aloof,
Flittered in the cool some azure damsel-fly,
910 Born of the simmering quiet, there to die.
Emerging whence, Apollo still, he spied
Mighty descents of forest; multiplied
Tuft on tuft, here, the frolic myrtle-trees,
There gendered the grave maple stocks at ease.
And, proud of its observer, straight the wood
Tried old surprises on him; black it stood
A sudden barrier ('twas a cloud passed o'er)
So dead and dense, the tiniest brute no more
Must pass; yet presently (the cloud dispatched)
920 Each clump, behold, was glistering detached
A shrub, oak-boles shrunk into ilex-stems!
Yet could not he denounce the stratagems
He saw through, till, hours thence, aloft would hang
White summer-lightnings; as it sank and sprang
To measure, that whole palpitating breast
Of heaven, 'twas Apollo, nature prest
At eve to worship.
     Time stole: by degrees
The Pythons perish off; his votaries
Sink to respectful distance; songs redeem
930 Their pains, but briefer; their dismissals seem
Emphatic; only girls are very slow
To disappear – his Delians! Some that glow
O' the instant, more with earlier loves to wrench
Away, reserves to quell, disdains to quench;
Alike in one material circumstance –
All soon or late adore Apollo! Glance
The bevy through, divine Apollo's choice,
His Daphne! 'We secure Count Richard's voice
In Este's counsels, good for Este's ends
940 As our Taurello,' say his faded friends,
'By granting him our Palma!' – the sole child,
They mean, of Agnes Este who beguiled
Ecelin, years before this Adelaide
Wedded and turned him wicked: 'but the maid
Rejects his suit,' those sleepy women boast.

She, scorning all beside, deserves the most
Sordello: so, conspicuous in his world
Of dreams sat Palma. How the tresses curled
Into a sumptuous swell of gold and wound
950   About her like a glory! even the ground
Was bright as with spilt sunbeams; breathe not, breathe
Not! – poised, see, one leg doubled underneath,
Its small foot buried in the dimpling snow,
Rests, but the other, listlessly below,
O'er the couch-side swings feeling for cool air,
The vein-streaks swollen a richer violet where
The languid blood lies heavily; yet calm
On her slight prop, each flat and outspread palm,
As but suspended in the act to rise
960   By consciousness of beauty, whence her eyes
Turn with so frank a triumph, for she meets
Apollo's gaze in the pine glooms.
                                        Time fleets:
That's worst! Because the pre-appointed age
Approaches. Fate is tardy with the stage
And crowd she promised. Lean he grows and pale,
Though restlessly at rest. Hardly avail
Fancies to soothe him. Time steals, yet alone
He tarries here! The earnest smile is gone.
How long this might continue matters not;
970   – For ever, possibly; since to the spot
None come: our lingering Taurello quits
Mantua at last, and light our lady flits
Back to her place disburthened of a care.
Strange – to be constant here if he is there!
Is it distrust? Oh, never! for they both
Goad Ecelin alike, Romano's growth
Is daily manifest, with Azzo dumb
And Richard wavering: let but Friedrich come,
Find matter for the minstrelsy's report
980   – Lured from the Isle and its young Kaiser's court
To sing us a Messina morning up,
And, double rillet of a drinking cup,
Sparkle along to ease the land of drouth,
Northward to Provence that, and thus far south
The other! What a method to apprise
Neighbours of births, espousals, obsequies,

Which in their very tongue the Troubadour
Records! and his performance makes a tour,
For Trouveres bear the miracle about,
990 Explain its cunning to the vulgar rout,
Until the Formidable House is famed
Over the country – as Taurello aimed,
Who introduced, although the rest adopt,
The novelty. Such games, her absence stopped,
Begin afresh now Adelaide, recluse
No longer, in the light of day pursues
Her plans at Mantua: whence an accident
Which, breaking on Sordello's mixed content
Opened, like any flash that cures the blind,
1000 The veritable business of mankind.

BOOK THE SECOND

The woods were long austere with snow: at last
Pink leaflets budded on the beech, and fast
Larches, scattered through pine-tree solitudes,
Brightened, 'as in the slumbrous heart o' the woods
Our buried year, a witch, grew young again
To placid incantations, and that stain
About were from her cauldron, green smoke blent
With those black pines' – so Eglamor gave vent
To a chance fancy. Whence a just rebuke
10 From his companion; brother Naddo shook
The solemnest of brows: 'Beware,' he said,
'Of setting up conceits in nature's stead!'
Forth wandered our Sordello. Naught so sure
As that today's adventure will secure
Palma, the visioned lady – only pass
O'er yon damp mound and its exhausted grass,
Under that brake where sundawn feeds the stalks
Of withered fern with gold, into those walks
Of pine and take her! Buoyantly he went.
20 Again his stooping forehead was besprent
With dew-drops from the skirting ferns. Then wide
Opened the great morass, shot every side
With flashing water through and through; a-shine,
Thick-steaming, all-alive. Whose shape divine,

Quivered i' the farthest rainbow-vapour, glanced
Athwart the flying herons? He advanced,
But warily; though Mincio leaped no more,
Each foot-fall burst up in the marish-floor
A diamond jet: and if he stopped to pick
30   Rose-lichen, or molest the leeches quick,
And circling blood-worms, minnow, newt or loach,
A sudden pond would silently encroach
This way and that. On Palma passed. The verge
Of a new wood was gained. She will emerge
Flushed, now, and panting, – crowds to see, – will own
She loves him – Boniface to hear, to groan,
To leave his suit! One screen of pine-trees still
Opposes: but – the startling spectacle –
Mantua, this time! Under the walls – a crowd
40   Indeed, real men and women, gay and loud
Round a pavilion. How he stood!

                          In truth
No prophecy had come to pass: his youth
In its prime now – and where was homage poured
Upon Sordello? – born to be adored,
And suddenly discovered weak, scarce made
To cope with any, cast into the shade
By this and this. Yet something seemed to prick
And tingle in his blood; a sleight – a trick –
And much would be explained. It went for naught –
50   The best of their endowments were ill bought
With his identity: nay, the conceit,
That this day's roving led to Palma's feet
Was not so vain – list! The word, 'Palma!' Steal
Aside, and die, Sordello; this is real,
And this – abjure!

                    What next? The curtains see
Dividing! She is there; and presently
He will be there – the proper You, at length –
In your own cherished dress of grace and strength:
Most like, the very Boniface!

                             Not so.
60   It was a showy man advanced; but though
A glad cry welcomed him, then every sound
Sank and the crowd disposed themselves around,
– 'This is not he,' Sordello felt; while, 'Place

For the best Troubadour of Boniface!'
Hollaed the Jongleurs, – 'Eglamor, whose lay
Concludes his patron's Court of Love today!'
Obsequious Naddo strung the master's lute
With the new lute-string, 'Elys,' named to suit
The song: he stealthily at watch, the while,
70 Biting his lip to keep down a great smile
Of pride: then up he struck. Sordello's brain
Swam; for he knew a sometime deed again;
So, could supply each foolish gap and chasm
The minstrel left in his enthusiasm,
Mistaking its true version – was the tale
Not of Apollo? Only, what avail
Luring her down, that Elys an he pleased,
If the man dared no further? Has he ceased
And, lo, the people's frank applause half done,
80 Sordello was beside him, had begun
(Spite of indignant twitchings from his friend
The Trouvere) the true lay with the true end,
Taking the other's names and time and place
For his. On flew the song, a giddy race,
After the flying story; word made leap
Out word, rhyme – rhyme; the lay could barely keep
Pace with the action visibly rushing past:
Both ended. Back fell Naddo more aghast
Than some Egyptian from the harassed bull
90 That wheeled abrupt and, bellowing, fronted full
His plague, who spied a scarab 'neath the tongue,
And found 'twas Apis' flank his hasty prong
Insulted. But the people – but the cries,
The crowding round, and proffering the prize!
– For he had gained some prize. He seemed to shrink
Into a sleepy cloud, just at whose brink
One sight withheld him. There sat Adelaide,
Silent; but at her knees the very maid
Of the North Chamber, her red lips as rich,
100 The same pure fleecy hair; one weft of which,
Golden and great, quite touched his cheek as o'er
She leant, speaking some six words and no more.
He answered something, anything; and she
Unbound a scarf and laid it heavily
Upon him, her neck's warmth and all. Again

Moved the arrested magic; in his brain
Noises grew, and a light that turned to glare,
And greater glare, until the intense flare
Engulfed him, shut the whole scene from his sense.
110   And when he woke 'twas many a furlong thence,
At home; the sun shining his ruddy wont;
The customary birds'-chirp; but his front
Was crowned – was crowned! Her scented scarf around
His neck! Whose gorgeous vesture heaps the ground?
A prize? He turned, and peeringly on him
Brooded the women-faces, kind and dim,
Ready to talk – 'The Jongleurs in a troop
Had brought him back, Naddo and Squarcialupe
And Tagliafer; how strange! a childhood spent
120   In taking, well for him, so brave a bent!
Since Eglamor,' they heard, 'was dead with spite,
And Palma chose him for her minstrel.'

                                                Light
Sordello rose – to think, now; hitherto
He had perceived. Sure, a discovery grew
Out of it all! Best live from first to last
The transport o'er again. A week he passed,
Sucking the sweet out of each circumstance,
From the bard's outbreak to the luscious trance
Bounding his own achievement. Strange! A man
130   Recounted an adventure, but began
Imperfectly; his own task was to fill
The frame-work up, sing well what he sung ill,
Supply the necessary points, set loose
As many incidents of little use
– More imbecile the other, not to see
Their relative importance clear as he!
But, for a special pleasure in the act
Of singing – had he ever turned, in fact,
From Elys, to sing Elys? – from each fit
140   Of rapture to contrive a song of it?
True, this snatch or the other seemed to wind
Into a treasure, helped himself to find
A beauty in himself; for, see, he soared
By means of that mere snatch, to many a hoard
Of fancies; as some falling cone bears soft
The eye along the fir-tree-spire, aloft

To a dove's nest. Then, how divine the cause
Why such performance should exact applause
From men, if they had fancies too? Did fate
150 Decree they found a beauty separate
In the poor snatch itself? – 'Take Elys, there,
– "Her head that's sharp and perfect like a pear,
So close and smooth are laid the few fine locks
Coloured like honey oozed from topmost rocks
Sun-blanched the livelong summer" – if they heard
Just those two rhymes, assented at my word,
And loved them as I love them who have run
These fingers through those pale locks, let the sun
Into the white cool skin – who first could clutch,
160 Then praise – I needs must be a god to such.
Or what if some, above themselves, and yet
Beneath me, like their Eglamor, have set
An impress on our gift? So, men believe
And worship what they know not, nor receive
Delight from. Have they fancies – slow, perchance,
Not at their beck, which indistinctly glance
Until, by song, each floating part be linked
To each, and all grow palpable, distinct?'
He pondered this.
                                    Meanwhile, sounds low and drear
170 Stole on him, and a noise of footsteps, near
And nearer, while the underwood was pushed
Aside, the larches grazed, the dead leaves crushed
At the approach of men. The wind seemed laid;
Only, the trees shrunk slightly and a shade
Came o'er the sky although 'twas midday yet:
You saw each half-shut downcast floweret
Flutter – 'a Roman bride, when they'd dispart
Her unbound tresses with the Sabine dart,
Holding that famous rape in memory still,
180 Felt creep into her curls the iron chill,
And looked thus,' Eglamor would say – indeed
'Tis Eglamor, no other, these precede
Home hither in the woods. ''Twere surely sweet
Far from the scene of one's forlorn defeat
To sleep!' judged Naddo, who in person led
Jongleurs and Trouveres, chanting at their head,
A scanty company; for, sooth to say,

Our beaten Troubadour had seen his day.
Old worshippers were something shamed, old friends
190 Nigh weary; still the death proposed amends.
'Let us but get them safely through my song
And home again!' quoth Naddo.
                                    All along,
This man (they rest the bier upon the sand)
– This calm corpse with the loose flowers in his hand,
Eglamor, lived Sordello's opposite.
For him indeed was Naddo's notion right,
And verse a temple-worship vague and vast,
A ceremony that withdrew the last
Opposing bolt, looped back the lingering veil
200 Which hid the holy place: should one so frail
Stand there without such effort? or repine
If much was blank, uncertain at the shrine
He knelt before, till, soothed by many a rite,
The power responded, and some sound or sight
Grew up, his own forever, to be fixed,
In rhyme, the beautiful, forever! – mixed
With his own life, unloosed when he should please,
Having it safe at hand, ready to ease
All pain, remove all trouble; every time
210 He loosed that fancy from its bonds of rhyme,
(Like Perseus when he loosed his naked love)
Faltering; so distinct and far above
Himself, these fancies! He, no genius rare,
Transfiguring in fire or wave or air
At will, but a poor gnome that, cloistered up
In some rock-chamber with his agate cup,
His topaz rod, his seed-pearl, in these few
And their arrangement finds enough to do
For his best art. Then, how he loved that art!
220 The calling marking him a man apart
From men – one not to care, take counsel for
Cold hearts, comfortless faces – (Eglamor
Was neediest of his tribe) – since verse, the gift,
Was his, and men, the whole of them, must shift
Without it, e'en content themselves with wealth
And pomp and power, snatching a life by stealth.
So, Eglamor was not without his pride!
The sorriest bat which cowers throughout noontide

While other birds are jocund, has one time
230 When moon and stars are blinded, and the prime
Of earth is his to claim, nor find a peer;
And Eglamor was noblest poet here –
He well knew, 'mid those April woods he cast
Conceits upon in plenty as he passed,
That Naddo might suppose him not to think
Entirely on the coming triumph: wink
At the one weakness! 'Twas a fervid child,
That song of his; no brother of the guild
Had e'er conceived its like. The rest you know,
240 The exaltation and the overthrow:
Our poet lost his purpose, lost his rank,
His life – to that it came. Yet envy sank
Within him, as he heard Sordello out,
And, for the first time, shouted – tried to shout
Like others, not from any zeal to show
Pleasure that way: the common sort did so,
What else was Eglamor? who, bending down
As they, placed his beneath Sordello's crown,
Printed a kiss on his successor's hand,
250 Left one great tear on it, then joined his band
– In time; for some were watching at the door:
Who knows what envy may effect? 'Give o'er,
Nor charm his lips, nor craze him!' (here one spied
And disengaged the withered crown) – 'Beside
His crown? How prompt and clear those verses rang
To answer yours! nay, sing them!' And he sang
Them calmly. Home he went; friends used to wait
His coming, zealous to congratulate;
But, to a man – so quickly runs report –
260 Could do no less than leave him, and escort
His rival. That eve, then, bred many a thought:
What must his future life be? was he brought
So low, who stood so lofty this Spring morn?
At length he said, 'Best sleep now with my scorn,
And by tomorrow I devise some plain
Expedient!' So, he slept, nor woke again.
They found as much, those friends, when they returned
O'erflowing with the marvels they had learned
About Sordello's paradise, his roves
270 Among the hills and vales and plains and groves,

Wherein, no doubt, this lay was roughly cast,
Polished by slow degrees, completed last
To Eglamor's discomfiture and death.
    Such form the chanters now, and, out of breath,
They lay the beaten man in his abode,
Naddo reciting that same luckless ode,
Doleful to hear. Sordello could explore
By means of it, however, one step more
In joy; and, mastering the round at length,
280 Learnt how to live in weakness as in strength,
When from his covert forth he stood, addressed
Eglamor, bade the tender ferns invest,
Primeval pines o'ercanopy his couch,
And, most of all, his fame – (shall I avouch
Eglamor heard it, dead though he might look,
And laughed as from his brow Sordello took
The crown, and laid on the bard's breast, and said
It was a crown, now, fit for poet's head?)
– Continue. Nor the prayer quite fruitless fell.
290 A plant they have, yielding a three-leaved bell
Which whitens at the heart ere noon, and ails
Till evening; evening gives it to her gales
To clear away with such forgotten things
As are an eyesore to the morn: this brings
Him to their mind, and bears his very name.
    So much for Eglamor. My own month came;
'Twas a sunrise of blossoming and May.
Beneath a flowering laurel thicket lay
Sordello; each new sprinkle of white stars
300 That smell fainter of wine than Massic jars
Dug up at Baiae, when the south wind shed
The ripest, made him happier; filleted
And robed the same, only a lute beside
Lay on the turf. Before him far and wide
The country stretched: Goito slept behind
– The castle and its covert, which confined
Him with his hopes and fears; so fain of old
To leave the story of his birth untold.
At intervals, 'spite the fantastic glow
310 Of his Apollo-life, a certain low
And wretched whisper, winding through the bliss,
Admonished, no such fortune could be his,

All was quite false and sure to fade one day:
The closelier drew he round him his array
Of brilliance to expel the truth. But when
A reason for his difference from men
Surprised him at the grave, he took no rest
While aught of that old life, superbly dressed
Down to its meanest incident, remained
320 A mystery: alas, they soon explained
Away Apollo! and the tale amounts
To this: when at Vicenza both her counts
Banished the Vivaresi kith and kin,
Those Maltraversi hung on Ecelin,
Reviled him as he followed; he for spite
Must fire their quarter, though that self-same night
Among the flames young Ecelin was born
Of Adelaide, there too, and barely torn
From the roused populace hard on the rear,
330 By a poor archer when his chieftain's fear
Grew high; into the thick Elcorte leapt,
Saved her, and died; no creature left except
His child to thank. And when the full escape
Was known – how men impaled from chine to nape
Unlucky Prata, all to pieces spurned
Bishop Pistore's concubines, and burned
Taurello's entire household, flesh and fell,
Missing the sweeter prey – such courage well
Might claim reward. The orphan, ever since,
340 Sordello, had been nurtured by his prince
Within a blind retreat where Adelaide –
(For, once this notable discovery made,
The past at every point was understood)
– Might harbour easily when times were rude,
When Azzo schemed for Palma, to retrieve
That pledge of Agnes Este – loth to leave
Mantua unguarded with a vigilant eye,
While there Taurello bode ambiguously –
He who could have no motive now to moil
350 For his own fortunes since their utter spoil –
As it were worth while yet (went the report)
To disengage himself from her. In short,
Apollo vanished; a mean youth, just named
His lady's minstrel, was to be proclaimed

– How shall I phrase it? – Monarch of the World!
For, on the day when that array was furled
Forever, and in place of one a slave
To longings, wild indeed, but longings save
In dreams as wild, suppressed – one daring not
360   Assume the mastery such dreams allot,
Until a magical equipment, strength,
Grace, wisdom, decked him too, – he chose at length,
Content with unproved wits and failing frame,
In virtue of his simple will, to claim
That mastery, no less – to do his best
With means so limited, and let the rest
Go by, – the seal was set: never again
Sordello could in his own sight remain
One of the many, one with hopes and cares
370   And interests nowise distinct from theirs,
Only peculiar in a thriveless store
Of fancies, which were fancies and no more;
Never again for him and for the crowd
A common law was challenged and allowed
If calmly reasoned of, howe'er denied
By a mad impulse nothing justified
Short of Apollo's presence. The divorce
Is clear: why needs Sordello square his course
By any known example? Men no more
380   Compete with him than tree and flower before.
Himself, inactive, yet is greater far
Than such as act, each stooping to his star,
Acquiring thence his function; he has gained
The same result with meaner mortals trained
To strength or beauty, moulded to express
Each the idea that rules him; since no less
He comprehends that function, but can still
Embrace the others, take of might his fill
With Richard as of grace with Palma, mix
390   Their qualities, or for a moment fix
On one; abiding free meantime, uncramped
By any partial organ, never stamped
Strong, and to strength turning all energies –
Wise, and restricted to becoming wise –
That is, he loves not, nor possesses One
Idea that, star-like over, lures him on

To its exclusive purpose. 'Fortunate!
This flesh of mine ne'er strove to emulate
A soul so various – took no casual mould
400 Of the first fancy and, contracted, cold,
Clogged her forever – soul averse to change
As flesh: whereas flesh leaves soul free to range,
Remains itself a blank, cast into shade,
Encumbers little, if it cannot aid.
So, range, free soul! – who, by self-consciousness,
The last drop of all beauty dost express –
The grace of seeing grace, a quintessence
For thee: while for the world, that can dispense
Wonder on men who, themselves, wonder – make
410 A shift to love at second-hand, and take
For idols those who do but idolize,
Themselves, – the world that counts men strong or wise,
Who, themselves, court strength, wisdom, – it shall bow
Surely in unexampled worship now,
Discerning me!' –
             (Dear monarch, I beseech,
Notice how lamentably wide a breach
Is here: discovering this, discover too
What our poor world has possibly to do
With it! As pigmy natures as you please –
420 So much the better for you; take your ease,
Look on, and laugh; style yourself God alone;
Strangle some day with a cross olive-stone!
All that is right enough: but why want us
To know that you yourself know thus and thus?)
'The world shall bow to me conceiving all
Man's life, who see its blisses, great and small,
Afar – not tasting any; no machine
To exercise my utmost will is mine:
Be mine mere consciousness! Let men perceive
430 What I could do, a mastery believe,
Asserted and established to the throng
By their selected evidence of song
Which now shall prove, whate'er they are, or seek
To be, I am – whose words, not actions speak,
Who change no standards of perfection, vex
With no strange forms created to perplex,
But just perform their bidding and no more,

At their own satiating-point give o'er,
While each shall love in me the love that leads
440   His soul to power's perfection.' Song, not deeds,
(For we get tired) was chosen. Fate would brook
Mankind no other organ; he would look
For not another channel to dispense
His own volition by, receive men's sense
Of its supremacy – would live content,
Obstructed else, with merely verse for vent.
Nor should, for instance, strength an outlet seek
And, striving, be admired: nor grace bespeak
Wonder, displayed in gracious attitudes:
450   Nor wisdom, poured forth, change unseemly moods;
But he would give and take on song's one point.
Like some huge throbbing stone that, poised a-joint,
Sounds, to affect on its basaltic bed,
Must sue in just one accent; tempests shed
Thunder, and raves the windstorm: only let
That key by any little noise be set –
The far benighted hunter's halloo pitch
On that, the hungry curlew chance to scritch
Or serpent hiss it, rustling through the rift,
460   However loud, however low – all lift
The groaning monster, stricken to the heart.
    Lo ye, the world's concernment, for its part,
And this, for his, will hardly interfere!
Its businesses in blood and blaze this year
But wile the hour away – a pastime slight
Till he shall step upon the platform: right!
And, now thus much is settled, cast in rough,
Proved feasible, be counselled! thought enough, –
Slumber, Sordello! any day will serve:
470   Were it a less digested plan! how swerve
Tomorrow? Meanwhile eat these sun-dried grapes,
And watch the soaring hawk there! Life escapes
Merrily thus.
                    He thoroughly read o'er
His truchman Naddo's missive six times more,
Praying him visit Mantua and supply
A famished world.
                    The evening star was high
When he reached Mantua, but his fame arrived

Before him: friends applauded, foes connived,
And Naddo looked an angel, and the rest
480 Angels, and all these angels would be blest
Supremely by a song – the thrice-renowned
Goito-manufacture. Then he found
(Casting about to satisfy the crowd)
That happy vehicle, so late allowed,
A sore annoyance; 'twas the song's effect
He cared for, scarce the song itself: reflect!
In the past life, what might be singing's use?
Just to delight his Delians, whose profuse
Praise, not the toilsome process which procured
490 That praise, enticed Apollo: dreams abjured,
No overleaping means for ends – take both
For granted or take neither! I am loth
To say the rhymes at last were Eglamor's;
But Naddo, chuckling, bade competitors
Go pine; 'the master certes meant to waste
No effort, cautiously had probed the taste
He'd please anon: true bard, in short, – disturb
His title if they could; nor spur nor curb,
Fancy nor reason, wanting in him; whence
500 The staple of his verses, common sense:
He built on man's broad nature – gift of gifts,
That power to build! The world contented shifts
With counterfeits enough, a dreary sort
Of warriors, statesmen, ere it can extort
Its poet-soul – that's, after all, a freak
(The having eyes to see and tongue to speak)
With our herd's stupid sterling happiness
So plainly incompatible that – yes –
Yes – should a son of his improve the breed
510 And turn out poet, he were cursed indeed!'
'Well, there's Goito and its woods anon,
If the worst happen; best go stoutly on
Now!' thought Sordello.
                          Ay, and goes on yet!
You pother with your glossaries to get
A notion of the Troubadour's intent
In rondel, tenzon, virlai or sirvent –
Much as you study arras how to twirl
His angelot, plaything of page and girl

Once; but you surely reach, at last, – or, no!
520 Never quite reach what struck the people so,
As from the welter of their time he drew
Its elements successively to view,
Followed all actions backward on their course,
And catching up, unmingled at the source,
Such a strength, such a weakness, added then
A touch or two, and turned them into men.
Virtue took form, nor vice refused a shape;
Here heaven opened, there was hell agape,
As Saint this simpered past in sanctity,
530 Sinner the other flared portentous by
A greedy people. Then why stop, surprised
At his success? The scheme was realized
Too suddenly in one respect: a crowd
Praising, eyes quick to see, and lips as loud
To speak, delicious homage to receive,
The woman's breath to feel upon his sleeve,
Who said, 'But Anafest – why asks he less
Than Lucio, in your verses? how confess,
It seemed too much but yestereve!' – the youth,
540 Who bade him earnestly, 'Avow the truth!
You love Bianca, surely, from your song;
I knew I was unworthy!' – soft or strong,
In poured such tributes ere he had arranged
Ethereal ways to take them, sorted, changed,
Digested. Courted thus at unawares,
In spite of his pretensions and his cares,
He caught himself shamefully hankering
After the obvious petty joys that spring
From true life, fain relinquish pedestal
550 And condescend with pleasures – one and all
To be renounced, no doubt; for, thus to chain
Himself to single joys and so refrain
From tasting their quintessence, frustrates, sure,
His prime design; each joy must he abjure
Even for love of it.
                    He laughed: what sage
But perishes if from his magic page
He look because, at the first line, a proof
'Twas heard salutes him from the cavern roof?
'On! Give yourself, excluding aught beside,

560 To the day's task; compel your slave provide
Its utmost at the soonest; turn the leaf
Thoroughly conned. These lays of yours, in brief –
Cannot men bear, now, something better? – fly
A pitch beyond this unreal pageantry
Of essences? the period sure has ceased
For such: present us with ourselves, at least,
Not portions of ourselves, mere loves and hates
Made flesh: wait not!'
      Awhile the poet waits
However. The first trial was enough:
570 He left imagining, to try the stuff
That held the imaged thing, and, let it writhe
Never so fiercely, scarce allowed a tithe
To reach the light – his Language. How he sought
The cause, conceived a cure, and slow re-wrought
That Language, – welding words into the crude
Mass from the new speech round him, till a rude
Armour was hammered out, in time to be
Approved beyond the Roman panoply
Melted to make it, – boots not. This obtained
580 With some ado, no obstacle remained
To using it; accordingly he took
An action with its actors, quite forsook
Himself to live in each, returned anon
With the result – a creature, and, by one
And one, proceeded leisurely to equip
Its limbs in harness of his workmanship.
'Accomplished! Listen, Mantuans!' Fond essay!
Piece after piece that armour broke away,
Because perceptions whole, like that he sought
590 To clothe, reject so pure a work of thought
As language: thought may take perception's place
But hardly co-exist in any case,
Being its mere presentment – of the whole
By parts, the simultaneous and the sole
By the successive and the many. Lacks
The crowd perception? painfully it tacks
Thought to thought, which Sordello, needing such,
Has rent perception into: its to clutch
And reconstruct – his office to diffuse,
600 Destroy: as hard, then, to obtain a Muse

As to become Apollo. 'For the rest,
E'en if some wondrous vehicle expressed
The whole dream, what impertinence in me
So to express it, who myself can be
The dream! nor, on the other hand, are those
I sing to, over-likely to suppose
A higher than the highest I present
Now, which they praise already: be content
Both parties, rather – they with the old verse,
610 And I with the old praise – far go, fare worse!'
A few adhering rivets loosed, upsprings
The angel, sparkles off his mail, which rings
Whirled from each delicatest limb it warps;
So might Apollo from the sudden corpse
Of Hyacinth have cast his luckless quoits.
He set to celebrating the exploits
Of Montfort o'er the Mountaineers.
                         Then came
The world's revenge: their pleasure, now his aim
Merely, – what was it? 'Not to play the fool
620 So much as learn our lesson in your school!'
Replied the world. He found that, every time
He gained applause by any ballad-rhyme,
His auditory recognized no jot
As he intended, and, mistaking not
Him for his meanest hero, ne'er was dunce
Sufficient to believe him – all, at once.
His will . . . conceive it caring for his will!
– Mantuans, the main of them, admiring still
How a mere singer, ugly, stunted, weak,
630 Had Montfort at completely (so to speak)
His fingers' ends; while past the praise-tide swept
To Montfort, either's share distinctly kept:
The true meed for true merit! – his abates
Into a sort he most repudiates,
And on them angrily he turns. Who were
The Mantuans, after all, that he should care
About their recognition, ay or no?
In spite of the convention months ago,
(Why blink the truth?) was not he forced to help
640 This same ungrateful audience, every whelp
Of Naddo's litter, make them pass for peers

With the bright band of old Goito years,
As erst he toiled for flower or tree? Why, there
Sat Palma! Adelaide's funereal hair
Ennobled the next corner. Ay, he strewed
A fairy dust upon that multitude,
Although he feigned to take them by themselves;
His giants dignified those puny elves,
Sublimed their faint applause. In short, he found
650 Himself still footing a delusive round,
Remote as ever from the self-display
He meant to compass, hampered every way
By what he hoped assistance. Wherefore then
Continue, make believe to find in men
A use he found not?
                              Weeks, months, years went by
And lo, Sordello vanished utterly,
Sundered in twain; each spectral part at strife
With each; one jarred against another life;
The Poet thwarting hopelessly the Man –
660 Who, fooled no longer, free in fancy ran
Here, there: let slip no opportunities
As pitiful, forsooth, beside the prize
To drop on him some no-time and acquit
His constant faith (the Poet-half's to wit –
That waiving any compromise between
No joy and all joy kept the hunger keen
Beyond most methods) – of incurring scoff
From the Man-portion – not to be put off
With self-reflectings by the Poet's scheme,
670 Though ne'er so bright. Who sauntered forth in dream,
Dressed any how, nor waited mystic frames,
Immeasurable gifts, astounding claims,
But just his sorry self? – who yet might be
Sorrier for aught he in reality
Achieved, so pinioned Man's the Poet-part,
Fondling, in turn of fancy, verse; the Art
Developing his soul a thousand ways –
Potent, by its assistance, to amaze
The multitude with majesties, convince
680 Each sort of nature that the nature's prince
Accosted it. Language, the makeshift, grew
Into a bravest of expedients, too;

Apollo, seemed it now, perverse had thrown
Quiver and bow away, the lyre alone
Sufficed. While, out of dream, his day's work went
To tune a crazy tenzon or sirvent –
So hampered him the Man-part, thrust to judge
Between the bard and the bard's audience, grudge
A minute's toil that missed its due reward!

690   But the complete Sordello, Man and Bard,
John's cloud-girt angel, this foot on the land,
That on the sea, with, open in his hand,
A bitter-sweeting of a book – was gone.
    Then, if internal struggles to be one,
Which frittered him incessantly piecemeal,
Referred, ne'er so obliquely, to the real
Intruding Mantuans! ever with some call
To action while he pondered, once for all,
Which looked the easier effort – to pursue

700   This course, still leap o'er paltry joys, yearn through
The present ill-appreciated stage
Of self-revealment, and compel the age
Know him – or else, forswearing bard-craft, wake
From out his lethargy and nobly shake
Off timid habits of denial, mix
With men, enjoy like men. Ere he could fix
On aught, in rushed the Mantuans; much they cared
For his perplexity! Thus unprepared,
The obvious if not only shelter lay

710   In deeds, the dull conventions of his day
Prescribed the like of him: why not be glad
'Tis settled Palma's minstrel, good or bad,
Submits to this and that established rule?
Let Vidal change, or any other fool,
His murrey-coloured robe for filamot,
And crop his hair; too skin-deep, is it not,
Such vigour? Then, a sorrow to the heart,
His talk! Whatever topics they might start
Had to be groped for in his consciousness

720   Straight, and as straight delivered them by guess.
Only obliged to ask himself, 'What was,'
A speedy answer followed; but, alas,
One of God's large ones, tardy to condense
Itself into a period; answers whence

A tangle of conclusions must be stripped
At any risk ere, trim to pattern clipped,
They matched rare specimens the Mantuan flock
Regaled him with, each talker from his stock
Of sorted-o'er opinions, every stage,
730 Juicy in youth or desiccate with age,
Fruits like the fig-tree's, rathe-ripe, rotten-rich,
Sweet-sour, all tastes to take: a practice which
He too had not impossibly attained,
Once either of those fancy-flights restrained;
(For, at conjecture how might words appear
To others, playing there what happened here,
And occupied abroad by what he spurned
At home, 'twas slipped, the occasion he returned
To seize:) he'd strike that lyre adroitly – speech,
740 Would but a twenty-cubit plectre reach;
A clever hand, consummate instrument,
Were both brought close; each excellency went
For nothing, else. The question Naddo asked,
Had just a lifetime moderately tasked
To answer, Naddo's fashion. More disgust
And more: why move his soul, since move it must
At minute's notice or as good it failed
To move at all? The end was, he retailed
Some ready-made opinion, put to use
750 This quip, that maxim, ventured reproduce
Gestures and tones – at any folly caught
Serving to finish with, nor too much sought
If false or true 'twas spoken; praise and blame
Of what he said grew pretty nigh the same
– Meantime awards to meantime acts: his soul,
Unequal to the compassing a whole,
Saw, in a tenth part, less and less to strive
About. And as for men in turn . . . contrive
Who could to take eternal interest
760 In them, so hate the worst, so love the best:
Though, in pursuance of his passive plan,
He hailed, decried, the proper way.

As Man

So figured he; and how as Poet? Verse
Came only not to a stand-still. The worse,
That his poor piece of daily work to do

Was – not sink under any rivals; who
Loudly and long enough, without these qualms,
Turned, from Bocafoli's stark-naked psalms,
To Plara's sonnets spoilt by toying with,
770 'As knops that stud some almug to the pith
Prickèd for gum, wry thence, and crinklèd worse
Than pursèd eyelids of a river-horse
Sunning himself o' the slime when whirrs the breese' –
Gad-fly, that is. He might compete with these!
But – but –

        'Observe a pompion-twine afloat;
Pluck me one cup from off the castle-moat!
Along with cup you raise leaf, stalk and root,
The entire surface of the pool to boot.
So could I pluck a cup, put in one song
780 A single sight, did not my hand, too strong,
Twitch in the least the root-strings of the whole.
How should externals satisfy my soul?'
'Why that's precise the error Squarcialupe'
(Hazarded Naddo) 'finds; "the man can't stoop
To sing us out," quoth he, "a mere romance;
He'd fain do better than the best, enhance
The subjects' rarity, work problems out
Therewith." Now, you're a bard, a bard past doubt,
And no philosopher; why introduce
790 Crotchets like these? fine, surely, but no use
In poetry – which still must be, to strike,
Based upon common sense; there's nothing like
Appealing to our nature! what beside
Was your first poetry? No tricks were tried
In that, no hollow thrills, affected throes!
"The man," said we, "tells his own joys and woes:
We'll trust him." Would you have your songs endure?
Build on the human heart! – why, to be sure
Yours is one sort of heart – but I mean theirs,
800 Ours, every one's, the healthy heart one cares
To build on! Central peace, mother of strength,
That's father of . . . nay, go yourself that length,
Ask those calm-hearted doers what they do
When they have got their calm! And is it true,
Fire rankles at the heart of every globe?
Perhaps. But these are matters one may probe

Too deeply for poetic purposes:
Rather select a theory that . . . yes,
Laugh! what does that prove? – stations you midway
810   And saves some little o'er-refining. Nay,
That's rank injustice done me! I restrict
The poet? Don't I hold the poet picked
Out of a host of warriors, statesmen . . . did
I tell you? Very like! As well you hid
That sense of power, you have! True bards believe
All able to achieve what they achieve –
That is, just nothing – in one point abide
Profounder simpletons than all beside.
Oh, ay! The knowledge that you are a bard
820   Must constitute your prime, nay sole, reward!'
So prattled Naddo, busiest of the tribe
Of genius-haunters – how shall I describe
What grubs or nips or rubs or rips – your louse
For love, your flea for hate, magnanimous,
Malignant, Pappacoda, Tagliafer,
Picking a sustenance from wear and tear
By implements it sedulous employs
To undertake, lay down, mete out, o'er-toise
Sordello? Fifty creepers to elude
830   At once! They settled staunchly; shame ensued:
Behold the monarch of mankind succumb
To the last fool who turned him round his thumb,
As Naddo styled it! 'Twas not worth oppose
The matter of a moment, gainsay those
He aimed at getting rid of; better think
Their thoughts and speak their speech, secure to slink
Back expeditiously to his safe place,
And chew the cud – what he and what his race
Were really, each of them. Yet even this
840   Conformity was partial. He would miss
Some point, brought into contact with them ere
Assured in what small segment of the sphere
Of his existence they attended him;
Whence blunders, falsehoods rectified – a grim
List – slur it over! How? If dreams were tried,
His will swayed sicklily from side to side,
Nor merely neutralized his waking act
But tended e'en in fancy to distract

The intermediate will, the choice of means.
850 He lost the art of dreaming: Mantuan scenes
Supplied a baron, say, he sang before,
Handsomely reckless, full to running-o'er
Of gallantries; 'abjure the soul, content
With body, therefore!' Scarcely had he bent
Himself in dream thus low, when matter fast
Cried out, he found, for spirit to contrast
And task it duly; by advances slight,
The simple stuff becoming composite,
Count Lori grew Apollo: best recall
860 His fancy! Then would some rough peasant-Paul,
Like those old Ecelin confers with, glance
His gay apparel o'er; that countenance
Gathered his shattered fancies into one,
And, body clean abolished, soul alone
Sufficed the grey Paulician: by and by,
To balance the ethereality,
Passions were needed; foiled he sank again.
    Meanwhile the world rejoiced ('tis time explain)
Because a sudden sickness set it free
870 From Adelaide. Missing the mother-bee,
Her mountain-hive Romano swarmed; at once
A rustle-forth of daughters and of sons
Blackened the valley. 'I am sick too, old,
Half-crazed I think; what good's the Kaiser's gold
To such an one? God help me! for I catch
My children's greedy sparkling eyes at watch –
"He bears that double breastplate on," they say,
"So many minutes less than yesterday!"
Beside, Monk Hilary is on his knees
880 Now, sworn to kneel and pray till God shall please
Exact a punishment for many things
You know, and some you never knew; which brings
To memory, Azzo's sister Beatrix
And Richard's Giglia are my Alberic's
And Ecelin's betrothed; the Count himself
Must get my Palma: Ghibellin and Guelf
Mean to embrace each other.' So began
Romano's missive to his fighting man
Taurello – on the Tuscan's death, away
890 With Friedrich sworn to sail from Naples' bay

Next month for Syria. Never thunder-clap
Out of Vesuvius' throat, like this mishap
Startled him. 'That accursed Vicenza! I
Absent; and she selects this time to die!
Ho, fellows, for Vicenza!' Half a score
Of horses ridden dead, he stood before
Romano in his reeking spurs: too late –
'Boniface urged me, Este could not wait,'
The chieftain stammered; 'let me die in peace –
900   Forget me! Was it I who craved increase
Of rule? Do you and Friedrich plot your worst
Against the Father: as you found me first
So leave me now. Forgive me! Palma, sure,
Is at Goito still. Retain that lure –
Only be pacified!'
                         The country rung
With such a piece of news: on every tongue,
How Ecelin's great servant, congeed off,
Had done a long day's service, so, might doff
The green and yellow, and recover breath
910   At Mantua, whither, – since Retrude's death,
(The girlish slip of a Sicilian bride
From Otho's house, he carried to reside
At Mantua till the Ferrarese should pile
A structure worthy her imperial style,
The gardens raise, the statues there enshrine,
She never lived to see) – although his line
Was ancient in her archives and she took
A pride in him, that city, nor forsook
Her child when he forsook himself and spent
920   A prowess on Romano surely meant
For his own growth – whither he ne'er resorts
If wholly satisfied (to trust reports)
With Ecelin. So, forward in a trice
Were shows to greet him. 'Take a friend's advice,'
Quoth Naddo to Sordello, 'nor be rash
Because your rivals (nothing can abash
Some folks) demur that we pronounced you best
To sound the great man's welcome; 'tis a test,
Remember! Strojavacca looks asquint,
930   The rough fat sloven; and there's plenty hint
Your pinions have received of late a shock –

Outsoar them, cobswan of the silver flock!
Sing well!' A signal wonder, song's no whit
Facilitated.
        Fast the minutes flit;
Another day, Sordello finds, will bring
The soldier, and he cannot choose but sing;
So, a last shift, quits Mantua – slow, alone:
Out of that aching brain, a very stone,
Song must be struck. What occupies that front?
940 Just how he was more awkward than his wont
The night before, when Naddo, who had seen
Taurello on his progress, praised the mien
For dignity no crosses could affect –
Such was a joy, and might not he detect
A satisfaction if established joys
Were proved imposture? Poetry annoys
Its utmost: wherefore fret? Verses may come
Or keep away! And thus he wandered, dumb
Till evening, when he paused, thoroughly spent,
950 On a blind hill-top: down the gorge he went,
Yielding himself up as to an embrace.
The moon came out; like features of a face,
A querulous fraternity of pines,
Sad blackthorn clumps, leafless and grovelling vines
Also came out, made gradually up
The picture; 'twas Goito's mountain-cup
And castle. He had dropped through one defile
He never dared explore, the Chief erewhile
Had vanished by. Back rushed the dream, enwrapped
960 Him wholly. 'Twas Apollo now they lapped,
Those mountains, not a pettish minstrel meant
To wear his soul away in discontent,
Brooding on fortune's malice. Heart and brain
Swelled; he expanded to himself again,
As some thin seedling spice-tree starved and frail,
Pushing between cat's head and ibis' tail
Crusted into the porphyry pavement smooth,
– Suffered remain just as it sprung, to soothe
The Soldan's pining daughter, never yet
970 Well in her chilly green-glazed minaret, –
When rooted up, the sunny day she died,
And flung into the common court beside

Its parent tree. Come home, Sordello! Soon
Was he low muttering, beneath the moon,
Of sorrow saved, of quiet evermore, –
Since from the purpose, he maintained before,
Only resulted wailing and hot tears.
Ah, the slim castle! dwindled of late years,
But more mysterious; gone to ruin – trails
980 Of vine through every loop-hole. Naught avails
The night as, torch in hand, he must explore
The maple chamber: did I say, its floor
Was made of intersecting cedar beams?
Worn now with gaps so large, there blew cold streams
Of air quite from the dungeon; lay your ear
Close and 'tis like, one after one, you hear
In the blind darkness water drop. The nests
And nooks retain their long ranged vesture-chests
Empty and smelling of the iris root
990 The Tuscan grated o'er them to recruit
Her wasted wits. Palma was gone that day,
Said the remaining women. Last, he lay
Beside the Caryaean group reserved and still.

    The Body, the Machine for Acting Will,
Had been at the commencement proved unfit;
That for Demonstrating, Reflecting it,
Mankind – no fitter: was the Will Itself
In fault?
          His forehead pressed the moonlit shelf
Beside the youngest marble maid awhile;
1000 Then, raising it, he thought, with a long smile,
'I shall be king again!' as he withdrew
The envied scarf; into the font he threw
His crown.
          Next day, no poet! 'Wherefore?' asked
Taurello, when the dance of Jongleurs, masked
As devils, ended; 'don't a song come next?'
The master of the pageant looked perplexed
Till Naddo's whisper came to his relief.
'His Highness knew what poets were: in brief,
Had not the tetchy race prescriptive right
1010 To peevishness, caprice? or, call it spite,
One must receive their nature in its length
And breadth, expect the weakness with the strength!'

- So phrasing, till, his stock of phrases spent,
The easy-natured soldier smiled assent,
Settled his portly person, smoothed his chin,
And nodded that the bull-bait might begin.

BOOK THE THIRD

And the font took them: let our laurels lie!
Braid moonfern now with mystic trifoly
Because once more Goito gets, once more,
Sordello to itself! A dream is o'er,
And the suspended life begins anew;
Quiet those throbbing temples, then, subdue
That cheek's distortion! Nature's strict embrace,
Putting aside the past, shall soon efface
Its print as well – factitious humours grown
10　Over the true – loves, hatreds not his own –
And turn him pure as some forgotten vest
Woven of painted byssus, silkiest
Tufting the Tyrrhene whelk's pearl-sheeted lip,
Left welter where a trireme let it slip
I' the sea, and vexed a satrap; so the stain
O' the world forsakes Sordello, with its pain,
Its pleasure: how the tinct loosening escapes,
Cloud after cloud! Mantua's familiar shapes
Die, fair and foul die, fading as they flit,
20　Men, women, and the pathos and the wit,
Wise speech and foolish, deeds to smile or sigh
For, good, bad, seemly or ignoble, die.
The last face glances through the eglantines,
The last voice murmurs, 'twixt the blossomed vines,
Of Men, of that machine supplied by thought
To compass self-perception with, he sought
By forcing half himself – an insane pulse
Of a god's blood, on clay it could convulse,
Never transmute – on human sights and sounds,
30　To watch the other half with; irksome bounds
It ebbs from to its source, a fountain sealed
Forever. Better sure be unrevealed
Than part revealed: Sordello well or ill
Is finished: then what further use of Will,

Point in the prime idea not realized,
An oversight? inordinately prized,
No less, and pampered with enough of each
Delight to prove the whole above its reach.
'To need become all natures, yet retain
40   The law of my own nature – to remain
Myself, yet yearn . . . as if that chestnut, think,
Should yearn for this first larch-bloom crisp and pink,
Or those pale fragrant tears where zephyrs stanch
March wounds along the fretted pine-tree branch!
Will and the means to show will, great and small,
Material, spiritual, – abjure them all
Save any so distinct, they may be left
To amuse, not tempt become! and, thus bereft,
Just as I first was fashioned would I be!
50   Nor, moon, is it Apollo now, but me
Thou visitest to comfort and befriend!
Swim thou into my heart, and there an end,
Since I possess thee! – nay, thus shut mine eyes
And know, quite know, by this heart's fall and rise,
When thou dost bury thee in clouds, and when
Out-standest: wherefore practise upon men
To make that plainer to myself?'
                       Slide here
Over a sweet and solitary year
Wasted; or simply notice change in him –
60   How eyes, once with exploring bright, grew dim
And satiate with receiving. Some distress
Was caused, too, by a sort of consciousness
Under the imbecility, – naught kept
That down; he slept, but was aware he slept,
So, frustrated: as who brainsick made pact
Erst with the overhanging cataract
To deafen him, yet still distinguished plain
His own blood's measured clicking at his brain.
   To finish. One declining Autumn day –
70   Few birds about the heaven chill and grey,
No wind that cared trouble the tacit woods –
He sauntered home complacently, their moods
According, his and nature's. Every spark
Of Mantua life was trodden out; so dark
The embers, that the Troubadour, who sung

Hundreds of songs, forgot, its trick his tongue,
Its craft his brain, how either brought to pass
Singing at all; that faculty might class
With any of Apollo's now. The year
80   Began to find its early promise sere
As well. Thus beauty vanishes; thus stone
Outlingers flesh: nature's and his youth gone,
They left the world to you, and wished you joy.
When, stopping his benevolent employ,
A presage shuddered through the welkin; harsh
The earth's remonstrance followed. 'Twas the marsh
Gone of a sudden. Mincio, in its place,
Laughed, a broad water, in next morning's face,
And, where the mists broke up immense and white
90   I' the steady wind, burned like a spilth of light
Out of the crashing of a myriad stars.
And here was nature, bound by the same bars
Of fate with him!
                    'No! youth once gone is gone:
Deeds, let escape, are never to be done.
Leaf-fall and grass-spring for the year; for us –
Oh forfeit I unalterably thus
My chance? nor two lives wait me, this to spend,
Learning save that? Nature has time, may mend
Mistake, she knows occasion will recur;
100   Landslip or seabreach, how affects it her
With her magnificent resources? – I
Must perish once and perish utterly.
Not any strollings now at even-close
Down the field-path, Sordello! by thorn-rows
Alive with lamp-flies, swimming spots of fire
And dew, outlining the black cypress' spire
She waits you at, Elys, who heard you first
Woo her, the snow-month through, but ere she durst
Answer 'twas April. Linden-flower-time-long
110   Her eyes were on the ground; 'tis July, strong
Now; and because white dust-clouds overwhelm
The woodside, here or by the village elm
That holds the moon, she meets you, somewhat pale,
But letting you lift up her coarse flax veil
And whisper (the damp little hand in yours)
Of love, heart's love, your heart's love that endures

Till death. Tush! No mad mixing with the rout
Of haggard ribalds wandering about
The hot torchlit wine-scented island-house
120 Where Friedrich holds his wickedest carouse,
Parading, – to the gay Palermitans,
Soft Messinese, dusk Saracenic clans
Nuocera holds, – those tall grave dazzling Norse,
High-cheeked, lank-haired, toothed whiter than the morse,
Queens of the caves of jet stalactites,
He sent his barks to fetch through icy seas,
The blind night seas without a saving star,
And here in snowy birdskin robes they are,
Sordello! – here, mollitious alcoves gilt
130 Superb as Byzant domes that devils built!
– Ah, Byzant, there again! no chance to go
Ever like august cheery Dandolo,
Worshipping hearts about him for a wall,
Conducted, blind eyes, hundred years and all,
Through vanquished Byzant where friends note for him
What pillar, marble massive, sardius slim,
'Twere fittest he transport to Venice' Square –
Flattered and promised life to touch them there
Soon, by those fervid sons of senators!
140 No more lifes, deaths, loves, hatreds, peaces, wars!
Ah, fragments of a whole ordained to be,
Points in the life I waited! what are ye
But roundels of a ladder which appeared
Awhile the very platform it was reared
To lift me on? – that happiness I find
Proofs of my faith in, even in the blind
Instinct which bade forego you all unless
Ye led me past yourselves. Ay, happiness
Awaited me; the way life should be used
150 Was to acquire, and deeds like you conduced
To teach it by a self-revealment, deemed
Life's very use, so long! Whatever seemed
Progress to that, was pleasure; aught that stayed
My reaching it – no pleasure. I have laid
The ladder down; I climb not; still, aloft
The platform stretches! Blisses strong and soft,
I dared not entertain, elude me; yet
Never of what they promised could I get

A glimpse till now! The common sort, the crowd,
160   Exist, perceive; with Being are endowed,
However slight, distinct from what they See,
However bounded; Happiness must be,
To feed the first by gleanings from the last,
Attain its qualities, and slow or fast
Become what they behold; such peace-in-strife,
By transmutation, is the Use of Life,
The Alien turning Native to the soul
Or body – which instructs me; I am whole
There and demand a Palma; had the world
170   Been from my soul to a like distance hurled,
'Twere Happiness to make it one with me:
Whereas I must, ere I begin to Be,
Include a world, in flesh, I comprehend
In spirit now; and this done, what's to blend
With? Naught is Alien in the world – my Will
Owns all already; yet can turn it – still
Less – Native, since my Means to correspond
With Will are so unworthy, 'twas my bond
To tread the very joys that tantalize
180   Most now, into a grave, never to rise.
I die then! Will the rest agree to die?
Next Age or no? Shall its Sordello try
Clue after clue, and catch at last the clue
I miss? – that's underneath my finger too,
Twice, thrice a day, perhaps, – some yearning traced
Deeper, some petty consequence embraced
Closer! Why fled I Mantua, then? – complained
So much my Will was fettered, yet remained
Content within a tether half the range
190   I could assign it? – able to exchange
My ignorance (I felt) for knowledge, and
Idle because I could thus understand –
Could e'en have penetrated to its core
Our mortal mystery, yet – fool – forbore,
Preferred elaborating in the dark
My casual stuff, by any wretched spark
Born of my predecessors, though one stroke
Of mine had brought the flame forth! Mantua's yoke,
My minstrel's-trade, was to behold mankind, –
200   My own concern was just to bring my mind

Behold, just extricate, for my acquist,
Each object suffered stifle in the mist
Which hazard, custom, blindness interpose
Betwixt things and myself.'
                                        Whereat he rose.
The level wind carried above the firs
Clouds, the irrevocable travellers,
Onward.
            'Pushed thus into a drowsy copse,
Arms twine about my neck, each eyelid drops
Under a humid finger; while there fleets,
210   Outside the screen, a pageant time repeats
Never again! To be deposed, immured
Clandestinely – still petted, still assured
To govern were fatiguing work – the Sight
Fleeting meanwhile! 'Tis noontide: wreak ere night
Somehow my will upon it, rather! Slake
This thirst somehow, the poorest impress take
That serves! A blasted bud displays you, torn,
Faint rudiments of the full flower unborn;
But who divines what glory coats o'erclasp
220   Of the bulb dormant in the mummy's grasp
Taurello sent?' ...
                        'Taurello? Palma sent
Your Trouvere,' (Naddo interposing leant
Over the lost bard's shoulder) – 'and, believe,
You cannot more reluctantly receive
Than I pronounce her message: we depart
Together. What avail a poet's heart
Verona's pomps and gauds? five blades of grass
Suffice him. News? Why, where your marish was,
On its mud-banks smoke rises after smoke
230   I' the valley, like a spout of hell new-broke.
Oh, the world's tidings! small your thanks, I guess,
For them. The father of our Patroness,
Has played Taurello an astounding trick,
Parts between Ecelin and Alberic
His wealth and goes into a convent: both
Wed Guelfs: the Count and Palma plighted troth
A week since at Verona: and they want
You doubtless to contrive the marriage-chant
Ere Richard storms Ferrara.' Then was told

240   The tale from the beginning – how, made bold
    By Salinguerra's absence, Guelfs had burned
    And pillaged till he unawares returned
    To take revenge: how Azzo and his friend
    Were doing their endeavour, how the end
    O' the siege was nigh, and how the Count, released
    From further care, would with his marriage-feast
    Inaugurate a new and better rule,
    Absorbing thus Romano.
                  'Shall I school
    My master,' added Naddo, 'and suggest
250   How you may clothe in a poetic vest
    These doings, at Verona? Your response
    To Palma! Wherefore jest? "Depart at once?"
    A good resolve! In truth, I hardly hoped
    So prompt an acquiescence. Have you groped
    Out wisdom in the wilds here? – thoughts may be
    Over-poetical for poetry.
    Pearl-white, you poets liken Palma's neck;
    And yet what spoils an orient like some speck
    Of genuine white, turning its own white grey?
260   You take me? Curse the cicala!'
                      One more day,
    One eve – appears Verona! Many a group,
    (You mind) instructed of the osprey's swoop
    On lynx and ounce, was gathering – Christendom
    Sure to receive, whate'er the end was, from
    The evening's purpose cheer or detriment,
    Since Friedrich only waited some event
    Like this, of Ghibellins establishing
    Themselves within Ferrara, ere, as King
    Of Lombardy, he'd glad descend there, wage
270   Old warfare with the Pontiff, disengage
    His barons from the burghers, and restore
    The rule of Charlemagne, broken of yore
    By Hildebrand.
                I' the palace, each by each,
    Sordello sat and Palma: little speech
    At first in that dim closet, face with face
    (Despite the tumult in the market-place)
    Exchanging quick low laughters: now would rush
    Word upon word to meet a sudden flush,

A look left off, a shifting lips' surmise –
280　But for the most part their two histories
Ran best through the locked fingers and linked arms.
And so the night flew on with its alarms
Till in burst one of Palma's retinue;
'Now, Lady!' gasped he. Then arose the two
And leaned into Verona's air, dead-still.
A balcony lay black beneath until
Out, 'mid a gush of torchfire, grey-haired men
Came on it and harangued the people: then
Sea-like that people surging to and fro
290　Shouted, 'Hale forth the carroch – trumpets, ho,
A flourish! Run it in the ancient grooves!
Back from the bell! Hammer – that whom behoves
May hear the League is up! Peal – learn who list,
Verona means not first of towns break tryst
Tomorrow with the League!'
　　　　　　　　　　　　Enough. Now turn –
Over the eastern cypresses: discern!
Is any beacon set a-glimmer?
　　　　　　　　　　　Rang
The air with shouts that overpowered the clang
Of the incessant carroch, even: 'Haste –
300　The candle's at the gateway! ere it waste,
Each soldier stand beside it, armed to march
With Tiso Sampier through the eastern arch!'
Ferrara's succoured, Palma!
　　　　　　　　　　　Once again
They sat together; some strange thing in train
To say, so difficult was Palma's place
In taking, with a coy fastidious grace
Like the bird's flutter ere it fix and feed.
But when she felt she held her friend indeed
Safe, she threw back her curls, began implant
310　Her lessons; telling of another want
Goito's quiet nourished than his own;
Palma – to serve him – to be served, alone
Importing; Agnes' milk so neutralized
The blood of Ecelin. Nor be surprised
If, while Sordello fain had captive led
Nature, in dream was Palma subjected
To some out-soul, which dawned not though she pined

Delaying, till its advent, heart and mind
Their life. 'How dared I let expand the force
320 Within me, till some out-soul, whose resource
It grew for, should direct it? Every law
Of life, its every fitness, every flaw,
Must One determine whose corporeal shape
Would be no other than the prime escape
And revelation to me of a Will
Orb-like o'ershrouded and inscrutable
Above, save at the point which, I should know,
Shone that myself, my powers, might overflow
So far, so much; as now it signified
330 Which earthly shape it henceforth chose my guide,
Whose mortal lip selected to declare
Its oracles, what fleshly garb would wear
– The first of intimations, whom to love;
The next, how love him. Seemed that orb, above
The castle-covert and the mountain-close,
Slow in appearing? – if beneath it rose
Cravings, aversions, – did our green precinct
Take pride in me, at unawares distinct
With this or that endowment, – how, repressed
340 At once, such jetting power shrank to the rest!
Was I to have a chance touch spoil me, leave
My spirit thence unfitted to receive
The consummating spell? – that spell so near
Moreover! "Waits he not the waking year?
His almond-blossoms must be honey-ripe
By this; to welcome him, fresh runnels stripe
The thawed ravines; because of him, the wind
Walks like a herald. I shall surely find
Him now!"
                    'And chief, that earnest April morn
350 Of Richard's Love-court, was it time, so worn
And white my cheek, so idly my blood beat,
Sitting that morn beside the Lady's feet
And saying as she prompted; till outburst
One face from all the faces. Not then first
I knew it; where in maple chamber glooms,
Crowned with what sanguine-heart pomegranate blooms,
Advanced it ever? Men's acknowledgement
Sanctioned my own: 'twas taken, Palma's bent, –

Sordello, – recognized, accepted.

'Dumb

360 Sat she still scheming. Ecelin would come
Gaunt, scared, "Cesano baffles me," he'd say:
"Better I fought it out, my father's way!
Strangle Ferrara in its drowning flats,
And you and your Taurello yonder! – what's
Romano's business there?" An hour's concern
To cure the froward Chief! – induce return
As heartened from those overmeaning eyes,
Wound up to persevere, – his enterprise
Marked out anew, its exigent of wit
370 Apportioned, – she at liberty to sit
And scheme against the next emergence, I –
To covet her Taurello-sprite, made fly
Or fold the wing – to con your horoscope
For leave command those steely shafts shoot ope,
Or straight assuage their blinding eagerness
In blank smooth snow. What semblance of success
To any of my plans for making you
Mine and Romano's? Break the first wall through,
Tread o'er the ruins of the Chief, supplant
380 His sons beside, still, vainest were the vaunt:
There, Salinguerra would obstruct me sheer,
And the insuperable Tuscan, here,
Stay me! But one wild eve that Lady died
In her lone chamber: only I beside:
Taurello far at Naples, and my sire
At Padua, Ecelin away in ire
With Alberic. She held me thus – a clutch
To make our spirits as our bodies touch –
And so began flinging the past up, heaps
390 Of uncouth treasure from their sunless sleeps
Within her soul; deeds rose along with dreams,
Fragments of many miserable schemes,
Secrets, more secrets, then – no, not the last –
'Mongst others, like a casual trick o' the past,
How . . . ay, she told me, gathering up her face,
All left of it, into one arch-grimace
To die with . . .

'Friend, 'tis gone! but not the fear
Of that fell laughing, heard as now I hear.

Nor faltered voice, nor seemed her heart grow weak
400 When i' the midst abrupt she ceased to speak
— Dead, as to serve a purpose, mark! — for in
Rushed o' the very instant Ecelin
(How summoned, who divines?) — looking as if
He understood why Adelaide lay stiff
Already in my arms; for "Girl, how must
I manage Este in the matter thrust
Upon me, how unravel your bad coil? —
Since" (he declared) "'tis on your brow — a soil
Like hers there!" then in the same breath, "he lacked
410 No counsel after all, had signed no pact
With devils, nor was treason here or there,
Goito or Vicenza, his affair:
He buried it in Adelaide's deep grave,
Would begin life afresh, now, — would not slave
For any Friedrich's nor Taurello's sake!
What booted him to meddle or to make
In Lombardy?" And afterward I knew
The meaning of his promise to undo
All she had done — why marriages were made,
420 New friendships entered on, old followers paid
With curses for their pains, — new friends' amaze
At height, when, passing out by Gate Saint Blaise,
He stopped short in Vicenza, bent his head
Over a friar's neck, — "had vowed," he said,
"Long since, nigh thirty years, because his wife
And child were saved there, to bestow his life
On God, his gettings on the Church."
                                        'Exiled
Within Goito, still one dream beguiled
My days and nights; 'twas found, the orb I sought
430 To serve, those glimpses came of Fomalhaut,
No other: but how serve it? — authorize
You and Romano mingle destinies?
And straight Romano's angel stood beside
Me who had else been Boniface's bride,
For Salinguerra 'twas, with neck low bent,
And voice lightened to music, (as he meant
To learn, not teach me,) who withdrew the pall
From the dead past and straight revived it all,
Making me see how first Romano waxed,

440 Wherefore he waned now, why, if I relaxed
My grasp (even I!) would drop a thing effete,
Frayed by itself, unequal to complete
Its course, and counting every step astray
A gain so much. Romano, every way
Stable, a Lombard House now – why start back
Into the very outset of its track?
This patching principle which late allied
Our House with other Houses – what beside
Concerned the apparition, the first Knight
450 Who followed Conrad hither in such plight
His utmost wealth was summed in his one steed?
For Ecelo, that prowler, was decreed
A task, in the beginning hazardous
To him as ever task can be to us;
But did the weather-beaten thief despair
When first our crystal cincture of warm air
That binds the Trevisan, – as its spice-belt
(Crusaders say) the tract where Jesus dwelt, –
Furtive he pierced, and Este was to face –
460 Despaired Saponian strength of Lombard grace?
Tried he at making surer aught made sure,
Maturing what already was mature?
No; his heart prompted Ecelo, "Confront
Este, inspect yourself. What's nature? Wont.
Discard three-parts your nature, and adopt
The rest as an advantage!" Old strength propped
The man who first grew Podestà among
The Vicentines, no less than, while there sprung
His palace up in Padua like a threat,
470 Their noblest spied a grace, unnoticed yet
In Conrad's crew. Thus far the object gained,
Romano was established – has remained –
"For are you not Italian, truly peers
With Este? *Azzo* better soothes our ears
Than *Alberic*? or is this lion's-crine
From over-mounts" (this yellow hair of mine)
"So weak a graft on Agnes Este's stock?"
(Thus went he on with something of a mock)
"Wherefore recoil, then, from the very fate
480 Conceded you, refuse to imitate
Your model farther? Este long since left

Being mere Este: as a blade its heft,
Este required the Pope to further him:
And you, the Kaiser – whom your father's whim
Foregoes or, better, never shall forego
If Palma dare pursue what Ecelo
Commenced, but Ecelin desists from: just
As Adelaide of Susa could intrust
Her donative, – her Piedmont given the Pope,
490 Her Alpine-pass for him to shut or ope
'Twixt France and Italy, – to the superb
Matilda's perfecting, – so, lest aught curb
Our Adelaide's great counter-project for
Giving her Trentine to the Emperor
With passage here from Germany, – shall you
Take it, – my slender plodding talent, too!"
– Urged me Taurello with his half-smile.
                                        'He
As Patron of the scattered family
Conveyed me to his Mantua, kept in bruit
500 Azzo's alliances and Richard's suit
Until, the Kaiser excommunicate,
"Nothing remains," Taurello said, "but wait
Some rash procedure: Palma was the link,
As Agnes' child, between us, and they shrink
From losing Palma: judge if we advance,
Your father's method, your inheritance!"
The day I was betrothed to Boniface
At Padua by Taurello's self, took place
The outrage of the Ferrarese: again,
510 The day I sought Verona with the train
Agreed for, – by Taurello's policy
Convicting Richard of the fault, since we
Were present to annul or to confirm, –
Richard, whose patience had outstayed its term,
Quitted Verona for the siege.
                              'And now
What glory may engird Sordello's brow
Through this? A month since at Oliero slunk
All that was Ecelin into a monk;
But how could Salinguerra so forget
520 His liege of thirty years as grudge even yet
One effort to recover him? He sent

Forthwith the tidings of this last event
To Ecelin – declared that he, despite
The recent folly, recognized his right
To order Salinguerra: "Should he wring
Its uttermost advantage out, or fling
This chance away? Or were his sons now Head
O' the House?" Through me Taurello's missive sped;
My father's answer will by me return.

530 Behold! "For him," he writes, "no more concern
With strife than, for his children, with fresh plots
Of Friedrich. Old engagements out he blots
For aye: Taurello shall no more subserve,
Nor Ecelin impose." Lest this unnerve
Taurello at this juncture, slack his grip
Of Richard, suffer the occasion slip, –
I, in his sons' default (who, mating with
Este, forsake Romano as the frith
Its mainsea for that firmland, sea makes head
540 Against) I stand, Romano, – in their stead
Assume the station they desert, and give
Still, as the Kaiser's representative,
Taurello licence he demands. Midnight –
Morning – by noon tomorrow, making light
Of the League's issue, we, in some gay weed
Like yours, disguised together, may precede
The arbitrators to Ferrara: reach
Him, let Taurello's noble accents teach
The rest! Then say if I have misconceived
550 Your destiny, too readily believed
The Kaiser's cause your own!'
                                                    And Palma's fled.
Though no affirmative disturbs the head,
A dying lamp-flame sinks and rises o'er,
Like the alighted planet Pollux wore,
Until, morn breaking, he resolves to be
Gate-vein of this heart's blood of Lombardy,
Soul of this body – to wield this aggregate
Of souls and bodies, and so conquer fate
Though he should live – a centre of disgust
560 Even – apart, core of the outward crust
He vivifies, assimilates. For thus
I bring Sordello to the rapturous

Exclaim at the crowd's cry, because one round
Of life was quite accomplished; and he found
Not only that a soul, whate'er its might,
Is insufficient to its own delight,
Both in corporeal organs and in skill
By means of such to body forth its Will –
And, after, insufficient to apprise
570   Men of that Will, oblige them recognize
The Hid by the Revealed – but that, – the last
Nor lightest of the struggles overpast, –
Will, he bade abdicate, which would not void
The throne, might sit there, suffer he enjoyed
Mankind, a varied and divine array
Incapable of homage, the first way,
Nor fit to render incidentally
Tribute connived at, taken by the by,
In joys. If thus with warrant to rescind
580   The ignominious exile of mankind –
Whose proper service, ascertained intact
As yet, (to be by him themselves made act,
Not watch Sordello acting each of them)
Was to secure – if the true diadem
Seemed imminent while our Sordello drank
The wisdom of that golden Palma, – thank
Verona's Lady in her citadel
Founded by Gaulish Brennus, legends tell:
And truly when she left him, the sun reared
590   A head like the first clamberer's who peered
A-top the Capitol, his face on flame
With triumph, triumphing till Manlius came.
Nor slight too much my rhymes – that spring, dispread,
Dispart, disperse, lingering overhead
Like an escape of angels! Rather say,
My transcendental platan! mounting gay
(An archimage so courts a novice-queen)
With tremulous silvered trunk, whence branches sheen
Laugh out, thick-foliaged next, a-shiver soon
600   With coloured buds, then glowing like the moon
One mild flame, – last a pause, a burst, and all
Her ivory limbs are smothered by a fall,
Bloom-flinders and fruit-sparkles and leaf-dust,
Ending the weird work prosecuted just

For her amusement; he decrepit, stark,
Dozes; her uncontrolled delight may mark
Apart –
　　　　Yet not so, surely never so
Only, as good my soul were suffered go
O'er the lagune: forth fare thee, put aside –
610　Entrance thy synod, as a god may glide
Out of the world he fills, and leave it mute
For myriad ages as we men compute,
Returning into it without a break
O' the consciousness! They sleep, and I awake
O'er the lagune, being at Venice.
　　　　　　　　　　Note,
In just such songs as Eglamor (say) wrote
With heart and soul and strength, for he believed
Himself achieving all to be achieved
By singer – in such songs you find alone
620　Completeness, judge the song and singer one,
And either purpose answered, his in it
Or its in him: while from true works (to wit
Sordello's dream-performances that will
Never be more than dreamed) escapes there still
Some proof, the singer's proper life was 'neath
The life his song exhibits, this a sheath
To that; a passion and a knowledge far
Transcending these, majestic as they are,
Smouldered; his lay was but an episode
630　In the bard's life: which evidence you owed
To some slight weariness, some looking-off
Or start-away. The childish skit or scoff
In 'Charlemagne,' (his poem, dreamed divine
In every point except one silly line
About the restiff daughters) – what may lurk
In that? 'My life commenced before this work,'
(So I interpret the significance
Of the bard's start aside and look askance)
'My life continues after: on I fare
640　With no more stopping, possibly, no care
To note the undercurrent, the why and how,
Where, when, o' the deeper life, as thus just now.
But, silent, shall I cease to live? Alas
For you! who sigh, "When shall it come to pass

We read that story? How will he compress
The future gains, his life's true business,
Into the better lay which – that one flout,
Howe'er inopportune it be, lets out –
Engrosses him already, though professed
650 To meditate with us eternal rest,
And partnership in all his life has found?'''
'Tis but a sailor's promise, weather-bound:
'Strike sail, slip cable, here the bark be moored
For once, the awning stretched, the poles assured!
Noontide above; except the wave's crisp dash,
Or buzz of colibri, or tortoise' splash,
The margin's silent: out with every spoil
Made in our tracking, coil by mighty coil,
This serpent of a river to his head
660 I' the midst! Admire each treasure, as we spread
The bank, to help us tell our history
Aright: give ear, endeavour to descry
The groves of giant rushes, how they grew
Like demons' endlong tresses we sailed through,
What mountains yawned, forests to give us vent
Opened, each doleful side, yet on we went
Till . . . may that beetle (shake your cap) attest
The springing of a land-wind from the West!'
– Wherefore? Ah yes, you frolic it today!
670 Tomorrow, and, the pageant moved away
Down to the poorest tent-pole, we and you
Part company: no other may pursue
Eastward your voyage, be informed what fate
Intends, if triumph or decline await
The tempter of the everlasting steppe.
    I muse this on a ruined palace-step
At Venice: why should I break off, nor sit
Longer upon my step, exhaust the fit
England gave birth to? Who's adorable
680 Enough reclaim a — no Sordello's Will
Alack! – be queen to me? That Bassanese
Busied among her smoking fruit-boats? These
Perhaps from our delicious Asolo
Who twinkle, pigeons o'er the portico
Not prettier, bind June lilies into sheaves
To deck the bridge-side chapel, dropping leaves

Soiled by their own loose gold-meal? Ah, beneath
The cool arch stoops she, brownest cheek! Her wreath
Endures a month – a half-month – if I make
690   A queen of her, continue for her sake
Sordello's story? Nay, that Paduan girl
Splashes with barer legs where a live whirl
In the dead black Giudecca proves sea-weed
Drifting has sucked down three, four, all indeed
Save one pale-red striped, pale-blue turbaned post
For gondolas.
           You sad dishevelled ghost
That pluck at me and point, are you advised
I breathe? Let stay those girls (e'en her disguised
– Jewels i' the locks that love no crownet like
700   Their native field-buds and the green wheat-spike,
So fair! – who left this end of June's turmoil,
Shook off, as might a lily its gold soil,
Pomp, save a foolish gem or two, and free
In dream, came join the peasants o'er the sea.)
Look they too happy, too tricked out? Confess
There is such niggard stock of happiness
To share, that, do one's uttermost, dear wretch,
One labours ineffectually to stretch
It o'er you so that mother and children, both
710   May equitably flaunt the sumpter-cloth!
Divide the robe yet farther: be content
With seeing just a score pre-eminent
Through shreds of it, acknowledged happy wights,
Engrossing what should furnish all, by rights!
For, these in evidence, you clearlier claim
A like garb for the rest, – grace all, the same
As these my peasants. I ask youth and strength
And health for each of you, not more – at length
Grown wise, who asked at home that the whole race
720   Might add the spirit's to the body's grace,
And all be dizened out as chiefs and bards.
But in this magic weather one discards
Much old requirement. Venice seems a type
Of Life – 'twixt blue and blue extends, a stripe,
As Life, the somewhat, hangs 'twixt naught and naught:
'Tis Venice, and 'tis Life – as good you sought
To spare me the Piazza's slippery stone

Or keep me to the unchoked canals alone,
As hinder Life the evil with the good
730 Which make up Living, rightly understood.
Only, do finish something! Peasants, queens,
Take them, made happy by whatever means,
Parade them for the common credit, vouch
That a luckless residue, we send to crouch
In corners out of sight, was just as framed
For happiness, its portion might have claimed
As well, and so, obtaining joy, had stalked
Fastuous as any! – such my project, balked
Already; I hardly venture to adjust
740 The first rags, when you find me. To mistrust
Me! – nor unreasonably. You, no doubt,
Have the true knack of tiring suitors out
With those thin lips on tremble, lashless eyes
Inveterately tear-shot: there, be wise,
Mistress of mine, there, there, as if I meant
You insult! – shall your friend (not slave) be shent
For speaking home? Beside, care-bit erased
Broken-up beauties ever took my taste
Supremely; and I love you more, far more
750 Than her I looked should foot Life's temple-floor.
Years ago, leagues at distance, when and where
A whisper came, 'Let others seek! – thy care
Is found, thy life's provision; if thy race
Should be thy mistress, and into one face
The many faces crowd?' Ah, had I, judge,
Or no, your secret? Rough apparel – grudge
All ornaments save tag or tassel worn
To hint we are not thoroughly forlorn –
Slouch bonnet, unloop mantle, careless go
760 Alone (that's saddest, but it must be so)
Through Venice, sing now and now glance aside,
Aught desultory or undignified, –
Then, ravishingest lady, will you pass
Or not each formidable group, the mass
Before the Basilic (that feast gone by,
God's great day of the Corpus Domini)
And, wistfully foregoing proper men,
Come timid up to me for alms? And then
The luxury to hesitate, feign do

770 Some unexampled grace! – when, whom but you
    Dare I bestow your own upon? And hear
    Further before you say, it is to sneer
    I call you ravishing; for I regret
    Little that she, whose early foot was set
    Forth as she'd plant it on a pedestal,
    Now, i' the silent city, seems to fall
    Toward me – no wreath, only a lip's unrest
    To quiet, surcharged eyelids to be pressed
    Dry of their tears upon my bosom. Strange
780 Such sad chance should produce in thee such change,
    My love! Warped souls and bodies! yet God spoke
    Of right-hand, foot and eye – selects our yoke,
    Sordello, as your poetship may find!
    So, sleep upon my shoulder, child, nor mind
    Their foolish talk; we'll manage reinstate
    Your old worth; ask moreover, when they prate
    Of evil men past hope, 'Don't each contrive,
    Despite the evil you abuse, to live? –
    Keeping, each losel, through a maze of lies,
790 His own conceit of truth? to which he hies
    By obscure windings, tortuous, if you will,
    But to himself not inaccessible;
    He sees truth, and his lies are for the crowd
    Who cannot see; some fancied right allowed
    His vilest wrong, empowered the losel clutch
    One pleasure from a multitude of such
    Denied him.' Then assert, 'All men appear
    To think all better than themselves, by here
    Trusting a crowd they wrong; but really,' say,
800 'All men think all men stupider than they,
    Since, save themselves, no other comprehends
    The complicated scheme to make amends
    – Evil, the scheme by which, through Ignorance,
    Good labours to exist.' A slight advance, –
    Merely to find the sickness you die through,
    And naught beside! but if one can't eschew
    One's portion in the common lot, at least
    One can avoid an ignorance increased
    Tenfold by dealing out hint after hint
810 How naught were like dispensing without stint
    The water of life – so easy to dispense

Beside, when one has probed the centre whence
Commotion's born – could tell you of it all!
' – Meantime, just meditate my madrigal
O' the mugwort that conceals a dewdrop safe!'
What, dullard? we and you in smothery chafe,
Babes, baldheads, stumbled thus far into Zin
The Horrid, getting neither out nor in,
A hungry sun above us, sands that bung
820   Our throats, – each dromedary lolls a tongue,
Each camel churns a sick and frothy chap,
And you, 'twixt tales of Potiphar's mishap,
And sonnets on the earliest ass that spoke,
– Remark, you wonder any one needs choke
With founts about! Potsherd him, Gibeonites!
While awkwardly enough your Moses smites
The rock, though he forego his Promised Land
Thereby, have Satan claim his carcass, and
Figure as Metaphysic Poet . . . ah,
830   Mark ye the dim first oozings? Meribah!
Then, quaffing at the fount my courage gained,
Recall – not that I prompt ye – who explained . . .
      'Presumptuous!' interrupts one. You, not I
'Tis, brother, marvel at and magnify
Such office: 'office,' quotha? can we get
To the beginning of the office yet?
What do we here? simply experiment
Each on the other's power and its intent
When elsewhere tasked, – if this of mine were trucked
840   For yours to either's good, – we watch construct,
In short, an engine: with a finished one,
What it can do, is all, – naught, how 'tis done.
But this of ours yet in probation, dusk
A kernel of strange wheelwork through its husk
Grows into shape by quarters and by halves;
Remark this tooth's spring, wonder what that valve's
Fall bodes, presume each faculty's device,
Make out each other more or less precise –
The scope of the whole engine's to be proved;
850   We die: which means to say, the whole's removed,
Dismounted wheel by wheel, this complex gin, –
To be set up anew elsewhere, begin
A task indeed, but with a clearer clime

Than the murk lodgement of our building-time.
And then, I grant you, it behoves forget
How 'tis done – all that must amuse us yet
So long: and, while you turn upon your heel,
Pray that I be not busy slitting steel
Or shredding brass, camped on some virgin shore
860 Under a cluster of fresh stars, before
I name a tithe o' the wheels I trust to do!
   So occupied, then, are we: hitherto,
At present, and a weary while to come,
The office of ourselves, – nor blind nor dumb,
And seeing somewhat of man's state, – has been,
For the worst of us, to say they so have seen;
For the better, what it was they saw; the best
Impart the gift of seeing to the rest:
'So that I glance,' says such an one, 'around,
870 And there's no face but I can read profound
Disclosures in; this stands for hope, that – fear,
And for a speech, a deed in proof, look here!
"Stoop, else the strings of blossom, where the nuts
O'erarch, will blind thee! Said I not? She shuts
Both eyes this time, so close the hazels meet!
Thus, prisoned in the Piombi, I repeat
Events one rove occasioned, o'er and o'er,
Putting 'twixt me and madness evermore
Thy sweet shape, Zanze! Therefore stoop!"
                      '"That's truth!"
880 (Adjudge you) "the incarcerated youth
Would say that!"
                 'Youth? Plara the bard? Set down
That Plara spent his youth in a grim town
Whose cramped ill-featured streets huddled about
The minster for protection, never out
Of its black belfry's shade and its bells' roar.
The brighter shone the suburb, – all the more
Ugly and absolute that shade's reproof
Of any chance escape of joy, – some roof,
Taller than they, allowed the rest detect, –
890 Before the sole permitted laugh (suspect
Who could, 'twas meant for laughter, that ploughed cheek's
Repulsive gleam!) when the sun stopped both peaks
Of the cleft belfry like a fiery wedge,

Then sank, a huge flame on its socket edge,
With leavings on the grey glass oriel-pane
Ghastly some minutes more. No fear of rain –
The minster minded that! in heaps the dust
Lay everywhere. This town, the minster's trust,
Held Plara; who, its denizen, bade hail
900 In twice twelve sonnets, Tempe's dewy vale.'
'"Exact the town, the minster and the street!"'
'As all mirth triumphs, sadness means defeat:
Lust triumphs and is gay, Love's triumphed o'er
And sad: but Lucio's sad. I said before,
Love's sad, not Lucio; one who loves may be
As gay his love has leave to hope, as he
Downcast that lusts' desire escapes the springe:
'Tis of the mood itself I speak, what tinge
Determines it, else colourless, – or mirth,
910 Or melancholy, as from heaven or earth.'
'"Ay, that's the variation's gist!"
                                        'Indeed?
Thus far advanced in safety then, proceed!
And having seen too what I saw, be bold
And next encounter what I do behold
(That's sure) but bid you take on trust!'
                                        Attack
The use and purpose of such sights! Alack,
Not so unwisely does the crowd dispense
On Salinguerras praise in preference
To the Sordellos: men of action, these!
920 Who, seeing just as little as you please,
Yet turn that little to account, – engage
With, do not gaze at, – carry on, a stage,
The work o' the world, not merely make report
The work existed ere their day! In short,
When at some future no-time a brave band
Sees, using what it sees, then shake my hand
In heaven, my brother! Meanwhile where's the hurt
Of keeping the Makers-see on the alert,
At whose defection mortals stare aghast
930 As though heaven's bounteous windows were slammed fast
Incontinent? Whereas all you, beneath,
Should scowl at, bruise their lips and break their teeth
Who ply the pulleys, for neglecting you:

And therefore have I moulded, made anew
A Man, and give him to be turned and tried,
Be angry with or pleased at. On your side,
Have ye times, places, actors of your own?
Try them upon Sordello when full-grown,
And then – ah then! If Hercules first parched
940 His foot in Egypt only to be marched
A sacrifice for Jove with pomp to suit,
What chance have I? The demigod was mute
Till, at the altar, where time out of mind
Such guests became oblations, chaplets twined
His forehead long enough, and he began
Slaying the slayers, nor escaped a man.
Take not affront, my gentle audience! whom
No Hercules shall make his hecatomb,
Believe, nor from his brows your chaplet rend –
950 That's your kind suffrage, yours, my patron-friend,
Whose great verse blares unintermittent on
Like your own trumpeter at Marathon, –
You who, Plataea and Salamis being scant,
Put up with Aetna for a stimulant –
And did well, I acknowledged, as he loomed
Over the midland sea last month, presumed
Long, lay demolished in the blazing West
At eve, while towards him tilting cloudlets pressed
Like Persian ships at Salamis. Friend, wear
960 A crest proud as desert while I declare
Had I a flawless ruby fit to wring
Tears of its colour from that painted king
Who lost it, I would, for that smile which went
To my heart, fling it in the sea, content,
Wearing your verse in place, an amulet
Sovereign against all passion, wear and fret!
My English Eyebright, if you are not glad
That, as I stopped my task awhile, the sad
Dishevelled form, wherein I put mankind
970 To come at times and keep my pact in mind,
Renewed me, – hear no crickets in the hedge,
Nor let a glowworm spot the river's edge
At home, and may the summer showers gush
Without a warning from the missel thrush!
So, to our business, now – the fate of such

As find our common nature – overmuch
Despised because restricted and unfit
To bear the burthen they impose on it –
Cling when they would discard it; craving strength
980 To leap from the allotted world, at length
They do leap, – flounder on without a term,
Each a god's germ, doomed to remain a germ
In unexpanded infancy, unless . . .
But that's the story – dull enough, confess!
There might be fitter subjects to allure;
Still, neither misconceive my portraiture
Nor undervalue its adornments quaint:
What seems a fiend perchance may prove a saint.
Ponder a story ancient pens transmit,
990 Then say if you condemn me or acquit.
    John the Beloved, banished Antioch
For Patmos, bade collectively his flock
Farewell, but set apart the closing eve
To comfort those his exile most would grieve,
He knew: a touching spectacle, that house
In motion to receive him! Xanthus' spouse
You missed, made panther's meat a month since; but
Xanthus himself (his nephew 'twas, they shut
'Twixt boards and sawed asunder), Polycarp,
1000 Soft Charicle, next year no wheel could warp
To swear by Caesar's fortune, with the rest
Were ranged; through whom the grey disciple pressed,
Busily blessing right and left, just stopped
To pat one infant's curls, the hangman cropped
Soon after, reached the portal. On its hinge
The door turns and he enters: what quick twinge
Ruins the smiling mouth, those wide eyes fix
Whereon, why like some spectral candlestick's
Branch the disciple's arms? Dead swooned he, woke
1010 Anon, heaved sigh, made shift to gasp, heart-broke,
'Get thee behind me, Satan! Have I toiled
To no more purpose? Is the gospel foiled
Here too, and o'er my son's, my Xanthus' hearth,
Portrayed with sooty garb and features swarth –
Ah Xanthus, am I to thy roof beguiled
To see the – the – the Devil domiciled?'
Whereto sobbed Xanthus, 'Father, 'tis yourself

Installed, a limning which our utmost pelf
Went to procure against tomorrow's loss;
1020 And that's no twy-prong, but a pastoral cross,
You're painted with!'
                              His puckered brows unfold –
And you shall hear Sordello's story told.

BOOK THE FOURTH

Meantime Ferrara lay in rueful case;
The lady-city, for whose sole embrace
Her pair of suitors struggled, felt their arms
A brawny mischief to the fragile charms
They tugged for – one discovering that to twist
Her tresses twice or thrice about his wrist
Secured a point of vantage – one, how best
He'd parry that by planting in her breast
His elbow spike – each party too intent
10 For noticing, howe'er the battle went,
The conqueror would but have a corpse to kiss.
'May Boniface be duly damned for this!'
– Howled some old Ghibellin, as up he turned,
From the wet heap of rubbish where they burned
His house, a little skull with dazzling teeth:
'A boon, sweet Christ – let Salinguerra seethe
In hell for ever, Christ, and let myself
Be there to laugh at him!' – moaned some young Guelf
Stumbling upon a shrivelled hand nailed fast
20 To the charred lintel of the doorway, last
His father stood within to bid him speed.
The thoroughfares were overrun with weed
– Docks, quitchgrass, loathy mallows no man plants.
     The stranger, none of its inhabitants
Crept out of doors to taste fresh air again,
And ask the purpose of a splendid train
Admitted on a morning; every town
Of the East League was come by envoy down
To treat for Richard's ransom: here you saw
30 The Vicentine, here snowy oxen draw
The Paduan carroch, its vermilion cross
On its white field. A-tiptoe o'er the fosse

Looked Legate Montelungo wistfully
After the flock of steeples he might spy
In Este's time, gone (doubts he) long ago
To mend the ramparts: sure the laggards know
The Pope's as good as here! They paced the streets
More soberly. At last, 'Taurello greets
The League,' announced a pursuivant, – 'will match
40   Its courtesy, and labours to dispatch
At earliest Tito, Friedrich's Pretor, sent
On pressing matters from his post at Trent,
With Mainard Count of Tyrol, – simply waits
Their going to receive the delegates.'
'Tito!' Our delegates exchanged a glance,
And, keeping the main way, admired askance
The lazy engines of outlandish birth,
Couched like a king each on its bank of earth –
Arbalist, manganel and catapult;
50   While stationed by, as waiting a result,
Lean silent gangs of mercenaries ceased
Working to watch the strangers. 'This, at least,
Were better spared; he scarce presumes gainsay
The League's decision! Get our friend away
And profit for the future: how else teach
Fools 'tis not safe to stray within claw's reach
Ere Salinguerra's final gasp be blown?
Those mere convulsive scratches find the bone.
Who bade him bloody the spent osprey's nare?'
60   The carrochs halted in the public square.
Pennons of every blazon once a-flaunt,
Men prattled, freelier that the crested gaunt
White ostrich with a horse-shoe in her beak
Was missing, and whoever chose might speak
'Ecelin' boldly out: so, – 'Ecelin
Needed his wife to swallow half the sin
And sickens by himself: the devil's whelp,
He styles his son, dwindles away, no help
From conserves, your fine triple-curded froth
70   Of virgin's blood, your Venice viper-broth –
Eh? Jubilate!' – 'Peace! no little word
You utter here that's not distinctly heard
Up at Oliero: he was absent sick
When we besieged Bassano – who, i' the thick

O' the work, perceived the progress Azzo made,
Like Ecelin, through his witch Adelaide?
She managed it so well that, night by night
At their bed-foot stood up a soldier-sprite,
First fresh, pale by-and-by without a wound,
80 And, when it came with eyes filmed as in swound,
They knew the place was taken.' – 'Ominous
That Ghibellins should get what cautelous
Old Redbeard sought from Azzo's sire to wrench
Vainly; Saint George contrived his town a trench
O' the marshes, an impermeable bar.'
' – Young Ecelin is meant the tutelar
Of Padua, rather; veins embrace upon
His hand like Brenta and Bacchiglion.'
What now? – 'The founts! God's bread, touch not a plank!
90 A crawling hell of carrion – every tank
Choke-full! – found out just now to Cino's cost –
The same who gave Taurello up for lost,
And, making no account of fortune's freaks,
Refused to budge from Padua then, but sneaks
Back now with Concorezzi: 'faith! they drag
Their carroch to San Vitale, plant the flag
On his own palace, so adroitly razed
He knew it not; a sort of Guelf folk gazed
And laughed apart; Cino disliked their air –
100 Must pluck up spirit, show he does not care –
Seats himself on the tank's edge – will begin
To hum, *za, za, Cavaler Ecelin* –
A silence; he gets warmer, clinks to chime,
Now both feet plough the ground, deeper each time,
At last, *za, za* and up with a fierce kick
Comes his own mother's face caught by the thick
Grey hair about his spur!'
                              Which means, they lift
The covering, Salinguerra made a shift
To stretch upon the truth; as well avoid
110 Further disclosures; leave them thus employed.
Our dropping Autumn morning clears apace,
And poor Ferrara puts a softened face
On her misfortunes. Let us scale this tall
Huge foursquare line of red brick garden-wall
Bastioned within by trees of every sort

On three sides, slender, spreading, long and short;
Each grew as it contrived, the poplar ramped,
The fig-tree reared itself, – but stark and cramped,
Made fools of, like tamed lions: whence, on the edge,
120 Running 'twixt trunk and trunk to smooth one ledge
Of shade, were shrubs inserted, warp and woof,
Which smothered up that variance. Scale the roof
Of solid tops, and o'er the slope you slide
Down to a grassy space level and wide,
Here and there dotted with a tree, but trees
Of rarer leaf, each foreigner at ease,
Set by itself: and in the centre spreads,
Borne upon three uneasy leopards' heads,
A laver, broad and shallow, one bright spirt
130 Of water bubbles in. The walls begirt
With trees leave off on either hand; pursue
Your path along a wondrous avenue
Those walls abut on, heaped of gleamy stone,
With aloes leering everywhere, grey-grown
From many a Moorish summer: how they wind
Out of the fissures! likelier to bind
The building than those rusted cramps which drop
Already in the eating sunshine. Stop,
You fleeting shapes above there! Ah, the pride
140 Or else despair of the whole country-side!
A range of statues, swarming o'er with wasps,
God, goddess, woman, man, the Greek rough-rasps
In crumbling Naples marble – meant to look
Like those Messina marbles Constance took
Delight in, or Taurello's self conveyed
To Mantua for his mistress, Adelaide, –
A certain font with caryatides
Since cloistered at Goito; only, these
Are up and doing, not abashed, a troop
150 Able to right themselves – who see you, stoop
Their arms o' the instant after you! Unplucked
By this or that, you pass; for they conduct
To terrace raised on terrace, and, between,
Creatures of brighter mould and braver mien
Than any yet, the choicest of the Isle
No doubt. Here, left a sullen breathing-while,
Up-gathered on himself the Fighter stood

For his last fight, and, wiping treacherous blood
Out of the eyelids just held ope beneath
160 Those shading fingers in their iron sheath,
Steadied his strengths amid the buzz and stir
Of the dusk hideous amphitheatre
At the announcement of his over-match
To wind the day's diversion up, dispatch
The pertinacious Gaul: while, limbs one heap,
The Slave, no breath in her round mouth, watched leap
Dart after dart forth, as her hero's car
Clove dizzily the solid of the war
– Let coil about his knees for pride in him.
170 We reach the farthest terrace, and the grim
San Pietro Palace stops us.
                  Such the state
Of Salinguerra's plan to emulate
Sicilian marvels, that his girlish wife
Retrude still might lead her ancient life
In her new home: whereat enlarged so much
Neighbours upon the novel princely touch
He took, – who here imprisons Boniface.
Here must the Envoys come to sue for grace;
And here, emerging from the labyrinth
180 Below, Sordello paused beside the plinth
Of the door-pillar.
              He had really left
Verona for the cornfields (a poor theft
From the morass) where Este's camp was made;
The Envoys' march, the Legate's cavalcade –
All had been seen by him, but scarce as when, –
Eager for cause to stand aloof from men
At every point save the fantastic tie
Acknowledged in his boyish sophistry, –
He made account of such. A crowd, – he meant
190 To task the whole of it; each part's intent
Concerned him therefore: and, the more he pried,
The less became Sordello satisfied
With his own figure at the moment. Sought
He respite from his task? Descried he aught
Novel in the anticipated sight
Of all these livers upon all delight?
This phalanx, as of myriad points combined,

Whereby he still had imaged the mankind
His youth was passed in dreams of rivalling,
200 His age – in plans to prove at least such thing
Had been so dreamed, – which now he must impress
With his own will, effect a happiness
By theirs, – supply a body to his soul
Thence, and become eventually whole
With them as he had hoped to be without –
Made these the mankind he once raved about?
Because a few of them were notable,
Should all be figured worthy note? As well
Expect to find Taurello's triple line
210 Of trees a single and prodigious pine.
Real pines rose here and there; but, close among,
Thrust into and mixed up with pines, a throng
Of shrubs, he saw, – a nameless common sort
O'erpast in dreams, left out of the report
And hurried into corners, or at best
Admitted to be fancied like the rest.
Reckon that morning's proper chiefs – how few!
And yet the people grew, the people grew,
Grew ever, as if the many there indeed,
220 More left behind and most who should succeed, –
Simply in virtue of their mouths and eyes,
Petty enjoyments and huge miseries, –
Mingled with, and made veritably great
Those chiefs: he overlooked not Mainard's state
Nor Concorezzi's station, but instead
Of stopping there, each dwindled to be head
Of infinite and absent Tyrolese
Or Paduans; startling all the more, that these
Seemed passive and disposed of, uncared for,
230 Yet doubtless on the whole (like Eglamor)
Smiling; for if a wealthy man decays
And out of store of robes must wear, all days,
One tattered suit, alike in sun and shade,
'Tis commonly some tarnished gay brocade
Fit for a feast-night's flourish and no more:
Nor otherwise poor Misery from her store
Of looks is fain upgather, keep unfurled
For common wear as she goes through the world,
The faint remainder of some worn-out smile

240 Meant for a feast-night's service merely. While
Crowd upon crowd rose on Sordello thus, –
(Crowds no way interfering to discuss,
Much less dispute, life's joys with one employed
In envying them, – or, if they aught enjoyed,
Where lingered something indefinable
In every look and tone, the mirth as well
As woe, that fixed at once his estimate
Of the result, their good or bad estate) –
Old memories returned with new effect:
250 And the new body, ere he could suspect,
Cohered, mankind and he were really fused,
The new self seemed impatient to be used
By him, but utterly another way
Than that anticipated: strange to say,
They were too much below him, more in thrall
Than he, the adjunct than the principal.
What booted scattered units? – here a mind
And there, which might repay his own to find,
And stamp, and use? – a few, howe'er august,
260 If all the rest were grovelling in the dust?
No: first a mighty equilibrium, sure,
Should he establish, privilege procure
For all, the few had long possessed! He felt
An error, an exceeding error melt:
While he was occupied with Mantuan chants,
Behoved him think of men, and take their wants,
Such as he now distinguished every side,
As his own want which might be satisfied, –
And, after that, think of rare qualities
270 Of his own soul demanding exercise.
It followed naturally, through no claim
On their part, which made virtue of the aim
At serving them, on his, – that, past retrieve,
He felt now in their toils, theirs – nor could leave
Wonder how, in the eagerness to rule,
Impress his will on mankind, he (the fool!)
Had never even entertained the thought
That this his last arrangement might be fraught
With incidental good to them as well,
280 And that mankind's delight would help to swell
His own. So, if he sighed, as formerly

Because the merry time of life must fleet,
'Twas deeplier now, – for could the crowds repeat
Their poor experiences? His hand that shook
Was twice to be deplored. 'The Legate, look!
With eyes, like fresh-blown thrush-eggs on a thread,
Faint-blue and loosely floating in his head,
Large tongue, moist open mouth; and this long while
That owner of the idiotic smile
290　Serves them!'
　　　　　　　　He fortunately saw in time
His fault however, and since the office prime
Includes the secondary – best accept
Both offices; Taurello, its adept,
Could teach him the preparatory one,
And how to do what he had fancied done
Long previously, ere take the greater task.
How render first these people happy? Ask
The people's friends: for there must be one good
One way to it – the Cause! He understood
300　The meaning now of Palma; why the jar
Else, the ado, the trouble wide and far
Of Guelfs and Ghibellins, the Lombard hope
And Rome's despair? – 'twixt Emperor and Pope
The confused shifting sort of Eden tale –
Hardihood still recurring, still to fail –
That foreign interloping fiend, this free
And native overbrooding deity:
Yet a dire fascination o'er the palms
The Kaiser ruined, troubling even the calms
310　Of paradise; or, on the other hand,
The Pontiff, as the Kaisers understand,
One snake-like cursed of God to love the ground,
Whose heavy length breaks in the noon profound
Some saving tree – which needs the Kaiser, dressed
As the dislodging angel of that pest:
Yet flames that pest bedropped, flat head, full fold,
With coruscating dower of dyes. 'Behold
The secret, so to speak, and master-spring
O' the contest! – which of the two Powers shall bring
320　Men good, perchance the most good: ay, it may
Be that! – the question, which best knows the way.'
　　　And hereupon Count Mainard strutted past

Out of San Pietro; never seemed the last
Of archers, slingers: and our friend began
To recollect strange modes of serving man –
Arbalist, catapult, brake, manganel,
And more. 'This way of theirs may, – who can tell? –
Need perfecting,' said he: 'let all be solved
At once! Taurello 'tis, the task devolved
On late: confront Taurello!'
                                                And at last
He did confront him. Scarce an hour had past
When forth Sordello came, older by years
Than at his entry. Unexampled fears
Oppressed him, and he staggered off, blind, mute
And deaf, like some fresh-mutilated brute,
Into Ferrara – not the empty town
That morning witnessed: he went up and down
Streets whence the veil had been stript shred by shred,
So that, in place of huddling with their dead
Indoors, to answer Salinguerra's ends,
Townsfolk make shift to crawl forth, sit like friends
With any one. A woman gave him choice
Of her two daughters, the infantile voice
Or the dimpled knee, for half a chain, his throat
Was clasped with; but an archer knew the coat –
Its blue cross and eight lilies, – bade beware
One dogging him in concert with the pair
Though thrumming on the sleeve that hid his knife.
Night set in early, autumn dews were rife,
They kindled great fires while the Leaguers' mass
Began at every carroch: he must pass
Between the kneeling people. Presently
The carroch of Verona caught his eye
With purple trappings; silently he bent
Over its fire, when voices violent
Began, 'Affirm not whom the youth was like
That struck me from the porch: I did not strike
Again: I too have chestnut hair; my kin
Hate Azzo and stand up for Ecelin.
Here, minstrel, drive bad thoughts away! Sing! Take
My glove for guerdon!' And for that man's sake
He turned: 'A song of Eglamor's!' – scarce named,
When, 'Our Sordello's rather!' – all exclaimed;

'Is not Sordello famousest for rhyme?'
He had been happy to deny, this time, –
Profess as heretofore the aching head
And failing heart, – suspect that in his stead
Some true Apollo had the charge of them,
Was champion to reward or to condemn,
370   So his intolerable risk might shift
Or share itself; but Naddo's precious gift
Of gifts, he owned, be certain! At the close –
'I made that,' said he to a youth who rose
As if to hear: 'twas Palma through the band
Conducted him in silence by her hand.

Back now for Salinguerra. Tito of Trent
Gave place to Palma and her friend, who went
In turn at Montelungo's visit: one
After the other were they come and gone, –
380   These spokesmen for the Kaiser and the Pope,
This incarnation of the People's hope,
Sordello, – all the say of each was said;
And Salinguerra sat, – himself instead
Of these to talk with, lingered musing yet.
'Twas a drear vast presence-chamber roughly set
In order for the morning's use; full face,
The Kaiser's ominous sign-mark had first place,
The crowned grim twy-necked eagle, coarsely-blacked
With ochre on the naked wall; nor lacked
390   Romano's green and yellow either side;
But the new token Tito brought had tried
The Legate's patience – nay, if Palma knew
What Salinguerra almost meant to do
Until the sight of her restored his lip
A certain half-smile, three months' chieftainship
Had banished! Afterward, the Legate found
No change in him, nor asked what badge he wound
And unwound carelessly. Now sat the Chief
Silent as when our couple left, whose brief
400   Encounter wrought so opportune effect
In thoughts he summoned not, nor would reject,
Though time 'twas now if ever, to pause – fix
On any sort of ending: wiles and tricks
Exhausted, judge! his charge, the crazy town,
Just managed to be hindered crashing down –

His last sound troops ranged – care observed to post
His best of the maimed soldiers innermost –
So much was plain enough, but somehow struck
Him not before. And now with this strange luck
410 Of Tito's news, rewarding his address
So well, what thought he of? – how the success
With Friedrich's rescript there, would either hush
Old Ecelin's scruples, bring the manly flush
To his young son's white cheek, or, last, exempt
Himself from telling what there was to tempt?
No: that this minstrel was Romano's last
Servant – himself the first! Could he contrast
The whole! – that minstrel's thirty years just spent
In doing naught, their notablest event
420 This morning's journey hither, as I told –
Who yet was lean, outworn and really old,
A stammering awkward man that scarce dared raise
His eye before the magisterial gaze –
And Salinguerra with his fears and hopes
Of sixty years, his Emperors and Popes,
Cares and contrivances, yet, you would say,
'Twas a youth nonchalantly looked away
Through the embrasure northward o'er the sick
Expostulating trees – so agile, quick
430 And graceful turned the head on the broad chest
Encased in pliant steel, his constant vest,
Whence split the sun off in a spray of fire
Across the room; and, loosened of its tire
Of steel, that head let breathe the comely brown
Large massive locks discoloured as if a crown
Encircled them, so frayed the basnet where
A sharp white line divided clean the hair;
Glossy above, glossy below, it swept
Curling and fine about a brow thus kept
440 Calm, laid coat upon coat, marble and sound:
This was the mystic mark the Tuscan found,
Mused of, turned over books about. Square-faced,
No lion more; two vivid eyes, enchased
In hollows filled with many a shade and streak
Settling from the bold nose and bearded cheek.
Nor might the half-smile reach them that deformed
A lip supremely perfect else – unwarmed,

Unwidened, less or more; indifferent
Whether on trees or men his thoughts were bent,
450 Thoughts rarely, after all, in trim and train
As now a period was fulfilled again:
Of such, a series made his life, compressed
In each, one story serving for the rest –
How his life-streams rolling arrived at last
At the barrier, whence, were it once overpast,
They would emerge, a river to the end, –
Gathered themselves up, paused, bade fate befriend,
Took the leap, hung a minute at the height,
Then fell back to oblivion infinite:
460 Therefore he smiled. Beyond stretched garden-grounds
Where late the adversary, breaking bounds,
Had gained him an occasion, that above,
That eagle, testified he could improve
Effectually. The Kaiser's symbol lay
Beside his rescript, a new badge by way
Of baldric; while, – another thing that marred
Alike emprise, achievement and reward, –
Ecelin's missive was conspicuous too.
    What past life did those flying thoughts pursue?
470 As his, few names in Mantua half so old;
But at Ferrara, where his sires enrolled
It latterly, the Adelardi spared
No pains to rival them: both factions shared
Ferrara, so that, counted out, 'twould yield
A product very like the city's shield,
Half black and white, or Ghibellin and Guelf
As after Salinguerra styled himself
And Este who, till Marchesalla died,
(Last of the Adelardi) – never tried
480 His fortune there: with Marchesalla's child
Would pass, – could Blacks and Whites be reconciled
And young Taurello wed Linguetta, – wealth
And sway to a sole grasp. Each treats by stealth
Already: when the Guelfs, the Ravennese
Arrive, assault the Pietro quarter, seize
Linguetta, and are gone! Men's first dismay
Abated somewhat, hurries down, to lay
The after indignation, Boniface,
This Richard's father. 'Learn the full disgrace

490 Averted, ere you blame us Guelfs, who rate
Your Salinguerra, your sole potentate
That might have been, 'mongst Este's valvassors –
Ay, Azzo's – who, not privy to, abhors
Our step; but we were zealous.' Azzo then
To do with! Straight a meeting of old men:
'Old Salinguerra dead, his heir a boy,
What if we change our ruler and decoy
The Lombard Eagle of the azure sphere
With Italy to build in, fix him here,
500 Settle the city's troubles in a trice?
For private wrong, let public good suffice!'
In fine, young Salinguerra's staunchest friends
Talked of the townsmen making him amends,
Gave him a goshawk, and affirmed there was
Rare sport, one morning, over the green grass
A mile or so. He sauntered through the plain,
Was restless, fell to thinking, turned again
In time for Azzo's entry with the bride;
Count Boniface rode smirking at their side;
510 'She brings him half Ferrara,' whispers flew,
'And all Ancona! If the stripling knew!'
    Anon the stripling was in Sicily
Where Heinrich ruled in right of Constance; he
Was gracious nor his guest incapable;
Each understood the other. So it fell,
One Spring, when Azzo, thoroughly at ease,
Had near forgotten by what precise degrees
He crept at first to such a downy seat,
The Count trudged over in a special heat
520 To bid him of God's love dislodge from each
Of Salinguerra's palaces, – a breach
Might yawn else, not so readily to shut,
For who was just arrived at Mantua but
The youngster, sword on thigh and tuft on chin,
With tokens for Celano, Ecelin,
Pistore, and the like! Next news, – no whit
Do any of Ferrara's domes befit
His wife of Heinrich's very blood: a band
Of foreigners assemble, understand
530 Garden-constructing, level and surround,
Build up and bury in. A last news crowned

The consternation: since his infant's birth,
He only waits they end his wondrous girth
Of trees that link San Pietro with Tomà,
To visit Mantua. When the Podestà
Ecelin, at Vicenza, called his friend
Taurello thither, what could be their end
But to restore the Ghibellins' late Head,
The Kaiser helping? He with most to dread
540 From vengeance and reprisal, Azzo, there
With Boniface beforehand, as aware
Of plots in progress, gave alarm, expelled
Both plotters: but the Guelfs in triumph yelled
Too hastily. The burning and the flight,
And how Taurello, occupied that night
With Ecelin, lost wife and son, I told:
– Not how he bore the blow, retained his hold,
Got friends safe through, left enemies the worst
O' the fray, and hardly seemed to care at first:
550 But afterward men heard not constantly
Of Salinguerra's House so sure to be!
Though Azzo simply gained by the event
A shifting of his plagues – the first, content
To fall behind the second and estrange
So far his nature, suffer such a change
That in Romano sought he wife and child,
And for Romano's sake seemed reconciled
To losing individual life, which shrunk
As the other prospered – mortised in his trunk;
560 Like a dwarf palm which wanton Arabs foil
Of bearing its own proper wine and oil,
By grafting into it the stranger-vine,
Which sucks its heart out, sly and serpentine,
Till forth one vine-palm feathers to the root,
And red drops moisten the insipid fruit.
Once Adelaide set on, – the subtle mate
Of the weak soldier, urged to emulate
The Church's valiant women deed for deed,
And paragon her namesake, win the meed
570 O' the great Matilda, – soon they overbore
The rest of Lombardy, – not as before
By an instinctive truculence, but patched
The Kaiser's strategy until it matched

The Pontiff's, sought old ends by novel means.
'Only, why is it Salinguerra screens
Himself behind Romano? – him we bade
Enjoy our shine i' the front, not seek the shade!'
– Asked Heinrich, somewhat of the tardiest
To comprehend. Nor Philip acquiesced
580 At once in the arrangement; reasoned, plied
His friend with offers of another bride,
A statelier function – fruitlessly: 'twas plain
Taurello through some weakness must remain
Obscure. And Otho, free to judge of both
– Ecelin the unready, harsh and loth,
And this more plausible and facile wight
With every point a-sparkle – chose the right,
Admiring how his predecessors harped
On the wrong man: 'thus,' quoth he, 'wits are warped
590 By outsides!' Carelessly, meanwhile, his life
Suffered its many turns of peace and strife
In many lands – you hardly could surprise
The man; who shamed Sordello (recognize!)
In this as much beside, that, unconcerned
What qualities were natural or earned,
With no ideal of graces, as they came
He took them, singularly well the same –
Speaking the Greek's own language, just because
Your Greek eludes you, leave the least of flaws
600 In contracts with him; while, since Arab lore
Holds the stars' secret – take one trouble more
And master it! 'Tis done, and now deter
Who may the Tuscan, once Jove trined for her,
From Friedrich's path! – Friedrich, whose pilgrimage
The same man puts aside, whom he'll engage
To leave next year John Brienne in the lurch,
Come to Bassano, see Saint Francis' church
And judge of Guido the Bolognian's piece
Which, – lend Taurello credit, – rivals Greece –
610 Angels, with aureoles like golden quoits
Pitched home, applauding Ecelin's exploits.
For elegance, he strung the angelot,
Made rhymes thereto; for prowess, clove he not
Tiso, last siege, from crest to crupper? Why
Detail you thus a varied mastery

But to show how Taurello, on the watch
For men, to read their hearts and thereby catch
Their capabilities and purposes,
Displayed himself so far as displayed these:
620   While our Sordello only cared to know
About men as a means whereby he'd show
Himself, and men had much or little worth
According as they kept in or drew forth
That self; the other's choicest instruments
Surmised him shallow.
                Meantime, malcontents
Dropped off, town after town grew wiser. 'How
Change the world's face?' asked people; 'as 'tis now
It has been, will be ever: very fine
Subjecting things profane to things divine,
630   In talk! This contumacy will fatigue
The vigilance of Este and the League!
The Ghibellins gain on us!' – as it happed.
Old Azzo and old Boniface, entrapped
By Ponte Alto, both in one month's space
Slept at Verona: either left a brace
Of sons – but, three years after, either's pair
Lost Guglielm and Aldobrand its heir:
Azzo remained and Richard – all the stay
Of Este and Saint Boniface, at bay
640   As 'twere. Then, either Ecelin grew old
Or his brain altered – not o' the proper mould
For new appliances – his old palm-stock
Endured no influx of strange strengths. He'd rock
As in a drunkenness, or chuckle low
As proud of the completeness of his woe,
Then weep real tears; – now make some mad onslaught
On Este, heedless of the lesson taught
So painfully, – now cringe for peace, sue peace
At price of past gain, bar of fresh increase
650   To the fortunes of Romano. Up at last
Rose Este, down Romano sank as fast.
And men remarked these freaks of peace and war
Happened while Salinguerra was afar:
Whence every friend besought him, all in vain,
To use his old adherent's wits again.
Not he! – 'who had advisers in his sons,

Could plot himself, nor needed any one's
Advice.' 'Twas Adelaide's remaining staunch
Prevented his destruction root and branch
660 Forthwith; but when she died, doom fell, for gay
He made alliances, gave lands away
To whom it pleased accept them, and withdrew
For ever from the world. Taurello, who
Was summoned to the convent, then refused
A word at the wicket, patience thus abused,
Promptly threw off alike his imbecile
Ally's yoke, and his own frank, foolish smile.
Soon a few movements of the happier sort
Changed matters, put himself in men's report
670 As heretofore; he had to fight, beside,
And that became him ever. So, in pride
And flushing of this kind of second youth,
He dealt a good-will blow. Este in truth
Lay prone – and men remembered, somewhat late,
A laughing old outrageous stifled hate
He bore to Este – how it would outbreak
At times spite of disguise, like an earthquake
In sunny weather – as that noted day
When with his hundred friends he tried to slay
680 Azzo before the Kaiser's face: and how,
On Azzo's calm refusal to allow
A liegeman's challenge, straight he too was calmed:
As if his hate could bear to lie embalmed,
Bricked up, the moody Pharaoh, and survive
All intermediate crumblings, to arrive
At earth's catastrophe – 'twas Este's crash
Not Azzo's he demanded, so, no rash
Procedure! Este's true antagonist
Rose out of Ecelin: all voices whist,
690 All eyes were sharpened, wits predicted. He
'Twas, leaned in the embrasure absently,
Amused with his own efforts, now, to trace
With his steel-sheathed forefinger Friedrich's face
I' the dust: but as the trees waved sere, his smile
Deepened, and words expressed its thought erewhile.
  'Ay, fairly housed at last, my old compeer?
That we should stick together, all the year
I kept Vicenza! – How old Boniface,

Old Azzo caught us in its market-place,
700   He by that pillar, I at this, – caught each
In mid-swing, more than fury of his speech,
Egging the rabble on to disavow
Allegiance to their Marquis – Bacchus, how
They boasted! Ecelin must turn their drudge,
Nor, if released, will Salinguerra grudge
Paying arrears of tribute due long since –
Bacchus! My man could promise then, nor wince:
The bones-and-muscles! Sound of wind and limb,
Spoke he the set excuse I framed for him:
710   And now he sits me, slavering and mute,
Intent on chafing each starved purple foot
Benumbed past aching with the altar slab:
Will no vein throb there when some monk shall blab
Spitefully to the circle of bald scalps,
"Friedrich's affirmed to be our side the Alps"
– Eh, brother Lactance, brother Anaclet?
Sworn to abjure the world, its fume and fret,
God's own now? Drop the dormitory bar,
Enfold the scanty grey serge scapular
720   Twice o'er the cowl to muffle memories out!
So! But the midnight whisper turns a shout,
Eyes wink, mouths open, pulses circulate
In the stone walls: the past, the world you hate
Is with you, ambush, open field – or see
The surging flame – we fire Vicenza – glee!
Follow, let Pilio and Bernardo chafe!
Bring up the Mantuans – through San Biagio – safe!
Ah, the mad people waken? Ah, they writhe
And reach us? If they block the gate? No tithe
730   Can pass – keep back, you Bassanese! The edge,
Use the edge – shear, thrust, hew, melt down the wedge,
Let out the black of those black upturned eyes!
Hell – are they sprinkling fire too? The blood fries
And hisses on your brass gloves as they tear
Those upturned faces choking with despair.
Brave! Slidder through the reeking gate! "How now?
You six had charge of her?" And then the vow
Comes, and the foam spirts, hair's plucked, till one shriek
(I hear it) and you fling – you cannot speak –
740   Your gold-flowered basnet to a man who haled

The Adelaide he dared scarce view unveiled
This morn, naked across the fire: how crown
The archer that exhausted lays you down
Your infant, smiling at the flame, and dies?
While one, while mine . . .

        'Bacchus! I think there lies
More than one corpse there' (and he paced the room)
' – Another cinder somewhere: 'twas my doom
Beside, my doom! If Adelaide is dead,
I live the same, this Azzo lives instead
750 Of that to me, and we pull, any how,
Este into a heap: the matter's now
At the true juncture slipping us so oft.
Ay, Heinrich died and Otho, please you, doffed
His crown at such a juncture! Still, if holds
Our Friedrich's purpose, if this chain enfolds
The neck of . . . who but this same Ecelin
That must recoil when the best days begin!
Recoil? that's naught; if the recoiler leaves
His name for me to fight with, no one grieves:
760 But he must interfere, forsooth, unlock
His cloister to become my stumbling-block
Just as of old! Ay, ay, there 'tis again –
The land's inevitable Head – explain
The reverences that subject us! Count
These Ecelins now! Not to say as fount,
Originating power of thought, – from twelve
That drop i' the trenches they joined hands to delve,
Six shall surpass him, but . . . why men must twine
Somehow with something! Ecelin's a fine
770 Clear name! 'Twere simpler, doubtless, twine with me
At once: our cloistered friend's capacity
Was of a sort! I had to share myself
In fifty portions, like an o'ertasked elf
That's forced illume in fifty points the vast
Rare vapour he's environed by. At last
My strengths, though sorely frittered, e'en converge
And crown . . . no, Bacchus, they have yet to urge
The man be crowned!

        'That aloe, an he durst,
Would climb! Just such a bloated sprawler first
780 I noted in Messina's castle-court

The day I came, when Heinrich asked in sport
If I would pledge my faith to win him back
His right in Lombardy: ''for, once bid pack
Marauders,'' he continued, ''in my stead
You rule, Taurello!'' and upon this head
Laid the silk glove of Constance – I see her
Too, mantled head to foot in miniver,
Retrude following!
    'I am absolved
From further toil: the empery devolved
790 On me, 'twas Tito's word: I have to lay
For once my plan, pursue my plan my way,
Prompt nobody, and render an account
Taurello to Taurello! Nay, I mount
To Friedrich: he conceives the post I kept,
– Who did true service, able or inept,
Who's worthy guerdon, Ecelin or I.
Me guerdoned, counsel follows: would he vie
With the Pope really? Azzo, Boniface
Compose a right-arm Hohenstauffen's race
800 Must break ere govern Lombardy. I point
How easy 'twere to twist, once out of joint,
The socket from the bone: my Azzo's stare
Meanwhile! for I, this idle strap to wear,
Shall – fret myself abundantly, what end
To serve? There's left me twenty years to spend
– How better than my old way? Had I one
Who laboured to o'erthrow my work – a son
Hatching with Azzo superb treachery,
To root my pines up and then poison me,
810 Suppose – 'twere worth while frustrate that! Beside,
Another life's ordained me: the world's tide
Rolls, and what hope of parting from the press
Of waves, a single wave through weariness
Gently lifted aside, laid upon shore?
My life must be lived out in foam and roar,
No question. Fifty years the province held
Taurello; troubles raised, and troubles quelled,
He in the midst – who leaves this quaint stone place,
These trees a year or two, then not a trace
820 Of him! How obtain hold, fetter men's tongues
Like this poor minstrel with the foolish songs –

To which, despite our bustle, he is linked?
– Flowers one may teaze, that never grow extinct.
Ay, that patch, surely, green as ever, where
I set Her Moorish lentisk, by the stair,
To overawe the aloes; and we trod
Those flowers, how call you such? – into the sod;
A stately foreigner – a world of pain
To make it thrive, arrest rough winds – all vain!
830   It would decline; these would not be destroyed:
And now, where is it? where can you avoid
The flowers? I frighten children twenty years
Longer! – which way, too, Ecelin appears
To thwart me, for his son's besotted youth
Gives promise of the proper tiger-tooth:
They feel it at Vicenza! Fate, fate, fate,
My fine Taurello! Go you, promulgate
Friedrich's decree, and here's shall aggrandise
Young Ecelin – your Prefect's badge! a prize
840   Too precious, certainly.
                              'How now? Compete
With my old comrade? shuffle from their seat
His children? Paltry dealing! Don't I know
Ecelin? now, I think, and years ago!
What's changed – the weakness? did not I compound
For that, and undertake to keep him sound
Despite it? Here's Taurello hankering
After a boy's preferment – this plaything
To carry, Bacchus!' And he laughed.
                                       Remark
Why schemes wherein cold-blooded men embark
850   Prosper, when your enthusiastic sort
Fail: while these last are ever stopping short –
(So much they should – so little they can do!)
The careless tribe see nothing to pursue
If they desist; meantime their scheme succeeds.
     Thoughts were caprices in the course of deeds
Methodic with Taurello; so, he turned, –
Enough amused by fancies fairly earned
Of Este's horror-struck submitted neck,
And Richard, the cowed braggart, at his beck, –
860   To his own petty but immediate doubt
If he could pacify the League without

Conceding Richard; just to this was brought
That interval of vain discursive thought!
As, shall I say, some Ethiop, past pursuit
Of all enslavers, dips a shackled foot
Burnt to the blood, into the drowsy black
Enormous watercourse which guides him back
To his own tribe again, where he is king;
And laughs because he guesses, numbering
870 The yellower poison-wattles on the pouch
Of the first lizard wrested from its couch
Under the slime (whose skin, the while, he strips
To cure his nostril with, and festered lips,
And eyeballs bloodshot through the desert-blast)
That he has reached its boundary, at last
May breathe; – thinks o'er enchantments of the South
Sovereign to plague his enemies, their mouth,
Eyes, nails, and hair; but, these enchantments tried
In fancy, puts them soberly aside
880 For truth, projects a cool return with friends,
The likelihood of winning mere amends
Ere long; thinks that, takes comfort silently,
Then, from the river's brink, his wrongs and he,
Hugging revenge close to their hearts, are soon
Off-striding for the Mountains of the Moon.

    Midnight: the watcher nodded on his spear,
Since clouds dispersing left a passage clear
For any meagre and discoloured moon
To venture forth; and such was peering soon
890 Above the harassed city – her close lanes
Closer, not half so tapering her fanes,
As though she shrunk into herself to keep
What little life was saved, more safely. Heap
By heap the watch-fires mouldered, and beside
The blackest spoke Sordello and replied
Palma with none to listen. ''Tis your cause:
What makes a Ghibellin? There should be laws –
(Remember how my youth escaped! I trust
To you for manhood, Palma! tell me just
900 As any child) – there must be laws at work
Explaining this. Assure me, good may lurk
Under the bad, – my multitude has part
In your designs, their welfare is at heart

With Salinguerra, to their interest
Refer the deeds he dwelt on, – so divest
Our conference of much that scared me. Why
Affect that heartless tone to Tito? I
Esteemed myself, yes, in my inmost mind
This morn, a recreant to my race – mankind
910 O'erlooked till now: why boast my spirit's force,
– Such force denied its object? why divorce
These, then admire my spirit's flight the same
As though it bore up, helped some half-orbed flame
Else quenched in the dead void, to living space?
That orb cast off to chaos and disgrace,
Why vaunt so much my unencumbered dance,
Making a feat's facilities enhance
Its marvel? But I front Taurello, one
Of happier fate, and all I should have done,
920 He does; the people's good being paramount
With him, their progress may perhaps account
For his abiding still; whereas you heard
The talk with Tito – the excuse preferred
For burning those five hostages, – and broached
By way of blind, as you and I approached,
I do believe.'

                    She spoke: then he, 'My thought
Plainlier expressed! All to your profit – naught
Meantime of these, of conquests to achieve
For them, of wretchedness he might relieve
930 While profiting your party. Azzo, too,
Supports a cause: what cause? Do Guelfs pursue
Their ends by means like yours, or better?'

                                              When
The Guelfs were proved alike, men weighed with men,
And deed with deed, blaze, blood, with blood and blaze,
Morn broke: 'Once more, Sordello, meet its gaze
Proudly – the people's charge against thee fails
In every point, while either party quails!
These are the busy ones: be silent thou!
Two parties take the world up, and allow
940 No third, yet have one principle, subsist
By the same injustice; whoso shall enlist
With either, ranks with man's inveterate foes.
So there is one less quarrel to compose:

The Guelf, the Ghibellin may be to curse –
I have done nothing, but both sides do worse
Than nothing. Nay, to me, forgotten, reft
Of insight, lapped by trees and flowers, was left
The notion of a service – ha ? What lured
Me here, what mighty aim was I assured
950   Must move Taurello ? What if there remained
A cause, intact, distinct from these, ordained
For me, its true discoverer ? '
                                        Some one pressed
Before them here, a watcher, to suggest
The subject for a ballad : 'They must know
The tale of the dead worthy, long ago
Consul of Rome – that's long ago for us,
Minstrels and bowmen, idly squabbling thus
In the world's corner – but too late no doubt,
For the brave time he sought to bring about.
960   – Not know Crescentius Nomentanus ? ' Then
He cast about for terms to tell him, when
Sordello disavowed it, how they used
Whenever their Superior introduced
A novice to the Brotherhood – ('for I
Was just a brown-sleeve brother, merrily
Appointed too,' quoth he, 'till Innocent
Bade me relinquish, to my small content,
My wife or my brown sleeves') – some brother spoke
Ere nocturns of Crescentius, to revoke
970   The edict issued, after his demise,
Which blotted fame alike and effigies,
All out except a floating power, a name
Including, tending to produce the same
Great act. Rome, dead, forgotten, lived at least
Within that brain, though to a vulgar priest
And a vile stranger, – two not worth a slave
Of Rome's, Pope John, King Otho, – fortune gave
The rule there : so, Crescentius, haply dressed
In white, called Roman Consul for a jest,
980   Taking the people at their word, forth stepped
As upon Brutus' heel, nor ever kept
Rome waiting, – stood erect, and from his brain
Gave Rome out on its ancient place again,
Ay, bade proceed with Brutus' Rome, Kings styled

Themselves mere citizens of, and, beguiled
Into great thoughts thereby, would choose the gem
Out of a lapfull, spoil their diadem
– The Senate's cipher was so hard to scratch!
He flashes like a phanal, all men catch
990   The flame, Rome's just accomplished! when returned
Otho, with John, the Consul's step had spurned,
And Hugo Lord of Este, to redress
The wrongs of each. Crescentius in the stress
Of adverse fortune bent. 'They crucified
Their Consul in the Forum; and abide
E'er since such slaves at Rome, that I – (for I
Was once a brown-sleeve brother, merrily
Appointed) – I had option to keep wife
Or keep brown sleeves, and managed in the strife
1000   Lose both. A song of Rome!'
                     And Rome, indeed,
Robed at Goito in fantastic weed,
The Mother-City of his Mantuan days,
Looked an established point of light whence rays
Traversed the world; for, all the clustered homes
Beside of men, seemed bent on being Romes
In their degree; the question was, how each
Should most resemble Rome, clean out of reach.
Nor, of the Two, did either principle
Struggle to change, but to possess Rome, – still
1010   Guelf Rome or Ghibellin Rome.
                     Let Rome advance!
Rome, as she struck Sordello's ignorance –
How could he doubt one moment? Rome's the Cause!
Rome of the Pandects, all the world's new laws –
Of the Capitol, of Castle Angelo;
New structures, that inordinately glow,
Subdued, brought back to harmony, made ripe
By many a relic of the archetype
Extant for wonder; every upstart church
That hoped to leave old temples in the lurch,
1020   Corrected by the Theatre forlorn
That, – as a mundane shell, its world late born, –
Lay and o'ershadowed it. These hints combined,
Rome typifies the scheme to put mankind
Once more in full possession of their rights.

'Let us have Rome again! On me it lights
To build up Rome – on me, the first and last:
For such a future was endured the past!'
And thus, in the grey twilight, forth he sprung
To give his thought consistency among
1030 The very People – let their facts avail
Finish the dream grown from the archer's tale.

BOOK THE FIFTH

Is it the same Sordello in the dusk
As at the dawn? – merely a perished husk
Now, that arose a power fit to build
Up Rome again? The proud conception chilled
So soon? Ay, watch that latest dream of thine
– A Rome indebted to no Palatine –
Drop arch by arch, Sordello! Art possessed
Of thy wish now, rewarded for thy quest
Today among Ferrara's squalid sons?
10 Are this and this and this the shining ones
Meet for the Shining City? Sooth to say,
Your favoured tenantry pursue their way
After a fashion! This companion slips
On the smooth causey, t'other blinkard trips
At his mooned sandal. 'Leave to lead the brawls
Here i' the atria?' No, friend! He that sprawls
On aught but a stibadium . . . what his dues
Who puts the lustral vase to such an use?
Oh, huddle up the day's disasters! March,
20 Ye runagates, and drop thou, arch by arch,
Rome!
          Yet before they quite disband – a whim –
Study mere shelter, now, for him, and him,
Nay, even the worst, – just house them! Any cave
Suffices: throw out earth! A loophole? Brave!
They ask to feel the sun shine, see the grass
Grow, hear the larks sing? Dead art thou, alas,
And I am dead! But here's our son excels
At hurdle-weaving any Scythian, fells
Oak and devises rafters, dreams and shapes
30 His dream into a door-post, just escapes

The mystery of hinges. Lie we both
Perdue another age. The goodly growth
Of brick and stone! Our building-pelt was rough,
But that descendant's garb suits well enough
A portico-contriver. Speed the years –
What's time to us? At last, a city rears
Itself! nay, enter – what's the grave to us?
Lo, our forlorn acquaintance carry thus
The head! Successively sewer, forum, cirque –
40   Last age, an aqueduct was counted work,
But now they tire the artificer upon
Blank alabaster, black obsidian,
– Careful, Jove's face be duly fulgurant,
And mother Venus' kiss-creased nipples pant
Back into pristine pulpiness, ere fixed
Above the baths. What difference betwixt
This Rome and ours – resemblance what, between
That scurvy dumb-show and this pageant sheen –
These Romans and our rabble? Use thy wit!
50   The work marched: step by step, – a workman fit
Took each, nor too fit, – to one task, one time, –
No leaping o'er the petty to the prime,
When just the substituting osier lithe
For brittle bulrush, sound wood for soft withe,
To further loam-and-roughcast-work a stage, –
Exacts an architect, exacts an age:
No tables of the Mauretanian tree
For men whose maple log's their luxury!
That way was Rome built. 'Better' (say you) 'merge
60   At once all workmen in the demiurge,
All epochs in a lifetime, every task
In one!' So should the sudden city bask
I' the day – while those we'd feast there, want the knack
Of keeping fresh-chalked gowns from speck and brack,
Distinguish not rare peacock from vile swan,
Nor Mareotic juice from Caecuban.
'Enough of Rome! 'Twas happy to conceive
Rome on a sudden, nor shall fate bereave
Me of that credit: for the rest, her spite
70   Is an old story – serves my folly right
By adding yet another to the dull
List of abortions – things proved beautiful

Could they be done, Sordello cannot do.'
　　He sat upon the terrace, plucked and threw
The powdery aloe-cusps away, saw shift
Rome's walls, and drop arch after arch, and drift
Mist-like afar those pillars of all stripe,
Mounds of all majesty. 'Thou archetype,
Last of my dreams and loveliest, depart!'
80　　And then a low voice wound into his heart:
'Sordello!' (low as some old Pythoness
Conceding to a Lydian King's distress
The cause of his long error – one mistake
Of her past oracle) 'Sordello, wake!
God has conceded two sights to a man –
One, of men's whole work, time's completed plan,
The other, of the minute's work, man's first
Step to the plan's completeness: what's dispersed
Save hope of that supreme step which, descried
90　　Earliest, was meant still to remain untried
Only to give you heart to take your own
Step, and there stay, leaving the rest alone?
Where is the vanity? Why count as one
The first step, with the last step? What is gone
Except Rome's aëry magnificence,
That last step you'd take first? – an evidence
You were God: be man now! Let those glances fall!
The basis, the beginning step of all,
Which proves you just a man – is that gone too?
100　　Pity to disconcert one versed as you
In fate's ill-nature! but its full extent
Eludes Sordello, even: the veil rent,
Read the black writing – that collective man
Outstrips the individual. Who began
The acknowledged greatnesses? Ay, your own art
Shall serve us: put the poet's mimes apart –
Close with the poet's self, and lo, a dim
Yet too plain form divides itself from him!
Alcamo's song enmeshes the lulled Isle,
110　　Woven into the echoes left erewhile
By Nina, one soft web of song: no more
Turning his name, then, flower-like o'er and o'er!
An elder poet in the younger's place;
Nina's the strength, but Alcamo's the grace:

Each neutralizes each then! Search your fill;
You get no whole and perfect Poet – still
New Ninas, Alcamos, till time's midnight
Shrouds all – or better say, the shutting light
Of a forgotten yesterday. Dissect
120 Every ideal workman – (to reject
In favour of your fearful ignorance
The thousand phantasms eager to advance,
And point you but to those within your reach) –
Were you the first who brought – (in modern speech)
The Multitude to be materialized?
That loose eternal unrest – who devised
An apparition i' the midst? The rout
Was checked, a breathless ring was formed about
That sudden flower: get round at any risk
130 The gold-rough pointel, silver-blazing disk
O' the lily! Swords across it! Reign thy reign
And serve thy frolic service, Charlemagne!
– The very child of over-joyousness,
Unfeeling thence, strong therefore: Strength by stress
Of Strength comes of that forehead confident,
Those widened eyes expecting heart's content,
A calm as out of just-quelled noise; nor swerves
For doubt, the ample cheek in gracious curves
Abutting on the upthrust nether lip:
140 He wills, how should he doubt then? Ages slip:
Was it Sordello pried into the work
So far accomplished, and discovered lurk
A company amid the other clans,
Only distinct in priests for castellans
And popes for suzerains (their rule confessed
Its rule, their interest its interest,
Living for sake of living – there an end, –
Wrapt in itself, no energy to spend
In making adversaries or allies) –
150 Dived you into its capabilities
And dared create, out of that sect, a soul
Should turn a multitude, already whole,
Into its body? Speak plainer! Is't so sure
God's church lives by a King's investiture?
Look to last step! A staggering – a shock –
What's mere sand is demolished, while the rock

Endures: a column of black fiery dust
Blots heaven – that help was prematurely thrust
Aside, perchance! – but air clears, naught's erased
160 Of the true outline. Thus much being firm based,
The other was a scaffold. See him stand
Buttressed upon his mattock, Hildebrand
Of the huge brain-mask welded ply o'er ply
As in a forge; it buries either eye
White and extinct, that stupid brow; teeth clenched,
The neck tight-corded, too, the chin deep-trenched,
As if a cloud enveloped him while fought
Under its shade, grim prizers, thought with thought
At dead-lock, agonizing he, until
170 The victor thought leap radiant up, and Will,
The slave with folded arms and drooping lids
They fought for, lean forth flame-like as it bids.
Call him no flower – a mandrake of the earth,
Thwarted and dwarfed and blasted in its birth,
Rather, – a fruit of suffering's excess,
Thence feeling, therefore stronger: still by stress
Of Strength, work Knowledge! Full three hundred years
Have men to wear away in smiles and tears
Between the two that nearly seemed to touch,
180 Observe you! quit one workman and you clutch
Another, letting both their trains go by –
The actors-out of either's policy,
Heinrich, on this hand, Otho, Barbaross,
Carry the three Imperial crowns across,
Aix' Iron, Mílan's Silver, and Rome's Gold –
While Alexander, Innocent uphold
On that, each Papal key – but, link on link,
Why is it neither chain betrays a chink?
How coalesce the small and great? Alack,
190 For one thrust forward, fifty such fall back!
Do the popes coupled there help Gregory
Alone? Hark – from the hermit Peter's cry
At Claremont, down to the first serf that says
Friedrich's no liege of his while he delays
Getting the Pope's curse off him! The Crusade –
Or trick of breeding Strength by other aid
Than Strength, is safe. Hark – from the wild harangue
Of Vimmercato, to the carroch's clang

Yonder! The League – or trick of turning Strength
200 Against Pernicious Strength, is safe at length.
Yet hark – from Mantuan Albert making cease
The fierce ones, to Saint Francis preaching peace
Yonder! God's Truce – or trick to supersede
The very Use of Strength, is safe. Indeed
We trench upon the future. Who is found
To take next step, next age – trail o'er the ground –
Shall I say, gourd-like? – not the flower's display
Nor the root's prowess, but the plenteous way
O' the plant – produced by joy and sorrow, whence
210 Unfeeling and yet feeling, strongest thence?
Knowledge by stress of merely Knowledge? No –
E'en were Sordello ready to forego
His life for this, 'twere overleaping work
Some one has first to do, howe'er it irk,
Nor stray a foot's breadth from the beaten road.
Who means to help must still support the load
Hildebrand lifted – "why hast Thou," he groaned,
"Imposed on me a burthen, Paul had moaned,
And Moses dropped beneath?" Much done – and yet
220 Doubtless that grandest task God ever set
On man, left much to do: at his arm's wrench,
Charlemagne's scaffold fell; but pillars blench
Merely, start back again – perchance have been
Taken for buttresses: crash every screen,
Hammer the tenons better, and engage
A gang about your work, for the next age
Or two, of Knowledge, part by Strength and part
By Knowledge! Then, indeed, perchance may start
Sordello on his race – would time divulge
230 Such secrets! If one step's awry, one bulge
Calls for correction by a step we thought
Got over long since, why, till that is wrought,
No progress! And the scaffold in its turn
Becomes, its service o'er, a thing to spurn.
Meanwhile, if your half-dozen years of life
In store dispose you to forego the strife,
Who takes exception? Only bear in mind
Ferrara's reached, Goito's left behind:
As you then were, as half yourself, desist!
240 – The warrior-part of you may, an it list,

Finding real faulchions difficult to poise,
Fling them afar and taste the cream of joys
By wielding such in fancy, – what is bard
Of you may spurn the vehicle that marred
Elys so much, and in free fancy glut
His sense, yet write no verses – you have but
To please yourself for law, and once could please
What once appeared yourself, by dreaming these
Rather than doing these, in days gone by.

250 But all is changed the moment you descry
Mankind as half yourself, – then, fancy's trade
Ends once and always: how may half evade
The other half? men are found half of you.
Out of a thousand helps, just one or two
Can be accomplished presently: but flinch
From these (as from the faulchion, raised an inch,
Elys, described a couplet) and make proof
Of fancy, – then, while one half lolls aloof
I' the vines, completing Rome to the tip-top –

260 See if, for that, your other half will stop
A tear, begin a smile! The rabble's woes,
Ludicrous in their patience as they chose
To sit about their town and quietly
Be slaughtered, – the poor reckless soldiery,
With their ignoble rhymes on Richard, how
"Polt-foot," sang they, "was in a pitfall now,"
Cheering each other from the engine-mounts, –
That crippled spawling idiot who recounts
How, lopped of limbs, he lay, stupid as stone,

270 Till the pains crept from out him one by one,
And wriggles round the archers on his head
To earn a morsel of their chestnut bread, –
And Cino, always in the self-same place
Weeping; beside that other wretch's case,
Eyepits to ear, one gangrene since he plied
The engine in his coat of raw sheep's hide
A double watch in the noon sun; and see
Lucchino, beauty, with the favours free,
Trim hacqueton, spruce beard and scented hair,

280 Campaigning it for the first time – cut there
In two already, boy enough to crawl
For latter orpine round the southern wall,

Tomà, where Richard's kept, because that whore
Marfisa, the fool never saw before,
Sickened for flowers this wearisomest siege:
And Tiso's wife – men liked their pretty liege,
Cared for her least of whims once, – Berta, wed
A twelvemonth gone, and, now poor Tiso's dead,
Delivering herself of his first child
290 On that chance heap of wet filth, reconciled
To fifty gazers!' – (Here a wind below
Made moody music augural of woe
From the pine barrier) – 'What if, now the scene
Draws to a close, yourself have really been
– You, plucking purples in Goito's moss
Like edges of a trabea (not to cross
Your consul-humour) or dry aloe-shafts
For fasces, at Ferrara – he, fate wafts,
This very age, her whole inheritance
300 Of opportunities? Yet you advance
Upon the last! Since talking is your trade,
There's Salinguerra left you to persuade:
Fail! then' –
           'No – no – which latest chance secure!'
Leaped up and cried Sordello: 'this made sure,
The past were yet redeemable; its work
Was – help the Guelfs, whom I, howe'er it irk,
Thus help!' He shook the foolish aloe-haulm
Out of his doublet, paused, proceeded calm
To the appointed presence. The large head
310 Turned on its socket; 'And your spokesman,' said
The large voice, 'is Elcorte's happy sprout?
Few such' – (so finishing a speech no doubt
Addressed to Palma, silent at his side)
' – My sober councils have diversified.
Elcorte's son! good: forward as you may,
Our lady's minstrel with so much to say!'
The hesitating sunset floated back,
Rosily traversed in the wonted track
The chamber, from the lattice o'er the girth
320 Of pines, to the huge eagle blacked in earth
Opposite, – outlined sudden, spur to crest,
That solid Salinguerra, and caressed
Palma's contour; 'twas day looped back night's pall;

Sordello had a chance left spite of all.
　　And much he made of the convincing speech
Meant to compensate for the past and reach
Through his youth's daybreak of unprofit, quite
To his noon's labour, so proceed till night
Leisurely! The great argument to bind

330　Taurello with the Guelf Cause, body and mind,
– Came the consummate rhetoric to that?
Yet most Sordello's argument dropped flat
Through his accustomed fault of breaking yoke,
Disjoining him who felt from him who spoke.
Was't not a touching incident – so prompt
A rendering the world its just accompt,
Once proved its debtor? Who'd suppose, before
This proof, that he, Goito's god of yore,
At duty's instance could demean himself

340　So memorably, dwindle to a Guelf?
Be sure, in such delicious flattery steeped,
His inmost self at the out-portion peeped,
Thus occupied; then stole a glance at those
Appealed to, curious if her colour rose
Or his lip moved, while he discreetly urged
The need of Lombardy becoming purged
At soonest of her barons; the poor part
Abandoned thus, missing the blood at heart
And spirit in brain, unseasonably off

350　Elsewhere! But, though his speech was worthy scoff,
Good-humoured Salinguerra, famed for tact
And tongue, who, careless of his phrase, ne'er lacked
The right phrase, and harangued Honorius dumb
At his accession, – looked as all fell plumb
To purpose and himself found interest
In every point his new instructor pressed
– Left playing with the rescript's white wax seal
To scrutinize Sordello head and heel.
He means to yield assent sure? No, alas!

360　All he replied was, 'What, it comes to pass
That poesy, sooner than politics,
Makes fade young hair?' To think such speech could fix
Taurello!
　　　　　Then a flash of bitter truth:
So fantasies could break and fritter youth

That he had long ago lost earnestness,
Lost will to work, lost power to even express
The need of working! Earth was turned a grave:
No more occasions now, though he should crave
Just one, in right of superhuman toil,
370 To do what was undone, repair such spoil,
Alter the past – nothing would give the chance!
Not that he was to die; he saw askance
Protract the ignominious years beyond
To dream in – time to hope and time despond,
Remember and forget, be sad, rejoice
As saved a trouble; he might, at his choice,
One way or other, idle life out, drop
No few smooth verses by the way – for prop,
A thyrsus, these sad people, all the same,
380 Should pick up, and set store by, – far from blame,
Plant o'er his hearse, convinced his better part
Survived him. 'Rather tear men out the heart
O' the truth!' – Sordello muttered, and renewed
His propositions for the Multitude.
    But Salinguerra, who at this attack
Had thrown great breast and ruffling corslet back
To hear the better, smilingly resumed
His task; beneath, the carroch's warning boomed;
He must decide with Tito; courteously
390 He turned then, even seeming to agree
With his admonisher – 'Assist the Pope,
Extend Guelf domination, fill the scope
O' the Church, thus based on All, by All, for All –
Change Secular to Evangelical' –
Echoing his very sentence: all seemed lost,
When suddenly he looked up, laughingly almost,
To Palma: 'This opinion of your friend's –
For instance, would it answer Palma's ends?
Best, were it not, turn Guelf, submit our Strength' –
400 (Here he drew out his baldric to its length)
– 'To the Pope's Knowledge – let our captive slip,
Wide to the walls throw ope our gates, equip
Azzo with ... what I hold here! Who'll subscribe
To a trite censure of the minstrel tribe
Henceforward? or pronounce, as Heinrich used,
"Spear-heads for battle, burr-heads for the joust!"

– When Constance, for his couplets, would promote
Alcamo, from a parti-coloured coat,
To holding her lord's stirrup in the wars.
410 Not that I see where couplet-making jars
With common sense: at Mantua I had borne
This chanted, better than their most forlorn
Of bull-baits, – that's indisputable!'
                                        Brave!
Whom vanity nigh slew, contempt shall save!
All's at an end: a Troubadour suppose
Mankind will class him with their friends or foes?
A puny uncouth ailing vassal think
The world and him bound in some special link?
Abrupt the visionary tether burst.
420 What were rewarded here, or what amerced
If a poor drudge, solicitous to dream
Deservingly, got tangled by his theme
So far as to conceit the knack or gift
Or whatsoe'er it be, of verse, might lift
The globe, a lever like the hand and head
Of – 'Men of Action,' as the Jongleurs said,
– 'The Great Men,' in the people's dialect?
    And not a moment did this scorn affect
Sordello: scorn the poet? They, for once,
430 Asking 'what was,' obtained a full response.
Bid Naddo think at Mantua – he had but
To look into his promptuary, put
Finger on a set thought in a set speech:
But was Sordello fitted thus for each
Conjecture? Nowise; since within his soul,
Perception brooded unexpressed and whole.
A healthy spirit like a healthy frame
Craves aliment in plenty – all the same,
Changes, assimilates its aliment.
440 Perceived Sordello, on a truth intent?
Next day no formularies more you saw
Than figs or olives in a sated maw.
'Tis Knowledge, whither such perceptions tend;
They lose themselves in that, means to an end,
The many old producing some one new,
A last unlike the first. If lies are true,
The Caliph's wheel-work man of brass receives

A meal, munched millet grains and lettuce leaves
Together in his stomach rattle loose;
450 You find them perfect next day to produce:
But ne'er expect the man, on strength of that,
Can roll an iron camel-collar flat
Like Haroun's self! I tell you, what was stored
Bit by bit through Sordello's life, outpoured
That eve, was, for that age, a novel thing:
And round those three the People formed a ring,
Of visionary judges whose award
He recognized in full – faces that barred
Henceforth return to the old careless life,
460 In whose great presence, therefore, his first strife
For their sake must not be ignobly fought;
All these, for once, approved of him, he thought,
Suspended their own vengeance, chose await
The issue of this strife to reinstate
Them in the right of taking it – in fact
He must be proved king ere they could exact
Vengeance for such king's defalcation. Last,
A reason why the phrases flowed so fast
Was in his quite forgetting for a time
470 Himself in his amazement that the rhyme
Disguised the royalty so much: he there –
And Salinguerra yet all-unaware
Who was the lord, who liegeman!
                                   'Thus I lay
On thine my spirit and compel obey
His lord, – my liegeman, – impotent to build
Another Rome, but hardly so unskilled
In what such builder should have been, as brook
One shame beyond the charge that I forsook
His function! Free me from that shame, I bend
480 A brow before, suppose new years to spend, –
Allow each chance, nor fruitlessly, recur –
Measure thee with the Minstrel, then, demur
At any crown he claims! That I must cede
Shamed now, my right to my especial meed –
Confess thee fitter help the world than I
Ordained its champion from eternity,
Is much: but to behold thee scorn the post
I quit in thy behalf – to hear thee boast

What makes my own despair!' And while he rung
490 The changes on this theme, the roof up-sprung,
The sad walls of the presence-chamber died
Into the distance, or embowering vied
With far-away Goito's vine-frontier;
And crowds of faces – (only keeping clear
The rose-light in the midst, his vantage-ground
To fight their battle from) – deep clustered round
Sordello, with good wishes no mere breath,
Kind prayers for him no vapour, since, come death
Come life, he was fresh-sinewed every joint,
500 Each bone new-marrowed as whom gods anoint
Though mortal to their rescue. Now let sprawl
The snaky volumes hither! Is Typhon all
For Hercules to trample – good report
From Salinguerra only to extort?
'So was I' (closed he his inculcating
A poet must be earth's essential king)
'So was I, royal so, and if I fail,
'Tis not the royalty, ye witness quail,
But one deposed who, caring not exert
510 Its proper essence, trifled malapert
With accidents instead – good things assigned
As heralds of a better thing behind –
And, worthy through display of these, put forth
Never the inmost all-surpassing worth
That constitutes him king precisely since
As yet no other spirit may evince
Its like: the power he took most pride to test,
Whereby all forms of life had been professed
At pleasure, forms already on the earth,
520 Was but a means to power beyond, whose birth
Should, in its novelty, be kingship's proof.
Now, whether he came near or kept aloof
The several forms he longed to imitate,
Not there the kingship lay, he sees too late.
Those forms, unalterable first as last,
Proved him her copier, not the protoplast
Of nature: what would come of being free,
By action to exhibit tree for tree,
Bird, beast, for beast and bird, or prove earth bore
530 One veritable man or woman more?

Means to an end, such proofs are: what the end?
Let essence, whatsoe'er it be, extend –
Never contract. Already you include
The multitude; then let the multitude
Include yourself; and the result were new:
Themselves before, the multitude turn you.
This were to live and move and have, in them,
Your being, and secure a diadem
You should transmit (because no cycle yearns
540 Beyond itself, but on itself returns)
When, the full sphere in wane, the world o'erlaid
Long since with you, shall have in turn obeyed
Some orb still prouder, some displayer, still
More potent than the last, of human will,
And some new king depose the old. Of such
Am I – whom pride of this elates too much?
Safe, rather say, 'mid troops of peers again;
I, with my words, hailed brother of the train
Deeds once sufficed: for, let the world roll back,
550 Who fails, through deeds howe'er diverse, retrack
My purpose still, my task? A teeming crust –
Air, flame, earth, wave at conflict! Then, needs must
Emerge some Calm embodied, these refer
The brawl to – yellow-bearded Jupiter?
No! Saturn; some existence like a pact
And protest against Chaos, some first fact
I' the faint of time. My deep of life, I know
Is unavailing e'en to poorly show' . . .
(For here the Chief immeasurably yawned)
560 . . . 'Deeds in their due gradation till Song dawned –
The fullest effluence of the finest mind,
All in degree, no way diverse in kind
From minds about it, minds which, more or less,
Lofty or low, move seeking to impress
Themselves on somewhat; but one mind has climbed
Step after step, by just ascent sublimed.
Thought is the soul of act, and, stage by stage,
Soul is from body still to disengage
As tending to a freedom which rejects
570 Such help and incorporeally affects
The world, producing deeds but not by deeds,
Swaying, in others, frames itself exceeds,

Assigning them the simpler tasks it used
To patiently perform till Song produced
Acts, by thoughts only, for the mind: divest
Mind of e'en Thought, and, lo, God's unexpressed
Will draws above us! All then is to win
Save that. How much for me, then? where begin
My work? About me, faces! and they flock,
580   The earnest faces. What shall I unlock
By song? behold me prompt, whate'er it be,
To minister: how much can mortals see
Of Life? No more than so? I take the task
And marshal you Life's elemental masque,
Show Men, on evil or on good lay stress,
This light, this shade make prominent, suppress
All ordinary hues that softening blend
Such natures with the level. Apprehend
Which sinner is, which saint, if I allot
590   Hell, Purgatory, Heaven, a blaze or blot,
To those you doubt concerning! I enwomb
Some wretched Friedrich with his red-hot tomb;
Some dubious spirit, Lombard Agilulph
With the black chastening river I engulph!
Some unapproached Matilda I enshrine
With languors of the planet of decline –
These, fail to recognize, to arbitrate
Between henceforth, to rightly estimate
Thus marshalled in the masque! Myself, the while,
600   As one of you, am witness, shrink or smile
At my own showing! Next age – what's to do?
The men and women stationed hitherto
Will I unstation, good and bad, conduct
Each nature to its farthest, or obstruct
At soonest, in the world: light, thwarted, breaks
A limpid purity to rainbow flakes,
Or shadow, massed, freezes to gloom: behold
How such, with fit assistance to unfold,
Or obstacles to crush them, disengage
610   Their forms, love, hate, hope, fear, peace make, war wage,
In presence of you all! Myself, implied
Superior now, as, by the platform's side,
I bade them do and suffer, – would last content
The world . . . no – that's too far! I circumvent

A few, my masque contented, and to these
Offer unveil the last of mysteries –
Man's inmost life shall have yet freer play:
Once more I cast external things away,
And natures composite, so decompose
620 That'... Why, he writes *Sordello!*

               'How I rose,
And how have you advanced! since evermore
Yourselves effect what I was fain before
Effect, what I supplied yourselves suggest,
What I leave bare yourselves can now invest.
How we attain to talk as brothers talk,
In half-words, call things by half-names, no balk
From discontinuing old aids. Today
Takes in account the work of Yesterday:
Has not the world a Past now, its adept
630 Consults ere he dispense with or accept
New aids? a single touch more may enhance,
A touch less turn to insignificance
Those structures' symmetry the past has strewed
The world with, once so bare. Leave the mere rude
Explicit details! 'tis but brother's speech
We need, speech where an accent's change gives each
The other's soul – no speech to understand
By former audience: need was then to expand,
Expatiate – hardly were we brothers! true –
640 Nor I lament my small remove from you,
Nor reconstruct what stands already. Ends
Accomplished turn to means: my art intends
New structure from the ancient: as they changed
The spoils of every clime at Venice, ranged
The horned and snouted Libyan god, upright
As in his desert, by some simple bright
Clay cinerary pitcher – Thebes as Rome,
Athens as Byzant rifled, till their Dome
From earth's reputed consummations razed
650 A seal, the all-transmuting Triad blazed
Above. Ah, whose that fortune? Ne'ertheless
E'en he must stoop contented to express
No tithe of what's to say – the vehicle
Never sufficient: but his work is still
For faces like the faces that select

The single service I am bound effect, –
That bid me cast aside such fancies, bow
Taurello to the Guelf cause, disallow
The Kaiser's coming – which with heart, soul, strength,
660 I labour for, this eve, who feel at length
My past career's outrageous vanity,
And would, as its amends, die, even die
Now I first estimate the boon of life,
If death might win compliance – sure, this strife
Is right for once – the People my support.'
    My poor Sordello! what may we extort
By this, I wonder? Palma's lighted eyes
Turned to Taurello who, long past surprise,
Began, 'You love him – what you'd say at large
670 Let me say briefly. First, your father's charge
To me, his friend, peruse: I guessed indeed
You were no stranger to the course decreed.
He bids me leave his children to the saints:
As for a certain project, he acquaints
The Pope with that, and offers him the best
Of your possessions to permit the rest
Go peaceably – to Ecelin, a stripe
Of soil the cursèd Vicentines will gripe,
– To Alberic, a patch the Trevisan
680 Clutches already; extricate, who can,
Treville, Villarazzi, Puissolo,
Loria and Cartiglione! – all must go,
And with them go my hopes. 'Tis lost, then! Lost
This eve, our crisis, and some pains it cost
Procuring; thirty years – as good I'd spent
Like our admonisher! But each his bent
Pursues: no question, one might live absurd
Oneself this while, by deed as he by word
Persisting to obtrude an influence where
690 'Tis made account of, much as . . . nay, you fare
With twice the fortune, youngster! – I submit,
Happy to parallel my waste of wit
With the renowned Sordello's: you decide
A course for me. Romano may abide
Romano, – Bacchus! After all, what dearth
Of Ecelins and Alberics on earth?
Say there's a prize in prospect, must disgrace

Betide competitors, unless they style
Themselves Romano? Were it worth my while
700 To try my own luck! But an obscure place
Suits me – there wants a youth to bustle, stalk
And attitudinize – some fight, more talk,
Most flaunting badges – how, I might make clear
Since Friedrich's very purposes lie here
– Here, pity they are like to lie! For me,
With station fixed unceremoniously
Long since, small use contesting; I am but
The liegeman – you are born the lieges: shut
That gentle mouth now! or resume your kin
710 In your sweet self; were Palma Ecelin
For me to work with! Could that neck endure
This bauble for a cumbrous garniture,
She should . . . or might one bear it for her? Stay –
I have not been so flattered many a day
As by your pale friend – Bacchus! The least help
Would lick the hind's fawn to a lion's whelp:
His neck is broad enough – a ready tongue
Beside: too writhled – but, the main thing, young –
I could . . . why, look ye!'
                                          And the badge was thrown
720 Across Sordello's neck: 'This badge alone
Makes you Romano's Head – becomes superb
On your bare neck, which would, on mine, disturb
The pauldron,' said Taurello. A mad act,
Nor even dreamed about before – in fact,
Not when his sportive arm rose for the nonce –
But he had dallied overmuch, this once,
With power: the thing was done, and he, aware
The thing was done, proceeded to declare –
(So like a nature made to serve, excel
730 In serving, only feel by service well!)
– That he would make Sordello that and more.
'As good a scheme as any. What's to pore
At in my face?' he asked – 'ponder instead
This piece of news; you are Romano's Head!
One cannot slacken pace so near the goal,
Suffer my Azzo to escape heart-whole
This time! For you there's Palma to espouse –
For me, one crowning trouble ere I house

Like my compeer.'
On which ensued a strange

740 And solemn visitation; there came change
O'er every one of them; each looked on each:
Up in the midst a truth grew, without speech.
And when the giddiness sank and the haze
Subsided, they were sitting, no amaze,
Sordello with the baldric on, his sire
Silent, though his proportions seemed aspire
Momently; and, interpreting the thrill, –
Night at its ebb, – Palma was found there still
Relating somewhat Adelaide confessed

750 A year ago, while dying on her breast, –
Of a contrivance, that Vicenza night
When Ecelin had birth. 'Their convoy's flight,
Cut off a moment, coiled inside the flame
That wallowed like a dragon at his game
The toppling city through – San Biagio rocks!
And wounded lies in her delicious locks
Retrude, the frail mother, on her face,
None of her wasted, just in one embrace
Covering her child: when, as they lifted her,

760 Cleaving the tumult, mighty, mightier
And mightiest Taurello's cry outbroke,
Leapt like a tongue of fire that cleaves the smoke,
Midmost to cheer his Mantuans onward – drown
His colleague Ecelin's clamour, up and down
The disarray: failed Adelaide see then
Who was the natural chief, the man of men?
Outstripping time, her infant there burst swathe,
Stood up with eyes haggard beyond the scathe
From wandering after his heritage

770 Lost once and lost for aye: and why that rage,
That deprecating glance? A new shape leant
On a familiar shape – gloatingly bent
O'er his discomfiture; 'mid wreaths it wore,
Still one outflamed the rest – her child's before
'Twas Salinguerra's for his child: scorn, hate,
Rage now might startle her when all too late!
Then was the moment! – rival's foot had spurned
Never that House to earth else! Sense returned –
The act conceived, adventured and complete,

780 They bore away to an obscure retreat
  Mother and child – Retrude's self not slain'
  (Nor even here Taurello moved) 'though pain
  Was fled; and what assured them most 'twas fled,
  All pain, was, if they raised the pale hushed head
  'Twould turn this way and that, waver awhile,
  And only settle into its old smile –
  (Graceful as the disquieted water-flag
  Steadying itself, remarked they, in the quag
  On either side their path) – when suffered look
790 Down on her child. They marched: no sign once shook
  The company's close litter of crossed spears
  Till, as they reached Goito, a few tears
  Slipped in the sunset from her long black lash,
  And she was gone. So far the action rash;
  No crime. They laid Retrude in the font,
  Taurello's very gift, her child was wont
  To sit beneath – constant as eve he came
  To sit by its attendant girls the same
  As one of them. For Palma, she would blend
800 With this magnific spirit to the end,
  That ruled her first; but scarcely had she dared
  To disobey the Adelaide who scared
  Her into vowing never to disclose
  A secret to her husband, which so froze
  His blood at half-recital, she contrived
  To hide from him Taurello's infant lived,
  Lest, by revealing that, himself should mar
  Romano's fortunes. And, a crime so far,
  Palma received that action: she was told
810 Of Salinguerra's nature, of his cold
  Calm acquiescence in his lot! But free
  To impart the secret to Romano, she
  Engaged to repossess Sordello of
  His heritage, and hers, and that way doff
  The mask, but after years, long years: while now,
  Was not Romano's sign-mark on that brow?'
   Across Taurello's heart his arms were locked:
  And when he did speak 'twas as if he mocked
  The minstrel, 'who had not to move,' he said,
820 'Nor stir – should fate defraud him of a shred
  Of his son's infancy? much less his youth!'

(Laughingly all this) – 'which to aid, in truth,
Himself, reserved on purpose, had not grown
Old, not too old – 'twas best they kept alone
Till now, and never idly met till now';
– Then, in the same breath, told Sordello how
All intimations of this eve's event
Were lies, for Friedrich must advance to Trent,
Thence to Verona, then to Rome, there stop,
830 Tumble the Church down, institute a-top
The Alps a Prefecture of Lombardy:
– 'That's now! – no prophesying what may be
Anon, with a new monarch of the clime,
Native of Gesi, passing his youth's prime
At Naples. Tito bids my choice decide
On whom . . .'
               'Embrace him, madman!' Palma cried,
Who through the laugh saw sweat-drops burst apace,
And his lips blanching: he did not embrace
Sordello, but he laid Sordello's hand
840 On his own eyes, mouth, forehead.
                        Understand,
This while Sordello was becoming flushed
Out of his whiteness; thoughts rushed, fancies rushed;
He pressed his hand upon his head and signed
Both should forbear him. 'Nay, the best's behind!'
Taurello laughed – not quite with the same laugh:
'The truth is, thus we scatter, ay, like chaff
These Guelfs, a despicable monk recoils
From: nor expect a fickle Kaiser spoils
Our triumph! – Friedrich? Think you, I intend
850 Friedrich shall reap the fruits of blood I spend
And brain I waste? Think you, the people clap
Their hands at my out-hewing this wild gap
For any Friedrich to fill up? 'Tis mine –
That's yours: I tell you, towards some such design
Have I worked blindly, yes, and idly, yes,
And for another, yes – but worked no less
With instinct at my heart; I else had swerved,
While now – look round! My cunning has preserved
Samminiato – that's a central place
860 Secures us Florence, boy, – in Pisa's case,
By land as she by sea; with Pisa ours,

And Florence, and Pistoia, one devours
The land at leisure! Gloriously dispersed –
Brescia, observe, Milan, Piacenza first
That flanked us (ah, you know not!) in the March;
On these we pile, as keystone of our arch,
Romagna and Bologna, whose first span
Covered the Trentine and the Valsugan;
Sofia's Egna by Bolgiano's sure!' ...
870 So he proceeded: half of all this, pure
Delusion, doubtless, nor the rest too true,
But what was undone he felt sure to do,
As ring by ring he wrung off, flung away
The pauldron-rings to give his sword-arm play –
Need of the sword now! That would soon adjust
Aught wrong at present; to the sword intrust
Sordello's whiteness, undersize: 'twas plain
He hardly rendered right to his own brain –
Like a brave hound, men educate to pride
880 Himself on speed or scent nor aught beside,
As though he could not, gift by gift, match men!
Palma had listened patiently: but when
'Twas time expostulate, attempt withdraw
Taurello from his child, she, without awe
Took off his iron arms from, one by one,
Sordello's shrinking shoulders, and, that done,
Made him avert his visage and relieve
Sordello (you might see his corslet heave
The while) who, loose, rose – tried to speak, then sank:
890 They left him in the chamber. All was blank.
And even reeling down the narrow stair
Taurello kept up, as though unaware
Palma was by to guide him, the old device
– Something of Milan – 'how we muster thrice
The Torriani's strength there; all along
Our own Visconti cowed them' – thus the song
Continued even while she bade him stoop,
Thrid somehow, by some glimpse of arrow-loop,
The turnings to the gallery below,
900 Where he stopped short as Palma let him go.
When he had sat in silence long enough
Splintering the stone bench, braving a rebuff
She stopped the truncheon; only to commence

One of Sordello's poems, a pretence
For speaking, some poor rhyme of 'Elys' hair
And head that's sharp and perfect like a pear,
So smooth and close are laid the few fine locks
Stained like pale honey oozed from topmost rocks
Sun-blanched the livelong summer' – from his worst

910 Performance, the Goito, as his first:
And that at end, conceiving from the brow
And open mouth no silence would serve now,
Went on to say the whole world loved that man
And, for that matter, thought his face, though wan,
Eclipsed the Count's – he sucking in each phrase
As if an angel spoke. The foolish praise
Ended, he drew her on his mailed knees, made
Her face a framework with his hands, a shade,
A crown, an aureole: there must she remain

920 (Her little mouth compressed with smiling pain
As in his gloves she felt her tresses twitch)
To get the best look at, in fittest niche
Dispose his saint. That done, he kissed her brow,
– 'Lauded her father for his treason now,'
He told her, 'only, how could one suspect
The wit in him? – whose clansman, recollect,
Was ever Salinguerra – she, the same,
Romano and his lady – so, might claim
To know all, as she should' – and thus begun

930 Schemes with a vengeance, schemes on schemes, 'not one
Fit to be told that foolish boy,' he said,
'But only let Sordello Palma wed,
– Then!'
　　　　'Twas a dim long narrow place at best:
Midway a sole grate showed the fiery West,
As shows its corpse the world's end some split tomb –
A gloom, a rift of fire, another gloom,
Faced Palma – but at length Taurello set
Her free; the grating held one ragged jet
Of fierce gold fire: he lifted her within

940 The hollow underneath – how else begin
Fate's second marvellous cycle, else renew
The ages than with Palma plain in view?
Then paced the passage, hands clenched, head erect,
Pursuing his discourse; a grand unchecked

Monotony made out from his quick talk
And the recurring noises of his walk;
– Somewhat too much like the o'ercharged assent
Of two resolved friends in one danger blent,
Who hearten each the other against heart;
950 Boasting there's naught to care for, when, apart
The boaster, all's to care for. He, beside
Some shape not visible, in power and pride
Approached, out of the dark, ginglingly near,
Nearer, passed close in the broad light, his ear
Crimson, eyeballs suffused, temples full-fraught,
Just a snatch of the rapid speech you caught,
And on he strode into the opposite dark,
Till presently the harsh heel's turn, a spark
I' the stone, and whirl of some loose embossed thong
960 That crashed against the angle aye so long
After the last, punctual to an amount
Of mailed great paces you could not but count, –
Prepared you for the pacing back again.
And by the snatches you might ascertain
That, Friedrich's Prefecture surmounted, left
By this alone in Italy, they cleft
Asunder, crushed together, at command
Of none, were free to break up Hildebrand,
Rebuild, he and Sordello, Charlemagne –
970 But garnished, Strength with Knowledge, 'if we deign
Accept that compromise and stoop to give
Rome law, the Caesar's Representative.'
Enough, that the illimitable flood
Of triumphs after triumphs, understood
In its faint reflux (you shall hear) sufficed
Young Ecelin for appanage, enticed
Him on till, these long quiet in their graves,
He found 'twas looked for that a whole life's braves
Should somehow be made good; so, weak and worn,
980 Must stagger up at Mílan, one grey morn
Of the to-come, and fight his latest fight.
But, Salinguerra's prophecy at height –
He voluble with a raised arm and stiff,
A blaring voice, a blazing eye, as if
He had our very Italy to keep
Or cast away, or gather in a heap

To garrison the better – ay, his word
Was, 'run the cucumber into a gourd,
Drive Trent upon Apulia' – at their pitch
990 Who spied the continents and islands which
Grew mulberry leaves and sickles, in the map –
(Strange that three such confessions so should hap
To Palma, Dante spoke with in the clear
Amorous silence of the Swooning-sphere, –
Cunizza, as he called her! Never ask
Of Palma more! She sat, knowing her task
Was done, the labour of it, – for, success
Concerned not Palma, passion's votaress.)
Triumph at height, and thus Sordello crowned –
1000 Above the passage suddenly a sound
Stops speech, stops walk: back shrinks Taurello, bids
With large involuntary asking lids,
Palma interpret. ''Tis his own foot-stamp –
Your hand! His summons! Nay, this idle damp
Befits not!' Out they two reeled dizzily.
'Visconti's strong at Mílan,' resumed he,
In the old, somewhat insignificant way –
(Was Palma wont, years afterward, to say)
As though the spirit's flight, sustained thus far,
1010 Dropped at that very instant.
                                    Gone they are –
Palma, Taurello; Eglamor anon,
Ecelin, – only Naddo's never gone!
– Labours, this moonrise, what the Master meant:
'Is Squarcialupo speckled? – purulent,
I'd say, but when was Providence put out?
He carries somehow handily about
His spite nor fouls himself!' Goito's vines
Stand like a cheat detected – stark rough lines,
The moon breaks through, a grey mean scale against
1020 The vault where, this eve's Maiden, thou remain'st
Like some fresh martyr, eyes fixed – who can tell?
As Heaven, now all's at end, did not so well,
Spite of the faith and victory, to leave
Its virgin quite to death in the lone eve.
While the persisting hermit-bee . . . ha! wait
No longer: these in compass, forward fate!

BOOK THE SIXTH

The thought of Eglamor's least like a thought,
And yet a false one, was, 'Man shrinks to naught
If matched with symbols of immensity;
Must quail, forsooth, before a quiet sky
Or sea, too little for their quietude':
And, truly, somewhat in Sordello's mood
Confirmed its speciousness, while eve slow sank
Down the near terrace to the farther bank,
And only one spot left from out the night
10   Glimmered upon the river opposite –
A breadth of watery heaven like a bay,
A sky-like space of water, ray for ray,
And star for star, one richness where they mixed
As this and that wing of an angel, fixed,
Tumultuary splendours folded in
To die. Nor turned he till Ferrara's din
(Say, the monotonous speech from a man's lip
Who lets some first and eager purpose slip
In a new fancy's birth – the speech keeps on
20   Though elsewhere its informing soul be gone)
– Aroused him, surely offered succour. Fate
Paused with this eve; ere she precipitate
Herself, – best put off new strange thoughts awhile,
That voice, those large hands, that portentous smile, –
What help to pierce the future as the past
Lay in the plaining city?
               And at last
The main discovery and prime concern,
All that just now imported him to learn,
Truth's self, like yonder slow moon to complete
30   Heaven, rose again, and, naked at his feet,
Lighted his old life's every shift and change,
Effort with counter-effort; nor the range
Of each looked wrong except wherein it checked,
Some other – which of these could he suspect,
Prying into them by the sudden blaze?
The real way seemed made up of all the ways –
Mood after mood of the one mind in him;
Tokens of the existence, bright or dim,

Of a transcendent all-embracing sense
40   Demanding only outward influence,
A soul, in Palma's phrase, above his soul,
Power to uplift his power, – such moon's control
Over such sea-depths, – and their mass had swept
Onward from the beginning and still kept
Its course: but years and years the sky above
Held none, and so, untasked of any love,
His sensitiveness idled, now amort,
Alive now, and, to sullenness or sport
Given wholly up, disposed itself anew
50   At every passing instigation, grew
And dwindled at caprice, in foam-showers spilt,
Wedge-like insisting, quivered now a gilt
Shield in the sunshine, now a blinding race
Of whitest ripples o'er the reef – found place
For much display; not gathered up and, hurled
Right from its heart, encompassing the world.
So had Sordello been, by consequence,
Without a function: others made pretence
To strength not half his own, yet had some core
60   Within, submitted to some moon, before
Them still, superior still whate'er their force, –
Were able therefore to fulfil a course,
Nor missed life's crown, authentic attribute.
To each who lives must be a certain fruit
Of having lived in his degree, – a stage,
Earlier or later in men's pilgrimage,
To stop at; and to this the spirits tend
Who, still discovering beauty without end,
Amass the scintillations, make one star
70   – Something unlike them, self-sustained, afar, –
And meanwhile nurse the dream of being blest
By winning it to notice and invest
Their souls with alien glory, some one day
Whene'er the nucleus, gathering shape alway,
Round to the perfect circle – soon or late,
According as themselves are formed to wait;
Whether mere human beauty will suffice
– The yellow hair and the luxurious eyes,
Or human intellect seem best, or each
80   Combine in some ideal form past reach

On earth, or else some shade of these, some aim,
Some love, hate even, take their place, the same,
So to be served – all this they do not lose,
Waiting for death to live, nor idly choose
What must be Hell – a progress thus pursued
Through all existence, still above the food
That's offered them, still fain to reach beyond
The widened range, in virtue of their bond
Of sovereignty. Not that a Palma's Love,
90   A Salinguerra's Hate, would equal prove
To swaying all Sordello: but why doubt
Some love meet for such strength, some moon without
Would match his sea ? – or fear, Good manifest,
Only the Best breaks faith ? – Ah but the Best
Somehow eludes us ever, still might be
And is not! Crave we gems ? No penury
Of their material round us! Pliant earth
And plastic flame – what balks the mage his birth
– Jacinth in balls or lodestone by the block?
100 Flinders enrich the strand, veins swell the rock;
Naught more! Seek creatures ? Life's i' the tempest, thought
Clothes the keen hill-top, mid-day woods are fraught
With fervours: human forms are well enough!
But we had hoped, encouraged by the stuff
Profuse at nature's pleasure, men beyond
These actual men! – and thus are over-fond
In arguing, from Good – the Best, from force
Divided – force combined, an ocean's course
From this our sea whose mere intestine pants
110 Might seem at times sufficient to our wants.
     External power! If none be adequate,
And he stand forth ordained (a prouder fate)
Himself a law to his own sphere ? 'Remove
All incompleteness!' for that law, that love ?
Nay, if all other laws be feints, – truth veiled
Helpfully to weak vision that had failed
To grasp aught but its special want, – for lure,
Embodied ? Stronger vision could endure
The unbodied want: no part – the whole of truth!
120 The People were himself; nor, by the ruth
At their condition, was he less impelled
To alter the discrepancy beheld,

Than if, from the sound whole, a sickly part
Subtracted were transformed, decked out with art,
Then palmed on him as alien woe – the Guelf
To succour, proud that he forsook himself.
All is himself; all service, therefore, rates
Alike, nor serving one part, immolates
The rest: but all in time! 'That lance of yours

130 Makes havoc soon with Malek and his Moors,
That buckler's lined with many a giant's beard
Ere long, our champion, be the lance upreared,
The buckler wielded handsomely as now!
But view your escort, bear in mind your vow,
Count the pale tracts of sand to pass ere that,
And, if you hope we struggle through the flat,
Put lance and buckler by! Next half-month lacks
Mere sturdy exercise of mace and axe
To cleave this dismal brake of prickly-pear

140 Which bristling holds Cydippe by the hair,
Lames barefoot Agathon: this felled, we'll try
The picturesque achievements by and by –
Next life!'
                Ay, rally, mock, O People, urge
Your claims! – for thus he ventured, to the verge,
Push a vain mummery which perchance distrust
Of his fast-slipping resolution thrust
Likewise: accordingly the Crowd – (as yet
He had unconsciously contrived forget
I' the whole, to dwell o' the points . . . one might assuage

150 The signal horrors easier than engage
With a dim vulgar vast unobvious grief.
Not to be fancied off, nor gained relief
In brilliant fits, cured by a happy quirk,
But by dim vulgar vast unobvious work
To correspond . . .) this Crowd then, forth they stood.
'And now content thy stronger vision, brood
On thy bare want; uncovered, turf by turf,
Study the corpse-face through the taint-worms' scurf!'
    Down sank the People's Then; uprose their Now.

160 These sad ones render service to! And how
Piteously little must that service prove
– Had surely proved in any case! for, move
Each other obstacle away, let youth

Become aware it had surprised a truth
'Twere service to impart – can truth be seized,
Settled forthwith, and, of the captive eased,
Its captor find fresh prey, since this alit
So happily, no gesture luring it,
The earnest of a flock to follow? Vain,
170 Most vain! a life to spend ere this he chain
To the poor crowd's complacence: ere the crowd
Pronounce it captured, he descries a cloud
Its kin of twice the plume; which he, in turn,
If he shall live as many lives, may learn
How to secure: not else. Then Mantua called
Back to his mind how certain bards were thralled
– Buds blasted, but of breath more like perfume
Than Naddo's staring nosegay's carrion bloom;
Some insane rose that burnt heart out in sweets,
180 A spendthrift in the spring, no summer greets;
Some Dularete, drunk with truths and wine,
Grown bestial, dreaming how become divine.
Yet to surmount this obstacle, commence
With the commencement, merits crowning! Hence
Must truth be casual truth, elicited
In sparks so mean, at intervals dispread
So rarely, that 'tis like at no one time
Of the world's story has not truth, the prime
Of truth, the very truth which, loosed, had hurled
190 The world's course right, been really in the world
– Content the while with some mean spark by dint
Of some chance-blow, the solitary hint
Of buried fire, which, rip earth's breast, would stream
Sky-ward!
            Sordello's miserable gleam
Was looked for at the moment: he would dash
This badge, and all it brought, to earth, – abash
Taurello thus, perhaps persuade him wrest
The Kaiser from his purpose, – would attest
His own belief, in any case. Before
200 He dashes it however, think once more!
For, were that little, truly service? 'Ay,
I' the end, no doubt; but meantime? Plain you spy
Its ultimate effect, but many flaws
Of vision blur each intervening cause.

Were the day's fraction clear as the life's sum
Of service, Now as filled as teems To-come
With evidence of good – nor too minute
A share to vie with evil! No dispute,
'Twere fitliest maintain the Guelfs in rule:
210 That makes your life's work: but you have to school
Your day's work on these natures circumstanced
Thus variously, which yet, as each advanced
Or might impede the Guelf rule, must be moved
Now, for the Then's sake, – hating what you loved,
Loving old hatreds! Nor if one man bore
Brand upon temples while his fellow wore
The aureole, would it task you to decide:
But, portioned duly out, the future vied
Never with the unparcelled present! Smite
220 Or spare so much on warrant all so slight?
The present's complete sympathies to break,
Aversions bear with, for a future's sake
So feeble? Tito ruined through one speck,
The Legate saved by his sole lightish fleck?
This were work, true, but work performed at cost
Of other work; aught gained here, elsewhere lost.
For a new segment spoil an orb half-done?
Rise with the People one step, and sink – one?
Were it but one step, less than the whole face
230 Of things, your novel duty bids erase!
Harms to abolish! What, the prophet saith,
The minstrel singeth vainly then? Old faith,
Old courage, only born because of harms,
Were not, from highest to the lowest, charms?
Flame may persist; but is not glare as staunch?
Where the salt marshes stagnate, crystals branch;
Blood dries to crimson; Evil's beautified
In every shape. Thrust Beauty then aside
And banish Evil! Wherefore? After all,
240 Is Evil a result less natural
Than Good? For overlook the seasons' strife
With tree and flower, – the hideous animal life,
(Of which who seeks shall find a grinning taunt
For his solution, and endure the vaunt
Of nature's angel, as a child that knows
Himself befooled, unable to propose

Aught better than the fooling) – and but care
For men, for the mere People then and there, –
In these, could you but see that Good and Ill
250 Claimed you alike! Whence rose their claim but still
From Ill, as fruit of Ill? What else could knit
You theirs but Sorrow? Any free from it
Were also free from you! Whose happiness
Could be distinguished in this morning's press
Of miseries? – the fool's who passed a gibe
"On thee," jeered he, "so wedded to thy tribe,
Thou carriest green and yellow tokens in
Thy very face that thou art Ghibellin!"
Much hold on you that fool obtained! Nay mount
260 Yet higher – and upon men's own account
Must Evil stay: for, what is joy? – to heave
Up one obstruction more, and common leave
What was peculiar, by such act destroy
Itself; a partial death is every joy;
The sensible escape, enfranchisement
Of a sphere's essence: once the vexed – content,
The cramped – at large, the growing circle – round,
All's to begin again – some novel bound
To break, some new enlargement to entreat;
270 The sphere though larger is not more complete.
Now for Mankind's experience: who alone
Might style the unobstructed world his own?
Whom palled Goito with its perfect things?
Sordello's self: whereas for Mankind springs
Salvation by each hindrance interposed.
They climb; life's view is not at once disclosed
To creatures caught up, on the summit left,
Heaven plain above them, yet of wings bereft:
But lower laid, as at the mountain's foot.
280 So, range on range, the girdling forests shoot
'Twixt your plain prospect and the throngs who scale
Height after height, and pierce mists, veil by veil,
Heartened with each discovery; in their soul,
The Whole they seek by Parts – but, found that Whole,
Could they revert, enjoy past gains? The space
Of time you judge so meagre to embrace
The Parts were more than plenty, once attained
The Whole, to quite exhaust it: naught were gained

But leave to look – not leave to do: Beneath
290   Soon sates the looker – look Above, and Death
Tempts ere a tithe of Life be tasted. Live
First, and die soon enough, Sordello! Give
Body and spirit the first right they claim,
And pasture soul on a voluptuous shame
That you, a pageant-city's denizen,
Are neither vilely lodged 'midst Lombard men –
Can force joy out of sorrow, seem to truck
Bright attributes away for sordid muck,
Yet manage from that very muck educe
300   Gold; then subject, nor scruple, to your cruce
The world's discardings! Though real ingots pay
Your pains, the clods that yielded them are clay
To all beside, – would clay remain, though quenched
Your purging-fire; who's robbed then? Had you wrenched
An ampler treasure forth! – As 'tis, they crave
A share that ruins you and will not save
Them. Why should sympathy command you quit
The course that makes your joy, nor will remit
Their woe? Would all arrive at joy? Reverse
310   The order (time instructs you) nor coerce
Each unit till, some predetermined mode,
The total be emancipate; men's road
Is one, men's times of travel many; thwart
No enterprising soul's precocious start
Before the general march! If slow or fast
All straggle up to the same point at last,
Why grudge your having gained, a month ago,
The brakes at balm-shed, asphodels in blow,
While they were landlocked? Speed their Then, but how
320   This badge would suffer you improve your Now!'
     His time of action for, against, or with
Our world (I labour to extract the pith
Of this his problem) grew, that even-tide,
Gigantic with its power of joy, beside
The world's eternity of impotence
To profit though at his whole joy's expense.
'Make nothing of my day because so brief?
Rather make more: instead of joy, use grief
Before its novelty have time subside!
330   Wait not for the late savour, leave untried

Virtue, the creaming honey-wine, quick squeeze
Vice like a biting spirit from the lees
Of life! Together let wrath, hatred, lust,
All tyrannies in every shape, be thrust
Upon this Now, which time may reason out
As mischiefs, far from benefits, no doubt;
But long ere then Sordello will have slipt
Away; you teach him at Goito's crypt,
There's a blank issue to that fiery thrill.
340 Stirring, the few cope with the many, still:
So much of sand as, quiet, makes a mass
Unable to produce three tufts of grass,
Shall, troubled by the whirlwind, render void
The whole calm glebe's endeavour: be employed!
And e'en though somewhat smart the Crowd for this,
Contribute each his pang to make your bliss,
'Tis but one pang – one blood-drop to the bowl
Which brimful tempts the sluggish asp uncowl
At last, stains ruddily the dull red cape,
350 And, kindling orbs grey as the unripe grape
Before, avails forthwith to disentrance
The portent, soon to lead a mystic dance
Among you! For, who sits alone in Rome?
Have those great hands indeed hewn out a home,
And set me there to live? Oh life, life-breath,
Life-blood, – ere sleep, come travail, life ere death!
This life stream on my soul, direct, oblique,
But always streaming! Hindrances? They pique:
Helps? such . . . but why repeat, my soul o'ertops
360 Each height, then every depth profoundlier drops?
Enough that I can live, and would live! Wait
For some transcendent life reserved by Fate
To follow this? Oh, never! Fate, I trust
The same, my soul to; for, as who flings dust,
Perchance (so facile was the deed) she chequed
The void with these materials to affect
My soul diversely: these consigned anew
To naught by death, what marvel if she threw
A second and superber spectacle
370 Before me? What may serve for sun, what still
Wander a moon above me? What else wind
About me like the pleasures left behind,

And how shall some new flesh that is not flesh
Cling to me? What's new laughter? Soothes the fresh
Sleep like sleep? Fate's exhaustless for my sake
In brave resource: but whether bids she slake
My thirst at this first rivulet, or count
No draught worth lip save from some rocky fount
Above i' the clouds, while here she's provident
380 Of pure loquacious pearl, the soft tree-tent
Guards, with its face of reate and sedge, nor fail
The silver globules and gold-sparkling grail
At bottom? Oh, 'twere too absurd to slight
For the hereafter the today's delight!
Quench thirst at this, then seek next well-spring: wear
Home-lilies ere strange lotus in my hair!
Here is the Crowd, whom I with freest heart
Offer to serve, contented for my part
To give life up in service, – only grant
390 That I do serve; if otherwise, why want
Aught further of me? If men cannot choose
But set aside life, why should I refuse
The gift? I take it – I, for one, engage
Never to falter through my pilgrimage –
Nor end it howling that the stock or stone
Were enviable, truly: I, for one,
Will praise the world, you style mere anteroom
To palace – be it so! shall I assume
– My foot the courtly gait, my tongue the trope,
400 My mouth the smirk, before the doors fly ope
One moment? What? with guarders row on row,
Gay swarms of varletry that come and go,
Pages to dice with, waiting-girls unlace
The plackets of, pert claimants help displace,
Heart-heavy suitors get a rank for, – laugh
At yon sleek parasite, break his own staff
'Cross Beetle-brows the Usher's shoulder, – why
Admitted to the presence by and by,
Should thought of having lost these make me grieve
410 Among new joys I reach, for joys I leave?
Cool citrine-crystals, fierce pyropus-stone,
Are floor-work there! But do I let alone
That black-eyed peasant in the vestibule
Once and for ever? – Floor-work? No such fool!

Rather, were heaven to forestall earth, I'd say
I, is it, must be blest? Then, my own way
Bless me! Giver firmer arm and fleeter foot,
I'll thank you: but to no mad wings transmute
These limbs of mine – our greensward was so soft!
420 Nor camp I on the thunder-cloud aloft:
We feel the bliss distinctlier, having thus
Engines subservient, not mixed up with us.
Better move palpably through heaven: nor, freed
Of flesh, forsooth, from space to space proceed
'Mid flying synods of worlds! No: in heaven's marge
Show Titan still, recumbent o'er his targe
Solid with stars – the Centaur at his game,
Made tremulously out in hoary flame!
　　'Life! Yet the very cup whose extreme dull
430 Dregs, even, I would quaff, was dashed, at full,
Aside so oft; the death I fly, revealed
So oft a better life this life concealed,
And which sage, champion, martyr, through each path
Have hunted fearlessly – the horrid bath,
The crippling-irons and the fiery chair.
'Twas well for them; let me become aware
As they, and I relinquish life, too! Let
What masters life disclose itself! Forget
Vain ordinances, I have one appeal –
440 I feel, am what I feel, know what I feel;
So much is truth to me. What Is, then? Since
One object, viewed diversely, may evince
Beauty and ugliness – this way attract,
That way repel, – why gloze upon the fact?
Why must a single of the sides be right?
What bids choose this and leave the opposite?
Where's abstract Right for me? – in youth endued
With Right still present, still to be pursued,
Through all the interchange of circles, rife
450 Each with its proper law and mode of life,
Each to be dwelt at ease in: where, to sway
Absolute with the Kaiser, or obey
Implicit with his serf of fluttering heart,
Or, like a sudden thought of God's, to start
Up, Brutus in the presence, then go shout
That some should pick the unstrung jewels out –

Each, well!'
        And, as in moments when the past
Gave partially enfranchisement, he cast
Himself quite through mere secondary states
460 Of his soul's essence, little loves and hates,
Into the mid deep yearnings overlaid
By these; as who should pierce hill, plain, grove, glade,
And on into the very nucleus probe
That first determined there exist a globe.
As that were easiest, half the globe dissolved,
So seemed Sordello's closing-truth evolved
By his flesh-half's break-up; the sudden swell
Of his expanding soul showed Ill and Well,
Sorrow and Joy, Beauty and Ugliness,
470 Virtue and Vice, the Larger and the Less,
All qualities, in fine, recorded here,
Might be but modes of Time and this one sphere,
Urgent on these, but not of force to bind
Eternity, as Time – as Matter – Mind,
If Mind, Eternity, should choose assert
Their attributes within a Life: thus girt
With circumstance, next change beholds them cinct
Quite otherwise – with Good and Ill distinct,
Joys, sorrows, tending to a like result –
480 Contrived to render easy, difficult,
This or the other course of . . . what new bond
In place of flesh may stop their flight beyond
Its new sphere, as that course does harm or good
To its arrangements. Once this understood,
As suddenly he felt himself alone,
Quite out of Time and this world: all was known.
What made the secret of his past despair?
– Most imminent when he seemed most aware
Of his own self-sufficiency: made mad
490 By craving to expand the power he had,
And not new power to be expanded? – just
This made it; Soul on Matter being thrust,
Joy comes when so much Soul is wreaked in Time
On Matter: let the Soul's attempt sublime
Matter beyond the scheme and so prevent
By more or less that deed's accomplishment,
And Sorrow follows: Sorrow how avoid?

Let the employer match the thing employed,
Fit to the finite his infinity,
500 And thus proceed for ever, in degree
Changed but in kind the same, still limited
To the appointed circumstance and dead
To all beyond. A sphere is but a sphere;
Small, Great, are merely terms we bandy here;
Since to the spirit's absoluteness all
Are like. Now, of the present sphere we call
Life, are conditions; take but this among
Many; the body was to be so long
Youthful, no longer: but, since no control
510 Tied to that body's purposes his soul,
She chose to understand the body's trade
More than the body's self – had fain conveyed
Her boundless to the body's bounded lot.
Hence, the soul permanent, the body not, –
Scarcely its minute for enjoying here, –
The soul must needs instruct her weak compeer,
Run o'er its capabilities and wring
A joy thence, she held worth experiencing:
Which, far from half discovered even, – lo,
520 The minute gone, the body's power let go
Apportioned to that joy's acquirement! Broke
Morning o'er earth, he yearned for all it woke –
From the volcano's vapour-flag, winds hoist
Black o'er the spread of sea, – down to the moist
Dale's silken barley-spikes sullied with rain,
Swayed earthwards, heavily to rise again –
The Small, a sphere as perfect as the Great
To the soul's absoluteness. Meditate
Too long on such a morning's cluster-chord
530 And the whole music it was framed afford, –
The chord's might half discovered, what should pluck
One string, his finger, was found palsy-struck.
And then no marvel if the spirit, shown
A saddest sight – the body lost alone
Through her officious proffered help, deprived
Of this and that enjoyment Fate contrived, –
Virtue, Good, Beauty, each allowed slip hence, –
Vain-gloriously were fain, for recompense,
To stem the ruin even yet, protract

540 The body's term, supply the power it lacked
From her infinity, compel it learn
These qualities were only Time's concern,
And body may, with spirit helping, barred –
Advance the same, vanquished – obtain reward,
Reap joy where sorrow was intended grow,
Of Wrong make Right, and turn Ill Good below.
And the result is, the poor body soon
Sinks under what was meant a wondrous boon,
Leaving its bright accomplice all aghast.

550 So much was plain then, proper in the past;
To be complete for, satisfy the whole
Series of spheres – Eternity, his soul
Needs must exceed, prove incomplete for, each
Single sphere – Time. But does our knowledge reach
No farther? Is the cloud of hindrance broke
But by the failing of the fleshly yoke,
Its loves and hates, as now when death lets soar
Sordello, self-sufficient as before,
Though during the mere space that shall elapse

560 'Twixt his enthralment in new bonds perhaps?
Must life be ever just escaped, which should
Have been enjoyed? – nay, might have been and would,
Each purpose ordered right – the soul's no whit
Beyond the body's purpose under it.
Like yonder breadth of watery heaven, a bay,
And that sky-space of water, ray for ray
And star for star, one richness where they mixed
As this and that wing of an angel, fixed,
Tumultuary splendours folded in

570 To die – would soul, proportioned thus, begin
Exciting discontent, or surelier quell
The body if, aspiring, it rebel?
But how so order life? Still brutalize
The soul, the sad world's way, with muffled eyes
To all that was before, all that shall be
After this sphere – all and each quality
Save some sole and immutable Great, Good
And Beauteous whither fate has loosed its hood
To follow? Never may some soul see All

580 – The Great Before and After, and the Small
Now, yet be saved by this the simplest lore,

And take the single course prescribed before,
As the king-bird with ages on his plumes
Travels to die in his ancestral glooms?
But where descry the Love that shall select
That course? Here is a soul whom, to affect,
Nature has plied with all her means, from trees
And flowers e'en to the Multitude! – and these,
Decides he save or no? One word to end!

590   Ah my Sordello, I this once befriend
And speak for you. Of a Power above you still
Which, utterly incomprehensible,
Is out of rivalry, which thus you can
Love, though unloving all conceived by man –
What need! And of – none the minutest duct
To that out-nature, naught that would instruct
And so let rivalry begin to live –
But of a Power its representative
Who, being for authority the same,

600   Communication different, should claim
A course, the first chose but this last revealed –
This Human clear, as that Divine concealed –
What utter need!

               What has Sordello found?
Or can his spirit go the mighty round,
End where poor Eglamor begun? So, says
Old fable, the two eagles went two ways
About the world: where, in the midst, they met,
Though on a shifting waste of sand, men set
Jove's temple. Quick, what has Sordello found?

610   For they approach – approach – that foot's rebound
Palma? No, Salinguerra though in mail;
They mount, have reached the threshold, dash the veil
Aside – and you divine who sat there dead,
Under his foot the badge: still, Palma said,
A triumph lingering in the wide eyes,
Wider than some spent swimmer's if he spies
Help from above in his extreme despair,
And, head far back on shoulder thrust, turns there
With short quick passionate cry: as Palma pressed

620   In one great kiss, her lips upon his breast,
It beat.

          By this, the hermit-bee has stopped

His day's toil at Goito: the new-cropped
Dead vine-leaf answers, now 'tis eve, he bit,
Twirled so, and filed all day: the mansion's fit,
God counselled for. As easy guess the word
That passed betwixt them, and become the third
To the soft small unfrighted bee, as tax
Him with one fault – so, no remembrance racks
Of the stone maidens and the font of stone
630 He, creeping through the crevice, leaves alone.
Alas, my friend, alas Sordello, whom
Anon they laid within that old font-tomb,
And, yet again, alas!
               And now is't worth
Our while bring back to mind, much less set forth
How Salinguerra extricates himself
Without Sordello? Ghibellin and Guelf
May fight their fiercest out? If Richard sulked
In durance or the Marquis paid his mulct,
Who cares, Sordello gone? The upshot, sure,
640 Was peace; our chief made some frank overture
That prospered; compliment fell thick and fast
On its disposer, and Taurello passed
With foe and friend for an outstripping soul,
Nine days at least. Then, – fairly reached the goal, –
He, by one effort, blotted the great hope
Out of his mind, nor further tried to cope
With Este, that mad evening's style, but sent
Away the Legate and the League, content
No blame at least the brothers had incurred,
650 – Dispatched a message to the Monk, he heard
Patiently first to last, scarce shivered at,
Then curled his limbs up on his wolfskin mat
And ne'er spoke more, – informed the Ferrarese
He but retained their rule so long as these
Lingered in pupilage, – and last, no mode
Apparent else of keeping safe the road
From Germany direct to Lombardy
For Friedrich, – none, that is, to guarantee
The faith and promptitude of who should next
660 Obtain Sofia's dowry, – sore perplexed –
(Sofia being youngest of the tribe
Of daughters, Ecelin was wont to bribe

The envious magnates with – nor, since he sent
Henry of Egna this fair child, had Trent
Once failed the Kaiser's purposes – 'we lost
Egna last year, and who takes Egna's post –
Opens the Lombard gate if Friedrich knock?')
Himself espoused the Lady of the Rock
In pure necessity, and, so destroyed
670 His slender last of chances, quite made void
Old prophecy, and spite of all the schemes
Overt and covert, youth's deeds, age's dreams,
Was sucked into Romano. And so hushed
He up this evening's work that, when 'twas brushed
Somehow against by a blind chronicle
Which, chronicling whatever woe befell
Ferrara, noted this the obscure woe
Of 'Salinguerra's sole son Giacomo
Deceased, fatuous and doting, ere his sire,'
680 The townsfolk rubbed their eyes, could but admire
Which of Sofia's five was meant.
                                        The chaps
Of earth's dead hope were tardy to collapse,
Obliterated not the beautiful
Distinctive features at a crash: but dull
And duller these, next year, as Guelfs withdrew
Each to his stronghold. Then (securely too
Ecelin at Campese slept; close by,
Who likes may see him in Solagna lie,
With cushioned head and gloved hand to denote
690 The cavalier he was) – then his heart smote
Young Ecelin at last; long since adult.
And, save Vicenza's business, what result
In blood and blaze? (So hard to intercept
Sordello till his plain withdrawal!) Stepped
Then its new lord on Lombardy. I' the nick
Of time when Ecelin and Alberic
Closed with Taurello, came precisely news
That in Verona half the souls refuse
Allegiance to the Marquis and the Count –
700 Have cast them from a throne they bid him mount,
Their Podestà, through his ancestral worth.
Ecelin flew there, and the town henceforth
Was wholly his – Taurello sinking back

From temporary station to a track
That suited. News received of this acquist,
Friedrich did come to Lombardy: who missed
Taurello then? Another year: they took
Vicenza, left the Marquis scarce a nook
For refuge, and, when hundreds two or three
710   Of Guelfs conspired to call themselves 'The Free,'
Opposing Alberic, – vile Bassanese, –
(Without Sordello!) – Ecelin at ease
Slaughtered them so observably, that oft
A little Salinguerra looked with soft
Blue eyes up, asked his sire the proper age
To get appointed his proud uncle's page.
More years passed, and that sire had dwindled down
To a mere showy turbulent soldier, grown
Better through age, his parts still in repute,
720   Subtle – how else? – but hardly so astute
As his contemporaneous friends professed;
Undoubtedly a brawler: for the rest,
Known by each neighbour, and allowed for, let
Keep his incorrigible ways, nor fret
Men who would miss their boyhood's bugbear: 'trap
The ostrich, suffer our bald osprey flap
A battered pinion!' – was the word. In fine,
One flap too much and Venice's marine
Was meddled with; no overlooking that!
730   She captured him in his Ferrara, fat
And florid at a banquet, more by fraud
Than force, to speak the truth; there's slender laud
Ascribed you for assisting eighty years
To pull his death on such a man; fate shears
The life-cord prompt enough whose last fine thread
You fritter: so, presiding his board-head,
The old smile, your assurance all went well
With Friedrich (as if he were like to tell!)
In rushed (a plan contrived before) our friends,
740   Made some pretence at fighting, some amends
For the shame done his eighty years – (apart
The principle, none found it in his heart
To be much angry with Taurello) – gained
Their galleys with the prize, and what remained
But carry him to Venice for a show?

      – Set him, as 'twere, down gently – free to go
      His gait, inspect our square, pretend observe
      The swallows soaring their eternal curve
      'Twixt Theodore and Mark, if citizens
750 Gathered importunately, fives and tens,
      To point their children the Magnifico,
      All but a monarch once in firm-land, go
      His gait among them now – 'it took, indeed,
      Fully this Ecelin to supersede
      That man,' remarked the seniors. Singular!
      Sordello's inability to bar
      Rivals the stage, that evening, mainly brought
      About by his strange disbelief that aught
      Was ever to be done, – this thrust the Twain
760 Under Taurello's tutelage, – whom, brain
      And heart and hand, he forthwith in one rod
      Indissolubly bound to baffle God
      Who loves the world – and thus allowed the thin
      Grey wizened dwarfish devil Ecelin,
      And massy-muscled big-boned Alberic
      (Mere man, alas!) to put his problem quick
      To demonstration – prove wherever's will
      To do, there's plenty to be done, or ill
      Or good. Anointed, then, to rend and rip –
770 Kings of the gag and flesh-hook, screw and whip,
      They plagued the world: a touch of Hildebrand
      (So far from obsolete!) made Lombards band
      Together, cross their coats as for Christ's cause,
      And saving Mílan win the world's applause.
      Ecelin perished: and I think grass grew
      Never so pleasant as in Valley Rù
      By San Zenon where Alberic in turn
      Saw his exasperated captors burn
      Seven children and their mother; then, regaled
780 So far, tied on to a wild horse, was trailed
      To death through raunce and bramble-bush. I take
      God's part and testify that 'mid the brake
      Wild o'er his castle on the pleasant knoll,
      You hear its one tower left, a belfry, toll –
      The earthquake spared it last year, laying flat
      The modern church beneath, – no harm in that!
      Chirrups the contumacious grasshopper,

Rustles the lizard and the cushats chirre
Above the ravage: there, at deep of day
790   A week since, heard I the old Canon say
He saw with his own eyes a barrow burst
And Alberic's huge skeleton unhearsed
Only five years ago. He added, 'June's
The month for carding off our first cocoons
The silkworms fabricate' – a double news,
Nor he nor I could tell the worthier. Choose!
    And Naddo gone, all's gone; not Eglamor!
Believe, I knew the face I waited for,
A guest my spirit of the golden courts!
800   Oh strange to see how, despite ill-reports,
Disuse, some wear of years, that face retained
Its joyous look of love! Suns waxed and waned,
And still my spirit held an upward flight,
Spiral on spiral, gyres of life and light
More and more gorgeous – ever that face there
The last admitted! crossed, too, with some care
As perfect triumph were not sure for all,
But, on a few, enduring damp must fall,
– A transient struggle, haply a painful sense
810   Of the inferior nature's clinging – whence
Slight starting tears easily wiped away,
Fine jealousies soon stifled in the play
Of irrepressible admiration – not
Aspiring, all considered, to their lot
Who ever, just as they prepare ascend
Spiral on spiral, wish thee well, impend
Thy frank delight at their exclusive track,
That upturned fervid face and hair put back!
    Is there no more to say? He of the rhymes –
820   Many a tale, of this retreat betimes,
Was born: Sordello die at once for men?
The Chroniclers of Mantua tired their pen
Telling how *Sordello Prince Visconti* saved
Mantua, and elsewhere notably behaved –
Who thus, by fortune ordering events,
Passed with posterity, to all intents,
For just the god he never could become.
As Knight, Bard, Gallant, men were never dumb
In praise of him: while what he should have been,

830 Could be, and was not – the one step too mean
For him to take, – we suffer at this day
Because of: Ecelin had pushed away
Its chance ere Dante could arrive and take
That step Sordello spurned, for the world's sake:
He did much – but Sordello's chance was gone.
Thus, had Sordello dared that step alone,
Apollo had been compassed: 'twas a fit
He wished should go to him, not he to it
– As one content to merely be supposed
840 Singing or fighting elsewhere, while he dozed
Really at home – one who was chiefly glad
To have achieved the few real deeds he had,
Because that way assured they were not worth
Doing, so spared from doing them henceforth –
A tree that covets fruitage and yet tastes
Never itself, itself. Had he embraced
Their cause then, men had plucked Hesperian fruit
And, praising that, just thrown him in to boot
All he was anxious to appear, but scarce
850 Solicitous to be. A sorry farce
Such life is, after all! Cannot I say
He lived for some one better thing? this way. –
Lo, on a heathy brown and nameless hill
By sparkling Asolo, in mist and chill,
Morning just up, higher and higher runs
A child barefoot and rosy. See! the sun's
On the square castle's inner-court's low wall
Like the chine of some extinct animal
Half turned to earth and flowers; and through the haze
860 (Save where some slender patches of grey maize
Are to be overleaped) that boy has crossed
The whole hill-side of dew and powder-frost
Matting the balm and mountain camomile.
Up and up goes he, singing all the while
Some unintelligible words to beat
The lark, God's poet, swooning at his feet,
So worsted is he at 'the few fine locks
Stained like pale honey oozed from topmost rocks
Sun-blanched the livelong summer,' – all that's left
870 Of the Goito lay! And thus bereft,
Sleep and forget, Sordello! In effect

He sleeps, the feverish poet – I suspect
Not utterly companionless; but, friends,
Wake up! The ghost's gone, and the story ends
I'd fain hope, sweetly; seeing, peri or ghoul,
That spirits are conjectured fair or foul,
Evil or good, judicious authors think,
According as they vanish in a stink
Or in a perfume. Friends, be frank! ye snuff
880 Civet, I warrant. Really? Like enough!
Merely the savour's rareness; any nose
May ravage with impunity a rose:
Rifle a musk-pod and 'twill ache like yours!
I'd tell you that same pungency ensures
An after-gust, but that were overbold.
Who would has heard Sordello's story told.

Pippa Passes:

A Drama

1841

I dedicate my best intentions, in this Poem,
admiringly to the author of *Ion*,
affectionately to Mr Sergeant Talfourd.

R.B.

London: 1841

PERSONS

Pippa
Ottima
Sebald
Foreign Students
Gottlieb
Schramm
Jules
Phene
Austrian Police
Bluphocks
Luigi and his Mother
Poor Girls
Monsignor and his Attendants

Pippa Passes

INTRODUCTION
NEW YEAR'S DAY AT ASOLO IN THE TREVISAN

Scene : A large mean airy chamber. A girl, PIPPA, *from the Silk-mills, springing out of bed.*

Day!
Faster and more fast,
O'er night's brim, day boils at last:
Boils, pure gold, o'er the cloud-cup's brim
Where spurting and suppressed it lay,
For not a froth-flake touched the rim
Of yonder gap in the solid grey
Of the eastern cloud, an hour away;
But forth one wavelet, then another, curled,
10   Till the whole sunrise, not to be suppressed,
Rose, reddened, and its seething breast
Flickered in bounds, grew gold, then overflowed the world.

Oh, Day, if I squander a wavelet of thee,
A mite of my twelve hours' treasure,
The least of thy gazes or glances,
(Be they grants thou art bound to or gifts above measure)
One of thy choices or one of thy chances,
(Be they tasks God imposed thee or freaks at thy pleasure)
– My Day, if I squander such labour or leisure,
20   Then shame fall on Asolo, mischief on me!

Thy long blue solemn hours serenely flowing,
Whence earth, we feel, gets steady help and good –
Thy fitful sunshine-minutes, coming, going,
As if earth turned from work in gamesome mood –
All shall be mine! But thou must treat me not
As prosperous ones are treated, those who live
At hand here, and enjoy the higher lot,
In readiness to take what thou wilt give,
And free to let alone what thou refusest;
30   For, Day, my holiday, if thou ill-usest
Me, who am only Pippa, – old-year's sorrow,
Cast off last night, will come again tomorrow:

Whereas, if thou prove gentle, I shall borrow
Sufficient strength of thee for new-year's sorrow.
All other men and women that this earth
Belongs to, who all days alike possess,
Make general plenty cure particular dearth,
Get more joy one way, if another, less:
Thou art my single day, God lends to leaven
40   What were all earth else, with a feel of heaven, –
Sole light that helps me through the year, thy sun's!
Try now! Take Asolo's Four Happiest Ones –
And let thy morning rain on that superb
Great haughty Ottima; can rain disturb
Her Sebald's homage? All the while thy rain
Beats fiercest on her shrub-house window-pane,
He will but press the closer, breathe more warm
Against her cheek; how should she mind the storm?
And, morning past, if midday shed a gloom
50   O'er Jules and Phene, – what care bride and groom
Save for their dear selves? 'Tis their marriage-day;
And while they leave church and go home their way,
Hand clasping hand, within each breast would be
Sunbeams and pleasant weather spite of thee.
Then, for another trial, obscure thy eve
With mist, – will Luigi and his mother grieve –
The lady and her child, unmatched, forsooth,
She in her age, as Luigi in his youth,
For true content? The cheerful town, warm, close
60   And safe, the sooner that thou art morose,
Receives them. And yet once again, outbreak
In storm at night on Monsignor, they make
Such stir about, – whom they expect from Rome
To visit Asolo, his brothers' home,
And say here masses proper to release
A soul from pain, – what storm dares hurt his peace?
Calm would he pray, with his own thoughts to ward
Thy thunder off, nor want the angels' guard.
But Pippa – just one such mischance would spoil
70   Her day that lightens the next twelvemonth's toil
At wearisome silk-winding, coil on coil!
    And here I let time slip for naught!
Aha, you foolhardy sunbeam, caught
With a single splash from my ewer!

You that would mock the best pursuer,
Was my basin over-deep?
One splash of water ruins you asleep,
And up, up, fleet your brilliant bits
Wheeling and counterwheeling,
80   Reeling, broken beyond healing:
Now grow together on the ceiling!
That will task your wits.
Whoever it was quenched fire first, hoped to see
Morsel after morsel flee
As merrily, as giddily . . .
Meantime, what lights my sunbeam on,
Where settles by degrees the radiant cripple?
Oh, is it surely blown, my martagon?
New-blown and ruddy as Saint Agnes' nipple,
90   Plump as the flesh-bunch on some Turk bird's poll!
Be sure if corals, branching 'neath the ripple
Of ocean, bud there, – fairies watch unroll
Such turban-flowers; I say, such lamps disperse
Thick red flame through that dusk green universe!
I am queen of thee, floweret!
And each fleshy blossom
Preserve I not – (safer
Than leaves that embower it,
Or shells that embosom)
100   – From weevil and chafer?
Laugh through my pane then; solicit the bee;
Gibe him, be sure; and, in midst of thy glee,
Love thy queen, worship me!

– Worship whom else? For am I not, this day,
Whate'er I please? What shall I please today?
My morn, noon, eve and night – how spend my day?
Tomorrow I must be Pippa who winds silk,
The whole year round, to earn just bread and milk:
But, this one day, I have leave to go,
110   And play out my fancy's fullest games;
I may fancy all day – and it shall be so –
That I taste of the pleasures, am called by the names
Of the Happiest Four in our Asolo!

See! Up the hill-side yonder, through the morning,
Some one shall love me, as the world calls love:
I am no less than Ottima, take warning!
The gardens, and the great stone house above,
And other house for shrubs, all glass in front,
Are mine; where Sebald steals, as he is wont,
120 To court me, while old Luca yet reposes:
And therefore, till the shrub-house door uncloses,
I ... what now? – give abundant cause for prate
About me – Ottima, I mean – of late,
Too bold, too confident she'll still face down
The spitefullest of talkers in our town.
How we talk in the little town below!
    But love, love, love – there's better love, I know!
This foolish love was only day's first offer;
I choose my next love to defy the scoffer:
130 For do not our Bride and Bridegroom sally
Out of Possagno church at noon?
Their house looks over Orcana valley:
Why should not I be the bride as soon
As Ottima? For I saw, beside,
Arrive last night that little bride –
Saw, if you call it seeing her, one flash
Of the pale snow-pure cheek and black bright tresses,
Blacker than all except the black eyelash;
I wonder she contrives those lids no dresses!
140 – So strict was she, the veil
Should cover close her pale
Pure cheeks – a bride to look at and scarce touch,
Scarce touch, remember, Jules! For are not such
Used to be tended, flower-like, every feature,
As if one's breath would fray the lily of a creature?
A soft and easy life these ladies lead:
Whiteness in us were wonderful indeed.
Oh, save that brow its virgin dimness,
Keep that foot its lady primness,
150 Let those ankles never swerve
From their exquisite reserve,
Yet have to trip along the streets like me,
All but naked to the knee!
How will she ever grant her Jules a bliss

So startling as her real first infant kiss?
Oh no, – not envy, this!

– Not envy, sure! – for if you gave me
Leave to take or to refuse,
In earnest, do you think I'd choose
160   That sort of new love to enslave me?
Mine should have lapped me round from the beginning;
As little fear of losing it as winning:
Lovers grow cold, men learn to hate their wives,
And only parents' love can last our lives.
At eve the Son and Mother, gentle pair,
Commune inside our turret: what prevents
My being Luigi? While that mossy lair
Of lizards through the winter-time is stirred
With each to each imparting sweet intents
170   For this new-year, as brooding bird to bird –
(For I observe of late, the evening walk
Of Luigi and his mother, always ends
Inside our ruined turret, where they talk,
Calmer than lovers, yet more kind than friends)
– Let me be cared about, kept out of harm,
And schemed for, safe in love as with a charm;
Let me be Luigi! If I only knew
What was my mother's face – my father, too!
   Nay, if you come to that, best love of all
180   Is God's; then why not have God's love befall
Myself as, in the palace by the Dome,
Monsignor? – who tonight will bless the home
Of his dead brother; and God bless in turn
That heart which beats, those eyes which mildly burn
With love for all men! I, tonight at least,
Would be that holy and beloved priest.

Now wait! – even I already seem to share
In God's love: what does New-year's hymn declare?
What other meaning do these verses bear?

190   *All service ranks the same with God:*
             If now, as formerly he trod
             Paradise, his presence fills

Our earth, each only as God wills
Can work – God's puppets, best and worst,
Are we ; there is no last nor first.

Say not 'a small event !' Why 'small' ?
Costs it more pain that this, ye call
A 'great event,' should come to pass,
Than that ? Untwine me from the mass
200 *Of deeds which make up life, one deed*
Power shall fall short in or exceed !

And more of it, and more of it ! – oh yes –
I will pass each, and see their happiness,
And envy none – being just as great, no doubt,
Useful to men, and dear to God, as they !
A pretty thing to care about
So mightily, this single holiday !
But let the sun shine ! Wherefore repine ?
– With thee to lead me, O Day of mine,
210 Down the grass path grey with dew,
Under the pine-wood, blind with boughs,
Where the swallow never flew
Nor yet cicala dared carouse –
No, dared carouse !
        [*She enters the street*]

PART I
MORNING

Scene : Up the Hill-side, inside the Shrub-House.
LUCA's *wife,* OTTIMA, *and her paramour, the German* SEBALD.

  SEBALD[*sings*]:

            Let the watching lids wink !
            Day's a-blaze with eyes, think !
            Deep into the night, drink !

OTTIMA: Night ? Such may be your Rhine-land nights perhaps;
    But this blood-red beam through the shutter's chink
    – We call such light, the morning: let us see !
    Mind how you grope your way, though ! How these tall

Naked geraniums straggle! Push the lattice
Behind that frame! – Nay, do I bid you? – Sebald,
10 It shakes the dust down on me! Why, of course
The slide-bolt catches. Well, are you content,
Or must I find you something else to spoil?
Kiss and be friends, my Sebald! Is't full morning?
Oh, don't speak then!
SEBALD: Ay, thus it used to be.
Ever your house was, I remember, shut
Till midday; I observed that, as I strolled
On mornings through the vale here; country girls
Were noisy, washing garments in the brook,
Hinds drove the slow white oxen up the hills:
20 But no, your house was mute, would ope no eye.
And wisely: you were plotting one thing there,
Nature, another outside. I looked up –
Rough white wood shutters, rusty iron bars,
Silent as death, blind in a flood of light.
Oh, I remember! – and the peasants laughed
And said, 'The old man sleeps with the young wife.'
This house was his, this chair, this window – his.
OTTIMA: Ah, the clear morning! I can see Saint Mark's;
That black streak is the belfry. Stop: Vicenza
30 Should lie ... there's Padua, plain enough, that blue!
Look o'er my shoulder, follow my finger!
SEBALD: Morning?
It seems to me a night with a sun added.
Where's dew, where's freshness? That bruised plant, I
  bruised
In getting through the lattice yestereve,
Droops as it did. See, here's my elbow's mark
I' the dust o' the sill.
OTTIMA: Oh, shut the lattice, pray!
SEBALD: Let me lean out. I cannot scent blood here,
Foul as the morn may be.
        There, shut the world out!
How do you feel now, Ottima? There, curse
40 The world and all outside! Let us throw off
This mask: how do you bear yourself? Let's out
With all of it.
OTTIMA: Best never speak of it.
SEBALD: Best speak again and yet again of it,

Till words cease to be more than words. 'His blood,'
For instance – let those two words mean 'His blood'
And nothing more. Notice, I'll say them now,
'His blood.'

OTTIMA: Assuredly if I repented
The deed –

SEBALD: Repent? Who should repent, or why?
What puts that in your head? Did I once say

50 That I repented?

OTTIMA: No, I said the deed . . .

SEBALD: 'The deed' and 'the event' – just now it was
'Our passion's fruit' – the devil take such cant!
Say, once and always, Luca was a wittol,
I am his cut-throat, you are . . .

OTTIMA: Here's the wine;
I brought it when we left the house above,
And glasses too – wine of both sorts. Black? White then?

SEBALD: But am not I his cut-throat? What are you?

OTTIMA: There trudges on his business from the Duomo
Benet the Capuchin, with his brown hood

60 And bare feet; always in one place at church,
Close under the stone wall by the south entry.
I used to take him for a brown cold piece
Of the wall's self, as out of it he rose
To let me pass – at first, I say, I used:
Now, so has that dumb figure fastened on me,
I rather should account the plastered wall
A piece of him, so chilly does it strike.
This, Sebald?

SEBALD: No, the white wine – the white wine!
Well, Ottima, I promised no new year

70 Should rise on us the ancient shameful way;
Nor does it rise. Pour on! To your black eyes!
Do you remember last damned New Year's day?

OTTIMA: You brought those foreign prints. We looked at them
Over the wine and fruit. I had to scheme
To get him from the fire. Nothing but saying
His own set wants the proof-mark, roused him up
To hunt them out.

SEBALD: 'Faith, he is not alive
To fondle you before my face.

OTTIMA: Do you

Fondle me then! Who means to take your life
80   For that, my Sebald?
SEBALD: Hark you, Ottima!
One thing to guard against. We'll not make much
One of the other – that is, not make more
Parade of warmth, childish officious coil,
Than yesterday: as if, sweet, I supposed
Proof upon proof were needed now, now first,
To show I love you – yes, still love you – love you
In spite of Luca and what's come to him
– Sure sign we had him ever in our thoughts,
White sneering old reproachful face and all!
90   We'll even quarrel, love, at times, as if
We still could lose each other, were not tied
By this: conceive you?
OTTIMA: Love!
SEBALD: Not tied so sure.
Because though I was wrought upon, have struck
His insolence back into him – am I
So surely yours? – therefore forever yours?
OTTIMA: Love, to be wise, (one counsel pays another)
Should we have – months ago, when first we loved,
For instance that May morning we two stole
Under the green ascent of sycamores –
100   If we had come upon a thing like that
Suddenly...
SEBALD: 'A thing' – there again – 'a thing!'
OTTIMA: Then, Venus' body, had we come upon
My husband Luca Gaddi's murdered corpse
Within there, at his couch-foot, covered close –
Would you have pored upon it? Why persist
In poring now upon it? For 'tis here
As much as there in the deserted house:
You cannot rid your eyes of it. For me,
Now he is dead I hate him worse: I hate...
110   Dare you stay here? I would go back and hold
His two dead hands, and say, 'I hate you worse,
Luca, than...'
SEBALD: Off, off – take your hands off mine,
'Tis the hot evening – off! oh, morning is it?
OTTIMA: There's one thing must be done; you know what thing.
Come in and help to carry. We may sleep

Anywhere in the whole wide house tonight.

SEBALD: What would come, think you, if we let him lie
Just as he is? Let him lie there until
The angels take him! He is turned by this
120   Off from his face beside, as you will see.

OTTIMA: This dusty pane might serve for looking-glass.
Three, four – four grey hairs! Is it so you said
A plait of hair should wave across my neck?
No – this way.

SEBALD: Ottima, I would give your neck,
Each splendid shoulder, both those breasts of yours,
That this were undone! Killing! Kill the world,
So Luca lives again! – ay, lives to sputter
His fulsome dotage on you – yes, and feign
Surprise that I return at eve to sup,
130   When all the morning I was loitering here –
Bid me dispatch my business and begone.
I would...

OTTIMA: See!

SEBALD: No, I'll finish. Do you think
I fear to speak the bare truth once for all?
All we have talked of, is, at bottom, fine
To suffer; there's a recompense in guilt;
One must be venturous and fortunate:
What is one young for, else? In age we'll sigh
O'er the wild reckless wicked days flown over;
Still, we have lived: the vice was in its place.
140   But to have eaten Luca's bread, have worn
His clothes, have felt his money swell my purse –
Do lovers in romances sin that way?
Why, I was starving when I used to call
And teach you music, starving while you plucked me
These flowers to smell!

OTTIMA: My poor lost friend!

SEBALD: He gave me
Life, nothing less: what if he did reproach
My perfidy, and threaten, and do more –
Had he no right? What was to wonder at?
He sat by us at table quietly:
150   Why must you lean across till our cheeks touched?
Could he do less than make pretence to strike?
'Tis not the crime's sake – I'd commit ten crimes

Greater, to have this crime wiped out, undone!
And you – O how feel you? Feel you for me?
OTTIMA: Well then, I love you better now than ever,
And best (look at me while I speak to you) –
Best for the crime; nor do I grieve, in truth,
This mask, this simulated ignorance,
This affectation of simplicity,
160 Falls off our crime; this naked crime of ours
May not now be looked over: look it down!
Great? let it be great; but the joys it brought,
Pay they or no its price? Come: they or it!
Speak not! The past, would you give up the past
Such as it is, pleasure and crime together?
Give up that noon I owned my love for you?
The garden's silence: even the single bee
Persisting in his toil, suddenly stopped,
And where he hid you only could surmise
170 By some campanula chalice set a-swing.
Who stammered – 'Yes, I love you'?
SEBALD: And I drew
Back; put far back your face with both my hands
Lest you should grow too full of me – your face
So seemed athirst for my whole soul and body!
OTTIMA: And when I ventured to receive you here,
Made you steal hither in the mornings –
SEBALD: When
I used to look up 'neath the shrub-house here,
Till the red fire on its glazed windows spread
To a yellow haze?
OTTIMA: Ah – my sign was, the sun
180 Inflamed the sere side of yon chestnut-tree
Nipped by the first frost.
SEBALD: You would always laugh
At my wet boots: I had to stride through grass
Over my ankles.
OTTIMA: Then our crowning night!
SEBALD: The July night?
OTTIMA: The day of it too, Sebald!
When heaven's pillars seemed o'erbowed with heat,
Its black-blue canopy suffered descend
Close on us both, to weigh down each to each,
And smother up all life except our life.

So lay we till the storm came.

SEBALD: How it came!

190 OTTIMA: Buried in woods we lay, you recollect;
Swift ran the searching tempest overhead;
And ever and anon some bright white shaft
Burned through the pine-tree roof, here burned and there,
As if God's messenger through the close wood screen
Plunged and replunged his weapon at a venture,
Feeling for guilty thee and me: then broke
The thunder like a whole sea overhead –

SEBALD: Yes!

OTTIMA: – While I stretched myself upon you, hands
To hands, my mouth to your hot mouth, and shook
200 All my locks loose, and covered you with them –
You, Sebald, the same you!

SEBALD: Slower, Ottima!

OTTIMA: And as we lay –

SEBALD: Less vehemently! Love me!
Forgive me! Take not words, mere words, to heart!
Your breath is worse than wine! Breathe slow, speak slow!
Do not lean on me!

OTTIMA: Sebald, as we lay,
Rising and falling only with our pants,
Who said, 'Let death come now! 'Tis right to die!
Right to be punished! Naught completes such bliss
But woe!' Who said that?

SEBALD: How did we ever rise?

210 Was't that we slept? Why did it end?

OTTIMA: I felt you
Taper into a point the ruffled ends
Of my loose locks 'twixt both your humid lips.
My hair is fallen now: knot it again!

SEBALD: I kiss you now, dear Ottima, now and now!
This way? Will you forgive me – be once more
My great queen?

OTTIMA: Bind it thrice about my brow;
Crown me your queen, your spirit's arbitress,
Magnificent in sin. Say that!

SEBALD: I crown you
My great white queen, my spirit's arbitress,
220 Magnificent . . .

[*From without is heard the voice of* PIPPA, *singing* –]

The year's at the spring
And day's at the morn;
Morning's at seven;
The hill-side's dew-pearled;
The lark's on the wing;
The snail's on the thorn:
God's in his heaven –
All's right with the world!

[PIPPA *passes*]

SEBALD: God's in his heaven! Do you hear that? Who spoke?
230   You, you spoke!
OTTIMA: Oh – that little ragged girl!
    She must have rested on the step: we give them
    But this one holiday the whole year round.
    Did you ever see our silk-mills – their inside?
    There are ten silk-mills now belong to you.
    She stoops to pick my double heartsease ... Sh!
    She does not hear: call you out louder!
SEBALD: Leave me!
    Go, get your clothes on – dress those shoulders!
OTTIMA: Sebald?
SEBALD: Wipe off that paint! I hate you.
OTTIMA: Miserable!
SEBALD: My God, and she is emptied of it now!
240   Outright now! – how miraculously gone
    All of the grace – had she not strange grace once?
    Why, the blank cheek hangs listless as it likes,
    No purpose holds the features up together,
    Only the cloven brow and puckered chin
    Stay in their places: and the very hair,
    That seemed to have a sort of life in it,
    Drops, a dead web!
OTTIMA: Speak to me – not of me!
SEBALD: – That round great full-orbed face, where not an angle
    Broke the delicious indolence – all broken!
250 OTTIMA: To me – not of me! Ungrateful, perjured cheat!
    A coward too: but ingrate's worse than all.
    Beggar – my slave – a fawning, cringing lie!
    Leave me! Betray me! I can see your drift!
    A lie that walks and eats and drinks!
SEBALD: My God!

Those morbid olive faultless shoulder-blades –
I should have known there was no blood beneath!

OTTIMA: You hate me then? You hate me then?

SEBALD: To think
She would succeed in her absurd attempt,
And fascinate by sinning, show herself

260   Superior – guilt from its excess superior
To innocence! That little peasant's voice
Has righted all again. Though I be lost,
I know which is the better, never fear,
Of vice or virtue, purity or lust,
Nature or trick! I see what I have done,
Entirely now! Oh I am proud to feel
Such torments – let the world take credit thence –
I, having done my deed, pay too its price!
I hate, hate – curse you! God's in his heaven!

OTTIMA: – Me!

270   Me! no, no, Sebald, not yourself – kill me!
Mine is the whole crime. Do but kill me – then
Yourself – then – presently – first hear me speak!
I always meant to kill myself – wait, you!
Lean on my breast – not as a breast; don't love me
The more because you lean on me, my own
Heart's Sebald! There, there, both deaths presently!

SEBALD: My brain is drowned now – quite drowned: all I feel
Is . . . is, at swift-recurring intervals,
A hurry-down within me, as of waters

280   Loosened to smother up some ghastly pit:
There they go – whirls from a black fiery sea!

OTTIMA: Not me – to him, O God, be merciful!

———

Talk by the way, while PIPPA *is passing from the hill-side to Orcana.* Foreign *Students of painting and sculpture, from Venice, assembled opposite the house of* JULES, *a young French statuary, at Possagno.*

FIRST STUDENT: Attention! My own post is beneath this window, but the pomegranate clump yonder will hide three or four of you with a little squeezing, and Schramm and his pipe must lie flat in the balcony. Four, five – who's a defaulter? We want everybody, for Jules must not be suffered to hurt his bride when the jest's found out.

SECOND STUDENT: All here! Only our poet's away – never
290 having much meant to be present, moonstrike him! The airs of that fellow, that Giovacchino! He was in violent love with himself, and had a fair prospect of thriving in his suit, so un-molested was it, – when suddenly a woman falls in love with him, too; and out of pure jealousy he takes himself off to Trieste, immortal poem and all: whereto is this prophetical epitaph appended already, as Bluphocks assures me, – '*Here a mammoth-poem lies, Fouled to death by butterflies.*' His own fault, the simpleton! Instead of cramp couplets, each like a knife in your entrails, he should write, says Bluphocks, both classically and
300 intelligibly. – *Aesculapius, an Epic. Catalogue of the drugs: Hebe's plaister – One strip Cools your lip. Phoebus' emulsion – One bottle Clears your throttle. Mercury's bolus – One box Cures . . .*

THIRD STUDENT: Subside, my fine fellow! If the marriage was over by ten o'clock, Jules will certainly be here in a minute with his bride.

SECOND STUDENT: Good! – only, so should the poet's muse have been universally acceptable, says Bluphocks, *et canibus nostris* . . . and Delia not better known to our literary dogs than the boy Giovacchino!

310 FIRST STUDENT: To the point, now. Where's Gottlieb, the new-comer? Oh, – listen, Gottlieb, to what has called down this piece of friendly vengeance on Jules, of which we now assemble to witness the winding-up. We are all agreed, all in a tale, observe, when Jules shall burst out on us in a fury by and by: I am spokesman – the verses that are to undeceive Jules bear my name of Lutwyche – but each professes himself alike insulted by this strutting stone-squarer, who came alone from Paris to Munich, and thence with a crowd of us to Venice and Possagno here, but proceeds in a day or two alone again – oh, alone
320 indubitably! – to Rome and Florence. He, forsooth, take up his portion with these dissolute, brutalized, heartless bunglers! – so he was heard to call us all: now, is Schramm brutalized, I should like to know? Am I heartless?

GOTTLIEB: Why, somewhat heartless; for, suppose Jules a coxcomb as much as you choose, still, for this mere coxcombry, you will have brushed off – what do folks style it? – the bloom of his life. Is it too late to alter? These love-letters now, you call his – I can't laugh at them.

FOURTH STUDENT: Because you never read the sham letters
330 of our inditing which drew forth these.

GOTTLIEB: His discovery of the truth will be frightful.

FOURTH STUDENT: That's the joke. But you should have
joined us at the beginning: there's no doubt he loves the girl –
loves a model he might hire by the hour!

GOTTLIEB: See here! 'He has been accustomed,' he writes,
'to have Canova's women about him, in stone, and the world's
women beside him, in flesh; these being as much below, as those
above, his soul's aspiration: but now he is to have the reality.'
There you laugh again! I say, you wipe off the very dew of his
340 youth.

FIRST STUDENT: Schramm! (Take the pipe out of his mouth,
somebody!) Will Jules lose the bloom of his youth?

SCHRAMM: Nothing worth keeping is ever lost in this world:
look at a blossom – it drops presently, having done its service
and lasted its time; but fruits succeed, and where would be the
blossom's place could it continue? As well affirm that your eye
is no longer in your body, because its earliest favourite, whatever
it may have first loved to look on, is dead and done with – as that
any affection is lost to the soul when its first object, whatever
350 happened first to satisfy it, is superseded in due course. Keep
but ever looking, whether with the body's eye or the mind's, and
you will soon find something to look on! Has a man done
wondering at women? – there follow men, dead and alive, to
wonder at. Has he done wondering at men? – there's God to
wonder at: and the faculty of wonder may be, at the same time,
old and tired enough with respect to its first object, and yet
young and fresh sufficiently, so far as concerns its novel one.
Thus...

FIRST STUDENT: Put Schramm's pipe into his mouth again!
360 There, you see! Well, this Jules ... a wretched fribble – oh, I
watched his disportings at Possagno, the other day! Canova's
gallery – you know: there he marches first resolvedly past great
works by the dozen without vouchsafing an eye: all at once he
stops full at the *Psiche-fanciulla* – cannot pass that old acquaintance without a nod of encouragement – 'In your new place,
beauty? Then behave yourself as well here as at Munich – I see
you!' Next he posts himself deliberately before the unfinished
Pietà for half an hour without moving, till up he starts of a
sudden, and thrusts his very nose into – I say, into – the group;
370 by which gesture you are informed that precisely the sole point

he had not fully mastered in Canova's practice was a certain method of using the drill in the articulation of the knee joint – and that, likewise, has he mastered at length! Good-bye, therefore, to poor Canova – whose gallery no longer needs detain his successor Jules, the predestinated novel thinker in marble!

FIFTH STUDENT: Tell him about the women: go on to the women!

FIRST STUDENT: Why, on that matter he could never be supercilious enough. How should we be other (he said) than the
380 poor devils you see, with those debasing habits we cherish? He was not to wallow in that mire, at least: he would wait, and love only at the proper time, and meanwhile put up with the *Psichefanciulla*. Now, I happened to hear of a young Greek – real Greek girl at Malamocco; a true Islander, do you see, with Alciphron's 'hair like sea-moss' – Schramm knows! – white and quiet as an apparition, and fourteen years old at farthest, – a daughter of Natalia, so she swears – that hag Natalia, who helps us to models at three *lire* an hour. We selected this girl for the heroine of our jest. So first, Jules received a scented letter –
390 somebody had seen his Tydeus at the Academy, and my picture was nothing to it: a profound admirer bade him persevere – would make herself known to him ere long. (Paolina, my little friend of the *Fenice*, transcribes divinely.) And in due time, the mysterious correspondent gave certain hints of her peculiar charms – the pale cheeks, the black hair – whatever, in short, had struck us in our Malamocco model: we retained her name, too – Phene, which is, by interpretation, sea-eagle. Now, think of Jules finding himself distinguished from the herd of us by such a creature! In his very first answer he proposed marrying his
400 monitress: and fancy us over these letters, two, three times a day, to receive and dispatch! I concocted the main of it: relations were in the way – secrecy must be observed – in fine, would he wed her on trust, and only speak to her when they were indissolubly united? St – st – Here they come!

SIXTH STUDENT: Both of them! Heaven's love, speak softly, speak within yourselves!

FIFTH STUDENT: Look at the bridegroom! Half his hair in storm and half in calm, – patted down over the left temple, – like a frothy cup one blows on to cool it: and the same old
410 blouse that he murders the marble in.

SECOND STUDENT: Not a rich vest like yours, Hannibal Scratchy! – rich, that your face may the better set it off.

SIXTH STUDENT: And the bride! Yes, sure enough, our
Phene! Should you have known her in her clothes? How
magnificently pale!

GOTTLIEB: She does not also take it for earnest, I hope?

FIRST STUDENT: Oh, Natalia's concern, that is! We settle
with Natalia.

SIXTH STUDENT: She does not speak – has evidently let out
420 no word. The only thing is, will she equally remember the rest
of her lesson, and repeat correctly all those verses which are to
break the secret to Jules?

GOTTLIEB: How he gazes on her! Pity – pity!

FIRST STUDENT: They go in: now, silence! You three, – not
nearer the window, mind, than that pomegranate: just where the
little girl, who a few minutes ago passed us singing, is seated!

PART II
NOON

Scene: Over Orcana. The house of JULES, *who crosses its threshold with*
PHENE: *she is silent, on which* JULES *begins –*

Do not die, Phene! I am yours now, you
Are mine now; let fate reach me how she likes,
If you'll not die: so, never die! Sit here –
My work-room's single seat. I over-lean
This length of hair and lustrous front; they turn
Like an entire flower upward: eyes, lips, last
Your chin – no, last your throat turns: 'tis their scent
Pulls down my face upon you. Nay, look ever
This one way till I change, grow you – I could
10 Change into you, beloved!
                          You by me,
And I by you; this is your hand in mine,
And side by side we sit: all's true. Thank God!
I have spoken: speak you!
                          O my life to come!
My Tydeus must be carved that's there in clay;
Yet how be carved, with you about the room?
Where must I place you? When I think that once
This room-full of rough block-work seemed my heaven
Without you! Shall I ever work again,

Get fairly into my old ways again,
20 Bid each conception stand while, trait by trait,
My hand transfers its lineaments to stone?
Will my mere fancies live near you, their truth –
The live truth, passing and repassing me,
Sitting beside me?
                    Now speak!
                          Only first,
See, all your letters! Was't not well contrived?
Their hiding-place is Psyche's robe; she keeps
Your letters next her skin: which drops out foremost?
Ah, – this that swam down like a first moonbeam
Into my world!
              Again those eyes complete
30 Their melancholy survey, sweet and slow,
Of all my room holds; to return and rest
On me, with pity, yet some wonder too:
As if God bade some spirit plague a world,
And this were the one moment of surprise
And sorrow while she took her station, pausing
O'er what she sees, finds good, and must destroy!
What gaze you at? Those? Books, I told you of;
Let your first word to me rejoice them, too:
This minion, a Coluthus, writ in red
40 Bistre and azure by Bessarion's scribe –
Read this line . . . no, shame – Homer's be the Greek
First breathed me from the lips of my Greek girl!
This Odyssey in coarse black vivid type
With faded yellow blossoms 'twixt page and page,
To mark great places with due gratitude;
'*He said, and on Antinous directed*
'*A bitter shaft*' . . . a flower blots out the rest!
Again upon your search? My statues, then!
– Ah, do not mind that – better that will look
50 When cast in bronze – an Almaign Kaiser, that,
Swart-green and gold, with truncheon based on hip.
This, rather, turn to! What, unrecognized?
I thought you would have seen that here you sit
As I imagined you, – Hippolyta,
Naked upon her bright Numidian horse.
Recall you this then? 'Carve in bold relief' –
So you commanded – 'carve, against I come,

A Greek, in Athens, as our fashion was,
Feasting, bay-filleted and thunder-free,
60   Who rises 'neath the lifted myrtle-branch.
"Praise those who slew Hipparchus!" cry the guests,
"While o'er thy head the singer's myrtle waves
As erst above our champion: stand up, all!"'
See, I have laboured to express your thought.
Quite round, a cluster of mere hands and arms,
(Thrust in all senses, all ways, from all sides,
Only consenting at the branch's end
They strain toward) serves for frame to a sole face,
The Praiser's, in the centre: who with eyes
70   Sightless, so bend they back to light inside
His brain where visionary forms throng up,
Sings, minding not that palpitating arch
Of hands and arms, nor the quick drip of wine
From the drenched leaves o'erhead, nor crowns cast off,
Violet and parsley crowns to trample on –
Sings, pausing as the patron-ghosts approve,
Devoutly their unconquerable hymn.
But you must say a 'well' to that – say 'well!'
Because you gaze – am I fantastic, sweet?
80   Gaze like my very life's-stuff, marble – marbly
Even to the silence! Why, before I found
The real flesh Phene, I inured myself
To see, throughout all nature, varied stuff
For better nature's birth by means of art:
With me, each substance tended to one form
Of beauty – to the human archetype.
On every side occurred suggestive germs
Of that – the tree, the flower – or take the fruit, –
Some rosy shape, continuing the peach,
90   Curved beewise o'er its bough; as rosy limbs,
Depending, nestled in the leaves; and just
From a cleft rose-peach the whole Dryad sprang.
But of the stuffs one can be master of,
How I divined their capabilities!
From the soft-rinded smoothe ing facile chalk
That yields your outline to the air's embrace,
Half-softened by a halo's pearly gloom;
Down to the crisp imperious steel, so sure
To cut its one confided thought clean out

100 Of all the world. But marble! – 'neath my tools
More pliable than jelly – as it were
Some clear primordial creature dug from depths
In the earth's heart, where itself breeds itself,
And whence all baser substance may be worked;
Refine it off to air, you may, – condense it
Down to the diamond; – is not metal there,
When o'er the sudden speck my chisel trips?
– Not flesh, as flake off flake I scale, approach,
Lay bare those bluish veins of blood asleep?
110 Lurks flame in no strange windings where, surprised
By the swift implement sent home at once,
Flushes and glowings radiate and hover
About its track?
                    Phene? what – why is this?
That whitening cheek, those still dilating eyes!
Ah, you will die – I knew that you would die!

                [PHENE *begins, on his having long remained silent*]
Now the end's coming; to be sure, it must
Have ended sometime! Tush, why need I speak
Their foolish speech? I cannot bring to mind
One half of it, beside; and do not care
120 For old Natalia now, nor any of them.
Oh, you – what are you? – if I do not try
To say the words Natalia made me learn,
To please your friends, – it is to keep myself
Where your voice lifted me, by letting that
Proceed: but can it? Even you, perhaps,
Cannot take up, now you have once let fall,
The music's life, and me along with that –
No, or you would! We'll stay, then, as we are:
Above the world.
                    You creature with the eyes!
130 If I could look for ever up to them,
As now you let me, – I believe, all sin,
All memory of wrong done, suffering borne,
Would drop down, low and lower, to the earth
Whence all that's low comes, and there touch and stay
– Never to overtake the rest of me,
All that, unspotted, reaches up to you,
Drawn by those eyes! What rises is myself,

Not me the shame and suffering; but they sink,
Are left, I rise above them. Keep me so,
140 Above the world!
                        But you sink, for your eyes
Are altering – altered! Stay – 'I love you, love' . . .
I could prevent it if I understood:
More of your words to me: was't in the tone
Or the words, your power?
                              Or stay – I will repeat
Their speech, if that contents you! Only change
No more, and I shall find it presently
Far back here, in the brain yourself filled up.
Natalia threatened me that harm should follow
Unless I spoke their lesson to the end,
150 But harm to me, I thought she meant, not you.
Your friends, – Natalia said they were your friends
And meant you well, – because, I doubted it,
Observing (what was very strange to see)
On every face, so different in all else,
The same smile girls like me are used to bear,
But never men, men cannot stoop so low;
Yet your friends, speaking of you, used that smile,
That hateful smirk of boundless self-conceit
Which seems to take possession of the world
160 And make of God a tame confederate,
Purveyor to their appetites . . . you know!
But still Natalia said they were your friends,
And they assented though they smiled the more,
And all came round me, – that thin Englishman
With light lank hair seemed leader of the rest;
He held a paper – 'What we want,' said he,
Ending some explanation to his friends –
'Is something slow, involved and mystical,
To hold Jules long in doubt, yet take his taste
170 And lure him on until, at innermost
Where he seeks sweetness' soul, he may find – this!
– As in the apple's core, the noisome fly:
For insects on the rind are seen at once,
And brushed aside as soon, but this is found
Only when on the lips or loathing tongue.'
And so he read what I have got by heart:

I'll speak it, – 'Do not die, love! I am yours.'
No – is not that, or like that, part of words
Yourself began by speaking? Strange to lose
180 What cost such pains to learn! Is this more right?

> *I am a painter who cannot paint;*
> *In my life, a devil rather than saint;*
> *In my brain, as poor a creature too:*
> *No end to all I cannot do!*
> *Yet do one thing at least I can –*
> *Love a man or hate a man*
> *Supremely: thus my lore began.*
> *Through the Valley of Love I went,*
> *In the lovingest spot to abide,*
190 > *And just on the verge where I pitched my tent,*
> *I found Hate dwelling beside.*
> *(Let the Bridegroom ask what the painter meant,*
> *Of his Bride, of the peerless Bride!)*
> *And further, I traversed Hate's grove,*
> *In the hatefullest nook to dwell;*
> *But lo, where I flung myself prone, couched Love*
> *Where the shadow threefold fell.*
> *(The meaning – those black bride's-eyes above,*
> *Not a painter's lip should tell!)*

200 'And here,' said he, 'Jules probably will ask,
"You have black eyes, Love, – you are, sure enough,
My peerless bride, – then do you tell indeed
What needs some explanation! What means this?"'
– And I am to go on, without a word –

> *So, I grew wise in Love and Hate,*
> *From simple that I was of late.*
> *Once, when I loved, I would enlace*
> *Breast, eyelids, hands, feet, form and face*
> *Of her I loved, in one embrace –*
210 > *As if by mere love I could love immensely!*
> *Once, when I hated, I would plunge*
> *My sword, and wipe with the first lunge*
> *My foe's whole life out like a sponge –*
> *As if by mere hate I could hate intensely!*

But now I am wiser, know better the fashion
How passion seeks aid from its opposite passion:
And if I see cause to love more, hate more
Than ever man loved, ever hated before –
And seek in the Valley of Love,
220   The nest, or the nook in Hate's Grove,
Where my soul may surely reach
The essence, naught less, of each,
The Hate of all Hates, the Love
Of all Loves, in the Valley or Grove, –
I find them the very warders
Each of the other's borders.
When I love most, Love is disguised
In Hate; and when Hate is surprised
In Love, then I hate most : ask
230   How Love smiles through Hate's iron casque,
Hate grins through Love's rose-braided mask, –
And how, having hated thee,
I sought long and painfully
To reach thy heart, nor prick
The skin but pierce to the quick –
Ask this, my Jules, and be answered straight
By thy bride – how the painter Lutwyche can hate !

[JULES *interposes*]
Lutwyche! Who else ? But all of them, no doubt,
Hated me: they at Venice – presently
240 Their turn, however! You I shall not meet:
If I dreamed, saying this would wake me.
                           Keep
What's here, the gold – we cannot meet again,
Consider! and the money was but meant
For two years' travel, which is over now,
All chance or hope or care or need of it.
This – and what comes from selling these, my casts
And books and medals, except . . . let them go
Together, so the produce keeps you safe
Out of Natalia's clutches! If by chance
250 (For all's chance here) I should survive the gang
At Venice, root out all fifteen of them,
We might meet somewhere, since the world is wide.
     [*From without is heard the voice of* PIPPA, *singing* –]

Give her but a least excuse to love me!
When – where –
How – can this arm establish her above me,
If fortune fixed her as my lady there,
There already, to eternally reprove me?
　　('Hist!' – said Kate the Queen;
　　But 'Oh!' – cried the maiden, binding her tresses,
260　　*''Tis only a page that carols unseen,*
　　Crumbling your hounds their messes!')

Is she wronged? – To the rescue of her honour,
My heart!
Is she poor? – What costs it to be styled a donor?
Merely an earth to cleave, a sea to part.
But that fortune should have thrust all this upon her!
　　('Nay, list!' – bade Kate the Queen;
　　And still cried the maiden, binding her tresses,
　　''Tis only a page that carols unseen,
270　　*Fitting your hawks their jesses!')*

[PIPPA *passes*]
[JULES *resumes*]
What name was that the little girl sang forth?
Kate? The Cornaro, doubtless, who renounced
The crown of Cyprus to be lady here
At Asolo, where still her memory stays,
And peasants sing how once a certain page
Pined for the grace of her so far above
His power of doing good to, 'Kate the Queen –
She never could be wronged, be poor,' he sighed,
'Need him to help her!'
　　　　　　　　　　Yes, a bitter thing
280 To see our lady above all need of us;
Yet so we look ere we will love; not I,
But the world looks so. If whoever loves
Must be, in some sort, god or worshipper,
The blessing or the blest one, queen or page,
Why should we always choose the page's part?
Here is a woman with utter need of me, –
I find myself queen here, it seems!
　　　　　　　　　　　　　How strange!
Look at the woman here with the new soul,

Like my own Psyche, – fresh upon her lips
290 Alit, the visionary butterfly,
Waiting my word to enter and make bright,
Or flutter off and leave all blank as first.
This body had no soul before, but slept
Or stirred, was beauteous or ungainly, free
From taint or foul with stain, as outward things
Fastened their image on its passiveness:
Now, it will wake, feel, live – or die again!
Shall to produce form out of unshaped stuff
Be Art – and further, to evoke a soul
300 From form be nothing? This new soul is mine!

Now, to kill Lutwyche, what would that do? – save
A wretched dauber, men will hoot to death
Without me, from their hooting. Oh, to hear
God's voice plain as I heard it first, before
They broke in with their laughter! I heard them
Henceforth, not God.
              To Ancona – Greece – some isle!
I wanted silence only; there is clay
Everywhere. One may do whate'er one likes
In Art: the only thing is, to make sure
310 That one does like it – which takes pains to know.
    Scatter all this, my Phene – this mad dream!
Who, what is Lutwyche, what Natalia's friends,
What the whole world except our love – my own,
Own Phene? But I told you, did I not,
Ere night we travel for your land – some isle
With the sea's silence on it? Stand aside –
I do but break these paltry models up
To begin Art afresh. Meet Lutwyche, I –
And save him from my statue meeting him?
320 Some unsuspected isle in the far seas!
Like a god going through his world, there stands
One mountain for a moment in the dusk,
Whole brotherhoods of cedars on its brow:
And you are ever by me while I gaze
– Are in my arms as now – as now – as now!
Some unsuspected isle in the far seas!
Some unsuspected isle in far-off seas!

Talk by the way, while PIPPA *is passing from Orcana to the Turret. Two or three of the Austrian Police loitering with* BLUPHOCKS, *an English vagabond, just in view of the Turret.*

BLUPHOCKS:* So, that is your Pippa, the little girl who passed us singing? Well, your Bishop's Intendant's money shall be
330 honestly earned: – now, don't make me that sour face because I bring the Bishop's name into the business; we know he can have nothing to do with such horrors: we know that he is a saint and all that a bishop should be, who is a great man beside. *Oh were but every worm a maggot, Every fly a grig, Every bough a Christmas faggot, Every tune a jig!* In fact, I have abjured all religions; but the last I inclined to, was the Armenian: for I have travelled, do you see, and at Koenigsberg, Prussia Improper (so styled because there's a sort of bleak hungry sun there), you might remark over a venerable house-porch, a certain Chaldee inscrip-
340 tion; and brief as it is, a mere glance at it used absolutely to change the mood of every bearded passenger. In they turned, one and all; the young and lightsome, with no irreverent pause, the aged and decrepit, with a sensible alacrity: 'twas the Grand Rabbi's abode, in short. Struck with curiosity, I lost no time in learning Syriac – (these are vowels, you dogs, – follow my stick's end in the mud – *Celarent, Darii, Ferio!*) and one morning presented myself, spelling-book in hand, a, b, c, – I picked it out letter by letter, and what was the purport of this miraculous posy? Some cherished legend of the past, you'll say – '*How*
350 *Moses hocus-pocussed Egypt's land with fly and locust,*' – or, '*How to Jonah sounded harshish, Get thee up and go to Tarshish,*' – or, '*How the angel meeting Balaam, Straight his ass returned a salaam,*' In no wise! '*Shackabrack – Boach – somebody or other – Isaach, Re-cei-ver, Pur-cha-ser and Ex-chan-ger of – Stolen Goods!*' So, talk to me of the religion of a bishop! I have renounced all bishops save Bishop Beveridge – mean to live so – and die – *As some Greek dog-sage, dead and merry, Hellward bound in Charon's wherry, With food for both worlds, under and upper, Lupine-seed and Hecate's supper, And never an obolus . . .*
360 (Though thanks to you, or this Intendant through you, or this Bishop through his Intendant – I possess a burning pocketful of zwanzigers) . . . *To pay the Stygian Ferry!*

---

* 'He maketh his sun to rise on the evil and on the good, and sendeth rain on the just and on the unjust.'

FIRST POLICEMAN: There is the girl, then; go and deserve them the moment you have pointed out to us Signor Luigi and his mother. [*To the rest*] I have been noticing a house yonder, this long while: not a shutter unclosed since morning!

SECOND POLICEMAN: Old Luca Gaddi's, that owns the silk-mills here: he dozes by the hour, wakes up, sighs deeply, says he should like to be Prince Metternich, and then dozes again, after
370 having bidden young Sebald, the foreigner, set his wife to playing draughts. Never molest such a household, they mean well.

BLUPHOCKS: Only, cannot you tell me something of this little Pippa, I must have to do with? One could make something of that name. Pippa – that is, short for Felippa – rhyming to *Panurge consults Hertrippa – Believest thou, King Agrippa?* Something might be done with that name.

SECOND POLICEMAN: Put into rhyme that your head and a ripe musk-melon would not be dear at half a *zwanziger!* Leave
380 this fooling, and look out; the afternoon's over or nearly so.

THIRD POLICEMAN: Where in this passport of Signor Luigi does our Principal instruct you to watch him so narrowly? There? What's there beside a simple signature? (That English fool's busy watching.)

SECOND POLICEMAN: Flourish all round – 'Put all possible obstacles in his way'; oblong dot at the end – 'Detain him till further advices reach you'; scratch at bottom – 'Send him back on pretence of some informality in the above'; ink-spirt on right-hand side (which is the case here) – 'Arrest him at once.'
390 Why and wherefore, I don't concern myself, but my instructions amount to this: if Signor Luigi leaves home tonight for Vienna – well and good, the passport deposed with us for our *visa* is really for his own use, they have misinformed the Office, and he means well; but let him stay over tonight – there has been the pretence we suspect, the accounts of his corresponding and holding intelligence with the Carbonari are correct, we arrest him at once, tomorrow comes Venice, and presently Spielberg. Bluphocks makes the signal, sure enough! That is he, entering the turret with his mother, no doubt.

PART III
EVENING

Scene : Inside the Turret on the Hill above Asolo.
LUIGI *and his* Mother *entering.*

MOTHER: If there blew wind, you'd hear a long sigh, easing
    The utmost heaviness of music's heart.
LUIGI: Here in the archway?
MOTHER: Oh no, no – in farther,
    Where the echo is made, on the ridge.
LUIGI: Here surely, then.
    How plain the tap of my heel as I leaped up!
    Hark – 'Lucius Junius!' The very ghost of a voice
    Whose body is caught and kept by . . . what are those?
    Mere withered wallflowers, waving overhead?
    They seem an elvish group with thin bleached hair
10   That lean out of their topmost fortress – look
    And listen, mountain men, to what we say,
    Hand under chin of each grave earthy face.
    Up and show faces all of you! – 'All of you!'
    That's the king dwarf with the scarlet comb; old Franz,
    Come down and meet your fate? Hark – 'Meet your fate!'
MOTHER: Let him not meet it, my Luigi – do not
    Go to his City! Putting crime aside,
    Half of these ills of Italy are feigned:
    Your Pellicos and writers for effect,
20   Write for effect.
LUIGI: Hush! Say A. writes, and B.
MOTHER: These A.s and B.s write for effect, I say.
    Then, evil is in its nature loud, while good
    Is silent; you hear each petty injury,
    None of his virtues; he is old beside,
    Quiet and kind, and densely stupid. Why
    Do A. and B. not kill him themselves?
LUIGI: They teach
    Others to kill him – me – and, if I fail,
    Others to succeed; now, if A. tried and failed,
    I could not teach that: mine's the lesser task.
30   Mother, they visit night by night . . .
MOTHER: – You, Luigi?

Ah, will you let me tell you what you are?
LUIGI: Why not? Oh, the one thing you fear to hint,
  You may assure yourself I say and say
  Ever to myself! At times – nay, even as now
  We sit – I think my mind is touched, suspect
  All is not sound: but is not knowing that,
  What constitutes one sane or otherwise?
  I know I am thus – so, all is right again.
  I laugh at myself as through the town I walk.
40 And see men merry as if no Italy
  Were suffering; then I ponder – 'I am rich,
  Young, healthy; why should this fact trouble me,
  More than it troubles these?' But it does trouble.
  No, trouble's a bad word: for as I walk
  There's springing and melody and giddiness,
  And old quaint turns and passages of my youth,
  Dreams long forgotten, little in themselves,
  Return to me – whatever may amuse me:
  And earth seems in a truce with me, and heaven
50 Accords with me, all things suspend their strife,
  The very cicala laughs 'There goes he, and there!
  Feast him, the time is short; he is on his way
  For the world's sake: feast him this once, our friend!'
  And in return for all this, I can trip
  Cheerfully up the scaffold-steps. I go
  This evening, mother!
MOTHER: But mistrust yourself –
  Mistrust the judgement you pronounce on him!
LUIGI: Oh, there I feel – am sure that I am right!
MOTHER: Mistrust your judgement then, of the mere means
60 To this wild enterprise. Say, you are right, –
  How should one in your state e'er bring to pass
  What would require a cool head, a cold heart,
  And a calm hand? You never will escape.
LUIGI: Escape? To even wish that, would spoil all.
  The dying is best part of it. Too much
  Have I enjoyed these fifteen years of mine,
  To leave myself excuse for longer life:
  Was not life pressed down, running o'er with joy,
  That I might finish with it ere my fellows
70 Who, sparelier feasted, make a longer stay?
  I was put at the board-head, helped to all

At first; I rise up happy and content.
God must be glad one loves his world so much.
I can give news of earth to all the dead
Who ask me: – last year's sunsets, and great stars
Which had a right to come first and see ebb
The crimson wave that drifts the sun away –
Those crescent moons with notched and burning rims
That strengthened into sharp fire, and there stood,
80   Impatient of the azure – and that day
In March, a double rainbow stopped the storm –
May's warm slow yellow moonlit summer nights –
Gone are they, but I have them in my soul!
MOTHER: (He will not go!)
LUIGI: You smile at me? 'Tis true, –
Voluptuousness, grotesqueness, ghastliness,
Environ my devotedness as quaintly
As round about some antique altar wreathe
The rose festoons, goats' horns, and oxen's skulls.
MOTHER: See now: you reach the city, you must cross
90   His threshold – how?
LUIGI: Oh, that's if we conspired!
Then would come pains in plenty, as you guess –
But guess not how the qualities most fit
For such an office, qualities I have,
Would little stead me, otherwise employed,
Yet prove of rarest merit only here.
Every one knows for what his excellence
Will serve, but no one ever will consider
For what his worst defect might serve: and yet
Have you not seen me range our coppice yonder
100   In search of a distorted ash? – I find
The wry spoilt branch a natural perfect bow.
Fancy the thrice-sage, thrice-precautioned man
Arriving at the palace on my errand!
No, no! I have a handsome dress packed up –
White satin here, to set off my black hair;
In I shall march – for you may watch your life out
Behind thick walls, make friends there to betray you;
More than one man spoils everything. March straight –
Only, no clumsy knife to fumble for.
110   Take the great gate, and walk (not saunter) on
Through guards and guards – I have rehearsed it all

Inside the turret here a hundred times.
Don't ask the way of whom you meet, observe!
But where they cluster thickliest is the door
Of doors; they'll let you pass – they'll never blab
Each to the other, he knows not the favourite,
Whence he is bound and what's his business now.
Walk in – straight up to him; you have no knife:
Be prompt, how should he scream? Then, out with you!

120   Italy, Italy, my Italy!
You're free, you're free! Oh mother, I could dream
They got about me – Andrea from his exile,
Pier from his dungeon, Gualtier from his grave!

MOTHER: Well, you shall go. Yet seems this patriotism
The easiest virtue for a selfish man
To acquire: he loves himself – and next, the world –
If he must love beyond, – but naught between:
As a short-sighted man sees naught midway
His body and the sun above. But you

130   Are my adored Luigi, ever obedient
To my least wish, and running o'er with love:
I could not call you cruel or unkind.
Once more, your ground for killing him! – then go!

LUIGI: Now do you try me, or make sport of me?
How first the Austrians got these provinces . . .
(If that is all, I'll satisfy you soon)
– Never by conquest but by cunning, for
That treaty whereby . . .

MOTHER: Well?

LUIGI: (Sure, he's arrived,
The tell-tale cuckoo: spring's his confidant,

140   And he lets out her April purposes!)
Or . . . better go at once to modern time,
He has . . . they have . . . in fact, I understand
But can't restate the matter; that's my boast:
Others could reason it out to you, and prove
Things they have made me feel.

MOTHER: Why go tonight?
Morn's for adventure. Jupiter is now
A morning-star. I cannot hear you, Luigi!

LUIGI: 'I am the bright and morning-star,' saith God –
And, 'to such an one I give the morning-star.'

150   The gift of the morning-star! Have I God's gift

Of the morning-star?

MOTHER: Chiara will love to see
That Jupiter an evening-star next June.

LUIGI: True, mother. Well for those who live through June!
Great noontides, thunder-storms, all glaring pomps
That triumph at the heels of June the god
Leading his revel through our leafy world.
Yes, Chiara will be here.

MOTHER: In June: remember,
Yourself appointed that month for her coming.

LUIGI: Was that low noise the echo?

MOTHER: The night-wind.

160   She must be grown – with her blue eyes upturned
As if life were one long and sweet surprise:
In June she comes.

LUIGI: We were to see together
The Titian at Treviso. There, again!

     [*From without is heard the voice of* PIPPA, *singing* –]

            A king lived long ago,
            In the morning of the world,
            When earth was nigher heaven than now:
            And the king's locks curled,
            Disparting o'er a forehead full
            As the milk-white space 'twixt horn and horn
170   *Of some sacrificial bull –*
            Only calm as a babe new-born:
            For he was got to a sleepy mood,
            So safe from all decrepitude,
            Age with its bane, so sure gone by,
            (The gods so loved him while he dreamed)
            That, having lived thus long, there seemed
            No need the king should ever die.

LUIGI: No need that sort of king should ever die!

            Among the rocks his city was:
180   *Before his palace, in the sun,*
            He sat to see his people pass,
            And judge them every one
            From its threshold of smooth stone.
            They haled him many a valley-thief

Caught in the sheep-pens, robber-chief
Swarthy and shameless, beggar-cheat,
Spy-prowler, or rough pirate found
On the sea-sand left aground;
And sometimes clung about his feet,
190 *With bleeding lip and burning cheek,*
A woman, bitterest wrong to speak
Of one with sullen thickset brows:
And sometimes from the prison-house
The angry priests a pale wretch brought,
Who through some chink had pushed and pressed
On knees and elbows, belly and breast,
Worm-like into the temple, – caught
He was by the very god,
Who ever in the darkness strode
200 *Backward and forward, keeping watch*
O'er his brazen bowls, such rogues to catch!
These, all and every one,
The king judged, sitting in the sun.

LUIGI: That king should still judge sitting in the sun!

His councillors, on left and right,
Looked anxious up, – but no surprise
Disturbed the king's old smiling eyes
Where the very blue had turned to white.
'Tis said, a Python scared one day
210 *The breathless city, till he came,*
With forky tongue and eyes on flame,
Where the old king sat to judge alway;
But when he saw the sweepy hair
Girt with a crown of berries rare
Which the god will hardly give to wear
To the maiden who singeth, dancing bare
In the altar-smoke by the pine-torch lights,
At his wondrous forest rites, –
Seeing this, he did not dare
220 *Approach that threshold in the sun,*
Assault the old king smiling there.
Such grace had kings when the world begun!

[PIPPA *passes*]

LUIGI: And such grace have they, now that the world ends!
    The Python at the city, on the throne,
    And brave men, God would crown for slaying him,
    Lurk in bye-corners lest they fall his prey.
    Are crowns yet to be won in this late time,
    Which weakness makes me hesitate to reach?
    'Tis God's voice calls: how could I stay? Farewell!

Talk by the way, while PIPPA *is passing from the Turret to
the Bishop's Brother's House, close to the Duomo Santa Maria.
Poor* Girls *sitting on the steps.*

230 FIRST GIRL: There goes a swallow to Venice – the stout seafarer!
    Seeing those birds fly, makes one wish for wings.
    Let us all wish; you wish first!
SECOND GIRL: I? This sunset
    To finish.
THIRD GIRL: That old – somebody I know,
    Greyer and older than my grandfather,
    To give me the same treat he gave last week –
    Feeding me on his knee with fig-peckers,
    Lampreys and red Breganze-wine, and mumbling
    The while some folly about how well I fare,
    Let sit and eat my supper quietly:
240 Since had he not himself been late this morning
    Detained at – never mind where, – had he not...
    'Eh, baggage, had I not!' –
SECOND GIRL: How she can lie!
THIRD GIRL: Look there – by the nails!
SECOND GIRL: What makes your fingers red?
THIRD GIRL: Dipping them into wine to write bad words with
    On the bright table: how he laughed!
FIRST GIRL: My turn.
    Spring's come and summer's coming. I would wear
    A long loose gown, down to the feet and hands,
    With plaits here, close about the throat, all day;
    And all night lie, the cool long nights, in bed;
250 And have new milk to drink, apples to eat,
    Deuzans and junetings, leather-coats... ah, I should say,
    This is away in the fields – miles!

THIRD GIRL: Say at once
    You'd be at home: she'd always be at home!
    Now comes the story of the farm among
    The cherry orchards, and how April snowed
    White blossoms on her as she ran. Why, fool,
    They've rubbed the chalk-mark out, how tall you were,
    Twisted your starling's neck, broken his cage,
    Made a dung-hill of your garden!
  FIRST GIRL: They, destroy
260 My garden since I left them? well – perhaps!
    I would have done so: so I hope they have!
    A fig-tree curled out of our cottage wall;
    They called it mine, I have forgotten why,
    It must have been there long ere I was born:
    Cric – cric – I think I hear the wasps o'erhead
    Pricking the papers strung to flutter there
    And keep off birds in fruit-time – coarse long papers,
    And the wasps eat them, prick them through and through.
  THIRD GIRL: How her mouth twitches! Where was I? – before
270 She broke in with her wishes and long gowns
    And wasps – would I be such a fool! – Oh, here!
    This is my way: I answer every one
    Who asks me why I make so much of him –
    (If you say, 'you love him' – straight 'he'll not be gulled!')
    'He that seduced me when I was a girl
    Thus high – had eyes like yours, or hair like yours,
    Brown, red, white,' – as the case may be: that pleases!
    See how that beetle burnishes in the path!
    There sparkles he along the dust: and, there –
280 Your journey to that maize-tuft spoiled at least!
  FIRST GIRL: When I was young, they said if you killed one
    Of those sunshiny beetles, that his friend
    Up there, would shine no more that day nor next.
  SECOND GIRL: When you were young? Nor are you young,
        that's true.
    How your plump arms, that were, have dropped away!
    Why, I can span them. Cecco beats you still?
    No matter, so you keep your curious hair.
    I wish they'd find a way to dye our hair
    Your colour – any lighter tint, indeed,
290 Than black: the men say they are sick of black,
    Black eyes, black hair!

FOURTH GIRL: Sick of yours, like enough.
Do you pretend you ever tasted lampreys
And ortolans? Giovita, of the palace,
Engaged (but there's no trusting him) to slice me
Polenta with a knife that had cut up
An ortolan.
SECOND GIRL: Why, there! Is not that Pippa
We are to talk to, under the window, – quick, –
Where the lights are?
FIRST GIRL: That she? No, or she would sing.
For the Intendant said . . .
THIRD GIRL: Oh, you sing first!
300   Then, if she listens and comes close . . . I'll tell you, –
Sing that song the young English noble made,
Who took you for the purest of the pure,
And meant to leave the world for you – what fun!
SECOND GIRL [sings]:

> You'll love me yet! – and I can tarry
>   Your love's protracted growing:
> June reared that bunch of flowers you carry,
>   From seeds of April's sowing.

> I plant a heartful now: some seed
>   At least is sure to strike,
310   And yield – what you'll not pluck indeed,
>   Not love, but, may be, like.

> You'll look at least on love's remains,
>   A grave's one violet:
> Your look? – that pays a thousand pains.
>   What's death? You'll love me yet!

THIRD GIRL [to PIPPA who approaches]: Oh, you may come
closer – we shall not eat you! Why, you seem the very person
that the great rich handsome Englishman has fallen so violently
in love with. I'll tell you all about it.

PART IV
NIGHT

Scene : Inside the Palace by the Duomo. MONSIGNOR, *dismissing his*
Attendants.

MONSIGNOR: Thanks, friends, many thanks! I chiefly desire
life now, that I may recompense every one of you. Most I know
something of already. What, a repast prepared? *Benedicto
benedicatur* . . . ugh, ugh! Where was I? Oh, as you were remarking, Ugo, the weather is mild, very unlike winter-weather: but
I am a Sicilian, you know, and shiver in your Julys here. To be
sure, when't was full summer at Messina, as we priests used to
cross in procession the great square on Assumption Day, you
might see our thickest yellow tapers twist suddenly in two, each
10 like a falling star, or sink down on themselves in a gore of wax.
But go, my friends, but go! [*To the* INTENDANT] Not you, Ugo!
[*The others leave the apartment*] I have long wanted to converse
with you, Ugo.

INTENDANT: Uguccio –

MONSIGNOR: . . . 'guccio Stefani, man! of Ascoli, Fermo and
Fossombruno; – what I do need instructing about, are these
accounts of your administration of my poor brother's affairs.
Ugh! I shall never get through a third part of your accounts:
take some of these dainties before we attempt it, however. Are
20 you bashful to that degree? For me, a crust and water suffice.

INTENDANT: Do you choose this especial night to question
me?

MONSIGNOR: This night, Ugo. You have managed my late
brother's affairs since the death of our elder brother: fourteen
years and a month, all but three days. On the Third of December,
I find him . . .

INTENDANT: If you have so intimate an acquaintance with
your brother's affairs, you will be tender of turning so far back:
they will hardly bear looking into, so far back.

30 MONSIGNOR: Ay, ay, ugh, ugh, – nothing but disappointments here below! I remark a considerable payment made to
yourself on this Third of December. Talk of disappointments!
There was a young fellow here, Jules, a foreign sculptor I did
my utmost to advance, that the Church might be a gainer by us
both: he was going on hopefully enough, and of a sudden he
notifies to me some marvellous change that has happened in his

notions of Art. Here's his letter, – 'He never had a clearly conceived Ideal within his brain till today. Yet since his hand could
manage a chisel, he has practised expressing other men's Ideals;
40 and, in the very perfection he has attained to, he foresees an
ultimate failure: his unconscious hand will pursue its prescribed
course of old years, and will reproduce with a fatal expertness
the ancient types, let the novel one appear never so palpably to
his spirit. There is but one method of escape: confiding the
virgin type to as chaste a hand, he will turn painter instead of
sculptor, and paint, not carve, its characteristics,' – strike out,
I dare say, a school like Correggio: how think you, Ugo?

INTENDANT: Is Correggio a painter?

MONSIGNOR: Foolish Jules! and yet, after all, why foolish?
50 He may – probably will – fail egregiously; but if there should
arise a new painter, will it not be in some such way, by a poet
now, or a musician (spirits who have conceived and perfected an
Ideal through some other channel), transferring it to this, and
escaping our conventional roads by pure ignorance of them; eh,
Ugo? If you have no appetite, talk at least, Ugo!

INTENDANT: Sir, I can submit no longer to this course of
yours. First, you select the group of which I formed one, – next
you thin it gradually, – always retaining me with your smile, –
and so do you proceed till you have fairly got me alone with you
60 between four stone walls. And now then? Let this farce, this
chatter end now: what is it you want with me?

MONSIGNOR: Ugo!

INTENDANT: From the instant you arrived, I felt your smile
on me as you questioned me about this and the other article in
those papers – why your brother should have given me this villa,
that *podere*, – and your nod at the end meant, – what?

MONSIGNOR: Possibly that I wished for no loud talk here.
If once you set me coughing, Ugo! –

INTENDANT: I have your brother's hand and seal to all I
70 possess: now ask me what for! what service I did him – ask me!

MONSIGNOR: I would better not: I should rip up old disgraces, let out my poor brother's weaknesses. By the way,
Maffeo of Forli (which, I forgot to observe, is your true name),
was the interdict ever taken off you, for robbing that church at
Cesena?

INTENDANT: No, nor needs be: for when I murdered your
brother's friend, Pasquale, for him . . .

MONSIGNOR: Ah, he employed you in that business, did he?

Well, I must let you keep, as you say, this villa and that *podere*,
for fear the world should find out my relations were of so indifferent a stamp? Maffeo, my family is the oldest in Messina,
and century after century have my progenitors gone on polluting
themselves with every wickedness under heaven: my own father
... rest his soul! – I have, I know, a chapel to support that it may
rest: my dear two dead brothers were, – what you know tolerably
well; I, the youngest, might have rivalled them in vice, if not in
wealth: but from my boyhood I came out from among them, and
so am not partaker of their plagues. My glory springs from
another source; or if from this, by contrast only, – for I, the
bishop, am the brother of your employers, Ugo. I hope to repair
some of their wrong, however; so far as my brothers' ill-gotten
treasure reverts to me, I can stop the consequences of his crime:
and not one *soldo* shall escape me. Maffeo, the sword we quiet
men spurn away, you shrewd knaves pick up and commit
murders with; what opportunities the virtuous forego, the
villainous seize. Because, to pleasure myself apart from other
considerations, my food would be millet-cake, my dress sack-
cloth, and my couch straw, – am I therefore to let you, the
offscouring of the earth, seduce the poor and ignorant by
appropriating a pomp these will be sure to think lessens the
abominations so unaccountably and exclusively associated with
it? Must I let villas and *poderi* go to you, a murderer and thief,
that you may beget by means of them other murderers and
thieves? No – if my cough would but allow me to speak!

INTENDANT: What am I to expect? You are going to punish
me?

MONSIGNOR: – Must punish you, Maffeo. I cannot afford to
cast away a chance. I have whole centuries of sin to redeem, and
only a month or two of life to do it in. How should I dare to
say ...

INTENDANT: 'Forgive us our trespasses'?

MONSIGNOR: My friend, it is because I avow myself a very
worm, sinful beyond measure, that I reject a line of conduct you
would applaud perhaps. Shall I proceed, as it were, a-pardoning?
– I? – who have no symptom of reason to assume that aught less
than my strenuousest efforts will keep myself out of mortal sin,
much less keep others out. No: I do trespass, but will not double
that by allowing you to trespass.

INTENDANT: And suppose the villas are not your brother's
to give, nor yours to take? Oh, you are hasty enough just now!

MONSIGNOR: 1, 2 – No. 3! – ay, can you read the substance of a letter, No. 3, I have received from Rome? It is precisely on the ground there mentioned, of the suspicion I have that a certain child of my late elder brother, who would have succeeded to his estates, was murdered in infancy by you, Maffeo, at the instigation of my late younger brother – that the Pontiff enjoins on me not merely the bringing that Maffeo to condign punishment, but the taking all pains, as guardian of the infant's heritage for the Church, to recover it parcel by parcel, howsoever,
130 whensoever, and wheresoever. While you are now gnawing those fingers, the police are engaged in sealing up your papers, Maffeo, and the mere raising my voice brings my people from the next room to dispose of yourself. But I want you to confess quietly, and save me raising my voice. Why, man, do I not know the old story? The heir between the succeeding heir, and this heir's ruffianly instrument, and their complot's effect, and the life of fear and bribes and ominous smiling silence? Did you throttle or stab my brother's infant? Come now!

INTENDANT: So old a story, and tell it no better? When did
140 such an instrument ever produce such an effect? Either the child smiles in his face; or, most likely, he is not fool enough to put himself in the employer's power so thoroughly: the child is always ready to produce – as you say – howsoever, wheresoever, and whensoever.

MONSIGNOR: Liar!

INTENDANT: Strike me? Ah, so might a father chastise! I shall sleep soundly tonight at least, though the gallows await me tomorrow; for what a life did I lead! Carlo of Cesena reminds me of his connivance, every time I pay his annuity; which
150 happens commonly thrice a year. If I remonstrate, he will confess all to the good bishop – you!

MONSIGNOR: I see through the trick, caitiff! I would you spoke truth for once. All shall be sifted, however – seven times sifted.

INTENDANT: And how my absurd riches encumbered me! I dared not lay claim to above half my possessions. Let me but once unbosom myself, glorify Heaven, and die!

Sir, you are no brutal dastardly idiot like your brother I frightened to death: let us understand one another. Sir, I will
160 make away with her for you – the girl – here close at hand; not the stupid obvious kind of killing; do not speak – know nothing of her nor of me! I see her every day – saw her this morning: of

course there is to be no killing; but at Rome the courtesans perish off every three years, and I can entice her thither – have indeed begun operations already. There's a certain lusty blue-eyed florid-complexioned English knave, I and the Police employ occasionally. You assent, I perceive – no, that's not it – assent I do not say – but you will let me convert my present havings and holdings into cash, and give me time to cross the
170 Alps? 'Tis but a little black-eyed pretty singing Felippa, gay silk-winding girl. I have kept her out of harm's way up to this present; for I always intended to make your life a plague to you with her. 'Tis as well settled once and for ever. Some women I have procured will pass Bluphocks, my handsome scoundrel, off for somebody; and once Pippa entangled! – you conceive? Through her singing? Is it a bargain?

[*From without is heard the voice of* PIPPA, *singing –*]

Overhead the tree-tops meet,
Flowers and grass spring 'neath one's feet;
There was naught above me, naught below,
180 *My childhood had not learned to know:*
For, what are the voices of birds
– Ay, and of beasts, – but words, our words,
Only so much more sweet?
The knowledge of that with my life begun.
But I had so near made out the sun,
And counted your stars, the seven and one,
Like the fingers of my hand:
Nay, I could all but understand
Wherefore through heaven the white moon ranges;
190 *And just when out of her soft fifty changes*
No unfamiliar face might overlook me –
Suddenly God took me.

[PIPPA *passes*]

MONSIGNOR [*springing up*]: My people – one and all – all – within there! Gag this villain – tie him hand and foot! He dares ... I know not half he dares – but remove him – quick! *Miserere mei, Domine!* Quick, I say!

[EPILOGUE]

Scene: PIPPA'*s chamber again. She enters it.*

The bee with his comb,
The mouse at her dray,
The grub in his tomb,
Wile winter away;
But the fire-fly and hedge-shrew and lob-worm, I pray,
How fare they?
Ha, ha, thanks for your counsel, my Zanze!
'Feast upon lampreys, quaff Breganze' –
The summer of life so easy to spend,
10 And care for tomorrow so soon put away!
But winter hastens at summer's end,
And fire-fly, hedge-shrew, lob-worm, pray,
How fare they?
No bidding me then to . . . what did Zanze say?
'Pare your nails pearlwise, get your small feet shoes
More like' . . . (what said she?) – 'and less like canoes!'
How pert that girl was! – would I be those pert
Impudent staring women! It had done me,
However, surely no such mighty hurt
20 To learn his name who passed that jest upon me:
No foreigner, that I can recollect,
Came, as she says, a month since, to inspect
Our silk-mills – none with blue eyes and thick rings
Of raw-silk-coloured hair, at all events.
Well, if old Luca keep his good intents,
We shall do better, see what next year brings.
I may buy shoes, my Zanze, not appear
More destitute than you perhaps next year!
Bluph . . . something! I had caught the uncouth name
30 But for Monsignor's people's sudden clatter
Above us – bound to spoil such idle chatter
As ours: it were indeed a serious matter
If silly talk like ours should put to shame
The pious man, the man devoid of blame,
The . . . ah but – ah but, all the same,
No mere mortal has a right
To carry that exalted air;

Best people are not angels quite:
While – not the worst of people's doings scare
40 The devil; so there's that proud look to spare!
     Which is mere counsel to myself, mind! for
I have just been the holy Monsignor:
And I was you too, Luigi's gentle mother,
And you too, Luigi! – how that Luigi started
Out of the turret – doubtlessly departed
On some good errand or another,
For he passed just now in a traveller's trim,
And the sullen company that prowled
About his path, I noticed, scowled
50 As if they had lost a prey in him.
And I was Jules the sculptor's bride,
And I was Ottima beside,
And now what am I? – tired of fooling.
Day for folly, night for schooling!
New-year's day is over and spent,
Ill or well, I must be content.
     Even my lily's asleep, I vow:
Wake up – here's a friend I've plucked you!
Call this flower a heartsease now!
60 Something rare, let me instruct you,
Is this, with petals triply swollen,
Three times spotted, thrice the pollen;
While the leaves and parts that witness
Old proportions and their fitness,
Here remain unchanged, unmoved now;
Call this pampered thing improved now!
Suppose there's a king of the flowers
And a girl-show held in his bowers –
'Look ye, buds, this growth of ours,'
70 Says he, 'Zanze from the Brenta,
I have made her gorge polenta
Till both cheeks are near as bouncing
As her . . . name there's no pronouncing!
See this heightened colour too,
For she swilled Breganze wine
Till her nose turned deep carmine;
'Twas but white when wild she grew.
And only by this Zanze's eyes
Of which we could not change the size,

80   The magnitude of all achieved
     Otherwise, may be perceived.'

     Oh what a drear dark close to my poor day!
     How could that red sun drop in that black cloud?
     Ah Pippa, morning's rule is moved away,
     Dispensed with, never more to be allowed!
     Day's turn is over, now arrives the night's.
     Oh lark, be day's apostle
     To mavis, merle and throstle,
     Bid them their betters jostle
90   From day and its delights!
     But at night, brother howlet, over the woods,
     Toll the world to thy chantry;
     Sing to the bats' sleek sisterhoods
     Full complines with gallantry:
     Then, owls and bats,
     Cowls and twats,
     Monks and nuns, in a cloister's moods,
     Adjourn to the oak-stump pantry!
          [*After she has begun to undress herself*]
     Now, one thing I should like to really know:
100 How near I ever might approach all these
     I only fancied being, this long day:
     – Approach, I mean, so as to touch them, so
     As to . . . in some way . . . move them – if you please,
     Do good or evil to them some slight way.
     For instance, if I wind
     Silk tomorrow, my silk may bind
          [*Sitting on the bedside*]
     And border Ottima's cloak's hem.
     Ah me, and my important part with them,
     This morning's hymn half promised when I rose!
110 True in some sense or other, I suppose.
          [*As she lies down*]
     God bless me! I can pray no more tonight.
     No doubt, some way or other, hymns say right.

         All service ranks the same with God –
         With God, whose puppets, best and worst,
         Are we : there is no last nor first.

      [*She sleeps*]

Dramatic Lyrics

1842

Cavalier Tunes *

I. MARCHING ALONG

I

Kentish Sir Byng stood for his King,
Bidding the crop-headed Parliament swing:
And, pressing a troop unable to stoop
And see the rogues flourish and honest folk droop,
Marched them along, fifty-score strong,
Great-hearted gentlemen, singing this song.

II

God for King Charles! Pym and such carles
To the Devil that prompts 'em their treasonous parles!
Cavaliers, up! Lips from the cup,
10 Hands from the pasty, nor bite take nor sup
Till you're –
    CHORUS. – *Marching along, fifty-score strong,*
        Great-hearted gentlemen, singing this song.

III

Hampden to hell, and his obsequies' knell
Serve Hazelrig, Fiennes, and young Harry as well!
England, good cheer! Rupert is near!
Kentish and loyalists, keep we not here
    CHORUS. – *Marching along, fifty-score strong,*
        Great-hearted gentlemen, singing this song?

IV

Then, God for King Charles! Pym and his snarls
20 To the Devil that pricks on such pestilent carles!
Hold by the right, you double your might;
So, onward to Nottingham, fresh for the fight,
    CHORUS. – *March we along, fifty-score strong,*
        Great-hearted gentlemen, singing this song!

---

*Such Poems as the majority in this volume might also come properly enough, I suppose, under the head of 'Dramatic Pieces'; being, though often Lyric in expression, always Dramatic in principle, and so many utterances of so many imaginary persons, not mine. – R.B.

II. GIVE A ROUSE

I

King Charles, and who'll do him right now?
King Charles, and who's ripe for fight now?
Give a rouse: here's, in hell's despite now,
King Charles!

II

Who gave me the goods that went since?
Who raised me the house that sank once?
Who helped me to gold I spent since?
Who found me in wine you drank once?
    CHORUS. – *King Charles, and who'll do him right now?*
10   *King Charles, and who's ripe for fight now?*
           Give a rouse: here's, in hell's despite now,
           King Charles!

III

To whom used my boy George quaff else,
By the old fool's side that begot him?
For whom did he cheer and laugh else,
While Noll's damned troopers shot him?
    CHORUS. – *King Charles, and who'll do him right now?*
           King Charles, and who's ripe for fight now?
           Give a rouse: here's, in hell's despite now,
20   *King Charles!*

III. BOOT AND SADDLE

I

Boot, saddle, to horse, and away!
Rescue my castle before the hot day
Brightens to blue from its silvery grey,
    CHORUS. – *Boot, saddle, to horse, and away!*

II

Ride past the suburbs, asleep as you'd say;
Many's the friend there, will listen and pray

'God's luck to gallants that strike up the lay –
    CHORUS. – *Boot, saddle, to horse, and away!*'

III

Forty miles off, like a roebuck at bay,
10 Flouts Castle Brancepeth the Roundheads' array:
Who laughs, 'Good fellows ere this, by my fay,
    CHORUS. – *Boot, saddle, to horse, and away!*'

IV

Who? My wife Gertrude; that, honest and gay,
Laughs when you talk of surrendering, 'Nay!
I've better counsellors; what counsel they?
    CHORUS. – *Boot, saddle, to horse, and away!*'

My Last Duchess

FERRARA

That's my last Duchess painted on the wall,
Looking as if she were alive. I call
That piece a wonder, now: Frà Pandolf's hands
Worked busily a day, and there she stands.
Will't please you sit and look at her? I said
'Frà Pandolf' by design, for never read
Strangers like you that pictured countenance,
The depth and passion of its earnest glance,
But to myself they turned (since none puts by
10 The curtain I have drawn for you, but I)
And seemed as they would ask me, if they durst,
How such a glance came there; so, not the first
Are you to turn and ask thus. Sir, 'twas not
Her husband's presence only, called that spot
Of joy into the Duchess' cheek: perhaps
Frà Pandolf chanced to say 'Her mantle laps
Over my lady's wrist too much,' or 'Paint
Must never hope to reproduce the faint
Half-flush that dies along her throat': such stuff
20 Was courtesy, she thought, and cause enough
For calling up that spot of joy. She had

A heart – how shall I say? – too soon made glad,
Too easily impressed; she liked whate'er
She looked on, and her looks went everywhere.
Sir, 'twas all one! My favour at her breast,
The dropping of the daylight in the West,
The bough of cherries some officious fool
Broke in the orchard for her, the white mule
She rode with round the terrace – all and each
30 Would draw from her alike the approving speech,
Or blush, at least. She thanked men, – good! but thanked
Somehow – I know not how – as if she ranked
My gift of a nine-hundred-years-old name
With anybody's gift. Who'd stoop to blame
This sort of trifling? Even had you skill
In speech – (which I have not) – to make your will
Quite clear to such an one, and say, 'Just this
Or that in you disgusts me; here you miss,
Or there exceed the mark' – and if she let
40 Herself be lessoned so, nor plainly set
Her wits to yours, forsooth, and made excuse,
– E'en then would be some stooping; and I choose
Never to stoop. Oh sir, she smiled, no doubt,
Whene'er I passed her; but who passed without
Much the same smile? This grew; I gave commands;
Then all smiles stopped together. There she stands
As if alive. Will't please you rise? We'll meet
The company below, then. I repeat,
The Count your master's known munificence
50 Is ample warrant that no just pretence
Of mine for dowry will be disallowed;
Though his fair daughter's self, as I avowed
At starting, is my object. Nay, we'll go
Together down, sir. Notice Neptune, though,
Taming a sea-horse, thought a rarity,
Which Claus of Innsbruck cast in bronze for me!

Count Gismond

AIX IN PROVENCE

I

Christ God who savest man, save most
   Of men Count Gismond who saved me!
Count Gauthier, when he chose his post,
   Chose time and place and company
To suit it; when he struck at length
My honour, 'twas with all his strength.

II

And doubtlessly ere he could draw
   All points to one, he must have schemed!
That miserable morning saw
10   Few half so happy as I seemed,
While being dressed in queen's array
To give our tourney prize away.

III

I thought they loved me, did me grace
   To please themselves; 'twas all their deed;
God makes, or fair or foul, our face;
   If showing mine so caused to bleed
My cousins' hearts, they should have dropped
A word, and straight the play had stopped.

IV

They, too, so beauteous! Each a queen
20   By virtue of her brow and breast;
Not needing to be crowned, I mean,
   As I do. E'en when I was dressed,
Had either of them spoke, instead
Of glancing sideways with still head!

V

But no: they let me laugh, and sing
   My birthday song quite through, adjust
The last rose in my garland, fling
   A last look on the mirror, trust

My arms to each an arm of theirs,
30 And so descend the castle-stairs –

VI

And come out on the morning-troop
   Of merry friends who kissed my cheek,
And called me queen, and made me stoop
   Under the canopy – (a streak
That pierced it, of the outside sun,
Powdered with gold its gloom's soft dun) –

VII

And they could let me take my state
   And foolish throne amid applause
Of all come there to celebrate
40   My queen's-day – Oh I think the cause
Of much was, they forgot no crowd
Makes up for parents in their shroud!

VIII

However that be, all eyes were bent
   Upon me, when my cousins cast
Theirs down; 'twas time I should present
   The victor's crown, but ... there, 'twill last
No long time ... the old mist again
Blinds me as then it did. How vain!

IX

See! Gismond's at the gate, in talk
50   With his two boys: I can proceed.
Well, at that moment, who should stalk
   Forth boldly – to my face, indeed –
But Gauthier, and he thundered 'Stay!'
And all stayed. 'Bring no crowns, I say!

X

'Bring torches! Wind the penance-sheet
   About her! Let her shun the chaste,
Or lay herself before their feet!
   Shall she whose body I embraced
A night long, queen it in the day?
60 For honour's sake no crowns, I say!'

XI

I? What I answered? As I live,
    I never fancied such a thing
As answer possible to give.
    What says the body when they spring
Some monstrous torture-engine's whole
Strength on it? No more says the soul.

XII

Till out strode Gismond; then I knew
    That I was saved. I never met
His face before, but, at first view,
70   I felt quite sure that God had set
Himself to Satan; who would spend
A minute's mistrust on the end?

XIII

He strode to Gauthier, in his throat
    Gave him the lie, then struck his mouth
With one back-handed blow that wrote
    In blood men's verdict there. North, South,
East, West, I looked. The lie was dead,
And damned, and truth stood up instead.

XIV

This glads me most, that I enjoyed
80   The heart of the joy, with my content
In watching Gismond unalloyed
    By any doubt of the event:
God took that on him – I was bid
Watch Gismond for my part: I did.

XV

Did I not watch him while he let
    His armourer just brace his greaves,
Rivet his hauberk, on the fret
    The while! His foot ... my memory leaves
No least stamp out, nor how anon
90 He pulled his ringing gauntlets on.

XVI

And e'en before the trumpet's sound
   Was finished, prone lay the false knight,
Prone as his lie, upon the ground:
   Gismond flew at him, used no sleight
O' the sword, but open-breasted drove,
Cleaving till out the truth he clove.

XVII

Which done, he dragged him to my feet
   And said 'Here die, but end thy breath
In full confession, lest thou fleet
100   From my first, to God's second death!
Say, hast thou lied?' And, 'I have lied
To God and her,' he said, and died.

XVIII

Then Gismond, kneeling to me, asked
   – What safe my heart holds, though no word
Could I repeat now, if I tasked
   My powers for ever, to a third
Dear even as you are. Pass the rest
Until I sank upon his breast.

XIX

Over my head his arm he flung
110   Against the world; and scarce I felt
His sword (that dripped by me and swung)
   A little shifted in its belt:
For he began to say the while
How South our home lay many a mile.

XX

So 'mid the shouting multitude
   We two walked forth to never more
Return. My cousins have pursued
   Their life, untroubled as before
I vexed them. Gauthier's dwelling-place
120 God lighten! May his soul find grace!

XXI
Our elder boy has got the clear
   Great brow; though when his brother's black
Full eye shows scorn, it ... Gismond here?
   And have you brought my tercel back?
I just was telling Adela
How many birds it struck since May.

Incident of the French Camp

I
You know, we French stormed Ratisbon:
   A mile or so away,
On a little mound, Napoleon
   Stood on our storming-day;
With neck out-thrust, you fancy how,
   Legs wide, arms locked behind,
As if to balance the prone brow
   Oppressive with its mind.

II
Just as perhaps he mused 'My plans
10   That soar, to earth may fall,
Let once my army-leader Lannes
   Waver at yonder wall,' –
Out 'twixt the battery-smokes there flew
   A rider, bound on bound
Full-galloping; nor bridle drew
   Until he reached the mound.

III
Then off there flung in smiling joy,
   And held himself erect
By just his horse's mane, a boy:
20   You hardly could suspect –
(So tight he kept his lips compressed,
   Scarce any blood came through)
You looked twice ere you saw his breast
   Was all but shot in two.

IV

'Well,' cried he, 'Emperor, by God's grace
   We've got you Ratisbon!
The Marshal's in the market-place,
   And you'll be there anon
To see your flag-bird flap his vans
30   Where I, to heart's desire,
Perched him!' The chief's eye flashed; his plans
   Soared up again like fire.

V

The chief's eye flashed; but presently
   Softened itself, as sheathes
A film the mother-eagle's eye
   When her bruisèd eaglet breathes;
'You're wounded!' 'Nay,' the soldier's pride
   Touched to the quick, he said:
'I'm killed, Sire!' And his chief beside,
40   Smiling the boy fell dead.

Soliloquy of the Spanish Cloister

I

Gr-r-r – there go, my heart's abhorrence!
   Water your damned flower-pots, do!
If hate killed men, Brother Lawrence,
   God's blood, would not mine kill you!
What? your myrtle-bush wants trimming?
   Oh, that rose has prior claims –
Needs its leaden vase filled brimming?
   Hell dry you up with its flames!

II

At the meal we sit together:
10   *Salve tibi!* I must hear
Wise talk of the kind of weather,
   Sort of season, time of year:
Not a plenteous cork-crop: scarcely
   Dare we hope oak-galls, I doubt:

What's the Latin name for 'parsley'?
What's the Greek name for Swine's Snout?

III

Whew! We'll have our platter burnished,
    Laid with care on our own shelf!
With a fire-new spoon we're furnished,
20   And a goblet for ourself,
Rinsed like something sacrificial
    Ere 'tis fit to touch our chaps –
Marked with L. for our initial!
    (He-he! There his lily snaps!)

IV

Saint, forsooth! While brown Dolores
    Squats outside the Convent bank
With Sanchicha, telling stories,
    Steeping tresses in the tank,
Blue-black, lustrous, thick like horsehairs,
30   – Can't I see his dead eye glow,
Bright as 'twere a Barbary corsair's?
    (That is, if he'd let it show!)

V

When he finishes refection,
    Knife and fork he never lays
Cross-wise, to my recollection,
    As do I, in Jesu's praise.
I the Trinity illustrate,
    Drinking watered orange-pulp –
In three sips the Arian frustrate;
40   While he drains his at one gulp.

VI

Oh, those melons? If he's able
    We're to have a feast! so nice!
One goes to the Abbot's table,
    All of us get each a slice.
How go on your flowers? None double?
    Not one fruit-sort can you spy?
Strange! – And I, too, at such trouble,
    Keep them close-nipped on the sly!

VII

There's a great text in Galatians,
50   Once you trip on it, entails
Twenty-nine distinct damnations,
    One sure, if another fails:
If I trip him just a-dying,
    Sure of heaven as sure can be,
Spin him round and send him flying
    Off to hell, a Manichee?

VIII

Or, my scrofulous French novel
    On grey paper with blunt type!
Simply glance at it, you grovel
60   Hand and foot in Belial's gripe:
If I double down its pages
    At the woeful sixteenth print,
When he gathers his greengages,
    Ope a sieve and slip it in't?

IX

Or, there's Satan! – one might venture
    Pledge one's soul to him, yet leave
Such a flaw in the indenture
    As he'd miss till, past retrieve,
Blasted lay that rose-acacia
70   We're so proud of! *Hy, Zy, Hine* ...
'St, there's Vespers! *Plena gratiâ
    Ave, Virgo!* Gr-r-r – you swine!

In a Gondola

He sings

I send my heart up to thee, all my heart
    In this my singing.
For the stars help me, and the sea bears part;
    The very night is clinging
Closer to Venice' streets to leave one space
    Above me, whence thy face
May light my joyous heart to thee its dwelling-place.

She speaks

Say after me, and try to say
My very words, as if each word
10   Came from you of your own accord,
In your own voice, in your own way:
'This woman's heart and soul and brain
Are mine as much as this gold chain
She bids me wear; which' (say again)
'I choose to make by cherishing
A precious thing, or choose to fling
Over the boat-side, ring by ring.'
And yet once more say . . . no word more!
Since words are only words. Give o'er!

20   Unless you call me, all the same,
Familiarly by my pet name,
Which if the Three should hear you call,
And me reply to, would proclaim
At once our secret to them all.
Ask of me, too, command me, blame –
Do, break down the partition-wall
'Twixt us, the daylight world beholds
Curtained in dusk and splendid folds!
What's left but – all of me to take?
30   I am the Three's: prevent them, slake
Your thirst! 'Tis said, the Arab sage,
In practising with gems, can loose
Their subtle spirit in his cruce
And leave but ashes: so, sweet mage,
Leave them my ashes when thy use
Sucks out my soul, thy heritage!

He sings

I
Past we glide, and past, and past!
  What's that poor Agnese doing
Where they make the shutters fast?
40   Grey Zanobi's just a-wooing
To his couch the purchased bride:
  Past we glide!

II

Past we glide, and past, and past!
  Why's the Pucci Palace flaring
Like a beacon to the blast?
  Guests by hundreds, not one caring
If the dear host's neck were wried:
  Past we glide!

She sings

I

The moth's kiss, first!
50 Kiss me as if you made believe
You were not sure, this eve,
How my face, your flower, had pursed
Its petals up; so, here and there
You brush it, till I grow aware
Who wants me, and wide ope I burst.

II

The bee's kiss, now!
Kiss me as if you entered gay
My heart at some noonday,
A bud that dares not disallow
60 The claim, so all is rendered up,
And passively its shattered cup
Over your head to sleep I bow.

He sings

I

What are we two?
I am a Jew,
And carry thee, farther than friends can pursue,
To a feast of our tribe;
Where they need thee to bribe
The devil that blasts them unless he imbibe
Thy . . . Scatter the vision for ever! And now,
70 As of old, I am I, thou art thou!

II
Say again, what we are?
The sprite of a star,
I lure thee above where the destinies bar
My plumes their full play
Till a ruddier ray
Than my pale one announce there is withering away
Some . . . Scatter the vision for ever! And now,
As of old, I am I, thou art thou!

He muses

Oh, which were best, to roam or rest?
80 The land's lap or the water's breast?
To sleep on yellow millet-sheaves,
Or swim in lucid shallows just
Eluding water-lily leaves,
An inch from Death's black fingers, thrust
To lock you, whom release he must;
Which life were best on Summer eves?

He speaks, musing

Lie back; could thought of mine improve you?
From this shoulder let there spring
A wing; from this, another wing;
90 Wings, not legs and feet, shall move you!
Snow-white must they spring, to blend
With your flesh, but I intend
They shall deepen to the end,
Broader, into burning gold,
Till both wings crescent-wise enfold
Your perfect self, from 'neath your feet
To o'er your head, where, lo, they meet
As if a million sword-blades hurled
Defiance from you to the world!

100 Rescue me thou, the only real!
And scare away this mad ideal
That came, nor motions to depart!
Thanks! Now, stay ever as thou art!

Still he muses

I

What if the Three should catch at last
Thy serenader? While there's cast
Paul's cloak about my head, and fast
Gian pinions me, Himself has past
His stylet through my back; I reel;
And . . . is it thou I feel?

II

110 They trail me, these three godless knaves,
Past every church that sains and saves,
Nor stop till, where the cold sea raves
By Lido's wet accursèd graves,
They scoop mine, roll me to its brink,
And . . . on thy breast I sink!

She replies, musing

Dip your arm o'er the boat-side, elbow-deep,
As I do: thus: were death so unlike sleep,
Caught this way? Death's to fear from flame or steel,
Or poison doubtless; but from water – feel!

120 Go find the bottom! Would you stay me? There!
Now pluck a great blade of that ribbon-grass
To plait in where the foolish jewel was,
I flung away: since you have praised my hair,
'Tis proper to be choice in what I wear.

He speaks

Row home? must we row home? Too surely
Know I where its front's demurely
Over the Giudecca piled;
Window just with window mating,
Door on door exactly waiting,
130 All's the set face of a child:
But behind it, where's a trace
Of the staidness and reserve,
And formal lines without a curve,

In the same child's playing-face?
No two windows look one way
O'er the small sea-water thread
Below them. Ah, the autumn day
I, passing, saw you overhead!
First, out a cloud of curtain blew,
140   Then a sweet cry, and last came you –
To catch your lory that must needs
Escape just then, of all times then,
To peck a tall plant's fleecy seeds,
And make me happiest of men.
I scarce could breathe to see you reach
So far back o'er the balcony
To catch him ere he climbed too high
Above you in the Smyrna peach
That quick the round smooth cord of gold,
150   This coiled hair on your head, unrolled,
Fell down you like a gorgeous snake
The Roman girls were wont, of old,
When Rome there was, for coolness' sake
To let lie curling o'er their bosoms.
Dear lory, may his beak retain
Ever its delicate rose stain
As if the wounded lotus-blossoms
Had marked their thief to know again!

Stay longer yet, for others' sake
160   Than mine! What should your chamber do?
– With all its rarities that ache
In silence while day lasts, but wake
At night-time and their life renew,
Suspended just to pleasure you
Who brought against their will together
These objects, and, while day lasts, weave
Around them such a magic tether
That dumb they look: your harp, believe,
With all the sensitive tight strings
170   Which dare not speak, now to itself
Breathes slumberously, as if some elf
Went in and out the chords, his wings
Make murmur wheresoe'er they graze,
As an angel may, between the maze

Of midnight palace-pillars, on
And on, to sow God's plagues, have gone
Through guilty glorious Babylon.
And while such murmurs flow, the nymph
Bends o'er the harp-top from her shell
180 As the dry limpet for the lymph
Come with a tune he knows so well.
And how your statues' hearts must swell!
And how your pictures must descend
To see each other, friend with friend!
Oh, could you take them by surprise,
You'd find Schidone's eager Duke
Doing the quaintest courtesies
To that prim saint by Haste-thee-Luke!
And, deeper into her rock den,
190 Bold Castelfranco's Magdalen
You'd find retreated from the ken
Of that robed counsel-keeping Ser –
As if the Tizian thinks of her,
And is not, rather, gravely bent
On seeing for himself what toys
Are these, his progeny invent,
What litter now the board employs
Whereon he signed a document
That got him murdered! Each enjoys
200 Its night so well, you cannot break
The sport up, so, indeed must make
More stay with me, for others' sake.

She speaks

I
Tomorrow, if a harp-string, say,
Is used to tie the jasmine back
That overfloods my room with sweets,
Contrive your Zorzi somehow meets
My Zanze! If the ribbon's black,
The Three are watching: keep away!
Your gondola – let Zorzi wreathe
210 A mesh of water-weeds about
Its prow, as if he unaware
Had struck some quay or bridge-foot stair!

That I may throw a paper out
As you and he go underneath.

There's Zanze's vigilant taper; safe are we.
Only one minute more tonight with me?
Resume your past self of a month ago!
Be you the bashful gallant, I will be
The lady with the colder breast than snow.
220 Now bow you, as becomes, nor touch my hand
More than I touch yours when I step to land,
And say, 'All thanks, Siora!' –
                                        Heart to heart
And lips to lips! Yet once more, ere we part,
Clasp me and make me thine, as mine thou art!
    [*He is surprised, and stabbed*]
It was ordained to be so, sweet! – and best
Comes now, beneath thine eyes, upon thy breast.
Still kiss me! Care not for the cowards! Care
Only to put aside thy beauteous hair
My blood will hurt! The Three, I do not scorn
230 To death, because they never lived: but I
Have lived indeed, and so – (yet one more kiss) – can die!

Artemis Prologizes

I am a goddess of the ambrosial courts,
And save by Here, Queen of Pride, surpassed
By none whose temples whiten this the world.
Through heaven I roll my lucid moon along;
I shed in hell o'er my pale people peace;
On earth I, caring for the creatures, guard
Each pregnant yellow wolf and fox-bitch sleek,
And every feathered mother's callow brood,
And all that love green haunts and loneliness.
10 Of men, the chaste adore me, hanging crowns
Of poppies red to blackness, bell and stem,
Upon my image at Athenai here;
And this dead Youth, Asclepios bends above,
Was dearest to me. He, my buskined step
To follow through the wild-wood leafy ways,

And chase the panting stag, or swift with darts
Stop the swift ounce, or lay the leopard low,
Neglected homage to another god:
Whence Aphrodite, by no midnight smoke
20 Of tapers lulled, in jealousy dispatched
A noisome lust that, as the gadbee stings,
Possessed his stepdame Phaidra for himself
The son of Theseus her great absent spouse.
Hippolutos exclaiming in his rage
Against the fury of the Queen, she judged
Life insupportable; and, pricked at heart
An Amazonian stranger's race should dare
To scorn her, perished by the murderous cord:
Yet, ere she perished, blasted in a scroll
30 The fame of him her swerving made not swerve.
And Theseus, read, returning, and believed,
And exiled, in the blindness of his wrath,
The man without a crime who, last as first,
Loyal, divulged not to his sire the truth.
Now Theseus from Poseidon had obtained
That of his wishes should be granted three,
And one he imprecated straight – 'Alive
May ne'er Hippolutos reach other lands!'
Poseidon heard, ai ai! And scarce the prince
40 Had stepped into the fixed boots of the car
That give the feet a stay against the strength
Of the Henetian horses, and around
His body flung the rein, and urged their speed
Along the rocks and shingles of the shore,
When from the gaping wave a monster flung
His obscene body in the coursers' path.
These, mad with terror, as the sea-bull sprawled
Wallowing about their feet, lost care of him
That reared them; and the master-chariot-pole
50 Snapping beneath their plunges like a reed,
Hippolutos, whose feet were trammelled fast,
Was yet dragged forward by the circling rein
Which either hand directed; nor they quenched
The frenzy of their flight before each trace,
Wheel-spoke and splinter of the woeful car,
Each boulder-stone, sharp stub and spiny shell,
Huge fish-bone wrecked and wreathed amid the sands

On that detested beach, was bright with blood
And morsels of his flesh: then fell the steeds
60 Head-foremost, crashing in their moonèd fronts,
Shivering with sweat, each white eye horror-fixed.
His people, who had witnessed all afar,
Bore back the ruins of Hippolutos.
But when his sire, too swoln with pride, rejoiced
(Indomitable as a man foredoomed)
That vast Poseidon had fulfilled his prayer,
I, in a flood of glory visible,
Stood o'er my dying votary and, deed
By deed, revealed, as all took place, the truth.
70 Then Theseus lay the woefullest of men,
And worthily; but ere the death-veils hid
His face, the murdered prince full pardon breathed
To his rash sire. Whereat Athenai wails.

So I, who ne'er forsake my votaries,
Lest in the cross-way none the honey-cake
Should tender, nor pour out the dog's hot life;
Lest at my fane the priests disconsolate
Should dress my image with some faded poor
Few crowns, made favours of, nor dare object
80 Such slackness to my worshippers who turn
Elsewhere the trusting heart and loaded hand,
As they had climbed Olumpos to report
Of Artemis and nowhere found her throne –
I interposed: and, this eventful night, –
(While round the funeral pyre the populace
Stood with fierce light on their black robes which bound
Each sobbing head, while yet their hair they clipped
O'er the dead body of their withered prince,
And, in his palace, Theseus prostrated
90 On the cold hearth, his brow cold as the slab
'Twas bruised on, groaned away the heavy grief –
As the pyre fell, and down the cross logs crashed
Sending a crowd of sparkles through the night,
And the gay fire, elate with mastery,
Towered like a serpent o'er the clotted jars
Of wine, dissolving oils and frankincense,
And splendid gums like gold), – my potency
Conveyed the perished man to my retreat

In the thrice-venerable forest here.
100 And this white-bearded sage who squeezes now
The berried plant, is Phoibos' son of fame,
Asclepios, whom my radiant brother taught
The doctrine of each herb and flower and root,
To know their secretest virtue and express
The saving soul of all: who so has soothed
With lavers the torn brow and murdered cheeks,
Composed the hair and brought its gloss again,
And called the red bloom to the pale skin back,
And laid the strips and jagged ends of flesh
110 Even once more, and slacked the sinew's knot
Of every tortured limb – that now he lies
As if mere sleep possessed him underneath
These interwoven oaks and pines. Oh cheer,
Divine presenter of the healing rod,
Thy snake, with ardent throat and lulling eye,
Twines his lithe spires around! I say, much cheer!
Proceed thou with thy wisest pharmacies!
And ye, white crowd of woodland sister-nymphs,
Ply, as the sage directs, these buds and leaves
120 That strew the turf around the twain! While I
Await, in fitting silence, the event.

Waring

I

I

What's become of Waring
Since he gave us all the slip,
Chose land-travel or seafaring,
Boots and chest or staff and scrip,
Rather than pace up and down
Any longer London town?

II

Who'd have guessed it from his lip
Or his brow's accustomed bearing,
On the night he thus took ship

10 Or started landward ? – little caring
For us, it seems, who supped together
(Friends of his too, I remember)
And walked home through the merry weather,
The snowiest in all December.
I left his arm that night myself
For what's-his-name's, the new prose-poet
Who wrote the book there, on the shelf –
How, forsooth, was I to know it
If Waring meant to glide away
20 Like a ghost at break of day ?
Never looked he half so gay !

III

He was prouder than the devil:
How he must have cursed our revel !
Ay and many other meetings,
Indoor visits, outdoor greetings,
As up and down he paced this London,
With no work done, but great works undone,
Where scarce twenty knew his name.
Why not, then, have earlier spoken,
30 Written, bustled ? Who's to blame
If your silence kept unbroken ?
'True, but there were sundry jottings,
Stray-leaves, fragments, blurs and blottings,
Certain first steps were achieved
Already which' – (is that your meaning ?)
'Had well borne out whoe'er believed
In more to come !' But who goes gleaning
Hedgeside chance-blades, while full-sheaved
Stand cornfields by him ? Pride, o'erweening
40 Pride alone, puts forth such claims
O'er the day's distinguished names.

IV

Meantime, how much I loved him,
I find out now I've lost him.
I who cared not if I moved him,
Who could so carelessly accost him,
Henceforth never shall get free
Of his ghostly company,

His eyes that just a little wink
As deep I go into the merit
50   Of this and that distinguished spirit –
His cheeks' raised colour, soon to sink,
As long I dwell on some stupendous
And tremendous (Heaven defend us!)
Monstr'-inform'-ingens-horrend-ous
Demoniaco-seraphic
Penman's latest piece of graphic.
Nay, my very wrist grows warm
With his dragging weight of arm.
E'en so, swimmingly appears,
60   Through one's after-supper musings,
Some lost lady of old years
With her beauteous vain endeavour
And goodness unrepaid as ever;
The face, accustomed to refusings,
We, puppies that we were . . . Oh never
Surely, nice of conscience, scrupled
Being aught like false, forsooth, to?
Telling aught but honest truth to?
What a sin, had we centupled
70   Its possessor's grace and sweetness!
No! she heard in its completeness
Truth, for truth's a weighty matter,
And truth, at issue, we can't flatter!
Well, 'tis done with; she's exempt
From damning us through such a sally;
And so she glides, as down a valley,
Taking up with her contempt,
Past our reach; and in, the flowers
Shut her unregarded hours.

v
80   Oh, could I have him back once more,
This Waring, but one half-day more!
Back, with the quiet face of yore,
So hungry for acknowledgement
Like mine! I'd fool him to his bent.
Feed, should not he, to heart's content?
I'd say, 'to only have conceived,
Planned your great works, apart from progress,

Surpasses little works achieved!'
I'd lie so, I should be believed.
90 I'd make such havoc of the claims
Of the day's distinguished names
To feast him with, as feasts an ogress
Her feverish sharp-toothed gold-crowned child!
Or as one feasts a creature rarely
Captured here, unreconciled
To capture; and completely gives
Its pettish humours license, barely
Requiring that it lives.

VI
Ichabod, Ichabod,
100 The glory is departed!
Travels Waring East away?
Who, of knowledge, by hearsay,
Reports a man upstarted
Somewhere as a god,
Hordes grown European-hearted,
Millions of the wild made tame
On a sudden at his fame?
In Vishnu-land what Avatar?
Or who in Moscow, toward the Czar,
110 With the demurest of footfalls
Over the Kremlin's pavement bright
With serpentine and syenite,
Steps, with five other Generals
That simultaneously take snuff,
For each to have pretext enough
And kerchiefwise unfold his sash
Which, softness' self, is yet the stuff
To hold fast where a steel chain snaps,
And leave the grand white neck no gash?
120 Waring in Moscow, to those rough
Cold northern natures born perhaps,
Like the lambwhite maiden dear
From the circle of mute kings
Unable to repress the tear,
Each as his sceptre down he flings,
To Dian's fane at Taurica,
Where now a captive priestess, she alway

Mingles her tender grave Hellenic speech
With theirs, tuned to the hailstone-beaten beach
130 As pours some pigeon, from the myrrhy lands
Rapt by the whirl-blast to fierce Scythian strands
Where breed the swallows, her melodious cry
Amid their barbarous twitter!
In Russia? Never! Spain were fitter!
Ay, most likely 'tis in Spain
That we and Waring meet again
Now, while he turns down that cool narrow lane
Into the blackness, out of grave Madrid
All fire and shine, abrupt as when there's slid
140 Its stiff gold blazing pall
From some black coffin-lid.
Or, best of all,
I love to think
The leaving us was just a feint;
Back here to London did he slink,
And now works on without a wink
Of sleep, and we are on the brink
Of something great in fresco-paint:
Some garret's ceiling, walls and floor,
150 Up and down and o'er and o'er
He splashes, as none splashed before
Since great Caldara Polidore.
Or Music means this land of ours
Some favour yet, to pity won
By Purcell from his Rosy Bowers, –
'Give me my so-long-promised son,
Let Waring end what I begun!'
Then down he creeps and out he steals
Only when the night conceals
160 His face; in Kent 'tis cherry-time,
Or hops are picking: or at prime
Of March he wanders as, too happy,
Years ago when he was young,
Some mild eve when woods grew sappy
And the early moths had sprung
To life from many a trembling sheath
Woven the warm boughs beneath;
While small birds said to themselves
What should soon be actual song,

170 And young gnats, by tens and twelves,
　　 Made as if they were the throng
　　 That crowd around and carry aloft
　　 The sound they have nursed, so sweet and pure,
　　 Out of a myriad noises soft,
　　 Into a tone that can endure
　　 Amid the noise of a July noon
　　 When all God's creatures crave their boon,
　　 All at once and all in tune,
　　 And get it, happy as Waring then,
180 Having first within his ken
　　 What a man might do with men:
　　 And far too glad, in the even-glow,
　　 To mix with the world he meant to take
　　 Into his hand, he told you, so –
　　 And out of it his world to make,
　　 To contract and to expand
　　 As he shut or oped his hand.
　　 Oh Waring, what's to really be?
　　 A clear stage and a crowd to see!
190 Some Garrick, say, out shall not he
　　 The heart of Hamlet's mystery pluck?
　　 Or, where most unclean beasts are rife,
　　 Some Junius – am I right? – shall tuck
　　 His sleeve, and forth with flaying-knife!
　　 Some Chatterton shall have the luck
　　 Of calling Rowley into life!
　　 Some one shall somehow run amuck
　　 With this old world for want of strife
　　 Sound asleep. Contrive, contrive
200 To rouse us, Waring! Who's alive?
　　 Our men scarce seem in earnest now.
　　 Distinguished names! – but 'tis, somehow,
　　 As if they played at being names
　　 Still more distinguished, like the games
　　 Of children. Turn our sport to earnest
　　 With a visage of the sternest!
　　 Bring the real times back, confessed
　　 Still better than our very best!

II

I
'When I last saw Waring...'
(How all turned to him who spoke!
You saw Waring? Truth or joke?
In land-travel or sea-faring?)

II
'We were sailing by Trieste
Where a day or two we harboured:
A sunset was in the West,
When, looking over the vessel's side,
One of our company espied
A sudden speck to larboard.
And as a sea-duck flies and swims
At once, so came the light craft up,
With its sole lateen sail that trims
And turns (the water round its rims
Dancing, as round a sinking cup)
And by us like a fish it curled,
And drew itself up close beside,
Its great sail on the instant furled,
And o'er its thwarts a shrill voice cried,
(A neck as bronzed as a Lascar's)
"Buy wine of us, you English Brig?
Or fruit, tobacco and cigars?
A pilot for you to Trieste?
Without one, look you ne'er so big,
They'll never let you up the bay!
We natives should know best."
I turned, and "just those fellows' way,"
Our captain said, "The 'long-shore thieves
Are laughing at us in their sleeves."

III
'In truth, the boy leaned laughing back;
And one, half-hidden by his side
Under the furled sail, soon I spied,
With great grass hat and kerchief black,
Who looked up with his kingly throat,
Said somewhat, while the other shook

His hair back from his eyes to look
Their longest at us; then the boat,
I know not how, turned sharply round,
Laying her whole side on the sea
As a leaping fish does; from the lee
Into the weather, cut somehow
250   Her sparkling path beneath our bow
And so went off, as with a bound,
Into the rosy and golden half
O' the sky, to overtake the sun
And reach the shore, like the sea-calf
Its singing cave; yet I caught one
Glance ere away the boat quite passed,
And neither time nor toil could mar
Those features: so I saw the last
Of Waring!' – You? Oh, never star
260   Was lost here but it rose afar!
Look East, where whole new thousands are!
In Vishnu-land what Avatar?

Rudel to the Lady of Tripoli

I

I know a Mount, the gracious Sun perceives
First, when he visits, last, too, when he leaves
The world; and, vainly favoured, it repays
The day-long glory of his steadfast gaze
By no change of its large calm front of snow.
And underneath the Mount, a Flower I know,
He cannot have perceived, that changes ever
At his approach; and, in the lost endeavour
To live his life, has parted, one by one,
10   With all a flower's true graces, for the grace
Of being but a foolish mimic sun,
With ray-like florets round a disk-like face.
Men nobly call by many a name the Mount
As over many a land of theirs its large
Calm front of snow like a triumphal targe
Is reared, and still with old names, fresh names vie,
Each to its proper praise and own account:
Men call the Flower, the Sunflower, sportively.

II

Oh, Angel of the East, one, one gold look
20 Across the waters to this twilight nook,
– The far sad waters, Angel, to this nook!

III

Dear Pilgrim, art thou for the East indeed?
Go! – saying ever as thou dost proceed,
That I, French Rudel, choose for my device
A sunflower outspread like a sacrifice
Before its idol. See! These inexpert
And hurried fingers could not fail to hurt
The woven picture; 'tis a woman's skill
Indeed; but nothing baffled me, so, ill
30 Or well, the work is finished. Say, men feed
On songs I sing, and therefore bask the bees
On my flower's breast as on a platform broad:
But, as the flower's concern is not for these
But solely for the sun, so men applaud
In vain this Rudel, he not looking here
But to the East – the East! Go, say this, Pilgrim dear!

Cristina

I

She should never have looked at me
    If she meant I should not love her!
There are plenty . . . men, you call such,
    I suppose . . . she may discover
All her soul to, if she pleases,
    And yet leave much as she found them:
But I'm not so, and she knew it
    When she fixed me, glancing round them.

II

What? To fix me thus meant nothing?
10 But I can't tell (there's my weakness)
What her look said! – no vile cant, sure,
    About 'need to strew the bleakness

Of some lone shore with its pearl-seed,
    That the sea feels' – no 'strange yearning
That such souls have, most to lavish
    Where there's chance of least returning.'

III
Oh, we're sunk enough here, God knows!
    But not quite so sunk that moments,
Sure though seldom, are denied us,
20   When the spirit's true endowments
Stand out plainly from its false ones,
    And apprise it if pursuing
Or the right way or the wrong way,
    To its triumph or undoing.

IV
There are flashes struck from midnights,
    There are fire-flames noondays kindle,
Whereby piled-up honours perish,
    Whereby swollen ambitions dwindle,
While just this or that poor impulse,
30   Which for once had play unstifled,
Seems the sole work of a life-time
    That away the rest have trifled.

V
Doubt you if, in some such moment,
    As she fixed me, she felt clearly,
Ages past the soul existed,
    Here an age 'tis resting merely,
And hence fleets again for ages,
    While the true end, sole and single,
It stops here for is, this love-way,
40   With some other soul to mingle?

VI
Else it loses what it lived for,
    And eternally must lose it;
Better ends may be in prospect,
    Deeper blisses (if you choose it),
But this life's end and this love-bliss

Have been lost here. Doubt you whether
This she felt as, looking at me,
  Mine and her souls rushed together?

VII

Oh, observe! Of course, next moment,
50   The world's honours, in derision
Trampled out the light for ever:
  Never fear but there's provision
Of the devil's to quench knowledge
  Lest we walk the earth in rapture!
– Making those who catch God's secret
  Just so much more prize their capture!

VIII

Such am I: the secret's mine now!
  She has lost me, I have gained her;
Her soul's mine: and thus, grown perfect,
60   I shall pass my life's remainder.
Life will just hold out the proving
  Both our powers, alone and blended:
And then, come next life quickly!
  This world's use will have been ended.

Johannes Agricola in Meditation

There's heaven above, and night by night
  I look right through its gorgeous roof;
No suns and moons though e'er so bright
  Avail to stop me; splendour-proof
I keep the broods of stars aloof:
For I intend to get to God,
  For 'tis to God I speed so fast,
For in God's breast, my own abode,
  Those shoals of dazzling glory passed,
10   I lay my spirit down at last.
I lie where I have always lain,
  God smiles as he has always smiled;
Ere suns and moons could wax and wane,
  Ere stars were thundergirt, or piled

The heavens, God thought on me his child;
Ordained a life for me, arrayed
   Its circumstances every one
To the minutest; ay, God said
   This head this hand should rest upon
20   Thus, ere he fashioned star or sun.
And having thus created me,
   Thus rooted me, he bade me grow,
Guiltless for ever, like a tree
   That buds and blooms, nor seeks to know
   The law by which it prospers so:
But sure that thought and word and deed
   All go to swell his love for me,
Me, made because that love had need
   Of something irreversibly
30   Pledged solely its content to be.
Yes, yes, a tree which must ascend,
   No poison-gourd foredoomed to stoop!
I have God's warrant, could I blend
   All hideous sins, as in a cup,
   To drink the mingled venoms up;
Secure my nature will convert
   The draught to blossoming gladness fast:
While sweet dews turn to the gourd's hurt,
   And bloat, and while they bloat it, blast,
40   As from the first its lot was cast.
For as I lie, smiled on, full-fed
   By unexhausted power to bless,
I gaze below on hell's fierce bed,
   And those its waves of flame oppress,
   Swarming in ghastly wretchedness;
Whose life on earth aspired to be
   One altar-smoke, so pure! – to win
If not love like God's love for me,
   At least to keep his anger in;
50   And all their striving turned to sin.
Priest, doctor, hermit, monk grown white
   With prayer, the broken-hearted nun,
The martyr, the wan acolyte,
   The incense-swinging child, – undone
   Before God fashioned star or sun!
God, whom I praise; how could I praise,

If such as I might understand,
Make out and reckon on his ways,
    And bargain for his love, and stand,
60   Paying a price, at his right hand?

Narrator is

Porphyria's Lover

The rain set early in tonight,
    The sullen wind was soon awake,   *— state of mind*
It tore the elm-tops down for spite,
    And did its worst to vex the lake: *Symbolism*
I listened with heart fit to break.
When glided in Porphyria; straight
    She shut the cold out and the storm,
And kneeled and made the cheerless grate
    Blaze up, and all the cottage warm;
10   Which done, she rose, and from her form
Withdrew the dripping cloak and shawl,
    And laid her soiled gloves by, untied
Her hat and let the damp hair fall,
    And, last, she sat down by my side
And called me. When no voice replied,
She put my arm about her waist,
    And made her smooth white shoulder bare,
And all her yellow hair displaced,
    And, stooping, made my cheek lie there,
20   And spread, o'er all, her yellow hair,
Murmuring how she loved me – she
    Too weak, for all her heart's endeavour,
To set its struggling passion free
    From pride, and vainer ties dissever,
    And give herself to me for ever.
But passion sometimes would prevail,
    Nor could tonight's gay feast restrain
A sudden thought of one so pale
    For love of her, and all in vain:
30   So, she was come through wind and rain.
Be sure I looked up at her eyes
    Happy and proud; at last I knew
Porphyria worshipped me; surprise   *delusion; insanity*

Made my heart swell, and still it grew
While I debated what to do.
That moment she was mine, mine, fair,
   Perfectly pure and good: I found
A thing to do, and all her hair
   In one long yellow string I wound
40   Three times her little throat around,
And strangled her. No pain felt she;
   I am quite sure she felt no pain.
As a shut bud that holds a bee,
   I warily oped her lids: again
Laughed the blue eyes without a stain.
And I untightened next the tress
   About her neck; her cheek once more
Blushed bright beneath my burning kiss:
   I propped her head up as before,
50   Only, this time my shoulder bore
Her head, which droops upon it still:
   The smiling rosy little head,
So glad it has its utmost will,
   That all it scorned at once is fled,
   And I, its love, am gained instead!
Porphyria's love: she guessed not how
   Her darling one wish would be heard.
And thus we sit together now,
   And all night long we have not stirred,
60   And yet God has not said a word!

Through the Metidja to Abd-el-Kadr

I

As I ride, as I ride,
With a full heart for my guide,
So its tide rocks my side,
As I ride, as I ride,
That, as I were double-eyed,
He, in whom our Tribes confide,
Is descried, ways untried
As I ride, as I ride.

II

As I ride, as I ride

10 To our Chief and his Allied,
Who dares chide my heart's pride
As I ride, as I ride?
Or are witnesses denied –
Through the desert waste and wide
Do I glide unespied
As I ride, as I ride?

III

As I ride, as I ride,
When an inner voice has cried,
The sands slide, nor abide

20 (As I ride, as I ride)
O'er each visioned homicide
That came vaunting (has he lied?)
To reside – where he died,
As I ride, as I ride.

IV

As I ride, as I ride,
Ne'er has spur my swift horse plied,
Yet his hide, streaked and pied,
As I ride, as I ride,
Shows where sweat has sprung and dried,

30 – Zebra-footed, ostrich-thighed –
How has vied stride with stride
As I ride, as I ride!

V

As I ride, as I ride,
Could I loose what Fate has tied,
Ere I pried, she should hide
(As I ride, as I ride)
All that's meant me – satisfied
When the Prophet and the Bride
Stop veins I'd have subside

40 As I ride, as I ride!

The Pied Piper of Hamelin;

A Child's Story
(Written for, and inscribed to, W.M. the Younger)

I

Hamelin Town's in Brunswick,
    By famous Hanover city;
The river Weser, deep and wide,
Washes its wall on the southern side;
A pleasanter spot you never spied;
    But, when begins my ditty,
Almost five hundred years ago,
To see the townsfolk suffer so
    From vermin, was a pity.

II

10   Rats!
They fought the dogs and killed the cats,
    And bit the babies in the cradles,
And ate the cheeses out of the vats,
    And licked the soup from the cooks' own ladles,
Split open the kegs of salted sprats,
Made nests inside men's Sunday hats,
And even spoiled the women's chats
        By drowning their speaking
        With shrieking and squeaking
20   In fifty different sharps and flats.

III

At last the people in a body
        To the Town Hall came flocking:
''Tis clear,' cried they, 'our Mayor's a noddy;
        And as for our Corporation – shocking
To think we buy gowns lined with ermine
For dolts that can't or won't determine
What's best to rid us of our vermin!
You hope, because you're old and obese,
To find in the furry civic robe ease?
30   Rouse up, sirs! Give your brains a racking
To find the remedy we're lacking,

Or, sure as fate, we'll send you packing!'
At this the Mayor and Corporation
Quaked with a mighty consternation.

IV

An hour they sat in council,
   At length the Mayor broke silence:
'For a guilder I'd my ermine gown sell,
   I wish I were a mile hence!
It's easy to bid one rack one's brain –
40 I'm sure my poor head aches again,
I've scratched it so, and all in vain.
Oh for a trap, a trap, a trap!'
Just as he said this, what should hap
At the chamber door but a gentle tap?
'Bless us,' cried the Mayor, 'what's that?'
(With the Corporation as he sat,
Looking little though wondrous fat;
Nor brighter was his eye, nor moister
Than a too-long-opened oyster,
50 Save when at noon his paunch grew mutinous
For a plate of turtle green and glutinous)
'Only a scraping of shoes on the mat?
Anything like the sound of a rat
Makes my heart go pit-a-pat!'

V

'Come in!' – the Mayor cried, looking bigger:
And in did come the strangest figure!
His queer long coat from heel to head
Was half of yellow and half of red,
And he himself was tall and thin,
60 With sharp blue eyes, each like a pin,
And light loose hair, yet swarthy skin,
No tuft on cheek nor beard on chin,
But lips where smiles went out and in;
There was no guessing his kith and kin:
And nobody could enough admire
The tall man and his quaint attire.
Quoth one: 'It's as my great-grandsire,
Starting up at the Trump of Doom's tone,
Had walked this way from his painted tombstone!'

VI

70 He advanced to the council-table:
   And, 'Please your honours,' said he, 'I'm able,
   By means of a secret charm, to draw
       All creatures living beneath the sun,
       That creep or swim or fly or run,
   After me so as you never saw!
   And I chiefly use my charm
   On creatures that do people harm,
   The mole and toad and newt and viper;
   And people call me the Pied Piper.'
80 (And here they noticed round his neck
       A scarf of red and yellow stripe,
   To match with his coat of the self-same check;
       And at the scarf's end hung a pipe;
   And his fingers, they noticed, were ever straying
   As if impatient to be playing
   Upon this pipe, as low it dangled
   Over his vesture so old-fangled.)
   'Yet,' said he, 'poor piper as I am,
   In Tartary I freed the Cham,
90   Last June, from his huge swarms of gnats;
   I eased in Asia the Nizam
       Of a monstrous brood of vampire-bats:
   And as for what your brain bewilders,
       If I can rid your town of rats
   Will you give me a thousand guilders?'
   'One? fifty thousand!' – was the exclamation
   Of the astonished Mayor and Corporation.

VII

   Into the street the Piper stept,
       Smiling first a little smile,
100 As if he knew what magic slept
       In his quiet pipe the while;
   Then, like a musical adept,
   To blow the pipe his lips he wrinkled,
   And green and blue his sharp eyes twinkled,
   Like a candle-flame where salt is sprinkled;
   And ere three shrill notes the pipe uttered,
   You heard as if an army muttered;
   And the muttering grew to a grumbling;

And the grumbling grew to a mighty rumbling;
110 And out of the houses the rats came tumbling.
Great rats, small rats, lean rats, brawny rats,
Brown rats, black rats, grey rats, tawny rats,
Grave old plodders, gay young friskers,
   Fathers, mothers, uncles, cousins,
Cocking tails and pricking whiskers,
   Families by tens and dozens,
Brothers, sisters, husbands, wives –
Followed the Piper for their lives.
From street to street he piped advancing,
120 And step for step they followed dancing,
Until they came to the river Weser,
   Wherein all plunged and perished!
– Save one who, stout as Julius Caesar,
Swam across and lived to carry
   (As he, the manuscript he cherished)
To Rat-land home his commentary:
Which was, 'At the first shrill notes of the pipe,
I heard a sound as of scraping tripe,
And putting apples, wondrous ripe,
130 Into a cider-press's gripe:
And a moving away of pickle-tub-boards,
And a leaving ajar of conserve-cupboards,
And a drawing the corks of train-oil-flasks,
And a breaking the hoops of butter-casks:
And it seemed as if a voice
   (Sweeter far than bý harp or bý psaltery
Is breathed) called out, "Oh rats, rejoice!
   The world is grown to one vast drysaltery!
So munch on, crunch on, take your nuncheon,
140 Breakfast, supper, dinner, luncheon!"
And just as a bulky sugar-puncheon,
All ready staved, like a great sun shone
Glorious scarce an inch before me,
Just as methought it said, "Come, bore me!"
– I found the Weser rolling o'er me.'

VIII
You should have heard the Hamelin people
Ringing the bells till they rocked the steeple.
'Go,' cried the Mayor, 'and get long poles,

Poke out the nests and block up the holes!
150 Consult with carpenters and builders,
And leave in our town not even a trace
Of the rats!' – when suddenly, up the face
Of the Piper perked in the market-place,
With a, 'First, if you please, my thousand guilders!'

IX

A thousand guilders! The Mayor looked blue;
So did the Corporation too.
For council dinners made rare havoc
With Claret, Moselle, Vin-de-Grave, Hock;
And half the money would replenish
160 Their cellar's biggest butt with Rhenish.
To pay this sum to a wandering fellow
With a gypsy coat of red and yellow!
'Beside,' quoth the Mayor with a knowing wink,
'Our business was done at the river's brink;
We saw with our eyes the vermin sink,
And what's dead can't come to life, I think.
So, friend, we're not the folks to shrink
From the duty of giving you something for drink,
And a matter of money to put in your poke;
170 But as for the guilders, what we spoke
Of them, as you very well know, was in joke.
Beside, our losses have made us thrifty.
A thousand guilders! Come, take fifty!'

X

The Piper's face fell, and he cried
'No trifling! I can't wait, beside!
I've promised to visit by dinner-time
Bagdat, and accept the prime
Of the Head-Cook's pottage, all he's rich in,
For having left, in the Caliph's kitchen,
180 Of a nest of scorpions no survivor:
With him I proved no bargain-driver,
With you, don't think I'll bate a stiver!
And folks who put me in a passion
May find me pipe after another fashion.'

XI

'How?' cried the Mayor, 'd'ye think I brook
Being worse treated than a Cook?
Insulted by a lazy ribald
With idle pipe and vesture piebald?
You threaten us, fellow? Do your worst,
190 Blow your pipe there till you burst!'

XII

Once more he stept into the street
    And to his lips again
    Laid his long pipe of smooth straight cane;
And ere he blew three notes (such sweet
Soft notes as yet musician's cunning
    Never gave the enraptured air)
There was a rustling that seemed like a bustling
Of merry crowds justling at pitching and hustling,
Small feet were pattering, wooden shoes clattering,
200 Little hands clapping and little tongues chattering,
And, like fowls in a farm-yard when barley is scattering,
Out came the children running.
All the little boys and girls,
With rosy cheeks and flaxen curls,
And sparkling eyes and teeth like pearls,
Tripping and skipping, ran merrily after
The wonderful music with shouting and laughter.

XIII

The Mayor was dumb, and the Council stood
As if they were changed into blocks of wood.
210 Unable to move a step, or cry
To the children merrily skipping by,
– Could only follow with the eye
That joyous crowd at the Piper's back.
But how the Mayor was on the rack,
And the wretched Council's bosoms beat,
As the Piper turned from the High Street
To where the Weser rolled its waters
Right in the way of their sons and daughters!
However he turned from South to West,
220 And to Koppelberg Hill his steps addressed,

And after him the children pressed;
Great was the joy in every breast.
'He never can cross that mighty top!
He's forced to let the piping drop,
And we shall see our children stop!'
When, lo, as they reached the mountain-side,
A wondrous portal opened wide,
As if a cavern was suddenly hollowed;
And the Piper advanced and the children followed,
230 And when all were in to the very last,
The door in the mountain-side shut fast.
Did I say, all? No! One was lame,
    And could not dance the whole of the way;
And in after years, if you would blame
    His sadness, he was used to say, –
'It's dull in our town since my playmates left!
I can't forget that I'm bereft
Of all the pleasant sights they see,
Which the Piper also promised me.
240 For he led us, he said, to a joyous land,
Joining the town and just at hand,
Where waters gushed and fruit-trees grew
And flowers put forth a fairer hue,
And everything was strange and new;
The sparrows were brighter than peacocks here,
And their dogs outran our fallow deer,
And honey-bees had lost their stings,
And horses were born with eagles' wings:
And just as I became assured
250 My lame foot would be speedily cured,
The music stopped and I stood still,
And found myself outside the hill,
Left alone against my will,
To go now limping as before,
And never hear of that country more!'

XIV
Alas, alas for Hamelin!
    There came into many a burgher's pate
    A text which says that heaven's gate
    Opes to the rich at as easy rate

260 As the needle's eye takes a camel in!
The mayor sent East, West, North and South,
To offer the Piper, by word of mouth,
    Wherever it was men's lot to find him,
Silver and gold to his heart's content,
If he'd only return the way he went,
    And bring the children behind him.
But when they saw 'twas a lost endeavour,
And Piper and dancers were gone for ever,
They made a decree that lawyers never
270 Should think their records dated duly
If, after the day of the month and year,
These words did not as well appear,
'And so long after what happened here
    On the Twenty-second of July,
Thirteen hundred and seventy-six':
And the better in memory to fix
The place of the children's last retreat,
They called it, the Pied Piper's Street –
Where any one playing on pipe or tabor
280 Was sure for the future to lose his labour.
Nor suffered they hostelry or tavern
    To shock with mirth a street so solemn;
But opposite the place of the cavern
    They wrote the story on a column,
And on the great church-window painted
The same, to make the world acquainted
How their children were stolen away,
And there it stands to this very day.
And I must not omit to say
290 That in Transylvania there's a tribe
Of alien people who ascribe
The outlandish ways and dress
On which their neighbours lay such stress,
To their fathers and mothers having risen
Out of some subterraneous prison
Into which they were trepanned
Long time ago in a mighty band
Out of Hamelin town in Brunswick land,
But how or why, they don't understand.

XV

300 So, Willy, let me and you be wipers
Of scores out with all men – especially pipers!
And, whether they pipe us free fróm rats or fróm mice,
If we've promised them aught, let us keep our promise!

Dramatic Romances and Lyrics

1845

I

I sprang to the stirrup, and Joris, and he;
I galloped, Dirck galloped, we galloped all three;
'Good speed!' cried the watch, as the gate-bolts undrew;
'Speed!' echoed the wall to us galloping through;
Behind shut the postern, the lights sank to rest,
And into the midnight we galloped abreast.

II

Not a word to each other; we kept the great pace
Neck by neck, stride by stride, never changing our place;
I turned in my saddle and made its girths tight,
10 Then shortened each stirrup, and set the pique right,
Rebuckled the cheek-strap, chained slacker the bit,
Nor galloped less steadily Roland a whit.

III

'Twas moonset at starting; but while we drew near
Lokeren, the cocks crew and twilight dawned clear;
At Boom, a great yellow star came out to see;
At Düffeld, 'twas morning as plain as could be;
And from Mecheln church-steeple we heard the half-chime,
So, Joris broke silence with, 'Yet there is time!'

IV

At Aershot, up leaped of a sudden the sun,
20 And against him the cattle stood black every one,
To stare through the mist at us galloping past,
And I saw my stout galloper Roland at last,
With resolute shoulders, each butting away
The haze, as some bluff river headland its spray:

V

And his low head and crest, just one sharp ear bent back
For my voice, and the other pricked out on his track;
And one eye's black intelligence, – ever that glance
O'er its white edge at me, his own master, askance!

And the thick heavy spume-flakes which aye and anon
30   His fierce lips shook upwards in galloping on.

VI

By Hasselt, Dirck groaned; and cried Joris, 'Stay spur!
Your Roos galloped bravely, the fault's not in her,
We'll remember at Aix' – for one heard the quick wheeze
Of her chest, saw the stretched neck and staggering knees,
And sunk tail, and horrible heave of the flank,
As down on her haunches she shuddered and sank.

VII

So, we were left galloping, Joris and I,
Past Looz and past Tongres, no cloud in the sky;
The broad sun above laughed a pitiless laugh,
40   'Neath our feet broke the brittle bright stubble like chaff;
Till over by Dalhem a dome-spire sprang white,
And 'Gallop,' gasped Joris, 'for Aix is in sight!'

VIII

'How they'll greet us!' – and all in a moment his roan
Rolled neck and croup over, lay dead as a stone;
And there was my Roland to bear the whole weight
Of the news which alone could save Aix from her fate,
With his nostrils like pits full of blood to the brim,
And with circles of red for his eye-sockets' rim.

IX

Then I cast loose my buffcoat, each holster let fall,
50   Shook off both my jack-boots, let go belt and all,
Stood up in the stirrup, leaned, patted his ear,
Called my Roland his pet-name, my horse without peer;
Clapped my hands, laughed and sang, any noise, bad or good,
Till at length into Aix Roland galloped and stood.

X

And all I remember is – friends flocking round
As I sat with his head 'twixt my knees on the ground;
And no voice but was praising this Roland of mine,
As I poured down his throat our last measure of wine,
Which (the burgesses voted by common consent)
60   Was no more than his due who brought good news from Ghent.

Pictor Ignotus

FLORENCE, 15—

I could have painted pictures like that youth's
    Ye praise so. How my soul springs up! No bar
Stayed me – ah, thought which saddens while it soothes!
    – Never did fate forbid me, star by star,
To outburst on your night with all my gift
    Of fires from God: nor would my flesh have shrunk
From seconding my soul, with eyes uplift
    And wide to heaven, or, straight like thunder, sunk
To the centre, of an instant; or around
10   Turned calmly and inquisitive, to scan
The licence and the limit, space and bound,
    Allowed to truth made visible in man.
And, like that youth ye praise so, all I saw,
    Over the canvas could my hand have flung,
Each face obedient to its passion's law,
    Each passion clear proclaimed without a tongue;
Whether Hope rose at once in all the blood,
    A-tiptoe for the blessing of embrace,
Or Rapture drooped the eyes, as when her brood
20   Pull down the nesting dove's heart to its place;
Or Confidence lit swift the forehead up,
    And locked the mouth fast, like a castle braved, –
O human faces, hath it spilt, my cup?
    What did ye give me that I have not saved?
Nor will I say I have not dreamed (how well!)
    Of going – I, in each new picture, – forth,
As, making new hearts beat and bosoms swell,
    To Pope or Kaiser, East, West, South, or North,
Bound for the calmly-satisfied great State,
30   Or glad aspiring little burgh, it went,
Flowers cast upon the car which bore the freight,
    Through old streets named afresh from the event,
Till it reached home, where learned age should greet
    My face, and youth, the star not yet distinct
Above his hair, lie learning at my feet! –
    Oh, thus to live, I and my picture, linked
With love about, and praise, till life should end,

And then not go to heaven, but linger here,
Here on my earth, earth's every man my friend, –
40   The thought grew frightful, 'twas so wildly dear!
But a voice changed it. Glimpses of such sights
    Have scared me, like the revels through a door
Of some strange house of idols at its rites!
    This world seemed not the world it was before:
Mixed with my loving trusting ones, there trooped
    ... Who summoned those cold faces that begun
To press on me and judge me? Though I stooped
    Shrinking, as from the soldiery a nun,
They drew me forth, and spite of me ... enough!
50   These buy and sell our pictures, take and give,
Count them for garniture and household-stuff,
    And where they live needs must our pictures live
And see their faces, listen to their prate,
    Partakers of their daily pettiness,
Discussed of, – 'This I love, or this I hate,
    This likes me more, and this affects me less!'
Wherefore I chose my portion. If at whiles
    My heart sinks, as monotonous I paint
These endless cloisters and eternal aisles
60   With the same series, Virgin, Babe and Saint,
With the same cold calm beautiful regard, –
    At least no merchant traffics in my heart;
The sanctuary's gloom at least shall ward
    Vain tongues from where my pictures stand apart:
Only prayer breaks the silence of the shrine
    While, blackening in the daily candle-smoke,
They moulder on the damp wall's travertine,
    'Mid echoes the light footstep never woke.
So, die my pictures! surely, gently die!
70   O youth, men praise so, – holds their praise its worth?
Blown harshly, keeps the trump its golden cry?
    Tastes sweet the water with such specks of earth?

The Italian in England

That second time they hunted me
From hill to plain, from shore to sea,
And Austria, hounding far and wide
Her blood-hounds through the country-side,
Breathed hot and instant on my trace, –
I made six days a hiding-place
Of that dry green old aqueduct
Where I and Charles, when boys, have plucked
The fire-flies from the roof above,
10 Bright creeping through the moss they love:
– How long it seems since Charles was lost!
Six days the soldiers crossed and crossed
The country in my very sight;
And when that peril ceased at night,
The sky broke out in red dismay
With signal fires; well, there I lay
Close covered o'er in my recess,
Up to the neck in ferns and cress,
Thinking on Metternich our friend,
20 And Charles's miserable end,
And much beside, two days; the third,
Hunger o'ercame me when I heard
The peasants from the village go
To work among the maize; you know,
With us in Lombardy, they bring
Provisions packed on mules, a string
With little bells that cheer their task,
And casks, and boughs on every cask
To keep the sun's heat from the wine;
30 These I let pass in jingling line,
And, close on them, dear noisy crew,
The peasants from the village, too;
For at the very rear would troop
Their wives and sisters in a group
To help, I knew. When these had passed,
I threw my glove to strike the last,
Taking the chance: she did not start,
Much less cry out, but stooped apart,
One instant rapidly glanced round,

40   And saw me beckon from the ground.
A wild bush grows and hides my crypt;
She picked my glove up while she stripped
A branch off, then rejoined the rest
With that; my glove lay in her breast.
Then I drew breath; they disappeared:
It was for Italy I feared.

An hour, and she returned alone
Exactly where my glove was thrown.
Meanwhile came many thoughts: on me
50   Rested the hopes of Italy.
I had devised a certain tale
Which, when 'twas told her, could not fail
Persuade a peasant of its truth;
I meant to call a freak of youth
This hiding, and give hopes of pay,
And no temptation to betray.
But when I saw that woman's face,
Its calm simplicity of grace,
Our Italy's own attitude
60   In which she walked thus far, and stood,
Planting each naked foot so firm,
To crush the snake and spare the worm –
At first sight of her eyes, I said,
'I am that man upon whose head
They fix the price, because I hate
The Austrians over us: the State
Will give you gold – oh, gold so much! –
If you betray me to their clutch,
And be your death, for aught I know,
70   If once they find you saved their foe.
Now, you must bring me food and drink,
And also paper, pen and ink,
And carry safe what I shall write
To Padua, which you'll reach at night
Before the duomo shuts; go in,
And wait till Tenebrae begin;
Walk to the third confessional,
Between the pillar and the wall,
And kneeling whisper, *Whence comes peace?*

80 Say it a second time, then cease;
   And if the voice inside returns,
   From Christ and Freedom; what concerns
   The cause of Peace? – for answer, slip
   My letter where you placed your lip;
   Then come back happy we have done
   Our mother service – I, the son,
   As you the daughter of our land!'

   Three mornings more, she took her stand
   In the same place, with the same eyes:
90 I was no surer of sunrise
   Than of her coming. We conferred
   Of her own prospects, and I heard
   She had a lover – stout and tall,
   She said – then let her eyelids fall,
   'He could do much' – as if some doubt
   Entered her heart, – then, passing out,
   'She could not speak for others, who
   Had other thoughts; herself she knew':
   And so she brought me drink and food.
100 After four days, the scouts pursued
   Another path; at last arrived
   The help my Paduan friends contrived
   To furnish me: she brought the news.
   For the first time I could not choose
   But kiss her hand, and lay my own
   Upon her head – 'This faith was shown
   To Italy, our mother; she
   Uses my hand and blesses thee.'
   She followed down to the sea-shore;
110 I left and never saw her more.

   How very long since I have thought
   Concerning – much less wished for – aught
   Beside the good of Italy,
   For which I live and mean to die!
   I never was in love; and since
   Charles proved false, what shall now convince
   My inmost heart I have a friend?
   However, if I pleased to spend

Real wishes on myself – say, three –
120 I know at least what one should be.
I would grasp Metternich until
I felt his red wet throat distil
In blood through these two hands. And next,
– Nor much for that am I perplexed –
Charles, perjured traitor, for his part,
Should die slow of a broken heart
Under his new employers. Last
– Ah, there, what should I wish? For fast
Do I grow old and out of strength.
130 If I resolved to seek at length
My father's house again, how scared
They all would look, and unprepared!
My brothers live in Austria's pay
– Disowned me long ago, men say;
And all my early mates who used
To praise me so – perhaps induced
More than one early step of mine –
Are turning wise: while some opine
'Freedom grows licence,' some suspect
140 'Haste breeds delay,' and recollect
They always said, such premature
Beginnings never could endure!
So, with a sullen 'All's for best,'
The land seems settling to its rest.
I think then, I should wish to stand
This evening in that dear, lost land,
Over the sea the thousand miles,
And know if yet that woman smiles
With the calm smile; some little farm
150 She lives in there, no doubt: what harm
If I sat on the door-side bench,
And, while her spindle made a trench
Fantastically in the dust,
Inquired of all her fortunes – just
Her children's ages and their names,
And what may be the husband's aims
For each of them. I'd talk this out,
And sit there, for an hour about,
Then kiss her hand once more, and lay
160 Mine on her head, and go my way.

So much for idle wishing – how
It steals the time! To business now.

The Englishman in Italy

PIANO DI SORRENTO

Fortù, Fortù, my beloved one,
    Sit here by my side,
On my knees put up both little feet!
    I was sure, if I tried,
I could make you laugh spite of Scirocco.
    Now, open your eyes,
Let me keep you amused till he vanish
    In black from the skies,
With telling my memories over
10   As you tell your beads;
All the Plain saw me gather, I garland
    – The flowers or the weeds.

Time for rain! for your long hot dry Autumn
    Had net-worked with brown
The white skin of each grape on the bunches,
    Marked like a quail's crown,
Those creatures you make such account of,
    Whose heads, – speckled white
Over brown like a great spider's back,
20   As I told you last night, –
Your mother bites off for her supper.
    Red-ripe as could be,
Pomegranates were chapping and splitting
    In halves on the tree:
And betwixt the loose walls of great flintstone,
    Or in the thick dust
On the path, or straight out of the rock-side,
    Wherever could thrust
Some burnt sprig of bold hardy rock-flower
30   Its yellow face up,
For the prize were great butterflies fighting,
    Some five for one cup.

So, I guessed, ere I got up this morning,
   What change was in store,
By the quick rustle-down of the quail-nets
   Which woke me before
I could open my shutter, made fast
   With a bough and a stone,
And look through the twisted dead vine-twigs,
40   Sole lattice that's known.
Quick and sharp rang the rings down the net-poles,
   While, busy beneath,
Your priest and his brother tugged at them,
   The rain in their teeth.
And out upon all the flat house-roofs
   Where split figs lay drying,
The girls took the frails under cover:
   Nor use seemed in trying
To get out the boats and go fishing,
50   For, under the cliff,
Fierce the black water frothed o'er the blind-rock.
   No seeing our skiff
Arrive about noon from Amalfi,
   – Our fisher arrive,
And pitch down his basket before us,
   All trembling alive
With pink and grey jellies, your sea-fruit;
   You touch the strange lumps,
And mouths gape there, eyes open, all manner
60   Of horns and of humps,
Which only the fisher looks grave at,
   While round him like imps
Cling screaming the children as naked
   And brown as his shrimps;
Himself too as bare to the middle
   – You see round his neck
The string and its brass coin suspended,
   That saves him from wreck.
But today not a boat reached Salerno,
70   So back, to a man,
Came our friends, with whose help in the vineyards
   Grape-harvest began.
In the vat, halfway up in our house-side,
   Like blood the juice spins,

While your brother all bare-legged is dancing
    Till breathless he grins
Dead-beaten in effort on effort
    To keep the grapes under,
Since still when he seems all but master,
80   In pours the fresh plunder
From girls who keep coming and going
    With basket on shoulder,
And eyes shut against the rain's driving;
    Your girls that are older, –
For under the hedges of aloe,
    And where, on its bed
Of the orchard's black mould, the love-apple
    Lies pulpy and red,
All the young ones are kneeling and filling
90   Their laps with the snails
Tempted out by this first rainy weather, –
    Your best of regales,
As tonight will be proved to my sorrow,
    When, supping in state,
We shall feast our grape-gleaners (two dozen,
    Three over one plate)
With lasagne so tempting to swallow
    In slippery ropes,
And gourds fried in great purple slices,
100   That colour of popes.
Meantime, see the grape bunch they've brought you:
    The rain-water slips
O'er the heavy blue bloom on each globe
    Which the wasp to your lips
Still follows with fretful persistence:
    Nay, taste, while awake,
This half of a curd-white smooth cheese-ball
    That peels, flake by flake,
Like an onion, each smoother and whiter;
110   Next, sip this weak wine
From the thin green glass flask, with its stopper,
    A leaf of the vine;
And end with the prickly-pear's red flesh
    That leaves through its juice
The stony black seeds on your pearl-teeth.
    Scirocco is loose!

Hark, the quick, whistling pelt of the olives
    Which, thick in one's track,
Tempt the stranger to pick up and bite them,
120   Though not yet half black!
How the old twisted olive trunks shudder,
    The medlars let fall
Their hard fruit, and the brittle great fig-trees
    Snap off, figs and all,
For here comes the whole of the tempest!
    No refuge, but creep
Back again to my side and my shoulder,
    And listen or sleep.

O how will your country show next week,
130   When all the vine-boughs
Have been stripped of their foliage to pasture
    The mules and the cows?
Last eve, I rode over the mountains;
    Your brother, my guide,
Soon left me, to feast on the myrtles
    That offered, each side,
Their fruit-balls, black, glossy and luscious, –
    Or strip from the sorbs
A treasure, or, rosy and wondrous,
140   Those hairy gold orbs!
But my mule picked his sure sober path out,
    Just stopping to neigh
When he recognized down in the valley
    His mates on their way
With the faggots and barrels of water;
    And soon we emerged
From the plain, where the woods could scarce follow;
    And still as we urged
Our way, the woods wondered, and left us,
150   As up still we trudged
Though the wild path grew wilder each instant,
    And place was e'en grudged
'Mid the rock-chasms and piles of loose stones
    Like the loose broken teeth
Of some monster which climbed there to die
    From the ocean beneath –
Place was grudged to the silver-grey fume-weed

That clung to the path,
And dark rosemary ever a-dying
160   That, 'spite the wind's wrath,
So loves the salt rock's face to seaward,
    And lentisks as staunch
To the stone where they root and bear berries,
    And . . . what shows a branch
Coral-coloured, transparent, with circlets
    Of pale sea-green leaves;
Over all trod my mule with the caution
    Of gleaners o'er sheaves,
Still, foot after foot like a lady,
170   Till, round after round,
He climbed to the top of Calvano,
    And God's own profound
Was above me, and round me the mountains,
    And under, the sea,
And within me my heart to bear witness
    What was and shall be.
Oh, heaven and the terrible crystal!
    No rampart excludes
Your eye from the life to be lived
180   In the blue solitudes.
Oh, those mountains, their infinite movement!
    Still moving with you;
For, ever some new head and breast of them
    Thrusts into view
To observe the intruder; you see it
    If quickly you turn
And, before they escape you, surprise them.
    They grudge you should learn
How the soft plains they look on, lean over
190   And love (they pretend)
– Cower beneath them, the flat sea-pine crouches,
    The wild fruit-trees bend,
E'en the myrtle-leaves curl, shrink and shut:
    All is silent and grave:
'Tis a sensual and timorous beauty,
    How fair! but a slave.
So, I turned to the sea; and there slumbered
    As greenly as ever
Those isles of the siren, your Galli;

200 No ages can sever
The Three, nor enable their sister
    To join them, – halfway
On the voyage, she looked at Ulysses –
    No farther today,
Though the small one, just launched in the wave,
    Watches breast-high and steady
From under the rock, her bold sister
    Swum halfway already.
Fortù, shall we sail there together
210 And see from the sides
Quite new rocks show their faces, new haunts
    Where the siren abides?
Shall we sail round and round them, close over
    The rocks, though unseen,
That ruffle the grey glassy water
    To glorious green?
Then scramble from splinter to splinter,
    Reach land and explore,
On the largest, the strange square black turret
220 With never a door,
Just a loop to admit the quick lizards;
    Then, stand there and hear
The birds' quiet singing, that tells us
    What life is, so clear?
– The secret they sang to Ulysses
    When, ages ago,
He heard and he knew this life's secret
    I hear and I know.

Ah, see! The sun breaks o'er Calvano;
230 He strikes the great gloom
And flutters it o'er the mount's summit
    In airy gold fume.
All is over. Look out, see the gypsy,
    Our tinker and smith,
Has arrived, set up bellows and forge,
    And down-squatted forthwith
To his hammering, under the wall there;
    One eye keeps aloof
The urchins that itch to be putting
240 His jews'-harps to proof,

While the other, through locks of curled wire,
    Is watching how sleek
Shines the hog, come to share in the windfall
    – Chew, abbot's own cheek!
All is over. Wake up and come out now,
    And down let us go,
And see the fine things got in order
    At church for the show
Of the Sacrament, set forth this evening.
250   Tomorrow's the Feast
Of the Rosary's Virgin, by no means
    Of Virgins the least,
As you'll hear in the off-hand discourse
    Which (all nature, no art)
The Dominican brother, these three weeks,
    Was getting by heart.
Not a pillar nor post but is dizened
    With red and blue papers;
All the roof waves with ribbons, each altar
260   A-blaze with long tapers;
But the great masterpiece is the scaffold
    Rigged glorious to hold
All the fiddlers and fifers and drummers
    And trumpeters bold,
Not afraid of Bellini nor Auber,
    Who, when the priest's hoarse,
Will strike us up something that's brisk
    For the feast's second course.
And then will the flaxen-wigged Image
270   Be carried in pomp
Through the plain, while in gallant procession
    The priests mean to stomp.
All round the glad church lie old bottles
    With gunpowder stopped,
Which will be, when the Image re-enters,
    Religiously popped;
And at night from the crest of Calvano
    Great bonfires will hang,
On the plain will the trumpets join chorus,
280   And more poppers bang.
At all events, come – to the garden
    As far as the wall;

    See me tap with a hoe on the plaster
       Till out there shall fall
    A scorpion with wide angry nippers!

     – 'Such trifles!' you say?
    Fortù, in my England at home,
       Men meet gravely today
    And debate, if abolishing Corn-laws
290   Be righteous and wise
    – If 'twere proper, Scirocco should vanish
       In black from the skies!

The Lost Leader

    I
Just for a handful of silver he left us,
    Just for a riband to stick in his coat –
Found the one gift of which fortune bereft us,
    Lost all the others she lets us devote;
They, with the gold to give, doled him out silver,
    So much was theirs who so little allowed:
How all our copper had gone for his service!
    Rags – were they purple, his heart had been proud!
We that had loved him so, followed him, honoured him,
10   Lived in his mild and magnificent eye,
Learned his great language, caught his clear accents,
    Made him our pattern to live and to die!
Shakespeare was of us, Milton was for us,
    Burns, Shelley, were with us, – they watch from their graves!
He alone breaks from the van and the freemen,
    – He alone sinks to the rear and the slaves!

    II
We shall march prospering, – not through his presence;
    Songs may inspirit us, – not from his lyre;
Deeds will be done, – while he boasts his quiescence,
20   Still bidding crouch whom the rest bade aspire:
Blot out his name, then, record one lost soul more,
    One task more declined, one more footpath untrod,
One more devils'-triumph and sorrow for angels,

One wrong more to man, one more insult to God!
Life's night begins: let him never come back to us!
   There would be doubt, hesitation and pain,
Forced praise on our part – the glimmer of twilight,
   Never glad confident morning again!
Best fight on well, for we taught him – strike gallantly,
30   Menace our heart ere we master his own;
Then let him receive the new knowledge and wait us,
   Pardoned in heaven, the first by the throne!

The Lost Mistress

I

All's over, then: does truth sound bitter
   As one at first believes?
Hark, 'tis the sparrows' good-night twitter
   About your cottage eaves!

II

And the leaf-buds on the vine are woolly,
   I noticed that, today;
One day more bursts them open fully
   – You know the red turns grey.

III

Tomorrow we meet the same then, dearest?
10   May I take your hand in mine?
Mere friends are we, – well, friends the merest
   Keep much that I resign:

IV

For each glance of the eye so bright and black,
   Though I keep with heart's endeavour, –
Your voice, when you wish the snowdrops back,
   Though it stay in my soul for ever! –

V

Yet I will but say what mere friends say,
   Or only a thought stronger;
I will hold your hand but as long as all may,
20   Or so very little longer!

Home-Thoughts, from Abroad

I
Oh, to be in England
Now that April's there,
And whoever wakes in England
Sees, some morning, unaware,
That the lowest boughs and the brushwood sheaf
Round the elm-tree bole are in tiny leaf,
While the chaffinch sings on the orchard bough
In England – now!

II
And after April, when May follows,
10 And the whitethroat builds, and all the swallows!
Hark, where my blossomed pear-tree in the hedge
Leans to the field and scatters on the clover
Blossoms and dewdrops – at the bent spray's edge –
That's the wise thrush; he sings each song twice over,
Lest you should think he never could recapture
The first fine careless rapture!
And though the fields look rough with hoary dew,
All will be gay when noontide wakes anew
The buttercups, the little children's dower
20 – Far brighter than this gaudy melon-flower!

Home-Thoughts, from the Sea

Nobly, nobly Cape Saint Vincent to the North-west died away;
Sunset ran, one glorious blood-red, reeking into Cadiz Bay;
Bluish 'mid the burning water, full in face Trafalgar lay;
In the dimmest North-east distance dawned Gibraltar grand and
    grey;
'Here and here did England help me: how can I help England?'
    – say,
Whoso turns as I, this evening, turn to God to praise and pray,
While Jove's planet rises yonder, silent over Africa.

The Bishop Orders His Tomb at Saint Praxed's Church

ROME, 15—

Vanity, saith the preacher, vanity!
Draw round my bed: is Anselm keeping back?
Nephews – sons mine ... ah God, I know not! Well –
She, men would have to be your mother once,
Old Gandolf envied me, so fair she was!
What's done is done, and she is dead beside,
Dead long ago, and I am Bishop since,
And as she died so must we die ourselves,
And thence ye may perceive the world's a dream.
10 Life, how and what is it? As here I lie
In this state-chamber, dying by degrees,
Hours and long hours in the dead night, I ask
'Do I live, am I dead?' Peace, peace seems all.
Saint Praxed's ever was the church for peace;
And so, about this tomb of mine. I fought
With tooth and nail to save my niche, ye know:
– Old Gandolf cozened me, despite my care;
Shrewd was that snatch from out the corner South
He graced his carrion with, God curse the same!
20 Yet still my niche is not so cramped but thence
One sees the pulpit o' the epistle-side,
And somewhat of the choir, those silent seats,
And up into the airy dome where live
The angels, and a sunbeam's sure to lurk:
And I shall fill my slab of basalt there,
And 'neath my tabernacle take my rest,
With those nine columns round me, two and two,
The odd one at my feet where Anselm stands:
Peach-blossom marble all, the rare, the ripe
30 As fresh-poured red wine of a mighty pulse.
– Old Gandolf with his paltry onion-stone,
Put me where I may look at him! True peach,
Rosy and flawless: how I earned the prize!
Draw close: that conflagration of my church
– What then? So much was saved if aught were missed!
My sons, ye would not be my death? Go dig
The white-grape vineyard where the oil-press stood,

Drop water gently till the surface sink,
And if ye find ... Ah God, I know not, I! ...
40 Bedded in store of rotten fig-leaves soft,
And corded up in a tight olive-frail,
Some lump, ah God, of *lapis lazuli*,
Big as a Jew's head cut off at the nape,
Blue as a vein o'er the Madonna's breast ...
Sons, all have I bequeathed you, villas, all,
That brave Frascati villa with its bath,
So, let the blue lump poise between my knees,
Like God the Father's globe on both his hands
Ye worship in the Jesu Church so gay,
50 For Gandolf shall not choose but see and burst!
Swift as a weaver's shuttle fleet our years:
Man goeth to the grave, and where is he?
Did I say basalt for my slab, sons? Black –
'Twas ever antique-black I meant! How else
Shall ye contrast my frieze to come beneath?
The bas-relief in bronze ye promised me,
Those Pans and Nymphs ye wot of, and perchance
Some tripod, thyrsus, with a vase or so,
The Saviour at his sermon on the mount,
60 Saint Praxed in a glory, and one Pan
Ready to twitch the Nymph's last garment off,
And Moses with the tables ... but I know
Ye mark me not! What do they whisper thee,
Child of my bowels, Anselm? Ah, ye hope
To revel down my villas while I gasp
Bricked o'er with beggar's mouldy travertine
Which Gandolf from his tomb-top chuckles at!
Nay, boys, ye love me – all of jasper, then!
'Tis jasper ye stand pledged to, lest I grieve
70 My bath must needs be left behind, alas!
One block, pure green as a pistachio-nut,
There's plenty jasper somewhere in the world –
And have I not Saint Praxed's ear to pray
Horses for ye, and brown Greek manuscripts,
And mistresses with great smooth marbly limbs?
– That's if ye carve my epitaph aright,
Choice Latin, picked phrase, Tully's every word,
No gaudy ware like Gandolf's second line –
Tully, my masters? Ulpian serves his need!

80 And then how I shall lie through centuries,
And hear the blessed mutter of the mass,
And see God made and eaten all day long,
And feel the steady candle-flame, and taste
Good strong thick stupefying incense-smoke!
For as I lie here, hours of the dead night,
Dying in state and by such slow degrees,
I fold my arms as if they clasped a crook,
And stretch my feet forth straight as stone can point,
And let the bedclothes, for a mortcloth, drop
90 Into great laps and folds of sculptor's-work:
And as yon tapers dwindle, and strange thoughts
Grow, with a certain humming in my ears,
About the life before I lived this life,
And this life too, popes, cardinals and priests,
Saint Praxed at his sermon on the mount,
Your tall pale mother with her talking eyes,
And new-found agate urns as fresh as day,
And marble's language, Latin pure, discreet,
– Aha, ELUCESCEBAT quoth our friend?
100 No Tully, said I, Ulpian at the best!
Evil and brief hath been my pilgrimage.
All *lapis*, all, sons! Else I give the Pope
My villas! Will ye ever eat my heart?
Ever your eyes were as a lizard's quick,
They glitter like your mother's for my soul,
Or ye would heighten my impoverished frieze,
Piece out its starved design, and fill my vase
With grapes, and add a vizor and a Term,
And to the tripod ye would tie a lynx
110 That in his struggle throws the thyrsus down,
To comfort me on my entablature
Whereon I am to lie till I must ask
'Do I live, am I dead?' There, leave me, there!
For ye have stabbed me with ingratitude
To death – ye wish it – God, ye wish it! Stone –
Gritstone, a-crumble! Clammy squares which sweat
As if the corpse they keep were oozing through –
And no more *lapis* to delight the world!
Well go! I bless ye. Fewer tapers there,
120 But in a row: and, going, turn your backs
– Ay, like departing altar-ministrants,

And leave me in my church, the church for peace,
    That I may watch at leisure if he leers –
Old Gandolf, at me, from his onion-stone,
    As still he envied me, so fair she was!

Garden Fancies

I. *The Flower's Name*

I

Here's the garden she walked across,
    Arm in my arm, such a short while since:
Hark, now I push its wicket, the moss
    Hinders the hinges and makes them wince!
She must have reached this shrub ere she turned,
    As back with that murmur the wicket swung;
For she laid the poor snail, my chance foot spurned,
    To feed and forget it the leaves among.

II

Down this side of the gravel-walk
10   She went while her robe's edge brushed the box:
And here she paused in her gracious talk
    To point me a moth on the milk-white phlox.
Roses, ranged in valiant row,
    I will never think that she passed you by!
She loves you noble roses, I know;
    But yonder, see, where the rock-plants lie!

III

This flower she stopped at, finger on lip,
    Stooped over, in doubt, as settling its claim;
Till she gave me, with pride to make no slip,
20   Its soft meandering Spanish name:
What a name! Was it love or praise?
    Speech half-asleep or song half-awake?
I must learn Spanish, one of these days,
    Only for that slow sweet name's sake.

IV

Roses, if I live and do well,
　I may bring her, one of these days,
To fix you fast with as fine a spell,
　Fit you each with his Spanish phrase;
But do not detain me now; for she lingers
30　　There, like sunshine over the ground,
And ever I see her soft white fingers
　　Searching after the bud she found.

V

Flower, you Spaniard, look that you grow not,
　Stay as you are and be loved for ever!
Bud, if I kiss you 'tis that you blow not:
　Mind, the shut pink mouth opens never!
For while it pouts, her fingers wrestle,
　Twinkling the audacious leaves between
Till round they turn and down they nestle –
40　　Is not the dear mark still to be seen?

VI

Where I find her not, beauties vanish;
　Whither I follow her, beauties flee;
Is there no method to tell her in Spanish
　June's twice June since she breathed it with me?
Come, bud, show me the least of her traces,
　Treasure my lady's lightest footfall!
– Ah, you may flout and turn up your faces –
　Roses, you are not so fair after all!

II. *Sibrandus Schafnaburgensis*

I

Plague take all your pedants, say I!
　He who wrote what I hold in my hand,
Centuries back was so good as to die,
　Leaving this rubbish to cumber the land;
This, that was a book in its time,
　Printed on paper and bound in leather,
Last month in the white of a matin-prime
　Just when the birds sang all together.

II

Into the garden I brought it to read,
10   And under the arbute and laurustine
Read it, so help me grace in my need,
    From title-page to closing line.
Chapter on chapter did I count,
    As a curious traveller counts Stonehenge;
Added up the mortal amount;
    And then proceeded to my revenge.

III

Yonder's a plum-tree with a crevice
    An owl would build in, were he but sage;
For a lap of moss, like a fine pont-levis
20   In a castle of the Middle Age,
Joins to a lip of gum, pure amber;
    When he'd be private, there might he spend
Hours alone in his lady's chamber:
    Into this crevice I dropped our friend.

IV

Splash, went he, as under he ducked,
    – At the bottom, I knew, rain-drippings stagnate:
Next, a handful of blossoms I plucked
    To bury him with, my bookshelf's magnate;
Then I went indoors, brought out a loaf,
30   Half a cheese, and a bottle of Chablis;
Lay on the grass and forgot the oaf
    Over a jolly chapter of Rabelais.

V

Now, this morning, betwixt the moss
    And gum that locked our friend in limbo,
A spider had spun his web across,
    And sat in the midst with arms akimbo:
So, I took pity, for learning's sake,
    And, *de profundis, accentibus laetis,*
Cantate! quoth I, as I got a rake;
40   And up I fished his delectable treatise.

VI

Here you have it, dry in the sun,
    With all the binding all of a blister,
And great blue spots where the ink has run,
    And reddish streaks that wink and glister
O'er the page so beautifully yellow:
    Oh, well have the droppings played their tricks!
Did he guess how toadstools grow, this fellow?
    Here's one stuck in his chapter six!

VII

How did he like it when the live creatures
50   Tickled and toused and browsed him all over,
And worm, slug, eft, with serious features,
    Came in, each one, for his right of trover?
– When the water-beetle with great blind deaf face
    Made of her eggs the stately deposit,
And the newt borrowed just so much of the preface
    As tiled in the top of his black wife's closet?

VIII

All that life and fun and romping,
    All that frisking and twisting and coupling,
While slowly our poor friend's leaves were swamping
60   And clasps were cracking and covers suppling!
As if you had carried sour John Knox
    To the play-house at Paris, Vienna or Munich,
Fastened him into a front-row box,
    And danced off the ballet with trousers and tunic.

IX

Come, old martyr! What, torment enough is it?
    Back to my room shall you take your sweet self.
Good-bye, mother-beetle; husband-eft, *sufficit!*
    See the snug niche I have made on my shelf!
A.'s book shall prop you up, B.'s shall cover you,
70   Here's C. to be grave with, or D. to be gay,
And with E. on each side, and F. right over you,
    Dry-rot at ease till the Judgement-day!

The Laboratory

Ancien Régime

I

Now that I, tying thy glass mask tightly,
May gaze through these faint smokes curling whitely,
As thou pliest thy trade in this devil's-smithy –
Which is the poison to poison her, prithee?

II

He is with her, and they know that I know
Where they are, what they do: they believe my tears flow
While they laugh, laugh at me, at me fled to the drear
Empty church, to pray God in, for them! – I am here.

III

Grind away, moisten and mash up thy paste,
10 Pound at thy powder, – I am not in haste!
Better sit thus, and observe thy strange things,
Than go where men wait me and dance at the King's.

IV

That in the mortar – you call it a gum?
Ah, the brave tree whence such gold oozings come!
And yonder soft phial, the exquisite blue,
Sure to taste sweetly, – is that poison too?

V

Had I but all of them, thee and thy treasures,
What a wild crowd of invisible pleasures!
To carry pure death in an ear-ring, a casket,
20 A signet, a fan-mount, a filigree basket!

VI

Soon, at the King's, a mere lozenge to give,
And Pauline should have just thirty minutes to live!
But to light a pastile, and Elise, with her head
And her breast and her arms and her hands, should drop dead!

VII

Quick – is it finished? The colour's too grim!
Why not soft like the phial's, enticing and dim?
Let it brighten her drink, let her turn it and stir,
And try it and taste, ere she fix and prefer!

VIII

What a drop! She's not little, no minion like me!
30 That's why she ensnared him: this never will free
The soul from those masculine eyes, – say, 'no!'
To that pulse's magnificent come-and-go.

IX

For only last night, as they whispered, I brought
My own eyes to bear on her so, that I thought
Could I keep them one half minute fixed, she would fall
Shrivelled; she fell not; yet this does it all!

X

Not that I bid you spare her the pain;
Let death be felt and the proof remain:
Brand, burn up, bite into its grace –
40 He is sure to remember her dying face!

XI

Is it done? Take my mask off! Nay, be not morose;
It kills her, and this prevents seeing it close:
The delicate droplet, my whole fortune's fee!
If it hurts her, beside, can it ever hurt me?

XII

Now, take all my jewels, gorge gold to your fill,
You may kiss me, old man, on my mouth if you will!
But brush this dust off me, lest horror it brings
Ere I know it – next moment I dance at the King's!

The Confessional

[Spain]

I

It is a lie – their Priests, their Pope,
Their Saints, their . . . all they fear or hope
Are lies, and lies – there! through my door
And ceiling, there! and walls and floor,
There, lies, they lie – shall still be hurled
Till spite of them I reach the world!

II

You think Priests just and holy men!
Before they put me in this den
I was a human creature too,
10   With flesh and blood like one of you,
A girl that laughed in beauty's pride
Like lilies in your world outside.

III

I had a lover – shame avaunt!
This poor wrenched body, grim and gaunt,
Was kissed all over till it burned,
By lips the truest, love e'er turned
His heart's own tint: one night they kissed
My soul out in a burning mist.

IV

So, next day when the accustomed train
20   Of things grew round my sense again,
'That is a sin,' I said: and slow
With downcast eyes to church I go,
And pass to the confession-chair,
And tell the old mild father there.

V

But when I falter Beltran's name,
'Ha?' quoth the father; 'much I blame
The sin; yet wherefore idly grieve?
Despair not – strenuously retrieve!

Nay, I will turn this love of thine
30   To lawful love, almost divine;

VI

'For he is young, and led astray,
This Beltran, and he schemes, men say,
To change the laws of church and state;
So, thine shall be an angel's fate,
Who, ere the thunder breaks, should roll
Its cloud away and save his soul.

VII

'For, when he lies upon thy breast,
Thou mayst demand and be possessed
Of all his plans, and next day steal
40   To me, and all those plans reveal,
That I and every priest, to purge
His soul, may fast and use the scourge.'

VIII

That father's beard was long and white,
With love and truth his brow seemed bright;
I went back, all on fire with joy,
And, that same evening, bade the boy
Tell me, as lovers should, heart-free,
Something to prove his love of me.

IX

He told me what he would not tell
50   For hope of heaven or fear of hell;
And I lay listening in such pride!
And, soon as he had left my side,
Tripped to the church by morning-light
To save his soul in his despite.

X

I told the father all his schemes,
Who were his comrades, what their dreams;
'And now make haste,' I said, 'to pray
The one spot from his soul away;
Tonight he comes, but not the same
60   Will look!' At night he never came.

XI

Nor next night: on the after-morn,
I went forth with a strength new-born.
The church was empty; something drew
My steps into the street; I knew
It led me to the market-place:
Where, lo, on high, the father's face!

XII

That horrible black scaffold dressed,
That stapled block . . . God sink the rest!
That head strapped back, that blinding vest,
70 Those knotted hands and naked breast,
Till near one busy hangman pressed,
And, on the neck these arms caressed . . .

XIII

No part in aught they hope or fear!
No heaven with them, no hell! – and here,
No earth, not so much space as pens
My body in their worst of dens
But shall bear God and man my cry,
Lies – lies, again – and still, they lie!

The Flight of the Duchess

I

You're my friend:
    I was the man the Duke spoke to;
    I helped the Duchess to cast off his yoke, too;
So here's the tale from beginning to end,
My friend!

II

Ours is a great wild country:
    If you climb to our castle's top,
    I don't see where your eye can stop;
For when you've passed the cornfield country,
10 Where vineyards leave off, flocks are packed,
And sheep-range leads to cattle-tract,

And cattle-tract to open-chase,
And open-chase to the very base
Of the mountain where, at a funeral pace,
Round about, solemn and slow,
One by one, row after row,
Up and up the pine-trees go,
So, like black priests up, and so
Down the other side again
20   To another greater, wilder country,
That's one vast red drear burnt-up plain,
Branched through and through with many a vein
Whence iron's dug, and copper's dealt;
    Look right, look left, look straight before, –
Beneath they mine, above they smelt,
    Copper-ore and iron-ore,
And forge and furnace mould and melt,
    And so on, more and ever more,
Till at the last, for a bounding belt,
30   Comes the salt sand hoar of the great sea-shore,
– And the whole is our Duke's country.

III
I was born the day this present Duke was –
    (And O, says the song, ere I was old!)
In the castle where the other Duke was –
    (When I was happy and young, not old!)
I in the kennel, he in the bower:
We are of like age to an hour.
My father was huntsman in that day;
Who has not heard my father say
40   That, when a boar was brought to bay,
Three times, four times out of five,
With his huntspear he'd contrive
To get the killing-place transfixed,
And pin him true, both eyes betwixt?
And that's why the old Duke would rather
He lost a salt-pit than my father,
And loved to have him ever in call;
That's why my father stood in the hall
When the old Duke brought his infant out
50   To show the people, and while they passed
The wondrous bantling round about,

Was first to start at the outside blast
As the Kaiser's courier blew his horn
Just a month after the babe was born.
'And,' quoth the Kaiser's courier, 'since
The Duke has got an heir, our Prince
 Needs the Duke's self at his side':
The Duke looked down and seemed to wince,
 But he thought of wars o'er the world wide,
60 Castles a-fire, men on their march,
The toppling tower, the crashing arch;
 And up he looked, and awhile he eyed
The row of crests and shields and banners
Of all achievements after all manners,
 And 'ay,' said the Duke with a surly pride.
 The more was his comfort when he died
At next year's end, in a velvet suit,
With a gilt glove on his hand, his foot
In a silken shoe for a leather boot,
70 Petticoated like a herald,
  In a chamber next to an ante-room,
  Where he breathed the breath of page and groom,
  What he called stink, and they, perfume:
– They should have set him on red Berold
Mad with pride, like fire to manage!
They should have got his cheek fresh tannage
Such a day as today in the merry sunshine!
Had they stuck on his fist a rough-foot merlin!
(Hark, the wind's on the heath at its game!
80 Oh for a noble falcon-lanner
To flap each broad wing like a banner,
And turn in the wind, and dance like flame!)
Had they broached a white-beer cask from Berlin!
– Or if you incline to prescribe mere wine
Put to his lips, when they saw him pine,
A cup of our own Moldavia fine,
Cotnar for instance, green as May sorrel
And ropy with sweet, – we shall not quarrel.

IV
So, at home, the sick tall yellow Duchess
90 Was left with the infant in her clutches,
She being the daughter of God knows who:

And now was the time to revisit her tribe.
Abroad and afar they went, the two,
   And let our people rail and gibe
At the empty hall and extinguished fire,
   As loud as we liked, but ever in vain,
Till after long years we had our desire,
   And back came the Duke and his mother again.

V

And he came back the pertest little ape
100 That ever affronted human shape;
Full of his travel, struck at himself.
   You'd say, he despised our bluff old ways?
– Not he! For in Paris they told the elf
   Our rough North land was the Land of Lays,
   The one good thing left in evil days;
Since the Mid-Age was the Heroic Time,
   And only in wild nooks like ours
Could you taste of it yet as in its prime,
   And see true castles, with proper towers,
110 Young-hearted women, old-minded men,
And manners now as manners were then.
So, all that the old Dukes had been, without knowing it,
This Duke would fain know he was, without being it;
'Twas not for the joy's self, but the joy of his showing it,
Nor for the pride's self, but the pride of our seeing it,
He revived all usages thoroughly worn-out,
The souls of them fumed-forth, the hearts of them torn-out:
And chief in the chase his neck he perilled
On a lathy horse, all legs and length,
120 With blood for bone, all speed, no strength;
– They should have set him on red Berold
With the red eye slow consuming in fire,
And the thin stiff ear like an abbey-spire!

VI

Well, such as he was, he must marry, we heard:
And out of a convent, at the word,
Came the lady, in time of spring.
– Oh, old thoughts they cling, they cling!
That day, I know, with a dozen oaths
I clad myself in thick hunting-clothes

130   Fit for the chase of urochs or buffle
      In winter-time when you need to muffle.
      But the Duke had a mind we should cut a figure,
          And so we saw the lady arrive:
      My friend, I have seen a white crane bigger!
          She was the smallest lady alive,
      Made in a piece of nature's madness,
      Too small, almost, for the life and gladness
          That over-filled her, as some hive
      Out of the bears' reach on the high trees
140   Is crowded with its safe merry bees:
      In truth, she was not hard to please!
      Up she looked, down she looked, round at the mead,
      Straight at the castle, that's best indeed
      To look at from outside the walls:
      As for us, styled the 'serfs and thralls,'
      She as much thanked me as if she had said it,
          (With her eyes, do you understand?)
      Because I patted her horse while I led it;
          And Max, who rode on her other hand,
150   Said, no bird flew past but she inquired
      What its true name was, nor ever seemed tired –
      If that was an eagle she saw hover,
      And the green and grey bird on the field was the plover.
      When suddenly appeared the Duke:
          And as down she sprung, the small foot pointed
      On to my hand, – as with a rebuke,
          And as if his backbone were not jointed,
      The Duke stepped rather aside than forward,
          And welcomed her with his grandest smile;
160   And, mind you, his mother all the while
      Chilled in the rear, like a wind to Nor'ward;
      And up, like a weary yawn, with its pulleys
      Went, in a shriek, the rusty portcullis;
      And, like a glad sky the north-wind sullies,
      The lady's face stopped its play,
      As if her first hair had grown grey;
      For such things must begin some one day.

      VII
      In a day or two she was well again;
      As who should say, 'You labour in vain!

170 This is all a jest against God, who meant
    I should ever be, as I am, content
    And glad in his sight; therefore, glad I will be.'
    So, smiling as at first went she.

VIII

She was active, stirring, all fire –
    Could not rest, could not tire –
    To a stone she might have given life!
        (I myself loved once, in my day)
    – For a shepherd's, miner's, huntsman's wife,
        (I had a wife, I know what I say)
180 Never in all the world such an one!
    And here was plenty to be done,
    And she that could do it, great or small,
    She was to do nothing at all.
    There was already this man in his post,
        This in his station, and that in his office,
    And the Duke's plan admitted a wife, at most,
        To meet his eye, with the other trophies,
    Now outside the hall, now in it,
        To sit thus, stand thus, see and be seen,
190 At the proper place in the proper minute,
        And die away the life between.
    And it was amusing enough, each infraction
        Of rule – (but for after-sadness that came)
    To hear the consummate self-satisfaction
        With which the young Duke and the old dame
    Would let her advise, and criticize,
    And, being a fool, instruct the wise,
        And, child-like, parcel out praise or blame:
    They bore it all in complacent guise,
200 As though an artificer, after contriving
    A wheel-work image as if it were living,
    Should find with delight it could motion to strike him!
    So found the Duke, and his mother like him:
    The lady hardly got a rebuff –
    That had not been contemptuous enough,
    With his cursed smirk, as he nodded applause,
    And kept off the old mother-cat's claws.

IX

So, the little lady grew silent and thin,
    Paling and ever paling,
210 As the way is with a hid chagrin;
    And the Duke perceived that she was ailing,
    And said in his heart, ''Tis done to spite me,
    But I shall find in my power to right me!'
    Don't swear, friend! The old one, many a year,
    Is in hell, and the Duke's self . . . you shall hear.

X

Well, early in autumn, at first winter-warning,
    When the stag had to break with his foot, of a morning,
    A drinking-hole out of the fresh tender ice
    That covered the pond till the sun, in a trice,
220 Loosening it, let out a ripple of gold,
    And another and another, and faster and faster,
    Till, dimpling to blindness, the wide water rolled:
    Then it so chanced that the Duke our master
    Asked himself what were the pleasures in season,
    And found, since the calendar bade him be hearty,
    He should do the Middle Age no treason
    In resolving on a hunting-party.
    Always provided, old books showed the way of it!
    What meant old poets by their strictures?
230 And when old poets had said their say of it,
    How taught old painters in their pictures?
    We must revert to the proper channels,
    Workings in tapestry, paintings on panels,
    And gather up woodcraft's authentic traditions:
    Here was food for our various ambitions,
    As on each case, exactly stated –
    To encourage your dog, now, the properest chirrup,
    Or best prayer to Saint Hubert on mounting your stirrup –
    We of the household took thought and debated.
240 Blessed was he whose back ached with the jerkin
    His sire was wont to do forest-work in;
    Blesseder he who nobly sunk 'ohs'
    And 'ahs' while he tugged on his grandsire's trunk-hose;
    What signified hats if they had no rims on,
    Each slouching before and behind like the scallop,
    And able to serve at sea for a shallop,

Loaded with lacquer and loopèd with crimson?
So that the deer now, to make a short rhyme on't,
　　What with our Venerers, Prickers and Verderers,
250　　Might hope for real hunters at length and not murderers,
And oh the Duke's tailor, he had a hot time on't!

XI

Now you must know that when the first dizziness
　　Of flap-hats and buff-coats and jack-boots subsided,
　　The Duke put this question, 'The Duke's part provided,
Had not the Duchess some share in the business?'
For out of the mouth of two or three witnesses
Did he establish all fit-or-unfitnesses:
And, after much laying of heads together,
Somebody's cap got a notable feather
260　By the announcement with proper unction
That he had discovered the lady's function;
Since ancient authors gave this tenet,
　　'When horns wind a mort and the deer is at siege,
Let the dame of the castle prick forth on her jennet,
　　And, with water to wash the hands of her liege
In a clean ewer with a fair toweling,
Let her preside at the disemboweling.'
Now, my friend, if you had so little religion
　　As to catch a hawk, some falcon-lanner,
270　　And thrust her broad wings like a banner
Into a coop for a vulgar pigeon;
And if day by day and week by week
　　You cut her claws, and sealed her eyes,
And clipped her wings, and tied her beak,
　　Would it cause you any great surprise
If, when you decided to give her an airing,
You found she needed a little preparing?
– I say, should you be such a curmudgeon,
If she clung to the perch, as to take it in dudgeon?
280　Yet when the Duke to his lady signified,
Just a day before, as he judged most dignified,
In what a pleasure she was to participate, –
　　And, instead of leaping wide in flashes,
　　Her eyes just lifted their long lashes,
As if pressed by fatigue even he could not dissipate,
And duly acknowledged the Duke's forethought,

But spoke of her health, if her health were worth aught,
Of the weight by day and the watch by night,
And much wrong now that used to be right,
290 So, thanking him, declined the hunting, –
Was conduct ever more affronting?
With all the ceremony settled –
  With the towel ready, and the sewer
  Polishing up his oldest ewer,
  And the jennet pitched upon, a picbald,
  Black-barred, cream-coated and pink eye-balled, –
No wonder if the Duke was nettled!
And when she persisted nevertheless, –
Well, I suppose here's the time to confess
300 That there ran half round our lady's chamber
A balcony none of the hardest to clamber;
And that Jacynth the tire-woman, ready in waiting,
Stayed in call outside, what need of relating?
And since Jacynth was like a June rose, why, a fervent
Adorer of Jacynth of course was your servant;
And if she had the habit to peep through the casement,
  How could I keep at any vast distance?
  And so, as I say, on the lady's persistence,
The Duke, dumb-stricken with amazement,
310 Stood for a while in a sultry smother,
  And then, with a smile that partook of the awful,
Turned her over to his yellow mother
  To learn what was held decorous and lawful;
And the mother smelt blood with a cat-like instinct,
As her cheek quick whitened through all its quince-tint.
Oh, but the lady heard the whole truth at once!
  What meant she? – Who was she? – Her duty and station,
The wisdom of age and the folly of youth, at once,
  Its decent regard and its fitting relation –
320 In brief, my friend, set all the devils in hell free
And turn them out to carouse in a belfry
And treat the priests to a fifty-part canon,
And then you may guess how that tongue of hers ran on!
Well, somehow or other it ended at last
And, licking her whiskers, out she passed;
And after her, – making (he hoped) a face
  Like Emperor Nero or Sultan Saladin,
Stalked the Duke's self with the austere grace

Of ancient hero or modern paladin,
330   From door to staircase – oh such a solemn
Unbending of the vertebral column!

XII

However, at sunrise our company mustered;
    And here was the huntsman bidding unkennel,
And there 'neath his bonnet the pricker blustered,
    With feather dank as a bough of wet fennel;
For the court-yard walls were filled with fog
You might have cut as an axe chops a log –
Like so much wool for colour and bulkiness;
And out rode the Duke in a perfect sulkiness,
340   Since, before breakfast, a man feels but queasily,
    And a sinking at the lower abdomen
    Begins the day with indifferent omen.
And lo, as he looked around uneasily,
The sun ploughed the fog up and drove it asunder
This way and that from the valley under;
    And, looking through the court-yard arch,
Down in the valley, what should meet him
    But a troop of Gypsies on their march?
No doubt with the annual gifts to greet him.

XIII

350   Now, in your land, Gypsies reach you, only
    After reaching all lands beside;
North they go, South they go, trooping or lonely,
    And still, as they travel far and wide,
Catch they and keep now a trace here, a trace there,
That puts you in mind of a place here, a place there.
But with us, I believe they rise out of the ground,
And nowhere else, I take it, are found
With the earth-tint yet so freshly embrowned:
Born, no doubt, like insects which breed on
360   The very fruit they are meant to feed on.
For the earth – not a use to which they don't turn it,
    The ore that grows in the mountain's womb,
    Or the sand in the pits like a honeycomb,
They sift and soften it, bake it and burn it –
Whether they weld you, for instance, a snaffle
With side-bars never a brute can baffle;

Or a lock that's a puzzle of wards within wards;
Or, if your colt's fore-foot inclines to curve inwards,
Horseshoes they hammer which turn on a swivel
370   And won't allow the hoof to shrivel.
Then they cast bells like the shell of the winkle
That keep a stout heart in the ram with their tinkle;
But the sand – they pinch and pound it like otters;
Commend me to Gypsy glass-makers and potters!
Glasses they'll blow you, crystal-clear,
Where just a faint cloud of rose shall appear,
As if in pure water you dropped and let die
A bruised black-blooded mulberry;
And that other sort, their crowning pride,
380   With long white threads distinct inside,
Like the lake-flower's fibrous roots which dangle
Loose such a length and never tangle,
Where the bold sword-lily cuts the clear waters,
And the cup-lily couches with all the white daughters:
Such are the works they put their hand to,
The uses they turn and twist iron and sand to.
And these made the troop, which our Duke saw sally
Toward his castle from out of the valley,
Men and women, like new-hatched spiders,
390   Come out with the morning to greet our riders.
And up they wound till they reached the ditch,
Whereat all stopped save one, a witch
That I knew, as she hobbled from the group,
By her gait directly and her stoop,
I, whom Jacynth was used to importune
To let that same witch tell us our fortune,
The oldest Gypsy then above ground;
And, sure as the autumn season came round,
She paid us a visit for profit or pastime,
400   And every time, as she swore, for the last time.
And presently she was seen to sidle
Up to the Duke till she touched his bridle,
So that the horse of a sudden reared up
As under its nose the old witch peered up
With her worn-out eyes, or rather eye-holes
Of no use now but to gather brine,
And began a kind of level whine
Such as they used to sing to their viols

When their ditties they go grinding
410   Up and down with nobody minding:
And then, as of old, at the end of the humming
Her usual presents were forthcoming
– A dog-whistle blowing the fiercest of trebles,
(Just a sea-shore stone holding a dozen fine pebbles,)
Or a porcelain mouth-piece to screw on a pipe-end, –
And so she awaited her annual stipend.
But this time, the Duke would scarcely vouchsafe
 A word in reply; and in vain she felt
 With twitching fingers at her belt
420   For the purse of sleek pine-marten pelt,
Ready to put what he gave in her pouch safe, –
Till, either to quicken his apprehension,
Or possibly with an after-intention,
She was come, she said, to pay her duty
To the new Duchess, the youthful beauty.
No sooner had she named his lady,
Than a shine lit up the face so shady,
And its smirk returned with a novel meaning –
For it struck him, the babe just wanted weaning;
430   If one gave her a taste of what life was and sorrow,
She, foolish today, would be wiser tomorrow;
And who so fit a teacher of trouble
As this sordid crone bent well-nigh double?
So, glancing at her wolf-skin vesture,
 (If such it was, for they grow so hirsute
 That their own fleece serves for natural fur-suit)
He was contrasting, 'twas plain from his gesture,
The life of the lady so flower-like and delicate
With the loathsome squalor of this helicat.
440   I, in brief, was the man the Duke beckoned
 From out of the throng, and while I drew near
He told the crone – as I since have reckoned
 By the way he bent and spoke into her ear
With circumspection and mystery –
The main of the lady's history,
Her frowardness and ingratitude:
And for all the crone's submissive attitude
I could see round her mouth the loose plaits tightening,
And her brow with assenting intelligence brightening,
450   As though she engaged with hearty goodwill

Whatever he now might enjoin to fulfil,
And promised the lady a thorough frightening.
And so, just giving her a glimpse
Of a purse, with the air of a man who imps
The wing of the hawk that shall fetch the hernshaw,
    He bade me take the Gypsy mother
    And set her telling some story or other
Of hill or dale, oak-wood or fernshaw,
To wile away a weary hour
460   For the lady left alone in her bower,
Whose mind and body craved exertion
And yet shrank from all better diversion.

XIV
Then clapping heel to his horse, the mere curveter,
    Out rode the Duke, and after his hollo
Horses and hounds swept, huntsman and servitor,
    And back I turned and bade the crone follow.
And what makes me confident what's to be told you
    Had all along been of this crone's devising,
Is, that, on looking round sharply, behold you,
470   There was a novelty quick as surprising:
For first, she had shot up a full head in stature,
    And her step kept pace with mine nor faltered,
As if age had foregone its usurpature,
    And the ignoble mien was wholly altered,
And the face looked quite of another nature,
And the change reached too, whatever the change meant,
Her shaggy wolf-skin cloak's arrangement:
For where its tatters hung loose like sedges,
Gold coins were glittering on the edges,
480   Like the band-roll strung with tomans
Which proves the veil a Persian woman's:
And under her brow, like a snail's horns newly
    Come out as after the rain he paces,
Two unmistakable eye-points duly
    Live and aware looked out of their places.
So, we went and found Jacynth at the entry
Of the lady's chamber standing sentry;
I told the command and produced my companion,
And Jacynth rejoiced to admit any one,
490   For since last night, by the same token,

Not a single word had the lady spoken:
They went in both to the presence together,
While I in the balcony watched the weather.

XV

And now, what took place at the very first of all,
I cannot tell, as I never could learn it:
Jacynth constantly wished a curse to fall
On that little head of hers and burn it
If she knew how she came to drop so soundly
   Asleep of a sudden and there continue
500 The whole time sleeping as profoundly
   As one of the boars my father would pin you
'Twixt the eyes where life holds garrison,
– Jacynth forgive me the comparison!
But where I begin my own narration
Is a little after I took my station
To breathe the fresh air from the balcony,
And, having in those days a falcon eye,
To follow the hunt through the open country,
   From where the bushes thinlier crested
510 The hillocks, to a plain where's not one tree.
   When, in a moment, my ear was arrested
By – was it singing, or was it saying,
Or a strange musical instrument playing
In the chamber? – and to be certain
I pushed the lattice, pulled the curtain,
And there lay Jacynth asleep,
Yet as if a watch she tried to keep,
In a rosy sleep along the floor
With her head against the door;
520 While in the midst, on the seat of state,
Was a queen – the Gypsy woman late,
With head and face down-bent
On the lady's head and face intent:
For, coiled at her feet like a child at ease,
The lady sat between her knees
And o'er them the lady's clasped hands met,
And on those hands her chin was set,
And her upturned face met the face of the crone
Wherein the eyes had grown and grown
530 As if she could double and quadruple

At pleasure the play of either pupil
    – Very like, by her hands' slow fanning,
As up and down like a gor-crow's flappers
They moved to measure, or bell-clappers.
    I said 'Is it blessing, is it banning,
Do they applaud you or burlesque you –
    Those hands and fingers with no flesh on?'
But, just as I thought to spring in to the rescue,
    At once I was stopped by the lady's expression:
540   For it was life her eyes were drinking
From the crone's wide pair above unwinking,
    – Life's pure fire received without shrinking,
Into the heart and breast whose heaving
Told you no single drop they were leaving,
    – Life, that filling her, passed redundant
    Into her very hair, back swerving
Over each shoulder, loose and abundant,
    As her head thrown back showed the white throat curving;
And the very tresses shared in the pleasure,
550   Moving to the mystic measure,
Bounding as the bosom bounded.
I stopped short, more and more confounded,
As still her cheeks burned and eyes glistened,
As she listened and she listened:
When all at once a hand detained me,
The selfsame contagion gained me,
And I kept time to the wondrous chime,
Making out words and prose and rhyme,
Till it seemed that the music furled
560   Its wings like a task fulfilled, and dropped
    From under the words it first had propped,
And left them midway in the world:
Word took word as hand takes hand,
I could hear at last, and understand,
And when I held the unbroken thread,
The Gypsy said: –

'And so at last we find my tribe.
    And so I set thee in the midst,
And to one and all of them describe
570   What thou said'st and what thou did'st,
Our long and terrible journey through,

And all thou art ready to say and do
In the trials that remain:
I trace them the vein and the other vein
That meet on thy brow and part again,
Making our rapid mystic mark;
   And I bid my people prove and probe
   Each eye's profound and glorious globe
Till they detect the kindred spark
580 In those depths so dear and dark,
Like the spots that snap and burst and flee,
Circling over the midnight sea.
And on that round young cheek of thine
   I make them recognize the tinge,
As when of the costly scarlet wine
   They drip so much as will impinge
And spread in a thinnest scale afloat
One thick gold drop from the olive's coat
Over a silver plate whose sheen
590 Still through the mixture shall be seen.
For so I prove thee, to one and all,
   Fit, when my people ope their breast,
To see the sign, and hear the call,
   And take the vow, and stand the test
   Which adds one more child to the rest –
When the breast is bare and the arms are wide,
And the world is left outside.
For there is probation to decree,
And many and long must the trials be
600 Thou shalt victoriously endure,
If that brow is true and those eyes are sure;
Like a jewel-finder's fierce assay
   Of the prize he dug from its mountain-tomb –
Let once the vindicating ray
   Leap out amid the anxious gloom,
And steel and fire have done their part
And the prize falls on its finder's heart;
So, trial after trial past,
Wilt thou fall at the very last
610 Breathless, half in trance
With the thrill of the great deliverance,
   Into our arms for evermore;
And thou shalt know, those arms once curled

About thee, what we knew before,
How love is the only good in the world.
Henceforth be loved as heart can love,
Or brain devise, or hand approve!
Stand up, look below,
It is our life at thy feet we throw
620 To step with into light and joy;
Not a power of life but we employ
To satisfy thy nature's want;
Art thou the tree that props the plant,
Or the climbing plant that seeks the tree –
Canst thou help us, must we help thee?
If any two creatures grew into one,
They would do more than the world has done:
Though each apart were never so weak,
Ye vainly through the world should seek
630 For the knowledge and the might
Which in such union grew their right:
So, to approach at least that end,
And blend, – as much as may be, blend
Thee with us or us with thee, –
As climbing plant or propping tree,
Shall some one deck thee, over and down
    Up and about, with blossoms and leaves?
Fix his heart's fruit for thy garland-crown,
    Cling with his soul as the gourd-vine cleaves,
640 Die on thy boughs and disappear
While not a leaf of thine is sere?
Or is the other fate in store,
And art thou fitted to adore,
To give thy wondrous self away,
And take a stronger nature's sway?
I foresee and could foretell
Thy future portion, sure and well:
But those passionate eyes speak true, speak true,
Let them say what thou shalt do!
650 Only be sure thy daily life,
In its peace or in its strife,
Never shall be unobserved;
    We pursue thy whole career,
    And hope for it, or doubt, or fear, –
Lo, hast thou kept thy path or swerved,

We are beside thee in all thy ways,
With our blame, with our praise,
Our shame to feel, our pride to show,
Glad, angry – but indifferent, no!
660 Whether it be thy lot to go,
For the good of us all, where the haters meet
In the crowded city's horrible street;
Or thou step alone through the morass
Where never sound yet was
Save the dry quick clap of the stork's bill,
For the air is still, and the water still,
When the blue breast of the dipping coot
Dives under, and all is mute.
So, at the last shall come old age,
670 Decrepit as befits that stage;
How else wouldst thou retire apart
With the hoarded memories of thy heart,
And gather all to the very least
Of the fragments of life's earlier feast,
Let fall through eagerness to find
The crowning dainties yet behind?
Ponder on the entire past
Laid together thus at last,
When the twilight helps to fuse
680 The first fresh with the faded hues,
And the outline of the whole,
As round eve's shades their framework roll,
Grandly fronts for once thy soul.
And then as, 'mid the dark, a gleam
Of yet another morning breaks,
And like the hand which ends a dream,
Death, with the might of his sunbeam,
Touches the flesh and the soul awakes,
Then –'
Ay, then indeed something would happen!
690 But what? For here her voice changed like a bird's;
There grew more of the music and less of the words;
Had Jacynth only been by me to clap pen
To paper and put you down every syllable
With those clever clerkly fingers,
All I've forgotten as well as what lingers
In this old brain of mine that's but ill able

To give you even this poor version
   Of the speech I spoil, as it were, with stammering
   – More fault of those who had the hammering
700 Of prosody into me and syntax,
   And did it, not with hobnails but tintacks!
   But to return from this excursion, –
   Just, do you mark, when the song was sweetest,
   The peace most deep and the charm completest,
   There came, shall I say, a snap –
      And the charm vanished!
      And my sense returned, so strangely banished,
   And, starting as from a nap,
   I knew the crone was bewitching my lady,
710 With Jacynth asleep; and but one spring made I
   Down from the casement, round to the portal,
      Another minute and I had entered, –
   When the door opened, and more than mortal
      Stood, with a face where to my mind centred
   All beauties I ever saw or shall see,
   The Duchess: I stopped as if struck by palsy.
   She was so different, happy and beautiful,
      I felt at once that all was best,
      And that I had nothing to do, for the rest,
720 But wait her commands, obey and be dutiful.
   Not that, in fact, there was any commanding;
      I saw the glory of her eye,
   And the brow's height and the breast's expanding,
      And I was hers to live or to die.
   As for finding what she wanted,
   You know God Almighty granted
   Such little signs should serve wild creatures
   To tell one another all their desires,
   So that each knows what his friend requires,
730 And does its bidding without teachers.
   I preceded her; the crone
   Followed silent and alone;
   I spoke to her, but she merely jabbered
      In the old style; both her eyes had slunk
      Back to their pits; her stature shrunk;
      In short, the soul in its body sunk
   Like a blade sent home to its scabbard.
   We descended, I preceding;

Crossed the court with nobody heeding;
740   All the world was at the chase,
    The courtyard like a desert-place,
    The stable emptied of its small fry;
    I saddled myself the very palfrey
    I remember patting while it carried her,
    The day she arrived and the Duke married her.
    And, do you know, though it's easy deceiving
    Oneself in such matters, I can't help believing
    The lady had not forgotten it either,
    And knew the poor devil so much beneath her
750   Would have been only too glad for her service
    To dance on hot ploughshares like a Turk dervise,
    But, unable to pay proper duty where owing it,
    Was reduced to that pitiful method of showing it:
    For though the moment I began setting
    His saddle on my own nag of Berold's begetting,
    (Not that I meant to be obtrusive)
        She stopped me, while his rug was shifting,
        By a single rapid finger's lifting,
    And, with a gesture kind but conclusive,
760   And a little shake of the head, refused me, –
    I say, although she never used me,
    Yet when she was mounted, the Gypsy behind her,
    And I ventured to remind her,
    I suppose with a voice of less steadiness
        Than usual, for my feeling exceeded me,
    – Something to the effect that I was in readiness
        Whenever God should please she needed me, –
    Then, do you know, her face looked down on me
    With a look that placed a crown on me,
770   And she felt in her bosom, – mark, her bosom –
    And, as a flower-tree drops its blossom,
    Dropped me ... ah, had it been a purse
    Of silver, my friend, or gold that's worse,
    Why, you see, as soon as I found myself
        So understood, – that a true heart so may gain
        Such a reward, – I should have gone home again,
    Kissed Jacynth, and soberly drowned myself!
    It was a little plait of hair
        Such as friends in a convent make
780   To wear, each for the other's sake, –

This, see, which at my breast I wear,
Ever did (rather to Jacynth's grudgement),
And ever shall, till the Day of Judgement.
And then, – and then, – to cut short, – this is idle,
    These are feelings it is not good to foster, –
I pushed the gate wide, she shook the bridle,
    And the palfrey bounded, – and so we lost her.

XVI

When the liquor's out why clink the cannikin?
I did think to describe you the panic in
790 The redoubtable breast of our master the mannikin,
And what was the pitch of his mother's yellowness,
    How she turned as a shark to snap the spare-rib
    Clean off, sailors say, from a pearl-diving Carib,
When she heard, what she called the flight of the feloness
– But it seems such child's play,
What they said and did with the lady away!
And to dance on, when we've lost the music,
Always made me – and no doubt makes you – sick.
Nay, to my mind, the world's face looked so stern
800 As that sweet form disappeared through the postern,
She that kept it in constant good humour,
It ought to have stopped; there seemed nothing to do more.
But the world thought otherwise and went on,
And my head's one that its spite was spent on:
Thirty years are fled since that morning,
And with them all my head's adorning.
Nor did the old Duchess die outright,
As you expect, of suppressed spite,
The natural end of every adder
810 Not suffered to empty its poison-bladder:
But she and her son agreed, I take it,
That no one should touch on the story to wake it,
For the wound in the Duke's pride rankled fiery,
So, they made no search and small inquiry –
And when fresh Gypsies have paid us a visit, I've
Noticed the couple were never inquisitive,
But told them they're folks the Duke don't want here,
And bade them make haste and cross the frontier.
Brief, the Duchess was gone and the Duke was glad of it,
820 And the old one was in the young one's stead,

And took, in her place, the household's head,
And a blessed time the household had of it!
And were I not, as a man may say, cautious
How I trench, more than needs, on the nauseous,
I could favour you with sundry touches
Of the paint-smutches with which the Duchess
Heightened the mellowness of her cheek's yellowness
(To get on faster) until at last her
Cheek grew to be one master-plaster
830   Of mucus and fucus from mere use of ceruse:
In short, she grew from scalp to udder
Just the object to make you shudder.

XVII
You're my friend –
What a thing friendship is, world without end!
How it gives the heart and soul a stir-up
    As if somebody broached you a glorious runlet,
    And poured out, all lovelily, sparklingly, sunlit,
Our green Moldavia, the streaky syrup,
Cotnar as old as the time of the Druids –
840   Friendship may match with that monarch of fluids;
Each supples a dry brain, fills you its ins-and-outs,
Gives your life's hour-glass a shake when the thin sand doubts
Whether to run on or stop short, and guarantees
Age is not all made of stark sloth and arrant ease.
I have seen my little lady once more,
    Jacynth, the Gypsy, Berold, and the rest of it,
For to me spoke the Duke, as I told you before;
    I always wanted to make a clean breast of it:
And now it is made – why, my heart's blood, that went trickle,
850   Trickle, but anon, in such muddy driblets,
Is pumped up brisk now, through the main ventricle,
    And genially floats me about the giblets.
I'll tell you what I intend to do:
I must see this fellow his sad life through –
He is our Duke, after all,
And I, as he says, but a serf and thrall.
My father was born here, and I inherit
    His fame, a chain he bound his son with;
Could I pay in a lump I should prefer it,
860   But there's no mine to blow up and get done with:

So, I must stay till the end of the chapter.
For, as to our middle-age-manners-adapter,
Be it a thing to be glad on or sorry on,
Some day or other, his head in a morion
And breast in a hauberk, his heels he'll kick up,
Slain by an onslaught fierce of hiccup.
And then, when red doth the sword of our Duke rust,
And its leathern sheath lie o'ergrown with a blue crust,
Then I shall scrape together my earnings;
870   For, you see, in the churchyard Jacynth reposes,
    And our children all went the way of the roses:
It's a long lane that knows no turnings.
One needs but little tackle to travel in;
    So, just one stout cloak shall I indue:
And for a staff, what beats the javelin
    With which his boars my father pinned you?
And then, for a purpose you shall hear presently,
    Taking some Cotnar, a tight plump skinful,
I shall go journeying, who but I, pleasantly!
880   Sorrow is vain and despondency sinful.
What's a man's age? He must hurry more, that's all;
    Cram in a day, what his youth took a year to hold:
    When we mind labour, then only, we're too old –
What age had Methusalem when he begat Saul?
And at last, as its haven some buffeted ship sees,
    (Come all the way from the north-parts with sperm oil)
    I hope to get safely out of the turmoil
And arrive one day at the land of the Gypsies,
And find my lady, or hear the last news of her
890   From some old thief and son of Lucifer,
His forehead chapleted green with wreathy hop,
Sunburned all over like an Aethiop.
And when my Cotnar begins to operate
And the tongue of the rogue to run at a proper rate,
And our wine-skin, tight once, shows each flaccid dent,
I shall drop in with – as if by accident –
'You never knew, then, how it all ended,
What fortune good or bad attended
The little lady your Queen befriended?'
900   – And when that's told me, what's remaining?
This world's too hard for my explaining.
The same wise judge of matters equine

Who still preferred some slim four-year-old
To the big-boned stock of mighty Berold,
And, for strong Cotnar, drank French weak wine,
He also must be such a lady's scorner!
   Smooth Jacob still robs homely Esau:
   Now up, now down, the world's one see-saw.
– So, I shall find out some snug corner
910 Under a hedge, like Orson the wood-knight,
Turn myself round and bid the world good-night;
And sleep a sound sleep till the trumpet's blowing
   Wakes me (unless priests cheat us laymen)
To a world where will be no further throwing
   Pearls before swine that can't value them. Amen!

Earth's Immortalities

Fame

See, as the prettiest graves will do in time,
Our poet's wants the freshness of its prime;
Spite of the sexton's browsing horse, the sods
Have struggled through its binding osier rods;
Headstone and half-sunk footstone lean awry,
Wanting the brick-work promised by-and-by;
How the minute grey lichens, plate o'er plate,
Have softened down the crisp-cut name and date!

Love

So, the year's done with!
   (*Love me for ever!*)
All March begun with,
   April's endeavour;
May-wreaths that bound me
   June needs must sever;
Now snows fall round me,
   Quenching June's fever –
   (*Love me for ever!*)

Song

I
Nay but you, who do not love her,
　Is she not pure gold, my mistress?
Holds earth aught – speak truth – above her?
　Aught like this tress, see, and this tress,
And this last fairest tress of all,
So fair, see, ere I let it fall?

II
Because, you spend your lives in praising;
　To praise, you search the wide world over:
Then why not witness, calmly gazing,
10　　If earth holds aught – speak truth – above her?
Above this tress, and this, I touch
But cannot praise, I love so much!

The Boy and the Angel

Morning, evening, noon and night,
'Praise God!' sang Theocrite.

Then to his poor trade he turned,
Whereby the daily meal was earned.

Hard he laboured, long and well;
O'er his work the boy's curls fell.

But ever, at each period,
He stopped and sang, 'Praise God!'

Then back again his curls he threw,
10　And cheerful turned to work anew.

Said Blaise, the listening monk, 'Well done;
I doubt not thou art heard, my son:

'As well as if thy voice today
Were praising God, the Pope's great way.

'This Easter Day, the Pope at Rome
Praises God from Peter's dome.'

Said Theocrite, 'Would God that I
Might praise him, that great way, and die!'

Night passed, day shone,
20 And Theocrite was gone.

With God a day endures alway,
A thousand years are but a day.

God said in heaven, 'Nor day nor night
Now brings the voice of my delight.'

Then Gabriel, like a rainbow's birth,
Spread his wings and sank to earth;

Entered, in flesh, the empty cell,
Lived there, and played the craftsman well;

And morning, evening, noon and night,
30 Praised God in place of Theocrite.

And from a boy, to youth he grew:
The man put off the stripling's hue:

The man matured and fell away
Into the season of decay:

And ever o'er the trade he bent,
And ever lived on earth content.

(He did God's will; to him, all one
If on the earth or in the sun.)

God said, 'A praise is in mine ear;
40 There is no doubt in it, no fear:

'So sing old worlds, and so
New worlds that from my footstool go.

'Clearer loves sound other ways:
I miss my little human praise.'

Then forth sprang Gabriel's wings, off fell
The flesh disguise, remained the cell.

'Twas Easter Day: he flew to Rome,
And paused above Saint Peter's dome.

In the tiring-room close by
50   The great outer gallery,

With his holy vestments dight,
Stood the new Pope, Theocrite:

And all his past career
Came back upon him clear,

Since when, a boy, he plied his trade,
Till on his life the sickness weighed;

And in his cell, when death drew near,
An angel in a dream brought cheer:

And rising from the sickness drear
60   He grew a priest, and now stood here.

To the East with praise he turned,
And on his sight the angel burned.

'I bore thee from thy craftsman's cell
And set thee here; I did not well.

'Vainly I left my angel-sphere,
Vain was thy dream of many a year.

'Thy voice's praise seemed weak; it dropped –
Creation's chorus stopped!

'Go back and praise again
70 The early way, while I remain.

'With that weak voice of our disdain,
Take up creation's pausing strain.

'Back to the cell and poor employ:
Resume the craftsman and the boy!'

Theocrite grew old at home;
A new Pope dwelt in Peter's dome.

One vanished as the other died:
They sought God side by side.

Meeting at Night

I
The grey sea and the long black land;
And the yellow half-moon large and low;
And the startled little waves that leap
In fiery ringlets from their sleep,
As I gain the cove with pushing prow,
And quench its speed i' the slushy sand.

II
Then a mile of warm sea-scented beach;
Three fields to cross till a farm appears;
A tap at the pane, the quick sharp scratch
10 And blue spurt of a lighted match,
And a voice less loud, through its joys and fears,
Than the two hearts beating each to each!

Parting at Morning

Round the cape of a sudden came the sea,
And the sun looked over the mountain's rim:
And straight was a path of gold for him,
And the need of a world of men for me.

Nationality in Drinks

I

My heart sank with our Claret-flask,
   Just now, beneath the heavy sedges
That serve this pond's black face for mask;
   And still at yonder broken edges
O' the hole, where up the bubbles glisten,
After my heart I look and listen.

II

Our laughing little flask, compelled
   Through depth to depth more bleak and shady;
As when, both arms beside her held,
10   Feet straightened out, some gay French lady
Is caught up from life's light and motion,
And dropped into death's silent ocean!

——————

Up jumped Tokay on our table,
Like a pygmy castle-warder,
Dwarfish to see, but stout and able,
Arms and accoutrements all in order;
And fierce he looked North, then, wheeling South,
Blew with his bugle a challenge to Drouth,
Cocked his flap-hat with the tosspot-feather,
20 Twisted his thumb in his red moustache,
Jingled his huge brass spurs together,
Tightened his waist with its Buda sash,
And then, with an impudence naught could abash,
Shrugged his hump-shoulder, to tell the beholder,
For twenty such knaves he should laugh but the bolder:

And so, with his sword-hilt gallantly jutting,
And dexter-hand on his haunch abutting,
Went the little man, Sir Ausbruch, strutting!

———————————

Here's to Nelson's memory!
30 'Tis the second time that I, at sea,
Right off Cape Trafalgar here,
Have drunk it deep in British Beer.
Nelson for ever – any time
Am I his to command in prose or rhyme!
Give me of Nelson only a touch,
And I save it, be it little or much:
Here's one our Captain gives, and so
Down at the word, by George, shall it go!
He says that at Greenwich they point the beholder
40 To Nelson's coat, 'still with tar on the shoulder:
For he used to lean with one shoulder digging,
Jigging, as it were, and zig-zag-zigging
Up against the mizen-rigging!'

Time's Revenges

I've a Friend, over the sea;
I like him, but he loves me.
It all grew out of the books I write;
They find such favour in his sight
That he slaughters you with savage looks
Because you don't admire my books.
He does himself though, – and if some vein
Were to snap tonight in this heavy brain,
Tomorrow month, if I lived to try,
10 Round should I just turn quietly,
Or out of the bedclothes stretch my hand
Till I found him, come from his foreign land
To be my nurse in this poor place,
And make my broth and wash my face
And light my fire and, all the while,
Bear with his old good-humoured smile
That I told him 'Better have kept away

Than come and kill me, night and day,
With, worse than fever throbs and shoots,
20 The creaking of his clumsy boots.'
I am as sure that this he would do,
As that Saint Paul's is striking two.
And I think I rather . . . woe is me!
– Yes, rather would see him than not see,
If lifting a hand could seat him there
Before me in the empty chair
Tonight, when my head aches indeed,
And I can neither think nor read
Nor make these purple fingers hold
30 The pen; this garret's freezing cold!

And I've a Lady – there he wakes,
The laughing fiend and prince of snakes
Within me, at her name, to pray
Fate send some creature in the way
Of my love for her, to be down-torn,
Upthrust and outward-borne,
So I might prove myself that sea
Of passion which I needs must be!
Call my thoughts false and my fancies quaint
40 And my style infirm and its figures faint,
All the critics say, and more blame yet,
And not one angry word you get.
But, please you, wonder I would put
My cheek beneath that lady's foot
Rather than trample under mine
The laurels of the Florentine,
And you shall see how the devil spends
A fire God gave for other ends!
I tell you, I stride up and down
50 This garret, crowned with love's best crown,
And feasted with love's perfect feast,
To think I kill for her, at least,
Body and soul and peace and fame,
Alike youth's end and manhood's aim,
– So is my spirit, as flesh with sin,
Filled full, eaten out and in
With the face of her, the eyes of her,
The lips, the little chin, the stir

Of shadow round her mouth; and she
60   – I'll tell you, – calmly would decree
That I should roast at a slow fire,
If that would compass her desire
And make her one whom they invite
To the famous ball tomorrow night.

There may be heaven; there must be hell;
Meantime, there is our earth here – well!

The Glove

(Peter Ronsard *loquitur*)

'Heigho!' yawned one day King Francis,
'Distance all value enhances!
When a man's busy, why, leisure
Strikes him as wonderful pleasure:
'Faith, and at leisure once is he?
Straightway he wants to be busy.
Here we've got peace; and aghast I'm
Caught thinking war the true pastime.
Is there a reason in metre?
10   Give us your speech, master Peter!'
I who, if mortal dare say so,
Ne'er am at loss with my Naso,
'Sire,' I replied, 'joys prove cloudlets:
Men are the merest Ixions' –
Here the King whistled aloud, 'Let's
– Heigho – go look at our lions!'
Such are the sorrowful chances
If you talk fine to King Francis.

And so, to the courtyard proceeding,
20   Our company, Francis was leading,
Increased by new followers tenfold
Before he arrived at the penfold;
Lords, ladies, like clouds which bedizen
At sunset the western horizon.
And Sir De Lorge pressed 'mid the foremost

With the dame he professed to adore most.
Oh, what a face! One by fits eyed
Her, and the horrible pit-side;
For the penfold surrounded a hollow
30   Which led where the eye scarce dared follow,
And shelved to the chamber secluded
Where Bluebeard, the great lion, brooded.
The King hailed his keeper, an Arab
As glossy and black as a scarab,
And bade him make sport and at once stir
Up and out of his den the old monster.
They opened a hole in the wire-work
Across it, and dropped there a firework,
And fled: one's heart's beating redoubled;
40   A pause, while the pit's mouth was troubled,
The blackness and silence so utter,
By the firework's slow sparkling and sputter;
Then earth in a sudden contortion
Gave out to our gaze her abortion.
Such a brute! Were I friend Clement Marot
(Whose experience of nature's but narrow,
And whose faculties move in no small mist
When he versifies David the Psalmist)
I should study that brute to describe you
50   *Illum Juda Leonem de Tribu.*
One's whole blood grew curdling and creepy
To see the black mane, vast and heapy,
The tail in the air stiff and straining,
The wide eyes, nor waxing nor waning,
As over the barrier which bounded
His platform, and us who surrounded
The barrier, they reached and they rested
On space that might stand him in best stead:
For who knew, he thought, what the amazement,
60   The eruption of clatter and blaze meant,
And if, in this minute of wonder,
No outlet, 'mid lightning and thunder,
Lay broad, and, his shackles all shivered,
The lion at last was delivered?
Ay, that was the open sky o'erhead!
And you saw by the flash on his forehead,
By the hope in those eyes wide and steady,

He was leagues in the desert already,
Driving the flocks up the mountain,
70 Or catlike couched hard by the fountain
To waylay the date-gathering negress:
So guarded he entrance or egress.
'How he stands!' quoth the King: 'we may well swear,
(No novice, we've won our spurs elsewhere
And so can afford the confession,)
We exercise wholesome discretion
In keeping aloof from his threshold,
Once hold you, those jaws want no fresh hold,
Their first would too pleasantly purloin
80 The visitor's brisket or surloin:
But who's he would prove so fool-hardy?
Not the best man of Marignan, pardie!'

The sentence no sooner was uttered,
Than over the rails a glove fluttered,
Fell close to the lion, and rested:
The dame 'twas, who flung it and jested
With life so, De Lorge had been wooing
For months past; he sat there pursuing
His suit, weighing out with nonchalance
90 Fine speeches like gold from a balance.

Sound the trumpet, no true knight's a tarrier!
De Lorge made one leap at the barrier,
Walked straight to the glove, – while the lion
Ne'er moved, kept his far-reaching eye on
The palm-tree-edged desert-spring's sapphire,
And the musky oiled skin of the Kaffir, –
Picked it up, and as calmly retreated,
Leaped back where the lady was seated,
And full in the face of its owner
100 Flung the glove.

                    'Your heart's queen, you dethrone her?
So should I!' – cried the King – ' 'twas mere vanity,
Not love, set that task to humanity!'
Lords and ladies alike turned with loathing
From such a proved wolf in sheep's clothing.

Not so, I; for I caught an expression
In her brow's undisturbed self-possession
Amid the Court's scoffing and merriment, –
As if from no pleasing experiment
She rose, yet of pain not much heedful
110 So long as the process was needful, –
As if she had tried in a crucible,
To what 'speeches like gold' were reducible,
And, finding the finest prove copper,
Felt the smoke in her face was but proper;
To know what she had *not* to trust to,
Was worth all the ashes and dust too.
She went out 'mid hooting and laughter;
Clement Marot stayed; I followed after,
And asked, as a grace, what it all meant?
120 If she wished not the rash deed's recalment?
'For I' – so I spoke – 'am a poet:
Human nature, – behoves that I know it!'

She told me, 'Too long had I heard
Of the deed proved alone by the word:
For my love – what De Lorge would not dare!
With my scorn – what De Lorge could compare!
And the endless descriptions of death
He would brave when my lip formed a breath,
I must reckon as braved, or, of course,
130 Doubt his word – and moreover, perforce,
For such gifts as no lady could spurn,
Must offer my love in return.
When I looked on your lion, it brought
All the dangers at once to my thought,
Encountered by all sorts of men,
Before he was lodged in his den, –
From the poor slave whose club or bare hands
Dug the trap, set the snare on the sands,
With no King and no Court to applaud,
140 By no shame, should he shrink, overawed,
Yet to capture the creature made shift,
That his rude boys might laugh at the gift,
– To the page who last leaped o'er the fence
Of the pit, on no greater pretence
Than to get back the bonnet he dropped,

Lest his pay for a week should be stopped.
So, wiser I judged it to make
One trial what "death for my sake"
Really meant, while the power was yet mine,
150 Than to wait until time should define
Such a phrase not so simply as I,
Who took it to mean just "to die."
The blow a glove gives is but weak:
Does the mark yet discolour my cheek?
But when the heart suffers a blow,
Will the pain pass so soon, do you know?'

I looked, as away she was sweeping,
And saw a youth eagerly keeping
As close as he dared to the doorway.
160 No doubt that a noble should more weigh
His life than befits a plebeian;
And yet, had our brute been Nemean –
(I judge by a certain calm fervour
The youth stepped with, forward to serve her)
– He'd have scarce thought you did him the worst turn
If you whispered 'Friend, what you'd get, first earn!'
And when, shortly after, she carried
Her shame from the Court, and they married,
To that marriage some happiness, maugre
170 The voice of the Court, I dared augur.

For De Lorge, he made women with men vie,
Those in wonder and praise, these in envy;
And in short stood so plain a head taller
That he wooed and won . . . how do you call her?
The beauty, that rose in the sequel
To the King's love, who loved her a week well.
And 'twas noticed he never would honour
De Lorge (who looked daggers upon her)
With the easy commission of stretching
180 His legs in the service, and fetching
His wife, from her chamber, those straying
Sad gloves she was always mislaying,
While the King took the closet to chat in, –
But of course this adventure came pat in.
And never the King told the story,

How bringing a glove brought such glory,
But the wife smiled – 'His nerves are grown firmer:
Mine he brings now and utters no murmur.'

Venienti occurrite morbo!
190 With which moral I drop my theorbo.

Christmas-Eve and Easter-Day

1850

Christmas-Eve

Out of the little chapel I burst
   Into the fresh night-air again.
Five minutes full, I waited first
   In the doorway, to escape the rain
That drove in gusts down the common's centre
   At the edge of which the chapel stands,
Before I plucked up heart to enter.
   Heaven knows how many sorts of hands
Reached past me, groping for the latch
10 Of the inner door that hung on catch
More obstinate the more they fumbled,
   Till, giving way at last with a scold
Of the crazy hinge, in squeezed or tumbled
   One sheep more to the rest in fold,
And left me irresolute, standing sentry
In the sheepfold's lath-and-plaster entry,
Six feet long by three feet wide,
Partitioned off from the vast inside –
   I blocked up half of it at least.
20 No remedy; the rain kept driving.
   They eyed me much as some wild beast,
That congregation, still arriving,
Some of them by the main road, white
A long way past me into the night,
Skirting the common, then diverging;
Not a few suddenly emerging
From the common's self through the paling-gaps,
– They house in the gravel-pits perhaps,
Where the road stops short with its safeguard border
30 Of lamps, as tired of such disorder; –
But the most turned in yet more abruptly
   From a certain squalid knot of alleys,
Where the town's bad blood once slept corruptly,
   Which now the little chapel rallies
And leads into day again, – its priestliness
Lending itself to hide their beastliness
So cleverly (thanks in part to the mason),
And putting so cheery a whitewashed face on

Those neophytes too much in lack of it,
40   That, where you cross the common as I did,
     And meet the party thus presided,
'Mount Zion' with Love-lane at the back of it,
They front you as little disconcerted
As, bound for the hills, her fate averted,
And her wicked people made to mind him,
Lot might have marched with Gomorrah behind him.

II

Well, from the road, the lanes or the common,
In came the flock: the fat weary woman,
Panting and bewildered, down-clapping
50   Her umbrella with a mighty report,
Grounded it by me, wry and flapping,
     A wreck of whalebones; then, with a snort,
Like a startled horse, at the interloper
(Who humbly knew himself improper,
But could not shrink up small enough)
– Round to the door, and in, – the gruff
Hinge's invariable scold
Making my very blood run cold.
Prompt in the wake of her, up-pattered
60   On broken clogs, the many-tattered
Little old-faced peaking sister-turned-mother
Of the sickly babe she tried to smother
Somehow up, with its spotted face,
From the cold, on her breast, the one warm place;
She too must stop, wring the poor ends dry
Of a draggled shawl, and add thereby
Her tribute to the door-mat, sopping
Already from my own clothes' dropping,
Which yet she seemed to grudge I should stand on:
70   Then, stooping down to take off her pattens,
She bore them defiantly, in each hand one,
Planted together before her breast
And its babe, as good as a lance in rest.
     Close on her heels, the dingy satins
Of a female something, past me flitted,
     With lips as much too white, as a streak
Lay far too red on each hollow cheek;
And it seemed the very door-hinge pitied

All that was left of a woman once,
80   Holding at least its tongue for the nonce.
Then a tall yellow man, like the Penitent Thief,
With his jaw bound up in a handkerchief,
And eyelids screwed together tight,
Led himself in by some inner light.
And, except from him, from each that entered,
    I got the same interrogation –
'What, you, the alien, you have ventured
    To take with us, the elect, your station?
A carer for none of it, a Gallio!' –
90   Thus, plain as print, I read the glance
At a common prey, in each countenance
    As of huntsman giving his hounds the tally-ho.
And, when the door's cry drowned their wonder,
    The draught, it always sent in shutting,
Made the flame of the single tallow candle
In the cracked square lantern I stood under,
    Shoot its blue lip at me, rebutting
As it were, the luckless cause of scandal:
I verily fancied the zealous light
100   (In the chapel's secret, too!) for spite
Would shudder itself clean off the wick,
With the airs of a Saint John's Candlestick.
There was no standing it much longer.
'Good folks,' thought I, as resolve grew stronger,
'This way you perform the Grand-Inquisitor
When the weather sends you a chance visitor?
You are the men, and wisdom shall die with you,
And none of the old Seven Churches vie with you!
But still, despite the pretty perfection
110   To which you carry your trick of exclusiveness,
And, taking God's word under wise protection,
    Correct its tendency to diffusiveness,
And bid one reach it over hot ploughshares, –
    Still, as I say, though you've found salvation,
If I should choose to cry, as now, "Shares!" –
    See if the best of you bars me my ration!
I prefer, if you please, for my expounder
Of the laws of the feast, the feast's own Founder;
Mine's the same right with your poorest and sickliest
120   Supposing I don the marriage vestiment:

So, shut your mouth and open your Testament,
And carve me my portion at your quickliest!'
Accordingly, as a shoemaker's lad
    With wizened face in want of soap,
    And wet apron wound round his waist like a rope,
(After stopping outside, for his cough was bad,
To get the fit over, poor gentle creature,
And so avoid disturbing the preacher)
– Passed in, I sent my elbow spikewise

130   At the shutting door, and entered likewise,
Received the hinge's accustomed greeting,
    And crossed the threshold's magic pentacle,
    And found myself in full conventicle,
– To wit, in Zion Chapel Meeting,
On the Christmas-Eve of 'Forty-nine,
    Which, calling its flock to their special clover,
    Found all assembled and one sheep over,
Whose lot, as the weather pleased, was mine.

III
I very soon had enough of it.

140   The hot smell and the human noises,
And my neighbour's coat, the greasy cuff of it,
    Were a pebble-stone that a child's hand poises,
Compared with the pig-of-lead-like pressure
    Of the preaching man's immense stupidity,
As he poured his doctrine forth, full measure,
    To meet his audience's avidity.
You needed not the wit of the Sibyl
    To guess the cause of it all, in a twinkling:
    No sooner our friend had got an inkling

150   Of treasure hid in the Holy Bible,
(Whene'er 'twas the thought first struck him,
How death, at unawares, might duck him
Deeper than the grave, and quench
The gin-shop's light in hell's grim drench)
Than he handled it so, in fine irreverence,
    As to hug the book of books to pieces:
And, a patchwork of chapters and texts in severance,
    Not improved by the private dog's-ears and creases,
Having clothed his own soul with, he'd fain see equipt yours, –

160   So tossed you again your Holy Scriptures.

And you picked them up, in a sense, no doubt:
   Nay, had but a single face of my neighbours
   Appeared to suspect that the preacher's labours
Were help which the world could be saved without,
'Tis odds but I might have borne in quiet
A qualm or two at my spiritual diet,
Or (who can tell?) perchance even mustered
   Somewhat to urge in behalf of the sermon:
But the flock sat on, divinely flustered,
170   Sniffing, methought, its dew of Hermon
With such content in every snuffle,
As the devil inside us loves to ruffle.
My old fat woman purred with pleasure,
   And thumb round thumb went twirling faster,
While she, to his periods keeping measure,
   Maternally devoured the pastor.
The man with the handkerchief untied it,
Showed us a horrible wen inside it,
Gave his eyelids yet another screwing,
180 And rocked himself as the woman was doing.
The shoemaker's lad, discreetly choking,
Kept down his cough. 'Twas too provoking!
My gorge rose at the nonsense and stuff of it;
   So, saying like Eve when she plucked the apple,
    'I wanted a taste, and now there's enough of it,'
I flung out of the little chapel.

IV
There was a lull in the rain, a lull
   In the wind too; the moon was risen,
And would have shone out pure and full,
190 But for the ramparted cloud-prison,
Block on block built up in the West,
For what purpose the wind knows best,
Who changes his mind continually.
And the empty other half of the sky
Seemed in its silence as if it knew
What, any moment, might look through
A chance gap in that fortress massy: –
   Through its fissures you got hints
   Of the flying moon, by the shifting tints,
200 Now, a dull lion-colour, now, brassy

Burning to yellow, and whitest yellow,
Like furnace-smoke just ere flames bellow,
All a-simmer with intense strain
To let her through, – then blank again,
At the hope of her appearance failing.
Just by the chapel, a break in the railing
Shows a narrow path directly across;
'Tis ever dry walking there, on the moss –
Besides, you go gently all the way uphill.
210   I stooped under and soon felt better;
My head grew lighter, my limbs more supple,
    As I walked on, glad to have slipt the fetter.
My mind was full of the scene I had left,
    That placid flock, that pastor vociferant,
    – How this outside was pure and different!
The sermon, now – what a mingled weft
Of good and ill! Were either less,
    Its fellow had coloured the whole distinctly;
But alas for the excellent earnestness,
220   And the truths, quite true if stated succinctly,
But as surely false, in their quaint presentment,
However to pastor and flock's contentment!
Say rather, such truths looked false to your eyes,
    With his provings and parallels twisted and twined,
Till how could you know them, grown double their size
    In the natural fog of the good man's mind,
Like yonder spots of our roadside lamps,
Haloed about with the common's damps?
Truth remains true, the fault's in the prover;
230   The zeal was good, and the aspiration;
And yet, and yet, yet, fifty times over,
    Pharaoh received no demonstration,
By his Baker's dream of Baskets Three,
Of the doctrine of the Trinity, –
Although, as our preacher thus embellished it,
Apparently his hearers relished it
With so unfeigned a gust – who knows if
They did not prefer our friend to Joseph?
But so it is everywhere, one way with all of them!
240   These people have really felt, no doubt,
A something, the motion they style the Call of them;
    And this is their method of bringing about,

By a mechanism of words and tones,
(So many texts in so many groans)
A sort of reviving and reproducing,
    More or less perfectly, (who can tell?)
The mood itself, which strengthens by using;
    And how that happens, I understand well.
A tune was born in my head last week,
250 Out of the thump-thump and shriek-shriek
    Of the train, as I came by it, up from Manchester;
And when, next week, I take it back again,
My head will sing to the engine's clack again,
    While it only makes my neighbour's haunches stir,
– Finding no dormant musical sprout
In him, as in me, to be jolted out.
'Tis the taught already that profits by teaching;
He gets no more from the railway's preaching
    Than, from this preacher who does the rail's office, I:
260 Whom therefore the flock cast a jealous eye on.
Still, why paint over their door 'Mount Zion,'
    To which all flesh shall come, saith the prophecy?

V
But wherefore be harsh on a single case?
    After how many modes, this Christmas-Eve,
Does the self-same weary thing take place?
    The same endeavour to make you believe,
And with much the same effect, no more:
    Each method abundantly convincing,
As I say, to those convinced before,
270 But scarce to be swallowed without wincing
By the not-as-yet-convinced. For me,
I have my own church equally:
And in this church my faith sprang first!
    (I said, as I reached the rising ground,
And the wind began again, with a burst
    Of rain in my face, and a glad rebound
From the heart beneath, as if, God speeding me,
I entered his church-door, nature leading me)
– In youth I looked to these very skies,
280 And probing their immensities,
    I found God there, his visible power;
        Yet felt in my heart, amid all its sense

Of the power, an equal evidence
That his love, there too, was the nobler dower.
For the loving worm within its clod,
Were diviner than a loveless god
Amid his worlds, I will dare to say.
　　You know what I mean: God's all, man's naught:
　　But also, God, whose pleasure brought
290　Man into being, stands away
　　As it were a handbreadth off, to give
Room for the newly-made to live,
And look at him from a place apart,
And use his gifts of brain and heart,
Given, indeed, but to keep for ever.
Who speaks of man, then, must not sever
Man's very elements from man,
Saying, 'But all is God's' – whose plan
Was to create man and then leave him
300　Able, his own word saith, to grieve him,
But able to glorify him too,
As a mere machine could never do,
That prayed or praised, all unaware
Of its fitness for aught but praise and prayer,
Made perfect as a thing of course.
Man, therefore, stands on his own stock
Of love and power as a pin-point rock:
And, looking to God who ordained divorce
Of the rock from his boundless continent,
310　Sees, in his power made evident,
Only excess by a million-fold
O'er the power God gave man in the mould.
For, note: man's hand, first formed to carry
A few pounds' weight, when taught to marry
Its strength with an engine's, lifts a mountain,
　　– Advancing in power by one degree;
　　And why count steps through eternity?
But love is the ever-springing fountain:
Man may enlarge or narrow his bed
320　For the water's play, but the water-head –
How can he multiply or reduce it?
　　As easy create it, as cause it to cease;
He may profit by it, or abuse it,
　　But 'tis not a thing to bear increase

As power does: be love less or more
  In the heart of man, he keeps it shut
  Or opes it wide, as he pleases, but
Love's sum remains what it was before.
So, gazing up, in my youth, at love
330 As seen through power, ever above
All modes which make it manifest,
My soul brought all to a single test –
That he, the Eternal First and Last,
Who, in his power, had so surpassed
All man conceives of what is might, –
Whose wisdom, too, showed infinite,
– Would prove as infinitely good;
Would never, (my soul understood,)
With power to work all love desires,
340 Bestow e'en less than man requires;
That he who endlessly was teaching,
Above my spirit's utmost reaching,
What love can do in the leaf or stone,
(So that to master this alone,
This done in the stone or leaf for me,
I must go on learning endlessly)
Would never need that I, in turn,
  Should point him out defect unheeded,
And show that God had yet to learn
350   What the meanest human creature needed,
– Not life, to wit, for a few short years,
Tracking his way through doubts and fears,
While the stupid earth on which I stay
  Suffers no change, but passive adds
  Its myriad years to myriads,
Though I, he gave it to, decay,
Seeing death come and choose about me,
And my dearest ones depart without me.
No: love which, on earth, amid all the shows of it,
360   Has ever been seen the sole good of life in it,
The love, ever growing there, spite of the strife in it,
  Shall arise, made perfect, from death's repose of it.
And I shall behold thee, face to face,
O God, and in thy light retrace
How in all I loved here, still wast thou!
Whom pressing to, then, as I fain would now,

I shall find as able to satiate
　The love, thy gift, as my spirit's wonder
Thou art able to quicken and sublimate,
370　With this sky of thine, that I now walk under,
And glory in thee for, as I gaze
Thus, thus! Oh, let men keep their ways
Of seeking thee in a narrow shrine –
Be this my way! And this is mine!

VI

For lo, what think you? suddenly
The rain and the wind ceased, and the sky
Received at once the full fruition
Of the moon's consummate apparition.
The black cloud-barricade was riven,
380　Ruined beneath her feet, and driven
Deep in the West; while, bare and breathless,
　North and South and East lay ready
For a glorious thing that, dauntless, deathless,
　Sprang across them and stood steady.
'Twas a moon-rainbow, vast and perfect,
From heaven to heaven extending, perfect
As the mother-moon's self, full in face.
It rose, distinctly at the base
　With its seven proper colours chorded,
390　Which still, in the rising, were compressed,
Until at last they coalesced,
　And supreme the spectral creature lorded
In a triumph of whitest white, –
Above which intervened the night.
But above night too, like only the next,
　The second of a wondrous sequence,
　Reaching in rare and rarer frequence,
Till the heaven of heavens were circumflexed,
Another rainbow rose, a mightier,
400　Fainter, flushier and flightier, –
Rapture dying along its verge.
Oh, whose foot shall I see emerge,
Whose, from the straining topmost dark,
On to the keystone of that arc?

VII

This sight was shown me, there and then, –
Me, one out of a world of men,
Singled forth, as the chance might hap
To another if, in a thunderclap
Where I heard noise and you saw flame,
410   Some one man knew God called his name.
For me, I think I said, 'Appear!
Good were it to be ever here.
If thou wilt, let me build to thee
Service-tabernacles three,
Where, forever in thy presence,
In ecstatic acquiescence,
Far alike from thriftless learning
And ignorance's undiscerning,
I may worship and remain!'
420   Thus at the show above me, gazing
With upturned eyes, I felt my brain
    Glutted with the glory, blazing
Throughout its whole mass, over and under,
Until at length it burst asunder,
And out of it bodily there streamed,
The too-much glory, as it seemed,
Passing from out me to the ground,
Then palely serpentining round
Into the dark with mazy error.

VIII

430   All at once I looked up with terror.
He was there.
He himself with his human air.
On the narrow pathway, just before.
I saw the back of him, no more –
He had left the chapel, then, as I.
I forgot all about the sky.
No face: only the sight
Of a sweepy garment, vast and white,
With a hem that I could recognize.
440   I felt terror, no surprise;
My mind filled with the cataract,
At one bound of the mighty fact.
'I remember, he did say

Doubtless that, to this world's end,
Where two or three should meet and pray,
    He would be in the midst, their friend;
Certainly he was there with them!'
    And my pulses leaped for joy
    Of the golden thought without alloy,
450 That I saw his very vesture's hem.
Then rushed the blood back, cold and clear,
With a fresh enhancing shiver of fear;
And I hastened, cried out while I pressed
To the salvation of the vest,
'But not so, Lord! It cannot be
That thou, indeed, art leaving me –
Me, that have despised thy friends!
Did my heart make no amends?
Thou art the love of God – above
460 His power, didst hear me place his love,
And that was leaving the world for thee.
Therefore thou must not turn from me
As I had chosen the other part!
Folly and pride o'ercame my heart.
Our best is bad, nor bears thy test;
Still, it should be our very best.
I thought it best that thou, the spirit,
    Be worshipped in spirit and in truth,
And in beauty, as even we require it –
470   Not in the forms burlesque, uncouth,
I left but now, as scarcely fitted
For thee: I knew not what I pitied.
But, all I felt there, right or wrong,
    What is it to thee, who curest sinning?
Am I not weak as thou art strong?
    I have looked to thee from the beginning,
Straight up to thee through all the world
Which, like an idle scroll, lay furled
To nothingness on either side:
480 And since the time thou wast descried,
Spite of the weak heart, so have I
Lived ever, and so fain would die,
Living and dying, thee before!
But if thou leavest me –'

IX

Less or more,
I suppose that I spoke thus.
When, – have mercy, Lord, on us!
The whole face turned upon me full.
    And I spread myself beneath it,
    As when the bleacher spreads, to seethe it
490 In the cleansing sun, his wool, –
Steeps in the flood of noontide whiteness
    Some defiled, discoloured web –
So lay I, saturate with brightness.
    And when the flood appeared to ebb,
Lo, I was walking, light and swift,
    With my senses settling fast and steadying,
But my body caught up in the whirl and drift
    Of the vesture's amplitude, still eddying
On, just before me, still to be followed,
500   As it carried me after with its motion:
What shall I say? – as a path were hollowed
    And a man went weltering through the ocean,
Sucked along in the flying wake
Of the luminous water-snake.
Darkness and cold were cloven, as through
I passed, upborne yet walking too.
And I turned to myself at intervals,
'So he said, so it befalls.
God who registers the cup
510   Of mere cold water, for his sake
To a disciple rendered up,
    Disdains not his own thirst to slake
At the poorest love was ever offered:
And because my heart I proffered,
With true love trembling at the brim,
He suffers me to follow him
For ever, my own way, – dispensed
From seeking to be influenced
By all the less immediate ways
520   That earth, in worships manifold,
Adopts to reach, by prayer and praise,
    The garment's hem, which, lo, I hold!'

X

And so we crossed the world and stopped.
  For where am I, in city or plain,
  Since I am 'ware of the world again?
And what is this that rises propped
With pillars of prodigious girth?
Is it really on the earth,
This miraculous Dome of God?
530 Has the angel's measuring-rod
Which numbered cubits, gem from gem,
'Twixt the gates of the New Jerusalem,
Meted it out, – and what he meted,
Have the sons of men completed?
– Binding, ever as he bade,
Columns in the colonnade
With arms wide open to embrace
The entry of the human race
To the breast of . . . what is it, yon building,
540 Ablaze in front, all paint and gilding,
With marble for brick, and stones of price
For garniture of the edifice?
Now I see; it is no dream;
It stands there and it does not seem:
For ever, in pictures, thus it looks,
And thus I have read of it in books
Often in England, leagues away,
And wondered how these fountains play,
Growing up eternally
550 Each to a musical water-tree,
Whose blossoms drop, a glittering boon,
Before my eyes, in the light of the moon,
To the granite lavers underneath.
Liar and dreamer in your teeth!
I, the sinner that speak to you,
Was in Rome this night, and stood, and knew
Both this and more. For see, for see,
The dark is rent, mine eye is free
To pierce the crust of the outer wall,
560 And I view inside, and all there, all,
As the swarming hollow of a hive,
The whole Basilica alive!
Men in the chancel, body and nave,

Men on the pillars' architrave,
Men on the statues, men on the tombs
With popes and kings in their porphyry wombs,
All famishing in expectation
Of the main-altar's consummation.
For see, for see, the rapturous moment
570 Approaches, and earth's best endowment
Blends with heaven's; the taper-fires
Pant up, the winding brazen spires
Heave loftier yet the baldachin;
The incense-gaspings, long kept in,
Suspire in clouds; the organ blatant
Holds his breath and grovels latent,
As if God's hushing finger grazed him,
(Like Behemoth when he praised him)
At the silver bell's shrill tinkling,
580 Quick cold drops of terror sprinkling
On the sudden pavement strewed
With faces of the multitude.
Earth breaks up, time drops away,
In flows heaven, with its new day
Of endless life, when He who trod,
Very man and very God,
This earth in weakness, shame and pain,
Dying the death whose signs remain
Up yonder on the accursed tree, –
590 Shall come again, no more to be
Of captivity the thrall,
But the one God, All in all,
Kings of kings, Lord of lords,
As His servant John received the words,
'I died, and live for evermore!'

XI
Yet I was left outside the door.
'Why sit I here on the threshold-stone
Left till He return, alone
Save for the garment's extreme fold
600 Abandoned still to bless my hold?'
My reason, to my doubt, replied,
As if a book were opened wide,
And at a certain page I traced

Every record undefaced,
Added by successive years, –
The harvestings of truth's stray ears
Singly gleaned, and in one sheaf
Bound together for belief.
Yes, I said – that he will go
610 And sit with these in turn, I know.
Their faith's heart beats, though her head swims
Too giddily to guide her limbs,
Disabled by their palsy-stroke
From propping mine. Though Rome's gross yoke
Drops off, no more to be endured,
Her teaching is not so obscured
By errors and perversities,
That no truth shines athwart the lies:
And he, whose eye detects a spark
620 Even where, to man's, the whole seems dark,
May well see flame where each beholder
Acknowledges the embers smoulder.
But I, a mere man, fear to quit
The clue God gave me as most fit
To guide my footsteps through life's maze,
Because himself discerns all ways
Open to reach him: I, a man
Able to mark where faith began
To swerve aside, till from its summit
630 Judgement drops her damning plummet,
Pronouncing such a fatal space
Departed from the founder's base:
He will not bid me enter too,
But rather sit, as now I do,
Awaiting his return outside.
– 'Twas thus my reason straight replied
And joyously I turned, and pressed
The garment's skirt upon my breast,
Until, afresh its light suffusing me,
640 My heart cried – What has been abusing me
That I should wait here lonely and coldly,
Instead of rising, entering boldly,
Baring truth's face, and letting drift
Her veils of lies as they choose to shift?

Do these men praise him? I will raise
My voice up to their point of praise!
I see the error; but above
The scope of error, see the love. –
Oh, love of those first Christian days!
650 – Fanned so soon into a blaze,
From the spark preserved by the trampled sect,
That the antique sovereign Intellect
Which then sat ruling in the world,
Like a change in dreams, was hurled
From the throne he reigned upon:
You looked up and he was gone.
Gone, his glory of the pen!
– Love, with Greece and Rome in ken,
Bade her scribes abhor the trick
660 Of poetry and rhetoric,
And exult with hearts set free,
In blessed imbecility
Scrawled, perchance, on some torn sheet
Leaving Sallust incomplete.
Gone, his pride of sculptor, painter!
– Love, while able to acquaint her
While the thousand statues yet
Fresh from chisel, pictures wet
From brush, she saw on every side,
670 Chose rather with an infant's pride
To frame those portents which impart
Such unction to true Christian Art.
Gone, music too! The air was stirred
By happy wings: Terpander's bird
(That, when the cold came, fled away)
Would tarry not the wintry day, –
As more-enduring sculpture must,
Till filthy saints rebuked the gust
With which they chanced to get a sight
680 Of some dear naked Aphrodite
They glanced a thought above the toes of,
By breaking zealously her nose off.
Love, surely, from that music's lingering,
Might have filched her organ-fingering,
Nor chosen rather to set prayings

To hog-grunts, praises to horse-neighings.
Love was the startling thing, the new:
Love was the all-sufficient too;
And seeing that, you see the rest:
690 As a babe can find its mother's breast
As well in darkness as in light,
Love shut our eyes, and all seemed right.
True, the world's eyes are open now:
– Less need for me to disallow
Some few that keep Love's zone unbuckled,
Peevish as ever to be suckled,
Lulled by the same old baby-prattle
With intermixture of the rattle,
When she would have them creep, stand steady
700 Upon their feet, or walk already,
Not to speak of trying to climb.
I will be wise another time,
And not desire a wall between us,
    When next I see a church-roof cover
So many species of one genus,
    All with foreheads bearing *lover*
Written above the earnest eyes of them;
    All with breasts that beat for beauty,
Whether sublimed, to the surprise of them,
710   In noble daring, steadfast duty,
The heroic in passion, or in action, –
Or, lowered for sense's satisfaction,
To the mere outside of human creatures,
Mere perfect form and faultless features.
What? with all Rome here, whence to levy
    Such contributions to their appetite,
With women and men in a gorgeous bevy,
    They take, as it were, a padlock, clap it tight
On their southern eyes, restrained from feeding
720 On the glories of their ancient reading,
On the beauties of their modern singing,
On the wonders of the builder's bringing,
On the majesties of Art around them, –
    And, all these loves, late struggling incessant,
When faith has at last united and bound them,
    They offer up to God for a present?

Why, I will, on the whole, be rather proud of it, –
And, only taking the act in reference
To the other recipients who might have allowed it,
730   I will rejoice that God had the preference.

XII

So I summed up my new resolves:
   Too much love there can never be.
And where the intellect devolves
   Its function on love exclusively,
I, a man who possesses both,
Will accept the provision, nothing loth,
– Will feast my love, then depart elsewhere,
That my intellect may find its share.
And ponder, O soul, the while thou departest,
740   And see thou applaud the great heart of the artist,
Who, examining the capabilities
   Of the block of marble he has to fashion
   Into a type of thought or passion, –
Not always, using obvious facilities,
Shapes it, as any artist can,
Into a perfect symmetrical man,
Complete from head to foot of the life-size,
Such as old Adam stood in his wife's eyes, –
But, now and then, bravely aspires to consummate
750   A Colossus by no means so easy to come at,
And uses the whole of his block for the bust,
   Leaving the mind of the public to finish it,
Since cut it ruefully short he must:
On the face alone he expends his devotion,
   He rather would mar than resolve to diminish it,
– Saying, 'Applaud me for this grand notion
Of what a face may be! As for completing it
   In breast and body and limbs, do that, you!'
All hail! I fancy how, happily meeting it,
760   A trunk and legs would perfect the statue,
Could man carve so as to answer volition.
   And how much nobler than petty cavils,
   Were a hope to find, in my spirit-travels,
Some artist of another ambition,
Who having a block to carve, no bigger,

Has spent his power on the opposite quest,
And believed to begin at the feet was best –
For so may I see, ere I die, the whole figure!

XIII

No sooner said than out in the night!
770 My heart beat lighter and more light:
And still, as before, I was walking swift,
 With my senses settling fast and steadying,
But my body caught up in the whirl and drift
 Of the vesture's amplitude, still eddying
On just before me, still to be followed,
 As it carried me after with its motion,
– What shall I say? – as a path were hollowed,
 And a man went weltering through the ocean,
Sucked along in the flying wake
780 Of the luminous water-snake.

XIV

Alone! I am left alone once more –
 (Save for the garment's extreme fold
 Abandoned still to bless my hold)
Alone, beside the entrance-door
Of a sort of temple, – perhaps a college,
– Like nothing I ever saw before
At home in England, to my knowledge.
The tall old quaint irregular town!
 It may be ... though which, I can't affirm ... any
790 Of the famous middle-age towns of Germany;
And this flight of stairs where I sit down,
Is it Halle, Weimar, Cassel, Frankfort
Or Göttingen, I have to thank for't?
It may be Göttingen, – most likely.
Through the open door I catch obliquely
Glimpses of a lecture-hall;
 And not a bad assembly neither,
 Ranged decent and symmetrical
 On benches, waiting what's to see there;
800 Which, holding still by the vesture's hem,
I also resolve to see with them,
Cautious this time how I suffer to slip
The chance of joining in fellowship

With any that call themselves his friends;
  As these folk do, I have a notion.
  But hist – a buzzing and emotion!
All settle themselves, the while ascends
By the creaking rail to the lecture-desk,
  Step by step, deliberate
810   Because of his cranium's over-freight,
Three parts sublime to one grotesque,
If I have proved an accurate guesser,
The hawk-nosed high-cheek-boned Professor.
I felt at once as if there ran
A shoot of love from my heart to the man –
That sallow virgin-minded studious
  Martyr to mild enthusiasm,
As he uttered a kind of cough-preludious
  That woke my sympathetic spasm,
820 (Beside some spitting that made me sorry)
And stood, surveying his auditory
With a wan pure look, well nigh celestial, –
  Those blue eyes had survived so much!
  While, under the foot they could not smutch,
Lay all the fleshly and the bestial.
Over he bowed, and arranged his notes,
Till the auditory's clearing of throats
Was done with, died into a silence;
  And, when each glance was upward sent,
830 Each bearded mouth composed intent,
And a pin might be heard drop half a mile hence, –
He pushed back higher his spectacles,
Let the eyes stream out like lamps from cells,
And giving his head of hair – a hake
  Of undressed tow, for colour and quantity –
One rapid and impatient shake,
  (As our own Young England adjusts a jaunty tie
When about to impart, on mature digestion,
Some thrilling view of the surplice-question)
840 – The Professor's grave voice, sweet though hoarse,
Broke into his Christmas-Eve discourse.

XV

And he began it by observing
 How reason dictated that men
Should rectify the natural swerving,
 By a reversion, now and then,
To the well-heads of knowledge, few
And far away, whence rolling grew
The life-stream wide whereat we drink,
Commingled, as we needs must think,
850 With waters alien to the source;
To do which, aimed this eve's discourse;
Since, where could be a fitter time
For tracing backward to its prime
This Christianity, this lake,
This reservoir, whereat we slake,
From one or other bank, our thirst?
So, he proposed inquiring first
Into the various sources whence
 This Myth of Christ is derivable;
860 Demanding from the evidence,
 (Since plainly no such life was liveable)
How these phenomena should class?
Whether 'twere best opine Christ was,
Or never was at all, or whether
He was and was not, both together –
It matters little for the name,
So the idea be left the same.
Only, for practical purpose' sake,
'Twas obviously as well to take
870 The popular story, – understanding
 How the ineptitude of the time,
And the penman's prejudice, expanding
 Fact into fable fit for the clime,
Had, by slow and sure degrees, translated it
 Into this myth, this Individuum, –
Which, when reason had strained and abated it
 Of foreign matter, left, for residuum,
A Man! – a right true man, however,
Whose work was worthy a man's endeavour:
880 Work, that gave warrant almost sufficient
 To his disciples, for rather believing
He was just omnipotent and omniscient,

As it gives to us, for as frankly receiving
His word, their tradition, – which, though it meant
Something entirely different
From all that those who only heard it,
In their simplicity thought and averred it,
Had yet a meaning quite as respectable:
For, among other doctrines delectable,
890 Was he not surely the first to insist on
     The natural sovereignty of our race? –
     Here the lecturer came to a pausing-place.
And while his cough, like a drouthy piston,
Tried to dislodge the husk that grew to him,
I seized the occasion of bidding adieu to him,
The vesture still within my hand.

XVI

I could interpret its command.
This time he would not bid me enter
The exhausted air-bell of the Critic.
900 Truth's atmosphere may grow mephitic
When Papist struggles with Dissenter,
Impregnating its pristine clarity,
  – One, by his daily fare's vulgarity,
    Its gust of broken meat and garlic;
  – One, by his soul's too-much presuming
To turn the frankincense's fuming
    And vapours of the candle star-like
Into the cloud her wings she buoys on.
    Each, that thus sets the pure air seething,
910   May poison it for healthy breathing –
But the Critic leaves no air to poison;
Pumps out with ruthless ingenuity
Atom by atom, and leaves you – vacuity.
Thus much of Christ does he reject?
And what retain? His intellect?
What is it I must reverence duly?
Poor intellect for worship, truly,
Which tells me simply what was told
    (If mere morality, bereft
920 Of the God in Christ, be all that's left)
Elsewhere by voices manifold;
With this advantage, that the stater

Made nowise the important stumble
Of adding, he, the sage and humble,
Was also one with the Creator.
You urge Christ's followers' simplicity:
But how does shifting blame, evade it?
Have wisdom's words no more felicity?
The stumbling-block, his speech – who laid it?
930 How comes it that for one found able
To sift the truth of it from fable,
Millions believe it to the letter?
Christ's goodness, then – does that fare better?
Strange goodness, which upon the score
Of being goodness, the mere due
Of man to fellow-man, much more
To God, – should take another view
Of its possessor's privilege,
And bid him rule his race! You pledge
940 Your fealty to such rule? What, all –
From heavenly John and Attic Paul,
And that brave weather-battered Peter,
Whose stout faith only stood completer
For buffets, sinning to be pardoned,
As, more his hands hauled nets, they hardened, –
All, down to you, the man of men,
Professing here at Göttingen,
Compose Christ's flock! They, you and I,
Are sheep of a good man! And why?
950 The goodness, – how did he acquire it?
Was it self-gained, did God inspire it?
Choose which; then tell me, on what ground
Should its possessor dare propound
His claim to rise o'er us an inch?
Were goodness all some man's invention,
Who arbitrarily made mention
What we should follow, and whence flinch, –
What qualities might take the style
Of right and wrong, – and had such guessing
960 Met with as general acquiescing
As graced the alphabet erewhile,
When A got leave an Ox to be,
No Camel (quoth the Jews) like G, –
For thus inventing thing and title

Worship were that man's fit requital.
But if the common conscience must
Be ultimately judge, adjust
Its apt name to each quality
Already known, – I would decree
970 Worship for such mere demonstration
    And simple work of nomenclature,
Only the day I praised, not nature,
    But Harvey, for the circulation.
I would praise such a Christ, with pride
And joy, that he, as none beside,
Had taught us how to keep the mind
God gave him, as God gave his kind,
Freer than they from fleshly taint:
I would call such a Christ our Saint,
980 As I declare our Poet, him
Whose insight makes all others dim:
A thousand poets pried at life,
And only one amid the strife
Rose to be Shakespeare: each shall take
His crown, I'd say, for the world's sake –
Though some objected – 'Had we seen
The heart and head of each, what screen
Was broken there to give them light,
While in ourselves it shuts the sight,
990 We should no more admire, perchance,
That these found truth out at a glance,
Than marvel how the bat discerns
Some pitch-dark cavern's fifty turns,
Led by a finer tact, a gift
He boasts, which other birds must shift
Without, and grope as best they can.'
No, freely I would praise the man, –
Nor one whit more, if he contended
That gift of his, from God descended.
1000 Ah friend, what gift of man's does not?
No nearer something, by a jot,
Rise an infinity of nothings
    Than one: take Euclid for your teacher:
Distinguish kinds: do crownings, clothings,
    Make that creator which was creature?
Multiply gifts upon man's head,

And what, when all's done, shall be said
But – the more gifted he, I ween!
 That one's made Christ, this other, Pilate,
1010 And this might be all that has been, –
 So what is there to frown or smile at?
What is left for us, save, in growth
Of soul, to rise up, far past both,
From the gift looking to the giver,
And from the cistern to the river,
And from the finite to infinity,
And from man's dust to God's divinity?

XVII
Take all in a word: the truth in God's breast
Lies trace for trace upon ours impressed:
1020 Though he is so bright and we so dim,
We are made in his image to witness him:
And were no eye in us to tell,
 Instructed by no inner sense,
The light of heaven from the dark of hell,
 That light would want its evidence, –
Though justice, good and truth were still
Divine, if, by some demon's will,
Hatred and wrong had been proclaimed
Law through the worlds, and right misnamed.
1030 No mere exposition of morality
Made or in part or in totality,
Should win you to give it worship, therefore:
And, if no better proof you will care for,
 – Whom do you count the worst man upon earth?
 Be sure, he knows, in his conscience, more
Of what right is, than arrives at birth
 In the best man's acts that we bow before:
This last knows better – true, but my fact is,
'Tis one thing to know, and another to practise.
1040 And thence I conclude that the real God-function
Is to furnish a motive and injunction
For practising what we know already.
And such an injunction and such a motive
As the God in Christ, do you waive, and 'heady,
High-minded,' hang your tablet-votive
Outside the fane on a finger-post?

Morality to the uttermost,
Supreme in Christ as we all confess,
Why need we prove would avail no jot
1050 To make him God, if God he were not?
What is the point where himself lays stress?
Does the precept run 'Believe in good,
In justice, truth, now understood
For the first time'? – or, 'Believe in me,
Who lived and died, yet essentially
Am Lord of Life'? Whoever can take
The same to his heart and for mere love's sake
Conceive of the love, – that man obtains
A new truth; no conviction gains
1060 Of an old one only, made intense
By a fresh appeal to his faded sense.

XVIII
Can it be that he stays inside?
    Is the vesture left me to commune with?
    Could my soul find aught to sing in tune with
Even at this lecture, if she tried?
Oh, let me at lowest sympathize
With the lurking drop of blood that lies
In the desiccated brain's white roots
Without throb for Christ's attributes,
1070 As the lecturer makes his special boast!
If love's dead there, it has left a ghost.
Admire we, how from heart to brain
    (Though to say so strike the doctors dumb)
One instinct rises and falls again,
    Restoring the equilibrium.
And how when the Critic had done his best,
And the pearl of price, at reason's test,
Lay dust and ashes levigable
On the Professor's lecture-table, –
1080 When we looked for the inference and monition
That our faith, reduced to such condition,
Be swept forthwith to its natural dust-hole, –
    He bids us, when we least expect it,
Take back our faith, – if it be not just whole,
    Yet a pearl indeed, as his tests affect it,
Which fact pays damage done rewardingly,

So, prize we our dust and ashes accordingly!
'Go home and venerate the myth
I thus have experimented with –
1090 This man, continue to adore him
Rather than all who went before him,
And all who ever followed after!' –
  Surely for this I may praise you, my brother!
Will you take the praise in tears or laughter?
  That's one point gained: can I compass another?
Unlearned love was safe from spurning –
Can't we respect your loveless learning?
Let us at least give learning honour!
What laurels had we showered upon her,
1100 Girding her loins up to perturb
Our theory of the Middle Verb;
Or Turk-like brandishing a scimitar
O'er anapaests in comic-trimeter;
Or curing the halt and maimed 'Iketides,'
While we lounged on at our indebted ease:
Instead of which, a tricksy demon
Sets her at Titus or Philemon!
When ignorance wags his ears of leather
And hates God's word, 'tis altogether;
1110 Nor leaves he his congenial thistles
To go and browse on Paul's Epistles.
– And you, the audience, who might ravage
The world wide, enviably savage,
Nor heed the cry of the retriever,
More than Herr Heine (before his fever), –
I do not tell a lie so arrant
  As say my passion's wings are furled up,
And, without plainest heavenly warrant,
  I were ready and glad to give the world up –
1120 But still, when you rub brow meticulous,
  And ponder the profit of turning holy
  If not for God's, for your own sake solely,
– God forbid I should find you ridiculous!
Deduce from this lecture all that eases you,
Nay, call yourselves, if the calling pleases you,
'Christians,' – abhor the deist's pravity, –
Go on, you shall no more move my gravity
Than, when I see boys ride a-cockhorse,

I find it in my heart to embarrass them
1130 By hinting that their stick's a mock horse,
And they really carry what they say carries them.

XIX
So sat I talking with my mind.
    I did not long to leave the door
    And find a new church, as before,
But rather was quiet and inclined
To prolong and enjoy the gentle resting
From further tracking and trying and testing.
'This tolerance is a genial mood!'
(Said I, and a little pause ensued).
1140 'One trims the bark 'twixt shoal and shelf,
    And sees, each side, the good effects of it,
A value for religion's self,
    A carelessness about the sects of it.
Let me enjoy my own conviction,
    Not watch my neighbour's faith with fretfulness,
Still spying there some dereliction
    Of truth, perversity, forgetfulness!
Better a mild indifferentism,
    Teaching that both our faiths (though duller
1150 His shine through a dull spirit's prism)
    Originally had one colour!
Better pursue a pilgrimage
    Through ancient and through modern times
    To many peoples, various climes,
Where I may see saint, savage, sage
Fuse their respective creeds in one
Before the general Father's throne!'

XX
– 'Twas the horrible storm began afresh!
The black night caught me in his mesh,
1160 Whirled me up, and flung me prone.
I was left on the college-step alone.
I looked, and far there, ever fleeting
Far, far away, the receding gesture,
And looming of the lessening vesture! –
Swept forward from my stupid hand,
While I watched my foolish heart expand

In the lazy glow of benevolence,
   O'er the various modes of man's belief.
I sprang up with fear's vehemence.
1170   Needs must there be one way, our chief
Best way of worship: let me strive
To find it, and when found, contrive
My fellows also take their share!
This constitutes my earthly care:
God's is above it and distinct.
For I, a man, with men am linked
And not a brute with brutes; no gain
That I experience, must remain
Unshared: but should my best endeavour
1180 To share it, fail – subsisteth ever
God's care above, and I exult
That God, by God's own ways occult,
May – doth, I will believe – bring back
All wanderers to a single track.
Meantime, I can but testify
God's care for me – no more, can I –
It is but for myself I know;
   The world rolls witnessing around me
   Only to leave me as it found me;
1190 Men cry there, but my ear is slow:
Their races flourish or decay
– What boots it, while yon lucid way
Loaded with stars divides the vault?
But soon my soul repairs its fault
When, sharpening sense's hebetude,
She turns on my own life! So viewed,
No mere mote's-breadth but teems immense
With witnessings of providence:
And woe to me if when I look
1200 Upon that record, the sole book
Unsealed to me, I take no heed
Of any warning that I read!
Have I been sure, this Christmas-Eve,
God's own hand did the rainbow weave,
Whereby the truth from heaven slid
Into my soul? – I cannot bid
The world admit he stooped to heal
My soul, as if in a thunder-peal

Where one heard noise, and one saw flame,
1210   I only knew he named my name:
But what is the world to me, for sorrow
Or joy in its censure, when tomorrow
It drops the remark, with just-turned head
Then, on again, 'That man is dead'?
Yes, but for me – my name called, – drawn
As a conscript's lot from the lap's black yawn,
He has dipt into on a battle-dawn:
Bid out of life by a nod, a glance, –
Stumbling, mute-mazed, at nature's chance, –
1220   With a rapid finger circled round,
Fixed to the first poor inch of ground
To fight from, where his foot was found;
Whose ear but a minute since lay free
To the wide camp's buzz and gossipry –
Summoned, a solitary man
To end his life where his life began,
From the safe glad rear, to the dreadful van!
Soul of mine, hadst thou caught and held
By the hem of the vesture! –

XXI

                         And I caught
1230   At the flying robe, and unrepelled
      Was lapped again in its folds full-fraught
With warmth and wonder and delight,
God's mercy being infinite.
For scarce had the words escaped my tongue,
When, at a passionate bound, I sprung,
Out of the wandering world of rain,
Into the little chapel again.

XXII

How else was I found there, bolt upright
      On my bench, as if I had never left it?
1240   – Never flung out on the common at night,
      Nor met the storm and wedge-like cleft it,
Seen the raree-show of Peter's successor,
Or the laboratory of the Professor!
For the Vision, that was true, I wist,
True as that heaven and earth exist.

There sat my friend, the yellow and tall,
 With his neck and its wen in the selfsame place;
Yet my nearest neighbour's cheek showed gall.
 She had slid away a contemptuous space:
1250 And the old fat woman, late so placable,
Eyed me with symptoms, hardly mistakable,
Of her milk of kindness turning rancid.
In short, a spectator might have fancied
That I had nodded, betrayed by slumber,
Yet kept my seat, a warning ghastly,
Through the heads of the sermon, nine in number,
And woke up now at the tenth and lastly.
But again, could such disgrace have happened?
 Each friend at my elbow had surely nudged it;
1260 And, as for the sermon, where did my nap end?
 Unless I heard it, could I have judged it?
Could I report as I do at the close,
First, the preacher speaks through his nose:
Second, his gesture is too emphatic:
 Thirdly, to waive what's pedagogic,
 The subject-matter itself lacks logic:
Fourthly, the English is ungrammatic.
Great news! the preacher is found no Pascal,
Whom, if I pleased, I might to the task call
1270 Of making square to a finite eye
 The circle of infinity,
 And find so all-but-just-succeeding!
Great news! the sermon proves no reading
Where bee-like in the flowers I bury me,
Like Taylor's the immortal Jeremy!
And now that I know the very worst of him,
What was it I thought to obtain at first of him?
Ha! Is God mocked, as he asks?
Shall I take on me to change his tasks,
1280 And dare, dispatched to a river-head
 For a simple draught of the element,
Neglect the thing for which he sent,
 And return with another thing instead? –
Saying, 'Because the water found
Welling up from underground,
Is mingled with the taints of earth,
While thou, I know, dost laugh at dearth,

And couldst, at wink or word, convulse
The world with the leap of a river-pulse, –
1290 Therefore I turned from the oozings muddy,
And bring thee a chalice I found, instead:
See the brave veins in the breccia ruddy!
One would suppose that the marble bled.
What matters the water? A hope I have nursed:
The waterless cup will quench my thirst.'
– Better have knelt at the poorest stream
That trickles in pain from the straitest rift!
For the less or the more is all God's gift,
Who blocks up or breaks wide the granite-seam.
1300 And here, is there water or not, to drink?
I then, in ignorance and weakness,
Taking God's help, have attained to think
My heart does best to receive in meekness
That mode of worship, as most to his mind,
Where earthly aids being cast behind,
His All in All appears serene
With the thinnest human veil between,
Letting the mystic lamps, the seven,
The many motions of his spirit,
1310 Pass, as they list, to earth from heaven.
For the preacher's merit or demerit,
It were to be wished the flaws were fewer
In the earthen vessel, holding treasure
Which lies as safe in a golden ewer;
But the main thing is, does it hold good measure?
Heaven soon sets right all other matters! –
Ask, else, these ruins of humanity,
This flesh worn out to rags and tatters,
This soul at struggle with insanity,
1320 Who thence take comfort – can I doubt? –
Which an empire gained, were a loss without.
May it be mine! And let us hope
That no worse blessing befall the Pope,
Turned sick at last of today's buffoonery,
Of posturings and petticoatings,
Beside his Bourbon bully's gloatings
In the bloody orgies of drunk poltroonery!
Nor may the Professor forego its peace
At Göttingen presently, when, in the dusk

1330   Of his life, if his cough, as I fear, should increase,
     Prophesied of by that horrible husk –
When thicker and thicker the darkness fills
The world through his misty spectacles,
And he gropes for something more substantial
     Than a fable, myth or personification, –
May Christ do for him what no mere man shall,
     And stand confessed as the God of salvation!
Meantime, in the still recurring fear
     Lest myself, at unawares, be found,
1340   While attacking the choice of my neighbours round,
With none of my own made – I choose here!
The giving out of the hymn reclaims me;
I have done: and if any blames me,
Thinking that merely to touch in brevity
     The topics I dwell on, were unlawful, –
Or worse, that I trench, with undue levity,
     On the bounds of the holy and the awful, –
I praise the heart, and pity the head of him,
And refer myself to THEE, instead of him,
1350 Who head and heart alike discernest,
     Looking below light speech we utter,
     When frothy spume and frequent sputter
Prove that the soul's depths boil in earnest!
May truth shine out, stand ever before us!
I put up pencil and join chorus
To Hepzibah Tune, without further apology,
     The last five verses of the third section
     Of the seventeenth hymn of Whitfield's Collection,
To conclude with the doxology.

Easter-Day

I
How very hard it is to be
A Christian! Hard for you and me,
– Not the mere task of making real
That duty up to its ideal,
Effecting thus, complete and whole,

A purpose of the human soul –
For that is always hard to do;
But hard, I mean, for me and you
To realize it, more or less,
10 With even the moderate success
Which commonly repays our strife
To carry out the aims of life.
'This aim is greater,' you will say,
'And so more arduous every way.'
– But the importance of their fruits
Still proves to man, in all pursuits,
Proportional encouragement.
'Then, what if it be God's intent
That labour to this one result
20 Should seem unduly difficult?'
Ah, that's a question in the dark –
And the sole thing that I remark
Upon the difficulty, this;
We do not see it where it is,
At the beginning of the race:
As we proceed, it shifts its place,
And where we looked for crowns to fall,
We find the tug's to come, – that's all.

II
At first you say, 'The whole, or chief
30 Of difficulties, is belief.
Could I believe once thoroughly,
The rest were simple. What? Am I
An idiot, do you think, – a beast?
Prove to me, only that the least
Command of God is God's indeed,
And what injunction shall I need
To pay obedience? Death so nigh,
When time must end, eternity
Begin, – and cannot I compute,
40 Weigh loss and gain together, suit
My actions to the balance drawn,
And give my body to be sawn
Asunder, hacked in pieces, tied
To horses, stoned, burned, crucified,

Like any martyr of the list?
How gladly! – if I make acquist,
Through the brief minute's fierce annoy,
Of God's eternity of joy.'

III

– And certainly you name the point
50 Whereon all turns: for could you joint
This flexile finite life once tight
Into the fixed and infinite,
You, safe inside, would spurn what's out,
With carelessness enough, no doubt –
Would spurn mere life: but when time brings
To their next stage your reasonings,
Your eyes, late wide, begin to wink
Nor see the path so well, I think.

IV

You say, 'Faith may be, one agrees,
60 A touchstone for God's purposes,
Even as ourselves conceive of them.
Could he acquit us or condemn
For holding what no hand can loose,
Rejecting when we can't but choose?
As well award the victor's wreath
To whosoever should take breath
Duly each minute while he lived –
Grant heaven, because a man contrived
To see its sunlight every day
70 He walked forth on the public way.
You must mix some uncertainty
With faith, if you would have faith be.
Why, what but faith, do we abhor
And idolize each other for –
Faith in our evil or our good,
Which is or is not understood
Aright by those we love or those
We hate, thence called our friends or foes?
Your mistress saw your spirit's grace,
80 When, turning from the ugly face,
I found belief in it too hard;
And she and I have our reward.

–Yet here a doubt peeps: well for us
Weak beings, to go using thus
A touchstone for our little ends,
Trying with faith the foes and friends;
– But God, bethink you! I would fain
Conceive of the Creator's reign
As based upon exacter laws
90   Than creatures build by with applause.
In all God's acts – (as Plato cries
He doth) – he should geometrize.
Whence, I desiderate . . .'

V

          I see!
You would grow as a natural tree,
Stand as a rock, soar up like fire.
The world's so perfect and entire,
Quite above faith, so right and fit!
Go there, walk up and down in it!
No. The creation travails, groans –
100 Contrive your music from its moans,
Without or let or hindrance, friend!
That's an old story, and its end
As old – you come back (be sincere)
With every question you put here
(Here where there once was, and is still,
We think, a living oracle,
Whose answers you stand carping at)
This time flung back unanswered flat, –
Beside, perhaps, as many more
110 As those that drove you out before,
Now added, where was little need.
Questions impossible, indeed,
To us who sat still, all and each
Persuaded that our earth had speech,
Of God's, writ down, no matter if
In cursive type or hieroglyph, –
Which one fact freed us from the yoke
Of guessing why He never spoke.
You come back in no better plight
120 Than when you left us, – am I right?

VI

So, the old process, I conclude,
Goes on, the reasoning's pursued
Further. You own, ''Tis well averred,
A scientific faith's absurd,
– Frustrates the very end 'twas meant
To serve. So, I would rest content
With a mere probability,
But, probable; the chance must lie
Clear on one side, – lie all in rough,
130 So long as there be just enough
To pin my faith to, though it hap
Only at points: from gap to gap
One hangs up a huge cùrtain so,
Grandly, nor seeks to have it go
Foldless and flat along the wall.
What care I if some interval
Of life less plainly may depend
On God? I'd hang there to the end;
And thus I should not find it hard
140 To be a Christian and debarred
From trailing on the earth, till furled
Away by death. – Renounce the world!
Were that a mighty hardship? Plan
A pleasant life, and straight some man
Beside you, with, if he thought fit,
Abundant means to compass it,
Shall turn deliberate aside
To try and live as, if you tried
You clearly might, yet most despise.
150 One friend of mine wears out his eyes,
Slighting the stupid joys of sense,
In patient hope that, ten years hence,
"Somewhat completer," he may say,
"My list of *coleoptera!*"
While just the other who most laughs
At him, above all epitaphs
Aspires to have his tomb describe
Himself as sole among the tribe
Of snuffbox-fanciers, who possessed
160 A Grignon with the Regent's crest.
So that, subduing, as you want,

Whatever stands predominant
Among my earthly appetites
For tastes and smells and sounds and sights,
I shall be doing that alone,
To gain a palm-branch and a throne.
Which fifty people undertake
To do, and gladly, for the sake
Of giving a Semitic guess,
170　Or playing pawns at blindfold chess.'

VII
Good: and the next thing is, – look round
For evidence enough! 'Tis found,
No doubt: as is your sort of mind,
So is your sort of search: you'll find
What you desire, and that's to be
A Christian. What says history?
How comforting a point it were
To find some mummy-scrap declare
There lived a Moses! Better still,
180　Prove Jonah's whale translatable
Into some quicksand of the seas,
Isle, cavern, rock, or what you please,
That faith might flap her wings and crow
From such an eminence! Or, no –
The human heart's best; you prefer
Making that prove the minister
To truth; you probe its wants and needs,
And hopes and fears, then try what creeds
Meet these most aptly, – resolute
190　That faith plucks such substantial fruit
Wherever these two correspond,
She little needs to look beyond,
And puzzle out who Orpheus was,
Or Dionysius Zagrias.
You'll find sufficient, as I say,
To satisfy you either way;
You wanted to believe; your pains
Are crowned – you do: and what remains?
'Renounce the world!' – Ah, were it done
200　By merely cutting one by one
Your limbs off, with your wise head last,

How easy were it! – how soon past,
If once in the believing mood!
'Such is man's usual gratitude,
Such thanks to God do we return,
For not exacting that we spurn
A single gift of life, forego
One real gain, – only taste them so
With gravity and temperance,
210 That those mild virtues may enhance
Such pleasures, rather than abstract –
Last spice of which, will be the fact
Of love discerned in every gift;
While, when the scene of life shall shift,
And the gay heart be taught to ache,
As sorrows and privations take
The place of joy, – the thing that seems
Mere misery, under human schemes,
Becomes, regarded by the light
220 Of love, as very near, or quite
As good a gift as joy before.
So plain is it that, all the more
A dispensation's merciful,
More pettishly we try and cull
Briers, thistles, from our private plot,
To mar God's ground where thorns are not!'

VIII
Do you say this, or I? – Oh, you!
Then, what, my friend? – (thus I pursue
Our parley) – you indeed opine
230 That the Eternal and Divine
Did, eighteen centuries ago,
In very truth . . . Enough! you know
The all-stupendous tale, – that Birth,
That Life, that Death! And all, the earth
Shuddered at, – all, the heavens grew black
Rather than see; all, nature's rack
And throe at dissolution's brink
Attested, – all took place, you think,
Only to give our joys a zest,
240 And prove our sorrows for the best?

We differ, then! Were I, still pale
And heartstruck at the dreadful tale,
Waiting to hear God's voice declare
What horror followed for my share,
As implicated in the deed,
Apart from other sins, – concede
That if He blacked out in a blot
My brief life's pleasantness, 'twere not
So very disproportionate!
250 Or there might be another fate –
I certainly could understand
(If fancies were the thing in hand)
How God might save, at that day's price,
The impure in their impurities,
Give licence formal and complete
To choose the fair and pick the sweet.
But there be certain words, broad, plain,
Uttered again and yet again,
Hard to mistake or overgloss –
260 Announcing this world's gain for loss,
And bidding us reject the same:
The whole world lieth (they proclaim)
In wickedness, – come out of it!
Turn a deaf ear, if you think fit,
But I who thrill through every nerve
At thought of what deaf ears deserve –
How do you counsel in the case?

IX
'I'd take, by all means, in your place,
The safe side, since it so appears:
270 Deny myself, a few brief years,
The natural pleasure, leave the fruit
Or cut the plant up by the root.
Remember what a martyr said
On the rude tablet overhead!
"I was born sickly, poor and mean,
A slave: no misery could screen
The holders of the pearl of price
From Caesar's envy; therefore twice
I fought with beasts, and three times saw

280   My children suffer by his law;
    At last my own release was earned:
    I was some time in being burned,
    But at the close a Hand came through
    The fire above my head, and drew
    My soul to Christ, whom now I see.
    Sergius, a brother, writes for me
    This testimony on the wall –
    For me, I have forgot it all."
    You say right; this were not so hard!
290   And since one nowise is debarred
    From this, why not escape some sins
    By such a method?'

x
                  Then begins
    To the old point revulsion new –
    (For 'tis just this I bring you to)
    If after all we should mistake,
    And so renounce life for the sake
    Of death and nothing else? You hear
    Each friend we jeered at, send the jeer
    Back to ourselves with good effect –
300   'There were my beetles to collect!
    My box – a trifle, I confess,
    But here I hold it, ne'ertheless!'
    Poor idiots, (let us pluck up heart
    And answer) we, the better part
    Have chosen, though 'twere only hope, –
    Nor envy moles like you that grope
    Amid your veritable muck,
    More than the grasshoppers would truck,
    For yours, their passionate life away,
310   That spends itself in leaps all day
    To reach the sun, you want the eyes
    To see, as they the wings to rise
    And match the noble hearts of them!
    Thus the contemner we contemn, –
    And, when doubt strikes us, thus we ward
    Its stroke off, caught upon our guard,
    – Not struck enough to overturn
    Our faith, but shake it – make us learn

What I began with, and, I wis,
320 End, having proved, – how hard it is
To be a Christian!

XI

        'Proved, or not,
Howe'er you wis, small thanks, I wot,
You get of mine, for taking pains
To make it hard to me. Who gains
By that, I wonder? Here I live
In trusting ease; and here you drive
At causing me to lose what most
Yourself would mourn for had you lost!'

XII

But, do you see, my friend, that thus
330 You leave Saint Paul for Aeschylus?
– Who made his Titan's arch-device
The giving men *blind hopes* to spice
The meal of life with, else devoured
In bitter haste, while lo, death loured
Before them at the platter's edge!
If faith should be, as I allege,
Quite other than a condiment
To heighten flavours with, or meant
(Like that brave curry of his Grace)
340 To take at need the victuals' place?
If, having dined, you would digest
Besides, and turning to your rest
Should find instead . . .

XIII

            Now, you shall see
And judge if a mere foppery
Pricks on my speaking! I resolve
To utter – yes, it shall devolve
On you to hear as solemn, strange
And dread a thing as in the range
Of facts, – or fancies, if God will –
350 E'er happened to our kind! I still
Stand in the cloud and, while it wraps
My face, ought not to speak perhaps;

Seeing that if I carry through
My purpose, if my words in you
Find a live actual listener,
My story, reason must aver
False after all – the happy chance!
While, if each human countenance
I meet in London day by day,
360 Be what I fear, – my warnings fray
No one, and no one they convert,
And no one helps me to assert
How hard it is to really be
A Christian, and in vacancy
I pour this story!

XIV
              I commence
By trying to inform you, whence
It comes that every Easter-night
As now, I sit up, watch, till light,
Upon those chimney-stacks and roofs,
370 Give, through my window-pane, grey proofs
That Easter-day is breaking slow.
On such a night three years ago,
It chanced that I had cause to cross
The common, where the chapel was,
Our friend spoke of, the other day –
You've not forgotten, I dare say.
I fell to musing of the time
So close, the blessed matin-prime
All hearts leap up at, in some guise –
380 One could not well do otherwise.
Insensibly my thoughts were bent
Toward the main point, I overwent
Much the same ground of reasoning
As you and I just now. One thing
Remained, however – one that tasked
My soul to answer; and I asked,
Fairly and frankly, what might be
That History, that Faith, to me
– Me there – not me in some domain
390 Built up and peopled by my brain,
Weighing its merits as one weighs

Mere theories for blame or praise,
– The kingcraft of the Lucumons,
Or Fourier's scheme, its pros and cons, –
But my faith there, or none at all.
'How were my case, now, did I fall
Dead here, this minute – should I lie
Faithful or faithless?' Note that I
Inclined thus ever! – little prone
400 For instance, when I lay alone
In childhood, to go calm to sleep
And leave a closet where might keep
His watch perdue some murderer
Waiting till twelve o'clock to stir,
As good authentic legends tell:
'He might: but how improbable!
How little likely to deserve
The pains and trial to the nerve
Of thrusting head into the dark!' –
410 Urged my old nurse, and bade me mark
Beside, that, should the dreadful scout
Really lie hid there, and leap out
At first turn of the rusty key,
Mine were small gain that she could see,
Killed not in bed but on the floor,
And losing one night's sleep the more.
I tell you, I would always burst
The door ope, know my fate at first.
This time, indeed, the closet penned
420 No such assassin: but a friend
Rather, peeped out to guard me, fit
For counsel, Common Sense, to wit,
Who said a good deal that might pass, –
Heartening, impartial too, it was,
Judge else: 'For, soberly now, – who
Should be a Christian if not you?'
(Hear how he smoothed me down.) 'One takes
A whole life, sees what course it makes
Mainly, and not by fits and starts –
430 In spite of stoppage which imparts
Fresh value to the general speed.
A life, with none, would fly indeed:
Your progressing is slower – right!

We deal with progress and not flight.
Through baffling senses passionate,
Fancies as restless, – with a freight
Of knowledge cumbersome enough
To sink your ship when waves grow rough,
Though meant for ballast in the hold, –
440 I find, 'mid dangers manifold,
The good bark answers to the helm
Where faith sits, easier to o'erwhelm
Than some stout peasant's heavenly guide,
Whose hard head could not, if it tried,
Conceive a doubt, nor understand
How senses hornier than his hand
Should 'tice the Christian off his guard.
More happy! But shall we award
Less honour to the hull which, dogged
450 By storms, a mere wreck, waterlogged,
Masts by the board, her bulwarks gone
And stanchions going, yet bears on, –
Than to mere life-boats, built to save,
And triumph o'er the breaking wave?
Make perfect your good ship as these,
And what were her performances!'
I added – 'Would the ship reach home!
I wish indeed "God's kingdom come –"
The day when I shall see appear
460 His bidding, as my duty, clear
From doubt! And it shall dawn, that day,
Some future season; Easter may
Prove, not impossibly, the time –
Yes, that were striking – fates would chime
So aptly! Easter-morn, to bring
The Judgement! – deeper in the spring
Than now, however, when there's snow
Capping the hills; for earth must show
All signs of meaning to pursue
470 Her tasks as she was wont to do
– The skylark, taken by surprise
As we ourselves, shall recognize
Sudden the end. For suddenly
It comes; the dreadfulness must be
In that; all warrants the belief –

"At night it cometh like a thief."
I fancy why the trumpet blows;
– Plainly, to wake one. From repose
We shall start up, at last awake
480 From life, that insane dream we take
For waking now, because it seems.
And as, when now we wake from dreams,
We laugh, while we recall them, "Fool,
To let the chance slip, linger cool
When such adventure offered! Just
A bridge to cross, a dwarf to thrust
Aside, a wicked mage to stab –
And, lo ye, I had kissed Queen Mab!"
So shall we marvel why we grudged
490 Our labour here, and idly judged
Of heaven, we might have gained, but lose!
Lose? Talk of loss, and I refuse
To plead at all! You speak no worse
Nor better than my ancient nurse
When she would tell me in my youth
I well deserved that shapes uncouth
Frighted and teased me in my sleep:
Why could I not in memory keep
Her precept for the evil's cure?
500 "Pinch your own arm, boy, and be sure
You'll wake forthwith!"'"

XV

              And as I said
This nonsense, throwing back my head
With light complacent laugh, I found
Suddenly all the midnight round
One fire. The dome of heaven had stood
As made up of a multitude
Of handbreadth cloudlets, one vast rack
Of ripples infinite and black,
From sky to sky. Sudden there went,
510 Like horror and astonishment,
A fierce vindictive scribble of red
Quick flame across, as if one said
(The angry scribe of Judgement) 'There –
Burn it!' And straight I was aware

That the whole ribwork round, minute
Cloud touching cloud beyond compute,
Was tinted, each with its own spot
Of burning at the core, till clot
Jammed against clot, and spilt its fire
520 Over all heaven, which 'gan suspire
As fanned to measure equable, –
Just so great conflagrations kill
Night overhead, and rise and sink,
Reflected. Now the fire would shrink
And wither off the blasted face
Of heaven, and I distinct might trace
The sharp black ridgy outlines left
Unburned like network – then, each cleft
The fire had been sucked back into,
530 Regorged, and out it surging flew
Furiously, and night writhed inflamed,
Till, tolerating to be tamed
No longer, certain rays world-wide
Shot downwardly. On every side
Caught past escape, the earth was lit;
As if a dragon's nostril split
And all his famished ire o'erflowed;
Then as he winced at his lord's goad,
Back he inhaled: whereat I found
540 The clouds into vast pillars bound,
Based on the corners of the earth,
Propping the skies at top: a dearth
Of fire i' the violet intervals,
Leaving exposed the utmost walls
Of time, about to tumble in
And end the world.

XVI
                    I felt begin
The Judgement-Day: to retrocede
Was too late now. 'In very deed,'
(I uttered to myself) 'that Day!'
550 The intuition burned away
All darkness from my spirit too:
There, stood I, found and fixed, I knew,
Choosing the world. The choice was made;

And naked and disguiseless stayed,
And unevadable, the fact.
My brain held all the same compact
Its senses, nor my heart declined
Its office; rather, both combined
To help me in this juncture. I
560 Lost not a second, – agony
Gave boldness: since my life had end
And my choice with it – best defend,
Applaud both! I resolved to say,
'So was I framed by thee, such way
I put to use thy senses here!
It was so beautiful, so near,
Thy world, – what could I then but choose
My part there? Nor did I refuse
To look above the transient boon
570 Of time; but it was hard so soon
As in a short life, to give up
Such beauty: I could put the cup
Undrained of half its fulness, by;
But, to renounce it utterly,
– That was too hard! Nor did the cry
Which bade renounce it, touch my brain
Authentically deep and plain
Enough to make my lips let go.
But Thou, who knowest all, dost know
580 Whether I was not, life's brief while,
Endeavouring to reconcile
Those lips (too tardily, alas!)
To letting the dear remnant pass,
One day, – some drops of earthly good
Untasted! Is it for this mood,
That Thou, whose earth delights so well,
Hast made its complement a hell?'

XVII
A final belch of fire like blood,
Overbroke all heaven in one flood
590 Of doom. Then fire was sky, and sky
Fire, and both, one brief ecstasy,
Then ashes. But I heard no noise
(Whatever was) because a voice

Beside me spoke thus, 'Life is done,
Time ends, Eternity's begun,
And thou art judged for evermore.'

XVIII

I looked up; all seemed as before;
Of that cloud-Tophet overhead
No trace was left: I saw instead
600   The common round me, and the sky
Above, stretched drear and emptily
Of life. 'Twas the last watch of night,
Except what brings the morning quite;
When the armed angel, conscience-clear,
His task nigh done, leans o'er his spear
And gazes on the earth he guards,
Safe one night more through all its wards,
Till God relieve him at his post.
'A dream – a waking dream at most!'
610   (I spoke out quick, that I might shake
The horrid nightmare off, and wake.)
'The world gone, yet the world is here?
Are not all things as they appear?
Is Judgement past for me alone?
– And where had place the great white throne?
The rising of the quick and dead?
Where stood they, small and great? Who read
The sentence from the opened book?'
So, by degrees, the blood forsook
620   My heart, and let it beat afresh;
I knew I should break through the mesh
Of horror, and breathe presently:
When, lo, again, the voice by me!

XIX

I saw ... Oh brother, 'mid far sands
The palm-tree-cinctured city stands,
Bright-white beneath, as heaven, bright-blue,
Leans o'er it, while the years pursue
Their course, unable to abate
Its paradisal laugh at fate!
630   One morn, – the Arab staggers blind
O'er a new tract of death, calcined

To ashes, silence, nothingness, –
And strives, with dizzy wits, to guess
Whence fell the blow. What if, 'twixt skies
And prostrate earth, he should surprise
The imaged vapour, head to foot,
Surveying, motionless and mute,
Its work, ere, in a whirlwind rapt
It vanish up again ? – So hapt
640 My chance. HE stood there. Like the smoke
Pillared o'er Sodom, when day broke, –
I saw Him. One magnific pall
Mantled in massive fold and fall
His dread, and coiled in snaky swathes
About His feet: night's black, that bathes
All else, broke, grizzled with despair,
Against the soul of blackness there.
A gesture told the mood within –
That wrapped right hand which based the chin,
650 That intense meditation fixed
On His procedure, – pity mixed
With the fulfilment of decree.
Motionless, thus, He spoke to me,
Who fell before His feet, a mass,
No man now.

XX
           'All is come to pass.
Such shows are over for each soul
They had respect to. In the roll
Of Judgement which convinced mankind
Of sin, stood many, bold and blind,
660 Terror must burn the truth into:
Their fate for them! – thou hadst to do
With absolute omnipotence,
Able its judgements to dispense
To the whole race, as every one
Were its sole object. Judgement done,
God is, thou art, – the rest is hurled
To nothingness for thee. This world,
This finite life, thou hast preferred,
In disbelief of God's plain word,
670 To heaven and to infinity.

Here the probation was for thee,
To show thy soul the earthly mixed
With heavenly, it must choose betwixt.
The earthly joys lay palpable, –
A taint, in each, distinct as well;
The heavenly flitted, faint and rare,
Above them, but as truly were
Taintless, so, in their nature, best.
Thy choice was earth: thou didst attest
680 'Twas fitter spirit should subserve
The flesh, than flesh refine to nerve
Beneath the spirit's play. Advance
No claim to their inheritance
Who chose the spirit's fugitive
Brief gleams, and yearned, "This were to live
Indeed, if rays, completely pure
From flesh that dulls them, could endure, –
Not shoot in meteor-light athwart
Our earth, to show how cold and swart
690 It lies beneath their fire, but stand
As stars do, destined to expand,
Prove veritable worlds, our home!"
Thou said'st, – "Let spirit star the dome
Of sky, that flesh may miss no peak,
No nook of earth, – I shall not seek
Its service further!" Thou art shut
Out of the heaven of spirit; glut
Thy sense upon the world: 'tis thine
For ever – take it!'

XXI

'How? Is mine,
700 The world?' (I cried, while my soul broke
Out in a transport.) 'Hast Thou spoke
Plainly in that? Earth's exquisite
Treasures of wonder and delight,
For me?'

XXII

The austere voice returned, –
'So soon made happy? Hadst thou learned
What God accounteth happiness,

Thou wouldst not find it hard to guess
What hell may be his punishment
For those who doubt if God invent
710 Better than they. Let such men rest
Content with what they judged the best.
Let the unjust usurp at will:
The filthy shall be filthy still:
Miser, there waits the gold for thee!
Hater, indulge thine enmity!
And thou, whose heaven self-ordained
Was, to enjoy earth unrestrained,
Do it! Take all the ancient show!
The woods shall wave, the rivers flow,
720 And men apparently pursue
Their works, as they were wont to do,
While living in probation yet.
I promise not thou shalt forget
The past, now gone to its account;
But leave thee with the old amount
Of faculties, nor less nor more,
Unvisited, as heretofore,
By God's free spirit, that makes an end.
So, once more, take thy world! Expend
730 Eternity upon its shows,
Flung thee as freely as one rose
Out of a summer's opulence,
Over the Eden-barrier whence
Thou art excluded. Knock in vain!'

XXIII
I sat up. All was still again.
I breathed free: to my heart, back fled
The warmth. 'But, all the world!' – I said.
I stooped and picked a leaf of fern,
And recollected I might learn
740 From books, how many myriad sorts
Of fern exist, to trust reports,
Each as distinct and beautiful
As this, the very first I cull.
Think, from the first leaf to the last!
Conceive, then, earth's resources! Vast
Exhaustless beauty, endless change

Of wonder! And this foot shall range
Alps, Andes, – and this eye devour
The bee-bird and the aloe-flower?

XXIV

750 Then the voice, 'Welcome so to rate
The arras-folds that variegate
The earth, God's antechamber, well!
The wise, who waited there, could tell
By these, what royalties in store
Lay one step past the entrance-door.
For whom, was reckoned, not too much,
This life's munificence? For such
As thou, – a race, whereof scarce one
Was able, in a million,
760 To feel that any marvel lay
In objects round his feet all day;
Scarce one, in many millions more,
Willing, if able, to explore
The secreter, minuter charm!
– Brave souls, a fern-leaf could disarm
Of power to cope with God's intent, –
Or scared if the south firmament
With north-fire did its wings refledge!
All partial beauty was a pledge
770 Of beauty in its plenitude:
But since the pledge sufficed thy mood,
Retain it! plenitude be theirs
Who looked above!'

XXV

Though sharp despairs
Shot through me, I held up, bore on.
'What matter though my trust were gone
From natural things? Henceforth my part
Be less with nature than with art!
For art supplants, gives mainly worth
To nature; 'tis man stamps the earth –
780 And I will seek his impress, seek
The statuary of the Greek,
Italy's painting – there my choice
Shall fix!'

XXVI

'Obtain it!' said the voice,
' – The one form with its single act,
Which sculptors laboured to abstract,
The one face, painters tried to draw,
With its one look, from throngs they saw.
And that perfection in their soul,
These only hinted at? The whole,
790 They were but parts of? What each laid
His claim to glory on? – afraid
His fellow-men should give him rank
By mere tentatives which he shrank
Smitten at heart from, all the more,
That gazers pressed in to adore!
"Shall I be judged by only these?"
If such his soul's capacities,
Even while he trod the earth, – think, now,
What pomp in Buonarroti's brow,
800 With its new palace-brain where dwells
Superb the soul, unvexed by cells
That crumbled with the transient clay!
What visions will his right hand's sway
Still turn to forms, as still they burst
Upon him? How will he quench thirst,
Titanically infantine,
Laid at the breast of the Divine?
Does it confound thee, – this first page
Emblazoning man's heritage? –
810 Can this alone absorb thy sight,
As pages were not infinite, –
Like the omnipotence which tasks
Itself to furnish all that asks
The soul it means to satiate?
What was the world, the starry state
Of the broad skies, – what, all displays
Of power and beauty intermixed,
Which now thy soul is chained betwixt, –
What else than needful furniture
820 For life's first stage? God's work, be sure,
No more spreads wasted, than falls scant!
He filled, did not exceed, man's want
Of beauty in this life. But through

Life pierce, – and what has earth to do,
Its utmost beauty's appanage,
With the requirement of next stage?
Did God pronounce earth "very good"?
Needs must it be, while understood
For man's preparatory state;
830 Naught here to heighten nor abate;
Transfer the same completeness here,
To serve a new state's use, – and drear
Deficiency gapes every side!
The good, tried once, were bad, retried.
See the enwrapping rocky niche,
Sufficient for the sleep in which
The lizard breathes for ages safe:
Split the mould – and as light would chafe
The creature's new world-widened sense,
840 Dazzled to death at evidence
Of all the sounds and sights that broke
Innumerous at the chisel's stroke, –
So, in God's eye, the earth's first stuff
Was, neither more nor less, enough
To house man's soul, man's need fulfil.
Man reckoned it immeasurable?
So thinks the lizard of his vault!
Could God be taken in default,
Short of contrivances, by you, –
850 Or reached, ere ready to pursue
His progress through eternity?
That chambered rock, the lizard's world,
Your easy mallet's blow has hurled
To nothingness for ever; so,
Has God abolished at a blow
This world, wherein his saints were pent, –
Who, though found grateful and content,
With the provision there, as thou,
Yet knew he would not disallow
860 Their spirit's hunger, felt as well, –
Unsated, – not unsatable,
As paradise gives proof. Deride
Their choice now, thou who sit'st outside!'

XXVII

I cried in anguish, 'Mind, the mind,
So miserably cast behind,
To gain what had been wisely lost!
Oh, let me strive to make the most
Of the poor stinted soul, I nipped
Of budding wings, else now equipped
870 For voyage from summer isle to isle!
And though she needs must reconcile
Ambition to the life on ground,
Still, I can profit by late found
But precious knowledge. Mind is best –
I will seize mind, forego the rest,
And try how far my tethered strength
May crawl in this poor breadth and length.
Let me, since I can fly no more,
At least spin dervish-like about
880 (Till giddy rapture almost doubt
I fly) through circling sciences,
Philosophies and histories!
Should the whirl slacken there, then verse,
Fining to music, shall asperse
Fresh and fresh fire-dew, till I strain
Intoxicate, half-break my chain!
Not joyless, though more favoured feet
Stand calm, where I want wings to beat
The floor. At least earth's bond is broke!'

XXVIII

890 Then, (sickening even while I spoke)
'Let me alone! No answer, pray,
To this! I know what Thou wilt say!
All still is earth's, – to know, as much
As feel its truths, which if we touch
With sense, or apprehend in soul,
What matter? I have reached the goal –
"Whereto does knowledge serve!" will burn
My eyes, too sure, at every turn!
I cannot look back now, nor stake
900 Bliss on the race, for running's sake.
The goal's a ruin like the rest!' –
'And so much worse thy latter quest,'

(Added the voice) 'that even on earth –
Whenever, in man's soul, had birth
Those intuitions, grasps of guess,
Which pull the more into the less,
Making the finite comprehend
Infinity, – the bard would spend
Such praise alone, upon his craft,
910   As, when wind-lyres obey the waft,
Goes to the craftsman who arranged
The seven strings, changed them and rechanged –
Knowing it was the South that harped.
He felt his song, in singing, warped;
Distinguished his and God's part: whence
A world of spirit as of sense
Was plain to him, yet not too plain,
Which he could traverse, not remain
A guest in: – else were permanent
920   Heaven on the earth its gleams were meant
To sting with hunger for full light, –
Made visible in verse, despite
The veiling weakness, – truth by means
Of fable, showing while it screens, –
Since highest truth, man e'er supplied,
Was ever fable on outside.
Such gleams made bright the earth an age;
Now the whole sun's his heritage!
Take up thy world, it is allowed,
930   Thou who hast entered in the cloud!'

XXIX
Then I – 'Behold, my spirit bleeds,
Catches no more at broken reeds, –
But lilies flower those reeds above:
I let the world go, and take love!
Love survives in me, albeit those
I love be henceforth masks and shows,
Not living men and women: still
I mind how love repaired all ill,
Cured wrong, soothed grief, made earth amends
940   With parents, brothers, children, friends!
Some semblance of a woman yet
With eyes to help me to forget,

Shall look on me; and I will match
Departed love with love, attach
Old memories to new dreams, nor scorn
The poorest of the grains of corn
I save from shipwreck on this isle,
Trusting its barrenness may smile
With happy foodful green one day,
950 More precious for the pains. I pray, –
Leave to love, only!'

XXX
                At the word,
The form, I looked to have been stirred
With pity and approval, rose
O'er me, as when the headsman throws
Axe over shoulder to make end –
I fell prone, letting Him expend
His wrath, while thus the inflicting voice
Smote me. 'Is this thy final choice?
Love is the best? 'Tis somewhat late!
960 And all thou dost enumerate
Of power and beauty in the world,
The mightiness of love was curled
Inextricably round about.
Love lay within it and without,
To clasp thee, – but in vain! Thy soul
Still shrunk from Him who made the whole,
Still set deliberate aside
His love! – Now take love! Well betide
Thy tardy conscience! Haste to take
970 The show of love for the name's sake,
Remembering every moment Who,
Beside creating thee unto
These ends, and these for thee, was said
To undergo death in thy stead
In flesh like thine: so ran the tale.
What doubt in thee could countervail
Belief in it? Upon the ground
"That in the story had been found
Too much love! How could God love so?"
980 He who in all his works below
Adapted to the needs of man,

Made love the basis of the plan, –
Did love, as was demonstrated:
While man, who was so fit instead
To hate, as every day gave proof, –
Man thought man, for his kind's behoof,
Both could and did invent that scheme
Of perfect love: 'twould well beseem
Cain's nature thou wast wont to praise,
990　Not tally with God's usual ways!'

XXXI
And I cowered deprecatingly –
'Thou Love of God! Or let me die,
Or grant what shall seem heaven almost!
Let me not know that all is lost,
Though lost it be – leave me not tied
To this despair, this corpse-like bride!
Let that old life seem mine – no more –
With limitation as before,
With darkness, hunger, toil, distress:
1000　Be all the earth a wilderness!
Only let me go on, go on,
Still hoping ever and anon
To reach one eve the Better Land!'

XXXII
Then did the form expand, expand –
I knew Him through the dread disguise
As the whole God within His eyes
Embraced me.

XXXIII
　　　　　　When I lived again,
The day was breaking, – the grey plain
I rose from, silvered thick with dew.
1010　Was this a vision? False or true?
Since then, three varied years are spent,
And commonly my mind is bent
To think it was a dream – be sure
A mere dream and distemperature –
The last day's watching: then the night, –
The shock of that strange Northern Light

Set my head swimming, bred in me
A dream. And so I live, you see,
Go through the world, try, prove, reject,
1020 Prefer, still struggling to effect
My warfare; happy that I can
Be crossed and thwarted as a man,
Not left in God's contempt apart,
With ghastly smooth life, dead at heart,
Tame in earth's paddock as her prize.
Thank God, she still each method tries
To catch me, who may yet escape,
She knows, – the fiend in angel's shape!
Thank God, no paradise stands barred
1030 To entry, and I find it hard
To be a Christian, as I said!
Still every now and then my head
Raised glad, sinks mournful – all grows drear
Spite of the sunshine, while I fear
And think, 'How dreadful to be grudged
No ease henceforth, as one that's judged,
Condemned to earth for ever, shut
From heaven!'
                    But Easter-Day breaks! But
Christ rises! Mercy every way
1040 Is infinite, – and who can say?

Men and Women

1855

Love Among the Ruins

I

Where the quiet-coloured end of evening smiles,
   Miles and miles
On the solitary pastures where our sheep
   Half-asleep
Tinkle homeward through the twilight, stray or stop
   As they crop –
Was the site once of a city great and gay,
   (So they say)
Of our country's very capital, its prince
10   Ages since
Held his court in, gathered councils, wielding far
   Peace or war.

II

Now, – the country does not even boast a tree,
   As you see,
To distinguish slopes of verdure, certain rills
   From the hills
Intersect and give a name to, (else they run
   Into one)
Where the domed and daring palace shot its spires
20   Up like fires
O'er the hundred-gated circuit of a wall
   Bounding all,
Made of marble, men might march on nor be pressed,
   Twelve abreast.

III

And such plenty and perfection, see, of grass
   Never was!
Such a carpet as, this summer-time, o'erspreads
   And embeds
Every vestige of the city, guessed alone,
30   Stock or stone –
Where a multitude of men breathed joy and woe
   Long ago;
Lust of glory pricked their hearts up, dread of shame
   Struck them tame;

And that glory and that shame alike, the gold
  Bought and sold.

IV

Now, – the single little turret that remains
  On the plains,
By the caper over-rooted, by the gourd
40   Overscored,
While the patching houseleek's head of blossom winks
  Through the chinks –
Marks the basement whence a tower in ancient time
  Sprang sublime,
And a burning ring, all round, the chariots traced
  As they raced,
And the monarch and his minions and his dames
  Viewed the games.

V

And I know, while thus the quiet-coloured eve
50   Smiles to leave
To their folding, all our many-tinkling fleece
  In such peace,
And the slopes and rills in undistinguished grey
  Melt away –
That a girl with eager eyes and yellow hair
  Waits me there
In the turret whence the charioteers caught soul
  For the goal,
When the king looked, where she looks now, breathless, dumb
60   Till I come.

VI

But he looked upon the city, every side,
  Far and wide,
All the mountains topped with temples, all the glades'
  Colonnades,
All the causeys, bridges, aqueducts, – and then,
  All the men!
When I do come, she will speak not, she will stand,
  Either hand
On my shoulder, give her eyes the first embrace

70   Of my face,
      Ere we rush, ere we extinguish sight and speech
          Each on each.

      VII
      In one year they sent a million fighters forth
          South and North,
      And they built their gods a brazen pillar high
          As the sky,
      Yet reserved a thousand chariots in full force –
          Gold, of course.
      Oh heart! oh blood that freezes, blood that burns!
80   Earth's returns
      For whole centuries of folly, noise and sin!
          Shut them in,
      With their triumphs and their glories and the rest!
          Love is best.

A Lovers' Quarrel

      I
      Oh, what a dawn of day!
      How the March sun feels like May!
          All is blue again
          After last night's rain,
      And the South dries the hawthorn-spray.
          Only, my Love's away!
      I'd as lief that the blue were grey.

      II
      Runnels, which rillets swell,
      Must be dancing down the dell,
10   With a foaming head
          On the beryl bed
      Paven smooth as a hermit's cell;
          Each with a tale to tell,
      Could my Love but attend as well.

III

Dearest, three months ago!
When we lived blocked-up with snow, –
   When the wind would edge
   In and in his wedge,
In, as far as the point could go –
20   Not to our ingle, though,
Where we loved each the other so!

IV

Laughs with so little cause!
We devised games out of straws.
   We would try and trace
   One another's face
In the ash, as an artist draws;
   Free on each other's flaws,
How we chattered like two church daws!

V

What's in the 'Times'? – a scold
30   At the Emperor deep and cold;
   He has taken a bride
   To his gruesome side,
That's as fair as himself is bold:
   There they sit ermine-stoled,
And she powders her hair with gold.

VI

Fancy the Pampas' sheen!
Miles and miles of gold and green
   Where the sunflowers blow
   In a solid glow,
40   And – to break now and then the screen –
   Black neck and eyeballs keen,
Up a wild horse leaps between!

VII

Try, will our table turn?
Lay your hands there light, and yearn
   Till the yearning slips
   Through the finger-tips

In a fire which a few discern,
  And a very few feel burn,
And the rest, they may live and learn!

VIII

50 Then we would up and pace,
For a change, about the place,
  Each with arm o'er neck:
  'Tis our quarter-deck,
We are seamen in woeful case.
  Help in the ocean-space!
Or, if no help, we'll embrace.

IX

See, how she looks now, dressed
In a sledging-cap and vest!
  'Tis a huge fur cloak –
60   Like a reindeer's yoke
Falls the lappet along the breast:
  Sleeves for her arms to rest,
Or to hang, as my Love likes best.

X

Teach me to flirt a fan
As the Spanish ladies can,
  Or I tint your lip
  With a burnt stick's tip
And you turn into such a man!
  Just the two spots that span
70 Half the bill of the young male swan.

XI

Dearest, three months ago
When the mesmerizer Snow
  With his hand's first sweep
  Put the earth to sleep:
'Twas a time when the heart could show
  All – how was earth to know,
'Neath the mute hand's to-and-fro?

XII

Dearest, three months ago
When we loved each other so,
80   Lived and loved the same
    Till an evening came
When a shaft from the devil's bow
    Pierced to our ingle-glow,
And the friends were friend and foe!

XIII

Not from the heart beneath –
'Twas a bubble born of breath,
    Neither sneer nor vaunt,
    Nor reproach nor taunt.
See a word, how it severeth!
90   Oh, power of life and death
In the tongue, as the Preacher saith!

XIV

Woman, and will you cast
For a word, quite off at last
    Me, your own, your You, –
    Since, as truth is true,
I was You all the happy past –
    Me do you leave aghast
With the memories We amassed?

XV

Love, if you knew the light
100   That your soul casts in my sight,
    How I look to you
    For the pure and true
And the beauteous and the right, –
    Bear with a moment's spite
When a mere mote threats the white!

XVI

What of a hasty word?
Is the fleshly heart not stirred
    By a worm's pin-prick
    Where its roots are quick?

110   See the eye, by a fly's foot blurred –
     Ear, when a straw is heard
    Scratch the brain's coat of curd!

XVII

Foul be the world or fair
More or less, how can I care?
   'Tis the world the same
   For my praise or blame,
And endurance is easy there.
   Wrong in the one thing rare –
Oh, it is hard to bear!

XVIII

120 Here's the spring back or close,
When the almond-blossom blows:
   We shall have the word
   In a minor third
There is none but the cuckoo knows:
   Heaps of the guelder-rose!
I must bear with it, I suppose.

XIX

Could but November come,
Were the noisy birds struck dumb
   At the warning slash
130   Of his driver's-lash –
I would laugh like the valiant Thumb
   Facing the castle glum
And the giant's fee-faw-fum!

XX

Then, were the world well stripped
Of the gear wherein equipped
   We can stand apart,
   Heart dispense with heart
In the sun, with the flowers unnipped, –
   Oh, the world's hangings ripped,
140 We were both in a bare-walled crypt!

XXI

Each in the crypt would cry
'But one freezes here! and why?
    When a heart, as chill,
    At my own would thrill
Back to life, and its fires out-fly?
    Heart, shall we live or die?
The rest, . . . settle by-and-by!'

XXII

So, she'd efface the score,
And forgive me as before.
150   It is twelve o'clock:
    I shall hear her knock
In the worst of a storm's uproar,
    I shall pull her through the door,
I shall have her for evermore!

Evelyn Hope

I

Beautiful Evelyn Hope is dead!
    Sit and watch by her side an hour.
That is her book-shelf, this her bed;
    She plucked that piece of geranium-flower,
Beginning to die too, in the glass;
    Little has yet been changed, I think:
The shutters are shut, no light may pass
    Save two long rays through the hinge's chink.

II

Sixteen years old when she died!
10   Perhaps she had scarcely heard my name;
It was not her time to love; beside,
    Her life had many a hope and aim,
Duties enough and little cares,
    And now was quiet, now astir,
Till God's hand beckoned unawares, –
    And the sweet white brow is all of her.

III

Is it too late then, Evelyn Hope?
    What, your soul was pure and true,
The good stars met in your horoscope,
20   Made you of spirit, fire and dew –
And, just because I was thrice as old
    And our paths in the world diverged so wide,
Each was naught to each, must I be told?
    We were fellow mortals, naught beside?

IV

No, indeed! for God above
    Is great to grant, as mighty to make,
And creates the love to reward the love:
    I claim you still, for my own love's sake!
Delayed it may be for more lives yet,
30   Through worlds I shall traverse, not a few:
Much is to learn, much to forget
    Ere the time be come for taking you.

V

But the time will come, – at last it will,
    When, Evelyn Hope, what meant (I shall say)
In the lower earth, in the years long still,
    That body and soul so pure and gay?
Why your hair was amber, I shall divine,
    And your mouth of your own geranium's red –
And what you would do with me, in fine,
40   In the new life come in the old one's stead.

VI

I have lived (I shall say) so much since then,
    Given up myself so many times,
Gained me the gains of various men,
    Ransacked the ages, spoiled the climes;
Yet one thing, one, in my soul's full scope,
    Either I missed or itself missed me:
And I want and find you, Evelyn Hope!
    What is the issue? let us see!

VII

I loved you, Evelyn, all the while.
50   My heart seemed full as it could hold?
There was place and to spare for the frank young smile,
    And the red young mouth, and the hair's young gold.
So, hush, – I will give you this leaf to keep:
    See, I shut it inside the sweet cold hand!
There, that is our secret: go to sleep!
    You will wake, and remember, and understand.

Up at a Villa – Down in the City

(As Distinguished by an Italian Person of Quality)

I

Had I but plenty of money, money enough and to spare,
The house for me, no doubt, were a house in the city-square;
Ah, such a life, such a life, as one leads at the window there!

II

Something to see, by Bacchus, something to hear, at least!
There, the whole day long, one's life is a perfect feast;
While up at a villa one lives, I maintain it, no more than a beast.

III

Well now, look at our villa! stuck like the horn of a bull
Just on a mountain-edge as bare as the creature's skull,
Save a mere shag of a bush with hardly a leaf to pull!
10   – I scratch my own, sometimes, to see if the hair's turned wool.

IV

But the city, oh the city – the square with the houses! Why?
They are stone-faced, white as a curd, there's something to take
        the eye!
Houses in four straight lines, not a single front awry;
You watch who crosses and gossips, who saunters, who hurries
        by;
Green blinds, as a matter of course, to draw when the sun gets
        high;
And the shops with fanciful signs which are painted properly.

V

What of a villa? Though winter be over in March by rights,
'Tis May perhaps ere the snow shall have withered well off the
    heights:
You've the brown ploughed land before, where the oxen steam
    and wheeze,
20 And the hills over-smoked behind by the faint grey olive-trees.

VI

Is it better in May, I ask you? You've summer all at once;
In a day he leaps complete with a few strong April suns.
'Mid the sharp short emerald wheat, scarce risen three fingers
    well,
The wild tulip, at end of its tube, blows out its great red bell
Like a thin clear bubble of blood, for the children to pick and sell.

VII

Is it ever hot in the square? There's a fountain to spout and
    splash!
In the shade it sings and springs; in the shine such foam-bows
    flash
On the horses with curling fish-tails, that prance and paddle and
    pash
Round the lady atop in her conch – fifty gazers do not abash,
30 Though all that she wears is some weeds round her waist in a
    sort of sash.

VIII

All the year long at the villa, nothing to see though you linger,
Except yon cypress that points like death's lean lifted forefinger.
Some think fireflies pretty, when they mix i' the corn and mingle,
Or thrid the stinking hemp till the stalks of it seem a-tingle.
Late August or early September, the stunning cicala is shrill,
And the bees keep their tiresome whine round the resinous firs on
    the hill.
Enough of the seasons, – I spare you the months of the fever and
    chill.

IX

Ere you open your eyes in the city, the blessed church-bells
    begin:
No sooner the bells leave off than the diligence rattles in:

40   You get the pick of the news, and it costs you never a pin.
    By-and-by there's the travelling doctor gives pills, lets blood,
        draws teeth;
    Or the Pulcinello-trumpet breaks up the market beneath.
    At the post-office such a scene-picture – the new play, piping hot!
    And a notice how, only this morning, three liberal thieves were
        shot.
    Above it, behold the Archbishop's most fatherly of rebukes,
    And beneath, with his crown and his lion, some little new law of
        the Duke's!
    Or a sonnet with flowery marge, to the Reverend Don So-and-so
    Who is Dante, Boccaccio, Petrarca, Saint Jerome and Cicero,
    'And moreover,' (the sonnet goes rhyming,) 'the skirts of Saint
        Paul has reached,
50   Having preached us those six Lent-lectures more unctuous than
        ever he preached.'
    Noon strikes, – here sweeps the procession! our Lady borne
        smiling and smart
    With a pink gauze gown all spangles, and seven swords stuck in
        her heart!
    Bang-whang-whang goes the drum, *tootle-te-tootle* the fife;
    No keeping one's haunches still: it's the greatest pleasure in life.

    x
    But bless you, it's dear – it's dear! fowls, wine, at double the rate.
    They have clapped a new tax upon salt, and what oil pays passing
        the gate
    It's a horror to think of. And so, the villa for me, not the city!
    Beggars can scarcely be choosers: but still – ah, the pity, the pity!
    Look, two and two go the priests, then the monks with cowls and
        sandals,
60   And the penitents dressed in white shirts, a-holding the yellow
        candles;
    One, he carries a flag up straight, and another a cross with
        handles,
    And the Duke's guard brings up the rear, for the better prevention
        of scandals:
    Bang-whang-whang goes the drum, *tootle-te-tootle* the fife.
    Oh, a day in the city-square, there is no such pleasure in life!

A Woman's Last Word

I
Let's contend no more, Love,
   Strive nor weep:
All be as before, Love,
   – Only sleep!

II
What so wild as words are?
   I and thou
In debate, as birds are,
   Hawk on bough!

III
See the creature stalking
10   While we speak!
Hush and hide the talking,
   Cheek on cheek!

IV
What so false as truth is,
   False to thee?
Where the serpent's tooth is
   Shun the tree –

V
Where the apple reddens
   Never pry –
Lest we lose our Edens,
20   Eve and I.

VI
Be a god and hold me
   With a charm!
Be a man and fold me
   With thine arm!

VII
Teach me, only teach, Love!
  As I ought
I will speak thy speech, Love,
  Think thy thought –

VIII
Meet, if thou require it,
30   Both demands,
Laying flesh and spirit
  In thy hands.

IX
That shall be tomorrow
  Not tonight:
I must bury sorrow
  Out of sight:

X
– Must a little weep, Love,
  (Foolish me!)
And so fall asleep, Love,
40   Loved by thee.

Fra Lippo Lippi

I am poor brother Lippo, by your leave!
You need not clap your torches to my face.
Zooks, what's to blame? you think you see a monk!
What, 'tis past midnight, and you go the rounds,
And here you catch me at an alley's end
Where sportive ladies leave their doors ajar?
The Carmine's my cloister: hunt it up,
Do, – harry out, if you must show your zeal,
Whatever rat, there, haps on his wrong hole,
10 And nip each softling of a wee white mouse,
Weke, weke, that's crept to keep him company!
Aha, you know your betters! Then, you'll take
Your hand away that's fiddling on my throat,
And please to know me likewise. Who am I?

Why, one, sir, who is lodging with a friend
Three streets off – he's a certain . . . how d'ye call?
Master – a . . . Cosimo of the Medici,
I' the house that caps the corner. Boh! you were best!
Remember and tell me, the day you're hanged,
20 How you affected such a gullet's-gripe!
But you, sir, it concerns you that your knaves
Pick up a manner nor discredit you:
Zooks, are we pilchards, that they sweep the streets
And count fair prize what comes into their net?
He's Judas to a tittle, that man is!
Just such a face! Why, sir, you make amends.
Lord, I'm not angry! Bid your hangdogs go
Drink out this quarter-florin to the health
Of the munificent House that harbours me
30 (And many more beside, lads! more beside!)
And all's come square again. I'd like his face –
His, elbowing on his comrade in the door
With the pike and lantern, – for the slave that holds
John Baptist's head a-dangle by the hair
With one hand ('Look you, now,' as who should say)
And his weapon in the other, yet unwiped!
It's not your chance to have a bit of chalk,
A wood-coal or the like? or you should see!
Yes, I'm the painter, since you style me so.
40 What, brother Lippo's doings, up and down,
You know them and they take you? like enough!
I saw the proper twinkle in your eye –
'Tell you, I liked your looks at very first.
Let's sit and set things straight now, hip to haunch.
Here's spring come, and the nights one makes up bands
To roam the town and sing out carnival,
And I've been three weeks shut within my mew,
A-painting for the great man, saints and saints
And saints again. I could not paint all night –
50 Ouf! I leaned out of window for fresh air.
There came a hurry of feet and little feet,
A sweep of lute-strings, laughs, and whiffs of song, –
Flower o' the broom,
Take away love, and our earth is a tomb!
Flower o' the quince,
I let Lisa go, and what good in life since?

Flower o' the thyme – and so on. Round they went.
Scarce had they turned the corner when a titter
Like the skipping of rabbits by moonlight, – three slim shapes,
60   And a face that looked up . . . zooks, sir, flesh and blood,
That's all I'm made of! Into shreds it went,
Curtain and counterpane and coverlet,
All the bed-furniture – a dozen knots,
There was a ladder! Down I let myself,
Hands and feet, scrambling somehow, and so dropped,
And after them. I came up with the fun
Hard by Saint Laurence, hail fellow, well met, –
Flower o' the rose,
If I've been merry, what matter who knows?
70   And so as I was stealing back again
To get to bed and have a bit of sleep
Ere I rise up tomorrow and go work
On Jerome knocking at his poor old breast
With his great round stone to subdue the flesh,
You snap me of the sudden. Ah, I see!
Though your eye twinkles still, you shake your head –
Mine's shaved – a monk, you say – the sting's in that!
If Master Cosimo announced himself,
Mum's the word naturally; but a monk!
80   Come, what am I a beast for? tell us, now!
I was a baby when my mother died
And father died and left me in the street.
I starved there, God knows how, a year or two
On fig-skins, melon-parings, rinds and shucks,
Refuse and rubbish. One fine frosty day,
My stomach being empty as your hat,
The wind doubled me up and down I went.
Old Aunt Lapaccia trussed me with one hand,
(Its fellow was a stinger as I knew)
90   And so along the wall, over the bridge,
By the straight cut to the convent. Six words there,
While I stood munching my first bread that month:
'So, boy, you're minded,' quoth the good fat father
Wiping his own mouth, 'twas refection-time, –
'To quit this very miserable world?
Will you renounce' . . . 'the mouthful of bread?' thought I;
By no means! Brief, they made a monk of me;
I did renounce the world, its pride and greed,

Palace, farm, villa, shop and banking-house,
100 Trash, such as these poor devils of Medici
Have given their hearts to – all at eight years old.
Well, sir, I found in time, you may be sure,
'Twas not for nothing – the good bellyful,
The warm serge and the rope that goes all round,
And day-long blessed idleness beside!
'Let's see what the urchin's fit for' – that came next.
Not overmuch their way, I must confess.
Such a to-do! They tried me with their books:
Lord, they'd have taught me Latin in pure waste!
110 *Flower o' the clove,*
All the Latin I construe is, 'amo' I love!
But, mind you, when a boy starves in the streets
Eight years together, as my fortune was,
Watching folk's faces to know who will fling
The bit of half-stripped grape-bunch he desires,
And who will curse or kick him for his pains, –
Which gentleman processional and fine,
Holding a candle to the Sacrament,
Will wink and let him lift a plate and catch
120 The droppings of the wax to sell again,
Or holla for the Eight and have him whipped, –
How say I? – nay, which dog bites, which lets drop
His bone from the heap of offal in the street, –
Why, soul and sense of him grow sharp alike,
He learns the look of things, and none the less
For admonition from the hunger-pinch.
I had a store of such remarks, be sure,
Which, after I found leisure, turned to use.
I drew men's faces on my copy-books,
130 Scrawled them within the antiphonary's marge,
Joined legs and arms to the long music-notes,
Found eyes and nose and chin for A's and B's,
And made a string of pictures of the world
Betwixt the ins and outs of verb and noun,
On the wall, the bench, the door. The monks looked black.
'Nay,' quoth the Prior, 'turn him out, d'ye say?
In no wise. Lose a crow and catch a lark.
What if at last we get our man of parts,
We Carmelites, like those Camaldolese
140 And Preaching Friars, to do our church up fine

And put the front on it that ought to be!'
And hereupon he bade me daub away.
Thank you! my head being crammed, the walls a blank,
Never was such prompt disemburdening.
First, every sort of monk, the black and white,
I drew them, fat and lean: then, folk at church,
From good old gossips waiting to confess
Their cribs of barrel-droppings, candle-ends, –
To the breathless fellow at the altar-foot,
150 Fresh from his murder, safe and sitting there
With the little children round him in a row
Of admiration, half for his beard and half
For that white anger of his victim's son
Shaking a fist at him with one fierce arm,
Signing himself with the other because of Christ
(Whose sad face on the cross sees only this
After the passion of a thousand years)
Till some poor girl, her apron o'er her head,
(Which the intense eyes looked through) came at eve
160 On tiptoe, said a word, dropped in a loaf,
Her pair of earrings and a bunch of flowers
(The brute took growling), prayed, and so was gone.
I painted all, then cried ''Tis ask and have;
Choose, for more's ready!' – laid the ladder flat,
And showed my covered bit of cloister-wall.
The monks closed in a circle and praised loud
Till checked, taught what to see and not to see,
Being simple bodies, – 'That's the very man!
Look at the boy who stoops to pat the dog!
170 That woman's like the Prior's niece who comes
To care about his asthma: it's the life!'
But there my triumph's straw-fire flared and funked;
Their betters took their turn to see and say:
The Prior and the learned pulled a face
And stopped all that in no time. 'How? what's here?
Quite from the mark of painting, bless us all!
Faces, arms, legs and bodies like the true
As much as pea and pea! it's devil's-game!
Your business is not to catch men with show,
180 With homage to the perishable clay,
But lift them over it, ignore it all,
Make them forget there's such a thing as flesh.

Your business is to paint the souls of men –
Man's soul, and it's a fire, smoke . . . no, it's not . . .
It's vapour done up like a new-born babe –
(In that shape when you die it leaves your mouth)
It's . . . well, what matters talking, it's the soul!
Give us no more of body than shows soul!
Here's Giotto, with his Saint a-praising God,
190 That sets us praising, – why not stop with him?
Why put all thoughts of praise out of our head
With wonder at lines, colours, and what not?
Paint the soul, never mind the legs and arms!
Rub all out, try at it a second time.
Oh, that white smallish female with the breasts,
She's just my niece . . . Herodias, I would say, –
Who went and danced and got men's heads cut off!
Have it all out!' Now, is this sense, I ask?
A fine way to paint soul, by painting body
200 So ill, the eye can't stop there, must go further
And can't fare worse! Thus, yellow does for white
When what you put for yellow's simply black,
And any sort of meaning looks intense
When all beside itself means and looks naught.
Why can't a painter lift each foot in turn,
Left foot and right foot, go a double step,
Make his flesh liker and his soul more like,
Both in their order? Take the prettiest face,
The Prior's niece . . . patron-saint – is it so pretty
210 You can't discover if it means hope, fear,
Sorrow or joy? won't beauty go with these?
Suppose I've made her eyes all right and blue,
Can't I take breath and try to add life's flash,
And then add soul and heighten them threefold?
Or say there's beauty with no soul at all –
(I never saw it – put the case the same –)
If you get simple beauty and naught else,
You get about the best thing God invents:
That's somewhat: and you'll find the soul you have missed,
220 Within yourself, when you return him thanks.
'Rub all out!' Well, well, there's my life, in short,
And so the thing has gone on ever since.
I'm grown a man no doubt, I've broken bounds:
You should not take a fellow eight years old

And make him swear to never kiss the girls.
I'm my own master, paint now as I please –
Having a friend, you see, in the Corner-house!
Lord, it's fast holding by the rings in front –
Those great rings serve more purposes than just
230 To plant a flag in, or tie up a horse!
And yet the old schooling sticks, the old grave eyes
Are peeping o'er my shoulder as I work,
The heads shake still – ' It's art's decline, my son!
You're not of the true painters, great and old;
Brother Angelico's the man, you'll find;
Brother Lorenzo stands his single peer:
Fag on at flesh, you'll never make the third!'
Flower o' the pine,
You keep your mistr . . . manners, and I'll stick to mine!
240 I'm not the third, then: bless us, they must know!
Don't you think they're the likeliest to know,
They with their Latin? So, I swallow my rage,
Clench my teeth, suck my lips in tight, and paint
To please them – sometimes do and sometimes don't;
For, doing most, there's pretty sure to come
A turn, some warm eve finds me at my saints –
A laugh, a cry, the business of the world –
(*Flower o' the peach,*
Death for us all, and his own life for each!)
250 And my whole soul revolves, the cup runs over,
The world and life's too big to pass for a dream,
And I do these wild things in sheer despite,
And play the fooleries you catch me at,
In pure rage! The old mill-horse, out at grass
After hard years, throws up his stiff heels so,
Although the miller does not preach to him
The only good of grass is to make chaff.
What would men have? Do they like grass or no –
May they or mayn't they? all I want's the thing
260 Settled for ever one way. As it is,
You tell too many lies and hurt yourself:
You don't like what you only like too much,
You do like what, if given you at your word,
You find abundantly detestable.
For me, I think I speak as I was taught;
I always see the garden and God there

A-making man's wife: and, my lesson learned,
The value and significance of flesh,
I can't unlearn ten minutes afterwards.

270   You understand me: I'm a beast, I know.
But see, now – why, I see as certainly
As that the morning-star's about to shine,
What will hap some day. We've a youngster here
Comes to our convent, studies what I do,
Slouches and stares and lets no atom drop:
His name is Guidi – he'll not mind the monks –
They call him Hulking Tom, he lets them talk –
He picks my practice up – he'll paint apace,
I hope so – though I never live so long,
280   I know what's sure to follow. You be judge!
You speak no Latin more than I, belike;
However, you're my man, you've seen the world
– The beauty and the wonder and the power,
The shapes of things, their colours, lights and shades,
Changes, surprises, – and God made it all!
– For what? Do you feel thankful, ay or no,
For this fair town's face, yonder river's line,
The mountain round it and the sky above,
Much more the figures of man, woman, child,
290   These are the frame to? What's it all about?
To be passed over, despised? or dwelt upon,
Wondered at? oh, this last of course! – you say.
But why not do as well as say, – paint these
Just as they are, careless what comes of it?
God's works – paint anyone, and count it crime
To let a truth slip. Don't object, 'His works
Are here already; nature is complete:
Suppose you reproduce her' – (which you can't)
'There's no advantage! you must beat her, then.'
300   For, don't you mark? we're made so that we love
First when we see them painted, things we have passed
Perhaps a hundred times nor cared to see;
And so they are better, painted – better to us,
Which is the same thing. Art was given for that;
God uses us to help each other so,
Lending our minds out. Have you noticed, now,
Your cullion's hanging face? A bit of chalk,

And trust me but you should, though! How much more,
If I drew higher things with the same truth!
310   That were to take the Prior's pulpit-place,
Interpret God to all of you! Oh, oh,
It makes me mad to see what men shall do
And we in our graves! This world's no blot for us,
Nor blank; it means intensely, and means good:
To find its meaning is my meat and drink.
'Ay, but you don't so instigate to prayer!'
Strikes in the Prior: 'when your meaning's plain
It does not say to folk – remember matins,
Or, mind you fast next Friday!' Why, for this
320   What need of art at all? A skull and bones,
Two bits of stick nailed crosswise, or, what's best,
A bell to chime the hour with, does as well.
I painted a Saint Laurence six months since
At Prato, splashed the fresco in fine style:
'How looks my painting, now the scaffold's down?'
I ask a brother: 'Hugely,' he returns –
'Already not one phiz of your three slaves
Who turn the Deacon off his toasted side,
But's scratched and prodded to our heart's content,
330   The pious people have so eased their own
With coming to say prayers there in a rage:
We get on fast to see the bricks beneath.
Expect another job this time next year,
For pity and religion grow i' the crowd –
Your painting serves its purpose!' Hang the fools!

– That is – you'll not mistake an idle word
Spoke in a huff by a poor monk, Got wot,
Tasting the air this spicy night which turns
The unaccustomed head like Chianti wine!
340   Oh, the church knows! don't misreport me, now!
It's natural a poor monk out of bounds
Should have his apt word to excuse himself:
And hearken how I plot to make amends.
I have bethought me: I shall paint a piece
... There's for you! Give me six months, then go, see
Something in Sant' Ambrogio's! Bless the nuns!
They want a cast o' my office. I shall paint

God in the midst, Madonna and her babe,
Ringed by a bowery flowery angel-brood,
350   Lilies and vestments and white faces, sweet
As puff on puff of grated orris-root
When ladies crowd to Church at midsummer.
And then i' the front, of course a saint or two –
Saint John, because he saves the Florentines,
Saint Ambrose, who puts down in black and white
The convent's friends and gives them a long day,
And Job, I must have him there past mistake,
The man of Uz (and Us without the z,
Painters who need his patience). Well, all these
360   Secured at their devotion, up shall come
Out of a corner when you least expect,
As one by a dark stair into a great light,
Music and talking, who but Lippo! I! –
Mazed, motionless and moonstruck – I'm the man!
Back I shrink – what is this I see and hear?
I, caught up with my monk's-things by mistake,
My old serge gown and rope that goes all round,
I, in this presence, this pure company!
Where's a hole, where's a corner for escape?
370   Then steps a sweet angelic slip of a thing
Forward, puts out a soft palm – 'Not so fast!'
– Addresses the celestial presence, 'nay –
He made you and devised you, after all,
Though he's none of you! Could Saint John there draw –
His camel-hair make up a painting-brush?
We come to brother Lippo for all that,
Iste perfecit opus!' So, all smile –
I shuffle sideways with my blushing face
Under the cover of a hundred wings
380   Thrown like a spread of kirtles when you're gay
And play hot cockles, all the doors being shut,
Till, wholly unexpected, in there pops
The hothead husband! Thus I scuttle off
To some safe bench behind, not letting go
The palm of her, the little lily thing
That spoke the good word for me in the nick,
Like the Prior's niece . . . Saint Lucy, I would say.
And so all's saved for me, and for the church

A pretty picture gained. Go, six months hence!
390 Your hand, sir, and good-bye: no lights, no lights!
The street's hushed, and I know my own way back,
Don't fear me! There's the grey beginning. Zooks!

A Toccata of Galuppi's

I

Oh Galuppi, Baldassaro, this is very sad to find!
I can hardly misconceive you; it would prove me deaf and blind;
But although I take your meaning, 'tis with such a heavy mind!

II

Here you come with your old music, and here's all the good it
     brings.
What, they lived once thus at Venice where the merchants were
     the kings,
Where Saint Mark's is, where the Doges used to wed the sea with
     rings?

III

Ay, because the sea's the street there; and 'tis arched by ... what
     you call
. . . Shylock's bridge with houses on it, where they kept the
     carnival:
I was never out of England – it's as if I saw it all.

IV

10 Did young people take their pleasure when the sea was warm in
     May?
Balls and masks begun at midnight, burning ever to midday,
When they made up fresh adventures for the morrow, do you say?

V

Was a lady such a lady, cheeks so round and lips so red, –
On her neck the small face buoyant, like a bell-flower on its bed,
O'er the breast's superb abundance where a man might base his
     head?

VI

Well, and it was graceful of them – they'd break talk off and afford
– She, to bite her mask's black velvet – he, to finger on his sword,
While you sat and played Toccatas, stately at the clavichord?

VII

What? Those lesser thirds so plaintive, sixths diminished, sigh
    on sigh,
20 Told them something? Those suspensions, those solutions –
    'Must we die?'
Those commiserating sevenths – 'Life might last! we can but
    try!'

VIII

'Were you happy?' – 'Yes.' – 'And are you still as happy?' –
    'Yes. And you?'
– 'Then, more kisses!' – 'Did *I* stop them, when a million
    seemed so few?'
Hark, the dominant's persistence till it must be answered to!

IX

So, an octave struck the answer. Oh, they praised you, I dare say!
'Brave Galuppi! that was music! good alike at grave and gay!
I can always leave off talking when I hear a master play!'

X

Then they left you for their pleasure: till in due time, one by one,
Some with lives that came to nothing, some with deeds as well
    undone,
30 Death stepped tacitly and took them where they never see the
    sun.

XI

But when I sit down to reason, think to take my stand nor swerve,
While I triumph o'er a secret wrung from nature's close reserve,
In you come with your cold music till I creep through every
    nerve.

XII

Yes, you, like a ghostly cricket, creaking where a house was
        burned:
'Dust and ashes, dead and done with, Venice spent what Venice
        earned.
The soul, doubtless, is immortal – where a soul can be discerned.

XIII

'Yours for instance: you know physics, something of geology,
Mathematics are your pastime; souls shall rise in their degree;
Butterflies may dread extinction, – you'll not die, it cannot be!

XIV

40 'As for Venice and her people, merely born to bloom and drop,
Here on earth they bore their fruitage, mirth and folly were the
        crop:
What of soul was left, I wonder, when the kissing had to stop?

XV

'Dust and ashes!' So you creak it, and I want the heart to scold.
Dear dead women, with such hair, too – what's become of all the
        gold
Used to hang and brush their bosoms? I feel chilly and grown
        old.

By the Fire-Side

I

How well I know what I mean to do
    When the long dark autumn-evenings come,
And where, my soul, is thy pleasant hue?
    With the music of all thy voices, dumb
In life's November too!

II

I shall be found by the fire, suppose,
    O'er a great wise book as beseemeth age,
While the shutters flap as the cross-wind blows
    And I turn the page, and I turn the page,
10 Not verse now, only prose!

III

Till the young ones whisper, finger on lip,
   'There he is at it, deep in Greek:
Now then, or never, out we slip
   To cut from the hazels by the creek
A mainmast for our ship!'

IV

I shall be at it indeed, my friends:
   Greek puts already on either side
Such a branch-work forth as soon extends
   To a vista opening far and wide,
20 And I pass out where it ends.

V

The outside-frame, like your hazel-trees:
   But the inside-archway widens fast,
And a rarer sort succeeds to these,
   And we slope to Italy at last
And youth, by green degrees.

VI

I follow wherever I am led,
   Knowing so well the leader's hand:
Oh woman-country, wooed not wed,
   Loved all the more by earth's male-lands,
30 Laid to their hearts instead!

VII

Look at the ruined chapel again
   Half-way up in the Alpine gorge!
Is that a tower, I point you plain,
   Or is it a mill, or an iron-forge
Breaks solitude in vain?

VIII

A turn, and we stand in the heart of things;
   The woods are round us, heaped and dim;
From slab to slab how it slips and springs,
   The thread of water single and slim,
40 Through the ravage some torrent brings!

IX

Does it feed the little lake below?
    That speck of white just on its marge
Is Pella; see, in the evening-glow,
    How sharp the silver spear-heads charge
When Alp meets heaven in snow!

X

On our other side is the straight-up rock;
    And a path is kept 'twixt the gorge and it
By boulder-stones where lichens mock
    The marks on a moth, and small ferns fit
50   Their teeth to the polished block.

XI

Oh the sense of the yellow mountain-flowers,
    And thorny balls, each three in one,
The chestnuts throw on our path in showers!
    For the drop of the woodland fruit's begun,
These early November hours,

XII

That crimson the creeper's leaf across
    Like a splash of blood, intense, abrupt,
O'er a shield else gold from rim to boss,
    And lay it for show on the fairy-cupped
60   Elf-needled mat of moss,

XIII

By the rose-flesh mushrooms, undivulged
    Last evening – nay, in today's first dew
Yon sudden coral nipple bulged,
    Where a freaked fawn-coloured flaky crew
Of toadstools peep indulged.

XIV

And yonder, at foot of the fronting ridge
    That takes the turn to a range beyond,
Is the chapel reached by the one-arched bridge
    Where the water is stopped in a stagnant pond
70   Danced over by the midge.

XV

The chapel and bridge are of stone alike,
　　Blackish-grey and mostly wet;
Cut hemp-stalks steep in the narrow dike.
　　See here again, how the lichens fret
And the roots of the ivy strike!

XVI

Poor little place, where its one priest comes
　　On a festa-day, if he comes at all,
To the dozen folk from their scattered homes,
　　Gathered within that precinct small
80　By the dozen ways one roams –

XVII

To drop from the charcoal-burners' huts,
　　Or climb from the hemp-dressers' low shed,
Leave the grange where the woodman stores his nuts,
　　Or the wattled cote where the fowlers spread
Their gear on the rock's bare juts.

XVIII

It has some pretension too, this front,
　　With its bit of fresco half-moon-wise
Set over the porch, Art's early wont:
　　'Tis John in the Desert, I surmise,
90　But has borne the weather's brunt –

XIX

Not from the fault of the builder, though,
　　For a pent-house properly projects
Where three carved beams make a certain show,
　　Dating – good thought of our architect's –
'Five, six, nine, he lets you know.

XX

And all day long a bird sings there,
　　And a stray sheep drinks at the pond at times;
The place is silent and aware;
　　It has had its scenes, its joys and crimes,
100　But that is its own affair.

XXI

My perfect wife, my Leonor,
　Oh heart, my own, oh eyes, mine too,
Whom else could I dare look backward for,
　With whom beside should I dare pursue
The path grey heads abhor?

XXII

For it leads to a crag's sheer edge with them;
　Youth, flowery all the way, there stops –
Not they; age threatens and they contemn,
　Till they reach the gulf wherein youth drops,
110 One inch from life's safe hem!

XXIII

With me, youth led ... I will speak now,
　No longer watch you as you sit
Reading by fire-light, that great brow
　And the spirit-small hand propping it,
Mutely, my heart knows how –

XXIV

When, if I think but deep enough,
　You are wont to answer, prompt as rhyme;
And you, too, find without rebuff
　Response your soul seeks many a time
120 Piercing its fine flesh-stuff.

XXV

My own, confirm me! If I tread
　This path back, is it not in pride
To think how little I dreamed it led
　To an age so blest that, by its side,
Youth seems the waste instead?

XXVI

My own, see where the years conduct!
　At first, 'twas something our two souls
Should mix as mists do; each is sucked
　In each now: on, the new stream rolls,
130 Whatever rocks obstruct.

XXVII

Think, when our one soul understands
   The great Word which makes all things new,
When earth breaks up and heaven expands,
   How will the change strike me and you
In the house not made with hands?

XXVIII

Oh I must feel your brain prompt mine,
   Your heart anticipate my heart,
You must be just before, in fine,
   See and make me see, for your part,
140 New depths of the divine!

XXIX

But who could have expected this
   When we two drew together first
Just for the obvious human bliss,
   To satisfy life's daily thirst
With a thing men seldom miss?

XXX

Come back with me to the first of all,
   Let us lean and love it over again,
Let us now forget and now recall,
   Break the rosary in a pearly rain,
150 And gather what we let fall!

XXXI

What did I say? – that a small bird sings
   All day long, save when a brown pair
Of hawks from the wood float with wide wings
   Strained to a bell: 'gainst noon-day glare
You count the streaks and rings.

XXXII

But at afternoon or almost eve
   'Tis better; then the silence grows
To that degree, you half believe
   It must get rid of what it knows,
160 Its bosom does so heave.

XXXIII

Hither we walked then, side by side,
    Arm in arm and cheek to cheek,
And still I questioned or replied,
    While my heart, convulsed to really speak,
Lay choking in its pride.

XXXIV

Silent the crumbling bridge we cross,
    And pity and praise the chapel sweet,
And care about the fresco's loss,
    And wish for our souls a like retreat,
170 And wonder at the moss.

XXXV

Stoop and kneel on the settle under,
    Look through the window's grated square:
Nothing to see! For fear of plunder,
    The cross is down and the altar bare,
As if thieves don't fear thunder.

XXXVI

We stoop and look in through the grate,
    See the little porch and rustic door,
Read duly the dead builder's date;
    Then cross the bridge that we crossed before,
180 Take the path again – but wait!

XXXVII

Oh moment, one and infinite!
    The water slips o'er stock and stone;
The West is tender, hardly bright:
    How grey at once is the evening grown –
One star, its chrysolite!

XXXVIII

We two stood there with never a third,
    But each by each, as each knew well:
The sights we saw and the sounds we heard,
    The lights and the shades made up a spell
190 Till the trouble grew and stirred.

XXXIX

Oh, the little more, and how much it is!
    And the little less, and what worlds away!
How a sound shall quicken content to bliss,
    Or a breath suspend the blood's best play,
And life be a proof of this!

XL

Had she willed it, still had stood the screen
    So slight, so sure, 'twixt my love and her:
I could fix her face with a guard between,
    And find her soul as when friends confer,
200 Friends – lovers that might have been.

XLI

For my heart had a touch of the woodland-time,
    Wanting to sleep now over its best.
Shake the whole tree in the summer-prime,
    But bring to the last leaf no such test!
'Hold the last fast!' runs the rhyme.

XLII

For a chance to make your little much,
    To gain a lover and lose a friend,
Venture the tree and a myriad such,
    When nothing you mar but the year can mend:
210 But a last leaf – fear to touch!

XLIII

Yet should it unfasten itself and fall
    Eddying down till it find your face
At some slight wind – best chance of all!
    Be your heart henceforth its dwelling-place
You trembled to forestall!

XLIV

Worth how well, those dark grey eyes,
    That hair so dark and dear, how worth
That a man should strive and agonize,
    And taste a veriest hell on earth
220 For the hope of such a prize!

XLV

You might have turned and tried a man,
   Set him a space to weary and wear,
And prove which suited more your plan,
   His best of hope or his worst despair,
Yet end as he began.

XLVI

But you spared me this, like the heart you are,
   And filled my empty heart at a word.
If two lives join, there is oft a scar,
   They are one and one, with a shadowy third;
230 One near one is too far.

XLVII

A moment after, and hands unseen
   Were hanging the night around us fast;
But we knew that a bar was broken between
   Life and life: we were mixed at last
In spite of the mortal screen.

XLVIII

The forests had done it; there they stood;
   We caught for a moment the powers at play:
They had mingled us so, for once and good,
   Their work was done – we might go or stay,
240 They relapsed to their ancient mood.

XLIX

How the world is made for each of us!
   How all we perceive and know in it
Tends to some moment's product thus,
   When a soul declares itself – to wit,
By its fruit, the thing it does!

L

Be hate that fruit or love that fruit,
   It forwards the general deed of man,
And each of the Many helps to recruit
   The life of the race by a general plan;
250 Each living his own, to boot.

LI

I am named and known by that moment's feat;
    There took my station and degree;
So grew my own small life complete,
    As nature obtained her best of me –
One born to love you, sweet!

LII

And to watch you sink by the fire-side now
    Back again, as you mutely sit
Musing by fire-light, that great brow
    And the spirit-small hand propping it,
260 Yonder, my heart knows how!

LIII

So, earth has gained by one man the more,
    And the gain of earth must be heaven's gain too;
And the whole is well worth thinking o'er
    When autumn comes: which I mean to do
One day, as I said before.

Any Wife to Any Husband

I

My love, this is the bitterest, that thou –
Who art all truth, and who dost love me now
    As thine eyes say, as thy voice breaks to say –
Shouldst love so truly, and couldst love me still
A whole long life through, had but love its will,
    Would death that leads me from thee brook delay.

II

I have but to be by thee, and thy hand
Will never let mine go, nor heart withstand
    The beating of my heart to reach its place.
10 When shall I look for thee and feel thee gone?
When cry for the old comfort and find none?
    Never, I know! Thy soul is in thy face.

III

Oh, I should fade – 'tis willed so! Might I save,
Gladly I would, whatever beauty gave
   Joy to thy sense, for that was precious too.
It is not to be granted. But the soul
Whence the love comes, all ravage leaves that whole;
   Vainly the flesh fades; soul makes all things new.

IV

It would not be because my eye grew dim
20 Thou couldst not find the love there, thanks to Him
   Who never is dishonoured in the spark
He gave us from his fire of fires, and bade
Remember whence it sprang, nor be afraid
   While that burns on, though all the rest grow dark.

V

So, how thou wouldst be perfect, white and clean
Outside as inside, soul and soul's demesne
   Alike, this body given to show it by!
Oh, three-parts through the worst of life's abyss,
What plaudits from the next world after this,
30   Couldst thou repeat a stroke and gain the sky!

VI

And is it not the bitterer to think
That, disengage our hands and thou wilt sink
   Although thy love was love in very deed?
I know that nature! Pass a festive day,
Thou dost not throw its relic-flower away
   Nor bid its music's loitering echo speed.

VII

Thou let'st the stranger's glove lie where it fell;
If old things remain old things all is well,
   For thou art grateful as becomes man best:
40 And hadst thou only heard me play one tune,
Or viewed me from a window, not so soon
   With thee would such things fade as with the rest.

VIII

I seem to see! We meet and part; 'tis brief;
The book I opened keeps a folded leaf,
    The very chair I sat on, breaks the rank;
That is a portrait of me on the wall –
Three lines, my face comes at so slight a call:
    And for all this, one little hour to thank!

IX

But now, because the hour through years was fixed,
50 Because our inmost beings met and mixed,
    Because thou once hast loved me – wilt thou dare
Say to thy soul and Who may list beside,
'Therefore she is immortally my bride;
    Chance cannot change my love, nor time impair.

X

'So, what if in the dusk of life that's left,
I, a tired traveller of my sun bereft,
    Look from my path when, mimicking the same,
The fire-fly glimpses past me, come and gone?
– Where was it till the sunset? where anon
60 It will be at the sunrise! What's to blame?'

XI

Is it so helpful to thee? Canst thou take
The mimic up, nor, for the true thing's sake,
    Put gently by such efforts at a beam?
Is the remainder of the way so long,
Thou need'st the little solace, thou the strong?
    Watch out thy watch, let weak ones doze and dream!

XII

– Ah, but the fresher faces! 'Is it true,'
Thou'lt ask, 'some eyes are beautiful and new?
    Some hair, – how can one choose but grasp such wealth?
70 And if a man would press his lips to lips
Fresh as the wilding hedge-rose-cup there slips
    The dew-drop out of, must it be by stealth?

XIII

'It cannot change the love still kept for Her,
More than if such a picture I prefer
    Passing a day with, to a room's bare side:
The painted form takes nothing she possessed,
Yet, while the Titian's Venus lies at rest,
    A man looks. Once more, what is there to chide?'

XIV

So must I see, from where I sit and watch,
80 My own self sell myself, my hand attach
    Its warrant to the very thefts from me –
Thy singleness of soul that made me proud.
Thy purity of heart I loved aloud,
    Thy man's-truth I was bold to bid God see!

XV

Love so, then, if thou wilt! Give all thou canst
Away to the new faces – disentranced,
    (Say it and think it) obdurate no more:
Re-issue looks and words from the old mint,
Pass them afresh, no matter whose the print
90   Image and superscription once they bore!

XVI

Re-coin thyself and give it them to spend, –
It all comes to the same thing at the end,
    Since mine thou wast, mine art and mine shalt be,
Faithful or faithless, sealing up the sum
Or lavish of my treasure, thou must come
    Back to the heart's place here I keep for thee!

XVII

Only, why should it be with stain at all?
Why must I, 'twixt the leaves of coronal,
    Put any kiss of pardon on thy brow?
100 Why need the other women know so much,
And talk together, 'Such the look and such
    The smile he used to love with, then as now!'

XVIII

Might I die last and show thee! Should I find
Such hardship in the few years left behind,
   If free to take and light my lamp, and go
Into thy tomb, and shut the door and sit,
Seeing thy face on those four sides of it
   The better that they are so blank, I know!

XIX

Why, time was what I wanted, to turn o'er
110 Within my mind each look, get more and more
   By heart each word, too much to learn at first;
And join thee all the fitter for the pause
'Neath the low doorway's lintel. That were cause
   For lingering, though thou called'st, if I durst!

XX

And yet thou art the nobler of us two:
What dare I dream of, that thou canst not do,
   Outstripping my ten small steps with one stride?
I'll say then, here's a trial and a task –
Is it to bear? – if easy, I'll not ask:
120   Though love fail, I can trust on in thy pride.

XXI

Pride? – when those eyes forestall the life behind
The death I have to go through! – when I find,
   Now that I want thy help most, all of thee!
What did I fear? Thy love shall hold me fast
Until the little minute's sleep is past
   And I wake saved. – And yet it will not be!

*An Epistle Containing the Strange Medical Experience of
Karshish, the Arab Physician*

   Karshish, the picker-up of learning's crumbs,
   The not-incurious in God's handiwork
   (This man's-flesh he hath admirably made,
   Blown like a bubble, kneaded like a paste,
   To coop up and keep down on earth a space
   That puff of vapour from his mouth, man's soul)

– To Abib, all-sagacious in our art,
Breeder in me of what poor skill I boast,
Like me inquisitive how pricks and cracks
10   Befall the flesh through too much stress and strain,
Whereby the wily vapour fain would slip
Back and rejoin its source before the term, –
And aptest in contrivance (under God)
To baffle it by deftly stopping such: –
The vagrant Scholar to his Sage at home
Sends greeting (health and knowledge, fame with peace)
Three samples of true snakestone – rarer still,
One of the other sort, the melon-shaped,
(But fitter, pounded fine, for charms than drugs)
20   And writeth now the twenty-second time.

My journeyings were brought to Jericho:
Thus I resume. Who studious in our art
Shall count a little labour unrepaid?
I have shed sweat enough, left flesh and bone
On many a flinty furlong of this land.
Also, the country-side is all on fire
With rumours of a marching hitherward:
Some say Vespasian cometh, some, his son.
A black lynx snarled and pricked a tufted ear;
30   Lust of my blood inflamed his yellow balls:
I cried and threw my staff and he was gone.
Twice have the robbers stripped and beaten me,
And once a town declared me for a spy;
But at the end, I reach Jerusalem,
Since this poor covert where I pass the night,
This Bethany, lies scarce the distance thence
A man with plague-sores at the third degree
Runs till he drops down dead. Thou laughest here!
'Sooth, it elates me, thus reposed and safe,
40   To void the stuffing of my travel-scrip
And share with thee whatever Jewry yields.
A viscid choler is observable
In tertians, I was nearly bold to say;
And falling-sickness hath a happier cure
Than our school wots of: there's a spider here
Weaves no web, watches on the ledge of tombs,
Sprinkled with mottles on an ash-grey back;

Take five and drop them . . . but who knows his mind,
The Syrian runagate I trust this to?
50 His service payeth me a sublimate
Blown up his nose to help the ailing eye.
Best wait: I reach Jerusalem at morn,
There set in order my experiences,
Gather what most deserves, and give thee all –
Or I might add, Judea's gum-tragacanth
Scales off in purer flakes, shines clearer-grained,
Cracks 'twixt the pestle and the porphyry,
In fine exceeds our produce. Scalp-disease
Confounds me, crossing so with leprosy –
60 Thou hadst admired one sort I gained at Zoar –
But zeal outruns discretion. Here I end.

Yet stay: my Syrian blinketh gratefully,
Protesteth his devotion is my price –
Suppose I write what harms not, though he steal?
I half resolve to tell thee, yet I blush,
What set me off a-writing first of all.
An itch I had, a sting to write, a tang!
For, be it this town's barrenness – or else
The Man had something in the look of him –
70 His case has struck me far more than 'tis worth.
So, pardon if – (lest presently I lose
In the great press of novelty at hand
The care and pains this somehow stole from me)
I bid thee take the thing while fresh in mind,
Almost in sight – for, wilt thou have the truth?
The very man is gone from me but now,
Whose ailment is the subject of discourse.
Thus then, and let thy better wit help all!

'Tis but a case of mania – subinduced
80 By epilepsy, at the turning-point
Of trance prolonged unduly some three days:
When, by the exhibition of some drug
Or spell, exorcization, stroke of art
Unknown to me and which 'twere well to know,
The evil thing out-breaking all at once
Left the man whole and sound of body indeed, –
But, flinging (so to speak) life's gates too wide,

Making a clear house of it too suddenly,
The first conceit that entered might inscribe
90   Whatever it was minded on the wall
So plainly at that vantage, as it were,
(First come, first served) that nothing subsequent
Attaineth to erase those fancy-scrawls
The just-returned and new-established soul
Hath gotten now so thoroughly by heart
That henceforth she will read or these or none.
And first – the man's own firm conviction rests
That he was dead (in fact they buried him)
– That he was dead and then restored to life
100   By a Nazarene physician of his tribe:
– 'Sayeth, the same bade 'Rise,' and he did rise.
'Such cases are diurnal,' thou wilt cry.
Not so this figment! – not, that such a fume,
Instead of giving way to time and health,
Should eat itself into the life of life,
As saffron tingeth flesh, blood, bones and all!
For see, how he takes up the after-life.
The man – it is one Lazarus a Jew,
Sanguine, proportioned, fifty years of age,
110   The body's habit wholly laudable,
As much, indeed, beyond the common health
As he were made and put aside to show.
Think, could we penetrate by any drug
And bathe the wearied soul and worried flesh,
And bring it clear and fair, by three days' sleep!
Whence has the man the balm that brightens all?
This grown man eyes the world now like a child.
Some elders of his tribe, I should premise,
Led in their friend, obedient as a sheep,
120   To bear my inquisition. While they spoke,
Now sharply, now with sorrow, – told the case, –
He listened not except I spoke to him,
But folded his two hands and let them talk,
Watching the flies that buzzed: and yet no fool.
And that's a sample how his years must go.
Look, if a beggar, in fixed middle-life,
Should find a treasure, – can he use the same
With straitened habits and with tastes starved small,
And take at once to his impoverished brain

130 The sudden element that changes things,
That sets the undreamed-of rapture at his hand
And puts the cheap old joy in the scorned dust?
Is he not such an one as moves to mirth –
Warily parsimonious, when no need,
Wasteful as drunkenness at undue times?
All prudent counsel as to what befits
The golden mean, is lost on such an one:
The man's fantastic will is the man's law.
So here – we call the treasure knowledge, say,
140 Increased beyond the fleshly faculty –
Heaven opened to a soul while yet on earth,
Earth forced on a soul's use while seeing heaven:
The man is witless of the size, the sum,
The value in proportion of all things,
Or whether it be little or be much.
Discourse to him of prodigious armaments
Assembled to besiege his city now,
And of the passing of a mule with gourds –
'Tis one! Then take it on the other side,
150 Speak of some trifling fact, – he will gaze rapt
With stupor at its very littleness,
(Far as I see) as if in that indeed
He caught prodigious import, whole results;
And so will turn to us the bystanders
In ever the same stupor (note this point)
That we too see not with his opened eyes.
Wonder and doubt come wrongly into play,
Preposterously, at cross-purposes.
Should his child sicken unto death, – why, look
160 For scarce abatement of his cheerfulness,
Or pretermission of the daily craft!
While a word, gesture, glance from that same child
At play or in the school or laid asleep,
Will startle him to an agony of fear,
Exasperation, just as like. Demand
The reason why – ''tis but a word,' object –
'A gesture' – he regards thee as our lord
Who lived there in the pyramid alone,
Looked at us (dost thou mind?) when, being young,
170 We both would unadvisedly recite
Some charm's beginning, from that book of his,

Able to bid the sun throb wide and burst
All into stars, as suns grown old are wont.
Thou and the child have each a veil alike
Thrown o'er your heads, from under which ye both
Stretch your blind hands and trifle with a match
Over a mine of Greek fire, did ye know!
He holds on firmly to some thread of life –
(It is the life to lead perforcedly)
180 Which runs across some vast distracting orb
Of glory on either side that meagre thread,
Which, conscious of, he must not enter yet –
The spiritual life around the earthly life:
The law of that is known to him as this,
His heart and brain move there, his feet stay here.
So is the man perplext with impulses
Sudden to start off crosswise, not straight on,
Proclaiming what is right and wrong across,
And not along, this black thread through the blaze –
190 'It should be' balked by 'here it cannot be.'
And oft the man's soul springs into his face
As if he saw again and heard again
His sage that bade him 'Rise' and he did rise.
Something, a word, a tick o' the blood within
Admonishes: then back he sinks at once
To ashes, who was very fire before,
In sedulous recurrence to his trade
Whereby he earneth him the daily bread;
And studiously the humbler for that pride,
200 Professedly the faultier that he knows
God's secret, while he holds the thread of life.
Indeed the especial marking of the man
Is prone submission to the heavenly will –
Seeing it, what it is, and why it is.
'Sayeth, he will wait patient to the last
For that same death which must restore his being
To equilibrium, body loosening soul
Divorced even now by premature full growth:
He will live, nay, it pleaseth him to live
210 So long as God please, and just how God please.
He even seeketh not to please God more
(Which meaneth, otherwise) than as God please.
Hence, I perceive not he affects to preach

The doctrine of his sect whate'er it be,
Make proselytes as madmen thirst to do:
How can he give his neighbour the real ground,
His own conviction? Ardent as he is –
Call his great truth a lie, why, still the old
'Be it as God please' reassureth him.
220 I probed the sore as thy disciple should:
'How, beast,' said I, 'this stolid carelessness
Sufficeth thee, when Rome is on her march
To stamp out like a little spark thy town,
Thy tribe, thy crazy tale and thee at once?'
He merely looked with his large eyes on me.
The man is apathetic, you deduce?
Contrariwise, he loves both old and young,
Able and weak, affects the very brutes
And birds – how say I? flowers of the field –
230 As a wise workman recognizes tools
In a master's workshop, loving what they make.
Thus is the man, as harmless as a lamb:
Only impatient, let him do his best,
At ignorance and carelessness and sin –
An indignation which is promptly curbed:
As when in certain travels I have feigned
To be an ignoramus in our art
According to some preconceived design,
And happed to hear the land's practitioners
240 Steeped in conceit sublimed by ignorance,
Prattle fantastically on disease,
Its cause and cure – and I must hold my peace!

Thou wilt object – Why have I not ere this
Sought out the sage himself, the Nazarene
Who wrought this cure, inquiring at the source,
Conferring with the frankness that befits?
Alas! it grieveth me, the learned leech
Perished in a tumult many years ago,
Accused, – our learning's fate, – of wizardry,
250 Rebellion, to the setting up a rule
And creed prodigious as described to me.
His death, which happened when the earthquake fell
(Prefiguring, as soon appeared, the loss
To occult learning in our lord the sage

Who lived there in the pyramid alone)
Was wrought by the mad people – that's their wont!
On vain recourse, as I conjecture it,
To his tried virtue, for miraculous help –
How could he stop the earthquake? That's their way!
260   The other imputations must be lies:
But take one, though I loathe to give it thee,
In mere respect for any good man's fame.
(And after all, our patient Lazarus
Is stark mad; should we count on what he says?
Perhaps not: though in writing to a leech
'Tis well to keep back nothing of a case.)
This man so cured regards the curer, then,
As – God forgive me! who but God himself,
Creator and sustainer of the world,
270   That came and dwelt in flesh on it awhile!
– 'Sayeth that such an one was born and lived,
Taught, healed the sick, broke bread at his own house,
Then died, with Lazarus by, for aught I know,
And yet was . . . what I said nor choose repeat,
And must have so avouched himself, in fact,
In hearing of this very Lazarus
Who saith – but why all this of what he saith?
Why write of trivial matters, things of price
Calling at every moment for remark?
280   I noticed on the margin of a pool
Blue-flowering borage, the Aleppo sort,
Aboundeth, very nitrous. It is strange!

Thy pardon for this long and tedious case,
Which, now that I review it, needs must seem
Unduly dwelt on, prolixly set forth!
Nor I myself discern in what is writ
Good cause for the peculiar interest
And awe indeed this man has touched me with.
Perhaps the journey's end, the weariness
290   Had wrought upon me first. I met him thus:
I crossed a ridge of short sharp broken hills
Like an old lion's cheek teeth. Out there came
A moon made like a face with certain spots
Multiform, manifold and menacing:
Then a wind rose behind me. So we met

In this old sleepy town at unaware,
The man and I. I send thee what is writ.
Regard it as a chance, a matter risked
To this ambiguous Syrian – he may lose,
300 Or steal, or give it thee with equal good.
Jerusalem's repose shall make amends
For time this letter wastes, thy time and mine;
Till when, once more thy pardon and farewell!

The very God! think, Abib; dost thou think?
So, the All-Great, were the All-Loving too –
So, through the thunder comes a human voice
Saying, 'O heart I made, a heart beats here!
Face, my hands fashioned, see it in myself!
Thou hast no power nor mayst conceive of mine,
310 But love I gave thee, with myself to love,
And thou must love me who have died for thee!'
The madman saith He said so: it is strange.

Mesmerism

I
All I believed is true!
  I am able yet
  All I want, to get
By a method as strange as new:
Dare I trust the same to you?

II
If at night, when doors are shut,
  And the wood-worm picks,
  And the death-watch ticks,
And the bar has a flag of smut,
10 And a cat's in the water-butt –

III
And the socket floats and flares,
  And the house-beams groan,
  And a foot unknown
Is surmised on the garret-stairs,
And the locks slip unawares –

IV

And the spider, to serve his ends,
   By a sudden thread,
   Arms and legs outspread,
On the table's midst descends,
20 Comes to find, God knows what friends! –

V

If since eve drew in, I say,
   I have sat and brought
   (So to speak) my thought
To bear on the woman away,
Till I felt my hair turn grey –

VI

Till I seemed to have and hold,
   In the vacancy
   'Twixt the wall and me,
From the hair-plait's chestnut gold
30 To the foot in its muslin fold –

VII

Have and hold, then and there,
   Her, from head to foot,
   Breathing and mute,
Passive and yet aware,
In the grasp of my steady stare –

VIII

Hold and have, there and then,
   All her body and soul
   That completes my whole,
All that women add to men,
40 In the clutch of my steady ken –

IX

Having and holding, till
   I imprint her fast
   On the void at last
As the sun does whom he will
By the calotypist's skill –

X

Then, – if my heart's strength serve,
   And through all and each
   Of the veils I reach
To her soul and never swerve,
50 Knitting an iron nerve –

XI

Command her soul to advance
   And inform the shape
   Which has made escape
And before my countenance
Answers me glance for glance –

XII

I, still with a gesture fit
   Of my hands that best
   Do my soul's behest,
Pointing the power from it,
60 While myself do steadfast sit –

XIII

Steadfast and still the same
   On my object bent,
   While the hands give vent
To my ardour and my aim
And break into very flame –

XIV

Then I reach, I must believe,
   Not her soul in vain,
   For to me again
It reaches, and past retrieve
70 Is wound in the toils I weave;

XV

And must follow as I require,
   As befits a thrall,
   Bringing flesh and all,
Essence and earth-attire,
To the source of the tractile fire:

XVI

Till the house called hers, not mine,
  With a growing weight
  Seems to suffocate
If she break not its leaden line
80 And escape from its close confine.

XVII

Out of doors into the night!
  On to the maze
  Of the wild wood-ways,
Not turning to left nor right
From the pathway, blind with sight –

XVIII

Making through rain and wind
  O'er the broken shrubs,
  'Twixt the stems and stubs,
With a still, composed, strong mind,
90 Nor a care for the world behind –

XIX

Swifter and still more swift,
  As the crowding peace
  Doth to joy increase
In the wide blind eyes uplift
Through the darkness and the drift!

XX

While I – to the shape, I too
  Feel my soul dilate
  Nor a whit abate,
And relax not a gesture due,
100 As I see my belief come true.

XXI

For, there! have I drawn or no
  Life to that lip?
  Do my fingers dip
In a flame which again they throw
On the cheek that breaks a-glow?

XXII

Ha! was the hair so first?
  What, unfilleted,
  Made alive, and spread
Through the void with a rich outburst,
110 Chestnut gold-interspersed?

XXIII

Like the doors of a casket-shrine,
  See, on either side,
  Her two arms divide
Till the heart betwixt makes sign,
Take me, for I am thine!

XXIV

'Now – now' – the door is heard!
  Hark, the stairs! and near –
  Nearer – and here –
'Now!' and at call the third
120 She enters without a word.

XXV

On doth she march and on
  To the fancied shape;
  It is, past escape,
Herself, now: the dream is done
And the shadow and she are one.

XXVI

First I will pray. Do Thou
  That ownest the soul,
  Yet wilt grant control
To another, nor disallow
130 For a time, restrain me now!

XXVII

I admonish me while I may,
  Not to squander guilt,
  Since require Thou wilt
At my hand its price one day!
What the price is, who can say?

A Serenade at the Villa

I
That was I, you heard last night,
   When there rose no moon at all,
Nor, to pierce the strained and tight
   Tent of heaven, a planet small:
Life was dead and so was light.

II
Not a twinkle from the fly,
   Not a glimmer from the worm;
When the crickets stopped their cry,
   When the owls forbore a term,
10 You heard music; that was I.

III
Earth turned in her sleep with pain,
   Sultrily suspired for proof:
In at heaven and out again,
   Lightning! – where it broke the roof,
Bloodlike, some few drops of rain.

IV
What they could my words expressed,
   O my love, my all, my one!
Singing helped the verses best,
   And when singing's best was done,
20 To my lute I left the rest.

V
So wore night; the East was grey,
   White the broad-faced hemlock-flowers:
There would be another day;
   Ere its first of heavy hours
Found me, I had passed away.

VI

What became of all the hopes,
  Words and song and lute as well?
Say, this struck you – 'When life gropes
  Feebly for the path where fell
30 Light last on the evening slopes,

VII

'One friend in that path shall be,
  To secure my step from wrong;
One to count night day for me,
  Patient through the watches long,
Serving most with none to see.'

VIII

Never say – as something bodes –
  'So, the worst has yet a worse!
When life halts 'neath double loads,
  Better the taskmaster's curse
40 Than such music on the roads!

IX

'When no moon succeeds the sun,
  Nor can pierce the midnight's tent
Any star, the smallest one,
  While some drops, where lightning rent,
Show the final storm begun –

X

'When the fire-fly hides its spot,
  When the garden-voices fail
In the darkness thick and hot, –
  Shall another voice avail,
50 That shape be where these are not?

XI

'Has some plague a longer lease,
  Proffering its help uncouth?
Can't one even die in peace?
  As one shuts one's eyes on youth,
Is that face the last one sees?'

XII

Oh how dark your villa was,
    Windows fast and obdurate!
How the garden grudged me grass
    Where I stood – the iron gate
60 Ground its teeth to let me pass!

My Star

All that I know
    Of a certain star
Is, it can throw
    (Like the angled spar)
Now a dart of red,
    Now a dart of blue;
Till my friends have said
    They would fain see, too,
My star that dartles the red and the blue!
10 Then it stops like a bird; like a flower, hangs furled:
    They must solace themselves with the Saturn above it.
What matter to me if their star is a world?
    Mine has opened its soul to me; therefore I love it.

Instans Tyrannus

I

Of the million or two, more or less,
I rule and possess,
One man, for some cause undefined,
Was least to my mind.

II

I struck him, he grovelled of course –
For, what was his force?
I pinned him to earth with my weight
And persistence of hate:
And he lay, would not moan, would not curse,
10 As his lot might be worse.

III

'Were the object less mean, would he stand
At the swing of my hand!
For obscurity helps him and blots
The hole where he squats.'
So, I set my five wits on the stretch
To inveigle the wretch.
All in vain! Gold and jewels I threw,
Still he couched there perdue;
I tempted his blood and his flesh,
20 Hid in roses my mesh,
Choicest cates and the flagon's best spilth:
Still he kept to his filth.

IV

Had he kith now or kin, were access
To his heart, did I press:
Just a son or a mother to seize!
No such booty as these.
Were it simply a friend to pursue
'Mid my million or two,
Who could pay me in person or pelf
30 What he owes me himself!
No: I could not but smile through my chafe:
For the fellow lay safe
As his mates do, the midge and the nit,
– Through minuteness, to wit.

V

Then a humour more great took its place
At the thought of his face,
The droop, the low cares of the mouth,
The trouble uncouth
'Twixt the brows, all that air one is fain
40 To put out of its pain.
And, 'no!' I admonished myself,
'Is one mocked by an elf,
Is one baffled by toad or by rat?
The gravamen's in that!
How the lion, who crouches to suit
His back to my foot,
Would admire that I stand in debate!

But the small turns the great
If it vexes you, – that is the thing!
50   Toad or rat vex the king?
Though I waste half my realm to unearth
Toad or rat, 'tis well worth!'

VI
So, I soberly laid my last plan
To extinguish the man.
Round his creep-hole, with never a break
Ran my fires for his sake;
Over-head, did my thunder combine
With my underground mine:
Till I looked from my labour content
60   To enjoy the event.

VII
When sudden . . . how think ye, the end?
Did I say 'without friend'?
Say rather, from marge to blue marge
The whole sky grew his targe
With the sun's self for visible boss,
While an Arm ran across
Which the earth heaved beneath like a breast
Where the wretch was safe prest!
Do you see? Just my vengeance complete,
70   The man sprang to his feet,
Stood erect, caught at God's skirts, and prayed!
– So, *I* was afraid!

A Pretty Woman

I
That fawn-skin-dappled hair of hers,
    And the blue eye
    Dear and dewy,
And that infantine fresh air of hers!

II

To think men cannot take you, Sweet,
  And enfold you,
  Ay, and hold you,
And so keep you what they make you, Sweet!

III

You like us for a glance, you know –
10   For a word's sake
  Or a sword's sake,
All's the same, whate'er the chance, you know.

IV

And in turn we make you ours, we say –
  You and youth too,
  Eyes and mouth too,
All the face composed of flowers, we say.

V

All's our own, to make the most of, Sweet –
  Sing and say for,
  Watch and pray for,
20 Keep a secret or go boast of, Sweet!

VI

But for loving, why, you would not, Sweet,
  Though we prayed you,
  Paid you, brayed you
In a mortar – for you could not, Sweet!

VII

So, we leave the sweet face fondly there:
  Be its beauty
  Its sole duty!
Let all hope of grace beyond, lie there!

VIII

And while the face lies quiet there,
30   Who shall wonder
  That I ponder
A conclusion? I will try it there.

IX

As, – why must one, for the love foregone,
    Scout mere liking?
    Thunder-striking
Earth, – the heaven, we looked above for, gone!

X

Why, with beauty, needs there money be,
    Love with liking?
    Crush the fly-king
40 In his gauze, because no honey-bee?

XI

May not liking be so simple-sweet,
    If love grew there
    'Twould undo there
All that breaks the cheek to dimples sweet?

XII

Is the creature too imperfect, say?
    Would you mend it
    And so end it?
Since not all addition perfects aye!

XIII

Or is it of its kind, perhaps,
50   Just perfection –
    Whence, rejection
Of a grace not to its mind, perhaps?

XIV

Shall we burn up, tread that face at once
    Into tinder,
    And so hinder
Sparks from kindling all the place at once?

XV

Or else kiss away one's soul on her?
    Your love-fancies!
    – A sick man sees
60 Truer, when his hot eyes roll on her!

XVI

Thus the craftsman thinks to grace the rose, –
  Plucks a mould-flower
  For his gold flower,
Uses fine things that efface the rose:

XVII

Rosy rubies make its cup more rose,
  Precious metals
  Ape the petals, –
Last, some old king locks it up, morose!

XVIII

Then how grace a rose? I know a way!
70　　Leave it, rather.
  Must you gather?
Smell, kiss, wear it – at last, throw away!

'Childe Roland to the Dark Tower Came'

(See Edgar's song in *Lear*)

I

My first thought was, he lied in every word,
  That hoary cripple, with malicious eye
  Askance to watch the working of his lie
On mine, and mouth scarce able to afford
Suppression of the glee, that pursed and scored
  Its edge, at one more victim gained thereby.

II

What else should he be set for, with his staff?
  What, save to waylay with his lies, ensnare
  All travellers who might find him posted there,
10　And ask the road? I guessed what skull-like laugh
Would break, what crutch 'gin write my epitaph
  For pastime in the dusty thoroughfare,

III

If at his counsel I should turn aside
   Into that ominous tract which, all agree,
   Hides the Dark Tower. Yet acquiescingly
I did turn as he pointed: neither pride
Nor hope rekindling at the end descried,
   So much as gladness that some end might be.

IV

For, what with my whole world-wide wandering,
20   What with my search drawn out through years, my hope
   Dwindled into a ghost not fit to cope
With that obstreperous joy success would bring, –
I hardly tried now to rebuke the spring
   My heart made, finding failure in its scope.

V

As when a sick man very near to death
   Seems dead indeed, and feels begin and end
   The tears and takes the farewell of each friend,
And hears one bid the other go, draw breath
Freelier outside, ('since all is o'er,' he saith,
30   'And the blow fallen no grieving can amend';)

VI

While some discuss if near the other graves
   Be room enough for this, and when a day
   Suits best for carrying the corpse away,
With care about the banners, scarves and staves:
And still the man hears all, and only craves
   He may not shame such tender love and stay.

VII

Thus, I had so long suffered in this quest,
   Heard failure prophesied so oft, been writ
   So many times among 'The Band' – to wit,
40 The knights who to the Dark Tower's search addressed
Their steps – that just to fail as they, seemed best,
   And all the doubt was now – should I be fit?

VIII

So, quiet as despair, I turned from him,
   That hateful cripple, out of his highway
   Into the path he pointed. All the day
Had been a dreary one at best, and dim
Was settling to its close, yet shot one grim
   Red leer to see the plain catch its estray.

IX

For mark! no sooner was I fairly found
50   Pledged to the plain, after a pace or two,
   Than, pausing to throw backward a last view
O'er the safe road, 'twas gone; grey plain all round:
Nothing but plain to the horizon's bound.
   I might go on; naught else remained to do.

X

So, on I went. I think I never saw
   Such starved ignoble nature; nothing throve:
   For flowers – as well expect a cedar grove!
But cockle, spurge, according to their law
Might propagate their kind, with none to awe,
60   You'd think; a burr had been a treasure-trove.

XI

No! penury, inertness and grimace,
   In some strange sort, were the land's portion. 'See
   Or shut your eyes,' said Nature peevishly,
'It nothing skills: I cannot help my case:
'Tis the Last Judgement's fire must cure this place,
   Calcine its clods and set my prisoners free.'

XII

If there pushed any ragged thistle-stalk
   Above its mates, the head was chopped; the bents
   Were jealous else. What made those holes and rents
70 In the dock's harsh swarth leaves, bruised as to balk
All hope of greenness? 'tis a brute must walk
   Pashing their life out, with a brute's intents.

XIII

As for the grass, it grew as scant as hair
    In leprosy; thin dry blades pricked the mud
    Which underneath looked kneaded up with blood.
One stiff blind horse, his every bone a-stare,
Stood stupefied, however he came there:
    Thrust out past service from the devil's stud!

XIV

Alive? he might be dead for aught I know,
80   With that red gaunt and colloped neck a-strain,
    And shut eyes underneath the rusty mane;
Seldom went such grotesqueness with such woe;
I never saw a brute I hated so;
    He must be wicked to deserve such pain.

XV

I shut my eyes and turned them on my heart.
    As a man calls for wine before he fights,
    I asked one draught of earlier, happier sights,
Ere fitly I could hope to play my part.
Think first, fight afterwards – the soldier's art:
90   One taste of the old time sets all to rights.

XVI

Not it! I fancied Cuthbert's reddening face
    Beneath its garniture of curly gold,
    Dear fellow, till I almost felt him fold
An arm in mine to fix me to the place,
That way he used. Alas, one night's disgrace!
    Out went my heart's new fire and left it cold.

XVII

Giles then, the soul of honour – there he stands
    Frank as ten years ago when knighted first.
    What honest man should dare (he said) he durst.
100   Good – but the scene shifts – faugh! what hangman-hands
Pin to his breast a parchment? His own bands
    Read it. Poor traitor, spit upon and curst!

XVIII

Better this present than a past like that;
   Back therefore to my darkening path again!
   No sound, no sight as far as eye could strain.
Will the night send a howlet or a bat?
I asked: when something on the dismal flat
   Came to arrest my thoughts and change their train.

XIX

A sudden little river crossed my path
110   As unexpected as a serpent comes.
   No sluggish tide congenial to the glooms;
This, as it frothed by, might have been a bath
For the fiend's glowing hoof – to see the wrath
   Of its black eddy bespate with flakes and spumes.

XX

So petty yet so spiteful! All along,
   Low scrubby alders kneeled down over it;
   Drenched willows flung them headlong in a fit
Of mute despair, a suicidal throng:
The river which had done them all the wrong,
120   Whate'er that was, rolled by, deterred no whit.

XXI

Which, while I forded, – good saints, how I feared
   To set my foot upon a dead man's cheek,
   Each step, or feel the spear I thrust to seek
For hollows, tangled in his hair or beard!
– It may have been a water-rat I speared,
   But, ugh! it sounded like a baby's shriek.

XXII

Glad was I when I reached the other bank.
   Now for a better country. Vain presage!
   Who were the strugglers, what war did they wage,
130   Whose savage trample thus could pad the dank
Soil to a plash? Toads in a poisoned tank,
   Or wild cats in a red-hot iron cage –

XXIII

The fight must so have seemed in that fell cirque.
What penned them there, with all the plain to choose?
No foot-print leading to that horrid mews,
None out of it. Mad brewage set to work
Their brains, no doubt, like galley-slaves the Turk
Pits for his pastime, Christians against Jews.

XXIV

And more than that – a furlong on – why, there!
140   What bad use was that engine for, that wheel,
Or brake, not wheel – that harrow fit to reel
Men's bodies out like silk? with all the air
Of Tophet's tool, on earth left unaware,
Or brought to sharpen its rusty teeth of steel.

XXV

Then came a bit of stubbed ground, once a wood,
Next a marsh, it would seem, and now mere earth
Desperate and done with; (so a fool finds mirth,
Makes a thing and then mars it, till his mood
Changes and off he goes!) within a rood –
150   Bog, clay and rubble, sand and stark black dearth.

XXVI

Now blotches rankling, coloured gay and grim,
Now patches where some leanness of the soil's
Broke into moss or substances like boils;
Then came some palsied oak, a cleft in him
Like a distorted mouth that splits its rim
Gaping at death, and dies while it recoils.

XXVII

And just as far as ever from the end!
Naught in the distance but the evening, naught
To point my footstep further! At the thought,
160   A great black bird, Apollyon's bosom-friend,
Sailed past, nor beat his wide wing dragon-penned
That brushed my cap – perchance the guide I sought.

XXVIII

For, looking up, aware I somehow grew,
  'Spite of the dusk, the plain had given place
  All round to mountains – with such name to grace
Mere ugly heights and heaps now stolen in view.
How thus they had surprised me, – solve it, you!
  How to get from them was no clearer case.

XXIX

Yet half I seemed to recognize some trick
170 Of mischief happened to me, God knows when –
  In a bad dream perhaps. Here ended, then,
Progress this way. When, in the very nick
Of giving up, one time more, came a click
  As when a trap shuts – you're inside the den!

XXX

Burningly it came on me all at once,
  This was the place! those two hills on the right,
  Crouched like two bulls locked horn in horn in fight;
While to the left, a tall scalped mountain . . . Dunce,
Dotard, a-dozing at the very nonce,
180 After a life spent training for the sight!

XXXI

What in the midst lay but the Tower itself?
  The round squat turret, blind as the fool's heart,
  Built of brown stone, without a counterpart
In the whole world. The tempest's mocking elf
Points to the shipman thus the unseen shelf
  He strikes on, only when the timbers start.

XXXII

Not see? because of night perhaps? – why, day
  Came back again for that! before it left,
  The dying sunset kindled through a cleft:
190 The hills, like giants at a hunting, lay,
  Chin upon hand, to see the game at bay, –
    'Now stab and end the creature – to the heft!'

XXXIII

Not hear? when noise was everywhere! it tolled
  Increasing like a bell. Names in my ears
  Of all the lost adventurers my peers, –
How such a one was strong, and such was bold,
And such was fortunate, yet each of old
  Lost, lost! one moment knelled the woe of years.

XXXIV

There they stood, ranged along the hill-sides, met
200   To view the last of me, a living frame
  For one more picture! in a sheet of flame
I saw them and I knew them all. And yet
Dauntless the slug-horn to my lips I set,
  And blew. '*Childe Roland to the Dark Tower came.*'

Respectability

I

Dear, had the world in its caprice
  Deigned to proclaim 'I know you both,
  Have recognized your plighted troth,
Am sponsor for you: live in peace!' –
How many precious months and years
  Of youth had passed, that speed so fast,
  Before we found it out at last,
The world, and what it fears?

II

How much of priceless life were spent
10   With men that every virtue decks,
  And women models of their sex,
Society's true ornament, –
Ere we dared wander, nights like this,
  Through wind and rain, and watch the Seine,
  And feel the Boulevart break again
To warmth and light and bliss?

III

I know! the world proscribes not love;
    Allows my finger to caress
    Your lips' contour and downiness,
20 Provided it supply a glove.
    The world's good word! – the Institute!
        Guizot receives Montalembert!
        Eh? Down the court three lampions flare:
    Put forward your best foot!

A Light Woman

I

So far as our story approaches the end,
    Which do you pity the most of us three? –
My friend, or the mistress of my friend
    With her wanton eyes, or me?

II

My friend was already too good to lose,
    And seemed in the way of improvement yet,
When she crossed his path with her hunting-noose
    And over him drew her net.

III

When I saw him tangled in her toils,
10   A shame, said I, if she adds just him
To her nine-and-ninety other spoils,
    The hundredth for a whim!

IV

And before my friend be wholly hers,
    How easy to prove to him, I said,
An eagle's the game her pride prefers,
    Though she snaps at a wren instead!

V

So, I gave her eyes my own eyes to take,
  My hand sought hers as in earnest need,
And round she turned for my noble sake,
20   And gave me herself indeed.

VI

The eagle am I, with my fame in the world,
  The wren is he, with his maiden face.
– You look away and your lip is curled?
  Patience, a moment's space!

VII

For see, my friend goes shaking and white;
  He eyes me as the basilisk:
I have turned, it appears, his day to night,
  Eclipsing his sun's disk.

VIII

And I did it, he thinks, as a very thief:
30 'Though I love her – that, he comprehends –
One should master one's passions, (love, in chief)
  And be loyal to one's friends!'

IX

And she, – she lies in my hand as tame
  As a pear late basking over a wall;
Just a touch to try and off it came;
  'Tis mine, – can I let it fall?

X

With no mind to eat it, that's the worst!
  Were it thrown in the road, would the case assist?
'Twas quenching a dozen blue-flies' thirst
40   When I gave its stalk a twist.

XI

And I, – what I seem to my friend, you see:
  What I soon shall seem to his love, you guess:
What I seem to myself, do you ask of me?
  No hero, I confess.

XII

'Tis an awkward thing to play with souls,
  And matter enough to save one's own:
Yet think of my friend, and the burning coals
  He played with for bits of stone!

XIII

One likes to show the truth for the truth;
50   That the woman was light is very true:
But suppose she says, – Never mind that youth!
  What wrong have I done to you?

XIV

Well, any how, here the story stays,
  So far at least as I understand;
And, Robert Browning, you writer of plays,
  Here's a subject made to your hand!

The Statue and the Bust

There's a palace in Florence, the world knows well,
And a statue watches it from the square,
And this story of both do our townsmen tell.

Ages ago, a lady there,
At the farthest window facing the East
Asked, 'Who rides by with the royal air?'

The bridesmaids' prattle around her ceased;
She leaned forth, one on either hand;
They saw how the blush of the bride increased –

10   They felt by its beats her heart expand –
As one at each ear and both in a breath
Whispered, 'The Great-Duke Ferdinand.'

That self-same instant, underneath,
The Duke rode past in his idle way,
Empty and fine like a swordless sheath.

Gay he rode, with a friend as gay,
Till he threw his head back – 'Who is she?'
– 'A bride the Riccardi brings home today.'

Hair in heaps lay heavily
20 Over a pale brow spirit-pure –
Carved like the heart of the coal-black tree,

Crisped like a war-steed's encolure –
And vainly sought to dissemble her eyes
Of the blackest black our eyes endure.

And lo, a blade for a knight's emprise
Filled the fine empty sheath of a man, –
The Duke grew straightway brave and wise.

He looked at her, as a lover can;
She looked at him, as one who awakes:
30 The past was a sleep, and her life began.

Now, love so ordered for both their sakes,
A feast was held that selfsame night
In the pile which the mighty shadow makes.

(For Via Larga is three-parts light,
But the palace overshadows one,
Because of a crime which may God requite!

To Florence and God the wrong was done,
Through the first republic's murder there
By Cosimo and his cursèd son.)

40 The Duke (with the statue's face in the square)
Turned in the midst of his multitude
At the bright approach of the bridal pair.

Face to face the lovers stood
A single minute and no more,
While the bridegroom bent as a man subdued –

Bowed till his bonnet brushed the floor –
For the Duke on the lady a kiss conferred,
As the courtly custom was of yore.

In a minute can lovers exchange a word?
50   If a word did pass, which I do not think,
Only one out of the thousand heard.

That was the bridegroom. At day's brink
He and his bride were alone at last
In a bedchamber by a taper's blink.

Calmly he said that her lot was cast,
That the door she had passed was shut on her
Till the final catafalque repassed.

The world meanwhile, its noise and stir,
Through a certain window facing the East,
60   She could watch like a convent's chronicler.

Since passing the door might lead to a feast,
And a feast might lead to so much beside,
He, of many evils, chose the least.

'Freely I choose too,' said the bride –
'Your window and its world suffice,'
Replied the tongue, while the heart replied –

'If I spend the night with that devil twice,
May his window serve as my loop of hell
Whence a damned soul looks on paradise!

70   'I fly to the Duke who loves me well,
Sit by his side and laugh at sorrow
Ere I count another ave-bell.

''Tis only the coat of a page to borrow,
And tie my hair in a horse-boy's trim,
And I save my soul – but not tomorrow' –

(She checked herself and her eye grew dim)
'My father tarries to bless my state:
I must keep it one day more for him.

'Is one day more so long to wait?
80 Moreover the Duke rides past, I know;
We shall see each other, sure as fate.'

She turned on her side and slept. Just so!
So we resolve on a thing and sleep:
So did the lady, ages ago.

That night the Duke said, 'Dear or cheap
As the cost of this cup of bliss may prove
To body or soul, I will drain it deep.'

And on the morrow, bold with love,
He beckoned the bridegroom (close on call,
90 As his duty bade, by the Duke's alcove)

And smiled ''Twas a very funeral,
Your lady will think, this feast of ours, –
A shame to efface, whate'er befall!

'What if we break from the Arno bowers,
And try if Petraja, cool and green,
Cure last night's fault with this morning's flowers?'

The bridegroom, not a thought to be seen
On his steady brow and quiet mouth,
Said, 'Too much favour for me so mean!

100 'But, alas! my lady leaves the South;
Each wind that comes from the Apennine
Is a menace to her tender youth:

'Nor a way exists, the wise opine,
If she quits her palace twice this year,
To avert the flower of life's decline.'

Quoth the Duke, 'A sage and a kindly fear.
Moreover Petraja is cold this spring:
Be our feast tonight as usual here!'

And then to himself – 'Which night shall bring
110   Thy bride to her lover's embraces, fool –
Or I am the fool, and thou art the king!

'Yet my passion must wait a night, nor cool –
For tonight the Envoy arrives from France
Whose heart I unlock with thyself, my tool.

'I need thee still and might miss perchance.
Today is not wholly lost, beside,
With its hope of my lady's countenance:

'For I ride – what should I do but ride?
And passing her palace, if I list,
120   May glance at its window – well betide!'

So said, so done: nor the lady missed
One ray that broke from the ardent brow,
Nor a curl of the lips where the spirit kissed.

Be sure that each renewed the vow,
No morrow's sun should arise and set
And leave them then as it left them now.

But next day passed, and next day yet,
With still fresh cause to wait one day more
Ere each leaped over the parapet.

130   And still, as love's brief morning wore,
With a gentle start, half smile, half sigh,
They found love not as it seemed before.

They thought it would work infallibly,
But not in despite of heaven and earth:
The rose would blow when the storm passed by.

Meantime they could profit in winter's dearth
By store of fruits that supplant the rose:
The world and its ways have a certain worth:

And to press a point while these oppose
140   Were simple policy; better wait:
We lose no friends and we gain no foes.

Meantime, worse fates than a lover's fate,
Who daily may ride and pass and look
Where his lady watches behind the grate!

And she – she watched the square like a book
Holding one picture and only one,
Which daily to find she undertook:

When the picture was reached the book was done,
And she turned from the picture at night to scheme
150   Of tearing it out for herself next sun.

So weeks grew months, years; gleam by gleam
The glory dropped from their youth and love,
And both perceived they had dreamed a dream;

Which hovered as dreams do, still above:
But who can take a dream for a truth?
Oh, hide our eyes from the next remove!

One day as the lady saw her youth
Depart, and the silver thread that streaked
Her hair, and, worn by the serpent's tooth,

160   The brow so puckered, the chin so peaked, –
And wondered who the woman was,
Hollow-eyed and haggard-cheeked,

Fronting her silent in the glass –
'Summon here,' she suddenly said,
Before the rest of my old self pass,

'Him, the Carver, a hand to aid,
Who fashions the clay no love will change,
And fixes a beauty never to fade.

'Let Robbia's craft so apt and strange
170 Arrest the remains of young and fair,
And rivet them while the seasons range.

'Make me a face on the window there,
Waiting as ever, mute the while,
My love to pass below in the square!

'And let me think that it may beguile
Dreary days which the dead must spend
Down in their darkness under the aisle,

'To say, "What matters it at the end?
I did no more while my heart was warm
180 Than does that image, my pale-faced friend."

'Where is the use of the lip's red charm,
The heaven of hair, the pride of the brow,
And the blood that blues the inside arm –

'Unless we turn, as the soul knows how,
The earthly gift to an end divine?
A lady of clay is as good, I trow.'

But long ere Robbia's cornice, fine,
With flowers and fruits which leaves enlace,
Was set where now is the empty shrine –

190 (And, leaning out of a bright blue space,
As a ghost might lean from a chink of sky,
The passionate pale lady's face –

Eyeing ever, with earnest eye
And quick-turned neck at its breathless stretch,
Some one who ever is passing by –)

The Duke had sighed like the simplest wretch
In Florence, 'Youth – my dream escapes!
Will its record stay?' And he bade them fetch

Some subtle moulder of brazen shapes –
200 'Can the soul, the will, die out of a man
Ere his body find the grave that gapes?

'John of Douay shall effect my plan,
Set me on horseback here aloft,
Alive, as the crafty sculptor can,

'In the very square I have crossed so oft:
That men may admire, when future suns
Shall touch the eyes to a purpose soft,

'While the mouth and the brow stay brave in bronze –
Admire and say, "When he was alive
210 How he would take his pleasure once!"

'And it shall go hard but I contrive
To listen the while, and laugh in my tomb
At idleness which aspires to strive.'

————————

So! While these wait the trump of doom,
How do their spirits pass, I wonder,
Nights and days in the narrow room?

Still, I suppose, they sit and ponder
What a gift life was, ages ago,
Six steps out of the chapel yonder.

220 Only they see not God, I know,
Nor all that chivalry of his,
The soldier-saints who, row on row,

Burn upward each to his point of bliss –
Since, the end of life being manifest,
He had burned his way through the world to this.

I hear you reproach, 'But delay was best,
For their end was a crime.' – Oh, a crime will do
As well, I reply, to serve for a test,

As a virtue golden through and through,
230 Sufficient to vindicate itself
And prove its worth at a moment's view!

Must a game be played for the sake of pelf?
Where a button goes, 'twere an epigram
To offer the stamp of the very Guelph.

The true has no value beyond the sham:
As well the counter as coin, I submit,
When your table's a hat, and your prize a dram.

Stake your counter as boldly every whit,
Venture as warily, use the same skill,
240 Do your best, whether winning or losing it,

If you choose to play! – is my principle.
Let a man contend to the uttermost
For his life's set prize, be it what it will!

The counter our lovers staked was lost
As surely as if it were lawful coin:
And the sin I impute to each frustrate ghost

Is – the unlit lamp and the ungirt loin,
Though the end in sight was a vice, I say.
You of the virtue (we issue join)
250 How strive you? *De te, fabula.*

Love in a Life

I
Room after room,
I hunt the house through
We inhabit together.
Heart, fear nothing, for, heart, thou shalt find her –

Next time, herself! – not the trouble behind her
Left in the curtain, the couch's perfume!
As she brushed it, the cornice-wreath blossomed anew:
Yon looking-glass gleamed at the wave of her feather.

II
Yet the day wears,
10   And door succeeds door;
I try the fresh fortune –
Range the wide house from the wing to the centre.
Still the same chance! she goes out as I enter.
Spend my whole day in the quest, – who cares?
But 'tis twilight, you see, – with such suites to explore,
Such closets to search, such alcoves to importune!

Life in a Love

Escape me?
Never –
Beloved!
While I am I, and you are you,
    So long as the world contains us both,
    Me the loving and you the loth,
While the one eludes, must the other pursue.
My life is a fault at last, I fear:
    It seems too much like a fate, indeed!
10   Though I do my best I shall scarce succeed.
But what if I fail of my purpose here?
It is but to keep the nerves at strain,
    To dry one's eyes and laugh at a fall,
And, baffled, get up and begin again, –
    So the chase takes up one's life, that's all.
While, look but once from your farthest bound
    At me so deep in the dust and dark,
No sooner the old hope goes to ground
    Than a new one, straight to the self-same mark,
20   I shape me –
Ever
Removed!

How It Strikes a Contemporary

I only knew one poet in my life:
And this, or something like it, was his way.

   You saw go up and down Valladolid,
A man of mark, to know next time you saw.
His very serviceable suit of black
Was courtly once and conscientious still,
And many might have worn it, though none did:
The cloak, that somewhat shone and showed the threads,
Had purpose, and the ruff, significance.
10 He walked and tapped the pavement with his cane,
Scenting the world, looking it full in face,
An old dog, bald and blindish, at his heels.
They turned up, now, the alley by the church,
That leads nowhither; now, they breathed themselves
On the main promenade just at the wrong time:
You'd come upon his scrutinizing hat,
Making a peaked shade blacker than itself
Against the single window spared some house
Intact yet with its mouldered Moorish work, –
20 Or else surprise the ferrel of his stick
Trying the mortar's temper 'tween the chinks
Of some new shop a-building, French and fine.
He stood and watched the cobbler at his trade,
The man who slices lemons into drink,
The coffee-roaster's brazier, and the boys
That volunteer to help him turn its winch.
He glanced o'er books on stalls with half an eye,
And fly-leaf ballads on the vendor's string,
And broad-edge bold-print posters by the wall.
30 He took such cognizance of men and things,
If any beat a horse, you felt he saw;
If any cursed a woman, he took note;
Yet stared at nobody, – you stared at him,
And found, less to your pleasure than surprise,
He seemed to know you and expect as much.
So, next time that a neighbour's tongue was loosed,
It marked the shameful and notorious fact,
We had among us, not so much a spy,

As a recording chief-inquisitor,
40   The town's true master if the town but knew!
We merely kept a governor for form,
While this man walked about and took account
Of all thought, said and acted, then went home,
And wrote it fully to our Lord the King
Who has an itch to know things, he knows why,
And reads them in his bedroom of a night.
Oh, you might smile! there wanted not a touch,
A tang of . . . well, it was not wholly ease
As back into your mind the man's look came.
50   Stricken in years a little, – such a brow
His eyes had to live under! – clear as flint
On either side the formidable nose
Curved, cut and coloured like an eagle's claw.
Had he to do with A.'s surprising fate?
When altogether old B. disappeared
And young C. got his mistress, – was't our friend,
His letter to the King, that did it all?
What paid the bloodless man for so much pains?
Our Lord the King has favourites manifold,
60   And shifts his ministry some once a month;
Our city gets new governors at whiles, –
But never word or sign, that I could hear,
Notified to this man about the streets
The King's approval of those letters conned
The last thing duly at the dead of night.
Did the man love his office? Frowned our Lord,
Exhorting when none heard – 'Beseech me not!
Too far above my people, – beneath me!
I set the watch, – how should the people know?
70   Forget them, keep me all the more in mind!'
Was some such understanding 'twixt the two?

I found no truth in one report at least –
That if you tracked him to his home, down lanes
Beyond the Jewry, and as clean to pace,
You found he ate his supper in a room
Blazing with lights, four Titians on the wall,
And twenty naked girls to change his plate!
Poor man, he lived another kind of life
In that new stuccoed third house by the bridge,

80 Fresh-painted, rather smart than otherwise!
    The whole street might o'erlook him as he sat,
    Leg crossing leg, one foot on the dog's back,
    Playing a decent cribbage with his maid
    (Jacynth, you're sure her name was) o'er the cheese
    And fruit, three red halves of starved winter-pears,
    Or treat of radishes in April. Nine,
    Ten, struck the church clock, straight to bed went he.

    My father, like the man of sense he was,
    Would point him out to me a dozen times;
90 ''St – 'St,' he'd whisper, 'the Corregidor!'
    I had been used to think that personage
    Was one with lacquered breeches, lustrous belt,
    And feathers like a forest in his hat,
    Who blew a trumpet and proclaimed the news,
    Announced the bull-fights, gave each church its turn,
    And memorized the miracle in vogue!
    He had a great observance from us boys;
    We were in error; that was not the man.

    I'd like now, yet had haply been afraid,
100 To have just looked, when this man came to die,
    And seen who lined the clean gay garret-sides
    And stood about the neat low truckle-bed,
    With the heavenly manner of relieving guard.
    Here had been, mark, the general-in-chief,
    Through a whole campaign of the world's life and death,
    Doing the King's work all the dim day long,
    In his old coat and up to knees in mud,
    Smoked like a herring, dining on a crust, –
    And, now the day was won, relieved at once!
110 No further show or need for that old coat,
    You are sure, for one thing! Bless us, all the while
    How sprucely we are dressed out, you and I!
    A second, and the angels alter that.
    Well, I could never write a verse, – could you?
    Let's to the Prado and make the most of time.

The Last Ride Together

I

I said – Then, dearest, since 'tis so,
Since now at length my fate I know,
Since nothing all my love avails,
Since all, my life seemed meant for, fails,
    Since this was written and needs must be –
My whole heart rises up to bless
Your name in pride and thankfulness!
Take back the hope you gave, – I claim
Only a memory of the same,
10 – And this beside, if you will not blame,
    Your leave for one more last ride with me.

II

My mistress bent that brow of hers;
Those deep dark eyes where pride demurs
When pity would be softening through,
Fixed me a breathing-while or two
    With life or death in the balance: right!
The blood replenished me again;
My last thought was at least not vain:
I and my mistress, side by side
20 Shall be together, breathe and ride,
    So, one day more am I deified.
    Who knows but the world may end tonight?

III

Hush! if you saw some western cloud
All billowy-bosomed, over-bowed
By many benedictions – sun's
And moon's and evening-star's at once –
    And so, you, looking and loving best,
Conscious grew, your passion drew
Cloud, sunset, moonrise, star-shine too,
30 Down on you, near and yet more near,
    Till flesh must fade for heaven was here! –
Thus leant she and lingered – joy and fear!
    Thus lay she a moment on my breast.

IV

Then we began to ride. My soul
Smoothed itself out, a long-cramped scroll
Freshening and fluttering in the wind.
Past hopes already lay behind.
 What need to strive with a life awry?
Had I said that, had I done this,
40 So might I gain, so might I miss.
Might she have loved me? just as well
She might have hated, who can tell!
Where had I been now if the worst befell?
 And here we are riding, she and I.

V

Fail I alone, in words and deeds?
Why, all men strive and who succeeds?
We rode; it seemed my spirit flew,
Saw other regions, cities new,
 As the world rushed by on either side.
50 I thought, – All labour, yet no less
Bear up beneath their unsuccess.
Look at the end of work, contrast
The petty done, the undone vast,
This present of theirs with the hopeful past!
 I hoped she would love me; here we ride.

VI

What hand and brain went ever paired?
What heart alike conceived and dared?
What act proved all its thought had been?
What will but felt the fleshly screen?
60 We ride and I see her bosom heave.
There's many a crown for who can reach.
Ten lines, a statesman's life in each!
The flag stuck on a heap of bones,
A soldier's doing! what atones?
They scratch his name on the Abbey-stones.
 My riding is better, by their leave.

VII

What does it all mean, poet? Well,
Your brains beat into rhythm, you tell
What we felt only; you expressed
70   You hold things beautiful the best,
    And pace them in rhyme so, side by side.
'Tis something, nay 'tis much: but then,
Have you yourself what's best for men?
Are you – poor, sick, old ere your time –
Nearer one whit your own sublime
Than we who never have turned a rhyme?
    Sing, riding's a joy! For me, I ride.

VIII

And you, great sculptor – so, you gave
A score of years to Art, her slave,
80   And that's your Venus, whence we turn
  To yonder girl that fords the burn!
    You acquiesce, and shall I repine?
What, man of music, you grown grey
With notes and nothing else to say,
Is this your sole praise from a friend,
'Greatly his opera's strains intend,
But in music we know how fashions end!'
    I gave my youth; but we ride, in fine.

IX

Who knows what's fit for us? Had fate
90   Proposed bliss here should sublimate
  My being – had I signed the bond –
  Still one must lead some life beyond,
    Have a bliss to die with, dim-descried.
This foot once planted on the goal,
This glory-garland round my soul,
Could I descry such? Try and test!
I sink back shuddering from the quest.
Earth being so good, would heaven seem best?
    Now, heaven and she are beyond this ride.

X
100 And yet – she has not spoke so long!
What if heaven be that, fair and strong
At life's best, with our eyes upturned
Whither life's flower is first discerned,
    We, fixed so, ever should so abide?
What if we still ride on, we two
With life for ever old yet new,
Changed not in kind but in degree,
The instant made eternity, –
And heaven just prove that I and she
110 Ride, ride together, for ever ride?

The Patriot

An Old Story

I
It was roses, roses, all the way,
    With myrtle mixed in my path like mad:
The house-roofs seemed to heave and sway,
    The church-spires flamed, such flags they had,
A year ago on this very day.

II
The air broke into a mist with bells,
    The old walls rocked with the crowd and cries.
Had I said, 'Good folk, mere noise repels –
    But give me your sun from yonder skies!'
10 They had answered, 'And afterward, what else?'

III
Alack, it was I who leaped at the sun
    To give it my loving friends to keep!
Naught man could do, have I left undone:
    And you see my harvest, what I reap
This very day, now a year is run.

IV

There's nobody on the house-tops now –
　　Just a palsied few at the windows set;
For the best of the sight is, all allow,
　　At the Shambles' Gate – or, better yet,
20　By the very scaffold's foot, I trow.

V

I go in the rain, and, more than needs,
　　A rope cuts both my wrists behind;
And I think, by the feel, my forehead bleeds,
　　For they fling, whoever has a mind,
Stones at me for my year's misdeeds.

VI

Thus I entered, and thus I go!
　　In triumphs, people have dropped down dead.
'Paid by the world, what dost thou owe
　　Me?' – God might question; now instead,
30　'Tis God shall repay: I am safer so.

Master Hugues of Saxe-Gotha

I

Hist, but a word, fair and soft!
　　Forth and be judged, Master Hugues!
Answer the question I've put you so oft:
　　What do you mean by your mountainous fugues?
See, we're alone in the loft, –

II

I, the poor organist here,
　　Hugues, the composer of note,
Dead though, and done with, this many a year:
　　Let's have a colloquy, something to quote,
10　Make the world prick up its ear!

III

See, the church empties apace:
   Fast they extinguish the lights.
Hallo there, sacristan! Five minutes' grace!
   Here's a crank pedal wants setting to rights,
Balks one of holding the bass.

IV

See, our huge house of the sounds,
   Hushing its hundreds at once,
Bids the last loiterer back to his bounds!
   – O you may challenge them, not a response
20 Get the church-saints on their rounds!

V

(Saints go their rounds, who shall doubt?
   – March, with the moon to admire,
Up nave, down chancel, turn transept about,
   Supervise all betwixt pavement and spire,
Put rats and mice to the rout –

VI

Aloys and Jurien and Just –
   Order things back to their place,
Have a sharp eye lest the candlesticks rust,
   Rub the church-plate, darn the sacrament-lace,
30 Clear the desk-velvet of dust.)

VII

Here's your book, younger folks shelve!
   Played I not off-hand and runningly,
Just now, your masterpiece, hard number twelve?
   Here's what should strike, could one handle it cunningly:
Help the axe, give it a helve!

VIII

Page after page as I played,
   Every bar's rest, where one wipes
Sweat from one's brow, I looked up and surveyed,
   O'er my three claviers, yon forest of pipes
40 Whence you still peeped in the shade.

IX

Sure you were wishful to speak?
    You, with brow ruled like a score,
Yes, and eyes buried in pits on each cheek,
    Like two great breves, as they wrote them of yore,
Each side that bar, your straight beak!

X

Sure you said – 'Good, the mere notes!
    Still, couldst thou take my intent,
Know what procured me our Company's votes –
    A master were lauded and sciolists shent,
50   Parted the sheep from the goats!'

XI

Well then, speak up, never flinch!
    Quick, ere my candle's a snuff
– Burnt, do you see? to its uttermost inch –
    I believe in you, but that's not enough:
Give my conviction a clinch!

XII

First you deliver your phrase
    – Nothing propound, that I see,
Fit in itself for much blame or much praise –
    Answered no less, where no answer needs be:
60   Off start the Two on their ways.

XIII

Straight must a Third interpose,
    Volunteer needlessly help;
In strikes a Fourth, a Fifth thrusts in his nose,
    So the cry's open, the kennel's a-yelp,
Argument's hot to the close.

XIV

One dissertates, he is candid;
    Two must discept, – has distinguished;
Three helps the couple, if ever yet man did;
    Four protests; Five makes a dart at the thing wished:
70   Back to One, goes the case bandied.

XV

One says his say with a difference;
   More of expounding, explaining!
All now is wrangle, abuse, and vociferance;
   Now there's a truce, all's subdued, self-restraining:
Five, though, stands out all the stiffer hence.

XVI

One is incisive, corrosive;
   Two retorts, nettled, curt, crepitant;
Three makes rejoinder, expansive, explosive;
   Four overbears them all, strident and strepitant:
80 Five ... O Danaïdes, O Sieve!

XVII

Now, they ply axes and crowbars;
   Now, they prick pins at a tissue
Fine as a skein of the casuist Escobar's
   Worked on the bone of a lie. To what issue?
Where is our gain at the Two-bars?

XVIII

Est fuga, volvitur rota.
   On we drift: where looms the dim port?
One, Two, Three, Four, Five, contribute their quota;
   Something is gained, if one caught but the import –
90 Show it us, Hugues of Saxe-Gotha!

XIX

What with affirming, denying,
   Holding, risposting, subjoining,
All's like ... it's like ... for an instance I'm trying ...
   There! See our roof, its gilt moulding and groining
Under those spider-webs lying!

XX

So your fugue broadens and thickens,
   Greatens and deepens and lengthens,
Till we exclaim – 'But where's music, the dickens?
   Blot ye the gold, while your spider-web strengthens
100 – Blacked to the stoutest of tickens?'

XXI

I for man's effort am zealous:
  Prove me such censure unfounded!
Seems it surprising a lover grows jealous –
  Hopes 'twas for something, his organ-pipes sounded,
Tiring three boys at the bellows?

XXII

Is it your moral of Life?
  Such a web, simple and subtle,
Weave we on earth here in impotent strife,
  Backward and forward each throwing his shuttle,
110 Death ending all with a knife?

XXIII

Over our heads truth and nature –
  Still our life's zigzags and dodges,
Ins and outs, weaving a new legislature –
  God's gold just shining its last where that lodges,
Palled beneath man's usurpature.

XXIV

So we o'ershroud stars and roses,
  Cherub and trophy and garland;
Nothings grow something which quietly closes
  Heaven's earnest eye: not a glimpse of the far land
120 Gets through our comments and glozes.

XXV

Ah but traditions, inventions,
  (Say we and make up a visage)
So many men with such various intentions,
  Down the past ages, must know more than this age!
Leave we the web its dimensions!

XXVI

Who thinks Hugues wrote for the deaf,
  Proved a mere mountain in labour?
Better submit; try again; what's the clef?
  'Faith, 'tis no trifle for pipe and for tabor –
130 Four flats, the minor in F.

XXVII

Friend, your fugue taxes the finger:
    Learning it once, who would lose it?
Yet all the while a misgiving will linger,
    Truth's golden o'er us although we refuse it –
Nature, through cobwebs we string her.

XXVIII

Hugues! I advise *meâ poenâ*
    (Counterpoint glares like a Gorgon)
Bid One, Two, Three, Four, Five, clear the arena!
    Say the word, straight I unstop the full-organ,
140 Blare out the *mode Palestrina*.

XXIX

While in the roof, if I'm right there,
    ... Lo you, the wick in the socket!
Hallo, you sacristan, show us a light there!
    Down it dips, gone like a rocket.
What, you want, do you, to come unawares,
Sweeping the church up for first morning-prayers,
And find a poor devil has ended his cares
At the foot of your rotten-runged rat-riddled stairs?
    Do I carry the moon in my pocket?

Bishop Blougram's Apology

No more wine? then we'll push back chairs and talk.
A final glass for me, though: cool, i' faith!
We ought to have our Abbey back, you see.
It's different, preaching in basilicas,
And doing duty in some masterpiece
Like this of brother Pugin's, bless his heart!
I doubt if they're half baked, those chalk rosettes,
Ciphers and stucco-twiddlings everywhere;
It's just like breathing in a lime-kiln: eh?
10 These hot long ceremonies of our church
Cost us a little – oh, they pay the price,
You take me – amply pay it! Now, we'll talk.

So, you despise me, Mr Gigadibs.
No deprecation, – nay, I beg you, sir!
Beside 'tis our engagement: don't you know,
I promised, if you'd watch a dinner out,
We'd see truth dawn together? – truth that peeps
Over the glasses' edge when dinner's done,
And body gets its sop and holds its noise
20 And leaves soul free a little. Now's the time:
Truth's break of day! You do despise me then.
And if I say, 'despise me,' – never fear!
I know you do not in a certain sense –
Not in my arm-chair, for example: here,
I well imagine you respect my place
(*Status*, *entourage*, worldly circumstance)
Quite to its value – very much indeed:
– Are up to the protesting eyes of you
In pride at being seated here for once –
30 You'll turn it to such capital account!
When somebody, through years and years to come,
Hints of the bishop, – names me – that's enough:
'Blougram? I knew him' – (into it you slide)
'Dined with him once, a Corpus Christi Day,
All alone, we two; he's a clever man:
And after dinner, – why, the wine you know, –
Oh, there was wine, and good! – what with the wine . . .
'Faith, we began upon all sorts of talk!
He's no bad fellow, Blougram; he had seen
40 Something of mine he relished, some review:
He's quite above their humbug in his heart,
Half-said as much, indeed – the thing's his trade.
I warrant, Blougram's sceptical at times:
How otherwise? I liked him, I confess!'
Che che, my dear sir, as we say at Rome,
Don't you protest now! It's fair give and take;
You have had your turn and spoken your home-truths:
The hand's mine now, and here you follow suit.

Thus much conceded, still the first fact stays –
50 You do despise me; your ideal of life
Is not the bishop's: you would not be I.
You would like better to be Goethe, now,
Or Buonaparte, or, bless me, lower still,

Count D'Orsay, – so you did what you preferred,
Spoke as you thought, and, as you cannot help,
Believed or disbelieved, no matter what,
So long as on that point, whate'er it was,
You loosed your mind, were whole and sole yourself.
– That, my ideal never can include,
60 Upon that element of truth and worth
Never be based! for say they make me Pope –
(They can't – suppose it for our argument!)
Why, there I'm at my tether's end, I've reached
My height, and not a height which pleases you:
An unbelieving Pope won't do, you say.
It's like those eerie stories nurses tell,
Of how some actor on a stage played Death,
With pasteboard crown, sham orb and tinselled dart,
And called himself the monarch of the world;
70 Then, going in the tire-room afterward,
Because the play was done, to shift himself,
Got touched upon the sleeve familiarly,
The moment he had shut the closet door,
By Death himself. Thus God might touch a Pope
At unawares, ask what his baubles mean,
And whose part he presumed to play just now.
Best be yourself, imperial, plain and true!

So, drawing comfortable breath again,
You weigh and find, whatever more or less
80 I boast of my ideal realized
Is nothing in the balance when opposed
To your ideal, your grand simple life,
Of which you will not realize one jot.
I am much, you are nothing; you would be all,
I would be merely much: you beat me there.

No, friend, you do not beat me: hearken why!
The common problem, yours, mine, every one's,
Is – not to fancy what were fair in life
Provided it could be, – but, finding first
90 What may be, then find how to make it fair
Up to our means: a very different thing!
No abstract intellectual plan of life
Quite irrespective of life's plainest laws,

But one, a man, who is man and nothing more,
May lead within a world which (by your leave)
Is Rome or London, not Fool's-paradise.
Embellish Rome, idealize away,
Make paradise of London if you can,
You're welcome, nay, you're wise.

                     A simile!
100 We mortals cross the ocean of this world
Each in his average cabin of a life;
The best's not big, the worst yields elbow-room.
Now for our six months' voyage – how prepare?
You come on shipboard with a landsman's list
Of things he calls convenient: so they are!
An India screen is pretty furniture,
A piano-forte is a fine resource,
All Balzac's novels occupy one shelf,
The new edition fifty volumes long;
110 And little Greek books, with the funny type
They get up well at Leipsic, fill the next:
Go on! slabbed marble, what a bath it makes!
And Parma's pride, the Jerome, let us add!
'Twere pleasant could Correggio's fleeting glow
Hang full in face of one where'er one roams,
Since he more than the others brings with him
Italy's self, – the marvellous Modenese! –
Yet was not on your list before, perhaps.
– Alas, friend, here's the agent . . . is't the name?
120 The captain, or whoever's master here –
You see him screw his face up; what's his cry
Ere you set foot on shipboard? 'Six feet square!'
If you won't understand what six feet mean,
Compute and purchase stores accordingly –
And if, in pique because he overhauls
Your Jerome, piano, bath, you come on board
Bare – why, you cut a figure at the first
While sympathetic landsmen see you off;
Not afterward, when long ere half seas over,
130 You peep up from your utterly naked boards
Into some snug and well-appointed berth,
Like mine for instance (try the cooler jug –
Put back the other, but don't jog the ice!)

And mortified you mutter 'Well and good;
He sits enjoying his sea-furniture;
'Tis stout and proper, and there's store of it:
Though I've the better notion, all agree,
Of fitting rooms up. Hang the carpenter,
Neat ship-shape fixings and contrivances –
140 I would have brought my Jerome, frame and all!'
And meantime you bring nothing: never mind –
You've proved your artist-nature: what you don't
You might bring, so despise me, as I say.

Now come, let's backward to the starting-place.
See my way: we're two college friends, suppose.
Prepare together for our voyage, then;
Each note and check the other in his work, –
Here's mine, a bishop's outfit; criticize!
What's wrong? why won't you be a bishop too?

150 Why first, you don't believe, you don't and can't,
(Not statedly, that is, and fixedly
And absolutely and exclusively)
In any revelation called divine.
No dogmas nail your faith; and what remains
But say so, like the honest man you are?
First, therefore, overhaul theology!
Nay, I too, not a fool, you please to think,
Must find believing every whit as hard:
And if I do not frankly say as much,
160 The ugly consequence is clear enough.

Now wait, my friend: well, I do not believe –
If you'll accept no faith that is not fixed,
Absolute and exclusive, as you say.
You're wrong – I mean to prove it in due time.
Meanwhile, I know where difficulties lie
I could not, cannot solve, nor ever shall,
So give up hope accordingly to solve –
(To you, and over the wine). Our dogmas then
With both of us, though in unlike degree,
170 Missing full credence – overboard with them!
I mean to meet you on your own premise:
Good, there go mine in company with yours!

And now what are we? unbelievers both,
Calm and complete, determinately fixed
Today, tomorrow and for ever, pray?
You'll guarantee me that? Not so, I think!
In no wise! all we've gained is, that belief,
As unbelief before, shakes us by fits,
Confounds us like its predecessor. Where's
180   The gain? how can we guard our unbelief,
Make it bear fruit to us? – the problem here.
Just when we are safest, there's a sunset-touch,
A fancy from a flower-bell, some one's death,
A chorus-ending from Euripides, –
And that's enough for fifty hopes and fears
As old and new at once as nature's self,
To rap and knock and enter in our soul,
Take hands and dance there, a fantastic ring,
Round the ancient idol, on his base again, –
190   The grand Perhaps! We look on helplessly.
There the old misgivings, crooked questions are –
This good God, – what he could do, if he would,
Would, if he could – then must have done long since:
If so, when, where and how? some way must be, –
Once feel about, and soon or late you hit
Some sense, in which it might be, after all.
Why not, 'The Way, the Truth, the Life'?

                                 – That way
Over the mountain, which who stands upon
Is apt to doubt if it be meant for a road;
200   While, if he views it from the waste itself,
Up goes the line there, plain from base to brow,
Not vague, mistakable! what's a break or two
Seen from the unbroken desert either side?
And then (to bring in fresh philosophy)
What if the breaks themselves should prove at last
The most consummate of contrivances
To train a man's eye, teach him what is faith?
And so we stumble at truth's very test!
All we have gained then by our unbelief
210   Is a life of doubt diversified by faith,
For one of faith diversified by doubt:
We called the chess-board white, – we call it black.

'Well,' you rejoin, 'the end's no worse, at least;
We've reason for both colours on the board:
Why not confess then, where I drop the faith
And you the doubt, that I'm as right as you?'

Because, friend, in the next place, this being so,
And both things even, – faith and unbelief
Left to a man's choice, – we'll proceed a step,
220 Returning to our image, which I like.

A man's choice, yes – but a cabin-passenger's –
The man made for the special life o' the world –
Do you forget him? I remember though!
Consult our ship's conditions and you find
One and but one choice suitable to all;
The choice, that you unluckily prefer,
Turning things topsy-turvy – they or it
Going to the ground. Belief or unbelief
Bears upon life, determines its whole course,
230 Begins at its beginning. See the world
Such as it is, – you made it not, nor I;
I mean to take it as it is, – and you,
Not so you'll take it, – though you get naught else.
I know the special kind of life I like,
What suits the most my idiosyncrasy,
Brings out the best of me and bears me fruit
In power, peace, pleasantness and length of days.
I find that positive belief does this
For me, and unbelief, no whit of this.
240 – For you, it does, however? – that, we'll try!
'Tis clear, I cannot lead my life, at least,
Induce the world to let me peaceably,
Without declaring at the outset, 'Friends,
I absolutely and peremptorily
Believe!' – I say, faith is my waking life:
One sleeps, indeed, and dreams at intervals,
We know, but waking's the main point with us
And my provision's for life's waking part.
Accordingly, I use heart, head and hand
250 All day, I build, scheme, study, and make friends;
And when night overtakes me, down I lie,
Sleep, dream a little, and get done with it,

The sooner the better, to begin afresh.
What's midnight doubt before the dayspring's faith?
You, the philosopher, that disbelieve,
That recognize the night, give dreams their weight –
To be consistent you should keep your bed,
Abstain from healthy acts that prove you man,
For fear you drowse perhaps at unawares!
260   And certainly at night you'll sleep and dream,
Live through the day and bustle as you please.
And so you live to sleep as I to wake,
To unbelieve as I to still believe?
Well, and the common sense o' the world calls you
Bed-ridden, – and its good things come to me.
Its estimation, which is half the fight,
That's the first-cabin comfort I secure:
The next . . . but you perceive with half an eye!
Come, come, it's best believing, if we may;
270   You can't but own that!

                    Next, concede again,
If once we choose belief, on all accounts
We can't be too decisive in our faith,
Conclusive and exclusive in its terms,
To suit the world which gives us the good things.
In every man's career are certain points
Whereon he dares not be indifferent;
The world detects him clearly, if he dare,
As baffled at the game, and losing life.
He may care little or he may care much
280   For riches, honour, pleasure, work, repose,
Since various theories of life and life's
Success are extant which might easily
Comport with either estimate of these;
And whoso chooses wealth or poverty,
Labour or quiet, is not judged a fool
Because his fellow would choose otherwise:
We let him choose upon his own account
So long as he's consistent with his choice.
But certain points, left wholly to himself,
290   When once a man has arbitrated on,
We say he must succeed there or go hang.
Thus, he should wed the woman he loves most

Or needs most, whatsoe'er the love or need –
For he can't wed twice. Then, he must avouch,
Or follow, at the least, sufficiently,
The form of faith his conscience holds the best,
Whate'er the process of conviction was:
For nothing can compensate his mistake
On such a point, the man himself being judge:
300 He cannot wed twice, nor twice lose his soul.

Well now, there's one great form of Christian faith
I happened to be born in – which to teach
Was given me as I grew up, on all hands,
As best and readiest means of living by;
The same on examination being proved
The most pronounced moreover, fixed, precise
And absolute form of faith in the whole world –
Accordingly, most potent of all forms
For working on the world. Observe, my friend!
310 Such as you know me, I am free to say,
In these hard latter days which hamper one,
Myself – by no immoderate exercise
Of intellect and learning, but the tact
To let external forces work for me,
– Bid the street's stones be bread and they are bread;
Bid Peter's creed, or rather, Hildebrand's,
Exalt me o'er my fellows in the world
And make my life an ease and joy and pride;
It does so, – which for me's a great point gained,
320 Who have a soul and body that exact
A comfortable care in many ways.
There's power in me and will to dominate
Which I must exercise, they hurt me else:
In many ways I need mankind's respect,
Obedience, and the love that's born of fear:
While at the same time, there's a taste I have,
A toy of soul, a titillating thing,
Refuses to digest these dainties crude.
The naked life is gross till clothed upon:
330 I must take what men offer, with a grace
As though I would not, could I help it, take!
An uniform I wear though over-rich –
Something imposed on me, no choice of mine;

No fancy-dress worn for pure fancy's sake
And despicable therefore! now folk kneel
And kiss my hand – of course the Church's hand.
Thus I am made, thus life is best for me,
And thus that it should be I have procured;
And thus it could not be another way,
340   I venture to imagine.

                You'll reply,
So far my choice, no doubt, is a success;
But were I made of better elements,
With nobler instincts, purer tastes, like you,
I hardly would account the thing success
Though it did all for me I say.

                But, friend,
We speak of what is; not of what might be,
And how 'twere better if 'twere otherwise.
I am the man you see here plain enough:
Grant I'm a beast, why, beasts must lead beasts' lives!
350   Suppose I own at once to tail and claws;
The tailless man exceeds me: but being tailed
I'll lash out lion fashion, and leave apes
To dock their stump and dress their haunches up.
My business is not to remake myself,
But make the absolute best of what God made.
Or – our first simile – though you prove me doomed
To a viler berth still, to the steerage-hole,
The sheep-pen or the pig-sty, I should strive
To make what use of each were possible;
360   And as this cabin gets upholstery,
That hutch should rustle with sufficient straw.

    But, friend, I don't acknowledge quite so fast
I fail of all your manhood's lofty tastes
Enumerated so complacently,
On the mere ground that you forsooth can find
In this particular life I choose to lead
No fit provision for them. Can you not?
Say you, my fault is I address myself
To grosser estimators than should judge?
370   And that's no way of holding up the soul,

Which, nobler, needs men's praise perhaps, yet knows
One wise man's verdict outweighs all the fools' –
Would like the two, but, forced to choose, takes that.
I pine among my million imbeciles
(You think) aware some dozen men of sense
Eye me and know me, whether I believe
In the last winking Virgin, as I vow,
And am a fool, or disbelieve in her
And am a knave, – approve in neither case,
380 Withhold their voices though I look their way:
Like Verdi when, at his worst opera's end
(The thing they gave at Florence, – what's its name?)
While the mad houseful's plaudits near out-bang
His orchestra of salt-box, tongs and bones,
He looks through all the roaring and the wreaths
Where sits Rossini patient in his stall.

Nay, friend, I meet you with an answer here –
That even your prime men who appraise their kind
Are men still, catch a wheel within a wheel,
390 See more in a truth than the truth's simple self,
Confuse themselves. You see lads walk the street
Sixty the minute; what's to note in that?
You see one lad o'erstride a chimney-stack;
Him you must watch – he's sure to fall, yet stands!
Our interest's on the dangerous edge of things.
The honest thief, the tender murderer,
The superstitious atheist, demirep
That loves and saves her soul in new French books –
We watch while these in equilibrium keep
400 The giddy line midway: one step aside,
They're classed and done with. I, then, keep the line
Before your sages, – just the men to shrink
From the gross weights, coarse scales and labels broad
You offer their refinement. Fool or knave?
Why needs a bishop be a fool or knave
When there's a thousand diamond weights between?
So, I enlist them. Your picked twelve, you'll find,
Profess themselves indignant, scandalized
At thus being held unable to explain
410 How a superior man who disbelieves
May not believe as well: that's Schelling's way!

It's through my coming in the tail of time,
Nicking the minute with a happy tact.
Had I been born three hundred years ago
They'd say, 'What's strange? Blougram of course believes';
And, seventy years since, 'disbelieves of course.'
But now, 'He may believe; and yet, and yet
How can he?' All eyes turn with interest.
Whereas, step off the line on either side –
420   You, for example, clever to a fault,
The rough and ready man who write apace,
Read somewhat seldomer, think perhaps even less –
You disbelieve! Who wonders and who cares?
Lord So-and-so – his coat bedropped with wax,
All Peter's chains about his waist, his back
Brave with the needlework of Noodledom –
Believes! Again, who wonders and who cares?
But I, the man of sense and learning too,
The able to think yet act, the this, the that,
430   I, to believe at this late time of day!
Enough; you see, I need not fear contempt.

  – Except it's yours! Admire me as these may,
You don't. But whom at least do you admire?
Present your own perfection, your ideal,
Your pattern man for a minute – oh, make haste,
Is it Napoleon you would have us grow?
Concede the means; allow his head and hand,
(A large concession, clever as you are)
Good! In our common primal element
440   Of unbelief (we can't believe, you know –
We're still at that admission, recollect!)
Where do you find – apart from, towering o'er
The secondary temporary aims
Which satisfy the gross taste you despise –
Where do you find his star? – his crazy trust
God knows through what or in what? it's alive
And shines and leads him, and that's all we want.
Have we aught in our sober night shall point
Such ends as his were, and direct the means
450   Of working out our purpose straight as his,
Nor bring a moment's trouble on success
With after-care to justify the same?

– Be a Napoleon, and yet disbelieve –
Why, the man's mad, friend, take his light away!
What's the vague good o' the world, for which you dare
With comfort to yourself blow millions up?
We neither of us see it! we do see
The blown-up millions – spatter of their brains
And writhing of their bowels and so forth,
460 In that bewildering entanglement
Of horrible eventualities
Past calculation to the end of time!
Can I mistake for some clear word of God
(Which were my ample warrant for it all)
His puff of hazy instinct, idle talk,
'The State, that's I,' quack-nonsense about crowns,
And (when one beats the man to his last hold)
A vague idea of setting things to rights,
Policing people efficaciously,
470 More to their profit, most of all to his own;
The whole to end that dismallest of ends
By an Austrian marriage, cant to us the Church,
And resurrection of the old *régime*?
Would I, who hope to live a dozen years,
Fight Austerlitz for reasons such and such?
No: for, concede me but the merest chance
Doubt may be wrong – there's judgement, life to come!
With just that chance, I dare not. Doubt proves right?
This present life is all? – you offer me
480 Its dozen noisy years, without a chance
That wedding an archduchess, wearing lace,
And getting called by divers new-coined names,
Will drive off ugly thoughts and let me dine,
Sleep, read and chat in quiet as I like!
Therefore I will not.

           Take another case;
Fit up the cabin yet another way.
What say you to the poets? shall we write
Hamlet, Othello – make the world our own,
Without a risk to run of either sort?
490 I can't! – to put the strongest reason first.
'But try,' you urge, 'the trying shall suffice;
The aim, if reached or not, makes great the life:

Try to be Shakespeare, leave the rest to fate!'
Spare my self-knowledge – there's no fooling me!
If I prefer remaining my poor self,
I say so not in self-dispraise but praise.
If I'm a Shakespeare, let the well alone;
Why should I try to be what now I am?
If I'm no Shakespeare, as too probable, –
500 His power and consciousness and self-delight
And all we want in common, shall I find –
Trying for ever? while on points of taste
Wherewith, to speak it humbly, he and I
Are dowered alike – I'll ask you, I or he,
Which in our two lives realizes most?
Much, he imagined – somewhat, I possess.
He had the imagination; stick to that!
Let him say, 'In the face of my soul's works
Your world is worthless and I touch it not
510 Lest I should wrong them' – I'll withdraw my plea.
But does he say so? look upon his life!
Himself, who only can, gives judgement there.
He leaves his towers and gorgeous palaces
To build the trimmest house in Stratford town;
Saves money, spends it, owns the worth of things,
Giulio Romano's pictures, Dowland's lute;
Enjoys a show, respects the puppets, too,
And none more, had he seen its entry once,
Than 'Pandulph, of fair Mílan cardinal.'
520 Why then should I who play that personage,
The very Pandulph Shakespeare's fancy made,
Be told that had the poet chanced to start
From where I stand now (some degree like mine
Being just the goal he ran his race to reach)
He would have run the whole race back, forsooth,
And left being Pandulph, to begin write plays?
Ah, the earth's best can be but the earth's best!
Did Shakespeare live, he could but sit at home
And get himself in dreams the Vatican,
530 Greek busts, Venetian paintings, Roman walls,
And English books, none equal to his own,
Which I read, bound in gold (he never did).
– Terni's fall, Naples' bay and Gothard's top –
Eh, friend? I could not fancy one of these;

But, as I pour this claret, there they are:
I've gained them – crossed Saint Gothard last July
With ten mules to the carriage and a bed
Slung inside; is my hap the worse for that?
We want the same things, Shakespeare and myself,
540 And what I want, I have: he, gifted more,
Could fancy he too had them when he liked,
But not so thoroughly that, if fate allowed,
He would not have them also in my sense.
We play one game; I send the ball aloft
No less adroitly that of fifty strokes
Scarce five go o'er the wall so wide and high
Which sends them back to me: I wish and get.
He struck balls higher and with better skill,
But at a poor fence level with his head,
550 And hit – his Stratford house, a coat of arms,
Successful dealings in his grain and wool, –
While I receive heaven's incense in my nose
And style myself the cousin of Queen Bess.
Ask him, if this life's all, who wins the game?

   Believe – and our whole argument breaks up.
Enthusiasm's the best thing, I repeat;
Only, we can't command it; fire and life
Are all, dead matter's nothing, we agree:
And be it a mad dream or God's very breath,
560 The fact's the same, – belief's fire, once in us,
Makes of all else mere stuff to show itself:
We penetrate our life with such a glow
As fire lends wood and iron – this turns steel,
That burns to ash – all's one, fire proves its power
For good or ill, since men call flare success.
But paint a fire, it will not therefore burn.
Light one in me, I'll find it food enough!
Why, to be Luther – that's a life to lead,
Incomparably better than my own.
570 He comes, reclaims God's earth for God, he says,
Sets up God's rule again by simple means,
Re-opens a shut book, and all is done.
He flared out in the flaring of mankind;
Such Luther's luck was: how shall such be mine?
If he succeeded, nothing's left to do:

And if he did not altogether – well,
Strauss is the next advance. All Strauss should be
I might be also. But to what result?
He looks upon no future: Luther did.
580 What can I gain on the denying side?
Ice makes no conflagration. State the facts,
Read the text right, emancipate the world –
The emancipated world enjoys itself
With scarce a thank-you: Blougram told it first
It could not owe a farthing, – not to him
More than Saint Paul! 'twould press its pay, you think?
Then add there's still that plaguy hundredth chance
Strauss may be wrong. And so a risk is run –
For what gain? not for Luther's, who secured
590 A real heaven in his heart throughout his life,
Supposing death a little altered things.

'Ay, but since really you lack faith,' you cry,
'You run the same risk really on all sides,
In cool indifference as bold unbelief.
As well be Strauss as swing 'twixt Paul and him.
It's not worth having, such imperfect faith,
No more available to do faith's work
Than unbelief like mine. Whole faith, or none!'

Softly, my friend! I must dispute that point.
600 Once own the use of faith, I'll find you faith.
We're back on Christian ground. You call for faith:
I show you doubt, to prove that faith exists.
The more of doubt, the stronger faith, I say,
If faith o'ercomes doubt. How I know it does?
By life and man's free will, God gave for that!
To mould life as we choose it, shows our choice:
That's our one act, the previous work's his own.
You criticize the soil? it reared this tree –
This broad life and whatever fruit it bears!
610 What matter though I doubt at every pore,
Head-doubts, heart-doubts, doubts at my fingers' ends,
Doubts in the trivial work of every day,
Doubts at the very bases of my soul
In the grand moments when she probes herself –
If finally I have a life to show,

The thing I did, brought out in evidence
Against the thing done to me underground
By hell and all its brood, for aught I know?
I say, whence sprang this? shows it faith or doubt?
620 All's doubt in me; where's break of faith in this?
It is the idea, the feeling and the love,
God means mankind should strive for and show forth
Whatever be the process to that end, –
And not historic knowledge, logic sound,
And metaphysical acumen, sure!
'What think ye of Christ,' friend? when all's done and said,
Like you this Christianity or not?
It may be false, but will you wish it true?
Has it your vote to be so if it can?
630 Trust you an instinct silenced long ago
That will break silence and enjoin you love
What mortified philosophy is hoarse,
And all in vain, with bidding you despise?
If you desire faith – then you've faith enough:
What else seeks God – nay, what else seek ourselves?
You form a notion of me, we'll suppose,
On hearsay; it's a favourable one:
'But still' (you add), 'there was no such good man,
Because of contradiction in the facts.
640 One proves, for instance, he was born in Rome,
This Blougram; yet throughout the tales of him
I see he figures as an Englishman.'
Well, the two things are reconcilable.
But would I rather you discovered that,
Subjoining – 'Still, what matter though they be?
Blougram concerns me naught, born here or there.'

Pure faith indeed – you know not what you ask!
Naked belief in God the Omnipotent,
Omniscient, Omnipresent, sears too much
650 The sense of conscious creatures to be borne.
It were the seeing him, no flesh shall dare.
Some think, Creation's meant to show him forth:
I say it's meant to hide him all it can,
And that's what all the blessèd evil's for.
Its use in Time is to environ us,
Our breath, our drop of dew, with shield enough

Against that sight till we can bear its stress.
Under a vertical sun, the exposed brain
And lidless eye and disimprisoned heart
660   Less certainly would wither up at once
Than mind, confronted with the truth of him.
But time and earth case-harden us to live;
The feeblest sense is trusted most; the child
Feels God a moment, ichors o'er the place,
Plays on and grows to be a man like us.
With me, faith means perpetual unbelief
Kept quiet like the snake 'neath Michael's foot
Who stands calm just because he feels it writhe.
Or, if that's too ambitious, – here's my box –
670   I need the excitation of a pinch
Threatening the torpor of the inside-nose
Nigh on the imminent sneeze that never comes.
'Leave it in peace' advise the simple folk:
Make it aware of peace by itching-fits,
Say I – let doubt occasion still more faith!

You'll say, once all believed, man, woman, child,
In that dear middle-age these noodles praise.
How you'd exult if I could put you back
Six hundred years, blot out cosmogony,
680   Geology, ethnology, what not,
(Greek endings, each the little passing-bell
That signifies some faith's about to die),
And set you square with Genesis again, –
When such a traveller told you his last news,
He saw the ark a-top of Ararat
But did not climb there since 'twas getting dusk
And robber-bands infest the mountain's foot!
How should you feel, I ask, in such an age,
How act? As other people felt and did;
690   With soul more blank than this decanter's knob,
Believe – and yet lie, kill, rob, fornicate
Full in belief's face, like the beast you'd be!

No, when the fight begins within himself,
A man's worth something. God stoops o'er his head,
Satan looks up between his feet – both tug –
He's left, himself, i' the middle: the soul wakes

And grows. Prolong that battle through his life!
Never leave growing till the life to come!
Here, we've got callous to the Virgin's winks
700 That used to puzzle people wholesomely:
Men have outgrown the shame of being fools.
What are the laws of nature, not to bend
If the Church bid them? – brother Newman asks.
Up with the Immaculate Conception, then –
On to the rack with faith! – is my advice.
Will not that hurry us upon our knees,
Knocking our breasts, 'It can't be – yet it shall!
Who am I, the worm, to argue with my Pope?
Low things confound the high things!' and so forth.
710 That's better than acquitting God with grace
As some folk do. He's tried – no case is proved,
Philosophy is lenient – he may go!

You'll say, the old system's not so obsolete
But men believe still: ay, but who and where?
King Bomba's lazzaroni foster yet
The sacred flame, so Antonelli writes;
But even of these, what ragamuffin saint
Believes God watches him continually,
As he believes in fire that it will burn,
720 Or rain that it will drench him? Break fire's law,
Sin against rain, although the penalty
Be just a singe or soaking? 'No,' he smiles;
'Those laws are laws that can enforce themselves.'

The sum of all is – yes, my doubt is great,
My faith's still greater, then my faith's enough.
I have read much, thought much, experienced much,
Yet would die rather than avow my fear
The Naples' liquefaction may be false,
When set to happen by the palace-clock
730 According to the clouds or dinner-time.
I hear you recommend, I might at least
Eliminate, decrassify my faith
Since I adopt it; keeping what I must
And leaving what I can – such points as this.
I won't – that is, I can't throw one away.
Supposing there's no truth in what I hold

About the need of trial to man's faith,
Still, when you bid me purify the same,
To such a process I discern no end.
740 Clearing off one excrescence to see two,
There's ever a next in size, now grown as big,
That meets the knife: I cut and cut again!
First cut the Liquefaction, what comes last
But Fichte's clever cut at God himself?
Experimentalize on sacred things!
I trust nor hand nor eye nor heart nor brain
To stop betimes: they all get drunk alike.
The first step, I am master not to take.

You'd find the cutting-process to your taste
750 As much as leaving growths of lies unpruned,
Nor see more danger in it, – you retort.
Your taste's worth mine; but my taste proves more wise
When we consider that the steadfast hold
On the extreme end of the chain of faith
Gives all the advantage, makes the difference
With the rough purblind mass we seek to rule:
We are their lords, or they are free of us,
Just as we tighten or relax our hold.
So, other matters equal, we'll revert
760 To the first problem – which, if solved my way
And thrown into the balance, turns the scale –
How we may lead a comfortable life,
How suit our luggage to the cabin's size.

Of course you are remarking all this time
How narrowly and grossly I view life,
Respect the creature-comforts, care to rule
The masses, and regard complacently
'The cabin,' in our old phrase. Well, I do.
I act for, talk for, live for this world now,
770 As this world prizes action, life and talk:
No prejudice to what next world may prove,
Whose new laws and requirements, my best pledge
To observe then, is that I observe these now,
Shall do hereafter what I do meanwhile.
Let us concede (gratuitously though)
Next life relieves the soul of body, yields

Pure spiritual enjoyment: well, my friend,
Why lose this life i' the meantime, since its use
May be to make the next life more intense?

780   Do you know, I have often had a dream
(Work it up in your next month's article)
Of man's poor spirit in its progress, still
Losing true life for ever and a day
Through ever trying to be and ever being –
In the evolution of successive spheres –
Before its actual sphere and place of life,
Halfway into the next, which having reached,
It shoots with corresponding foolery
Halfway into the next still, on and off!
790   As when a traveller, bound from North to South,
Scouts fur in Russia: what's its use in France?
In France spurns flannel: where's its need in Spain?
In Spain drops cloth, too cumbrous for Algiers!
Linen goes next, and last the skin itself,
A superfluity at Timbuctoo.
When, through his journey, was the fool at ease?
I'm at ease now, friend; worldly in this world,
I take and like its way of life; I think
My brothers, who administer the means,
800   Live better for my comfort – that's good too;
And God, if he pronounce upon such life,
Approves my service, which is better still.
If he keep silence, – why, for you or me
Or that brute beast pulled-up in today's 'Times,'
What odds is't, save to ourselves, what life we lead?

You meet me at this issue: you declare, –
All special-pleading done with – truth is truth,
And justifies itself by undreamed ways.
You don't fear but it's better, if we doubt,
810   To say so, act up to our truth perceived
However feebly. Do then, – act away!
'Tis there I'm on the watch for you. How one acts
Is, both of us agree, our chief concern:
And how you'll act is what I fain would see
If, like the candid person you appear,
You dare to make the most of your life's scheme

As I of mine, live up to its full law
Since there's no higher law that counterchecks.
Put natural religion to the test
820 You've just demolished the revealed with – quick,
Down to the root of all that checks your will,
All prohibition to lie, kill and thieve,
Or even to be an atheistic priest!
Suppose a pricking to incontinence –
Philosophers deduce you chastity
Or shame, from just the fact that at the first
Whoso embraced a woman in the field,
Threw club down and forewent his brains beside,
So, stood a ready victim in the reach
830 Of any brother savage, club in hand;
Hence saw the use of going out of sight
In wood or cave to prosecute his loves:
I read this in a French book t'other day.
Does law so analysed coerce you much?
Oh, men spin clouds of fuzz where matters end,
But you who reach where the first thread begins,
You'll soon cut that! – which means you can, but won't,
Through certain instincts, blind, unreasoned-out,
You dare not set aside, you can't tell why,
840 But there they are, and so you let them rule.
Then, friend, you seem as much a slave as I,
A liar, conscious coward and hypocrite,
Without the good the slave expects to get,
In case he has a master after all!
You own your instincts? why, what else do I,
Who want, am made for, and must have a God
Ere I can be aught, do aught? – no mere name
Want, but the true thing with what proves its truth,
To wit, a relation from that thing to me,
850 Touching from head to foot – which touch I feel,
And with it take the rest, this life of ours!
I live my life here; yours you dare not live.

– Not as I state it, who (you please subjoin)
Disfigure such a life and call it names,
While, to your mind, remains another way
For simple men: knowledge and power have rights,
But ignorance and weakness have rights too.

There needs no crucial effort to find truth
If here or there or anywhere about:
860 We ought to turn each side, try hard and see,
And if we can't, be glad we've earned at least
The right, by one laborious proof the more,
To graze in peace earth's pleasant pasturage.
Men are not angels, neither are they brutes:
Something we may see, all we cannot see.
What need of lying? I say, I see all,
And swear to each detail the most minute
In what I think a Pan's face – you, mere cloud:
I swear I hear him speak and see him wink,
870 For fear, if once I drop the emphasis,
Mankind may doubt there's any cloud at all.
You take the simple life – ready to see,
Willing to see (for no cloud's worth a face) –
And leaving quiet what no strength can move,
And which, who bids you move? who has the right?
I bid you; but you are God's sheep, not mine:
'*Pastor est tui Dominus.*' You find
In this the pleasant pasture of our life
Much you may eat without the least offence,
880 Much you don't eat because your maw objects,
Much you would eat but that your fellow-flock
Open great eyes at you and even butt,
And thereupon you like your mates so well
You cannot please yourself, offending them;
Though when they seem exorbitantly sheep,
You weigh your pleasure with their butts and bleats
And strike the balance. Sometimes certain fears
Restrain you, real checks since you find them so;
Sometimes you please yourself and nothing checks:
890 And thus you graze through life with not one lie,
And like it best.

> But do you, in truth's name?
If so, you beat – which means you are not I –
Who needs must make earth mine and feed my fill
Not simply unbutted at, unbickered with,
But motioned to the velvet of the sward
By those obsequious wethers' very selves.
Look at me, sir; my age is double yours:

At yours, I knew beforehand, so enjoyed,
What now I should be – as, permit the word,
900   I pretty well imagine your whole range
And stretch of tether twenty years to come.
We both have minds and bodies much alike:
In truth's name, don't you want my bishopric,
My daily bread, my influence and my state?
You're young. I'm old; you must be old one day;
Will you find then, as I do hour by hour,
Women their lovers kneel to, who cut curls
From your fat lap-dog's ear to grace a brooch –
Dukes, who petition just to kiss your ring –
910   With much beside you know or may conceive?
Suppose we die tonight: well, here am I,
Such were my gains, life bore this fruit to me,
While writing all the same my articles
On music, poetry, the fictile vase
Found at Albano, chess, Anacreon's Greek.
But you – the highest honour in your life,
The thing you'll crown yourself with, all your days,
Is – dining here and drinking this last glass
I pour you out in sign of amity
920   Before we part for ever. Of your power
And social influence, worldly worth in short,
Judge what's my estimation by the fact,
I do not condescend to enjoin, beseech,
Hint secrecy on one of all these words!
You're shrewd and know that should you publish one
The world would brand the lie – my enemies first,
Who'd sneer – 'the bishop's an arch-hypocrite
And knave perhaps, but not so frank a fool.'
Whereas I should not dare for both my ears
930   Breathe one such syllable, smile one such smile,
Before the chaplain who reflects myself –
My shade's so much more potent than your flesh.
What's your reward, self-abnegating friend?
Stood you confessed of those exceptional
And privileged great natures that dwarf mine –
A zealot with a mad ideal in reach,
A poet just about to print his ode,
A statesman with a scheme to stop this war,
An artist whose religion is his art –

940 I should have nothing to object: such men
Carry the fire, all things grow warm to them,
Their drugget's worth my purple, they beat me.
But you, – you're just as little those as I –
You, Gigadibs, who, thirty years of age,
Write stately for Blackwood's Magazine,
Believe you see two points in Hamlet's soul
Unseized by the Germans yet – which view you'll print –
Meantime the best you have to show being still
That lively lightsome article we took

950 Almost for the true Dickens, – what's its name?
'The Slum and Cellar, or Whitechapel life
Limned after dark!' it made me laugh, I know,
And pleased a month, and brought you in ten pounds.
– Success I recognize and compliment,
And therefore give you, if you choose, three words
(The card and pencil-scratch is quite enough)
Which whether here, in Dublin or New York,
Will get you, prompt as at my eyebrow's wink,
Such terms as never you aspired to get

960 In all our own reviews and some not ours.
Go write your lively sketches! be the first
'Blougram, or The Eccentric Confidence' –
Or better simply say, 'The Outward-bound.'
Why, men as soon would throw it in my teeth
As copy and quote the infamy chalked broad
About me on the church-door opposite.
You will not wait for that experience though,
I fancy, howsoever you decide,
To discontinue – not detesting, not

970 Defaming, but at least – despising me!

Over his wine so smiled and talked his hour
Sylvester Blougram, styled *in partibus*
Episcopus, nec non – (the deuce knows what
It's changed to by our novel hierarchy)
With Gigadibs the literary man,
Who played with spoons, explored his plate's design,
And ranged the olive-stones about its edge,
While the great bishop rolled him out a mind
Long crumpled, till creased consciousness lay smooth.

980 For Blougram, he believed, say, half he spoke.
The other portion, as he shaped it thus
For argumentatory purposes,
He felt his foe was foolish to dispute.
Some arbitrary accidental thoughts
That crossed his mind, amusing because new,
He chose to represent as fixtures there,
Invariable convictions (such they seemed
Beside his interlocutor's loose cards
Flung daily down, and not the same way twice)
990 While certain hell-deep instincts, man's weak tongue
Is never bold to utter in their truth
Because styled hell-deep ('tis an old mistake
To place hell at the bottom of the earth)
He ignored these, – not having in readiness
Their nomenclature and philosophy:
He said true things, but called them by wrong names.
'On the whole,' he thought, 'I justify myself
On every point where cavillers like this
Oppugn my life: he tries one kind of fence,
1000 I close, he's worsted, that's enough for him.
He's on the ground: if ground should break away
I take my stand on, there's a firmer yet
Beneath it, both of us may sink and reach.
His ground was over mine and broke the first:
So, let him sit with me this many a year!'

He did not sit five minutes. Just a week
Sufficed his sudden healthy vehemence.
Something had struck him in the 'Outward-bound'
Another way than Blougram's purpose was:
1010 And having bought, not cabin-furniture
But settler's-implements (enough for three)
And started for Australia – there, I hope,
By this time he has tested his first plough,
And studied his last chapter of Saint John.

Memorabilia

I

Ah, did you once see Shelley plain,
  And did he stop and speak to you
And did you speak to him again?
  How strange it seems and new!

II

But you were living before that,
  And also you are living after;
And the memory I started at –
  My starting moves your laughter.

III

I crossed a moor, with a name of its own
10   And a certain use in the world no doubt,
Yet a hand's-breadth of it shines alone
  'Mid the blank miles round about:

IV

For there I picked up on the heather
  And there I put inside my breast
A moulted feather, an eagle-feather!
  Well, I forget the rest.

Andrea del Sarto

(Called 'The Faultless Painter')

But do not let us quarrel any more,
No, my Lucrezia; bear with me for once:
Sit down and all shall happen as you wish.
You turn your face, but does it bring your heart?
I'll work then for your friend's friend, never fear,
Treat his own subject after his own way,
Fix his own time, accept too his own price,
And shut the money into this small hand
When next it takes mine. Will it? tenderly?

10 Oh, I'll content him, – but tomorrow, Love!
  I often am much wearier than you think,
  This evening more than usual, and it seems
  As if – forgive now – should you let me sit
  Here by the window with your hand in mine
  And look a half-hour forth on Fiesole,
  Both of one mind, as married people use,
  Quietly, quietly the evening through,
  I might get up tomorrow to my work
  Cheerful and fresh as ever. Let us try.
20 Tomorrow, how you shall be glad for this!
  Your soft hand is a woman of itself,
  And mine the man's bared breast she curls inside.
  Don't count the time lost, neither; you must serve
  For each of the five pictures we require:
  It saves a model. So! keep looking so –
  My serpentining beauty, rounds on rounds!
  – How could you ever prick those perfect ears,
  Even to put the pearl there! oh, so sweet –
  My face, my moon, my everybody's moon,
30 Which everybody looks on and calls his,
  And, I suppose, is looked on by in turn,
  While she looks – no one's: very dear, no less.
  You smile? why, there's my picture ready made,
  There's what we painters call our harmony!
  A common greyness silvers everything, –
  All in a twilight, you and I alike
  – You, at the point of your first pride in me
  (That's gone you know), – but I, at every point;
  My youth, my hope, my art, being all toned down
40 To yonder sober pleasant Fiesole.
  There's the bell clinking from the chapel-top;
  That length of convent-wall across the way
  Holds the trees safer, huddled more inside;
  The last monk leaves the garden; days decrease,
  And autumn grows, autumn in everything.
  Eh? the whole seems to fall into a shape
  As if I saw alike my work and self
  And all that I was born to be and do,
  A twilight-piece. Love, we are in God's hand.
50 How strange now, looks the life he makes us lead;
  So free we seem, so fettered fast we are!

I feel he laid the fetter: let it lie!
This chamber for example – turn your head –
All that's behind us! You don't understand
Nor care to understand about my art,
But you can hear at least when people speak:
And that cartoon, the second from the door
– It is the thing, Love! so such things should be –
Behold Madonna! – I am bold to say.

60 I can do with my pencil what I know,
What I see, what at bottom of my heart
I wish for, if I ever wish so deep –
Do easily, too – when I say, perfectly,
I do not boast, perhaps: yourself are judge,
Who listened to the Legate's talk last week,
And just as much they used to say in France.
At any rate 'tis easy, all of it!
No sketches first, no studies, that's long past:
I do what many dream of, all their lives,

70 – Dream? strive to do, and agonize to do,
And fail in doing. I could count twenty such
On twice your fingers, and not leave this town,
Who strive – you don't know how the others strive
To paint a little thing like that you smeared
Carelessly passing with your robes afloat, –
Yet do much less, so much less, Someone says,
(I know his name, no matter) – so much less!
Well, less is more, Lucrezia: I am judged.
There burns a truer light of God in them,

80 In their vexed beating stuffed and stopped-up brain,
Heart, or whate'er else, than goes on to prompt
This low-pulsed forthright craftsman's hand of mine.
Their works drop groundward, but themselves, I know,
Reach many a time a heaven that's shut to me,
Enter and take their place there sure enough,
Though they come back and cannot tell the world.
My works are nearer heaven, but I sit here.
The sudden blood of these men! at a word –
Praise them, it boils, or blame them, it boils too.

90 I, painting from myself and to myself,
Know what I do, am unmoved by men's blame
Or their praise either. Somebody remarks
Morello's outline there is wrongly traced,

His hue mistaken; what of that? or else,
Rightly traced and well ordered; what of that?
Speak as they please, what does the mountain care?
Ah, but a man's reach should exceed his grasp,
Or what's a heaven for? All is silver-grey
Placid and perfect with my art: the worse!
100 I know both what I want and what might gain,
And yet how profitless to know, to sigh
'Had I been two, another and myself,
Our head would have o'erlooked the world!' No doubt.
Yonder's a work now, of that famous youth
The Urbinate who died five years ago.
('Tis copied, George Vasari sent it me.)
Well, I can fancy how he did it all,
Pouring his soul, with kings and popes to see,
Reaching, that heaven might so replenish him,
110 Above and through his art – for it gives way;
That arm is wrongly put – and there again –
A fault to pardon in the drawing's lines,
Its body, so to speak: its soul is right,
He means right – that, a child may understand.
Still, what an arm! and I could alter it:
But all the play, the insight and the stretch –
Out of me, out of me! And wherefore out?
Had you enjoined them on me, given me soul,
We might have risen to Rafael, I and you!
120 Nay, Love, you did give all I asked, I think –
More than I merit, yes, by many times.
But had you – oh, with the same perfect brow,
And perfect eyes, and more than perfect mouth,
And the low voice my soul hears, as a bird
The fowler's pipe, and follows to the snare –
Had you, with these the same, but brought a mind!
Some women do so. Had the mouth there urged
'God and the glory! never care for gain.
The present by the future, what is that?
130 Live for fame, side by side with Agnolo!
Rafael is waiting: up to God, all three!'
I might have done it for you. So it seems:
Perhaps not. All is as God over-rules.
Beside, incentives come from the soul's self;
The rest avail not. Why do I need you?

What wife had Rafael, or has Agnolo?
In this world, who can do a thing, will not;
And who would do it, cannot, I perceive:
Yet the will's somewhat – somewhat, too, the power –
140 And thus we half-men struggle. At the end,
God, I conclude, compensates, punishes.
'Tis safer for me, if the award be strict,
That I am something underrated here,
Poor this long while, despised, to speak the truth.
I dared not, do you know, leave home all day,
For fear of chancing on the Paris lords.
The best is when they pass and look aside;
But they speak sometimes; I must bear it all.
Well may they speak! That Francis, that first time,
150 And that long festal year at Fontainebleau!
I surely then could sometimes leave the ground,
Put on the glory, Rafael's daily wear,
In that humane great monarch's golden look, –
One finger in his beard or twisted curl
Over his mouth's good mark that made the smile,
One arm about my shoulder, round my neck,
The jingle of his gold chain in my ear,
I painting proudly with his breath on me,
All his court round him, seeing with his eyes,
160 Such frank French eyes, and such a fire of souls
Profuse, my hand kept plying by those hearts, –
And, best of all, this, this, this face beyond,
This in the background, waiting on my work,
To crown the issue with a last reward!
A good time, was it not, my kingly days?
And had you not grown restless . . . but I know –
'Tis done and past; 'twas right, my instinct said;
Too live the life grew, golden and not grey,
And I'm the weak-eyed bat no sun should tempt
170 Out of the grange whose four walls make his world.
How could it end in any other way?
You called me, and I came home to your heart.
The triumph was – to reach and stay there; since
I reached it ere the triumph, what is lost?
Let my hands frame your face in your hair's gold,
You beautiful Lucrezia that are mine!
'Rafael did this, Andrea painted that;

The Roman's is the better when you pray,
But still the other's Virgin was his wife –'
180 Men will excuse me. I am glad to judge
Both pictures in your presence; clearer grows
My better fortune, I resolve to think.
For, do you know, Lucrezia, as God lives,
Said one day Agnolo, his very self,
To Rafael . . . I have known it all these years . . .
(When the young man was flaming out his thoughts
Upon a palace-wall for Rome to see,
Too lifted up in heart because of it)
'Friend, there's a certain sorry little scrub
190 Goes up and down our Florence, none cares how,
Who, were he set to plan and execute
As you are, pricked on by your popes and kings,
Would bring the sweat into that brow of yours!'
To Rafael's! – And indeed the arm is wrong.
I hardly dare . . . yet, only you to see,
Give the chalk here – quick, thus the line should go!
Ay, but the soul! he's Rafael! rub it out!
Still, all I care for, if he spoke the truth,
(What he? why, who but Michel Agnolo?
200 Do you forget already words like those?)
If really there was such a chance, so lost, –
Is, whether you're – not grateful – but more pleased.
Well, let me think so. And you smile indeed!
This hour has been an hour! Another smile?
If you would sit thus by me every night
I should work better, do you comprehend?
I mean that I should earn more, give you more.
See, it is settled dusk now; there's a star;
Morello's gone, the watch-lights show the wall,
210 The cue-owls speak the name we call them by.
Come from the window, love, – come in, at last,
Inside the melancholy little house
We built to be so gay with. God is just.
King Francis may forgive me: oft at nights
When I look up from painting, eyes tired out,
The walls become illumined, brick from brick
Distinct, instead of mortar, fierce bright gold,
That gold of his I did cement them with!
Let us but love each other. Must you go?

220 That Cousin here again? he waits outside?
Must see you – you, and not with me? Those loans?
More gaming debts to pay? you smiled for that?
Well, let smiles buy me! have you more to spend?
While hand and eye and something of a heart
Are left me, work's my ware, and what's it worth?
I'll pay my fancy. Only let me sit
The grey remainder of the evening out,
Idle, you call it, and muse perfectly
How I could paint, were I but back in France,
230 One picture, just one more – the Virgin's face,
Not yours this time! I want you at my side
To hear them – that is, Michel Agnolo –
Judge all I do and tell you of its worth.
Will you? Tomorrow, satisfy your friend.
I take the subjects for his corridor,
Finish the portrait out of hand – there, there,
And throw him in another thing or two
If he demurs; the whole should prove enough
To pay for this same Cousin's freak. Beside,
240 What's better and what's all I care about,
Get you the thirteen scudi for the ruff!
Love, does that please you? Ah, but what does he,
The Cousin! what does he to please you more?

I am grown peaceful as old age tonight.
I regret little, I would change still less.
Since there my past life lies, why alter it?
The very wrong to Francis! – it is true
I took his coin, was tempted and complied,
And built this house and sinned, and all is said.
250 My father and my mother died of want.
Well, had I riches of my own? you see
How one gets rich! Let each one bear his lot.
They were born poor, lived poor, and poor they died:
And I have laboured somewhat in my time
And not been paid profusely. Some good son
Paint my two hundred pictures – let him try!
No doubt, there's something strikes a balance. Yes,
You loved me quite enough, it seems tonight.
This must suffice me here. What would one have?
260 In heaven, perhaps, new chances, one more chance –

Four great walls in the New Jerusalem,
Meted on each side by the angel's reed,
For Leonard, Rafael, Agnolo and me
To cover – the three first without a wife,
While I have mine! So – still they overcome
Because there's still Lucrezia, – as I choose.

Again the Cousin's whistle! Go, my Love.

Before

I

Let them fight it out, friend! things have gone too far.
God must judge the couple: leave them as they are
– Whichever one's the guiltless, to his glory,
And whichever one the guilt's with, to my story!

II

Why, you would not bid men, sunk in such a slough,
Strike no arm out further, stick and stink as now,
Leaving right and wrong to settle the embroilment,
Heaven with snaky hell, in torture and entoilment?

III

Who's the culprit of them? How must he conceive
10   God – the queen he caps to, laughing in his sleeve,
''Tis but decent to profess oneself beneath her:
Still, one must not be too much in earnest, either!'

IV

Better sin the whole sin, sure that God observes;
Then go live his life out! Life will try his nerves,
When the sky, which noticed all, makes no disclosure,
And the earth keeps up her terrible composure.

V

Let him pace at pleasure, past the walls of rose,
Pluck their fruits when grape-trees graze him as he goes!
For he 'gins to guess the purpose of the garden,
20   With the sly mute thing, beside there, for a warden.

VI

What's the leopard-dog-thing, constant at his side,
A leer and lie in every eye of its obsequious hide?
When will come an end to all the mock obeisance,
And the price appear that pays for the misfeasance?

VII

So much for the culprit. Who's the martyred man?
Let him bear one stroke more, for be sure he can!
He that strove thus evil's lump with good to leaven,
Let him give his blood at last and get his heaven!

VIII

All or nothing, stake it! Trusts he God or no?
30 Thus far and no farther? farther? be it so!
Now, enough of your chicane of prudent pauses,
Sage provisos, sub-intents and saving-clauses!

IX

Ah, 'forgive' you bid him? While God's champion lives,
Wrong shall be resisted: dead, why, he forgives.
But you must not end my friend ere you begin him;
Evil stands not crowned on earth, while breath is in him.

X

Once more – Will the wronger, at this last of all,
Dare to say, 'I did wrong,' rising in his fall?
No? – Let go, then! Both the fighters to their places!
40 While I count three, step you back as many paces!

After

Take the cloak from his face, and at first
    Let the corpse do its worst!

How he lies in his rights of a man!
    Death has done all death can.
And, absorbed in the new life he leads,
    He recks not, he heeds

Nor his wrong nor my vengeance; both strike
  On his senses alike,
And are lost in the solemn and strange
10 Surprise of the change.

Ha, what avails death to erase
  His offence, my disgrace?
I would we were boys as of old
  In the field, by the fold:
His outrage, God's patience, man's scorn
  Were so easily borne!

I stand here now, he lies in his place:
  Cover the face!

In Three Days

I

So, I shall see her in three days
And just one night, but nights are short,
Then two long hours, and that is morn.
See how I come, unchanged, unworn!
Feel, where my life broke off from thine,
How fresh the splinters keep and fine, –
Only a touch and we combine!

II

Too long, this time of year, the days!
But nights, at least the nights are short.
10 As night shows where her one moon is,
A hand's-breadth of pure light and bliss,
So life's night gives my lady birth
And my eyes hold her! What is worth
The rest of heaven, the rest of earth?

III

O loaded curls, release your store
Of warmth and scent, as once before
The tingling hair did, lights and darks
Outbreaking into fairy sparks,

When under curl and curl I pried
After the warmth and scent inside,
Through lights and darks how manifold –
20 The dark inspired, the light controlled!
As early Art embrowns the gold.

IV
What great fear, should one say, 'Three days
That change the world might change as well
Your fortune; and if joy delays,
Be happy that no worse befell!'
What small fear, if another says,
'Three days and one short night beside
May throw no shadow on your ways;
But years must teem with change untried,
30 With chance not easily defied,
With an end somewhere undescried.'
No fear! – or if a fear be born
This minute, it dies out in scorn.
Fear? I shall see her in three days
And one night, now the nights are short,
Then just two hours, and that is morn.

In a Year

I
Never any more,
    While I live,
Need I hope to see his face
    As before.
Once his love grown chill,
    Mine may strive:
Bitterly we re-embrace,
    Single still.

II
Was it something said,
10   Something done,
Vexed him? was it touch of hand,
    Turn of head?

Strange! that very way
   Love begun:
I as little understand
   Love's decay.

III

When I sewed or drew,
   I recall
How he looked as if I sung,
20   – Sweetly too.
If I spoke a word,
   First of all
Up his cheek the colour sprung,
   Then he heard.

IV

Sitting by my side,
   At my feet,
So he breathed but air I breathed,
   Satisfied!
I, too, at love's brim
30   Touched the sweet:
I would die if death bequeathed
   Sweet to him.

V

'Speak, I love thee best!'
   He exclaimed:
'Let thy love my own foretell!'
   I confessed:
'Clasp my heart on thine
   Now unblamed,
Since upon thy soul as well
40   Hangeth mine!'

VI

Was it wrong to own,
   Being truth?
Why should all the giving prove
   His alone?
I had wealth and ease,
   Beauty, youth:

Since my lover gave me love,
   I gave these.

VII

That was all I meant,
50   – To be just,
And the passion I had raised,
   To content.
Since he chose to change
   Gold for dust,
If I gave him what he praised
   Was it strange?

VIII

Would he loved me yet,
   On and on,
While I found some way undreamed
60   – Paid my debt!
Gave more life and more,
   Till, all gone,
He should smile 'She never seemed
   Mine before.

IX

'What, she felt the while,
   Must I think?
Love's so different with us men!'
   He should smile:
'Dying for my sake –
70   White and pink!
Can't we touch these bubbles then
   But they break?'

X

Dear, the pang is brief,
   Do thy part,
Have thy pleasure! How perplexed
   Grows belief!
Well, this cold clay clod
   Was man's heart:
Crumble it, and what comes next?
80   Is it God?

Old Pictures in Florence

I

The morn when first it thunders in March,
    The eel in the pond gives a leap, they say:
As I leaned and looked over the aloed arch
    Of the villa-gate this warm March day,
No flash snapped, no dumb thunder rolled
    In the valley beneath where, white and wide
And washed by the morning water gold,
    Florence lay out on the mountain-side.

II

River and bridge and street and square
10   Lay mine, as much at my beck and call,
Through the live translucent bath of air,
    As the sights in a magic crystal ball.
And of all I saw and of all I praised,
    The most to praise and the best to see
Was the startling bell-tower Giotto raised:
    But why did it more than startle me?

III

Giotto, how, with that soul of yours,
    Could you play me false who loved you so?
Some slights if a certain heart endures
20   Yet it feels, I would have your fellows know!
I' faith, I perceive not why I should care
    To break a silence that suits them best,
But the thing grows somewhat hard to bear
    When I find a Giotto join the rest.

IV

On the arch where olives overhead
    Print the blue sky with twig and leaf,
(That sharp-curled leaf which they never shed)
    'Twixt the aloes, I used to lean in chief,
And mark through the winter afternoons,
30   By a gift God grants me now and then,
In the mild decline of those suns like moons,
    Who walked in Florence, besides her men.

V

They might chirp and chaffer, come and go
    For pleasure or profit, her men alive –
My business was hardly with them, I trow,
    But with empty cells of the human hive;
– With the chapter-room, the cloister-porch,
    The church's apsis, aisle or nave,
Its crypt, one fingers along with a torch,
40   Its face set full for the sun to shave.

VI

Wherever a fresco peels and drops,
    Wherever an outline weakens and wanes
Till the latest life in the painting stops,
    Stands One whom each fainter pulse-tick pains:
One, wishful each scrap should clutch the brick,
    Each tinge not wholly escape the plaster,
– A lion who dies of an ass's kick,
    The wronged great soul of an ancient Master.

VII

For oh, this world and the wrong it does!
50   They are safe in heaven with their backs to it,
The Michaels and Rafaels, you hum and buzz
    Round the works of, you of the little wit!
Do their eyes contract to the earth's old scope,
    Now that they see God face to face,
And have all attained to be poets, I hope?
    'Tis their holiday now, in any case.

VIII

Much they reck of your praise and you!
    But the wronged great souls – can they be quit
Of a world where their work is all to do,
60   Where you style them, you of the little wit,
Old Master This and Early the Other,
    Not dreaming that Old and New are fellows:
A younger succeeds to an elder brother,
    Da Vincis derive in good time from Dellos.

IX

And here where your praise might yield returns,
 And a handsome word or two give help,
Here, after your kind, the mastiff girns
 And the puppy pack of poodles yelp.
What, not a word for Stefano there,
70 Of brow once prominent and starry,
Called Nature's Ape and the world's despair
 For his peerless painting? (See Vasari.)

X

There stands the Master. Study, my friends,
 What a man's work comes to! So he plans it,
Performs it, perfects it, makes amends
 For the toiling and moiling, and then, *sic transit!*
Happier the thrifty blind-folk labour,
 With upturned eye while the hand is busy,
Not sidling a glance at the coin of their neighbour!
80 'Tis looking downward that makes one dizzy.

XI

'If you knew their work you would deal your dole.'
 May I take upon me to instruct you?
When Greek Art ran and reached the goal,
 Thus much had the world to boast *in fructu* –
The Truth of Man, as by God first spoken,
 Which the actual generations garble,
Was re-uttered, and Soul (which Limbs betoken)
 And Limbs (Soul informs) made new in marble.

XII

So, you saw yourself as you wished you were,
90 As you might have been, as you cannot be;
Earth here, rebuked by Olympus there:
 And grew content in your poor degree
With your little power, by those statues' godhead,
 And your little scope, by their eyes' full sway,
And your little grace, by their grace embodied,
 And your little date, by their forms that stay.

XIII

You would fain be kinglier, say, than I am?
　Even so, you will not sit like Theseus.
You would prove a model? The Son of Priam
100　Has yet the advantage in arms' and knees' use.
You're wroth – can you slay your snake like Apollo?
　You're grieved – still Niobe's the grander!
You live – there's the Racers' frieze to follow:
　You die – there's the dying Alexander.

XIV

So, testing your weakness by their strength,
　Your meagre charms by their rounded beauty,
Measured by Art in your breadth and length,
　You learned – to submit is a mortal's duty.
– When I say 'you' 'tis the common soul,
110　The collective, I mean: the race of Man
That receives life in parts to live in a whole,
　And grow here according to God's clear plan.

XV

Growth came when, looking your last on them all,
　You turned your eyes inwardly one fine day
And cried with a start – What if we so small
　Be greater and grander the while than they?
Are they perfect of lineament, perfect of stature?
　In both, of such lower types are we
Precisely because of our wider nature;
120　For time, theirs – ours, for eternity.

XVI

Today's brief passion limits their range;
　It seethes with the morrow for us and more.
They are perfect – how else? they shall never change:
　We are faulty – why not? we have time in store.
The Artificer's hand is not arrested
　With us; we are rough-hewn, nowise polished:
They stand for our copy, and, once invested
　With all they can teach, we shall see them abolished.

XVII

'Tis a life-long toil till our lump be leaven –
130   The better! What's come to perfection perishes.
Things learned on earth, we shall practise in heaven:
    Works done least rapidly, Art most cherishes.
Thyself shalt afford the example, Giotto!
    Thy one work, not to decrease or diminish,
Done at a stroke, was just (was it not?) 'O!'
    Thy great Campanile is still to finish.

XVIII

Is it true that we are now, and shall be hereafter,
    But what and where depend on life's minute?
Hails heavenly cheer or infernal laughter
140   Our first step out of the gulf or in it?
Shall Man, such step within his endeavour,
    Man's face, have no more play and action
Than joy which is crystallized for ever,
    Or grief, an eternal petrifaction?

XIX

On which I conclude, that the early painters,
    To cries of 'Greek Art and what more wish you?' –
Replied, 'To become now self-acquainters,
    And paint man man, whatever the issue!
Make new hopes shine through the flesh they fray,
150   New fears aggrandize the rags and tatters:
To bring the invisible full into play!
    Let the visible go to the dogs – what matters?'

XX

Give these, I exhort you, their guerdon and glory
    For daring so much, before they well did it.
The first of the new, in our race's story,
    Beats the last of the old; 'tis no idle quiddit.
The worthies began a revolution,
    Which if on earth you intend to acknowledge,
Why, honour them now! (ends my allocution)
160   Nor confer your degree when the folk leave college.

XXI

There's a fancy some lean to and others hate –
　That, when this life is ended, begins
New work for the soul in another state,
　Where it strives and gets weary, loses and wins:
Where the strong and the weak, this world's congeries,
　Repeat in large what they practised in small,
Through life after life in unlimited series;
　Only the scale's to be changed, that's all.

XXII

Yet I hardly know. When a soul has seen
170　By the means of Evil that Good is best,
And, through earth and its noise, what is heaven's serene, –
　When our faith in the same has stood the test –
Why, the child grown man, you burn the rod,
　The uses of labour are surely done;
There remaineth a rest for the people of God:
　And I have had troubles enough, for one.

XXIII

But at any rate I have loved the season
　Of Art's spring-birth so dim and dewy;
My sculptor is Nicolo the Pisan,
180　My painter – who but Cimabue?
Nor ever was man of them all indeed,
　From these to Ghiberti and Ghirlandajo,
Could say that he missed my critic-meed.
　So, now to my special grievance – heigh ho!

XXIV

Their ghosts still stand, as I said before,
　Watching each fresco flaked and rasped,
Blocked up, knocked out, or whitewashed o'er:
　– No getting again what the church has grasped!
The works on the wall must take their chance;
190　'Works never conceded to England's thick clime!'
(I hope they prefer their inheritance
　Of a bucketful of Italian quick-lime.)

XXV

When they go at length, with such a shaking
    Of heads o'er the old delusion, sadly
Each master his way through the black streets taking,
    Where many a lost work breathes though badly –
Why don't they bethink them of who has merited?
    Why not reveal, while their pictures dree
Such doom, how a captive might be out-ferreted?
200   Why is it they never remember me?

XXVI

Not that I expect the great Bigordi,
    Nor Sandro to hear me, chivalric, bellicose;
Nor the wronged Lippino; and not a word I
    Say of a scrap of Frà Angelico's:
But are you too fine, Taddeo Gaddi,
    To grant me a taste of your intonaco,
Some Jerome that seeks the heaven with a sad eye?
    Not a churlish saint, Lorenzo Monaco?

XXVII

Could not the ghost with the close red cap,
210   My Pollajolo, the twice a craftsman,
Save me a sample, give me the hap
    Of a muscular Christ that shows the draughtsman?
No Virgin by him the somewhat petty,
    Of finical touch and tempera crumbly –
Could not Alesso Baldovinetti
    Contribute so much, I ask him humbly?

XXVIII

Margheritone of Arezzo,
    With the grave-clothes garb and swaddling barret
(Why purse up mouth and beak in a pet so,
220   You bald old saturnine poll-clawed parrot?)
Not a poor glimmering Crucifixion,
    Where in the foreground kneels the donor?
If such remain, as is my conviction,
    The hoarding it does you but little honour.

XXIX

They pass; for them the panels may thrill,
    The tempera grow alive and tinglish;
Their pictures are left to the mercies still
    Of dealers and stealers, Jews and the English,
Who, seeing mere money's worth in their prize,
230   Will sell it to somebody calm as Zeno
At naked High Art, and in ecstasies
    Before some clay-cold vile Carlino!

XXX

No matter for these! But Giotto, you,
    Have you allowed, as the town-tongues babble it, –
Oh, never! it shall not be counted true –
    That a certain precious little tablet
Which Buonarroti eyed like a lover, –
    Was buried so long in oblivion's womb
And, left for another than I to discover,
240   Turns up at last! and to whom? – to whom?

XXXI

I, that have haunted the dim San Spirito,
    (Or was it rather the Ognissanti?)
Patient on altar-step planting a weary toe!
    Nay, I shall have it yet! *Detur amanti!*
My Koh-i-noor – or (if that's a platitude)
    Jewel of Giamschid, the Persian Sofi's eye;
So, in anticipative gratitude,
    What if I take up my hope and prophesy?

XXXII

When the hour grows ripe, and a certain dotard
250   Is pitched, no parcel that needs invoicing,
To the worse side of the Mont Saint Gothard,
    We shall begin by way of rejoicing;
None of that shooting the sky (blank cartridge),
    Nor a civic guard, all plumes and lacquer,
Hunting Radetzky's soul like a partridge
    Over Morello with squib and cracker.

XXXIII

This time we'll shoot better game and bag 'em hot –
   No mere display at the stone of Dante,
But a kind of sober Witanagemot
260   (Ex: 'Casa Guidi,' *quod videas ante*)
Shall ponder, once Freedom restored to Florence,
   How Art may return that departed with her.
Go, hated house, go each trace of the Lorraine's,
   And bring us the days of Orgagna hither!

XXXIV

How we shall prologize, how we shall perorate,
   Utter fit things upon art and history,
Feel truth at blood-heat and falsehood at zero rate,
   Make of the want of the age no mystery;
Contrast the fructuous and sterile eras,
270   Show – monarchy ever its uncouth cub licks
Out of the bear's shape into Chimera's,
   While Pure Art's birth is still the republic's.

XXXV

Then one shall propose in a speech (curt Tuscan,
   Expúrgate and sober, with scarcely an '*issimo*,')
To end now our half-told tale of Cambuscan,
   And turn the bell-tower's *alt* to *altissimo*:
And fine as the beak of a young beccaccia
   The Campanile, the Duomo's fit ally,
Shall soar up in gold full fifty braccia,
280   Completing Florence, as Florence Italy.

XXXVI

Shall I be alive that morning the scaffold
   Is broken away, and the long-pent fire,
Like the golden hope of the world, unbaffled
   Springs from its sleep, and up goes the spire
While 'God and the People' plain for its motto,
   Thence the new tricolour flaps at the sky?
At least to foresee that glory of Giotto
   And Florence together, the first am I!

In a Balcony

PERSONS

Norbert
Constance
The Queen

CONSTANCE *and* NORBERT

NORBERT: Now!
CONSTANCE: Not now!
NORBERT: Give me them again, those hands:
 Put them upon my forehead, how it throbs!
 Press them before my eyes, the fire comes through!
 You cruellest, you dearest in the world,
 Let me! The Queen must grant whate'er I ask –
 How can I gain you and not ask the Queen?
 There she stays waiting for me, here stand you;
 Some time or other this was to be asked;
 Now is the one time – what I ask, I gain:
10 Let me ask now, Love!
CONSTANCE: Do, and ruin us.
NORBERT: Let it be now, Love! All my soul breaks forth.
 How I do love you! Give my love its way!
 A man can have but one life and one death,
 One heaven, one hell. Let me fulfil my fate –
 Grant me my heaven now! Let me know you mine,
 Prove you mine, write my name upon your brow,
 Hold you and have you, and then die away,
 If God please, with completion in my soul!
CONSTANCE: I am not yours then? How content this man!
20 I am not his – who change into himself,
 Have passed into his heart and beat its beats,
 Who give my hands to him, my eyes, my hair,
 Give all that was of me away to him –
 So well, that now, my spirit turned his own,
 Takes part with him against the woman here,
 Bids him not stumble at so mere a straw
 As caring that the world be cognizant

How he loves her and how she worships him.
You have this woman, not as yet that world.

30   Go on, I bid, nor stop to care for me
By saving what I cease to care about,
The courtly name and pride of circumstance –
The name you'll pick up and be cumbered with
Just for the poor parade's sake, nothing more;
Just that the world may slip from under you –
Just that the world may cry 'So much for him –
The man predestined to the heap of crowns:
There goes his chance of winning one, at least!'

NORBERT: The world!

CONSTANCE: You love it. Love me quite as well,

40   And see if I shall pray for this in vain!
Why must you ponder what it knows or thinks?

NORBERT: You pray for – what, in vain?

CONSTANCE: Oh my heart's heart,
How I do love you, Norbert! That is right:
But listen, or I take my hands away!
You say, 'let it be now': you would go now
And tell the Queen, perhaps six steps from us,
You love me – so you do, thank God!

NORBERT: Thank God!

CONSTANCE: Yes, Norbert, – but you fain would tell your love,
And, what succeeds the telling, ask of her

50   My hand. Now take this rose and look at it,
Listening to me. You are the minister,
The Queen's first favourite, nor without a cause.
Tonight completes your wonderful year's-work
(This palace-feast is held to celebrate)
Made memorable by her life's success,
The junction of two crowns, on her sole head,
Her house had only dreamed of anciently:
That this mere dream is grown a stable truth,
Tonight's feast makes authentic. Whose the praise?

60   Whose genius, patience, energy, achieved
What turned the many heads and broke the hearts?
You are the fate, your minute's in the heaven.
Next comes the Queen's turn. 'Name your own reward!'
With leave to clench the past, chain the to-come,
Put out an arm and touch and take the sun
And fix it ever full-faced on your earth,

Possess yourself supremely of her life, –
You choose the single thing she will not grant;
Nay, very declaration of which choice
70   Will turn the scale and neutralize your work:
At best she will forgive you, if she can.
You think I'll let you choose – her cousin's hand?
NORBERT: Wait. First, do you retain your old belief
The Queen is generous, – nay, is just?
CONSTANCE: There, there!
So men make women love them, while they know
No more of women's hearts than . . . look you here,
You that are just and generous beside,
Make it your own case! For example now,
I'll say – I let you kiss me, hold my hands –
80   Why? do you know why? I'll instruct you, then –
The kiss, because you have a name at court;
This hand and this, that you may shut in each
A jewel, if you please to pick up such.
That's horrible? Apply it to the Queen –
Suppose I am the Queen to whom you speak:
'I was a nameless man; you needed me:
Why did I proffer you my aid? there stood
A certain pretty cousin at your side.
Why did I make such common cause with you?
90   Access to her had not been easy else.
You give my labour here abundant praise?
'Faith, labour, which she overlooked, grew play.
How shall your gratitude discharge itself?
Give me her hand!'
NORBERT: And still I urge the same.
Is the Queen just? just – generous or no!
CONSTANCE: Yes, just. You love a rose; no harm in that:
But was it for the rose's sake or mine
You put it in your bosom? mine, you said –
Then, mine you still must say or else be false.
100 You told the Queen you served her for herself;
If so, to serve her was to serve yourself,
She thinks, for all your unbelieving face!
I know her. In the hall, six steps from us,
One sees the twenty pictures; there's a life
Better than life, and yet no life at all.
Conceive her born in such a magic dome,

Pictures all round her! why, she sees the world,
Can recognize its given things and facts,
The fight of giants or the feast of gods,
110   Sages in senate, beauties at the bath,
Chases and battles, the whole earth's display,
Landscape and sea-piece, down to flowers and fruit –
And who shall question that she knows them all,
In better semblance than the things outside?
Yet bring into the silent gallery
Some live thing to contrast in breath and blood,
Some lion, with the painted lion there –
You think she'll understand composedly?
– Say, 'that's his fellow in the hunting-piece
120   Yonder, I've turned to praise a hundred times'?
Not so. Her knowledge of our actual earth,
Its hopes and fears, concerns and sympathies,
Must be too far, too mediate, too unreal.
The real exists for us outside, not her:
How should it, with that life in these four walls –
That father and that mother, first to last
No father and no mother – friends, a heap,
Lovers, no lack – a husband in due time,
And every one of them alike a lie!
130   Things painted by a Rubens out of naught
Into what kindness, friendship, love should be;
All better, all more grandiose than the life,
Only no life; mere cloth and surface-paint,
You feel, while you admire. How should she feel?
Yet now that she has stood thus fifty years
The sole spectator in that gallery,
You think to bring this warm real struggling love
In to her of a sudden, and suppose
She'll keep her state untroubled? Here's the truth –
140   She'll apprehend truth's value at a glance,
Prefer it to the pictured loyalty?
You only have to say, 'so men are made,
For this they act; the thing has many names,
But this the right one: and now, Queen, be just!'
Your life slips back; you lose her at the word:
You do not even for amends gain me.
He will not understand; oh, Norbert, Norbert,
Do you not understand?

NORBERT: The Queen's the Queen:
    I am myself – no picture, but alive
150 In every nerve and every muscle, here
    At the palace-window o'er the people's street,
    As she in the gallery where the pictures glow:
    The good of life is precious to us both.
    She cannot love; what do I want with rule?
    When first I saw your face a year ago
    I knew my life's good, my soul heard one voice –
    'The woman yonder, there's no use of life
    But just to obtain her! heap earth's woes in one
    And bear them – make a pile of all earth's joys
160 And spurn them, as they help or help not this;
    Only, obtain her!' How was it to be?
    I found you were the cousin of the Queen;
    I must then serve the Queen to get to you.
    No other way. Suppose there had been one,
    And I, by saying prayers to some white star
    With promise of my body and my soul,
    Might gain you, – should I pray the star or no?
    Instead, there was the Queen to serve! I served,
    Helped, did what other servants failed to do.
170 Neither she sought nor I declared my end.
    Her good is hers, my recompense be mine, –
    I therefore name you as that recompense.
    She dreamed that such a thing could never be?
    Let her wake now. She thinks there was more cause
    In love of power, high fame, pure loyalty?
    Perhaps she fancies men wear out their lives
    Chasing such shades. Then, I've a fancy too;
    I worked because I want you with my soul:
    I therefore ask your hand. Let it be now!
180 CONSTANCE: Had I not loved you from the very first,
    Were I not yours, could we not steal out thus
    So wickedly, so wildly, and so well,
    You might become impatient. What's conceived
    Of us without here, by the folk within?
    Where are you now? immersed in cares of state –
    Where am I now? intent on festal robes –
    We two, embracing under death's spread hand!
    What was this thought for, what that scruple of yours
    Which broke the council up? – to bring about

190 One minute's meeting in the corridor!
And then the sudden sleights, strange secrecies,
Complots inscrutable, deep telegraphs,
Long-planned chance-meetings, hazards of a look,
'Does she know? does she not know? saved or lost?'
A year of this compression's ecstasy
All goes for nothing! you would give this up
For the old way, the open way, the world's,
His way who beats, and his who sells his wife!
What tempts you? – their notorious happiness
200 Makes you ashamed of ours? The best you'll gain
Will be – the Queen grants all that you require,
Concedes the cousin, rids herself of you
And me at once, and gives us ample leave
To live like our five hundred happy friends.
The world will show us with officious hand
Our chamber-entry, and stand sentinel
Where we so oft have stolen across its traps!
Get the world's warrant, ring the falcons' feet,
And make it duty to be bold and swift,
210 Which long ago was nature. Have it so!
We never hawked by rights till flung from fist?
Oh, the man's thought! no woman's such a fool.
 NORBERT: Yes, the man's thought and my thought, which is
   more –
One made to love you, let the world take note!
Have I done worthy work? be love's the praise,
Though hampered by restrictions, barred against
By set forms, blinded by forced secrecies!
Set free my love, and see what love can do
Shown in my life – what work will spring from that!
220 The world is used to have its business done
On other grounds, find great effects produced
For power's sake, fame's sake, motives in men's mouth.
So, good: but let my low ground shame their high!
Truth is the strong thing. Let man's life be true!
And love's the truth of mine. Time prove the rest!
I choose to wear you stamped all over me,
Your name upon my forehead and my breast,
You, from the sword's blade to the ribbon's edge,
That men may see, all over, you in me –
230 That pale loves may die out of their pretence

In face of mine, shames thrown on love fall off.
Permit this, Constance! Love has been so long
Subdued in me, eating me through and through,
That now 'tis all of me and must have way.
Think of my work, that chaos of intrigues,
Those hopes and fears, surprises and delays,
That long endeavour, earnest, patient, slow,
Trembling at last to its assured result:
Then think of this revulsion! I resume
240   Life after death, (it is no less than life,
After such long unlovely labouring days)
And liberate to beauty life's great need
O' the beautiful, which, while it prompted work,
Suppressed itself erewhile. This eve's the time,
This eve intense with yon first trembling star
We seem to pant and reach; scarce aught between
The earth that rises and the heaven that bends;
All nature self-abandoned, every tree
Flung as it will, pursuing its own thoughts
250   And fixed so, every flower and every weed,
No pride, no shame, no victory, no defeat;
All under God, each measured by itself.
These statues round us stand abrupt, distinct,
The strong in strength, the weak in weakness fixed,
The Muse for ever wedded to her lyre,
Nymph to her fawn, and Silence to her rose:
See God's approval on his universe!
Let us do so – aspire to live as these
In harmony with truth, ourselves being true!
260   Take the first way, and let the second come!
My first is to possess myself of you;
The music sets the march-step – forward, then!
And there's the Queen, I go to claim you of,
The world to witness, wonder and applaud.
Our flower of life breaks open. No delay!
CONSTANCE: And so shall we be ruined, both of us.
Norbert, I know her to the skin and bone:
You do not know her, were not born to it,
To feel what she can see or cannot see.
270   Love, she is generous, – ay, despite your smile,
Generous as you are: for, in that thin frame
Pain-twisted, punctured through and through with cares,

There lived a lavish soul until it starved,
Debarred of healthy food. Look to the soul –
Pity that, stoop to that, ere you begin
(The true man's-way) on justice and your rights,
Exactions and acquittance of the past!
Begin so – see what justice she will deal!
We women hate a debt as men a gift.
280   Suppose her some poor keeper of a school
Whose business is to sit through summer months
And dole out children leave to go and play,
Herself superior to such lightness – she
In the arm-chair's state and pedagogic pomp –
To the life, the laughter, sun and youth outside:
We wonder such a face looks black on us?
I do not bid you wake her tenderness,
(That were vain truly – none is left to wake)
But let her think her justice is engaged
290   To take the shape of tenderness, and mark
If she'll not coldly pay its warmest debt!
Does she love me, I ask you? not a whit:
Yet, thinking that her justice was engaged
To help a kinswoman, she took me up –
Did more on that bare ground than other loves
Would do on greater argument. For me,
I have no equivalent of such cold kind
To pay her with, but love alone to give
If I give anything. I give her love:
300   I feel I ought to help her, and I will.
So, for her sake, as yours, I tell you twice
That women hate a debt as men a gift.
If I were you, I could obtain this grace –
Could lay the whole I did to love's account,
Nor yet be very false as courtiers go –
Declaring my success was recompense;
It would be so, in fact: what were it else?
And then, once loose her generosity, –
Oh, how I see it! – then, were I but you,
310   To turn it, let it seem to move itself,
And make it offer what I really take,
Accepting just, in the poor cousin's hand,
Her value as the next thing to the Queen's –
Since none love Queens directly, none dare that,

And a thing's shadow or a name's mere echo
Suffices those who miss the name and thing!
You pick up just a ribbon she has worn,
To keep in proof how near her breath you came.
Say, I'm so near I seem a piece of her –
320 Ask for me that way – (oh, you understand)
You'd find the same gift yielded with a grace,
Which, if you make the least show to extort . . .
– You'll see! and when you have ruined both of us,
Dissertate on the Queen's ingratitude!
NORBERT: Then, if I turn it that way, you consent?
'Tis not my way; I have more hope in truth:
Still, if you won't have truth – why, this indeed,
Were scarcely false, as I'd express the sense.
Will you remain here?
CONSTANCE: O best heart of mine,
330 How I have loved you! then, you take my way?
Are mine as you have been her minister,
Work out my thought, give it effect for me,
Paint plain my poor conceit and make it serve?
I owe that withered woman everything –
Life, fortune, you, remember! Take my part –
Help me to pay her! Stand upon your rights?
You, with my rose, my hands, my heart on you?
Your rights are mine – you have no rights but mine.
NORBERT: Remain here. How you know me!
CONSTANCE: Ah, but still –
    [*He breaks from her : she remains. Dance-music from within*]

    [*Enter the* QUEEN]
340 QUEEN: Constance? She is here as he said. Speak quick!
    Is it so? Is it true or false? One word!
    CONSTANCE: True.
    QUEEN: Mercifullest Mother, thanks to thee!
    CONSTANCE: Madam?
    QUEEN: I love you, Constance, from my soul.
    Now say once more, with any words you will,
    'Tis true, all true, as true as that I speak.
    CONSTANCE: Why should you doubt it?
    QUEEN: Ah, why doubt? why doubt?
    Dear, make me see it! Do you see it so?
    None see themselves; another sees them best.

You say 'why doubt it?' – you see him and me.
350   It is because the Mother has such grace
That if we had but faith – wherein we fail –
Whate'er we yearn for would be granted us;
Yet still we let our whims prescribe despair,
Our fancies thwart and cramp our will and power,
And while, accepting life, abjure its use.
Constance, I had abjured the hope of love
And being loved, as truly as yon palm
The hope of seeing Egypt from that plot.
CONSTANCE: Heaven!
QUEEN: But it was so, Constance, it was so!
360   Men say – or do men say it? fancies say –
'Stop here, your life is set, you are grown old.
Too late – no love for you, too late for love –
Leave love to girls. Be queen: let Constance love.'
One takes the hint – half meets it like a child,
Ashamed at any feelings that oppose.
'Oh love, true, never think of love again!
I am a queen: I rule, not love forsooth.'
So it goes on; so a face grows like this,
Hair like this hair, poor arms as lean as these,
370   Till, – nay, it does not end so, I thank God!
CONSTANCE: I cannot understand –
QUEEN: The happier you!
Constance, I know not how it is with men:
For women (I am a woman now like you)
There is no good of life but love – but love!
What else looks good, is some shade flung from love;
Love gilds it, gives it worth. Be warned by me,
Never you cheat yourself one instant! Love,
Give love, ask only love, and leave the rest!
O Constance, how I love you!
CONSTANCE: I love you.
380 QUEEN: I do believe that all is come through you.
I took you to my heart to keep it warm
When the last chance of love seemed dead in me;
I thought your fresh youth warmed my withered heart.
Oh, I am very old now, am I not?
Not so! it is true and it shall be true!
CONSTANCE: Tell it me: let me judge if true or false.
QUEEN: Ah, but I fear you! you will look at me

And say, 'she's old, she's grown unlovely quite
Who ne'er was beauteous: men want beauty still.'
390 Well, so I feared – the curse! so I felt sure!
CONSTANCE: Be calm. And now you feel not sure, you say?
QUEEN: Constance, he came, – the coming was not strange –
Do not I stand and see men come and go?
I turned a half-look from my pedestal
Where I grow marble – 'one young man the more!
He will love some one; that is naught to me:
What would he with my marble stateliness?'
Yet this seemed somewhat worse than heretofore;
The man more gracious, youthful, like a god,
400 And I still older, with less flesh to change –
We two those dear extremes that long to touch.
It seemed still harder when he first began
To labour at those state-affairs, absorbed
The old way for the old end – interest.
Oh, to live with a thousand beating hearts
Around you, swift eyes, serviceable hands,
Professing they've no care but for your cause,
Thought but to help you, love but for yourself, –
And you the marble statue all the time
410 They praise and point at as preferred to life,
Yet leave for the first breathing woman's smile,
First dancer's, gypsy's or street baladine's!
Why, how I have ground my teeth to hear men's speech
Stifled for fear it should alarm my ear,
Their gait subdued lest step should startle me,
Their eyes declined, such queendom to respect,
Their hands alert, such treasure to preserve,
While not a man of them broke rank and spoke,
Wrote me a vulgar letter all of love,
420 Or caught my hand and pressed it like a hand!
There have been moments, if the sentinel
Lowering his halbert to salute the queen,
Had flung it brutally and clasped my knees,
I would have stooped and kissed him with my soul.
CONSTANCE: Who could have comprehended?
QUEEN: Ay, who – who?
Why, no one, Constance, but this one who did.
Not they, not you, not I. Even now perhaps
It comes too late – would you but tell the truth.

CONSTANCE: I wait to tell it.

QUEEN: Well, you see, he came,
430   Outfaced the others, did a work this year
  Exceeds in value all was ever done,
  You know – it is not I who say it – all
  Say it. And so (a second pang and worse)
  I grew aware not only of what he did,
  But why so wondrously. Oh, never work
  Like his was done for work's ignoble sake –
  Souls need a finer aim to light and lure!
  I felt, I saw, he loved – loved somebody.
  And Constance, my dear Constance, do you know,
440   I did believe this while 'twas you he loved.

CONSTANCE: Me, madam?

QUEEN: It did seem to me, your face
  Met him where'er he looked: and whom but you
  Was such a man to love? It seemed to me,
  You saw he loved you, and approved his love,
  And both of you were in intelligence.
  You could not loiter in that garden, step
  Into this balcony, but I straight was stung
  And forced to understand. It seemed so true,
  So right, so beautiful, so like you both,
450   That all this work should have been done by him
  Not for the vulgar hope of recompense,
  But that at last – suppose, some night like this –
  Borne on to claim his due reward of me,
  He might say 'Give her hand and pay me so.'
  And I (O Constance, you shall love me now!)
  I thought, surmounting all the bitterness,
  – 'And he shall have it. I will make her blest,
  My flower of youth, my woman's self that was,
  My happiest woman's self that might have been!
460   These two shall have their joy and leave me here.'
  Yes – yes!

CONSTANCE: Thanks!

QUEEN: And the word was on my lips
  When he burst in upon me. I looked to hear
  A mere calm statement of his just desire
  For payment of his labour. When – O heaven,
  How can I tell you? lightning on my eyes
  And thunder in my ears proved that first word

Which told 'twas love of me, of me, did all –
He loved me – from the first step to the last,
Loved me!
CONSTANCE: You hardly saw, scarce heard him speak
470   Of love: what if you should mistake?
QUEEN: No, no –
No mistake! Ha, there shall be no mistake!
He had not dared to hint the love he felt –
You were my reflex – (how I understood!)
He said you were the ribbon I had worn,
He kissed my hand, he looked into my eyes,
And love, love came at end of every phrase.
Love is begun; this much is come to pass:
The rest is easy. Constance, I am yours!
I will learn, I will place my life on you,
480   Teach me but how to keep what I have won!
Am I so old? This hair was early grey;
But joy ere now has brought hair brown again,
And joy will bring the cheek's red back, I feel.
I could sing once too; that was in my youth.
Still, when men paint me, they declare me . . . yes,
Beautiful – for the last French painter did!
I know they flatter somewhat; you are frank –
I trust you. How I loved you from the first!
Some queens would hardly seek a cousin out
490   And set her by their side to take the eye:
I must have felt that good would come from you.
I am not generous – like him – like you!
But he is not your lover after all:
It was not you he looked at. Saw you him?
You have not been mistaking words or looks?
He said you were the reflex of myself.
And yet he is not such a paragon
To you, to younger women who may choose
Among a thousand Norberts. Speak the truth!
500   You know you never named his name to me:
You know, I cannot give him up – ah God,
Not up now, even to you!
CONSTANCE: Then calm yourself.
QUEEN: See, I am old – look here, you happy girl!
I will not play the fool, deceive – ah, whom?
'Tis all gone: put your cheek beside my cheek

And what a contrast does the moon behold!
But then I set my life upon one chance,
The last chance and the best – am *I* not left,
My soul, myself? All women love great men
510   If young or old; it is in all the tales:
Young beauties love old poets who can love –
Why should not he, the poems in my soul,
The passionate faith, the pride of sacrifice,
Life-long, death-long? I throw them at his feet.
Who cares to see the fountain's very shape,
Whether it be a Triton's or a Nymph's
That pours the foam, makes rainbows all around?
You could not praise indeed the empty conch;
But I'll pour floods of love and hide myself.
520   How I will love him! Cannot men love love?
Who was a queen and loved a poet once
Humpbacked, a dwarf? ah, women can do that!
Well, but men too; at least, they tell you so.
They love so many women in their youth,
And even in age they all love whom they please;
And yet the best of them confide to friends
That 'tis not beauty makes the lasting love –
They spend a day with such and tire the next:
They like soul, – well then, they like phantasy,
530   Novelty even. Let us confess the truth,
Horrible though it be, that prejudice,
Prescription . . . curses! they will love a queen.
They will, they do: and will not, does not – he?
CONSTANCE: How can he? You are wedded: 'tis a name
We know, but still a bond. Your rank remains,
His rank remains. How can he, nobly souled
As you believe and I incline to think,
Aspire to be your favourite, shame and all?
QUEEN: Hear her! There, there now – could she love like me?
540   What did I say of smooth-cheeked youth and grace?
See all it does or could do! so youth loves!
Oh, tell him, Constance, you could never do
What I will – you, it was not born in! I
Will drive these difficulties far and fast
As yonder mists curdling before the moon.
I'll use my light too, gloriously retrieve
My youth from its enforced calamity,

Dissolve that hateful marriage, and be his,
His own in the eyes alike of God and man.
550 CONSTANCE: You will do – dare do . . . pause on what you say!
QUEEN: Hear her! I thank you, sweet, for that surprise.
You have the fair face: for the soul, see mine!
I have the strong soul: let me teach you, here.
I think I have borne enough and long enough,
And patiently enough, the world remarks,
To have my own way now, unblamed by all.
It does so happen (I rejoice for it)
This most unhoped-for issue cuts the knot.
There's not a better way of settling claims
560 Than this; God sends the accident express:
And were it for my subjects' good, no more,
'Twere best thus ordered. I am thankful now,
Mute, passive, acquiescent. I receive,
And bless God simply, or should almost fear
To walk so smoothly to my ends at last.
Why, how I baffle obstacles, spurn fate!
How strong I am! Could Norbert see me now!
CONSTANCE: Let me consider. It is all too strange.
QUEEN: You, Constance, learn of me; do you, like me!
570 You are young, beautiful: my own, best girl,
You will have many lovers, and love one –
Light hair, not hair like Norbert's, to suit yours:
Taller than he is, since yourself are tall.
Love him, like me! Give all away to him;
Think never of yourself; throw by your pride,
Hope, fear, – your own good as you saw it once,
And love him simply for his very self.
Remember, I (and what am I to you?)
Would give up all for one, leave throne, lose life,
580 Do all but just unlove him! He loves me.
CONSTANCE: He shall.
QUEEN: You, step inside my inmost heart!
Give me your own heart: let us have one heart!
I'll come to you for counsel; 'this he says,
This he does; what should this amount to, pray?
Beseech you, change it into current coin!
Is that worth kisses? Shall I please him there?'
And then we'll speak in turn of you – what else?
Your love, according to your beauty's worth,

For you shall have some noble love, all gold:
590 Whom choose you? we will get him at your choice.
– Constance, I leave you. Just a minute since,
I felt as I must die or be alone
Breathing my soul into an ear like yours:
Now, I would face the world with my new life,
Wear my new crown. I'll walk around the rooms,
And then come back and tell you how it feels.
How soon a smile of God can change the world!
How we are made for happiness – how work
Grows play, adversity a winning fight!
600 True, I have lost so many years: what then?
Many remain: God has been very good.
You, stay here! 'Tis as different from dreams,
From the mind's cold calm estimate of bliss,
As these stone statues from the flesh and blood.
The comfort thou hast caused mankind, God's moon!
        [*She goes out, leaving* CONSTANCE. *Dance-music from
        within*]

[NORBERT *enters*]
NORBERT: Well? we have but one minute and one word!
CONSTANCE: I am yours, Norbert!
NORBERT: Yes, mine.
CONSTANCE: Not till now!
    You were mine. Now I give myself to you.
NORBERT: Constance?
CONSTANCE: Your own! I know the thriftier way
610 Of giving – haply, 'tis the wiser way.
    Meaning to give a treasure, I might dole
    Coin after coin out (each, as that were all,
    With a new largess still at each despair)
    And force you keep in sight the deed, preserve
    Exhaustless till the end my part and yours,
    My giving and your taking; both our joys
    Dying together. Is it the wiser way?
    I choose the simpler; I give all at once.
    Know what you have to trust to, trade upon!
620 Use it, abuse it, – anything but think
    Hereafter, 'Had I known she loved me so,
    And what my means, I might have thriven with it.'
    This is your means. I give you all myself.

NORBERT: I take you and thank God.

CONSTANCE: Look on through years!

   We cannot kiss, a second day like this;

   Else were this earth no earth.

NORBERT: With this day's heat

   We shall go on through years of cold.

CONSTANCE: So, best!

   – I try to see those years – I think I see.

   You walk quick and new warmth comes; you look back

630   And lay all to the first glow – not sit down

   For ever brooding on a day like this

   While seeing embers whiten and love die.

   Yes, love lives best in its effect; and mine,

   Full in its own life, yearns to live in yours.

NORBERT: Just so. I take and know you all at once.

   Your soul is disengaged so easily,

   Your face is there, I know you; give me time,

   Let me be proud and think you shall know me.

   My soul is slower: in a life I roll

640   The minute out whereto you condense yours –

   The whole slow circle round you I must move,

   To be just you. I look to a long life

   To decompose this minute, prove its worth.

   'Tis the sparks' long succession one by one

   Shall show you, in the end, what fire was crammed

   In that mere stone you struck: how could you know,

   If it lay ever unproved in your sight,

   As now my heart lies? your own warmth would hide

   Its coldness, were it cold.

CONSTANCE: But how prove, how?

650 NORBERT: Prove in my life, you ask?

CONSTANCE: Quick, Norbert – how?

NORBERT: That's easy told. I count life just a stuff

   To try the soul's strength on, educe the man.

   Who keeps one end in view makes all things serve.

   As with the body – he who hurls a lance

   Or heaps up stone on stone, shows strength alike:

   So must I seize and task all means to prove

   And show this soul of mine, you crown as yours,

   And justify us both.

CONSTANCE: Could you write books,

   Paint pictures! One sits down in poverty

660   And writes or paints, with pity for the rich.

NORBERT: And loves one's painting and one's writing, then,
     And not one's mistress! All is best, believe,
     And we best as no other than we are.
     We live, and they experiment on life –
     Those poets, painters, all who stand aloof
     To overlook the farther. Let us be
     The thing they look at! I might take your face
     And write of it and paint it – to what end?
     For whom? what pale dictatress in the air

670   Feeds, smiling sadly, her fine ghost-like form
     With earth's real blood and breath, the beauteous life
     She makes despised for ever? You are mine,
     Made for me, not for others in the world,
     Nor yet for that which I should call my art,
     The cold calm power to see how fair you look.
     I come to you; I leave you not, to write
     Or paint. You are, I am: let Rubens there
     Paint us!

CONSTANCE: So, best!

NORBERT: I understand your soul.
     You live, and rightly sympathize with life,

680   With action, power, success. This way is straight;
     And time were short beside, to let me change
     The craft my childhood learnt: my craft shall serve.
     Men set me here to subjugate, enclose,
     Manure their barren lives, and force thence fruit
     First for themselves, and afterward for me
     In the due tithe; the task of some one soul,
     Through ways of work appointed by the world.
     I am not bid create – men see no star
     Transfiguring my brow to warrant that –

690   But find and bind and bring to bear their wills.
     So I began: tonight sees how I end.
     What if it see, too, power's first outbreak here
     Amid the warmth, surprise and sympathy,
     And instincts of the heart that teach the head?
     What if the people have discerned at length
     The dawn of the next nature, novel brain
     Whose will they venture in the place of theirs,
     Whose work, they trust, shall find them as novel ways
     To untried heights which yet he only sees?

700 I felt it when you kissed me. See this Queen,
This people – in our phrase, this mass of men –
See how the mass lies passive to my hand
Now that my hand is plastic, with you by
To make the muscles iron! Oh, an end
Shall crown this issue as this crowns the first!
My will be on this people! then, the strain,
The grappling of the potter with his clay,
The long uncertain struggle, – the success
And consummation of the spirit-work,

710 Some vase shaped to the curl of the god's lip,
While rounded fair for human sense to see
The Graces in a dance men recognize
With turbulent applause and laughs of heart!
So triumph ever shall renew itself;
Ever shall end in efforts higher yet,
Ever begin ...

CONSTANCE: I ever helping?

NORBERT: Thus!

    [*As he embraces her, the* QUEEN *enters*]

CONSTANCE: Hist, madam! So have I performed my part.
You see your gratitude's true decency,
Norbert? A little slow in seeing it!

720 Begin, to end the sooner! What's a kiss?

NORBERT: Constance?

CONSTANCE: Why, must I teach it you again?
You want a witness to your dulness, sir?
What was I saying these ten minutes long?
Then I repeat – when some young handsome man
Like you has acted out a part like yours,
Is pleased to fall in love with one beyond,
So very far beyond him, as he says –
So hopelessly in love that but to speak
Would prove him mad, – he thinks judiciously,

730 And makes some insignificant good soul,
Like me, his friend, adviser, confidant,
And very stalking-horse to cover him
In following after what he dares not face.
When his end's gained – (sir, do you understand?)
When she, he dares not face, has loved him first,
– May I not say so, madam? – tops his hope,
And overpasses so his wildest dream,

With glad consent of all, and most of her
The confidant who brought the same about –
740 Why, in the moment when such joy explodes,
I do hold that the merest gentleman
Will not start rudely from the stalking-horse,
Dismiss it with a 'There, enough of you!'
Forget it, show his back unmannerly:
But like a liberal heart will rather turn
And say, 'A tingling time of hope was ours;
Betwixt the fears and falterings, we two lived
A chanceful time in waiting for the prize:
The confidant, the Constance, served not ill.
750 And though I shall forget her in due time,
Her use being answered now, as reason bids,
Nay as herself bids from her heart of hearts, –
Still, she has rights, the first thanks go to her,
The first good praise goes to the prosperous tool,
And the first – which is the last – rewarding kiss.'
NORBERT: Constance, it is a dream – ah, see, you smile!
CONSTANCE: So, now his part being properly performed,
Madam, I turn to you and finish mine
As duly; I do justice in my turn.
760 Yes, madam, he has loved you – long and well;
He could not hope to tell you so – 'twas I
Who scrved to prove your soul accessible,
I led his thoughts on, drew them to their place
When they had wandered else into despair,
And kept love constant toward its natural aim.
Enough, my part is played; you stoop half-way
And meet us royally and spare our fears:
'Tis like yourself. He thanks you, so do I.
Take him – with my full heart! my work is praised
770 By what comes of it. Be you happy, both!
Yourself – the only one on earth who can –
Do all for him, much more than a mere heart
Which though warm is not useful in its warmth
As the silk vesture of a queen! fold that
Around him gently, tenderly. For him –
For him, – he knows his own part!
NORBERT: Have you done?
I take the jest at last. Should I speak now?
Was yours the wager, Constance, foolish child,

Or did you but accept it? Well – at least
780 You lose by it.
    CONSTANCE: Nay, madam, 'tis your turn!
Restrain him still from speech a little more,
And make him happier as more confident!
Pity him, madam, he is timid yet!
Mark, Norbert! Do not shrink now! Here I yield
My whole right in you to the Queen, observe!
With her go put in practice the great schemes
You teem with, follow the career else closed –
Be all you cannot be except by her!
Behold her! – Madam, say for pity's sake
790 Anything – frankly say you love him! Else
He'll not believe it: there's more earnest in
His fear than you conceive: I know the man!
    NORBERT: I know the woman somewhat, and confess
I thought she had jested better: she begins
To overcharge her part. I gravely wait
Your pleasure, madam: where is my reward?
    QUEEN: Norbert, this wild girl (whom I recognize
Scarce more than you do, in her fancy-fit,
Eccentric speech and variable mirth,
800 Not very wise perhaps and somewhat bold,
Yet suitable, the whole night's work being strange)
– May still be right: I may do well to speak
And make authentic what appears a dream
To even myself. For, what she says, is true:
Yes, Norbert – what you spoke just now of love,
Devotion, stirred no novel sense in me,
But justified a warmth felt long before.
Yes, from the first – I loved you, I shall say:
Strange! but I do grow stronger, now 'tis said.
810 Your courage helps mine: you did well to speak
Tonight, the night that crowns your twelvemonths' toil:
But still I had not waited to discern
Your heart so long, believe me! From the first
The source of so much zeal was almost plain,
In absence even of your own words just now
Which hazarded the truth. 'Tis very strange,
But takes a happy ending – in your love
Which mine meets: be it so! as you chose me,
So I choose you.

NORBERT: And worthily you choose.

820 I will not be unworthy your esteem,
No, madam. I do love you; I will meet
Your nature, now I know it. This was well.
I see, – you dare and you are justified:
But none had ventured such experiment,
Less versed than you in nobleness of heart,
Less confident of finding such in me.
I joy that thus you test me ere you grant
The dearest richest beauteousest and best
Of women to my arms: 'tis like yourself.

830 So – back again into my part's set words –
Devotion to the uttermost is yours,
But no, you cannot, madam, even you,
Create in me the love our Constance does.
Or – something truer to the tragic phrase –
Not yon magnolia-bell superb with scent
Invites a certain insect – that's myself –
But the small eye-flower nearer to the ground.
I take this lady.

CONSTANCE: Stay – not hers, the trap –
Stay, Norbert – that mistake were worst of all!

840 He is too cunning, madam! It was I,
I, Norbert, who . . .

NORBERT: You, was it, Constance? Then,
But for the grace of this divinest hour
Which gives me you, I might not pardon here!
I am the Queen's; she only knows my brain:
She may experiment upon my heart
And I instruct her too by the result.
But you, sweet, you who know me, who so long
Have told my heart-beats over, held my life
In those white hands of yours, – it is not well!

850 CONSTANCE: Tush! I have said it, did I not say it all?
The life, for her – the heart-beats, for her sake!

NORBERT: Enough! my cheek grows red, I think. Your test?
There's not the meanest woman in the world,
Not she I least could love in all the world,
Whom, did she love me, had love proved itself,
I dare insult as you insult me now.
Constance, I could say, if it must be said,
'Take back the soul you offer, I keep mine!'

But – 'Take the soul still quivering on your hand,
860   The soul so offered, which I cannot use,
And, please you, give it to some playful friend,
For– what's the trifle he requites me with?'
I, tempt a woman, to amuse a man,
That two may mock her heart if it succumb?
No: fearing God and standing 'neath his heaven,
I would not dare insult a woman so,
Were she the meanest woman in the world,
And he, I cared to please, ten emperors!
CONSTANCE: Norbert!
NORBERT: I love once as I live but once.
870   What case is this to think or talk about?
I love you. Would it mend the case at all
If such a step as this killed love in me?
Your part were done: account to God for it!
But mine – could murdered love get up again,
And kneel to whom you please to designate,
And make you mirth? It is too horrible.
You did not know this, Constance? now you know
That body and soul have each one life, but one:
And here's my love, here, living, at your feet.
880   CONSTANCE: See the Queen! Norbert – this one more last
        word –
If thus you have taken jest for earnest – thus
Loved me in earnest . . .
NORBERT: Ah, no jest holds here!
Where is the laughter in which jests break up,
And what this horror that grows palpable?
Madam – why grasp you thus the balcony?
Have I done ill? Have I not spoken truth?
How could I other? Was it not your test,
To try me, what my love for Constance meant?
Madam, your royal soul itself approves,
890   The first, that I should choose thus! so one takes
A beggar, – asks him, what would buy his child?
And then approves the expected laugh of scorn
Returned as something noble from the rags.
Speak, Constance, I'm the beggar! Ha, what's this?
You two glare each at each like panthers now.
Constance, the world fades; only you stand there!
You did not, in tonight's wild whirl of things,

Sell me – your soul of souls, for any price?
No – no – 'tis easy to believe in you!
900   Was it your love's mad trial to o'ertop
Mine by this vain self-sacrifice? well, still –
Though I might curse, I love you. I am love
And cannot change: love's self is at your feet!
   [*The* QUEEN *goes out*]
CONSTANCE: Feel my heart; let it die against your own!
NORBERT: Against my own. Explain not; let this be!
   This is life's height.
CONSTANCE: Yours, yours, yours!
NORBERT: You and I –
   Why care by what meanders we are here
   I' the centre of the labyrinth? Men have died
   Trying to find this place, which we have found.
910   CONSTANCE: Found, found!
NORBERT: Sweet, never fear what she can do!
   We are past harm now.
CONSTANCE: On the breast of God.
   I thought of men – as if you were a man.
   Tempting him with a crown!
NORBERT: This must end here:
   It is too perfect.
CONSTANCE: There's the music stopped.
   What measured heavy tread? It is one blaze
   About me and within me.
NORBERT: Oh, some death
   Will run its sudden finger round this spark
   And sever us from the rest!
CONSTANCE: And so do well.
   Now the doors open.
NORBERT: 'Tis the guard comes.
CONSTANCE: Kiss!

Saul

I

Said Abner, 'At last thou art come! Ere I tell, ere thou speak,
Kiss my cheek, wish me well!' Then I wished it, and did kiss his
    cheek.
And he, 'Since the King, O my friend, for thy countenance sent,
Neither drunken nor eaten have we; nor until from his tent
Thou return with the joyful assurance the King liveth yet,
Shall our lip with the honey be bright, with the water be wet.
For out of the black mid-tent's silence, a space of three days,
Not a sound hath escaped to thy servants, of prayer nor of praise,
To betoken that Saul and the Spirit have ended their strife,
10 And that, faint in his triumph, the monarch sinks back upon life.

II

'Yet now my heart leaps, O beloved! God's child with his dew
On thy gracious gold hair, and those lilies still living and blue
Just broken to twine round thy harp-strings, as if no wild heat
Were now raging to torture the desert!'

III

                   Then I, as was meet,
Knelt down to the God of my fathers, and rose on my feet,
And ran o'er the sand burnt to powder. The tent was unlooped;
I pulled up the spear that obstructed, and under I stooped;
Hands and knees on the slippery grass-patch, all withered and
    gone,
That extends to the second enclosure, I groped my way on
20 Till I felt where the foldskirts fly open. Then once more I
    prayed,
And opened the foldskirts and entered, and was not afraid
But spoke, 'Here is David, thy servant!' And no voice replied.
At the first I saw naught but the blackness; but soon I descried
A something more black than the blackness – the vast, the
    upright
Main prop which sustains the pavilion: and slow into sight
Grew a figure against it, gigantic and blackest of all.
Then a sunbeam, that burst through the tent-roof, showed Saul.

IV

He stood as erect as that tent-prop, both arms stretched out wide
On the great cross-support in the centre, that goes to each side;
30 He relaxed not a muscle, but hung there as, caught in his pangs
And waiting his change, the king-serpent all heavily hangs,
Far away from his kind, in the pine, till deliverance come
With the spring-time, – so agonized Saul, drear and stark, blind
    and dumb.

V

Then I tuned my harp, – took off the lilies we twine round its
    chords
Lest they snap 'neath the stress of the noontide – those sunbeams
    like swords!
And I first played the tune all our sheep know, as, one after one,
So docile they come to the pen-door till folding be done.
They are white and untorn by the bushes, for lo, they have fed
Where the long grasses stifle the water within the stream's bed;
40 And now one after one seeks its lodging, as star follows star
Into eve and the blue far above us, – so blue and so far!

VI

– Then the tune, for which quails on the cornland will each leave
    his mate
To fly after the player; then, what makes the crickets elate
Till for boldness they fight one another: and then, what has
    weight
To set the quick jerboa a-musing outside his sand house –
There are none such as he for a wonder, half bird and half
    mouse!
God made all the creatures and gave them our love and our fear,
To give sign, we and they are his children, one family here.

VII

Then I played the help-tune of our reapers, their wine-song,
    when hand
50 Grasps at hand, eye lights eye in good friendship, and great
    hearts expand
And grow one in the sense of this world's life. – And then, the
    last song
When the dead man is praised on his journey – 'Bear, bear him
    along

With his few faults shut up like dead flowerets! Are balm-seeds
    not here
To console us? The land has none left such as he on the bier.
Oh, would we might keep thee, my brother!' – And then, the
    glad chaunt
Of the marriage, – first go the young maidens, next, she whom
    we vaunt
As the beauty, the pride of our dwelling. – And then, the great
    march
Wherein man runs to man to assist him and buttress an arch
Naught can break; who shall harm them, our friends? – Then,
    the chorus intoned
60 As the Levites go up to the altar in glory enthroned.
But I stopped here: for here in the darkness Saul groaned.

VIII

And I paused, held my breath in such silence, and listened apart;
And the tent shook, for mighty Saul shuddered: and sparkles
    'gan dart
From the jewels that woke in his turban, at once with a start,
All its lordly male-sapphires, and rubies courageous at heart.
So the head: but the body still moved not, still hung there erect.
And I bent once again to my playing, pursued it unchecked,
As I sang, –

IX

    'Oh, our manhood's prime vigour! No spirit feels waste,
Not a muscle is stopped in its playing nor sinew unbraced.
70 Oh, the wild joys of living! the leaping from rock up to rock,
The strong rending of boughs from the fir-tree, the cool silver
    shock
Of the plunge in a pool's living water, the hunt of the bear,
And the sultriness showing the lion is couched in his lair.
And the meal, the rich dates yellowed over with gold dust divine,
And the locust-flesh steeped in the pitcher, the full draught of
    wine,
And the sleep in the dried river-channel where bulrushes tell
That the water was wont to go warbling so softly and well.
How good is man's life, the mere living! how fit to employ
All the heart and the soul and the senses for ever in joy!
80 Hast thou loved the white locks of thy father, whose sword thou
    didst guard

When he trusted thee forth with the armies, for glorious reward?
Didst thou see the thin hands of thy mother, held up as men sung
The low song of the nearly-departed, and hear her faint tongue
Joining in while it could to the witness, "Let one more attest,
I have lived, seen God's hand through a lifetime, and all was for
    best"?
Then they sung through their tears in strong triumph, not much,
    but the rest.
And thy brothers, the help and the contest, the working whence
    grew
Such result as, from seething grape-bundles, the spirit strained
    true:
And the friends of thy boyhood – that boyhood of wonder and
    hope,
90 Present promise and wealth of the future beyond the eye's
    scope, –
Till lo, thou art grown to a monarch; a people is thine;
And all gifts, which the world offers singly, on one head combine!
On one head, all the beauty and strength, love and rage (like the
    throe
That, a-work in the rock, helps its labour and lets the gold go)
High ambition and deeds which surpass it, fame crowning them,
    – all
Brought to blaze on the head of one creature – King Saul!'

X

And lo, with that leap of my spirit, – heart, hand, harp and voice,
Each lifting Saul's name out of sorrow, each bidding rejoice
Saul's fame in the light it was made for – as when, dare I say,
100 The Lord's army, in rapture of service, strains through its array,
And upsoareth the cherubim-chariot – 'Saul!' cried I, and
    stopped,
And waited the thing that should follow. Then Saul, who hung
    propped
By the tent's cross-support in the centre, was struck by his name.
Have ye seen when Spring's arrowy summons goes right to the
    aim,
And some mountain, the last to withstand her, that held (he
    alone,
While the vale laughed in freedom and flowers) on a broad bust
    of stone

A year's snow bound about for a breastplate, – leaves grasp of the
    sheet?
Fold on fold all at once it crowds thunderously down to his feet,
And there fronts you, stark, black, but alive yet, your mountain
    of old,
110 With his rents, the successive bequeathings of ages untold –
Yea, each harm got in fighting your battles, each furrow and scar
Of his head thrust 'twixt you and the tempest – all hail, there
    they are!
– Now again to be softened with verdure, again hold the nest
Of the dove, tempt the goat and its young to the green on his
    crest
For their food in the ardours of summer. One long shudder
    thrilled
All the tent till the very air tingled, then sank and was stilled
At the King's self left standing before me, released and aware.
What was gone, what remained? All to traverse, 'twixt hope and
    despair;
Death was past, life not come: so he waited. Awhile his right
    hand
120 Held the brow, helped the eyes left too vacant forthwith to
    remand
To their place what new objects should enter: 'twas Saul as
    before.
I looked up and dared gaze at those eyes, nor was hurt any more
Than by slow pallid sunsets in autumn, ye watch from the shore,
At their sad level gaze o'er the ocean – a sun's slow decline
Over hills which, resolved in stern silence, o'erlap and entwine
Base with base to knit strength more intensely: so, arm folded
    arm
O'er the chest whose slow heavings subsided.

XI

                        What spell or what charm,
(For, awhile there was trouble within me) what next should I
    urge
To sustain him where song had restored him? – Song filled to the
    verge
130 His cup with the wine of this life, pressing all that it yields
Of mere fruitage, the strength and the beauty: beyond, on what
    fields,
Glean a vintage more potent and perfect to brighten the eye

And bring blood to the lip, and commend them the cup they put
    by?
He saith, 'It is good'; still he drinks not: he lets me praise life,
Gives assent, yet would die for his own part.

XII

                 Then fancies grew rife
Which had come long ago on the pasture, when round me the
    sheep
Fed in silence – above, the one eagle wheeled slow as in sleep;
And I lay in my hollow and mused on the world that might lie
'Neath his ken, though I saw but the strip 'twixt the hill and the
    sky:
140 And I laughed – 'Since my days are ordained to be passed with
    my flocks,
Let me people at least, with my fancies, the plains and the rocks,
Dream the life I am never to mix with, and image the show
Of mankind as they live in those fashions I hardly shall know!
Schemes of life, its best rules and right uses, the courage that
    gains,
And the prudence that keeps what men strive for.' And now
    these old trains
Of vague thought came again; I grew surer; so, once more the
    string
Of my harp made response to my spirit, as thus –

XIII

                 'Yea, my King,'
I began – 'thou dost well in rejecting mere comforts that spring
From the mere mortal life held in common by man and by brute:
150 In our flesh grows the branch of this life, in our soul it bears
    fruit.
Thou hast marked the slow rise of the tree, – how its stem
    trembled first
Till it passed the kid's lip, the stag's antler; then safely outburst
The fan-branches all round; and thou mindest when these too,
    in turn
Broke a-bloom and the palm-tree seemed perfect: yet more was
    to learn,
E'en the good that comes in with the palm-fruit. Our dates shall
    we slight,

When their juice brings a cure for all sorrow? or care for the
    plight
Of the palm's self whose slow growth produced them? Not so!
    stem and branch
Shall decay, nor be known in their place, while the palm-wine
    shall staunch
Every wound of man's spirit in winter. I pour thee such wine.
160 Leave the flesh to the fate it was fit for! the spirit be thine!
By the spirit, when age shall o'ercome thee, thou still shalt enjoy
More indeed, than at first when inconscious, the life of a boy.
Crush that life, and behold its wine running! Each deed thou
    hast done
Dies, revives, goes to work in the world; until e'en as the sun
Looking down on the earth, though clouds spoil him, though
    tempests efface,
Can find nothing his own deed produced not, must everywhere
    trace
The results of his past summer-prime, – so, each ray of thy will,
Every flash of thy passion and prowess, long over, shall thrill
Thy whole people, the countless, with ardour, till they too give
    forth
170 A like cheer to their sons, who in turn, fill the South and the
    North
With the radiance thy deed was the germ of. Carouse in the past!
But the license of age has its limit; thou diest at last:
As the lion when age dims his eyeball, the rose at her height
So with man – so his power and his beauty for ever take flight.
No! Again a long draught of my soul-wine! Look forth o'er the
    years!
Thou hast done now with eyes for the actual; begin with the
    seer's!
Is Saul dead? In the depth of the vale make his tomb – bid arise
A grey mountain of marble heaped four-square, till, built to the
    skies,
Let it mark where the great First King slumbers: whose fame
    would ye know?
180 Up above see the rock's naked face, where the record shall go
In great characters cut by the scribe, – Such was Saul, so he did;
With the sages directing the work, by the populace chid, –
For not half, they'll affirm, is comprised there! Which fault to
    amend,

In the grove with his kind grows the cedar, whereon they shall
　　spend
(See, in tablets 'tis level before them) their praise, and record
With the gold of the graver, Saul's story, – the statesman's great
　　word
Side by side with the poet's sweet comment. The river's a-wave
With smooth paper-reeds grazing each other when prophet-
　　winds rave:
So the pen gives unborn generations their due and their part
190　In thy being! Then, first of the mighty, thank God that thou art!'

XIV

And behold while I sang . . . but O Thou who didst grant me that
　　day,
And before it not seldom hast granted thy help to essay,
Carry on and complete an adventure, – my shield and my sword
In that act where my soul was thy servant, thy word was my
　　word, –
Still be with me, who then at the summit of human endeavour
And scaling the highest, man's thought could, gazed hopeless as
　　ever
On the new stretch of heaven above me – till, mighty to save,
Just one lift of thy hand cleared that distance – God's throne
　　from man's grave!
Let me tell out my tale to its ending – my voice to my heart
200　Which can scarce dare believe in what marvels last night I took
　　part,
As this morning I gather the fragments, alone with my sheep,
And still fear lest the terrible glory evanish like sleep!
For I wake in the grey dewy covert, while Hebron upheaves
The dawn struggling with night on his shoulder, and Kidron
　　retrieves
Slow the damage of yesterday's sunshine.

XV
　　　　　　　　　　　　　　　　I say then, – my song
While I sang thus, assuring the monarch, and ever more strong
Made a proffer of good to console him – he slowly resumed
His old motions and habitudes kingly. The right-hand replumed
His black locks to their wonted composure, adjusted the swathes
210　Of his turban, and see – the huge sweat that his countenance
　　bathes,

He wipes off with the robe; and he girds now his loins as of yore,
And feels slow for the armlets of price, with the clasp set before.
He is Saul, ye remember in glory, – ere error had bent
The broad brow from the daily communion; and still, though
    much spent
Be the life and the bearing that front you, the same, God did
    choose,
To receive what a man may waste, desecrate, never quite lose.
So sank he along by the tent-prop till, stayed by the pile
Of his armour and war-cloak and garments, he leaned there
    awhile,
And sat out my singing, – one arm round the tent-prop, to raise
220 His bent head, and the other hung slack – till I touched on the
    praise
I foresaw from all men in all time, to the man patient there;
And thus ended, the harp falling forward. Then first I was 'ware
That he sat, as I say, with my head just above his vast knees
Which were thrust out on each side around me, like oak-roots
    which please
To encircle a lamb when it slumbers. I looked up to know
If the best I could do had brought solace: he spoke not, but slow
Lifted up the hand slack at his side, till he laid it with care
Soft and grave, but in mild settled will, on my brow: through my
    hair
The large fingers were pushed, and he bent back my head, with
    kind power –
230 All my face back, intent to peruse it, as men do a flower.
Thus held he me there with his great eyes that scrutinized mine –
And oh, all my heart how it loved him! but where was the sign?
I yearned – 'Could I help thee, my father, inventing a bliss,
I would add, to that life of the past, both the future and this;
I would give thee new life altogether, as good, ages hence,
As this moment, – had love but the warrant, love's heart to
    dispense!'

XVI
Then the truth came upon me. No harp more – no song more!
    outbroke –

XVII

'I have gone the whole round of creation: I saw and I spoke:
I, a work of God's hand for that purpose, received in my brain
240 And pronounced on the rest of his handwork – returned him
      again
His creation's approval or censure: I spoke as I saw:
I report, as a man may of God's work – all's love, yet all's law.
Now I lay down the judgeship he lent me. Each faculty tasked
To perceive him, has gained an abyss, where a dew-drop was
      asked.
Have I knowledge? confounded it shrivels at Wisdom laid bare.
Have I forethought? how purblind, how blank, to the Infinite
      Care!
Do I task any faculty highest, to image success?
I but open my eyes, – and perfection, no more and no less,
In the kind I imagined, full-fronts me, and God is seen God
250 In the star, in the stone, in the flesh, in the soul and the clod.
And thus looking within and around me, I ever renew
(With that stoop of the soul which in bending upraises it too)
The submission of man's nothing-perfect to God's all-complete,
As by each new obeisance in spirit, I climb to his feet.
Yet with all this abounding experience, this deity known,
I shall dare to discover some province, some gift of my own.
There's a faculty pleasant to exercise, hard to hood-wink,
I am fain to keep still in abeyance, (I laugh as I think)
Lest, insisting to claim and parade in it, wot ye, I worst
260 E'en the Giver in one gift. – Behold, I could love if I durst!
But I sink the pretension as fearing a man may o'ertake
God's own speed in the one way of love: I abstain for love's sake.
– What, my soul? see thus far and no farther? when doors great
      and small,
Nine-and-ninety flew ope at our touch, should the hundredth
      appal?
In the least things have faith, yet distrust in the greatest of all?
Do I find love so full in my nature, God's ultimate gift,
That I doubt his own love can compete with it? Here, the parts
      shift?
Here, the creature surpass the Creator, – the end, what Began?
Would I fain in my impotent yearning do all for this man,
270 And dare doubt he alone shall not help him, who yet alone can?
Would it ever have entered my mind, the bare will, much less
      power,

To bestow on this Saul what I sang of, the marvellous dower
Of the life he was gifted and filled with? to make such a soul,
Such a body, and then such an earth for insphering the whole?
And doth it not enter my mind (as my warm tears attest)
These good things being given, to go on, and give one more, the
  best?
Ay, to save and redeem and restore him, maintain at the height
This perfection, – succeed with life's dayspring, death's minute
  of night?
Interpose at the difficult minute, snatch Saul the mistake,
280 Saul the failure, the ruin he seems now, – and bid him awake
From the dream, the probation, the prelude, to find himself set
Clear and safe in new light and new life, – a new harmony yet
To be run, and continued, and ended – who knows? – or endure!
The man taught enough, by life's dream, of the rest to make sure;
By the pain-throb, triumphantly winning intensified bliss,
And the next world's reward and repose, by the struggles in this.

XVIII

'I believe it! 'Tis thou, God, that givest, 'tis I who receive:
In the first is the last, in thy will is my power to believe.
All's one gift: thou canst grant it moreover, as prompt to my
  prayer
290 As I breathe out this breath, as I open these arms to the air.
From thy will, stream the worlds, life and nature, thy dread
  Sabaoth:
I will? – the mere atoms despise me! Why am I not loth
To look that, even that in the face too? Why is it I dare
Think but lightly of such impuissance? What stops my despair?
This; – 'tis not what man Does which exalts him, but what man
  Would do!
See the King – I would help him but cannot, the wishes fall
  through.
Could I wrestle to raise him from sorrow, grow poor to enrich,
To fill up his life, starve my own out, I would – knowing which,
I know that my service is perfect. Oh, speak through me now!
300 Would I suffer for him that I love? So wouldst thou – so wilt
  thou!
So shall crown thee the topmost, ineffablest, uttermost crown –
And thy love fill infinitude wholly, nor leave up nor down
One spot for the creature to stand in! It is by no breath,
Turn of eye, wave of hand, that salvation joins issue with death!

As thy Love is discovered almighty, almighty be proved
Thy power, that exists with and for it, of being Beloved!
He who did most, shall bear most; the strongest shall stand the
    most weak.
'Tis the weakness in strength, that I cry for! my flesh, that I seek
In the Godhead! I seek and I find it. O Saul, it shall be
310 A Face like my face that receives thee; a Man like to me,
Thou shalt love and be loved by, for ever: a Hand like this hand
Shall throw open the gates of new life to thee! See the Christ
    stand!'

XIX

I know not too well how I found my way home in the night.
There were witnesses, cohorts about me, to left and to right,
Angels, powers, the unuttered, unseen, the alive, the aware:
I repressed, I got through them as hardly, as strugglingly there,
As a runner beset by the populace famished for news –
Life or death. The whole earth was awakened, hell loosed with
    her crews;
And the stars of night beat with emotion, and tingled and shot
320 Out in fire the strong pain of pent knowledge: but I fainted not,
For the Hand still impelled me at once and supported, suppressed
All the tumult, and quenched it with quiet, and holy behest,
Till the rapture was shut in itself, and the earth sank to rest.
Anon at the dawn, all that trouble had withered from earth –
Not so much, but I saw it die out in the day's tender birth;
In the gathered intensity brought to the grey of the hills;
In the shuddering forests' held breath; in the sudden wind-
    thrills;
In the startled wild beasts that bore off, each with eye sidling
    still
Though averted with wonder and dread; in the birds stiff and
    chill
330 That rose heavily, as I approached them, made stupid with awe:
E'en the serpent that slid away silent, – he felt the new law.
The same stared in the white humid faces upturned by the
    flowers;
The same worked in the heart of the cedar and moved the vine-
    bowers:
And the little brooks witnessing murmured, persistent and low,
With their obstinate, all but hushed voices – 'E'en so, it is so!'

'De Gustibus –'

I
Your ghost will walk, you lover of trees,
 (If our loves remain)
 In an English lane,
By a cornfield-side a-flutter with poppies.
Hark, those two in the hazel coppice –
A boy and a girl, if the good fates please,
 Making love, say, –
 The happier they!
Draw yourself up from the light of the moon,
10 And let them pass, as they will too soon,
 With the bean-flowers' boon,
 And the blackbird's tune,
 And May, and June!

II
What I love best in all the world
Is a castle, precipice-encurled,
In a gash of the wind-grieved Apennine.
Or look for me, old fellow of mine,
(If I get my head from out the mouth
O' the grave, and loose my spirit's bands,
20 And come again to the land of lands) –
In a sea-side house to the farther South,
Where the baked cicala dies of drouth,
And one sharp tree – 'tis a cypress – stands,
By the many hundred years red-rusted,
Rough iron-spiked, ripe fruit-o'ercrusted,
My sentinel to guard the sands
To the water's edge. For, what expands
Before the house, but the great opaque
Blue breadth of sea without a break?
30 While, in the house, for ever crumbles
Some fragment of the frescoed walls,
From blisters where a scorpion sprawls.
A girl bare-footed brings, and tumbles
Down on the pavement, green-flesh melons,
And says there's news today – the king
Was shot at, touched in the liver-wing,

Goes with his Bourbon arm in a sling:
– She hopes they have not caught the felons.
Italy, my Italy!
40 Queen Mary's saying serves for me –
      (When fortune's malice
      Lost her – Calais) –
Open my heart and you will see
Graved inside of it, 'Italy.'
Such lovers old are I and she:
So it always was, so shall ever be!

Women and Roses

I

I dream of a red-rose tree.
And which of its roses three
Is the dearest rose to me?

II

Round and round, like a dance of snow
In a dazzling drift, as its guardians, go
Floating the women faded for ages,
Sculptured in stone, on the poet's pages.
Then follow women fresh and gay,
Living and loving and loved today.
10 Last, in the rear, flee the multitude of maidens,
Beauties yet unborn. And all, to one cadence,
They circle their rose on my rose tree.

III

Dear rose, thy term is reached,
Thy leaf hangs loose and bleached:
Bees pass it unimpeached.

IV

Stay then, stoop, since I cannot climb,
You, great shapes of the antique time!
How shall I fix you, fire you, freeze you,
Break my heart at your feet to please you?
20 Oh, to possess and be possessed!

Hearts that beat 'neath each pallid breast!
Once but of love, the poesy, the passion,
Drink but once and die! – In vain, the same fashion,
They circle their rose on my rose tree.

V
Dear rose, thy joy's undimmed,
Thy cup is ruby-rimmed,
Thy cup's heart nectar-brimmed.

VI
Deep, as drops from a statue's plinth
The bee sucked in by the hyacinth,
30   So will I bury me while burning,
Quench like him at a plunge my yearning,
Eyes in your eyes, lips on your lips!
Fold me fast where the cincture slips,
Prison all my soul in eternities of pleasure,
Girdle me for once! But no – the old measure,
They circle their rose on my rose tree.

VII
Dear rose without a thorn,
Thy bud's the babe unborn:
First streak of a new morn.

VIII
40   Wings, lend wings for the cold, the clear!
What is far conquers what is near.
Roses will bloom nor want beholders,
Sprung from the dust where our flesh moulders.
What shall arrive with the cycle's change?
A novel grace and a beauty strange.
I will make an Eve, be the artist that began her,
Shaped her to his mind! – Alas! in like manner
They circle their rose on my rose tree.

Protus

Among these latter busts we count by scores,
Half-emperors and quarter-emperors,
Each with his bay-leaf fillet, loose-thonged vest,
Loric and low-browed Gorgon on the breast, –
One loves a baby face, with violets there,
Violets instead of laurel in the hair,
As those were all the little locks could bear.

Now read here. 'Protus ends a period
Of empery beginning with a god;
10 Born in the porphyry chamber at Byzant,
Queens by his cradle, proud and ministrant:
And if he quickened breath there, 'twould like fire
Pantingly through the dim vast realm transpire.
A fame that he was missing spread afar:
The world, from its four corners, rose in war,
Till he was borne out on a balcony
To pacify the world when it should see.
The captains ranged before him, one, his hand
Made baby points at, gained the chief command.
20 And day by day more beautiful he grew
In shape, all said, in feature and in hue,
While young Greek sculptors, gazing on the child,
Became with old Greek sculpture reconciled.
Already sages laboured to condense
In easy tomes a life's experience:
And artists took grave counsel to impart
In one breath and one hand-sweep, all their art –
To make his graces prompt as blossoming
Of plentifully-watered palms in spring:
30 Since well beseems it, whoso mounts the throne,
For beauty, knowledge, strength, should stand alone,
And mortals love the letters of his name.'

– Stop! Have you turned two pages? Still the same.
New reign, same date. The scribe goes on to say
How that same year, on such a month and day,
'John the Pannonian, groundedly believed
A blacksmith's bastard, whose hard hand reprieved

The Empire from its fate the year before, –
Came, had a mind to take the crown, and wore
40 The same for six years (during which the Huns
Kept off their fingers from us), till his sons
Put something in his liquor' – and so forth.
Then a new reign. Stay – 'Take at its just worth'
(Subjoins an annotator) 'what I give
As hearsay. Some think, John let Protus live
And slip away. 'Tis said, he reached man's age
At some blind northern court; made, first a page,
Then tutor to the children; last, of use
About the hunting-stables. I deduce
50 He wrote the little tract "On worming dogs,"
Whereof the name in sundry catalogues
Is extant yet. A Protus of the race
Is rumoured to have died a monk in Thrace, –
And if the same, he reached senility.'

Here's John the Smith's rough-hammered head. Great eye,
Gross jaw and griped lips do what granite can
To give you the crown-grasper. What a man!

Holy-Cross Day

On which the Jews were forced to attend an annual Christian sermon in Rome

['Now was come about Holy-Cross Day, and now must my lord preach his first sermon to the Jews: as it was of old cared for in the merciful bowels of the Church, that, so to speak, a crumb at least from her conspicuous table here in Rome should be, though but once yearly, cast to the famishing dogs, under-trampled and bespitten-upon beneath the feet of the guests. And a moving sight in truth, this, of so many of the besotted blind restif and ready-to-perish Hebrews! now maternally brought – nay (for He saith "Compel them to come in") haled, as it were, by the head and hair, and against their obstinate hearts, to partake of the heavenly grace. What awakening, what striving with tears, what working of a yeasty conscience! Nor was my lord wanting to himself on so apt an occasion; witness the abundance of conversions which did incontinently reward him: though not to my lord be altogether the glory.' – *Diary by the Bishop's Secretary*, 1600.]

What the Jews really said, on thus being driven to church, was rather to this effect: –

I

Fee, faw, fum! bubble and squeak!
Blessedest Thursday's the fat of the week.
Rumble and tumble, sleek and rough,
Stinking and savoury, smug and gruff,
Take the church-road, for the bell's due chime
Gives us the summons – 'tis sermon-time!

II

Boh, here's Barnabas! Job, that's you?
Up stumps Solomon – bustling too?
Shame, man! greedy beyond your years
To handsel the bishop's shaving-shears?
Fair play's a jewel! Leave friends in the lurch?
Stand on a line ere you start for the church!

III

Higgledy piggledy, packed we lie,
Rats in a hamper, swine in a sty,
Wasps in a bottle, frogs in a sieve,
Worms in a carcase, fleas in a sleeve.
Hist! square shoulders, settle your thumbs
And buzz for the bishop – here he comes.

IV

Bow, wow, wow – a bone for the dog!
I liken his Grace to an acorned hog.
What, a boy at his side, with the bloom of a lass,
To help and handle my lord's hour-glass!
Didst ever behold so lithe a chine?
His cheek hath laps like a fresh-singed swine.

V

Aaron's asleep – shove hip to haunch,
Or somebody deal him a dig in the paunch!
Look at the purse with the tassel and knob,
And the gown with the angel and thingumbob!
What's he at, quotha? reading his text!
Now you've his curtsey – and what comes next.

VI

See to our converts – you doomed black dozen –
No stealing away – nor cog nor cozen!
You five, that were thieves, deserve it fairly;
You seven, that were beggars, will live less sparely;
You took your turn and dipped in the hat,
Got fortune – and fortune gets you; mind that!

VII

Give your first groan – compunction's at work;
And soft! from a Jew you mount to a Turk.
Lo, Micah, – the selfsame beard on chin
40 He was four times already converted in!
Here's a knife, clip quick – it's a sign of grace –
Or he ruins us all with his hanging-face.

VIII

Whom now is the bishop a-leering at?
I know a point where his text falls pat.
I'll tell him tomorrow, a word just now
Went to my heart and made me vow
I meddle no more with the worst of trades –
Let somebody else pay his serenades.

IX

Groan all together now, whee – hee – hee!
50 It's a-work, it's a-work, ah, woe is me!
It began, when a herd of us, picked and placed,
Were spurred through the Corso, stripped to the waist;
Jew brutes, with sweat and blood well spent
To usher in worthily Christian Lent.

X

It grew, when the hangman entered our bounds,
Yelled, pricked us out to his church like hounds:
It got to a pitch, when the hand indeed
Which gutted my purse would throttle my creed:
And it overflows when, to even the odd,
60 Men I helped to their sins help me to their God.

XI

But now, while the scapegoats leave our flock,
And the rest sit silent and count the clock,
Since forced to muse the appointed time
On these precious facts and truths sublime, –
Let us fitly employ it, under our breath,
In saying Ben Ezra's Song of Death.

XII

For Rabbi Ben Ezra, the night he died,
Called sons and sons' sons to his side,
And spoke, 'This world has been harsh and strange;
70 Something is wrong: there needeth a change.
But what, or where? at the last or first?
In one point only we sinned, at worst.

XIII

'The Lord will have mercy on Jacob yet,
And again in his border see Israel set.
When Judah beholds Jerusalem,
The stranger-seed shall be joined to them:
To Jacob's House shall the Gentiles cleave.
So the Prophet saith and his sons believe.

XIV

'Ay, the children of the chosen race
80 Shall carry and bring them to their place:
In the land of the Lord shall lead the same,
Bondsmen and handmaids. Who shall blame,
When the slaves enslave, the oppressed ones o'er
The oppressor triumph for evermore?

XV

'God spoke, and gave us the word to keep,
Bade never fold the hands nor sleep
'Mid a faithless world, – at watch and ward,
Till Christ at the end relieve our guard.
By His servant Moses the watch was set:
90 Though near upon cock-crow, we keep it yet.

XVI

'Thou! if thou wast He, who at mid-watch came,
By the starlight, naming a dubious name!
And if, too heavy with sleep – too rash
With fear – O Thou, if that martyr-gash
Fell on Thee coming to take thine own,
And we gave the Cross, when we owed the Throne –

XVII

'Thou art the Judge. We are bruisèd thus.
But, the Judgement over, join sides with us!
Thine too is the cause! and not more thine
100   Than ours, is the work of these dogs and swine,
Whose life laughs through and spits at their creed!
Who maintain Thee in word, and defy Thee in deed!

XVIII

'We withstood Christ then? Be mindful how
At least we withstand Barabbas now!
Was our outrage sore? But the worst we spared,
To have called these – Christians, had we dared!
Let defiance to them pay mistrust of Thee,
And Rome make amends for Calvary!

XIX

'By the torture, prolonged from age to age,
110   By the infamy, Israel's heritage,
By the Ghetto's plague, by the garb's disgrace,
By the badge of shame, by the felon's place,
By the branding-tool, the bloody whip,
And the summons to Christian fellowship, –

XX

'We boast our proof that at least the Jew
Would wrest Christ's name from the Devil's crew.
Thy face took never so deep a shade
But we fought them in it, God our aid!
A trophy to bear, as we march, thy band,
120   South, East, and on to the Pleasant Land!'

[*Pope Gregory XVI abolished this bad business of the Sermon.*
– R. B.]

The Guardian-Angel

A Picture at Fano

I

Dear and great Angel, wouldst thou only leave
    That child, when thou hast done with him, for me!
Let me sit all the day here, that when eve
    Shall find performed thy special ministry,
And time come for departure, thou, suspending
Thy flight, mayst see another child for tending,
    Another still, to quiet and retrieve.

II

Then I shall feel thee step one step, no more,
    From where thou standest now, to where I gaze,
10 – And suddenly my head is covered o'er
    With those wings, white above the child who prays
Now on that tomb – and I shall feel thee guarding
Me, out of all the world; for me, discarding
    Yon heaven thy home, that waits and opes its door.

III

I would not look up thither past thy head
    Because the door opes, like that child, I know,
For I should have thy gracious face instead,
    Thou bird of God! And wilt thou bend me low
Like him, and lay, like his, my hands together,
20 And lift them up to pray, and gently tether
    Me, as thy lamb there, with thy garment's spread?

IV

If this was ever granted, I would rest
    My head beneath thine, while thy healing hands
Close-covered both my eyes beside thy breast,
    Pressing the brain, which too much thought expands,
Back to its proper size again, and smoothing
Distortion down till every nerve had soothing,
    And all lay quiet, happy and suppressed.

V

How soon all worldly wrong would be repaired!
30   I think how I should view the earth and skies
And sea, when once again my brow was bared
    After thy healing, with such different eyes.
O world, as God has made it! All is beauty:
And knowing this, is love, and love is duty.
    What further may be sought for or declared?

VI

Guercino drew this angel I saw teach
    (Alfred, dear friend!) – that little child to pray,
Holding the little hands up, each to each
    Pressed gently, – with his own head turned away
40 Over the earth where so much lay before him
Of work to do, though heaven was opening o'er him,
    And he was left at Fano by the beach.

VII

We were at Fano, and three times we went
    To sit and see him in his chapel there,
And drink his beauty to our soul's content
    – My angel with me too: and since I care
For dear Guercino's fame (to which in power
And glory comes this picture for a dower,
    Fraught with a pathos so magnificent) –

VIII

50 And since he did not work thus earnestly
    At all times, and has else endured some wrong –
I took one thought his picture struck from me,
    And spread it out, translating it to song.
My love is here. Where are you, dear old friend?
How rolls the Wairoa at your world's far end?
    This is Ancona, yonder is the sea.

Cleon

'As certain also of your own poets have said' –

Cleon the poet (from the sprinkled isles,
Lily on lily, that o'erlace the sea,
And laugh their pride when the light wave lisps 'Greece') –
To Protus in his Tyranny: much health!

They give thy letter to me, even now:
I read and seem as if I heard thee speak.
The master of thy galley still unlades
Gift after gift; they block my court at last
And pile themselves along its portico
10 Royal with sunset, like a thought of thee:
And one white she-slave from the group dispersed
Of black and white slaves (like the chequer-work
Pavement, at once my nation's work and gift,
Now covered with this settle-down of doves),
One lyric woman, in her crocus vest
Woven of sea-wools, with her two white hands
Commends to me the strainer and the cup
Thy lip hath bettered ere it blesses mine.

Well-counselled, king, in thy munificence!
20 For so shall men remark, in such an act
Of love for him whose song gives life its joy,
Thy recognition of the use of life;
Nor call thy spirit barely adequate
To help on life in straight ways, broad enough
For vulgar souls, by ruling and the rest.
Thou, in the daily building of thy tower, –
Whether in fierce and sudden spasms of toil,
Or through dim lulls of unapparent growth,
Or when the general work 'mid good acclaim
30 Climbed with the eye to cheer the architect, –
Didst ne'er engage in work for mere work's sake –
Had'st ever in thy heart the luring hope
Of some eventual rest a-top of it,
Whence, all the tumult of the building hushed,
Thou first of men mightst look out to the East:

The vulgar saw thy tower, thou sawest the sun.
For this, I promise on thy festival
To pour libation, looking o'er the sea,
Making this slave narrate thy fortunes, speak
40　Thy great words, and describe thy royal face –
Wishing thee wholly where Zeus lives the most,
Within the eventual element of calm.

　Thy letter's first requirement meets me here.
It is as thou hast heard: in one short life
I, Cleon, have effected all those things
Thou wonderingly dost enumerate.
That epos on thy hundred plates of gold
Is mine, – and also mine the little chant,
So sure to rise from every fishing-bark
50　When, lights at prow, the seamen haul their net.
The image of the sun-god on the phare,
Men turn from the sun's self to see, is mine;
The Poecile, o'er-storied its whole length,
As thou didst hear, with painting, is mine too.
I know the true proportions of a man
And woman also, not observed before;
And I have written three books on the soul,
Proving absurd all written hitherto,
And putting us to ignorance again.
60　For music, – why, I have combined the moods,
Inventing one. In brief, all arts are mine;
Thus much the people know and recognize,
Throughout our seventeen islands. Marvel not.
We of these latter days, with greater mind
Than our forerunners, since more composite,
Look not so great, beside their simple way,
To a judge who only sees one way at once,
One mind-point and no other at a time, –
Compares the small part of a man of us
70　With some whole man of the heroic age,
Great in his way – not ours, nor meant for ours.
And ours is greater, had we skill to know:
For, what we call this life of men on earth,
This sequence of the soul's achievements here
Being, as I find much reason to conceive,
Intended to be viewed eventually

As a great whole, not analysed to parts,
But each part having reference to all, –
How shall a certain part, pronounced complete,
80 Endure effacement by another part?
Was the thing done? – then, what's to do again?
See, in the chequered pavement opposite,
Suppose the artist made a perfect rhomb,
And next a lozenge, then a trapezoid –
He did not overlay them, superimpose
The new upon the old and blot it out,
But laid them on a level in his work,
Making at last a picture; there it lies.
So, first the perfect separate forms were made,
90 The portions of mankind; and after, so,
Occurred the combination of the same.
For where had been a progress, otherwise?
Mankind, made up of all the single men, –
In such a synthesis the labour ends.
Now mark me! those divine men of old time
Have reached, thou sayest well, each at one point
The outside verge that rounds our faculty;
And where they reached, who can do more than reach?
It takes but little water just to touch
100 At some one point the inside of a sphere,
And, as we turn the sphere, touch all the rest
In due succession: but the finer air
Which not so palpably nor obviously,
Though no less universally, can touch
The whole circumference of that emptied sphere,
Fills it more fully than the water did;
Holds thrice the weight of water in itself
Resolved into a subtler element.
And yet the vulgar call the sphere first full
110 Up to the visible height – and after, void;
Not knowing air's more hidden properties.
And thus our soul, misknown, cries out to Zeus
To vindicate his purpose in our life:
Why stay we on the earth unless to grow?
Long since, I imaged, wrote the fiction out,
That he or other god descended here
And, once for all, showed simultaneously
What, in its nature, never can be shown,

Piecemeal or in succession; – showed, I say,
120 The worth both absolute and relative
Of all his children from the birth of time,
His instruments for all appointed work.
I now go on to image, – might we hear
The judgement which should give the due to each,
Show where the labour lay and where the ease,
And prove Zeus' self, the latent everywhere!
This is a dream: – but no dream, let us hope,
That years and days, the summers and the springs,
Follow each other with unwaning powers.
130 The grapes which dye thy wine are richer far,
Through culture, than the wild wealth of the rock;
The suave plum than the savage-tasted drupe;
The pastured honey-bee drops choicer sweet;
The flowers turn double, and the leaves turn flowers;
That young and tender crescent-moon, thy slave,
Sleeping above her robe as buoyed by clouds,
Refines upon the women of my youth.
What, and the soul alone deteriorates?
I have not chanted verse like Homer, no –
140 Nor swept string like Terpander, no – nor carved
And painted men like Phidias and his friend:
I am not great as they are, point by point.
But I have entered into sympathy
With these four, running these into one soul,
Who, separate, ignored each other's art.
Say, is it nothing that I know them all?
The wild flower was the larger; I have dashed
Rose-blood upon its petals, pricked its cup's
Honey with wine, and driven its seed to fruit,
150 And show a better flower if not so large:
I stand myself. Refer this to the gods
Whose gift alone it is! which, shall I dare
(All pride apart) upon the absurd pretext
That such a gift by chance lay in my hand,
Discourse of lightly or depreciate?
It might have fallen to another's hand: what then?
I pass too surely: let at least truth stay!

And next, of what thou followest on to ask.
This being with me as I declare, O king,
160 My works, in all these varicoloured kinds,
So done by me, accepted so by men –
Thou askest, if (my soul thus in men's hearts)
I must not be accounted to attain
The very crown and proper end of life?
Inquiring thence how, now life closeth up,
I face death with success in my right hand:
Whether I fear death less than dost thyself
The fortunate of men? 'For' (writest thou)
'Thou leavest much behind, while I leave naught.
170 Thy life stays in the poems men shall sing,
The pictures men shall study; while my life,
Complete and whole now in its power and joy,
Dies altogether with my brain and arm,
Is lost indeed; since, what survives myself?
The brazen statue to o'erlook my grave,
Set on the promontory which I named.
And that – some supple courtier of my heir
Shall use its robed and sceptred arm, perhaps,
To fix the rope to, which best drags it down.
180 I go then: triumph thou, who dost not go!'

Nay, thou art worthy of hearing my whole mind.
Is this apparent, when thou turn'st to muse
Upon the scheme of earth and man in chief,
That admiration grows as knowledge grows?
That imperfection means perfection hid,
Reserved in part, to grace the after-time?
If, in the morning of philosophy,
Ere aught had been recorded, nay perceived,
Thou, with the light now in thee, couldst have looked
190 On all earth's tenantry, from worm to bird,
Ere man, her last, appeared upon the stage –
Thou wouldst have seen them perfect, and deduced
The perfectness of others yet unseen.
Conceding which, – had Zeus then questioned thee
'Shall I go on a step, improve on this,
Do more for visible creatures than is done?'
Thou wouldst have answered, 'Ay, by making each
Grow conscious in himself – by that alone.

All's perfect else: the shell sucks fast the rock,
200 The fish strikes through the sea, the snake both swims
And slides, forth range the beasts, the birds take flight,
Till life's mechanics can no further go –
And all this joy in natural life is put
Like fire from off thy finger into each,
So exquisitely perfect is the same.
But 'tis pure fire, and they mere matter are;
It has them, not they it: and so I choose
For man, thy last premeditated work
(If I might add a glory to the scheme)
210 That a third thing should stand apart from both,
A quality arise within his soul,
Which, intro-active, made to supervise
And feel the force it has, may view itself,
And so be happy.' Man might live at first
The animal life: but is there nothing more?
In due time, let him critically learn
How he lives; and, the more he gets to know
Of his own life's adaptabilities,
The more joy-giving will his life become.
220 Thus man, who hath this quality, is best.

But thou, king, hadst more reasonably said:
'Let progress end at once, – man make no step
Beyond the natural man, the better beast,
Using his senses, not the sense of sense.'
In man there's failure, only since he left
The lower and inconscious forms of life.
We called it an advance, the rendering plain
Man's spirit might grow conscious of man's life,
And, by new lore so added to the old,
230 Take each step higher over the brute's head.
This grew the only life, the pleasure-house,
Watch-tower and treasure-fortress of the soul,
Which whole surrounding flats of natural life
Seemed only fit to yield subsistence to;
A tower that crowns a country. But alas,
The soul now climbs it just to perish there!
For thence we have discovered ('tis no dream –
We know this, which we had not else perceived)
That there's a world of capability

240   For joy, spread round about us, meant for us,
      Inviting us; and still the soul craves all,
      And still the flesh replies, 'Take no jot more
      Than ere thou clombst the tower to look abroad!
      Nay, so much less as that fatigue has brought
      Deduction to it.' We struggle, fain to enlarge
      Our bounded physical recipiency,
      Increase our power, supply fresh oil to life,
      Repair the waste of age and sickness: no,
      It skills not! life's inadequate to joy,
250   As the soul sees joy, tempting life to take.
      They praise a fountain in my garden here
      Wherein a Naiad sends the water-bow
      Thin from her tube; she smiles to see it rise.
      What if I told her, it is just a thread
      From that great river which the hills shut up,
      And mock her with my leave to take the same?
      The artificer has given her one small tube
      Past power to widen or exchange – what boots
      To know she might spout oceans if she could?
260   She cannot lift beyond her first thin thread:
      And so a man can use but a man's joy
      While he sees God's. Is it for Zeus to boast,
      'See, man, how happy I live, and despair –
      That I may be still happier – for thy use!'
      If this were so, we could not thank our lord,
      As hearts beat on to doing; 'tis not so –
      Malice it is not. Is it carelessness?
      Still, no. If care – where is the sign? I ask,
      And get no answer, and agree in sum,
270   O king, with thy profound discouragement,
      Who seest the wider but to sigh the more.
      Most progress is most failure: thou sayest well.

      The last point now: – thou dost except a case –
      Holding joy not impossible to one
      With artist-gifts – to such a man as I
      Who leave behind me living works indeed;
      For, such a poem, such a painting lives.
      What? dost thou verily trip upon a word,
      Confound the accurate view of what joy is
280   (Caught somewhat clearer by my eyes than thine)

With feeling joy? confound the knowing how
And showing how to live (my faculty)
With actually living? – Otherwise
Where is the artist's vantage o'er the king?
Because in my great epos I display
How divers men young, strong, fair, wise, can act –
Is this as though I acted? if I paint,
Carve the young Phoebus, am I therefore young?
Methinks I'm older that I bowed myself
290 The many years of pain that taught me art!
Indeed, to know is something, and to prove
How all this beauty might be enjoyed, is more:
But, knowing naught, to enjoy is something too.
Yon rower, with the moulded muscles there,
Lowering the sail, is nearer it than I.
I can write love-odes: thy fair slave's an ode.
I get to sing of love, when grown too grey
For being beloved: she turns to that young man,
The muscles all a-ripple on his back.
300 I know the joy of kingship: well, thou art king!

'But,' sayest thou – (and I marvel, I repeat
To find thee trip on such a mere word) 'what
Thou writest, paintest, stays; that does not die:
Sappho survives, because we sing her songs,
And Aeschylus, because we read his plays!'
Why, if they live still, let them come and take
Thy slave in my despite, drink from thy cup,
Speak in my place. Thou diest while I survive?
Say rather that my fate is deadlier still,
310 In this, that every day my sense of joy
Grows more acute, my soul (intensified
By power and insight) more enlarged, more keen;
While every day my hairs fall more and more,
My hand shakes, and the heavy years increase –
The horror quickening still from year to year,
The consummation coming past escape
When I shall know most, and yet least enjoy –
When all my works wherein I prove my worth,
Being present still to mock me in men's mouths,
320 Alive still, in the praise of such as thou,
I, I the feeling, thinking, acting man,

The man who loved his life so over-much,
Sleep in my urn. It is so horrible,
I dare at times imagine to my need
Some future state revealed to us by Zeus,
Unlimited in capability
For joy, as this is in desire for joy,
– To seek which, the joy-hunger forces us:
That, stung by straitness of our life, made strait
330 On purpose to make prized the life at large –
Freed by the throbbing impulse we call death,
We burst there as the worm into the fly,
Who, while a worm still, wants his wings. But no!
Zeus has not yet revealed it; and alas,
He must have done so, were it possible!

　　Live long and happy, and in that thought die:
Glad for what was! Farewell. And for the rest,
I cannot tell thy messenger aright
Where to deliver what he bears of thine
340 To one called Paulus; we have heard his fame
Indeed, if Christus be not one with him –
I know not, nor am troubled much to know.
Thou canst not think a mere barbarian Jew,
As Paulus proves to be, one circumcised,
Hath access to a secret shut from us?
Thou wrongest our philosophy, O king,
In stooping to inquire of such an one,
As if his answer could impose at all!
He writeth, doth he? well, and he may write.
350 Oh, the Jew findeth scholars! certain slaves
Who touched on this same isle, preached him and Christ;
And (as I gathered from a bystander)
Their doctrine could be held by no sane man.

The Twins

'Give' and 'It-shall-be-given-unto-you.'

I

Grand rough old Martin Luther
   Bloomed fables – flowers on furze,
The better the uncouther:
   Do roses stick like burrs?

II

A beggar asked an alms
   One day at an abbey-door,
Said Luther; but, seized with qualms,
   The abbot replied, 'We're poor!

III

'Poor, who had plenty once,
10   When gifts fell thick as rain:
But they give us naught, for the nonce,
   And how should we give again?'

IV

Then the beggar, 'See your sins!
   Of old, unless I err,
Ye had brothers for inmates, twins,
   Date and Dabitur.

V

'While Date was in good case
   Dabitur flourished too:
For Dabitur's lenten face
20   No wonder if Date rue.

VI

'Would ye retrieve the one?
   Try and make plump the other!
When Date's penance is done,
   Dabitur helps his brother.

VII

'Only, beware relapse!'
   The Abbot hung his head.
This beggar might be perhaps
   An angel, Luther said.

Popularity

I

Stand still, true poet that you are!
   I know you; let me try and draw you.
Some night you'll fail us: when afar
   You rise, remember one man saw you,
Knew you, and named a star!

II

My star, God's glow-worm! Why extend
   That loving hand of his which leads you,
Yet locks you safe from end to end
   Of this dark world, unless he needs you,
10 Just saves your light to spend?

III

His clenched hand shall unclose at last,
   I know, and let out all the beauty:
My poet holds the future fast,
   Accepts the coming ages' duty,
Their present for this past.

IV

That day, the earth's feast-master's brow
   Shall clear, to God the chalice raising;
'Others give best at first, but thou
   Forever set'st our table praising,
20 Keep'st the good wine till now!'

V

Meantime, I'll draw you as you stand,
    With few or none to watch and wonder:
I'll say – a fisher, on the sand
    By Tyre the old, with ocean-plunder,
A netful, brought to land.

VI

Who has not heard how Tyrian shells
    Enclosed the blue, that dye of dyes
Whereof one drop worked miracles,
    And coloured like Astarte's eyes
30 Raw silk the merchant sells?

VII

And each bystander of them all
    Could criticize, and quote tradition
How depths of blue sublimed some pall
    – To get which, pricked a king's ambition;
Worth sceptre, crown and ball.

VIII

Yet there's the dye, in that rough mesh,
    The sea has only just o'erwhispered!
Live whelks, each lip's beard dripping fresh,
    As if they still the water's lisp heard
40 Through foam the rock-weeds thresh.

IX

Enough to furnish Solomon
    Such hangings for his cedar-house,
That, when gold-robed he took the throne
    In that abyss of blue, the Spouse
Might swear his presence shone

X

Most like the centre-spike of gold
    Which burns deep in the blue-bell's womb,
What time, with ardours manifold,
    The bee goes singing to her groom,
50 Drunken and overbold.

XI

Mere conchs! not fit for warp or woof!
    Till cunning come to pound and squeeze
And clarify, – refine to proof
    The liquor filtered by degrees,
While the world stands aloof.

XII

And there's the extract, flasked and fine,
    And priced and salable at last!
And Hobbs, Nobbs, Stokes and Nokes combine
    To paint the future from the past,
60 Put blue into their line.

XIII

Hobbs hints blue, – straight he turtle eats:
    Nobbs prints blue, – claret crowns his cup:
Nokes outdares Stokes in azure feats, –
    Both gorge. Who fished the murex up?
What porridge had John Keats?

The Heretic's Tragedy

A Middle-Age Interlude

ROSA MUNDI; SEU, FULCITE ME FLORIBUS. A CONCEIT OF MASTER
GYSBRECHT, CANON-REGULAR OF SAINT JODOCUS-BY-THE-BAR, YPRES
CITY. CANTUQUE, *Virgilius.* AND HATH OFTEN BEEN SUNG AT HOCK-TIDE
AND FESTIVALS. GAVISUS ERAM, *Jessides.*

(It would seem to be a glimpse from the burning of Jacques du Bourg-Molay, at
Paris, A.D. 1314; as distorted by the refraction from Flemish brain to brain, during
the course of a couple of centuries.)

———

I

PREADMONISHETH THE ABBOT DEODAET
The Lord, we look to once for all,
    Is the Lord we should look at, all at once:
He knows not to vary, saith Saint Paul,
    Nor the shadow of turning, for the nonce.

See him no other than as he is!
  Give both the infinitudes their due –
Infinite mercy, but, I wis,
    As infinite a justice too.
      [*Organ: plagal-cadence*]
    As infinite a justice too.

II
ONE SINGETH

10 John, Master of the Temple of God,
  Falling to sin the Unknown Sin,
What he bought of Emperor Aldabrod,
  He sold it to Sultan Saladin:
Till, caught by Pope Clement, a-buzzing there,
  Hornet-prince of the mad wasps' hive,
And clipt of his wings in Paris square,
    They bring him now to be burned alive.
      [*And wanteth there grace of lute or clavicithern, ye shall say to
      confirm him who singeth –*]
    We bring John now to be burned alive.

III

In the midst is a goodly gallows built;
20 'Twixt fork and fork, a stake is stuck;
But first they set divers tumbrils a-tilt,
  Make a trench all round with the city muck;
Inside they pile log upon log, good store;
  Faggots no few, blocks great and small,
Reach a man's mid-thigh, no less, no more, –
    For they mean he should roast in the sight of all.

CHORUS
  We mean he should roast in the sight of all.

IV

Good sappy bavins that kindle forthwith;
  Billets that blaze substantial and slow;
30 Pine-stump split deftly, dry as pith;
  Larch-heart that chars to a chalk-white glow:
Then up they hoist me John in a chafe,
  Sling him fast like a hog to scorch,

Spit in his face, then leap back safe,
　　Sing 'Laudes' and bid clap-to the torch.

CHORUS
　　Laus Deo – who bids clap-to the torch.

V
John of the Temple, whose fame so bragged,
　　Is burning alive in Paris square!
How can he curse, if his mouth is gagged?
40　　Or wriggle his neck, with a collar there?
Or heave his chest, which a band goes round?
　　Or threat with his fist, since his arms are spliced?
Or kick with his feet, now his legs are bound?
　　– Thinks John, I will call upon Jesus Christ.
　　　[Here one crosseth himself]

VI
Jesus Christ – John had bought and sold,
　　Jesus Christ – John had eaten and drunk;
To him, the Flesh meant silver and gold.
　　(*Salvâ reverentiâ*)
Now it was, 'Saviour, bountiful lamb,
50　　I have roasted thee Turks, though men roast me!
See thy servant, the plight wherein I am!
　　Art thou a saviour? Save thou me!'

CHORUS
　　'Tis John the mocker cries, 'Save thou me!'

VII
Who maketh God's menace an idle word?
　　– Saith, it no more means what it proclaims,
Than a damsel's threat to her wanton bird? –
　　For she too prattles of ugly names.
– Saith, he knoweth but one thing, – what he knows?
　　That God is good and the rest is breath;
60 Why else is the same styled Sharon's rose?
　　Once a rose, ever a rose, he saith.

CHORUS
　　O, John shall yet find a rose, he saith!

VIII

Alack, there be roses and roses, John!
    Some, honied of taste like your leman's tongue:
Some, bitter; for why? (roast gaily on!)
    Their tree struck root in devil's-dung.
When Paul once reasoned of righteousness
    And of temperance and of judgement to come,
Good Felix trembled, he could no less:
70   John, snickering, crooked his wicked thumb.

CHORUS
    What cometh to John of the wicked thumb?

IX

Ha ha, John plucketh now at his rose
    To rid himself of a sorrow at heart!
Lo, – petal on petal, fierce rays unclose;
    Anther on anther, sharp spikes outstart;
And with blood for dew, the bosom boils;
    And a gust of sulphur is all its smell;
And lo, he is horribly in the toils
    Of a coal-black giant flower of hell!

CHORUS
80   What maketh heaven, That maketh hell.

X

So, as John called now, through the fire amain,
    On the Name, he had cursed with, all his life –
To the Person, he bought and sold again –
    For the Face, with his daily buffets rife –
Feature by feature It took its place:
    And his voice, like a mad dog's choking bark,
At the steady whole of the Judge's face –
    Died. Forth John's soul flared into the dark.

SUBJOINETH THE ABBOT DEODAET
God help all poor souls lost in the dark!

Two in the Campagna

I

I wonder do you feel today
   As I have felt since, hand in hand,
We sat down on the grass, to stray
   In spirit better through the land,
This morn of Rome and May?

II

For me, I touched a thought, I know,
   Has tantalized me many times,
(Like turns of thread the spiders throw
   Mocking across our path) for rhymes
10   To catch at and let go.

III

Help me to hold it! First it left
   The yellowing fennel, run to seed
There, branching from the brickwork's cleft,
   Some old tomb's ruin: yonder weed
Took up the floating weft,

IV

Where one small orange cup amassed
   Five beetles, – blind and green they grope
Among the honey-meal: and last,
   Everywhere on the grassy slope
20   I traced it. Hold it fast!

V

The champaign with its endless fleece
   Of feathery grasses everywhere!
Silence and passion, joy and peace,
   An everlasting wash of air –
Rome's ghost since her decease.

VI

Such life here, through such lengths of hours,
   Such miracles performed in play,
Such primal naked forms of flowers,
   Such letting nature have her way
30 While heaven looks from its towers!

VII

How say you? Let us, O my dove,
   Let us be unashamed of soul,
As earth lies bare to heaven above!
   How is it under our control
To love or not to love?

VIII

I would that you were all to me,
   You that are just so much, no more.
Nor yours nor mine, nor slave nor free!
   Where does the fault lie? What the core
40 O' the wound, since wound must be?

IX

I would I could adopt your will,
   See with your eyes, and set my heart
Beating by yours, and drink my fill
   At your soul's springs, – your part my part
In life, for good and ill.

X

No. I yearn upward, touch you close,
   Then stand away. I kiss your cheek,
Catch your soul's warmth, – I pluck the rose
   And love it more than tongue can speak –
50 Then the good minute goes.

XI

Already how am I so far
   Out of that minute? Must I go
Still like the thistle-ball, no bar,
   Onward, whenever light winds blow,
Fixed by no friendly star?

XII

Just when I seemed about to learn!
   Where is the thread now? Off again!
The old trick! Only I discern –
   Infinite passion, and the pain
60 Of finite hearts that yearn.

A Grammarian's Funeral

Shortly after the Revival of Learning in Europe

Let us begin and carry up this corpse,
   Singing together.
Leave we the common crofts, the vulgar thorpes
   Each in its tether
Sleeping safe on the bosom of the plain,
   Cared-for till cock-crow:
Look out if yonder be not day again
   Rimming the rock-row!
That's the appropriate country; there, man's thought,
10 Rarer, intenser,
Self-gathered for an outbreak, as it ought,
   Chafes in the censer.
Leave we the unlettered plain its herd and crop;
   Seek we sepulture
On a tall mountain, cited to the top,
   Crowded with culture!
All the peaks soar, but one the rest excels;
   Clouds overcome it;
No! yonder sparkle is the citadel's
20 Circling its summit.
Thither our path lies; wind we up the heights:
   Wait ye the warning?
Our low life was the level's and the night's;
   He's for the morning.
Step to a tune, square chests, erect each head,
   'Ware the beholders!
This is our master, famous calm and dead,
   Borne on our shoulders.

Sleep, crop and herd! sleep, darkling thorpe and croft,
30 Safe from the weather!
He, whom we convoy to his grave aloft,
  Singing together,
He was a man born with thy face and throat,
  Lyric Apollo!
Long he lived nameless: how should spring take note
  Winter would follow?
Till lo, the little touch, and youth was gone!
  Cramped and diminished,
Moaned he, 'New measures, other feet anon!
40 My dance is finished?'
No, that's the world's way: (keep the mountain-side,
  Make for the city!)
He knew the signal, and stepped on with pride
  Over men's pity;
Left play for work, and grappled with the world
  Bent on escaping:
'What's in the scroll,' quoth he, 'thou keepest furled?
  Show me their shaping,
Theirs who most studied man, the bard and sage, –
50 Give!' – So, he gowned him,
Straight got by heart that book to its last page:
  Learned, we found him.
Yea, but we found him bald too, eyes like lead,
  Accents uncertain:
'Time to taste life,' another would have said,
  'Up with the curtain!'
This man said rather, 'Actual life comes next?
  Patience a moment!
Grant I have mastered learning's crabbed text,
60 Still there's the comment.
Let me know all! Prate not of most or least,
  Painful or easy!
Even to the crumbs I'd fain eat up the feast,
  Ay, nor feel queasy.'
Oh, such a life as he resolved to live,
  When he had learned it,
When he had gathered all books had to give!
  Sooner, he spurned it.
Image the whole, then execute the parts –
70 Fancy the fabric

Quite, ere you build, ere steel strike fire from quartz,
    Ere mortar dab brick!

(Here's the town-gate reached: there's the market-place
    Gaping before us.)
Yea, this in him was the peculiar grace
    (Hearten our chorus!)
That before living he'd learn how to live –
    No end to learning:
Earn the means first – God surely will contrive
80   Use for our earning.
Others mistrust and say, 'But time escapes:
    Live now or never!'
He said, 'What's time? Leave Now for dogs and apes!
    Man has Forever.'
Back to his book then: deeper drooped his head:
    Calculus racked him:
Leaden before, his eyes grew dross of lead:
    Tussis attacked him.
'Now, master, take a little rest!' – not he!
90   (Caution redoubled,
Step two abreast, the way winds narrowly!)
    Not a whit troubled
Back to his studies, fresher than at first,
    Fierce as a dragon
He (soul-hydroptic with a sacred thirst)
    Sucked at the flagon.
Oh, if we draw a circle premature,
    Heedless of far gain,
Greedy for quick returns of profit, sure
100   Bad is our bargain!
Was it not great? did not he throw on God,
    (He loves the burthen) –
God's task to make the heavenly period
    Perfect the earthen?
Did not he magnify the mind, show clear
    Just what it all meant?
He would not discount life, as fools do here,
    Paid by instalment.
He ventured neck or nothing – heaven's success
110   Found, or earth's failure:
'Wilt thou trust death or not?' He answered 'Yes:

Hence with life's pale lure!'
That low man seeks a little thing to do,
   Sees it and does it:
This high man, with a great thing to pursue,
   Dies ere he knows it.
That low man goes on adding one to one,
   His hundred's soon hit:
This high man, aiming at a million,
120   Misses an unit.
That, has the world here – should he need the next,
   Let the world mind him!
This, throws himself on God, and unperplexed
   Seeking shall find him.
So, with the throttling hands of death at strife,
   Ground he at grammar;
Still, through the rattle, parts of speech were rife:
   While he could stammer
He settled *Hoti's* business – let it be! –
130   Properly based *Oun* –
Gave us the doctrine of the enclitic *De*,
   Dead from the waist down.
Well, here's the platform, here's the proper place:
   Hail to your purlieus,
All ye highfliers of the feathered race,
   Swallows and curlews!
Here's the top-peak; the multitude below
   Live, for they can, there:
This man decided not to Live but Know –
140   Bury this man there?
Here – here's his place, where meteors shoot, clouds form,
   Lightnings are loosened,
Stars come and go! Let joy break with the storm,
   Peace let the dew send!
Lofty designs must close in like effects:
   Loftily lying,
Leave him – still loftier than the world suspects,
   Living and dying.

One Way of Love

I

All June I bound the rose in sheaves.
Now, rose by rose, I strip the leaves
And strew them where Pauline may pass.
She will not turn aside? Alas!
Let them lie. Suppose they die?
The chance was they might take her eye.

II

How many a month I strove to suit
These stubborn fingers to the lute!
Today I venture all I know.
10   She will not hear my music? So!
Break the string; fold music's wing:
Suppose Pauline had bade me sing!

III

My whole life long I learned to love.
This hour my utmost art I prove
And speak my passion – heaven or hell?
She will not give me heaven? 'Tis well!
Lose who may – I still can say,
Those who win heaven, blest are they!

Another Way of Love

I

June was not over
   Though past the full,
And the best of her roses
   Had yet to blow,
   When a man I know
(But shall not discover,
   Since ears are dull,
   And time discloses)
Turned him and said with a man's true air,
10   Half sighing a smile in a yawn, as 'twere, –
'If I tire of your June, will she greatly care?'

II

> Well, dear, in-doors with you!
>> True! serene deadness
> Tries a man's temper.
>> What's in the blossom
>> June wears on her bosom?
> Can it clear scores with you?
>> Sweetness and redness.
>> *Eadem semper!*
20 Go, let me care for it greatly or slightly!
> If June mend her bower now, your hand left unsightly
> By plucking the roses, – my June will do rightly.

III

>> And after, for pastime,
>> If June be refulgent
>> With flowers in completeness,
>>> All petals, no prickles,
>>> Delicious as trickles
>> Of wine poured at mass-time, –
>> And choose One indulgent
30 >> To redness and sweetness:
> Or if, with experience of man and of spider,
> June use my June-lightning, the strong insect-ridder,
> And stop the fresh film-work, – why, June will consider.

'Transcendentalism: A Poem in Twelve Books'

> Stop playing, poet! May a brother speak?
> 'Tis you speak, that's your error. Song's our art:
> Whereas you please to speak these naked thoughts
> Instead of draping them in sights and sounds.
> – True thoughts, good thoughts, thoughts fit to treasure up!
> But why such long prolusion and display,
> Such turning and adjustment of the harp,
> And taking it upon your breast, at length,
> Only to speak dry words across its strings?
10 Stark-naked thought is in request enough:
> Speak prose and hollo it till Europe hears!

The six-foot Swiss tube, braced about with bark,
Which helps the hunter's voice from Alp to Alp –
Exchange our harp for that, – who hinders you?

But here's your fault; grown men want thought, you think;
Thought's what they mean by verse, and seek in verse.
Boys seek for images and melody,
Men must have reason – so, you aim at men.
Quite otherwise! Objects throng our youth, 'tis true;
20 We see and hear and do not wonder much:
If you could tell us what they mean, indeed!
As German Boehme never cared for plants
Until it happed, a-walking in the fields,
He noticed all at once that plants could speak,
Nay, turned with loosened tongue to talk with him.
That day the daisy had an eye indeed –
Colloquized with the cowslip on such themes!
We find them extant yet in Jacob's prose.
But by the time youth slips a stage or two
30 While reading prose in that tough book he wrote
(Collating and emendating the same
And settling on the sense most to our mind),
We shut the clasps and find life's summer past.
Then, who helps more, pray, to repair our loss –
Another Boehme with a tougher book
And subtler meanings of what roses say, –
Or some stout Mage like him of Halberstadt,
John, who made things Boehme wrote thoughts about?
He with a 'look you!' vents a brace of rhymes,
40 And in there breaks the sudden rose herself,
Over us, under, round us every side,
Nay, in and out the tables and the chairs
And musty volumes, Boehme's book and all, –
Buries us with a glory, young once more,
Pouring heaven into this shut house of life.

So come, the harp back to your heart again!
You are a poem, though your poem's naught.
The best of all you showed before, believe,
Was your own boy-face o'er the finer chords
50 Bent, following the cherub at the top
That points to God with his paired half-moon wings.

Misconceptions

I

This is a spray the Bird clung to,
   Making it blossom with pleasure,
Ere the high tree-top she sprung to,
   Fit for her nest and her treasure.
   Oh, what a hope beyond measure
Was the poor spray's, which the flying feet hung to, –
So to be singled out, built in, and sung to!

II

This is a heart the Queen leant on,
   Thrilled in a minute erratic,
10   Ere the true bosom she bent on,
   Meet for love's regal dalmatic.
   Oh, what a fancy ecstatic
Was the poor heart's, ere the wanderer went on –
Love to be saved for it, proffered to, spent on!

One Word More

TO E.B.B.
1855

I

There they are, my fifty men and women
Naming me the fifty poems finished!
Take them, Love, the book and me together:
Where the heart lies, let the brain lie also.

II

Rafael made a century of sonnets,
Made and wrote them in a certain volume
Dinted with the silver-pointed pencil
Else he only used to draw Madonnas:
These, the world might view – but one, the volume.
10 Who that one, you ask? Your heart instructs you.
Did she live and love it all her life-time?

Did she drop, his lady of the sonnets,
Die, and let it drop beside her pillow
Where it lay in place of Rafael's glory,
Rafael's cheek so duteous and so loving –
Cheek, the world was wont to hail a painter's,
Rafael's cheek, her love had turned a poet's?

III
You and I would rather read that volume,
(Taken to his beating bosom by it)
20 Lean and list the bosom-beats of Rafael,
Would we not? than wonder at Madonnas –
Her, San Sisto names, and Her, Foligno,
Her, that visits Florence in a vision,
Her, that's left with lilies in the Louvre –
Seen by us and all the world in circle.

IV
You and I will never read that volume.
Guido Reni, like his own eye's apple
Guarded long the treasure-book and loved it.
Guido Reni dying, all Bologna
30 Cried, and the world cried too, 'Ours, the treasure!'
Suddenly, as rare things will, it vanished.

V
Dante once prepared to paint an angel:
Whom to please? You whisper 'Beatrice.'
While he mused and traced it and retraced it,
(Peradventure with a pen corroded
Still by drops of that hot ink he dipped for,
When, his left-hand i' the hair o' the wicked,
Back he held the brow and pricked its stigma,
Bit into the live man's flesh for parchment,
40 Loosed him, laughed to see the writing rankle,
Let the wretch go festering through Florence) –
Dante, who loved well because he hated,
Hated wickedness that hinders loving,
Dante standing, studying his angel, –
In there broke the folk of his Inferno.
Says he – 'Certain people of importance'
(Such he gave his daily dreadful line to)

'Entered and would seize, forsooth, the poet.'
Says the poet – 'Then I stopped my painting.'

VI

50 You and I would rather see that angel,
Painted by the tenderness of Dante,
Would we not? – than read a fresh Inferno.

VII

You and I will never see that picture.
While he mused on love and Beatrice,
While he softened o'er his outlined angel,
In they broke, those 'people of importance':
We and Bice bear the loss for ever.

VIII

What of Rafael's sonnets, Dante's picture?
This: no artist lives and loves, that longs not
60 Once, and only once, and for one only,
(Ah, the prize!) to find his love a language
Fit and fair and simple and sufficient –
Using nature that's an art to others,
Not, this one time, art that's turned his nature.
Ay, of all the artists living, loving,
None but would forego his proper dowry, –
Does he paint? he fain would write a poem, –
Does he write? he fain would paint a picture,
Put to proof art alien to the artist's,
70 Once, and only once, and for one only,
So to be the man and leave the artist,
Gain the man's joy, miss the artist's sorrow.

IX

Wherefore? Heaven's gift takes earth's abatement!
He who smites the rock and spreads the water,
Bidding drink and live a crowd beneath him,
Even he, the minute makes immortal,
Proves, perchance, but mortal in the minute,
Desecrates, belike, the deed in doing.
While he smites, how can he but remember,
80 So he smote before, in such a peril,
When they stood and mocked – 'Shall smiting help us?'

When they drank and sneered – 'A stroke is easy!'
When they wiped their mouths and went their journey,
Throwing him for thanks – 'But drought was pleasant.'
Thus old memories mar the actual triumph;
Thus the doing savours of disrelish;
Thus achievement lacks a gracious somewhat;
O'er-importuned brows becloud the mandate,
Carelessness or consciousness – the gesture.

90   For he bears an ancient wrong about him,
Sees and knows again those phalanxed faces,
Hears, yet one time more, the 'customed prelude –
'How shouldst thou, of all men, smite, and save us?'
Guesses what is like to prove the sequel –
'Egypt's flesh-pots – nay, the drought was better.'

X
Oh, the crowd must have emphatic warrant!
Theirs, the Sinai-forehead's cloven brilliance,
Right-arm's rod-sweep, tongue's imperial fiat.
Never dares the man put off the prophet.

XI
100   Did he love one face from out the thousands,
(Were she Jethro's daughter, white and wifely,
Were she but the Aethiopian bondslave,)
He would envy yon dumb patient camel,
Keeping a reserve of scanty water
Meant to save his own life in the desert;
Ready in the desert to deliver
(Kneeling down to let his breast be opened)
Hoard and life together for his mistress.

XII
I shall never, in the years remaining,
110   Paint you pictures, no, nor carve you statues,
Make you music that should all-express me;
So it seems: I stand on my attainment.
This of verse alone, one life allows me;
Verse and nothing else have I to give you.
Other heights in other lives, God willing:
All the gifts from all the heights, your own, Love!

XIII

Yet a semblance of resource avails us –
Shade so finely touched, love's sense must seize it.
Take these lines, look lovingly and nearly,
120 Lines I write the first time and the last time.
He who works in fresco, steals a hair-brush,
Curbs the liberal hand, subservient proudly,
Cramps his spirit, crowds its all in little,
Makes a strange art of an art familiar,
Fills his lady's missal-marge with flowerets.
He who blows through bronze, may breathe through silver,
Fitly serenade a slumbrous princess.
He who writes, may write for once as I do.

XIV

Love, you saw me gather men and women,
130 Live or dead or fashioned by my fancy,
Enter each and all, and use their service,
Speak from every mouth, – the speech, a poem.
Hardly shall I tell my joys and sorrows,
Hopes and fears, belief and disbelieving:
I am mine and yours – the rest be all men's,
Karshish, Cleon, Norbert and the fifty.
Let me speak this once in my true person,
Not as Lippo, Roland or Andrea,
Though the fruit of speech be just this sentence:
140 Pray you, look on these my men and women,
Take and keep my fifty poems finished;
Where my heart lies, let my brain lie also!
Poor the speech; be how I speak, for all things.

XV

Not but that you know me! Lo, the moon's self!
Here in London, yonder late in Florence,
Still we find her face, the thrice-transfigured.
Curving on a sky imbrued with colour,
Drifted over Fiesole by twilight,
Came she, our new crescent of a hair's-breadth.
150 Full she flared it, lamping Samminiato,
Rounder 'twixt the cypresses and rounder,
Perfect till the nightingales applauded.
Now, a piece of her old self, impoverished,

Hard to greet, she traverses the houseroofs,
Hurries with unhandsome thrift of silver,
Goes dispiritedly, glad to finish.

XVI

What, there's nothing in the moon noteworthy?
Nay: for if that moon could love a mortal,
Use, to charm him (so to fit a fancy),
160   All her magic ('tis the old sweet mythos)
She would turn a new side to her mortal,
Side unseen of herdsman, huntsman, steersman –
Blank to Zoroaster on his terrace,
Blind to Galileo on his turret,
Dumb to Homer, dumb to Keats – him, even!
Think, the wonder of the moonstruck mortal –
When she turns round, comes again in heaven,
Opens out anew for worse or better!
Proves she like some portent of an iceberg
170   Swimming full upon the ship it founders,
Hungry with huge teeth of splintered crystals?
Proves she as the paved work of a sapphire
Seen by Moses when he climbed the mountain?
Moses, Aaron, Nadab and Abihu
Climbed and saw the very God, the Highest,
Stand upon the paved work of a sapphire.
Like the bodied heaven in his clearness
Shone the stone, the sapphire of that paved work,
When they ate and drank and saw God also!

XVII

180   What were seen? None knows, none ever shall know.
Only this is sure – the sight were other,
Not the moon's same side, born late in Florence,
Dying now impoverished here in London.
God be thanked, the meanest of his creatures
Boasts two soul-sides, one to face the world with,
One to show a woman when he loves her!

XVIII

This I say of me, but think of you, Love!
This to you – yourself my moon of poets!
Ah, but that's the world's side, there's the wonder,

190   Thus they see you, praise you, think they know you!
      There, in turn I stand with them and praise you –
      Out of my own self, I dare to phrase it.
      But the best is when I glide from out them,
      Cross a step or two of dubious twilight,
      Come out on the other side, the novel
      Silent silver lights and darks undreamed of,
      Where I hush and bless myself with silence.

XIX
      Oh, their Rafael of the dear Madonnas,
      Oh, their Dante of the dread Inferno,
200   Wrote one song – and in my brain I sing it,
      Drew one angel – borne, see, on my bosom!

R.B.

Dramatis Personae

1864

James Lee's Wife

I James Lee's Wife Speaks at the Window

I

Ah, Love, but a day
  And the world has changed!
The sun's away,
  And the bird estranged;
The wind has dropped,
  And the sky's deranged:
Summer has stopped.

II

Look in my eyes!
  Wilt thou change too?
10 Should I fear surprise?
  Shall I find aught new
In the old and dear,
  In the good and true,
With the changing year?

III

Thou art a man,
  But I am thy love.
For the lake, its swan;
  For the dell, its dove;
And for thee – (oh, haste!)
20 Me, to bend above,
Me, to hold embraced.

II By the Fireside

I

Is all our fire of shipwreck wood,
  Oak and pine?
Oh, for the ills half-understood,
  The dim dead woe
  Long ago

Befallen this bitter coast of France!
Well, poor sailors took their chance;
   I take mine.

II

30 A ruddy shaft our fire must shoot
    O'er the sea:
Do sailors eye the casement – mute,
    Drenched and stark,
    From their bark –
And envy, gnash their teeth for hate
O' the warm safe house and happy freight
    – Thee and me?

III

God help you, sailors, at your need!
    Spare the curse!
40 For some ships, safe in port indeed,
    Rot and rust,
    Run to dust,
All through worms i' the wood, which crept,
Gnawed our hearts out while we slept:
    That is worse.

IV

Who lived here before us two?
    Old-world pairs.
Did a woman ever – would I knew! –
    Watch the man
50   With whom began
Love's voyage full-sail, – (now, gnash your teeth!)
When planks start, open hell beneath
    Unawares?

III In the Doorway

I

The swallow has set her six young on the rail,
    And looks sea-ward:
The water's in stripes like a snake, olive-pale
    To the leeward, –

On the weather-side, black, spotted white with the wind.
'Good fortune departs, and disaster's behind,' –
60 Hark, the wind with its wants and its infinite wail!

II

Our fig-tree, that leaned for the saltness, has furled
    Her five fingers,
Each leaf like a hand opened wide to the world
    Where there lingers
No glint of the gold, Summer sent for her sake:
How the vines writhe in rows, each impaled on its stake!
My heart shrivels up and my spirit shrinks curled.

III

Yet here are we two; we have love, house enough,
    With the field there,
70 This house of four rooms, that field red and rough,
    Though it yield there,
For the rabbit that robs, scarce a blade or a bent;
If a magpie alight now, it seems an event;
And they both will be gone at November's rebuff.

IV

But why must cold spread? but wherefore bring change
    To the spirit,
God meant should mate his with an infinite range,
    And inherit
His power to put life in the darkness and cold?
80 Oh, live and love worthily, bear and be bold!
Whom Summer made friends of, let Winter estrange!

IV Along the Beach

I

I will be quiet and talk with you,
    And reason why you are wrong.
You wanted my love – is that much true?
And so I did love, so I do:
    What has come of it all along?

II

I took you – how could I otherwise?
　　For a world to me, and more;
For all, love greatens and glorifies
90　Till God's a-glow, to the loving eyes,
　　In what was mere earth before.

III

Yes, earth – yes, mere ignoble earth!
　　Now do I mis-state, mistake?
Do I wrong your weakness and call it worth?
Expect all harvest, dread no dearth,
　　Seal my sense up for your sake?

IV

Oh, Love, Love, no, Love! not so, indeed!
　　You were just weak earth, I knew:
With much in you waste, with many a weed,
100　And plenty of passions run to seed,
　　But a little good grain too.

V

And such as you were, I took you for mine:
　　Did not you find me yours,
To watch the olive and wait the vine,
And wonder when rivers of oil and wine
　　Would flow, as the Book assures?

VI

Well, and if none of these good things came,
　　What did the failure prove?
The man was my whole world, all the same,
110　With his flowers to praise or his weeds to blame,
　　And, either or both, to love.

VII*

Yet this turns now to a fault – there! there!
　　That I do love, watch too long,
And wait too well, and weary and wear;
And 'tis all an old story, and my despair
　　Fit subject for some new song:

VIII

'How the light, light love, he has wings to fly
　　At suspicion of a bond:
My wisdom has bidden your pleasure good-bye,
120　Which will turn up next in a laughing eye,
　　And why should you look beyond?'

V   On the Cliff

I

I leaned on the turf,
I looked at a rock
Left dry by the surf;
For the turf, to call it grass were to mock:
Dead to the roots, so deep was done
The work of the summer sun.

II

And the rock lay flat
As an anvil's face:
130　No iron like that!
Baked dry; of a weed, of a shell, no trace:
Sunshine outside, but ice at the core,
Death's altar by the lone shore.

III

On the turf, sprang gay
With his films of blue,
No cricket, I'll say,
But a warhorse, barded and chanfroned too,
The gift of a quixote-mage to his knight,
Real fairy, with wings all right.

IV

140　On the rock, they scorch
Like a drop of fire
From a brandished torch,
Fall two red fans of a butterfly:
No turf, no rock: in their ugly stead,
See, wonderful blue and red!

V

Is it not so
With the minds of men?
The level and low,
The burnt and bare, in themselves; but then
150 With such a blue and red grace, not theirs, –
Love settling unawares!

VI Reading a Book, Under the Cliff

I

'Still ailing, Wind? Wilt be appeased or no?
 Which needs the other's office, thou or I?
Dost want to be disburthened of a woe,
 And can, in truth, my voice untie
Its links, and let it go?

II

'Art thou a dumb wronged thing that would be righted,
 Entrusting thus thy cause to me? Forbear!
No tongue can mend such pleadings; faith, requited
160 With falsehood, – love, at last aware
Of scorn, – hopes, early blighted, –

III

'We have them; but I know not any tone
 So fit as thine to falter forth a sorrow:
Dost think men would go mad without a moan,
 If they knew any way to borrow
A pathos like thy own?

IV

'Which sigh wouldst mock, of all the sighs? The one
 So long escaping from lips starved and blue,
That lasts while on her pallet-bed the nun
170 Stretches her length; her foot comes through
The straw she shivers on;

V

'You had not thought she was so tall: and spent,
  Her shrunk lids open, her lean fingers shut
Close, close, their sharp and livid nails indent
  The clammy palm; then all is mute:
That way, the spirit went.

VI

'Or wouldst thou rather that I understand
  Thy will to help me? – like the dog I found
Once, pacing sad this solitary strand,
180 Who would not take my food, poor hound,
But whined and licked my hand.'

––––––––––

VII

All this, and more, comes from some young man's pride
  Of power to see, – in failure and mistake,
Relinquishment, disgrace, on every side, –
  Merely examples for his sake,
Helps to his path untried:

VIII

Instances he must – simply recognize?
  Oh, more than so! – must, with a learner's zeal,
Make doubly prominent, twice emphasize,
190 By added touches that reveal
The god in babe's disguise.

IX

Oh, he knows what defeat means, and the rest!
  Himself the undefeated that shall be:
Failure, disgrace, he flings them you to test, –
  His triumph, in eternity
Too plainly manifest!

X

Whence, judge if he learn forthwith what the wind
  Means in its moaning – by the happy prompt
Instinctive way of youth, I mean; for kind
200 Calm years, exacting their accompt
Of pain, mature the mind:

XI

And some midsummer morning, at the lull
   Just about daybreak, as he looks across
A sparkling foreign country, wonderful
   To the sea's edge for gloom and gloss,
Next minute must annul, –

XII

Then, when the wind begins among the vines,
   So low, so low, what shall it say but this?
'Here is the change beginning, here the lines
210   Circumscribe beauty, set to bliss
The limit time assigns.'

XIII

Nothing can be as it has been before;
   Better, so call it, only not the same.
To draw one beauty into our hearts' core,
   And keep it changeless! such our claim;
So answered, – Never more!

XIV

Simple? Why this is the old woe o' the world;
   Tune, to whose rise and fall we live and die.
Rise with it, then! Rejoice that man is hurled
220   From change to change unceasingly,
His soul's wings never furled!

XV

That's a new question; still replies the fact,
   Nothing endures: the wind moans, saying so;
We moan in acquiescence: there's life's pact,
   Perhaps probation – do *I* know?
God does: endure his act!

XVI

Only, for man, how bitter not to grave
   On his soul's hands' palms one fair good wise thing
Just as he grasped it! For himself, death's wave;
230   While time first washes – ah, the sting! –
O'er all he'd sink to save.

VII   Among the Rocks

I

Oh, good gigantic smile o' the brown old earth,
    This autumn morning! How he sets his bones
To bask i' the sun, and thrusts out knees and feet
For the ripple to run over in its mirth;
    Listening the while, where on the heap of stones
The white breast of the sea-lark twitters sweet.

II

That is the doctrine, simple, ancient, true;
    Such is life's trial, as old earth smiles and knows.
240 If you loved only what were worth your love,
Love were clear gain, and wholly well for you:
    Make the low nature better by your throes!
Give earth yourself, go up for gain above!

VIII   Beside the Drawing-Board

I

'As like as a Hand to another Hand!'
    Whoever said that foolish thing,
Could not have studied to understand
    The counsels of God in fashioning,
Out of the infinite love of his heart,
This Hand, whose beauty I praise, apart
250 From the world of wonder left to praise,
If I tried to learn the other ways
Of love in its skill, or love in its power.
    'As like as a Hand to another Hand':
    Who said that, never took his stand,
Found and followed, like me, an hour,
The beauty in this, – how free, how fine
To fear, almost, – of the limit-line!
As I looked at this, and learned and drew,
    Drew and learned, and looked again,
260 While fast the happy minutes flew,
    Its beauty mounted into my brain,
    And a fancy seized me; I was fain

To efface my work, begin anew,
Kiss what before I only drew;
Ay, laying the red chalk 'twixt my lips,
    With soul to help if the mere lips failed,
    I kissed all right where the drawing ailed,
Kissed fast the grace that somehow slips
Still from one's soul-less finger-tips.

II

270 'Tis a clay cast, the perfect thing,
    From Hand live once, dead long ago:
Princess-like it wears the ring
    To fancy's eye, by which we know
That here at length a master found
    His match, a proud lone soul its mate,
As soaring genius sank to ground,
    And pencil could not emulate
The beauty in this, – how free, how fine
To fear almost! – of the limit-line.
280 Long ago the god, like me
The worm, learned, each in our degree:
Looked and loved, learned and drew,
    Drew and learned and loved again,
While fast the happy minutes flew,
    Till beauty mounted into his brain
And on the finger which outvied
    His art he placed the ring that's there,
Still by fancy's eye descried,
    In token of a marriage rare:
290   For him on earth, his art's despair,
For him in heaven, his soul's fit bride.

III

Little girl with the poor coarse hand
    I turned from to a cold clay cast –
I have my lesson, understand
    The worth of flesh and blood at last.
Nothing but beauty in a Hand?
    Because he could not change the hue,
    Mend the lines and make them true
To this which met his soul's demand, –

300 Would Da Vinci turn from you?
I hear him laugh my woes to scorn –
'The fool forsooth is all forlorn
Because the beauty, she thinks best,
Lived long ago or was never born, –
Because no beauty bears the test
In this rough peasant Hand! Confessed!
"Art is null and study void!"
   So sayest thou? So said not I,
   Who threw the faulty pencil by,
310 And years instead of hours employed,
Learning the veritable use
   Of flesh and bone and nerve beneath
   Lines and hue of the outer sheath,
If haply I might reproduce
One motive of the powers profuse,
Flesh and bone and nerve that make
   The poorest coarsest human hand
   An object worthy to be scanned
A whole life long for their sole sake.
320 Shall earth and the cramped moment-space
Yield the heavenly crowning grace?
Now the parts and then the whole!
Who art thou, with stinted soul
   And stunted body, thus to cry
"I love, – shall that be life's strait dole?
   I must live beloved or die!"
This peasant hand that spins the wool
   And bakes the bread, why lives it on,
   Poor and coarse with beauty gone, –
330 What use survives the beauty?' Fool!

Go, little girl with the poor coarse hand!
I have my lesson, shall understand.

IX   On Deck

I
There is nothing to remember in me,
   Nothing I ever said with a grace,
Nothing I did that you care to see,

Nothing I was that deserves a place
In your mind, now I leave you, set you free.

II

Conceded! In turn, concede to me,
 Such things have been as a mutual flame.
340 Your soul's locked fast; but, love for a key,
 You might let it loose, till I grew the same
In your eyes, as in mine you stand: strange plea!

III

For then, then, what would it matter to me
 That I was the harsh ill-favoured one?
We both should be like as pea and pea;
 It was ever so since the world begun:
So, let me proceed with my reverie.

IV

How strange it were if you had all me,
 As I have all you in my heart and brain,
350 You, whose least word brought gloom or glee,
 Who never lifted the hand in vain –
Will hold mine yet, from over the sea!

V

Strange, if a face, when you thought of me,
 Rose like your own face present now,
With eyes as dear in their due degree,
 Much such a mouth, and as bright a brow,
Till you saw yourself, while you cried ''Tis She!'

VI

Well, you may, you must, set down to me
 Love that was life, life that was love;
360 A tenure of breath at your lips' decree,
 A passion to stand as your thoughts approve,
A rapture to fall where your foot might be.

VII

But did one touch of such love for me
 Come in a word or a look of yours,
Whose words and looks will, circling, flee

Round me and round while life endures, –
Could I fancy 'As I feel, thus feels he';

VIII

Why, fade you might to a thing like me,
  And your hair grow these coarse hanks of hair,
370 Your skin, this bark of a gnarled tree, –
    You might turn myself! – should I know or care
  When I should be dead of joy, James Lee?

Gold Hair:

A Story of Pornic

I

Oh, the beautiful girl, too white,
  Who lived at Pornic, down by the sea,
Just where the sea and the Loire unite!
  And a boasted name in Brittany
She bore, which I will not write.

II

Too white, for the flower of life is red;
  Her flesh was the soft seraphic screen
Of a soul that is meant (her parents said)
  To just see earth, and hardly be seen,
10 And blossom in heaven instead.

III

Yet earth saw one thing, one how fair!
  One grace that grew to its full on earth:
Smiles might be sparse on her cheek so spare,
  And her waist want half a girdle's girth,
But she had her great gold hair.

IV

Hair, such a wonder of flix and floss,
  Freshness and fragrance – floods of it, too!
Gold, did I say? Nay, gold's mere dross:
  Here, Life smiled, 'Think what I meant to do!'
20 And Love sighed, 'Fancy my loss!'

V

So, when she died, it was scarce more strange
　Than that, when delicate evening dies,
And you follow its spent sun's pallid range,
　There's a shoot of colour startles the skies
With sudden, violent change, –

VI

That, while the breath was nearly to seek,
　As they put the little cross to her lips,
She changed; a spot came out on her cheek,
　A spark from her eye in mid-eclipse,
30　And she broke forth, 'I must speak!'

VII

'Not my hair!' made the girl her moan –
　'All the rest is gone or to go;
But the last, last grace, my all, my own,
　Let it stay in the grave, that the ghosts may know!
Leave my poor gold hair alone!'

VIII

The passion thus vented, dead lay she;
　Her parents sobbed their worst on that;
All friends joined in, nor observed degree:
　For indeed the hair was to wonder at,
40　As it spread – not flowing free,

IX

But curled around her brow, like a crown,
　And coiled beside her cheeks, like a cap,
And calmed about her neck – ay, down
　To her breast, pressed flat, without a gap
I' the gold, it reached her gown.

X

All kissed that face, like a silver wedge
　'Mid the yellow wealth, nor disturbed its hair:
E'en the priest allowed death's privilege,
　As he planted the crucifix with care
50　On her breast, 'twixt edge and edge.

XI

And thus was she buried, inviolate
　Of body and soul, in the very space
By the altar; keeping saintly state
　In Pornic church, for her pride of race,
Pure life and piteous fate.

XII

And in after-time would your fresh tear fall,
　Though your mouth might twitch with a dubious smile,
As they told you of gold, both robe and pall,
　How she prayed them leave it alone awhile,
60　So it never was touched at all.

XIII

Years flew; this legend grew at last
　The life of the lady; all she had done,
All been, in the memories fading fast
　Of lover and friend, was summed in one
Sentence survivors passed:

XIV

To wit, she was meant for heaven, not earth;
　Had turned an angel before the time:
Yet, since she was mortal, in such dearth
　Of frailty, all you could count a crime
70　Was – she knew her gold hair's worth.

XV

At little pleasant Pornic church,
　It chanced, the pavement wanted repair,
Was taken to pieces: left in the lurch,
　A certain sacred space lay bare,
And the boys began research.

XVI

'Twas the space where our sires would lay a saint,
　A benefactor, – a bishop, suppose,
A baron with armour-adornments quaint,
　Dame with chased ring and jewelled rose,
80　Things sanctity saves from taint;

XVII

So we come to find them in after-days
    When the corpse is presumed to have done with gauds
Of use to the living, in many ways:
    For the boys get pelf, and the town applauds,
And the church deserves the praise.

XVIII

They grubbed with a will: and at length – *O cor*
    Humanum, pectora caeca, and the rest! –
They found – no gaud they were prying for,
    No ring, no rose, but – who would have guessed? –
90 A double Louis-d'or!

XIX

Here was a case for the priest: he heard,
    Marked, inwardly digested, laid
Finger on nose, smiled, 'There's a bird
    Chirps in my ear': then, 'Bring a spade,
Dig deeper!' – he gave the word.

XX

And lo, when they came to the coffin-lid,
    Or rotten planks which composed it once,
Why, there lay the girl's skull wedged amid
    A mint of money, it served for the nonce
100 To hold in its hair-heaps hid!

XXI

Hid there? Why? Could the girl be wont
    (She the stainless soul) to treasure up
Money, earth's trash and heaven's affront?
    Had a spider found out the communion-cup,
Was a toad in the christening-font?

XXII

Truth is truth: too true it was.
    Gold! She hoarded and hugged it first,
Longed for it, leaned o'er it, loved it – alas –
    Till the humour grew to a head and burst,
110 And she cried, at the final pass, –

XXIII

'Talk not of God, my heart is stone!
    Nor lover nor friend – be gold for both!
Gold I lack; and, my all, my own,
    It shall hide in my hair. I scarce die loth
If they let my hair alone!'

XXIV

Louis-d'or, some six times five,
    And duly double, every piece.
Now do you see? With the priest to shrive,
    With parents preventing her soul's release
120 By kisses that kept alive, –

XXV

With heaven's gold gates about to ope,
    With friends' praise, gold-like, lingering still,
An instinct had bidden the girl's hand grope
    For gold, the true sort – 'Gold in heaven, if you will;
But I keep earth's too, I hope.'

XXVI

Enough! The priest took the grave's grim yield:
    The parents, they eyed that price of sin
As if *thirty pieces* lay revealed
    On the place *to bury strangers in,*
130 The hideous Potter's Field.

XXVII

But the priest bethought him: ' "Milk that's spilt"
    – You know the adage! Watch and pray!
Saints tumble to earth with so slight a tilt!
    It would build a new altar; that, we may!'
And the altar therewith was built.

XXVIII

Why I deliver this horrible verse?
    As the text of a sermon, which now I preach:
Evil or good may be better or worse
    In the human heart, but the mixture of each
140 Is a marvel and a curse.

XXIX

The candid incline to surmise of late
    That the Christian faith proves false, I find;
For our Essays-and-Reviews' debate
    Begins to tell on the public mind,
And Colenso's words have weight:

XXX

I still, to suppose it true, for my part,
    See reasons and reasons; this, to begin:
'Tis the faith that launched point-blank her dart
    At the head of a lie – taught Original Sin,
150   The Corruption of Man's Heart.

The Worst of It

I

Would it were I had been false, not you!
    I that am nothing, not you that are all:
I, never the worse for a touch or two
    On my speckled hide; not you, the pride
Of the day, my swan, that a first fleck's fall
    On her wonder of white must unswan, undo!

II

I had dipped in life's struggle and, out again,
    Bore specks of it here, there, easy to see,
When I found my swan and the cure was plain;
10   The dull turned bright as I caught your white
On my bosom: you saved me – saved in vain
    If you ruined yourself, and all through me!

III

Yes, all through the speckled beast that I am,
    Who taught you to stoop; you gave me yourself,
And bound your soul by the vows that damn:
    Since on better thought you break, as you ought,
Vows – words, no angel set down, some elf
    Mistook, – for an oath, an epigram!

IV

Yes, might I judge you, here were my heart,
20   And a hundred its like, to treat as you pleased!
I choose to be yours, for my proper part,
    Yours, leave or take, or mar me or make;
If I acquiesce, why should you be teased
    With the conscience-prick and the memory-smart?

V

But what will God say? Oh, my sweet,
    Think, and be sorry you did this thing
Though earth were unworthy to feel your feet,
    There's a heaven above may deserve your love:
Should you forfeit heaven for a snapt gold ring
30   And a promise broke, were it just or meet?

VI

And I to have tempted you! I, who tried
    Your soul, no doubt, till it sank! Unwise,
I loved and was lowly, loved and aspired,
    Loved, grieving or glad, till I made you mad,
And you meant to have hated and despised –
    Whereas, you deceived me nor inquired!

VII

She, ruined? How? No heaven for her?
    Crowns to give, and none for the brow
That looked like marble and smelt like myrrh?
40   Shall the robe be worn, and the palm-branch borne,
And she go graceless, she graced now
    Beyond all saints, as themselves aver?

VIII

Hardly! That must be understood!
    The earth is your place of penance, then;
And what will it prove? I desire your good,
    But, plot as I may, I can find no way
How a blow should fall, such as falls on men,
    Nor prove too much for your womanhood.

IX

It will come, I suspect, at the end of life,
50   When you walk alone, and review the past;
And I, who so long shall have done with strife,
    And journeyed my stage and earned my wage
And retired as was right, – I am called at last
    When the devil stabs you, to lend the knife.

X

He stabs for the minute of trivial wrong,
    Nor the other hours are able to save,
The happy, that lasted my whole life long:
    For a promise broke, not for first words spoke,
The true, the only, that turn my grave
60   To a blaze of joy and a crash of song.

XI

Witness beforehand! Off I trip
    On a safe path gay through the flowers you flung:
My very name made great by your lip,
    And my heart a-glow with the good I know
Of a perfect year when we both were young,
    And I tasted the angels' fellowship.

XII

And witness, moreover . . . Ah, but wait!
    I spy the loop whence an arrow shoots!
It may be for yourself, when you meditate,
70   That you grieve – for slain ruth, murdered truth.
'Though falsehood escape in the end, what boots?
    How truth would have triumphed!' – you sigh too late.

XIII

Ay, who would have triumphed like you, I say!
    Well, it is lost now; well, you must bear,
Abide and grow fit for a better day:
    You should hardly grudge, could I be your judge!
But hush! For you, can be no despair:
    There's amends: 'tis a secret: hope and pray!

XIV

For I was true at least – oh, true enough!
80   And, Dear, truth is not as good as it seems!
Commend me to conscience! Idle stuff!
   Much help is in mine, as I mope and pine,
And skulk through day, and scowl in my dreams
   At my swan's obtaining the crow's rebuff.

XV

Men tell me of truth now – 'False!' I cry:
   Of beauty – 'A mask, friend! Look beneath!'
We take our own method, the devil and I,
   With pleasant and fair and wise and rare:
And the best we wish to what lives, is – death;
90   Which even in wishing, perhaps we lie!

XVI

Far better commit a fault and have done –
   As you, Dear! – for ever; and choose the pure,
And look where the healing waters run,
   And strive and strain to be good again,
And a place in the other world ensure,
   All glass and gold, with God for its sun.

XVII

Misery! What shall I say or do?
   I cannot advise, or, at least, persuade:
Most like, you are glad you deceived me – rue
100   No whit of the wrong: you endured too long,
Have done no evil and want no aid,
   Will live the old life out and chance the new.

XVIII

And your sentence is written all the same,
   And I can do nothing, – pray, perhaps:
But somehow the world pursues its game, –
   If I pray, if I curse, – for better or worse:
And my faith is torn to a thousand scraps,
   And my heart feels ice while my words breathe flame.

XIX

Dear, I look from my hiding-place.
110   Are you still so fair? Have you still the eyes?
Be happy! Add but the other grace,
    Be good! Why want what the angels vaunt?
I knew you once: but in Paradise,
    If we meet, I will pass nor turn my face.

Dîs Aliter Visum; or, Le Byron de Nos Jours

I

Stop, let me have the truth of that!
    Is that all true? I say, the day
Ten years ago when both of us
    Met on a morning, friends – as thus
We meet this evening, friends or what? –

II

Did you – because I took your arm
    And sillily smiled, 'A mass of brass
That sea looks, blazing underneath!'
    While up the cliff-road edged with heath,
10 We took the turns nor came to harm –

III

Did you consider 'Now makes twice
    That I have seen her, walked and talked
With this poor pretty thoughtful thing,
    Whose worth I weigh: she tries to sing;
Draws, hopes in time the eye grows nice;

IV

'Reads verse and thinks she understands;
    Loves all, at any rate, that's great,
Good, beautiful; but much as we
    Down at the bath-house love the sea,
20 Who breathe its salt and bruise its sands:

V

'While . . . do but follow the fishing-gull
  That flaps and floats from wave to cave!
There's the sea-lover, fair my friend!
  What then? Be patient, mark and mend!
Had you the making of your skull?'

VI

And did you, when we faced the church
  With spire and sad slate roof, aloof
From human fellowship so far,
  Where a few graveyard crosses are,
30 And garlands for the swallows' perch, –

VII

Did you determine, as we stepped
  O'er the lone stone fence, 'Let me get
Her for myself, and what's the earth
  With all its art, verse, music, worth –
Compared with love, found, gained, and kept?

VIII

'Schumann's our music-maker now;
  Has his march-movement youth and mouth?
Ingres's the modern man that paints;
  Which will lean on me, of his saints?
40 Heine for songs; for kisses, how?'

IX

And did you, when we entered, reached
  The votive frigate, soft aloft
Riding on air this hundred years,
  Safe-smiling at old hopes and fears, –
Did you draw profit while she preached?

X

Resolving, 'Fools we wise men grow!
  Yes, I could easily blurt out curt
Some question that might find reply
  As prompt in her stopped lips, dropped eye,
50 And rush of red to cheek and brow:

XI

'Thus were a match made, sure and fast,
    'Mid the blue weed-flowers round the mound
Where, issuing, we shall stand and stay
    For one more look at baths and bay,
Sands, sea-gulls, and the old church last –

XII

'A match 'twixt me, bent, wigged and lamed,
    Famous, however, for verse and worse,
Sure of the Fortieth spare Arm-chair
    When gout and glory seat me there,
60 So, one whose love-freaks pass unblamed, –

XIII

'And this young beauty, round and sound
    As a mountain-apple, youth and truth
With loves and doves, at all events
    With money in the Three per Cents;
Whose choice of me would seem profound: –

XIV

'She might take me as I take her.
    Perfect the hour would pass, alas!
Climb high, love high, what matter? Still,
    Feet, feelings, must descend the hill:
70 An hour's perfection can't recur.

XV

'Then follows Paris and full time
    For both to reason: "Thus with us!"
She'll sigh, "Thus girls give body and soul
    At first word, think they gain the goal,
When 'tis the starting-place they climb!

XVI

'"My friend makes verse and gets renown;
    Have they all fifty years, his peers?
He knows the world, firm, quiet and gay;
    Boys will become as much one day:
80 They're fools; he cheats, with beard less brown.

XVII

'"For boys say, *Love me or I die!*
   He did not say, *The truth is, youth
I want, who am old and know too much;
      I'd catch youth: lend me sight and touch!
Drop heart's blood where life's wheels grate dry!"*

XVIII

'While I should make rejoinder' – (then
   It was, no doubt, you ceased that least
Light pressure of my arm in yours)
      '"I can conceive of cheaper cures
90 For a yawning-fit o'er books and men.

XIX

'"What? All I am, was, and might be,
   All, books taught, art brought, life's whole strife,
Painful results since precious, just
      Were fitly exchanged, in wise disgust,
For two cheeks freshened by youth and sea?

XX

'"All for a nosegay! – what came first;
   With fields on flower, untried each side;
I rally, need my books and men,
      And find a nosegay": drop it, then,
100 No match yet made for best or worst!'

XXI

That ended me. You judged the porch
   We left by, Norman; took our look
At sea and sky, wondered so few
      Find out the place for air and view;
Remarked the sun began to scorch;

XXII

Descended, soon regained the baths,
   And then, good-bye! Years ten since then:
Ten years! We meet: you tell me, now,
      By a window-seat for that cliff-brow,
110 On carpet-stripes for those sand-paths.

XXIII

Now I may speak: you fool, for all
   Your lore! Who made things plain in vain?
What was the sea for? What, the grey
   Sad church, that solitary day,
Crosses and graves and swallows' call?

XXIV

Was there naught better than to enjoy?
   No feat which, done, would make time break,
And let us pent-up creatures through
   Into eternity, our due?
120 No forcing earth teach heaven's employ?

XXV

No wise beginning, here and now,
   What cannot grow complete (earth's feat)
And heaven must finish, there and then?
   No tasting earth's true food for men,
Its sweet in sad, its sad in sweet?

XXVI

No grasping at love, gaining a share
   O' the sole spark from God's life at strife
With death, so, sure of range above
   The limits here? For us and love,
130 Failure; but, when God fails, despair.

XXVII

This you call wisdom? Thus you add
   Good unto good again, in vain?
You loved, with body worn and weak;
   I loved, with faculties to seek:
Were both loves worthless since ill-clad?

XXVIII

Let the mere star-fish in his vault
   Crawl in a wash of weed, indeed,
Rose-jacinth to the finger-tips:
   He, whole in body and soul, outstrips
140 Man, found with either in default.

XXIX

But what's whole, can increase no more,
    Is dwarfed and dies, since here's its sphere.
The devil laughed at you in his sleeve!
    You knew not? That I well believe;
Or you had saved two souls: nay, four.

XXX

For Stephanie sprained last night her wrist,
    Ankle or something. 'Pooh,' cry you?
At any rate she danced, all say,
    Vilely; her vogue has had its day.
150 Here comes my husband from his whist.

Too Late

I

Here was I with my arm and heart
    And brain, all yours for a word, a want
Put into a look – just a look, your part, –
    While mine, to repay it . . . vainest vaunt,
Were the woman, that's dead, alive to hear,
    Had her lover, that's lost, love's proof to show!
But I cannot show it; you cannot speak
    From the churchyard neither, miles removed,
Though I feel by a pulse within my cheek,
10   Which stabs and stops, that the woman I loved
Needs help in her grave and finds none near,
    Wants warmth from the heart which sends it – so!

II

Did I speak once angrily, all the drear days
    You lived, you woman I loved so well,
Who married the other? Blame or praise,
    Where was the use then? Time would tell,
And the end declare what man for you,
    What woman for me, was the choice of God.
But, Edith dead! no doubting more!
20   I used to sit and look at my life
As it rippled and ran till, right before,

A great stone stopped it: oh, the strife
Of waves at the stone some devil threw
   In my life's midcurrent, thwarting God!

III

But either I thought, 'They may churn and chide
   Awhile, my waves which came for their joy
And found this horrible stone full-tide:
   Yet I see just a thread escape, deploy
Through the evening-country, silent and safe,
30   And it suffers no more till it finds the sea.'
Or else I would think, 'Perhaps some night
   When new things happen, a meteor-ball
May slip through the sky in a line of light,
   And earth breathe hard, and landmarks fall,
And my waves no longer champ nor chafe,
   Since a stone will have rolled from its place: let be!'

IV

But, dead! All's done with: wait who may,
   Watch and wear and wonder who will.
Oh, my whole life that ends today!
40   Oh, my soul's sentence, sounding still,
'The woman is dead that was none of his;
   And the man that was none of hers may go!'
There's only the past left: worry that!
   Wreak, like a bull, on the empty coat,
Rage, its late wearer is laughing at!
   Tear the collar to rags, having missed his throat;
Strike stupidly on – 'This, this and this,
   Where I would that a bosom received the blow!'

V

I ought to have done more: once my speech,
50   And once your answer, and there, the end,
And Edith was henceforth out of reach!
   Why, men do more to deserve a friend,
Be rid of a foe, get rich, grow wise,
   Nor, folding their arms, stare fate in the face.
Why, better even have burst like a thief
   And borne you away to a rock for us two,
In a moment's horror, bright, bloody and brief:

Then changed to myself again – 'I slew
Myself in that moment; a ruffian lies
60 Somewhere: your slave, see, born in his place!'

VI

What did the other do? You be judge!
 Look at us, Edith! Here are we both!
Give him his six whole years: I grudge
 None of the life with you, nay, loathe
Myself that I grudged his start in advance
 Of me who could overtake and pass.
But, as if he loved you! No, not he,
 Nor anyone else in the world, 'tis plain:
Who ever heard that another, free
70 As I, young, prosperous, sound and sane,
Poured life out, proffered it – 'Half a glance
 Of those eyes of yours and I drop the glass!'

VII

Handsome, were you? 'Tis more than they held,
 More than they said; I was 'ware and watched:
I was the 'scapegrace, this rat belled
 The cat, this fool got his whiskers scratched:
The others? No head that was turned, no heart
 Broken, my lady, assure yourself!
Each soon made his mind up; so and so
80 Married a dancer, such and such
Stole his friend's wife, stagnated slow,
 Or maundered, unable to do as much,
And muttered of peace where he had no part:
 While, hid in the closet, laid on the shelf, –

VIII

On the whole, you were let alone, I think!
 So, you looked to the other, who acquiesced;
My rival, the proud man, – prize your pink
 Of poets! A poet he was! I've guessed:
He rhymed you his rubbish nobody read,
90 Loved you and doved you – did not I laugh!
There was a prize! But we both were tried.
 Oh, heart of mine, marked broad with her mark,
Tekel, found wanting, set aside,

Scorned! See, I bleed these tears in the dark
Till comfort come and the last be bled:
   He? He is tagging your epitaph.

IX

If it would only come over again!
   – Time to be patient with me, and probe
This heart till you punctured the proper vein,
   Just to learn what blood is: twitch the robe
From that blank lay-figure your fancy draped,
   Prick the leathern heart till the – verses spurt!
And late it was easy; late, you walked
   Where a friend might meet you; Edith's name
Arose to one's lip if one laughed or talked;
   If I heard good news, you heard the same;
When I woke, I knew that your breath escaped;
   I could bide my time, keep alive, alert.

X

And alive I shall keep and long, you will see!
   I knew a man, was kicked like a dog
From gutter to cesspool; what cared he
   So long as he picked from the filth his prog?
He saw youth, beauty and genius die,
   And jollily lived to his hundredth year.
But I will live otherwise: none of such life!
   At once I begin as I mean to end.
Go on with the world, get gold in its strife,
   Give your spouse the slip and betray your friend!
There are two who decline, a woman and I,
   And enjoy our death in the darkness here.

XI

I liked that way you had with your curls
   Wound to a ball in a net behind:
Your cheek was chaste as a quaker-girl's,
   And your mouth – there was never, to my mind,
Such a funny mouth, for it would not shut;
   And the dented chin too – what a chin!
There were certain ways when you spoke, some words
   That you know you never could pronounce:
You were thin, however; like a bird's

130 Your hand seemed – some would say, the pounce
  Of a scaly-footed hawk – all but!
   The world was right when it called you thin.

XII
But I turn my back on the world: I take
 Your hand, and kneel, and lay to my lips.
Bid me live, Edith! Let me slake
 Thirst at your presence! Fear no slips:
'Tis your slave shall pay, while his soul endures,
 Full due, love's whole debt, *summum jus*.
My queen shall have high observance, planned
140 Courtship made perfect, no least line
Crossed without warrant. There you stand,
 Warm too, and white too: would this wine
Had washed all over that body of yours,
 Ere I drank it, and you down with it, thus!

Abt Vogler

(After he has been extemporizing upon the musical instrument of his invention)

I
Would that the structure brave, the manifold music I build,
 Bidding my organ obey, calling its keys to their work,
Claiming each slave of the sound, at a touch, as when Solomon
   willed
 Armies of angels that soar, legions of demons that lurk,
Man, brute, reptile, fly, – alien of end and of aim,
 Adverse, each from the other heaven-high, hell-deep
   removed, –
Should rush into sight at once as he named the ineffable Name,
 And pile him a palace straight, to pleasure the princess he
   loved!

II

Would it might tarry like his, the beautiful building of mine,
10   This which my keys in a crowd pressed and importuned to
          raise!
    Ah, one and all, how they helped, would dispart now and now
          combine,
        Zealous to hasten the work, heighten their master his praise!
    And one would bury his brow with a blind plunge down to hell,
        Burrow awhile and build, broad on the roots of things,
    Then up again swim into sight, having based me my palace well,
        Founded it, fearless of flame, flat on the nether springs.

III

And another would mount and march, like the excellent minion
          he was,
        Ay, another and yet another, one crowd but with many a crest,
    Raising my rampired walls of gold as transparent as glass,
20   Eager to do and die, yield each his place to the rest:
    For higher still and higher (as a runner tips with fire,
        When a great illumination surprises a festal night –
    Outlining round and round Rome's dome from space to spire)
        Up, the pinnacled glory reached, and the pride of my soul was
          in sight.

IV

In sight? Not half! for it seemed, it was certain, to match man's
          birth,
        Nature in turn conceived, obeying an impulse as I;
    And the emulous heaven yearned down, made effort to reach the
          earth,
        As the earth had done her best, in my passion, to scale the sky:
    Novel splendours burst forth, grew familiar and dwelt with mine,
30   Not a point nor peak but found and fixed its wandering star;
    Meteor-moons, balls of blaze: and they did not pale nor pine,
        For earth had attained to heaven, there was no more near nor
          far.

V

Nay more; for there wanted not who walked in the glare and
          glow,
        Presences plain in the place; or, fresh from the Protoplast,
    Furnished for ages to come, when a kindlier wind should blow,

Lured now to begin and live, in a house to their liking at last;
Or else the wonderful Dead who have passed through the body
and gone,
But were back once more to breathe in an old world worth
their new:
What never had been, was now; what was, as it shall be anon;
40   And what is, – shall I say, matched both? for I was made
perfect too.

VI

All through my keys that gave their sounds to a wish of my soul,
All through my soul that praised as its wish flowed visibly
forth,
All through music and me! For think, had I painted the whole,
Why, there it had stood, to see, nor the process so wonder-
worth:
Had I written the same, made verse – still, effect proceeds from
cause,
Ye know why the forms are fair, ye hear how the tale is told;
It is all triumphant art, but art in obedience to laws,
Painter and poet are proud in the artist-list enrolled: –

VII

But here is the finger of God, a flash of the will that can,
50   Existent behind all laws, that made them and, lo, they are!
And I know not if, save in this, such gift be allowed to man,
That out of three sounds he frame, not a fourth sound, but a
star.
Consider it well: each tone of our scale in itself is naught;
It is everywhere in the world – loud, soft, and all is said:
Give it to me to use! I mix it with two in my thought:
And, there! Ye have heard and seen: consider and bow the
head!

VIII

Well, it is gone at last, the palace of music I reared;
Gone! and the good tears start, the praises that come too slow;
For one is assured at first, one scarce can say that he feared,
60   That he even gave it a thought, the gone thing was to go.
Never to be again! But many more of the kind
As good, nay, better perchance: is this your comfort to me?

To me, who must be saved because I cling with my mind
　　To the same, same self, same love, same God: ay, what was,
　　　　shall be.

IX

Therefore to whom turn I but to thee, the ineffable Name?
　　Builder and maker, thou, of houses not made with hands!
What, have fear of change from thee who art ever the same?
　　Doubt that thy power can fill the heart that thy power expands?
There shall never be one lost good! What was, shall live as
　　　　before;
70　The evil is null, is naught, is silence implying sound;
What was good shall be good, with, for evil, so much good more;
　　On the earth the broken arcs; in the heaven, a perfect round.

X

All we have willed or hoped or dreamed of good shall exist;
　　Not its semblance, but itself; no beauty, nor good, nor power
Whose voice has gone forth, but each survives for the melodist
　　When eternity affirms the conception of an hour.
The high that proved too high, the heroic for earth too hard,
　　The passion that left the ground to lose itself in the sky,
Are music sent up to God by the lover and the bard;
80　Enough that he heard it once: we shall hear it by-and-by.

XI

And what is our failure here but a triumph's evidence
　　For the fulness of the days? Have we withered or agonized?
Why else was the pause prolonged but that singing might issue
　　　　thence?
　　Why rushed the discords in but that harmony should be
　　　　prized?
Sorrow is hard to bear, and doubt is slow to clear,
　　Each sufferer says his say, his scheme of the weal and woe:
But God has a few of us whom he whispers in the ear;
　　The rest may reason and welcome: 'tis we musicians know.

XII

Well, it is earth with me; silence resumes her reign:
90　I will be patient and proud, and soberly acquiesce.
Give me the keys. I feel for the common chord again,
　　Sliding by semitones, till I sink to the minor, – yes,

And I blunt it into a ninth, and I stand on alien ground,
 Surveying awhile the heights I rolled from into the deep;
Which, hark, I have dared and done, for my resting-place is
  found,
 The C Major of this life: so, now I will try to sleep.

Rabbi Ben Ezra

I

 Grow old along with me!
 The best is yet to be,
The last of life, for which the first was made:
 Our times are in His hand
 Who saith 'A whole I planned,
Youth shows but half; trust God: see all nor be afraid!'

II

 Not that, amassing flowers,
 Youth sighed 'Which rose make ours,
Which lily leave and then as best recall?'
10 Not that, admiring stars,
 It yearned 'Nor Jove, nor Mars;
Mine be some figured flame which blends, transcends them all!'

III

 Not for such hopes and fears
 Annulling youth's brief years,
Do I remonstrate: folly wide the mark!
 Rather I prize the doubt
 Low kinds exist without,
Finished and finite clods, untroubled by a spark.

IV

 Poor vaunt of life indeed,
20 Were man but formed to feed
On joy, to solely seek and find and feast:
 Such feasting ended, then
 As sure an end to men;
Irks care the crop-full bird? Frets doubt the maw-crammed
  beast?

V

Rejoice we are allied
To That which doth provide
And not partake, effect and not receive!
A spark disturbs our clod;
Nearer we hold of God
30 Who gives, than of His tribes that take, I must believe.

VI

Then, welcome each rebuff
That turns earth's smoothness rough,
Each sting that bids nor sit nor stand but go!
Be our joys three-parts pain!
Strive, and hold cheap the strain;
Learn, nor account the pang; dare, never grudge the throe!

VII

For thence, – a paradox
Which comforts while it mocks, –
Shall life succeed in that it seems to fail:
40 What I aspired to be,
And was not, comforts me:
A brute I might have been, but would not sink i' the scale.

VIII

What is he but a brute
Whose flesh has soul to suit,
Whose spirit works lest arms and legs want play?
To man, propose this test –
Thy body at its best,
How far can that project thy soul on its lone way?

IX

Yet gifts should prove their use:
50 I own the Past profuse
Of power each side, perfection every turn:
Eyes, ears took in their dole,
Brain treasured up the whole;
Should not the heart beat once 'How good to live and learn'?

x

Not once beat 'Praise be Thine!
    I see the whole design,
I, who saw power, see now love perfect too:
    Perfect I call Thy plan:
    Thanks that I was a man!
60 Maker, remake, complete, – I trust what Thou shalt do!'

xi

For pleasant is this flesh;
    Our soul, in its rose-mesh
Pulled ever to the earth, still yearns for rest;
    Would we some prize might hold
    To match those manifold
Possessions of the brute, – gain most, as we did best!,

xii

Let us not always say
    'Spite of this flesh today
I strove, made head, gained ground upon the whole!'
70 As the bird wings and sings,
    Let us cry 'All good things
Are ours, nor soul helps flesh more, now, than flesh helps soul!'

xiii

Therefore I summon age
    To grant youth's heritage,
Life's struggle having so far reached its term:
    Thence shall I pass, approved
    A man, for aye removed
From the developed brute; a god though in the germ.

xiv

And I shall thereupon
80 Take rest, ere I be gone
Once more on my adventure brave and new:
    Fearless and unperplexed,
    When I wage battle next,
What weapons to select, what armour to indue.

XV

> Youth ended, I shall try
> My gain or loss thereby;
> Leave the fire ashes, what survives is gold:
> And I shall weigh the same,
> Give life its praise or blame:

90 Young, all lay in dispute; I shall know, being old.

XVI

> For note, when evening shuts,
> A certain moment cuts
> The deed off, calls the glory from the grey:
> A whisper from the west
> Shoots – 'Add this to the rest,
> Take it and try its worth: here dies another day.'

XVII

> So, still within this life,
> Though lifted o'er its strife,
> Let me discern, compare, pronounce at last,

100 'This rage was right i' the main,
> That acquiescence vain:
> The Future I may face now I have proved the Past.'

XVIII

> For more is not reserved
> To man, with soul just nerved
> To act tomorrow what he learns today:
> Here, work enough to watch
> The Master work, and catch
> Hints of the proper craft, tricks of the tool's true play.

XIX

> As it was better, youth

110 Should strive, through acts uncouth,
> Toward making, than repose on aught found made:
> So, better, age, exempt
> From strife, should know, than tempt
> Further. Thou waitedest age: wait death nor be afraid!

XX

Enough now, if the Right
And Good and Infinite
Be named here, as thou callest thy hand thine own,
    With knowledge absolute,
    Subject to no dispute
120 From fools that crowded youth, nor let thee feel alone.

XXI

Be there, for once and all,
Severed great minds from small,
Announced to each his station in the Past!
    Was I, the world arraigned,
    Were they, my soul disdained,
Right? Let age speak the truth and give us peace at last!

XXII

Now, who shall arbitrate?
Ten men love what I hate,
Shun what I follow, slight what I receive;
130   Ten, who in ears and eyes
    Match me: we all surmise,
They this thing, and I that: whom shall my soul believe?

XXIII

Not on the vulgar mass
Called 'work,' must sentence pass,
Things done, that took the eye and had the price;
    O'er which, from level stand,
    The low world laid its hand,
Found straightway to its mind, could value in a trice:

XXIV

But all, the world's coarse thumb
140 And finger failed to plumb,
So passed in making up the main account;
    All instincts immature,
    All purposes unsure,
That weighed not as his work, yet swelled the man's amount:

XXV

Thoughts hardly to be packed
Into a narrow act,
Fancies that broke through language and escaped;
All I could never be,
All, men ignored in me,
150 This, I was worth to God, whose wheel the pitcher shaped.

XXVI

Ay, note that Potter's wheel,
That metaphor! and feel
Why time spins fast, why passive lies our clay, –
Thou, to whom fools propound,
When the wine makes its round,
'Since life fleets, all is change; the Past gone, seize today!'

XXVII

Fool! All that is, at all,
Lasts ever, past recall;
Earth changes, but thy soul and God stand sure:
160 What entered into thee,
That was, is, and shall be:
Time's wheel runs back or stops: Potter and clay endure.

XXVIII

He fixed thee 'mid this dance
Of plastic circumstance,
This Present, thou, forsooth, wouldst fain arrest:
Machinery just meant
To give thy soul its bent,
Try thee and turn thee forth, sufficiently impressed.

XXIX

What though the earlier grooves
170 Which ran the laughing loves
Around thy base, no longer pause and press?
What though, about thy rim,
Skull-things in order grim
Grow out, in graver mood, obey the sterner stress?

XXX

Look not thou down but up!
   To uses of a cup,
The festal board, lamp's flash and trumpet's peal,
   The new wine's foaming flow,
   The Master's lips a-glow!
180 Thou, heaven's consummate cup, what need'st thou with earth's
       wheel?

XXXI

But I need, now as then,
   Thee, God, who mouldest men;
And since, not even while the whirl was worst,
   Did I, – to the wheel of life
   With shapes and colours rife,
Bound dizzily, – mistake my end, to slake Thy thirst:

XXXII

So, take and use Thy work:
   Amend what flaws may lurk,
What strain o' the stuff, what warpings past the aim!
190 My times be in Thy hand!
   Perfect the cup as planned!
Let age approve of youth, and death complete the same!

A Death in the Desert

[Supposed of Pamphylax the Antiochene:
It is a parchment, of my rolls the fifth,
Hath three skins glued together, is all Greek
And goeth from *Epsilon* down to *Mu*:
Lies second in the surnamed Chosen Chest,
Stained and conserved with juice of terebinth,
Covered with cloth of hair, and lettered *Xi*,
From Xanthus, my wife's uncle, now at peace:
Mu and *Epsilon* stand for my own name.
10 I may not write it, but I make a cross
To show I wait His coming, with the rest,
And leave off here: beginneth Pamphylax.]

I said, 'If one should wet his lips with wine,
And slip the broadest plantain-leaf we find,
Or else the lappet of a linen robe,
Into the water-vessel, lay it right,
And cool his forehead just above the eyes,
The while a brother, kneeling either side,
Should chafe each hand and try to make it warm, –
20 He is not so far gone but he might speak.'

This did not happen in the outer cave,
Nor in the secret chamber of the rock
Where, sixty days since the decree was out,
We had him, bedded on a camel-skin,
And waited for his dying all the while;
But in the midmost grotto: since noon's light
Reached there a little, and we would not lose
The last of what might happen on his face.

I at the head, and Xanthus at the feet,
30 With Valens and the Boy, had lifted him,
And brought him from the chamber in the depths,
And laid him in the light where we might see:
For certain smiles began about his mouth,
And his lids moved, presageful of the end.

Beyond, and half way up the mouth o' the cave,
The Bactrian convert, having his desire,
Kept watch, and made pretence to graze a goat
That gave us milk, on rags of various herb,
Plantain and quitch, the rocks' shade keeps alive:
40 So that if any thief or soldier passed,
(Because the persecution was aware)
Yielding the goat up promptly with his life,
Such man might pass on, joyful at a prize,
Nor care to pry into the cool o' the cave.
Outside was all noon and the burning blue.

'Here is wine,' answered Xanthus, – dropped a drop;
I stooped and placed the lap of cloth aright,
Then chafed his right hand, and the Boy his left:
But Valens had bethought him, and produced

50 And broke a ball of nard, and made perfume.
Only, he did – not so much wake, as – turn
And smile a little, as a sleeper does
If any dear one call him, touch his face –
And smiles and loves, but will not be disturbed.

Then Xanthus said a prayer, but still he slept:
It is the Xanthus that escaped to Rome,
Was burned, and could not write the chronicle.

Then the Boy sprang up from his knees, and ran,
Stung by the splendour of a sudden thought,
60 And fetched the seventh plate of graven lead
Out of the secret chamber, found a place,
Pressing with finger on the deeper dints,
And spoke, as 'twere his mouth proclaiming first,
'I am the Resurrection and the Life.'

Whereat he opened his eyes wide at once,
And sat up of himself, and looked at us;
And thenceforth nobody pronounced a word:
Only, outside, the Bactrian cried his cry
Like the lone desert-bird that wears the ruff,
70 As signal we were safe, from time to time.

First he said, 'If a friend declared to me,
This my son Valens, this my other son,
Were James and Peter, – nay, declared as well
This lad was very John, – I could believe!
– Could, for a moment, doubtlessly believe:
So is myself withdrawn into my depths,
The soul retreated from the perished brain
Whence it was wont to feel and use the world
Through these dull members, done with long ago.
80 Yet I myself remain; I feel myself:
And there is nothing lost. Let be, awhile!'

[This is the doctrine he was wont to teach,
How divers persons witness in each man,
Three souls which make up one soul: first, to wit,
A soul of each and all the bodily parts,

Seated therein, which works, and is what Does,
And has the use of earth, and ends the man
Downward: but, tending upward for advice,
Grows into, and again is grown into
90 By the next soul, which, seated in the brain,
Useth the first with its collected use,
And feeleth, thinketh, willeth, – is what Knows:
Which, duly tending upward in its turn,
Grows into, and again is grown into
By the last soul, that uses both the first,
Subsisting whether they assist or no,
And, constituting man's self, is what Is –
And leans upon the former, makes it play,
As that played off the first: and, tending up,
100 Holds, is upheld by, God, and ends the man
Upward in that dread point of intercourse,
Nor needs a place, for it returns to Him.
What Does, what Knows, what Is; three souls, one man.
I give the glossa of Theotypas.]

And then, 'A stick, once fire from end to end;
Now, ashes save the tip that holds a spark!
Yet, blow the spark, it runs back, spreads itself
A little where the fire was: thus I urge
The soul that served me, till it task once more
110 What ashes of my brain have kept their shape,
And these make effort on the last o' the flesh,
Trying to taste again the truth of things –'
(He smiled) – 'their very superficial truth;
As that ye are my sons, that it is long
Since James and Peter had release by death,
And I am only he, your brother John,
Who saw and heard, and could remember all.
Remember all! It is not much to say.
What if the truth broke on me from above
120 As once and oft-times? Such might hap again:
Doubtlessly He might stand in presence here,
With head wool-white, eyes flame, and feet like brass,
The sword and the seven stars, as I have seen –
I who now shudder only and surmise
"How did your brother bear that sight and live?"

'If I live yet, it is for good, more love
Through me to men: be naught but ashes here
That keep awhile my semblance, who was John, –
Still, when they scatter, there is left on earth
130   No one alive who knew (consider this!)
– Saw with his eyes and handled with his hands
That which was from the first, the Word of Life.
How will it be when none more saith "I saw"?

'Such ever was love's way: to rise, it stoops.
Since I, whom Christ's mouth taught, was bidden teach,
I went, for many years, about the world,
Saying "It was so; so I heard and saw,"
Speaking as the case asked: and men believed.
Afterward came the message to myself
140   In Patmos isle; I was not bidden teach,
But simply listen, take a book and write,
Nor set down other than the given word,
With nothing left to my arbitrament
To choose or change: I wrote, and men believed.
Then, for my time grew brief, no message more,
No call to write again, I found a way,
And, reasoning from my knowledge, merely taught
Men should, for love's sake, in love's strength believe;
Or I would pen a letter to a friend
150   And urge the same as friend, nor less nor more:
Friends said I reasoned rightly, and believed.
But at the last, why, I seemed left alive
Like a sea-jelly weak on Patmos strand,
To tell dry sea-beach gazers how I fared
When there was mid-sea, and the mighty things;
Left to repeat, "I saw, I heard, I knew,"
And go all over the old ground again,
With Antichrist already in the world,
And many Antichrists, who answered prompt
160   "Am I not Jasper as thyself art John?
Nay, young, whereas through age thou mayst forget:
Wherefore, explain, or how shall we believe?"
I never thought to call down fire on such,
Or, as in wonderful and early days,
Pick up the scorpion, tread the serpent dumb;
But patient stated much of the Lord's life

Forgotten or misdelivered, and let it work:
Since much that at the first, in deed and word,
Lay simply and sufficiently exposed,
170 Had grown (or else my soul was grown to match,
Fed through such years, familiar with such light,
Guarded and guided still to see and speak)
Of new significance and fresh result;
What first were guessed as points, I now knew stars,
And named them in the Gospel I have writ.
For men said, "It is getting long ago:
Where is the promise of His coming?" – asked
These young ones in their strength, as loth to wait,
Of me who, when their sires were born, was old.
180 I, for I loved them, answered, joyfully,
Since I was there, and helpful in my age;
And, in the main, I think such men believed.
Finally, thus endeavouring, I fell sick,
Ye brought me here, and I supposed the end,
And went to sleep with one thought that, at least,
Though the whole earth should lie in wickedness,
We had the truth, might leave the rest to God.
Yet now I wake in such decrepitude
As I had slidden down and fallen afar,
190 Past even the presence of my former self,
Grasping the while for stay at facts which snap,
Till I am found away from my own world,
Feeling for foot-hold through a blank profound,
Along with unborn people in strange lands,
Who say – I hear said or conceive they say –
"Was John at all, and did he say he saw?
Assure us, ere we ask what he might see!"

'And how shall I assure them? Can they share
– They, who have flesh, a veil of youth and strength
200 About each spirit, that needs must bide its time,
Living and learning still as years assist
Which wear the thickness thin, and let man see –
With me who hardly am withheld at all,
But shudderingly, scarce a shred between,
Lie bare to the universal prick of light?
Is it for nothing we grow old and weak,
We whom God loves? When pain ends, gain ends too.

To me, that story – ay, that Life and Death
Of which I wrote "it was" – to me, it is;
210 – Is, here and now: I apprehend naught else.
Is not God now i' the world His power first made?
Is not His love at issue still with sin
Visibly when a wrong is done on earth?
Love, wrong, and pain, what see I else around?
Yea, and the Resurrection and Uprise
To the right hand of the throne – what is it beside,
When such truth, breaking bounds, o'erfloods my soul,
And, as I saw the sin and death, even so
See I the need yet transiency of both,
220 The good and glory consummated thence?
I saw the power; I see the Love, once weak,
Resume the Power: and in this word "I see,"
Lo, there is recognized the Spirit of both
That moving o'er the spirit of man, unblinds
His eye and bids him look. These are, I see;
But ye, the children, His beloved ones too,
Ye need, – as I should use an optic glass
I wondered at erewhile, somewhere i' the world,
It had been given a crafty smith to make;
230 A tube, he turned on objects brought too close,
Lying confusedly insubordinate
For the unassisted eye to master once:
Look through his tube, at distance now they lay,
Become succinct, distinct, so small, so clear!
Just thus, ye needs must apprehend what truth
I see, reduced to plain historic fact,
Diminished into clearness, proved a point
And far away: ye would withdraw your sense
From out eternity, strain it upon time,
240 Then stand before that fact, that Life and Death,
Stay there at gaze, till it dispart, dispread,
As though a star should open out, all sides,
Grow the world on you, as it is my world.

'For life, with all it yields of joy and woe,
And hope and fear, – believe the aged friend, –
Is just our chance o' the prize of learning love,
How love might be, hath been indeed, and is;
And that we hold thenceforth to the uttermost

Such prize despite the envy of the world,
250 And, having gained truth, keep truth: that is all.
But see the double way wherein we are led,
How the soul learns diversely from the flesh!
With flesh, that hath so little time to stay,
And yields mere basement for the soul's emprise,
Expect prompt teaching. Helpful was the light,
And warmth was cherishing and food was choice
To every man's flesh, thousand years ago,
As now to yours and mine; the body sprang
At once to the height, and stayed: but the soul, – no!
260 Since sages who, this noontide, meditate
In Rome or Athens, may descry some point
Of the eternal power, hid yestereve;
And, as thereby the power's whole mass extends,
So much extends the aether floating o'er,
The love that tops the might, the Christ in God.
Then, as new lessons shall be learned in these
Till earth's work stop and useless time run out,
So duly, daily, needs provision be
For keeping the soul's prowess possible,
270 Building new barriers as the old decay,
Saving us from evasion of life's proof,
Putting the question ever, "Does God love,
And will ye hold that truth against the world?"
Ye know there needs no second proof with good
Gained for our flesh from any earthly source:
We might go freezing, ages, – give us fire,
Thereafter we judge fire at its full worth,
And guard it safe through every chance, ye know!
That fable of Prometheus and his theft,
280 How mortals gained Jove's fiery flower, grows old
(I have been used to hear the pagans own)
And out of mind; but fire, howe'er its birth,
Here is it, precious to the sophist now
Who laughs the myth of Aeschylus to scorn,
As precious to those satyrs of his play,
Who touched it in gay wonder at the thing.
While were it so with the soul, – this gift of truth
Once grasped, were this our soul's gain safe, and sure
To prosper as the body's gain is wont, –
290 Why, man's probation would conclude, his earth

Crumble; for he both reasons and decides,
Weighs first, then chooses: will he give up fire
For gold or purple once he knows its worth?
Could he give Christ up were His worth as plain?
Therefore, I say, to test man, the proofs shift,
Nor may he grasp that fact like other fact,
And straightway in his life acknowledge it,
As, say, the indubitable bliss of fire.
Sigh ye, "It had been easier once than now"?
300 To give you answer I am left alive;
Look at me who was present from the first!
Ye know what things I saw; then came a test,
My first, befitting me who so had seen:
"Forsake the Christ thou sawest transfigured, Him
Who trod the sea and brought the dead to life?
What should wring this from thee!" – ye laugh and ask.
What wrung it? Even a torchlight and a noise,
The sudden Roman faces, violent hands,
And fear of what the Jews might do! Just that,
310 And it is written, "I forsook and fled":
There was my trial, and it ended thus.
Ay, but my soul had gained its truth, could grow:
Another year or two, – what little child,
What tender woman that had seen no least
Of all my sights, but barely heard them told,
Who did not clasp the cross with a light laugh,
Or wrap the burning robe round, thanking God?
Well, was truth safe for ever, then? Not so.
Already had begun the silent work
320 Whereby truth, deadened of its absolute blaze,
Might need love's eye to pierce the o'erstretched doubt.
Teachers were busy, whispering "All is true
As the aged ones report; but youth can reach
Where age gropes dimly, weak with stir and strain,
And the full doctrine slumbers till today."
Thus, what the Roman's lowered spear was found,
A bar to me who touched and handled truth,
Now proved the glozing of some new shrewd tongue,
This Ebion, this Cerinthus or their mates,
330 Till imminent was the outcry "Save our Christ!"
Whereon I stated much of the Lord's life
Forgotten or misdelivered, and let it work.

Such work done, as it will be, what comes next?
What do I hear say, or conceive men say,
"Was John at all, and did he say he saw?
Assure us, ere we ask what he might see!"

'Is this indeed a burthen for late days,
And may I help to bear it with you all,
Using my weakness which becomes your strength?
340 For if a babe were born inside this grot,
Grew to a boy here, heard us praise the sun,
Yet had but yon sole glimmer in light's place, –
One loving him and wishful he should learn,
Would much rejoice himself was blinded first
Month by month here, so made to understand
How eyes, born darkling, apprehend amiss:
I think I could explain to such a child
There was more glow outside than gleams he caught,
Ay, nor need urge "I saw it, so believe!"
350 It is a heavy burthen you shall bear
In latter days, new lands, or old grown strange,
Left without me, which must be very soon.
What is the doubt, my brothers? Quick with it!
I see you stand conversing, each new face,
Either in fields, of yellow summer eves,
On islets yet unnamed amid the sea;
Or pace for shelter 'neath a portico
Out of the crowd in some enormous town
Where now the larks sing in a solitude;
360 Or muse upon blank heaps of stone and sand
Idly conjectured to be Ephesus:
And no one asks his fellow any more
"Where is the promise of His coming?" but
"Was he revealed in any of His lives,
As Power, as Love, as Influencing Soul?"

'Quick, for time presses, tell the whole mind out,
And let us ask and answer and be saved!
My book speaks on, because it cannot pass;
One listens quietly, nor scoffs but pleads
370 "Here is a tale of things done ages since;
What truth was ever told the second day?
Wonders, that would prove doctrine, go for naught.

Remains the doctrine, love; well, we must love,
And what we love most, power and love in one,
Let us acknowledge on the record here,
Accepting these in Christ: must Christ then be?
Has He been? Did not we ourselves make Him?
Our mind receives but what it holds, no more.
First of the love, then; we acknowledge Christ –
380 A proof we comprehend His love, a proof
We had such love already in ourselves,
Knew first what else we should not recognize.
'Tis mere projection from man's inmost mind,
And, what he loves, thus falls reflected back,
Becomes accounted somewhat out of him;
He throws it up in air, it drops down earth's,
With shape, name, story added, man's old way.
How prove you Christ came otherwise at least?
Next try the power: He made and rules the world:
390 Certes there is a world once made, now ruled,
Unless things have been ever as we see.
Our sires declared a charioteer's yoked steeds
Brought the sun up the east and down the west,
Which only of itself now rises, sets,
As if a hand impelled it and a will, –
Thus they long thought, they who had will and hands:
But the new question's whisper is distinct,
Wherefore must all force needs be like ourselves?
We have the hands, the will; what made and drives
400 The sun is force, is law, is named, not known,
While will and love we do know; marks of these,
Eye-witnesses attest, so books declare –
As that, to punish or reward our race,
The sun at undue times arose or set
Or else stood still: what do not men affirm?
But earth requires as urgently reward
Or punishment today as years ago,
And none expects the sun will interpose:
Therefore it was mere passion and mistake,
410 Or erring zeal for right, which changed the truth.
Go back, far, farther, to the birth of things;
Ever the will, the intelligence, the love,
Man's! – which he gives, supposing he but finds,
As late he gave head, body, hands and feet,

To help these in what forms he called his gods.
First, Jove's brow, Juno's eyes were swept away,
But Jove's wrath, Juno's pride continued long;
As last, will, power, and love discarded these,
So law in turn discards power, love, and will.
420 What proveth God is otherwise at least?
All else, projection from the mind of man!"

'Nay, do not give me wine, for I am strong,
But place my gospel where I put my hands.

'I say that man was made to grow, not stop;
That help, he needed once, and needs no more,
Having grown but an inch by, is withdrawn:
For he hath new needs, and new helps to these.
This imports solely, man should mount on each
New height in view; the help whereby he mounts,
430 The ladder-rung his foot has left, may fall,
Since all things suffer change save God the Truth.
Man apprehends Him newly at each stage
Whereat earth's ladder drops, its service done;
And nothing shall prove twice what once was proved.
You stick a garden-plot with ordered twigs
To show inside lie germs of herbs unborn,
And check the careless step would spoil their birth;
But when herbs wave, the guardian twigs may go,
Since should ye doubt of virtues, question kinds,
440 It is no longer for old twigs ye look,
Which proved once underneath lay store of seed,
But to the herb's self, by what light ye boast,
For what fruit's signs are. This book's fruit is plain,
Nor miracles need prove it any more.
Doth the fruit show? Then miracles bade 'ware
At first of root and stem, saved both till now
From trampling ox, rough boar and wanton goat.
What? Was man made a wheelwork to wind up,
And be discharged, and straight wound up anew?
450 No! – grown, his growth lasts; taught, he ne'er forgets:
May learn a thousand things, not twice the same.

'This might be pagan teaching: now hear mine.

'I say, that as the babe, you feed awhile,
Becomes a boy and fit to feed himself,
So, minds at first must be spoon-fed with truth:
When they can eat, babe's-nurture is withdrawn.
I fed the babe whether it would or no:
I bid the boy or feed himself or starve.
I cried once, "That ye may believe in Christ,
460 Behold this blind man shall receive his sight!"
I cry now, "Urgest thou, *for I am shrewd*
And smile at stories how John's word could cure –
Repeat that miracle and take my faith?"
I say, that miracle was duly wrought
When, save for it, no faith was possible.
Whether a change were wrought i' the shows o' the world,
Whether the change came from our minds which see
Of shows o' the world so much as and no more
Than God wills for His purpose, – (what do I
470 See now, suppose you, there where you see rock
Round us?) – I know not; such was the effect,
So faith grew, making void more miracles
Because too much: they would compel, not help.
I say, the acknowledgement of God in Christ
Accepted by thy reason, solves for thee
All questions in the earth and out of it,
And has so far advanced thee to be wise.
Wouldst thou unprove this to re-prove the proved?
In life's mere minute, with power to use that proof,
480 Leave knowledge and revert to how it sprung?
Thou hast it; use it and forthwith, or die!

'For I say, this is death and the sole death,
When a man's loss comes to him from his gain,
Darkness from light, from knowledge ignorance,
And lack of love from love made manifest;
A lamp's death when, replete with oil, it chokes;
A stomach's when, surcharged with food, it starves.
With ignorance was surety of a cure.
When man, appalled at nature, questioned first
490 "What if there lurk a might behind this might?"
He needed satisfaction God could give,
And did give, as ye have the written word:
But when he finds might still redouble might,

Yet asks, "Since all is might, what use of will?"
– Will, the one source of might, – he being man
With a man's will and a man's might, to teach
In little how the two combine in large, –
That man has turned round on himself and stands,
Which in the course of nature is, to die.

500 'And when man questioned, "What if there be love
Behind the will and might, as real as they?" –
He needed satisfaction God could give,
And did give, as ye have the written word:
But when, beholding that love everywhere,
He reasons, "Since such love is everywhere,
And since ourselves can love and would be loved,
We ourselves make the love, and Christ was not," –
How shall ye help this man who knows himself,
That he must love and would be loved again,
510 Yet, owning his own love that proveth Christ,
Rejecteth Christ through very need of Him?
The lamp o'erswims with oil, the stomach flags
Loaded with nurture, and that man's soul dies.

'If he rejoin, "But this was all the while
A trick; the fault was, first of all, in thee,
Thy story of the places, names and dates,
Where, when and how the ultimate truth had rise,
– Thy prior truth, at last discovered none,
Whence now the second suffers detriment.
520 What good of giving knowledge if, because
O' the manner of the gift, its profit fail?
And why refuse what modicum of help
Had stopped the after-doubt, impossible
I' the face of truth – truth absolute, uniform?
Why must I hit of this and miss of that,
Distinguish just as I be weak or strong,
And not ask of thee and have answer prompt,
Was this once, was it not once? – then and now
And evermore, plain truth from man to man.
530 Is John's procedure just the heathen bard's?
Put question of his famous play again
How for the ephemerals' sake Jove's fire was filched,
And carried in a cane and brought to earth:

The fact is in the fable, cry the wise,
Mortals obtained the boon, so much is fact,
Though fire be spirit and produced on earth.
As with the Titan's, so now with thy tale:
Why breed in us perplexity, mistake,
Nor tell the whole truth in the proper words?"

540 'I answer, Have ye yet to argue out
The very primal thesis, plainest law,
– Man is not God but hath God's end to serve,
A master to obey, a course to take,
Somewhat to cast off, somewhat to become?
Grant this, then man must pass from old to new,
From vain to real, from mistake to fact,
From what once seemed good, to what now proves best.
How could man have progression otherwise?
Before the point was mooted "What is God?"
550 No savage man inquired "What am myself?"
Much less replied, "First, last, and best of things."
Man takes that title now if he believes
Might can exist with neither will nor love,
In God's case – what he names now Nature's Law –
While in himself he recognizes love
No less than might and will: and rightly takes.
Since if man prove the sole existent thing
Where these combine, whatever their degree,
However weak the might or will or love,
560 So they be found there, put in evidence, –
He is as surely higher in the scale
Than any might with neither love nor will,
As life, apparent in the poorest midge,
(When the faint dust-speck flits, ye guess its wing)
Is marvellous beyond dead Atlas' self –
Given to the nobler midge for resting-place!
Thus, man proves best and highest – God, in fine,
And thus the victory leads but to defeat,
The gain to loss, best rise to the worst fall,
570 His life becomes impossible, which is death.

'But if, appealing thence, he cower, avouch
He is mere man, and in humility
Neither may know God nor mistake himself;

I point to the immediate consequence
And say, by such confession straight he falls
Into man's place, a thing nor God nor beast,
Made to know that he can know and not more:
Lower than God who knows all and can all,
Higher than beasts which know and can so far
580 As each beast's limit, perfect to an end,
Nor conscious that they know, nor craving more;
While man knows partly but conceives beside,
Creeps ever on from fancies to the fact,
And in this striving, this converting air
Into a solid he may grasp and use,
Finds progress, man's distinctive mark alone,
Not God's, and not the beasts': God is, they are,
Man partly is and wholly hopes to be.
Such progress could no more attend his soul
590 Were all it struggles after found at first
And guesses changed to knowledge absolute,
Than motion wait his body, were all else
Than it the solid earth on every side,
Where now through space he moves from rest to rest.
Man, therefore, thus conditioned, must expect
He could not, what he knows now, know at first;
What he considers that he knows today,
Come but tomorrow, he will find misknown;
Getting increase of knowledge, since he learns
600 Because he lives, which is to be a man,
Set to instruct himself by his past self:
First, like the brute, obliged by facts to learn,
Next, as man may, obliged by his own mind,
Bent, habit, nature, knowledge turned to law.
God's gift was that man should conceive of truth
And yearn to gain it, catching at mistake,
As midway help till he reach fact indeed.
The statuary ere he mould a shape
Boasts a like gift, the shape's idea, and next
610 The aspiration to produce the same;
So, taking clay, he calls his shape thereout,
Cries ever "Now I have the thing I see":
Yet all the while goes changing what was wrought,
From falsehood like the truth, to truth itself.
How were it had he cried "I see no face,

No breast, no feet i' the ineffectual clay"?
Rather commend him that he clapped his hands,
And laughed "It is my shape and lives again!"
Enjoyed the falsehood, touched it on to truth,
620 Until yourselves applaud the flesh indeed
In what is still flesh-imitating clay.
Right in you, right in him, such way be man's!
God only makes the live shape at a jet.
Will ye renounce this pact of creatureship?
The pattern on the Mount subsists no more,
Seemed awhile, then returned to nothingness;
But copies, Moses strove to make thereby,
Serve still and are replaced as time requires:
By these, make newest vessels, reach the type!
630 If ye demur, this judgement on your head,
Never to reach the ultimate, angels' law,
Indulging every instinct of the soul
There where law, life, joy, impulse are one thing!

'Such is the burthen of the latest time.
I have survived to hear it with my ears,
Answer it with my lips: does this suffice?
For if there be a further woe than such,
Wherein my brothers struggling need a hand,
So long as any pulse is left in mine,
640 May I be absent even longer yet,
Plucking the blind ones back from the abyss,
Though I should tarry a new hundred years!'

But he was dead; 'twas about noon, the day
Somewhat declining: we five buried him
That eve, and then, dividing, went five ways,
And I, disguised, returned to Ephesus.

By this, the cave's mouth must be filled with sand.
Valens is lost, I know not of his trace;
The Bactrian was but a wild childish man,
650 And could not write nor speak, but only loved:
So, lest the memory of this go quite,
Seeing that I tomorrow fight the beasts,
I tell the same to Phoebas, whom believe!
For many look again to find that face,

Beloved John's to whom I ministered,
Somewhere in life about the world; they err:
Either mistaking what was darkly spoke
At ending of his book, as he relates,
Or misconceiving somewhat of this speech
660 Scattered from mouth to mouth, as I suppose.
Believe ye will not see him any more
About the world with his divine regard!
For all was as I say, and now the man
Lies as he lay once, breast to breast with God.

[Cerinthus read and mused; one added this:

'If Christ, as thou affirmest, be of men
Mere man, the first and best but nothing more, –
Account Him, for reward of what He was,
Now and for ever, wretchedest of all.
670 For see; Himself conceived of life as love,
Conceived of love as what must enter in,
Fill up, make one with His each soul He loved:
Thus much for man's joy, all men's joy for Him.
Well, He is gone, thou sayest, to fit reward.
But by this time are many souls set free,
And very many still retained alive:
Nay, should His coming be delayed awhile,
Say, ten years longer (twelve years, some compute)
See if, for every finger of thy hands,
680 There be not found, that day the world shall end,
Hundreds of souls, each holding by Christ's word
That He will grow incorporate with all,
With me as Pamphylax, with him as John,
Groom for each bride! Can a mere man do this?
Yet Christ saith, this He lived and died to do.
Call Christ, then, the illimitable God,
Or lost!'

But 'twas Cerinthus that is lost.]

Caliban upon Setebos; or, Natural Theology in the Island

'Thou thoughtest that I was altogether such a one as thyself.'

['Will sprawl, now that the heat of day is best,
Flat on his belly in the pit's much mire,
With elbows wide, fists clenched to prop his chin.
And, while he kicks both feet in the cool slush,
And feels about his spine small eft-things course,
Run in and out each arm, and make him laugh:
And while above his head a pompion-plant,
Coating the cave-top as a brow its eye,
Creeps down to touch and tickle hair and beard,
10 And now a flower drops with a bee inside,
And now a fruit to snap at, catch and crunch, –
He looks out o'er yon sea which sunbeams cross
And recross till they weave a spider-web
(Meshes of fire, some great fish breaks at times)
And talks to his own self, howe'er he please,
Touching that other, whom his dam called God.
Because to talk about Him, vexes – ha,
Could He but know! and time to vex is now,
When talk is safer than in winter-time.
20 Moreover Prosper and Miranda sleep
In confidence he drudges at their task,
And it is good to cheat the pair, and gibe,
Letting the rank tongue blossom into speech.]

Setebos, Setebos, and Setebos!
'Thinketh, He dwelleth i' the cold o' the moon.

'Thinketh He made it, with the sun to match,
But not the stars; the stars came otherwise;
Only made clouds, winds, meteors, such as that:
Also this isle, what lives and grows thereon,
30 And snaky sea which rounds and ends the same.

'Thinketh, it came of being ill at ease:
He hated that He cannot change His cold,
Nor cure its ache. 'Hath spied an icy fish
That longed to 'scape the rock-stream where she lived,

And thaw herself within the lukewarm brine
O' the lazy sea her stream thrusts far amid,
A crystal spike 'twixt two warm walls of wave;
Only, she ever sickened, found repulse
At the other kind of water, not her life,
40 (Green-dense and dim-delicious, bred o' the sun)
Flounced back from bliss she was not born to breathe,
And in her old bounds buried her despair,
Hating and loving warmth alike: so He.

'Thinketh, He made thereat the sun, this isle,
Trees and the fowls here, beast and creeping thing.
Yon otter, sleek-wet, black, lithe as a leech;
Yon auk, one fire-eye in a ball of foam,
That floats and feeds; a certain badger brown
He hath watched hunt with that slant white-wedge eye
50 By moonlight; and the pie with the long tongue
That pricks deep into oakwarts for a worm,
And says a plain word when she finds her prize,
But will not eat the ants; the ants themselves
That build a wall of seeds and settled stalks
About their hole – He made all these and more,
Made all we see, and us, in spite: how else?
He could not, Himself, make a second self
To be His mate; as well have made Himself:
He would not make what he mislikes or slights,
60 An eyesore to Him, or not worth His pains:
But did, in envy, listlessness or sport,
Make what Himself would fain, in a manner, be –
Weaker in most points, stronger in a few,
Worthy, and yet mere playthings all the while,
Things He admires and mocks too, – that is it.
Because, so brave, so better though they be,
It nothing skills if He begin to plague.
Look now, I melt a gourd-fruit into mash,
Add honeycomb and pods, I have perceived,
70 Which bite like finches when they bill and kiss, –
Then, when froth rises bladdery, drink up all,
Quick, quick, till maggots scamper through my brain;
Last, throw me on my back i' the seeded thyme,
And wanton, wishing I were born a bird.
Put case, unable to be what I wish,

I yet could make a live bird out of clay:
Would not I take clay, pinch my Caliban
Able to fly? – for, there, see, he hath wings,
And great comb like the hoopoe's to admire,
80 And there, a sting to do his foes offence,
There, and I will that he begin to live,
Fly to yon rock-top, nip me off the horns
Of grigs high up that make the merry din,
Saucy through their veined wings, and mind me not.
In which feat, if his leg snapped, brittle clay,
And he lay stupid-like, – why, I should laugh;
And if he, spying me, should fall to weep,
Beseech me to be good, repair his wrong,
Bid his poor leg smart less or grow again, –
90 Well, as the chance were, this might take or else
Not take my fancy: I might hear his cry,
And give the mankin three sound legs for one,
Or pluck the other off, leave him like an egg,
And lessoned he was mine and merely clay.
Were this no pleasure, lying in the thyme,
Drinking the mash, with brain become alive,
Making and marring clay at will? So He.

'Thinketh, such shows nor right nor wrong in Him,
Nor kind, nor cruel: He is strong and Lord.
100 'Am strong myself compared to yonder crabs
That march now from the mountain to the sea,
'Let twenty pass, and stone the twenty-first,
Loving not, hating not, just choosing so.
'Say, the first straggler that boasts purple spots
Shall join the file, one pincer twisted off;
'Say, this bruised fellow shall receive a worm,
And two worms he whose nippers end in red;
As it likes me each time, I do: so He.

Well then, 'supposeth He is good i' the main,
110 Placable if His mind and ways were guessed,
But rougher than His handiwork, be sure!
Oh, He hath made things worthier than Himself,
And envieth that, so helped, such things do more
Than He who made them! What consoles but this?
That they, unless through Him, do naught at all,

And must submit: what other use in things?
'Hath cut a pipe of pithless elder-joint
That, blown through, gives exact the scream o' the jay
When from her wing you twitch the feathers blue:
120 Sound this, and little birds that hate the jay
Flock within stone's throw, glad their foe is hurt:
Put case such pipe could prattle and boast forsooth
'I catch the birds, I am the crafty thing,
I make the cry my maker cannot make
With his great round mouth; he must blow through mine!'
Would not I smash it with my foot? So He.

But wherefore rough, why cold and ill at ease?
Aha, that is a question! Ask, for that,
What knows, – the something over Setebos
130 That made Him, or He, may be, found and fought,
Worsted, drove off and did to nothing, perchance.
There may be something quiet o'er His head,
Out of His reach, that feels nor joy nor grief,
Since both derive from weakness in some way.
I joy because the quails come; would not joy
Could I bring quails here when I have a mind:
This Quiet, all it hath a mind to, doth.
'Esteemeth stars the outposts of its couch,
But never spends much thought nor care that way.
140 It may look up, work up, – the worse for those
It works on! 'Careth but for Setebos
The many-handed as a cuttle-fish,
Who, making Himself feared through what He does,
Looks up, first, and perceives he cannot soar
To what is quiet and hath happy life;
Next looks down here, and out of very spite
Makes this a bauble-world to ape yon real,
These good things to match those as hips do grapes.
'Tis solace making baubles, ay, and sport.
150 Himself peeped late, eyed Prosper at his books
Careless and lofty, lord now of the isle:
Vexed, 'stitched a book of broad leaves, arrow-shaped,
Wrote thereon, he knows what, prodigious words;
Has peeled a wand and called it by a name;
Weareth at whiles for an enchanter's robe
The eyed skin of a supple oncelot;

And hath an ounce sleeker than youngling mole,
A four-legged serpent he makes cower and couch,
Now snarl, now hold its breath and mind his eye,
160 And saith she is Miranda and my wife:
'Keeps for his Ariel a tall pouch-bill crane
He bids go wade for fish and straight disgorge;
Also a sea-beast, lumpish, which he snared,
Blinded the eyes of, and brought somewhat tame,
And split its toe-webs, and now pens the drudge
In a hole o' the rock and calls him Caliban;
A bitter heart that bides its time and bites.
'Plays thus at being Prosper in a way,
Taketh his mirth with make-believes: so He.

170 His dam held that the Quiet made all things
Which Setebos vexed only: 'holds not so.
Who made them weak, meant weakness He might vex.
Had He meant other, while His hand was in,
Why not make horny eyes no thorn could prick,
Or plate my scalp with bone against the snow,
Or overscale my flesh 'neath joint and joint,
Like an orc's armour? Ay, – so spoil His sport!
He is the One now: only He doth all.

'Saith, He may like, perchance, what profits Him.
180 Ay, himself loves what does him good; but why?
'Gets good no otherwise. This blinded beast
Loves whoso places flesh-meat on his nose,
But, had he eyes, would want no help, but hate
Or love, just as it liked him: He hath eyes.
Also it pleaseth Setebos to work,
Use all His hands, and exercise much craft,
By no means for the love of what is worked.
'Tasteth, himself, no finer good i' the world
When all goes right, in this safe summer-time,
190 And he wants little, hungers, aches not much,
Than trying what to do with wit and strength.
'Falls to make something: 'piled yon pile of turfs,
And squared and stuck there squares of soft white chalk,
And, with a fish-tooth, scratched a moon on each,
And set up endwise certain spikes of tree,
And crowned the whole with a sloth's skull a-top,

Found dead i' the woods, too hard for one to kill.
No use at all i' the work, for work's sole sake;
'Shall some day knock it down again: so He.

200 'Saith He is terrible: watch His feats in proof!
One hurricane will spoil six good months' hope.
He hath a spite against me, that I know,
Just as He favours Prosper, who knows why?
So it is, all the same, as well I find.
'Wove wattles half the winter, fenced them firm
With stone and stake to stop she-tortoises
Crawling to lay their eggs here: well, one wave,
Feeling the foot of Him upon its neck,
Gaped as a snake does, lolled out its large tongue,
210 And licked the whole labour flat: so much for spite.
'Saw a ball flame down late (yonder it lies)
Where, half an hour before, I slept i' the shade:
Often they scatter sparkles: there is force!
'Dug up a newt He may have envied once
And turned to stone, shut up inside a stone.
Please Him and hinder this? – What Prosper does?
Aha, if He would tell me how! Not He!
There is the sport: discover how or die!
All need not die, for of the things o' the isle
220 Some flee afar, some dive, some run up trees;
Those at His mercy, – why, they please Him most
When ... when ... well, never try the same way twice!
Repeat what act has pleased, He may grow wroth.
You must not know His ways, and play Him off,
Sure of the issue. 'Doth the like himself:
'Spareth a squirrel that it nothing fears
But steals the nut from underneath my thumb,
And when I threat, bites stoutly in defence:
'Spareth an urchin that contrariwise,
230 Curls up into a ball, pretending death
For fright at my approach: the two ways please.
But what would move my choler more than this,
That either creature counted on its life
Tomorrow and next day and all days to come,
Saying, forsooth, in the inmost of its heart,
'Because he did so yesterday with me,
And otherwise with such another brute,

So must he do henceforth and always.' – Ay?
Would teach the reasoning couple what 'must' means!
240 'Doth as he likes, or wherefore Lord? So He.

'Conceiveth all things will continue thus,
And we shall have to live in fear of Him
So long as He lives, keeps His strength: no change,
If He have done His best, make no new world
To please Him more, so leave off watching this, –
If He surprise not even the Quiet's self
Some strange day, – or, suppose, grow into it
As grubs grow butterflies: else, here are we,
And there is He, and nowhere help at all.

250 'Believeth with the life, the pain shall stop.
His dam held different, that after death
He both plagued enemies and feasted friends:
Idly! He doth His worst in this our life,
Giving just respite lest we die through pain,
Saving last pain for worst, – with which, an end.
Meanwhile, the best way to escape His ire
Is, not to seem too happy. 'Sees, himself,
Yonder two flies, with purple films and pink,
Bask on the pompion-bell above: kills both.
260 'Sees two black painful beetles roll their ball
On head and tail as if to save their lives:
Moves them the stick away they strive to clear.

Even so, 'would have Him misconceive, suppose
This Caliban strives hard and ails no less,
And always, above all else, envies Him;
Wherefore he mainly dances on dark nights,
Moans in the sun, gets under holes to laugh,
And never speaks his mind save housed as now:
Outside, 'groans, curses. If He caught me here,
270 O'erheard this speech, and asked 'What chucklest at?'
'Would, to appease Him, cut a finger off,
Or of my three kid yearlings burn the best,
Or let the toothsome apples rot on tree,
Or push my tame beast for the orc to taste:
While myself lit a fire, and made a song
And sung it, '*What I hate, be consecrate*

To celebrate Thee and Thy state, no mate
For Thee ; what see for envy in poor me ?'
Hoping the while, since evils sometimes mend,
280   Warts rub away and sores are cured with slime,
That some strange day, will either the Quiet catch
And conquer Setebos, or likelier He
Decrepit may doze, doze, as good as die.
[What, what ? A curtain o'er the world at once!
Crickets stop hissing; not a bird – or, yes,
There scuds His raven that has told Him all!
It was fool's play, this prattling! Ha! The wind
Shoulders the pillared dust, death's house o' the move,
And fast invading fires begin! White blaze –
290   A tree's head snaps – and there, there, there, there, there,
His thunder follows! Fool to gibe at Him!
Lo! 'Lieth flat and loveth Setebos!
'Maketh his teeth meet through his upper lip,
Will let those quails fly, will not eat this month
One little mess of whelks, so he may 'scape!]

Confessions

I
What is he buzzing in my ears?
   'Now that I come to die,
Do I view the world as a vale of tears?'
   Ah, reverend sir, not I!

II
What I viewed there once, what I view again
   Where the physic bottles stand
On the table's edge, – is a suburb lane,
   With a wall to my bedside hand.

III
That lane sloped, much as the bottles do,
10   From a house you could descry
O'er the garden-wall: is the curtain blue
   Or green to a healthy eye?

IV

To mine, it serves for the old June weather
   Blue above lane and wall;
And that farthest bottle labelled 'Ether'
   Is the house o'ertopping all.

V

At a terrace, somewhere near the stopper,
   There watched for me, one June,
A girl: I know, sir, it's improper,
20   My poor mind's out of tune.

VI

Only, there was a way ... you crept
   Close by the side, to dodge
Eyes in the house, two eyes except:
   They styled their house 'The Lodge.'

VII

What right had a lounger up their lane?
   But, by creeping very close,
With the good wall's help, – their eyes might strain
   And stretch themselves to Oes,

VIII

Yet never catch her and me together,
30   As she left the attic, there,
By the rim of the bottle labelled 'Ether,'
   And stole from stair to stair,

IX

And stood by the rose-wreathed gate. Alas,
   We loved, sir – used to meet:
How sad and bad and mad it was –
   But then, how it was sweet!

May and Death

I

I wish that when you died last May,
    Charles, there had died along with you
Three parts of spring's delightful things;
    Ay, and, for me, the fourth part too.

II

A foolish thought, and worse, perhaps!
    There must be many a pair of friends
Who, arm in arm, deserve the warm
    Moon-births and the long evening-ends.

III

So, for their sake, be May still May!
10   Let their new time, as mine of old,
Do all it did for me: I bid
    Sweet sights and sounds throng manifold.

IV

Only, one little sight, one plant,
    Woods have in May, that starts up green
Save a sole streak which, so to speak,
    Is spring's blood, spilt its leaves between, –
V
That, they might spare; a certain wood
    Might miss the plant; their loss were small:
But I, – whene'er the leaf grows there,
20   Its drop comes from my heart, that's all.

Deaf and Dumb

A Group by Woolner

Only the prism's obstruction shows aright
The secret of a sunbeam, breaks its light
Into the jewelled bow from blankest white,
    So may a glory from defect arise:

Only by Deafness may the vexed Love wreak
Its insuppressive sense on brow and cheek,
Only by Dumbness adequately speak
  As favoured mouth could never, through the eyes.

Prospice

Fear death ? – to feel the fog in my throat,
  The mist in my face,
When the snows begin, and the blasts denote
  I am nearing the place,
The power of the night, the press of the storm,
  The post of the foe;
Where he stands, the Arch Fear in a visible form,
  Yet the strong man must go:
For the journey is done and the summit attained,
10 And the barriers fall,
Though a battle's to fight ere the guerdon be gained,
  The reward of it all.
I was ever a fighter, so – one fight more,
  The best and the last!
I would hate that death bandaged my eyes, and forbore,
  And bade me creep past.
No! let me taste the whole of it, fare like my peers
  The heroes of old,
Bear the brunt, in a minute pay glad life's arrears
20 Of pain, darkness and cold.
For sudden the worst turns the best to the brave,
  The black minute's at end,
And the elements' rage, the fiend-voices that rave,
  Shall dwindle, shall blend,
Shall change, shall become first a peace out of pain,
  Then a light, then thy breast,
O thou soul of my soul! I shall clasp thee again,
  And with God be the rest!

Eurydice to Orpheus

A Picture by Leighton

> But give them me, the mouth, the eyes, the brow!
> Let them once more absorb me! One look now
>   Will lap me round for ever, not to pass
> Out of its light, though darkness lie beyond:
> Hold me but safe again within the bond
>   Of one immortal look! All woe that was,
> Forgotten, and all terror that may be,
> Defied, – no past is mine, no future: look at me!

Youth and Art

I

> It once might have been, once only:
>   We lodged in a street together,
> You, a sparrow on the housetop lonely,
>   I, a lone she-bird of his feather.

II

> Your trade was with sticks and clay,
>   You thumbed, thrust, patted and polished,
> Then laughed 'They will see some day
>   Smith made, and Gibson demolished.'

III

> My business was song, song, song;
> I chirped, cheeped, trilled and twittered,
> 'Kate Brown's on the boards ere long,
>   And Grisi's existence embittered!'

IV

> I earned no more by a warble
>   Than you by a sketch in plaster;
> You wanted a piece of marble,
>   I needed a music-master.

V

We studied hard in our styles,
    Chipped each at a crust like Hindoos,
    For air looked out on the tiles,
20   For fun watched each other's windows.

VI

You lounged, like a boy of the South,
    Cap and blouse – nay, a bit of beard too;
Or you got it, rubbing your mouth
    With fingers the clay adhered to.

VII

And I – soon managed to find
    Weak points in the flower-fence facing,
Was forced to put up a blind
    And be safe in my corset-lacing.

VIII

No harm! It was not my fault
30   If you never turned your eye's tail up
As I shook upon E *in alt*,
    Or ran the chromatic scale up:

IX

For spring bade the sparrows pair,
    And the boys and girls gave guesses,
And stalls in our street looked rare
    With bulrush and watercresses.

X

Why did not you pinch a flower
    In a pellet of clay and fling it?
Why did not I put a power
40   Of thanks in a look, or sing it?

XI

I did look, sharp as a lynx,
    (And yet the memory rankles)
When models arrived, some minx
    Tripped up-stairs, she and her ankles.

XII

But I think I gave you as good!
　'That foreign fellow, – who can know
How she pays, in a playful mood,
　For his tuning her that piano?'

XIII

Could you say so, and never say
50　'Suppose we join hands and fortunes,
And I fetch her from over the way,
　Her, piano, and long tunes and short tunes?'

XIV

No, no: you would not be rash,
　Nor I rasher and something over:
You've to settle yet Gibson's hash,
　And Grisi yet lives in clover.

XV

But you meet the Prince at the Board,
　I'm queen myself at *bals-paré*,
I've married a rich old lord,
60　And you're dubbed knight and an R.A.

XVI

Each life unfulfilled, you see;
　It hangs still, patchy and scrappy:
We have not sighed deep, laughed free,
　Starved, feasted, despaired, – been happy.

XVII

And nobody calls you a dunce,
　And people suppose me clever:
This could but have happened once,
　And we missed it, lost it for ever.

A Face

If one could have that little head of hers
    Painted upon a background of pale gold,
Such as the Tuscan's early art prefers!
    No shade encroaching on the matchless mould
Of those two lips, which should be opening soft
    In the pure profile; not as when she laughs,
For that spoils all: but rather as if aloft
    Yon hyacinth, she loves so, leaned its staff's
Burthen of honey-coloured buds to kiss
10 And capture 'twixt the lips apart for this.
Then her lithe neck, three fingers might surround,
How it should waver on the pale gold ground
Up to the fruit-shaped, perfect chin it lifts!

I know, Correggio loves to mass, in rifts
Of heaven, his angel faces, orb on orb
Breaking its outline, burning shades absorb:
But these are only massed there, I should think,
    Waiting to see some wonder momently
    Grow out, stand full, fade slow against the sky
20 (That's the pale ground you'd see this sweet face by),
    All heaven, meanwhile, condensed into one eye
Which fears to lose the wonder, should it wink.

A Likeness

Some people hang portraits up
In a room where they dine or sup:
    And the wife clinks tea-things under,
And her cousin, he stirs his cup,
    Asks, 'Who was the lady, I wonder?'
''Tis a daub John bought at a sale,'
    Quoth the wife, – looks black as thunder:
'What a shade beneath her nose!
Snuff-taking, I suppose, –'
10 Adds the cousin, while John's corns ail.

Or else, there's no wife in the case,
But the portrait's queen of the place,
Alone 'mid the other spoils
Of youth, – masks, gloves and foils,
And pipe-sticks, rose, cherry-tree, jasmine,
    And the long whip, the tandem-lasher,
And the cast from a fist ('not, alas! mine,
    But my master's, the Tipton Slasher'),
And the cards where pistol-balls mark ace,
20 And a satin shoe used for cigar-case,
And the chamois-horns ('shot in the Chablais')
    And prints – Rarey drumming on Cruiser,
    And Sayers, our champion, the bruiser,
And the little edition of Rabelais:
Where a friend, with both hands in his pockets,
    May saunter up close to examine it,
    And remark a good deal of Jane Lamb in it,
'But the eyes are half out of their sockets;
That hair's not so bad, where the gloss is,
30 But they've made the girl's nose a proboscis:
Jane Lamb, that we danced with at Vichy!
What, is not she Jane? Then, who is she?'

All that I own is a print,
An etching, a mezzotint;
'Tis a study, a fancy, a fiction,
Yet a fact (take my conviction)
Because it has more than a hint
    Of a certain face, I never
Saw elsewhere touch or trace of
40 In women I've seen the face of:
    Just an etching, and, so far, clever.

I keep my prints, an imbroglio,
Fifty in one portfolio.
When somebody tries my claret,
We turn round chairs to the fire,
Chirp over days in a garret,
    Chuckle o'er increase of salary,
Taste the good fruits of our leisure,
Talk about pencil and lyre,
50   And the National Portrait Gallery:

Then I exhibit my treasure.
After we've turned over twenty,
　　And the debt of wonder my crony owes
　　Is paid to my Marc Antonios,
He stops me – '*Festina lentè!*
What's that sweet thing there, the etching?'
How my waistcoat-strings want stretching,
　　How my cheeks grow red as tomatoes,
How my heart leaps! But hearts, after leaps, ache.

60 'By the by, you must take, for a keepsake,
　　That other, you praised, of Volpato's.'
The fool! would he try a flight further and say –
He never saw, never before today,
What was able to take his breath away,
A face to lose youth for, to occupy age
With the dream of, meet death with, – why, I'll not engage
But that, half in a rapture and half in a rage,
I should toss him the thing's self – ''Tis only a duplicate,
A thing of no value! Take it, I supplicate!'

Mr Sludge, '*The Medium*'

Now, don't, sir! Don't expose me! Just this once!
This was the first and only time, I'll swear, –
Look at me, – see, I kneel, – the only time,
I swear, I ever cheated, – yes, by the soul
Of Her who hears – (your sainted mother, sir!)
All, except this last accident, was truth –
This little kind of slip! – and even this,
It was your own wine, sir, the good champagne,
(I took it for Catawba, you're so kind)
10 Which put the folly in my head!

　　　　　　　　　'Get up?'
You still inflict on me that terrible face?
You show no mercy? – Not for Her dear sake,
The sainted spirit's, whose soft breath even now

Blows on my cheek – (don't you feel something, sir?)
You'll tell?

        Go tell, then! Who the devil cares
What such a rowdy chooses to . . .
                            Aie – aie – aie!
Please, sir! your thumbs are through my windpipe, sir!
Ch – ch!

        Well, sir, I hope you've done it now!
Oh Lord! I little thought, sir, yesterday,
20 When your departed mother spoke those words
Of peace through me, and moved you, sir, so much,
You gave me – (very kind it was of you)
These shirt-studs – (better take them back again,
Please, sir) – yes, little did I think so soon
A trifle of trick, all through a glass too much
Of his own champagne, would change my best of friends
Into an angry gentleman!

                Though, 'twas wrong.
I don't contest the point; your anger's just:
Whatever put such folly in my head,
30 I know 'twas wicked of me. There's a thick
Dusk undeveloped spirit (I've observed)
Owes me a grudge – a negro's, I should say,
Or else an Irish emigrant's; yourself
Explained the case so well last Sunday, sir,
When we had summoned Franklin to clear up
A point about those shares i' the telegraph:
Ay, and he swore . . . or might it be Tom Paine? . . .
Thumping the table close by where I crouched,
He'd do me soon a mischief: that's come true!

40 Why, now your face clears! I was sure it would!
Then, this one time . . . don't take your hand away,
Through yours I surely kiss your mother's hand . . .
You'll promise to forgive me? – or, at least,
Tell nobody of this? Consider, sir!
What harm can mercy do? Would but the shade
Of the venerable dead-one just vouchsafe

A rap or tip! What bit of paper's here?
Suppose we take a pencil, let her write,
Make the least sign, she urges on her child
50 Forgiveness? There now! Eh? Oh! 'Twas your foot,
And not a natural creak, sir?

               Answer, then!
Once, twice, thrice . . . see, I'm waiting to say 'thrice!'
All to no use? No sort of hope for me?
It's all to post to Greeley's newspaper?

What? If I told you all about the tricks?
Upon my soul! – the whole truth, and naught else,
And how there's been some falsehood – for your part,
Will you engage to pay my passage out,
And hold your tongue until I'm safe on board?
60 England's the place, not Boston – no offence!
I see what makes you hesitate: don't fear!
I mean to change my trade and cheat no more,
Yes, this time really it's upon my soul!
Be my salvation! – under Heaven, of course.
I'll tell some queer things. Sixty Vs must do.
A trifle, though, to start with! We'll refer
The question to this table?

               How you're changed!
Then split the difference; thirty more, we'll say.
Ay, but you leave my presents! Else I'll swear
70 'Twas all through those: you wanted yours again,
So, picked a quarrel with me, to get them back!
Tread on a worm, it turns, sir! If I turn,
Your fault! 'Tis you'll have forced me! Who's obliged
To give up life yet try no self-defence?
At all events, I'll run the risk. Eh?

               Done!
May I sit, sir? This dear old table, now!
Please, sir, a parting egg-nog and cigar!
I've been so happy with you! Nice stuffed chairs,
And sympathetic sideboards; what an end
80 To all the instructive evenings! (It's alight.)

Well, nothing lasts, as Bacon came and said.
Here goes, – but keep your temper, or I'll scream!

Fol-lol-the-rido-liddle-iddle-ol!
You see, sir, it's your own fault more than mine;
It's all your fault, you curious gentlefolk!
You're prigs, – excuse me, – like to look so spry,
So clever, while you cling by half a claw
To the perch whereon you puff yourselves at roost,
Such piece of self-conceit as serves for perch
90 Because you chose it, so it must be safe.
Oh, otherwise you're sharp enough! You spy
Who slips, who slides, who holds by help of wing,
Wanting real foothold, – who can't keep upright
On the other perch, your neighbour chose, not you:
There's no outwitting you respecting him!
For instance, men love money – that, you know
And what men do to gain it: well, suppose
A poor lad, say a help's son in your house,
Listening at keyholes, hears the company
100 Talk grand of dollars, V-notes, and so forth,
How hard they are to get, how good to hold,
How much they buy, – if, suddenly, in pops he –
'*I've* got a V-note!' – what do you say to him?
What's your first word which follows your last kick?
'Where did you steal it, rascal?' That's because
He finds you, fain would fool you, off your perch,
Not on the special piece of nonsense, sir,
Elected your parade-ground: let him try
Lies to the end of the list, – 'He picked it up,
110 His cousin died and left it him by will,
The President flung it to him, riding by,
An actress trucked it for a curl of his hair,
He dreamed of luck and found his shoe enriched,
He dug up clay, and out of clay made gold' –
How would you treat such possibilities?
Would not you, prompt, investigate the case
With cow-hide? 'Lies, lies, lies,' you'd shout: and why?
Which of the stories might not prove mere truth?
This last, perhaps, that clay was turned to coin!
120 Let's see, now, give him me to speak for him!
How many of your rare philosophers,

In plaguy books I've had to dip into,
Believed gold could be made thus, saw it made
And made it? Oh, with such philosophers
You're on your best behaviour! While the lad –
With him, in a trice, you settle likelihoods,
Nor doubt a moment how he got his prize:
In his case, you hear, judge and execute,
All in a breath: so would most men of sense.

130 But let the same lad hear you talk as grand
At the same keyhole, you and company,
Of signs and wonders, the invisible world;
How wisdom scouts our vulgar unbelief
More than our vulgarest credulity;
How good men have desired to see a ghost,
What Johnson used to say, what Wesley did,
Mother Goose thought, and fiddle-diddle-dee: –
If he break in with, 'Sir, *I* saw a ghost!'
Ah, the ways change! He finds you perched and prim;
140 It's a conceit of yours that ghosts may be:
There's no talk now of cow-hide. 'Tell it out!
Don't fear us! Take your time and recollect!
Sit down first: try a glass of wine, my boy!
And, David, (is not that your Christian name?)
Of all things, should this happen twice – it may –
Be sure, while fresh in mind, you let us know!'
Does the boy blunder, blurt out this, blab that,
Break down in the other, as beginners will?
All's candour, all's considerateness – 'No haste!
150 Pause and collect yourself! We understand!
That's the bad memory, or the natural shock,
Or the unexplained *phenomena*!'

                    Egad,
The boy takes heart of grace; finds, never fear,
The readiest way to ope your own heart wide,
Show – what I call your peacock-perch, pet post
To strut, and spread the tail, and squawk upon!
'Just as you thought, much as you might expect!
There be more things in heaven and earth, Horatio,' . . .
And so on. Shall not David take the hint,
160 Grow bolder, stroke you down at quickened rate?

If he ruffle a feather, it's 'Gently, patiently!
Manifestations are so weak at first!
Doubting, moreover, kills them, cuts all short,
Cures with a vengeance!'

               There, sir, that's your style!
You and your boy – such pains bestowed on him,
Or any headpiece of the average worth,
To teach, say, Greek, would perfect him apace,
Make him a Person ('Porson?' thank you, sir!)
Much more, proficient in the art of lies.

170   You never leave the lesson! Fire alight,
Catch you permitting it to die! You've friends;
There's no withholding knowledge, – least from those
Apt to look elsewhere for their souls' supply:
Why should not you parade your lawful prize?
Who finds a picture, digs a medal up,
Hits on a first edition, – he henceforth
Gives it his name, grows notable: how much more,
Who ferrets out a 'medium'? 'David's yours,
You highly-favoured man? Then, pity souls

180   Less privileged! Allow us share your luck!'
So, David holds the circle, rules the roast,
Narrates the vision, peeps in the glass ball,
Sets-to the spirit-writing, hears the raps,
As the case may be.

              Now mark! To be precise –
Though I say, 'lies' all these, at this first stage,
'Tis just for science' sake: I call such grubs
By the name of what they'll turn to, dragonflies.
Strictly, it's what good people style untruth;
But yet, so far, not quite the full-grown thing:

190   It's fancying, fable-making, nonsense-work –
What never meant to be so very bad –
The knack of story-telling, brightening up
Each dull old bit of fact that drops its shine.
One does see somewhat when one shuts one's eyes,
If only spots and streaks; tables do tip
In the oddest way of themselves: and pens, good Lord,
Who knows if you drive them or they drive you?
'Tis but a foot in the water and out again;

Not that duck-under which decides your dive.
200 Note this, for it's important: listen why.

I'll prove, you push on David till he dives
And ends the shivering. Here's your circle, now:
Two-thirds of them, with heads like you their host,
Turn up their eyes, and cry, as you expect,
'Lord, who'd have thought it!' But there's always one
Looks wise, compassionately smiles, submits
'Of your veracity no kind of doubt,
But – do you feel so certain of that boy's?
Really, I wonder! I confess myself
210 More chary of my faith!' That's galling, sir!
What, he the investigator, he the sage,
When all's done? Then, you just have shut your eyes,
Opened your mouth, and gulped down David whole,
You! Terrible were such catastrophe!
So, evidence is redoubled, doubled again,
And doubled besides; once more, 'He heard, we heard,
You and they heard, your mother and your wife,
Your children and the stranger in your gates:
Did they or did they not?' So much for him,
220 The black sheep, guest without the wedding-garb,
The doubting Thomas! Now's your turn to crow:
'He's kind to think you such a fool: Sludge cheats?
Leave you alone to take precautions!'
                              Straight
The rest join chorus. Thomas stands abashed,
Sips silent some such beverage as this,
Considers if it be harder, shutting eyes
And gulping David in good fellowship,
Than going elsewhere, getting, in exchange,
With no egg-nog to lubricate the food,
230 Some just as tough a morsel. Over the way,
Holds Captain Sparks his court: is it better there?
Have not you hunting-stories, scalping-scenes,
And Mexican War exploits to swallow plump
If you'd be free o' the stove-side, rocking-chair,
And trio of affable daughters?
                              Doubt succumbs!
Victory! All your circle's yours again!
Out of the clubbing of submissive wits,

David's performance rounds, each chink gets patched,
Every protrusion of a point's filed fine,
240 All's fit to set a-rolling round the world,
And then return to David finally,
Lies seven-feet thick about his first half-inch.
Here's a choice birth o' the supernatural,
Poor David's pledged to! You've employed no tool
That laws exclaim at, save the devil's own,
Yet screwed him into henceforth gulling you
To the top o' your bent, – all out of one half-lie!

You hold, if there's one half or a hundredth part
Of a lie, that's his fault, – his be the penalty!
250 I dare say! You'd prove firmer in his place?
You'd find the courage, – that first flurry over,
That mild bit of romancing-work at end, –
To interpose with 'It gets serious, this;
Must stop here. Sir, I saw no ghost at all.
Inform your friends I made ... well, fools of them,
And found you ready-made. I've lived in clover
These three weeks: take it out in kicks of me!'
I doubt it. Ask your conscience! Let me know,
Twelve months hence, with how few embellishments
260 You've told almighty Boston of this passage
Of arms between us, your first taste o' the foil
From Sludge who could not fence, sir! Sludge, your boy!
I lied, sir, – there! I got up from my gorge
On offal in the gutter, and preferred
Your canvas-backs: I took their carver's size,
Measured his modicum of intelligence,
Tickled him on the cockles of his heart
With a raven feather, and next week found myself
Sweet and clean, dining daintily, dizened smart,
270 Set on a stool buttressed by ladies' knees,
Every soft smiler calling me her pet,
Encouraging my story to uncoil
And creep out from its hole, inch after inch,
'How last night, I no sooner snug in bed,
Tucked up, just as they left me, – than came raps!
While a light whisked' ... 'Shaped somewhat like a star?'
'Well, like some sort of stars, ma'am.' – 'So we thought!
And any voice? Not yet? Try hard, next time,

If you can't hear a voice; we think you may:
280 At least, the Pennsylvanian "mediums" did.'
Oh, next time comes the voice! 'Just as we hoped!'
Are not the hopers proud now, pleased, profuse
O' the natural acknowledgement?

                        Of course!
So, off we push, illy-oh-yo, trim the boat,
On we sweep with a cataract ahead,
We're midway to the Horseshoe: stop, who can,
The dance of bubbles gay about our prow!
Experiences become worth waiting for,
Spirits now speak up, tell their inmost mind,
290 And compliment the 'medium' properly,
Concern themselves about his Sunday coat,
See rings on his hand with pleasure. Ask yourself
How you'd receive a course of treats like these!
Why, take the quietest hack and stall him up,
Cram him with corn a month, then out with him
Among his mates on a bright April morn,
With the turf to tread; see if you find or no
A caper in him, if he bucks or bolts!
Much more a youth whose fancies sprout as rank
300 As toadstool-clump from melon-bed. 'Tis soon,
'Sirrah, you spirit, come, go, fetch and carry,
Read, write, rap, rub-a-dub, and hang yourself!'
I'm spared all further trouble; all's arranged;
Your circle does my business; I may rave
Like an epileptic dervish in the books,
Foam, fling myself flat, rend my clothes to shreds;
No matter: lovers, friends and countrymen
Will lay down spiritual laws, read wrong things right
By the rule o' reverse. If Francis Verulam
310 Styles himself Bacon, spells the name beside
With a y and a k, says he drew breath in York,
Gave up the ghost in Wales when Cromwell reigned,
(As, sir, we somewhat fear he was apt to say,
Before I found the useful book that knows)
Why, what harm's done? The circle smiles apace,
'It was not Bacon, after all, you see!
We understand; the trick's but natural:
Such spirits' individuality

Is hard to put in evidence: they incline
320 To gibe and jeer, these undeveloped sorts.
You see, their world's much like a gaol broke loose,
While this of ours remains shut, bolted, barred,
With a single window to it. Sludge, our friend,
Serves as this window, whether thin or thick,
Or stained or stainless; he's the medium-pane
Through which, to see us and be seen, they peep:
They crowd each other, hustle for a chance,
Tread on their neighbour's kibes, play tricks enough!
Does Bacon, tired of waiting, swerve aside?
330 Up in his place jumps Barnum – "I'm your man,
I'll answer you for Bacon!" Try once more!'

Or else it's – 'What's a "medium"? He's a means,
Good, bad, indifferent, still the only means
Spirits can speak by; he may misconceive,
Stutter and stammer, – he's their Sludge and drudge,
Take him or leave him; they must hold their peace,
Or else, put up with having knowledge strained
To half-expression through his ignorance.
Suppose, the spirit Beethoven wants to shed
340 New music he's brimful of; why, he turns
The handle of this organ, grinds with Sludge,
And what he poured in at the mouth o' the mill
As a Thirty-third Sonata, (fancy now!)
Comes from the hopper as bran-new Sludge, naught else,
The Shakers' Hymn in G, with a natural F,
Or the "Stars and Stripes" set to consecutive fourths.'

Sir, where's the scrape you did not help me through,
You that are wise? And for the fools, the folk
Who came to see, – the guests, (observe that word!)
350 Pray do you find guests criticize your wine,
Your furniture, your grammar, or your nose?
Then, why your 'medium'? What's the difference?
Prove your madeira red-ink and gamboge, –
Your Sludge, a cheat – then, somebody's a goose
For vaunting both as genuine. 'Guests!' Don't fear!
They'll make a wry face, nor too much of that,
And leave you in your glory.

'No, sometimes
They doubt and say as much!' Ay, doubt they do!
And what's the consequence? 'Of course they doubt' –
360 (You triumph) 'that explains the hitch at once!
Doubt posed our "medium," puddled his pure mind;
He gave them back their rubbish: pitch chaff in,
Could flour come out o' the honest mill?' So, prompt
Applaud the faithful: cases flock in point,
'How, when a mocker willed a "medium" once
Should name a spirit James whose name was George,
"James" cried the "medium," – 'twas the test of truth!'
In short, a hit proves much, a miss proves more.

Does this convince? The better: does it fail?
370 Time for the double-shotted broadside, then –
The grand means, last resource. Look black and big!
'You style us idiots, therefore – why stop short?
Accomplices in rascality: this we hear
In our own house, from our invited guest
Found brave enough to outrage a poor boy
Exposed by our good faith! Have you been heard?
Now, then, hear us; one man's not quite worth twelve.
You see a cheat? Here's some twelve see an ass:
Excuse me if I calculate: good day!'
380 Out slinks the sceptic, all the laughs explode,
Sludge waves his hat in triumph!

                                        Or – he don't.
There's something in real truth (explain who can!)
One casts a wistful eye at, like the horse
Who mopes beneath stuffed hay-racks and won't munch
Because he spies a corn-bag: hang that truth,
It spoils all dainties proffered in its place!
I've felt at times when, cockered, cosseted
And coddled by the aforesaid company,
Bidden enjoy their bullying, – never fear,
390 But o'er their shoulders spit at the flying man, –
I've felt a child; only, a fractious child
That, dandled soft by nurse, aunt, grandmother,
Who keep him from the kennel, sun and wind,
Good fun and wholesome mud, – enjoined be sweet,
And comely and superior, – eyes askance

The ragged sons o' the gutter at their game,
Fain would be down with them i' the thick o' the filth,
Making dirt-pies, laughing free, speaking plain,
And calling granny the grey old cat she is.

400 I've felt a spite, I say, at you, at them,
Huggings and humbug – gnashed my teeth to mark
A decent dog pass! It's too bad, I say,
Ruining a soul so!

                 But what's 'so,' what's fixed,
Where may one stop? Nowhere! The cheating's nursed
Out of the lying, softly and surely spun
To just your length, sir! I'd stop soon enough:
But you're for progress. 'All old, nothing new?
Only the usual talking through the mouth,
Or writing by the hand? I own, I thought

410 This would develop, grow demonstrable,
Make doubt absurd, give figures we might see,
Flowers we might touch. There's no one doubts you, Sludge!
You dream the dreams, you see the spiritual sights,
The speeches come in your head, beyond dispute.
Still, for the sceptics' sake, to stop all mouths,
We want some outward manifestation! – well,
The Pennsylvanians gained such; why not Sludge?
He may improve with time!'

                 Ay, that he may!
He sees his lot: there's no avoiding fate.

420 'Tis a trifle at first. 'Eh, David? Did you hear?
You jogged the table, your foot caused the squeak,
This time you're . . . joking, are you not, my boy?'
'N-n-no!' – and I'm done for, bought and sold henceforth.
The old good easy jog-trot way, the . . . eh?
The . . . not so very false, as falsehood goes,
The spinning out and drawing fine, you know, –
Really mere novel-writing of a sort,
Acting, or improvising, make-believe,
Surely not downright cheatery, – any how,

430 'Tis done with and my lot cast; Cheat's my name:
The fatal dash of brandy in your tea
Has settled what you'll have the souchong's smack:
The caddy gives way to the dram-bottle.

Then, it's so cruel easy! Oh, those tricks
That can't be tricks, those feats by sleight of hand,
Clearly no common conjurer's! – no indeed!
A conjurer? Choose me any craft i' the world
A man puts hand to; and with six months' pains,
I'll play you twenty tricks miraculous
440 To people untaught the trade: have you seen glass blown,
Pipes pierced? Why, just this biscuit that I chip,
Did you ever watch a baker toss one flat
To the oven? Try and do it! Take my word,
Practise but half as much, while limbs are lithe,
To turn, shove, tilt a table, crack your joints,
Manage your feet, dispose your hands aright,
Work wires that twitch the curtains, play the glove
At end o' your slipper, – then put out the lights
And . . . there, there, all you want you'll get, I hope!
450 I found it slip, easy as an old shoe.

Now, lights on table again! I've done my part,
You take my place while I give thanks and rest.
'Well, Judge Humgruffin, what's your verdict, sir?
You, hardest head in the United States, –
Did you detect a cheat here? Wait! Let's see!
Just an experiment first, for candour's sake!
I'll try and cheat you, Judge! The table tilts:
Is it I that move it? Write! I'll press your hand:
Cry when I push, or guide your pencil, Judge!'
460 Sludge still triumphant! 'That a rap, indeed?
That, the real writing? Very like a whale!
Then, if, sir you – a most distinguished man,
And, were the Judge not here, I'd say, . . . no matter!
Well, sir, if you fail, you can't take us in, –
There's little fear that Sludge will!'

                      Won't he, ma'am?
But what if our distinguished host, like Sludge,
Bade God bear witness that he played no trick,
While you believed that what produced the raps
Was just a certain child who died, you know,
470 And whose last breath you thought your lips had felt?
Eh? That's a capital point, ma'am: Sludge begins
At your entreaty with your dearest dead,

The little voice set lisping once again,
The tiny hand made feel for yours once more,
The poor lost image brought back, plain as dreams,
Which image, if a word had chanced recall,
The customary cloud would cross your eyes,
Your heart return the old tick, pay its pang!
A right mood for investigation, this!

480 One's at one's ease with Saul and Jonathan,
Pompey and Caesar: but one's own lost child . . .
I wonder, when you heard the first clod drop
From the spadeful at the grave-side, felt you free
To investigate who twitched your funeral scarf
Or brushed your flounces? Then, it came of course
You should be stunned and stupid; then, (how else?)
Your breath stopped with your blood, your brain struck work.
But now, such causes fail of such effects,
All's changed, – the little voice begins afresh,
490 Yet you, calm, consequent, can test and try
And touch the truth. 'Tests? Didn't the creature tell
Its nurse's name, and say it lived six years,
And rode a rocking-horse? Enough of tests!
Sludge never could learn that!'

                      He could not, eh?
You compliment him. 'Could not?' Speak for yourself!
I'd like to know the man I ever saw
Once, – never mind where, how, why, when, – once saw,
Of whom I do not keep some matter in mind
He'd swear I 'could not' know, sagacious soul!
500 What? Do you live in this world's blow of blacks,
Palaver, gossipry, a single hour
Nor find one smut has settled on your nose,
Of a smut's worth, no more, no less? – one fact
Out of the drift of facts, whereby you learn
What someone was, somewhere, somewhen, somewhy?
You don't tell folk – 'See what has stuck to me!
Judge Humgruffin, our most distinguished man,
Your uncle was a tailor, and your wife
Thought to have married Miggs, missed him, hit you!' –
510 Do you, sir, though you see him twice a-week?
'No,' you reply, 'what use retailing it?
Why should I?' But, you see, one day you *should*,

Because one day there's much use, – when this fact
Brings you the Judge upon both gouty knees
Before the supernatural; proves that Sludge
Knows, as you say, a thing he 'could not' know:
Will not Sludge thenceforth keep an outstretched face
The way the wind drives?

       'Could not!' Look you now,
I'll tell you a story! There's a whiskered chap,
520 A foreigner, that teaches music here
And gets his bread, – knowing no better way:
He says, the fellow who informed of him
And made him fly his country and fall West
Was a hunchback cobbler, sat, stitched soles and sang,
In some outlandish place, the city Rome,
In a cellar by their Broadway, all day long;
Never asked questions, stopped to listen or look,
Nor lifted nose from lapstone; let the world
Roll round his three-legged stool, and news run in
530 The ears he hardly seemed to keep pricked up.
Well, that man went on Sundays, touched his pay,
And took his praise from government, you see;
For something like two dollars every week,
He'd engage tell you some one little thing
Of some one man, which led to many more,
(Because one truth leads right to the world's end)
And make you that man's master – when he dined
And on what dish, where walked to keep his health
And to what street. His trade was, throwing thus
540 His sense out, like an ant-eater's long tongue,
Soft, innocent, warm, moist, impassible,
And when 'twas crusted o'er with creatures – slick,
Their juice enriched his palate. 'Could not Sludge!'

I'll go yet a step further, and maintain,
Once the imposture plunged its proper depth
I' the rotten of your natures, all of you, –
(If one's not mad nor drunk, and hardly then)
It's impossible to cheat – that's, be found out!
Go tell your brotherhood this first slip of mine,
550 All today's tale, how you detected Sludge,
Behaved unpleasantly, till he was fain confess,

And so has come to grief! You'll find, I think,
Why Sludge still snaps his fingers in your face.
There now, you've told them! What's their prompt reply?
'Sir, did that youth confess he had cheated me,
I'd disbelieve him. He may cheat at times;
That's in the "medium"-nature, thus they're made,
Vain and vindictive, cowards, prone to scratch.
And so all cats are; still, a cat's the beast
560   You coax the strange electric sparks from out,
By rubbing back its fur; not so a dog,
Nor lion, nor lamb: 'tis the cat's nature, sir!
Why not the dog's? Ask God, who made them beasts!
D' ye think the sound, the nicely-balanced man
(Like me' – aside) – 'like you yourself,' – (aloud)
'– He's stuff to make a "medium"? Bless your soul,
'Tis these hysteric, hybrid half-and-halfs,
Equivocal, worthless vermin yield the fire!
We take such as we find them, 'ware their tricks,
570   Wanting their service. Sir, Sludge took in you –
How, I can't say, not being there to watch:
He was tried, was tempted by your easiness, –
He did not take in me!'

                    Thank you for Sludge!
I'm to be grateful to such patrons, eh,
When what you hear's my best word? 'Tis a challenge;
'Snap at all strangers, half-tamed prairie-dog,
So you cower duly at your keeper's beck!
Cat, show what claws were made for, muffling them
Only to me! Cheat others if you can,
580   Me, if you dare!' And, my wise sir, I dared –
Did cheat you first, made you cheat others next,
And had the help o' your vaunted manliness
To bully the incredulous. You used me?
Have not I used you, taken full revenge,
Persuaded folk they knew not their own name,
And straight they'd own the error! Who was the fool
When, to an awe-struck wide-eyed open-mouthed
Circle of sages, Sludge would introduce
Milton composing baby-rhymes, and Locke
590   Reasoning in gibberish, Homer writing Greek
In noughts and crosses, Asaph setting psalms

To crotchet and quaver? I've made a spirit squeak
In sham voice for a minute, then outbroke
Bold in my own, defying the imbeciles –
Have copied some ghost's pothooks, half a page,
Then ended with my own scrawl undisguised.
'All right! The ghost was merely using Sludge,
Suiting itself from his imperfect stock!'
Don't talk of gratitude to me! For what?
600 For being treated as a showman's ape,
Encouraged to be wicked and make sport,
Fret or sulk, grin or whimper, any mood
So long as the ape be in it and no man –
Because a nut pays every mood alike.
Curse your superior, superintending sort,
Who, since you hate smoke, send up boys that climb
To cure your chimney, bid a 'medium' lie
To sweep you truth down! Curse your women too,
Your insolent wives and daughters, that fire up
610 Or faint away if a male hand squeeze theirs,
Yet, to encourage Sludge, may play with Sludge
As only a 'medium,' only the kind of thing
They must humour, fondle ... oh, to misconceive
Were too preposterous! But I've paid them out!
They've had their wish – called for the naked truth,
And in she tripped, sat down and bade them stare:
They had to blush a little and forgive!
'The fact is, children talk so; in next world
All our conventions are reversed, – perhaps
620 Made light of: something like old prints, my dear!
The Judge has one, he brought from Italy,
A metropolis in the background, – o'er a bridge,
A team of trotting roadsters, – cheerful groups
Of wayside travellers, peasants at their work,
And, full in front, quite unconcerned, why not?
Three nymphs conversing with a cavalier,
And never a rag among them: "fine," folk cry –
And heavenly manners seem not much unlike!
Let Sludge go on; we'll fancy it's in print!'

630 If such as came for wool, sir, went home shorn,
Where is the wrong I did them? 'Twas their choice;
They tried the adventure, ran the risk, tossed up

And lost, as some one's sure to do in games;
They fancied I was made to lose, – smoked glass
Useful to spy the sun through, spare their eyes:
And had I proved a red-hot iron plate
They thought to pierce, and, for their pains, grew blind,
Whose were the fault but theirs? While, as things go,
Their loss amounts to gain, the more's the shame!
640 They've had their peep into the spirit-world,
And all this world may know it! They've fed fat
Their self-conceit which else had starved: what chance
Save this, of cackling o'er a golden egg
And compassing distinction from the flock,
Friends of a feather? Well, they paid for it,
And not prodigiously; the price o' the play,
Not counting certain pleasant interludes,
Was scarce a vulgar play's worth. When you buy
The actor's talent, do you dare propose
650 For his soul beside? Whereas my soul you buy!
Sludge acts Macbeth, obliged to be Macbeth,
Or you'll not hear his first word! Just go through
That slight formality, swear himself's the Thane,
And thenceforth he may strut and fret his hour,
Spout, spawl, or spin his target, no one cares!
Why hadn't I leave to play tricks, Sludge as Sludge?

Enough of it all! I've wiped out scores with you –
Vented your fustian, let myself be streaked
Like tom-fool with your ochre and carmine,
660 Worn patchwork your respectable fingers sewed
To metamorphose somebody, – yes, I've earned
My wages, swallowed down my bread of shame,
And shake the crumbs off – where but in your face?

As for religion – why, I served it, sir!
I'll stick to that! With my *phenomena*
I laid the atheist sprawling on his back,
Propped up Saint Paul, or, at least, Swedenborg!
In fact, it's just the proper way to balk
These troublesome fellows – liars, one and all,
670 Are not these sceptics? Well, to baffle them,
No use in being squeamish: lie yourself!
Erect your buttress just as wide o' the line,

Your side, as they build up the wall on theirs;
Where both meet, midway in a point, is truth
High overhead: so, take your room, pile bricks,
Lie! Oh, there's titillation in all shame!
What snow may lose in white, snow gains in rose!
Miss Stokes turns – Rahab, – nor a bad exchange!
Glory be on her, for the good she wrought,
680 Breeding belief anew 'neath ribs of death,
Browbeating now the unabashed before,
Ridding us of their whole life's gathered straws
By a live coal from the altar! Why, of old,
Great men spent years and years in writing books
To prove we've souls, and hardly proved it then:
Miss Stokes with her live coal, for you and me!
Surely, to this good issue, all was fair –
Not only fondling Sludge, but, even suppose
He let escape some spice of knavery, – well,
690 In wisely being blind to it! Don't you praise
Nelson for setting spy-glass to blind eye
And saying . . . what was it – that he could not see
The signal he was bothered with? Ay, indeed!

I'll go beyond: there's a real love of a lie,
Liars find ready-made for lies they make,
As hand for glove, or tongue for sugar-plum.
At best, 'tis never pure and full belief;
Those furthest in the quagmire, – don't suppose
They strayed there with no warning, got no chance
700 Of a filth-speck in their face, which they clenched teeth,
Bent brow against! Be sure they had their doubts,
And fears, and fairest challenges to try
The floor o' the seeming solid sand! But no!
Their faith was pledged, acquaintance too apprised,
All but the last step ventured, kerchiefs waved,
And Sludge called 'pet': 'twas easier marching on
To the promised land, join those who, Thursday next,
Meant to meet Shakespeare; better follow Sludge –
Prudent, oh sure! – on the alert, how else? –
710 But making for the mid-bog, all the same!
To hear your outcries, one would think I caught
Miss Stokes by the scruff o' the neck, and pitched her flat,
Foolish-face-foremost! Hear these simpletons,

That's all I beg, before my work's begun,
Before I've touched them with my finger-tip!
Thus they await me (do but listen, now!
It's reasoning, this is, – I can't imitate
The baby voice, though) 'In so many tales
Must be some truth, truth though a pin-point big,
720 Yet, some: a single man's deceived, perhaps –
Hardly, a thousand: to suppose one cheat
Can gull all these, were more miraculous far
Than aught we should confess a miracle' –
And so on. Then the Judge sums up – (it's rare)
Bids you respect the authorities that leap
To the judgement-seat at once, – why don't you note
The limpid nature, the unblemished life,
The spotless honour, indisputable sense
Of the first upstart with his story? What –
730 Outrage a boy on whom you ne'er till now
Set eyes, because he finds raps trouble him?

Fools, these are: ay, and how of their opposites
Who never did, at bottom of their hearts,
Believe for a moment? – Men emasculate,
Blank of belief, who played, as eunuchs use,
With superstition safely, – cold of blood,
Who saw what made for them i' the mystery,
Took their occasion, and supported Sludge
– As proselytes? No, thank you, far too shrewd!
740 – But promisers of fair play, encouragers
O' the claimant; who in candour needs must hoist
Sludge up on Mars' Hill, get speech out of Sludge
To carry off, criticize, and cant about!
Didn't Athens treat Saint Paul so? – at any rate,
It's 'a new thing' philosophy fumbles at.

Then there's the other picker-out of pearl
From dung-heaps, – ay, your literary man,
Who draws on his kid gloves to deal with Sludge
Daintily and discreetly, – shakes a dust
750 O' the doctrine, flavours thence, he well knows how,
The narrative or the novel, – half-believes,
All for the book's sake, and the public's stare,
And the cash that's God's sole solid in this world!

Look at him! Try to be too bold, too gross
For the master! Not you! He's the man for muck;
Shovel it forth, full-splash, he'll smooth your brown
Into artistic richness, never fear!
Find him the crude stuff; when you recognize
Your lie again, you'll doff your hat to it,
760 Dressed out for company! 'For company,'
I say, since there's the relish of success:
Let all pay due respect, call the lie truth,
Save the soft silent smirking gentleman
Who ushered in the stranger: you must sigh
'How melancholy, he, the only one
Fails to perceive the bearing of the truth
Himself gave birth to!' – There's the triumph's smack!
That man would choose to see the whole world roll
I' the slime o' the slough, so he might touch the tip
770 Of his brush with what I call the best of browns –
Tint ghost-tales, spirit-stories, past the power
Of the outworn umber and bistre!

                                      Yet I think
There's a more hateful form of foolery –
The social sage's, Solomon of saloons
And philosophic diner-out, the fribble
Who wants a doctrine for a chopping-block
To try the edge of his faculty upon,
Prove how much common sense he'll hack and hew
I' the critical minute 'twixt the soup and fish!
780 These were my patrons: these, and the like of them
Who, rising in my soul now, sicken it, –
These I have injured! Gratitude to these?
The gratitude, forsooth, of a prostitute
To the greenhorn and the bully – friends of hers,
From the wag that wants the queer jokes for his club,
To the snuff-box-decorator, honest man,
Who just was at his wits' end where to find
So genial a Pasiphae! All and each
Pay, compliment, protect from the police:
790 And how she hates them for their pains, like me!
So much for my remorse at thanklessness
Toward a deserving public!

But, for God?
Ay, that's a question! Well, sir, since you press –
(How you do tease the whole thing out of me!
I don't mean you, you know, when I say 'them':
Hate you, indeed! But that Miss Stokes, that Judge!
Enough, enough – with sugar: thank you, sir!)
Now for it, then! Will you believe me, though?
You've heard what I confess; I don't unsay
800 A single word: I cheated when I could,
Rapped with my toe-joints, set sham hands at work,
Wrote down names weak in sympathetic ink,
Rubbed odic lights with ends of phosphor-match,
And all the rest; believe that: believe this,
By the same token, though it seem to set
The crooked straight again, unsay the said,
Stick up what I've knocked down; I can't help that.
It's truth! I somehow vomit truth today.
This trade of mine – I don't know, can't be sure
810 But there was something in it, tricks and all!
Really, I want to light up my own mind.
They were tricks, – true, but what I mean to add
Is also true. First, – don't it strike you, sir?
Go back to the beginning, – the first fact
We're taught is, there's a world beside this world,
With spirits, not mankind, for tenantry;
That much within that world once sojourned here,
That all upon this world will visit there,
And therefore that we, bodily here below,
820 Must have exactly such an interest
In learning what may be the ways o' the world
Above us, as the disembodied folk
Have (by all analogic likelihood)
In watching how things go in the old home
With us, their sons, successors, and what not.
Oh yes, with added powers probably,
Fit for the novel state, – old loves grown pure,
Old interests understood aright, – they watch!
Eyes to see, ears to hear, and hands to help,
830 Proportionate to advancement: they're ahead,
That's all – do what we do, but noblier done –
Use plate, whereas we eat our meals off delf,
(To use a figure).

Concede that, and I ask
Next what may be the mode of intercourse
Between us men here, and those once-men there?
First comes the Bible's speech; then, history
With the supernatural element, – you know –
All that we sucked in with our mothers' milk,
Grew up with, got inside of us at last,
840 Till it's found bone of bone and flesh of flesh.
See now, we start with the miraculous,
And know it used to be, at all events:
What's the first step we take, and can't but take,
In arguing from the known to the obscure?
Why this: 'What was before, may be today.
Since Samuel's ghost appeared to Saul, of course
My brother's spirit may appear to me.'
Go tell your teacher that! What's his reply?
What brings a shade of doubt for the first time
850 O'er his brow late so luminous with faith?
'Such things have been,' says he, 'and there's no doubt
Such things may be: but I advise mistrust
Of eyes, ears, stomach, and, more than all, your brain,
Unless it be of your great-grandmother,
Whenever they propose a ghost to you!'
The end is, there's a composition struck;
'Tis settled, we've some way of intercourse
Just as in Saul's time; only, different:
How, when and where, precisely, – find it out!
860 I want to know, then, what's so natural
As that a person born into this world
And seized on by such teaching, should begin
With firm expectancy and a frank look-out
For his own allotment, his especial share
I' the secret, – his particular ghost, in fine?
I mean, a person born to look that way,
Since natures differ: take the painter-sort,
One man lives fifty years in ignorance
Whether grass be green or red, – 'No kind of eye
870 For colour,' say you; while another picks
And puts away even pebbles, when a child,
Because of bluish spots and pinky veins –
'Give him forthwith a paint-box!' Just the same
Was I born ... 'medium,' you won't let me say, –

Well, seer of the supernatural
Everywhen, everyhow and everywhere, –
Will that do?

           I and all such boys of course
Started with the same stock of Bible-truth;
Only, – what in the rest you style their sense,
880 Instinct, blind reasoning but imperative,
This, betimes, taught them the old world had one law
And ours another: 'New world, new laws,' cried they:
'None but old laws, seen everywhere at work,'
Cried I, and by their help explained my life
The Jews' way, still a working way to me.
Ghosts made the noises, fairies waved the lights,
Or Santa Claus slid down on New Year's Eve
And stuffed with cakes the stocking at my bed,
Changed the worn shoes, rubbed clean the fingered slate
890 O' the sum that came to grief the day before.

This could not last long: soon enough I found
Who had worked wonders thus, and to what end:
But did I find all easy, like my mates?
Henceforth no supernatural any more?
Not a whit: what projects the billiard-balls?
'A cue,' you answer: 'Yes, a cue,' said I;
'But what hand, off the cushion, moved the cue?
What unseen agency, outside the world,
Prompted its puppets to do this and that,
900 Put cakes and shoes and slates into their mind,
These mothers and aunts, nay even schoolmasters?'

Thus high I sprang, and there have settled since.
Just so I reason, in sober earnest still,
About the greater godsends, what you call
The serious gains and losses of my life.
What do I know or care about your world
Which either is or seems to be? This snap
O' my fingers, sir! My care is for myself;
Myself am whole and sole reality
910 Inside a raree-show and a market-mob
Gathered about it: that's the use of things.
'Tis easy saying they serve vast purposes,

Advantage their grand selves: be it true or false,
Each thing may have two uses. What's a star?
A world, or a world's sun: doesn't it serve
As taper also, time-piece, weather-glass,
And almanac? Are stars not set for signs
When we should shear our sheep, sow corn, prune trees?
The Bible says so.

           Well, I add one use
920 To all the acknowledged uses, and declare
If I spy Charles's Wain at twelve tonight,
It warns me, 'Go, nor lose another day,
And have your hair cut, Sludge!' You laugh: and why?
Were such a sign too hard for God to give?'
No: but Sludge seems too little for such grace:
Thank you, sir! So you think, so does not Sludge!
When you and good men gape at Providence,
Go into history and bid us mark
Not merely powder-plots prevented, crowns
930 Kept on kings' heads by miracle enough,
But private mercies – oh, you've told me, sir,
Of such interpositions! How yourself
Once, missing on a memorable day
Your handkerchief – just setting out, you know, –
You must return to fetch it, lost the train,
And saved your precious self from what befell
The thirty-three whom Providence forgot.
You tell, and ask me what I think of this?
Well, sir, I think then, since you needs must know,
940 What matter had you and Boston city to boot
Sailed skyward, like burnt onion-peelings? Much
To you, no doubt: for me – undoubtedly
The cutting of my hair concerns me more,
Because, however sad the truth may seem,
Sludge is of all-importance to himself.
You set apart that day in every year
For special thanksgiving, were a heathen else:
Well, I who cannot boast the like escape,
Suppose I said 'I don't thank Providence
950 For my part, owing it no gratitude'?
'Nay, but you owe as much' – you'd tutor me,
'You, every man alive, for blessings gained

In every hour o' the day, could you but know!
I saw my crowning mercy: all have such,
Could they but see!' Well, sir, why don't they see?
'Because they won't look, – or perhaps, they can't.'
Then, sir, suppose I can, and will, and do
Look, microscopically as is right,
Into each hour with its infinitude
960 Of influences at work to profit Sludge?
For that's the case: I've sharpened up my sight
To spy a providence in the fire's going out,
The kettle's boiling, the dime's sticking fast
Despite the hole i' the pocket. Call such facts
Fancies, too petty a work for Providence,
And those same thanks which you exact from me
Prove too prodigious payment: thanks for what,
If nothing guards and guides us little men?

No, no, sir! You must put away your pride,
970 Resolve to let Sludge into partnership!
I live by signs and omens: looked at the roof
Where the pigeons settle – 'If the further bird,
The white, takes wing first, I'll confess when thrashed;
Not, if the blue does' – so I said to myself
Last week, lest you should take me by surprise:
Off flapped the white, – and I'm confessing, sir!
Perhaps 'tis Providence's whim and way
With only me, i' the world: how can you tell?
'Because unlikely!' Was it likelier, now,
980 That this our one out of all worlds beside,
The what-d'you-call-'em millions, should be just
Precisely chosen to make Adam for,
And the rest o' the tale? Yet the tale's true, you know:
Such undeserving clod was graced so once;
Why not graced likewise undeserving Sludge?

Are we merit-mongers, flaunt we filthy rags?
All you can bring against my privilege
Is, that another way was taken with you, –
Which I don't question. It's pure grace, my luck:
990 I'm broken to the way of nods and winks,
And need no formal summoning. You've a help;
Holloa his name or whistle, clap your hands,

Stamp with your foot or pull the bell: all's one,
He understands you want him, here he comes.
Just so, I come at the knocking: you, sir, wait
The tongue o' the bell, nor stir before you catch
Reason's clear tingle, nature's clapper brisk,
Or that traditional peal was wont to cheer
Your mother's face turned heavenward: short of these
1000 There's no authentic intimation, eh?
Well, when you hear, you'll answer them, start up
And stride into the presence, top of toe,
And there find Sludge beforehand, Sludge that sprang
At noise o' the knuckle on the partition-wall!

I think myself the more religious man.
Religion's all or nothing; it's no mere smile
O' contentment, sigh of aspiration, sir –
No quality o' the finelier-tempered clay
Like its whiteness or its lightness; rather, stuff
1010 O' the very stuff, life of life, and self of self.
I tell you, men won't notice; when they do,
They'll understand. I notice nothing else:
I'm eyes, ears, mouth of me, one gaze and gape,
Nothing eludes me, everything's a hint,
Handle and help. It's all absurd, and yet
There's something in it all, I know: how much?
No answer! What does that prove? Man's still man,
Still meant for a poor blundering piece of work
When all's done; but, if somewhat's done, like this,
1020 Or not done, is the case the same? Suppose
I blunder in my guess at the true sense
O' the knuckle-summons, nine times out of ten, –
What if the tenth guess happen to be right?
If the tenth shovel-load of powdered quartz
Yield me the nugget? I gather, crush, sift all,
Pass o'er the failure, pounce on the success.

To give you a notion, now – (let who wins, laugh!)
When first I see a man, what do I first?
Why, count the letters which make up his name,
1030 And as their number chances, even or odd,
Arrive at my conclusion, trim my course:
Hiram H. Horsefall is your honoured name,

And haven't I found a patron, sir, in you?
'Shall I cheat this stranger?' I take apple-pips,
Stick one in either canthus of my eye,
And if the left drops first – (your left, sir, stuck)
I'm warned, I let the trick alone this time.
You, sir, who smile, superior to such trash,
You judge of character by other rules:
1040 Don't your rules sometimes fail you? Pray, what rule
Have you judged Sludge by hitherto?

                                 Oh, be sure,
You, everybody blunders, just as I,
In simpler things than these by far! For see:
I knew two farmers, – one, a wiseacre
Who studied seasons, rummaged almanacs,
Quoted the dew-point, registered the frost,
And then declared, for outcome of his pains,
Next summer must be dampish: 'twas a drought.
His neighbour prophesied such drought would fall,
1050 Saved hay and corn, made cent. per cent. thereby,
And proved a sage indeed: how came his lore?
Because one brindled heifer, late in March,
Stiffened her tail of evenings, and somehow
He got into his head that drought was meant!

I don't expect all men can do as much:
Such kissing goes by favour. You must take
A certain turn of mind for this, – a twist
I' the flesh, as well. Be lazily alive,
Open-mouthed, like my friend the ant-eater,
1060 Letting all nature's loosely-guarded motes
Settle and, slick, be swallowed! Think yourself
The one i' the world, the one for whom the world
Was made, expect it tickling at your mouth!
Then will the swarm of busy buzzing flies,
Clouds of coincidence, break egg-shell, thrive,
Breed, multiply, and bring you food enough.

I can't pretend to mind your smiling, sir!
Oh, what you mean is this! Such intimate way,
Close converse, frank exchange of offices,
1070 Strict sympathy of the immeasurably great

With the infinitely small, betokened here
By a course of signs and omens, raps and sparks, –
How does it suit the dread traditional text
O' the 'Great and Terrible Name'? Shall the Heaven of
    Heavens
Stoop to such child's play?

                        Please, sir, go with me
A moment, and I'll try to answer you.
The '*Magnum et terribile*' (is that right?)
Well, folk began with this in the early day;
And all the acts they recognized in proof
1080 Were thunders, lightnings, earthquakes, whirlwinds, dealt
Indisputably on men whose death they caused.
There, and there only, folk saw Providence
At work, – and seeing it, 'twas right enough
All heads should tremble, hands wring hands amain,
And knees knock hard together at the breath
O' the Name's first letter; why, the Jews, I'm told,
Won't write it down, no, to this very hour,
Nor speak aloud: you know best if't be so.
Each ague-fit of fear at end, they crept
1090 (Because somehow people once born must live)
Out of the sound, sight, swing and sway o' the Name,
Into a corner, the dark rest of the world,
And safe space where as yet no fear had reached;
'Twas there they looked about them, breathed again,
And felt indeed at home, as we might say.
The current o' common things, the daily life,
This had their due contempt; no Name pursued
Man from the mountain-top where fires abide,
To his particular mouse-hole at its foot
1100 Where he ate, drank, digested, lived in short:
Such was man's vulgar business, far too small
To be worth thunder: 'small,' folk kept on, 'small,'
With much complacency in those great days!
A mote of sand, you know, a blade of grass –
What was so despicable as mere grass,
Except perhaps the life o' the worm or fly
Which fed there? These were 'small' and men were great.
Well, sir, the old way's altered somewhat since,
And the world wears another aspect now:

1110 Somebody turns our spyglass round, or else
Puts a new lens in it: grass, worm, fly grow big:
We find great things are made of little things,
And little things go lessening till at last
Comes God behind them. Talk of mountains now?
We talk of mould that heaps the mountain, mites
That throng the mould, and God that makes the mites.
The Name comes close behind a stomach-cyst,
The simplest of creations, just a sac
That's mouth, heart, legs and belly at once, yet lives
1120 And feels, and could do neither, we conclude,
If simplified still further one degree:
The small becomes the dreadful and immense!
Lightning, forsooth? No word more upon that!
A tin-foil bottle, a strip of greasy silk,
With a bit of wire and knob of brass, and there's
Your dollar's-worth of lightning! But the cyst –
The life of the least of the little things?

          No, no!
Preachers and teachers try another tack,
Come near the truth this time: they put aside
1130 Thunder and lightning: 'That's mistake,' they cry,
'Thunderbolts fall for neither fright nor sport,
But do appreciable good, like tides,
Changes o' the wind, and other natural facts –
"Good" meaning good to man, his body or soul.
Mediate, immediate, all things minister
To man, – that's settled: be our future text
"We are His children!"' So, they now harangue
About the intention, the contrivance, all
That keeps up an incessant play of love, –
See the Bridgewater book.

1140   Amen to it!
Well, sir, I put this question: I'm a child?
I lose no time, but take you at your word:
How shall I act a child's part properly?
Your sainted mother, sir, – used you to live
With such a thought as this a-worrying you?
'She has it in her power to throttle me,
Or stab or poison: she may turn me out.

Or lock me in, – nor stop at this today,
But cut me off tomorrow from the estate
1150 I look for' – (long may you enjoy it, sir!)
'In brief, she may unchild the child I am.'
You never had such crotchets? Nor have I!
Who, frank confessing childship from the first,
Cannot both fear and take my ease at once,
So, don't fear, – know what might be, well enough,
But know too, child-like, that it will not be,
At least in my case, mine, the son and heir
O' the kingdom, as yourself proclaim my style.

But do you fancy I stop short at this?
1160 Wonder if suit and service, son and heir
Needs must expect, I dare pretend to find?
If, looking for signs proper to such an one,
I straight perceive them irresistible?
Concede that homage is a son's plain right,
And, never mind the nods and raps and winks,
'Tis the pure obvious supernatural
Steps forward, does its duty: why, of course!
I have presentiments; my dreams come true:
I fancy a friend stands whistling all in white
1170 Blithe as a boblink, and he's dead I learn.
I take dislike to a dog my favourite long,
And sell him; he goes mad next week and snaps.
I guess that stranger will turn up today
I have not seen these three years; there's his knock.
I wager 'sixty peaches on that tree!' –
That I pick up a dollar in my walk,
That your wife's brother's cousin's name was George –
And win on all points. Oh, you wince at this?
You'd fain distinguish between gift and gift,
1180 Washington's oracle and Sludge's itch
O' the elbow when at whist he ought to trump?
With Sludge it's too absurd? *Fine, draw the line
Somewhere, but, sir, your somewhere is not mine!*

Bless us, I'm turning poet! It's time to end.
How you have drawn me out, sir! All I ask
Is – am I heir or not heir? If I'm he,
Then, sir, remember, that same personage

(To judge by what we read i' the newspaper)
Requires, beside one nobleman in gold
1190 To carry up and down his coronet,
Another servant, probably a duke,
To hold egg-nog in readiness: why want
Attendance, sir, when helps in his father's house
Abound, I'd like to know?

                 Enough of talk!
My fault is that I tell too plain a truth.
Why, which of those who say they disbelieve,
Your clever people, but has dreamed his dream,
Caught his coincidence, stumbled on his fact
He can't explain, (he'll tell you smilingly)
1200 Which he's too much of a philosopher
To count as supernatural, indeed,
So calls a puzzle and problem, proud of it, –
Bidding you still be on your guard, you know,
Because one fact don't make a system stand,
Nor prove this an occasional escape
Of spirit beneath the matter: that's the way!
Just so wild Indians picked up, piece by piece,
The fact in California, the fine gold
That underlay the gravel – hoarded these,
1210 But never made a system stand, nor dug!
So wise men hold out in each hollowed palm
A handful of experience, sparkling fact
They can't explain; and since their rest of life
Is all explainable, what proof in this?
Whereas I take the fact, the grain of gold,
And fling away the dirty rest of life,
And add this grain to the grain each fool has found
O' the million other such philosophers, –
Till I see gold, all gold and only gold,
1220 Truth questionless though unexplainable,
And the miraculous proved the commonplace!
The other fools believed in mud, no doubt –
Failed to know gold they saw: was that so strange?
Are all men born to play Bach's fiddle-fugues,
'Time' with the foil in carte, jump their own height,
Cut the mutton with the broadsword, skate a five,
Make the red hazard with the cue, clip nails

While swimming, in five minutes row a mile,
Pull themselves three feet up with the left arm,
1230   Do sums of fifty figures in their head,
And so on, by the scores of instances?
The Sludge with luck, who sees the spiritual facts
His fellows strive and fail to see, may rank
With these, and share the advantage.

                                      Ay, but share
The drawback! Think it over by yourself;
I have not heart, sir, and the fire's gone grey.
Defect somewhere compénsates for success,
Everyone knows that. Oh, we're equals, sir!
The big-legged fellow has a little arm
1240   And a less brain, though big legs win the race:
Do you suppose I 'scape the common lot?
Say, I was born with flesh so sensitive,
Soul so alert, that, practice helping both,
I guess what's going on outside the veil,
Just as a prisoned crane feels pairing-time
In the islands where his kind are, so must fall
To capering by himself some shiny night,
As if your back-yard were a plot of spice –
Thus am I 'ware o' the spirit-world: while you,
1250   Blind as a beetle that way, – for amends,
Why, you can double fist and floor me, sir!
Ride that hot hardmouthed horrid horse of yours,
Laugh while it lightens, play with the great dog,
Speak your mind though it vex some friend to hear,
Never brag, never bluster, never blush, –
In short, you've pluck, when I'm a coward – there!
I know it, I can't help it, – folly or no,
I'm paralysed, my hand's no more a hand,
Nor my head a head, in danger: you can smile
1260   And change the pipe in your cheek. Your gift's not mine.
Would you swap for mine? No! but you'd add my gift
To yours: I dare say! I too sigh at times,
Wish I were stouter, could tell truth nor flinch,
Kept cool when threatened, did not mind so much
Being dressed gaily, making strangers stare,
Eating nice things; when I'd amuse myself,
I shut my eyes and fancy in my brain

I'm – now the President, now Jenny Lind,
Now Emerson, now the Benicia Boy –
1270 With all the civilized world a-wondering
And worshipping. I know it's folly and worse;
I feel such tricks sap, honeycomb the soul,
But I can't cure myself: despond, despair,
And then, hey, presto, there's a turn o' the wheel,
Under comes uppermost, fate makes full amends;
Sludge knows and sees and hears a hundred things
You all are blind to, – I've my taste of truth,
Likewise my touch of falsehood, – vice no doubt,
But you've your vices also: I'm content.

1280 What, sir? You won't shake hands? 'Because I cheat!'
'You've found me out in cheating!' That's enough
To make an apostle swear! Why, when I cheat,
Mean to cheat, do cheat, and am caught in the act,
Are you, or, rather, am I sure o' the fact?
(There's verse again, but I'm inspired somehow.)
Well then I'm not sure! I may be, perhaps,
Free as a babe from cheating: how it began,
My gift, – no matter; what 'tis got to be
In the end now, that's the question; answer that!
1290 Had I seen, perhaps, what hand was holding mine,
Leading me whither, I had died of fright:
So, I was made believe I led myself.
If I should lay a six-inch plank from roof
To roof, you would not cross the street, one step,
Even at your mother's summons: but, being shrewd,
If I paste paper on each side the plank
And swear 'tis solid pavement, why, you'll cross
Humming a tune the while, in ignorance
Beacon Street stretches a hundred feet below:
1300 I walked thus, took the paper-cheat for stone.
Some impulse made me set a thing o' the move
Which, started once, ran really by itself;
Beer flows thus, suck the siphon; toss the kite,
It takes the wind and floats of its own force.
Don't let truth's lump rot stagnant for the lack
Of a timely helpful lie to leaven it!
Put a chalk-egg beneath the clucking hen,
She'll lay a real one, laudably deceived.

Daily for weeks to come. I've told my lie,
And seen truth follow, marvels none of mine;
All was not cheating, sir, I'm positive!
I don't know if I move your hand sometimes
When the spontaneous writing spreads so far,
If my knee lifts the table all that height,
Why the inkstand don't fall off the desk a-tilt,
Why the accordion plays a prettier waltz
Than I can pick out on the pianoforte,
Why I speak so much more than I intend,
Describe so many things I never saw.
I tell you, sir, in one sense, I believe
Nothing at all, – that everybody can,
Will, and does cheat: but in another sense
I'm ready to believe my very self –
That every cheat's inspired, and every lie
Quick with a germ of truth.

                                    You ask perhaps
Why I should condescend to trick at all
If I know a way without it? This is why!
There's a strange secret sweet self-sacrifice
In any desecration of one's soul
To a worthy end, – isn't it Herodotus
(I wish I could read Latin!) who describes
The single gift o' the land's virginity,
Demanded in those old Egyptian rites,
(I've but a hazy notion – help me, sir!)
For one purpose in the world, one day in a life,
One hour in a day – thereafter, purity,
And a veil thrown o'er the past for evermore!
Well, now, they understood a many things
Down by Nile city, or wherever it was!
I've always vowed, after the minute's lie,
And the end's gain, – truth should be mine henceforth.
This goes to the root o' the matter, sir, – this plain
Plump fact: accept it and unlock with it
The wards of many a puzzle!

                                    Or, finally,
Why should I set so fine a gloss on things?
What need I care? I cheat in self-defence,

And there's my answer to a world of cheats!
Cheat? To be sure, sir! What's the world worth else?
Who takes it as he finds, and thanks his stars?
1350 Don't it want trimming, turning, furbishing up
And polishing over? Your so-styled great men,
Do they accept one truth as truth is found,
Or try their skill at tinkering? What's your world?
Here are you born, who are, I'll say at once,
Of the luckiest kind, whether in head and heart,
Body and soul, or all that helps them both.
Well, now, look back: what faculty of yours
Came to its full, had ample justice done
By growing when rain fell, biding its time,
1360 Solidifying growth when earth was dead,
Spiring up, broadening wide, in seasons due?
Never! You shot up and frost nipped you off,
Settled to sleep when sunshine bade you sprout;
One faculty thwarted its fellow: at the end,
All you boast is 'I had proved a topping tree
In other climes' – yet this was the right clime
Had you foreknown the seasons. Young, you've force
Wasted like well-streams: old, – oh, then indeed,
Behold a labyrinth of hydraulic pipes
1370 Through which you'd play off wondrous waterwork;
Only, no water's left to feed their play.
Young, – you've a hope, an aim, a love: it's tossed
And crossed and lost: you struggle on, some spark
Shut in your heart against the puffs around,
Through cold and pain; these in due time subside,
Now then for age's triumph, the hoarded light
You mean to loose on the altered face of things, –
Up with it on the tripod! It's extinct.
Spend your life's remnant asking, which was best,
1380 Light smothered up that never peeped forth once,
Or the cold cresset with full leave to shine?
Well, accept this too, – seek the fruit of it
Not in enjoyment, proved a dream on earth,
But knowledge, useful for a second chance,
Another life, – you've lost this world – you've gained
Its knowledge for the next. What knowledge, sir,
Except that you know nothing? Nay, you doubt
Whether 'twere better have made you man or brute,

If aught be true, if good and evil clash.
1390 No foul, no fair, no inside, no outside,
There's your world!

     Give it me! I slap it brisk
With harlequin's pasteboard sceptre: what's it now?
Changed like a rock-flat, rough with rusty weed,
At first wash-over o' the returning wave!
All the dry dead impracticable stuff
Starts into life and light again; this world
Pervaded by the influx from the next.
I cheat, and what's the happy consequence?
You find full justice straightway dealt you out,
1400 Each want supplied, each ignorance set at ease,
Each folly fooled. No life-long labour now
As the price of worse than nothing! No mere film
Holding you chained in iron, as it seems,
Against the outstretch of your very arms
And legs i' the sunshine moralists forbid!
What would you have? Just speak and, there, you see!
You're supplemented, made a whole at last,
Bacon advises, Shakespeare writes you songs,
And Mary Queen of Scots embraces you.
1410 Thus it goes on, not quite like life perhaps,
But so near, that the very difference piques,
Shows that e'en better than this best will be –
This passing entertainment in a hut
Whose bare walls take your taste since, one stage more,
And you arrive at the palace: all half real,
And you, to suit it, less than real beside,
In a dream, lethargic kind of death in life,
That helps the interchange of natures, flesh
Transfused by souls, and such souls! Oh, 'tis choice!
1420 And if at whiles the bubble, blown too thin,
Seem nigh on bursting, – if you nearly see
The real world through the false, – what *do* you see?
Is the old so ruined? You find you're in a flock
O' the youthful, earnest, passionate – genius, beauty,
Rank and wealth also, if you care for these:
And all depose their natural rights, hail you,
(That's me, sir) as their mate and yoke-fellow,
Participate in Sludgehood – nay, grow mine,

I veritably possess them – banish doubt,
1430 And reticence and modesty alike!
Why, here's the Golden Age, old Paradise
Or new Eutopia! Here's true life indeed,
And the world well won now, mine for the first time!

And all this might be, may be, and with good help
Of a little lying shall be: so, Sludge lies!
Why, he's at worst your poet who sings how Greeks
That never were, in Troy which never was,
Did this or the other impossible great thing!
He's Lowell – it's a world (you smile applause),
1440 Of his own invention – wondrous Longfellow,
Surprising Hawthorne! Sludge does more than they,
And acts the books they write: the more his praise!

But why do I mount to poets? Take plain prose –
Dealers in common sense, set these at work,
What can they do without their helpful lies?
Each states the law and fact and face o' the thing
Just as he'd have them, finds what he thinks fit,
Is blind to what missuits him, just records
What makes his case out, quite ignores the rest.
1450 It's a History of the World, the Lizard Age,
The Early Indians, the Old Country War,
Jerome Napoleon, whatsoever you please,
All as the author wants it. Such a scribe
You pay and praise for putting life in stones,
Fire into fog, making the past your world.
There's plenty of 'How did you contrive to grasp
The thread which led you through this labyrinth?
How build such solid fabric out of air?
How on so slight foundation found this tale,
1460 Biography, narrative?' or, in other words,
'How many lies did it require to make
The portly truth you here present us with?'
'Oh,' quoth the penman, purring at your praise,
''Tis fancy all; no particle of fact:
I was poor and threadbare when I wrote that book
"Bliss in the Golden City." I, at Thebes?
We writers paint out of our heads, you see!'
'– Ah, the more wonderful the gift in you,

The more creativeness and godlike craft!'
1470 But I, do I present you with my piece,
      It's 'What, Sludge? When my sainted mother spoke
      The verses Lady Jane Grey last composed
      About the rosy bower in the seventh heaven
      Where she and Queen Elizabeth keep house, –
      You made the raps? 'Twas your invention that?
      Cur, slave and devil!' – eight fingers and two thumbs
      Stuck in my throat!

                          Well, if the marks seem gone
      'Tis because stiffish cocktail, taken in time,
      Is better for a bruise than arnica.

1480 There, sir! I bear no malice: 'tisn't in me.
      I know I acted wrongly: still, I've tried
      What I could say in my excuse, – to show
      The devil's not all devil . . . I don't pretend,
      He's angel, much less such a gentleman
      As you, sir! And I've lost you, lost myself,
      Lost all-l-l-l- . . .

                          No – are you in earnest, sir?
      O yours, sir, is an angel's part! I know
      What prejudice prompts, and what's the common course
      Men take to soothe their ruffled self-conceit:
1490 Only you rise superior to it all!
      No, sir, it don't hurt much; it's speaking long
      That makes me choke a little: the marks will go!
      What? Twenty V-notes more, and outfit too,
      And not a word to Greeley? One – one kiss
      O' the hand that saves me! You'll not let me speak,
      I well know, and I've lost the right, too true!
      But I must say, sir, if She hears (she does)
      Your sainted . . . Well, sir, – be it so! That's, I think,
      My bed-room candle. Good night! Bl-l-less you, sir!

                          ————————

1500 R-r-r, you brute-beast and blackguard! Cowardly scamp!
      I only wish I dared burn down the house
      And spoil your sniggering! Oh what, you're the man?

You're satisfied at last? You've found out Sludge?
We'll see that presently: my turn, sir, next!
I too can tell my story: brute, – do you hear? –
You throttled your sainted mother, that old hag,
In just such a fit of passion: no, it was . . .
To get this house of hers, and many a note
Like these . . . I'll pocket them, however . . . five,
1510 Ten, fifteen . . . ay, you gave her throat the twist,
Or else you poisoned her! Confound the cuss!
Where was my head? I ought to have prophesied
He'll die in a year and join her: that's the way.

I don't know where my head is: what had I done?
How did it all go? I said he poisoned her,
And hoped he'd have grace given him to repent,
Whereon he picked this quarrel, bullied me
And called me cheat: I thrashed him, – who could help?
He howled for mercy, prayed me on his knees
1520 To cut and run and save him from disgrace:
I do so, and once off, he slanders me.
An end of him! Begin elsewhere anew!
Boston's a hole, the herring-pond is wide,
V-notes are something, liberty still more.
Beside, is he the only fool in the world?

Apparent Failure

'We shall soon lose a celebrated building.' *Paris Newspaper*

I

No, for I'll save it! Seven years since,
    I passed through Paris, stopped a day
To see the baptism of your Prince;
    Saw, made my bow, and went my way:
Walking the heat and headache off,
    I took the Seine-side, you surmise,
Thought of the Congress, Gortschakoff,
    Cavour's appeal and Buol's replies,
So sauntered till – what met my eyes?

II

10 Only the Doric little Morgue!
    The dead-house where you show your drowned:
Petrarch's Vaucluse makes proud the Sorgue,
    Your Morgue has made the Seine renowned.
One pays one's debt in such a case;
    I plucked up heart and entered, – stalked,
Keeping a tolerable face
    Compared with some whose cheeks were chalked:
Let them! No Briton's to be balked!

III

First came the silent gazers; next,
20   A screen of glass, we're thankful for;
Last, the sight's self, the sermon's text;
    The three men who did most abhor
Their life in Paris yesterday,
    So killed themselves: and now, enthroned
Each on his copper couch, they lay
    Fronting me, waiting to be owned.
I thought, and think, their sin's atoned.

IV

Poor men, God made, and all for that!
    The reverence struck me; o'er each head
30 Religiously was hung its hat,
    Each coat dripped by the owner's bed,
Sacred from touch: each had his berth,
    His bounds, his proper place of rest,
Who last night tenanted on earth
    Some arch, where twelve such slept abreast, –
Unless the plain asphalt seemed best.

V

How did it happen, my poor boy?
    You wanted to be Buonaparte
And have the Tuileries for toy,
40   And could not, so it broke your heart?
You, old one by his side, I judge,
    Were, red as blood, a socialist,
A leveller! Does the Empire grudge
    You've gained what no Republic missed?
Be quiet, and unclench your fist!

VI

And this – why, he was red in vain,
  Or black, – poor fellow that is blue!
What fancy was it turned your brain?
  Oh, women were the prize for you!
50 Money gets women, cards and dice
  Get money, and ill-luck gets just
The copper couch and one clear nice
  Cool squirt of water o'er your bust,
The right thing to extinguish lust!

VII

It's wiser being good than bad;
  It's safer being meek than fierce:
It's fitter being sane than mad.
  My own hope is, a sun will pierce
The thickest cloud earth ever stretched;
60   That, after Last, returns the First,
Though a wide compass round be fetched;
  That what began best, can't end worst,
Nor what God blessed once, prove accurst.

Epilogue

First Speaker, as David

I

On the first of the Feast of Feasts,
  The Dedication Day,
When the Levites joined the Priests
  At the Altar in robed array,
Gave signal to sound and say, –

II

When the thousands, rear and van,
  Swarming with one accord
Became as a single man
  (Look, gesture, thought and word)
10 In praising and thanking the Lord, –

III

When the singers lift up their voice,
  And the trumpets made endeavour,
Sounding, 'In God rejoice!'
  Saying, 'In Him rejoice
Whose mercy endureth for ever!' –

IV

Then the Temple filled with a cloud,
  Even the House of the Lord;
Porch bent and pillar bowed:
  For the presence of the Lord,
20 In the glory of His cloud,
  Had filled the House of the Lord.

Second Speaker, as Renan

Gone now! All gone across the dark so far,
  Sharpening fast, shuddering ever, shutting still,
Dwindling into the distance, dies that star
  Which came, stood, opened once! We gazed our fill
With upturned faces on as real a Face
  That, stooping from grave music and mild fire,
Took in our homage, made a visible place
  Through many a depth of glory, gyre on gyre,
30 For the dim human tribute. Was this true?
  Could man indeed avail, mere praise of his,
To help by rapture God's own rapture too,
  Thrill with a heart's red tinge that pure pale bliss?
Why did it end? Who failed to beat the breast,
  And shriek, and throw the arms protesting wide,
When a first shadow showed the star addressed
  Itself to motion, and on either side
The rims contracted as the rays retired;
  The music, like a fountain's sickening pulse,
40 Subsided on itself; awhile transpired
  Some vestige of a Face no pangs convulse,
No prayers retard; then even this was gone,
  Lost in the night at last. We, lone and left
Silent through centuries, ever and anon
  Venture to probe again the vault bereft

Of all now save the lesser lights, a mist
  Of multitudinous points, yet suns, men say –
And this leaps ruby, this lurks amethyst,
  But where may hide what came and loved our clay?
50 How shall the sage detect in yon expanse
  The star which chose to stoop and stay for us?
Unroll the records! Hailed ye such advance
  Indeed, and did your hope evanish thus?
Watchers of twilight, is the worst averred?
  We shall not look up, know ourselves are seen,
Speak, and be sure that we again are heard,
  Acting or suffering, have the disk's serene
Reflect our life, absorb an earthly flame,
  Nor doubt that, were mankind inert and numb,
60 Its core had never crimsoned all the same,
  Nor, missing ours, its music fallen dumb?
Oh, dread succession to a dizzy post,
  Sad sway of sceptre whose mere touch appals,
Ghastly dethronement, cursed by those the most
  On whose repugnant brow the crown next falls!

Third Speaker

I

Witless alike of will and way divine,
How heaven's high with earth's low should intertwine!
Friends, I have seen through your eyes: now use mine!

II

Take the least man of all mankind, as I;
70 Look at his head and heart, find how and why
He differs from his fellows utterly:

III

Then, like me, watch when nature by degrees
Grows alive round him, as in Arctic seas
(They said of old) the instinctive water flees

IV

Toward some elected point of central rock,
As though, for its sake only, roamed the flock
Of waves about the waste: awhile they mock

V

With radiance caught for the occasion, – hues
Of blackest hell now, now such reds and blues
80 As only heaven could fitly interfuse, –

VI

The mimic monarch of the whirlpool, king
O' the current for a minute: then they wring
Up by the roots and oversweep the thing,

VII

And hasten off, to play again elsewhere
The same part, choose another peak as bare,
They find and flatter, feast and finish there.

VIII

When you see what I tell you, – nature dance
About each man of us, retire, advance,
As though the pageant's end were to enhance

IX

90 His worth, and – once the life, his product, gained –
Roll away elsewhere, keep the strife sustained,
And show thus real, a thing the North but feigned –

X

When you acknowledge that one world could do
All the diverse work, old yet ever new,
Divide us, each from other, me from you, –

XI

Why, where's the need of Temple, when the walls
O' the world are that? What use of swells and falls
From Levites' choir, Priests' cries, and trumpet-calls?

XII

That one Face, far from vanish, rather grows,
100 Or decomposes but to recompose,
Become my universe that feels and knows.

Balaustion's Adventure: including a Transcript from Euripides

1871

To the Countess Cowper

If I mention the simple truth: that this poem absolutely owes its existence to you, – who not only suggested, but imposed on me as a task, what has proved the most delightful of May-month amusements – I shall seem honest, indeed, but hardly prudent; for, how good and beautiful ought such a poem to be!

Euripides might fear little; but I, also, have an interest in the performance; and what wonder if I beg you to suffer that it make, in another and far easier sense, its nearest possible approach to those Greek qualities of goodness and beauty, by laying itself gratefully at your feet?

R. B.

London: 23 July 1871

> Our Euripides, the human,
>> With his droppings of warm tears,
> And his touches of things common
>> Till they rose to touch the spheres.

About that strangest, saddest, sweetest song
I, when a girl, heard in Kameiros once,
And, after, saved my life by? Oh, so glad
To tell you the adventure!
     Petalé,
Phullis, Charopé, Chrusion! You must know,
This 'after' fell in that unhappy time
When poor reluctant Nikias, pushed by fate,
Went falteringly against Syracuse;
And there shamed Athens, lost her ships and men,
10 And gained a grave, or death without a grave.
I was at Rhodes – the isle, not Rhodes the town,
Mine was Kameiros – when the news arrived:
Our people rose in tumult, cried 'No more
Duty to Athens, let us join the League
And side with Sparta, share the spoil, – at worst,
Abjure a headship that will ruin Greece!'
And so, they sent to Knidos for a fleet
To come and help revolters. Ere help came, –
Girl as I was, and never out of Rhodes
20 The whole of my first fourteen years of life,
But nourished with Ilissian mother's-milk, –
I passionately cried to who would hear
And those who loved me at Kameiros – 'No!
Never throw Athens off for Sparta's sake –
Never disloyal to the life and light
Of the whole world worth calling world at all!
Rather go die at Athens, lie outstretched
For feet to trample on, before the gate
Of Diomedes or the Hippadai,
30 Before the temples and among the tombs,
Than tolerate the grim felicity
Of harsh Lakonia! Ours the fasts and feasts,
Choës and Chutroi; ours the sacred grove,

Agora, Dikasteria, Poikilé,
Pnux, Keramikos; Salamis in sight,
Psuttalia, Marathon itself, not far!
Ours the great Dionusiac theatre,
And tragic triad of immortal fames,
Aischulos, Sophokles, Euripides!
40 To Athens, all of us that have a soul,
Follow me!' And I wrought so with my prayer,
That certain of my kinsfolk crossed the strait
And found a ship at Kaunos; well-disposed
Because the Captain – where did he draw breath
First but within Psuttalia? Thither fled
A few like-minded as ourselves. We turned
The glad prow westward, soon were out at sea,
Pushing, brave ship with the vermilion cheek,
Proud for our heart's true harbour. But a wind
50 Lay ambushed by Point Malea of bad fame,
And leapt out, bent us from our course. Next day
Broke stormless, so broke next blue day and next.
'But whither bound in this white waste?' we plagued
The pilot's old experience: 'Cos or Crete?'
Because he promised us the land ahead.
While we strained eyes to share in what he saw,
The Captain's shout startled us; round we rushed:
What hung behind us but a pirate-ship
Panting for the good prize! 'Row! harder row!
60 Row for dear life!' the Captain cried: ''tis Crete,
Friendly Crete looming large there! Beat this craft
That's but a keles, one-benched pirate-bark,
Lokrian, or that bad breed off Thessaly!
Only, so cruel are such water-thieves,
No man of you, no woman, child, or slave,
But falls their prey, once let them board our boat!'
So, furiously our oarsmen rowed and rowed;
And when the oars flagged somewhat, dash and dip,
As we approached the coast and safety, so
70 That we could hear behind us plain the threats
And curses of the pirate panting up
In one more throe and passion of pursuit, –
Seeing our oars flag in the rise and fall,
I sprang upon the altar by the mast
And sang aloft, – some genius prompting me, –

That song of ours which saved at Salamis:
'O sons of Greeks, go, set your country free,
Free your wives, free your children, free the fanes
O' the Gods, your fathers founded, – sepulchres
80 They sleep in! Or save all, or all be lost!'
Then, in a frenzy, so the noble oars
Churned the black water white, that well away
We drew, soon saw land rise, saw hills grow up,
Saw spread itself a sea-wide town with towers,
Not fifty stadia distant; and, betwixt
A large bay and a small, the islet-bar,
Even Ortugia's self – oh, luckless we!
For here was Sicily and Syracuse:
We ran upon the lion from the wolf.
90 Ere we drew breath, took counsel, out there came
A galley, hailed us. 'Who asks entry here
In war-time? Are you Sparta's friend or foe?'
'Kaunians' – our Captain judged his best reply,
'The mainland-seaport that belongs to Rhodes;
Rhodes that casts in her lot now with the League,
Forsaking Athens, – you have heard belike!'
'Ay, but we heard all Athens in one ode
Just now! we heard her in that Aischulos!
You bring a boatful of Athenians here,
100 Kaunians although you be: and prudence bids,
For Kaunos' sake, why, carry them unhurt
To Kaunos, if you will: for Athens' sake,
Back must you, though ten pirates blocked the bay!
We want no colony from Athens here,
With memories of Salamis, forsooth,
To spirit up our captives, that pale crowd
I' the quarry, whom the daily pint of corn
Keeps in good order and submissiveness.'
Then the grey Captain prayed them by the Gods,
110 And by their own knees, and their fathers' beards,
They should not wickedly thrust suppliants back,
But save the innocent on traffic bound –
Or, may be, some Athenian family
Perishing of desire to die at home, –
From that vile foe still lying on its oars,
Waiting the issue in the distance. Vain!
Words to the wind! And we were just about

To turn and face the foe, as some tired bird
Barbarians pelt at, drive with shouts away
120 From shelter in what rocks, however rude,
She makes for, to escape the kindled eye,
Split beak, crook'd claw o' the creature, cormorant
Or ossifrage, that, hardly baffled, hangs
Afloat i' the foam, to take her if she turn.
So were we at destruction's very edge,
When those o' the galley, as they had discussed
A point, a question raised by somebody,
A matter mooted in a moment, – 'Wait!'
Cried they (and wait we did, you may be sure).
130 'That song was veritable Aischulos,
Familiar to the mouth of man and boy,
Old glory: how about Euripides?
The newer and not yet so famous bard,
He that was born upon the battle-day
While that song and the salpinx sounded him
Into the world, first sound, at Salamis –
Might you know any of his verses too?'

Now, some one of the Gods inspired this speech:
Since ourselves knew what happened but last year –
140 How, when Gulippos gained his victory
Over poor Nikias, poor Demosthenes,
And Syracuse condemned the conquered force
To dig and starve i' the quarry, branded them –
Freeborn Athenians, brute-like in the front
With horse-head brands, – ah, 'Region of the Steed'! –
Of all these men immersed in misery,
It was found none had been advantaged so
By aught in the past life he used to prize
And pride himself concerning, – no rich man
150 By riches, no wise man by wisdom, no
Wiser man still (as who loved more the Muse)
By storing, at brain's edge and tip of tongue,
Old glory, great plays that had long ago
Made themselves wings to fly about the world, –
Not one such man was helped so at his need
As certain few that (wisest they of all)
Had, at first summons, oped heart, flung door wide
At the new knocking of Euripides,

Nor drawn the bolt with who cried 'Decadence!
160 And, after Sophokles, be nature dumb!'
Such, – and I see in it God Bacchos' boon
To souls that recognized his latest child,
He who himself, born latest of the Gods,
Was stoutly held impostor by mankind, –
Such were in safety: any who could speak
A chorus to the end, or prologize,
Roll out a rhesis, wield some golden length
Stiffened by wisdom out into a line,
Or thrust and parry in bright monostich,
170 Teaching Euripides to Syracuse –
Any such happy man had prompt reward:
If he lay bleeding on the battle-field
They staunched his wounds and gave him drink and food;
If he were slave i' the house, for reverence
They rose up, bowed to who proved master now,
And bade him go free, thank Euripides!
Ay, and such did so: many such, he said,
Returning home to Athens, sought him out,
The old bard in the solitary house,
180 And thanked him ere they went to sacrifice.
I say, we knew that story of last year!

Therefore, at mention of Euripides,
The Captain crowed out 'Euoi, praise the God!
Oöp, boys, bring our owl-shield to the fore!
Out with our Sacred Anchor! Here she stands,
Balaustion! Strangers, greet the lyric girl!
Euripides? Babai! what a word there 'scaped
Your teeth's enclosure, quoth my grandsire's song!
Why, fast as snow in Thrace, the voyage through,
190 Has she been falling thick in flakes of him!
Frequent as figs at Kaunos, Kaunians said.
Balaustion, stand forth and confirm my speech!
Now it was some whole passion of a play;
Now, peradventure, but a honey-drop
That slipt its comb i' the chorus. If there rose
A star, before I could determine steer
Southward or northward – if a cloud surprised
Heaven, ere I fairly hollaed "Furl the sail! –"
She had at fingers' end both cloud and star;

200   Some thought that perched there, tame and tunable,
Fitted with wings; and still, as off it flew,
"So sang Euripides," she said, "so sang
The meteoric poet of air and sea,
Planets and the pale populace of heaven,
The mind of man, and all that's made to soar!"
And so, although she has some other name,
We only call her Wild-pomegranate-flower,
Balaustion; since, where'er the red bloom burns
I' the dull dark verdure of the bounteous tree,
210   Dethroning, in the Rosy Isle, the rose,
You shall find food, drink, odour, all at once;
Cool leaves to bind about an aching brow,
And, never much away, the nightingale.
Sing them a strophe, with the turn-again,
Down to the verse that ends all, proverb-like,
And save us, thou Balaustion, bless the name!'

But I cried 'Brother Greek! better than so, –
Save us, and I have courage to recite
The main of a whole play from first to last;
220   That strangest, saddest, sweetest song of his,
ALKESTIS; which was taught, long years ago
At Athens, in Glaukinos' archonship,
But only this year reached our Isle o' the Rose.
I saw it, at Kameiros, played the same,
They say, as for the right Lenean feast
In Athens; and beside the perfect piece –
Its beauty and the way it makes you weep, –
There is much honour done your own loved God
Herakles, whom you house i' the city here
230   Nobly, the Temple wide Greece talks about!
I come a suppliant to your Herakles!
Take me and put me on his temple-steps
To tell you his achievement as I may,
And, that told, he shall bid you set us free!'

Then, because Greeks are Greeks, and hearts are hearts,
And poetry is power, – they all outbroke
In a great joyous laughter with much love:
'Thank Herakles for the good holiday!
Make for the harbour! Row, and let voice ring,

240 "In we row, bringing more Euripides!'"
All the crowd, as they lined the harbour now,
'More of Euripides!' – took up the cry.
We landed; the whole city, soon astir,
Came rushing out of gates in common joy
To the suburb temple; there they stationed me
O' the topmost step: and plain I told the play,
Just as I saw it; what the actors said,
And what I saw, or thought I saw the while,
At our Kameiros theatre, clean-scooped
250 Out of a hill-side, with the sky above
And sea before our seats in marble row:
Told it, and, two days more, repeated it,
Until they sent us on our way again
With good words and great wishes.

                      Oh, for me –
A wealthy Syracusan brought a whole
Talent and bade me take it for myself:
I left it on the tripod in the fane,
– For had not Herakles a second time
Wrestled with Death and saved devoted ones? –
260 Thank-offering to the hero. And a band
Of captives, whom their lords grew kinder to
Because they called the poet countryman,
Sent me a crown of wild-pomegranate-flower:
So, I shall live and die Balaustion now.
But one – one man – one youth, – three days, each day, –
(If, ere I lifted up my voice to speak,
I gave a downward glance by accident)
Was found at foot o' the temple. When we sailed,
There, in the ship too, was he found as well,
270 Having a hunger to see Athens too.
We reached Peiraieus; when I landed – lo,
He was beside me. Anthesterion-month
Is just commencing: when its moon rounds full,
We are to marry. O Euripides!

I saw the master: when we found ourselves
(Because the young man needs must follow me)
Firm on Peiraieus, I demanded first
Whither to go and find him. Would you think?
The story how he saved us made some smile:

280 They wondered strangers were exorbitant
In estimation of Euripides.
He was not Aischulos nor Sophokles:
– 'Then, of our younger bards who boast the bay,
Had I sought Agathon, or Iophon,
Or, what now had it been Kephisophon?
A man that never kept good company,
The most unsociable of poet-kind,
All beard that was not freckle in his face!'

I soon was at the tragic house, and saw
290 The master, held the sacred hand of him
And laid it to my lips. Men love him not:
How should they? Nor do they much love his friend
Sokrates: but those two have fellowship:
Sokrates often comes to hear him read,
And never misses if he teach a piece.
Both, being old, will soon have company,
Sit with their peers above the talk. Meantime,
He lives as should a statue in its niche;
Cold walls enclose him, mostly darkness there,
300 Alone, unless some foreigner uncouth
Breaks in, sits, stares an hour, and so departs,
Brain-stuffed with something to sustain his life,
Dry to the marrow 'mid much merchandise.
How should such know and love the man?
                                        Why, mark!
Even when I told the play and got the praise,
There spoke up a brisk little somebody,
Critic and whippersnapper, in a rage
To set things right: 'The girl departs from truth!
Pretends she saw what was not to be seen,
310 Making the mask of the actor move, forsooth!
"Then a fear flitted o'er the wife's white face," –
"Then frowned the father," – "then the husband shook," –
"Then from the festal forehead slipt each spray,
And the heroic mouth's gay grace was gone"; –
As she had seen each naked fleshly face,
And not the merely-painted mask it wore!'
Well, is the explanation difficult?
What's poetry except a power that makes?
And, speaking to one sense, inspires the rest,

320 Pressing them all into its service; so
     That who sees painting, seems to hear as well
     The speech that's proper for the painted mouth;
     And who hears music, feels his solitude
     Peopled at once – for how count heart-beats plain
     Unless a company, with hearts which beat,
     Come close to the musician, seen or no?
     And who receives true verse at eye or ear,
     Takes in (with verse) time, place, and person too,
     So, links each sense on to its sister-sense,
330 Grace-like: and what if but one sense of three
     Front you at once? The sidelong pair conceive
     Through faintest touch of finest finger-tips, –
     Hear, see and feel, in faith's simplicity,
     Alike, what one was sole recipient of:
     Who hears the poem, therefore, sees the play.

     Enough and too much! Hear the play itself!
     Under the grape-vines, by the streamlet-side,
     Close to Baccheion; till the cool increase,
     And other stars steal on the evening-star,
340 And so, we homeward flock i' the dusk, we five!
     You will expect, no one of all the words
     O' the play but is grown part now of my soul,
     Since the adventure. 'Tis the poet speaks:
     But if I, too, should try and speak at times,
     Leading your love to where my love, perchance,
     Climbed earlier, found a nest before you knew –
     Why, bear with the poor climber, for love's sake!
     Look at Baccheion's beauty opposite,
     The temple with the pillars at the porch!
350 See you not something beside masonry?
     What if my words wind in and out the stone
     As yonder ivy, the God's parasite?
     Though they leap all the way the pillar leads,
     Festoon about the marble, foot to frieze,
     And serpentiningly enrich the roof,
     Toy with some few bees and a bird or two, –
     What then? The column holds the cornice up.

There slept a silent palace in the sun,
With plains adjacent and Thessalian peace –
360 Pherai, where King Admetos ruled the land.

Out from the portico there gleamed a God,
Apollon: for the bow was in his hand,
The quiver at his shoulder, all his shape
One dreadful beauty. And he hailed the house
As if he knew it well and loved it much:
'O Admeteian domes, where I endured,
Even the God I am, to drudge awhile,
Do righteous penance for a reckless deed,
Accepting the slaves' table thankfully!'
370 Then told how Zeus had been the cause of all,
Raising the wrath in him which took revenge
And slew those forgers of the thunderbolt
Wherewith Zeus blazed the life from out the breast
Of Phoibos' son Asklepios (I surmise,
Because he brought the dead to life again)
And so, for punishment, must needs go slave,
God as he was, with a mere mortal lord:
– Told how he came to King Admetos' land,
And played the ministrant, was herdsman there,
380 Warding all harm away from him and his
Till now; 'For, holy as I am,' said he,
'The lord I chanced upon was holy too:
Whence I deceived the Moirai, drew from death
My master, this same son of Pheres, – ay,
The Goddesses conceded him escape
From Hades, when the fated day should fall,
Could he exchange lives, find some friendly one
Ready, for his sake, to content the grave.
But trying all in turn, the friendly list,
390 Why, he found no one, none who loved so much,
Nor father, nor the agèd mother's self
That bore him, no, not any save his wife,
Willing to die instead of him and watch
Never a sunrise nor a sunset more:
And she is even now within the house,
Upborne by pitying hands, the feeble frame
Gasping its last of life out; since today
Destiny is accomplished, and she dies,

And I, lest here pollution light on me,
400   Leave, as ye witness, all my wonted joy
In this dear dwelling. Ay, – for here comes Death
Close on us of a sudden! who, pale priest
Of the mute people, means to bear his prey
To the house of Hades. The symmetric step!
How he treads true to time and place and thing,
Dogging day, hour and minute, for death's-due!'

And we observed another Deity,
Half in, half out the portal, – watch and ward, –
Eyeing his fellow: formidably fixed,
410   Yet faltering too at who affronted him,
As somehow disadvantaged, should they strive.
Like some dread heapy blackness, ruffled wing,
Convulsed and cowering head that is all eye,
Which proves a ruined eagle who, too blind
Swooping in quest o' the quarry, fawn or kid,
Descried deep down the chasm 'twixt rock and rock,
Has wedged and mortised, into either wall
O' the mountain, the pent earthquake of his power;
So lies, half hurtless yet still terrible,
420   Just when – who stalks up, who stands front to front,
But the great lion-guarder of the gorge,
Lord of the ground, a stationed glory there?
Yet he too pauses ere he try the worst
O' the frightful unfamiliar nature, new
To the chasm, indeed, but elsewhere known enough,
Among the shadows and the silences
Above i' the sky: so each antagonist
Silently faced his fellow and forbore.
Till Death shrilled, hard and quick, in spite and fear:

430   'Ha ha, and what mayst thou do at the domes,
Why hauntest here, thou Phoibos? Here again
At the old injustice, limiting our rights,
Balking of honour due us Gods o' the grave?
Was't not enough for thee to have delayed
Death from Admetos, – with thy crafty art
Cheating the very Fates, – but thou must arm
The bow-hand and take station, press 'twixt me
And Pelias' daughter, who then saved her spouse, –

Did just that, now thou comest to undo, –
440 Taking his place to die, Alkestis here?'

But the God sighed 'Have courage! All my arms,
This time, are simple justice and fair words.'

Then each plied each with rapid interchange:

'What need of bow, were justice arms enough?'

'Ever it is my wont to bear the bow.'

'Ay, and with bow, not justice, help this house!'

'I help it, since a friend's woe weighs me too.'

'And now, – wilt force from me this second corpse?'

'By force I took no corpse at first from thee.'

450 'How then is he above ground, not beneath?'

'He gave his wife instead of him, thy prey.'

'And prey, this time at least, I bear below!'

'Go take her! – for I doubt persuading thee . . .'

'To kill the doomed one? What my function else?'

'No! Rather, to dispatch the true mature.'

'Truly I take thy meaning, see thy drift!'

'Is there a way then she may reach old age?'

'No way! I glad me in my honours too!'

'But, young or old, thou tak'st one life, no more!'

460 'Younger they die, greater my praise redounds!'

'If she die old, – the sumptuous funeral!'

'Thou layest down a law the rich would like.'

'How so? Did wit lurk there and 'scape thy sense?'

'Who could buy substitutes would die old men.'

'It seems thou wilt not grant me, then, this grace?'

'This grace I will not grant: thou know'st my ways.'

'Ways harsh to men, hateful to Gods, at least!'

'All things thou canst not have: my rights for me!'

And then Apollon prophesied, – I think,
470 More to himself than to impatient Death,
Who did not hear or would not heed the while, –
For he went on to say 'Yet even so,
Cruel above the measure, thou shalt clutch
No life here! Such a man do I perceive
Advancing to the house of Pheres now,
Sent by Eurustheus to bring out of Thrace,
The winter world, a chariot with its steeds!
He indeed, when Admetos proves the host,
And he the guest, at the house here, – he it is
480 Shall bring to bear such force, and from thy hands
Rescue this woman. Grace no whit to me
Will that prove, since thou dost thy deed the same,
And earnest too my hate, and all for naught!'

But how should Death or stay or understand?
Doubtless, he only felt the hour was come,
And the sword free; for he but flung some taunt –
'Having talked much, thou wilt not gain the more!
This woman, then, descends to Hades' hall
Now that I rush on her, begin the rites
490 O' the sword; for sacred, to us Gods below,
That head whose hair this sword shall sanctify!'

And,.in the fire-flash of the appalling sword,
The uprush and the outburst, the onslaught
Of Death's portentous passage through the door,
Apollon stood a pitying moment-space:
I caught one last gold gaze upon the night
Nearing the world now: and the God was gone,
And mortals left to deal with misery,
As in came stealing slow, now this, now that
500 Old sojourner throughout the country-side,
Servants grown friends to those unhappy here:
And, cloudlike in their increase, all these griefs
Broke and began the over-brimming wail,
Out of a common impulse, word by word.

'What now may mean the silence at the door?
Why is Admetos' mansion stricken dumb?
Not one friend near, to say if we should mourn
Our mistress dead, or if Alkestis lives
And sees the light still, Pelias' child – to me,
510 To all, conspicuously the best of wives
That ever was toward husband in this world!
Hears anyone or wail beneath the roof,
Or hands that strike each other, or the groan
Announcing all is done and naught to dread?
Still not a servant stationed at the gates!
O Paian, that thou wouldst dispart the wave
O' the woe, be present! Yet, had woe o'erwhelmed
The housemates, they were hardly silent thus:
It cannot be, the dead is forth and gone.
520 Whence comes thy gleam of hope? I dare not hope:
What is the circumstance that heartens thee?
How could Admetos have dismissed a wife
So worthy, unescorted to the grave?
Before the gates I see no hallowed vase
Of fountain-water, such as suits death's door;
Nor any clipt locks strew the vestibule,
Though surely these drop when we grieve the dead,
Nor hand sounds smitten against youthful hand,
The women's way. And yet – the appointed time –
530 How speak the word? – this day is even the day
Ordained her for departing from its light.

O touch calamitous to heart and soul!
Needs must one, when the good are tortured so,
Sorrow, – one reckoned faithful from the first.'

Then their souls rose together, and one sigh
Went up in cadence from the common mouth:
How 'Vainly – anywhither in the world
Directing or land-labour or sea-search –
To Lukia or the sand-waste, Ammon's seat –
540 Might you set free their hapless lady's soul
From the abrupt Fate's footstep instant now.
Not a sheep-sacrificer at the hearths
Of Gods had they to go to: one there was
Who, if his eyes saw light still, – Phoibos' son, –
Had wrought so she might leave the shadowy place
And Hades' portal; for he propped up Death's
Subdued ones till the Zeus-flung thunder-flame
Struck him; and now what hope of life were hailed
With open arms? For, all the king could do
550 Is done already, – not one God whereof
The altar fails to reek with sacrifice:
And for assuagement of these evils – naught!'

But here they broke off, for a matron moved
Forth from the house: and, as her tears flowed fast,
They gathered round. 'What fortune shall we hear?
For mourning thus, if aught affect thy lord,
We pardon thee: but lives the lady yet
Or has she perished? – that we fain would know!'

'Call her dead, call her living, each style serves,'
560 The matron said: 'though grave-ward bowed, she breathed;
Nor knew her husband what the misery meant
Before he felt it: hope of life was none:
The appointed day pressed hard; the funeral pomp
He had prepared too.'
                    When the friends broke out:
'Let her in dying know herself at least
Sole wife, of all the wives 'neath the sun wide,
For glory and for goodness!' – 'Ah, how else
Than best? who controverts the claim?' quoth she:

     'What kind of creature should the woman prove
570 That has surpassed Alkestis? – surelier shown
     Preference for her husband to herself
     Than by determining to die for him?
     But so much all our city knows indeed:
     Hear what she did indoors and wonder then!
     For, when she felt the crowning day was come,
     She washed with river-waters her white skin,
     And, taking from the cedar closets forth
     Vesture and ornament, bedecked herself
     Nobly, and stood before the hearth, and prayed:
580 "Mistress, because I now depart the world,
     Falling before thee the last time, I ask –
     Be mother to my orphans! wed the one
     To a kind wife, and make the other's mate
     Some princely person: nor, as I who bore
     My children perish, suffer that they too
     Die all untimely, but live, happy pair,
     Their full glad life out in the fatherland!"
     And every altar through Admetos' house
     She visited and crowned and prayed before,
590 Stripping the myrtle-foliage from the boughs,
     Without a tear, without a groan, – no change
     At all to that skin's nature, fair to see,
     Caused by the imminent evil. But this done –
     Reaching her chamber, falling on her bed,
     There, truly, burst she into tears and spoke:
     "O bride-bed, where I loosened from my life
     Virginity for that same husband's sake
     Because of whom I die now – fare thee well!
     Since nowise do I hate thee: me alone
600 Hast thou destroyed; for, shrinking to betray
     Thee and my spouse, I die: but thee, O bed,
     Some other woman shall possess as wife –
     Truer, no! but of better fortune, say!"
     – So falls on, kisses it till all the couch
     Is moistened with the eyes' sad overflow.
     But, when of many tears she had her fill,
     She flings from off the couch, goes headlong forth,
     Yet, – forth the chamber, – still keeps turning back
     And casts her on the couch again once more.
610 Her children, clinging to their mother's robe,

Wept meanwhile: but she took them in her arms,
And, as a dying woman might, embraced
Now one and now the other: 'neath the roof,
All of the household servants wept as well,
Moved to compassion for their mistress; she
Extended her right hand to all and each,
And there was no one of such low degree
She spoke not to nor had an answer from.
Such are the evils in Admetos' house.
620 Dying, – why, he had died; but, living, gains
Such grief as this he never will forget!'

And when they questioned of Admetos, 'Well –
Holding his dear wife in his hands, he weeps;
Entreats her not to give him up, and seeks
The impossible, in fine: for there she wastes
And withers by disease, abandoned now,
A mere dead weight upon her husband's arm.
Yet, none the less, although she breathe so faint,
Her will is to behold the beams o' the sun:
630 Since never more again, but this last once,
Shall she see sun, its circlet or its ray.
But I will go, announce your presence, – friends
Indeed; since 'tis not all so love their lords
As seek them in misfortune, kind the same:
But you are the old friends I recognize.'

And at the word she turned again to go:
The while they waited, taking up the plaint
To Zeus again: 'What passage from this strait?
What loosing of the heavy fortune fast
640 About the palace? Will such help appear,
Or must we clip the locks and cast around
Each form already the black peplos' fold?
Clearly the black robe, clearly! All the same,
Pray to the Gods! – like Gods' no power so great!
O thou king Paian, find some way to save!
Reveal it, yea, reveal it! Since of old
Thou found'st a cure, why, now again become
Releaser from the bonds of Death, we beg,
And give the sanguinary Hades pause!'
650 So the song dwindled into a mere moan,

How dear the wife, and what her husband's woe;
When suddenly –
                              'Behold, behold!' breaks forth:
'Here is she coming from the house indeed!
Her husband comes, too! Cry aloud, lament,
Pheraian land, this best of women, bound –
So is she withered by disease away –
For realms below and their infernal king!
Never will we affirm there's more of joy
Than grief in marriage; making estimate
660 Both from old sorrows anciently observed,
And this misfortune of the king we see –
Admetos who, of bravest spouse bereaved,
Will live life's remnant out, no life at all!'

So wailed they, while a sad procession wound
Slow from the innermost o' the palace, stopped
At the extreme verge of the platform-front:
There opened, and disclosed Alkestis' self,
The consecrated lady, borne to look
Her last – and let the living look their last –
670 She at the sun, we at Alkestis.
                              We!
For would you note a memorable thing?
We grew to see in that severe regard, –
Hear in that hard dry pressure to the point,
Word slow pursuing word in monotone, –
What Death meant when he called her consecrate
Henceforth to Hades. I believe, the sword –
Its office was to cut the soul at once
From life, – from something in this world which hides
Truth, and hides falsehood, and so lets us live
680 Somehow. Suppose a rider furls a cloak
About a horse's head; unfrightened, so,
Between the menace of a flame, between
Solicitation of the pasturage,
Untempted equally, he goes his gait
To journey's end: then pluck the pharos off!
Show what delusions steadied him i' the straight
O' the path, made grass seem fire and fire seem grass,
All through a little bandage o'er the eyes!
As certainly with eyes unbandaged now

690   Alkestis looked upon the action here,
     Self-immolation for Admetos' sake;
     Saw, with a new sense, all her death would do,
     And which of her survivors had the right,
     And which the less right, to survive thereby.
     For, you shall note, she uttered no one word
     Of love more to her husband, though he wept
     Plenteously, waxed importunate in prayer –
     Folly's old fashion when its seed bears fruit.
     I think she judged that she had bought the ware
700   O' the seller at its value, – nor praised him
     Nor blamed herself, but, with indifferent eye,
     Saw him purse money up, prepare to leave
     The buyer with a solitary bale –
     True purple – but in place of all that coin,
     Had made a hundred others happy too,
     If so willed fate or fortune! What remained
     To give away, should rather go to these
     Than one with coin to clink and contemplate.
     Admetos had his share and might depart,
710   The rest was for her children and herself.
     (Charopé makes a face: but wait awhile!)
     She saw things plain as Gods do: by one stroke
     O' the sword that rends the life-long veil away.
     (Also Euripides saw plain enough:
     But you and I, Charopé! – you and I
     Will trust his sight until our own grow clear.)

     'Sun, and thou light of day, and heavenly dance
     O' the fleet cloud-figure!' (so her passion paused,
     While the awe-stricken husband made his moan,
720   Muttered now this now that ineptitude:
     'Sun that sees thee and me, a suffering pair,
     Who did the Gods no wrong whence thou shouldst die!')
     Then, as if caught up, carried in their course,
     Fleeting and free as cloud and sunbeam are,
     She missed no happiness that lay beneath:
     'O thou wide earth, from these my palace roofs,
     To distant nuptial chambers once my own
     In that Iolkos of my ancestry!' –
     There the flight failed her. 'Raise thee, wretched one!
730   Give us not up! Pray pity from the Gods!'

Vainly Admetos: for 'I see it – see
The two-oared boat! The ferryer of the dead,
Charon, hand hard upon the boatman's-pole,
Calls me – even now calls – "Why delayest thou?
Quick! Thou obstructest all made ready here
For prompt departure: quick, then!"'
                                        'Woe is me!

A bitter voyage this to undergo,
Even i' the telling! Adverse Powers above,
How do ye plague us!'
                        Then a shiver ran:
740   'He has me – seest not? – hales me, – who is it? –
To the hall o' the Dead – ah, who but Hades' self,
He, with the wings there, glares at me, one gaze
All that blue brilliance, under the eyebrow!
What wilt thou do? Unhand me! Such a way
I have to traverse, all unhappy one!'

'Way – piteous to thy friends, but, most of all,
Me and thy children: ours assuredly
A common partnership in grief like this!'

Whereat they closed about her; but 'Let be!
750   Leave, let me lie now! Strength forsakes my feet.
Hades is here, and shadowy on my eyes
Comes the night creeping. Children – children, now
Indeed, a mother is no more for you!
Farewell, O children, long enjoy the light!'

'Ah me, the melancholy word I hear,
Oppressive beyond every kind of death!
No, by the Deities, take heart nor dare
To give me up – no, by our children too
Made orphans of! But rise, be resolute,
760   Since, thou departed, I no more remain!
For in thee are we bound up, to exist
Or cease to be – so we adore thy love!'

– Which brought out truth to judgement. At this word
And protestation, all the truth in her
Claimed to assert itself: she waved away
The blue-eyed black-wing'd phantom, held in check

The advancing pageantry of Hades there,
And, with no change in her own countenance,
She fixed her eyes on the protesting man,
770 And let her lips unlock their sentence, – so!

'Admetos, – how things go with me thou seest, –
I wish to tell thee, ere I die, what things
I will should follow. I – to honour thee,
Secure for thee, by my own soul's exchange,
Continued looking on the daylight here –
Die for thee – yet, if so I pleased, might live,
Nay, wed what man of Thessaly I would,
And dwell i' the dome with pomp and queenliness.
I would not, – would not live bereft of thee,
780 With children orphaned, neither shrank at all,
Though having gifts of youth wherein I joyed.
Yet, who begot thee and who gave thee birth,
Both of these gave thee up; no less, a term
Of life was reached when death became them well,
Ay, well – to save their child and glorious die:
Since thou wast all they had, nor hope remained
Of having other children in thy place.
So, I and thou had lived out our full time,
Nor thou, left lonely of thy wife, wouldst groan
790 With children reared in orphanage: but thus
Some God disposed things, willed they so should be.
Be they so! Now do thou remember this,
Do me in turn a favour – favour, since
Certainly I shall never claim my due,
For nothing is more precious than a life:
But a fit favour, as thyself wilt say,
Loving our children here no less than I,
If head and heart be sound in thee at least.
Uphold them, make them masters of my house,
800 Nor wed and give a step-dame to the pair,
Who, being a worse wife than I, through spite
Will raise her hand against both thine and mine.
Never do this at least, I pray to thee!
For hostile the new-comer, the step-dame,
To the old brood – a very viper she
For gentleness! Here stand they, boy and girl;
The boy has got a father, a defence

Tower-like, he speaks to and has answer from:
But thou, my girl, how will thy virginhood
810 Conclude itself in marriage fittingly?
Upon what sort of sire-found yoke-fellow
Art thou to chance? with all to apprehend –
Lest, casting on thee some unkind report,
She blast thy nuptials in the bloom of youth.
For neither shall thy mother watch thee wed,
Nor hearten thee in childbirth, standing by
Just when a mother's presence helps the most!
No, for I have to die: and this my ill
Comes to me, nor tomorrow, no, nor yet
820 The third day of the month, but now, even now,
I shall be reckoned among those no more.
Farewell, be happy! And to thee, indeed,
Husband, the boast remains permissible
Thou hadst a wife was worthy! and to you,
Children; as good a mother gave you birth.'

'Have courage!' interposed the friends, 'For him
I have no scruple to declare – all this
Will he perform, except he fail of sense.'

'All this shall be – shall be!' Admetos sobbed:
830 'Fear not! And, since I had thee living, dead
Alone wilt thou be called my wife: no fear
That some Thessalian ever styles herself
Bride, hails this man for husband in thy place!
No woman, be she of such lofty line
Or such surpassing beauty otherwise!
Enough of children: gain from these I have,
Such only may the Gods grant! since in thee
Absolute is our loss, where all was gain.
And I shall bear for thee no year-long grief,
840 But grief that lasts while my own days last, love!
Love! For my hate is she who bore me, now:
And him I hate, my father: loving-ones
Truly, in word not deed! But thou didst pay
All dearest to thee down, and buy my life,
Saving me so! Is there not cause enough
That I who part with such companionship
In thee, should make my moan? I moan, and more:

For I will end the feastings – social flow
O' the wine friends flock for, garlands and the Muse
850 That graced my dwelling. Never now for me
To touch the lyre, to lift my soul in song
At summons of the Lydian flute; since thou
From out my life hast emptied all the joy!
And this thy body, in thy likeness wrought
By some wise hand of the artificers,
Shall lie disposed within my marriage-bed:
This I will fall on, this enfold about,
Call by thy name, – my dear wife in my arms
Even though I have not, I shall seem to have –
860 A cold delight, indeed, but all the same
So should I lighten of its weight my soul!
And, wandering my way in dreams perchance,
Thyself wilt bless me: for, come when they will,
Even by night our loves are sweet to see.
But were the tongue and tune of Orpheus mine,
So that to Koré crying, or her lord,
In hymns, from Hades I might rescue thee –
Down would I go, and neither Plouton's dog
Nor Charon, he whose oar sends souls across,
870 Should stay me till again I made thee stand
Living, within the light! But, failing this,
There, where thou art, await me when I die,
Make ready our abode, my house-mate still!
For in the self-same cedar, me with thee
Will I provide that these our friends shall place,
My side lay close by thy side! Never, corpse
Although I be, would I division bear
From thee, my faithful one of all the world!'

So he stood sobbing: nowise insincere,
880 But somehow child-like, like his children, like
Childishness the world over. What was new
In this announcement that his wife must die?
What particle of pain beyond the pact
He made, with eyes wide open, long ago –
Made and was, if not glad, content to make?
Now that the sorrow, he had called for, came,
He sorrowed to the height: none heard him say,
However, what would seem so pertinent,

'To keep this pact, I find surpass my power:
890 Rescind it, Moirai! Give me back her life,
And take the life I kept by base exchange!
Or, failing that, here stands your laughing-stock
Fooled by you, worthy just the fate o' the fool
Who makes a pother to escape the best
And gain the worst you wiser Powers allot!'
No, not one word of this: nor did his wife
Despite the sobbing, and the silence soon
To follow, judge so much was in his thought –
Fancy that, should the Moirai acquiesce,
900 He would relinquish life nor let her die.
The man was like some merchant who, in storm,
Throws the freight over to redeem the ship:
No question, saving both were better still.
As it was, – why, he sorrowed, which sufficed.
So, all she seemed to notice in his speech
Was what concerned her children. Children, too,
Bear the grief and accept the sacrifice.
Rightly rules nature: does the blossomed bough
O' the grape-vine, or the dry grape's self, bleed wine?

910 So, bending to her children all her love,
She fastened on their father's only word
To purpose now, and followed it with this.
'O children, now yourselves have heard these things –
Your father saying he will never wed
Another woman to be over you,
Nor yet dishonour me!'

     'And now at least
I say it, and I will accomplish too!'

'Then, for such promise of accomplishment,
Take from my hand these children!'

      'Thus I take –
920 Dear gift from the dear hand!'

      'Do thou become
Mother, now, to these children in my place!'

'Great the necessity I should be so,
At least, to these bereaved of thee!'

                          'Child – child!
Just when I needed most to live, below
Am I departing from you both!'

                          'Ah me!
And what shall I do, then, left lonely thus?'

'Time will appease thee: who is dead is naught.'

'Take me with thee – take, by the Gods below!'

'We are sufficient, we who die for thee.'

930 'Oh, Powers, ye widow me of what a wife!'

'And truly the dimmed eye draws earthward now!'

'Wife, if thou leav'st me, I am lost indeed!'

'She once was – now is nothing, thou mayst say.'

'Raise thy face nor forsake thy children thus!'

'Ah, willingly indeed I leave them not!
But – fare ye well, my children!'

                          'Look on them –
Look!'

        'I am nothingness.'

                          'What dost thou? Leav'st ...'

'Farewell!'
            And in the breath she passed away.
'Undone – me miserable!' moaned the king,
940 While friends released the long-suspended sigh
'Gone is she: no wife for Admetos more!'

Such was the signal: how the woe broke forth,
Why tell? – or how the children's tears ran fast
Bidding their father note the eyelids' stare
Hands' droop, each dreadful circumstance of death.

'Ay, she hears not, she sees not: I and you,
'Tis plain, are stricken hard and have to bear!'
Was all Admetos answered; for, I judge,
He only now began to taste the truth:
950 The thing done lay revealed, which undone thing,
Rehearsed for fact by fancy, at the best,
Never can equal. He had used himself
This long while (as he muttered presently)
To practise with the terms, the blow involved
By the bargain, sharp to bear, but bearable
Because of plain advantage at the end.
Now that, in fact not fancy, the blow fell –
Needs must he busy him with the surprise.
'Alkestis – not to see her nor be seen,
960 Hear nor be heard of by her, any more
Today, tomorrow, to the end of time –
Did I mean this should buy my life?' thought he.

So, friends came round him, took him by the hand,
Bade him remember our mortality,
Its due, its doom: how neither was he first,
Nor would be last, to thus deplore the loved.

'I understand' slow the words came at last.
'Nor of a sudden did the evil here
Fly on me: I have known it long ago,
970 Ay, and essayed myself in misery;
Nothing is new. You have to stay, you friends,
Because the next need is to carry forth
The corpse here: you must stay and do your part,
Chant proper paean to the God below;
Drink-sacrifice he likes not. I decree
That all Thessalians over whom I rule
Hold grief in common with me; let them shear
Their locks, and be the peplos black they show!
And you who to the chariot yoke your steeds,
980 Or manage steeds one-frontleted, – I charge,

Clip from each neck with steel the mane away!
And through my city, nor of flute nor lyre
Be there a sound till twelve full moons succeed.
For I shall never bury any corpse
Dearer than this to me, nor better friend:
One worthy of all honour from me, since
Me she has died for, she and she alone.'

With that, he sought the inmost of the house,
He and his dead, to get grave's garniture,
990 While the friends sang the paean that should peal.
'Daughter of Pelias, with farewell from me,
I' the house of Hades have thy unsunned home!
Let Hades know, the dark-haired deity, –
And he who sits to row and steer alike,
Old corpse-conductor, let him know he bears
Over the Acherontian lake, this time,
I' the two-oared boat, the best – oh, best by far
Of womankind! For thee, Alkestis Queen!
Many a time those haunters of the Muse
1000 Shall sing thee to the seven-stringed mountain-shell,
And glorify in hymns that need no harp,
At Sparta when the cycle comes about,
And that Karneian month wherein the moon
Rises and never sets the whole night through:
So too at splendid and magnificent
Athenai. Such the spread of thy renown,
And such the lay that, dying, thou hast left
Singer and sayer. O that I availed
Of my own might to send thee once again
1010 From Hades' hall, Kokutos' stream, by help
O' the oar that dips the river, back to day!'

So, the song sank to prattle in her praise:
'Light, from above thee, lady, fall the earth,
Thou only one of womankind to die,
Wife for her husband! If Admetos take
Anything to him like a second spouse –
Hate from his offspring and from us shall be
His portion, let the king assure himself!
No mind his mother had to hide in earth
1020 Her body for her son's sake, nor his sire

Had heart to save whom he begot, – not they,
The white-haired wretches! only thou it was,
I' the bloom of youth, didst save him and so die!
Might it be mine to chance on such a mate
And partner! For there's penury in life
Of such allowance: were she mine at least,
So wonderful a wife, assuredly
She would companion me throughout my days
And never once bring sorrow!'
                                        A great voice –
1030   'My hosts here!'
                              Oh, the thrill that ran through us!
Never was aught so good and opportune
As that great interrupting voice! For see!
Here maundered this dispirited old age
Before the palace; whence a something crept
Which told us well enough without a word
What was a-doing inside, – every touch
O' the garland on those temples, tenderest
Disposure of each arm along its side,
Came putting out what warmth i' the world was left.
1040   Then, as it happens at a sacrifice
When, drop by drop, some lustral bath is brimmed:
Into the thin and clear and cold, at once
They slaughter a whole wine-skin: Bacchos' blood
Sets the white water all a-flame; even so,
Sudden into the midst of sorrow, leapt
Along with the gay cheer of that great voice,
Hope, joy, salvation: Herakles was here!
Himself, o' the threshold, sent his voice on first
To herald all that human and divine
1050   I' the weary happy face of him, – half God,
Half man, which made the god-part God the more.

'Hosts mine,' he broke upon the sorrow with,
'Inhabitants of this Pheraian soil,
Chance I upon Admetos inside here?'
The irresistible sound wholesome heart
O' the hero, – more than all the mightiness
At labour in the limbs that, for man's sake,
Laboured and meant to labour their life long, –
This drove back, dried up sorrow at its source.

1060 How could it brave the happy weary laugh
Of who had bantered sorrow 'Sorrow here?
What have you done to keep your friend from harm?
Could no one give the life I see he keeps?
Or, say there's sorrow here past friendly help,
Why waste a word or let a tear escape
While other sorrows wait you in the world,
And want the life of you, though helpless here?'
Clearly there was no telling such an one
How, when their monarch tried who loved him more
1070 Than he loved them, and found they loved, as he,
Each man, himself, and held, no otherwise,
That, of all evils in the world, the worst
Was – being forced to die, whate'er death gain:
How all this selfishness in him and them
Caused certain sorrow which they sang about, –
I think that Herakles, who held his life
Out on his hand, for any man to take –
I think his laugh had marred their threnody.

'He is in the house' they answered. After all,
1080 They might have told the story, talked their best
About the inevitable sorrow here,
Nor changed nor checked the kindly nature, – no!
So long as men were merely weak, not bad,
He loved men: were they Gods he used to help?
'Yea, Pheres' son is in-doors, Herakles.
But say, what sends thee to Thessalian soil,
Brought by what business to this Pherai town?'

'A certain labour that I have to do
Eurustheus the Tirunthian,' laughed the God.

1090 'And whither wendest – on what wandering
Bound now?' (they had an instinct, guessed what meant
Wanderings, labours, in the God's light mouth.)

'After the Thrakian Diomedes' car
With the four horses.'

                    'Ah, but canst thou that?
Art inexperienced in thy host to be?'

'All-inexperienced: I have never gone
As yet to the land o' the Bistones.'

                'Then, look
By no means to be master of the steeds
Without a battle!'
            'Battle there may be:
1100   I must refuse no labour, all the same.'

'Certainly, either having slain a foe
Wilt thou return to us, or, slain thyself,
Stay there!'
        'And, even if the game be so,
The risk in it were not the first I run.'

'But, say thou overpower the lord o' the place,
What more advantage dost expect thereby?'

'I shall drive off his horses to the king.'

'No easy handling them to bit the jaw!'

'Easy enough; except, at least, they breathe
1110   Fire from their nostrils!'
              'But they mince up men
With those quick jaws!'
              'You talk of provender
For mountain-beasts, and not mere horses' food!'

'Thou mayst behold their mangers caked with gore!'

'And of what sire does he who bred them boast
Himself the son?'
          'Of Ares, king o' the targe –
Thrakian, of gold throughout.'
              Another laugh.
'Why, just the labour, just the lot for me
Dost thou describe in what I recognize!
Since hard and harder, high and higher yet,
1120   Truly this lot of mine is like to go
If I must needs join battle with the brood

Of Ares: ay, I fought Lukaon first,
And again, Kuknos: now engage in strife
This third time, with such horses and such lord.
But there is nobody shall ever see
Alkmené's son shrink foemen's hand before!'

– 'Or ever hear him say' (the Chorus thought)
'That death is terrible; and help us so
To chime in – "terrible beyond a doubt,
1130   And, if to thee, why, to ourselves much more:
Know what has happened, then, and sympathize"!'
Therefore they gladly stopped the dialogue,
Shifted the burthen to new shoulder straight,
As, 'Look where comes the lord o' the land, himself,
Admetos, from the palace!' they outbroke
In some surprise, as well as much relief.
What had induced the king to waive his right
And luxury of woe in loneliness?

Out he came quietly; the hair was clipt,
1140   And the garb sable; else no outward sign
Of sorrow as he came and faced his friend.
Was truth fast terrifying tears away?
'Hail, child of Zeus, and sprung from Perseus too!'
The salutation ran without a fault.

'And thou, Admetos, King of Thessaly!'

'Would, as thou wishest me, the grace might fall!
But my good-wisher, that thou art, I know.'

'What's here? these shorn locks, this sad show of thee?'

'I must inter a certain corpse today.'

1150   'Now, from thy children God avert mischance!'

'They live, my children; all are in the house!'

'Thy father – if 'tis he departs indeed,
His age was ripe at least.'

'My father lives,
And she who bore me lives too, Herakles.'

'It cannot be thy wife Alkestis gone?'

'Two-fold the tale is, I can tell of her.'

'Dead dost thou speak of her, or living yet?'

'She is – and is not: hence the pain to me!'

'I learn no whit the more, so dark thy speech!'

1160 'Know'st thou not on what fate she needs must fall?'

'I know she is resigned to die for thee.'

'How lives she still, then, if submitting so?'

'Eh, weep her not beforehand! wait till then!'

'Who is to die is dead; doing is done.'

'To be and not to be are thought diverse.'

'Thou judgest this – I, that way, Herakles!'

'Well, but declare what causes thy complaint!
Who is the man has died from out thy friends?'

'No man: I had a woman in my mind.'

1170 'Alien, or someone born akin to thee?'

'Alien: but still related to my house.'

'How did it happen then that here she died?'

'Her father dying left his orphan here.'

'Alas, Admetos – would we found thee gay,
Not grieving!'

'What as if about to do
Subjoinest thou that comment?'

                          'I shall seek
Another hearth, proceed to other hosts.'

'Never, O king, shall that be! No such ill
Betide me!'

                    'Nay, to mourners should there come
1180 A guest, he proves importunate!'
                                'The dead –
Dead are they: but go thou within my house!'

''Tis base carousing beside friends who mourn.'

'The guest-rooms, whither we shall lead thee, lie
Apart from ours.'
                    'Nay, let me go my way!
Ten thousandfold the favour I shall thank!'

'It may not be thou goest to the hearth
Of any man but me!' so made an end
Admetos, softly and decisively,
Of the altercation. Herakles forbore:
1190 And the king bade a servant lead the way,
Open the guest-rooms ranged remote from view
O' the main hall; tell the functionaries, next,
They had to furnish forth a plenteous feast,
And then shut close the doors o' the hall, midway,
'Because it is not proper friends who feast
Should hear a groaning or be grieved,' quoth he.

Whereat the hero, who was truth itself,
Let out the smile again, repressed awhile
Like fountain-brilliance one forbids to play.
1200 He did too many grandnesses, to note
Much in the meaner things about his path:
And stepping there, with face towards the sun,
Stopped seldom to pluck weeds or ask their names.
Therefore he took Admetos at the word:
This trouble must not hinder any more

A true heart from good will and pleasant ways.
And so, the great arm, which had slain the snake,
Strained his friend's head a moment in embrace
On that broad breast beneath the lion's hide,
1210 Till the king's cheek winced at the thick rough gold;
And then strode off, with who had care of him,
To the remote guest-chamber: glad to give
Poor flesh and blood their respite and relief
In the interval 'twixt fight and fight again –
All for the world's sake. Our eyes followed him,
Be sure, till those mid-doors shut us outside.
The king, too, watched great Herakles go off
All faith, love, and obedience to a friend.

And when they questioned him, the simple ones,
1220 'What dost thou? Such calamity to face,
Lies full before thee – and thou art so bold
As play the host, Admetos? Hast thy wits?'
He replied calmly to each chiding tongue:
'But if from house and home I forced away
A coming guest, wouldst thou have praised me more?
No, truly! since calamity were mine,
Nowise diminished; while I showed myself
Unhappy and inhospitable too:
So adding to my ills this other ill,
1230 That mine were styled a stranger-hating house.
Myself have ever found this man the best
Of entertainers when I went his way
To parched and thirsty Argos.'
                                    'If so be –
Why didst thou hide what destiny was here,
When one came that was kindly, as thou say'st?'

'He never would have willed to cross my door
Had he known aught of my calamities.
And probably to some of you I seem
Unwise enough in doing what I do;
1240 Such will scarce praise me: but these halls of mine
Know not to drive off and dishonour guests.'

And so, the duty done, he turned once more
To go and busy him about his dead.
As for the sympathizers left to muse,
There was a change, a new light thrown on things,
Contagion from the magnanimity
O' the man whose life lay on his hand so light,
As up he stepped, pursuing duty still
'Higher and harder,' as he laughed and said.
1250 Somehow they found no folly now in the act
They blamed erewhile: Admetos' private grief
Shrank to a somewhat pettier obstacle
I' the way o' the world: they saw good days had been,
And good days, peradventure, still might be,
Now that they overlooked the present cloud
Heavy upon the palace opposite.
And soon the thought took words and music thus.

'Harbour of many a stranger, free to friend,
Ever and always, O thou house o' the man
1260 We mourn for! Thee, Apollon's very self,
The lyric Puthian, deigned inhabit once,
Become a shepherd here in thy domains,
And pipe, adown the winding hill-side paths,
Pastoral marriage-poems to thy flocks
At feed: while with them fed in fellowship,
Through joy i' the music, spot-skin lynxes; ay,
And lions too, the bloody company,
Came, leaving Othrus' dell; and round thy lyre,
Phoibos, there danced the speckle-coated fawn,
1270 Pacing on lightsome fetlock past the pines
Tress-topped, the creature's natural boundary,
Into the open everywhere; such heart
Had she within her, beating joyous beats,
At the sweet reassurance of thy song!
Therefore the lot o' the master is, to live
In a home multitudinous with herds,
Along by the fair-flowing Boibian lake,
Limited, that ploughed land and pasture-plain,
Only where stand the sun's steeds, stabled west
1280 I' the cloud, by that mid-air which makes the clime
Of those Molossoi: and he rules as well
O'er the Aigaian, up to Pelion's shore, –

Sea-stretch without a port! Such lord have we:
And here he opens house now, as of old,
Takes to the heart of it a guest again:
Though moist the eyelid of the master, still
Mourning his dear wife's body, dead but now!'

And they admired: nobility of soul
Was self-impelled to reverence, they saw:
1290 The best men ever prove the wisest too:
Something instinctive guides them still aright.
And on each soul this boldness settled now,
That one, who reverenced the Gods so much,
Would prosper yet: (or – I could wish it ran –
Who venerates the Gods, i' the main will still
Practise things honest though obscure to judge).
They ended, for Admetos entered now;
Having disposed all duteously indoors,
He came into the outside world again,
1300 Quiet as ever: but a quietude
Bent on pursuing its descent to truth,
As who must grope until he gain the ground
O' the dungeon doomed to be his dwelling now.
Already high o'er head was piled the dusk,
When something pushed to stay his downward step,
Pluck back despair just reaching its repose.
He would have bidden the kind presence there
Observe that, – since the corpse was coming out,
Cared for in all things that befit the case,
1310 Carried aloft, in decency and state,
To the last burial place and burning pile, –
'Twere proper friends addressed, as custom prompts,
Alkestis bound on her last journeying.

'Ay, for we see thy father' they subjoined
'Advancing as the agèd foot best may;
His servants, too: each bringing in his hand
Adornments for thy wife, all pomp that's due
To the downward-dwelling people.' And in truth,
By slow procession till they filled the stage,
1320 Came Pheres, and his following, and their gifts.
You see, the worst of the interruption was,
It plucked back, with an over-hasty hand,

Admetos from descending to the truth,
(I told you) – put him on the brink again,
Full i' the noise and glare where late he stood:
With no fate fallen and irrevocable,
But all things subject still to chance and change:
And that chance – life, and that change – happiness.
And with the low strife came the little mind:
1330 He was once more the man might gain so much,
Life too and wife too, would his friends but help!
All he felt now was that there faced him one
Supposed the likeliest, in emergency,
To help: and help, by mere self-sacrifice
So natural, it seemed as if the sire
Must needs lie open still to argument,
Withdraw the rash decision, not to die
But rather live, though death would save his son: –
Argument like the ignominious grasp
1340 O' the drowner whom his fellow grasps as fierce,
Each marvelling that the other needs must hold
Head out of water, though friend choke thereby.

And first the father's salutation fell.
Burthened, he came, in common with his child,
Who lost, none would gainsay, a good chaste spouse:
Yet such things must be borne, though hard to bear.
'So, take this tribute of adornment, deep
In the earth let it descend along with her!
Behoves we treat the body with respect
1350 – Of one who died, at least, to save thy life,
Kept me from being childless, nor allowed
That I, bereft of thee, should peak and pine
In melancholy age! she, for the sex,
All of her sisters, put in evidence,
By daring such a feat, that female life
Might prove more excellent than men suppose.
O thou Alkestis!' out he burst in fine,
'Who, while thou savedst this my son, didst raise
Also myself from sinking, – hail to thee!
1360 Well be it with thee even in the house
Of Hades! I maintain, if mortals must
Marry, this sort of marriage is the sole
Permitted those among them who are wise!'

So his oration ended. Like hates like:
Accordingly Admetos, – full i' the face
Of Pheres, his true father, outward shape
And inward fashion, body matching soul, –
Saw just himself when years should do their work
And reinforce the selfishness inside
1370 Until it pushed the last disguise away:
As when the liquid metal cools i' the mould,
Stands forth a statue: bloodless, hard, cold bronze.
So, in old Pheres, young Admetos showed,
Pushed to completion: and a shudder ran,
And his repugnance soon had vent in speech:
Glad to escape outside, nor, pent within,
Find itself there fit food for exercise.

'Neither to this interment called by me
Comest thou, nor thy presence I account
1380 Among the covetable proofs of love.
As for thy tribute of adornment, – no!
Ne'er shall she don it, ne'er in debt to thee
Be buried! What is thine, that keep thou still!
Then it behoved thee to commiserate
When I was perishing: but thou – who stood'st
Foot-free o' the snare, wast acquiescent then
That I, the young, should die, not thou, the old –
Wilt thou lament this corpse thyself hast slain?
Thou wast not, then, true father to this flesh;
1390 Nor she, who makes profession of my birth
And styles herself my mother, neither she
Bore me: but, come of slave's blood, I was cast
Stealthily 'neath the bosom of thy wife!
Thou showedst, put to touch, the thing thou art,
Nor I esteem myself born child of thee!
Otherwise, thine is the preëminence
O'er all the world in cowardice of soul:
Who, being the old man thou art, arrived
Where life should end, didst neither will nor dare
1400 Die for thy son, but left the task to her,
The alien woman, whom I well might think
Own, only mother both and father too!
And yet a fair strife had been thine to strive,
– Dying for thy own child; and brief for thee

In any case, the rest of time to live;
While I had lived, and she, our rest of time,
Nor I been left to groan in solitude.
Yet certainly all things which happy man
Ought to experience, thy experience grasped.
1410 Thou wast a ruler through the bloom of youth,
And I was son to thee, recipient due
Of sceptre and demesne, – no need to fear
That dying thou shouldst leave an orphan house
For strangers to despoil. Nor yet wilt thou
Allege that as dishonouring, forsooth,
Thy length of days, I gave thee up to die, –
I, who have held thee in such reverence!
And in exchange for it, such gratitude
Thou, father, – thou award'st me, mother mine!
1420 Go, lose no time, then, in begetting sons
Shall cherish thee in age, and, when thou diest,
Deck up and lay thee out as corpses claim!
For never I, at least, with this my hand
Will bury thee: it is myself am dead
So far as lies in thee. But if I light
Upon another saviour, and still see
The sunbeam, – his, the child I call myself,
His, the old age that claims my cherishing.
How vainly do these aged pray for death,
1430 Abuse the slow drag of senility!
But should death step up, nobody inclines
To die, nor age is now the weight it was!'

You see what all this poor pretentious talk
Tried at, – how weakness strove to hide itself
In bluster against weakness, – the loud word
To hide the little whisper, not so low
Already in that heart beneath those lips!
Ha, could it be, who hated cowardice
Stood confessed craven, and who lauded so
1440 Self-immolating love, himself had pushed
The loved one to the altar in his place?
Friends interposed, would fain stop further play
O' the sharp-edged tongue: they felt love's champion here
Had left an undefended point or two,
The antagonist might profit by; bade 'Pause!

Enough the present sorrow! Nor, O son,
Whet thus against thyself thy father's soul!'

Ay, but old Pheres was the stouter stuff!
Admetos, at the flintiest of the heart,
1450 Had so much soft in him as held a fire:
The other was all iron, clashed from flint
Its fire, but shed no spark and showed no bruise.
Did Pheres crave instruction as to facts?
He came, content, the ignoble word, for him,
Should lurk still in the blackness of each breast,
As sleeps the water-serpent half surmised:
Not brought up to the surface at a bound,
By one touch of the idly-probing spear,
Reed-like against unconquerable scale.
1460 He came pacific, rather, as strength should,
Bringing the decent praise, the due regret,
And each banality prescribed of old.
Did he commence 'Why let her die for you?'
And rouse the coiled and quiet ugliness
'What is so good to man as man's own life?'
No: but the other did: and, for his pains,
Out, full in face of him, the venom leapt.

'And whom dost thou make bold, son – Ludian slave,
Or Phrugian whether, money made thy ware,
1470 To drive at with revilings? Know'st thou not
I, a Thessalian, from Thessalian sire
Spring and am born legitimately free?
Too arrogant art thou; and, youngster words
Casting against me, having had thy fling,
Thou goest not off as all were ended so!
I gave thee birth indeed and mastership
I' the mansion, brought thee up to boot: there ends
My owing, nor extends to die for thee!
Never did I receive it as a law
1480 Hereditary, no, nor Greek at all,
That sires in place of sons were bound to die.
For, to thy sole and single self wast thou
Born, with whatever fortune, good or bad;
Such things as bear bestowment, those thou hast;
Already ruling widely, broad-lands, too,

Doubt not but I shall leave thee in due time:
For why? My father left me them before.
Well then, where wrong I thee? – of what defraud?
Neither do thou die for this man, myself,
Nor let him die for thee! – is all I beg.   1490
Thou joyest seeing daylight: dost suppose
Thy father joys not too? Undoubtedly,
Long I account the time to pass below,
And brief my span of days; yet sweet the same:
Is it otherwise to thee who, impudent,
Didst fight off this same death, and livest now
Through having sneaked past fate apportioned thee,
And slain thy wife so? Cryest cowardice
On me, I wonder, thou – whom, poor poltroon,
A very woman worsted, daring death   1500
Just for the sake of thee, her handsome spark?
Shrewdly hast thou contrived how not to die
For evermore now: 'tis but still persuade
The wife, for the time being, to take thy place!
What, and thy friends who would not do the like,
These dost thou carp at, craven thus thyself?
Crouch and be silent, craven! Comprehend
That, if thou lovest so that life of thine,
Why, everybody loves his own life too:
So, good words, henceforth! If thou speak us ill,   1510
Many and true an ill thing shalt thou hear!'

There you saw leap the hydra at full length!
Only, the old kept glorying the more,
The more the portent thus uncoiled itself,
Whereas the young man shuddered head to foot,
And shrank from kinship with the creature. Why
Such horror, unless what he hated most,
Vaunting itself outside, might fairly claim
Acquaintance with the counterpart at home?
I would the Chorus here had plucked up heart,   1520
Spoken out boldly and explained the man,
If not to men, to Gods. That way, I think,
Sophokles would have led their dance and song.
Here, they said simply 'Too much evil spoke
On both sides!' As the young before, so now
They bade the old man leave abusing thus.

'Let him speak, – I have spoken!' said the youth:
And so died out the wrangle by degrees
In wretched bickering. 'If thou wince at fact,
1530 Behoved thee not prove faulty to myself!'

'Had I died for thee I had faulted more!'

'All's one, then, for youth's bloom and age to die?'

'Our duty is to live one life, not two!'

'Go then, and outlive Zeus, for aught I care!'

'What, curse thy parents with no sort of cause?'

'Curse, truly! All thou lovest is long life!'

'And dost not thou, too, all for love of life,
Carry out now, in place of thine, this corpse?'

'Monument, rather, of thy cowardice,
1540 Thou worst one!'
                    'Not for me she died, I hope!
That, thou wilt hardly say!'
                              'No, simply this:
Would, some day, thou mayst come to need myself!'

'Meanwhile, woo many wives – the more will die!'

'And so shame thee who never dared the like!'

'Dear is this light o' the sun-god – dear, I say!'

'Proper conclusion for a beast to draw!'

'One thing is certain: there's no laughing now,
As out thou bearest the poor dead old man!'

'Die when thou wilt, thou wilt die infamous!'

1550 'And once dead, whether famed or infamous,
I shall not care!'

                    'Alas and yet again!
How full is age of impudency!'
                                        'True!
Thou couldst not call thy young wife impudent:
She was found foolish merely.'
                                    'Get thee gone!
And let me bury this my dead!'
                                    'I go.
Thou buriest her whom thou didst murder first;
Whereof there's some account to render yet
Those kinsfolk by the marriage-side! I think,
Brother Akastos may be classed with me,
1560 Among the beasts, not men, if he omit
Avenging upon thee his sister's blood!'

'Go to perdition, with thy housemate too!
Grow old all childlessly, with child alive,
Just as ye merit! for to me, at least,
Beneath the same roof ne'er do ye return.
And did I need by heralds' help renounce
The ancestral hearth, I had renounced the same!
But we – since this woe, lying at our feet
I' the path, is to be borne – let us proceed
1570 And lay the body on the pyre.'
                                    I think,
What, through this wretched wrangle, kept the man
From seeing clear – beside the cause I gave –
Was, that the woe, himself described as full
I' the path before him, there did really lie –
Not roll into the abyss of dead and gone.
How, with Alkestis present, calmly crowned,
Was she so irrecoverable yet –
The bird, escaped, that's just on bough above,
The flower, let flutter half-way down the brink?
1580 Not so detached seemed lifelessness from life
But – one dear stretch beyond all straining yet –
And he might have her at his heart once more,
When, in the critical minute, up there comes
The father and the fact, to trifle time!

'To the pyre!' an instinct prompted: pallid face,
And passive arm and pointed foot, when these
No longer shall absorb the sight, O friends,
Admetos will begin to see indeed
Who the true foe was, where the blows should fall!

1590   So, the old selfish Pheres went his way,
Case-hardened as he came; and left the youth,
(Only half-selfish now, since sensitive)
To go on learning by a light the more,
As friends moved off, renewing dirge the while:

'Unhappy in thy daring! Noble dame,
Best of the good, farewell! With favouring face
May Hermes the infernal, Hades too,
Receive thee! And if there, – ay, there, – some touch
Of further dignity await the good,
1600   Sharing with them, mayst thou sit throned by her
The Bride of Hades, in companionship!'

Wherewith, the sad procession wound away,
Made slowly for the suburb sepulchre.
And lo, – while still one's heart, in time and tune,
Paced after that symmetric step of Death
Mute-marching, to the mind's eye, at the head
O' the mourners – one hand pointing out their path
With the long pale terrific sword we saw,
The other leading, with grim tender grace,
1610   Alkestis quieted and consecrate, –
Lo, life again knocked laughing at the door!
The world goes on, goes ever, in and through,
And out again o' the cloud. We faced about,
Fronted the palace where the mid-hall-gate
Opened – not half, nor half of half, perhaps –
Yet wide enough to let out light and life,
And warmth and bounty and hope and joy, at once.
Festivity burst wide, fruit rare and ripe
Crushed in the mouth of Bacchos, pulpy-prime,
1620   All juice and flavour, save one single seed
Duly ejected from the God's nice lip,
Which lay o' the red edge, blackly visible –
To wit, a certain ancient servitor:

On whom the festal jaws o' the palace shut,
So, there he stood, a much-bewildered man.
Stupid? Nay, but sagacious in a sort:
Learned, life long, i' the first outside of things,
Though bat for blindness to what lies beneath
And needs a nail-scratch ere 'tis laid you bare.
1630 This functionary was the trusted one
We saw deputed by Admetos late
To lead in Herakles and help him, soul
And body, to such snatched repose, snapped-up
Sustainment, as might do away the dust
O' the last encounter, knit each nerve anew
For that next onset sure to come at cry
O' the creature next assailed, – nay, should it prove
Only the creature that came forward now
To play the critic upon Herakles!

1640 'Many the guests' – so he soliloquized
In musings burdensome to breast before,
When it seemed not too prudent tongue should wag –
'Many, and from all quarters of this world,
The guests I now have known frequent our house,
For whom I spread the banquet; but than this,
Never a worse one did I yet receive
At the hearth here! One who seeing, first of all,
The master's sorrow, entered gate the same,
And had the hardihood to house himself.
1650 Did things stop there! But, modest by no means,
He took what entertainment lay to hand,
Knowing of our misfortune, – did we fail
In aught of the fit service, urged us serve
Just as a guest expects! And in his hands
Taking the ivied goblet, drinks and drinks
The unmixed product of black mother-earth,
Until the blaze o' the wine went round about
And warmed him: then he crowns with myrtle sprigs
His head, and howls discordance – twofold lay
1660 Was thereupon for us to listen to –
This fellow singing, namely, nor restrained
A jot by sympathy with sorrows here –
While we o' the household mourned our mistress – mourned,
That is to say, in silence – never showed

The eyes, which we kept wetting, to the guest –
For there Admetos was imperative.
And so, here am I helping make at home
A guest, some fellow ripe for wickedness,
Robber or pirate, while she goes her way
1670 Out of our house: and neither was it mine
To follow in procession, nor stretch forth
Hand, wave my lady dear a last farewell,
Lamenting who to me and all of us
Domestics was a mother: myriad harms
She used to ward away from everyone,
And mollify her husband's ireful mood.
I ask then, do I justly hate or no
This guest, this interloper on our grief?'

'Hate him and justly!' Here's the proper judge
1680 Of what is due to the house from Herakles!
This man of much experience saw the first
O' the feeble duckings-down at destiny,
When King Admetos went his rounds, poor soul,
A-begging somebody to be so brave
As die for one afraid to die himself –
'Thou, friend? Thou, love? Father or mother, then!
None of you? What, Alkestis must Death catch?
O best of wives, one woman in the world!
But nowise droop: our prayers may still assist:
1690 Let us try sacrifice: if those avail
Nothing and Gods avert their countenance,
Why, deep and durable our grief will be!'
Whereat the house, this worthy at its head,
Re-echoed 'deep and durable our grief!'
This sage, who justly hated Herakles,
Did he suggest once 'Rather I than she!'
Admonish the Turannos – 'Be a man!
Bear thine own burden, never think to thrust
Thy fate upon another and thy wife!
1700 It were a dubious gain could death be doomed
That other, and no passionatest plea
Of thine, to die instead, have force with fate;
Seeing thou lov'st Alkestis: what were life
Unlighted by the loved one? But to live –
Not merely live unsolaced by some thought,

Some word so poor – yet solace all the same –
As "Thou i' the sepulchre, Alkestis, say!
Would I, or would not I, to save thy life,
Die, and die on, and die for evermore?"

1710 No! but to read red-written up and down
The world "This is the sunshine, this the shade,
This is some pleasure of earth, sky or sea,
Due to that other, dead that thou mayst live!"
Such were a covetable gain to thee?
Go die, fool, and be happy while 'tis time!'
One word of counsel in this kind, methinks,
Had fallen to better purpose than Ai, ai,
Pheu, pheu, e, papai, and a pother of praise
O' the best, best, best one! Nothing was to hate

1720 In King Admetos, Pheres, and the rest
O' the household down to his heroic self!
This was the one thing hateful: Herakles
Had flung into the presence, frank and free,
Out from the labour into the repose,
Ere out again and over head and ears
I' the heart of labour, all for love of men:
Making the most o' the minute, that the soul
And body, strained to height a minute since,
Might lie relaxed in joy, this breathing-space,

1730 For man's sake more than ever; till the bow,
Restrung o' the sudden, at first cry for help,
Should send some unimaginable shaft
True to the aim and shatteringly through
The plate-mail of a monster, save man so.
He slew the pest o' the marish yesterday:
Tomorrow he would bit the flame-breathed steeds
That fed on man's-flesh: and this day between –
Because he held it natural to die,
And fruitless to lament a thing past cure,

1740 So, took his fill of food, wine, song and flowers,
Till the new labour claimed him soon enough, –
'Hate him and justly!'
                              True, Charopé mine!
The man surmised not Herakles lay hid
I' the guest; or, knowing it, was ignorant
That still his lady lived – for Herakles;
Or else judged lightness needs must indicate

This or the other caitiff quality:
And therefore – had been right if not so wrong!
For who expects the sort of him will scratch
1750 A nail's depth, scrape the surface just to see
What peradventure underlies the same?

So, he stood petting up his puny hate,
Parent-wise, proud of the ill-favoured babe.
Not long! A great hand, careful lest it crush,
Startled him on the shoulder: up he stared,
And over him, who stood but Herakles!
There smiled the mighty presence, all one smile
And no touch more of the world-weary God,
Through the brief respite. Just a garland's grace
1760 About the brow, a song to satisfy
Head, heart and breast, and trumpet-lips at once,
A solemn draught of true religious wine,
And, – how should I know? – half a mountain goat
Torn up and swallowed down, – the feast was fierce
But brief: all cares and pains took wing and flew,
Leaving the hero ready to begin
And help mankind, whatever woe came next,
Even though what came next should be naught more
Than the mean querulous mouth o' the man, remarked
1770 Pursing its grievance up till patience failed
And the sage needs must rush out, as we saw
To sulk outside and pet his hate in peace.
By no means would the Helper have it so:
He who was just about to handle brutes
In Thrace, and bit the jaws which breathed the flame, –
Well, if a good laugh and a jovial word
Could bridle age which blew bad humours forth,
That were a kind of help, too!
                              'Thou, there!' hailed
This grand benevolence the ungracious one –
1780 'Why look'st so solemn and so thought-absorbed?
To guests a servant should not sour-faced be,
But do the honours with a mind urbane.
While thou, contrariwise, beholding here
Arrive thy master's comrade, hast for him
A churlish visage, all one beetle-brow –
Having regard to grief that's out-of-door!

Come hither, and so get to grow more wise!
Things mortal – know'st the nature that they have?
No, I imagine! whence could knowledge spring?
1790 Give ear to me, then! For all flesh to die,
Is nature's due; nor is there any one
Of mortals with assurance he shall last
The coming morrow: for, what's born of chance
Invisibly proceeds the way it will,
Not to be learned, no fortune-teller's prize.
This, therefore, having heard and known through me,
Gladden thyself! Drink! Count the day-by-day
Existence thine, and all the other – chance!
Ay, and pay homage also to by far
1800 The sweetest of divinities for man,
Kupris! Benignant Goddess will she prove!
But as for aught else, leave and let things be!
And trust my counsel, if I seem to speak
To purpose – as I do, apparently.
Wilt not thou, then, – discarding overmuch
Mournfulness, do away with this shut door,
Come drink along with me, be-garlanded
This fashion? Do so, and – I well know what –
From this stern mood, this shrunk-up state of mind,
1810 The pit-pat fall o' the flagon-juice down throat
Soon will dislodge thee from bad harbourage!
Men being mortal should think mortal-like:
Since to your solemn, brow-contracting sort,
All of them, – so I lay down law at least, –
Life is not truly life but misery.'

Whereto the man with softened surliness:
'We know as much: but deal with matters, now,
Hardly befitting mirth and revelry.'

'No intimate, this woman that is dead:
1820 Mourn not too much! For, those o' the house itself,
Thy masters live, remember!'

                              'Live indeed?
Ah, thou know'st naught o' the woe within these walls!'

'I do – unless thy master spoke me false
Somehow!'
      'Ay, ay, too much he loves a guest,
Too much, that master mine!' so muttered he.

'Was it improper he should treat me well,
Because an alien corpse was in the way?'

'No alien, but most intimate indeed!'

'Can it be, some woe was, he told me not?'

1830   'Farewell and go thy way! Thy cares for thee –
To us, our master's sorrow is a care.'

'This word begins no tale of alien woe!'

'Had it been other woe than intimate,
I could have seen thee feast, nor felt amiss.'

'What! have I suffered strangely from my host?'

'Thou cam'st not at a fit reception-time:
With sorrow here beforehand: and thou seest
Shorn hair, black robes.'
        'But who is it that's dead?
Some child gone? or the agèd sire perhaps?'

1840   'Admetos' wife, then! she has perished, guest!'

'How sayest? And did ye house me, all the same?'

'Ay: for he had thee in that reverence
He dared not turn thee from his door away!'

'O hapless, and bereft of what a mate!'

'All of us now are dead, not she alone!'

'But I divined it! seeing, as I did,
His eye that ran with tears, his close-clipt hair,
His countenance! Though he persuaded me,

Saying it was a stranger's funeral
1850 He went with to the grave: against my wish,
He forced on me that I should enter doors,
Drink in the hall o' the hospitable man
Circumstanced so! And do I revel yet
With wreath on head? But – thou to hold thy peace
Nor tell me what a woe oppressed my friend!
Where is he gone to bury her? Where am I
To go and find her?'
                              'By the road that leads
Straight to Larissa, thou wilt see the tomb,
Out of the suburb, a carved sepulchre.'

1860 So said he, and therewith dismissed himself
Inside to his lamenting: somewhat soothed,
However, that he had adroitly spoilt
The mirth of the great creature: oh, he marked
The movement of the mouth, how lip pressed lip,
And either eye forgot to shine, as, fast,
He plucked the chaplet from his forehead, dashed
The myrtle-sprays down, trod them underfoot!
And all the joy and wonder of the wine
Withered away, like fire from off a brand
1870 The wind blows over – beacon though it be,
Whose merry ardour only meant to make
Somebody all the better for its blaze,
And save lost people in the dark: quenched now!

Not long quenched! As the flame, just hurried off
The brand's edge, suddenly renews its bite,
Tasting some richness caked i' the core o' the tree, –
Pine, with a blood that's oil, – and triumphs up
Pillar-wise to the sky and saves the world:
So, in a spasm and splendour of resolve,
1880 All at once did the God surmount the man.

'O much-enduring heart and hand of mine!
Now show what sort of son she bore to Zeus,
That daughter of Elektruon, Tiruns' child,
Alkmené! for that son must needs save now
The just-dead lady: ay, establish here
I' the house again Alkestis, bring about

Comfort and succour to Admetos so!
I will go lie in wait for Death, black-stoled
King of the corpses! I shall find him, sure,
1890   Drinking, beside the tomb, o' the sacrifice:
And if I lie in ambuscade, and leap
Out of my lair, and seize – encircle him
Till one hand join the other round about –
There lives not who shall pull him out from me,
Rib-mauled, before he let the woman go!
But even say I miss the booty, – say,
Death comes not to the boltered blood, – why then,
Down go I, to the unsunned dwelling-place
Of Koré and the king there, – make demand,
1900   Confident I shall bring Alkestis back,
So as to put her in the hands of him
My host, that housed me, never drove me off:
Though stricken with sore sorrow, hid the stroke,
Being a noble heart and honouring me!
Who of Thessalians, more than this man, loves
The stranger? Who, that now inhabits Greece?
Wherefore he shall not say the man was vile
Whom he befriended, – native noble heart!'

So, one look upward, as if Zeus might laugh
1910   Approval of his human progeny, –
One summons of the whole magnific frame,
Each sinew to its service, – up he caught,
And over shoulder cast, the lion-shag,
Let the club go, – for had he not those hands?
And so went striding off, on that straight way
Leads to Larissa and the suburb tomb.
Gladness be with thee, Helper of our world!
I think this is the authentic sign and seal
Of Godship, that it ever waxes glad,
1920   And more glad, until gladness blossoms, bursts
Into a rage to suffer for mankind,
And recommence at sorrow: drops like seed
After the blossom, ultimate of all.
Say, does the seed scorn earth and seek the sun?
Surely it has no other end and aim
Than to drop, once more die into the ground,

Taste cold and darkness and oblivion there:
And thence rise, tree-like grow through pain to joy,
More joy and most joy, – do man good again.

1930 So, to the struggle off strode Herakles.
When silence closed behind the lion-garb,
Back came our dull fact settling in its place,
Though heartiness and passion half-dispersed
The inevitable fate. And presently
In came the mourners from the funeral,
One after one, until we hoped the last
Would be Alkestis and so end our dream.
Could they have really left Alkestis lone
I' the wayside sepulchre! Home, all save she!
1940 And when Admetos felt that it was so,
By the stand-still: when he lifted head and face
From the two hiding hands and peplos' fold,
And looked forth, knew the palace, knew the hills,
Knew the plains, knew the friendly frequence there,
And no Alkestis any more again,
Why, the whole woe billow-like broke on him.

'O hateful entry, hateful countenance
O' the widowed halls!' – he moaned. 'What was to be?
Go there? Stay here? Speak, not speak? All was now
1950 Mad and impossible alike; one way
And only one was sane and safe – to die:
Now he was made aware how dear is death,
How lovable the dead are, how the heart
Yearns in us to go hide where they repose,
When we find sunbeams do no good to see,
Nor earth rests rightly where our footsteps fall.
His wife had been to him the very pledge,
Sun should be sun, earth – earth; the pledge was robbed,
Pact broken, and the world was left no world.'
1960 He stared at the impossible mad life:
Stood, while they urged 'Advance – advance! Go deep
Into the utter dark, thy palace-core!'
They tried what they called comfort, 'touched the quick
Of the ulceration in his soul,' he said,
With memories, – 'once thy joy was thus and thus!'

True comfort were to let him fling himself
Into the hollow grave o' the tomb, and so
Let him lie dead along with all he loved.

One bade him note that his own family
1970 Boasted a certain father whose sole son,
Worthy bewailment, died: and yet the sire
Bore stoutly up against the blow and lived;
For all that he was childless now, and prone
Already to grey hairs, far on in life.
Could such a good example miss effect?
Why fix foot, stand so, staring at the house,
Why not go in, as that wise kinsman would?

'O that arrangement of the house I know!
How can I enter, how inhabit thee
1980 Now that one cast of fortune changes all?
Oh me, for much divides the then from now!
Then – with those pine-tree torches, Pelian pomp
And marriage-hymns, I entered, holding high
The hand of my dear wife; while many-voiced
The revelry that followed me and her
That's dead now, – friends felicitating both,
As who were lofty-lineaged, each of us
Born of the best, two wedded and made one;
Now – wail is wedding-chant's antagonist,
1990 And, for white peplos, stoles in sable state
Herald my way to the deserted couch!'

The one word more they ventured was 'This grief
Befell thee witless of what sorrow means,
Close after prosperous fortune: but, reflect!
Thou hast saved soul and body. Dead, thy wife –
Living, the love she left. What's novel here?
Many the man, from whom Death long ago
Loosed the life-partner!'
                              Then Admetos spoke:
Turned on the comfort, with no tears, this time.
2000 He was beginning to be like his wife.
I told you of that pressure to the point,
Word slow pursuing word in monotone,

Alkestis spoke with; so Admetos, now,
Solemnly bore the burden of the truth.
And as the voice of him grew, gathered strength,
And groaned on, and persisted to the end,
We felt how deep had been descent in grief,
And with what change he came up now to light,
And left behind such littleness as tears.

2010 'Friends, I account the fortune of my wife
Happier than mine, though it seem otherwise:
For, her indeed no grief will ever touch,
And she from many a labour pauses now,
Renowned one! Whereas I, who ought not live,
But do live, by evading destiny,
Sad life am I to lead, I learn at last!
For how shall I bear going in-doors here?
Accosting whom? By whom saluted back,
Shall I have joyous entry? Whither turn?
2020 Inside, the solitude will drive me forth,
When I behold the empty bed – my wife's –
The seat she used to sit upon, the floor
Unsprinkled as when dwellers loved the cool,
The children that will clasp my knees about,
Cry for their mother back: these servants too
Moaning for what a guardian they have lost!
Inside my house such circumstance awaits.
Outside, – Thessalian people's marriage-feasts
And gatherings for talk will harass me,
2030 With overflow of women everywhere;
It is impossible I look on them –
Familiars of my wife and just her age!
And then, whoever is a foe of mine,
And lights on me – why, this will be his word –
"See there! alive ignobly, there he skulks
That played the dastard when it came to die,
And, giving her he wedded, in exchange,
Kept himself out of Hades safe and sound,
The coward! Do you call that creature – man?
2040 He hates his parents for declining death,
Just as if he himself would gladly die!"
This sort of reputation shall I have,

Beside the other ills enough in store.
Ill-famed, ill-faring, – what advantage, friends,
Do you perceive I gain by life for death?'

That was the truth. Vexed waters sank to smooth:
'Twas only when the last of bubbles broke,
The latest circlet widened all away
And left a placid level, that up swam
2050 To the surface the drowned truth, in dreadful change.
So, through the quiet and submission, – ay,
Spite of some strong words – (for you miss the tone)
The grief was getting to be infinite –
Grief, friends fell back before. Their office shrank
To that old solace of humanity –
'Being born mortal, bear grief! Why born else?'
And they could only meditate anew.

'They, too, upborne by airy help of song,
And haply science, which can find the stars,
2060 Had searched the heights: had sounded depths as well
By catching much at books where logic lurked,
Yet nowhere found they aught could overcome
Necessity: not any medicine served,
Which Thrakian tablets treasure, Orphic voice
Wrote itself down upon: nor remedy
Which Phoibos gave to the Asklepiadai;
Cutting the roots of many a virtuous herb
To solace overburdened mortals. None!
Of this sole goddess, never may we go
2070 To altar nor to image: sacrifice
She hears not. All to pray for is – "Approach!
But, oh, no harder on me, awful one,
Than heretofore! Let life endure thee still!
For, whatsoever Zeus' nod decree, that same
In concert with thee hath accomplishment.
Iron, the very stuff o' the Chaluboi,
Thou, by sheer strength, dost conquer and subdue;
Nor, of that harsh abrupt resolve of thine,
Any relenting is there!"
                                        'O my king!
2080 Thee also, in the shackles of those hands,
Not to be shunned, the Goddess grasped! Yet, bear!

Since never wilt thou lead from underground
The dead ones, wail thy worst! If mortals die, –
The very children of immortals, too,
Dropped 'mid our darkness, these decay as sure!
Dear indeed was she while among us: dear,
Now she is dead, must she for ever be:
Thy portion was to clasp, within thy couch,
The noblest of all women as a wife.
2090   Nor be the tomb of her supposed some heap
That hides mortality: but like the Gods
Honoured, a veneration to a world
Of wanderers! Oft the wanderer, struck thereby,
Who else had sailed past in his merchant-ship,
Ay, he shall leave ship, land, long wind his way
Up to the mountain-summit, till there break
Speech forth "So, this was she, then, died of old
To save her husband! now, a deity
She bends above us. Hail, benignant one!
2100   Give good!" Such voices so will supplicate.

'But – can it be? Alkmené's offspring comes,
Admetos! – to thy house advances here!'

I doubt not, they supposed him decently
Dead somewhere in that winter world of Thrace –
Vanquished by one o' the Bistones, or else
Victim to some mad steed's voracity –
For did not friends prognosticate as much?
It were a new example to the point,
That 'children of immortals, dropped by stealth
2110   Into our darkness, die as sure as we!'
A case to quote and comfort people with:
But, as for lamentation, ai and pheu,
Right-minded subjects kept them for their lord.

Ay, he it was advancing! In he strode,
And took his stand before Admetos, – turned
Now by despair to such a quietude,
He neither raised his face nor spoke, this time,
The while his friend surveyed him steadily.
That friend looked rough with fighting: had he strained
2120   Worst brute to breast was ever strangled yet?

Somehow, a victory – for there stood the strength,
Happy, as always; something grave, perhaps;
The great vein-cordage on the fret-worked front,
Black-swollen, beaded yet with battle-dew
The yellow hair o' the hero! – his big frame
A-quiver with each muscle sinking back
Into the sleepy smooth it leaped from late.
Under the great guard of one arm, there leant
A shrouded something, live and woman-like,
2130 Propped by the heart-beats 'neath the lion-coat.
When he had finished his survey, it seemed,
The heavings of the heart began subside,
The helpful breath returned, and last the smile
Shone out, all Herakles was back again,
As the words followed the saluting hand.

'To friendly man, behoves we freely speak,
Admetos! – nor keep buried, deep in breast,
Blame we leave silent. I assuredly
Judged myself proper, if I should approach
2140 By accident calamities of thine,
To be demonstrably thy friend: but thou
Told'st me not of the corpse then claiming care,
That was thy wife's, but didst install me guest
I' the house here, as though busied with a grief
Indeed, but then, mere grief beyond thy gate:
And so, I crowned my head, and to the Gods
Poured my libations in thy dwelling-place,
With such misfortune round me. And I blame –
Certainly blame thee, having suffered thus!
2150 But still I would not pain thee, pained enough:
So let it pass! Wherefore I seek thee now,
Having turned back again though onward bound,
That I will tell thee. Take and keep for me
This woman, till I come thy way again,
Driving before me, having killed the king
O' the Bistones, that drove of Thrakian steeds:
In such case, give the woman back to me!
But should I fare, – as fare I fain would not,
Seeing I hope to prosper and return, –
2160 Then, I bequeath her as thy household slave.
She came into my hands with good hard toil!

For, what find I, when started on my course,
But certain people, a whole country-side,
Holding a wrestling-bout? as good to me
As a new labour: whence I took, and here
Come keeping with me, this, the victor's prize.
For, such as conquered in the easy work,
Gained horses which they drove away: and such
As conquered in the harder, – those who boxed
2170 And wrestled, – cattle; and, to crown the prize,
A woman followed. Chancing as I did,
Base were it to forego this fame and gain!
Well, as I said, I trust her to thy care:
No woman I have kidnapped, understand!
But good hard toil has done it: here I come!
Some day, who knows? even thou wilt praise the feat!'

Admetos raised his face and eyed the pair:
Then, hollowly and with submission, spoke,
And spoke again, and spoke time after time,
2180 When he perceived the silence of his friend
Would not be broken by consenting word.
As a tired slave goes adding stone to stone
Until he stop some current that molests,
So poor Admetos piled up argument
Vainly against the purpose all too plain
In that great brow acquainted with command.

'Nowise dishonouring, nor amid my foes
Ranking thee, did I hide my wife's ill fate;
But it were grief superimposed on grief,
2190 Shouldst thou have hastened to another home.
My own woe was enough for me to weep!
But, for this woman, – if it so may be, –
Bid some Thessalian, – I entreat thee, king! –
Keep her, – who has not suffered like myself!
Many of the Pheraioi welcome thee.
Be no reminder to me of my ills!
I could not, if I saw her come to live,
Restrain the tear! Inflict on me diseased
No new disease: woe bends me down enough!
2200 Then, where could she be sheltered in my house,
Female and young too? For that she is young,

The vesture and adornment prove. Reflect!
Should such an one inhabit the same roof
With men? And how, mixed up, a girl, with youths,
Shall she keep pure, in that case? No light task
To curb the May-day youngster, Herakles!
I only speak because of care for thee.
Or must I, in avoidance of such harm,
Make her to enter, lead her life within
2210 The chamber of the dead one, all apart?
How shall I introduce this other, couch
This where Alkestis lay? A double blame
I apprehend: first, from the citizens –
Lest some tongue of them taunt that I betray
My benefactress, fall into the snare
Of a new fresh face: then, the dead one's self, –
Will she not blame me likewise? Worthy, sure,
Of worship from me! circumspect my ways,
And jealous of a fault, are bound to be.
2220 But thou, – O woman, whosoe'er thou art, –
Know, thou hast all the form, art like as like
Alkestis, in the bodily shape! Ah me!
Take, – by the Gods, – this woman from my sight,
Lest thou undo me, the undone before!
Since I seem – seeing her – as if I saw
My own wife! And confusions cloud my heart,
And from my eyes the springs break forth! Ah me
Unhappy – how I taste for the first time
My misery in all its bitterness!'

2230 Whereat the friends conferred: 'The chance, in truth,
Was an untoward one – none said otherwise.
Still, what a God comes giving, good or bad,
That, one should take and bear with. Take her, then!'

Herakles, – not unfastening his hold
On that same misery, beyond mistake
Hoarse in the words, convulsive in the face, –
'I would that I had such a power,' said he,
'As to lead up into the light again
Thy very wife, and grant thee such a grace.'

2240 'Well do I know thou wouldst: but where the hope?
       There is no bringing back the dead to light.'

       'Be not extravagant in grief, no less!
       Bear it, by augury of better things!'

       ''Tis easier to advise "bear up," than bear!'

       'But how carve way i' the life that lies before,
       If bent on groaning ever for the past?'

       'I myself know that: but a certain love
       Allures me to the choice I shall not change.'

       'Ay, but, still loving dead ones, still makes weep.'

2250 'And let it be so! She has ruined me,
       And still more than I say: that answers all.'

       'Oh, thou hast lost a brave wife: who disputes?'

       'So brave a one – that he whom thou behold'st
       Will never more enjoy his life again!'

       'Time will assuage! The evil yet is young!'

       'Time, thou mayst say, will; if time mean – to die.'

       'A wife – the longing for new marriage-joys
       Will stop thy sorrow!'
                              'Hush, friend, – hold thy peace!
       What hast thou said! I could not credit ear!'

2260 'How then? Thou wilt not marry, then, but keep
       A widowed couch?'
                              'There is not anyone
       Of womankind shall couch with whom thou seest!'

       'Dost think to profit thus in any way
       The dead one?'
                              'Her, wherever she abide,
       My duty is to honour.'

                'And I praise –
Indeed I praise thee! Still, thou hast to pay
The price of it, in being held a fool!'

'Fool call me – only one name call me not!
Bridegroom!'
              'No: it was praise, I portioned thee,
2270 Of being good true husband to thy wife!'

'When I betray her, though she is no more,
May I die!'
          And the thing he said was true:
For out of Herakles a great glow broke.
There stood a victor worthy of a prize:
The violet-crown that withers on the brow
Of the half-hearted claimant. Oh, he knew
The signs of battle hard fought and well won,
This queller of the monsters! – knew his friend
Planted firm foot, now, on the loathly thing
2280 That was Admetos late! 'would die,' he knew,
Ere let the reptile raise its crest again.
If that was truth, why try the true friend more?

'Then, since thou canst be faithful to the death,
Take, deep into thy house, my dame!' smiled he.

'Not so! – I pray, by thy Progenitor!'

'Thou wilt mistake in disobeying me!'

'Obeying thee, I have to break my heart!'

'Obey me! Who knows but the favour done
May fall into its place as duty too?'

2290 So, he was humble, would decline no more
Bearing a burden: he just sighed 'Alas!
Wouldst thou hadst never brought this prize from game!'

'Yet, when I conquered there, thou conqueredst!'

'All excellently urged! Yet – spite of all,
Bear with me! let the woman go away!'

'She shall go, if needs must: but ere she go,
See if there *is* need!'
                        'Need there is! At least,
Except I make thee angry with me, so!'

'But I persist, because I have my spice
2300 Of intuition likewise: take the dame!'

'Be thou the victor, then! But certainly
Thou dost thy friend no pleasure in the act!'

'Oh, time will come when thou shalt praise me! Now –
Only obey!'
                'Then, servants, since my house
Must needs receive this woman, take her there!'

'I shall not trust this woman to the care
Of servants.'
                'Why, conduct her in, thyself,
If that seem preferable!'
                        'I prefer,
With thy good leave, to place her in thy hands!'

2310 'I would not touch her! Entry to the house –
That, I concede thee.'
                        'To thy sole right hand,
I mean to trust her!'
                        'King! Thou wrenchest this
Out of me by main force, if I submit!'

'Courage, friend! Come, stretch hand forth! Good! Now touch
The stranger-woman!'
                        'There! A hand I stretch –
As though it meant to cut off Gorgon's head!'

'Hast hold of her?'
                'Fast hold.'
                                'Why, then, hold fast
And have her! and, one day, asseverate

Thou wilt, I think, thy friend, the son of Zeus,
2320 He was the gentle guest to entertain!
Look at her! See if she, in any way,
Present thee with resemblance of thy wife!'

Ah, but the tears come, find the words at fault!
There is no telling how the hero twitched
The veil off: and there stood, with such fixed eyes
And such slow smile, Alkestis' silent self!
It was the crowning grace of that great heart,
To keep back joy: procrastinate the truth
Until the wife, who had made proof and found
2330 The husband wanting, might essay once more,
Hear, see, and feel him renovated now –
Able to do, now, all herself had done,
Risen to the height of her: so, hand in hand,
The two might go together, live and die.

Beside, when he found speech, you guess the speech.
He could not think he saw his wife again:
It was some mocking God that used the bliss
To make him mad! Till Herakles must help:
Assure him that no spectre mocked at all;
2340 He was embracing whom he buried once.
Still, – did he touch, might he address the true, –
True eye, true body of the true live wife?

And Herakles said, smiling, 'All was truth.
Spectre? Admetos had not made his guest
One who played ghost-invoker, or such cheat!
Oh, he might speak and have response, in time!
All heart could wish was gained now – life for death:
Only, the rapture must not grow immense:
Take care, nor wake the envy of the Gods!'

2350 'Oh thou, of greatest Zeus true son,' – so spoke
Admetos when the closing word must come,
'Go ever in a glory of success,
And save, that sire, his offspring to the end!
For thou hast – only thou – raised me and mine
Up again to this light and life!' Then asked
Tremblingly, how was trod the perilous path

Out of the dark into the light and life:
How it had happened with Alkestis there.

And Herakles said little, but enough –
2360 How he engaged in combat with that king
O' the demons: how the field of contest lay
By the tomb's self: how he sprang from ambuscade,
Captured Death, caught him in that pair of hands.

But all the time, Alkestis moved not once
Out of the set gaze and the silent smile;
And a cold fear ran through Admetos' frame:
'Why does she stand and front me, silent thus?'

Herakles solemnly replied 'Not yet
Is it allowable thou hear the things
2370 She has to tell thee; let evanish quite
That consecration to the lower Gods,
And on our upper world the third day rise!
Lead her in, meanwhile; good and true thou art,
Good, true, remain thou! Practise piety
To stranger-guests the old way! So, farewell!
Since forth I fare, fulfil my urgent task
Set by the king, the son of Sthenelos.'

Fain would Admetos keep that splendid smile
Ever to light him. 'Stay with us, thou heart!
2380 Remain our house-friend!'

                                    'At some other day!
Now, of necessity, I haste!' smiled he.

'But mayst thou prosper, go forth on a foot
Sure to return! Through all the tetrarchy
Command my subjects that they institute
Thanksgiving-dances for the glad event,
And bid each altar smoke with sacrifice!
For we are minded to begin a fresh
Existence, better than the life before;
Seeing I own myself supremely blest.'

2390   Whereupon all the friendly moralists
      Drew this conclusion: chirped, each beard to each:
      'Manifold are thy shapings, Providence!
      Many a hopeless matter Gods arrange.
      What we expected never came to pass:
      What we did not expect, Gods brought to bear;
      So have things gone, this whole experience through!'

      Ah, but if you had seen the play itself!
      They say, my poet failed to get the prize:
      Sophokles got the prize, – great name! They say,
2400   Sophokles also means to make a piece,
      Model a new Admetos, a new wife:
      Success to him! One thing has many sides.
      The great name! But no good supplants a good,
      Nor beauty undoes beauty. Sophokles
      Will carve and carry a fresh cup, brimful
      Of beauty and good, firm to the altar-foot,
      And glorify the Dionusiac shrine:
      Not clash against this crater in the place
      Where the God put it when his mouth had drained,
2410   To the last dregs, libation life-blood-like,
      And praised Euripides for evermore –
      The Human with his droppings of warm tears.

      Still, since one thing may have so many sides,
      I think I see how, – far from Sophokles, –
      You, I, or anyone might mould a new
      Admetos, new Alkestis. Ah, that brave
      Bounty of poets, the one royal race
      That ever was, or will be, in this world!
      They give no gift that bounds itself and ends
2420   I' the giving and the taking: theirs so breeds
      I' the heart and soul o' the taker, so transmutes
      The man who only was a man before,
      That he grows godlike in his turn, can give –
      He also: share the poets' privilege,
      Bring forth new good, new beauty, from the old.
      As though the cup that gave the wine, gave, too,
      The God's prolific giver of the grape,
      That vine, was wont to find out, fawn around

His footstep, springing still to bless the dearth,
2430 At bidding of a Mainad. So with me:
For I have drunk this poem, quenched my thirst,
Satisfied heart and soul – yet more remains!
Could we too make a poem? Try at least,
Inside the head, what shape the rose-mists take!

When God Apollon took, for punishment,
A mortal form and sold himself a slave
To King Admetos till a term should end, –
Not only did he make, in servitude,
Such music, while he fed the flocks and herds,
2440 As saved the pasturage from wrong or fright,
Curing rough creatures of ungentleness:
Much more did that melodious wisdom work
Within the heart o' the master: there, ran wild
Many a lust and greed that grow to strength
By preying on the native pity and care,
Would else, all undisturbed, possess the land.

And these, the God so tamed, with golden tongue,
That, in the plenitude of youth and power,
Admetos vowed himself to rule thenceforth
2450 In Pherai solely for his people's sake,
Subduing to such end each lust and greed
That dominates the natural charity.

And so the struggle ended. Right ruled might:
And soft yet brave, and good yet wise, the man
Stood up to be a monarch; having learned
The worth of life, life's worth would he bestow
On all whose lot was cast, to live or die,
As he determined for the multitude.
So stands a statue: pedestalled sublime,
2460 Only that it may wave the thunder off,
And ward, from winds that vex, a world below.

And then, – as if a whisper found its way
E'en to the sense o' the marble, – 'Vain thy vow!
The royalty of its resolve, that head
Shall hide within the dust ere day be done:
That arm, its outstretch of beneficence,

Shall have a speedy ending on the earth:
Lie patient, prone, while light some cricket leaps
And takes possession of the masterpiece,
2470 To sit, sing louder as more near the sun.
For why? A flaw was in the pedestal;
Who knows? A worm's work! Sapped, the certain fate
O' the statue is to fall, and thine to die!'

Whereat the monarch, calm, addressed himself
To die, but bitterly the soul outbroke –
'O prodigality of life, blind waste
I' the world, of power profuse without the will
To make life do its work, deserve its day!
My ancestors pursued their pleasure, poured
2480 The blood o' the people out in idle war,
Or took occasion of some weary peace
To bid men dig down deep or build up high,
Spend bone and marrow that the king might feast
Entrenched and buttressed from the vulgar gaze.
Yet they all lived, nay, lingered to old age:
As though Zeus loved that they should laugh to scorn
The vanity of seeking other ends
In rule than just the ruler's pastime. They
Lived; I must die.'

And, as some long last moan
2490 Of a minor suddenly is propped beneath
By note which, new-struck, turns the wail, that was,
In a wonder and a triumph, so
Began Alkestis: 'Nay, thou art to live!
The glory that, in the disguise of flesh,
Was helpful to our house, – he prophesied
The coming fate: whereon, I pleaded sore
That he, – I guessed a God, who to his couch
Amid the clouds must go and come again,
While we were darkling, – since he loved us both,
2500 He should permit thee, at whatever price,
To live and carry out to heart's content
Soul's purpose, turn each thought to very deed,
Nor let Zeus lose the monarch meant in thee.'

To which Apollon, with a sunset smile,
Sadly – 'And so should mortals arbitrate!
It were unseemly if they aped us Gods,
And, mindful of our chain of consequence,
Lost care of the immediate earthly link:
Forwent the comfort of life's little hour,
2510 In prospect of some cold abysmal blank
Alien eternity, – unlike the time
They know, and understand to practise with, –
No, – our eternity – no heart's blood, bright
And warm outpoured in its behoof, would tinge
Never so palely, warm a whit the more:
Whereas retained and treasured – left to beat
Joyously on, a life's length, in the breast
O' the loved and loving – it would throb itself
Through, and suffuse the earthly tenement,
2520 Transform it, even as your mansion here
Is love-transformed into a temple-home
Where I, a God, forget the Olumpian glow,
I' the feel of human richness like the rose:
Your hopes and fears, so blind and yet so sweet
With death about them. Therefore, well in thee
To look, not on eternity, but time:
To apprehend that, should Admetos die,
All, we Gods purposed in him, dies as sure:
That, life's link snapping, all our chain is lost.
2530 And yet a mortal glance might pierce, methinks,
Deeper into the seeming dark of things,
And learn, no fruit, man's life can bear, will fade:
Learn, if Admetos die now, so much more
Will pity for the frailness found in flesh,
Will terror at the earthly chance and change
Frustrating wisest scheme of noblest soul,
Will these go wake the seeds of good asleep
Throughout the world: as oft a rough wind sheds
The unripe promise of some field-flower, – true!
2540 But loosens too the level, and lets breathe
A thousand captives for the year to come.
Nevertheless, obtain thy prayer, stay fate!
Admetos lives – if thou wilt die for him!'

'So was the pact concluded that I die,
And thou live on, live for thyself, for me,
For all the world. Embrace and bid me hail,
Husband, because I have the victory –
Am, heart, soul, head to foot, one happiness!'

Whereto Admetos, in a passionate cry,
2550 'Never, by that true word Apollon spoke!
All the unwise wish is unwished, oh wife!
Let purposes of Zeus fulfil themselves,
If not through me, then through some other man!
Still, in myself he had a purpose too,
Inalienably mine, to end with me:
This purpose – that, throughout my earthly life,
Mine should be mingled and made up with thine, –
And we two prove one force and play one part
And do one thing. Since death divides the pair,
2560 'Tis well that I depart and thou remain
Who wast to me as spirit is to flesh:
Let the flesh perish, be perceived no more,
So thou, the spirit that informed the flesh,
Bend yet awhile, a very flame above
The rift I drop into the darkness by, –
And bid remember, flesh and spirit once
Worked in the world, one body, for man's sake.
Never be that abominable show
Of passive death without a quickening life –
2570 Admetos only, no Alkestis now!'

Then she: 'O thou Admetos, must the pile
Of truth on truth, which needs but one truth more
To tower up in completeness, trophy-like,
Emprise of man, and triumph of the world,
Must it go ever to the ground again
Because of some faint heart or faltering hand,
Which we, that breathless world about the base,
Trusted should carry safe to altitude,
Superimpose o' the summit, our supreme
2580 Achievement, our victorious coping-stone?
Shall thine, Beloved, prove the hand and heart
That fail again, flinch backward at the truth
Would cap and crown the structure this last time, –

Precipitate our monumental hope
And strew the earth ignobly yet once more?
See how, truth piled on truth, the structure wants,
Waits just the crowning truth I claim of thee!
Wouldst thou, for any joy to be enjoyed,
For any sorrow that thou mightst escape,
2590 Unwill thy will to reign a righteous king?
Nowise! And were there two lots, death and life, –
Life, wherein good resolve should go to air,
Death, whereby finest fancy grew plain fact
I' the reign of thy survivor, – life or death?
Certainly death, thou choosest. Here stand I
The wedded, the beloved one: hadst thou loved
Her who less worthily could estimate
Both life and death than thou? Not so should say
Admetos, whom Apollon made come court
2600 Alkestis in a car, submissive brutes
Of blood were yoked to, symbolizing soul
Must dominate unruly sense in man.
Then, shall Admetos and Alkestis see
Good alike, and alike choose, each for each,
Good, – and yet, each for other, at the last,
Choose evil? What? thou soundest in my soul
To depths below the deepest, reachest good
In evil, that makes evil good again,
And so allottest to me that I live
2610 And not die – letting die, not thee alone,
But all true life that lived in both of us?
Look at me once ere thou decree the lot!'

Therewith her whole soul entered into his,
He looked the look back, and Alkestis died.

And even while it lay, i' the look of him,
Dead, the dimmed body, bright Alkestis' soul
Had penetrated through the populace
Of ghosts, was got to Koré, – throned and crowned
The pensive queen o' the twilight, where she dwells
2620 Forever in a muse, but half away
From flowery earth she lost and hankers for, –
And there demanded to become a ghost
Before the time.

Whereat the softened eyes
Of the lost maidenhood that lingered still
Straying among the flowers in Sicily,
Sudden was startled back to Hades' throne
By that demand: broke through humanity
Into the orbed omniscience of a God,
Searched at a glance Alkestis to the soul,
2630   And said – while a long slow sigh lost itself
I' the hard and hollow passage of a laugh:

'Hence, thou deceiver! This is not to die,
If, by the very death which mocks me now,
The life, that's left behind and past my power,
Is formidably doubled. Say, there fight
Two athletes, side by side, each athlete armed
With only half the weapons, and no more,
Adequate to a contest with their foe:
If one of these should fling helm, sword and shield
2640   To fellow – shieldless, swordless, helmless late –
And so leap naked o'er the barrier, leave
A combatant equipped from head to heel,
Yet cry to the other side "Receive a friend
Who fights no longer!" "Back, friend, to the fray!"
Would be the prompt rebuff; I echo it.
Two souls in one were formidable odds:
Admetos must not be himself and thou!'

And so, before the embrace relaxed a whit,
The lost eyes opened, still beneath the look;
2650   And lo, Alkestis was alive again,
And of Admetos' rapture who shall speak?

So, the two lived together long and well.
But never could I learn, by word of scribe
Or voice of poet, rumour wafts our way,
That – of the scheme of rule in righteousness,
The bringing back again the Golden Age,
Which, rather than renounce, our pair would die –
That ever one faint particle came true,
With both alive to bring it to effect:
2660   Such is the envy Gods still bear mankind!

So might our version of the story prove,
And no Euripidean pathos plague
Too much my critic-friend of Syracuse.

'Besides your poem failed to get the prize:
(That is, the first prize: second prize is none).
Sophokles got it!' Honour the great name!
All cannot love two great names; yet some do:
I know the poetess who graved in gold,
Among her glories that shall never fade,
2670 This style and title for Euripides,
The Human with his droppings of warm tears.

I know, too, a great Kaunian painter, strong
As Herakles, though rosy with a robe
Of grace that softens down the sinewy strength:
And he has made a picture of it all.
There lies Alkestis dead, beneath the sun,
She longed to look her last upon, beside
The sea, which somehow tempts the life in us
To come trip over its white waste of waves,
2680 And try escape from earth, and fleet as free.
Behind the body, I suppose there bends
Old Pheres in his hoary impotence;
And women-wailers, in a corner crouch
– Four, beautiful as you four – yes, indeed! –
Close, each to other, agonizing all,
As fastened, in fear's rhythmic sympathy,
To two contending opposite. There strains
The might o' the hero 'gainst his more than match,
– Death, dreadful not in thew and bone, but like
2690 The envenomed substance that exudes some dew
Whereby the merely honest flesh and blood
Will fester up and run to ruin straight,
Ere they can close with, clasp and overcome
The poisonous impalpability
That simulates a form beneath the flow
Of those grey garments; I pronounce that piece
Worthy to set up in our Poikilé!

And all came, – glory of the golden verse,
And passion of the picture, and that fine

2700   Frank outgush of the human gratitude
        Which saved our ship and me, in Syracuse, –
        Ay, and the tear or two which slipt perhaps
        Away from you, friends, while I told my tale,
        – It all came of this play that gained no prize!
        Why crown whom Zeus has crowned in soul before?

Prince Hohenstiel-Schwangau, Saviour of Society

1871

"Ὕδραν φονεύσας, μυρίων τ᾿ ἄλλων πόνων
διῆλθον ἀγέλας . . .
τὸ λοίσθιον δὲ τόνδ᾿ ἔτλην τάλας πόνον,
. . . δῶμα θριγκῶσαι κακοῖς.

I slew the Hydra, and from labour passed
To labour – tribes of labours! Till, at last,
Attempting one more labour, in a trice,
Alack, with ills I *crowned the edifice*.

Prince Hohenstiel-Schwangau, Saviour of Society

You have seen better days, dear? So have I –
And worse too, for they brought no such bud-mouth
As yours to lisp 'You wish you knew me!' Well,
Wise men, 'tis said, have sometimes wished the same,
And wished and had their trouble for their pains.
Suppose my Oedipus should lurk at last
Under a pork-pie hat and crinoline,
And, latish, pounce on Sphinx in Leicester Square?
Or likelier, what if Sphinx in wise old age,
10 Grown sick of snapping foolish people's heads,
And jealous for her riddle's proper rede, –
Jealous that the good trick which served the turn
Have justice rendered it, nor class one day
With friend Home's stilts and tongs and medium-ware, –
What if the once redoubted Sphinx, I say,
(Because night draws on, and the sands increase,
And desert-whispers grow a prophecy)
Tell all to Corinth of her own accord,
Bright Corinth, not dull Thebes, for Laïs' sake,
20 Who finds me hardly grey, and likes my nose,
And thinks a man of sixty at the prime?
Good! It shall be! Revealment of myself!
But listen, for we must co-operate;
I don't drink tea: permit me the cigar!

First, how to make the matter plain, of course –
What was the law by which I lived. Let's see:
Ay, we must take one instant of my life
Spent sitting by your side in this neat room:
Watch well the way I use it, and don't laugh!
30 Here's paper on the table, pen and ink:
Give me the soiled bit – not the pretty rose!
See! having sat an hour, I'm rested now,
Therefore want work: and spy no better work
For eye and hand and mind that guides them both,
During this instant, than to draw my pen
From blot One – thus – up, up to blot Two – thus –
Which I at last reach, thus, and here's my line

Five inches long and tolerably straight:
Better to draw than leave undrawn, I think,
40 Fitter to do than let alone, I hold,
Though better, fitter, by but one degree.
Therefore it was that, rather than sit still
Simply, my right-hand drew it while my left
Pulled smooth and pinched the moustache to a point.

Now I permit your plump lips to unpurse:
'So far, one possibly may understand
Without recourse to witchcraft!' True, my dear.
Thus folks begin with Euclid, – finish, how?
Trying to square the circle! – at any rate,
50 Solving abstruser problems than this first
'How find the nearest way 'twixt point and point.'
Deal but with moral mathematics so –
Master one merest moment's work of mine,
Even this practising with pen and ink, –
Demónstrate why I rather plied the quill
Than left the space a blank, – you gain a fact,
And God knows what a fact's worth! So proceed
By inference from just this moral fact
– I don't say, to that plaguy quadrature
60 'What the whole man meant, whom you wish you knew,'
But, what meant certain things he did of old,
Which puzzled Europe, – why, you'll find them plain,
This way, not otherwise: I guarantee,
Understand one, you comprehend the rest.
Rays from all round converge to any point:
Study the point then ere you track the rays!
The size o' the circle's nothing; subdivide
Earth, and earth's smallest grain of mustard-seed,
You count as many parts, small matching large,
70 If you can use the mind's eye: otherwise,
Material optics, being gross at best,
Prefer the large and leave our mind the small –
And pray how many folk have minds can see?
Certainly you – and somebody in Thrace
Whose name escapes me at the moment. You –
Lend me your mind then! Analyse with me
This instance of the line 'twixt blot and blot
I rather chose to draw than leave a blank,

Things else being equal. You are taught thereby
80 That 'tis my nature, when I am at ease,
Rather than idle out my life too long,
To want to do a thing – to put a thought,
Whether a great thought or a little one,
Into an act, as nearly as may be.
Make what is absolutely new – I can't,
Mar what is made already well enough –
I won't: but turn to best account the thing
That's half-made – that I can. Two blots, you saw
I knew how to extend into a line
90 Symmetric on the sheet they blurred before –
Such little act sufficed, this time, such thought.

Now, we'll extend rays, widen out the verge,
Describe a larger circle; leave this first
Clod of an instance we began with, rise
To the complete world many clods effect.
Only continue patient while I throw,
Delver-like, spadeful after spadeful up,
Just as truths come, the subsoil of me, mould
Whence spring my moods: your object, – just to find,
100 Alike from handlift and from barrow-load,
What salts and silts may constitute the earth –
If it be proper stuff to blow man glass,
Or bake him pottery, bear him oaks or wheat –
What's born of me, in brief; which found, all's known.
If it were genius did the digging-job,
Logic would speedily sift its product smooth
And leave the crude truths bare for poetry;
But I'm no poet, and am stiff i' the back.
What one spread fails to bring, another may.
110 In goes the shovel and out comes scoop – as here!

I live to please myself. I recognize
Power passing mine, immeasurable, God –
Above me, whom He made, as heaven beyond
Earth – to use figures which assist our sense.
I know that He is there as I am here,
By the same proof, which seems no proof at all,
It so exceeds familiar forms of proof.
Why 'there,' not 'here'? Because, when I say 'there,'

I treat the feeling with distincter shape
120 That space exists between us: I, – not He, –
Live, think, do human work here – no machine,
His will moves, but a being by myself,
His, and not He who made me for a work,
Watches my working, judges its effect,
But does not interpose. He did so once,
And probably will again some time – not now,
Life being the minute of mankind, not God's,
In a certain sense, like time before and time
After man's earthly life, so far as man
130 Needs apprehend the matter. Am I clear?
Suppose I bid a courier take tonight
(. . . Once for all, let me talk as if I smoked
Yet in the Residenz, a personage:
I must still represent the thing I was,
Galvanically make dead muscle play,
Or how shall I illustrate muscle's use?)
I could then, last July, bid courier take
Message for me, post-haste, a thousand miles.
I bid him, since I have the right to bid,
140 And, my part done so far, his part begins;
He starts with due equipment, will and power,
Means he may use, misuse, not use at all,
At his discretion, at his peril too.
I leave him to himself: but, journey done,
I count the minutes, call for the result
In quickness and the courier quality,
Weigh its worth, and then punish or reward
According to proved service; not before.
Meantime, he sleeps through noontide, rides till dawn
150 Sticks to the straight road, tries the crooked path,
Measures and manages resource, trusts, doubts
Advisers by the wayside, does his best
At his discretion, lags or launches forth,
(He knows and I know) at his peril too.
You see? Exactly thus men stand to God:
I with my courier, God with me. Just so
I have His bidding to perform; but mind
And body, all of me, though made and meant
For that sole service, must consult, concert
160 With my own self and nobody beside,

How to effect the same: God helps not else.
'Tis I who, with my stock of craft and strength,
Choose the directer cut across the hedge,
Or keep the foot-track that respects a crop.
Lie down and rest, rise up and run, – live spare,
Feed free, – all that's my business: but, arrive,
Deliver message, bring the answer back,
And make my bow, I must: then God will speak,
Praise me or haply blame as service proves.
170 To other men, to each and everyone,
Another law! what likelier? God, perchance,
Grants each new man, by some as new a mode,
Intercommunication with Himself,
Wreaking on finiteness infinitude;
By such a series of effects, gives each
Last His own imprint: old yet ever new
The process: 'tis the way of Deity.
How it succeeds, He knows: I only know
That varied modes of creatureship abound,
180 Implying just as varied intercourse
For each with the creator of them all.
Each has his own mind and no other's mode.
What mode may yours be? I shall sympathize!
No doubt, you, good young lady that you are,
Despite a natural naughtiness or two,
Turn eyes up like a Pradier Magdalen
And see an outspread providential hand
Above the owl's-wing aigrette – guard and guide –
Visibly o'er your path, about your bed,
190 Through all your practisings with London-town.
It points, you go; it stays fixed, and you stop;
You quicken its procedure by a word
Spoken, a thought in silence, prayer and praise.
Well, I believe that such a hand may stoop,
And such appeals to it may stave off harm,
Pacify the grim guardian of this Square,
And stand you in good stead on quarter-day:
Quite possible in your case; not in mine.
'Ah, but I choose to make the difference,
200 Find the emancipation?' No, I hope!
If I deceive myself, take noon for night,
Please to become determinedly blind

To the true ordinance of human life,
Through mere presumption – that is my affair,
And truly a grave one; but as grave I think
Your affair, yours, the specially observed, –
Each favoured person that perceives his path
Pointed him, inch by inch, and looks above
For guidance, through the mazes of this world,
210 In what we call its meanest life-career
– Not how to manage Europe properly,
But how keep open shop, and yet pay rent,
Rear household, and make both ends meet, the same.
I say, such man is no less tasked than I
To duly take the path appointed him
By whatsoever sign he recognize.
Our insincerity on both our heads!
No matter what the object of a life,
Small work or large, – the making thrive a shop,
220 Or seeing that an empire take no harm, –
There are known fruits to judge obedience by.
You've read a ton's weight, now, of newspaper –
Lives of me, gabble about the kind of prince –
You know my work i' the rough; I ask you, then,
Do I appear subordinated less
To hand-impulsion, one prime push for all,
Than little lives of men, the multitude
That cried out, every quarter of an hour,
For fresh instructions, did or did not work,
230 And praised in the odd minutes?

                  Eh, my dear?
Such is the reason why I acquiesced
In doing what seemed best for me to do,
So as to please myself on the great scale,
Having regard to immortality
No less than life – did that which head and heart
Prescribed my hand, in measure with its means
Of doing – used my special stock of power –
Not from the aforesaid head and heart alone,
But every sort of helpful circumstance,
240 Some problematic and some nondescript:
All regulated by the single care
I' the last resort – that I made thoroughly serve

The when and how, toiled where was need, reposed
As resolutely at the proper point,
Braved sorrow, courted joy, to just one end:
Namely, that just the creature I was bound
To be, I should become, nor thwart at all
God's purpose in creation. I conceive
No other duty possible to man, –
250 Highest mind, lowest mind, – no other law
By which to judge life failure or success:
What folk call being saved or cast away.

Such was my rule of life: I worked my best
Subject to ultimate judgement, God's not man's.

Well then, this settled, – take your tea, I beg,
And meditate the fact, 'twixt sip and sip, –
This settled – why I pleased myself, you saw,
By turning blot and blot into a line,
O' the little scale, – we'll try now (as your tongue
260 Tries the concluding sugar-drop) what's meant
To please me most o' the great scale. Why, just now,
With nothing else to do within my reach,
Did I prefer making two blots one line
To making yet another separate
Third blot, and leaving those I found unlinked?
It meant, I like to use the thing I find,
Rather than strive at unfound novelty:
I make the best of the old, nor try for new.
Such will to act, such choice of action's way,
270 Constitute – when at work on the great scale,
Driven to their farthest natural consequence
By all the help from all the means – my own
Particular faculty of serving God,
Instinct for putting power to exercise
Upon some wish and want o' the time, I prove
Possible to mankind as best I may.
This constitutes my mission, – grant the phrase, –
Namely, to rule men – men within my reach,
To order, influence and dispose them so
280 As render solid and stabilify
Mankind in particles, the light and loose,
For their good and my pleasure in the act.

Such good accomplished proves twice good to me –
Good for its own sake, as the just and right,
And, in the effecting also, good again
To me its agent, tasked as suits my taste.

Is this much easy to be understood
At first glance? Now begin the steady gaze!

My rank – (if I must tell you simple truth –
290   Telling were else not worth the whiff o' the weed
I lose for the tale's sake) – dear, my rank i' the world
Is hard to know and name precisely: err
I may, but scarcely over-estimate
My style and title. Do I class with men
Most useful to their fellows? Possibly, –
Therefore, in some sort, best; but, greatest mind
And rarest nature? Evidently no.
A conservator, call me, if you please,
Not a creator nor destroyer: one
300   Who keeps the world safe. I profess to trace
The broken circle of society,
Dim actual order, I can redescribe
Not only where some segment silver-true
Stays clear, but where the breaks of black commence
Baffling you all who want the eye to probe –
As I make out yon problematic thin
White paring of your thumb-nail outside there,
Above the plaster-monarch on his steed –
See an inch, name an ell, and prophesy
310   O' the rest that ought to follow, the round moon
Now hiding in the night of things: that round,
I labour to demonstrate moon enough
For the month's purpose, – that society,
Render efficient for the age's need:
Preserving you in either case the old,
Nor aiming at a new and greater thing,
A sun for moon, a future to be made
By first abolishing the present law:
No such proud task for me by any means!
320   History shows you men whose master-touch
Not so much modifies as makes anew:
Minds that transmute nor need restore at all.

A breath of God made manifest in flesh
Subjects the world to change, from time to time,
Alters the whole conditions of our race
Abruptly, not by unperceived degrees
Nor play of elements already there,
But quite new leaven, leavening the lump,
And liker, so, the natural process. See!
330 Where winter reigned for ages – by a turn
I' the time, some star-change, (ask geologists)
The ice-tracts split, clash, splinter and disperse,
And there's an end of immobility,
Silence, and all that tinted pageant, base
To pinnacle, one flush from fairyland
Dead-asleep and deserted somewhere, – see! –
As a fresh sun, wave, spring and joy outburst.
Or else the earth it is, time starts from trance,
Her mountains tremble into fire, her plains
340 Heave blinded by confusion: what result?
New teeming growth, surprises of strange life
Impossible before, a world broke up
And re-made, order gained by law destroyed.
Not otherwise, in our society
Follow like portents, all as absolute
Regenerations: they have birth at rare
Uncertain unexpected intervals
O' the world, by ministry impossible
Before and after fulness of the days:
350 Some dervish desert-spectre, swordsman, saint,
Law-giver, lyrist, – oh, we know the names!
Quite other these than I. Our time requires
No such strange potentate, – who else would dawn, –
No fresh force till the old have spent itself.
Such seems the natural economy.
To shoot a beam into the dark, assists:
To make that beam do fuller service, spread
And utilize such bounty to the height,
That assists also, – and that work is mine.
360 I recognize, contémplate, and approve
The general compact of society,
Not simply as I see effected good,
But good i' the germ, each chance that's possible
I' the plan traced so far: all results, in short,

For better or worse of the operation due
To those exceptional natures, unlike mine,
Who, helping, thwarting, conscious, unaware,
Did somehow manage to so far describe
This diagram left ready to my hand,
370 Waiting my turn of trial. I see success,
See failure, see what makes or mars throughout.
How shall I else but help complete this plan
Of which I know the purpose and approve,
By letting stay therein what seems to stand,
And adding good thereto of easier reach
Today than yesterday?

        So much, no more!
Whereon, 'No more than that?' – inquire aggrieved
Half of my critics: 'nothing new at all?
The old plan saved, instead of a sponged slate
380 And fresh-drawn figure?' – while, 'So much as that?'
Object their fellows of the other faith:
'Leave uneffaced the crazy labyrinth
Of alteration and amendment, lines
Which every dabster felt in duty bound
To signalize his power of pen and ink
By adding to a plan once plain enough?
Why keep each fool's bequeathment, scratch and blur
Which overscrawl and underscore the piece –
Nay, strengthen them by touches of your own?'

390 Well, that's my mission, so I serve the world,
Figure as man o' the moment, – in default
Of somebody inspired to strike such change
Into society – from round to square,
The ellipsis to the rhomboid, how you please,
As suits the size and shape o' the world he finds.
But this I can, – and nobody my peer, –
Do the best with the least change possible:
Carry the incompleteness on, a stage,
Make what was crooked straight, and roughness smooth,
400 And weakness strong: wherein if I succeed,
It will not prove the worst achievement, sure,
In the eyes at least of one man, one I look
Nowise to catch in critic company:

To-wit, the man inspired, the genius' self
Destined to come and change things thoroughly.
He, at least, finds his business simplified,
Distinguishes the done from undone, reads
Plainly what meant and did not mean this time
We live in, and I work on, and transmit
410 To such successor: he will operate
On good hard substance, not mere shade and shine.
Let all my critics, born to idleness
And impotency, get their good, and have
Their hooting at the giver: I am deaf –
Who find great good in this society,
Great gain, the purchase of great labour. Touch
The work I may and must, but – reverent
In every fall o' the finger-tip, no doubt.
Perhaps I find all good there's warrant for
420 I' the world as yet: nay, to the end of time, –
Since evil never means part company
With mankind, only shift side and change shape.
I find advance i' the main, and notably
The Present an improvement on the Past,
And promise for the Future – which shall prove
Only the Present with its rough made smooth,
Its indistinctness emphasized; I hope
No better, nothing newer for mankind,
But something equably smoothed everywhere,
430 Good, reconciled with hardly-quite-as-good,
Instead of good and bad each jostling each.
'And that's all?' Ay, and quite enough for me!
We have toiled so long to gain what gain I find
I' the Present, – let us keep it! We shall toil
So long before we gain – if gain God grant –
A Future with one touch of difference
I' the heart of things, and not their outside face, –
Let us not risk the whiff of my cigar
For Fourier, Comte, and all that ends in smoke!

440 This I see clearest probably of men
With power to act and influence, now alive:
Juster than they to the true state of things;
In consequence, more tolerant that, side
By side, shall co-exist and thrive alike

In the age, the various sorts of happiness
Moral, mark! – not material – moods o' the mind
Suited to man and man his opposite:
Say, minor modes of movement – hence to there,
Or thence to here, or simply round about –
450 So long as each toe spares its neighbour's kibe,
Nor spoils the major march and main advance.
The love of peace, care for the family,
Contentment with what's bad but might be worse –
Good movements these! and good, too, discontent,
So long as that spurs good, which might be best,
Into becoming better, anyhow:
Good – pride of country, putting hearth and home
I' the background, out of undue prominence:
Good – yearning after change, strife, victory,
460 And triumph. Each shall have its orbit marked,
But no more, – none impede the other's path
In this wide world, – though each and all alike
Save for me, fain would spread itself through space
And leave its fellow not an inch of way.
I rule and regulate the course, excite,
Restrain: because the whole machine should march
Impelled by those diversely-moving parts,
Each blind to aught beside its little bent.
Out of the turnings round and round inside,
470 Comes that straightforward world-advance, I want,
And none of them supposes God wants too
And gets through just their hindrance and my help.
I think that to have held the balance straight
For twenty years, say, weighing claim and claim,
And giving each its due, no less no more,
This was good service to humanity,
Right usage of my power in head and heart,
And reasonable piety beside.
Keep those three points in mind while judging me!
480 You stand, perhaps, for some one man, not men, –
Represent this or the other interest,
Nor mind the general welfare, – so, impugn
My practice and dispute my value: why?
You man of faith, I did not tread the world
Into a paste, and thereof make a smooth
Uniform mound whereon to plant your flag,

The lily-white, above the blood and brains!
Nor yet did I, you man of faithlessness,
So roll things to the level which you love,
490 That you could stand at ease there and survey
The universal Nothing undisgraced
By pert obtrusion of some old church-spire
I' the distance! Neither friend would I content,
Nor, as the world were simply meant for him,
Thrust out his fellow and mend God's mistake.
Why, you two fools, – my dear friends all the same, –
Is it some change o' the world and nothing else
Contents you? Should whatever was, not be?
How thanklessly you view things! There's the root
500 Of the evil, source of the entire mistake:
You see no worth i' the world, nature and life,
Unless we change what is to what may be,
Which means, – may be, i' the brain of one of you!
'Reject what is?' – all capabilities –
Nay, you may style them chances if you choose –
All chances, then, of happiness that lie
Open to anybody that is born,
Tumbles into this life and out again, –
All that may happen, good and evil too,
510 I' the space between, to each adventurer
Upon this 'sixty, Anno Domini:
A life to live – and such a life! a world
To learn, one's lifetime in, – and such a world!
How did the foolish ever pass for wise
By calling life a burden, man a fly
Or worm or what's most insignificant?
'O littleness of man!' deplores the bard;
And then, for fear the Powers should punish him,
'O grandeur of the visible universe
520 Our human littleness contrasts withal!
O sun, O moon, ye mountains and thou sea,
Thou emblem of immensity, thou this,
That, and the other, – what impertinence
In man to eat and drink and walk about
And have his little notions of his own,
The while some wave sheds foam upon the shore!'
First of all, 'tis a lie some three-times thick:
The bard, – this sort of speech being poetry, –

The bard puts mankind well outside himself
530 And then begins instructing them: 'This way
I and my friend the sea conceive of you!
What would you give to think such thoughts as ours
Of you and the sea together?' Down they go
On the humbled knees of them: at once they draw
Distinction, recognize no mate of theirs
In one, despite his mock humility,
So plain a match for what he plays with. Next,
The turn of the great ocean-playfellow,
When the bard, having Bond Street very far
540 From ear-shot, cares not to ventriloquize,
But tells the sea its home-truths: 'You, my match?
You, all this terror and immensity
And what not? Shall I tell you what you are?
Just fit to hitch into a stanza, so
Wake up and set in motion who's asleep
O' the other side of you in England, else
Unaware, as folk pace their Bond Street now,
Somebody here despises them so much!
Between us, – they are the ultimate! to them
550 And their perception go these lordly thoughts:
Since what were ocean – mane and tail, to boot –
Mused I not here, how make thoughts thinkable?
Start forth my stanza and astound the world!
Back, billows, to your insignificance!
Deep, you are done with!'

                Learn, my gifted friend,
There are two things i' the world, still wiser folk
Accept – intelligence and sympathy.
You pant about unutterable power
I' the ocean, all you feel but cannot speak?
560 Why, that's the plainest speech about it all.
You did not feel what was not to be felt.
Well, then, all else but what man feels is naught –
The wash o' the liquor that o'erbrims the cup
Called man, and runs to waste adown his side,
Perhaps to feed a cataract, – who cares?
I'll tell you: all the more I know mankind,
The more I thank God, like my grandmother,
For making me a little lower than

The angels, honour-clothed and glory-crowned
570 This is the honour, – that no thing I know,
Feel or conceive, but I can make my own
Somehow, by use of hand or head or heart:
This is the glory, – that in all conceived,
Or felt or known, I recognize a mind
Not mine but like mine, – for the double joy, –
Making all things for me and me for Him.
There's folly for you at this time of day!
So think it! and enjoy your ignorance
Of what – no matter for the worthy's name –
580 Wisdom set working in a noble heart,
When he, who was earth's best geometer
Up to that time of day, consigned his life
With its results into one matchless book,
The triumph of the human mind so far,
All in geometry man yet could do:
And then wrote on the dedication-page
In place of name the universe applauds,
'But, God, what a geometer art Thou!'
I suppose Heaven is, through Eternity,
590 The equalizing, ever and anon,
In momentary rapture, great with small,
Omniscience with intelligency, God
With man, – the thunder-glow from pole to pole
Abolishing, a blissful moment-space,
Great cloud alike and small cloud, in one fire –
As sure to ebb as sure again to flow
When the new receptivity deserves
The new completion. There's the Heaven for me.
And I say, therefore, to live out one's life
600 I' the world here, with the chance, – whether by pain
Or pleasure be the process, long or short
The time, august or mean the circumstance
To human eye, – of learning how set foot
Decidedly on some one path to Heaven,
Touch segment in the circle whence all lines
Lead to the centre equally, red lines
Or black lines, so they but produce themselves –
This, I do say, – and here my sermon ends, –
This makes it worth our while to tenderly
610 Handle a state of things which mend we might,

Mar we may, but which meanwhile helps so far.
Therefore my end is – save society!

'And that's all?' twangs the never-failing taunt
O' the foe – 'No novelty, creativeness,
Mark of the master that renews the age?'
'Nay, all that?' rather will demur my judge
I look to hear some day, nor friend nor foe –
'Did you attain, then, to perceive that God
Knew what He undertook when He made things?'
620 Ay: that my task was to co-operate
Rather than play the rival, chop and change
The order whence comes all the good we know,
With this, – good's last expression to our sense, –
That there's a further good conceivable
Beyond the utmost earth can realize:
And, therefore, that to change the agency,
The evil whereby good is brought about –
Try to make good do good as evil does –
Were just as if a chemist, wanting white,
630 And knowing black ingredients bred the dye,
Insisted these too should be white forsooth!
Correct the evil, mitigate your best,
Blend mild with harsh, and soften black to grey
If grey may follow with no detriment
To the eventual perfect purity!
But as for hazarding the main result
By hoping to anticipate one half
In the intermediate process, – no, my friends!
This bad world, I experience and approve;
640 Your good world, – with no pity, courage, hope,
Fear, sorrow, joy, – devotedness, in short,
Which I account the ultimate of man,
Of which there's not one day nor hour but brings,
In flower or fruit, some sample of success,
Out of this same society I save –
None of it for me! That I might have none,
I rapped your tampering knuckles twenty years.
Such was the task imposed me, such my end.

Now for the means thereto. Ah, confidence –
650 Keep we together or part company?
This is the critical minute! 'Such my end?'
Certainly; how could it be otherwise?
Can there be question which was the right task –
To save or to destroy society?
Why, even prove that, by some miracle,
Destruction were the proper work to choose,
And that a torch best remedies what's wrong
I' the temple, whence the long procession wound
Of powers and beauties, earth's achievements all,
660 The human strength that strove and overthrew, –
The human love that, weak itself, crowned strength, –
The instinct crying 'God is whence I came!' –
The reason laying down the law 'And such
His will i' the world must be!' – the leap and shout
Of genius 'For I hold His very thoughts,
The meaning of the mind of Him!' – nay, more,
The ingenuities, each active force
That turning in a circle on itself
Looks neither up nor down but keeps the spot,
670 Mere creature-like, and, for religion, works,
Works only and works ever, makes and shapes
And changes, still wrings more of good from less,
Still stamps some bad out, where was worst before,
So leaves the handiwork, the act and deed,
Were it but house and land and wealth, to show
Here was a creature perfect in the kind –
Whether as bee, beaver, or behemoth,
What's the importance? he has done his work
For work's sake, worked well, earned a creature's praise; –
680 I say, concede that same fane, whence deploys
Age after age, all this humanity,
Diverse but ever dear, out of the dark
Behind the altar into the broad day
By the portal – enter, and concede there mocks
Each lover of free motion and much space
A perplexed length of apse and aisle and nave, –
Pillared roof and carvèd screen, and what care I? –
Which irk the movement and impede the march, –
Nay, possibly, bring flat upon his nose
690 At some odd break-neck angle, by some freak

Of old-world artistry, that personage
Who, could he but have kept his skirts from grief
And catching at the hooks and crooks about,
Had stepped out on the daylight of our time
Plainly the man of the age, – still, still, I bar
Excessive conflagration in the case.
'Shake the flame freely!' shout the multitude:
The architect approves I stuck my torch
Inside a good stout lantern, hung its light
700 Above the hooks and crooks, and ended so.
To save society was well: the means
Whereby to save it, – there begins the doubt
Permitted you, imperative on me;
Were mine the best means? Did I work aright
With powers appointed me? – since powers denied
Concern me nothing.

                Well, my work reviewed
Fairly, leaves more hope than discouragement.
First, there's the deed done: what I found, I leave, –
What tottered, I kept stable: if it stand
710 One month, without sustainment, still thank me
The twenty years' sustainer! Now, observe,
Sustaining is no brilliant self-display
Like knocking down or even setting up:
Much bustle these necessitate; and still
To vulgar eye, the mightier of the myth
Is Hercules, who substitutes his own
For Atlas' shoulder and supports the globe
A whole day, – not the passive and obscure
Atlas who bore, ere Hercules was born,
720 And is to go on bearing that same load
When Hercules turns ash on Oeta's top.
'Tis the transition-stage, the tug and strain,
That strike men: standing still is stupid-like.
My pressure was too constant on the whole
For any part's eruption into space
'Mid sparkles, crackling, and much praise of me.
I saw that, in the ordinary life,
Many of the little make a mass of men
Important beyond greatness here and there;
730 As certainly as, in life exceptional,

When old things terminate and new commence,
A solitary great man's worth the world.
God takes the business into His own hands
At such time: who creates the novel flower
Contrives to guard and give it breathing-room:
I merely tend the corn-field, care for crop,
And weed no acre thin to let emerge
What prodigy may stifle there perchance,
– No, though my eye have noted where he lurks.
740 Oh those mute myriads that spoke loud to me –
The eyes that craved to see the light, the mouths
That sought the daily bread and nothing more,
The hands that supplicated exercise,
Men that had wives, and women that had babes,
And all these making suit to only live!
Was I to turn aside from husbandry,
Leave hope of harvest for the corn, my care,
To play at horticulture, rear some rose
Or poppy into perfect leaf and bloom
750 When, 'mid the furrows, up was pleased to sprout
Some man, cause, system, special interest
I ought to study, stop the world meanwhile?
'But I am Liberty, Philanthropy,
Enlightenment, or Patriotism, the power
Whereby you are to stand or fall!' cries each:
'Mine and mine only be the flag you flaunt!'
And, when I venture to object 'Meantime,
What of yon myriads with no flag at all –
My crop which, who flaunts flag must tread across?'
760 'Now, this it is to have a puny mind!'
Admire my mental prodigies: 'down – down –
Ever at home o' the level and the low,
There bides he brooding! Could he look above,
With less of the owl and more of the eagle eye,
He'd see there's no way helps the little cause
Like the attainment of the great. Dare first
The chief emprise; dispel yon cloud between
The sun and us; nor fear that, though our heads
Find earlier warmth and comfort from his ray,
770 What lies about our feet, the multitude,
Will fail of benefaction presently.
Come now, let each of us awhile cry truce

To special interests, make common cause
Against the adversary – or perchance
Mere dullard to his own plain interest!
Which of us will you choose? – since needs must be
Some one o' the warring causes you incline
To hold, i' the main, has right and should prevail:
Why not adopt and give it prevalence?
780   Choose strict Faith or lax Incredulity, –
King, Caste and Cultus – or the Rights of Man,
Sovereignty of each Proudhon o'er himself,
And all that follows in just consequence!
Go free the stranger from a foreign yoke;
Or stay, concentrate energy at home;
Succeed! – when he deserves, the stranger will.
Comply with the Great Nation's impulse, print
By force of arms, – since reason pleads in vain,
And, 'mid the sweet compulsion, pity weeps, –
790   Hohenstiel-Schwangau on the universe!
Snub the Great Nation, cure the impulsive itch
With smartest fillip on a restless nose
Was ever launched by thumb and finger! Bid
Hohenstiel-Schwangau first repeal the tax
On pig-tails and pomatum, and then mind
Abstruser matters for next century!
Is your choice made? Why then, act up to choice!
Leave the illogical touch now here now there
I' the way of work, the tantalizing help
800   First to this, then the other opposite:
The blowing hot and cold, sham policy,
Sure ague of the mind and nothing more,
Disease of the perception or the will,
That fain would hide in a fine name! Your choice,
Speak it out and condemn yourself thereby!'

Well, Leicester Square is not the Residenz:
Instead of shrugging shoulder, turning friend
The deaf ear, with a wink to the police –
I'll answer – by a question, wisdom's mode.
810   How many years, o' the average, do men
Live in this world? Some score, say computists.
Quintuple me that term and give mankind
The likely hundred, and with all my heart

I'll take your task upon me, work your way,
Concentrate energy on some one cause:
Since, counseller, I also have my cause,
My flag, my faith in its effect, my hope
In its eventual triumph for the good
O' the world. And once upon a time, when I
820 Was like all you, mere voice and nothing more,
Myself took wings, soared sunward, and thence sang
'Look where I live i' the loft, come up to me,
Groundlings, nor grovel longer! gain this height,
And prove you breathe here better than below!
Why, what emancipation far and wide
Will follow in a trice! They too can soar,
Each tenant of the earth's circumference
Claiming to elevate humanity,
They also must attain such altitude,
830 Live in the luminous circle that surrounds
The planet, not the leaden orb itself.
Press out, each point, from surface to yon verge
Which one has gained and guaranteed your realm!'
Ay, still my fragments wander, music-fraught,
Sighs of the soul, mine once, mine now, and mine
For ever! Crumbled arch, crushed aqueduct,
Alive with tremors in the shaggy growth
Of wild-wood, crevice-sown, that triumphs there
Imparting exultation to the hills!
840 Sweep of the swathe when only the winds walk
And waft my words above the grassy sea
Under the blinding blue that basks o'er Rome, –
Hear ye not still – 'Be Italy again'?
And ye, what strikes the panic to your heart?
Decrepit council-chambers, – where some lamp
Drives the unbroken black three paces off
From where the greybeards huddle in debate,
Dim cowls and capes, and midmost glimmers one
Like tarnished gold, and what they say is doubt,
850 And what they think is fear, and what suspends
The breath in them is not the plaster-patch
Time disengages from the painted wall
Where Rafael moulderingly bids adieu,
Nor tick of the insect turning tapestry
Which a queen's finger traced of old, to dust;

But some word, resonant, redoubtable,
Of who once felt upon his head a hand
Whereof the head now apprehends his foot.
'Light in Rome, Law in Rome, and Liberty
860 O' the soul in Rome – the free Church, the free State!
Stamp out the nature that's best typified
By its embodiment in Peter's Dome,
The scorpion-body with the greedy pair
Of outstretched nippers, either colonnade
Agape for the advance of heads and hearts!'
There's one cause for you! one and only one,
For I am vocal through the universe,
I' the workshop, manufactory, exchange
And market-place, sea-port and custom-house
870 O' the frontier: listen if the echoes die –
'Unfettered commerce! Power to speak and hear,
And print and read! The universal vote!
Its rights for labour!' This, with much beside,
I spoke when I was voice and nothing more,
But altogether such an one as you
My censors. 'Voice, and nothing more, indeed!'
Re-echoes round me: 'that's the censure, there's
Involved the ruin of you soon or late!
Voice, – when its promise beat the empty air:
880 And nothing more, – when solid earth's your stage,
And we desiderate performance, deed
For word, the realizing all you dreamed
In the old days: now, for deed, we find at door
O' the council-chamber posted, mute as mouse,
Hohenstiel-Schwangau, sentry and safeguard
O' the greybeards all a-chuckle, cowl to cape,
Who challenge Judas, – that's endearment's style, –
To stop their mouths or let escape grimace,
While they keep cursing Italy and him.
890 The power to speak, hear, print and read is ours?
Ay, we learn where and how, when clapped inside
A convict-transport bound for cool Cayenne!
The universal vote we have: its urn,
We also have where votes drop, fingered-o'er
By the universal Prefect. Say, Trade's free
And Toil turned master out o' the slave it was:
What then? These feed man's stomach, but his soul

Craves finer fare, nor lives by bread alone,
As somebody says somewhere. Hence you stand
900 Proved and recorded either false or weak,
Faulty in promise or performance: which?'

Neither, I hope. Once pedestalled on earth,
To act not speak, I found earth was not air.
I saw that multitude of mine, and not
The nakedness and nullity of air
Fit only for a voice to float in free.
Such eyes I saw that craved the light alone,
Such mouths that wanted bread and nothing else,
Such hands that supplicated handiwork,
910 Men with the wives, and women with the babes,
Yet all these pleading just to live, not die!
Did I believe one whit less in belief,
Take truth for falsehood, wish the voice revoked
That told the truth to heaven for earth to hear?
No, this should be, and shall; but when and how?
At what expense to these who average
Your twenty years of life, my computists?
'Not bread alone' but bread before all else
For these: the bodily want serve first, said I;
920 If earth-space and the life-time help not here,
Where is the good of body having been?
But, helping body, if we somewhat balk
The soul of finer fare, such food's to find
Elsewhere and afterward – all indicates,
Even this self-same fact that soul can starve
Yet body still exist its twenty years:
While, stint the body, there's an end at once
O' the revel in the fancy that Rome's free,
And superstition's fettered, and one prints
930 Whate'er one pleases and who pleases reads
The same, and speaks out and is spoken to,
And divers hundred thousand fools may vote
A vote untampered with by one wise man,
And so elect Barabbas deputy
In lieu of his concurrent. I who trace
The purpose written on the face of things,
For my behoof and guidance – (whoso needs
No such sustainment, sees beneath my signs,

Proves, what I take for writing, penmanship,
940 Scribble and flourish with no sense for me
O' the sort I solemnly go spelling out, –
Let him! there's certain work of mine to show
Alongside his work: which gives warranty
Of shrewder vision in the workman – judge!)
I who trace Providence without a break
I' the plan of things, drop plumb on this plain print
Of an intention with a view to good,
That man is made in sympathy with man
At outset of existence, so to speak;
950 But in dissociation, more and more,
Man from his fellow, as their lives advance
In culture; still humanity, that's born
A mass, keeps flying off, fining away
Ever into a multitude of points,
And ends in isolation, each from each:
Peerless above i' the sky, the pinnacle, –
Absolute contact, fusion, all below
At the base of being. How comes this about?
This stamp of God characterizing man
960 And nothing else but man in the universe –
That, while he feels with man (to use man's speech)
I' the little things of life, its fleshly wants
Of food and rest and health and happiness,
Its simplest spirit-motions, loves and hates,
Hopes, fears, soul-cravings on the ignoblest scale,
O' the fellow-creature, – owns the bond at base, –
He tends to freedom and divergency
In the upward progress, plays the pinnacle
When life's at greatest (grant again the phrase!
970 Because there's neither great nor small in life).
'Consult thou for thy kind that have the eyes
To see, the mouths to eat, the hands to work,
Men with the wives, and women with the babes!'
Prompts Nature. 'Care thou for thyself alone
I' the conduct of the mind God made thee with!
Think, as if man had never thought before!
Act, as if all creation hung attent
On the acting of such faculty as thine,
To take prime pattern from thy masterpiece!'
980 Nature prompts also: neither law obeyed

To the uttermost by any heart and soul
We know or have in record: both of them
Acknowledged blindly by whatever man
We ever knew or heard of in this world.
'Will you have why and wherefore, and the fact
Made plain as pikestaff?' modern Science asks.
'That mass man sprung from was a jelly-lump
Once on a time; he kept an after-course
Through fish and insect, reptile, bird and beast,
990 Till he attained to be an ape at last
Or last but one. And if this doctrine shock
In aught the natural pride' ... Friend, banish fear,
The natural humility replies!
Do you suppose, even I, poor potentate,
Hohenstiel-Schwangau, who once ruled the roast, –
I was born able at all points to ply
My tools? or did I have to learn my trade,
Practise as exile ere perform as prince?
The world knows something of my ups and downs:
1000 But grant me time, give me the management
And manufacture of a model me,
Me fifty-fold, a prince without a flaw, –
Why, there's no social grade, the sordidest,
My embryo potentate should blink and scape.
King, all the better he was cobbler once,
He should know, sitting on the throne, how tastes
Life to who sweeps the doorway. But life's hard,
Occasion rare; you cut probation short,
And, being half-instructed, on the stage
1010 You shuffle through your part as best you can,
And bless your stars, as I do. God takes time.
I like the thought He should have lodged me once
I' the hole, the cave, the hut, the tenement,
The mansion and the palace; made me learn
The feel o' the first, before I found myself
Loftier i' the last, not more emancipate;
From first to last of lodging, I was I,
And not at all the place that harboured me.
Do I refuse to follow farther yet
1020 I' the backwardness, repine if tree and flower,
Mountain or streamlet were my dwelling-place
Before I gained enlargement, grew mollusc?

As well account that way for many a thrill
Of kinship, I confess to, with the powers
Called Nature: animate, inanimate,
In parts or in the whole, there's something there
Man-like that somehow meets the man in me.
My pulse goes altogether with the heart
O' the Persian, that old Xerxes, when he stayed
His march to conquest of the world, a day
I' the desert, for the sake of one superb
Plane-tree which queened it there in solitude:
Giving her neck its necklace, and each arm
Its armlet, suiting soft waist, snowy side,
With cincture and apparel. Yes, I lodged
In those successive tenements; perchance
Taste yet the straitness of them while I stretch
Limb and enjoy new liberty the more.
And some abodes are lost or ruinous;
Some, patched-up and pieced-out, and so transformed
They still accommodate the traveller
His day of lifetime. O you count the links,
Descry no bar of the unbroken man?
Yes, – and who welds a lump of ore, suppose
He likes to make a chain and not a bar,
And reach by link on link, link small, link large,
Out to the due length – why, there's forethought still
Outside o' the series, forging at one end,
While at the other there's – no matter what
The kind of critical intelligence
Believing that last link had last but one
For parent, and no link was, first of all,
Fitted to anvil, hammered into shape.
Else, I accept the doctrine, and deduce
This duty, that I recognize mankind,
In all its height and depth and length and breadth.
Mankind i' the main have little wants, not large:
I, being of will and power to help, i' the main,
Mankind, must help the least wants first. My friend,
That is, my foe, without such power and will,
May plausibly concentrate all he wields,
And do his best at helping some large want,
Exceptionally noble cause, that's seen
Subordinate enough from where I stand.

1030
1040
1050
1060

As he helps, I helped once, when like himself,
Unable to help better, work more wide;
And so would work with heart and hand today,
Did only computists confess a fault,
And multiply the single score by five,
1070 Five only, give man's life its hundred years.
Change life, in me shall follow change to match!
Time were then, to work here, there, everywhere,
By turns and try experiment at ease!
Full time to mend as well as mar: why wait
The slow and sober uprise all around
O' the building? Let us run up, right to roof,
Some sudden marvel, piece of perfectness,
And testify what we intend the whole!
Is the world losing patience? 'Wait!' say we:
1080 'There's time: no generation needs to die
Unsolaced; you've a century in store!'
But, no: I sadly let the voices wing
Their way i' the upper vacancy, nor test
Truth on this solid as I promised once.
Well, and what is there to be sad about?
The world's the world, life's life, and nothing else.
'Tis part of life, a property to prize,
That those o' the higher sort engaged i' the world,
Should fancy they can change its ill to good,
1090 Wrong to right, ugliness to beauty: find
Enough success in fancy turning fact,
To keep the sanguine kind in countenance
And justify the hope that busies them:
Failure enough, – to who can follow change
Beyond their vision, see new good prove ill
I' the consequence, see blacks and whites of life
Shift square indeed, but leave the chequered face
Unchanged i' the main, – failure enough for such,
To bid ambition keep the whole from change,
1100 As their best service. I hope naught beside.
No, my brave thinkers, whom I recognize,
Gladly, myself the first, as, in a sense,
All that our world's worth, flower and fruit of man!
Such minds myself award supremacy
Over the common insignificance,
When only Mind's in question, – Body bows

To quite another government, you know.
Be Kant crowned king o' the castle in the air!
Hans Slouch, – his own, and children's mouths to feed
1110 I' the hovel on the ground, – wants meat, nor chews
'The Critique of Pure Reason' in exchange.

But, now, – suppose I could allow your claims
And quite change life to please you, – would it please?
Would life comport with change and still be life?
Ask, now, a doctor for a remedy:
There's his prescription. Bid him point you out
Which of the five or six ingredients saves
The sick man. 'Such the efficacity?
Then why not dare and do things in one dose
1120 Simple and pure, all virtue, no alloy
Of the idle drop and powder?' What's his word?
The efficacity, neat, were neutralized:
It wants dispersing and retarding, – nay
Is put upon its mettle, plays its part
Precisely through such hindrance everywhere,
Finds some mysterious give and take i' the case,
Some gain by opposition, he foregoes
Should he unfetter the medicament.
So with this thought of yours that fain would work
1130 Free in the world: it wants just what it finds –
The ignorance, stupidity, the hate,
Envy and malice and uncharitableness
That bar your passage, break the flow of you
Down from those happy heights where many a cloud
Combined to give you birth and bid you be
The royalest of rivers: on you glide
Silverly till you reach the summit-edge,
Then over, on to all that ignorance,
Stupidity, hate, envy, bluffs and blocks,
1140 Posted to fret you into foam and noise.
What of it? Up you mount in minute mist,
And bridge the chasm that crushed your quietude,
A spirit-rainbow, earthborn jewelry
Outsparkling the insipid firmament
Blue above Terni and its orange-trees.
Do not mistake me! You, too, have your rights!
Hans must not burn Kant's house above his head

Because he cannot understand Kant's book:
And still less must Hans' pastor burn Kant's self
1150 Because Kant understands some books too well.
But, justice seen to on this little point,
Answer me, is it manly, is it sage
To stop and struggle with arrangements here
It took so many lives, so much of toil,
To tinker up into efficiency?
Can't you contrive to operate at once, –
Since time is short and art is long, – to show
Your quality i' the world, whate'er you boast,
Without this fractious call on folks to crush
1160 The world together just to set you free,
Admire the capers you will cut perchance,
Nor mind the mischief to your neighbours?

         'Age!
Age and experience bring discouragement,'
You taunt me: I maintain the opposite.
Am I discouraged who, – perceiving health,
Strength, beauty, as they tempt the eye of soul,
Are uncombinable with flesh and blood, –
Resolve to let my body live its best,
And leave my soul what better yet may be
1170 Or not be, in this life or afterward?
 – In either fortune, wiser than who waits
Till magic art procure a miracle.
In virtue of my very confidence
Mankind ought to outgrow its babyhood,
I prescribe rocking, deprecate rough hands,
While thus the cradle holds it past mistake.
Indeed, my task's the harder – equable
Sustainment everywhere, all strain, no push –
Whereby friends credit me with indolence,
1180 Apathy, hesitation. 'Stand stock-still
If able to move briskly? "All a-strain" –
So must we compliment your passiveness?
Sound asleep, rather!'

       Just the judgement passed
Upon a statue, luckless like myself,
I saw at Rome once! 'Twas some artist's whim

To cover all the accessories close
I' the group, and leave you only Laocoön
With neither sons nor serpents to denote
The purpose of his gesture. Then a crowd
1190 Was called to try the question, criticize
Wherefore such energy of legs and arms,
Nay, eyeballs, starting from the socket. One –
I give him leave to write my history –
Only one said 'I think the gesture strives
Against some obstacle we cannot see.'
All the rest made their minds up. ' 'Tis a yawn
Of sheer fatigue subsiding to repose:
The statue's "Somnolency" clear enough!'

There, my arch stranger-friend, my audience both
1200 And arbitress, you have one half your wish,
At least: you know the thing I tried to do!
All, so far, to my praise and glory – all
Told as befits the self-apologist, –
Who ever promises a candid sweep
And clearance of those errors miscalled crimes
None knows more, none laments so much as he,
And ever rises from confession, proved
A god whose fault was – trying to be man.
Just so, fair judge, – if I read smile aright –
1210 I condescend to figure in your eyes
As biggest heart and best of Europe's friends,
And hence my failure. God will estimate
Success one day; and, in the meantime – you!

I dare say there's some fancy of the sort
Frolicking round this final puff I send
To die up yonder in the ceiling-rose, –
Some consolation-stakes, we losers win!
A plague of the return to 'I – I – I
Did this, meant that, hoped, feared the other thing!'
1220 Autobiography, adieu! The rest
Shall make amends, be pure blame, history
And falsehood: not the ineffective truth,
But Thiers-and-Victor-Hugo exercise.
Hear what I never was, but might have been
I' the better world where goes tobacco-smoke!

Here lie the dozen volumes of my life:
(Did I say 'lie'? the pregnant word will serve).
Cut on to the concluding chapter, though!
Because the little hours begin to strike.
1230 Hurry Thiers-Hugo to the labour's end!

Something like this the unwritten chapter reads.

Exemplify the situation thus!
Hohenstiel-Schwangau, being, no dispute,
Absolute mistress, chose the Assembly, first,
To serve her: chose this man, its President
Afterward, to serve also, – specially
To see that folk did service one and all.
And now the proper term of years was out
When the Head-servant must vacate his place,
1240 And nothing lay so patent to the world
As that his fellow-servants one and all
Were – mildly to make mention – knaves or fools,
Each of them with his promise flourished full
I' the face of you by word and impudence,
Or filtered slyly out by nod and wink
And nudge upon your sympathetic rib –
That not one minute more did knave or fool
Mean to keep faith and serve as he had sworn
Hohenstiel-Schwangau, once her Head away.
1250 Why should such swear except to get the chance,
When time should ripen and confusion bloom,
Of putting Hohenstielers-Schwangauese
To the true use of human property –
Restoring souls and bodies, this to Pope,
And that to King, that other to his planned
Perfection of a Share-and-share-alike,
That other still, to Empire absolute
In shape of the Head-servant's very self
Transformed to Master whole and sole? each scheme
1260 Discussible, concede one circumstance –
That each scheme's parent were, beside himself,
Hohenstiel-Schwangau, not her serving-man
Sworn to do service in the way she chose
Rather than his way: way superlative,
Only, – by some infatuation, – his

And his and his and everyone's but hers
Who stuck to just the Assembly and the Head.
I make no doubt the Head, too, had his dream
Of doing sudden duty swift and sure
1270 On all that heap of untrustworthiness –
Catching each vaunter of the villainy
He meant to perpetrate when time was ripe,
Once the Head-servant fairly out of doors, –
And, caging here a knave and there a fool,
Cry 'Mistress of your servants, these and me,
Hohenstiel-Schwangau! I, their trusty Head,
Pounce on a pretty scheme concocting here
That's stopped, extinguished by my vigilance.
Your property is safe again: but mark!
1280 Safe in these hands, not yours, who lavish trust
Too lightly. Leave my hands their charge awhile!
I know your business better than yourself:
Let me alone about it! Some fine day,
Once we are rid of the embarrassment,
You shall look up and see your longings crowned!'
Such fancy might have tempted him be false,
But this man chose truth and was wiser so.
He recognized that for great minds i' the world
There is no trial like the appropriate one
1290 Of leaving little minds their liberty
Of littleness to blunder on through life,
Now, aiming at right ends by foolish means,
Now, at absurd achievement through the aid
Of good and wise endeavour – to acquiesce
In folly's life-long privilege, though with power
To do the little minds the good they need,
Despite themselves, by just abolishing
Their right to play the part and fill the place
I' the scheme of things He schemed who made alike
1300 Great minds and little minds, saw use for each.
Could the orb sweep those puny particles
It just half-lights at distance, hardly leads
I' the leash – sweep out each speck of them from space
They anticize in with their days and nights
And whirlings round and dancings off, forsooth,
And all that fruitless individual life
One cannot lend a beam to but they spoil –

Sweep them into itself and so, one star,
Preponderate henceforth i' the heritage
1310 Of heaven! No! in less senatorial phrase,
The man endured to help, not save outright
The multitude by substituting him
For them, his knowledge, will and way, for God's:
Nor change the world, such as it is, and was
And will be, for some other, suiting all
Except the purpose of the maker. No!
He saw that weakness, wickedness will be,
And therefore should be: that the perfect man
As we account perfection – at most pure
1320 O' the special gold, whate'er the form it take,
Head-work or heart-work, fined and thrice-refined
I' the crucible of life, whereto the powers
Of the refiner, one and all, are flung
To feed the flame, he saw that e'en the block
Such perfect man holds out triumphant, breaks
Into some poisonous ore, gold's opposite,
At the very purest, so compensating
Man's Adversary – what if we believe? –
For earlier stern exclusion of his stuff.
1330 See the sage, with the hunger for the truth,
And see his system that's all true, except
The one weak place that's stanchioned by a lie!
The moralist who walks with head erect
I' the crystal clarity of air so long,
Until a stumble, and the man's one mire!
Philanthropy undoes the social knot
With axe-edge, makes love room 'twixt head and trunk:
Religion – but, enough, the thing's too clear!
Well, if these sparks break out i' the greenest tree,
1340 Our topmost of performance, yours and mine,
What will be done i' the dry ineptitude
Of ordinary mankind, bark and bole,
All seems ashamed of but their mother-earth?
Therefore throughout Head's term of servitude
He did the appointed service, and forebore
Extraneous action that were duty else,
Done by some other servant, idle now
Or mischievous: no matter, each his own –
Own task, and, in the end, own praise or blame!

1350   He suffered them strut, prate and brag their best,
   Squabble at odds on every point save one,
   And there shake hands, – agree to trifle time,
   Obstruct advance with, each, his cricket-cry
   'Wait till the Head be off the shoulders here!
   Then comes my King, my Pope, my Autocrat,
   My Socialist Republic to her own –
   To-wit, that property of only me,
   Hohenstiel-Schwangau who conceits herself
   Free, forsooth, and expects I keep her so!'

1360   – Nay, suffered when, perceiving with dismay
   Head's silence paid no tribute to their noise,
   They turned on him. 'Dumb menace in that mouth,
   Malice in that unstridulosity!
   He cannot but intend some stroke of state
   Shall signalize his passage into peace
   Out of the creaking, – hinder transference
   O' the Hohenstielers-Schwangauese to king,
   Pope, autocrat, or socialist republic! That's
   Exact the cause his lips unlocked would cry!

1370   Therefore be stirring: brave, beard, bully him!
   Dock, by the million, of its friendly joints,
   The electoral body short at once! who did,
   May do again, and undo us beside.
   Wrest from his hands the sword for self-defence,
   The right to parry any thrust in play
   We peradventure please to meditate!'
   And so forth; creak, creak, creak: and ne'er a line
   His locked mouth oped the wider, till at last
   O' the long degraded and insulting day,

1380   Sudden the clock told it was judgement-time.
   Then he addressed himself to speak indeed
   To the fools, not knaves: they saw him walk straight down
   Each step of the eminence, as he first engaged,
   And stand at last o' the level, – all he swore.
   'People, and not the people's varletry,
   This is the task you set myself and these!
   Thus I performed my part of it, and thus
   They thwarted me throughout, here, here, and here:
   Study each instance! yours the loss, not mine.

1390   What they intend now is demonstrable
   As plainly: here's such man, and here's such mode

Of making you some other than the thing
You, wisely or unwisely, choose to be,
And only set him up to keep you so.
Do you approve this? Yours the loss, not mine.
Do you condemn it? There's a remedy.
Take me – who know your mind, and mean your good,
With clearer brain and stouter arm than they,
Or you, or haply anybody else –
1400 And make me master for the moment! Choose
What time, what power you trust me with: I too
Will choose as frankly ere I trust myself
With time and power: they must be adequate
To the end and aim, since mine the loss, with yours,
If means be wanting; once their worth approved,
Grant them, and I shall forthwith operate –
Ponder it well! – to the extremest stretch
O' the power you trust me: if with unsuccess,
God wills it, and there's nobody to blame.'

1410 Whereon the people answered with a shout
'The trusty one! no tricksters any more!'
How could they other? He was in his place.

What followed? Just what he foresaw, what proved
The soundness of both judgements, – his, o' the knaves
And fools, each trickster with his dupe, – and theirs,
The people's, in what head and arm could help.
There was uprising, masks dropped, flags unfurled,
Weapons outflourished in the wind, my faith!
Heavily did he let his fist fall plumb
1420 On each perturber of the public peace,
No matter whose the wagging head it broke –
From bald pate craft and greed and impudence
Of night-hawk at first chance to prowl and prey
For glory and a little gain beside,
Passing for eagle in the dusk of the age, –
To florid head-top, foamy patriotism
And tribunitial daring, breast laid bare
Through confidence in rectitude, with hand
On private pistol in the pocket: these
1430 And all the dupes of these, who lent themselves
As dust and feather do, to help offence

O' the wind that whirls them at you, then subsides
In safety somewhere, leaving filth afloat,
Annoyance you may brush from eyes and beard, –
These he stopped: bade the wind's spite howl or whine
Its worst outside the building, wind conceives
Meant to be pulled together and become
Its natural playground so. What foolishness
Of dust or feather proved importunate
1440   And fell 'twixt thumb and finger, found them gripe
To detriment of bulk and buoyancy.
Then followed silence and submission. Next,
The inevitable comment came on work
And work's cost: he was censured as profuse
Of human life and liberty: too swift
And thorough his procedure, who had lagged
At the outset, lost the opportunity
Through timid scruples as to right and wrong.
'There's no such certain mark of a small mind'
1450   (So did Sagacity explain the fault)
'As when it needs must square away and sink
To its own small dimensions, private scale
Of right and wrong, – humanity i' the large,
The right and wrong of the universe, forsooth!
This man addressed himself to guard and guide
Hohenstiel-Schwangau. When the case demands
He frustrate villainy in the egg, unhatched,
With easy stamp and minimum of pang
E'en to the punished reptile, "There's my oath
1460   Restrains my foot," objects our guide and guard,
"I must leave guardianship and guidance now:
Rather than stretch one handbreadth of the law,
I am bound to see it break from end to end.
First show me death i' the body politic:
Then prescribe pill and potion, what may please
Hohenstiel-Schwangau! all is for her sake:
'Twas she ordained my service should be so.
What if the event demónstrate her unwise,
If she unwill the thing she willed before?
1470   I hold to the letter and obey the bond
And leave her to perdition loyally."
Whence followed thrice the expenditure we blame
Of human life and liberty: for want

O' the by-blow, came deliberate butcher's-work!'
'Elsewhere go carry your complaint!' bade he.
'Least, largest, there's one law for all the minds,
Here or above: be true at any price!
'Tis just o' the great scale, that such happy stroke
Of falsehood would be found a failure. Truth
1480 Still stands unshaken at her base by me,
Reigns paramount i' the world, for the large good
O' the long late generations, – I and you
Forgotten like this buried foolishness!
Not so the good I rooted in its grave.'

This is why he refused to break his oath,
Rather appealed to the people, gained the power
To act as he thought best, then used it, once
For all, no matter what the consequence
To knaves and fools. As thus began his sway,
1490 So, through its twenty years, one rule of right
Sufficed him: govern for the many first,
The poor mean multitude, all mouths and eyes:
Bid the few, better favoured in the brain,
Be patient nor presume on privilege,
Help him or else be quiet, – never crave
That he help them, – increase, forsooth, the gulf
Yawning so terribly 'twixt mind and mind
I' the world here, which his purpose was to block
At bottom, were it by an inch, and bridge,
1500 If by a filament, no more, at top.
Equalize things a little! And the way
He took to work that purpose out, was plain
Enough to intellect and honesty
And – superstition, style it if you please,
So long as you allow there was no lack
O' the quality imperative in man –
Reverence. You see deeper? thus saw he,
And by the light he saw, must walk: how else
Was he to do his part? a man's, with might
1510 And main, and not a faintest touch of fear,
Sure he was in the hand of God who comes
Before and after, with a work to do
Which no man helps nor hinders. Thus the man, –
So timid when the business was to touch

The uncertain order of humanity,
Imperil, for a problematic cure
Of grievance on the surface, any good
I' the deep of things, dim yet discernible –
This same man, so irresolute before,
1520 Show him a true excrescence to cut sheer,
A devil's-graft on God's foundation-stock,
Then – no complaint of indecision more!
He wrenched out the whole canker, root and branch,
Deaf to who cried that earth would tumble in
At its four corners if he touched a twig.
Witness that lie of lies, arch-infamy,
When the Republic, with her life involved
In just this law – 'Each people rules itself
Its own way, not as any stranger please' –
1530 Turned, and for first proof she was living, bade
Hohenstiel-Schwangau fasten on the throat
Of the first neighbour that claimed benefit
O' the law herself established: 'Hohenstiel
For Hohenstielers! Rome, by parity
Of reasoning, for Romans? That's a jest
Wants proper treatment, – lancet-puncture suits
The proud flesh: Rome ape Hohenstiel forsooth!'
And so the siege and slaughter and success
Whereof we nothing doubt that Hohenstiel
1540 Will have to pay the price, in God's good time
Which does not always fall on Saturday
When the world looks for wages. Anyhow,
He found this infamy triumphant. Well:
Sagacity suggested, make this speech!
'The work was none of mine: suppose wrong wait,
Stand over for redressing? Mine for me,
My predecessors' work on their own head!
Meantime there's plain advantage, should we leave
Things as we find them. Keep Rome manacled
1550 Hand and foot: no fear of unruliness!
Her foes consent to even seem our friends
So long, no longer. Then, there's glory got
By boldness and bravado to the world:
The disconcerted world must grin and bear
The old saucy writing, "Grunt thereat who may,
So shall things be, for such my pleasure is –

Hohenstiel-Schwangau's." How that reads in Rome
I' the Capitol where Brennus broke his pate,
And lends a flourish to our journalists!'
1560 Only, it was nor read nor flourished of,
Since, not a moment did such glory stay
Excision of the canker! Out it came,
Root and branch, with much roaring, and some blood,
And plentiful abuse of him from friend
And foe. Who cared? Not Nature who assuaged
The pain and set the patient on his legs
Promptly: the better! had it been the worse,
'Tis Nature you must try conclusions with,
Not he, since nursing canker kills the sick
1570 For certain, while to cut may cure, at least.
'Ah,' groaned a second time Sagacity,
'Again the little mind, precipitate,
Rash, rude, when even in the right, as here!
The great mind knows the power of gentleness,
Only tries force because persuasion fails.
Had this man, by prelusive trumpet-blast,
Signified "Truth and Justice mean to come,
Nay, fast approach your threshold! Ere they knock,
See that the house be set in order, swept
1580 And garnished, windows shut, and doors thrown wide!
The free State comes to visit the free Church:
Receive her! or ... or ... never mind what else!"
Thus moral suasion heralding brute force,
How had he seen the old abuses die,
And new life kindle here, there, everywhere,
Roused simply by that mild yet potent spell –
Beyond or beat of drum or stroke of sword –
Public opinion!'

'How, indeed?' he asked,
'When all to see, after some twenty years,
1590 Were your own fool-face waiting for the sight,
Faced by as wide a grin from ear to ear
O' the knaves who, while the fools were waiting, worked –
Broke yet another generation's heart –
Twenty years' respite helping! Teach your nurse
"Compliance with, before you suck, the teat!"
Find what that means, and meanwhile hold your tongue!'

Whereof the war came which he knew must be.

Now, this had proved the dry-rot of the race
He ruled o'er, that, i' the old day, when was need
1600 They fought for their own liberty and life,
Well did they fight, none better: whence, such love
Of fighting somehow still for fighting's sake
Against no matter whose the liberty
And life, so long as self-conceit should crow
And clap the wing, while justice sheathed her claw, –
That what had been the glory of the world
When thereby came the world's good, grew its plague
Now that the champion-armour, donned to dare
The dragon once, was clattered up and down
1610 Highway and by-path of the world at peace,
Merely to mask marauding, or for sake
O' the shine and rattle that apprised the fields
Hohenstiel-Schwangau was a fighter yet,
And would be, till the weary world suppressed
Her peccant humours out of fashion now.
Accordingly the world spoke plain at last,
Promised to punish who next played with fire.

So, at his advent, such discomfiture
Taking its true shape of beneficence,
1620 Hohenstiel-Schwangau, half-sad and part-wise,
Sat: if with wistful eye reverting oft
To each pet weapon, rusty on its peg,
Yet, with a sigh of satisfaction too
That, peacefulness become the law, herself
Got the due share of godsends in its train,
Cried shame and took advantage quietly.
Still, so the dry-rot had been nursed into
Blood, bones and marrow, that, from worst to best,
All, – clearest brains and soundest hearts save here, –
1630 All had this lie acceptable for law
Plain as the sun at noonday – 'War is best,
Peace is worst; peace we only tolerate
As needful preparation for new war:
War may be for whatever end we will –
Peace only as the proper help thereto.
Such is the law of right and wrong for us

Hohenstiel-Schwangau: for the other world,
As naturally, quite another law.
Are we content? The world is satisfied.
1640 Discontent? Then the world must give us leave
To strike right, left, and exercise our arm
Torpid of late through overmuch repose,
And show its strength is still superlative
At somebody's expense in life or limb:
Which done, – let peace succeed and last a year!'
Such devil's-doctrine so was judged God's law,
We say, when this man stepped upon the stage,
That it had seemed a venial fault at most
Had he once more obeyed Sagacity.
1650 'You come i' the happy interval of peace,
The favourable weariness from war:
Prolong it! artfully, as if intent
On ending peace as soon as possible.
Quietly so increase the sweets of ease
And safety, so employ the multitude,
Put hod and trowel so in idle hands,
So stuff and stop up wagging jaws with bread,
That selfishness shall surreptitiously
Do wisdom's office, whisper in the ear
1660 Of Hohenstiel-Schwangau, there's a pleasant feel
In being gently forced down, pinioned fast
To the easy arm-chair by the pleading arms
O' the world beseeching her to there abide
Content with all the harm done hitherto,
And let herself be petted in return,
Free to re-wage, in speech and prose and verse,
The old unjust wars, nay – in verse and prose
And speech, – to vaunt new victories shall prove
A plague o' the future, – so that words suffice
1670 For present comfort, and no deeds denote
That – tired of illimitable line on line
Of boulevard-building, tired o' the theatre
With the tuneful thousand in their thrones above,
For glory of the male intelligence,
And Nakedness in her due niche below,
For illustration of the female use –
That she, 'twixt yawn and sigh, prepares to slip
Out of the arm-chair, wants fresh blood again

From over the boundary, to colour-up
1680 The sheeny sameness, keep the world aware
Hohenstiel-Schwangau's arm needs exercise
Despite the petting of the universe!
Come, you're a city-builder: what's the way
Wisdom takes when time needs that she entice
Some fierce tribe, castled on the mountain-peak,
Into the quiet and amenity
O' the meadow-land below? By crying "Done
With fight now, down with fortress?" Rather – "Dare
On, dare ever, not a stone displace!"
1690 Cries Wisdom: "Cradle of our ancestors,
Be bulwark, give our children safety still!
Who of our children please may stoop and taste
O' the valley-fatness, unafraid, – for why?
At first alarm they have thy mother-ribs
To run upon for refuge: foes forget
Scarcely that Terror on her vantage-coign,
Couchant supreme among the powers of air,
Watches – prepared to pounce – the country wide!
Meanwhile the encouraged valley holds its own,
1700 From the first hut's adventure in descent,
Half home, half hiding place, – to dome and spire
Befitting the assured metropolis:
Nor means offence to the fort which caps the crag,
All undismantled of a turret-stone,
And bears the banner-pole that creaks at times
Embarrassed by the old emblazonment,
When festal days are to commemorate:
Otherwise left untenanted, no doubt,
Since, never fear, our myriads from below
1710 Would rush, if needs were, man the walls again,
Renew the exploits of the earlier time
At moment's notice! But till notice sound,
Inhabit we in ease and opulence!"
And so, till one day thus a notice sounds,
Not trumpeted, but in a whisper-gust
Fitfully playing through mute city streets
At midnight weary of day's feast and game –
"Friends, your famed fort's a ruin past repair!
Its use is – to proclaim it had a use
1720 Obsolete long since. Climb and study there

How to paint barbican and battlement
I' the scenes of our new theatre! We fight
Now – by forbidding neighbours to sell steel
Or buy wine, not by blowing out their brains!
Moreover, while we let time sap the strength
O' the walls omnipotent in menace once,
Neighbours would seem to have prepared surprise –
Run up defences in a mushroom-growth,
For all the world like what we boasted: brief –
1730   Hohenstiel-Schwangau's policy is peace!" '

Ay, so Sagacity advised him filch
Folly from fools: handsomely substitute
The dagger o' lath, while gay they sang and danced,
For that long dangerous sword they liked to feel,
Even at feast-time, clink and make friends start.
No! he said 'Hear the truth, and bear the truth,
And bring the truth to bear on all you are
And do, assured that only good comes thence
Whate'er the shape good take! While I have rule,
1740   Understand! – war for war's sake, war for sake
O' the good war gets you as war's sole excuse,
Is damnable and damned shall be. You want
Glory? Why so do I, and so does God.
Where is it found, – in this paraded shame, –
One particle of glory? Once you warred
For liberty against the world, and won:
There was the glory. Now, you fain would war
Because the neighbour prospers overmuch, –
Because there has been silence half-an-hour,
1750   Like Heaven on earth, without a cannon-shot
Announcing Hohenstielers-Schwangauese
Are minded to disturb the jubilee, –
Because the loud tradition echoes faint,
And who knows but posterity may doubt
If the great deeds were ever done at all,
Much less believe, were such to do again,
So the event would follow: therefore, prove
The old power, at the expense of somebody!
Oh Glory, – gilded bubble, bard and sage
1760   So nickname rightly, – would thy dance endure
One moment, would thy vaunting make believe

Only one eye thy ball was solid gold,
Hadst thou less breath to buoy thy vacancy
Than a whole multitude expends in praise,
Less range for roaming than from head to head
Of a whole people? Flit, fall, fly again,
Only, fix never where the resolute hand
May prick thee, prove the glassy lie thou art!
Give me real intellect to reason with,
1770 No multitude, no entity that apes
One wise man, being but a million fools!
How and whence wishest glory, thou wise one?
Wouldst get it, – didst thyself guide Providence, –
By stinting of his due each neighbour round
In strength and knowledge and dexterity
So as to have thy littleness grow large
By all those somethings once, turned nothings now,
As children make a molehill mountainous
By scooping out a trench around their pile,
1780 And saving so the mudwork from approach?
Quite otherwise the cheery game of life,
True yet mimetic warfare, whereby man
Does his best with his utmost, and so ends
A victor most of all in fair defeat.
Who thinks, – would he have no one think beside?
Who knows, who does, – save his must learning die
And action cease? Why, so our giant proves
No better than a dwarf, once rivalry
Prostrate around him. Let the whole race stand
1790 For him to try conclusions fairly with!
Show me the great man would engage his peer
Rather by grinning "Cheat, thy gold is brass!"
Than granting "Perfect piece of purest ore!
Still, is it less good mintage, this of mine?"
Well, and these right and sound results of soul
I' the strong and healthy one wise man, – shall such
Be vainly sought for, scornfully renounced
I' the multitude that make the entity –
The people? – to what purpose, if no less,
1800 In power and purity of soul, below
The reach of the unit than, by multiplied
Might of the body, vulgarized the more,
Above, in thick and threefold brutishness?

See! you accept such one wise man, myself:
Wiser or less wise, still I operate
From my own stock of wisdom, nor exact
Of other sort of natures you admire,
That whoso rhymes a sonnet pays a tax,
Who paints a landscape dips brush at his cost,
1810 Who scores a septett true for strings and wind
Mulcted must be – else how should I impose
Properly, attitudinize aright,
Did such conflicting claims as these divert
Hohenstiel-Schwangau from observing me?
Therefore, what I find facile, you be sure,
With effort or without it, you shall dare –
You, I aspire to make my better self
And truly the Great Nation. No more war
For war's sake, then! and, – seeing, wickedness
1820 Springs out of folly, – no more foolish dread
O' the neighbour waxing too inordinate
A rival, through his gain of wealth and ease!
What? – keep me patient, Powers! – the people here,
Earth presses to her heart, nor owns a pride
Above her pride i' the race all flame and air
And aspiration to the boundless Great,
The incommensurably Beautiful –
Whose very falterings groundward come of flight
Urged by a pinion all too passionate
1830 For heaven and what it holds of gloom and glow:
Bravest of thinkers, bravest of the brave
Doers, exalt in Science, rapturous
In Art, the – more than all – magnetic race
To fascinate their fellows, mould mankind
Hohenstiel-Schwangau-fashion, – these, what? – these
Will have to abdicate their primacy
Should such a nation sell them steel untaxed,
And such another take itself, on hire
For the natural sen'night, somebody for lord
1840 Unpatronized by me whose back was turned?
Or such another yet would fain build bridge,
Lay rail, drive tunnel, busy its poor self
With its appropriate fancy: so there's – flash –
Hohenstiel-Schwangau up in arms at once!
Genius has somewhat of the infantine:

But of the childish, not a touch nor taint
Except through self-will, which, being foolishness,
Is certain, soon or late, of punishment
Which Providence avert! – and that it may
1850 Avert what both of us would so deserve,
No foolish dread o' the neighbour, I enjoin!
By consequence, no wicked war with him,
While I rule!

        Does that mean – no war at all
When just the wickedness I here proscribe
Comes, haply, from the neighbour? Does my speech
Precede the praying that you beat the sword
To ploughshare, and the spear to pruning-hook,
And sit down henceforth under your own vine
And fig-tree through the sleepy summer month,
1860 Letting what hurly-burly please explode
On the other side the mountain-frontier? No,
Beloved! I foresee and I announce
Necessity of warfare in one case,
For one cause: one way, I bid broach the blood
O' the world. For truth and right, and only right
And truth, – right, truth, on the absolute scale of God,
No pettiness of man's admeasurement, –
In such case only, and for such one cause,
Fight your hearts out, whatever fate betide
1870 Hands energetic to the uttermost!
Lie not! Endure no lie which needs your heart
And hand to push it out of mankind's path –
No lie that lets the natural forces work
Too long ere lay it plain and pulverized –
Seeing man's life lasts only twenty years!
And such a lie, before both man and God,
Proving, at this time present, Austria's rule
O'er Italy, – for Austria's sake the first,
Italy's next, and our sake last of all,
1880 Come with me and deliver Italy!
Smite hip and thigh until the oppressor leave
Free from the Adriatic to the Alps
The oppressed one! We were they who laid her low
In the old bad day when Villainy braved Truth
And Right, and laughed "Henceforward, God deposed,

Satan we set to rule for evermore
I' the world!" – whereof to stop the consequence,
And for atonement of false glory there
Gaped at and gabbled over by the world,
I purpose to get God enthroned again
1890 For what the world will gird at as sheer shame
I' the cost of blood and treasure. "All for naught –
Not even, say, some patch of province, splice
O' the frontier? – some snug honorarium-fee
Shut into glove and pocketed apace?"
(Questions Sagacity) "in deference
To the natural susceptibility
Of folks at home, unwitting of that pitch
You soar to, and misdoubting if Truth, Right
1900 And the other such augustnesses repay
Expenditure in coin o' the realm, – but prompt
To recognize the cession of Savoy
And Nice as marketable value!" No,
Sagacity, go preach to Metternich,
And, sermon ended, stay where he resides!
Hohenstiel-Schwangau, you and I must march
The other road! war for the hate of war,
Not love, this once!' So Italy was free.

What else noteworthy and commendable
1910 I' the man's career? – that he was resolute
No trepidation, much less treachery
On his part, should imperil from its poise
The ball o' the world, heaved up at such expense
Of pains so far, and ready to rebound,
Let but a finger maladroitly fall,
Under pretence of making fast and sure
The inch gained by late volubility,
And run itself back to the ancient rest
At foot o' the mountain. Thus he ruled, gave proof
1920 The world had gained a point, progressive so,
By choice, this time, as will and power concurred,
O' the fittest man to rule; not chance of birth,
Or such-like dice-throw. Oft Sagacity
Was at his ear: 'Confirm this clear advance,
Support this wise procedure! You, elect
O' the people, mean to justify their choice

And out-king all the kingly imbeciles;
But that's just half the enterprise: remains
You find them a successor like yourself,
1930 In head and heart and eye and hand and aim,
Or all done's undone; and whom hope to mould
So like you as the pupil Nature sends,
The son and heir's completeness which you lack?
Lack it no longer! Wed the pick o' the world,
Where'er you think you find it. Should she be
A queen, – tell Hohenstielers-Schwangauese
"So do the old enthroned decrepitudes
Acknowledge, in the rotten hearts of them,
Their knell is knolled, they hasten to make peace
1940 With the new order, recognize in me
Your right to constitute what king you will,
Cringe therefore crown in hand and bride on arm,
To both of us: we triumph, I suppose!"
Is it the other sort of rank? – bright eye,
Soft smile, and so forth, all her queenly boast?
Undaunted the exordium – "I, the man
O' the people, with the people mate myself:
So stand, so fall. Kings, keep your crowns and brides!
Our progeny (if Providence agree)
1950 Shall live to tread the baubles underfoot
And bid the scarecrows consort with their kin.
For son, as for his sire, be the free wife
In the free state!"'

That is, Sagacity
Would prop up one more lie, the most of all
Pernicious fancy that the son and heir
Receives the genius from the sire, himself
Transmits as surely, – ask experience else!
Which answers, – never was so plain a truth
As that God drops his seed of heavenly flame
1960 Just where He wills on earth: sometimes where man
Seems to tempt – such the accumulated store
Of faculties – one spark to fire the heap;
Sometimes where, fire-ball-like, it falls upon
The naked unpreparedness of rock,
Burns, beaconing the nations through their night.
Faculties, fuel for the flame? All helps

Come, ought to come, or come not, crossed by chance,
From culture and transmission. What's your want
I' the son and heir? Sympathy, aptitude,
1970 Teachableness, the fuel for the flame?
You'll have them for your pains: but the flame's self,
The novel thought of God shall light the world?
No, poet, though your offspring rhyme and chime
I' the cradle, – painter, no, for all your pet
Draws his first eye, beats Salvatore's boy, –
And thrice no, statesman, should your progeny
Tie bib and tucker with no tape but red,
And make a foolscap-kite of protocols!
Critic and copyist and bureaucrat
1980 To heart's content! The seed o' the apple-tree
Brings forth another tree which bears a crab:
'Tis the great gardener grafts the excellence
On wildings where he will.

                              'How plain I view,
Across those misty years 'twixt me and Rome' –
(Such the man's answer to Sagacity)
'The little wayside temple, half-way down
To a mild river that makes oxen white
Miraculously, un-mouse-colours skin,
Or so the Roman country people dream!
1990 I view that sweet small shrub-embedded shrine
On the declivity, was sacred once
To a transmuting Genius of the land,
Could touch and turn its dunnest natures bright,
– Since Italy means the Land of the Ox, we know.
Well, how was it the due succession fell
From priest to priest who ministered i' the cool
Calm fane o' the Clitumnian god? The sire
Brought forth a son and sacerdotal sprout,
Endowed instinctively with good and grace
2000 To suit the gliding gentleness below –
Did he? Tradition tells another tale.
Each priest obtained his predecessor's staff,
Robe, fillet and insignia, blamelessly,
By springing out of ambush, soon or late,
And slaying him: the initiative rite
Simply was murder, save that murder took,

I' the case, another and religious name.
So it was once, is now, shall ever be
With genius and its priesthood in this world:
2010 The new power slays the old – but handsomely.
There he lies, not diminished by an inch
Of stature that he graced the altar with,
Though somebody of other bulk and build
Cries "What a goodly personage lies here
Reddening the water where the bulrush roots!
May I conduct the service in his place,
Decently and in order, as did he,
And, as he did not, keep a wary watch
When meditating 'neath yon willow shade!"
2020 Find out your best man, sure the son of him
Will prove best man again, and, better still
Somehow than best, the grandson-prodigy!
You think the world would last another day
Did we so make us masters of the trick
Whereby the works go, we could pre-arrange
Their play and reach perfection when we please?
Depend on it, the change and the surprise
Are part o' the plan: 'tis we wish steadiness;
Nature prefers a motion by unrest,
2030 Advancement through this force which jostles that.
And so, since much remains i' the world to see,
Here's the world still, affording God the sight.'
Thus did the man refute Sagacity
Ever at this old whisper in his ear:
'Here are you picked out, by a miracle,
And placed conspicuously enough, folks say
And you believe, by Providence outright
Taking a new way – nor without success –
To put the world upon its mettle: good!
2040 But Fortune alternates with Providence;
Resource is soon exhausted. Never count
On such a happy hit occurring twice!
Try the old method next time!'

                       'Old enough,'
(At whisper in his ear, the laugh outbroke)
'And mode the most discredited of all,
By just the men and women who make boast

They are kings and queens thereby! Mere self-defence
Should teach them, on one chapter of the law
Must be no sort of trifling – chastity:
2050 They stand or fall, as their progenitors
Were chaste or unchaste. Now, run eye around
My crowned acquaintance, give each life its look
And no more, – why, you'd think each life was led
Purposely for example of what pains
Who leads it took to cure the prejudice,
And prove there's nothing so unprovable
As who is who, what son of what a sire,
And, – inferentially, – how faint the chance
That the next generation needs to fear
2060 Another fool o' the selfsame type as he
Happily regnant now by right divine
And luck o' the pillow! No: select your lord
By the direct employment of your brains
As best you may, – bad as the blunder prove,
A far worse evil stank beneath the sun
When some legitimate blockhead managed so
Matters that high time was to interfere,
Though interference came from hell itself
And not the blind mad miserable mob
2070 Happily ruled so long by pillow-luck
And divine right, – by lies in short, not truth.
And meanwhile use the allotted minute ...'

——————————

One, –
Two, three, four, five – yes, five the *pendule* warns!
Eh? Why, this wild work wanders past all bound
And bearing! Exile, Leicester Square, the life
I' the old gay miserable time, rehearsed,
Tried on again like cast clothes, still to serve
At a pinch, perhaps? 'Who's who?' was aptly asked,
Since certainly I am not I! since when?
2080 Where is the bud-mouthed arbitress? A nod
Out-Homering Homer! Stay – there flits the clue
I fain would find the end of! Yes, – 'Meanwhile,
Use the allotted minute!' Well, you see,
(Veracious and imaginary Thiers,
Who map out thus the life I might have led,

But did not, – all the worse for earth and me –
Doff spectacles, wipe pen, shut book, decamp!)
You see 'tis easy in heroics! Plain
Pedestrian speech shall help me perorate.
2090 Ah, if one had no need to use the tongue!
How obvious and how easy 'tis to talk
Inside the soul, a ghostly dialogue –
Instincts with guesses, – instinct, guess, again
With dubious knowledge, half-experience: each
And all the interlocutors alike
Subordinating, – as decorum bids,
Oh, never fear! but still decisively, –
Claims from without that take too high a tone,
– ('God wills this, man wants that, the dignity
2100 Prescribed a prince would wish the other thing') –
Putting them back to insignificance
Beside one intimatest fact – myself
Am first to be considered, since I live
Twenty years longer and then end, perhaps!
But, where one ceases to soliloquize,
Somehow the motives, that did well enough
I' the darkness, when you bring them into light
Are found, like those famed cave-fish, to lack eye
And organ for the upper magnitudes.
2110 The other common creatures, of less fine
Existence, that acknowledge earth and heaven,
Have it their own way in the argument.
Yes, forced to speak, one stoops to say – one's aim
Was – what it peradventure should have been:
To renovate a people, mend or end
That bane come of a blessing meant the world –
Inordinate culture of the sense made quick
By soul, – the lust o' the flesh, lust of the eye,
And pride of life, – and, consequent on these,
2120 The worship of that prince o' the power o' the air
Who paints the cloud and fills the emptiness
And bids his votaries, famishing for truth,
Feed on a lie.

      Alack, one lies oneself
Even in the stating that one's end was truth,
Truth only, if one states as much in words!

Give me the inner chamber of the soul
For obvious easy argument! 'tis there
One pits the silent truth against a lie –
Truth which breaks shell a careless simple bird,
2130 Nor wants a gorget nor a beak filed fine,
Steel spurs, and the whole armoury o' the tongue,
To equalize the odds. But, do your best,
Words have to come: and somehow words deflect
As the best cannon ever rifled will.

'Deflect' indeed! nor merely words from thoughts
But names from facts: 'Clitumnus' did I say?
As if it had been his ox-whitening wave
Whereby folk practised that grim cult of old –
The murder of their temple's priest by who
2140 Would qualify for his succession. Sure –
Nemi was the true lake's style. Dream had need
Of the ox-whitening piece of prettiness
And so confused names, well known once awake.

So, i' the Residenz yet, not Leicester Square,
Alone, – no such congenial intercourse! –
My reverie concludes, as dreaming should,
With daybreak: nothing done and over yet,
Except cigars! The adventure thus may be,
Or never needs to be at all: who knows?
2150 My Cousin-Duke, perhaps, at whose hard head
– Is it, now – is this letter to be launched,
The sight of whose grey oblong, whose grim seal,
Set all these fancies floating for an hour?

Twenty years are good gain, come what come will!
Double or quits! The letter goes! Or stays?

Appendix 1: Browning's 'Introductory Essay'
['*Essay on Shelley*']

The 'Introductory Essay' was published in 1852 by Edward Moxon in *Letters of Percy Bysshe Shelley*, a book swiftly withdrawn from publication when the letters were discovered to be forgeries. Browning's essay, written late in 1851, has generally been regarded as an important expression of his feeling about the poet who had so strongly influenced him, and as even more significant as expressive of fundamentals in Browning's aesthetic. There is, however, strong disagreement about a number of points of central importance in the statement, disagreement focused clearly in Philip Drew, 'Browning's *Essay on Shelley*', *Victorian Poetry* I, 1963, 1–6, and T. J. Collins, 'Browning's *Essay on Shelley*: In Context', *Victorian Poetry* II, 1964, 119–24; Drew treats the essay again in his *The Poetry of Browning: A Critical Introduction*, 5–11, as does Collins in *Browning's Moral-Aesthetic Theory*, 113-22.

Introductory Essay

An opportunity having presented itself for the acquisition of a series of un-edited letters by Shelley, all more or less directly supplementary to and illustrative of the collection already published by Mr Moxon, that gentleman has decided on securing them. They will prove an acceptable addition to a body of correspondence, the value of which towards a right understanding of its author's purpose and work, may be said to exceed that of any similar con-tribution exhibiting the worldly relations of a poet whose genius has operated by a different law.

Doubtless we accept gladly the biography of an objective poet, as the phrase now goes; one whose endeavour has been to reproduce things external (whether the phenomena of the scenic universe, or the manifested action of the human heart and brain) with an immediate reference, in every case, to the common eye and apprehension of his fellow men, assumed capable of receiving and profiting by this reproduction. It has been obtained through the poet's double faculty of seeing external objects more clearly, widely, and deeply, than is possible to the average mind, at the same time that he is so acquainted and in sympathy with its narrower comprehension as to be careful to supply it with no other materials than it can combine into an intelligible whole. The auditory of such a poet will include, not only the intelligences which, save for such assistance, would have missed the deeper meaning and enjoyment of the original objects, but also the spirits of a like endowment with his own, who, by means of his abstract, can forthwith pass to the reality it was made from, and either corroborate their impressions of things known already, or supply themselves with new from whatever shows in the inex-haustible variety of existence may have hitherto escaped their knowledge. Such a poet is properly the ποιητης, the fashioner; and the thing fashioned, his poetry, will of necessity be substantive, projected from himself and distinct. We are ignorant what the inventor of 'Othello' conceived of that fact as he beheld it in completeness, how he accounted for it, under what known law he registered its nature, or to what unknown law he traced its coincidence. We learn only what he intended we should learn by that particular exercise of his power, – the fact itself, – which, with its infinite significances, each of us receives for the first time as a creation, and is here-after left to deal with, as, in proportion to his own intelligence, he best may. We are ignorant, and would fain be otherwise.

Doubtless, with respect to such a poet, we covet his biography. We desire to look back upon the process of gathering together in a lifetime, the materials of the work we behold entire; of elaborating, perhaps under difficulty and with hindrance, all that is familiar to our admiration in the apparent facility of success. And the inner impulse of this effort and operation, what induced it? Did a soul's delight in its own extended sphere of vision set it, for the gratification of an insuppressible power, on labour, as other men are set on rest? Or did a sense of duty or of love lead it to communicate its own sensations to mankind? Did an irresistible sympathy with men compel it to bring down and suit its own provision of knowledge and beauty to their narrow scope? Did the personality of such an one stand like an open watch-tower in the midst of the territory it is erected to gaze on, and were the storms and calms, the stars and meteors, its watchman was wont to report of, the habitual variegation of his every-day life, as they glanced across its open roof or lay reflected on its four-square parapet? Or did some sunken and darkened chamber of imagery witness, in the artificial illumination of every storied compartment we are permitted to contemplate, how rare and precious were the outlooks through here and there an embrasure upon a world beyond, and how blankly would have pressed on the artificer the boundary of his daily life, except for the amorous diligence with which he had rendered permanent by art whatever came to diversify the gloom? Still, fraught with instruction and interest as such details undoubtedly are, we can, if needs be, dispense with them. The man passes, the work remains. The work speaks for itself, as we say: and the biography of the worker is no more necessary to an understanding or enjoyment of it, than is a model or anatomy of some tropical tree, to the right tasting of the fruit we are familiar with on the market-stall, – or a geologist's map and stratification, to the prompt recognition of the hill-top, our landmark of every day.

We turn with stronger needs to the genius of an opposite tendency – the subjective poet of modern classification. He, gifted like the objective poet with the fuller perception of nature and man, is impelled to embody the thing he perceives, not so much with reference to the many below as to the one above him, the supreme Intelligence which apprehends all things in their absolute truth, – an ultimate view ever aspired to, if but partially attained, by the poet's own soul. Not what man sees, but what God sees – the *Ideas* of Plato, seeds of creation lying burningly on the Divine Hand – it is toward these that he struggles. Not with the combination of humanity in action, but with the primal elements of humanity he has to do; and he digs where he stands, – preferring to seek them in his own soul as the nearest reflex of that absolute Mind, according to the intuitions of which he desires to perceive and speak. Such a poet does not deal habitually with the picturesque groupings and tempestuous tossings of the forest-trees, but with their roots and fibres naked to the chalk and stone. He does not paint pictures and hang them on the walls, but rather carries them on the retina of his own eyes: we must look deep into his human eyes, to see those pictures on them. He is rather a seer, accordingly, than a fashioner, and what he produces will be less a work than an effluence. That effluence cannot be easily considered in abstraction from his personality, – being indeed the very radiance and aroma of his personality, projected from it but not separated. Therefore, in our approach to the poetry, we necessarily approach the personality of the poet; in apprehending it we apprehend him, and certainly we cannot love it without loving him. Both for love's and for understanding's sake we desire to know him, and as readers of his poetry must be readers of his biography also.

I shall observe, in passing, that it seems not so much from any essential distinction in the faculty of the two poets or in the nature of the objects contemplated by either, as in the more immediate adaptability of these objects to the distinct purpose of each, that the objective poet, in his appeal to the aggregate human mind, chooses to deal with the doings of men, (the result of which dealing, in its pure form, when even description, as suggesting a describer, is dispensed with, is what we call dramatic poetry), while the subjective poet, whose study has been himself, appealing through himself to the absolute Divine mind, prefers to dwell upon those external scenic appearances which strike out most abundantly and uninterruptedly his inner light and power, selects that silence of the earth and sea in which he can best hear the beating of his individual heart, and leaves the noisy, complex, yet imperfect exhibitions of nature in the manifold experience of man around him, which serve only to distract and suppress the working of his brain. These opposite tendencies of genius will be more readily descried in their artistic effect than in their moral spring and cause. Pushed to an extreme and manifested as a deformity, they will be seen plainest of all in the fault of either artist, when subsidiarily to the human interest of his work his occasional illustrations from scenic nature are introduced as in the earlier works of the originative painters – men and women filling the foreground with consummate mastery, while mountain, grove and rivulet show like an anticipatory revenge on that succeeding race of landscape-painters whose 'figures' disturb the perfection of their earth and sky. It would be idle to inquire, of these two kinds of poetic faculty in operation, which is the higher or even rarer endowment. If the subjective might seem to be the ultimate requirement of every age, the objective, in the strictest state, must still retain its original value. For it is with this world, as starting point and basis alike, that we shall always have to concern ourselves: the world is not to be learned and thrown aside, but reverted to and relearned. The spiritual comprehension may be infinitely subtilized, but the raw material it operates upon, must remain. There may be no end of the poets who communicate to us what they see in an object with reference to their own individuality; what it was before they saw it, in reference to the aggregate human mind, will be as desirable to know as ever. Nor is there any reason why these two modes of poetic faculty may not issue hereafter from the same poet in successive perfect works, examples of which, according to what are now considered the exigences of art, we have hitherto possessed in distinct individuals only. A mere running-in of the one faculty upon the other, is, of course, the ordinary circumstance. Far more rarely it happens that either is found so decidedly prominent and superior, as to be pronounced comparatively pure: while of the perfect shield, with the gold and the silver side set up for all comers to challenge, there has yet been no instance. Either faculty in its eminent state is doubtless conceded by Providence as a best gift to men, according to their especial want. There is a time when the general eye has, so to speak, absorbed its fill of the phenomena around it, whether spiritual or material, and desires rather to learn the exacter significance of what it possesses, than to receive any augmentation of what is possessed. Then is the opportunity for the poet of loftier vision, to lift his fellows, with their half-apprehensions, up to his own sphere, by intensifying the import of details and rounding the universal meaning. The influence of such an achievement will not soon die out. A tribe of successors (Homerides) working more or less in the same spirit, dwell on his discoveries and reinforce his doctrine; till, at unawares, the world is found to be subsisting wholly on the shadow of a reality, on sentiments diluted from passions, on the tradition of a fact, the convention of a moral, the straw of last year's harvest. Then is the imperative call for the appearance of another sort of poet, who shall at once replace this intellectual rumination of food swallowed long ago, by a supply of the fresh and living swathe; getting at new substance by breaking up the assumed wholes into parts of independent and unclassed value, careless of the un-known laws for re-combining them (it will be the business of yet another poet to suggest those hereafter), prodigal of objects for men's outer and not inner sight, shaping for their uses a new and different creation from the last, which it displaces by the right of life over death, – to endure until, in the inevitable process, its very sufficiency to itself shall require, at length, an exposition of its affinity to something higher, – when the positive yet conflicting facts shall again precipitate themselves under a harmonizing law, and one more degree will be apparent for a poet to climb in that mighty ladder, of which, however cloud-involved and undefined may glimmer the topmost step, the world dares no longer doubt that its gradations ascend.

Such being the two kinds of artists, it is naturally, as I have shown, with the biography of the subjective poet that we have the deeper concern. Apart from his recorded life altogether, we might fail to determine with satisfactory pre-cision to what class his productions belong, and what amount of praise is assignable to the producer. Certainly, in the face of any conspicuous achieve-ment of genius, philosophy, no less than sympathetic instinct, warrants our belief in a great moral purpose having mainly inspired even where it does not visibly look out of the same. Greatness in a work suggests an adequate instrumentality; and none of the lower incitements, however they may avail to initiate or even effect many considerable displays of power, simulating the nobler inspiration to which they are mistakenly referred, have been found able, under the ordinary conditions of humanity, to task themselves to the end of so exacting a performance as a poet's complete work. As soon will the galvan-ism that provokes to violent action the muscles of a corpse, induce it to cross the chamber steadily: sooner. The love of displaying power for the display's sake, the love of riches, of distinction, of notoriety, – the desire of a triumph over rivals, and the vanity in the applause of friends, – each and all of such whetted appetites grow intenser by exercise and increasingly sagacious as to the best and readiest means of self-appeasement, – while for any of their ends, whether the money or the pointed finger of the crowd, or the flattery and hate to heart's content, there are cheaper prices to pay, they will all find soon enough, than the bestowment of a life upon a labour, hard, slow, and not sure. Also, assuming the proper moral aim to have produced a work, there are many and various states of an aim: it may be more intense than clear-sighted, or too easily satisfied with a lower field of activity than a steadier aspiration would reach. All the bad poetry in the world (accounted poetry, that is, by its affinities) will be found to result from some one of the infinite degrees of discrepancy between the attributes of the poet's soul, occasioning a want of correspondency between his work and the verities of nature, – issuing in poetry, false under whatever form, which shows a thing not as it is to mankind generally, nor as it is to the particular describer, but as it is supposed to be for some unreal neutral mood, midway between both and of value to neither, and living its brief minute simply through the indolence of whoever accepts it or his incapacity to denounce a cheat. Although of such depths of failure there can be no question here we must in every case betake ourselves to the review of a poet's life ere we determine some of the nicer questions concerning his poetry, – more especially if the performance we seek to estimate aright, has been obstructed and cut short of completion by circumstances, – a disastrous youth or a premature death. We may learn from the biography whether his spirit invariably saw and spoke from the last height to which it had attained. An absolute vision is not for this world, but we are permitted a continual approximation to it, every degree of which in the individual, provided it exceed the attainment of the masses, must procure him a clear advantage. Did the poet ever attain to a higher platform than where he rested and exhibited a result? Did he know more than he spoke of?

I concede however, in respect to the subject of our study as well as some few other illustrious examples, that the unmistakable quality of the verse would be evidence enough, under usual circumstances, not only of the kind and degree of the intellectual but of the moral constitution of Shelley: the whole personality of the poet shining forward from the poems, without much need of going further to seek it. The 'Remains' – produced within a period of ten years, and at a season of life when other men of at all comparable genius have hardly done more than prepare the eye for future sight and the tongue for speech – present us with the complete enginery of a poet, as signal in the excellence of its several adaptitudes as transcendent in the combination of effects, – examples, in fact, of the whole poet's function of beholding with an understanding keenness the universe, nature and man, in their actual state of perfection in imperfection, – of the whole poet's virtue of being untempted by the manifold partial developments of beauty and good on every side, into leaving them the ultimates he found them, – induced by the facility of the gratification of his own sense of those qualities, or by the pleasure of acquiescence in the shortcomings of his predecessors in art, and the pain of disturbing their conventionalisms, – the whole poet's virtue, I repeat, of looking higher than any manifestation yet made of both beauty and good, in order to suggest from the utmost actual realization of the one a corresponding capability in the other, and out of the calm, purity and energy of nature, to reconstitute and store up for the forthcoming stage of man's being, a gift in repayment of that former gift, in which man's own thought and passion had been lavished by the poet on the else-incompleted magnificence of the sunrise, the else-uninterpreted mystery of the lake, – so drawing out, lifting up, and assimilating this ideal of a future man, thus descried as possible, to the present reality of the poet's soul already arrived at the higher state of development, and still aspirant to elevate and extend itself in conformity with its still-improving perceptions of, no longer the eventual Human, but the actual Divine. In conjunction with which noble and rare powers, came the sub-ordinate power of delivering these attained results to the world in an embodi-ment of verse more closely answering to and indicative of the process of the informing spirit, (failing as it occasionally does, in art, only to succeed in highest art), – with a diction more adequate to the task in its natural and acquired richness, its material colour and spiritual transparency, – the whole being moved by and suffused with a music at once of the soul and the sense, expressive both of an external might of sincere passion and an internal fitness and consonancy, – than can be attributed to any other writer whose record is among us. Such was the spheric poetical faculty of Shelley, as its own self-sufficing central light, radiating equally through immaturity and accomplish-ment, through many fragments and occasional completion, reveals it to a competent judgement.

But the acceptance of this truth by the public, has been retarded by certain objections which cast us back on the evidence of biography, even with Shelley's poetry in our hands. Except for the particular character of these objections, indeed, the non-appreciation of his contemporaries would simply class, now that it is over, with a series of experiences which have necessarily happened and needlessly been wondered at, ever since the world began, and concerning which any present anger may well be moderated, no less in justice to our forerunners than in policy to ourselves. For the misapprehensiveness of his age is exactly what a poet is sent to remedy; and the interval between his operation and the generally perceptible effect of it, is no greater, less indeed, than in many other departments of the great human effort. The 'E pur si muove' of the astronomer was as bitter a word as any uttered before or since by a poet over his rejected living work, in that depth of conviction which is so like despair.

But in this respect was the experience of Shelley peculiarly unfortunate – that the disbelief in him as a man, even preceded the disbelief in him as a writer; the misconstruction of his moral nature preparing the way for the misappreciation of his intellectual labours. There existed from the beginning, – simultaneous with, indeed anterior to his earliest noticeable works, and not brought forward to counteract any impression they had succeeded in making, – certain charges against his private character and life, which, if substantiated to their whole breadth, would materially disturb, I do not attempt to deny, our reception and enjoyment of his works, however wonderful the artistic qualities of these. For we are not sufficiently supplied with instances of genius of his order, to be able to pronounce certainly how many of its constituent parts have been tasked and strained to the production of a given lie, and how high and pure a mood of the creative mind may be dramatically simulated as the poet's habitual and exclusive one. The doubts, therefore, arising from such a question, required to be set at rest, as they were effectually, by those

early authentic notices of Shelley's career and the corroborative accompani-
ment of his letters, in which not only the main tenor and principal result of
his life, but the purity and beauty of many of the processes which had conduced to them, were made apparent enough for the general reader's purpose,
– whoever lightly condemned Shelley first, on the evidence of reviews and
gossip, as lightly acquitting him now, on that of memoirs and correspondence.
Still, it is advisable to lose no opportunity of strengthening and completing
the chain of biographical testimony; much more, of course, for the sake of the
poet's original lovers, whose volunteered sacrifice of particular principle in
favour of absorbing sympathy we might desire to dispense with, than for the
sake of his foolish haters, who have long since diverted upon other objects
their obtuseness or malignancy. A full life of Shelley should be written at once,
while the materials for it continue in reach; not to minister to the curiosity of
the public, but to obliterate the last stain of that false life which was forced on
the public's attention before it had any curiosity on the matter, – a biography,
composed in harmony with the present general disposition to have faith in
him, yet not shrinking from a candid statement of all ambiguous passages,
through a reasonable confidence that the most doubtful of them will be found
consistent with a belief in the eventual perfection of his character, according
to the poor limits of our humanity. Nor will men persist in confounding, any
more than God confounds, with genuine infidelity and an atheism of the
heart, those passionate, impatient struggles of a boy towards distant truth and
love, made in the dark, and ended by one sweep of the natural seas before the
full moral sunrise could shine out on him. Crude convictions of boyhood,
conveyed in imperfect and inapt forms of speech, – for such things all boys
have been pardoned. There are growing-pains, accompanied by temporary
distortion, of the soul also. And it would be hard indeed upon this young
Titan of genius, murmuring in divine music his human ignorances, through
his very thirst for knowledge, and his rebellion, in mere aspiration to law, if
the melody itself substantiated the error, and the tragic cutting short of life
perpetuated into sins, such faults as, under happier circumstances, would
have been left behind by the consent of the most arrogant moralist, forgotten
on the lowest steps of youth.

The responsibility of presenting to the public a biography of Shelley, does
not, however lie with me: I have only to make it a little easier by arranging
these few supplementary letters, with a recognition of the value of the whole
collection. This value I take to consist in a most truthful conformity of the
Correspondence, in its limited degree, with the moral and intellectual character
of the writer as displayed in the highest manifestations of his genius. Letters
and poems are obviously an act of the same mind, produced by the same law,
only differing in the application to the individual or collective understanding.
Letters and poems may be used indifferently as the basement of our opinion
upon the writer's character; the finished expression of a sentiment in the
poems, giving light and significance to the rudiments of the same in the
letters, and these, again, in their incipiency and unripeness, authenticating
the exalted mood and reattaching it to the personality of the writer. The

musician speaks on the note he sings with; there is no change in the scale, as he diminishes the volume into familiar intercourse. There is nothing of that jarring between the man and the author, which has been found so amusing or so melancholy; no dropping of the tragic mask, as the crowd melts away; no mean discovery of the real motives of a life's achievement, often, in other lives, laid bare as pitifully as when, at the close of a holiday, we catch sight of the internal lead-pipes and wood-valves, to which, and not to the ostensible conch and dominant Triton of the fountain, we have owed our admired waterwork. No breaking out, in household privacy, of hatred anger and scorn, incongruous with the higher mood and suppressed artistically in the book: no brutal return to self-delighting, when the audience of philanthropic schemes is out of hearing: no indecent stripping off the grander feeling and rule of life as too costly and cumbrous for every-day wear. Whatever Shelley was, he was with an admirable sincerity. It was not always truth that he thought and spoke; but in the purity of truth he spoke and thought always. Everywhere is apparent his belief in the existence of Good, to which Evil is an accident; his faithful holding by what he assumed to be the former, going everywhere in company with the tenderest pity for those acting or suffering on the opposite hypothesis. For he was tender, though tenderness is not always the character-istic of very sincere natures; he was eminently both tender and sincere. And not only do the same affection and yearning after the well-being of his kind, appear in the letters as in the poems, but they express themselves by the same theories and plans, however crude and unsound. There is no reservation of a subtler, less costly, more serviceable remedy for his own ill, than he has pro-posed for the general one; nor does he ever contemplate an object on his own account, from a less elevation than he uses in exhibiting it to the world. How shall we help believing Shelley to have been, in his ultimate attainment, the splendid spirit of his own best poetry, when we find even his carnal speech to agree faithfully, at faintest as at strongest, with the tone and rhythm of his most oracular utterances?

For the rest, these new letters are not offered as presenting any new feature of the poet's character. Regarded in themselves, and as the substantive pro-ductions of a man, their importance would be slight. But they possess interest beyond their limits, in confirming the evidence just dwelt on, of the poetical mood of Shelley being only the intensification of his habitual mood; the same tongue only speaking, for want of the special excitement to sing. The very first letter, as one instance for all, strikes the key-note of the predominating sentiment of Shelley throughout his whole life – his sympathy with the oppressed. And when we see him at so early an age, casting out, under the influence of such a sympathy, letters and pamphlets on every side, we accept it as the simple exemplification of the sincerity, with which, at the close of his life, he spoke of himself, as –

> One whose heart a stranger's tear might wear
> As water-drops the sandy fountain stone;
> Who loved and pitied all things, and could moan
> For woes which others hear not, and could see

> The absent with the glass of phantasy,
> And near the poor and trampled sit and weep,
> Following the captive to his dungeon deep –
> One who was as a nerve o'er which do creep
> The else-unfelt oppressions of this earth.

Such sympathy with his kind was evidently developed in him to an extraordinary and even morbid degree, at a period when the general intellectual powers it was impatient to put in motion, were immature or deficient.

I conjecture, from a review of the various publications of Shelley's youth, that one of the causes of his failure at the outset, was the peculiar *practicalness* of his mind, which was not without a determinate effect on his progress in theorizing. An ordinary youth, who turns his attention to similar subjects, discovers falsities, incongruities, and various points for amendment, and, in the natural advance of the purely critical spirit unchecked by considerations of remedy, keeps up before his young eyes so many instances of the same error and wrong, that he finds himself unawares arrived at the startling conclusion that all must be changed – or nothing: in the face of which plainly impossible achievement, he is apt (looking perhaps a little more serious by the time he touches at the decisive issue), to feel, either carelessly or considerately, that his own attempting a single piece of service would be worse than useless even, and to refer the whole task to another age and person – safe in proportion to his incapacity. Wanting words to speak, he has never made a fool of himself by speaking. But, in Shelley's case, the early fervour and power to *see*, was accompanied by as precocious a fertility to *contrive*: he endeavoured to realize as he went on idealizing; every wrong had simultaneously its remedy, and, out of the strength of his hatred for the former, he took the strength of his confidence in the latter – till suddenly he stood pledged to the defence of a set of miserable little expedients, just as if they represented great principles, and to an attack upon various great principles, really so, without leaving himself time to examine whether, because they were antagonistical to the remedy he had suggested, they must therefore be identical or even essentially connected with the wrong he sought to cure, – playing with blind passion into the hands of his enemies, and dashing at whatever red cloak was held forth to him, as the cause of the fireball he had last been stung with – mistaking Churchdom for Christianity, and for marriage, 'the sale of love' and the law of sexual oppression.

Gradually, however, he was leaving behind him this low practical dexterity, unable to keep up with his widening intellectual perception; and, in exact proportion as he did so, his true power strengthened and proved itself. Gradually he was raised above the contemplation of spots and the attempt at effacing them, to the great Abstract Light, and, through the discrepancy of the creation, to the sufficiency of the First Cause. Gradually he was learning that the best way of removing abuses is to stand fast by truth. Truth is one, as they are manifold; and innumerable negative effects are produced by the upholding of one positive principle. I shall say what I think, – had Shelley lived he would have finally ranged himself with the Christians; his very instinct for helping the weaker side (if numbers make strength), his very 'hate of hate,' which at first mistranslated itself into delirious Queen Mab notes and the like, would have got clearer-sighted by exercise. The preliminary step to following Christ, is the leaving the dead to bury their dead – not clamouring on His doctrine for an especial solution of difficulties which are referable to the general problem of the universe. Already he had attained to a profession of 'a worship to the Spirit of good within, which requires (before it sends that inspiration forth, which impresses its likeness upon all it creates) devoted and disinterested homage, *as Coleridge says*,' – and Paul likewise. And we find in one of his last exquisite fragments, avowedly a record of one of his own mornings and its experience, as it dawned on him at his soul and body's best in his boat on the Serchio – that as surely as

> The stars burnt out in the pale blue air,
> And the thin white moon lay withering there –
> Day had kindled the dewy woods,
> And the rocks above, and the stream below,
> And the vapours in their multitudes,
> And the Apennine's shroud of summer snow –
> Day had awakened all things that be;

just so surely, he tells us (stepping forward from this delicious dance-music, choragus-like, into the grander measure befitting the final enunciation),

> All rose to do the task He set to each,
> Who shaped us to his ends and not our own;
> The million rose to learn, and One to teach
> What none yet ever knew or can be known.

No more difference than this, from David's pregnant conclusion so long ago!

Meantime, as I call Shelley a moral man, because he was true, simple-hearted, and brave, and because what he acted corresponded to what he knew, so I call him a man of religious mind, because every audacious negative cast up by him against the Divine, was interpenetrated with a mood of reverence and adoration, – and because I find him everywhere taking for granted some of the capital dogmas of Christianity, while most vehemently denying their historical basement. There is such a thing as an efficacious knowledge of and belief in the politics of Junius, or the poetry of Rowley, though a man should at the same time dispute the title of Chatterton to the one, and consider the author of the other, as Byron wittily did, 'really, truly, nobody at all.'* There is even such a thing, we come to learn wonderingly in these very letters, as a

---

* Or, to take our illustrations from the writings of Shelley himself, there is such a thing as admirably appreciating a work by Andrea Verocchio, – and fancifully characterizing the Pisan Torre Guelfa by the Ponte a Mare, black against the sunsets, – and consummately painting the islet of San Clemente with its penitentiary for rebellious priests, to the west between Venice and the Lido – while you believe the

profound sensibility and adaptitude for art, while the science of the percipient is so little advanced as to admit of his stronger admiration for Guido (and Carlo Dolce!) than for Michael Angelo. A Divine Being has Himself said, that 'a word against the Son of man shall be forgiven to a man,' while 'a word against the Spirit of God' (implying a general deliberate preference of perceived evil to perceived good) 'shall not be forgiven to a man.' Also, in religion, one earnest and unextorted assertion of belief should outweigh, as a matter of testimony, many assertions of unbelief. The fact that there is a gold-region is established by the finding of one lump, though you miss the vein never so often.

He died before his youth ended. In taking the measure of him as a man, he must be considered on the whole and at his ultimate spiritual stature, and not be judged of at the immaturity and by the mistakes of ten years before: that, indeed, would be to judge of the author of 'Julian and Maddalo' by 'Zastrozzi.' Let the whole truth be told of his worst mistake. I believe, for my own part, that if anything could now shame or grieve Shelley, it would be an attempt to vindicate him at the expense of another.

In forming a judgement, I would, however, press on the reader the simple justice of considering tenderly his constitution of body as well as mind, and how unfavourable it was to the steady symmetries of conventional life; the body, in the torture of incurable disease, refusing to give repose to the bewildered soul, tossing in its hot fever of the fancy, – and the laudanum-bottle making but a perilous and pitiful truce between these two. He was constantly subject to 'that state of mind' (I quote his own note to 'Hellas') 'in which ideas may be supposed to assume the force of sensation, through the confusion of thought with the objects of thought, and excess of passion animating the creations of the imagination': in other words, he was liable to remarkable delusions and hallucinations. The nocturnal attack in Wales, for instance, was assuredly a delusion; and I venture to express my own conviction, derived from a little attention to the circumstances of either story, that the idea of the enamoured lady following him to Naples, and of the 'man in the cloak' who struck him at the Pisan post-office, were equally illusory, – the mere projection, in fact, from himself, of the image of his own love and hate.

> To thirst and find no fill – to wail and wander
> With short unsteady steps – to pause and ponder –
> To feel the blood run through the veins and tingle
> When busy thought and blind sensation mingle, –
> To nurse the image of *unfelt caresses*
> Till dim imagination just possesses
> The half-created shadow –

---

first to be a fragment of an antique sarcophagus, – the second, Ugolino's Tower of Famine (the vestiges of which should be sought for in the Piazza de' Cavalieri) – and the third (as I convinced myself last summer at Venice), San Servolo with its mad-house – which, far from being 'windowless,' is as full of windows as a barrack.

of unfelt caresses, – and of unfelt blows as well: to such conditions was his genius subject. It was not at Rome only (where he heard a mystic voice exclaiming, 'Cenci, Cenci,' in reference to the tragic theme which occupied him at the time), – it was not at Rome only that he mistook the cry of 'old rags.' The habit of somnambulism is said to have extended to the very last days of his life.

Let me conclude with a thought of Shelley as a poet. In the hierarchy of creative minds, it is the presence of the highest faculty that gives first rank, in virtue of its kind, not degree; no pretension of a lower nature, whatever the completeness of development or variety of effect, impeding the precedency of the rarer endowment though only in the germ. The contrary is sometimes maintained; it is attempted to make the lower gifts (which are potentially included in the higher faculty) of independent value, and equal to some exercise of the special function. For instance, should not a poet possess common sense? Then the possession of abundant common sense implies a step towards becoming a poet. Yes; such a step as the lapidary's, when, strong in the fact of carbon entering largely into the composition of the diamond, he heaps up a sack of charcoal in order to compete with the Koh-i-noor. I pass at once, therefore, from Shelley's minor excellencies to his noblest and predominating characteristic.

This I call his simultaneous perception of Power and Love in the absolute, and of Beauty and Good in the concrete, while he throws, from his poet's station between both, swifter, subtler, and more numerous films for the connexion of each with each, than have been thrown by any modern artificer of whom I have knowledge; proving how, as he says,

> The spirit of the worm within the sod,
> In love and worship blends itself with God.

I would rather consider Shelley's poetry as a sublime fragmentary essay towards a presentment of the correspondency of the universe to Deity, of the natural to the spiritual, and of the actual to the ideal, than I would isolate and separately appraise the worth of many detachable portions which might be acknowledged as utterly perfect in a lower moral point of view, under the mere conditions of art. It would be easy to take my stand on successful instances of objectivity in Shelley: there is the unrivalled 'Cenci'; there is the 'Julian and Maddalo' too; there is the magnificent 'Ode to Naples': why not regard, it may be said, the less organized matter as the radiant elemental foam and solution, out of which would have been evolved, eventually, creations as perfect even as those? But I prefer to look for the highest attainment, not simply the high, – and, seeing it, I hold by it. There is surely enough of the work 'Shelley' to be known enduringly among men, and, I believe, to be accepted of God, as human work may; and around the imperfect proportions of such, the most elaborated productions of ordinary art must arrange themselves as inferior illustrations.

It is because I have long held these opinions in assurance and gratitude, that I catch at the opportunity offered to me of expressing them here; knowing that the alacrity to fulfil an humble office conveys more love than the acceptance of the honour of a higher one, and that better, therefore, than the signal service it was the dream of my boyhood to render to his fame and memory, may be the saying of a few, inadequate words upon these scarcely more important supplementary letters of SHELLEY.

Paris, 4 December 1851

Appendix 2: Browning's Rearrangement of the Poems Originally Published in 1842, 1845 and 1855

The poems published in *Dramatic Lyrics* (1842) and *Dramatic Romances and Lyrics* (1845) were collected in *1849* in their original order under the title *Dramatic Romances and Lyrics*. Two poems were omitted: 'Claret and Tokay' and the second part of 'Home-Thoughts, from Abroad' (later called 'Here's to Nelson's Memory'). These were restored in *1863*, grouped together under the title of 'Nationality in Drinks'. In the first volume of *1863*, Browning collected and redistributed all these poems and those from *Men and Women* (1855) in three groupings: 'Lyrics', 'Romances' and 'Men, and Women'. The same divisions were repeated in *1868* and *1888–9*. In *1863* they were as follows:

Lyrics
Cavalier Tunes
    I. Marching Along
    II. Give a Rouse
   III. Boot and Saddle
The Lost Leader
'How They Brought the Good News from Ghent to Aix'
Through the Metidja to Abd-el-Kadr
Nationality in Drinks [including 'Here's to Nelson's Memory']
Garden Fancies
    I. The Flower's Name
    II. Sibrandus Schafnaburgensis
   III. Soliloquy of the Spanish Cloister [separated from 'Garden Fancies' in *1868*]
The Laboratory
The Confessional
Cristina
The Lost Mistress
Earth's Immortalities
Meeting at Night
Parting at Morning
Song ['Nay but you, who do not love her']
A Woman's Last Word
Evelyn Hope
Love among the Ruins
A Lovers' Quarrel
Up at a Villa – Down in the City
A Toccata of Galuppi's
Old Pictures in Florence
'De gustibus –'
Home-Thoughts, from Abroad
Home-Thoughts, from the Sea

Saul
My Star
By the Fire-Side
Any Wife to Any Husband
Two in the Campagna
Misconceptions
A Serenade at the Villa
One Way of Love
Another Way of Love
A Pretty Woman
Respectability
Love in a Life
Life in a Love
In three Days
In a Year
Women and Roses
Before
After
The Guardian-Angel
Memorabilia
Popularity
Master Hugues of Saxe-Gotha

Romances
Incident of the French Camp
The Patriot
My Last Duchess
Count Gismond
The Boy and the Angel
Instans Tyrannus
Mesmerism
The Glove
Time's Revenges
The Italian in England
The Englishman in Italy
In a Gondola
Waring
The Twins
A Light Woman
The Last Ride together
The Pied Piper of Hamelin
The Flight of the Duchess
A Grammarian's Funeral
Johannes Agricola in Meditation [moved to 'Men, and Women' in *1868*, following
    'An Epistle']
The Heretic's Tragedy
Holy-Cross Day
Protus
The Statue and the Bust
Porphyria's Lover
'Childe Roland to the Dark Tower Came'

Men, and Women
'Transcendentalism': A Poem in Twelve Books
How it Strikes a Contemporary
Artemis Prologizes
An Epistle Containing the Strange Medical Experience of Karshish, the Arab
    Physician
Pictor Ignotus
Fra Lippo Lippi
Andrea del Sarto
The Bishop Orders His Tomb at Saint Praxed's Church
Bishop Blougram's Apology
Cleon
Rudel to the Lady of Tripoli
One Word More.

Notes

Browning's editions are often referred to in the notes by the dates of publication. Collected-edition references are:

1849 the two-volume *Poems*, Chapman & Hall, 1849
1863 the three-volume *The Poetical Works*, Chapman & Hall, 1863
1868 the six-volume *The Poetical Works*, Smith, Elder, 1868
1888 the sixteen-volume *The Poetical Works*, Smith, Elder, 1888–9 (the first impression of this edition)

Some secondary works are referred to by authors' or editors' surnames and short titles. Reference to the bibliography in 'Further Reading' should make these self-explanatory. Other abbreviations used are:

BIS   *Browning Institute Studies*
BNL   *Browning Newsletter*
BSN   *Browning Society Notes*
ELH   *English Literary History*
JEGP   *Journal of English and Germanic Philology*
MLN   *Modern Language Notes*
MLQ   *Modern Language Quarterly*
MLR   *Modern Language Review*
MP   *Modern Philology*
N&Q   *Notes and Queries*
OED   *Oxford English Dictionary*
PMLA   *Publications of the Modern Language Association*
PQ   *Philological Quarterly*
SBHC   *Studies in Browning and His Circle*
SP   *Studies in Philology*
TLS   *Times Literary Supplement*
TQ   *University of Toronto Quarterly*
VNL   *Victorian Newsletter*
VP   *Victorian Poetry*
VS   *Victorian Studies*

References to Shakespeare are to the Globe edition; to classical literature, normally to the Loeb edition; to *The Ring and the Book*, to the Penguin English Poets edition.

Dedication

The dedication for *1888* appeared originally in *1863* and was reprinted in *1868*. John Forster (1812–76), best known for his biography of Dickens, was the early supporter and friend of Browning.

Pauline

Published anonymously early in March 1833 by Saunders and Otley, the expenses being borne by Browning's aunt. It was written between 22 October 1832 and January 1833. The place and date printed at the end of the poem, 'Richmond: 22 October 1832', were those of the poem's conception, as Browning's note in the copy of *Pauline* that J. S. Mill annotated for a projected review records: 'Kean was acting there: I saw him in Richard III that night, and conceived the childish plan already mentioned: there is an allusion to Kean, page 47 [lines 669–75]. I don't know whether I had not made up my mind to *act*, as well as to make verses, music, and God knows what, – que de châteaux en Espagne [what castles in Spain]!' The 'childish scheme already mentioned' in Mill's copy is in Browning's note opposite the poem's opening there:

'The following Poem was written in pursuance of a foolish plan which occupied me mightily for a time, and which had for its object the enabling me to assume and realize I know not how many different characters; – meanwhile the world was never to grasp that "Brown, Smith, Jones, and Robinson" (as the spelling books have it), the respective authors of this poem, the other novel, such an opera, such a speech etc. etc. were no other than one and the same individual. The present abortion was the work of the *Poet* of the batch, who would have been more legitimately *myself* than most of the others; but I surrounded him with all manner of (to my then notion) poetical accessories, and had planned quite a delightful life for him.

'Only this crab remains of the shapely Tree of Life in this Fool's Paradise of mine.
R.B.'

The 'confessional' nature of *Pauline* is characteristic of its period, but the poem reflects clearly, and not only in the direct tributes to the 'Sun-treader', the impact of that vital influence on the young Browning, Shelley, and especially of his *Alastor* (1816). Most scholars have agreed that *Pauline* is essentially autobiographical, and that if the shadowy heroine has any live model it is probably Eliza Flower, or possibly her sister Sarah, or a fusion of the two – the friendship of the Flower sisters, wards of W. J. Fox (one of Browning's first literary supporters) and both some years older than Browning, meant much to him.

Pauline attracted little attention; Browning told T. J. Wise over fifty years later (Hood, *Letters*, 251) that it sold not one copy. Only twenty-odd copies now survive, of which the most famous, now in the Forster collection of the Victoria and Albert Museum, is J. S. Mill's review copy, which, shortly after Mill had annotated it, was returned to Browning, who himself wrote in it notes and replies to Mill's comments. Some of the two writers' notes are quoted below; they have special interest since Browning himself lent support to what, largely as a result of the influence of W. C. DeVane, became the traditional view that Mill's remarks decisively affected the poet's career, inciting him to turn to more dramatic and less self-revelatory poetry (the traditional view is vigorously challenged in M. Miyoshi, 'Mill and "Pauline": The Myth and Some Facts', *VS* IX, 1965, 154–63; see also O. P. Govil, 'A Note on Mill and Browning's *Pauline*', *VP* IV, 1966, 287–91). Mill sums up his feeling about the poem at the end of the volume:

'With considerable poetic powers, this writer seems to me possessed with a more intense and morbid self-consciousness than I ever knew in any sane human being – I should think it a *sincere confession*, though of a most unloveable state, if the 'Pauline' were not evidently a mere phantom. All about her is full of inconsistency – he neither loves her nor fancies he loves her yet insists upon *talking* love to her – if she *existed* and loved him, he treats her most ungenerously and unfeelingly. All his aspirings and yearnings and regrets point to other things, never to her – then, he *pays her off* towards the end by a piece of flummery, amounting to the modest request that she will love him and live with him and give herself up to him *without* his *loving her*, *moyennant quoi* [in return for which] he will think her and call her everything that is handsome and he promises her that she shall find it mighty pleasant. Then he leaves off by saying he knows he shall have changed his mind by tomorrow, and despise "these intents which seem so fair", but that having been thus visited once no doubt he will again – and is therefore "in perfect joy" [–] bad luck to him! as the Irish say.

'A cento of most beautiful passages might be made from this poem – and the psychological history of himself is powerful and truthful, *truth-like* certainly all but the last stage. *That* he evidently has not yet got into. The self-seeking and self-worshipping state is well described – beyond that I should think the writer had made, as yet, only the next step: viz. into despising his own state. I even question whether part even of that self-disdain is not *assumed*. He is evidently *dissatisfied*, and feels part of the badness of his state, but he does not write as if it were purged out of him – if he once could muster a hearty hatred of this selfishness, it would *go* – as it is, he feels only the *lack* of good, not the positive *evil*. He feels not remorse, but only disappointment. A mind in that state can only be regenerated by some new passion, and I know not what to wish for him, but that he may meet with a *real* Pauline.

'Meanwhile he should not attempt to shew how a person may be *recovered* from this morbid state – for *he* is hardly convalescent, and "what should we speak of but that which we know?"' See W. S. Peterson and F. L. Standley, 'The J. S. Mill Marginalia in Robert Browning's *Pauline*: A History and Transcription', *Papers of the Bibliographical Society of America* LXVI, 1972, 135–70.

Browning came to regard *Pauline* with an extreme distaste illustrated in the prefatory material to *1868* and *1888*, and in his initial note in the Mill *Pauline* quoted above. D. G. Rossetti transcribed the British Museum copy in 1847, and guessed that Browning had written it; but, despite increasing awareness of the poem and its authorship, Browning was reluctant to show it to Elizabeth Barrett, excluded it from *1849* and *1863*, and (apparently mainly to forestall pirated versions, but also at the urging of his new publisher) reprinted it only in *1868*, prefacing it with the depreciatory comment reprinted and supplemented in *1888*. The poem was much more extensively revised for *1868* and *1888* than Browning's comments reveal, though the verbal and punctuational changes are almost invariably within individual lines; the number of lines remained constant, one line (404) being added, and another (457ʌ8) being deleted. T. J. Wise published a facsimile of the first edition in 1886, and the 1833 text has several times been reprinted. N. H. Wallis's edition (1931) compares the texts of 1833, 1868 and 1888. The manuscript is not extant.

Biographers tend to deal with *Pauline* in detail, but there are few critical studies. Some treatments are: Collins, *Browning's Moral-Aesthetic Theory*, 3–16; Cook, *Browning's Lyrics*, 3–14; Hair, *Browning's Experiments*, 4–19; M. Hancher, 'The Dramatic Situation of Browning's "Pauline"', *Yearbook of English Studies* I, 1971, 149–59; P. Honan, 'Browning's *Pauline*: The Artistic Safety Device', *VNL* 18, 1960, 23–4; Jack, *Browning's Major Poetry*, 11–21; John Maynard, *Browning's Youth*, 193–237; W. L. Phelps, 'Notes on Browning's *Pauline*', *MLN* XLVII, 1932, 292–9; R. Preyer, 'Robert Browning: A Reading of the Early Narratives', *ELH* XXVI, 1959, 531–48 (in Drew, *Robert Browning*, 157–75; and Litzinger and Knickerbocker, *The Browning Critics*, 343–63,); C. de L. Ryals, 'Browning's *Pauline*: The Question of Genre', *Genre* IX, 1974, 231–45.

The French motto, 'I am no longer what I was,/Nor would I ever know how to be that again', is from a poem, *De lui-même*, wrongly attributed to the French court poet and rebel, Clément Marot (1496 ?–1544); its theme is Shelleyan and is frequently embodied in *Pauline*. The Latin introduction is abbreviated and adapted from the opening pages of *De occulta philosophia*, a defence of magic by the German physician and mystic, Heinrich Cornelius Agrippa von Nettesheim (1486–1535): 'I have no doubt that the title of our book may by its unusual character entice very many to read it, and that among them some of biased opinions, with weak minds – many even hostile and churlish – will attack our genius, who in the rashness of their ignorance will cry out, almost before they have read the title, that we are teaching forbidden things, are scattering the seeds of heresies, that we are an annoyance to righteous ears, to enlightened minds an object of offence; so taking care for their consciences that neither Apollo, nor all the Muses, nor an angel from heaven could save me from their execration. To these I now give counsel not to read our book, neither to understand it nor remember it; for it is harmful, poisonous; the gate of Hell is in this book; it speaks of stones – let them beware lest by them it beat out their brains. But if you who come to its perusal with unprejudiced minds will exercise as much discernment and prudence as bees in gathering honey, then read with safety. For I think you will receive not a little of instruction and a great deal of enjoyment. On the other hand, if you find things which do not please you, pass over them and make no use of them. FOR I DO NOT RECOMMEND THESE THINGS TO YOU: I MERELY TELL YOU OF THEM. Yet do not on that account reject the rest. Therefore if anything has been said rather freely, forgive my youth; I wrote this work when I was less than a youth.' (F. A. Pottle's translation.) Mill wrote in the Mill *Pauline*, 'Too much pretension in this motto'; Browning's comment about the pretentiousness first appeared in *1888*. Browning explained to Wise (Hood, *Letters*, 256): 'V.A. XX. is the Latin abbreviation of *Vixi annos* [*viginti*] – "I was twenty years old" – that is, the imaginary subject of the poem was of that age.' Browning himself was twenty, but in 1867 he insisted: 'the poem was purely dramatic and intended to head a series of "Men and Women" such as I have afterwards introduced to the world under somewhat better auspices'.

18   Mill remarked, 'not, I think, an appropriate image – and it throws considerable obscurity over the meaning of the passage.' Mill wrote 'same remark' beside line 27.
83   *faithful found*   'So spake the Seraph Abdiel, faithful found/Among the faithless, faithful only he' (*Paradise Lost* V, 893).

91 *wide*] *1833, this edition*; wild *1868–88*.

102 *white swan* possibly suggested by the eagle who visited the imprisoned Cythna in Shelley's *Laon and Cythna* VII, 14, or by the white swan of *Alastor* 275–90.

112–14 Mill remarked, 'a curious idealization of self-worship. Very fine though.'

114 *radiant form* Shelley often uses the two words in close conjunction.

142 *HIS award* Mill remarked, 'what does this mean? His opinion of yourself? only at the fourth reading of the poem, I found out what this meant'; Browning answered, 'The award of fame to Him – The late acknowledgement of Shelley's genius.'

147–9 Mill remarked, 'bad simile [–] the spider does not detest or scorn the light'.

151 *Sun-treader* Shelley (1792–1822), whose verse, first read in 1826, strongly affected the young Browning. Shelley is the poet referred to in the preceding verse paragraph, and is celebrated also in subsequent passages in *Pauline* (see Pottle, *Shelley and Browning*). The phrase 'Sun-treader', echoed in lines 201 and 1020, suggests the ethereal quality of Shelley's idealism and imagery.

163–7 Mill wrote 'beautiful' beside these lines. Other later passages are similarly commended (173–80, 222–9, 230–35, 766–80, for instance).

171 *a star to men* Compare *Paracelsus* I, 527.

192 *I am not what I have been to thee* Browning's initial enthusiasm for Shelley, and for his 'atheism' in particular, had waned somewhat by 1833.

194 *loneliness*] loveliness *1833, 1868*.

196 *bloom*] bleed *1833, 1868*.

199 Mill remarked 'obscurely expressed'. He marked several further passages 'where the meaning is so obscurely expressed as not to be easily understood'.

203] I am proud to feel I would have thrown up all *1833, 1868*.

203–5 *I proudly feel . . . as thou art* Compare 'Memorabilia'.

215–18 Mill remarked, 'the obscurity of this is the greater fault as the meaning if I can *guess* it right is really poetical'.

238 *own*] old *1833*.

252 *whilst ebbing day dies soft* 'While barrèd clouds bloom the soft-dying day' (Keats, 'To Autumn', 25).

260–67 Mill crossed out the lines, and remarked, 'this only says you shall see what you shall see; and is more prose than poetry'.

284 *imagination* Mill remarked, 'not imagination but *I*magination. The absence of that capital letter obscures the meaning.' Browning made the change in the Mill *Pauline*, but not in any later editions.

293 *halted*] wasted, *1833*; wasted *1868*.

315] For I still find them – turning my wild youth *1833*; For I still find them turning my wild youth *1868*.

319 *wisest ancient books* Browning read voraciously in his father's large library, and was early introduced to the classical worlds evoked in the following lines (see 'Development' in Volume II of the present edition).

321–5 *a god . . . Tenedos* If Browning has particular figures in mind, the god may well be Apollo in pursuit of Daphne; the giant, Atlas, the Titan, holding the heavens on his shoulders; the old hunter, Peleus, father of Achilles; the chief, one of the Greek leaders who sailed to the small island of Tenedos, near Troy, when the Trojan Horse had been introduced into Troy, and at the end of the War.

331 *clustered isles in the blue sea* islands in the Aegean, perhaps the Cyclades. Browning's Cleon (line 1) refers to the Sporades as 'the sprinkled isles'.

334 *Swift-footed* Hermes, the gods' winged-footed messenger.

335 *Proserpine* (Persephone), wife of Pluto, King of the Underworld.

342   Mill remarked, 'what times? your own imaginative times? or the antique times themselves?' The answer is clearly the latter.

351-2   *all world's wrong /That*]   which so long /Have *1833, 1868.*

352   *cleansed my soul.*]   I was restored, *1833*; I was restored. *1868.*

365-7   *music (which is earnest of a heaven . . . revealed,)*   For the feeling, compare 'Abt Vogler'. Browning was a keen student of music.

376]   No wish to paint, no yearning – but I sang. *1833*; No wish to paint, no yearning; but I sang. *1868.*

387   *my own fancies justified*]   and my powers exemplified *1833, 1868.*

389   *With them*]   And then *1833, 1868.*

391   *To rival what I wondered at*   As a boy Browning wrote verses imitative of Romantic poets, especially Byron. Only two of these poems survive: 'The Dance of Death' and 'The First-Born of Egypt'.

392   *if*]   so *1833*; so, *1868.* Mill remarked, 'This writer seems to use "*so*" according to the colloquial vulgarism in the sense of "therefore" or "accordingly" – from which occasionally comes great obscurity and ambiguity – as here.' Browning replied by adding a comma after 'so' and by remarking, 'The *recurrence* of "*so*" thus employed is as vulgar as you please: but the usage itself of "*so* in the sense of accordingly" is perfectly authorized, – take an instance or two, from Milton.' He then cites examples from *Paradise Lost.*

396   *future*]   coming, *1833*; coming *1868.* (Mill found the phrasing obscure.)

403   *White Way*   Milky Way.

403-4]   The white way for a star. / * * * * *1833.*

404   *man*   identified by Mrs Orr as Plato (see line 436), but Shelley is almost certainly meant. Presumably, Shelley led the speaker to Plato.

413-14]   To gather every breathing of his songs. / And woven with them there were words, which seemed *1833*; To gather every breathing of his songs: / And woven with them there were words which seemed *1868.*

417   *leapt as still I sought*]   beat, as I went on, *1833*; beat as I went on *1868.*

418   *soul*]   mind *1833, 1868.*

423   *voice . . . shame*]   hands . . . dim *1833, 1868.*

444]   Men, and their cares, and hopes, and fears, and joys; *1833*; Men and their cares and hopes and fears and joys; *1868.*

448-88   Mill described the passage as 'finely painted and evidently from experience'.

457]   And fairy bowers – all his search is vain. / Well I remember * * * * *1833*; And fairy bowers, all his search is vain. *1868.*

471-2   *God is gone | And some dark spirit sitteth in his seat*   Perhaps suggested by Shelley's Demogorgon; compare 'I see a mighty darkness / Filling the seat of power' (*Prometheus Unbound* II.4.2-3).

479   *Arab birds*   possibly pelicans, but probably birds of paradise.

488]   Smiling * * * * * * *1833*; Smiling. . . . . *1868.*

488   *vanity of vanities*   'Vanity of vanities, saith the Preacher, vanity of vanities; all is vanity' (Ecclesiastes i 2).

495   *knowledge*]   feeling *1833, 1868.*

505   *erst*   formerly (archaism).

516   *Dearer*]   Brighter *1833, 1868.*

525   *straight encircle men*]   would encircle me *1833, 1868.*

527   *One branch from the gold forest*   While editors refer to the golden bough of *Aeneid* VI, the context here makes the allusion unlikely.

534   *like a swift wind*   The context supports the suggestion of Shelley's 'Ode to the West Wind'.

554 *trust some love is true*] trust in love so really *1833, 1868.*

556 *him I*] souls I'd *1833, 1868.*

557] In beauty – I'd be sad to equal them; *1833*; In beauty; I'd be sad to equal them; *1868.*

560] Pauline, my sweet friend, thou dost not forget *1833, 1868.*

563 *past glory*] opinion *1833, 1868.*

564 *seemed defiant*] was most happy *1833, 1868.*

567–8 *that king | Treading the purple calmly to his death* Agamemnon, King of Argos, returned home after the Trojan War, trod the purple carpet reserved for the gods, and was murdered by Aegisthus and Clytemnestra. In the Mill *Pauline*, Browning quotes in Greek two lines (956–7) from the *Agamemnon* of Aeschylus, in which the King agrees to tread the purple pathway.

572 *him sitting alone in blood* Ajax, covered in blood from the sheep and cattle he has slain in his madness. In the Mill *Pauline*, Browning quotes in Greek lines 322–4 and 342–3 of the *Ajax* of Sophocles.

573–4 *the boy | With his white breast* Orestes, son of Agamemnon and Clytemnestra, who slew his mother. In the Mill *Pauline*, Browning quotes in Greek lines 1021–3 and 1026–7 of the *Choephori* of Aeschylus.

580 *much*] what *1833, 1868.*

604 *soul*] mind *1833, 1868.*

606 *an aim, pursue success*] a sect, or a pursuit, *1833*; a sect or a pursuit *1868.*

616 *the world,*] them all, *1833*; them all *1868.*

624 *harpy* winged monster, with head and breasts of a woman, of classical myth.

629–30 *wild eyes . . . left alone* reminiscent of Keats's 'La Belle Dame sans Merci'.

634] And thus I know this earth is not my sphere, *1833, 1868.*

635] For I cannot so narrow me, but that *1833*; For I cannot so narrow me but that *1868.*

636 *Soul still exceeds*] I still exceed *1833, 1868.*

637 *outsoars*] would pass *1833, 1868.*

641 *Love chained*] All love *1833, 1868.*

  were love, set free,] must be that love *1833, 1868.*

641–3 *what were love . . . seraphim* Compare David's experience in 'Saul'.

642 *pass*] quell *1833, 1868.*

648–9 Mill remarked, 'inconsistent with what precedes'.

653] All my sad weaknesses, this wavering will, *1833, 1868.*

656 *Andromeda* The first of Browning's many references to what was for him a central myth, one re-enacted in Caponsacchi's rescue of Pompilia and in his own rescue of Elizabeth Barrett (see W. C. DeVane, 'The Virgin and the Dragon'). Andromeda was left by her father chained to a rock at the sea-edge to be devoured by a monster, but was saved by Perseus. An engraving of a painting by Polidoro da Caravaggio (1490–1543) hung above the young Browning's desk (the engraving is reproduced in H. C. Duffin's *Amphibian*).

659 *fixed*] dark *1833, 1868.*

666 *I . . . some god*] You . . . that God *1833, 1868.*

669 *mind*] soul *1833, 1868.*

669–75 When Edmund Kean (1787–1833), one of the greatest of English actors, so impressed Browning as Richard III in 1832, he was very near the end of his career.

675] And I rise triumphing over my decay. *1833, 1868.*

705 *throes*] tales *1833, 1868.*

761 *lymph* water.

811 Browning's note, like his use of the French and Latin mottoes, perhaps reflects

the special influence of Shelley. 'I am very much afraid that my poor friend is not always to be perfectly understood in what remains to be read of this strange fragment, but he is less fitted than anyone else to clarify what from its nature can ever be only dream and confusion. Besides I am not sure whether in seeking better to integrate certain parts, one would not risk damaging the only merit to which so singular a production can pretend, that of giving a precise enough idea of the kind that has only been sketched. This unpretentious beginning, this stirring of the passions which first increases and then gradually subsides, these impulses of the soul, this sudden return on himself, and, above all, the exceptional nature of my friend's spirit, make changes almost impossible. The reasons he advances elsewhere, and others still more powerful, have made me appreciate this composition that I should otherwise have advised him to burn. I do not believe any the less in the grand principle of all composition – that principle of Shakespeare, of Raphael, of Beethoven, from which it follows that the concentration of ideas owes much more to their conception than to their execution: I have every reason to fear that the first of these qualities is still strange to my friend, and I very much doubt that a doubling of effort would make him acquire the second. The best thing would be to burn this; but what can one do?

'I believe that in what follows he refers to a certain examination that he once made of the soul, or rather of his own soul, to discover the succession of goals which it would be possible for him to attain, and of which each, once obtained, would be a sort of plateau from which one could discern other ends, other projects, other pleasures, that should in their turn be surmounted. The conclusion was that oblivion and sleep ought to end everything. This idea, which I do not perfectly grasp, is perhaps as unintelligible to him as to me.'

831   Mill remarked, 'Why should this follow the description of scenery?'

851   *Olivet*   the ridge, overlooking Gethsemane, east of Jerusalem.

860   Mill remarked, 'strange transition'.

875   *song proves one word has*]   I feel that thou hast *1833, 1868*.

876]   And that I still may hope to win it back. *1833, 1868*.

884   *chronicled*]   shadowed out *1833, 1868*.

885   *shadow this*]   tell this my *1833, 1868*.

886   *recognize*]   feel all dim the shift *1833, 1868*.

887–8]   Of thought. These are my last thoughts; I discern / Faintly immortal life, and truth, and good. *1833*; Of thought; these are my last thoughts; I discern / Faintly immortal life and truth and good. *1868*.

891   *Despite the … love looks*]   With fears and … I look *1833, 1868*.

900   *Pauline from heights above*]   dear thing to kiss and love *1833, 1868*.

902   *the more*]   for it *1833, 1868*.

908   *éxtreme*   final. The accentuation is Shelleyan.

916   *some grand*]   the dim *1833, 1868*.

919–21   *isle … home*   Odysseus and his crew, having eaten of the lotos on Circe's island, lost their desire to return to Ithaca (*Odyssey* IX).

924   *Words are wild and*]   I am very *1833, 1868*.

930–34]   A key to music's mystery, when mind fails,
          A reason, a solution and a clue.
          You see I have thrown off my prescribed rules:
          I hope in myself – and hope, and pant, and love –
          You'll find me better – know me more than when *1833*.
          A key to music's mystery when mind fails,
          A reason, a solution and a clue!
          You see I have thrown off my prescribed rules:

> I hope in myself – and hope and pant and love.
> You'll find me better, know me more than when *1868*.

932   Mill remarked 'poor'.

949   *his liege*] thy sweet *1833*, *1868*.

964   *fair pale sister*   Antigone. In the Mill *Pauline*, Browning quotes in Greek lines 523 and 916–20 of the *Antigone* of Sophocles.

974–5   *I shall be | Prepared*   Mill remarked, 'he is always talking of being *prepared* – what for!' Browning replied, 'Why, "that's tellings", as schoolboys say.'

976]   And all old loves shall come to us – but changed *1833*; And all old loves shall come to us, but changed *1868*.

980–82]   And then when I am firm we'll seek again
> My own land, and again I will approach
> My old designs, and calmly look on all *1833*, *1868* (with comma after 'firm').

988   *may*]   will *1833*, *1868*.

992   *With this avowal, these intents*]   This verse, and these intents which seem *1833*, *1868*.

1019   *prophet*]   lover, *1833*; lover *1868*.

1025   *If such must*]   When such shall *1833*, *1868*.

1029–31   *| Richmond : 22 October 1832*   Mill remarked, 'this transition from speaking to Pauline to writing a letter to the public with *place* and *date*, is quite horrible'. Browning replied with the reference to Kean given above.

Paracelsus

The poem, the first to appear under Browning's name, was published on 15 August 1835 by Effingham Wilson, the expenses being borne by Browning's father. The subject was suggested in the summer of 1834 by the friend to whom Browning dedicated the poem, Comte Amédée de Ripert-Monclar (1807–71), unofficial Bourbon representative to the French émigrés in London (the dedication is not in the manuscript or *1849*). The poem was written between early October 1834 and 15 March 1835.

The printers' manuscript is now in the Forster and Dyce collection of the Library of the Victoria and Albert Museum. The punctuation of Browning's manuscript, notably idiosyncratic especially in the first half of the poem, was subjected to considerable house-styling (some of it indicated on the manuscript) to an extent neither needed nor evidenced with other extant Browning manuscripts; the differences between manuscript and *1835* in punctuation and capitalization are very considerable. Verbal differences are, however, few: there are a few misprints (corrected by Browning in his own copy of *1835* now in the University of London Library) and a mere handful of other verbal changes of negligible importance, none of them affecting more than three words. DeVane (*Handbook*, 49) errs (as more often than not on textual matters) in stating that Browning added almost a hundred lines while *Paracelsus* was in press, for not one line was added – or subtracted. There being no significant verbal differences between the manuscript and *1835*, the variant notes that follow generally ignore the manuscript.

Browning revised the poem extensively for *1849*. Two copies of *1835* which were used to prepare the revision, both of them very close, except for punctuation, to *1849* in their readings, are now in the Beinecke Library of Yale University and the Berg Collection of the New York Public Library – in the Berg copy Browning noted that he began corrections in Pisa in the spring of 1847. The *1849* version deletes or shortens some *1835* passages, and adds new ones. An unusually high proportion of *1849* revisions was discarded when Browning revised the poem extensively again for *1863*. Further revisions were made for *1868* and *1888*, but these are relatively insignificant, and in the three later printings the number of lines remained constant (4,151). There are 4,099 lines in the manuscript and *1835*, 4,178 in *1849*.

Like the speaker of *Pauline* (see especially lines 604–49 of that poem), Browning's Faust-like hero is in significant ways like Browning himself (for an extreme biographical reading, see Miller, *Robert Browning*, where the garden of Part I is associated with Browning's in Camberwell, and *Festus* and *Michal* with Browning's *father* and *mother*). It is generally agreed that Browning's hero at least projects some aspects of the young Browning's personal and poetic problems, and that the dramatic form is in part a response to Mill's equation of the speaker of *Pauline* with the poet. Be this as it may, Shelley (especially *Alastor*) again markedly influences Browning, and Aprile is generally held to be modelled on Shelley (Aprile, Festus and Michal are Browning's inventions). While DeVane (*Handbook*, 55) is surely right in seeing the young poet as himself the main source of the poem, the 'drapery' for the treatment of Paracelsus (1493–1541, born Theophrastus Bombast von Hohenstein) derived mainly from three works in the library of Browning's father: the entry in the *Biographie Universelle* (1822), from which much of Browning's appended Note is taken; the three-volume edition (and especially the preface) of the *Works* of Paracelsus (1658) edited by Frederick Botiskius, which is also used in the Note; and Melchior Adam's *Vitae Germanorum Medicorum* (1620). The sources are treated freely, and the long Note that Browning appended to all printings of the poem reflects an erudition which is, to one's relief, more ostentatious than real. Browning might have prefaced *Paracelsus*, as he did *Sordello*, by remarking: 'The historical decoration was purposely of no more importance than a background requires; and my stress lay on the incidents in the development of a soul.'

The poem brought Browning a modicum of fame, and ensured him access to the great. He always remained proud of it.

Among treatments of the poem are: Collins, *Browning's Moral-Aesthetic Theory*, 17–43; Cook, *Browning's Lyrics*, 15–26; M. D. Hawthorne, '*Paracelsus* Once Again: A Study in Imagery', *BIS* III, 1975, 41–60; Jack, *Browning's Major Poetry*, 22–39; F. E. L. Priestley, 'The Ironic Pattern of Browning's *Paracelsus*', *TQ* XXXIV, 1964, 68–81; Raymond, 'Browning's Conception of Love as Represented in "Paracelsus"', in his *The Infinite Moment*, 156–75.

1835 had a preface dated 15 March 1835 (also in the manuscript, but excluded from all subsequent printings): 'I am anxious that the reader should not, at the very outset – mistaking my performance for one of a class with which it has nothing in common – judge it by principles on which it was never moulded, and subject it to a standard to which it was never meant to conform. I therefore anticipate his discovery, that it is an attempt, probably more novel than happy, to reverse the method usually adopted by writers whose aim it is to set forth any phenomenon of the mind or the passions, by the operation of persons and events; and that, instead of having recourse to an external machinery of incidents to create and evolve the crisis I desire to produce, I have ventured to display somewhat minutely the mood itself in its rise and progress, and have suffered the agency by which it is influenced and determined, to be generally discernible in its effects alone, and subordinate throughout, if not altogether excluded: and this for a reason. I have endeavoured to write a poem, not a drama; the canons of the drama are well known, and I cannot but think that, inasmuch as they have immediate regard to stage representation, the peculiar advantages they hold out are really such only so long as the purpose for which they were at first instituted is kept in view. I do not very well understand what is called a Dramatic Poem, wherein all those restrictions only submitted to on account of compensating good in the original scheme are scrupulously retained, as though for some special fitness in themselves – and all new facilities placed at an author's disposal by the vehicle he selects, as pertinaciously rejected. It is certain, however, that a work like mine depends more immediately on the intelligence and sympathy of the reader for its success – indeed were my scenes stars it must be his co-operating fancy which, supplying all chasms, shall connect the scattered lights into one constellation – a Lyre or a Crown. I trust for his indulgence towards a poem which had not been imagined six months ago; and that even should he think slightingly of the present (an experiment I am in no case likely to repeat) he will not be prejudiced against other productions which may follow in a more popular, and perhaps less difficult form.'

PART I

Würzburg   the city in north-west Bavaria on the Main river.
1512]   1507   *1835*.
60   *Saint Saviour's*   The church appears to be fictional.
105   *Trithemius*   John Tritheim (1462–1516), historian and theologian, Abbot of Saint James in Würzburg, and Paracelsus's teacher.
120   *Einsiedeln*   the Swiss town, south-east of Zurich, near Paracelsus's birthplace.
170]   These points are no mere visionary truths:
>   But, once determined, it remains alone
>   To act upon them straight as best we may: *1835*.
The sentiment is frequent in Browning. Compare, for instance, 'Bishop Blougram's Apology', 271–2, 290–91.
173ₓ4]   A broad plan, vague and ill defined enough,
>   But courting censure and imploring aid: *1835*.
190   *Folly of man*]   Lusts of the world *1849*.
237   *soul and those intents*]   soul: accordingly
>   I could go further back, and trace each bough
>   Of this wide-branching tree even to its birth;
>   Each full-grown passion to its outspring faint;
>   But I shall only dwell upon the intents *1835*.
305ₓ6]   There is a curse upon the earth; let man *1835*.
311–12]   Though I doubt much if he consent that we
>   Discover this great secret, I know well
>   You will allege no other comprehends
>   The work in question save its labourer:
>   I shall assume the aim improved; and you
>   That I am implicated in the issue
>   Not simply as your friend, but as yourself –
>   As though it were my task that you perform,
>   And some plague dogged my heels till it were done.
>   Suppose this owned then; you are born to KNOW.
>   (You will heed well your answers, for my faith *1835*.
In the University of London copy, Browning changed 'improved' to 'approved' (the MS. reading) in the fifth line above.
338]   Where error is not, but success is sure. *1835*.
347   *geier-eagle*   Leviticus xi 18 refers to the gier-eagle (the spelling Browning used

till *1868*) as one of the birds that 'are an abomination'. 'Geier' is German for 'hawk'.

357-8   *Black Arts,* | *Great Works, the Secret and Sublime* respectively, Black Magic, the alchemical process of forming the Philosopher's Stone, and a reference to the alchemists' deliberate cultivation of mystery.

382-4   *periods . . . palaces,*]   periods; I renounce

> All hope of learning further on this head;
> And what I next advance holds good as well
> With one assured that all these things are true;
> For might not such seek out a fast retreat – *1835*.

394   *new-hearted*]   and untired *MS.*; and untried *1835*; and earnest *1849*; and untired *1863*.

400-414]   *not in 1835*.

417   *Stagirite*   Aristotle, born at Stagira.

417-18]   If in this wild rejection you regard

> Mankind and their award of fame – 'tis clear, *1835*.

481   *riveled . . . burgonet*   shrivelled . . . an open helmet.

518]   *not in 1835*.

527   *a star to men*   The same phrase is used of Shelley in *Pauline*, 171.

548   *brow was sealed his own*]   fate was sealed for ever *1835*.

599‸600]   So free from all past sin – that it was heard . . . *1835*.

606]   *not in 1835*.

648‸9]   Once more (since I am forced to speak as one

> Who has full liberty at his discretion) *1835*.

651   *gold and apes*   Solomon's navy brought 'gold, and silver, ivory, and apes, and peacocks' (1 Kings x 22).

715]   Were wide awake, I should have made all sure

> For my departure that remains to do;
> So answer not, while I run lightly o'er
> The topics you have urged tonight. It seems *1835*.

757]   *not in 1835*.

759]   It issues proudly? seeing that the soul

> Is deathless (we know well) but oftener cooped
> A prisoner and a thrall, than a throned power; *1835*.

763-4]   *not in 1835*.

770   *One man*   Christopher Smart (1722–71), the English poet who, Browning believed, had in madness once been divinely inspired and had written then his *Song to David* (1763), a poem Browning greatly admired.

775]   Seeing all this why should I pine in vain

> Attempts to win some day the august form
> Of Truth to stand before me, and compel
> My dark unvalued frame to change its nature,
> And straight become suffused with light – at best
> For my sole good – leaving the world to seek
> Salvation out as it best may, or follow
> The same long thorny course? No, I will learn
> How to set free the soul alike in all, *1835*.

801   *amaranth*   the flower traditionally associated by poets with immortality.

811   *Mayne*   Würzburg is on the Main river.

812   *schistous*   readily splittable.

832]   Festus, I plunge! *1835*.

PART II

4] *not in 1835.*

21–2] *not in 1835.*

23 *Make up the sum*] Within this roll *1835.*

25 *arch-genethliac* leading caster of horoscopes.

65] *not in 1835.*

78–9] Oh, were it but in failure, to have rest! *1849.*

79 *I hoped that once!*] *not in 1835.*

79ᴧ80] 'Tis little wonder truly; things go on
And at their worst they end or mend – 'tis time
To look about, with matters at this pass: *1835.*

107–8] Ordained life; there alone I cannot doubt,
That only way I may be satisfied. *1849.*

113–16] In what it should be, more than what it was –
Consenting that whatever passions slept,
Whatever impulses lay unmatured,
Should wither in the germ, – but scarce foreseeing
That the soil, doomed thus to perpetual waste, *1849.*

136 *But let grow*] Which have grown *1835.*

139 *lusts*] loves *1835.*

160] *not in 1849.*

166–9] Yet all was then o'erlooked, though noted now. *1835.*

168] Men saw the robe – I saw the august form. *1849.*

171ᴧ2] Of youth, and common life, and liberty, *Berg MS.*

179ᴧ80] Who knows which are the wise and which the fools ? *1849.*

180 *pride*] us, *1835.*

182–3] He who stoops lowest may find most – in short,
I am here; and all seems natural; I start not:
And never having glanced behind to know *1849.*

202 *mockery*] murrain *MS. first reading.*

223] *not in 1835.*

242 *frequence* assembled throng (archaism).

265] Had reached me: stars would write his will in heaven,
As once when a labarum was not deemed *1849.*

265–6 *fire-labarum . . . old founder of these walls* The labarum was the military standard of Constantine the Great, who made Christianity the official religion of the Roman Empire and Byzantium (later Constantinople), its capital. Going to battle, Constantine had seen in the sky a flaming cross inscribed *In hoc signo vinces* (Latin – 'Under this sign you will conquer').

270ᴧ71] Though such were meant to follow as its fruit, *1849.*

273 'And he that sat upon the throne said, Behold, I make all things new' (Revelation xxi 5).

273] *not in 1835.*

280] *not in 1849.*

281–96] *not in 1835.*

302–4] Lost one, come! the last *1835.*

311–14] *not in 1835.*

319–22] Not one of the sweet race? *1835.*

330–31] O come, come! *1835.*

334-5 *ruin . . . undoing* The rhyme is, in *1835*, correct, and reflects then current pronunciation.

338-9] Sharp sorrow, far from . . . *1835*.

339ᴧ40] A spirit better armed, succeeding me? *1849*.

341] *not in 1835*.

347-51] Ay, look on me! shall I be king or no? *1835*.

365ᴧ6] Even as thou sayest, succeeding to my place, *1849*.

366 *Reaping my sowing* 'whatsoever a man soweth, that shall he also reap' (Galatians vi 7).

368-9] *not in 1835*.

402] *not in 1835*.

407-17] *not in 1835*.

434 *clothe in*] *1835, this edition*; clothe it in *1849–88*.

435-6] The lines are transposed in *1835*.

451 Compare 'Rocks, caves, lakes, fens, bogs, dens, and shades of death' (*Paradise Lost* II, 621).

453 *wyvern* two-footed winged dragon.

471 *tent-tree* species of screw-pine.

475-7 *to pérfect . . . chasms with music* Compare the penultimate sentence of the *1835* preface.

519 *malachite* mineral used for ornaments.

521 *Cressets* metal vessels holding combustibles for torches.

558 *hind* peasant.

606ᴧ7] Didst not perceive, spoiled by the subtle ways
        Of intricate but instantaneous thought,
        That common speech was useless to its ends –
        That language, wedded from the first to thought,
        Will strengthen as it strengthens; but, divorced,
        Will dwindle, while thought widens more and more? . . . *1835*.

638] *not in 1835*.

648 *perfect poet*] PERFECT POET *1835–63*.

649] Who in His grand love acts his own conceptions. *Yale MS.*; Who in creation acts his own conceptions. *Berg MS., 1849*.

649ᴧ50] Shall man refuse to be aught less than God?
        Man's weakness is his glory – for the strength
        Which raises him to heaven and near God's self,
        Came spite of it: God's strength his glory is,
        For thence came with our weakness sympathy
        Which brought God down to earth, a man like us. *1849*.

The passage, which, with different punctuation, is also in the Berg and Yale manuscripts, is an important early statement of a central Browning theme.

661] The line in *1835* appeared in capital letters through a compositor's error.

PART III

Basil The city (Basel) in what is now north-west Switzerland was in 1526 a major centre of culture. The historical Paracelsus was there from the end of November 1526 to early 1528, and lectured at the University.

100-101 *gannet . . . lake* The sea-bird does not in fact nest in trees.

128 (note) 'Citrinula (flammula), a herb well known to Paracelsus' (Latin).

Gerhard Dorn, sixteenth-century German chemist and alchemist, was a follower of Paracelsus.

147-8 *fill | The chair* Paracelsus took up his position in March 1527.

183 *garnishry* Defining the word as 'garnishment', 'adornment', *OED* describes it as a nonce-word. The only recorded usages are Browning's, here and in *The Ring and the Book* IV, 545.

204 *sand-blind* partially blind.

211 *Rhasis* tenth-century Arab physician.

222-3 *the fallen prince . . . unchanged in semblance* Lucifer. The form of Milton's Satan 'had yet not lost / All her original brightness, nor appeared / Less than archangel ruined' (*Paradise Lost* I, 591-3).

269] Its progress. Nor was this the scheme of one
    Enamoured of a lot unlike the world's,
    And thus far sure from common casualty –
    (Folly of follies!) in that, thus, the mind
    Became the only arbiter of fate.
    No; what I termed and might conceive my choice,
    Already had been rooted in my soul –
    Had long been part and portion of myself. *1835*.

293 *Oecolampadius* Johannes Oecolampadius (1482–1531), German reformer, associated with Zwingli in the Reformation. He held a chair in theology at Basil, and apparently arranged Paracelsus's lecturing appointment there.

294 *Castellanus* Pierre Duchatel, who helped Frobenius.

295 *Munsterus* Sebastian Munster, scholar and follower of Luther, went to the University of Basil in 1529, lecturing in Hebrew and theology.

Frobenius Johannes Froben, important printer at the University of Basil, and associate of Erasmus and other noted figures. Paracelsus treated him successfully in 1526, but he died in 1527.

296-8] And staring, and expectant, – then, I say,
    'Tis like that the poor zany of the show,
    Your friend, will choose to put his trappings off
    Before them, bid adieu to cap and bells
    And motley with a grace but seldom judged *1849*.

305 *foul vapours* 'foul and pestilent congregation of vapours' (*Hamlet* II.2.315).

335 *soul]* spirit *1835*; mind *1849*.

344 *Our Luther's burning tongue* By 1526, Luther was no longer a Roman Catholic, and his reform views were having sweeping effects.

378-86, 388] *not in 1835*.

391 *rear-mice* bats.

394 *Lachen* village north-east of Einsiedeln.

399-400] Your earnest will unfaltering: if you still
    Remain unchanged, and if, in spite of all,
    You have experienced the defeat you tell – *1835*.
    Your earnest will unfaltering, if you still
    Remain unchanged, and if, in spite of this,
    You have experienced a defeat that proves
    Your aims for ever unattainable – *1849*.

411ʌ12] I am quite competent to answer all
    Demands, in any such capacity – *1835*.

437 *sudary* a cloth used to remove sweat.

441 *suffumigation* therapeutic application of smoke to the body.

446 *cross-grained* contrarious, intractable.

450 *Placarded* The first usage of the word in this sense recorded by *OED* is dated 1818.

480–82 *Erasmus* The great Dutch Humanist (1467–1536) had settled in Basil where his works were printed by Frobenius, at whose suggestion he wrote to Paracelsus in 1526 about treatment for his gallstones.

492 *mortal* Pelops, son of Tantalus. Demeter ate part of his shoulder. Paracelsus's knowledge is inaccurate, and he appears to confuse Pelops and Asclepius.

564ᴧ5] Nay, was assured no such could be for me, *1835*.

574–5] *not in 1835*.

579ᴧ80] And let the next world's knowledge dawn on this; *1849*.

597ᴧ8] Whatever that may be – but not till then. *1835*.

603 *Here I stand* 'Here I stand; I can do no otherwise' (Luther, at the Diet of Worms).

635ᴧ6] That really come to learn for learning's sake; *1849*.

670] Its nature in the next career they try. *1835*.

695ᴧ6] To catch Aprile's spirit, as I hoped, *1849*.

714 *addressed a frock* donned (archaism – *OED* 4b) a coat.

744] How sweet the gardens where he slept last night, . . . *MS. first reading.*

750ᴧ51] As calmly, as sincerely, as I may; *1835*.

765 *men*] me *1835*.

862] But I know too what sort of soul is prone
        To errors of that stamp – sins like to spring
        From one alone whose life has passed the bounds *1835*.

866 *traces of decay* sunspots.

867 *Praeclare! Optime!* 'Excellent! Splendid!' (Latin).

869ᴧ70] And that his flittering words should soothe me better
          Than fulsome tributes: not that that is strange: *1835*.

870ᴧ71] I ne'er supposed that since *I* failed no other
          Needs hope success: I act as though each one
          Who hears me may aspire: now mark me well: *1835*.

875 *multitudinous* 'multitudinous seas' (*Macbeth* II.1.63).

888] And whoso wills, is very free to make
        That use of me which I disdained to make
        Of my forerunners – (vanity, perchance;
        But had I deemed their learning wonder-worth,
        I had been other than I am) – to mount *1835*.

907 *Ulysses' bow, Achilles' shield* their most distinctive weapons in Homer.

907–10] With Hercules' club, Achilles' shield, Ulysses'
          Bow – a choice sight to scare the crows away! *1835*.

932] *not in 1835*.

946–7 *Aëtius . . . Averröes* The seven are all physicians whose works strongly influenced medical theory and practice in Paracelsus's time. They are, respectively, a sixth-century physician, a fourth-century Greek physician, the enormously influential second-century physician, the tenth-century Arab physician, the tenth-century Syrian physician, the greatest of Arab physicians (980–1037), the twelfth-century Arab physician and philosopher.

955 *Zuinglius* Ulrich Zwingli (1484–1531), the leading Swiss reformer.

959 *Wittenberg* the city of Saxony, on the Elbe, home of Luther's University and cradle of the Reformation.

960–61 *the differences of late | With Carolostadius* Andreas Bodenstein ('Carlstadt') originally taught Luther at the University of Wittenberg. Later he became a Luther disciple, but broke with him to influence Zwingli. The main 'differences' were over the doctrine of transubstantiation.

989   *mischance*]   despair *1835–49*.

993–5   *gangs of peasants . . . the elector*   The Peasants' War, a revolt stimulated by Reformation ideals, erupted in 1524, and spread over Suabia (the region in south-west Germany) and then more widely. Thomas Münzer had established a theocratic Anabaptist state in central Germany. The revolt was suppressed and Münzer executed in 1525 by the Duke of Brunswick, the Landgrave of Hesse and the Elector of Saxony.

PART IV

Oporinus   printer, scholar, and student of Paracelsus. In 1528 he followed Paracelsus to Colmar, but soon afterwards he left his service.

1   *Sic itur ad astra*   'Thus one journeys to the stars' (Latin).

Von Visenburg   Like Torinus (line 2) and Pütter (line 7), he seems to be a Browning invention.

5   *Liechtenfels*   a canon whom Paracelsus saved from death by gout, and who then refused to pay the promised fee.

9   *scathe*   harm (archaic and dialectal).

10   *mantling*   sparkling.

28]   *not in 1835*.

82–3   *Saul is among | The prophets*   See 1 Samuel x 10–12.

86]   I had huge praise, and doubtless might have grown
    Grey in the exposition of such antics,
    Had my stock lasted long enough; but such
    Was not my purpose: one can ne'er keep down *1835*.

108–9]   *not in 1835*.

115   *Quid multa?*   'Why many words?' (Latin).

120   *patient merit*   *Hamlet* III.1.74.

139   *blains*   bodily inflammatory swellings or sores.

142–3]   – I say that, could you see as I could show, *1849*.

152–5]   *not in 1849*.

190   *stripes*   strips.

190–92   *Heap cassia . . . dull nard*   The sweet-smelling substances mentioned are all used in ointments.

194]   *not in 1835*.

203   *mothed*   *OED* records only Browning's usage here.

213   *Luther's psalms*   Some of Luther's hymns are based on the psalms; he translated the Bible.

225]   *not in 1835*.

241]   *not in 1835*.

244   *earthliest sensualest*   characteristic Browning superlatives.

246–7   *My soul . . . gained?*   'For what shall it profit a man, if he shall gain the whole world, and lose his own soul?' (Mark viii 36).

246–8]   And gain is gain, however small: nor should,
    On the other hand, those honeyed pleasures follow *1835*.

267]   *not in 1835*.

287]   Provoke it: I ne'er sought to domineer;
    The mere asserting my supremacy

Has little mortified their self-conceit;
I took my natural station and no more: *1835*.

295–300]   Hiding the fact – and, had I been but wise,
Had ne'er concerned myself with scruples, nor
Communicated aught to such a race;
But been content to own myself a man, *1835*.

302ᴧ3]   Still, one thing I have learned – not to despair: *1849*.

306   *empiric*   charlatan.

310   *Fiat experientia corpore vili*   'The experiment is to be performed on a valueless body' (Latin).

310]   *not in 1835*.

400ᴧ401]   Mere hopes of bliss for proofs that bliss will be, *1849*.

407–8]   *not in 1835*.

434–49   *Have I, you ask … the wind's.*]   *not in 1835*.

459]   *not in 1835*.

466]   *not in 1835*.

489–90]   Not so the isles our voyage must find
Should meet our longing eye; *1835*.

523ᴧ4]   May still be read on that deserted rock, *1849–63*.

539   *rest by lying there*]   boyhood's carelessness *1835*.

561ᴧ2]   God made you and knows what you may become – *1849*.

588–94   *The serviceable spirits … lamp's rubbing*   Aladdin in the *Arabian Nights* summons up spirits to serve him by rubbing a lamp.

602]   Can be concerned, or I am much deceived: *1835*.

618   *John the thief*   The historical Paracelsus suspected Oporinus of stealing his secrets.

630   *tetter, morphew, furfair*   a skin disease, a leprous or scurfy eruption, scurf. Compare *Hamlet* I.5. 70–72.

672   *julep*   sweet medicinal drink.

690–93   *while we fight the prize … perish for your sport*   Paracelsus sees himself as gladiator.

PART V

Scene   Melchior Adam records that Paracelsus died in the Hospital of Saint Sebastian in Salzburg in north Austria.

44]   *not in 1835*.

49]   *not in 1835*.

95ᴧ6]   Let me speak to him in another's name. *1849–63*.

123–5   *Jove strikes the Titans … crown the work*   The Giants (or the Titans) piled Mount Ossa on Mount Pelion to scale Olympus and attack Jove, but were defeated.

126–8   *Phaeton … thunder*   Phaeton, son of Apollo, took over the chariot of the sun for one day, but drove so erratically that Jove killed him with a thunderbolt.

134ᴧ5]   You that hate men and all who wish their good – *1849*.

161–5]   *not in 1835*.

174]   *not in 1835*.

181–2   *Galen of Pergamos … face to face*   Browning annotated line 182 in *1835*: 'He did in effect affirm that he had disputed with Galen in the vestibule of hell.' The famous Greek physician was born in Pergamos (or Pergamum) in north-west Asia Minor.

183–5]   *not in 1835*.

186–92 *Oh, emptiness... After the shade!*] *not in 1835.*

187 *Persic Zoroaster* the Persian religious prophet, probably of the sixth century B.C., founder of Zoroastrianism.

201] *not in 1835.*

287 *wormwood* the bitter aromatic herb; figuratively, something bitter to the soul.

346] *not in 1835.*

386 *phares* lighthouses.

388 *Their theft shall be their bale*] Men look up to the sun *1849.*

    bale used here in the obsolete sense of 'great fire' or in the archaic Scottish sense of 'signal-fire'. (Browning uses many Scotticisms, many of them being doubtless an inheritance from his Scottish mother.)

417 *ay, leaning so!*] *not in 1835.*

440 *marl* a kind of soil.

484 *canes* stems of certain grasses or reeds.

485 *fan-trees, tamarisks* respectively, fan-palms and delicate evergreen shrubs.

554 *Azoth* Pictures of Paracelsus, like one that Browning used as frontispiece for the manuscript of his poem, show him with his famous long sword on the hilt of which is engraved 'Azoth'. The word is the alchemists' for 'mercury'; and is also the name for Paracelsus's 'universal remedy', as Browning's note indicates: the 'universal remedy' was probably opium, though Paracelsus pretended otherwise.

574–5]   Pardon from Him, who calls me to Himself
        To teach me better and exalt me higher! *1835.*

607]   And, grappling strenuously with Fate, compel her *1835.*

626]   Were saved me, though the lion heart repines not
        At working through such lets its purpose out. *1835.*

638]   I knew, I felt, not as one knows or feels
        Aught else; a vast perception unexpressed, *1835.*

642 In *1835* the line is annotated: ' "Paracelse faisait profession du Panthéisme le plus grossier." – Renauldin.' ('Paracelsus professed the grossest Pantheism'.) The quotation is from the entry on Paracelsus in the *Biographie Universelle.*

653 *The centre-fire*... The passage beginning with this line, as DeVane (*Handbook,* 55) observes, owes much to *Paradise Lost* (V, 403–505) and Pope's *Essay on Man* (I, 207–80), and little to Paracelsus. In 1881 Browning claimed: 'all that seems *proved* in Darwin's scheme was a conception familiar to me from the beginning: see in *Paracelsus* the progressive development from senseless matter to organized, until man's appearance' (Hood, *Letters,* 199). Browning was not an expert on Darwin.

656 *outbranches* *OED* calls the word 'very rare': Browning's usage here is the first recorded.

662 *cyclops-like* that is, essentially at least, 'one-eyed' – from the one-eyed monsters of classical myth. Used here with reference to volcano craters.

666 *psaltress* female player of the ancient and medieval stringed instrument, the psaltery.

666–81 *But spring-wind . . . rapture* Compare Lucretius, *De Rerum Natura* I, 10–20.

673 *dorrs* insects that fly with loud humming noises. Perhaps bees or beetles; probably here may-bugs, or june-bugs.

691–2]   (So would a spirit deem, intent on watching
        The purpose of the world from its faint rise
        To its mature development) – some point
        Whereto those wandering rays should all converge – *1835.*

701 *stains* spots of colour different from their grounds (see *OED* 2d).

706]   Anticipations, hints of these and more *1835*.

707–8   *everywhere about . . . higher*]   everywhere – all seek / An object to possess and stamp their own; *1835*.

709   *superior*]   forthcoming *1835*.

717]   The clear dawn of those qualities shines out, *1835*.

743   *man is not Man as yet.*]   man is not man as yet: *1835*; man's self is not yet Man! *1849–63*.

820ₐ21]   Although my own name led the brightness in: *1835*.

825   *work*]   tools *1849–63*.

836]   *not in 1835*.

851]   *not in 1835*.

852   *poor melodious wretch*   'pulled the poor wretch from her melodious lay' (*Hamlet* IV.7.184).

898]   *not in 1835*.

NOTE   Browning's note, appended to the poem in all his editions, underwent considerable revision. It is here reprinted verbatim from *1888*: to edit it is to meddle with what DeVane (*Handbook*, 55) calls 'a rather handsome exhibition of erudition', and to annotate it is to risk confounding confusion even though the 'erudition' tends to evaporate under scrutiny. Translations of the passages in Latin (they are not especially helpful to an understanding of *Paracelsus*) are available in Appendix E of I. Jack's Oxford Standard Authors edition.

Sordello

First published on 7 March 1840 by Edward Moxon at the expense of Browning's father. In 1845–7 Browning gave some thought to revising *Sordello* for republication, but it was not included in *1849*. In the winter of 1855–6 he tried unsuccessfully to revise the poem; it was not until *1863* that it was restored to the canon. For *1863* the inadequate and often curious punctuation of *1840*, where in particular the shortage of quotation marks frequently creates problems for readers, had been tidied up; eighty-five lines had been added and other extensive revisions effected, though Browning declared that only 'some few alterations' had been made. There were further changes, very few of them of much significance, for *1868* and again for *1888*. Running titles, designed to elucidate the action, were included in *1863* and *1868* (and are reprinted in this edition in the headnote to each book). The running titles were dropped in *1888*; no other significant revision failed to be incorporated in succeeding editions, though Browning in these did uncharacteristically make a very occasional return to an earlier reading. The manuscript has apparently perished, but a proof copy with modest holograph revisions is in the Boston Public Library.

In *1863* the poem was dedicated to J. Milsand, Browning's close French friend to whose memory he dedicated the *Parleyings* in 1887. The dedication, one of Browning's most important, was slightly revised for *1868*, and reprinted in *1888*.

The poem was begun before *Paracelsus*, shortly after the publication of *Pauline* in March 1833, and work on it, the longest of his poems except for *The Ring and the Book*, proceeded with varying degrees of intensity for over six years. Browning's conception of the poem, his sense of its main direction, varied over this period; and may have been affected by the appearance of a six-part poem on *Sordello* by one Mrs William Busk, though the work is of so abysmal a quality (it reminds one irresistibly of Chaucer's *Sir Thopas*) that it could hardly have effected the major shift in Browning's view of his work that is postulated by some scholars. What is obvious is that Browning found writing the poem difficult, and that his poetic intention was often not clear in his own mind, and it is probable that he was disturbed by the clear parallels between, and inevitable duplication of material in, *Pauline, Paracelsus* and *Sordello*. The announcement in his play *Strafford*, published on 1 May 1837, that *Sordello* was 'nearly ready' was clearly optimistic; on 26 May 1839 Browning claimed to Macready that *Sordello* was finished. (W. C. DeVane attempts to chart the poem's probable progress over the six or seven years in '*Sordello*'s Story Retold', *SP* XXVII, 1930, 1–24, and in his *Handbook*, 71–87.)

There is much of Browning himself in Sordello, and Browning obviously used his hero to grapple with questions of major importance to him. Consequently *Sordello* often reminds one of much in the earlier poems, and among its more important sources is Browning himself, a fact implied in the 1863 dedication: 'The historical decoration was purposely of no more importance than a background requires; and my stress lay on the incidents in the development of a soul: little else is worth study.' Despite that claim, however, *Sordello* stresses the historical too, and Browning made much greater use of it than in his two earlier long poems. For information about Sordello, Dante's guide in *Purgatory* (vi–ix), Browning is chiefly indebted to Volume XLIII of that standard multi-volume reference work of his youth, the *Biographie Universelle*, which had begun to appear in 1811; he consulted the work also for other things in his poem. Most of Browning's materials on the Ecelins of the House of Romano come from Volumes I and II of Giambattista Verci's *Storia degli Ecelini* (3 volumes, Bassano, 1779), and his other main historical sources are materials in Volumes VIII and XX of L. Muratori's *Rerum Italicarum Scriptores*, a collection of chronicles (25 volumes, Milan, 1723–51); the seventh volume of the same editor's *Annali d'Italia* (12 volumes, Milan, 1744–9); the second and third volumes of A. Frizzi's five-volume *Memorie per la storia di Ferrara raccolte* (Ferrara, 1793); G. B. Pigna's *Historia de' Principi d'Este* (Venice, 1572); L. Ughi's two-volume *Dizionario Storico degli Uomini Illustri Ferraresi* (Ferrara, 1804); and the second and third volumes of J. C. L. Simonde de Sismondi's sixteen-volume *Républiques Italiennes* (Paris, 1809–18). S. W. Holmes's authoratitive article, 'The Sources of Browning's *Sordello*', *SP* XXXIV, 1937, 467–96, gives full details. Browning familiarized himself with much of the territory of his poem on his visit to north-eastern Italy in 1838.

Browning's sources are confused, contradictory and shadowy. He felt free to invent details: it is unlikely that Sordello or Salinguerra ever knew the other existed; the name of Sordello's love was Cunizza, a lusty lady married five times and daughter of Ecelin the Monk and Adelaide, while Palma was the name of her half-sister, daughter of Ecelin and Agnes Este; Retrude was not the daughter of Henry and Constance of Sicily. He felt free to treat chronology with abandon: the poem's Ecelin the Monk dies about ten years earlier than his historical counterpart; events around Ferrara of 1220–24 are – with the odd exception – compressed into 1224. When sources contradicted one another, Browning chose the account that best suited his needs: some sources have Sordello dying at ninety, others have him dying young and violently.

Fifteen years after *Sordello* was published, 157 copies had been sold, despite which it became notorious for its obscurity, and greatly damaged Browning's reputation; stories about early readers' responses to it are legion. Even Elizabeth Barrett had problems with it, and Ezra Pound, who found the poem a model of lucidity, is probably the only person who has ever seriously claimed to have understood *Sordello*. It was, however, popular with the Pre-Raphaelites, and may have special nterest as what G. K. Chesterton called it: 'the most glorious compliment that has ever been paid to the average man'.

Many of the poem's difficulties stem from Browning's apparent assumption that his readers would be intimately familiar with the historical background of his poem. *Sordello* is set in a northern Italy torn by civil war in the first half of the thirteenth century, a period of huge confusion. And a reader is not helped by the further confusions of Browning, who, himself confused, confounds confusion by changing facts and muddling characters, places and chronology. The two opposing factions in the civil wars were the Guelfs (Guelphs) and Ghibellins (Ghibellines) – the notes here use Browning's spellings of names but initially record also the standard names or spellings in parentheses. The names of the two factions derived from opposing ones in Germany; but in Italy the term 'Guelf' was applied to the Papal party, 'Ghibellin' to the Imperial. Each term, however, is often applied to a person or group whose association with either side is more apparent than real; again, cities theoretically supporting one side were themselves deeply divided between the two factions.

The poem's first reported historical incident, the capture of Verona's Count Richard, occurred in 1224. At this time Honorius III was Pope, and Friedrich (Frederick) II was Holy Roman Emperor. The Guelf leader in Lombardy and Venetia was Azzo VII (1205–64) of the House of Este (Este is a few miles south-west of Padua, but Azzo's main residence was Ferrara). The Ghibellin leader, Ecelin the Monk, or Ecelin II (*c.* 1150–1234) of the House of Romano (Romano is near Bassano, north of Padua), had retired to a monastery in 1221, dividing his lands between his sons, Ecelin III (1194–1259) – the Tyrant, or the Ferocious, or the Terrible – and his brother Alberico. The effective leader of the Ghibellins was Taurello Salinguerra (his first name is variously spelled in Browning's sources) (*c.* 1160–1245), who led the faction in Ferrara.

Still useful is A. J. Whyte's edition (1913). The pioneering annotation in the Florentine edition is highly selective and often erroneous. Text and textual apparatus of the Ohio edition (Volume II, 1970) are inaccurate, and the annotation is arbitrarily selective and riddled with error. Among treatments are: Collins, *Robert Browning's Moral-Aesthetic Theory*, 45–77; R. R. Columbus and C. Kemper, 'Sordello and the Speaker: A Problem in Identity', *VP* II, 1964, 25–67; Cook, *Browning's Lyrics*, 27–49; E. Dowden, 'Mr. Browning's *Sordello*', in his *Transcripts and Studies*, Kegan, Paul, Trench, 1888, 474–525 (Browning commended Dowden's treatment); Griffin and Minchin, *Life*, 89–103; E. Hilton, 'Browning's *Sordello* as a Study of the Will', *PMLA* LXIX, 1954, 1127–34; S. W. Holmes, 'Browning's *Sordello* and Jung: Browning's *Sordello* in the Light of Jung's Theory of Types', *PMLA* LVI, 1941, 758–96; S. W. Holmes, 'Browning: Semantic Stutterer', *PMLA* LX, 1945, 231–55; P. Honan, 'Browning's Poetic Laboratory: The Uses of *Sordello*', *MP* LVI, 1959, 162–6; A. P. Johnson, '*Sordello*: Apollo, Bacchus, and the Pattern of Italian History', *VP* VII, 1969, 321–38; M. Mason, 'The Importance of *Sordello*', in I. Armstrong (ed.), *The Major Victorian Poets*, Routledge & Kegan Paul, 1969, 125–51; L. Poston, 'Browning's Political Skepticism: *Sordello* and the Plays', *PMLA* LXXXVIII, 1973, 260–70; D. Stempel, 'Browning's *Sordello*: The Art of the Makers-See', *PMLA* LXXX, 1965, 554–61; L. Stevenson, 'The Key Poem of the Victorian Age', in M. F. Schulz, with W. D. Templeman and C. R. Metzger (eds.), *Essays in American and English Literature Presented to Bruce Robert McElderry Jr.*, Ohio University Press, 1967, 260–89; H. F. Tucker, 'Browning, Eglamor and Closure in *Sordello*', *SBHC* IV, 1976, 54–70; M. G. Yetman, 'Exorcising Shelley Out of Browning: *Sordello* and the Problem of Poetic Identity', *VP* XIII, 1975, 79–98.

BOOK THE FIRST

Book I was only slightly revised after *1840*; no lines were added or deleted. In *1863* and *1868* running titles were used. The *1868* version is: 'A Quixotic attempt. Why the poet himself addresses his audience – few living, many dead. Shelley departing, Verona appears. How her Guelfs are discomfited. Why they entreat the Lombard League, in their changed fortune at Ferrara: for the times grow stormy again. The Ghibellins' wish: the Guelfs' wish. How Ecelo's House grew Head of those, as Azzo Lord of Este heads these. Count Richard's palace at Verona. Of the couple found therein, one belongs to Dante; his birthplace. A vault inside the castle at Goito, and what Sordello would see there. His boyhood in the domain of Ecelin. How a poet's soul comes into play. What denotes such a soul's progress. How poets class at length – for honour, or shame – which may the gods avert from Sordello, now in childhood. The delights of his childish fancy, which could blow out a great bubble, being secure awhile from intrusion. But it comes; and new-born judgement decides that he needs sympathizers. He therefore creates such a company; each of which, leading its own life, has qualities impossible to a boy, so, only to be appropriated in fancy, and practised on till the real come. He means to be perfect – say, Apollo: and Apollo must one day find Daphne. But when will this dream turn truth? For the time is ripe, and he ready.'

4–7 *the friendless-people's friend ... Arm* Don Quixote, seeing a cloud of dust raised by sheep, thought it Alifanfaron's army chased by the Garomantean King, Pentapolin, who entered battle with his right sleeve tucked up (*Don Quixote* I, iv).

11 *Verona* The northern city, for the most part a centre of Guelf strength, was constantly a focal point for conflict in the Middle Ages.

25 *Fresh-chapleted* wearing fresh garlands.

26 *unexampled* unprecedented.

30 *Motley on back and pointing-pole in hand* Court jesters wore motley, and Browning sometimes 'enters' the poem to comment, perhaps, as Stempel suggests, assuming the role of lecturer with diorama.

36 *quick* living.

60 *thou, spirit* that of Shelley.

65–8 *thunder-phrase ... shield* Aeschylus fought against the Persians at Marathon (490 B.C.).

67 *griding* grating.

68 *Braying* pounding into small pieces.

69 *Sidney's self, the starry paladin* Sir Philip Sidney's sonnet sequence was called *Astrophil and Stella* ('Star-lover' and 'Star'); a 'paladin' champions a noble cause.

70 *intense* strained.

   sounding summoning musically.

78–80 *The Second Friedrich wore | The purple, and the Third Honorius filled | The holy chair* Friedrich (Frederick) II (1194–1250) became Holy Roman Emperor in 1220 and leader of the Ghibellin cause. He feuded constantly with Honorius III, Pope from 1216 to 1227, and leader of the Guelf cause.

85 *A single eye* that of Sordello.

102–6 *Count Richard of Saint Boniface . . . Ferrara* Richard, a Guelf (of San Bonifazio), ruled Verona, under the leader of the Guelf cause in northern Italy, Azzo VII of the House of Este. In 1224 Salinguerra captured Richard by treachery.

108 *proper* own.

110 *Lombard League* The League of fifteen cities, including Verona, was revived in 1226; it supported the Guelf cause.

115 *pavis* large shield. The Este arms had an eagle against a blue or purple ground.

117 *play* compete against.

119 *patron* Emperor, Friedrich II.

121 *Duke o' the Rood* Azzo VII. The leader of the Lombard League was Knight of the Holy Cross (or Rood).

123 *hill-cat* Ecelin II. His seat at Romano was in hilly country south of the Alps.

126 *feeds her fat* 'Advantage feeds him fat while men delay' (*1 Henry IV* III.2.181).

   lion Azzo VII. The lion is associated with Verona (controlled by the Este family), and with the Pope.

127 *in wane* in decline ('Like a moon in wane, faded' – Keats, *Lamia* I, 136).

128 *osprey* 'sea-eagle'.

131 *Kaiser* Friedrich II.

138 *Pontiff* the Pope, Honorius III.

138-9 *Ecelin . . . Oliero* Ecelin II ('The Monk') had retired to the monastery at Oliero, a village near Romano, about this time, leaving the leadership of the Ghibellin cause to his son.

145-6 *Cino Bocchimpane . . . Buccio Virtù* imaginary characters. One of Browning's sources, however, mentions the Bucchimpane family as a leading one in Ferrara.

146 *God's wafer* a mild oath, alluding to the communion wafer.

147 *Tutti Santi* 'All the saints' (Italian).

150 *Podestà* chief magistrate of a city. To ensure greater impartiality, he was invariably a citizen of another city. The appointment was usually directly or indirectly arranged by the main leaders of the day.

154 *palaces are burned* Salinguerra was driven from Ferrara in 1221, and his two palaces burned.

155 *our*] your *1840*. An example of a kind of revision frequent in *Sordello*: the second-person possessive pronoun and the definite article are often changed to first-person singular or plural possessive pronouns, the result being that the narrator of *1863-88* is less objective and more involved than in *1840*.

166 *ounce* a name applied to various cat-like animals; here, probably, 'leopard'.

172 *Men fed on men* Ferrara was under siege in 1222 and 1224. Browning seems to assume that the siege had been continuous. At any rate, the cannibalism is not in Browning's sources.

   At length] Astute *1840*.

193 *Hohenstaufen* Friedrich II's family name.

   Hohenstaufen] *this edition*; Hohenstauffen *1840-88*.

194-9 John of Brienne was titular King of Jerusalem and son-in-law of Friedrich II, whom he had urged to keep his promise to lead a Crusade, a promise that Friedrich postponed implementing, partly, at least, because he feared that his absence would allow the Papal forces to retrieve the gains made by Otho (Otto) IV and Barbaross (Frederick I, 'Barbarossa' – 'Red-beard'), Friedrich II's immediate predecessors as Holy Roman Emperor.

199 *fear* that Friedrich would not lead a Crusade.

200 *excommunicate that very year* Friedrich was excommunicated in 1227 by Gregory IX, Papal successor to Honorius III.

201 *triple-bearded Teuton* Friedrich I, Barbaross. Legend had it that he lived on, and would reveal himself when his beard had three times grown around a table.

222 *wreck* In the extended metaphor here, the Ghibellins are associated with rocks and cliffs, the Guelfs with chokeweed. The 'wreck' is Lombardy.

225 *mantling* forming a scum upon.

240 *ambiguous stranger-guest* The House of Romano was Saxon in origin.

244 *Arpo or Yoland* Arpo (Arpone), a Saxon, is said to have come with Conrad II, Holy Roman Emperor (1027–39), and founded the House of Romano. 'Yoland' appears to be Browning's invention: some writers call the Romano founder Ecelino d'Olanda.

247 *Trevisan* the area around Treviso in the Venetian plain.

248 *Conrad* Conrad III, the Suabian, German King (1138–52) – he was succeeded by his nephew, Friedrich I, Barbaross.

249 *Ecelo* son of Arpo (died 1091).

251-2 *Godego ... Loria* fiefs under Romano control.

253 *Suabian's fief* Suabia (Swabia) was the large duchy north of Lombardy. Conrad III and Friedrich I were Suabians.

254 *Lombard chief* Ecelin I (the Stammerer), historically grandson of Ecelo (in Browning's version, son of Ecelo), father of Ecelin II (the Monk).

256 *Trent* the city in northern Italy, controlling the route into Italy through the Brenner pass.

257 *Roncaglia* On his first visit to Italy in 1154, Friedrich I held a Diet on this plain near Piacenza.

258 *Tyrol* the County, almost wholly Alpine and including the Brenner Pass, in what is now western Austria.

259 *Asolan and Euganean hills* respectively, the hills around Asolo, about thirty miles north-west of Venice, and the group between Padua and Este.

260 *Rhetian and the Julian* ranges of the Alps respectively to the north of Lombardy and the north-east of Venetia.

261 *Ecelin* Ecelin II (the Monk), the 'hillcat' of line 123.

270 *griesliest* archaic form (Spenser's form) of 'grisliest'.

271 *Signory* the governing body of an Italian city-state (*signoria*).

274-5 *Otho ... Your Este* Otho (Otto) IV was Emperor 1209–15. He was tenuously related by blood to the House of Este. The point of his vaunt is that if he (being an Estian) or his representative, Ecelin, should supplant the Italian head of the House of Este, the Ghibellin Este would then have beaten the Guelf Este.

276 *this Ecelin* Ecelin III (the Tyrant, the Ferocious).

281 *the man's-flesh went*] men's flesh is meant *1840*.

284-5 *a tree ... Successively* Salinguerra is the bole, and his sons, dying, the boughs.

288 *surcoat* medieval outer garment.

290 *writhen* twisted.

290-92] Ecelin lifts two writhen hands to pray
At Oliero's convent now: so, place
For Azzo, Lion of the ... why disgrace *1840*.

292 *Why disgrace* Why try to disgrace.

294-5 *Atii ... Hun* The sixteenth-century historian Pigna begins the Este pedigree with Caio Atio. He tells too of Este bravery in repulsing Attila the Hun in 452.

296 *trumpeting* denouncing. Ecelin II was a heretic, a Paterine opposed to clerical corruption.

297 *Styled Patron* The area mentioned was only technically under Papal control.

  Rovigo's Polesine Rovigo is about fifteen miles north-east of Ferrara, and a few miles south of Este. The Polesine is the lower valley of the Po river, south of Rovigo.

298   *Ancona's march*   Ancona, the Italian port-city on the Adriatic, is the capital of the region of the Marches, but the reference here is to the more confined area of the fief around Ancona.

306   *Father Porphyry*   an imaginary monk whose name comes from the Greek for 'purple'.

308   *Hildebrand*   Pope Gregory VII (1073-85).

310   *Twenty-four*   Verona was ruled by a Podestà, but local 'consuls' served under him.

311   *his*   Richard's.

313   *clapping*   banging.

314   *cressets*   containers for combustibles, torches.

317   *carroch*   Browning's englishing of *carroccio*, the sacred, heavily decorated car of state accompanying an Italian city-state army and carrying its standard. It is booming because the alarm is being sounded from it.

332-3   *wise | And lulling words*   See *Sordello* III, 319-551.

337   *outcry*   See *Sordello* III, 276-303.

342-5   *half-burnt taper . . . wedding-robe*   an Armenian wedding-custom.

343   *Erst*   formerly (archaism).

346   *Gate-vein*   the *Vena portae*, the great abdominal vein. The line is repeated later (III, 556).

348   *thy forerunner, Florentine*   Dante praised Sordello for his contribution to the Italian language in *De Vulgari Eloquentia*. Sordello features largely in *Purgatorio* vi-ix, where he guides Dante and Vergil.

352   *sempiternal*   everlasting.

362   *argentine*   silver.

364   *sea whose fire was mixt with glass*   'And I saw as it were a sea of glass mingled with fire' (Revelation xv 2).

366-72   *Dante . . . lie*   Dante's Inferno, Purgatorio and Paradiso are respectively imaged.

369   *óbscure*   Browning uses the word here with the accentuation of Shakespeare and Milton, and in a now old-fashioned sense of 'dark and dismal'.

371   *amaranths*   fabled never-fading flowers, emblematic of immortality.

374   *Mantua*   The city of eastern Lombardy is on the Mincio river twenty-odd miles south of Verona. The city's main square is named after Sordello, who, according to some stories, relieved the city from its three-year siege by Ecelin III in 1253.

381   *Goito*   The village is about ten miles north-west of Mantua. It has a red-brick medieval tower called the 'Torre Sordello', but the castle may well be Browning's conjecture.

388   *lapwings*   The lapwing is a kind of plover.

397   *Arab's wisdom*   Though Arab culture strongly affected medieval Europe, Browning is probably referring particularly to Arab astrology, in which Adelaide was deeply interested.

402   *bacchanals*   Bacchic revellers.

412   *Caryatides*   female figures used as architectural columns.

422   *buried vestal*   In ancient Rome, vestal virgins tended the fire of Vesta. If they were unchaste, they were incarcerated to die of starvation.

429   *constant as eve he came*   repeated in V, 797, where we learn a fact unknown to Sordello: that his mother, Retrude, was buried beneath the font.

434   *globed*   Gold was refined in globes.

446   *eastward*]   southward *1840*.

454 *broidered* embroidered.

458 *Ecelin* Ecelin I (the Stammerer); in Browning's poem, the son (historically the grandson) of Ecelo (died 1091).

459 *Auria, and their Child* wife of Ecelin the Stammerer, and their second son, Ecelin the Monk.

460 *Agnes* Agnes Este, first of Ecelin the Monk's four wives. The historical Agnes had a daughter, Palma, whose name (and mother) Browning gives to her half-sister, Cunizza, daughter of Adelaide.

Tuscan that survives Adelaide da Mangone, fourth wife of Ecelin the Monk, and mother, among others, of Ecelin the Tyrant and (historically, though not in *Sordello*) Cunizza (Browning's Palma).

516 *legend* If a particular one is meant, it may be that in Hesiod's *Theogony*.

559 *Emprise* enterprise.

574 *Pisan pair* Nicolo (Nicola) Pisano (*c*. 1225–*c*. 1284), architect and founder of a school of sculpture combining classical and Gothic, and his son, Giovanni (*c*. 1250–*c*. 1320).

576 *Guidone* About Guido of Siena, thirteenth-century painter, almost nothing is known. As Browning suggests, however, he may, like Nicolo, have been a formative influence on the new art to come.

578 *Saint Eufemia* probably a reference to the church of the name in Verona.

580 *moon*] noon-sun *1840*. The change was suggested by Browning's friend, Alfred Domett, whose annotated copy of *Sordello* is in the British Library. Browning seems to have heeded Domett's scattered criticisms, though Domett himself later grossly exaggerated his own influence on Browning's revisions.

589 *may*] shall *1840*.

592–603 *So they found . . . gifts of gold* In A.D. 164, Lucius Verus, co-Emperor with the philosopher Marcus Aurelius Antoninus, commanded Roman forces that sacked Seleucia, north of Babylon. It is said that soldiers searching the temple of Apollo ('Loxian' is one of Apollo's epithets) opened a box and released a plague on the Empire.

595–6] Its pride, in rummaging the rarities,
    A cabinet; be sure, who made the prize *1840*.

632 *palmer-worm* a hairy caterpillar.

637 *not a shard dissheathed* that is, his wings, like those of the palmer-worm, are still sheathed in their casing.

657 *orpine* succulent herbaceous plant.

660 *Chief* Salinguerra.

665–6 *spider . . . height* Browning has a particular spider (a species of orb-weaver) in mind, but commits an arachnological inexactitude in having her shoot threads from depth to height.

667 *barbican* an outer fortification.

680 *Stead* to serve.

693 *Naddo* He represents conventional common sense throughout *Sordello*. It has been suggested that he may be based in part on John Forster.

fern-seed It was supposed to make one invisible; 'we have the receipt of fern-seed, we walk invisible' (*1 Henry IV* II.1.96).

707 *fleering* mocking, grinning.

708 *crane* cranium (an archaism).

709 *Lay bare*] Protrudes *1840*.

759 *Conceited* fancied.

763 *now dared*] availed *1840*.

768 *Lord, liegeman, valvassor and suzerain* four feudal social grades.

813 *Imperial Vicar* Ecelin the Monk became Otho IV's vicegerent in 1209.

816 *Trentine-pass* the pass through the Trent valley, south of the Brenner river.

819 *The Guelf's paid stabber* In 1209 Ecelin accused Azzo of seizing his arm in the Square of Saint Mark in Venice as he was attacked by assassins.

841 *Malek* a name for any Saracen chief.

868 *Miramoline* 'Commander of the Faithful' (Arabic).

871–3 *bough . . . Canaan* See 194–9 and note. John of Brienne, titular King of Jerusalem, sent Friedrich II a palm-branch to remind him of his promise to lead a crusade.

881–3 *dispread . . . angels* repeated in III, 593–5.

887 *Eglamor* the fictional troubadour over whom Sordello later triumphs.

900 *purfle* ornament the edge of.

902 *sheen* here, the adjective: 'shining'.

903 *runnel* small brook.

907 *crenelled* notched (an architectural term).

909 *damsel-fly* a kind of slender dragon-fly (*demoiselle* in French); probably a Browning coinage.

920 *behold*] forsooth *1840*.

921 *ilex* probably, here, holly.

928 *Pythons* The young Apollo slew the monster Python.

932 *Delians* Delos, the Aegean island, was the birthplace of Apollo and sacred to him.

937 *divine* verb, not adjective.

938 *Daphne* the nymph, beloved of Apollo, who became a laurel tree.

   Count Richard Richard of Saint Boniface (whose capture was reported in lines 102–9) is, in *Sordello*, husband of Palma, daughter of Ecelin the Monk by his first wife, Agnes Este (Adelaide the Tuscan was his fourth wife). (Historically, Richard's wife – and Sordello's love – was Cunizza, half-sister of Palma and child of Adelaide.)

950 *glory* halo.

951 *spilt*] shed *1840*.

980 *Isle* Sicily. Friedrich II was born there, and was King of Sicily (1197) before he became King of Germany (1212) and Emperor (1220).

981 *Messina* the port-city in north-east Sicily.

982 *rillet* tiny brook.

984 *Provence* the County (in the south-east of modern France) of the Holy Roman Empire in which the Troubadours and their poetry and music flourished in the later Middle Ages.

987 *their very tongue* the vernacular.

989 *Trouveres* The distinction between troubadours and trouveres is one that varies from writer to writer. Browning makes little distinction, but here he seems to see the troubadour as composer, the trouvere as performer.

991 *Formidable House* that of Romano.

BOOK THE SECOND

Revisions to Book II after *1840* were fairly minor. No lines were added or deleted. The running titles for *1868* were: 'This bubble of fancy, when greatest and brightest, bursts. At a court of love, a minstrel sings. Sordello, before Palma, conquers him, receives the prize, and ruminates. How had he been superior to Eglamor? This is answered by Eglamor himself: one who belonged to what he loved, loving his art and rewarded by it, ending with what had possessed him. Eglamor done with, Sordello begins. Who he really was, and why at Goito. He, so little, would fain be so much: leaves the dream he may be something, for the fact that he can do nothing, yet is able to imagine everything, if the world esteem this equivalent. He has loved song's results, not song; so, must effect this to obtain those. He succeeds a little, but fails more; tries again, is no better satisfied, and declines from the ideal of song. What is the world's recognition worth? How, poet no longer in unity with man, the whole visible Sordello goes wrong with those too hard for half of him, of whom he is also too contemptuous. He pleases neither himself nor them: which the best judges account for. Their criticisms give small comfort: and his own degradation is complete. Adelaide's death: what happens on it: and a trouble it occasions Sordello. He chances upon his old environment, sees but failure in all done since, and resolves to desist from the like.'

12   *conceits*   fancies.
15   *visioned*]   forest- *1840*.
20   *besprent*   besprinkled.
28   *marish*   marsh.
30   *Rose-lichen*   a kind of lichen.
31   *loach*   a kind of small river-fish.
65   *Jongleurs*   entertainers of the Middle Ages, often closely associated with the troubadours and trouveres.
66   *Court of Love*   here, a kind of Tournament of Song.
68   *Elys*   El-lys, the Lily.
77   *an*   if (archaism).
89–93   *some Egyptian ... Insulted*   The scarab (beetle) identifies the bull as a sacred one in ancient Egypt. Apis was the bull of Memphis, sacred to Osiris.
118–19   *Squarcialupe | And Tagliafer*   jongleurs. The former, lines 783–8 suggest, is also a trouvere. *Squarciare* and *lupo* are Italian for 'tear' and 'wolf'.
145   *soft*]   oft *1840*.
149   *Did*]   Can *1840*; Could *1863–8*.
177–80   *a Roman bride . . . iron chill*   The Roman capture or rape of the Sabine women was recalled in the Roman wedding-custom of separating a bride's hair with a spear-point.
211   *Perseus . . . love*   one of Browning's many references to the Greek myth in which Perseus released Andromeda from a rock to which she had been chained as food for a monster.
234   *Conceits*   fancies.
290   *plant*   probably the day-lily, though there is no plant called 'eglamor'.
296   *My own month*   Browning was born in May.
300–301   *Massic jars | Dug up at Baiae*   Part of the Roman resort of Baiae, west of Naples, was later submerged by the sea; jars that had contained Massic wine have been recovered there.
322–39   *at Vicenza . . . reward*   From the city, lying between Padua and Verona, the Ghibellins, including the then podestà, Ecelin the Monk, and Salinguerra, were expelled in 1194. The incident is a central one in *Sordello*, and laid foundations for struggle between the Houses of Este and Romano. See for other accounts: IV, 535–46, 725–46; and V, 751–94.
322   *both her counts*   The two counts have not been positively identified, but in IV, 541–2, Browning writes of Azzo and Richard as the two expelling Guelfs.

323 *Vivaresi* the leading Ghibellin family in Vicenza.

324 *Maltraversi* the leading Guelf family in Vicenza.

327 *Ecelin* Ecelin the Tyrant was born in 1194.

331 *Elcorte* The *Biographie Universelle* records that Sordello was said to be the son of a poor knight, Elcort.

335 *Prata* probably fictional.

336 *Pistore* He was among those expelled, and he drowned soon afterwards.

345–8] When Este schemes for Palma – would retrieve
              That pledge, when Mantua is not fit to leave
              Longer unguarded with a vigilant eye,
              Taurello bides there so ambiguously *1840*.

349 *moil* toil.

402 *As flesh : whereas flesh leaves soul*] As that. Whereas it left her *1840*; As that: whereas it left her *1863–8*.

405 *free*] my *1840–68*.

412 *counts men strong or*] loves the soul as strong, as *1840*; loves souls as strong or *1863–8*.

413] Whose love is Strength, is Wisdom, – such shall bow *1840*; Who, themselves, love strength, wisdom, – it shall bow *1863–8*.

434 *whose words, not actions speak*] who take no pains to speak *1840–68*.

437 *just*] mean *1840*; will *1863–8*.

440 *power's*] its *1840–68*.

445 *supremacy – would live*] existing,[; *1868*] but would be *1840–68*.

453 *basaltic* Basalt is a blackish rock.

455 *windstorm*] landstorm *1840–63*.

458 *scritch* screech (archaism).

474 *truchman* interpreter.

511 *and its woods anon,*] to retire upon *1840*.

516 *rondel, tenzon, virlai or sirvent* A rondel (earlier form of 'rondeau') is a short poem, the form of which was differently defined at various times. A tenzon (or tenson) was a 'contention' in verse between two troubadours. A virlai (or virelay – *OED* does not record Browning's form of the word) was a short lyric with short lines and two rhymes, which in fact did not exist in Sordello's time. A sirvent was a troubadour lay, generally satirical.

518 *angelot* a musical instrument, somewhat like a lute.

536 *The woman's*] Bianca's *1840*.

549 *true*] real *1840–63*.

574–9 *slow re-wrought . . . make it* Dante praised Sordello for his contributions to a new vernacular.

615 *Hyacinth* a youth beloved of Apollo. Zephyr, jealous of Apollo, blew Apollo's quoit so that it killed the youth.

617 *Montfort* Simon de Montfort (father of the famous English baron) led the Crusade against the heretical Albigenses in southern France early in the thirteenth century.

643 *erst* formerly (archaism).

691–3 *John's cloud-girt angel . . . a book* 'And I saw another mighty angel come down from heaven, clothed with a cloud . . . And he had in his hand a little book open: and he set his right foot upon the sea, and his left foot on the earth . . . And I took the little book out of the angel's hand, and ate it up; and it was in my mouth sweet as honey: and as soon as I had eaten it, my belly was bitter' (Revelation x 1–2, 10).

714 *Vidal* The troubadour Pierre Vidal (*fl.* 1200) is attacked in some of Sordello's verses.

715 *murrey-coloured* dark red.

    filamot the colour of a dead leaf (*feuillemort*).

731 *rathe* early.

740 *twenty-cubit plectre* a gigantic wand for striking the strings of the lyre (one cubit is 18–22 inches).

768 *Turned*] Tuned *1840–68*.

    Bocafoli Browning's invented name for an over-simple poet.

769 *Plara* Browning's invented name for an over-elaborate poet. See the following lines, and III, 881–900.

770 *knops* knobs (archaism).

    almug a kind of tree, probably sandalwood. The name is a Biblical error (1 Kings x 11) for 'algum'.

772 *river-horse* hippopotamus.

773 *whirrs* emits a vibratory sound.

    breese gad-fly.

774 *Gad-fly, that is. He*] Ha, ha! Of course he *1840*.

775 *pompion* pumpkin.

791–2 *strike, | Based upon common sense* 'Kenyon . . . says my common sense strikes him, and its contrast with my muddy metaphysical poetry' (Browning letter to Elizabeth Barrett of 24 May 1845).

825 *Pappacoda* an invented name ('Paste-tail') for a jongleur.

828 *o'er-toise* 'to measure out in toises' (*OED*: a nonce-word). A toise is a French measure of nearly two metres.

844 *falsehoods rectified*] which untruths must cure *proof copy* (corrected to *1840* reading: falsehoods rectify).

859 *Count Lori* Browning's invented name for Sordello's initial choice of hero.

860 *peasant-Paul* a Paulician heretic. The Albigenses were Paulicians, and Ecelin the Monk was accused of being one.

864 *body clean abolished* In the Paulician heresy, body was evil.

879 *Monk Hilary* He is fictional.

883–5 *Beatrix . . . Ecelin's betrothed* Beatrix (Beatrice) of Este (sister of Azzo VII of Este, the Guelf leader) was the first of the two wives of Alberic (Alberico), Ecelin the Monk's younger son. Giglia, daughter of Richard of Saint Boniface, was the first of the four wives of Ecelin the Tyrant.

888 *Romano* Ecelin II (the Monk).

890 *Friedrich sworn to sail* Salinguerra's being with Friedrich, and Friedrich's oath to sail at this particular time are not historical.

892 *Vesuvius* the volcano near Naples.

    throat] mount *1840*.

907 *congeed off* given leave to go.

909 *green and yellow* the colours of the House of Romano and of the Ghibellins.

910 *Retrude* Salinguerra's first wife. Almost nothing is known of her. Browning invented her connection with Otho's house, and transferred her five children (reported by Browning's source Frizzi) to Salinguerra's second wife, Sofia. Browning invents too, of course, her being Sordello's mother.

919 *Her child* Sordello.

929 *Strojavacca* a fictional troubadour.

932 *cobswan* male swan.

966 *ibis* The wading bird was, like the cat, sacred in ancient Egypt.

969 *Soldan* Sultan.

989 *iris root* used for perfumes and medicines.

990 *recruit* restore the health of.

993 *Caryaean*] *this edition*; Carian *1840–88*. Caria was an ancient region in southwest Asia Minor. Browning has erred here, confusing Caria with Caryae, the town near Sparta from which comes the word 'Caryatides', used (I, 412) in describing the group round the font.

1016 *bull-bait* the old 'sport' in which a tethered bull was attacked by dogs.

BOOK THE THIRD

Revisions of *1840* for *1863* of Book III were extensive; and twenty-eight lines were added. The running titles for *1868* were: 'Nature may triumph therefore; for her son, lately alive, dies again, – was found and is lost. But Nature is one thing, Man another – having multifarious sympathies, he may neither renounce nor satisfy; in the process to which is pleasure, while renunciation ensures despair. There is yet a way of escaping this; which he now takes by obeying Palma: who thereupon becomes his associate. As her own history will account for, – a reverse to, and completion of, his. How she ever aspired for his sake, circumstances helping or hindering. How success at last seemed possible, by the intervention of Salinguerra: who remedied ill wrought by Ecelin, and had a project for her own glory, which she would change to Sordello's. Thus then, having completed a circle, the poet may pause and breathe, being really in the flesh at Venice, and watching his own life sometimes, because it is pleasant to be young, would but suffering humanity allow! – which instigates to tasks like this, and doubtlessly compensates them, as those who desist should remember. Let the poet take his own part, then, should any object that he was dull beside his sprightlier predecessors. One ought not blame but praise this; at all events, his own audience may: what if things brighten, who knows? Whereupon, with a story to the point, he takes up the thread of discourse.'

2 *Braid moonfern now with mystic trifoly* Moonfern (moonwort) is a kind of fern, and trifoly (a form of 'trefoil') a clover. Presumably the braiding of the two has medicinal or magical value; the concoction is apparently Browning's.

12 *byssus* the filament by which some shellfish fasten themselves to rocks. The filaments have been spun into exceptionally fine cloths.

13 *Tyrrhene whelk* the shellfish from which the purple dye is made (see 'Popularity').

14 *trireme* an ancient ship or galley with three tiers of oars.

15 *satrap* a Persian provincial governor.

17 *tinct* dye.

25 *Of Men, of that*] This May of the *1840*.

67 *still distinguished plain*] may distinguish now *1840*; still distinguished slow *1863–8*.

68 *brain*] brow *1840–68*.

71 *tacit* silent.

86 *earth's remonstrance* Most chronicles date the earthquake in September 1222, and associate it with a comet.

90 *spilth* spilling.

119–23 *island-house . . . Nuocera holds* Friedrich had a villa near Palermo in Sicily. Palermitans and Messinese are the inhabitants of Palermo and Messina on the island. Friedrich established two major Saracen colonies, at Nocera (Nocera Inferiore, in ancient times Nuceria, twenty-three miles east and south of Naples), and Lucera (near Foggia); *Nuocera* is probably an error for the former. The Normans had been a strong force in Sicily for two centuries.

124 *morse* walrus.

129 *mollitious* softly luxurious.

130 *Byzant* Byzantine. The style, because pagan, was often thought devilish.

132-7 *Dandolo . . . Venice' Square* Enrico Dandolo (*c.* 1108–1205), elected Doge in 1192, conquered Constantinople (Byzantium) in 1203-4, when over ninety and blind, and brought many of its treasures back to Venice.

136 *sardius* a precious stone that Browning apparently confuses with a building stone.

155 *ladder*] roundels *1840*.

201 *acquist* acquiring.

203] Convention, hazard, blindness could impose *1840*; Which hazard, use and blindness could impose *1863-8*.

204] In their relation to myself.

> He rose. *1840* (so also, with quotation marks after 'myself', *1863-8*).

220 *bulb dormant* In ancient Egypt, hyacinth bulbs were buried with mummified corpses.

227 *gauds* showy ceremonies.

228 *marish* marsh.

239-51 *Then was told . . . These doings, at Verona?*] not in *1840*.

258 *orient* pearl.

262-3 *osprey . . . lynx and ounce* Salinguerra (see I, 128), Azzo VII, and Richard of Saint Boniface (see I, 166).

272-3 *The rule . . . Hildebrand* Charlemagne claimed the Emperor protected the Church; Hildebrand (Pope Gregory VII) asserted Papal power.

277 *rush*] gush *1840*.

302 *Tiso Sampier* member of a family hostile to Ecelin; in IV, 613-14, Salinguerra is said to have killed another Tiso. (The latter was killed in Ferrara in 1222 after Salinguerra's treachery to Azzo.)

318 *Delaying, till its advent,*] Delaying still (pursued she) *1840*.

321-2 *Every law | Of life* Domett criticized the passage beginning with these words as '*expressed* in far too *abstract* a manner'.

359] She said.

> And day by day the Tuscan dumb *1840*.
>
>   Sordello, accepted.
>
>   'And the Tuscan dumb *1863-8*.

360 *Sat she still scheming*] Sat scheming, scheming *1840-68*.

361 *Cesano baffles me* He, or it, baffles editors too. The Florentine edition identifies it with the city on the Savio river alluded to in *Inferno* xxvii, 52-4; but that city's name is Cesena (as it is in *Pippa Passes*). The Ohio edition seems to agree with the Florentine: it misquotes the Dante passage (one that refers to the city's being on the Savio) in the translation of 'Dorothy Sayer' [*sic*], but then confounds confusion by locating the place between Como and Milan, nearly 200 miles from the Savio. That this town should baffle Ecelin seems unlikely. It is most likely that the word 'Cesano' is Browning's error or an unnoted misprint for either 'Celsano' (one spelling of the name of a member of the Maltraversi family, the leading Guelf family involved in the expulsion of Ecelin from Vicenza in 1194), or, more probably, 'Celano'. The town of Celano was razed by Friedrich in 1222; see also IV, 525n.

378-80] Romano's lord? That Chief – her children too – *1840*.

422 *Gate Saint Blaise* No such gate seems to have existed. In IV, 727, Browning seems to think of San Biagio (a church) as the gate involved.

430 *Fomalhaut* a bright star. Browning's reasons for citing it remain unexplained.

437-9 *who withdrew ... Making me see]* not in *1840*.

449 *first Knight* in I, 244, called Arpo or Yoland. Here, apparently, Ecelo.

450 *Conrad* Conrad II, Holy Roman Emperor 1027-39.

460 *Saponian* almost certainly an error or uncorrected misprint for 'Saxonian'.

467 *The man* Ecelin the Stammerer, father of Ecelin the Monk (and in Browning's genealogy son of Ecelo), was Podestà of Vicenza.

475 *Alberic* Historically, Ecelin the Stammerer's father was Alberico.

  crine head of hair.

476 *over-mounts* 'beyond the mountains' (*OED*, which cites only Browning's usages here and in 'A Bean-Stripe', 239, in *Ferishtah's Fancies*).

488-9 *Adelaide of Susa ... Pope* Adelaide (1020-91), as widow of Oddone of Savoy, governed Piedmont towards the end of her life; she did not in fact give Piedmont to Matilda.

492 *Matilda* The Countess of Tuscany (1046-1115) left all her possessions to the Holy See.

  so, lest aught curb] lest aught disturb *1840*.

493 *Adelaide's great counter-project* Adelaide the Tuscan's project to do for the Emperor something like what Adelaide of Susa and Matilda did for the Pope.

499 *in bruit* in public circulation. Browning's use appears slightly unidiomatic. The phrase seems to mean here 'bruited about'.

501 *excommunicate* out-of-touch (not 'excommunicated'). Friedrich was occupied with Sicily and southern Italy; see I, 130-37.

517 *at Oliero slunk]* Oliero sunk *1840*.

538 *frith* firth.

546 *disguised together* One erroneous account had it that Beatrice, sister of Cunizza (Browning's Palma), pursued Sordello disguised as a page.

554 *Pollux* The son of Leda and Zeus, like his twin-brother Castor, was a protector of seamen to whom in storms he appeared in the form of the electrical phenomenon known as Saint Elmo's fire.

556 The line repeats I, 346; the gate-vein is the great abdominal vein.

563 *exclaim* exclamation. Johnson called the noun 'now disused'; Browning's is the last recorded *OED* usage.

587 *Verona's Lady* Palma.

588-92 *Gaulish Brennus ... Manlius came* About 390 B.C. Brennus, the Gaulish general, overran Italy and captured Rome, but not its Capitol, commanded by Manlius.

593-5 *dispread ... angels* repeating I, 881-3.

596 *platan* plane tree.

597 *archimage* chief magician.

598 *sheen* shining.

603 *flinders* splinters.

609 *lagune* lagoon.

610 *Entrance* the verb (put into a trance).

614 *I awake* For the rest of Book III, Browning speaks in his own person in the 'digression'. He may have had the poem drafted up to this point when he first visited Italy (and Venice) in 1838.

615] O'er the lagune.
            Sordello said once, note ['Note *1863*] *1840–63.*

625 *proper* own.

633 '*Charlemagne*' The historical Sordello wrote no such poem.

634 *silly*] restive *1840.*

635 *restiff* a seldom used alternative form of 'restive'.

637–8] *not in 1840.*

641–3] To jot down (says the bard) the why and how
            And where and when of life as I do now:
            But shall I cease to live for that? Alas *1840.*

646 *gains*] years *1840.*

651–2] *not in 1840.*

656 *colibri* a kind of humming-bird (the word is singular).

668 *land-wind* wind blowing off the land.

676 *muse this on a ruined*] sung this on an empty *1840.*

681 *Bassanese* native of Bassano, the town about forty miles north-west of Venice
on the Brenta river, a centre of Romano power.

683 *Asolo* the hill-town, beloved by Browning, thirty-odd miles north-west of
Venice, and about ten miles east of Bassano. *Pippa Passes* is set there; it gave its name
to his final volume; and his son died there.

693 *Giudecca* the large Venetian canal.

704] Came join the peasants o'er the kissing sea.) *1840.*

710 *sumpter-cloth* covering for a baggage animal.

715–23] (At home we dizen scholars, chiefs and kings,
            But in this magic weather hardly clings
            The old garb gracefully: Venice, a type *1840.*

721 *dizened out* dressed up.

728–32] Or stay me thrid her cross canals alone,
            As hinder Life what seems the single good
            Sole purpose, one thing to be understood
            Of Life) – best, be they Peasants, be they Queens,
            Take them, I say, made happy any means, *1840.*

729] *not in proof copy.*

738 *Fastuous* ostentatious, haughty (rare).

746 *shent* reproached.

750 *looked* expected.

765 *Basilic* the Basilica of Saint Mark.

766 *day of the Corpus Domini* Corpus Christi Day, the festival kept on the
Thursday after Trinity Sunday.

789 *losel* scamp, vagabond (archaism).

790 *conceit* conception.

815 *mugwort* a plant.

816 *smothery chafe* temper threatening to smother (both words are archaisms).

817–18 *Zin | The Horrid* the waterless desert into which Moses led the Children of
Israel (Numbers xx).

819 *that bung*] among *1840.*

822 *Potiphar's mishap* Potiphar, an officer of Pharaoh, favoured his servant
Joseph, but imprisoned him when he was falsely accused of attempted rape by
Potiphar's wife (Genesis xxxix).

823 *the earliest ass that spoke* Balaam's ass (Numbers xxii 28).

825 *Potsherd him, Gibeonites* A potsherd is a broken piece of earthenware.

Browning's use of the word (now an archaism) as a verb is probably unique. The Gibeonites became the hewers of wood and drawers of water for the children of Israel (Joshua ix–x).

826–7 *Moses smites . . . Promised Land*   Moses 'smote the rock' and got water for the Children of Israel; consequently the Lord denied him the Promised Land (Numbers xx, 9–12).

828 *have Satan claim his carcass*   See Jude 9.

829 *Metaphysic Poet*   Browning's point is that the philosophical poet (Moses or Browning, for instance) will have problems with his audience.

830 *Meribah*   Moses' name for the place where he smote the rock (Numbers xx 13; Exodus xvii 7).

835 *quotha*   said he (an equivalent in force to 'forsooth!').

844 *wheelwork*   a set of connected wheels forming part of a machine.

849 *proved*   tested.

851 *gin*   engine.

854 *lodgement*   foothold.

876 *Piombi*   prison-cells in Venice's Ducal Palace.

879 *Zanze*]   Elys *1840*.

880 *Adjudge*]   Applaud *1840*.

881 *Plara*   the over-elaborate bard first referred to in II, 769.

895 *oriel-pane*   a projecting upper-storey window-pane.

900 *Tempe's dewy vale*   Apollo's seat, the ideally beautiful valley in Thessaly.

904 *Lucio*   See II, 538.

907 *springe*   snare.

917 *does*]   hastes *1840*.

939–46 *Hercules . . . a man*   Hercules was about to be sacrificed by Busiris, King of Egypt, when he loosed his bonds and slew his captors.

948 *hecatomb*   a great public sacrifice.

950 *my patron friend*,]   nay, yours, my friend *1840*. ('Landor was the Friend, and his praise was prompt, both private and public' [Browning to Furnivall, 16 December 1881 – Hood, *Letters*, 206–7]. Browning appreciated the verse tribute of W. S. Landor [1775–1864] of 1845, admired him greatly, and became his close friend.)

952 *your own*]   any *1840*.

952–4 *trumpeter . . . stimulant*   Aeschylus, whom Landor praised and who fought at the battle of Marathon (490 B.C.), possibly at Plataea (479 B.C.), and probably at Salamis (480 B.C.). The battle of Salamis is central in *The Persians* (472 B.C.), the play which Aeschylus produced in Sicily at the new city of Aetna (founded 476 B.C.), in honour of which city he wrote his lost play *The Women of Aetna*.

953]   He'll testify who when Plataeas grew scant *1840*.

955 *he*   the Sicilian volcano, Mount Aetna (Etna).

956 *midland sea*   the Mediterranean.

last month]   that morn *1840*.

presumed   expected.

957 *Long, lay*]   All day, *1840*.

962–4 *that painted king . . . the sea*   King Polycrates of Samos, legend says, threw a jewel into the sea, but found it again in the belly of a fish presented to him. One of Landor's *Imaginary Conversations* involves Polycrates.

966 *all passion, wear*]   low-thoughtedness *1840*.

967 *English Eyebright*   Euphrasia Fanny Haworth, a minor poet, Browning's friend. Browning wrote to her (24 July 1838): 'I called you, "Eyebright" – meaning a simple and sad sort of translation of "Euphrasia" into my own language: folks

would know who Euphrasia, or Fanny was, – and *I* should not know Ianthe or Clemanthe' (Hood, *Letters*, 2). See also DeVane and Knickerbocker, *New Letters*, 18.

975 *So, to our business, now* –] For, Eyebright, what I sing's *1840*.

983–6] In unexpanded infancy, assure / Yourself, nor misconceive my portraiture *1840*.

991–2 *John the Beloved . . . Patmos* Saint John, the apostle 'whom Jesus loved', was exiled to Patmos, the Aegean island (Revelation i 9). The Bible does not say that he actually went there.

996 *motion* excitement.

Xanthus a fictional follower of Saint John. A fictional character of the same name attends John in 'A Death in the Desert'.

999 *Polycarp* A disciple of John, Polycarp, Bishop of Smyrna, was martyred by fire about 155.

1000 *Charicle* The character is apparently Browning's invention.

wheel a wheel for torturing.

1001 *Caesar* the Emperor.

1011 *Get thee behind me, Satan* 'And Jesus answered and said unto him, Get thee behind me, Satan '(Luke iv 8).

1018 *limning* painting.

pelf money.

1020 *twy-prong* two-pronged fork (presumably, the Devil's pitch-fork).

BOOK THE FOURTH

Revisions of *1840* for *1863* were extensive, and thirty-one lines were added. The running titles for *1868* were: 'Men suffered much, whichever of the parties was victor. How Guelfs criticize Ghibellin work as unusually energetic in this case. How, passing through the rare garden, Salinguerra contrived for a purpose, Sordello ponders all seen and heard, finds in men no machine for his sake, but a thing with a life of its own, and rights hitherto ignored by him, – a fault he is now anxious to repair, since he apprehends its full extent, and would fain have helped some way. But Salinguerra is also preoccupied; resembling Sordello in nothing else. How he was made in body and spirit, and what had been his career of old. The original check to his fortunes, which he was in the way to retrieve, when a fresh calamity destroyed all. He sank into a secondary personage, with the appropriate graces of such. But Ecelin, he set in front, falling, Salinguerra must again come forward, – why and how, is let out in soliloquy. Ecelin, he did all for, is a monk now, just when the prize awaits somebody – himself, if it were only worthwhile, as it may be – but also, as it may not be – the supposition he most inclines to; being contented with mere vengeance. Sordello, taught what Ghibellins are, and what Guelfs, approves of neither. Have men a cause distinct from both? Who was the famed Roman Crescentius? How if, in the reintegration of Rome, be typified the triumph of mankind?'

23 *quitchgrass* couch grass.

loathy loathsome.

mallows common wild plants.

24 *stranger, none* a good example of Browning's frequent use of a comma for 'that'.

28 *East League* the eastern cities of the Lombard League.

30–32 *snowy oxen . . . white field* The details come from Verci.

32 *fosse* moat.

33 *Legate Montelungo* the Papal representative in the negotiations.

34 *flock of steeples*   One of Browning's sources refers to thirty-two towers as being destroyed in Ferrara.

39 *pursuivant*   state messenger.

40 *labours*   In his copy of the poem, Domett wrote: 'is *labouring*? Here little carelessnesses make his style so obscure –'.

41–3 *Tito, Friedrich's Pretor . . . Mainard Count of Tyrol*   Sodegerio de Tito, appointed Podestà (or Praetor) of Trent by Friedrich II. Count Mainard is another historical figure.

49 *Arbalist, manganel*   crossbow and stone-throwing machine respectively.

59 *nare*   nostril.

61 *blazon*   description (*OED* 4 – an improper transferred sense).

   a-flaunt   in a flaunting state.

62–3 *the crested gaunt | White ostrich with a horse-shoe in her beak*   the Romano crest (described thus by Verci).

65 *Ecelin*   the Monk.

68 *son*   Ecelin III, the Tyrant, the Ferocious.

69 *conserves . . . viper-broth*   The speaker takes seriously the rumour that Adelaide was a witch.

71 *Jubilate*   'Rejoice' (Psalm lxvi, 1).

80 *swound*   swoon.

82 *cautelous*   wily.

83 *Redbeard*   Barbaross, Friedrich I, Holy Roman Emperor 1155–90, tried in vain to take Alessandria, the city founded by the Lombard League in 1168 in south-east Piedmont.

84 *Saint George*   patron saint of Ferrara.

88 *Brenta and Bacchiglion*   The former is the river in Romano territory flowing through Bassano; the latter is a tributary of it.

91 *Cino*   presumably the Cino of I, 145; the incident is apparently fictional.

95 *Concorezzi*   Robertas da Concorezzo was Podestà of Padua.

96 *San Vitale*   in the south-east of Ferrara, next to the San Pietro area.

102 *za, za, Cavaler Ecelin*   Ecelin's war-cry (the detail comes from Rolandino).

117 *ramped*   grew quickly.

129 *laver*   basin of a fountain.

133 *gleamy*   lighted up by gleams.

134 *aloes*   fleshy evergreens, very common in Italy.

137 *cramps*   metal bars for holding buildings together.

142 *rough-rasps*   abrades roughly.

143–4 *Naples marble . . . Messina marbles*   older marble from Naples imitative of the newer, stronger marble from Messina.

144 *Constance*   heiress of Sicily, wife of Heinrich (Henry) VI, Emperor 1191–7.

147 *font with caryatides*   see I, 410–15.

150 *stoop*   lower.

155 *Isle*   Sicily.

157 *Fighter*   the statue of a gladiator fighting the Gaul (line 165).

166 *Slave*   another statue.

168 *the solid*   'the unbroken mass, the main part or body' (*OED* 4).

171 *San Pietro Palace*   Salinguerra's main palace was in the south-east of Ferrara.

180 *Sordello paused*]   two minstrels pause *1840* (the two minstrels are Sordello and Palma).

   plinth   base-block.

230 *like*]   quoth *1840*.

271]   And like demand it longer: nor a claim *1840*.

279-82]   With good to them as well, and he should be
          Rejoiced thereat; and if, as formerly,
          He sighed the merry time of life must fleet, *1840*.

281   the only unrhymed line in *Sordello*.

312   Genesis iii 14.

313   *Whose heavy length*]   With lulling eye *1840*.

324   *slingers*   soldiers armed with slings.

326   *brake*   crossbow, or similar instrument for hurling.

346   *blue cross and eight lilies*   Romano arms (the details come from Verci).

380-84]   *not in 1840*.

386-7]   In order for this morning's use; you met *1840*.

387   *sign-mark*   badge.

388-9   *crowned grim twy-necked eagle ... ochre*   Friedrich II's 'sign-mark'.

390   *Romano's green and yellow*   Romano's colours (see II, 909).

412   *rescript*   imperial edict: the offer, through Tito, that Salinguerra become Friedrich's Vicar-General in northern Italy. The offer is not historical.

433   *tire*   attire.

436   *basnet*   light globular helmet.

454-9]   *not in 1840*.

462   *occasion, that*]   *this edition*; occasion That *1840*, occasion, That *1863-88*. (The capital 'T' seems impossible, but even with this edition's emendation the meaning is not clear, and the text appears to be corrupt.)

466   *baldric*   shoulder-sash.

467   *emprise*   enterprise.

472   *Adelardi*   the leading Guelf family in Ferrara – Salinguerra's counterparts.

478   *Marchesalla*   Browning's spelling and identification are erroneous: the daughter's (not the father's) name was Marchesella (not Linguetta), and Browning otherwise departs from history. His sources are confused and contradictory, but his story, though largely unhistorical, is clear (his main source here is Frizzi). The head of the Guelf Adelardi family dies (in 1184), leaving his daughter Linguetta as his heir. Salinguerra is to marry her and thus bring peace through the uniting of the two factions. The Guelfs from Ravenna, however, carry off Linguetta and marry her to Azzo d'Este, the Guelf leader in northern Italy (Azzo VI). The Ferrarese agree to Este rule. Salinguerra goes off to Sicily where he marries Retrude, daughter of the Emperor, and then returns as the Emperor's emissary to the Ghibellin leaders in northern Italy.

481   *Blacks and Whites*   As indicated in lines 475-6, Ferrara's shield is half black, half white; Browning makes the colours symbolic of Ghibellin and Guelf.

489   *This Richard's father*]   No meaner spokesman *1840*.

492   *valvassors*   feudal tenants, ranking below barons.

496-7]   *not in 1840*.

498   *Lombard Eagle of the azure sphere*   the Este crest.

500-501]   This deemed – the other owned upon advice –
          A third reflected on the matter twice – *1840*.

504   *goshawk*   short-winged hawk, used for hunting.

513   *Heinrich ruled in right of Constance*   The marriage of Heinrich VI, Emperor 1190-97, to Constance, heiress to Sicily, extended the Empire.

525   *Celano*   The Count of Celano had his seat near Ferrara. He is said to have murdered Azzo VII's brother.

526   *Pistore*   the Bishop of Vicenza, killed in 1194 (see II, 336).

534   *Tomà*   Bastion of San Tomaso in Ferrara (Richard of Saint Boniface's prison).

537-40]   Regaled him at Vicenza, Este, there *1840*.

543]   A party which abetted him, but yelled *1840*.

   Both plotters   Ecelin and Salinguerra.

559   *mortised*   fixed firmly.

559-63]   A very pollard mortised in a trunk

                Which Arabs out of wantonness contrive

                Shall dwindle that the alien stock may thrive *1840*.

564   *feathers*   grows in a feathery form (*OED* 8).

569-70   *namesake . . . Matilda*   Adelaide of Susa, and the Countess of Tuscany (see III, 488-92).

576-7]   *not in 1840*.

578   *Heinrich*   Heinrich VI died in 1197; Browning's character seems to have lived somewhat longer.

579   *Philip*   brother of Heinrich VI, and contender with Otho IV for the Emperorship.

584   *Otho*   Otho (Otto) IV, the rival King of Germany, and, later (1209-15), Emperor.

600-602]   In contracts, while, through Arab lore, deter *1840*.

603   *Jove trined*   The planet Jupiter assumed a favourable position.

606   *John Brienne*   King of Jerusalem (see I, 194).

607-11   *Saint Francis' church . . . Pitched home*   San Francesco, built by Ecelin I (the Stammerer) about 1177, after his return from a Crusade, is said to have had a tomb painted by Guido, and frescoes illustrating Ecelin's deeds. The Church is still used, but tomb and frescoes do not survive.

612   *For elegance, he*]   In Painimrie. He *1840*.

   angelot   a kind of lute.

614   *Tiso*   Tisolino de Campo Sampiero, killed in Ferrara in 1222 after an act of treachery by Salinguerra, was a close friend of Azzo (see III, 302).

632]   Observe! accordingly, their basement sapped, *1840*.

633-4   *Old Azzo and old Boniface . . . Ponte Alto*   Azzo VI and Ludovico of Saint Boniface (fathers of Azzo VII and Count Richard) died in 1212 after the battle of Ponte Alto.

637   *Guglielm and Aldobrand*   brothers of Richard of Saint Boniface and Azzo VII respectively.

660]   Forthwith; Goito green above her, gay *1840*.

666   *Promptly threw off alike*]   At Este's mercy through *1840*.

675   *hate*   Domett asks in his copy: 'for stealing Linguetta?' Browning writes in reply, 'burning his son and'.

678-82   *that noted day . . . calmed*   The incident is historical.

679   *tried to*]   offered *1840*.

689   *whist*   were silent (archaism).

690   *He*   Domett writes 'Who'; Browning replies 'Sᵃ'.

698   *Vicenza*]   Verona *1840-63*. (Vicenza was the place he 'kept', but the incident described occurred in Verona.)

703   *Marquis*   Azzo VI.

716   *Lactance . . . Anaclet*   Browning's inventions.

719   *scapular*   monk's short cloak.

725-36   *The surging flame . . . reeking gate*   Ecelin was driven from Vicenza in 1194

(Salinguerra's presence is Browning's invention) by Guelfs led by Pilio da Celsone and Giacomo de Bernardi. San Biagio was a church near a city gate. Much of Vicenza was destroyed by fire.

736   *Slidder*   slide, slip (dialectal).

737   *vow*   Ecelin's vow (see III, 424-7) 'to bestow his life / On God, his gettings on the Church'.

743   *archer*   Elcorte.

754-5]   Browning changed the rhyming words to the indicative from the subjunctive ('hold' and 'enfold', *1840-88*) for the second impression of *1888* (dated 1889).

787   *miniver*   kind of fur.

802   *stare*   condition of horror (*OED* 2).

821   *minstrel*   Sordello.

823   *teaze*   shred.

825   *lentisk*   mastic tree – not native to Italy, and therefore a 'stately foreigner' (line 828).

836   *feel it*]   prattle, *1840*.

856   *Methodic*   methodical (obsolete usage).

859   *Richard, the cowed braggart,*]   Boniface completely *1840*.

870   *wattles*   fleshy lobes or flaps of skin.

913-14]   As though it bore a burden, which could tame
       No pinion, from dead void to living space ? *1840*.

916   *so much my unencumbered*]   complacently my frantic *1840*.

920   *people's good being*]   multitude aye *1840*.

923   *preferred*   proffered (an archaic use of the word).

927   *to your*]   Friedrich's *1840*.

930   *your party*]   that Friedrich *1840*.

936   *charge*   Browning notes in Domett's copy: 'The charge your conscience prefers on the people's account (or) what you feel they might justly charge you with, – the having neglected their cause.'

950-52]   Moved Salinguerra ? If a Cause remained
       Intact, distinct from these, and fate ordained,
       For all the past, that Cause for me ?
                                    One pressed *1840*.

960   *Crescentius Nomentanus*   In the later tenth century he tried to revive the old Roman republic, was himself elected consul, and tried to create his own Popes. Browning's information about him comes from *Biographie Universelle* X.

965   *brown-sleeve brother*   Presumably the brown sleeves mark the novice? Browning may have meant the speaker to be a Franciscan; the order was founded, however, only seven years before Innocent's death, and Franciscans originally wore grey.

966   *Innocent*   Innocent III, Pope 1198-1216, was a reformer in many areas.

969   *nocturns*   divisions of the office of matins.

977   *Pope John, King Otho*   John XV, Otho (Otto) III.

981   *Brutus*   Junius Brutus, in legend the leader of the republican revolt and first consul of Rome (509 B.C.).

986-8   *choose the gem . . . scratch*   The point is obscure. Perhaps part of the point is that Crescentius chose the consulate (the gem) for himself, but did not revive the Senate, their secret being so hard to scratch (scribble – *OED* 10) or reproduce.

989   *phanal*   beacon (archaism).

991   *John*   John XVI had been set up by Crescentius as anti-Pope; in fact it was Pope Gregory V, exiled by Crescentius, who returned with Otho in the year 998.

992   *Hugo Lord of Este*   If he existed, he was not of the Este family that leads the Guelfs in *Sordello*.

994–5   *crucified | Their Consul*   Crescentius was killed in 998; Browning gives one version of what happened to him.

995   *Forum*   the old Roman Forum, commercial centre of old Rome.

1010–12]   For Friedrich or Honorius.

Rome's the Cause! *1840*.

1013   *Pandects*   the compendium of Roman civil law made in the sixth century by order of Justinian.

1014   *Capitol*   the highest of Rome's hills.

Castle Angelo   the famous castle built on the Mausoleum of Hadrian. It was the Papal fortress in the Middle Ages. Crescentius took refuge here when attacked by Otho III in 998.

1016–19]   *not in 1840*.

1020   *the Theatre*   the Colosseum, the amphitheatre of ancient Rome.

1022]   – Verona, that's beside it. These combined, *1840*.

1030]   The People's self, and let their truth avail *1840*.

BOOK THE FIFTH

Revisions of *1840* for *1863* were extensive, and twenty-two lines were added. The running titles for *1868* were: 'Mankind triumph of a sudden? Why, the work should be one of ages, if performed equally and thoroughly; and a man can but do a man's portion. The last of each series of workmen sums up in himself all predecessors. We just see Charlemagne, Hildebrand, in composite work they end and name. If associates trouble you, stand off! – should the new sympathies allow you. Time having been lost, choose quick! He takes his first step as a Guelf; but to will and to do are different: he may sleep on the bed he has made. Scorn flings cold water in his face, arouses him at last, to some purpose, and thus gets the utmost out of him. He asserts the poet's rank and right, basing these on their proper ground, recognizing true dignity in service, whether successively that of epoist, dramatist, or, so to call him, analyst, who turns in due course synthetist. This for one day: now, serve as Guelf! Salinguerra, dislodged from his post, in moving, opens a door to Sordello, who is declared Salinguerra's son, hidden hitherto by Adelaide's policy. How the discovery moves Salinguerra, and Sordello the finally-determined, – the Devil putting forth his potency: since Sordello, who began by rhyming, may, even from the depths of failure, yet spring to the summit of success, if he consent to oppress the world. Just this decided, as it now may be, [*as it now may be*, not in *1863*] and we have done.'

6   *Palatine*   palace or ruler.

14   *causey*   causeway.

   blinkard   person with imperfect sight.

15   *mooned*   crescent-shaped.

16   *atria*   courts.

17   *stibadium*   semi-circular sofa (Latin – not in *OED*).

   stibadium ... what his dues]   stibadium suffers ... goose, *1840*.

18   *lustral vase*   vase holding purificatory water.

20   *runagates*   renegades.

28   *hurdle*   rectangular frame, interwoven with twigs and so on, used in building.

   Scythian   nomad of the region north of the Black Sea.

32   *Perdue*   concealed.

33 *pelt*] In *proof copy*, the printer queried the word. Browning noted 'Pelt – a raw hide – all right.'

39 *cirque* circus.

42 *obsidian* a glassy volcanic rock.

43 *fulgurant* flashing like lightning.

48 *sheen* shining.

53 *osier* willow twig.

54 *withe* pliant twig.

57 *Mauretanian*] *this edition*; Mauritanian *1840–88*.

Mauretanian tree the citrus or citrum (not citron) tree, the wood of which came from north Africa and was highly prized for Roman tables.

60 *demiurge* creator of the world.

64 *brack* flaw in cloth.

66 *Mareotic . . . Caecuban* respectively, the fine Egyptian wine; and the originally fine, but in later days ordinary, Italian wine.

75 *cusps* sharp points of leaves.

81–4 *Pythoness . . . oracle* Browning presumably takes the word 'Pythoness' as applied to the Pythia (Apollo's priestess at Delphi – originally called Pytho) from Byron, *Don Juan* VI, cxvii. Croesus, King of Lydia in Asia Minor, was told by the Delphic Oracle that if he crossed the river Halys he would overthrow an empire; he crossed it, and destroyed his own empire. After his defeat he was told he might have asked which empire was meant.

85–92] *not in 1840*.

97 *were God : be man now!*] were . . . no matter. *1840*.

109 *Alcamo* Cielo d'Alcamo, thirteenth-century Sicilian poet.

111 *Nina* Sicilian woman poet, predecessor of Alcamo. She wrote love poems to a poet called Dante da Maiano, and called herself the Nina of Dante.

116] Search further and the past presents you still *1840*.

118–20] Concluding, – better say its evenlight
   Of yesterday. You, now, in this respect
   Of benefitting [*sic*] people (to reject *1840*.

127–8 *The rout | Was checked* It seems almost certain that Browning is here thinking of Clovis I, King of the Franks 481–511, who was converted to Christianity in 496, and became its champion. He united the Franks, beat the Visigoths, and laid the foundations for such later rulers as Charlemagne (line 132), the first Holy Roman Emperor (800–814).

129 *flower* the fleur-de-lys, which, legend has it, was made the heraldic flower of France by Clovis I.

130 *pointel* pistil, style or stamen (obsolete).

133 *child of over-joyousness* Charlemagne was perhaps illegitimate.

134–9 *Strength . . . lip* Browning had seen the famous portrait of Charlemagne at Aix, and recalls it here.

144 *castellans* governors of castles.

145 *suzerains* feudal lords.

154 *a King's investiture* Until 1122 the Emperors claimed the right to invest clerics.

162 *Hildebrand* Pope Gregory VII (1073–85) fought lay investiture.

168 *prizers* prizefighters (archaism).

173 *Call him no flower – a*] – A root, the crippled *1840*.

mandrake poisonous plant of the potato family; the forked root is said to resemble a human.

177   *Full three hundred years*   Charlemagne became King of the Franks in 768, Hildebrand became Pope in 1073. (Not the three [in fact, four] centuries between the accession of Charlemagne and the action of *Sordello*, as claimed in the Ohio edition).

183   *Heinrich*   in all probability, Heinrich (Henry) V (Emperor 1111–25), who in 1122 gave up the Emperor's claims to the right to invest clerics. See the notes on lines 154 and 162.

   Otho   Otho (Otto) IV (Emperor 1209–15), who was deposed.

   Barbaross   Friedrich (Frederick) I (Emperor 1155–90), who recognized Alexander III as Pope in 1176.

185   *Aix' Iron, Milan's Silver, and Rome's Gold*   the crowns (to speak approximately) of Germany, Italy, the Empire. Some sources agree with Browning, others reverse the metals of Aix-la-Chapelle and Milan.

186   *Alexander*   identified as Alexander II by Florentine and Ohio editions, but the reference is certainly to Alexander III (Pope 1159–81), who received the recognition of Barbaross after the Battle of Legnano in 1176.

   Innocent   Innocent III (Pope 1198–1216), whose reign saw the zenith of Papal temporal and spiritual supremacy.

187   *each Papal key*   two keys, one gold and one silver, of the Kingdom of Heaven. Saint Peter (see Matthew xvi 19) is always represented with them, and they are crossed on the Papal arms.

191   *Gregory*   Gregory IX, Pope 1227–41, who excommunicated Friedrich II, sought peace in northern Italy, and was friend to Saint Francis.

191–2]   The couple there alone help Gregory?
       Hark – from the hermit Peter's thin sad cry *1840.*

192–3   *hermit Peter . . . Claremont*   Peter the Hermit preached the First Crusade, and was given Papal support at Claremont in south-east France (1095).

195   *Pope's curse*   Gregory IX excommunicated Friedrich II shortly after his accession to the Papacy in 1227.

198   *Vimmercato*   Vimercate is a town near Milan, where a call went up for a league against Friedrich I. In 1226 the Lombard League was revived against Friedrich II.

201   *Mantuan Albert*   In 1207 the preaching of Fra Alberto da Mantua in Ferrara led to the reconciliation of a number of feuding families.

202   *Saint Francis*   Saint Francis of Assisi (*c.* 1182–1226).

205   *trench*   encroach.

207–8]   *not in 1840.*
   flower . . . root   See V, 129 and 173.

215]   No end's in sight yet of that second road: *1840.*

218   *Paul*   Saint Paul the Apostle.

222   *blench*   shrink back.

225   *tenons*   projections which fit into mortises to join two pieces.

241   *faulchions*   swords.

246   *sense, yet write no verses – you*]   sense on her free beauties – we *1840.*

249–52]   Rather than doing these: now – fancy's trade
       Is ended, mind, nor one half may evade *1840.*

266   *Polt-foot*   club-foot.

268   *spawling*   spitting (archaism).

273   *Cino*   See I, 145.

278   *Lucchino*   probably Browning's invention.

279   *hacqueton*   stuffed jacket worn under mail.

282   *orpine*   succulent herbaceous plant.

284   *Marfisa*   probably Browning's invention.

292   *augural of*   betokening.

296   *trabea*   toga with purple stripes, worn by Romans of rank.

298   *fasces*   bundle of rods with an axe in the middle, Roman symbol of authority.

307   *haulm*   stalks.

364   *could*]   shall *1840*.

379   *thyrsus*   staff or spear borne by Bacchus (Dionysus) and his votaries.

386   *corslet*   cuirass.

406   *burr*   broad iron ring on a tilting-spear, just behind the place for the hand.

423   *conceit*   fancy.

432   *promptuary*   notebook with information in summary form.

441   *formularies*   books of formulae or precedents.

447   *Caliph's wheel-work man of brass*   Haroun al-Raschid, Caliph of Baghdad (786–809) of *Arabian Nights* fame, had robots among his mechanical contrivances.
   Caliph's wheel-work]   Caliph Haroun's *1840*.

457–62]   *not in 1840*.

483   *crown*]   *1840–63*; crowd *1868–88*.

488–9   *to hear thee boast | What makes my own despair*]   as aught's to boast / Unless you help the world *1840*.

502   *Typhon*   the monster with a hundred dragon heads and a body covered with serpents, killed by Zeus. He fathered many monsters of which two were killed by Hercules.

523–4]   *not in 1840*.

526   *protoplast*   'the first former, fashioner, or creator' (*OED* 2).

537–8   *to live and move and have, in them, | Your being*   'For in him we live, and move, and have our being' (Acts xvii 28).

552   *Air, flame, earth, wave*   alluding to the old theory of the four elements.

555   *Saturn*   Saturn (Cronus) was Jupiter's father, and is often associated with the Golden Age.

577   *draws*]   dawns *1840–63*.

577–9   *All then is to win | Save that. How much for me, then? where begin | My work?*]   But so much to win / Ere that! A lesser round of steps within / The last. *1840*.

590]   Your Hell, the Purgatory, Heaven ye wot, *1840*.

592   *red-hot tomb*   Dante assigns Friedrich II to a burning tomb (*Inferno* x, 119).

593   *Lombard Agilulph*   King of the Lombards (592–615), a 'dubious spirit' because while friendly to the Church he remained an Arian. He is not mentioned by Dante.

595   *Matilda*   the lady who succeeds Vergil as Dante's guide (*Purgatorio* xxviii) and who is in Beatrice's train.

596   *planet of decline*   Venus.

605–6   *light . . . flakes*   Browning's first use in verse of his characteristic prism image.

607   *massed*]   helped *1840*.

620]   That . . . but enough! Why fancy how I rose, *1840*.

645   *Libyan god*   Set, Egyptian god of evil.

647   *cinerary*   for containing ashes of the dead.
   Thebes   the Egyptian city which, like the other cities mentioned here, provided spoil for Venice.

648   *Dome Duomo* (Italian for 'cathedral'): Saint Mark's.

649–50   *razed | A seal*   erased the former special identifying mark (because transmuted in the new harmony of Saint Mark's).

650 *Triad* a puzzle – possibly Browning remembered, incorrectly, three domes on Saint Mark's (there are five).

657] Nor murmur, bid me, still as poet, bow *1840*.

664 *If death might win compliance*] So death might bow Taurello *1840*.

677 *stripe* long narrow strip of land.

679 *Alberic* younger brother (Alberico) of Ecelin the Tyrant.

681–2 *Treville . . . Cartiglione* villages in the Romano territory.

697–700 Revision broke the couplets.

698–700] Betide competitors? An obscure place *1840*.

712 *garniture* ornament.

718 *writhled* wrinkled (obsolete).

721 *becomes superb*] the Lombard's Curb *1840*.

723 *pauldron* shoulder-plate.

755 *San Biagio* the church near a northern gate of Vicenza (see IV, 727).

771 *new shape* Adelaide.

778 *House*] brow *1840–68*.

788 *quag* marshy spot.

790] Downward: they marched: no sign of life once shook *1840*.

797–9 *constant . . . one of them* See I, 429–31.

834 *Gesi* Jesi, near Ancona; birthplace of Friedrich II.

859 *Samminiato* San Miniato, a hill near Florence.

862 *Pistoia* city north-west of Florence.

864 *Brescia* city about fifty miles east of Milan.

   Piacenza city nearly forty miles south-east of Milan.

865 *March* the area (Italian *Marche*) in north-central Italy between Apennines and Adriatic.

867–8 *Romagna . . . Bologna . . . Trentine . . . Valsugan* Romagna is the region lying between Florence and Bologna, the city fifty miles to the north. The Trentine Pass is in Trentino province in the north of Italy, and the Sugana valley lies just east of the city of Trent.

869 *Sofia's Egna by Bolgiano* Sofia was the third daughter of Ecelin the Monk and Adelaide. Her first husband was Henry of Egna, her second Salinguerra. Bolgiano (Bolzano) is north of Trent.

895 *Torriani* unidentified (the Florentine and Ohio identifications seem unlikely).

896 *Visconti* Milanese family of Ghibellin nobility. Some of Browning's sources say that Sordello was a member of the family.

898 *Thrid* thread (archaism).

   arrow-loop loop-hole for archers.

905–9 *Elys' hair . . . summer* See I, 151–5, and VI, 867–9.

945 *Monotony* monotone.

948 *blent* blended.

953 *ginglingly* jinglingly (the only example cited in *OED*).

960 *angle* corner.

961 *punctual* exactly timed (*OED* 5c).

976 *appanage* provision for maintenance.

978 *braves* bravado.

989 *Apulia* region in south-east Italy.

989–91 *at their pitch . . . in the map* Unannotated by editors and scholars, the passage strikes this editor as incomprehensible.

993–5 *Palma . . . her* Dante meets Cunizza (whom Browning calls Palma) in Venus, the third Heaven in Paradise (*Paradise* ix, 13–66).

1012 – *only Naddo's never*] Alberic . . . ah, Naddo's *1840*.
1014 *Squarcialupo* See II, 118 (where the name is 'Squarcialupe').

BOOK THE SIXTH

Revisions of *1840* for *1863* were extensive, but of less significance than their bulk would suggest. Four lines were added. The running titles for *1868* were: 'At the close of a day or a life, past procedure is fitliest reviewed, as more appreciable in its entirety. Strong, he needed external strength: even now, where can he perceive such? Internal strength must suffice then, his sympathy with the people, to wit; of which, try now the inherent force! How much of man's ill may be removed? How much of ill ought to be removed? – if removed, at what cost to Sordello? Men win little thereby; he loses all: for he can infinitely enjoy himself, freed from a problematic obligation, and accepting life on its own terms, which, yet, others have renounced: how? Because there is a life beyond life, and with new conditions of success, nor such as, in this, produce failure. But, even here, is failure inevitable? Or may failure here [Or failure here may *1863*] be success also when induced by love? Sordello knows: but too late: an insect knows sooner. On his disappearance from the stage, the next aspirant can press forward; Salinguerra's part lapsing to Ecelin, who, with his brother, played it out, and went home duly to their reward. Good will – ill luck, get second prize: what least one may I award Sordello? This – that must perforce content him, as no prize at all, has contented me.'

1–7 *The thought . . . speciousness* As in *Prince Hohenstiel-Schwangau*, 517–55, and *Fifine at the Fair*, 1105–28, the criticism is directed at the sentiments in Byron's *Childe Harold* IV, clxxix–clxxxiii.
15 *Tumultuary* haphazard.
26 *plaining* mourning (archaism).
99 *Jacinth* sapphire.
100 *Flinders* splinters.
116 *Helpfully to weak*] In mercy to each *1840–68*.
127–8 *all service, therefore, rates | Alike* 'All service ranks the same with God' (*Pippa Passes*, Epilogue 113).
130 *Malek* a name for any Saracen chief (see I, 841).
132 *our champion*] Porphyrio *1840*.
140–41 *Cydippe . . . Agathon* No classical allusion is involved.
141–3 *this felled . . . rally, mock*,] *not in 1840*.
145 *mummery* absurd play-acting.
158 *taint-worms* worms supposed to infect cattle (archaism).
181 *Dularete* a fictional bard.
209] The Guelfs were fitliest maintained in rule? *1840*.
249] Of which 'tis easy saying Good and Ill *1840*.
257 *green and yellow* the Ecelin colours.
273 *palled* cloyed.
300 *cruce* crucible.
307] Yourselves? – imperiously command I quit *1840*.
318 *brakes at balm-shed* ferns at the time (autumn) when balm is distilled.
344 *glebe* earth.
348 *asp uncowl* small hooded serpent put back its hood.
365 *chequed* checkered. (In *proof copy* the word had been changed to 'checked'. Browning corrected to 'chequed', noting '*a different word*'.)

380 *pure*] (taste) *1840*.

381 *reate* water-crowfoot (archaism).

382 *grail* gravel.

404 *plackets* petticoats.

411 *citrine* quartz.

 pyropus garnet.

426 *Titan* the constellation Orion, with its hunter.

427 *Centaur* the constellation Sagittarius, with its centaur shooting an arrow.

455–6 *Brutus . . . jewels out* The allusion is possibly to the Brutus who expelled the Tarquins from Rome (he feigned idiocy in his uncle's presence), but probably to the Brutus who helped kill Julius Caesar (the crown jewels being unstrung because Caesar had not become Emperor).

461 *deep*] vague *1840*.

477 *cinct* girt.

489] Of greatness in the Past – naught turned him mad *1840*.

531–2] The lines are added by Browning to the *proof copy*.

583 *king-bird* There seems little reason for the phoenix of the Florentine and Ohio editions. *OED* conjectures the eagle, which, unlike the phoenix, is king of the birds, 'Bird of Jove', and frequent royal emblem. Spenser alludes to the eagle's rising from the ocean wave, 'Where he hath left his plumes all hoary grey, / And decks himself with feathers youthly gay' (*Faerie Queene* I, xi, 34). And see lines 606–9.

602] To which all rivalry with this appealed *proof copy*.

605] At length, end where our souls begun? as says *1840*.

606 *eagles*] doves *1840*.

606–9 *Old fable . . . Jove's temple* One of the eagles of Zeus flew west, one east. They met at Delphi, the centre of the world, and site of Apollo's temple.

621 *hermit-bee* See V, 1025.

638 *mulct* compelled payment.

661–8 *Sofia . . . Lady of the Rock* See V, 869. Sofia was the third of Ecelin the Monk's four daughters, and widow of Henry of Egna. The 'Lombard gate' is the Trentine Pass.

675–9 *chronicle . . . his sire* The anonymous *Chronica Parva Ferrariensis*, one of the major sources of *Sordello*, gives Browning the quotation.

681 *Sofia's five* Sofia had one child by Salinguerra. The historical Retrude had five by him.

687–90 *Ecelin . . . cavalier he was* Ecelin the Monk died at Campese, just north of Bassano, and a tomb at nearby Solagna is reputedly his.

691–2 *Young Ecelin . . . Vicenza* Ecelin the Tyrant was, by the standards of the day, late in making his military debut, one which came near Vicenza.

698–703 *in Verona . . . wholly his* Some fact and a good deal of condensation. Verona revolted in 1225 and expelled its podestà, but it was some years before Ecelin really controlled the city. The following 'history' is similar in quality.

730 *She captured him* Salinguerra was captured in 1240 and taken to Venice where he died five years later.

749 *Theodore and Mark* Two columns in Saint Mark's Square bear an effigy of Saint Theodore, and a winged lion of Saint Mark.

751 *Magnifico* Venetian noble, grandee.

752 *firm-land* solid earth (*terra firma* – Latin).

759 *Twain* Ecelin the Tyrant and his brother Alberic.

771 *They plagued the world* Their cruelties, Ecelin's especially, were prodigious: thousands died of torture alone.

775 *Ecelin perished* Taken prisoner in a campaign against Milan in 1259, Ecelin tore his bandages off, refused food, and died.

776–81 *in Valley Rù . . . bramble-bush* In 1260 Alberic was betrayed, and captured at his castle in San Zenone, between Bassano and Asolo. His wife and two daughters were tortured and burned alive and his six sons torn to pieces in his presence; he was then tortured and dragged to his death.

778 *exasperated* incensed.

779 *regaled* The word's irony is intensified by the pun on 'regal'.

781 *raunce* bramble.

783 *the pleasant*] Zenone's *1840*.

785 *earthquake* On 20 July 1836, nearly two years before Browning's visit, there were three violent shocks in the area. There were earthquakes also in 1846; but no others of importance before 1863.

785–6] *not in 1840.*

787 *contumacious* rebellious.

788 *cushats* a kind of pigeon or dove.

chirre Browning's spelling is not given in *OED*, which defines 'chirr' as 'to make the trilled sound characteristic of grasshoppers, etc.'.

792 *skeleton unhearsed* Medieval skeletons still surface occasionally in the area; Browning may well be recording a story he heard in 1838.

794 *carding* combing. Asolo was famous for its silks (see *Pippa Passes*).

804 *gyres* spirals.

822–4 *Chroniclers of Mantua . . . Mantua* The main chronicler alluded to here is Platina, whose *Historiae Mantuanae* says Sordello was of the Visconti family. Some chroniclers say that he raised Ecelin the Tyrant's siege of Mantua in 1253.

823 *Telling how Sordello*] Relating how a *1840*.

835 *chance*] step *1840*.

836 *dared*] ta'en *1840*.

837] He had been perfect Phoebus – that bright fit *proof copy*.

845] He'd be a tree of fruitage, which yet tastes *proof copy*.

847 *Hesperian fruit* the apples of the garden of the Hesperides, a kind of Paradise in classical mythology.

857 *low*] green *1840*.

858 *chine* spine.

extinct] fossil *1840*.

863 *balm* kind of herb.

camomile chrysanthemum-like plant.

867–70 *the few . . . Goito lay* See II, 153–5, and V, 907–9.

875 *peri or ghoul* In Persian mythology, peris are beautiful good fairies or angels (originally they were evil). In Moslem countries, ghouls are evil spirits that prey on human corpses.

879 *snuff* draw into the nostrils.

880 *Civet* musky-smelling substance used in perfumes.

883 *musk-pod* It is just possible that Browning is thinking of the seed-containers of one of the plants with a musky odour that bear the name musk (opposing that plant to the rose). It is, however, altogether probable that the reference is to the musk-gland of certain animals, an anal gland (as with civet – line 880) from which the strong aroma comes.

885 *after-gust* subsequent enjoyable savour.

Pippa Passes

First published in April 1841 in a sixteen-page pamphlet that initially sold for six-pence, *Pippa Passes* was the first of a series of eight pamphlets printed in double columns in a cheap format recommended by Edward Moxon, who published them at the expense of Browning's father. Browning called the series *Bells and Pomegranates*, explaining in No. VIII that by the title he meant 'to indicate an endeavour towards something like an alternation, or mixture, of music with discoursing, sound with sense, poetry with thought; which looks too ambitious, thus expressed, so the symbol was preferred'. He added that 'such is actually one of the most familiar of the many Rabbinical (and Patristic) acceptations of the phrase'. The symbolism stems from Exodus xxviii 33.

At Pisa early in 1847 Browning revised the poem, and in *1849* the introduction was heavily revised, the first interlude and, even more, the Jules–Phene episode considerably expanded, and other parts slightly revised. Punctuation underwent extensive revision for *1863*, *1868* and *1888*, but verbal changes after *1849* were comparatively few. The MS. may well be extant in private hands.

The song of Part III, 'A king lived long ago . . .', is a revision of a poem first published in the *Monthly Repository* in November 1835. It has been suggested that the scene between Luigi and his mother may have been drafted during Browning's voyage to Italy in the spring of 1838. The probability is, however, that most of *Pippa Passes* was written shortly after Browning completed *Sordello* on 26 May 1839; it was advertised as almost ready on 7 March 1840.

Mrs Orr records (*Handbook*, 55) that 'Browning was walking alone, in a wood near Dulwich, when the image flashed upon him of some one walking thus alone through life; one apparently too obscure to leave a trace of his or her passage, yet exercising a lasting though unconscious influence at every step of it; and the image shaped itself into the little silk-winder of Asolo, Felippa, or Pippa.' The Ottima–Sebald episode reminds one of much in *Macbeth*, and the Jules–Phene episode is indebted to Lytton's *Lady of Lyons* (1838) and its source (see F. A. Faverty, 'The Source of the Jules–Phene Episode in *Pippa Passes*', *SP* XXXVIII, 1952, 97–105; and T. Otten, 'What Browning Never Learned from Bulwer-Lytton', *Research Studies*[Washington State University] XXXVII, 1969, 338–42). It is also indebted to Diderot's novel *Jacques le Fataliste* (1796) (see C. W. Jennings, 'Diderot: A Suggested Source of the Jules–Phene Episode in *Pippa Passes*', *English Language Notes* I, 1964, 32–6). Elizabeth Barrett referred in 1841 to a general debt to Landor. More essentially, however, the play is a product of Browning's first visit to Italy in 1838 (and a kind of by-product of *Sordello*), when he fell in love with 'delicious Asolo', the ancient hill-town thirty-odd miles north-west of Venice which rises from the Venetian plain to overlook the Euganean Hills to the south and the foothills of the Alps to the north – all the play's locations are from direct observation. In later years Browning revisited Asolo a number of times (its main street is named after him), he called his final volume *Asolando*, and his son was to live and die there. The most operatic of his works, *Pippa Passes* may have been conceived by Browning as the opera he had planned to write; he suggested to Eliza Flower that she write music for the play's lyrics. Though what emerged was a closet-drama, the play has several times been performed.

The poem has been much discussed. Among essays are: J. M. Ariail, 'Is "Pippa Passes" a Dramatic Failure?', *SP* XXXVII, 1940, 120–29; Cook, *Browning's Lyrics*, 54–68; M. E. Glen, 'The Meaning and Structure of *Pippa Passes*', *TQ* XXIV, 1955, 410–26; Honan, *Browning's Characters*, 79–92; J. Korg, 'A Reading of *Pippa*

Passes', *VP* VI, 1968, 5-19; D. Kramer, 'Character and Theme in *Pippa Passes*', *VP* II, 1964, 241-9; J. M. Purcell, 'The Dramatic Failure of "Pippa Passes"', *SP* XXXVI, 1939, 77-87; E. W. Slinn, ' "God a Tame Confederate": The Reader's Dual Vision in *Pippa Passes*', *TQ* XLV, 1976, 158-73.

In *1841* the dedication was led up to by an 'advertisement' beginning: 'Two or three years ago I wrote a Play [*Strafford*, 1837], about which the chief matter I much care to recollect at present is, that a Pit-full of goodnatured people applauded it: – ever since, I have been desirous of doing something in the same way that should better reward their attention. What follows I mean for the first of a series of Dramatical Pieces, to come out at intervals, and I amuse myself by fancying that the cheap mode in which they appear will for once help me to a sort of Pit-audience again.' Sir Thomas Noon Talfourd (1795-1854), to whom *Pippa Passes* (like *Pickwick Papers*) is dedicated, was lawyer, judge and man of letters, now best known for his friendship with Lamb. Macready produced his classical tragedy, *Ion*, in 1836, the production being followed by a famous dinner at Talfourd's, attended by Browning and other major literary figures.

INTRODUCTION

New Year's Day   The poem seems confused as to the time of year. A number of references (to flowers, the cuckoo, and the time of sunrise, for instance) suggest that Browning may have thought of the old New Year's Day, March 25; but the Monsignor's third speech in Part IV indicates that the date is 1 January.

Asolo in the Trevisan   For Asolo, see above. The Trevisan is the region round the city of Treviso, about twenty miles south-east of Asolo and about fifteen north-west of Venice. The area was ruled at the time by Austria. Asolo was celebrated for its silk industry, which Browning's son later attempted to revive.

21-4]   *not in 1841.*

26-7]   As happy tribes – so happy tribes! who live
At hand – the common, other creatures' lot – *1841.*

30-42]   Day, 'tis but Pippa thou ill-usest
If thou prove sullen, me, whose old year's sorrow
Who except thee can chase before tomorrow,
Seest thou, my day? Pippa's – who mean to borrow
Only of thee strength against new year's sorrow: *1841.*

41   *sun's*   punning on 'son's'.

45-55]   Her Sebald's homage? And if noon shed gloom
O'er Jules and Phene – what care bride and groom
Save for their dear selves? Then, obscure thy eve *1841.*

59-61]   For true content? And once again, outbreak *1841.*

67-8]   *not in 1841.*

70   *Her day that lightens the*]   Bethink thee, utterly *1841.*

88   *martagon*   a flower, the Turk's-cap lily.

89]   New-blown, though! – ruddy as a nipple, *1841.*

Saint Agnes   the fourth-century young Roman martyred for refusing marriage.

90   *Turk bird*   turkey.

100   *weevil and chafer*   kinds of beetle.

107-13]   *not in 1841.*

131   *Possagno church*   designed by the sculptor Canova (1757-1822), a native of Possagno; the town is about five miles north of Asolo across the Organa (or Orcana) valley.

146–7] *not in 1841.*
163–4] *not in 1841.*
171–4] *not in 1841.*
181 *Dome* that is, *Duomo*: Italian for 'Cathedral'.
183–5] Of his dead brother! I, tonight at least, *1841.*
189] *not in 1841.*
203–5] I pass, will be alike important – prove
            That true! oh yes – the brother,
            The bride, the lover, and the mother, –
            Only to pass whom will remove –
            Whom a mere look at half will cure
            The Past, and help me to endure
            The Coming . . . I am just as great, no doubt,
            As they!   *1841.*
213 *cicala* cicada, locust.

PART I MORNING

4–7] Night? What, a Rhineland night, then? How these tall *1841.*
19 *Hinds* farm workmen.
28 *Saint Mark's* the cathedral of Venice.
29 *Vicenza* city about twenty-five miles south-west of Asolo.
30 *Padua* city about twenty-five miles south of Asolo.
56 *Black* red. Ottima, like the Macbeths, tends to avoid words that bear too directly on the murder.
59 *the Capuchin, with his brown hood* The Capuchins are an order of friars; they wear brown habits.
76 *proof-mark* a mark on a print to indicate that it is one of the first run off, and thus of higher value than a print lacking it.
83 *coil* fuss.
102 *Venus' body* the Italian oath, *corpo di Venere*.
119–20 *He is turned by this | Off from his face beside* Murder victims, it is sometimes believed, look to Heaven for revenge.
139, 142, 149] *not in 1841.*
170 *campanula* bellflower.
186 *suffered]* seemed let *1841–63.*
191–7 Browning is perhaps recalling the storm in *King Lear*.
235 *heartsease* pansy, or pansy-like flower.
255 *morbid* here (see *OED* 3), painted with flesh-like delicacy.
290 *moonstrike* usage not recorded by *OED*.
294 *Trieste* the port-city east of Venice.
300–302 *Aesculapius . . . Hebe . . . Phoebus . . . Mercury . . . bolus* respectively, god of medicine; goddess of youth and spring and cupbearer to the gods; Apollo, father of Aesculapius, and god of healing among other things; messenger of the gods; pill (in this case, for the pox).
307 *et canibus nostris* 'and to our dogs'. The student alludes to Vergil's *Eclogues* III, 66–7; Delia can see her lover because she is known to the watchdogs.
360 *fribble* frivolous person.
364 *Psiche-fanciulla* Canova's celebrated statue of Psyche (the Soul) as a girl with a butterfly (emblematic of her soul). Canova made a copy of the statue.

368 *Pietà* Canova worked his statue (Mary with Christ's body) for the Church in Possagno.

384 *Malamocco* island and town near Venice.

385 *Alciphron's 'hair like sea-moss'* The reference is to the *Letters* 3,1, of the second-century Greek writer.

388 *lire* plural of *lira*, the Italian currency unit.

390 *Tydeus* Greek hero, one of the seven against Thebes.
Academy the art museum in Venice.

393 *Fenice* the Phoenix, a Venice theatre.

411 *Hannibal Scratchy* Annibale Caracci, Italian painter (1560–1609).

PART II NOON

5 *front* forehead.

26 *Psyche* the beautiful legendary lover of Cupid.

29–37] Into my world!
                               Those? Books I told you of. *1841.*

39 *Coluthus* Alexandrian poet of the sixth century.

40 *Bistre* dark-brown.
Bessarion fifteenth-century cardinal, discoverer of a Coluthus poem.

42] *not in 1841.*

46–7 *He said . . . shaft* *Odyssey* XXII, 10. Odysseus killed Antinous, his wife's leading suitor.

48] *not in 1841.*

50 *Almaign Kaiser* German Emperor.

54 *Hippolyta* queen of the Amazons.

55 *Numidian* Numidia is an ancient North-African country.

58–9] A Greek, bay-filleted and thunder-free, *1841.*

59 *bay-filleted* crowned with bay (laurel) leaves, thought to protect against lightning.

61 *Hipparchus* Greek tyrant, stabbed to death in 514 B.C. by men who hid their daggers in myrtle-boughs.

61–4] Whose turn arrives to praise Harmodius.' – Praise him! *1841.*

63 *erst* formerly (archaism).

69] (Place your own face) – the Praiser's, who with eyes *1841.*

71‿2] (Gaze – I am your Harmodius dead and gone,) *1841.*

92 *Dryad* wood-nymph.

97, 114] *not in 1841.*

129–40] Above the world –
                               Now you sink – for your eyes *1841.*

151–76] *not in 1841.*

181–5] The Bard said, do one thing I can – *1841.*

191–3] Dwelt Hate beside –
         (And the bridegroom asked what the bard's smile meant
         Of his bride.)   *1841.*

197–9] Next cell.
         (For not I, said the bard, but those black bride's eyes above
         Should tell!)   *1841.*

205–6, 210, 214–16] *not in 1841.*

222‿3] (Here he said, if you interrupted me
         With, 'There must be some error, – who induced you

To speak this jargon?' – I was to reply
Simply – 'Await till . . . until . . .' I must say
Last rhyme again –)
. . . The essence, naught less, of each – *1841*.

232–7]   Of thy bride, Giulio!
(Then you, 'Oh, not mine –
Preserve the real name of the foolish song!'
But I must answer, 'Giulio – Jules – 'tis Jules!)
Thus I, Jules, hating thee
Sought long and painfully . . . *1841*.

258   *Kate the Queen*   Caterina Cornaro (*c.* 1454–1510), Venetian queen of Cyprus, was forced to abdicate and set up court in the castle of Asolo.

259, 268]   *not in 1841*.

270   *jesses*   straps around hawk's leg.

271]   *not in 1841*.

274–82]   At Asolo – and whosoever loves *1841*.

285–6, 288–97]   *not in 1841*.

303–6]   Without me.
To Ancona – Greece – some isle! *1841*.

306   *Ancona*   port-city on Italian east coast.

328   *Bluphocks*＊   Browning's note quotes Matthew v 45.

328–32   So . . . beside.]   *not in 1841*.

329   *Intendant*   steward of estate.

334   *grig*   cricket or grasshopper.

336   *Armenian*   The Armenian Church split from the Catholic in the fourth century.

337   *Koenigsberg*   capital of Prussia at the time; now Kaliningrad.
Prussia Improper   Prussia Proper was East Prussia.

339   *Chaldee*   (or Chaldean), a Semitic language.

345   *Syriac*   an Aramaic language.

346   *Celarent, Darii, Ferio*   part of a mnemonic for valid syllogism forms.

350   *Moses . . . locust*   As God's agent, Moses brought a plague of locusts into Egypt because Pharaoh had refused to let the children of Israel go. Exodus x 13–15.

350–51   *How to Jonah . . . Tarshish*   The Lord commanded Jonah to go to Nineveh, but he tried to flee to Tarshish. Jonah i 1–3.

352–3   *How the angel meeting Balaam . . . salaam*   Numbers xxii 22–34.

353–5   *Shackabrack . . . Stolen Goods*   The translation of the Chaldean inscription adds little to the sum of human knowledge.

356   *Bishop Beveridge*   Calvinist divine and writer (1636–1707), with a pun on 'beverage'. A 'Bishop' (*OED* 8) is a sweet alcoholic punch.

357   *Greek dog-sage*   Cynic philosopher.

358   *Charon's wherry*   Charon ferried the souls of the dead across the river Styx in Hades. He was paid with an obolus, a Greek coin.

359   *Hecate*   underworld goddess, sometimes propitiated by food placed at cross-roads.

359﹐60   *obolus . . . (Though thanks]*   (it might be got in somehow) *Though Cerberus should gobble us – To pay the Stygian ferry – or you might say, Never an obol To pay for the coble . . . 1841*.

362   *zwanzigers*   Austrian coins.

362–5   *zwanzigers) . . . [To the rest]*   *not in 1841*.

369   *Metternich*   reactionary Chancellor of Austria from 1809 to 1848.

376   *Panurge consults Hertrippa*   In Rabelais' *Gargantua and Pantagruel* (III, xxv), Panurge consults Herr Trippa about marriage. (Herr Trippa is almost certainly the Cornelius Agrippa quoted in the warning before *Pauline*.)

Believest thou, King Agrippa?   Saint Paul asks the question (Acts xxvi 27) of the King of Judea.

392   *deposed* deposited.

visa police endorsement on a passport.

396   *Carbonari*   a secret society dedicated to Italian freedom.

397   *Spielberg*   notorious Austrian prison.

PART III   EVENING

Scene   Asolo's thousand-year-old turret or fortress (La Rocca) dominates the town from its hill.

5ᴧ6]   Aristogeiton! 'ristogeiton' – plain *1841*.

6   *Lucius Junius*   The legendary Lucius Junius Brutus avenged the rape of Lucrece, and led the revolt that expelled the Tarquins from Rome in 510 B.C.

7–8]   Whose flesh is caught and kept by those withered wall-flowers, *1841*.

14   *old Franz*]   now hark *1849–63*. Francis I, Austrian Emperor, 1804–35.

14–16]   That's the king with the scarlet comb: come down! – 'Come down.'
       MOTHER: Do not kill that Man, my Luigi – do not *1841*.

19   *Pellicos*   Silvio Pellico, dramatist and member of the Carbonari, was imprisoned in Spielberg from 1820 to 1830. His book on his imprisonment was published in 1832. The date of the action of *Pippa Passes* is probably 1834.

122–3   *Andrea . . . Pier . . . Gualtier*   fictional Italian patriots.

128   *midway* midway between.

135   *How first the Austrians got these provinces*   The Congress of Vienna awarded the northern Italian provinces to Austria in 1815.

137   *conquest but by cunning*]   warfare but by treaty *1841*.

146   *Jupiter*   largest and second-brightest of the planets.

148   'I am the root and the offspring of David, and the bright and morning star' (Revelation xxii 16).

149   'And I will give him ['he that overcometh, and keepeth my works to the end'] the morning star' (Revelation ii 28).

163   *The Titian at Treviso*   Titian (Venetian painter, *c.* 1485–1576) altar-piece of the Annunciation in a chapel of the Duomo.

164–222   The song appeared in three sections in the *Monthly Repository*, N.S. IX, November 1835, 707–8, as a poem called 'The King'. Revisions for *1841* were fairly extensive.

174   *bane*]   pine *1835*.

175   *The gods so*]   As though gods *1835*.

187   *rough*]   some *1835–41*.

189–92]   *not in 1835*.

209   *Python*   The original Python guarded the Delphic Oracle until slain by Apollo. Subsequent Pythons are evil dragons.

213   *sweepy*]   silver *1835*.

218ᴧ19]   But which the god's self granted him
       For setting free each felon limb
       Faded because of murder done; – *1835*.
       But which the God's self granted him
       For setting free each felon limb

Because of earthly murder done
Faded till other hope was none; – *1841*.

222]   *not in 1835, 1841.*

223–9]   *Luigi.*   Farewell, farewell – how could I stay? Farewell! *1841.*

226   *bye-corners*   out-of-the-way corners.

231, 234]   *not in 1841.*

236   *fig-peckers*   birds (*beccafichi*) feeding mainly on fig-trees.

237   *Breganze*   Breganza is a village a few miles west of Asolo.

239]   *not in 1841.*

251   *Deuzans and junetings, leather-coats*   kinds of apple.

293   *ortolans*   small birds. A delicacy (see Prologue to *Ferishtah's Fancies*).

295   *Polenta*   a mush generally made from cornmeal.

312]   To look upon . . . my whole remains, *1841*.

317-20   *Why, you seem . . . all about it.]   not in 1841.*

PART IV   NIGHT

3-4   *Benedicto benedicatur*   Latin grace: 'May it be blessed with a blessing.'

7   *Messina*   port-city in Sicily.

8   *Assumption Day*   15 August, celebration of the ascension to Heaven of the Virgin Mary.

12   *The others leave the apartment.]   The others leave the apartment, where a table with refreshments is prepared. 1841.*

15-16   *Ascoli, Fermo and Fossombruno*   cities of north-central Italy, near the east coast.

40-41   *in the very perfection . . . he foresees an ultimate failure*   a constant Browning theme; see, especially, 'Andrea del Sarto'.

47   *Correggio*   famous Italian painter (*c.* 1489-1534).

65-6   *villa, that podere]*   manor, that liberty *1841.*
   podere   farm.

73   *Forli*   city of north-central Italy.

75   *Cesena*   town near Forli.

93   *soldo*   small coin (equivalent, say, of cent or penny).

126   *younger]   not in 1841-63.*
   Pontiff   Pope.

136   *complot*   conspiracy.

176   *Through her singing? Is it a bargain?]   not in 1841.*

176,7]   MON: Why, if she sings, one might . . . *1841.*

181]   What are the voices of birds *1841.*

186   *seven and one*   the seven Pleiades, and Aldeboran ('the follower').

195-6   *Miserere mei, Domine!*   'Lord, have mercy upon me!' (Latin).

[EPILOGUE]

2   *dray*   nest.

5   *lob-worm*   lugworm, a large seashore worm.

17   *How pert that girl was!]*   Pert as a sparrow . . . *1841.*

24   *raw-silk-coloured]*   English-coloured *1841-63.*

32-3, 47-50, 56]   *not in 1841.*

70   *Brenta*   river flowing south through Bassano, about ten miles west of Asolo.

88   *mavis, merle and throstle*   song-thrush, blackbird and thrush.

91   *howlet*   owl (archaic form).

94   *complines*   the last daily prayers.

96   *twats*   a notorious gaffe. Browning wrote (Hood, *Letters*, 252) that he thought the word referred to 'a distinctive part of a nun's attire that might fitly pair off with the cowl appropriated to a monk'. Browning misunderstood the reference in *Vanity of Vanities* (1660), 50–51: 'They talk't of his having a Cardinalls Hat, / They'd send him as soon an Old Nuns Twat'. *OED* discreetly describes the word as '*low. Obs.*' and refers one to Bailey's 1727 definition: '*pudendum muliebre*'; it cites and explains Browning's error.

110ʌ11]   Though I passed by them all, and felt no sign. *1849–63.*

113   *All service ranks the same with God* –   'all service, therefore, rates / Alike' (*Sordello* VI, 127–8).

113-15]   *All service is the same with God –*
            Whose puppets, best and worst,
            Are we...[She sleeps. 1841.

Dramatic Lyrics

Dramatic Lyrics, the third pamphlet published at the expense of Browning's father in the series of *Bells and Pomegranates*, appeared in the second half of November 1842. It was made up of sixteen poems, two of which had been published before. All sixteen were subsequently reprinted in all collected editions. Browning had originally planned *Bells and Pomegranates* to include plays, but Edward Moxon, his publisher, urged him to publish some shorter pieces, most of which Browning had already at hand, as likely to be more popular (see Browning's letter of 22 May 1842 in Kenyon, *Browning and Domett*, 36). The poems were written between 1834 and 1842.

In *1849*, under the title of *Dramatic Romances and Lyrics*, Browning republished these poems and those of *Dramatic Romances and Lyrics* (1845) in their original order. In *1863*, however, he redistributed the poems of *Dramatic Lyrics*, *Dramatic Romances*, and *Men and Women* (1855) in three groupings: 'Lyrics', 'Romances', and 'Men, and Women'. The same groupings were retained in *1868* and *1888*. In the new arrangement, 'Lyrics' included fifty poems, most of them from the 1855 *Men and Women*, and only six from the original *Dramatic Lyrics*. Seven of the original poems were included in 'Romances', three went to 'Men, and Women' (Appendix 2 in Volume I gives details of the redistribution, which is not followed in this edition). After 1842 revisions were slight.

Though it included some poems that subsequently became popular and famous, *Dramatic Lyrics* originally attracted little attention. It is now generally regarded as marking an important stage in Browning's career, foreshadowing much of his later work and its more distinctive and valuable qualities.

Browning's note to *Dramatic Lyrics* was the 'advertisement' in *1842*.

CAVALIER TUNES

Probably written in 1842, the bicentenary of the outbreak of the Civil Wars in England between the Royalist or Cavalier forces of Charles I and the Parliamentary or Roundhead forces. The 'Tunes' are a kind of by-product of Browning's work on Strafford in 1836–7 when he helped with Forster's *Life* and published his own play, *Strafford*. They are indebted to Scott's *Woodstock* (1826) (see R. L. Lowe in *N & Q* CXCVII, 1952, 103–4). The manuscript, on paper watermarked 1836, is at Yale, and its appearance suggests that the three poems were written about the same time. The 'Tunes' remained in 'Lyrics' in later collections.

I   Marching Along

1   *Kentish Sir Byng*   probably a Browning invention, though the surname of Byng has Kentish associations. Kent was a Royalist county.
2   *crop-headed Parliament*   Royalists wore their hair long, Parliamentarians (Roundheads), short.
3   *pressing*   enlisting, impressing.
7   *Pym*   John Pym, leading Parliamentarian until his death in 1643. He had led the attack on Strafford.
   carles   churls.
8   *parles*   obsolete form of 'parleys' – here 'speeches' or 'words'.
13   *Hampden*   John Hampden, leading Parliamentarian, killed in battle in 1643.
14   *Hazelrig,*]   Rudyard, and *MS.*, *1842*.
   Hazelrig, Fiennes, and young Harry   Sir Arthur Hazelrig, Nathaniel Fiennes and Henry Vane were leading Parliamentarians. *Young* Harry because his father, Sir Henry, was Charles's Secretary of State.
15   *Rupert*   Prince Rupert of Bavaria, nephew of Charles I, and a leading Cavalier general.
22   *Nottingham*   The King's raising of his standard here in central England in August 1842 marked the beginning of the Civil Wars.

II   Give a Rouse

Rouse   cheer.
8   *found*   kept.
16   *Noll's damned troopers*   Oliver Cromwell's famed Ironsides. The toast clearly belongs to a later stage of the Wars.

III   Boot and Saddle

Title]   MY WIFE GERTRUDE *MS.*, *1842*.
4   *Boot, saddle, to horse, and away!*   'sound, boot and saddle – to horse and away' (Scott, *Woodstock*).
10   *Brancepeth*]   Barham *MS. first reading*. Brancepeth is just south-west of Durham in north-east England, Barham is in eastern Kent.
11   *fay*   faith.

MY LAST DUCHESS

In *1842* the poem was grouped with 'II. France' (later called 'Count Gismond') under the general title of 'Italy and France' as 'I. Italy'. In *1849* it had its present title, and in *1863* it was reassigned to 'Romances'. The poem is another by-product of *Sordello*, and perhaps too of the 'Essay on Chatterton' (purportedly an essay on Tasso); as L. S. Friedland showed in 'Ferrara and *My Last Duchess*', *SP* XXXIII, 1936, 656–84, the Duke is modelled on Alfonso II, fifth Duke of Ferrara, and the last of the Este family with which Browning had dealt in *Sordello*, and patron of Tasso. Alfonso II was born in 1533, and married Lucrezia de Medici, then fourteen, in 1558. She died in 1561, and poison was suspected. In 1565 the Duke married the daughter of Ferdinand I, Count of Tyrol, whose capital was Innsbruck. The emissary conducting the negotiations for her marriage was one Nikolaus Madruz.

The poem was almost certainly written in the summer or early autumn of 1842. It has been exhaustively discussed. One book is entirely devoted to it: R. J. Berman, *Browning's Duke*, Richards Rosen Press, 1972. L. R. Stevens (*VNL* 28, 1965, 25-6) suggests the influence of Wanley's *Wonders of the Little World* (1678); L. Stevenson (*MLN* LXXIV, 1959, 489-92) suggests that of Byron's *Parisina*. Criticism includes: J. Adler, 'Structure and Meaning in Browning's "My Last Duchess"', *VP* XV, 1977, 219-27; B. R. Jerman, 'Browning's Witless Duke', *PMLA* LXXII, 1957, 488-93 (in Litzinger and Knickerbocker, *The Browning Critics,* 329-35); Langbaum, *The Poetry of Experience,* 82-5; L. Perrine, 'Browning's Shrewd Duke', *PMLA* LXXIV, 1959, 157-9; B. N. Pipes, Jr, 'The Portrait of "My Last Duchess"', *VS* III, 1960, 381-6; W. D. Shaw, 'Browning's Duke as Theatrical Producer', *VNL* 29, 1966, 18-22.

3 *Frà Pandolf* probably an imaginary painter of an imaginary painting. There are extant portraits of Lucrezia de Medici (see Berman).
30 *approving*] forward *1842.*
36 *to*] could *1842.*
45 *I gave commands* According to H. Corson (*An Introduction to the Study of Robert Browning's Poetry*, 3rd edn, Heath, 1903, viii), Browning said, 'I meant that the commands were that she should be put to death ... Or he might have had her shut up in a convent.' Browning said also that the Duke used his wife's shallowness 'as an excuse – mainly to himself – for taking revenge on one who had unwittingly wounded his absurdly pretentious vanity, by failing to recognize his superiority in even the most trifling matters'.
56 *Claus of Innsbruck* probably Browning's invention. The Austrian city was a centre for bronze sculpting in the sixteenth century.

COUNT GISMOND

The poem was paired with 'Italy' (later 'My Last Duchess') in *1842*, and entitled 'II. France'. In *1849* it was separated from 'My Last Duchess' and given its present title. In *1863* it was included in 'Romances'.

Aix is the old capital of Provence in south-east France. The characters and incident are generally thought to originate with Browning; however, F. Allen, 'Ariosto and Browning: A Reexamination of "Count Gismond"', *VP* XI, 1973, 15-25, suggests a debt to the Genevra–Airodant episode in Ariosto's *Orlando Furioso* and the Hero–Claudio material in *Much Ado*. Conventional straightforward readings of the poem are ingeniously challenged by J. V. Hagopian (*PQ* XL, 1961, 153-5), Sister Marcella M. Holloway (*SP* LX, 1963, 549-53), and J. W. Tilton and R. D Tuttle (*SP* LIX, 1962, 83-95); M. Timko, 'Ah, Did You Once See Browning Plain?', pleads for sanity.

48] Blinds me ... but the true mist was rain. *1842.*
52 *boldly*] calmly *1842.*
86 *greaves* armour from knee to ankle.
87 *hauberk* coat of chain mail.
 on the fret in an agitated manner.
124 *tercel* male falcon.

INCIDENT OF THE FRENCH CAMP

In *1842* the poem was called 'I – Camp (French)' and grouped with 'II – Cloister (Spanish)' (the poem later called 'Soliloquy of the Spanish Cloister'), under the general title of 'Camp and Cloister'. The poems were separated and present titles adopted in *1849*. The poem was included in 'Romances' in *1863*. Napoleon had an impressive second burial in December 1841, and the poem was probably written in 1842. The manuscript of the first stanza is in the Ashley Library of the British Library.

Mrs Orr (*Handbook*, 300) said the poem was based on fact, though its hero was man, not boy; a possible source in Excellmanns' life of Napoleon is cited by DeVane, *Handbook*, 112. The French stormed Ratisbon (Regensburg, on the Danube in Bavaria) on 23 April 1809. Marshal Lannes, Duke of Montebello, fatally wounded a month later, fought bravely at Ratisbon.

7   *prone*   bent downwards.
29 *flag-bird*   the eagle, Napoleon's emblem.
    vans   wings.

SOLILOQUY OF THE SPANISH CLOISTER

In *1842*, the poem was called 'II – Cloister (Spanish)' and grouped with 'I – Camp (French)' (the poem later called 'Incident of the French Camp') under the general title of 'Camp and Cloister'. The poems were separated in *1849* and the present titles adopted. In *1863* the poem was No. III of a group called 'Garden Fancies' (I and II were 'The Flower's Name' and 'Sibrandus Schafnaburgensis'). In *1868* that grouping also was dissolved, but the poem remained in 'Lyrics'. Date of composition is unknown, though DeVane (*Handbook*, 114) suggests a date after the completion of *Sordello* in May 1839 when Browning was reading Elizabethan plays. J. U. Rundle (*N&Q* CXCVI, 1951, 252) suggests the influence of Burns's 'Holy Willie's Prayer'. Discussions, often very solemn, are voluminous; among them are: D. Sonstroem, 'Animal and Vegetable in the Spanish Cloister', *VP* VI, 1968, 70–73; M. K. Starkman, 'The Manichee in the Cloister: A Reading of Browning's "Soliloquy of the Spanish Cloister"', *MLN* LXXV, 1960, 399–405.

3   *Brother Lawrence*   perhaps a Spanish cousin of another inveterate and dim-witted gardener, Friar Laurence in *Romeo and Juliet*?
10 *Salve tibi!*   'Hail to thee!' (Latin).
14 *oak-galls*   growths on diseased oak-leaves, valuable for their tannin.
15 *What's the Latin name for 'parsley'?*   petroselinum.
16 *Swine's Snout*   dandelion; in Latin, *rostrum porcinum*.
22 *chaps*   'chops': cheeks or jaws.
31 *Barbary corsair*   The Barbary coast of north-west Africa was famous for its pirates.
33 *refection*   a light meal.
39 *Arian*   heretical follower of the fourth-century Arius who denied the equality of Christ with God and the doctrine of the Trinity.
49–51 *great text in Galatians . . . damnations*   There being no such text, much mathematical ingenuity and ink have been lavished on the lines. Browning, who acknowledged his error in a letter of 26 April 1888 (see *SIB* II, No. 1, 1974, 62), may have had in mind as 'text' Deuteronomy xxviii 15–45, but 'Galatians' is a better

rhyme word and the poet wrote that he 'was not careful to be correct'. The strange suggestion that 'twenty-nine' is used for an indefinite number has been made.

56 *Manichee* a heretic who believes that the Universe reveals a constant fight between balanced forces of Good and Evil.

60 *Belial's gripe* the Devil's grip.

62 *woeful* wretched.

66] Pledge one's soul yet slily leave *1842*.

70 *Hy, Zy, Hine* probably the most-discussed three words in Browning. Onomatopoeic rendering (or distortion) of the bell sounds? Invocation to Satan as part of a pact to blast the rose-acacia? Slurred version of a Mass refrain burlesquing the Old-French version of praise for an ass? Nonsense words to conjure demons? Malicious snarl? Scholarship continues. For perhaps the most convincing explanation, see J. F. Loucks, '"Hy, Zy, Hine" and Peter of Abano', *VP* XII, 1974, 165–9: the words are nonsense words and derive from a conjuration of Mars in a medieval manual of magic formulae, the *Heptameron*, or *Elementa Magica*, ascribed to Peter of Abano, and the monk is rehearsing 'the words he must memorize for use at a later time in closing the deal to blast the rose acacia'.

71 *Vespers* evening prayer.

71–2 *Plena gratiâ | Ave, Virgo* 'Full of grace, Hail, Virgin' (Latin – normal order would be *Ave Maria, gratia plena*).

IN A GONDOLA

The first few lines were composed impromptu probably late in 1841 as a catalogue entry for Maclise's picture, *The Serenade*, exhibited in 1842. The opening lines were based on Forster's description of the painting; when Browning actually saw it, he added to them. The picture, very popular in its day, is now in the Armstrong Browning Library, and is reproduced in *BNL* 5, 1970, 21. The poem's stage directions were added in *1849*, and other slight revisions made. In *1863* it was included in 'Romances'. Browning had visited Venice in 1838.

33 *cruce* crucible.

34 *mage* magus, magician.

44 *Pucci Palace* probably a Browning invention.

47 *wried* wrung.

72 *sprite* spirit.

87 *thought of mine*] I *1842*.

104 *What if the Three should*] He and the Couple *1842*.

107 *Himself* the Lady's husband.

108 *stylet* stiletto.

111 *sains* blesses (obsolete or Scottish).

113 *Lido's wet accursèd graves* As heretics, Jews were buried on the island shielding Venice from the sea. The graves were washed at high tide.

127 *Giudecca* one of Venice's largest channels.

141 *lory* small parrot.

148 *Smyrna peach* The city in Asia Minor was known for fine fruit; presumably the tree is from the city.

175–6] Of pillars on God's quest have gone *1842*.

177 *Babylon* traditionally a city of luxury and sin.

180 *limpet* a marine mollusc.

186 *Schidone's eager Duke* Bartolommeo Schidone (1560–1616) was a minor

painter of Modena. The painting is probably a Browning invention, but Schidone's patron was the Duke of Modena.

188   *Haste-thee-Luke*   englishing of the nickname (*Luca fa presto*) of the Neapolitan painter, Luca Giordano (1632-1705).

190   *Castelfranco's Magdalen*   The Venetian painter Giorgione (1478?-1510) was born at Castelfranco. The painting is probably a Browning invention.

192   *Ser*   seer.

193   *Tizian*   Titian (*c.* 1485-1576), Venetian painter.

222   *Siora*   Venetian form of *Signora* ('Madam').

ARTEMIS PROLOGIZES

Revisions for *1849* were extensive but relatively insignificant. *1849* virtually established the final text, though later punctuational revisions were fairly numerous. In *1863* the poem was put into 'Men, and Women'. At the end of the first proof of the poem (in Harvard's Widener Library) is a note: 'I had better say perhaps that the above is nearly all retained of a tragedy I composed, much against my endeavour, while in bed with a fever two years ago: it went farther into the story of Hippolytus and Aricia, but when I got well, putting only thus much down at once, I soon forgot the remainder, – which came nearer the mark, I think.' Browning deleted the last seven words on the proof, and ultimately the whole note. The illness referred to was of December 1840–January 1841.

The poem forms the prologue to a projected sequel to the *Hippolytus* of Euripides, much of the plot of which is recapitulated here. Prompted by Aphrodite, goddess of erotic love, Phaedra, wife of Theseus, fell in love with her stepson Hippolytus. Her love being unrequited, she hanged herself but left a document accusing Hippolytus of unnatural love for her. Theseus asked Poseidon, god of the sea, to kill his son. Poseidon sent a monster which caused the horses of Hippolytus to panic, and Hippolytus was fatally wounded. Artemis then told Theseus the truth, and father and dying son were reconciled. Both Vergil (*Aeneid* VII) and Ovid (*Metamorphoses* XV) had it, however, that Aesculapius (Asclepius) healed Hippolytus and that Artemis took him to Italy, where he fell in love with Aricia, one of Artemis' many nymphs. Browning's version occurs as Hippolytus is being healed. The virgin Artemis (Diana) is goddess of the moon and of hunting. She speaks here as healer, balancing the destructive Aphrodite who introduces the play of Euripides.

The poem is the first to use Browning's characteristic Greek spellings; he stated the reasons for using them in his preface to his transcript of the *Agamemnon*. The poem was a special favourite of Matthew Arnold.

1   *ambrosial courts*   Olympian courts. Ambrosia was the food of the gods.

2   *Here*   Hera (Juno), Queen of the gods.

12   *Athenai*   Athens.

13   *Asclepios*   Asclepius, god of healing and medicine, son of Apollo.

14   *buskined*   half-booted.

17   *ounce*   snow leopard, jaguar.

21   *gadbee*   gadfly.

27   *Amazonian*   Hippolytus was son of Hippolyta, Queen of the Amazons.

39   *ai, ai*   'woe, woe' (Greek).

40   *car*   chariot.

42   *Henetian*   from a district in Asia Minor.

75   *cross-way*   Artemis, as Trivia, was worshipped at cross-ways.

87 *their hair they clipped* alluding to a Greek rite expressive of woe.
102 *radiant brother* Phoebus Apollo, twin of Artemis.
106 *lavers* waters of spiritual cleansing.
114–15 *healing rod, | Thy snake* traditionally associated with Asclepius.

WARING

A few minor changes were made for *1849* and later editions. In *1863* the poem was included in 'Romances'. The name Browning took from a King's Messenger he met in Russia in 1834, but the poem is what a mutual friend called it, 'a fancy portrait of a very dear friend', Alfred Domett (1811–87), who left England on 30 April 1842 for New Zealand (where he was later briefly Prime Minister). In the second set of proofs (in Harvard's Widener Library), Browning wrote above the printed title 'Alfred Domett or'. The poem was thus written in the summer of 1842. Domett, lawyer and minor poet, became a close friend of Browning about 1840 (see Kenyon, *Robert Browning and Alfred Domett*, and E. A. Horsman's edition of Domett's *Diary*). Domett is referred to in 'The Guardian Angel' (written 1848), and possibly in 'Popularity' (1855) and 'Time's Revenges' (1845). The poem's details are highly fanciful. See J. F. McCarthy, 'Browning's "Waring": The Real Subject of the "Fancy Portrait"', *VP* IX, 1971, 371–82.

27 *done ... undone* reminiscent of Donne's playing with his name in 'A Hymn to God the Father'.
34 *first steps* Domett had published in *Blackwood's* and his poems were printed in *Poems* (1833) and *Venice* (1839).
38 *chance-blades* The combination is unrecorded in *OED*.
54–5 *Monstr'-inform'-ingens-horrend-ous | Demoniaco-seraphic* Mock-heroic notes are struck frequently in 'Waring'. Here Browning varies Vergil's description of the huge monster, Polyphemus, in *Aeneid* III, 658: '*Monstrum horrendum, informe, ingens*'. The Vergilian passage is often used to exemplify the elision of -um before a vowel in scansion.
61 *lost lady* If real, she is as yet unidentified.
87 *your great works* 'You can do anything' (Browning to Domett, 22 May 1842).
88 *little works*] all we've yet *1842–63*.
99–100 *Ichabod, Ichabod, | The glory is departed* 'And she named the child Ichabod, saying, The glory is departed from Israel' (1 Samuel iv 21).
108 *Vishnu-land ... Avatar* India ... incarnation. Vishnu is a Hindu deity and saviour, several times incarnated on earth.
109 *Czar* 'Waring' was written in the year of the retreat from Kabul, when thousands of Britons were massacred. Afghanistan was the scene of Russian–British conflict.
111 *Kremlin* Moscow's walled citadel.
112 *serpentine and syenite* two kinds of rock.
122 *lamb-white maiden* Iphigenia. As Agamemnon prepared to sacrifice his daughter, Artemis bore her off to Tauris (the Crimea and Scythian strands) to become a priestess at the goddess's (Diana's) shrine.
130 *myrrhy* the first usage recorded by *OED*.
131 *Rapt by the whirl-blast* swept on by the whirlwind (Cumberland dialect; used by Wordsworth and Shelley).
152 *Caldara Polidore* Polidoro Caldara da Caravaggio (*c.* 1492–1543), Italian painter of frescoes under Raphael.

153–7] *not in 1842.*

155 *Purcell from his Rosy Bowers* Henry Purcell, English composer (1659–95), was setting *From Rosy Bowers* at the time of his death.

190 *Garrick* David Garrick (1717–79), celebrated English actor.

191 *The heart of Hamlet's mystery pluck?* 'You would pluck out the heart of my mystery' (*Hamlet* III.2.382).

193 *Junius* pseudonym of Whig controversialist (1769–92).

195–6 *Some Chatterton . . . Rowley into life* Thomas Chatterton (1752–70), main subject of Browning's celebratory essay written in the early summer of 1842, English poet, creator of the Rowley Poems which he claimed were the work of a fifteenth-century monk.

213 *Trieste* the port-city east of Venice.

215–51 The lines are vaguely reminiscent of much in Coleridge's 'Rime of the Ancient Mariner'.

228 *Lascar's* East Indian sailor's.

RUDEL TO THE LADY OF TRIPOLI

Entitled 'Rudel and the Lady of Tripoli', the poem was paired in *1842* with 'Cristina' under the general title of 'Queen-Worship'. In *1849* the pairing was broken, and the poem's first part extensively revised. In *1863* it was included in 'Men, and Women', just before Browning's tribute to his wife in 'One Word More'. It was perhaps written in 1838 or 1839 as a by-product of Browning's interest, whetted by *Sordello*, in troubadour literature. The legend is widely known and no special source for Browning's poem has been distinguished. A possibility is Mrs Dobson's note in her *History of the Troubadours*, 22–5, a work Browning consulted for *Sordello*. One of Rudel's poems, 'On Distant Love', may also have influenced Browning's lines.

In the legend, Rudel, a twelfth-century troubadour prince in Provence, fell in love with the Princess of Tripoli, a small duchy in Syria. As is appropriate for a courtly lover, he had not met her, and she was married. The poem is set shortly before the trip to Tripoli on which Rudel fell ill, was momentarily revived as his Love held his hand, expired appropriately in her arms, and got himself lavishly buried. The flower, sun and mountain symbolism is traditional troubadour material. See Cook, *Browning's Lyrics*, 83–6.

1 *gracious]* *not in 1842.*
3 *vainly favoured]* *not in 1842.*
4 *steadfast]* *not in 1842.*
5 *front]* steadfast front *1842.*
6 *And underneath the Mount]* *not in 1842.*
15 *Calm front of snow]* Calm steadfast front *1842.*

CRISTINA

In *1842* the poem was paired with 'Rudel and the Lady of Tripoli' under the general title of 'Queen-Worship'. The grouping was broken in *1849*. In *1863* the poem was included in 'Lyrics'. Slight revisions were made for *1849*, in which the final text was virtually established.

Maria Christina (1806–78), young fourth wife of old Ferdinand VII (and a noted coquette) was Queen of Spain (1829–33) and then Regent (1833–40) for her daughter.

In 1840 she was forced to leave Spain temporarily when her secret marriage to one Muñoz was revealed; Browning's poem may well belong to the same year.

For a challenge to the conventional view that the poem embodies Browning's 'doctrine' of elective affinities (or his belief – reflected in his life and art – in love at or before first sight), see, with the suggestion that the speaker is not sane, C. S. Kilby, 'Browning's *Cristina*', *Explicator* II, November 1943, Item 16.

61-4] That just holds out the proving
    Our powers, alone and blended –
    And then, come next life quickly,
      This life will have been ended! *1842*.

JOHANNES AGRICOLA IN MEDITATION

First published, entitled 'Johannes Agricola', in the *Monthly Repository*, new series X, January 1836, 45-6, immediately following 'Porphyria', each poem signed 'Z.' like others Browning published in Fox's journal. Slightly revised, it was reprinted in *Dramatic Lyrics* in 1842, grouped with its earlier companion under the general title 'Madhouse Cells'. Neither poem was otherwise titled: this poem was simply 'I' and the other, 'II'. In *1849* it assumed its final title, and as 'I. – Madhouse Cell' was again grouped with 'Porphyria's Lover' ('II. – Madhouse Cell'). In *1863* both poems were classified as 'Romances'; perhaps significantly, 'Johannes Agricola in Meditation' immediately preceded 'The Heretic's Tragedy'. In *1868* it joined 'Men and Women', the only poem reassigned after *1863*; perhaps significantly, it there follows 'An Epistle'.

Griffin and Minchin (73) state, without evidence, that the poem and its companion were written in Saint Petersburg in April–May 1834, but in 1863 Browning wrote that 'Porphyria's Lover' was written in London in 1836. Both dates are probably wrong; the poem probably belongs to 1835 since (a) in the headnote given below, Browning changed the date in his quotation from 1538 to 1535, and (b) the poem stems from Browning's reading for *Paracelsus* and probably especially from Adam's *Vitae Germanorum Medicorum*. Johannes Schnitter or Schneider (1494–1566) adopted the name Agricola; he founded Antinomianism, a doctrine roughly defined in the headnote Browning printed in *1836*: 'Antinomians, so denominated for rejecting the Law as a thing of no use under the Gospel dispensation: they say, that good works do not further, nor evil works hinder salvation; that the child of God cannot sin, that God never chastiseth him, that murder, drunkenness, &c. are sins in the wicked but not in him, that the child of grace being once assured of salvation, afterwards never doubteth ... that God doth not love any man for his holiness, that sanctification is no evidence of justification, &c. Pontanus, in his Catalogue of Heresies, says John Agricola was the author of this sect, A.D. 1535.' – *Dictionary of all Religions*, 1704.

Browning had no sympathy (as *Paracelsus*, for instance, makes clear) with doctrines of predestination, eternal damnation, salvation by faith alone, election and so on.

29 *irreversibly*] irrevocably *1836-68*.
42] With unexhausted blessedness *1836*.
46 *life*] like *1836*.

PORPHYRIA'S LOVER

First published as 'Porphyria' in the *Monthly Repository*, new series X, January 1836, 43–4, immediately before 'Johannes Agricola', each poem signed 'Z.', like others Browning published in Fox's journal. With slight revisions it was reprinted in 1842 in *Dramatic Lyrics* with its earlier companion under the general title of 'Madhouse Cells'. Neither poem was otherwise titled: this poem was simply 'II' and the other, 'I'. In *1849* it assumed its final title, and as 'II. – Madhouse Cell' was again grouped with 'Johannes Agricola in Meditation' ('I. – Madhouse Cell'). In *1863* the poems were separated, though both poems were included in 'Romances', the division in which this poem remained.

The remark of Lady Ritchie (*Records of Tennyson, Ruskin and Browning*, 1892, 221) that the poem was written in Russia probably lies behind the unsubstantiated claim of Griffin and Minchin (73) that the poem was written in Saint Petersburg in April–May 1834. In 1863 Browning wrote that he composed it in London in 1836; it probably belongs with 'Johannes Agricola' to 1835.

Two sources have been identified: John Wilson's '"Extracts from Gosschen's Diary" No. I', *Blackwood's* III, 1818, 596–8, and 'Barry Cornwall's' poem 'Marcian Colonna' (1820) (see M. Mason, 'Browning and the Dramatic Monologue', in *Robert Browning*, ed. I. Armstrong, 255–8). Essays include: D. Eggenschwiler, 'Psychological Complexity in "Porphyria's Lover"', *VP* VIII, 1970, 39–48; C. R. Tracy, 'Porphyria's Lover', *MLN* LII, 1937, 579–80.

32 *Happy and proud*] Proud – very proud *1836*; Proud, very proud *1842–9*.
50 *my*] *my*[italics] *1836, 1849–63*; my *1842, 1868–88*.
58–60 'She died, and spoke no word: and still he sate / Beside her like an image' ('Marcian Colonna').

THROUGH THE METIJDA TO ABD-EL-KADR

In *1863* the poem was included in 'Lyrics'. The text has remained virtually unchanged. It was composed on horseback in the summer of 1842.

Abd-el-Kadr ('Servant of the Mighty One') (1808–83), Emir of Mascara, a popular hero of the day, fought for Algerian independence from France for ten years. In the summer of 1842 he suffered severe defeats. Browning's speaker is riding to his relief through the Metijda, the plain south-west of Algiers.

23 *reside*] abide *1842* (despite Browning's change to 'reside' in two sets of proofs).
38 *the Prophet and the Bride* Mohammed and Ayeshah.

THE PIED PIPER OF HAMELIN

First published in *Dramatic Lyrics* in 1842, it was a late addition when Browning learned that the projected pamphlet was not filled; the poem is not in the first set of proofs in Harvard's Widener Library, but is in the second set. DeVane (*Handbook*, 128) errs in stating that the manuscript is at Baylor University. Six lines were added in *1849* (DeVane, *Handbook*, 127, errs in stating that two lines disappeared), but other revisions then and in future printings were slight. In *1863* it was included in 'Romances'.

The poem was probably written early in May 1842 (and/or perhaps in late April). William ('Willie') Macready, oldest son of the tragedian, was ill in May, and

Browning gave him this poem (and possibly 'The Cardinal and the Dog', eventually published in 1889) to read and illustrate.

Browning's sources for the poem have been much discussed (see, especially, A. Dickson, 'Browning's Source for *The Pied Piper of Hamelin*', *SP* XXIII, 1926, 327–36). Browning said that Wanley's *Wonders of the Little World* (1678) gave him his materials. But the closest parallels are with Richard Verstegen's *Restitution of Decayed Intelligence in Antiquities* (1605), which Browning later denied having read before composing his poem. That Browning had almost surely read or heard about the legend as reported by Verstegen is clear from details used in the poem, and that other sources were involved has been conclusively shown. Browning's father had begun his own version of the poem, but 'stopped short' until his son's version was complete (Mr Browning's version, later completed, is in *The Bookman* of May 1912). The question of the legend's origins has been much discussed – inconclusively but fascinatingly. On the poem see M. Millhauser, 'Poet and Burgher: A Comic Variation on a Serious Theme', *VP* VII, 1969, 163–8.

1–3 *Hamelin ... Weser*   Hamelin is on the Weser river in north-west Germany, about twenty-five miles from Hanover. It is in Hanover, not Brunswick, an error found in Verstegen.

4 *southern*   in fact, western.

27 *best*]   like *1842*.

28–9]   *not in 1842*.

48–51]   *not in 1842*.

89 *Tartary ... Cham*   Tartary, east of the Caspian Sea, was ruled by a Khan (Cham).

91 *Nizam*   beginning in the eighteenth century, the name given to the ruler of Hyderabad, India.

95 *guilders*   the basic Netherlands monetary unit, roughly in today's values twelve pence or twenty-five cents.

123–5 *Julius Caesar ... manuscript*   alluding to the legend that when Caesar's ship was captured at Alexandria, he swam ashore carrying the manuscript of his *Commentaries on the Gallic Wars*.

133 *train-oil-flasks*   whale-oil-flasks.

136 *psaltery*   ancient musical stringed instrument.

138 *drysaltery*   place where pickles, sauces and oils are sold (the usage antedates the earliest recorded usage in *OED* – by Dickens).

139 *nuncheon*   light refreshment (dialectal).

141 *puncheon*   huge cask.

158 *Claret ... Hock*   wines ('Grave' is an error for 'Graves').

160 *Rhenish*   a Rhine wine.

169 *poke*   pocket or small bag.

177 *Bagdat*   Baghdad.

179 *Caliph*   ruler of a Mohammedan country.

182 *stiver*   a Dutch coin of little value.

220 *Koppelberg Hill*   real but not 'mighty'; and east, not west, of Hamelin.

246 *fallow*   light-brown.

258–60 *A text ... camel in*   'It is easier for a camel to go through the eye of a needle, than for a rich man to enter into the kingdom of God' (Matthew xix 24).

269–75 *decree ... seventy-six*   Hamelin did date its records from the event in 1284. Browning's date of 1376 is Verstegen's.

285 *church-window painted*   in 1572.

290   *Transylvania*   district in east-central Europe (detail from Verstegen).
296   *trepanned*   ensnared (archaism).

Dramatic Romances and Lyrics

First published on 6 November 1845, *Dramatic Romances and Lyrics* was the seventh pamphlet printed at the expense of Browning's father in the series of *Bells and Pomegranates*, and, like *Dramatic Lyrics*, it was published partly 'for popularity's sake', a motive strengthened by Elizabeth Barrett's approval of it. The pamphlet held twenty-one poems, a few of which had been published in one form or another in journals, and all of which were retained in the canon. In *1849* all the poems except 'Claret and Tokay' were republished in their original order following the poems from *Dramatic Lyrics* under the general title of *Dramatic Romances and Lyrics*. In *1863* six poems from the original *Dramatic Romances and Lyrics* were put among the 'Romances', thirteen were put in 'Lyrics', and two in 'Men, and Women' (the Appendix to Volume II of the present edition gives details). Generally, revisions after *1845* were slight, the most obvious exception being with 'Saul', which was completed for, and published in, *Men and Women* in 1855 (where it is included in this edition – in 1845 the fragment followed 'Claret and Tokay'). With minor exceptions, none of the poems survives in manuscript, but some knowledge of manuscript readings can be gleaned from Elizabeth Barrett's comments on a number of the poems that she read in manuscript or proof. Of these comments, some are given below; most of them were first published in *New Poems* (1914). The manuscript of these comments is in the Library of Wellesley College, along with the love letters, which allude frequently to the poems of *1845*.

    With one or two possible exceptions, the poems were composed between 1842 and 1845. Though the pamphlet included some of Browning's best and most characteristic work, it attracted little attention when first published. The pamphlet bore a dedication, dated November 1845: 'Inscribed to John Kenyon, Esq., in the hope that a recollection of his own successful *Rhymed Plea for Tolerance* may induce him to admit good-naturedly this humbler prose one of his very sincere friend, R.B.' Kenyon (1784–1856), philanthropist and minor poet, was friend to both Robert Browning and Elizabeth Barrett, and left them £11,000 in his will. The volume Browning refers to was published in 1833. The *1863* and *1868* collections expressed the wish that the redistributed poems might 'obtain the honour of an association with his memory'.

'HOW THEY BROUGHT THE GOOD NEWS FROM GHENT TO AIX'

First published in *Dramatic Romances and Lyrics*, 6 November 1845. In *1863* it was included in 'Lyrics'. After *1845* it was but slightly revised, the two verbal changes being trifling. The poem was probably written late in August 1844 on Browning's second voyage to Italy, despite statements by the poet much later in life that it was written on the first voyage in 1838 'off the African coast'. More accurate seems the neglected remark attributed to Browning by the anonymous author of 'Reminiscences of Mr Browning' in the *Pall Mall Gazette* of 31 December 1889, one that dates the poem in August 1844: 'I was in a sailing vessel slowly making my way from Sicily to Naples in calm weather. I had a good horse at home in my stables, and I thought to myself how much I should like a breezy gallop. As I could not ride on board ship, I determined to enjoy a ride in imagination; so I galloped all through the night with the steed Roland, which brought the goods news to Ghent[*sic*].'

In a letter of 7 March 1884 (*New Letters*, 300) Browning remarked that 'the places mentioned were remembered or guessed at loosely enough'. The poet had twice been in Flanders but the geographical inexactitudes are clear enough: Roland galloped about 120 miles, several more than necessary (or possible?). As Browning pointed out to many inquirers, the journey and situation are not historical. Ghent is in the north-west of modern Belgium, Aix-la-Chapelle (now Aachen) now in Germany near the Belgian and Dutch borders. The other places mentioned are more or less between the two points. There survives an 1889 recording, on an Edison cylinder, of Browning reciting – and having trouble remembering – the poem's opening lines.

3-5] Good speed cried the watch as the east gate undrew;
      Good speed from the wall, to us galloping through.
      The gate shut the porter, the light sank to rest *MS*. (as recorded by Elizabeth
      Barrett).

10 *pique* much discussed. Misspelling of 'peak'? Pommel? A coinage for 'spur' (French *piquer* to spur)?

14 *dawned*] seemed *MS*. (as recorded by Elizabeth Barrett: 'I doubt about "twilight seeming clear". Is it a happy expression?').

55-60] Elizabeth Barrett's comment makes clear that the stanza was extensively revised in MS. where it included (presumably as its fifth line): 'That they saved to have drunk our duke's health in but grieved'. She criticized 'but grieved'.

PICTOR IGNOTUS

First published in *Dramatic Romances and Lyrics*, 6 November 1845. The revised *1849* version in most respects established the final text. In *1863* the poem preceded, with obvious appropriateness, 'Fra Lippo Lippi' and 'Andrea del Sarto' in 'Men, and Women'. It was probably written in Florence late in 1844. Just how sympathetic the speaker is intended to be has been debated: see P. F. Jamieson, 'Browning's *Pictor Ignotus*, Florence, 15—', *Explicator* XI, 1952, Item 8. J. B. Bullen, 'Browning's "Pictor Ignotus" and Vasari's "Life of Fra Bartolommeo di San Marco"', *Review of English Studies* XXIII, 1972, 313-19, convincingly suggests that Browning's model is Fra Bartolommeo (*c*. 1475-1517), described by Vasari as 'of a timid and even cowardly disposition', who opposed some of the new tendencies in art. M. H. Bright, 'Browning's Celebrated Pictor Ignotus', *ELN* XIII, 1976, 192-4, denies Bullen's case; see also the rejoinders of Bullen and Bright, 206-15.

The designation 'Pictor Ignotus' (Latin, 'painter unknown') is used in many art museums. 'Ignotus' also means 'obscure', and the ambiguity is of a kind to appeal to Browning. On the poem see Jack, *Browning's Major Poetry*, 208-13; F. Kaplan, *Miracles of Rare Device*, Wayne State University Press, 1972, 109-15.

1 *youth* probably Raphael (1483-1520), friend, teacher, and pupil of Fra Bartolommeo.

22 *braved* threatened.

23 *O human faces*] Men, women, children *1845*.

27] Ever new hearts made beat and bosoms swell *MS*. (as recorded by Elizabeth Barrett, who adds, 'The construction seems to be entangled a little by this line; and the reader pauses, he clears meaning to himself. Why not clear it for him by writing the line thus, for instance?

      New hearts being made to beat, and breasts to swell.
Or something better which will strike you.').

31 *car* chariot.

33] And thus to reach my home, where Age should greet *MS.* (as recorded by Elizabeth Barrett, who suggests the *1845* reading: Of reaching thus my home, where Age should greet).

34 *not*] as *1845*.

41 *voice* probably, Bullen suggests, that of Savonarola.

47 *Though I stooped*] As asquat *1845*.

48–9 *Shrinking ... enough* In 1498 Bartolommeo was in the convent of San Marco when it was stormed, and its Prior, Savonarola, taken to prison.

50 *These buy and sell our pictures*] These men may buy us, sell us *MS.* (as recorded by Elizabeth Barrett, who adds, 'meaning pictures, by "us". But the reader cannot see it till afterwards, and gets confused.').

67 *travertine* limestone.

THE ITALIAN IN ENGLAND

'Italy in England' was first published in *Dramatic Romances and Lyrics*, 6 November 1845. It was renamed in *1849*, and was included in 'Romances' in *1863*. Revisions after first publication were very slight. Date of composition is uncertain (editors cite Elizabeth Barrett's comment that she had a rough manuscript of the poem on 13 August, but generally neglect the fact that she has the title wrong and is referring to 'England in Italy'). 1845 is, however, the probable date.

The poem is set near Padua, and Browning may have thought of the revolt against the Austrians in northern Italy of 1823. His imagination may also have been stimulated by a Naples revolt in 1844, shortly before he arrived there. Browning's Italian teacher in London was an Italian refugee. Mazzini admired the poem, and his life and personality may indeed have suggested it.

19 *Metternich* reactionary Austrian Chancellor from 1809–48.

75 *duomo* cathedral (Italian).

76 *Tenebrae* a Holy Week service.

122 *I felt his red wet throat distil*] I felt his throat, and had my will *MS.* (as recorded by Elizabeth Barrett, who remarks, 'is not "had my will" a little wrong? – *I would what I would*. There is a weakness in the expression. Is there not?').

THE ENGLISHMAN IN ITALY

'England in Italy' was first published in *Dramatic Romances and Lyrics*, 6 November 1845. It was renamed in *1849*, and in *1863* joined its companion-poem in 'Romances'. After first publication, revision, while fairly extensive, was of little significance.

Browning was on the Sorrento Plain (*Piano*) near Naples early in October 1844, but the date of composition of the poem is uncertain; on 13 August 1845 Elizabeth Barrett had an incomplete version 'unfinished and in a rough state', which lacked the final section added between 13 August and 13 October. Relevant is much of Browning's letter to Elizabeth Barrett of 3 May 1845; so is Shelley's 'Ode to the West Wind'. Elizabeth Barrett commented on the poem in some detail (see *New Poems*, 145–9, from which come the MS. readings cited below).

1 *Fortù* a young girl.

5 *Scirocco* more usually, Sirocco: a hot and dry south wind in autumn.

7–8] While I lull you asleep till he's o'er
    With his black in the skies. *MS*.
Miss Barrett disliked the conjunction of the two contractions, and suggested, as 'more active': 'Till he carries / His black from the skies.'

10 *beads* of the Rosary.

13] 'Twas time, for your long dry autumn. *MS*. (Miss Barrett was disturbed by the rhythm.)

14 *net-worked* The verb is not recorded in *OED*.

34] What was in store. *MS*. (Miss Barrett suggested, for rhythmical reasons, 'What change' or 'What fate'.)

47 *frails* rush-baskets.

51 *blind-rock* hidden rock.

53 *Amalfi* town near Sorrento.

66] Miss Barrett suggested a change for rhythmical reasons, but Browning made none.

69 *Salerno* city a few miles east of Sorrento.

85 *aloe* a genus of plants, including several varieties. Here the spiked shrub or tree is referred to.

87 *love-apple* tomato.

92 *regales* choice dainties.

107 *cheese-ball* not in *OED*. Probably a ball of mozzarella cheese, for which Sorrento is well-known. Possibly, however, Browning means 'chesboll', an obsolete equivalent to 'chibol', a kind of leek or onion, with the word being applied to the bulb of the sweet fennel, much used in salads in Italy.

122 *medlars* trees with small hard fruit, roughly apple-like.

138 *sorbs* service-trees.

140 *orbs* of the strawberry tree, to judge from Browning's letter of 3 May 1845 in which he misquotes Shelley, *Marenghi* xiii: 'When one should find those globes of deep red gold – Which in the woods the strawberry-tree doth bear, Suspended in their emerald atmosphere.'

157 *fume-weed* not in *OED*. Fumitory (common European herb)?

162 *lentisks* mastic trees, small evergreens.

171 *Calvano* Browning thought that he might have had the name wrong. There is a Vico Alvano, a small mountain in the area, and 'Calvano' probably represents a local pronunciation Browning had heard (he alludes to 'Monte Calvano' in his letter of 3 May 1845).

177 *the terrible crystal* of one of the Ptolemaic spheres. Ezekiel i 22.

183] 'For' was added after Miss Barrett had criticized the line's rhythm.

189–90] How the soft plains they look on and love so
    As they would pretend *MS*.

198] Browning added Miss Barrett's suggested 'As'.

199 *Galli* three islands in the Gulf of Salerno. Browning visited them on 4 October. They are said to be the islands from which the Sirens tempted Odysseus (*Odyssey* XII–XIII); see *Aeneid* V, 864. Browning follows others, Spenser for instance, in having five Sirens.

200] Years cannot sever. *MS*.

201 *sister* Vivaro Rock, half-way between the Galli and the mainland.

205 *small one* Isca Rock, just off-shore.

213] Oh to sail round them, close over *MS*.

215 *glassy*] sea *MS*. (Miss Barrett suggested 'ocean'.)

219]   The square black tower on the largest. *MS*.

turret   the remains of a fourteenth-century tower on the largest of the Galli, La Praia.

230]   'He' was added at Miss Barrett's suggestion.

250–55   *Feast | Of the Rosary's Virgin … Dominican*   feast held on the first Sunday in October to celebrate the anniversary of the Turkish defeat at Lepanto on 7 October 1571. Saint Dominic is said to have instituted the devotion of the Rosary. The Feast occurred while Browning was in Sorrento in 1844.

257   *dizened*   bedizened, festooned.

265   *Bellini … Auber*   Italian composer (1801–35), and French composer (1782–1871).

269   *Image*   that of the Virgin.

272   *stomp*   'Used by Browning (to obtain a rime) for *stump* or *stamp*' (*OED*). In North America, the word is, however, in frequent use.

289   *Corn-laws*   Browning rarely mentions contemporary politics directly. Here he condemns the Laws (repealed in June 1846, and which were being much discussed in autumn 1845) which by restricting the import of corn made bread expensive.

THE LOST LEADER

First published in *Dramatic Romances and Lyrics*, 6 November 1845. It was included in 'Lyrics' in *1863*. After 1845 Browning made a few revisions, mostly to the second section. Date of composition is unknown. In a letter of 24 February 1875 (Hood, *Letters*, 166–7), Browning wrote: 'I *did* in my hasty youth presume to use the great and venerable personality of Wordsworth as a sort of painter's model; one from which this or the other particular feature may be selected and turned to account: had I intended more, above all, such a boldness as portraying the entire man, I should not have talked about "handfuls of silver and bits of ribbon". These never influenced the change of politics in the great poet; whose defection, nevertheless, accompanied as it was by a regular face-about of his special party, was to my juvenile apprehension, and even mature consideration, an event to deplore.' There are similar reflections in a letter of 7 September 1875 (Orr, *Life*, 123). Browning had met Wordsworth; he was distressed at Wordsworth's increasing conservatism, one given a kind of symbolic form in his acceptance of a civil-list pension in October 1842, and the Laureateship on 4 April 1843. The poem's attitude towards Wordsworth is rather like Shelley's in his sonnet 'To Wordsworth' (1816), and, as DeVane and others have suggested, like Pym's (in *Strafford* V. ii) towards Wentworth (Strafford).

1–2   *handful of silver … riband*   glancing at Judas's thirty pieces of silver, and at Wordsworth's pension and Laureateship.

18   *inspirit*]   excite *1845*.

22   *more declined, one more*]   unaccepted, one *1845*.

30   *Menace our heart*]   Strike our face hard *1845*; Aim at our heart *1849*.
   master]   shatter *1845*; pierce through *1849*.

THE LOST MISTRESS

First published in *Dramatic Romances and Lyrics*, 6 November 1845. In *1863* it was included in 'Lyrics'. It was probably written in 1845 after Browning had declared himself too precipitately to Elizabeth Barrett. She found the fourth stanza difficult in manuscript and after publication, and Browning revised it for *1849*. Other revisions were trifling.

13–16]   For though no glance of the eyes so black
                   But I keep with heart's endeavour, –
              If you only wish the snowdrops back
                   That shall stay in my soul for ever! – *1845*.

HOME–THOUGHTS, FROM ABROAD

First published in *Dramatic Romances and Lyrics*, 6 November 1845, where it was the first part of a three-part poem entitled 'Home-Thoughts, from Abroad'; none of the parts had another title. In *1849* this poem, slightly revised, was separated from 'Here's to Nelson's Memory' and 'Home-Thoughts, from the Sea'. In a letter of 4 October 1845, Miss Barrett had disapproved of the yoking (Browning promised to devise titles), and the manuscript of this poem (now in the Pierpont Morgan Library – for a photograph of the *MS.*, see *BNL* 3, 1969, 33) suggests that the three poems were not originally thought of as one anyway. In *1863* the poem was included in 'Lyrics'. The date of composition is unknown. Browning's Italian visit of 1838 was a summer visit, that of 1844 an autumn one.

3   *whoever*]   who *MS.*, 1845.
7   *orchard*]   fruit-tree *MS.*
17   *look*]   are *MS.*, *1845*.

HOME–THOUGHTS, FROM THE SEA

First published in *Dramatic Romances and Lyrics*, 6 November 1845, as the untitled third part of 'Home-Thoughts, from Abroad'. In *1849* it was separated from the other parts and given its title. In *1863* it was included in 'Lyrics'. Revisions were slight. The date of composition is unknown. Griffin and Minchin (*Life*, 127) suggested 27 April 1838 on the first voyage to Italy, presumably on the evidence of a reference in Browning's diary (the leaf is now in the University of Toronto Library) to Cape Saint Vincent as being sixteen miles to the north-west at noon on that date. The dating was challenged by Kenyon (Centenary Edition III, xxi) and rejected by DeVane (*Handbook*, 165); the poem may well, like 'Here's to Nelson's Memory', belong to the second voyage to Italy in 1844.

1   *Nobly, nobly*]   Nobly *1845*.
    Cape Saint Vincent   at the south-west point of Portugal. Scene of Nelson's victory in 1797.
2   *Cadiz Bay*   off south-west Spain.
3   *Trafalgar*   cape in southern Spain; scene of Nelson's greatest victory (1805) and death.
7   *While Jove's planet rises yonder, silent*]   Yonder where Jove's planet rises silent *1845*.
    Jove's planet   Jupiter.

THE BISHOP ORDERS HIS TOMB AT SAINT PRAXED'S CHURCH

Entitled 'The Tomb at Saint Praxed's', the poem first appeared in *Hood's Magazine* III, March 1845, 237–9, and then in *Dramatic Romances and Lyrics*, 6 November 1845, the latter printing establishing the text verbally. The poem was retitled in *1849*, and in *1863* it was included in 'Men, and Women' immediately before 'Bishop Blougram's Apology'.

The Basilica of Santa Prassede is near Maria Maggiore in Rome, and is named after the second-century virgin saint who gave her wealth to the poor and the Church. Browning first visited it in October 1844, and the poem was sent to *Hood's* on 18 February 1845. It is generally dated in the winter of 1844–5, but it may well antedate Browning's second visit to Italy in the autumn of 1844: (a) the actual church is – in a way not characteristic of Browning – very different in detail and total effect from the one in the poem; (b) Browning's covering letter to *Hood's* may imply an earlier date: 'I pick it out as being a pet of mine, and just the thing for the time – what with the Oxford business [the Tractarian Movement]'; (c) L. Stevenson, 'The Pertinacious Victorian Poets', *TQ* XXI, 1952, 241, suggested, attractively, that Browning may have taken as model for his Bishop the uncle of the main model for the Duke of Ferrara of 'My Last Duchess', Cardinal Ippolito d'Este the Younger. (Other models have been proposed, most notably one in the *Vita di Vespasiano Gonzaga* by Ireneo Affò [1780] – see J. D. Rea, '"My Last Duchess"', *SP* XXIX, 1932, 120–22). Various models for the tomb have been suggested, but the poem's irony almost demands that there be none since the Bishop's 'orders' were clearly not going to be obeyed. B. Melchiori suggests that Browning is indebted for many details in his Church to that important book for him, Gerard de Lairesse's *The Art of Painting in All its Branches*, 1778 (see *Browning's Poetry of Reticence*, 20–39).

Ruskin's praise of the poem (in *Modern Painters* IV, xx, 34) is well known: 'I know no other piece of modern English, prose or poetry, in which there is so much told, as in these lines, of the Renaissance spirit, – its worldliness, inconsistency, pride, hypocrisy, ignorance of itself, love of art, of luxury, and of good Latin. It is nearly all that I said of the central Renaissance in thirty pages of the *Stones of Venice* put into as many lines, Browning's being also the antecedent work.' The poem was a favourite of Elizabeth Barrett's and has been one for most readers. It has been exhaustively discussed. Some treatments are: R. A. Greenberg, 'Ruskin, Pugin, and the Contemporary Context of "The Bishop Orders His Tomb"', *PMLA* LXXXIV, 1969, 1588–94; King, *The Bow and the Lyre*, 52–75; G. M. Laws, Jr, 'Death and Browning's Dying Bishop', in *Romantic and Victorian*, ed. W. P. Elledge and R. L. Hoffman, Fairleigh Dickinson University Press, 1971, 318–28; L. Poston, 'Ritual in "The Bishop Orders His Tomb"', *VNL* 17, 1960, 27–8.

1   *Vanity, saith the preacher, vanity*   'Vanity of vanities, saith the Preacher, vanity of vanities; all is vanity' (Ecclesiastes i 2).

17   *cozened*   tricked.
   cozened me]   came me in *Hood's*. (Miss Barrett suggested the phrase be changed.)
18–19   For a shrewd snatch out of the corner south
       To grace his carrion with, God curse the same! *Hood's*.

21   *epistle-side*   the right side (facing the altar), from which the Epistle is read during Mass.

23   *airy dome*   The real Church has two small domes, neither 'airy'.

25   *basalt*   a black stone.

26   *tabernacle*   canopy over a tomb.

26–7 *tabernacle . . . nine columns* Compare the tabernacle ordered of Moses by the Lord (Exodus xxv–xxvii, and especially xxvi 30–37). Nine pillars are there ordered for the veil and hanging.

31 *onion-stone* translating the Italian *cipollino*: a cheap marble, so-called because it peels easily.

41 *frail* basket.

42 *lapis lazuli* semi-precious blue stone.

43 *Jew's head* presumably the head of John the Baptist.

46 *Frascati* beautiful town near Rome.

48–9 *God the Father's globe . . . Jesu Church* Rome's Chiesa del Gesù (completed 1575) has an altar (completed 1697) with a representation of the Trinity in which an angel, not God, holds a huge globe of lapis lazuli.

51 *Swift as a weaver's shuttle fleet our years* 'My days are swifter than a weaver's shuttle, and are spent without hope' (Job vii 6).

52 *Man goeth to the grave, and where is he?* 'so he that goeth down to the grave shall come up no more' (Job vii 9); 'man giveth up the ghost, and where is he?' (Job xiv 10).

54 *antique-black* translating *nero antico*: a black stone, more valuable than basalt.

57 *Pans* Pan, god of fields and forests, and often licentious.

   wot know (archaism).

58 *tripod, thyrsus* three-legged stool associated with priestesses of Apollo; and staff of Dionysus (Bacchus), god of wine, orgies, fertility, and other good things.

60 *glory* halo.

62 *tables* tablets. Exodus xxiv–xxxvi.

65 *revel down* squander.

66 *travertine* limestone.

68 *jasper* kind of quartz (the wall of the Heavenly City is made of it).

70 *bath* large bathing pool.

77 *Tully* Marcus Tullius Cicero (106–43 B.C.), Roman master of rhetoric.

79 *Ulpian* Domitius Ulpianus (170–228), a later and inferior writer.

87 *crook* Bishop's pastoral staff. In an obsolete usage the word also means 'piece of trickery'.

89 *mortcloth* pall.

95 *Saint Praxed at his sermon on the mount* Compare line 59. The Bishop's mind is here confused; he mixes the female Saint Praxed with Christ. There may also be a hint that the Bishop is unaware that his Church's saint is female. Browning wrote that 'the blunder as to the sermon is the result of the dying man's haziness; he would not reveal himself as he does but for that'. Nevertheless, the odd critic still accuses Browning, rather than the Bishop, of an error here – one of the critical problems for a reader of Browning is knowing always when errors are dramatic (the speaker's) and when not (the poet's).

99 *Elucescebat* 'He was illustrious'; Ciceronian Latin would be *elucebat*.

101 *Evil and brief hath been my pilgrimage* 'The days of the years of my pilgrimage are an hundred and thirty years: few and evil have the days of the years of my life been' (Genesis xlvii 9).

106–8] *not in Hood's.*

108 *vizor and a Term* mask and a pedestal bust.

109 *lynx* Lynxes frequently attend Dionysus.

111 *entablature* a misuse of the word – for 'entablement' (platform supporting a statue)?

116 *Gritstone* cheap sandstone.

GARDEN FANCIES

The two poems were first published in *Hood's Magazine* II, July 1844, 45–8. Revised versions appeared in *Dramatic Romances and Lyrics*, 6 November 1845, where the final text is virtually established. In *1863* the poems were included in 'Lyrics'; in that edition only, 'Soliloquy of the Spanish Cloister' became a third part. Both poems were probably composed shortly before initial publication.

I *The Flower's Name*

It has been suggested that the poem celebrates Browning's mother's garden at Hatcham, New Cross. On the poem, see Cook, *Browning's Lyrics*, 89–91.

10 *box* shrub.

14 *I will never think that*] Think will I never *1844–5*.

15 *you*] *not in 1844–5*.

16] But this – so surely this met her eye! *1844*. (Miss Barrett disliked the singular 'eye'.)

18 *as*] *not in 1844*.

20 *Spanish name* perhaps *azucena*, a white lily traditionally used in Renaissance Spanish literature in praising lady-loves.

33 *look that you*] look you *1844*. (Miss Barrett suggested the change.)

36 *Mind, the shut pink*] Mind the pink shut *1844*; Mind that the pink *1845*. (Miss Barrett disliked the 'clogged' line.)

48 *you are not*] are you *1844*. (Miss Barrett suggested the affirmative.)

II *Sibrandus Schafnaburgensis*

Sibrandus of Aschafenburg is mentioned in Wanley's *Wonders of the Little World* (1678), a work that profoundly influenced Browning. The poem is based on fact.

4 *cumber*] bother *1844–5*.

7 *matin-prime* early morning.

10 *arbute and laurustine* evergreen shrubs.

14 *Stonehenge* the place of huge stones near Salisbury.

19 *pont-levis* drawbridge.

30 *Chablis* French white wine.

32 *Rabelais* The sixteenth-century French humanist was a Browning favourite.

38–9 *de profundis, accentibus laetis, / Cantate!* 'From the depths, in happy accents, sing!' (Latin). A Browning invention? 'Out of the depths have I cried unto thee, O Lord' (Psalm cxxx 1).

50 *toused* pulled roughly about (obsolete).

52 *right of trover* finder's right to keep a treasure.

61 *John Knox* the puritanical Scottish religious leader (1505–72).

67 *sufficit* 'enough' (Latin).

THE LABORATORY

First published in *Hood's Magazine* I, June 1844, 513–14, and revised for *Dramatic Romances and Lyrics*, 6 November 1845, with 'The Confessional' as its companion under the general title of 'France and Spain'. After *1845* Browning made further verbal changes. In *1849* the two poems were separated; in *1863* the poem was included in 'Lyrics'.

Browning's heroine may be based on the famous seventeenth-century poisoner, the Marquise de Brinvilliers (whose lover, rumour had it, died when his mask fell off as he was preparing poison). The date of composition is unknown. The poem was the subject of Rossetti's first water-colour, which had as title Browning's fourth line.

Ancien Régime The term ('Old Order') used with reference to pre-Revolution France.

1] Now that I have tied thy glass mask on tightly, *1844*. (Miss Barrett criticized the poem's rhythms, especially in the opening lines.)
23 *pastile* roll of paste, burned for perfume.
29 *minion* an unusual use of the word; here, 'delicate person'.
31 *masculine*] *1845, 1863–8*; strong, great *1844, 1849*. (Miss Barrett criticized the 'perplexed' rhythm.)
47 *it brings*] there springs *1844*. (The expression seemed 'clogged' and 'forced' to Miss Barrett.)

THE CONFESSIONAL

First published in *Dramatic Romances and Lyrics*, 6 November 1845, under the general title of 'France and Spain' with 'The Laboratory'. Subsequent revisions were minor. In *1849* it was separated from its earlier companion; it was included in 'Lyrics' in *1863*. The date of composition is unknown.

44 *seemed*] was *MS*. (as recorded by Miss Barrett, who suggested the change).
66] And lo! – there, smiled the father's face. *MS*. (as recorded by Miss Barrett, who criticized a lack of realism).
68 *stapled* with the iron collar of the garotte.

THE FLIGHT OF THE DUCHESS

The first nine sections of the poem were published, unnumbered, in *Hood's Magazine* III, April 1845, 313–18, and were reprinted, virtually unchanged, with the added sections in *Dramatic Romances and Lyrics*, 6 November 1845. In *1863* the poem was included in 'Romances'. After *1845* revisions were trifling – DeVane (*Handbook*, 172) errs in stating that eleven lines were lost, since none was lost – or found.

The evidence for dates of composition is sketchy and inconclusive; for detailed conjecture, see DeVane, *Handbook*, 172–6. Browning may have begun the poem as early as 1842, but the bulk of it was almost certainly written in 1845. Browning wrote in 1883 that the idea of the poem grew out of a line he heard as a boy, 'Following the Queen of the Gypsies, O!' He originally conceived of the poem as one focussing on 'the Gypsy's description of the life the Lady was to lead with her future Gypsy lover' (see his letter to Elizabeth Barrett of 25 July 1845). Interrupted in writing, Browning lost the feel of his poem, and gave the fragment to *Hood's*. Later, a remark that 'The deer had already to break the ice in the pond' stimulated Browning's imagination in another direction.

E. Snyder and F. Palmer, Jr, 'New Light on the Brownings', *Quarterly Review* CCLXIX, 1937, 48–63, drew attention to Elizabeth Barrett's criticisms of the poem (as yet unpublished, the manuscript is in the Library of Wellesley College, along with those on which Kenyon in *New Poems* based his inaccurate transcripts of Miss Barrett's comments on other of the *Dramatic Romances and Lyrics*). Snyder and Palmer exaggerated, but they made clear that Elizabeth Barrett's comments were detailed and voluminous and that Browning responded by revising his earlier readings to accommodate most of her suggestions. Snyder and Palmer also suggested that the poem had unusual biographical significance: that Browning used the poem, casting Elizabeth Barrett in the role of the Duchess, to plead indirectly with her to flee her father. Independently, F. M. Smith argued that same point in *SP* XXXIX, 1942, 102–17 and 693–5. The argument has been generally accepted as probably valid, and is not seriously affected by doubts about dates of writing – that Browning may have used the poem as suggested does not necessarily imply that he wrote it for that reason. What is sure is that the poem greatly affected Elizabeth Barrett: it is referred to more often than any other poem in the love letters, and her comments in the Wellesley MS. are unusually detailed. It is also sure that the lady imperilled by a dastardly male is common in Browning's works: the Duke of this poem may, for instance, have had a relative in Ferrara or Arezzo. It has been suggested that Browning owes a general debt to Thomas Hood's comic puns and to Barham's *Ingoldsby Legends* (First Series, 1840).

12   *chase*   hunting-ground.
51   *bantling*   infant.
76   *tannage*   tanning.
78   *merlin*   kind of hawk.
80   *falcon-lanner*   long-tailed hawk.
86   *Moldavia*   wine from the area, Moldavia, to the north of Romania.
87   *Cotnar*   Cotnari is a Moldavian village and wine-centre.
88   *ropy*   sticky, stringy.
119   *lathy*   lath-like, long and thin.
130   *urochs ... buffle*   Lithuanian bison ... buffalo.
201   *wheel-work*   mechanical.
217–19   *stag ... pond*   The remark, Browning said, that prompted him to complete the poem was that the deer had already to break the ice in the pond.
225–7]   Finding the calendar bade him be hearty, / Did resolve on a hunting party – *MS.* (as recorded by Elizabeth Barrett, who commented: 'Does not that first line seem as if it were meditating a rhyme for the second? ... there is something forced in the expression, or appears to *me* to be so. And then the second line ... is it not too short to the ear?').
229]   Oh, and old books, they knew the way of it!   *MS.* (as recorded by Elizabeth Barrett, who said she liked the abruptness, but that people would complain of obscurity – Browning had changed 'taught' to 'knew', and Elizabeth Barrett suggested the 'showed' that Browning adopted).
238   *Saint Hubert*   patron saint of hunting.
240   *jerkin*   close-fitting jacket.
243   *trunk-hose*   full breeches extending from waist to middle of thigh.
244]   What meant a hat if it had no rims on *MS.* (as recorded by Elizabeth Barrett, who criticized 'What meant' and 'rims on').
246   *shallop*   small open boat.
249   *Venerers, Prickers and Verderers*   hunters (earliest recorded usage in *OED*), riders, and game wardens.
253   *flap-hats and buff-coats and jack-boots*   hats with flaps or a flapping brim, and coats of buff-leather, and heavy top-boots reaching above the knee.
263   *wind a mort*   sound a call to indicate the killing of game.
       at siege   gone to ground (idiom unrecorded in *OED*).
264   *jennet*   small Spanish horse.
273   *sealed*   rendered blind, or, more probably, a misspelling of 'seeled': stitched up (falconry term).

293 *sewer* attendant, steward.

302 *tire-woman* lady's maid.

322 *fifty-part canon* Browning, in a letter of 28 December 1886, wrote: '"A canon", in music, is a piece wherein the subject is repeated – in various keys: and being strictly obeyed in the repetition, becomes the "Canon" – the imperative *law* – to what follows. Fifty of such parts would be indeed a notable peal: to manage three is enough of an achievement for a good musician.'

329 *paladin* paragon of knighthood.

365 *snaffle* horse-bit.

371 *winkle* periwinkle.

420 *pine-marten* weasel-like animal of northern forests.

439 *helicat* hell-cat (not recorded in *OED*).

454 *imps* ingrafts feathers in.

455 *hernshaw* heron.

458 *fernshaw* fern thicket.

463 *curveter* leaping horse (*OED*: 'nonce-word').

480 *band-roll* banderole: here, inscribed ribbon (form of word not in *OED*).
 tomans Persian coins.

533 *gor-crow* carrion (common) crow.

535 *banning* cursing.

608–41 Robert Browning to Elizabeth Barrett?

743 *palfrey* saddle-horse.

788 *clink the cannikin* 'And let me the canikin clink, clink' (*Othello* II. 3.71). A cannikin is a small drinking vessel.

793 *Carib* Indian of the *West* Indies (geographical confusion).

794 *feloness* recorded by *OED* as 'rare'; probably a nonce-word.

830 *fucus . . . ceruse* brown algae . . . white lead used as pigment.

839 *Druids* ancient Celtic priests.

864 *morion* helmet.

865 *hauberk* coat of mail.

872 *It's a long lane that knows no turnings* proverbial.

884 *Methusalem* Methuselah lived to be 969 (Genesis v 27), but it is not known that he begat Saul.

907 *Smooth Jacob still robs homely Esau* Genesis xxv 31–4. Esau sold his birth-right for a mess of pottage. 'Smooth' – clean-shaven (Esau was hairy).

910 *Orson* In the old French romance, the twin of Valentine was born in the woods and brought up like a bear. Called 'the Wild Man of the Forest', he was ultimately reclaimed by Valentine.

914–15 *throwing| Pearls before swine* 'neither cast ye your pearls before swine' (Matthew vii 6).

EARTH'S IMMORTALITIES

The two poems, untitled, were first published in *Dramatic Romances and Lyrics*, 6 November 1845. In *1849* the subtitles (or speakers' designations) were given. In *1863* 'Earth's Immortalities' was put in 'Lyrics'. Browning made no verbal changes in the poems. The date of composition is unknown, but DeVane (*Handbook*, 176–7) suggests that the former may have been prompted by Browning's visit to Shelley's grave in the autumn of 1844, and that the first line of 'Love' suggests a dating of December 1844. Elizabeth Barrett called them 'new' (new to her?) on 29 October 1845. On the poem, see Cook, *Browning's Lyrics*, 93–7.

Fame 4   *osier rods*   willow branches.
Love 2   In a letter of 22 February 1889, Browning called the refrain 'a mournful comment on the short duration of the conventional "For Ever!"'

SONG

First published in *Dramatic Romances and Lyrics*, 6 November 1845; in *1863* it was included in 'Lyrics'. Revisions were slight. Date of composition is unknown. Elizabeth Barrett praised it as 'new' (new to her?) on 29 October 1845.

5   *last fairest*]   one last *1845*.

THE BOY AND THE ANGEL

First published in *Hood's Magazine* II, August 1844, 140–42. Elizabeth Barrett made detailed criticisms of it, and the poem was considerably revised when reprinted in *Dramatic Romances and Lyrics*, 6 November 1845. With further revisions, it was included in 'Romances' in *1863*, where the final text was virtually established. Date of composition is unknown – perhaps Easter 1844? The story appears to be Browning's invention, and no Theocrite has been Pope.

1]   Morning, noon, eve, and night, *1844*. (The change was suggested by Miss Barrett.)
13   *well as*]   not in *1844*. (The change was suggested by Miss Barrett.)
24   *Now brings the*]   Brings one *1844*. (Miss Barrett criticized the couplet.)
25   *Gabriel*   an archangel; 'Chief of the angelic guards' in *Paradise Lost*.
27   *in flesh*]   not in *1844*. (Miss Barrett criticized the couplet's short lines.)
28   *Lived there*]   not in *1844*.
36   *on earth*]   not in *1844*.
37–8]   not in *1844–5*.
46   *disguise*]   not in *1844*. (Miss Barrett criticized the line.)
48   *Saint Peter's*]   the *1844*.
51   *dight*   dressed.
55–8]   not in *1844*.
62   *on his sight*]   in *1844*. (Miss Barrett wondered if *in* was clear.)
63–4]   not in *1844*.
66]   Vainly hast thou lived many a year; *1844*.
67–8]   not in *1844*.
71–4]   Be again the boy all curled;
       I will finish with the world.' *1844*.
(Miss Barrett criticized the couplet and suggested a need for expansion.)
76   *A new Pope*]   Gabriel *1844*.

MEETING AT NIGHT and PARTING AT MORNING

First published in *Dramatic Romances and Lyrics*, 6 November 1845, entitled 'I. Night', and 'II. Morning', under the general title 'Night and Morning'. The poems were given their final separate titles in *1849*, and in *1863* both poems were grouped in 'Lyrics'. Revisions were minor. Date of composition is unknown. Elizabeth Barrett called them 'new' (new to her?) in her letter of 29 October 1845. In a letter of 22 February 1889 replying to a question about the final line of 'Parting at Morning',

Browning wrote: 'it is *his* confession of how fleeting is the belief (implied in the first part) that such raptures are self-sufficient and enduring – as for the time they appear'. In line 3 of the latter poem, the 'him' is, if Browning interprets his work correctly, the sun. On the poems, see J. D. Boyd, in *BSN* V, No. 3, 1975, 14–20; Cook, *Browning's Lyrics*, 99–103; R. W. Condee, in *Explicator* XII, 1954, Item 23; K. Kroeber, in *VP* III, 1965, 101–7; F. R. Leavis, in *Scrutiny* XIII, 1945, 130–31, reprinted in *The Living Principle*, Oxford University Press, 1975, 120–22; J. McNally, in *VP* V, 1967, 219–24.

NATIONALITY IN DRINKS

The first two parts of the final poem were in the same number of *Hood's Magazine* I, June 1844, 525, called 'Claret and Tokay'. They were reprinted in *Dramatic Romances and Lyrics*, 6 November 1845, where the third part, 'Here's to Nelson's Memory', was first published as the untitled second part of 'Home-Thoughts, from Abroad'. All three parts were dropped completely in *1849*, probably, to some extent at least, because of Mrs Browning's reservations. The three parts finally came together in 'Lyrics' in *1863* under the final title, with subtitles 'Claret' 'Tokay', and 'Beer' ('Nelson'). In *1868* the subtitles were dropped. Revisions were very minor. Claret is a dry red Bordeaux wine, and Tokay is a sweet, strong, fuller-bodied Hungarian. See E. C. McAleer in *Explicator* XX, 1961, Item 34.

14 *pygmy castle-warder* figure on the label of a Tokay bottle?

18 *Drouth* drought.

19 *flap-hat* hat with flaps or a flapping brim.

tosspot drunkard.

22 *Buda* the old capital of Hungary (Budapest dates from 1873).

28 *Sir Ausbruch*] from Ausbruch *1844–5*. Browning corrects an error: Ausbruch is not a place, but indicates high quality.

30 *second time* Browning passed Cape Trafalgar for the second time in late August 1844 on his second voyage to Italy. Trafalgar in 1805 saw Nelson's greatest victory and his death.

39 *Greenwich* east of London on the Thames. Nelson relics, including two coats, neither of them with a tarred shoulder, were at Greenwich Hospital. The coat Nelson wore on the day he was killed was presented to the Hospital about 1 August 1845. Nelson lost his right arm in 1797. The story here is not apparently confirmed elsewhere. See J. F. Loucks in *SBHC* IV, Fall 1976, 71–2.

[SAUL

The first nine sections of the poem followed 'Nationality in Drinks' in *1845*. The poem is printed in *Men and Women* in this edition.]

TIME'S REVENGES

First published in *Dramatic Romances and Lyrics*, 6 November 1845. In *1863* it was included in 'Romances'. Apart from the couplet deleted in *1849*, revisions were minor, and were mainly prompted by Elizabeth Barrett's reservations. Date of composition is unknown; 1845 is as likely as any. The title alludes to *Twelfth Night* V. 1.385; 'And thus the whirligig of time brings in his revenges.'

1   *Friend*   Browning, it has been suggested, may have been thinking of Domett.

7   *does himself though*]   does though *MS.* (as recorded by Miss Barrett, who suggested the change).

10]   I should just turn round nor ope an eye *MS.* (as recorded by Miss Barrett, who disliked the line, and 'lived to try' in line 9).

22   *Saint Paul's*   the London cathedral.

27   *head aches*   Browning suffered often from headaches.

46   *Florentine*   Dante.

54ₐ5]   As all my genius, all my learning / Leave me, where there's no returning, *1845* (Miss Barrett thought the second line 'somewhat weak and indefinite'). DeVane (*Handbook*, 180) errs in saying that two new lines were substituted.

63]   And purchase her the dear invite *MS.* (as recorded by Miss Barrett, who protested 'zealously' against the vulgarism).

THE GLOVE

First published in *Dramatic Romances and Lyrics*, 6 November 1845. In *1863* it was included in 'Romances'. Revisions were minor (DeVane, *Handbook*, 181, errs in stating that *1849* added two lines, and in his line-count). The poem was probably written in the summer of 1845. It is based on an old story, but the particular version behind the poem is Leigh Hunt's brief ballad, 'The Glove and the Lions' (1836), a version in which the lady's vanity is rewarded by a royally approved glove in the face. In Browning's poem, the twist is all Browning's. DeVane argues other debts (see *Handbook*, 181-5, and *Browning's "Parleyings"*, 83-91).

Peter Ronsard loquitur   Latin: 'Peter Ronsard speaks'. Ronsard (1524-85) was the leading French court poet of his time.

1   *Francis*   Francis I was King of France 1515-47.

7   *peace*   that of 1538-43.

12   *Naso*   Publius Ovidius Naso (Ovid), Roman poet.

13-14   *joys . . . Ixions*   Ixion (see Browning's poem of 1883) made love to a cloud, thinking it Hera, and Zeus then bound him for ever to a turning wheel of fire.

23   *bedizen*   deck.

25   *De Lorge*   Jacques de Montgomery, sire de Lorges (died 1562).

32   *Bluebeard*   the sobriquet of the notorious mass-murderer.

34   *scarab*   large black beetle.

45   *Clement Marot*   court poet (1496-1544) and translator of the Psalms under Francis I: reputed author of the motto of *Pauline*.

50   *Illum Juda Leonem de Tribu*   Latin: 'behold, the lion of the tribe of Judah' (Revelation v 5).

82   *Marignan*   battle of 1515, near Milan, won by Francis I.
    pardie!   by God!

96   *Kaffir*   Kaffirs are known for their skill as lion-hunters in Africa.

101-2   *'twas mere vanity, / Not love, set that task to humanity*   'No love', quoth he, 'but vanity, sets love a task like that' (Hunt, 'The Glove and the Lions', 24).

162   *Nemean*   Heracles killed the famed Nemean lion.

169   *maugre*   in spite of (archaism).

189   *Venienti occurrite morbo!*   'Meet the disease at its first stage!' (Persius, *Satires* III, 64).

190   *theorbo*   a large kind of lute.

Christmas-Eve and Easter-Day

The volume, the only one published in the first nine years of Browning's marriage, and only the second published at publisher's risk, appeared on 1 April (Easter Monday) 1850. Revisions for later collected editions were extensive, but few are of major significance. The printers' manuscript is in the Forster and Dyce Collection of the Victoria and Albert Museum Library. The poems were written in Florence in the few months preceding publication; the first reference to the 'new poem' is Mrs Browning's on 9 January 1850.

The poems are in some ways prompted by the death of Browning's pious mother in March 1849, the birth of his son in the same month, and the strong religious convictions of his wife, who, like his mother, was a passionate Dissenter. It seems reasonable to assume that Browning is working out his own religious beliefs in the poems, after a long period in which those beliefs had been far from settled; and Browning speaks here more directly (as his wife had urged him to do) than is customary. While, however, the religious views of the 'I' and the poet bear close resemblances, they are not identical: as Mrs Browning pointed out, for instance, the 'I' of 'Easter-Day' is more ascetic than her husband. Elizabeth Barrett's first letter of 15 August 1846 may have influenced 'Christmas-Eve'; relevant, for instance, are these remarks: 'Well – there is enough to dissent from among the dissenters . . . you feel moreover bigotry and ignorance pressing on you on all sides, till you gasp for breath like one strangled – But better this, even, than what is elsewhere . . . Public and social prayer is right and desirable – and I would prefer, as a matter of custom, to pray in one of those chapels, where the minister is simple-minded and not controversial . . . The Unitarians seem to me to throw over what is most beautiful in the Christian Doctrine; but the Formulists, on the other side, stir up a dust, in which it appears excusable not to see. When the veil of the body falls, how shall we look into each other's faces, astonished, . . . after one glance at God's!' Probably, too, incidents and people of the York Street Chapel that Browning had attended contributed something to the Zion Chapel of 'Christmas-Eve'; its minister, George Clayton, had, for example, infuriated the young Browning. Clayton, however, was a sophisticated man, and there is no reason to doubt the essential truth in Browning's insistence that the incidents were all imaginary – 'save the lunar rainbow – I saw that'. Browning had almost certainly read Strauss's *Das Leben Jesu* in the 1846 translation of Marian Evans (George Eliot), and its arguments lie behind the Göttingen sections of 'Christmas-Eve'.

Two hundred copies of the volume sold in the first two weeks, but most of the rest were remaindered and were still being sold in the 1860s.

Essays useful for background are DeVane, *Handbook*, 194–205; J. Maynard, 'Robert Browning's Evangelical Heritage', *BIS* III, 1975, 1–16; and W. O. Raymond, 'Browning and Higher Criticism', in his *The Infinite Moment*, 19–51. See also Collins, *Robert Browning's Moral-Aesthetic Theory*, 93–113; Drew, *Poetry of Browning*, 201–12; P. J. Guskin, 'Ambiguities in the Structure and Meaning of Browning's *Christmas-Eve*', *VP* IV, 1966, 21–8.

CHRISTMAS-EVE

17 *Six . . . three*] Four . . . two *MS.*, *1850–88*. (Browning made the change for the second impression of the final collected edition.)

17 *Six feet long by three feet wide* probably a hit at Wordsworth's notorious couplet: 'I've measured it from side to side: / 'Tis three feet long, and two feet wide' (*The Thorn*, iii).

46   *Lot . . . Gomorrah behind him*   Genesis xix 15–29.

70   *pattens*   clogs.

73   *rest*   lance-support on medieval armour.

81   *Penitent Thief*   the one who suffered with Christ at the Crucifixion; Luke xxiii 40–43.

84   *inner light*   the guiding special knowledge believed in by many Dissenters.

89   *Gallio*   indifferent person (Acts xviii 17).

92   *tally-ho*   cry to urge on hounds.

102   *Saint John's Candlestick*   Saint John used seven candlesticks to represent the 'seven churches which are in Asia' (Revelation i 12–20).

105   *Grand-Inquisitor*   of the Spanish Inquisition.

107   *You are the men, and wisdom shall die with you*   'No doubt but ye are the people, and wisdom shall die with you' (Job xii 2).

108   *old Seven Churches*   Revelation i 20.

118   *the laws . . . Founder*   Matthew xxii gives the Parable of the Feast.

120   *vestiment*   vestment. See Matthew xxii 11–13.

122   *quickliest*   archaic, and characteristic Browning, superlative.

132   *pentacle*   five-pointed star, often having supposed occult significance.

133   *conventicle*   gathering of Dissenters.

138   *weather*   punning on 'wether'.

143   *pig*   ingot.

147   *Sibyl*   classical prophetess.

157   *in severance*   disconnected.

170   *dew of Hermon*   'As the dew of Hermon, and as the dew that descended upon the mountains of Zion' (Psalm cxxxiii 3).

216–17   *mingled weft / Of good and ill*   'The web of our life is of a mingled yarn, good and ill together' (*All's Well* IV. 3.83).

221   *presentment*   presentation.

232–8   *Pharaoh . . . Joseph*   Genesis xl 16–22.

241   *the motion they style the Call*   that is, God's Call or Summons.

262   *To which all flesh shall come, saith the prophecy*   'Praise waiteth for thee, O God, in Sion . . . unto thee shall all flesh come' (Psalm lxv 1–2).

285–6   *loving worm . . . god*   'The spirit of the worm beneath the sod / In love and worship, blends itself with God' (Shelley, *Epipsychidion*, 128–9). Shelley's lines are quoted in the 'Essay on Shelley'.

332–74   *My soul . . . this is mine*   While the fifth section contains much of the essence of Browning's expressed faith, these lines express much that is central in the 'Saul' of 1855 in particular.

389   *chorded*   combining harmoniously (*OED*, citing this usage, states that the use of the word to refer to colours is rare).

398   *circumflexed*   arched over with something bent round (*OED* 1b).

400   *flushier . . . flightier*   *OED* does not include 'flushier', and suggests that 'flightier' here may be unique.

413–14   *let me build . . . three*   'let us make three tabernacles' (Mark ix 5).

438   *sweepy*   sweeping.

445–6   *Where two or three . . . the midst*   'For where two or three are gathered together in my name, there am I in the midst of them' (Matthew xviii 20).

467–8   *the spirit, / Be worshipped in spirit and in truth*   'God is a Spirit: and they that worship him must worship him in spirit and in truth' (John iv 24).

509–11 *the cup ... disciple* Matthew x 42.

529 *Dome of God* Saint Peter's Basilica, Rome.

530–32 *angel's measuring-rod ... New Jerusalem* Revelation xxi 15–7.

548 *fountains* the two fountains flanking the Egyptian obelisk in the square before Saint Peter's.

553 *lavers* fountain-basins (archaism).

564 *architrave* epistyle: the stone on top of a pillar that supports the frieze; the lowest part of an entablature.

566 *porphyry* beautiful hard rock.

573 *baldachin* canopy over an altar.

578 *Behemoth* the animal of Job xl 15–24.

579 *silver bell* rung at the elevation of the Host; people then kneel.

595 *I died, and live for evermore* 'I am he that liveth, and was dead; and, behold, I am alive for evermore' (Revelation i 18).

629–32 *summit ... base* alluding to the Leaning Tower of Pisa.

658 *ken* sight (obsolete usage).

664 *Sallust* Roman historian (86–34 B.C.). Only fragments of his work survive.
　Sallust] Livy *MS., 1850.*

674 *Terpander's bird* the nightingale. Terpander was the father of Greek music (sixth century B.C.).

680 *Aphrodite* (Venus) goddess of erotic love.

731–813] The lines in the manuscript are in Mrs Browning's hand.

750 *Colossus* The original Colossus, at Rhodes, was one of the Seven Wonders.

769ₓ70] And still as we swept through storm and night, *MS., 1850.*

792–3 *Halle ... Göttingen* all German centres of culture. David Friedrich Strauss (1808–74), whose views are satirised in what follows (Browning had little use for the so-called Higher Criticism) had no connection with the celebrated University at Göttingen.

794–5 *likely ... obliquely* The rhyme, in 1850, is exact.

834 *hake* The word presumably is meant to mean something like 'bunch'; *OED* records no sense possible here.

835 *undressed tow* unkempt flax.

837 *Young England* a group of Tory politicians of the 1840s; a kind of political equivalent of the Oxford or Tractarian movement.

839 *surplice-question* The term hits at arguments between High-Church and Low-Church parties over matters of ritual including vestments and so on.

875 *Individuum* indivisible unit.

893 *drouthy* droughty.

900 *mephitic* foul.

941 *Attic* Attica is the area around Athens.

962–3 *A ... G* The Hebrew letter Aleph (A) was represented by an ox; 'Gimel' (G) means 'Camel'.

966–1017] The lines are in Mrs Browning's hand in the manuscript.

973 *Harvey* William Harvey (1578–1657) discovered the circulation of the blood.

1003 *Euclid* the great Greek mathematician of the third century B.C.

1054–6 *Believe in me ... Lord of Life* See John xiv 1, Revelation i 18.

1078 *levigable* that can be reduced to powder.

1101 *Middle Verb* a reflexive form.

1104 *Iketides* *The Suppliants* of Aeschylus, only fragments of which survive.

1106–7 *a tricksy demon ... Philemon* The point is that scholarly approaches suitable for literary studies are adopted towards biblical texts; in fact, the Higher

Criticism did develop in part from applying techniques of literary scholarship to the Bible.

1115   *Heine (before his fever)*   The German poet (1797–1856) became very ill in 1848, but the point is obscure.

1126   *pravity*   depravity.

1128   *ride a-cockhorse*   'riding' a stick, leg, or foot, pretending it to be a horse.

1242   *raree-show*   peepshow.

1244   *wist*   knew (archaism).

1253–1359]   The lines in the manuscript are in Mrs Browning's hand.

1268   *Pascal*   the French theologian, mathematician, writer (1623–62).

1270–71   *square . . . infinity*   To square the circle is to attempt an impossibility; here Pascal's mathematical and theological genius cannot succeed in the 'task'.

1275   *Taylor*   Jeremy Taylor, the great English sermon-writer (1613–67).

1292   *breccia*   Browning uses the word in a sense really archaic before his time to refer to a kind of marble.

1313   *earthen vessel, holding treasure*   2 Corinthians iv 7.

1323   *Pope*   Pius IX had fled Rome in November 1849 disguised as a servant. He returned on 12 April 1850.

1326   *Bourbon bully*   Ferdinand II of Naples and Sicily ('King Bomba').

1356   *Hepzibah Tune*   unidentified – a Browning invention?

1358   *Whitfield's Collection*   George Whit(e)field (1714–70), early follower of Wesley, as a strict Calvinist later split from him. His *Collection of Hymns for Social Worship* was first published in 1753, and went through many editions. In early editions 'the seventeenth hymn' is appropriate for Browning's context (Isaac Watts's 'O God, how endless is thy Love') but has only three stanzas. Browning's references probably have no special significance.

1359   *doxology*   hymn of praise to God.

EASTER-DAY

46   *acquist*   acquisition.

91–2   *Plato . . . geometrize*   Plutarch's *Symposiacs* viii, 2, quotes Plato as saying 'God always plays the geometer.'

94–7]   You would grow smoothly as a tree,
            Soar heavenward, straightly up like fire –
            God bless you – there's your world entire
            Needing no faith, if you think fit; *MS., 1850.*

98   *walk up and down*   Zechariah x 12.

154   *coleoptera*   order of insects.

160   *Grignon with the Regent's crest*   a snuff-box made by the eighteenth-century metal-worker, Pierre Grignon, bearing the crest of the Regent, the Duke of Orleans.

166   *gain a palm-branch*   that is, triumph; victorious gladiators were given palm-branches.

169   *Semitic guess*   guess about the meaning of something in a Semitic language.

180   *Jonah's whale*   the 'great fish' that swallowed Jonah (Jonah i 17).

183   *flap]*   clap *MS., 1850–68.*

193   *Orpheus*   the great musician of Greek legend, central figure of a mystic religion having parallels with Christianity, Orphicism; he was torn to pieces by Thracian women.

194   *Dionysius Zagrias*   a prominent figure in Orphicism, son of Zeus and Persephone, torn to pieces by the Titans.

277–8 *pearl of price* ... *Caesar*   'pearl of great price' (Matthew xiii 46) .. Emperor.

279 *fought with beasts*   Saint Paul 'fought with beasts' (1 Corinthians xv 32).

286 *Sergius*   Sergius Paulus, proconsul in Cyprus, friendly to Paul (Acts xiii 7)?

322 *wis* ... *wot*   think ... know (archaisms).

330 *leave Saint Paul for Aeschylus*   leave Saint Paul's faith in immortality for the 'blind hopes' of the Titan Prometheus of Aeschylus.

332 *blind hopes*   Aeschylus, *Prometheus Bound*, 255.

382 *overwent*   traversed.

393 *Lucumons*   ancient Etruscan priest-king patriarchs.

394 *Fourier's scheme*   François Fourier (1772–1837), socialist writer, advocated communes.

403 *perdue*   hidden.

411 *scout*   spy, skulker.

447 *'tice*   entice.

458 *God's kingdom come*   'Thy kingdom come' (Lord's Prayer).

476 *At night it cometh like a thief*   'But the day of the Lord will come as a thief in the night' (2 Peter iii 10).

487 *mage*   magus, magician.

488 *Queen Mab*   here, apparently, Queen of the fairies; usually the 'fairies' midwife' delivering the brain of dreams, as in *Romeo and Juliet*, I. 4.53.

498–9 *in memory keep | Her precept*   'These few precepts in thy memory' (*Hamlet* I. 3.58).

520 *'gan suspire*   began to breathe.

598 *Tophet*   place of burning (Isaiah xxx 33), often roughly synonymous with Hell.

609 *a waking dream*   'Was it a vision or a waking dream?' (Keats, 'Ode to a Nightingale', 79). Both 'Christmas-Eve' and 'Easter-Day' often suggest, if only faintly, that Browning had been reading Keats.

615 *great white throne*   'And I saw a great white throne, and him that sat on it, from whose face the earth and the heaven fled away; and there was found no place for them' (Revelation xx 11).

616 *quick and dead*   'Who shall give account to him that is ready to judge the quick and the dead' (1 Peter iv 5).

617–18 *Where stood they, small and great? Who read | The sentence from the opened book?*   'And I saw the dead, small and great, stand before God; and the books were opened: and another book was opened, which is the book of life: and the dead were judged out of those things which were written in the books, according to their works' (Revelation xx 12).

625 *palm-tree-cinctured city*   In a letter of 7 June 1887 Browning wrote: 'the "Palm-cinctured City" is merely typical, – "such a thing might be, and doubtless has been" – enough for an illustration, that's all' (T. J. Collins, 'Letters from Robert Browning To the Rev. J. D. Williams, 1874–1889', *BIS* IV, 1976, 46).

640–41 *smoke | Pillared o'er Sodom*   Genesis xix 28.

697–8 *glut | Thy sense*   'glut thy sorrow on a morning rose' (Keats, 'Ode on Melancholy', 15).

712–13 *Let the unjust usurp at will : | The filthy shall be filthy still*   'He that is unjust, let him be unjust still: and he which is filthy, let him be filthy still' (Revelation xxii 11).

749 *bee-bird*   humming-bird.

767ₐ8] About seven lines of manuscript have been cut out here, presumably by Browning himself.

799 *Buonarroti*   Michelangelo.

827 *very good* Genesis i 31.

840] One minute after you dispense *MS.*, *1850*; One minute after day dispense *1863–8*.

841 *Of all the sounds*] The thousand sounds *MS.*, *1850–68*.

842 *Innumerous*] In, on him, *MS.*, *1850–63*; In on him *1868*.

910 *wind-lyres* Almost certainly, Browning refers to the Aeolian harp and is mistranslating the German *Windharfe* (wind harp). Probably a unique use of the word.

waft breath of wind.

932ᴧ3] Able to wound it, not sustain –
But let me not choose all in vain! *MS. first reading.*

937 *living*] loving *MS.*, *1850–68*.

943' *look on*] live with *MS.*, *1850–63*.

945 *Old memories to new dreams*] Its fragments to my whole *MS.*, *1850–68*.

1010 *Was this a vision?* 'Was it a vision or a waking dream?' (Keats, 'Ode to a Nightingale', 79).

Men and Women

The two volumes of *Men and Women* were published by Chapman and Hall on 10 November 1855. In later collections, all fifty-one poems in the collection were reprinted, sometimes after fairly extensive revision. In *1863* 'In a Balcony' became independent, and the other poems were rearranged in three groupings together with poems from *Dramatic Lyrics* and *Dramatic Romances and Lyrics*: thirty poems went to 'Lyrics', twelve to 'Romances', eight to 'Men, and Women' (details of the groupings are in the Appendix to Volume II of the present edition). The same groupings were retained in *1868* and *1888* under the titles of 'Dramatic Lyrics', 'Dramatic Romances' and 'Men and Women'. Of the poems printed in *1855* only 'The Twins' (1854) and the first nine sections of 'Saul' had appeared before.

The volume title probably alludes to the twenty-sixth sonnet in Mrs Browning's *Sonnets from the Portuguese* (1850), the opening lines of which are: 'I lived with visions for my company / Instead of men and women, years ago'. The dates of composition of most poems in *Men and Women* are unknown, and difficult or impossible to determine with any precision. The dedication to (and the epilogue of) the collection, 'One Word More', was the last written (September 1855). 'The Guardian-Angel' (July 1848) may have been the first written, and it is the only poem that can positively be said, despite frequent conjectures masquerading as facts, to have been written before 1853. On 5 June 1854 Browning wrote to his friend John Forster that the poems were 'not written before last year' (*New Letters*, 77), and it is almost certain that the vast mass of the poems in *Men and Women* was written in 1853–5. On 24 February 1853 Browning wrote of 'writing – a first step towards popularity for me – lyrics with more music and painting than before, so as to get people to hear and see' (W. Thomas, 'Deux lettres inédités de Robert Browning à Joseph Milsand', *Revue Germanique* XII, 1921, 253). Mrs Browning described her husband as being at work on 24 August 1853, and in September 1854 she is reported to have said that her husband was ready to publish and that he had considered publication in the Summer of 1854. Browning, however, continued work on the collection. On 12 July 1855 he brought the manuscript, which has apparently perished, to London. There are, however, extant MSS. of a handful of the poems. Further MS. readings are also preserved in a set of proofs in the Huntington Library (see W. S. Peterson, 'The Proofs of Browning's *Men and Women*', *SBHC* III, No. 2, 1975, 23–39).

With the possible exception of *The Ring and the Book*, *Men and Women* is the most highly regarded of all Browning's works. Now agreed to be one of Victorian England's most distinguished books, it had little impact at the time: of the fairly small run (2,000?), many copies were still available a decade later, and there was no second edition. Browning continued to be known as his wife's husband.

There are two important editions of *Men and Women* published in this century; both reprint the text of 1855: B. Worsfold's of 1904, and P. Turner's of 1972. J. R. Watson collected some essays in a Macmillan casebook (1974) on the *Men and Women* of the later grouping; and M. Willy offers a brief introduction in *A Critical Commentary on Browning's 'Men and Women'*, Macmillan, 1968. Books on Browning normally focus heavily on the poems of *Men and Women*. See also R. A. Foakes, *The Romantic Assertion*, Methuen, 1958, 138–48; and W. Irvine, 'Four Monologues in Browning's *Men and Women*', *VP* II, 1964, 155–64 ('Lippo', 'Blougram', 'Karshish', 'Cleon').

LOVE AMONG THE RUINS

First published as the first poem of *Men and Women* on 10 November 1855. In *1863* it was included in 'Lyrics'. In these printings it was divided into fourteen stanzas of six lines each; for *1868* Browning made the final division into seven stanzas of twelve lines each. There were no verbal revisions after *1855*. A manuscript, entitled 'Sicilian Pastoral', is in Harvard's Houghton Library; see J. Maynard, 'Browning's "Sicilian Pastoral"', *Harvard Library Bulletin* XX, 1972, 436–43.

DeVane (*Handbook*, 212) states that the poem was written in an apartment on the Champs Elysées on 3 January 1853, but one of the two references he cites does not support his statement, and the other contradicts it (see J. Parr, 'The Date and Composition of Browning's *Love Among the Ruins*', *PQ* XXXII, 1953, 443–6, and J. Huebenthal's note in *VP* IV, 1966, 51–4). F. J. Furnivall (*BSP* I, 159), probably reporting Browning, stated that the poet wrote '*Love Among the Ruins*, *Women and Roses*, and *Childe Roland* in three successive days 1, 2 and 3 January 1852'; but the date of composition remains uncertain, especially since Furnivall was never addicted to accuracy and since Browning wrote on 5 June 1854 that the *Men and Women* poems were not written before 1853. Parr's suggestion that the poem was written in Florence in 1853 is as reasonable as any, and it has implicit support in Whiting, *The Brownings*, 261.

Despite the MS. title, the setting of the poem derives in part from visits to the Campagna, the countryside around Rome. In part it comes from Browning's reading about ancient ruined cities, notably Nineveh and Babylon (see J. Parr, 'The Site and Ancient City of Browning's *Love Among the Ruins*', *PMLA* LXVIII, 1953, 128–37). Debts have also been suggested to such writings as Herodotus' description of Babylon, Revelation, Ralegh's *History of the World*, and Spenser's *Complaints* (see R. K. R. Thornton, in *N & Q* CCXIII, 1968, 178–9). For criticism, see W. Cadbury, 'Lyric and Anti-Lyric Forms', *TQ* XXXIV, 1964, 49–67 (reprinted in Tracy, *Browning's Mind and Art*, 32–50), and Cook, *Browning's Lyrics*, 163–73.

7 *a city great and gay* 'all that in this world is great or gay, / Doth as a vapour vanish, and decay' (Spenser, *Ruines of Time*, 55–6).
9 *Of*] Was *MS*.
11 *gathered ... wielding far*] had his ... sent afar *MS*.
19 *shot its spires* 'sharpèd steeples high shot up in air' (Spenser, *Ruines of Rome*, 16).

21 *hundred-gated*   Babylon and the Egyptian Thebes were reputed to have had a hundred gates.

39 *By the caper over-rooted*]   Which the caper roots a-top of *MS.*
  caper   a small shrub.

41 *houseleek*   a flowering plant that generally grows on walls or roofs.

43 *Marks*]   Was *MS.*

61 *he looked upon the city*]   the city he looked out on *MS.*

65 *causeys*   causeways.

77 *Yet reserved a thousand*]   And yet mustered five-score *MS.*

79 *freezes*]   The *MS.* shows Browning debating between the first reading *freezes* and the second reading *tingles*.

84 *Love is best.*]   *This* is best! *MS.*; Love is best! *1855–63.*

A LOVERS' QUARREL

First published in *Men and Women* on 10 November 1855; in *1863* it was included in 'Lyrics'. Revisions after 1855 were trifling. The poem was probably written in Florence in March 1853. The Brownings disagreed about Napoleon III, and about spiritualism, a major fad in Florence in 1852–3. On the poem, see Cook, *Browning's Lyrics*, 138–41.

7 *as lief that*   rather.

8 *rillets*   small rivulets.

11 *beryl*   light-green.

20 *ingle*   fireplace.

30 *Emperor*   Napoleon III of France married on 30 January 1853; *The Times* criticized the extravagance.

36 *Pampas*   the plains of South America.

43 *will our table turn?*   that is, in a spiritualist ritual. Mrs Browning believed in spiritualism, her husband did not.

64 *flirt*   open and close quickly, or wave smartly (*OED*).

69 *two spots*   of the nostrils.

90–91 'Death and life are in the power of the tongue' (Proverbs xviii 21).

105 *threats*   threatens (archaism).

123 *minor third*   The interval in the cuckoo's notes increases as spring progresses. The time of the minor third is towards the middle of spring.

125 *guelder-rose*   a variety of cranberry.

131–3   The giant's speech is from the folk-tale of Jack the Giant-killer. Jack, unlike Tom Thumb, is valiant; Browning probably confused two stories.

EVELYN HOPE

First published in *Men and Women* on 10 November 1855; in *1863* it was included in 'Lyrics'. Later revisions were trifling. The date of composition is unknown.

UP AT A VILLA – DOWN IN THE CITY

First published in *Men and Women* on 10 November 1855; in *1863* it was included in 'Lyrics'. Later revisions were trifling. The date of writing is unknown; the setting is Tuscan. D. C. Allen (*Andrew Marvell*, 123) suggests a debt to Martial. See Cook, *Browning's Lyrics*, 178–80.

4 *Bacchus* (Dionysus) god of wine, associated with revels.

9 *shag* tangled mass.

28 *pash* strike with hoofs.

34 *thrid* thread (archaism).

39 *diligence* stage-coach.

42 *Pulcinello-trumpet* the trumpet announcing the puppet-show. (Pulcinello is a kind of Punch-figure.)

46 *Duke* the Tuscan Grand-Duke, Leopold II.

48–9 That is, roughly, the priest combines great philosophical poet, fiction writer, love poet, translator, rhetorician and preacher.

52 *seven swords* representing the Virgin's Seven Sorrows.

56 *new tax . . . gate* In Italy, taxes on salt and on produce entering cities were fairly heavy.

A WOMAN'S LAST WORD

First published in *Men and Women* on 10 November 1855; in *1863* it was included in 'Lyrics'. There were no verbal changes after 1855. Date of composition is unknown. That a woman always gets the last word had been further popularized by Mrs Caudle in Douglas Jerrold's *Mrs Caudle's Curtain Lectures*, first published in 1845. See M. R. Sullivan, 'Irony in "A Woman's Last Word"', *BSN* V, No. 2, 1975, 14–17.

FRA LIPPO LIPPI

First published in *Men and Women* on 10 November 1855. In *1863* it remained in 'Men, and Women'. Revisions after 1855 were trifling. The poem was probably written in Florence in the first half of 1853. Its main and only really essential source, apart from Browning's familiarity with the paintings of Fra Filippo Lippi (*c.* 1406–69), is Vasari's *Lives of the Artists*, which gave many of the facts, and supports the general tenor, of Browning's poem.

It is generally agreed that Lippo's artistic creed reflects much in Browning's, and that he is really a kind of spokesman for the poet, paralleling in his comments much that Browning had said in his essay on Shelley. In the reorganized 'Men, and Women' of *1863* and later collected editions, 'Andrea del Sarto', an obvious companion poem, followed 'Pictor Ignotus' and 'Fra Lippo Lippi'. Among a host of essays on this perennial favourite are: Jack, *Browning's Major Poetry*, 213–24; J. L. Kendall, 'Lippo's Vision', *VNL* 18, 1960, 18–21; King, *The Bow and the Lyre*, 32–51; W. D. Shaw, 'Character and Philosophy in "Fra Lippo Lippi"', *VP* II, 1964, 127–32.

3 *Zooks* abbreviation of 'Gadzooks' (God's hooks), a mild oath.

7 *Carmine* the monastery of the religious order of the Carmelites in Florence. Vasari says Lippo left the order at the age of seventeen.

17 *Cosimo of the Medici* the Florentine ruler and patron of the arts.

18 *house* the Medici-Riccardi Palace, built 1444–60.

    caps crowns.

28 *florin* a word applied imprecisely to various continental coins.

34 *John Baptist* Vasari mentions the saint as a subject painted by Lippo; his frescoes of the saint are at Prato.

41   *take*   catch the fancy of (*OED* 10).

47   *mew*   cage.

52   *whifts*   whiffs.

53–7   The three-line Tuscan folksong beginning with a reference to a flower is called a *stornello*.

67   *Saint Laurence*   the church of San Lorenzo.

73   *Jerome*   the highly ascetic saint (340–420) whom Lippo painted for Cosimo in his *Virgin Adoring the Child with Saint Hilarion*. The work is now in the Uffizi in Florence (for a photograph, see *SIB* I, No. 2, 1973, 34).

75   *snap*   seize.

81–2   Vasari says Lippo was orphaned at the age of two, and then for six years brought up by his aunt, Mona Lapaccia.

121   *Eight*   the eight magistrates of Florence.

130   *antiphonary*   book with choral music.

135   *looked black*]   were mazed *Huntington proof*.

139   *Camaldolese*   The religious order had a convent near Florence.

140   *Preaching Friars*   Dominicans.

146   *fat and lean*]   good and bad *Huntington proof*.

148   *cribs*   petty thefts.

160   *dropped*]   threw *Huntington proof*.

170   *niece*   almost certainly not a relation, but one with whom he has relations.

172   *funked*   expired in smoke.

186   *when you die it leaves your mouth*   There is an old doctrine (referred to again in 'An Epistle', 6) that the soul departs from the body in the form of vapour with the last breath.

189   *Giotto*   the great Florentine painter and architect (1267–1337).

196   *Herodias*   mother of Salome, who, after dancing for Herod, asked him for the head of John the Baptist (Matthew xiv). The same error is in Vasari.

229   *Those great rings*   The iron rings referred to still survive.

235   *Angelico*   Fra Angelico (1387–1455), one of the most ethereal of painters. J. Parr, 'Browning's *Fra Lippo Lippi*, Vasari's Masaccio, and Mrs. Jameson', *English Language Notes* V, 1968, 277–83, suggests that the contrast between Lippo and Fra Angelico may have been suggested by the writings of the Brownings' friend, Mrs Jameson.

236   *Lorenzo*   Lorenzo Monaco (*c*. 1370–*c*. 1425), painter, Fra Angelico's master.

237   *Fag*   toil.

250   *the cup runs over*   'my cup runneth over' (Psalm xxiii, 5).

276   *Guidi*   Tomasso Guidi, Masaccio (1401–28?), was, despite Browning's protests to the contrary, Lippo's teacher, not pupil. The error stems from footnotes in the Brownings' edition of Vasari – see J. Parr, 'Browning's *Fra Lippo Lippi*, Baldinucci, and the Milanesi Edition of Vasari', *English Language Notes* III, 1966, 197–201.

313   *blot*]   trap *Huntington proof*.

323–4   *Saint Laurence . . . Prato*   The saint was roasted to death in 258. Some of Lippo's best work was done in the town near Florence. The painting is probably invented, though Lippo did treat Saint Laurence at least twice.

327   *phiz*   face (slang).

328   *turn*]   turned *Huntington proof*.

337   *wot*   knows (archaism).

346   *Sant'Ambrogio's*   a convent in Florence for which Lippo painted his *Coronation*

of the Virgin (now in the Uffizi), the painting described in the following lines. It was, Vasari says, this painting that got Cosimo interested in Lippo. (A photograph faces page 202 in Griffin and Minchin, *Life*.)

347 *cast o' my office* sample of my work.

351 *orris-root* iris-root. Some kinds are used in perfumes.

354 *Saint John* the patron-saint of Florence.

355 *Saint Ambrose* Lippo seems confused. Saint Ambrose, patron-saint of Sant'Ambrogio, was the fourth-century Archbishop of Milan, but Lippo seems to mean Ambrose the Camaldulian (1386–1439), friend of Cosimo de Medici and translator of Greek theologians, born near Florence.

358 *Uz* Job i 1.

364 *Mazed* bewildered (archaism).

370 *slip* Saint Lucy, a figure in *The Coronation of the Virgin*.

375 *camel-hair* Saint John wore camel hair (Matthew iii 4; Mark i 6).

377 *Iste perfecit opus* Latin (actually, *Is perfecit opus*): 'This man arranged the work'. In Browning's time, the words, occurring on a scroll in the painting, were thought to mean 'This man did the work'; the figure then thought to be Lippo himself, as in the poem, is now known to be the Canon Maringhi who commissioned the painting in 1441.

380 *kirtles* skirts.

381 *hot cockles* technically a rustic game; here a euphemism for vigorous amorous activity.

387 *Saint Lucy* The martyr was a virgin; the Prior's 'niece' is almost certainly not.

A TOCCATA OF GALUPPI'S

First published in *Men and Women* on 10 November 1855; in *1863* it was included in 'Lyrics'. Revisions after 1855 were trifling. Date of composition is unknown. J. C. Maxwell (*N & Q*, n.s. XX, 1973, 270) suggests that it was not written before 1850, the date of publication of Thackeray's poem in the same metre on King Canute in *Rebecca and Rowena*.

A toccata (*toccare*, 'to touch' in Italian) is a fast-moving keyboard piece, often written to display technical prowess. Baldassare Galuppi (1706–85), the Venetian composer, is known mainly for his light operas, for many of which Goldoni was librettist. He visited England in 1741, and had considerable influence on English music. In 1887 Browning wrote that he had two manuscript volumes of Galuppi 'toccata-pieces' which he described as 'apparently a slighter form of the Sonata to be "touched" lightly off'. The poem and its intention have been much discussed. Essays include: Cook, *Browning's Lyrics*, 173–8; E. F. Harden, 'A New Reading of Browning's "A Toccata of Galuppi's"', *VP* XI, 1973, 330–36.

1 *Baldassaro* an error for 'Baldassare'.

6 *Saint Mark's . . . wed the sea with rings* Saint Mark's is the cathedral of Venice. The Dukes of Venice used annually to symbolize the maritime power of the city by wedding it to the sea in a ceremony in which a ring was cast into the sea.

8 *Shylock's bridge* the Rialto.

18 *clavichord* a stringed keyboard instrument, ancestor of the modern piano.

19 *lesser thirds* This technical term and those that follow are, in terms of their effects, given their traditional associations within the poem itself. Here, 'lesser' means 'minor'; a 'third' is a chord of two notes four semitones apart.

sixths diminished   A 'sixth' is a chord made up of two notes nine semitones apart; 'diminished' (by two semitones) it becomes one of two notes seven semitones apart. It is going a little far to suggest that 'mentioning diminished sixths in this off-hand way is rather like casually speaking of breakfasting off roc's egg as a matter of every-day occurrence' (see H. E. Greene, 'Browning's Knowledge of Music', *PMLA* LXII, 1947, 1097). It would seem that by 'diminished' Browning may have meant 'minor'.

20 *suspensions*   A suspension is a note held from one chord to another, first pro-ducing a discord, and then resolving concordantly.

solutions   resolutions. A 'resolution' (technical term) is a concord following a discord.

21 *sevenths*   chords of two notes eleven semitones apart, producing mild dissonances.

24 *the dominant's persistence till it must be answered to*   A 'dominant' is 'the note in a mode or scale which, in traditional harmonic procedures, most urgently demands resolution upon the tonic' (Grove): it is the fifth note above the tonic or key-note.

25 *octave*   The octave, being a perfect consonance, gives the 'answer' to (resolves) the dominant.

30 *tacitly*   punning on *'tacet'* (Latin: 'it is silent'), the word indicating an ex-tended rest for a player on an orchestral score.

43 *want*   lack.

BY THE FIRE-SIDE

First published in *Men and Women* on 10 November 1855. In *1863* it was included in 'Lyrics'. After 1855 there were a few verbal revisions, and many in punctuation. The poem is traditionally thought to have been written late in 1853, after a summer in which the Brownings had occupied a house near Lucca, from which they had made a number of trips, including one in mid-September with their friends, the Storys, to Prato Fiorito, which, it has been said, provides most of the details for the setting of the poem. The poem, however, may have been written as early as 1847, since the locale has been clearly shown to be based on information given in a guidebook con-sulted by the Brownings in planning a tour, which they never made, to the Lake of Orta, and perhaps also on descriptions by friends (see J. S. Lindsay, 'The Central Episode of Browning's *By the Fire-Side*', *SP* XXXIX, 1942, 571-9, and D. Robertson, 'Browning on the Colle di Colma', *BSN* V, No. 2, 1975, 6-13). Probable are the traditional date, and a composite landscape of the imagination rather than a factual one. While biographical elements are subdued, the poem is one of Browning's rare more personal utterances, and the portrait of 'Leonor' is one of Mrs Browning. In a letter of 6 April 1888 (see *SBHC* II, No. 1, 1974, 62), Browning wrote of the poem: 'all but the personality is fictitious – that is, the portraiture only is intended to be like – the circumstances are a mere imaginary framework'. Among discussions are: I. Armstrong, 'Browning and the Grotesque Style', *The Major Victorian Poets: Reconsiderations*, 105-11; Cook, *Browning's Lyrics*, 214-27; Jacob Korg, 'Browning's Art and "By the Fire-Side"', *VP* XV, 1977, 147-58; G. Tillotson, 'A Word for Browning,' *Sewanee Review* LXXII, 1964, 389-97.

22 *widens*]   narrows *1855-63*.
43 *Pella*   village in north-west Italy.
45 *Alp*   Monte Rosa?
58 *boss*   the protuberance at the centre of a shield.

64 *freaked* streaked.
74 *fret* eat into.
77 *festa* 'feast' (Italian).
84 *wattled cote* rough shelter of woven sticks.
92 *pent-house* projecting cover.
95 *'Five, six, nine* 1569.
101 *Leonor* the name of the good wife in Beethoven's opera *Fidelio*.
113-14 *that great brow | And the spirit-small hand propping it* Mrs Browning in a characteristic pose.
132 *The great Word which makes all things new* 'And he that sat upon the throne said, Behold, I make all things new' (Revelation xxi 5).
135 *house not made with hands* quoting 2 Corinthians v 1.
171 *settle* bench.
182 *stock* log, stump.
185 *chrysolite* a yellow or green semi-precious stone.
237 *moment*] second *1855–63*.
251 *moment's*] hour's *1855–63*.

ANY WIFE TO ANY HUSBAND

First published in *Men and Women* on 10 November 1855. In *1863*, it was included in 'Lyrics'. Revisions were trifling. The date of writing is unknown. It has been suggested that the poem was prompted by Browning's father's being sued for breach-of-promise in 1852, three years after the death of Browning's mother.

18 *soul makes all things new* 'Behold, I make all things new' (Revelation xxi 5).
71 *wilding* growing wild.
77 *Titian's Venus* Probably Titian's *Venus of Urbino* (1538), in the Uffizi in Florence.
94 *sealing up the sum* 'Thou sealest up the sum, full of wisdom, and perfect in beauty' (Ezekiel xxviii 12).

AN EPISTLE . . . OF KARSHISH

First published in *Men and Women* on 10 November 1855; in *1863–88* it was retained in 'Men and Women'. After 1855, revisions were extensive, but of minor significance. The date of writing is unknown. 'Cleon' is a companion poem.

Karshish and his master Abib are Browning's inventions. The story of Lazarus is in John xi 1–44. The poem is set in A.D. 66 or 69–70. On it, see W. L. Guerin, 'Irony and Tension in Browning's "Karshish"', *VP* I, 1963, 132–9; and R. A. King, Jr, 'Karshish Encounters Himself: An Interpretation of Browning's "Epistle"', *Concerning Poetry* I, 1968, 23–33.

1 *Karshish* Arabic for 'one who gathers', or, roughly, 'the picker-up of learning's crumbs' (see M. Wright's letter in *TLS*, 1 May 1953, 285).
6 Karshish refers to the old doctrine that the soul leaves the body with the last breath in the form of vapour. Compare 'Fra Lippo Lippi', 186.
15 *vagrant* wandering.
17 *snakestone* a stone used in treating snake bites.
20 Karshish's formal opening to his epistle is rather like that to a Pauline one –

compare the opening to Romans (see R. D. Altick, 'Browning's "Karshish" and Saint Paul', *MLN* LXXII, 1957, 494–6).

21 *Jericho* the city east of Jerusalem.

28 *Vespasian* Roman Emperor (70–79). He invaded Palestine in 66; his son Titus, in 70.

30 *balls* eyeballs.

32 Compare 2 Corinthians xi 25–6.

36 *Bethany* a small village near Jerusalem, the home of Lazarus.

40 *scrip* small bag.

42 *viscid choler* sticky bile.

43 *tertians* fevers recurring every other day.

44 *falling-sickness* epilepsy.

49 *runagate* renegade, vagabond.

50 *payeth me* payeth me for.
   sublimate product of a refining process.

55 *gum-tragacanth* a salve.

57 *porphyry* a hard rock.

60 *Zoar* town north of the Dead Sea.

67 *tang* sting.

79 *subinduced* brought about as a result of something else.

81 *three days* actually four days (John xi 17, 39); Karshish errs often in 'facts'.

82 *exhibition* administration.

89 *conceit* fancy.

103 *fume* hallucination.

106 *saffron* drug from the plant of the same name.

109 *Sanguine* robust.
   fifty Karshish's 'facts' are often wrong: Lazarus would have been well over sixty.

110 *laudable* healthy (a medical term).

112 *As* as if (a frequent meaning in Browning).

161 *pretermission* neglecting.

169 *mind* remember.

177 *Greek fire* an incendiary mixture, not used till the seventh century. Browning may have meant burning oil.

194 *tick* pulse-beat.

213 *affects* aspires.

222 *Sufficeth* may it satisfy (archaism).

228 *affects* has affection for (archaism).

240 *conceit* fancy (but perhaps used ambiguously for 'vanity' also).
   sublimed refined.

248–59 The historical facts have become garbled. The 'earthquake' (line 252) is reported in Matthew xxvii 51.

251 *prodigious* monstrous.

281 *borage* herb, anciently used medicinally.
   Aleppo town in northern Syria.

304–12 The thought and feeling of the conclusion parallel those in 'Saul'.

312 *He* The capital letter may be enough in itself to refute the traditional arguments that Karshish (like Cleon) rejects the new religion.

MESMERISM

First published in *Men and Women* on 10 November 1855; in *1863* it was included in 'Romances'. Revisions after 1855 were trifling. Date of writing is unknown, but similarities to 'A Lovers' Quarrel' make a date of March 1853 a reasonable guess. Mesmerism was a topic of much interest in the decade before *Men and Women* (Arnold had seen his Scholar-Gypsy of 1853 as the first mesmerist). Mrs Browning believed in it, Browning disliked it. Jack, *Browning's Major Poetry*, 159-61, suggests that the speaker may be insane and the action imaginary. J. C. Austin suggests a debt to Hawthorne's *The House of the Seven Gables* in 'The Hawthorne and Browning Acquaintance: Including an Unpublished Browning Letter', *VNL* 20, 1961, 13-18.

26 *to have and hold* 'to have and to hold' (marriage service).
45 *calotypist* photographer.
75 *tractile* capable of being drawn out.

A SERENADE AT THE VILLA

First published in *Men and Women* on 10 November 1855. In *1863* it was included in 'Lyrics'. After 1855 revisions were trifling. Date of composition is unknown. Arthur Symons suggested the influence of a song from Sidney's *Astrophil and Stella* with the same metre and subject. There has been some disagreement as to the poem's attitude towards the speaker, and as to whether he is dead or alive. On the poem, see Cook, *Browning's Lyrics*, 135-8, and J. Maynard in *BSN* VI, No. 1, 1976, 3-10.

6 *fly* fire-fly.
7 *worm* glow-worm.
9 *forbore a term* were quiet for a while.

MY STAR

First published in *Men and Women* on 10 November 1855. In *1863* it was included in 'Lyrics'. After 1855 there were minor revisions only in punctuation. The date of composition is unknown. The *MS.* in the Boston Public Library reported in *Robert Browning : A Bibliography*, 13, is, as suggested there, a late souvenir autograph. On 9 November 1845 Browning wrote to Elizabeth Barrett: 'Dearest, I believed in your glorious genius and knew it for a true star from the moment I saw it, – long before I had the blessing of knowing it was MY star, with my fortune and futurity in it'; that the poem pays tribute to Mrs Browning is almost universally agreed. Most readers have, however, not limited the poem's symbolism only to her, especially since Browning often uses imagery of white light and the colours composing it with reference to poetry and its creation. On the poem, see Cook, *Browning's Lyrics*, 204-8; and J. F. Loucks, Jr, 'New Light on "My Star"', *BSN* IV, No. 2, 1974, 25-7.

4 *angled spar* crystalline mineral substance with sparkling facets.
9 *dartles* darts, shoots forth repeatedly. Perhaps a Browning neologism.
11 *Saturn* the second largest planet, and a bright one.

INSTANS TYRANNUS

First published in *Men and Women* on 10 November 1855. In *1863* it was included in 'Romances'. After 1855 revisions were trifling. Date of composition is unknown. The title, 'The Threatening Tyrant', is from Horace, *Odes* III, iii, 3; and details come from the same ode, in which Horace says that the just man cannot be frightened by a threatening tyrant or Jove's thunder and lightning, or a falling sky.

18 *perdue*   concealed.
21 *spilth*   effusion.
33 *nit*   young louse.
44 *gravamen*   grievance.
47 *admire*   wonder.
64 *targe*   shield.
65 *boss*   protuberance at the centre of a shield.

A PRETTY WOMAN

First published in *Men and Women* on 10 November 1855. In *1863* it was included in 'Lyrics'. After 1855 there were no verbal changes. The date of composition is uncertain; DeVane (*Handbook*, 228) suggests 1847, proposing that the poem's model was Gerardine Bate, niece of the Brownings' friend, Mrs Anna Jameson. Miss Bate visited the Brownings in April 1847, irritated Browning, and was described by Mrs Browning as 'just pretty and no more at most'.

23 *brayed*   ground.
34 *Scout*   reject with disdain.
61 *grace the rose*   gild the lily.

'CHILDE ROLAND TO THE DARK TOWER CAME'

First published in *Men and Women* on 10 November 1855. In *1863* it was included in 'Romances'; after 1855 revisions were few and minor. The date of writing is uncertain (see J. Huebenthal's note in *VP* IV, 1966, 51–4), despite DeVane's statement (*Handbook*, 229) that Browning himself gave the date of 2 January 1852 (Browning did not). F. J. Furnivall (*Browning Society's Papers* I, 159), probably citing Browning himself, gives 3 January 1852 as the date, and Griffin and Minchin (*Life*, 189) echo him. The information given by L. Whiting (*The Brownings*, 251), if correct, makes the accepted date impossible, since she reports Browning as saying he wrote the poem in Florence (in 1866, however, he wrote that he composed it in Paris). The one thing that seems likely from the conflicting evidence is that Browning wrote 'Childe Roland' the day after he wrote 'Women and Roses'. The poet recalled that he had written the poem in one day.

Often questioned about the poem, Browning said that it came upon him 'as a kind of dream' that had to be written, that he did not know what it meant, that he was 'very fond' of it, that it was 'only a fantasy' with 'no allegorical intention'. Asked if it meant that 'he that endureth to the end shall be saved', Browning replied 'Just about that'. The debt to *King Lear* he acknowledged in the title. He also pointed to the influence of a horse from a tapestry (now in Vizcaya in Miami) in his living-room, a painting seen in Paris, a strange tower in Massa-Carrara among low hills. Scholars have suggested scores of other debts: to the Bible (see L. M. Thompson, 'Biblical Influence in *Childe Roland to the Dark Tower Came*', *Papers on Language and Literature* III, 1967, 339-53), to fairy-tale and folk-lore (and perhaps especially the stories of Jack the Giant-Killer and Jack and the Bean-Stalk), to medieval literature generally and Malory's story of Gareth of Orkney, to *Pilgrim's Progress*, to Gerard de Lairesse on *The Art of Painting* (see W. C. DeVane, 'The Landscape of Browning's *Childe Roland*', *PMLA* XL, 1925, 426-32), to *Inferno* (see R. Sullivan, 'Browning's "Childe Roland" and Dante's "Inferno"', *VP* V, 1967, 296-302), to Wordsworth's 'Peter Bell' (see T. P. Harrison, 'Browning's *Childe Roland* and Wordsworth', *Tennessee Studies in Literature* VI, 1961, 119-23), to Keats, to Poe's 'Metzengerstein', to Shelley. Among other source studies are: C. C. Clarke, 'Humor and Wit in "Childe Roland"', *MLQ* XXIII, 1962, 323-36; and H. Golder, 'Browning's *Childe Roland*', *PMLA* XXXIX, 1924, 358-76. Critical studies multiply. Among them are: D. V. Erdman, 'Browning's Industrial Nightmare', *PQ* XXXVI, 1957, 417-35; Jack, *Browning's Major Poetry*, 179-94; E. R. Kintgen, 'Childe Roland and the Perversity of the Mind', *VP* IV, 1966, 253-8; Langbaum, *Poetry of Experience*, 92-9; J. S. Meyers, '"Childe Roland to the Dark Tower Came": A Nightmare Confrontation with Death', *VP* VIII, 1970, 335-9; P. Raisor, 'The Failure of Browning's Childe Roland', *Tennessee Studies in Literature* XVIII, 1972, 99-110; C. Short, 'Childe Roland, Pedestrian', *VP* VI, 1968, 175-7; J. W. Willoughby, 'Browning's "Childe Roland to the Dark Tower Came"', *VP* I, 1963, 291-9; C. R. Woodward, 'The Road to the Dark Tower: An Interpretation of Browning's "Childe Roland"', *Studies in Honor of John C. Hodges and Alwin Thaler*, ed. R. B. Davis and J. L. Lievsay, University of Tennessee Press, 1961, 93-9.

Title The title quotes Edgar (in his role as the madman, Poor Tom) in *King Lear* III. 4.187 (Browning originally thought the Fool spoke the words). A childe is a candidate for knighthood.

25-36 'As virtuous men pass mildly away, / And whisper to their souls, to go, / Whilst some of their sad friends do say, / The breath goes now, and some say, no' (Donne, 'A Valediction: forbidding Mourning', 1-4) – see R. L. Lowe in *N&Q* CXCVIII, 1953, 491-2. 'I could no more, but lay like one in trance, / That hears his burial talked of by his friends, / And cannot speak, nor move, nor make one sign, / But lies and dreads his doom' (Tennyson, 'The Princess' VII, 136-9) – see C. Ricks in *N&Q*, n.s. XIV, 1967, 374.
48 *estray* stray animal.
58 *cockle, spurge* weeds.
64 *nothing skills* is no use.
66 *Calcine* burn to ashes.
68 *bents* coarse grasses.
72 *Pashing* trampling (dialectal).
76 *stiff blind horse* While Browning said that the portrait of the horse derived from a tapestry he owned, B. Melchiori argues convincingly also for the influence of the tapestry horse in Poe's 'Metzengerstein' (see *Browning's Poetry of Reticence*, 208-13).
80 *colloped* cut up like pieces of meat? An unusual usage: *OED* defines the participial adjective, 'Having collops or thick folds of fat or flesh'. That is clearly not the meaning here. Browning seems to have formed his participial adjective from the noun in its sense of 'a slice of meat' (*OED* 2b). Even for Browning, the use of language in 'Childe Roland' is unusually unusual.

99 'I dare do all that may become a man; / Who dares do more is none' (*Macbeth* I. 7.46–7).

106 *howlet* owl (dialectal).

114 *bespate* bespattered (archaism).

130 *pad* tread down (dialectal in this sense).

131 *plash* puddle.

133 *cirque* circus, or circular space, or natural amphitheatre.

135 *mews* The word means 'stables', but is used here to mean 'place of confinement' (mew).

141 *brake* heavy harrow for crushing clods.

143 *Tophet* the Biblical valley of burning; symbolic of Hell.

145 *stubbed* abounding in stubs (*OED*'s first recorded usage in this sense).

147–8 *a fool finds mirth, / Makes a thing and then mars it* 'Making and marring' ('Caliban upon Setebos', 97).

149 *rood* a quarter of an acre.

160 *Apollyon* the Devil (Revelation ix 11), and a monster with 'wings like a dragon' in *Pilgrim's Progress*.

161 *penned* winged.

182 *blind as the fool's heart* 'The fool hath said in his heart, There is no God. They are corrupt, they have done abominable works, there is none that doeth good' (Psalm xiv, 1).

187–204 There are clear debts here to *Inferno* xxxi, and to the end of *Jack the Giant-Killer*.

203 *slug-horn* 'Slughorn' is an early form of 'slogan'. Probably Browning was misled by Chatterton into thinking it meant 'trumpet', but the suggestion of 'slogan' has point, and the use of language here is like that in the poem generally. The situation here, given the hero's name, leads many readers to recall Roland and his horn (which he three times refused to sound until it was too late) at Roncesvalles.

RESPECTABILITY

First published in *Men and Women* on 10 November 1855; in *1863* it was included in 'Lyrics'. After 1855 there were minor changes in punctuation only. The reference in line 22 suggests a date soon after 5 February 1852. See L. Perrine, 'Browning's "Respectability"', *College English* XIV, 1953, 347–8.

15 *Boulevart* Boulevard.

21 *Institute* The French Academy is a branch of the Institute of France.

22 *Guizot receives Montalembert* On 5 February 1852, at a ceremony at which Browning was apparently present, François Guizot had to welcome his enemy Charles Montalembert into the French Academy.

23 *lampions* small oil-burning lamps, in the courtyard of the Institute.

A LIGHT WOMAN

First published in *Men and Women* on 10 November 1855; in *1863* it was included in 'Lyrics'. Changes after 1855 were very minor. The date of writing is unknown.

26 *basilisk* the fabulous monster, which killed with a look.

34 *late*] hung *1855*.

55 *writer of plays* Until *Men and Women*, Browning had published more volumes of plays than poems.

THE STATUE AND THE BUST

First published in *Men and Women* on 10 November 1855; in *1863* it was included in 'Romances'. After 1855 revisions were fairly extensive, but of minor significance. The date of composition is unknown. It has been suggested that the story probably had special appeal for Browning because of his strong belief that it would have been wrong had he and Elizabeth Barrett not married, and/or because of the extended platonic relation of J. S. Mill and Harriet Taylor (the two finally married in 1851).

In a hitherto neglected letter of 22 April 1888 to Edmund Yates (printed in the *World*, 18 December 1889), Browning wrote: 'the fiction in the poem . . . comprises everything but the (legendary) fact that the lady was shut up there by a jealous husband, and that the Duke commemorated his riding past her window by the statue's erection, as you see it; so my old friend Kirkup, preeminently learned in such legends, told me. There are niches in the palace wall where such a bust *might* have been placed, "and if not, why not?" "The poets are such liars", says the veracious Byron.' The equestrian statue of Ferdinand de Medici (1549–1608), who became Grand-Duke of Florence in 1587, dominates the Piazza Annunziata in Florence (Griffin and Minchin, *Life*, facing page 198, has a photograph). It is the work of John of Douay (line 202), better known as Giovanni da Bologna (1524–1608). The bust is fictional. About the two palaces in the poem, Browning himself does not appear to be clear, and the result has been interminable confusion – DeVane's attempt (*Handbook*, 234) to clear things up makes them worse. The palace of line 33, where the Duke holds his feast, is the one now called the Medici-Riccardi Palace. It stands on the Via Larga (line 34), now called the Via Cavour, is the palace from which Lippo escaped, is famous, and plays little part in 'The Statue and the Bust'. The other palace (line 1), the one from which the Lady looks out on the Duke and in which she is imprisoned, is, probably, the one now known as the Budini-Gattai. It is not famous (despite line 1), and Browning does not seem to distinguish it clearly from the other palace.

Among essays are: B. Litzinger, 'Browning's "The Statue and the Bust" Once More', in *Studies in Honor of John C. Hodges and Alwin Thaler*, ed. R. B. Davis and J. L. Lievsay, University of Tennessee Press, 1961, 87–92; and W. O. Raymond, '*The Statue and the Bust*', in his *The Infinite Moment*, 214–35 (reprinted in Tracy, *Browning's Mind and Art*, 143–62).

18 *the Riccardi* a leading Florentine family.

21 *coal-black tree* ebony.

22 *encolure* a nonce-word, here used to mean 'mane' (it is the French word for the neck of a horse).

23 *dissemble* simulate by imitation (an obsolete usage).

25 *emprise* enterprise.

36 *crime* the suppression of Florentine liberty following the return of Cosimo de Medici in 1434. The cursed son's name was Piero; Browning probably meant the grandson, Lorenzo the Magnificent.

57 *catafalque* structure supporting a coffin or corpse.

68 *loop* loop-hole.

72 *ave-bell* the bell calling to evening prayer.

94 *Arno* the river on which Florence stands.

95 *Petraja* Ferdinand had a villa here, just north of Florence.

100 *leaves* comes from.

140 *simple* foolish.

143 *pass*] lean *1855*.

149 *the picture at*] it all *1855*.

151 *years*] *not in Huntington proof.*

159 *serpent's tooth* The phrase, normally associated with ingratitude (*King Lear* I. 4.310), has other associations here.

163 *Fronting* confronting.

169 *Robbia* name of a family of Florentine sculptors, the most notable of whom was Luca della Robbia (1400–1482). Della Robbia ware became famous.

191 *lean*] *not in 1855.*

203 *Set*] Mould *1855*.

213 *idleness*] indolence *1855*.

219 *chapel* church of the Santissima Annunziata.

220 *Only*] Surely *1855*.

  know] trow *Huntington proof.*

221 *chivalry* band of knights.

225 *burned*] cut *1855*.

234 *Guelph* A *Guelpho* or *Grosso Guelpho* was a fourteenth-century Florentine coin.

237 *When your table's a hat* for rolling dice on?

  dram a very light weight, that is, a trifling stake.

239 *warily*] truly *1855–63*.

247 *the unlit lamp and the ungirt loin* Luke xii 35–7. Probably also relevant are the unlit lamps of the foolish virgins (Matthew xxv), and 'gird up the loins of your mind' (1 Peter i 13).

248 *vice*] crime *1855*.

250 *De te, fabula* 'The story is about you' (Horace, *Satires* I, i, 69–70).

LOVE IN A LIFE

First published in *Men and Women* on 10 November 1855; in *1863* it was included in 'Lyrics'. After 1855 there were minor punctuation changes only. Date of composition is unknown. The poem's imagery is characteristic of Browning; a parallel is provided by his letter to Elizabeth Barrett of 5 April 1846: 'Oh, how different it all *might* be! In this House of Life – where I go, you go, – where I ascend you run before, – where I descend, it is after you. Now, one might have a *piece* of Ba, but a very little of her, and make it up into a Lady and a Mistress, and find her a room to her mind . . . visit her there . . . and then, – after a time, leave her there and go . . . whither one liked – after, to me, the most melancholy fashion in the world. How different with us! If it were *not*, indeed – what a mad folly would marriage be!' On the poem, see Cook, *Browning's Lyrics*, 143–7.

LIFE IN A LOVE

First published in *Men and Women* on 10 November 1855; in *1863* it joined its companion in 'Lyrics'. After 1855 there were two minor verbal changes, and some in punctuation. On the poem, see Cook, *Browning's Lyrics*, 143–7.

18 *goes*] drops *1855*.

HOW IT STRIKES A CONTEMPORARY

First published in *Men and Women* on 10 November 1855; it remained with 'Men and Women'. After 1855 there were several revisions, none of much significance although the allegory was made less obtrusive by reducing the number of capital letters. Date of composition is unknown, but the poem may have been written soon after Browning completed his essay on Shelley late in 1851. For the title, Browning is indebted to 'How It Strikes a Stranger', a story by Jane Taylor (1783–1824) which Browning later used for 'Rephan' (1889); a 'corrégidor de Valladolid' and a house-keeper called Jacinte appear in LeSage's *Le Gil Blas de la Jeunesse*. Carlyle has been suggested as the model for the poem's hero. The poem is one of Browning's most important poetic statements about the nature of his art.

3   *Valladolid*   town about 100 miles north-west of Madrid.
12   *old dog*   rather like Mrs Browning's Flush.
28   *fly-leaf*   broadside; printed on one sheet.
39–44   The lines recall Lear's speech to Cordelia on their way to prison, and especially the reference to 'God's spies' (V. 3.17). On 10 December 1855 Browning wrote to Ruskin: 'A poet's affair is with God, to whom he is accountable, and of whom is his reward.'
48   *tang*   sting.
73–7   *his home . . . change his plate*   'there's no denying the deep delight of playing the Eastern Jew's part here in this London – they go about, you know by travel-books, with the tokens of extreme destitution and misery, and steal by blind ways and by-paths to some blank dreary house, one obscure door in it – which being well shut behind them, they grope on through a dark corridor or so, and then, a blaze follows the lifting a curtain or the like, for they are in a palace-hall with fountains and light, and marble and gold, of which the envious are never to dream' (Robert Browning to Elizabeth Barrett, 9 July 1845).
76   *Titians*   paintings by Titian, the Venetian artist (*c.* 1485–1577).
90   *Corregidor*   Chief Magistrate.
96   *memorized*   memorialized.
115   *Prado*   Promenade.

THE LAST RIDE TOGETHER

First published in *Men and Women* on 10 November 1855; in *1863* it was included in 'Romances'. After 1855 there were no verbal revisions. Date of composition is unknown. Possible significances of *ride* have been explored; one commentator fancies that the poem is about sexual intercourse. I. Orenstein associates the lady with the Muse in 'A Fresh Interpretation of "The Last Ride Together"', *Baylor Browning Interests* 18, 1961, 3–10. The poem is one of Browning's most-loved lyrics. J. K. Stephen wrote a celebrated parody in which the lady replies to Mr B.

65   They honour him with burial in Westminster Abbey.
90   *sublimate*   refine, exalt.

THE PATRIOT

First published in *Men and Women* on 10 November 1855; it was included in 'Romances' in *1863*. Except for the sixth stanza, which was heavily revised, changes after 1855 were extremely minor. The original title was 'The Old Story' (Huntington proof). Date of composition is unknown, but the poem may belong to the spring of 1849 after the Battle of Novara and the collapse of the Italian struggle for freedom. The 'Old' of the title has the sense of 'Recurring'; no particular story lies behind the poem. On it, see D. J. DeLaura, 'The Religious Imagery in Browning's "The Patriot"', *VNL* 21, 1962, 16–18.

19 *Shambles* slaughter-house.
26 *entered*] entered Brescia *1855*. (The change was probably made to avoid the identification, denied by Browning, of his hero with Arnold of Brescia, hanged in 1155.)
30 *repay:*] requite! *1855*.

MASTER HUGUES OF SAXE-GOTHA

First published in *Men and Women* on 10 November 1855; in *1863* it was included in 'Lyrics'. After 1855 revisions were minor. Date of composition is unknown, but it may well have been 1853. Master Hugues is fictional; his name, despite frequent spellings and pronunciations to the contrary, conveniently rhymes with 'fugues'. Saxe-Gotha, a duchy in central Germany, was near the birthplace of J. S. Bach (1685–1750), but Browning in a letter of 30 June 1887 said that his composer of fugues was not 'meant for the glorious Bach' but for 'one of the dry-as-dust imitators who would elaborate . . . [a trifling subject] for a dozen pages altogether' (see H. E. Greene, 'Browning's Knowledge of Music', *PMLA* LXII, 1947, 1095–9). A fugue is a composition in which a 'subject' is introduced, repeated, and complexly developed. In 1886 Browning, who himself played the organ, said 'that he had no allegorical intent in his head when he wrote the poem; that it was composed in an organ-loft and was merely the expression of a fugue – the construction of which he understood . . . because he had composed fugues himself: it was an involved labyrinth of entanglement *leading to nothing* – the only allegory in it was the possible reflection of the labyrinth of human life. That was all . . .' (L. C. Collins, *Life and Memoirs of J. C. Collins*, 1912). On the poem see R. D. Altick, 'The Symbolism of Browning's "Master Hugues of Saxe-Gotha"', *VP* III, 1965, 1–7.

16 *house of the sounds* organ.
26 *Aloys and Jurien and Just* presumably the Church's saints.
29 *sacrament-lace* the lace of the altar-cloth.
35 *helve* handle.
39 *claviers* keyboards.
42 *ruled like a score* furrowed as with horizontal lines on a musical score.
44 *breves* double long notes used to be written as solid black rectangles.
45 *bar* vertical line at the end of a bar.
48 *Company's votes* the ones that made Hugues church organist.
49 *sciolists shent* people with superficial knowledge shamed.
52 *snuff* charred part of a wick.
56 *phrase* 'subject' of the fugue.
57 *propound* The *proposta* is the 'subject'.
60 *Two* The 'subject' is answered by the second 'voice'. This fugue is a 'five-voiced' one.
67 *discept* disagree.
73 *vociferance* clamour.

77 *crepitant* crackling.

79 *strepitant* noisy (the first recorded usage in *OED*).

80 *O Danaides, O Sieve* The legendary daughters of Danaus, having killed their husbands on their wedding night, were condemned to pour water into sieves forever.

83 *Escobar* the Jesuit casuist (1589–1669) from whose name was formed the French word for 'equivocate'.

85 *Two-bars* A double bar marks the end of a section or composition.

86 *Est fuga, volvitur rota* 'It's a fugue [or 'flight'], the wheel turns' (Latin). Given the speaker's exasperation, he may well be thinking of the wheel on which Ixion was bound in Hades.

92 *risposting* riposting (the *risposta* is the 'answer' in a fugue).

94 *groining* groin, the edge formed by the intersection of two vaults (*OED* does not record the word in this sense).

100 *tickens* ticking.

127 *mountain in labour* 'Mountains will be in labour, the birth will be a single laughable little mouse' (Horace, *Art of Poetry*, 139).

135 *cobwebs we string*] dust-clouds we fling *1855*.

136 *meâ poenâ* 'at my risk' (Latin).

137 *Gorgon* Greek mythical female whose face turned men to stone.

140 *mode Palestrina* The organist Palestrina (1525–94), most distinguished of Renaissance composers, wrote mainly unaccompanied choral works (he probably never wrote for the organ). Browning defined his meaning in a letter of 30 June 1887: 'The "mode Palestrina" has no reference to organ-playing; it was the name given by old Italian writers on Composition to a certain simple and severe style like that of the Master; just as, according to Byron, "the word Miltonic means sublime."'

148 *runged*] planked *1855*.

149 *carry the moon in my pocket* 'If Caesar can hide the sun from us with a blanket, or put the moon in his pocket, we will pay him tribute for light' (*Cymbeline* III. 1.43–5).

BISHOP BLOUGRAM'S APOLOGY

First published in *Men and Women* on 10 November 1855; afterwards it remained in 'Men and Women' and underwent some revision. Details within the poem support DeVane's suggestion (*Handbook*, 241) that the poem was begun in 1850–51, and given final form about the middle of 1854.

Browning himself stated that Cardinal Wiseman (1801–65) had served as a model for Blougram. Wiseman became Roman Catholic Archbishop of Westminster and head of the Roman Catholic Church in England in 1850; the appointment had created much controversy. The fictional Bishop is, however, not a realistic portrait of the real one – and the old persistent myth that Wiseman himself reviewed the poem was finally exploded by E. R. Houghton (*VNL* 33, 1968, 46). Elements of John Henry Newman too, it is generally agreed, went into Browning's Bishop (see C. R. Tracy, 'Bishop Blougram', *MLR* XXXIV, 1939, 422–5). With the Oxford Movement in full flower and with a wealth of topical allusions not altogether characteristic of Browning, the poem is firmly set in its own time and place. For the view that the poem is indebted to Emerson's 'Montaigne; Or, the Skeptic', in *Representative Men* (1850), see C. E. Tanzy, 'Browning, Emerson, and Bishop Blougram', *VS* I, 1958, 255–66.

The names of protagonist and antagonist are suggestive. 'Blougram' may remind one of a leading nineteenth-century figure who may have contributed to Browning's portrait, Lord Brougham (1778–1868), the magnificent orator and debater, arrogant and eccentric, of whom Rogers remarked, 'There goes Solon, Lycurgus, Demosthenes, Archimedes, Sir Isaac Newton, Lord Chesterfield, and a great many more in one post-chaise.' The heavy, closed and normally four-wheeled carriage is named after him, while a 'gig' is a light, open, two-wheeled carriage. The name 'Gigadibs' is, quite apart from its triviality and silliness of sound, otherwise suggestive: a 'gig' is a fish-spear, to 'dib' is to fish. *OED* also defines 'gig' as 'a whipping top', 'a set of feathers', 'a flighty, giddy girl', 'a fancy, joke, whim', 'fun, merriment, glee', 'a squeaking noise'. *OED* definitions of 'dib' and 'dibs' include 'a small hollow', 'a game played by children', 'a counter used in playing at cards, etc. as a substitute for money', 'a slang term for money', 'a puddle', 'to dibble'.

The word 'Apology' in the title is probably deliberately ambiguous, having the senses of 'statement of regret for error' and 'justification'. Critical argument about the poem has concentrated mainly on suggesting which of the senses dominates: the two poles are represented by, say, Chesterton's view of 'a vulgar, fashionable priest, justifying his own cowardice' (page 201), and F. E. L. Priestley's of the Bishop as one whose argument is dictated by the vulgar nature of his petty opponent ('Blougram's Apologetics', *TQ* XV, 139–47; reprinted in Litzinger and Knickerbocker, *The Browning Critics*, 167–80). Chesterton's often-cited statement that Browning had said the poem was not a satire ('there is nothing hostile about it') has been shown to be apocryphal. What Browning probably did say is that Blougram 'was not treated ungenerously' (see Sir Charles Duffy, *My Life in Two Hemispheres* II, 1898, 259–61, from which it appears, incidentally, that Browning may have pronounced his character's name 'Blogram').

Among the more important critical treatments are: Susan Hardy Aiken, 'Bishop Blougram and Carlyle', *VP* XVI, 1978, 323–40; Drew, *Poetry of Browning*, 122–43; King, *The Bow and the Lyre*, 76–99; R. G. Laird, ' "He Did Not Sit Five Minutes": The Conversion of Gigadibs', *TQ* XLV, 1976, 295–313; Julia Marcus, 'Bishop Blougram and the Literary Men', *VS* XXI, 1978, 171–95; R. E. Palmer, Jr, 'The Uses of Character in "Bishop Blougram's Apology" ', *MP* LVIII, 1960, 108–18, and Priestley's essay.

3   *Abbey*   Westminster Abbey, taken over by Henry VIII.
6   *Pugin*   A. W. N. Pugin (1812–52), a convert to Roman Catholicism, and an architect of the Gothic Revival.
21   *Truth's*]   'Tis *1855–88*. (Browning made the revision for the second impression of *1888*.)
26   *Status, entourage*   rank, household.
34   *Corpus Christi Day*   commemorating the celebration of the Eucharist, the Thursday after Trinity Sunday.
38   '*Faith*   in faith.
45   *Che che*   an Italian exclamation; here, roughly, 'Come, come!'
54   *D'Orsay*   Count D'Orsay (1801–52), famous Victorian dandy.
70   *tire-room*   dressing room.
78   *comfortable*   used in the archaic or obsolete sense of sustaining or inspiriting.
108–9   *Balzac's novels*   A set of the French novelist (1799–1850) in fifty-five volumes began to appear in 1856; it had been advertised in 1855.
111   *Leipsic*   The Teubner series of classical works began to appear in 1849.
113   *Parma's pride, the Jerome*   The picture of Saint Jerome is in the Ducal Academy in Parma.
114   *Correggio*   The Italian painter (*c.* 1489–1534) studied in Modena (line 117).
125   *overhauls*   hauls overboard.

182-3 'The sound of distant music or a plaintive note, a passing word, or the momentary scent of a flower, or the sound of a bell, or the retiring of the day, or the falling leaf of autumn . . . all these will touch a chord' (Isaac Williams, *The Passion*, 1848, 434). Williams (1802-65) participated in the Oxford Movement.

184 *Euripides* Browning's favourite Greek dramatist.

190 *The grand Perhaps* 'I go to seek a grand perhaps (*un grand peut-être*)' – attributed to Rabelais on his death-bed.

197 *The Way, the Truth, the Life* 'Jesus saith unto him, I am the way, the truth, and the life' (John xiv 6).

199 *it be meant for*] it's indeed *1855*; it be indeed *1863-8*.

269 *may*] can *1855*.

283 *Comport* accord.

291 *go hang*] be lost *Huntington proof*.

315 'If thou be the Son of God, command that these stones be made bread' (Matthew iv 3).

316 *Peter's creed, or rather, Hildebrand's* Saint Peter was the first Pope; Hildebrand (Gregory VII, Pope 1073-85) fought for Papal temporal power.

353 *haunches*] buttocks *Huntington proof*.

369 *should judge*] I need *1855-63*.

377 *winking Virgin* Newman defended the belief that the Virgin's eyes move in some pictures.

381 *Verdi . . . worst opera* The allusion is probably to the *Macbeth* of Verdi (1813-1901), first produced at Florence in 1847.

386 *Rossini* The composer (1792-1868) was in Florence in 1847.

388 *prime men* journalists.

397 *demirep* woman of doubtful reputation.

411 *Schelling* the German Idealist philosopher (1775-1854). He stressed the ultimate compatibility of apparently incompatible ideas.

425 *Peter's chains* Saint Peter's chains were miraculously removed by an angel (Acts xii 7).

426 *Brave* splendid.

Noodledom The word was coined by Sydney Smith in 1810.

465 *puff* bombast.

466 *The State, that's I* 'L'État, c'est moi' was said by Louis XIV, not Napoleon.

472 *Austrian marriage* Napoleon married Marie Louise of Austria in 1810.

473 *resurrection of the old régime* The *ancien régime* was the period before the French Revolution; Napoleon was crowned Emperor in 1804.

475 *Austerlitz* Napoleon's victory of 1805 over the Russians and Austrians.

513 *towers and gorgeous palaces* 'The cloud-capped towers, the gorgeous palaces' (*The Tempest* IV. 1.152).

514 *trimmest house* New Place, bought by Shakespeare in 1597.

516 *Giulio Romano* Italian painter (*c.* 1492-1546), referred to anachronistically in *The Winter's Tale* (V. 2.106).

Dowland The English lutanist and composer (1563-1626) is mentioned in *The Passionate Pilgrim*, a book attributed to Shakespeare.

519 *Pandulph, of fair Milan cardinal* a quotation from Shakespeare's Pandulph, powerful spokesman for expediency, in *King John* (III. 1.138).

533 *Terni's fall* the waterfall north of Rome.

Gothard's top The Saint Gothard is the major pass between Switzerland and Italy.

538 *hap* fate.

550 *coat of arms* Shakespeare's father received his coat of arms in 1596.

553   *cousin of Queen Bess*   close acquaintance of Queen Elizabeth I.

572   *Re-opens a shut book*   has the Bible translated.

577   *Strauss*   The author of the *Life of Jesus* (1835) here represents, as in 'Christmas Eve', the Higher Criticism in Biblical studies.

585   *farthing*   the least valuable of English coins (a quarter of a penny).

592   *you lack*]   I lack *1855*.

593   *You*]   I *1855*.

608   *soil*]   *1855–68*; soul *1888*.

626   '*What think ye of Christ*'   Matthew xxii 42.

640   *born in Rome*   Wiseman was born in Seville; he served in Rome 1828–40.

664   *ichors*   liquids issuing from wounds to help healing.

667   *Michael*   The archangel who threw Satan out of Heaven is often represented astride a snake or dragon.

669   *box*   snuff-box.

681   *Greek endings*   suffixes like -*logy* (study).

685   *Ararat*   the mountain in Turkey where Noah's ark landed (Genesis viii 4).

703   *Newman*   John Henry Newman, who had become a Roman Catholic in 1845, was a strong spokesman for miracles.

704   *Immaculate Conception*   The Pope proclaimed the Doctrine (that the Virgin was free from original sin with Christ's birth) in 1854. Browning seems to have shared a general misunderstanding of the Doctrine which confuses it with the perpetual Virginity (see J. Britton, S.J., in *Explicator* XVII, 1959, Item 50).

715   *King Bomba*   nickname of Ferdinand II, King of the Two Sicilies 1810–59.
       lazzaroni   beggars.

716   *Antonelli*   Cardinal Antonelli, secretary to Pius IX.

728   *Naples' liquefaction*   In 1851 in *Lectures on the Present Position of Catholics*, Newman defended the belief that some of the blood of the patron saint of Naples, Saint Januarius, liquefies regularly.

732   *decrassify*   remove the crass from, purify (a Blougram neologism).

744   *Fichte's clever cut*   The German philosopher (1762–1814) thought God an idea created by man.

770   *prizes*]   calls for *1855–63*.

791   *Scouts*   mocks at.

819   *natural religion*   one based on natural things, not on revelation.

833   *French book*   possibly Balzac's *Physiologie du Mariage* (R. E. N. Dodge in *TLS*, 21 March 1935, 176); probably Diderot's *Supplément au Voyage de Bougainville* (O. Maurer, 'Bishop Blougram's French Book', *VP* VI, 1968, 177–9).

864]   Men are not gods, but, properly, are brutes. *1855*.

868   *Pan's*]   man's *1855*.

877   *Pastor est tui Dominus*   'The Lord is your shepherd' (Latin). 'The Lord is my shepherd' (Psalm xxiii, 1).

914   *fictile*   moulded.

915   *Albano*   a few miles south-east of Rome, site of Roman ruins.
       Anacreon   Greek lyric poet of the sixth century B.C.

938   *this war*   The Crimean War began in March 1854.

942   *drugget*   coarse material.
       purple   the colour of rulers.

945   *Blackwood's Magazine*   the leading and powerful magazine.

947   *Germans*   German criticism of Shakespeare was dominant in much of the nineteenth century.

951   *Whitechapel*   district in eastern London.

957   *Dublin*   Wiseman founded the *Dublin Review* in 1836; Brougham had helped to found (and contributed extensively to) the *Edinburgh Review*.

972-3   *in partibus | Episcopus, nec non*   'Bishop in regions, and also' (Latin). In 1850 Wiseman ceased to be titular Archbishop of Melipotamus *in partibus infidelium* (in unbelieving regions), and became Archbishop of Westminster.

979]   *not in 1855-68*.

999   *fence*   swordsmanship.

1014   The point of the line has been much disputed. Gigadibs has read the primary rather than the secondary sources? He has been studying the Gospels intensively? Revolted by people like Blougram, Gigadibs has fled (like the hero of Clough's *Bothie*, 1849) to Australia? He has read an after-dinner speech in the last chapter of John of a kind very different from Blougram's?

MEMORABILIA

First published as the last poem in the first volume of *Men and Women* on 10 November 1855, and included in 'Lyrics' in *1863*. Later revisions were minor. The poem may have been written soon after the essay on Shelley was completed in late 1851. H. Reynolds gives a description and facsimile of what may be an early draft of the poem, titled 'Incident in a Life', in *Christian Science Monitor*, 17 September 1956, 8.

One well-known account of the incident that probably led to the poem is that of W. G. Kingsland, who reports Browning as saying: 'I was one day in the shop of Hodgson, the well-known London bookseller, when a stranger came in, who, in the course of conversation with the bookseller, spoke of something that Shelley had once said to him. Suddenly the stranger paused, and burst into laughter as he observed me staring at him with blanched face; and ... I still vividly remember how strangely the presence of a man who had seen and spoken with Shelley affected me.' A different account is, however, given in an unpublished letter of 30 March 1881 (now in the Pforzheimer Library) to Buxton Forman. Here Browning writes that the man who saw Shelley plain was a composite of a bookseller whom Browning met only once and who happened to mention seeing the poet, and of a friend who was with Browning in the shop and was surprised by Browning's amazement. DeVane (*Handbook*, 244) suggests a date of 1851 for the incident but gives no reasons; Browning wrote, however, that he was a boy at the time. The young Browning's reverence for Shelley had diminished by 1855, and was profoundly affected when Browning later learned, probably in 1858, more biographical details. The Latin title of the poem means 'Memorable things'.

9   *moor*   Browning wrote that it was imaginary.

10   *certain*]   *not in 1855*.

15   *eagle-feather*   Perhaps suggested by some such passage as this (from Shelley's 'Ode to Liberty', 5-8): 'My soul spurned the chains of its dismay, / And in the rapid plumes of song / Clothed itself, sublime and strong, / (As a young eagle soars the morning clouds among)'.

ANDREA DEL SARTO

First published as the first poem of the second volume of *Men and Women* on 10 November 1855. In *1863-88* it remained in 'Men and Women', now placed after its companion poem, 'Fra Lippo Lippi'. Revisions after 1855 were minor. The word 'Painter' was added to the subtitle in proof.

The poem's origin probably lies in the request by John Kenyon, the Brownings' friend, for a copy (not a photograph) of a painting in the Pitti Palace in Florence, then supposed to be del Sarto's portrait of himself and his wife; it is now known to be two portraits joined together, is no longer attributed to del Sarto, is not thought to depict the painter or his wife, and has been relegated to storage. Unable to get a copy of the painting, Browning instead sent the poem, which was probably written in 1853. Browning was generally familiar with the paintings of del Sarto (1486–1531), and the particular painting behind this poem is clearly a major source (a photograph of it faces page 200 in Griffin and Minchin, *Life*). As with 'Fra Lippo Lippi', the main source is Vasari's *Lives of the Artists*, which gives most of the facts, and supports the general tenor, of Browning's poem (Vasari may have been Andrea's pupil). Browning may have consulted Baldinucci's *Notizie*, and may be indebted to Musset's play *André del Sarto* (1833) – see B. Melchiori's note in *VP* IV, 1966, 132–6. J. Markus has argued that the poem is influenced by the break-up of the marriage of Browning's friend, the artist William Page, and Mrs Page in '"Andrea del Sarto (Called 'The Faultless Painter')" and William Page (Called "The American Titian")', *BIS* II, 1974, 1–24.

Andrea was called 'del Sarto' because his father was a tailor, and 'the Faultless Painter' (*Il Pittore senza Errori*) because of his technique. He married the widowed Lucrezia in 1513; she often served as his model. In 1518–19 he was in the French court of Francis I. The poem is set in 1525, six years before Andrea died of the plague. Recent authorities see as valid Browning's (and Vasari's) basic judgement about Andrea, but generally see his treatment (one that twists Vasari's materials at times) as being somewhat unfair (see D. B. Maceachen's attack on Browning's 'libel' in *VP* VIII, 1970, 61–4). Mrs Miller's fancy, presented briefly in her biography (175–6), that the poem owes much to Browning's feeling that his wife was stifling his genius is notorious.

The poem, often judged to be Browning's finest achievement, has been much discussed. Among essays are: R. D. Altick, '"Andrea del Sarto": The Kingdom of Hell is Within', in Tracy, *Browning's Mind and Art*, 18–31; E. Bieman, 'An Eros Manqué: Browning's "Andrea del Sarto"', *Studies in English Literature* X, 1970, 651–68; Cook, *Browning's Lyrics*, 126–35; M. L. D'Avanzo, 'King Francis, Lucrezia, and the Figurative Language of "Andrea del Sarto"', *Texas Studies in Literature and Language* IX, 1958, 523–36; F. Kaplan *Miracles of Rare Device*, Wayne State University Press, 1972, 94–108; King, *The Bow and the Lyre*, 11–31; Langbaum, *The Poetry of Experience*, 148–54.

15 *Fiesole*   the hill-town just north-east of Florence.

35 *common greyness*   according to modern scholars, not so much a characteristic of Andrea's art as of the effects of time and light.

57 *cartoon*   sketch for a painting.

76 *Someone*   Michelangelo.

83–4   'My words fly up, my thoughts remain below: / Words without thoughts never to heaven go' (*Hamlet* III. 3.97–8).

93 *Morello*   mountain north of Florence.

96]   *not in 1855.*

105 *the Urbinate*   Raphael (1483–1520) was born at Urbino.

106 *Vasari*   Giorgio Vasari (1512–74), main source for Browning's poem, was introduced to Andrea by Michelangelo.

130 *Agnolo* Michelangelo (Michel Agnolo Buonarroti) (1475–1564).
150 *Fontainebleau* the town south-east of Paris where Francis I built the royal palace.
160 *frank* with a pun on Frank (the Franks gave France its name).
178 *the Roman* Raphael worked in Rome for the last twelve years of his life.
210 *cue-owls* scops-owls. Browning anglicizes the Italian name imitative of the birds' cries (*ciù*). A neologism which Mrs Browning picked up in *Aurora Leigh* (1856).
241 *scudi* Roman coins.
250 Vasari says that Andrea abandoned his own parents for Lucrezia's relatives.
261–2 *Four great walls... angel's reed* Revelation xxi 10–21.
263 *Leonard* Leonardo da Vinci (1452–1519).

BEFORE

First published in *Men and Women* on 10 November 1855. In *1863* it was included in 'Lyrics'; after 1855 revisions were minor. The date of writing is unknown. In letters of April 1846 Browning had supported duelling, while Miss Barrett had opposed it. The initial opposition and Browning's move to his wife's views are reflected in 'Before' and its companion. On the poem, see Drew, *Poetry of Browning*, 82–3.

8 *entoilment* state of being trapped (the only usage recorded in *OED*).
10 *caps* doffs his cap.
18 *grape-trees* grape-vines.
24 *misfeasance* transgression (a legal term).
27 *evil's lump with good to leaven* 'Know ye not that a little leaven leaveneth the whole lump' (1 Corinthians v 6).
32 *sub-intents* subordinate purposes (not in *OED*).

AFTER

First published in *Men and Women* on 10 November 1855. In *1863* it was included in 'Lyrics'; after 1855 there were minor revisions in punctuation only. The date of writing is unknown. In letters of April 1846 Browning had supported duelling, while Miss Barrett had opposed it. The initial opposition and Browning's move to his wife's views are reflected in 'After' and its companion.

18 *Cover the face* 'Cover her face; mine eyes dazzle; she died young' (Webster, *Duchess of Malfi* IV. 2.267).

IN THREE DAYS

First published in *Men and Women* on 10 November 1855. In *1863* it was included in 'Lyrics'. After 1855 there were a few changes in punctuation and one verbal change. The date of composition is unknown, though Mrs Miller suggests in her biography (170n.) that it may have been written about 23 July 1852 when, for the only time in their married life, Browning and his wife were separated for a few days. On the poem, see Cook, *Browning's Lyrics*, 211–14.

IN A YEAR

First published in *Men and Women* on 10 November 1855. In *1863* it joined its companion in 'Lyrics'; after 1855 revisions were trifling. The date of writing is unknown.

OLD PICTURES IN FLORENCE

First published in *Men and Women* on 10 November 1855. The Huntington proof shows the original title as 'Opus Magistri Jocti'. In *1863* the poem was included in 'Lyrics'. After 1855 Browning revised the poem extensively but not very significantly. The poem may well have been begun in 1850, when the Brownings were excitedly collecting old pictures in Florence, but most of the work on it would seem to belong to the spring of 1853. Vasari's *Lives of the Artists* and Browning's direct exposure to Italian art, and especially Florentine art, are the poem's major sources.

Browning speaks here in his own person in a way not characteristic of most of his work. The poem expands on themes of perennial interest to him, especially on the 'philosophy of the imperfect' (to which the unfinished bell-tower of Giotto in the centre of Florence gives body).

3   *aloed*   covered with aloes, a kind of lily (only example in this sense in *OED*).

15   *bell-tower Giotto raised*   Giotto di Bondone (1267–1337), the greatest early Florentine artist, designed the campanile shortly before his death. Nearly a hundred yards high, it is generally regarded as the world's most beautiful campanile, and as among the greatest examples of Gothic art. His plans included a spire which has never been placed on 'Giotto's Tower'.

28   *in chief*   as my favourite spot.

33   *chaffer*   haggle about price.

38   *apsis*   apse.

51   *Michaels*   paintings by Michelangelo.

59   *their work is all*   all their work is *Huntington proof*.

64   *Dellos*   Dello di Niccolo Delli was a minor fifteenth-century artist.

67   *girns*   snarls (Scotticism).

69–72   *Stefano . . . Vasari*   Stefano Fiorentino (1301–50), pupil of Giotto, highly praised by Vasari, and known as the Ape of Nature for his realism.

76   *sic transit 'sic transit gloria mundi'*:   'thus passes the world's glory' (Latin).

84   *in fructu*   'as fruit' (Latin).

86   *actual*   present.

91–2   *Earth here, rebuked by Olympus there : | And*]   And bringing your own shortcomings there, | You *1855* (in *Huntington proof* the printed *1855* reading is changed in Browning's hand to: Earth-here rebuked by Olympus there – And).

98   *Theseus*   mythical King of Athens, and Greek hero.

99   *Son of Priam*   either Hector or Paris, both sons of the Trojan King. If Browning has specific works in mind, he may be thinking, as with Theseus, of representations on the Parthenon. One famous Greek sculpture depicted Paris as a kneeling archer.

101   *Apollo*   The Greek god of poetry killed the Python when still a child.

102   *Niobe*   The Queen of Thebes grieved because the gods killed all her children. The Uffizi has a Greek sculpture of her.

103   *Racers' frieze*   the Procession of Horsemen on the Parthenon frieze.

104   *Alexander*   presumably Alexander the Great.

108 *a mortal's*] the worsted's *1855*.

127 *for our copy* to be copied by us.

129 'A little leaven leaveneth the whole lump' (Galatians v 9).

135 *O* Giotto (the famous story is told by Vasari), asked for a sample of his skill by a Papal envoy, immediately drew with one stroke a perfect circle.

149 *fray* rub away.

156 *quiddit* quiddity: captious nicety in argument.

159 *allocution* formal address.

179 *Nicolo the Pisan* early Italian sculptor and architect (*c.* 1225–*c.* 1284).

180 *Cimabue* Giovanni Cimabue (1240–1302), great early Italian painter, reputedly the teacher of Giotto.

182 *Ghiberti* Lorenzo Ghiberti (1381–1455), Florentine sculptor, best known for the 'Gate of Paradise', the eastern doors of Florence's Baptistery.

  Ghirlandajo Domenico Bigordi or Ghirlandaio (1449–94), Florentine fresco painter and teacher of Michelangelo.

198 *dree* suffer (Scotticism or archaism).

201 *Bigordi* Ghirlandaio.

202 *Sandro* Botticelli (Alessandro dei Filipepi) (1444–1510), Florentine painter.

203 *wronged Lippino* Filippino Lippi (1457–1504), son of Fra Filippo Lippi, painter, 'wronged' presumably either because paintings of his were attributed to others or because he was illegitimate.

204 *Frà Angelico* Florentine painter (1387–1455).

205 *Taddeo Gaddi* fourteenth-century Florentine painter, pupil of Giotto.

206 *intonaco* plaster background for fresco painting.

207 *Jerome* the fourth-century saint, and a favourite subject for painters.

208 *Lorenzo Monaco* Florentine painter (*c.* 1370–*c.* 1425).

209–10 *close red cap,* | *My Pollajolo* Antonio Pollaiulo (*c.* 1432–98), Florentine artist, painted what Browning thought was a self-portrait in which the subject wears a 'close red cap'. He is 'twice a craftsman' presumably because he turned from goldsmith's work to painting.

211 *hap* chance.

212 *muscular Christ* Browning probably alludes to Pollaiulo's *Christ at the Column*, depicted on a panel owned by the Brownings.

215 *Alesso Baldovinetti* Florentine painter (1427–99).

217 *Margheritone of Arezzo* Margarito of Arezzo, thirteenth-century Sienese painter, is treated with some disdain by Vasari, and by Mrs Browning in *Casa Guidi Windows* (1851).

218 *barret* biretta, a priest's flat cap.

220 *poll-clawed parrot* 'poll clawed like a parrot' (*2 Henry IV* II. 4.282).

226 *tinglish* the only recorded usage in *OED*.

227 *Their pictures*] Works rot or *Huntington proof*.

230 *Zeno* founder of the Stoic philosophy.

232 *Carlino* a painting by Carlo Dolci (1616–86), Florentine painter.

236 *tablet* Browning in a letter of 1886 described this as 'a famous "Last Supper" ' (page 232), mentioned by Vasari, and gone astray long ago from the Church of S. Spirito: it turned up, according to report, in some obscure corner, while I was in Florence, and was at once acquired by a stranger'.

237 *Buonarroti* Michelangelo.

241 *San Spirito* church in Florence.

242 *Ognissanti* church in Florence.

244 *Detur amanti* 'It is to be given to one who loves it' (Latin).

245 *Koh-i-noor* 'Mountain of Light', the famous diamond given to Queen Victoria in 1849.

246 *Giamschid* a legendary Persian king, owner of a remarkable ruby.

Persian Sofi's eye 'Sophy' is the former title of Persian kings. In Byron's *Giaour* (479), Soul, from Leila's eye, beams 'Bright as the jewel of Giamschid'.

251 *Mont Saint Gothard* mountain in the Alps.

255 *Radetzky* Count Radetzky (1766-1858), Austrian general, was governor of Upper Italy (1849-57). He is the 'dotard' of line 249.

256 *Morello* mountain north of Florence.

258 *stone of Dante* 'the stone / Called Dante's, – a plain flat stone scarce discerned / From others in the pavement, – whereupon / He used to bring his quiet chair out, turned to Brunelleschi's church, and pour alone/ The lava of his spirit when it burned' (Mrs Browning, *Casa Guidi Windows* I). She goes on to see it as a focal point for the exiled Dante's thoughts of his city, and to say, 'thy favourite stone's elected right / As tryst-place for the Tuscans to foresee / Their earliest chartas from'.

259 *Witanagemot* governing council in Anglo-Saxon England.

260 *Casa Guidi* Mrs Browning's long poem, *Casa Guidi Windows* (1851); it pressed the cause of Italian freedom.

quod videas ante 'which you may have seen before' (Latin).

263 *Lorraine* The Austrian emperors were of the house of Habsburg-Lorraine.

264 *Orgagna* Andrea di Cione, fourteenth-century Florentine artist, generally known as Orcagna.

269 *fructuous* fruitful.

271 *Chimera* legendary fire-breathing monster.

274 *issimo* the superlative ending for Italian adjectives.

275 *half-told tale of Cambuscan* Chaucer's unfinished 'Squire's Tale': 'Or call up him that left half told / The story of Cambuscan bold' (Milton, 'Il Penseroso', 109-10).

276 *alt to altissimo* 'high to highest' (Italian).

277 *beccaccia* woodcock (Italian). The only recorded usage in *OED*.

279 *braccia* A braccio is an Italian measure of length, a cubit, or nearly two feet. Giotto's plans called for a fifty-braccia spire on the campanile.

285 *'God and the People'* the motto of Mazzini.

286 *tricolour* The flag of Italy is green, white and red.

287-8] Why, to hail him, the vindicated Giotto / Thanking God for it all, the first am I! *Huntington proof*; Foreseeing the day that vindicates Giotto / And Florence together, the first am I! *1855*.

IN A BALCONY

First published in *Men and Women* on 10 November 1855. In *1863* it was included with 'Tragedies and Other Plays'. In *1868* (and *1888*) it was made independent, in both editions appearing in a volume with, but not as part of, 'Dramatis Personae'. After *1855* it was extensively revised, an unusually large number of changes being made for *1888*, but the total results are not of much significance. In *1855* the poem was in three parts (1-339, 340-605, 606-919). The divisions were permanently dropped in *1863*, in which edition alone the title had '*A Scene*' added to it.

In *1868* and *1888* Browning dates the play 1853, and indicates that it was written in Bagni di Lucca. The Brownings stayed there between July and October 1853, and the fairly successful revival of *Colombe's Birthday* in London in April 1853 may well have prompted further dramatic experiment. Though written as a closet drama, the work has been staged several times. The plot and characters are Browning's own. It has been suggested that the contrasting views of Constance and Norbert as to the right approach to the Queen reflect those of Elizabeth Barrett and Browning as to their approach to Mr Barrett in 1846.

On the play, see P. G. Mudford, 'The Artistic Consistency of Browning's *In a Balcony*', *VP* VII, 1969, 31–40; and E. E. Stoll, 'Browning's *In a Balcony*', *MLQ* III, 1942, 407–17 (reprinted in his *From Shakespeare to Joyce*, Doubleday Doran, 1944, 328–38; and in Drew, *Robert Browning*, 178–88).

17   *Hold you and have you*   'to have and to hold' (marriage service).

106 *dome* mansion.

130 *Rubens* the great Flemish artist (1577–1640).

333 *conceit* concept.

342 *Mother* the Virgin Mary.

355] And so accepting life, abjure ourselves! *1855*; And so, accepting life, abjure ourselves. *1863–8*.

358 *plot*] turf *1855*.

400 *change* give up in exchange.

411 *smile*] cheek *1855–68*.

412 *baladine* female public dancer.

422 *halbert* halberd, long-handled weapon with head combining spear-point and axe.

445 *in intelligence* mutually aware of the situation.

465 *lightning*] cloud was *1855–68*.

466 *proved*] at *1855–68*.

504 *deceive – ah, whom?*] deceive myself; *1855–68*.

513] The love, the passionate faith, the sacrifice, *1855–68*.

514 *Life-long, death-long*] The constancy *1855–68*.

516 *Triton* merman-like sea-god.

605 *God's moon* love. (As moon reflects sun, so love reflects God.)

645–6 *fire was crammed | In that mere stone you struck* 'fire i' the flint / Shows not till it be struck' (*Timon of Athens* I. 1.22–3).

686 *soul*] man *1855–68*.

690] But bind in one and carry out their wills. *1855–68*.

696 *novel brain*] the new man *1855–68*.

698] And whom they trust to find them out new ways *1855*.
      And who, they trust, shall find them out new ways *1863–8*.

699 *To untried heights*] To the new heights *1855*; To heights as new *1863–8*.

707–10 The image is developed in 'Rabbi Ben Ezra', 145–92.

709 *And consummation*] In that uprising *1855*.

711 *human sense*] lower men *1855–68*.

712 *men*] they *1855*; all *1863–8*.

742 *stalking-horse* something serving to hide one's intention.

765 *constant* The heroine's name is clearly used punningly.

795 *overcharge her part* overact.

816 *hazarded*] opened out *1855–68*.

837 *eye-flower* Perhaps eyebright, the scarlet pimpernel.

919 The question as to what happens at the play's end has been much discussed. Browning himself said, 'The queen had a large and passionate temperament, which had only once been touched and brought into intense life. She would have died, as by a knife in her heart. The guard would have come to carry away her dead body.' And

he thought it might be well to add stage directions, 'and have it seen that they were carrying her [the queen] across the back of the stage' (K. de K. Bronson, 'Browning in Venice', *Century Magazine* LXIII, 1902, 578).

SAUL

The first nine sections of 'Saul' were first published on 6 November 1845 in *Dramatic Romances and Lyrics*, with a note ('End of Part the First') to indicate that the poem was incomplete. The same sections, again unnumbered (though in manuscript the fragment was divided into four parts), were reprinted with some revisions in *1849*. In both printings, each long line of the final text was printed as two lines (with the divisions in the obvious places). On 10 November 1855 when the completed poem was printed in *Men and Women*, 239 lines (the last ten sections) had been added, and the poem's length more than tripled; the first nine sections, and especially the last few lines of the ninth, had been extensively revised. In *1855*, as in later printings, the verse paragraphs were numbered, and the long lines used. After *1855* punctuation revisions were extensive, verbal revisions few and insignificant. In *1863* the poem appeared in 'Lyrics'.

The fragment published in 1845 was probably written in that year: Browning later indicated that he reread Christopher Smart's *Song to David* (1763) in 1845 (he had first been impressed by it in 1827). On 3 May 1845 Browning told Miss Barrett that he would one day show her 'Saul'; by 27 August she had read it and urged its completion. Browning, however, could not finish it; and it would seem clear that he had not worked out his religious ideas in a way that would have allowed him to finish it. Thus he adopted Miss Barrett's suggestion of 9 September that he publish the fragment. When he later completed the poem is not known; *Christmas-Eve and Easter-Day* shows that by 1850 Browning's religious views were such as to make completion of 'Saul' possible. Thematically, 'Saul' has much in common with 'An Epistle . . . of Karshish', and 1853 seems a likely date for both poems.

The Biblical source is 1 Samuel xvi 14-23. Smart's *Song to David*, as Browning says in his 'Parleying with Christopher Smart', led him in 1845 to other of Smart's works including the preface in which Smart writes of the 'fine subject' suggested to him of 'David's playing to King Saul when he was troubled with the evil spirit'. The story was well known to the nineteenth century and other sources have been suggested, including a letter of Wordsworth published in 1851 which may have influenced the arguments for a future life in sections XV–XVIII (see M. M. Bevington, *VNL* 20, 1961, 19–21). The only other significant and demonstrable source is, however, Thomas Wyatt's *Seven Penitential Psalms*, especially important in its influence on the structure of 'Saul' (see J. A. S. McPeek, 'The Shaping of Saul', *JEGP* XLIV, 1945, 360–66). Other important treatments include: E. Bieman, 'The Ongoing Testament in Browning's "Saul"', *TQ* XLIII, 1974, 151–68; A. W. Crawford, 'Browning's "Saul"', *Queen's Quarterly* XXXIV, 1927, 448–54; C. Dahl and J. L. Brewer, 'Browning's "Saul" and the Fourfold Vision: A Neoplatonic-Hermetic Approach', *BIS* III, 1975, 101–18; W. Hellstrom, 'Time and Type in Browning's *Saul*', *ELH* XXXIII, 1966, 370–89; King, *The Bow and the Lyre*, 100–123; W. D. Shaw, 'The Analogical Argument of Browning's "Saul"', *VP* II, 1964, 277–82.

The poem was a favourite of the Pre-Raphaelites, and of Browning, who, asked to name four representative poems of moderate length, selected 'Saul' as one of two lyrics. Miss Barrett also admired it; without exception, Browning changed passages she criticized (see *New Poems*, 155–9), in most cases adopting her suggested change (as indicated in notes that follow).

1 *Abner* the captain of Saul's 'host' (1 Samuel xxvi 5), Saul's cousin.

4 *until*] till *MS*. (Browning followed Miss Barrett's suggestion, one designed 'to break the course of monosyllables'.)

7] For in the black midtent silence / Three drear days, *MS*. (Miss Barrett wrote, 'the short line is too short to the ear – not to say that "drear days" conspires against "dread ways" found afterwards'.)

9 *ended their strife*] gone their dread ways *1845*.

10] *not in 1845*.

12 *lilies still living and blue* In a letter of 16 March 1846 to Miss Barrett, Browning wrote 'lilies are of all colours in Palestine – . . . the water lily, lotos, which I think I meant, is *blue* altogether'.

13 *Just broken*] As thou brak'st them *1845–9*.

19 *extends*] leads *1845–9*.

24] Something more black than the blackness – / The vast, upright *MS*. (Browning adopted Miss Barrett's suggestions to improve the rhythm.)

27 *that burst through the tent-roof*] burst through the blind tent-roof *MS*. (Browning adopted the suggestion of Miss Barrett, who found 'blind' a clogging – and repeated – epithet, and who thought the earlier rapidity of rhythm gave greater force to 'showed Saul'.)

30 *He relaxed*] So he bent *1845–9*.

33 *stark*] black *1845*.

37 *So docile*] Docile *MS*. (Browning adopted Miss Barrett's suggestion.)

40 *And now*] *not in MS*. (Browning adopted Miss Barrett's suggestion.)

41 *eve and*] *not in MS*. (Browning adopted Miss Barrett's suggestion.)

45 *jerboa* a rodent with long back legs for leaping.

51 *last*] low *1845*.

55 *Oh*] *not in MS*. (Miss Barrett's suggestion: 'it throws a wail into the line, and swells the rhythm rightly, I think'.)

57 *As*] *not in MS*. (Browning adopted Miss Barrett's suggestion.)

59 *friends*] brothers *1845*.

60 *Levites* Those assisting the priests in the Temple were traditionally chosen from the tribe of Levi.

61 *stopped here*] stopped *MS*. (Browning adopted Miss Barrett's suggestion.)

65 *male* very blue.

　　courageous lively (the word's etymological roots lie in the Latin *cor*, 'heart').

66 *still moved*] stirred *MS*. (Miss Barrett suggested 'that stirred'.)

71 *The strong rending of boughs from the fir-tree*] The rending their boughs from the palm-trees *1845–9*.

72 *hunt*] haunt *1849*.

77 *so*] *not in MS*. (Elizabeth Barrett suggested 'right'.)

78 *life, the*] life here, *1845–9*.

81 *with the armies*] to the wolf hunt *1845–9*.

84 *Joining*] Join *MS*. (Browning adopted Miss Barrett's suggestion.)

90 *Present*] And *MS*.; And the *1845*. (Browning adopted Miss Barrett's suggestion, but reverted to the MS. reading in *1849*.)

　　of] for *MS*.; in *1845–9*.

92 *And all gifts, which*] Oh all, all *1845*; Oh all gifts *1849*.

93–6] On one head the joy and the pride,
　　　　Even rage like the throe
　　That opes the rock, helps its glad labour,
　　　　And lets the gold go –

> And ambition that sees a sun lead it [– *1849*]
> > Oh, all of these – all
> Combine to unite in one creature
> > – Saul! *1845–9*.

97–335] *not in 1845–9*.

100 *Strains* feels high tension.

101 *cherubim-chariot* Ezekiel x 3–17.

162 *inconscious* unconscious (rare).

179 *First King* Saul was the first king of Israel.

188 *paper-reeds* plants from which papyrus is made.

200 *last*] that *1855*.

203 *Hebron* mountain and city south of Jerusalem, the home of David.

204 *Kidron* brook or gully near Jerusalem.

204–5 *retrieves/ Slow the damage* probably influenced by Horace, *Odes* IV, vii, 13; see J. C. Maxwell in *VP* III, 1965, 144.

213 *error* Saul had disobeyed God (1 Samuel xv).

245 *Wisdom*] wisdom *1855*.

291 *Sabaoth* hosts or armies.

292 *not*] not in *1855*.

327 *held breath*] new awe *1855–63*.

'DE GUSTIBUS –'

First published in *Men and Women* on 10 November 1855. In *1863* it was included in 'Lyrics'. After *1855* revisions were minor. The date of composition is unknown. The title is from the Latin proverb, '*De gustibus non est disputandum*': 'About tastes there's no arguing' (*not* 'There's no accounting for tastes').

4 *cornfield* field of grain (English usage, not North American).

28 *Before*] Without *1855*.

35 *king* Ferdinand II, the Bourbon King of the Two Sicilies (King 'Bomba').

36 *liver-wing* right arm.

40 *Queen Mary's saying* 'When I am dead and opened, you shall find "Calais" lying in my heart.' (The saying, known to every English schoolboy, referred to her grief at the loss of Calais, last British possession in France, in 1558, just before Mary Tudor's death.)

46 *shall ever*] it still shall *1855*. Browning left Italy for England in 1861.

WOMEN AND ROSES

First published in *Men and Women* on 10 November 1855. In *1863* it was included in 'Lyrics'. After 1855 there were eight verbal changes, and a few in punctuation. The date of composition is uncertain despite the precision of DeVane's invention (*Handbook*, 259) of 1 January 1852, a date not supported by any evidence and contradicted by some. The evidence for dating is contradictory (see J. Huebenthal's note in *VP* IV, 1966, 51–4). Late in 1887 Browning is reported to have said, 'One year in Florence I had been rather lazy; I resolved that I would write something every day. Well, the first day I wrote about some roses, suggested by a magnificent basket that some one had sent my wife. The next day *Childe Roland* came upon me as a kind of dream' (Whiting, *The Brownings*, 261). In 1866, however, Browning said he wrote 'Childe Roland' in Paris; if so, 'Women and Roses' belongs to January 1852. On balance, 1853 seems the likely date, a day before 'Childe Roland'. There is no support for the frequently made statement (see DeVane, *Handbook*, 259) that *this* poem records a vivid (or any other kind of) dream. What is sure is that the meaning of the poem has occasioned dispute, and that (like many other poems of Browning) it is most uncharacteristic of its author. On it, see Cook, *Browning's Lyrics*, 181–92; L. Poston III, '"A Novel Grace and a Beauty Strange": Browning's "Women and Roses"', *BSN* IV, No. 3, 1974, 15–17; G. Tillotson, 'A Word for Browning', *Sewanee Review* LXXII, 1964, 389–97.

15 *unimpeached* unentangled.

PROTUS

First published in *Men and Women* on 10 November 1855. In *1863* the poem was included in 'Romances'. After 1855 revisions were trifling. The date of writing is unknown, but the poem may date from the Brownings' visit to Rome from December 1853 to May 1854. The characters are imaginary. Browning is, of course, casting an ironic eye on later Roman emperors.

2 *Half-emperors and quarter-emperors* After 285 there were usually two or more emperors.
4 *Loric and low-browed Gorgon* The Roman *lorica* (Browning anglicizes the word) was a leather cuirass. The breast is decorated with a Gorgon's head, low-browed because of the snaky hair designed to petrify opponents.
9 *god* Augustus, first Roman emperor, was deified in A.D. 14.
10 *porphyry* a hard richly coloured rock.
  Byzant Byzantium, site of the new capital of the Roman Empire after 330.
36 *Pannonian* from the Roman province south and west of the Danube.
49–50 *hunting-stables ... dogs* Pannonia was famous for its hunting-dogs.
53 *Thrace* Roman province in the eastern Balkans.

HOLY-CROSS DAY

First published in *Men and Women* on 10 November 1855. In *1863* it was included in 'Romances'. Revisions after 1855 were trifling. As with 'Protus', it seems reasonable to assume that the poem is a product of the Brownings' stay in Rome, December 1853 to May 1854.
  Holy Cross Day is 14 September, but in fact the sermons were not annual but frequent events. They were introduced by Pope Gregory XIII in 1584 and abolished by Pope Gregory XVI in 1846 ('*Pope Gregory XVI*' in the final note of the poem read 'The present Pope' in *1855*). Evelyn's *Diary* for 7 January 1645 records the Jews' sitting at the sermon 'with so much malice in their countenances, spitting, coughing, humming, and motion, that it is almost impossible they should hear a word from the preacher' – the passage may have suggested the spirit of the opening of Browning's poem, and the 'quotation' from the Secretary's Diary, which is, of course, by Browning. The concluding stanzas are often said to have been based on the *Song of Death* of Rabbi Ben Ezra (1092–1167), but the supposed *Song* is probably Browning's invention. On the poem see B. Melchiori, *Browning's Poetry of Reticence*, 90–113.

Epigraph 3–5 *crumb ... dogs* Matthew xv 22–7.
Epigraph 8 "*Compel them to come in*" Luke xiv 23.

1   *Fee, faw, fum*   possibly an echo of the Giant in stories of Jack the Giant-killer; in some versions the Giant goes on to smell the blood of a Christian man.
    bubble and squeak   a mixture of meat and cabbage which, in England, masquerades as food.
2   *Blessedest Thursday*   presumably, the Thursday before Lent.
4   *smug and gruff*   smooth and rough.
10   *handsel*   use first.
    shaving-shears   To be shaved (see line 41) is to display one's conversion.
20   *acorned*   full of acorns – 'full-acorned boar' (*Cymbeline* II. 5.16).
22   *hour-glass*   to time the sermon.
23   *chine*   backbone.
24   *laps*   folds of skin.
29   *quotha*   forsooth.
31   *doomed black dozen*   the 'converts'.
32   *cog … cozen*   cheat … trick.
38   *from a Jew you mount to a Turk*   move some way up the scale of Christian regard.
52   *Corso*   then the main street of Rome.
66   *Ben Ezra's Song of Death*   Ben Ezra was the Spanish Jew and scholar (1092–1167) whom Browning used as a spokesman in 'Rabbi Ben Ezra' (1864). The *Song of Death* that follows is in all probability not a translation but original Browning. In 1888 Browning wrote to Furnivall: 'in *Holy Cross Day*, Ben Ezra is not supposed to acknowledge Christ as the Messiah because he resorts to the obvious argument "even on your own showing, and accepting for the moment the authority of your accepted Lawgiver, you are condemned by His precepts – let alone ours"' (Hood, *Letters*, 287–8).
73–8   'For the Lord will have mercy on Jacob, and will yet choose Israel, and set them in their own land; and the strangers shall be joined with them, and they shall cleave to the house of Jacob' (Isaiah xiv 1).
85–90   Mark xiii 32–7.
91   *He*   Jesus.
104   *Barabbas*   the murderer whom Pilate released after giving the mob their choice between Barabbas and Jesus.
111   *Ghetto*   the area to which Jews were confined (*Borghetto* is Italian for 'little town').
120   *Pleasant Land*   Jeremiah iii 19.

THE GUARDIAN-ANGEL

First published in *Men and Women* on 10 November 1855. In *1863* it was included in 'Lyrics'. Revisions after 1855 were trifling. The poem was written in Ancona in the last week of July 1848, when the Brownings had just seen what Mrs Browning called 'a divine picture' in the Church of San Agostino in Fano, the town a few miles north of Ancona on the east coast of Italy. Giovanni Francesco Barbieri (1591–1666), Guercino ('Squinter'), was a Bolognese artist of some distinction; Browning's initial enthusiasm for his picture at Fano would seem later to have moderated. (A photograph of *The Guardian-Angel* faces page 166 in Griffin and Minchin's *Life*.) Browning had seen his work in England, at Dulwich, with his old friend Alfred Domett, whom he addresses in the poem. This is the only poem of Browning's known to have been written in the first three years of his marriage.

2   *child*   In the painting, the Angel guards a young child standing on a tomb.

4 *performed thy special ministry* 'performs its secret ministry' (Coleridge, 'Frost at Midnight', 1).

18 *bird of God* Dante, *Purgatorio* ii, 38 (and elsewhere).

33–5 Browning may be recalling the last lines of Keats's 'Ode on a Grecian Urn'.

40 'The world was all before them' (Milton, *Paradise Lost* XII, 646).

46 *My angel* Mrs Browning.

51 *wrong* perhaps a reference to hostile remarks about Guercino in Ruskin's *Modern Painters*, and/or in a book by the Brownings' friend, Mrs Jameson, about which they had remonstrated with her.

55 *Wairoa* river in New Zealand, where Alfred Domett had gone.

CLEON

First published in *Men and Women* on 10 November 1855. In later collections it stayed in 'Men and Women'. Revisions after 1855 were trifling. The poem is a companion to 'An Epistle . . . of Karshish', and would seem to have been written after it; its date may well be 1854. It has affinities with Arnold's *Empedocles on Etna*, which had been published in 1852 but withdrawn in 1853; in 1867 it was reprinted at the request of Browning. Browning's epigraph comes from Acts xvii 28: 'For in him we live, and move, and have our being; as certain also of your own poets have said, For we are also his offspring.' Cleon and Protus are fictional; the time of the poem is about A.D. 52.

The poem's relationship to *Empedocles on Etna* is explored in A. W. Crawford, 'Browning's "Cleon"', *JEGP* XXVI, 1927, 485–90. E. C. McAleer sees the poem as a critique of Positivism in 'Browning's "Cleon" and Auguste Comte', *Comparative Literature* VIII, 1956, 142–5. For criticism, see R. A. King, Jr, 'Browning: "Mage" and "Maker" – A Study in Poetic Purpose and Method', *VNL* 20, 1961, 22–5 (reprinted in Drew, *Robert Browning*, 189–98).

1 *sprinkled isles* probably the Sporades: scattered islands in the Aegean Sea. In *Pauline* 331, 'clustered isles' (probably the Cyclades) are referred to.

4 *Tyranny* The word is used in its Greek sense as a description of a kind of rule, and without its modern implications.

14 *settle-down* flock settling down (*OED* describes it as a nonce word).

15 *crocus* saffron.

16 *sea-wools* wools dyed with sea-purple.

43 *requirement* request, inquiry.

47 *epos . . . plates* epic poem . . . tablets.

51 *sun-god on the phare* statue of Apollo on the lighthouse.

53 *Poecile* the painted Portico at Athens.

60 *moods* modes (types of musical scale).

83 *rhomb* rhombus, equilateral parallelogram.

84 *lozenge* diamond-shaped figure.

   trapezoid trapezium (British usage), four-sided figure without any parallel sides.

132 *suave . . . drupe* sweet . . . wild plum.

138 *soul* Cleon uses the word in a sense lacking in spirituality and therefore ironic to Christian readers, to mean, roughly, 'inner essence' or 'consciousness'.

140 *Terpander* seventh-century B.C. founder of Greek music.

141 *Phidias and his friend* the Greek sculptor of the fifth century B.C., and (probably) Pericles, the great Athenian statesman, or (possibly) Polygnotus, the painter.

191 *man, her last,*] man had yet *1855–63*.

212   *intro-active*   internally active; apparently a neologism.
224   *sense of sense*   analytic self-consciousness.
226   *inconscious*   unconscious (rare).
231   *pleasure-house*   'I built my soul a lordly pleasure-house' (Tennyson, 'The Palace of Art', 1). Browning is probably thinking of Tennyson's isolated 'Soul' in the lines that follow.
243   *clombst*   climbed (archaic form).
246   *recipiency*   receptivity.
249   *skills*   avails (archaism).
252   *Naiad*   (statue of a) water-nymph.
258   *boots*   use (archaism).
273–335   In replying to Protus' suggestion about a kind of immortality, Cleon would seem to be replying also to the widely held views of the Utilitarians and Comtists in Victorian England.
288   *Phoebus*   Apollo, god of the sun and poetry.
304   *Sappho*   Greek lyric poet of the seventh century B.C.
330   *prized*]   sweet *1855*.
332   *fly*   butterfly (emblem of the soul).
333   *wants*   lacks – but perhaps used ambiguously here.
340   *Paulus*   Saint Paul.

THE TWINS

First published in a small pamphlet, *Two Poems*, with Mrs Browning's 'A Plea for the Ragged Schools of London', on or about 19 April 1854. The pamphlet was sold at a bazaar to raise money for a 'refuge for young destitute girls'; the poems were a response to a request from Arabel Barrett (see DeVane and Knickerbocker, *New Letters*, 70–72). In *1854* the poem is dated 30 March 1854. With one verbal change and a few revisions in punctuation, it was reprinted in *Men and Women* on 10 November 1855. In *1863* it was included in 'Romances'. The manuscript is in the Pierpont Morgan Library.

The story is an old one, but Browning found it in Luther's *Table-Talk*, where it illustrates 'Give, and it shall be given unto you' (Luke vi 38; in the Vulgate, '*Date, et dabitur vobis*').

24   *helps*]   joins *MS.*, *1854*.
28   *Luther said*   not in the parable. Luther remarks later in *Table-Talk* that angels perform tasks that even mendicants would not.

POPULARITY

First published in *Men and Women* on 10 November 1855. In *1863* it was included in 'Lyrics'. After 1855 there were a few verbal and punctuational changes. The date of composition is unknown, but the poem may possibly have been prompted by Milnes's *Life, Letters, and Literary Remains of John Keats* (1848). The subject of the poem has generally been taken to be John Keats, an identification perhaps made difficult by the use of the third person in the poem's final line after the poet has been addressed in the other sixty-four lines in the second person. B. Worsfold, in his edition of *Men and Women* (II, 313) proposed Alfred Domett, a suggestion endorsed by Drew, *Poetry of Browning*, 84–7. In a valuable note (*VP* I, 1963, 65–6), R. D. Altick persuasively argues that the poet addressed is 'a projection of Browning himself' and that a sonnet praising Keats in Milnes's *Life* (I, 254) was quite possibly in Browning's mind, helping to prompt 'Popularity'. Certainly Browning's sense of his own originality and lack of popularity was very strong. Finally, of course, it is not necessary and may well be undesirable to particularize in reference what was probably intended to be general. On the poem see Cook, *Browning's Lyrics*, 232-4, and Drew, *Poetry of Browning*, 84-7.

4   *one man*   If Browning did have Domett in mind as his subject, the reference is probably to Browning himself - 'never star / Was lost here but it rose afar' ('Waring', 258-9). If Keats is the subject, Shelley may be meant (in *Adonais* Keats becomes a star) or the author of the sonnet in Milnes's *Life* ('Star of high promise! Not to this dark age / Do thy mild light and loveliness belong'). If the subject is a projection of Browning himself, the referent might be any one of such people as Fox, Domett, Forster.

18-20   'When the ruler of the feast had tasted the water that was made wine . . . [he] called the bridegroom, And saith unto him, Every man at the beginning doth set forth good wine; and when men have well drunk, then that which is worse: but thou hast kept the good wine until now' (John ii 9-10).

24   *Tyre*   the ancient Phoenician port-city in the eastern Mediterranean.

26-30   The Phoenicians discovered that some Tyrian shellfish contained a liquid that turned purple in air and made a superior dye. Astarte was the Phoenician goddess of love.

33   *sublimed some pall*   made sublime some cloak.

42   *hangings*   possibly suggested by those in Esther i 6.
   cedar-house   1 Kings vii 2-3.

44   *Spouse*   Pharaoh's daughter, Solomon's wife.

48   *What time*   a Miltonism.

52   *cunning come*]   art comes, – comes *1855*.

53   *proof*   greater purity.

58   *Hobbs, Nobbs, Stokes and Nokes*   The names of literary hacks are invented.

60   *line*   punning, as Altick points out, on the word in the artist's sense, as a line of verse, as a commercial term, as 'lineage'.

64   *murex*   a kind of whelk from which the dye comes.

65   That is, the innovative Keats did not benefit from his discovery; only his imitators did.

THE HERETIC'S TRAGEDY

First published in *Men and Women* on 10 November 1855. In *1863* it was included in 'Romances'. After 1855 changes were trifling. The date of composition is unknown.

The work is described as an 'interlude', a dramatic form that flourished in the sixteenth and seventeenth centuries, and that is brief and generally farcical. Chatterton used the term in two of his subtitles, and Browning's form may owe a debt to the young poet whose work he so much admired. Browning attributes his interlude to an imaginary Master Gysbrecht. His 'conceit' (fancy) is entitled (to translate the Latin) 'Rose of the World; or, Support Me with Flowers'. *Cantuque, Virgilius*: 'and in song, a Vergil' (Master Gysbrecht is a master-poet). *Hock-tide*: the second Monday and Tuesday after Easter were holidays. The garbled Latin at the end of the poem's 'title-page' means 'I had rejoiced, The Son of Jesse' – the scribe is trying to quote Psalm cxxii 1 (by David, son of Jesse), but making a hash of it. The English note was signed 'R.B.' in *1855*.

The poem's hero (mistakenly called 'John' in the interlude itself) is Jacques du Bourg-Molay, last Grand Master of the Knights Templar, an order which, during the Crusades, had exercised enormous power and acquired great wealth. The order was repressed by Philip IV of France with the support of Pope Clement V; the Grand Master was tortured in prison into confession, and finally burned in Paris, in March 1314.

3   *Saint Paul*   an error; the Abbot paraphrases James i 17.

8͵9   *plagal-cadence*   a cadence in which the subdominant chord immediately precedes the tonic. The cadence is a closing one.

12   *Aldabrod*   The gentleman never existed.

13   *Saladin*   The Sultan died fifty years before Jacques was born.

17͵18   *clavicithern*   early keyboard instrument.

28   *bavins*   bundles of brushwood.

29   *Billets*   short thick sticks of firewood.

32   *chafe*   fury.

35   *Laudes*   Lauds, a Church service including psalms of praise.

36   *Laus Deo*   'Praise to God' (Latin).

42   *threat*   threaten (archaism).

48   *Salvâ reverentiâ*   'a saving reverence' (Latin); that is, a bow or genuflection is called for.

60   *Sharon's rose*   Song of Solomon ii 1.

64   *leman*   lover.

67-9   'And as he [Paul] reasoned of righteousness, temperance, and judgement to come, Felix [Governor of Judea] trembled' (Acts xxiv 25).

75   *Anther*   pollen-bearing part of a stamen.

TWO IN THE CAMPAGNA

First published in *Men and Women* on 10 November 1855. In *1863* it was included in 'Lyrics'. The poem was virtually unchanged after 1855. It was probably written in May 1854, a month in which the Brownings spent what Mrs Browning called 'some exquisite hours on the Campagna'. The countryside around Rome is also featured in 'Love Among the Ruins'. Among essays are: R. D. Altick, 'Lovers' Finiteness: Browning's "Two in the Campagna"', *Papers on Language and Literature* III, 1967, 75-80; Cook, *Browning's Lyrics*, 149-61.

15   *weft*   web.

21   *champaign*   campagna.

33   *As earth lies bare to heaven above*   probable allusion to the myth in which Zeus came to Danaë in a shower of gold: 'Now lies the Earth all Danaë to the stars' (Tennyson, *The Princess* VII, 168).

48   *pluck the rose*   'When I have plucked the rose, / I cannot give it vital growth again, / It needs must wither' (*Othello* V. 2.13-5).

55   *Fixed*   guided (by a 'fix' on a star).

    Fixed by no friendly star   'it [Love] is an ever-fixèd mark / That looks on tempests and is never shaken; / It is the star to every wandering bark' (Shakespeare, Sonnet 116).

A GRAMMARIAN'S FUNERAL

First published in *Men and Women* on 10 November 1855. In *1863* it was included in 'Romances'. There were a few minor revisions after 1855. The date of composition is unknown. There has been much discussion as to whether the grammarian is praised or satirized. A page in Browning's autograph transcribing the last twelve lines in the Berg Collection of the New York Public Library, dated 1 November 1869; headed 'In memoriam Johannis Conington', it would indicate that – at the very least – Browning did not mean the poem to be entirely satirical (John Conington was the industrious Oxford scholar, 1825–69). Many models for the grammarian have been presented, among them Isaac Casaubon (1559–1614), Thomas Linacre (*c.* 1460–1524), the sixteenth-century German physician Jacobus Milichius, and Erasmus himself (1466–1536) – no case as yet is convincing. The poem seems to be indebted for form, and in part subject, to an obscure poem by John Davies of Hereford of about 1610, 'Invention's Life, Death, and Funeral'.

Treatments include: R. D. Altick, '*A Grammarian's Funeral*: Browning's Praise of Folly', *Studies in English Literature* III, 1963, 449–60; R. L. Kelly, 'Dactyls and Curlews: Satire in "A Grammarian's Funeral"', *VP* V, 1967, 105–12; G. Monteiro, 'A Proposal for Settling the Grammarian's Estate', *VP* III, 1965, 266–70; R. C. Schweik, 'The Structure of "A Grammarian's Funeral"', *College English* XXII, 1961, 411–12; M. J. Svaglic, 'Browning's Grammarian: Apparent Failure or Real?', *VP* V, 1967, 93–104.

3 *crofts* small farms, or small fields.
  thorpes country villages.
14 *sepulture* burial.
22 *warning* the signal to begin.
50 *gowned him* donned the symbol of academic life.
86 *Calculus* gallstones.
88 *Tussis* bronchial coughing.
95 *hydroptic* excessively thirsty.
120 *Misses an unit* misses by only a unit.
127 *rattle* death-rattle.
129 *Hoti* 'that' (Greek particle).
130 *Oun* 'then' (Greek particle).
131 *enclitic De* 'towards' (Greek suffix). Browning wrote to Tennyson in 1863 that he wanted his grammarian working on 'the biggest of the littlenesses'.
132 *waist* punning on 'waste'.
134 *purlieus* haunts.

ONE WAY OF LOVE

First published in *Men and Women* on 10 November 1855. In *1863* it was included in 'Lyrics'. After 1855 there were minor changes in punctuation only. The date of composition is unknown.

ANOTHER WAY OF LOVE

First published in *Men and Women* on 10 November 1855. In *1863* it was included with its companion in 'Lyrics'. After 1855 there were minor revisions. The date of composition is unknown.

17   *Clear scores*   settle accounts.

19   *Eadem semper*   'always the same' (Latin).

21   *mend*   improve.

33   *And stop the fresh film-work*]   To stop the fresh spinning *1855*; And stop the fresh spinning *1863*.

   film-work   cobweb.

'TRANSCENDENTALISM: A POEM IN TWELVE BOOKS'

First published in *Men and Women* on 10 November 1855. It later remained in 'Men and Women' as the first poem, presumably designed as prefatory to a group for which its subject-matter otherwise scarcely qualifies it. There were minor revisions after 1855. The date of composition may well be 1853, when the Brownings were reading Swedenborg, who was interested in Boehme. Inevitably, various models, including Wordsworth, have been suggested for the prosy poet chastised in this poem; R. D. Altick suggests that Browning is chastising the earlier Browning (and that he is indebted to Carlyle): 'Browning's "Transcendentalism"', *JEGP* LVIII, 1959, 24-8.

4   *draping them in sights and sounds*   'I am writing – a first step towards popularity for me – lyrics with more music and painting than before, so as to get people to hear and see' (Browning to his friend J. Milsand, 24 February 1853).

6   *prolusion*   prologue or preliminary flourish.

12   *Swiss tube*   alpenhorn.

22   *German*]   Swedish *1855-63* (Edward Dowden suggested the correction in 1866).
   Boehme   Jacob Boehme (1575–1624), the German shoemaker and mystic. It was probably in a translation of 1764 of Boehme's *Works* that Browning read about Boehme's communion with 'the Herbs and Grass of the field', when 'in his inward Light he saw into their Essences, Use and Properties'. What, if any, particular 'tough book' (line 30) Browning may have had in mind is not known, but the context suggests *De Signatura Rerum*.

26   *the daisy had an eye*   'Daisy' means 'day's eye'.

37-8   John of Halberstadt was an obscure German canon of the fifteenth century, whose name Browning would have met in Wanley's *Wonders of the Little World*, a favourite childhood book. There he is remarkable chiefly for being turned into a black horse, and is said to have 'performed a number of prestigious feats almost incredible'. His skill with rose-growing is apparently Browning's invention.

48   *showed*]   did *1855-63*.

49   *finer*   thinner. The harp's higher notes come from thinner strings placed nearest the harpist's head.

MISCONCEPTIONS

First published in *Men and Women* on 10 November 1855. In *1863* the poem was included in 'Lyrics'. After 1855 the only changes were in indentation. The date of composition is unknown.

11   *dalmatic*   royal coronation robe.

ONE WORD MORE

First published in *Men and Women* on 10 November 1855. Later it remained with the collection, with a note to explain that it had originally been appended to the larger ollection bearing that titl e. Changes after 1855 were minor. The printer's manuscript is in the Pierpont Morgan Library; there the poem is called 'A Last Word, to E.B.B.'. In changing the title, Browning probably was mindful of the unfortunate echo of 'A Woman's Last Word'; in choosing the new one, he may well have thought of his wife's remark in a letter of 31 August 1845 as she discouraged his love: 'Therefore we must leave this subject – and I must trust you to leave it without one word more.' Between manuscript and *1855* there were many revisions, which were clearly made in proof. The poem, a favourite of all lovers of the Brownings, was written in London while the other poems of *Men and Women* were in the printer's hands; the manuscript dates the poem 22 September 1855. It seems altogether probable that Browning wished to dedicate the collection to his wife (especially after her *Sonnets from the Portuguese*, first published in 1850), and that 'One Word More' stemmed from his thinking about an appropriate form for the dedication. Browning stressed the unusually intensely personal nature of the poem by signing it 'R.B.' in editions after 1855 (after his wife's death). On the poem, see Cook, *Browning's Lyrics*, 229-38.

1 *fifty* The poem is the fifty-first in *Men and Women*.
4 *Where the heart lies, let the brain lie also.* 'where your treasure is, there will your heart be also' (Matthew vi 21). The line is echoed in 142.
   lies] is *MS*.
5 *Rafael made a century of sonnets* Browning was long said to have erred here. But Baldinucci, *Notizie* (used elsewhere by Browning), refers to 'the famous book of a hundred sonnets from the hand of Raphael, which Guido had bought in Rome' (F. Page, *TLS*, 25 May 1940, 255). Raphael, the great Italian painter (1483-1520), was a special favourite of Browning's.
9-10 *but one ... Who that one*] one eye ... Whose that eye *cancelled MS. readings.* (Did Browning recall his wife's earlier strictures against his reference to a single eye in 'The Flower's Name', 16?)
12 *lady of the sonnets* probably the reputed model, whose name may have been Margherita, for some of Raphael's paintings, including *La Fornarina*. Baldinucci refers to a mistress whom Raphael 'loved until his death', and Vasari also records the devotion.
22 *San Sisto* the *Sistine Madonna* at Dresden.
   Foligno the *Madonna di Foligno* in the Vatican.
23 the *Madonna del Granduco* in the Pitti Palace, Florence.
24-5 *La Belle Jardinière* in the Louvre, Paris. The upper part of the picture is semi-circular.
27 *Guido Reni* Bolognese painter (1575-1642). Baldinucci records that Raphael's sonnets disappeared at the time of Reni's death.
28 *Guarded long*] Laid away *MS*.
30 *cried too*] with it *MS*.
32 On the first anniversary of Beatrice's death, Dante wrote, 'I was drawing an angel upon my tablets, ... I turned my eyes and saw at my side certain people of importance' (*Vita Nuova*, xxxv). Beatrice (abbreviated 'Bice') is Dante's platonic love and heroine in the *Divine Comedy* and the *Vita Nuova*.
35 *pen corroded* The phrase and the following lines refer to Dante's attacks on enemies in *Inferno* (probably begun, in fact, about ten years after Beatrice's death).
37 *Inferno* xxxii, 97-104.
42 *who loved well*] the who loved *MS*.
46 See 32n.
48-9 The points about seizing and stopping are Browning's, not Dante's.

54 *love and Beatrice*]   heaven and on Bice *cancelled MS. reading.*

58]   The one line formed section VIII in *MS.* and *1855.*

60 *for one*]   but once *MS.*

64 *one time, art*]   time, an art *MS.*

65 *Ay,*]   Out *MS.*

72 *Gain*]   Save *MS.*

73 *Wherefore? Heaven's*]   Ah, – for heaven's *MS.*

74 *He who smites the rock*   Moses. Exodus xvii 6; Numbers xx 11.

77 *but*]   his *MS., 1855–63.*

82 *sneered*]   smiled *MS.*

85 *actual*   present (the usual meaning in Browning).

89ₐ90]   Make precipitate or more retarding *cancelled MS. reading.*

95   The children of Israel 'murmured against Moses and Aaron in the wilderness' and 'said unto them, Would to God we had died by the hand of the Lord in the land of Egypt, when we sat by the flesh pots' (Exodus xvi 2–3).

97–8   While Moses was in a 'clift' of Mount Sinai, God showed him His glory (Exodus xxxiii 17–23). His face shone as he returned with the Ten Commandments (Exodus xxxiv 30).

98 *rod-sweep, tongue's imperial fiat*]   rod-sweep and tongue's regal fiat *MS.*

101 *Jethro's daughter*   Zipporah, wife of Moses (Exodus ii 21, iii 1).

102 *Aethiopian bondslave*   wife of Moses (Numbers xii 1).

103 *He would*]   Why – he'd *MS.*

119 *these lines*]   this verse *MS.*

120   Only in 'One Word More' did Browning use unrhymed trochaic pentameter.
Lines]   Verse *MS.*

121 *a hair*]   an oil *MS.*

125 *missal-marge*   margin of a prayer-book.

136 *Karshish*]   Karshook *MS., 1855–68.* The error was first corrected in the Tauchnitz edition of 1872, and then in late reprints of *1868.* 'Ben Karshook's Wisdom' had been written in April 1854, but was not published until 1856; presumably Browning simply confused names. In 'The Return of the Druses' (1843), one of the Druses is called Karshook.

Norbert   the hero of 'In a Balcony'.

142 *lies*]   is *MS.* (Compare 4 and note.)

146 *thrice-transfigured*   perhaps new, full, and waning; perhaps Browning alludes to the (roughly) three lunar months that have passed between the Brownings' departure from Florence and the writing of the poem.

148 *Fiesole*   small hill-town a few miles north-east of Florence.

150 *Samminiato*   San Miniato, a church on a hill south-east of Florence.

151 *Rounder*]   Rounded *MS.*

160 *mythos*   the story of the love of Diana, the moon goddess, for Endymion.

163 *Zoroaster on his terrace*   Zoroaster (Zarathustra), sixth-century(?) religious figure and astronomer. The ziggurat was a terraced temple tower pyramidal in form with extensive terrace space at each storey.

164 *Galileo on his turret*   The leading Renaissance scientist (1564–1642) made discoveries about the moon. The 'turret' is probably the Leaning Tower of Pisa from which Galileo conducted experiments.

165 *Homer*   The *Homeric Hymns* (translated by Shelley) include one addressed to the moon.

Keats   Keats told the story of *Endymion* (1818), which includes an invocation to the moon (iii 40–71).

172-3] Proves she as when Moses climbed the mountain,
    Saw the paved-work of a stone, a sapphire, *MS*.

172-9 'Then went up Moses, and Aaron, Nadab, and Abihu, and seventy of the elders of Israel: And they saw the God of Israel: and there was under his feet as it were a paved work of a sapphire stone, and as it were the body of heaven in his clearness. And upon the nobles of the children of Israel he laid not his hand: also they saw God, and did eat and drink!' (Exodus xxiv 9-11).

186 *when*] if *MS*.

192ᴧ3] Seeing – mine with all the eyes – our wonder. *MS*.

197 *silence*] beauty *MS*.

198-201] part of the preceding section in *MS*., not a separate section.

Dramatis Personae

Dramatis Personae, with its eighteen poems, was first published on 28 May 1864 by Chapman and Hall. Thirty lines of 'James Lee' had been published in 1836, and 'May and Death' in 1857. With these exceptions, the poems were new, though 'Prospice' and the sixth section of 'James Lee' had appeared a few days before in the *Atlantic Monthly*, and 'Gold Hair' a month or so before in the same journal. A second printing was called for, and the revised second edition was published later in 1864. Two brief occasional poems, 'Deaf and Dumb' and 'Eurydice to Orpheus', were added to *Dramatis Personae* when it appeared with substantial revisions in *1868*. Further revisions for *1888* were trifling. The title of course means 'Persons of the Drama' and is the Latin phrase often prefixed to the names of a play's characters.

Browning appears to have written very little in the four years or so after the publication of *Men and Women*. In May 1860 Mrs Browning reported: 'he has been writing a good deal this winter – working at a long poem which I have not seen a line of, and producing short lyrics which I *have* seen, and may declare worthy of him'. Nevertheless, for a poet as productive as Browning could be, the winter of 1859-60 seems to have produced little, and the next eighteen months or so virtually nothing. In March 1861 Mrs Browning optimistically wrote of her husband's plans for working on a new volume in the summer, but her death on 29 June further delayed progress. Browning planned a volume for April or May in 1863, but publication of *Dramatis Personae* was held back so as not to interfere with the collected edition of *1863* (the first *Selections* published in the same year also sold well). In the meantime Browning added further work to the volume that appeared in 1864. The printers' manuscript, very clean except for 'Mr Sludge', is in the Pierpont Morgan Library, and a proof-copy with extensive corrections, which were incorporated in the published text, is in the Beinecke Library of Yale University.

Except for the rather special case of *A Blot in the 'Scutcheon* (1843), *Dramatis Personae* was Browning's first work to go into a second edition. For him, sales were reasonably good; Browning, in his fifties, was beginning to attract a fair number of readers. In 1868, however, Chapman and Hall still had 550 copies on hand.

There is only one twentieth-century edition of significance, that of F. B. Pinion (1969); its text is based substantially on the first edition. A brief essay on the volume as a whole is L. Poston III, *Loss and Gain: An Essay on Browning's 'Dramatis Personae'*, University of Nebraska, 1974.

JAMES LEE'S WIFE

'James Lee' was first published in *Dramatis Personae* on 28 May 1864. The first six stanzas of VI had appeared in the *Monthly Repository*, n.s. X, May 1836, 270-71, called 'Lines' and signed 'Z.', Browning's regular pseudonym for contributions to the journal. The whole section had appeared in the *Atlantic Monthly* for June 1864, published a few days before *Dramatis Personae*. The text (two section-titles excepted) was not revised for the second edition, but there were minor revisions and very substantial additions in *1868*, in which the final text was virtually established. The poem's title was changed to 'James Lee's Wife' in *1868*. Two section titles were changed: I (originally 'At the Window'), and VI (originally 'Under the Cliff') were given their final titles in the second edition. In the manuscript there are no titles, the sections being merely numbered; Browning made many revisions in proof. On 31 December 1864 the poet wrote, somewhat misleadingly, 'I misled you into thinking the couple were "prolétaire" – but I meant them for just the opposite – people newly-married, trying to realize a dream of being sufficient to each other, in a foreign land (where you can try such an experiment) and finding it break up, – the man being tired *first*, – and tired precisely of the love: – but I have expressed it all insufficiently, and will break the chain up, one day, and leave so many separate little round rings to roll each its way, if it can' (Curle, *Robert Browning and Julia Wedgwood*, 123).

It is almost certain that most of the poem was written in southern Brittany, where Browning spent the summers of 1862 and 1863, staying near Pornic in Sainte Marie, then a sea-coast hamlet (the view from the house provided the fig-tree and field of III, as well as the doorway). Most of the poem was probably composed in 1862, and the mood doubtless reflects a frequent one of Browning himself at the time. The poem may also reflect the general influence of Meredith's *Modern Love* and *Ode to the Spirit of Earth in Autumn* (both published in April 1862); and, especially in V, of Tennyson's *Maud*.

Swinburne's parody is called 'James Lee and John Jones'. See P. M. Ball, *The Heart's Desire*, Athlone Press, 1976, 144-66; Cook, *Browning's Lyrics*, 247-61; F. E. Faverty, 'Browning's Debt to Meredith in *James Lee's Wife*', in *Essays in American and English Literature Presented to Bruce Robert McElderry, Jr.*, ed. M. F. Schulz, Ohio University Press, 1968, 290-305; Poston, *Loss and Gain*, 1-8; G. Sandstrom, '"James Lee's Wife" – and Browning's', *VP* IV, 1966, 259-70.

21₋2 *Title* 'By the Fire-Side' is the title of a poem in *Men and Women*.

72 *bent* coarse grass stalk.

95 *harvest*] beauty *MS*.

105-6 *rivers of oil and wine . . . Book assures* The Bible does not in fact speak of rivers of oil and wine; possibly Browning had in mind Deuteronomy viii 7-10, or Joel ii 24: 'the fats [troughs] shall overflow with wine and oil'.

121 *you*] love *MS*.

126 *Dead*] Red *MS*.

137 *barded and chanfroned* breast-plated and with frontlets of armour (*OED* does not record Browning's form of the word 'chamfrond').

138 *quixote-mage* magician or wise man with Don Quixote qualities.

143 *fans* wings.

174 *Close,*] So *MS.*, *1836*.

182 *young man* Robert Browning, at age twenty-three.

195 *eternity*] *cancelled MS. reading, 1864-88*; serenity *MS*.

196 *Too*] So *MS*.

200 *Calm*] Long *MS.*
203 *about*] before *MS.*
208 *say*] mean *MS.*, *1864.*
219 *with*] through *MS.*
227 *grave* engrave.
229 *himself,*] ourselves; *MS.*
230 *washes*] ripples *MS.*
231 *he'd*] we'd *MS.*
234 *knees*] arms *MS.*
238 *ancient,*] old and *MS.*
242 *Make the low nature better*] Give the low nature comfort *MS.*
243 *Give earth*] Leave it *MS.*
257 *limit-line* outline.
270–330] *not in MS., 1864.*
274 *master* Leonardo da Vinci.
315 *powers profuse*] mechanism *1868.*
325 *strait dole* small allowance.
331–2] The couplet forms part 2 (of VIII) in *1864.*
340 *Your*] My *MS.*
  a] your *MS.*
341 *it*] mine *MS.*
345 *be*] turn *MS.*
352 *Will hold mine yet*] Which still holds mine *MS.*
365 *flee*] free *MS.*
372 *When*] For *MS.*

GOLD HAIR

First published in the *Atlantic Monthly* XIII, May 1864, 596–9, and then in *Dramatis Personae* on 28 May 1864. The poem was extensively revised in proof; and the first edition was in turn revised, most notable being the adding of fifteen lines (101–15) in the second edition. Further minor changes were made for *1888*. Browning wrote the poem probably in 1862 at Sainte Marie; in a letter of 18 August 1862 (McAleer, *Dearest Isa*, 119) he refers to having written, the day before, a poem of 120 lines, and the reference is probably to 'Gold Hair' (though it may be to 'James Lee'). The story is outlined in F.-J. Carou's *Histoire de Pornic* (1859) ⌐7–9; the present editor owns a transcription by Sarianna Browning of the story. The gold was found in 1782 in the hair of one Mlle Beaulon des Roussières. Most of the details in the poem are not in the source. Until the second edition, the subtitle was 'A Legend of Pornic'.

2 *Pornic* a small port-town in southern Brittany at the mouth of the river Loire.
14 *want* lack.
16 *flix and floss*] gloom and gloss *MS.*
  flix The word is usually applied to the fur of animals (in a transferred sense, *OED* records only Browning's usage here).
  floss fluff.
17 *floods*] heaps *MS.*
38 *degree* the order of things ('the planets and this centre / Observe degree, priority and place' – *Troilus and Cressida* I. 3.86–7).
46 *silver*] fine white *MS.*

61 *flew*]   came *MS*.

74]   A sacred space in the midst lay bare *MS*.

75 *research*]   their search *MS*.

79 *chased*   engraved or embossed.

82 *gauds*   trinkets.

84 *pelf*   booty.

85 *deserves*]   receives *MS*.

86–7 *O cor | Humanum, pectora caeca*   'O human heart, blind breasts' – a misquotation from Lucretius, *De Rerum Natura* II, 14.

90 *Louis-d'or*   a gold coin.

91–2 *heard, | Marked, inwardly digested*   'read, mark, learn, and inwardly digest' (Collect for second Sunday in Advent, *Book of Common Prayer*).

93 *smiled*]   said *MS*.

  There's a]   A little *MS.*, *1864–8*.

101–15] *not in MS.*, *1864*. (The stanzas were written for the second edition to meet George Eliot's criticism that the lady's motivation was not clear enough. George Eliot's copy of *1864* is in Harvard's Houghton Library with the three stanzas added in Browning's hand – there is only one minor verbal difference between the stanzas in her copy and those that appear in the second edition of *1864*.)

109 *humour*   in the sense of the older psychology and physiology (with their four humours), with reference to the 'humour' or bodily fluid that was thought to control health and temperament.

116 *six times five*   Browning's source refers only to 'une grande quantité'.

122 *friends*]   Earth's *MS*.

123 *An*]   What *MS.*, *1864 (1)*.

124 *if you will*]   I hope *MS.*, *1864 (1)*.

124–5   See Matthew vi 19–21.

125 *earth's too, I hope*]   this, if God will *MS.*; earth's, if God will *1864 (1)*.

128–30 *thirty pieces . . . Potter's Field*   Judas got thirty pieces of silver for betraying Christ. With them, the chief priests bought 'the potter's field, to bury strangers in' (Matthew xxvii 7).

131–2 *Milk that's spilt . . . adage*   'There's no use crying over spilt milk.'

141 *candid incline*]   public inclines *MS*.

142 *proves*]   may be *MS.*, *1864–8*.

143 *Essays-and-Reviews' debate*   In 1860 *Essays and Reviews*, with seven articles by members of the Broad Church party, initiated the Higher Criticism in England and caused an uproar.

144 *public*]   candid *MS*.

145 *Colenso*   John William Colenso (1814–83), Bishop of Natal, published the first volume of his *Critical Examination of the Pentateuch* in 1862; the work questioned Biblical historical facts, and increased uproar.

146 *still, to*]   still must *MS*.

149 *lie*   that man is innately good. The point here is not characteristic of Browning's thought.

THE WORST OF IT

First published in *Dramatis Personae* on 28 May 1864. Verbal differences between manuscript and *1864* are trifling; there were no verbal changes after *1864*. The date of composition is unknown, but the poem may have been one of those lyrics that Mrs Browning, in May 1861, had reported having seen.

40 Revelation vii 9.
68 *loop* loophole.
112 *want* lack.

DÎS ALITER VISUM; OR, LE BYRON DE NOS JOURS

First published in *Dramatis Personae* on 28 May 1864. There are few changes between the manuscript and *1864*; after *1864* the only changes were in punctuation. The date of composition is unknown, though the setting of the French coast may point to the summers of 1858, 1862 or 1863 as possibilities. The title is from *Aeneid* II, 428: 'The gods' thought was [or seemed] otherwise.' The subtitle, 'The Byron of Our Days', probably points to the contrast between Byron and the present 'hero'. DeVane (*Handbook*, 289) suggests the possible influence of Byron's 'The Dream'. On the poem see F. Kaplan, *Miracles of Rare Device,* Wayne State University Press, 1972, 115–23.

15 *nice* discriminating.
19 *bath-house* changing-room.
36 *Schumann* German composer (1810–56).
38 *Ingres* French painter (1780–1867).
40 *Heine* German poet (1797–1856).
42 *votive frigate* a ship model given to the Church to fulfil a vow.
58 *Fortieth spare Arm-chair* election to the French Academy (which has forty members).
63 *loves and doves* 'Loved you and doved you' ('Too Late', 90).
64 *Three per Cents* safe government bonds (Consols) paying three per cent.
100 *best or worst* 'for better, for worse' (marriage service).
102 *Norman* The Pornic church was Norman (a kind of Romanesque architecture of the eleventh and twelfth centuries).
131 *wisdom*] progress *MS*.
135] Both loves worth nothing since ill-clad! *MS*.
138 *jacinth* brown, red, or orange.

TOO LATE

First published in *Dramatis Personae* on 28 May 1864. The manuscript and *1864* differ only slightly; after *1864* there were trifling changes in punctuation, and one trivial verbal change. The date of composition is unknown. Thematically the poem (and its title) are representative of much in *Dramatis Personae*. See J. F. Loucks, 'On Two Late Interpretations of "Too Late"', *BSN* IV, No. 3, 1974, 24–6; L. Perrine, 'Browning's "Too Late": A Re-Interpretation', *VP* VII, 1969, 339–45.

43 *worry* pull or tear at, with the teeth.
75–6 *belled | The cat* took the risk for others.
87 *pink* paragon.
90 *Loved you and doved you* 'loves and doves' ('Dîs Aliter Visum', 63).
93 *Tekel, found wanting* '*Tekel*' was one of the words written on the wall at Belshazzar's feast and interpreted 'Thou art weighed in the balances, and art found wanting' (Daniel v 27).
96 *tagging* stringing together.
102 *leathern* leather.

112 *prog* 'grub' (slang for 'food').

121-6 Mrs Miller notes the similarity between the faces of Edith and Julia Wedgwood, whom Browning had met probably in 1863.

138 *summum jus* 'the highest law' (Latin).

ABT VOGLER

First published in *Dramatis Personae* on 28 May 1864. The manuscript and *1864* differ slightly a few times; after *1864* changes are trivial. The date of writing is unknown. Abbé Georg Joseph Vogler (1749–1814), German composer, organist, theorist, teacher and noted extemporizer, had been the master of John Relfe, Browning's music teacher. A person of importance in his day, he is, except for this poem, now almost unknown. The 'musical instrument of his invention' is the orchestrion, a kind of large organ. 'Abt Vogler' was one of the two lyrics Browning chose when asked to name four poems that would represent him fairly. See Whitla, *The Central Truth*, 80–88.

1 *brave* splendid.

3 *Solomon* Solomon was reputed to be able to control spirits with a seal that bore God's 'ineffable name' (line 7).

8 *princess* Pharaoh's daughter (1 Kings vii 8).

16 *nether springs* perhaps referring to the belief that the earth rested on a great deep.

19 *rampired* strengthened against attack, ramparted (archaism).

23 *Rome's dome* Saint Peter's was lighted on special occasions.

33 *wanted* lacked.

34 *fresh from the Protoplast* just created; 'the Protoplast' is 'the first former, fashioner, or creator' (*OED* 2).

63 *must*] hope to *cancelled MS. reading*; shall *MS.*

66 *houses not made with hands* 'For we know that if our earthly house of this tabernacle were dissolved, we have a building of God, an house not made with hands, eternal in the heavens' (2 Corinthians v 1).

74 *semblance*] likeness *MS.* (The second 'nor' was not in the first edition, probably a printers' error in the line.)

82 *fulness of the days* Ephesians i 10.

91 *common chord* three-note chord made up of the first, third and fifth notes in the scale.

92 *Sliding by semitones, till I sink to the minor* 'the refuge of the destitute amateur improviser' (Sir Charles Stanford). Vogler is modulating from the key of the 'common chord' to its relative minor key (probably from C Major to A Minor).

93 *blunt* flatten one note.

ninth one note more than the octave.

alien ground the discord of the ninth. The ground is 'alien' also because Vogler pioneered the use of the ninth in his system of harmony (Grove).

95 *hark*] see *MS.*

dared and done 'Determined, dared and done' (Smart, *Song to David*, final line).

96 *The C Major of this life* the level of ordinary living (the chord has no sharps or flats). Probably Vogler is also returning to the key in which his improvisation began.

RABBI BEN EZRA

First published in *Dramatis Personae* on 28 May 1864. The poem was fairly heavily revised in proof, but after *1864* there was only one verbal change; no lines were indented until *1888*. The date of composition is unknown, but is unlikely to be before 1862 when Browning probably read FitzGerald's *Rubáiyát* (1859). Much in 'Rabbi Ben Ezra' suggests that Browning is replying to FitzGerald, but he may also have had Arnold's *Empedocles on Etna* (1852) very much in mind (Arnold's 'Growing Old' of 1867 probably replies in turn to Browning's poem). On his deathbed, Thomas Hardy asked for 'Rabbi Ben Ezra'.

It is generally agreed that the Rabbi is a spokesman for Browning himself or for Browning as he would wish to be. Abraham Ibn Ezra (Abenezra) (1092–1167), a Spanish Jew, spent the latter part of his life travelling in exile; he was a most distinguished scholar and a man of genius in several areas. Browning had referred to him in 'Holy-Cross Day', and there 'translated' his *Song of Death*, but Browning's knowledge of the man was probably sketchy. At one time 'Rabbi Ben Ezra' was one of Browning's most popular works; it epitomizes many central Browning themes. See D. Fleisher, '"Rabbi Ben Ezra', 49–72: A New Key to an Old Crux', *VP* I, 1963, 46–52.

45 *want* lack.
57 *see now love*] shall see Love *MS*.
84 *indue* put on.
85 *try* test, or try to find out.
87 *Leave*] Be *MS.*, *1864*, *1864* (*2 edn*).
102 *proved* tested.
113 *tempt* attempt.
141 *passed* ignored.
150 The image that begins here and that dominates the conclusion of the poem is a common one: that of God as potter and man as pot. In Browning's handling, the wheel becomes earthly time and circumstance, and the clay is man's spiritual being. It has often been suggested that the image is in part unfortunate for Browning's purposes in that it tends to suggest an absence of human free will. FitzGerald's *Rubáiyát* uses the image, and Biblical examples include Jeremiah xviii 2–6, and Romans ix 21, but Browning was probably, especially since Ben Ezra had written a commentary on Isaiah, most conscious of Isaiah lxiv 8: 'we are the clay, and thou [Lord] our potter'.
153 *spins fast*] turns round *MS*.
154–6 *fools propound . . . seize today* an obvious hit at the *Rubáiyát*.
156 *all*] earth *MS*.
159 *changes*] passes *MS*.
164 *plastic* fashioning.
168 *Try* test.
174 *sterner stress* heavier pressure.
191 *the cup*] Thy work *MS*.

A DEATH IN THE DESERT

First published in *Dramatis Personae* on 28 May 1864. Extensive revisions were made in proof; after *1864* revisions were minor. The date of composition is unknown, but it is probable that some at least of the poem was written not long before publication:

Browning read Renan's *La Vie de Jésus* in November 1863, and the poem has usually been seen as a reply to Renan, while Strauss's *New Life of Jesus*, which may have influenced 'A Death in the Desert', was published in January 1864 (Strauss's earlier *Life* Browning had read long before). In *The Poetry of Browning*, 212–22, Philip Drew suggests also the strong influence of Ludwig Feuerbach's *Das Wesen des Christentums* (1841), translated by George Eliot as *The Essence of Religion* (1853). Browning's favourite gospel was John, the one that insists most strongly on God as God of Love; the Higher Criticism attacked the authenticity of the gospel, and Browning deals in the poem with many of the general and specific points raised by it, though he is not particularly concerned with the historicity of biblical events but with the value for every individual of the Christ story. To the latter point the Higher Criticism is essentially irrelevant, but Browning feared that historical 'fact' might trample on spiritual truth. On the poem, see Poston, *Loss and Gain*, 17–24; Raymond, *The Infinite Moment*, 32–51; and Whitla, *The Central Truth*, 30–39. Crucially important, and not just for this poem, is E. Shaffer, 'Browning's St. John: The Casuistry of the Higher Criticism', *VS* XVI, 1972, 205–22, expanded in her '*Kubla Khan' and 'The Fall of Jerusalem'*, Cambridge University Press, 1975, 191–224.

There is an old tradition that John died in his nineties about the year 100, and that he is buried at Ephesus. Cerinthus excepted, the other characters in the poem are fictional, as are the circumstances in which John dies.

1   *Pamphylax*   The name means 'all-guarding'.
   Antiochene   of Antioch. Saint Paul established churches at each of the two cities (in modern Syria and Turkey) bearing the name.
2   *parchment*   Rolls of parchment or papyrus were the equivalent of later books.
4   *Epsilon down to Mu*   the fifth and twelfth letters of the Greek alphabet: the Greeks used letters for numbers.
6   *terebinth*   turpentine.
7   *Xi*   the fourteenth Greek letter.
11   *His coming*   Christ's Second Coming was thought imminent by the early Christians.
23   *decree*   presumably of the Emperor Trajan, that Christians be killed.
29   *Xanthus*   Browning gave the name to John's follower ('son') in *Sordello* III, 996–1021.
36   *Bactrian*   Bactria was in central Asia, north-west of modern India.
39   *quitch*   a tough grass.
50   *nard*   spikenard, the herb from which the ointment and the perfume are made.
64   'I am the resurrection and the life: he that believeth in me, though he were dead, yet shall he live' (John xi 25).
69   *desert-bird that wears the ruff*   vulture.
73   *James and Peter*   the two Apostles, Saint James (John's brother) and Saint Peter.
82   *doctrine he was wont to teach*   The doctrine is hardly John's, and is perhaps more closely related to Plato's doctrine of the three souls. It is, however, Browning's doctrine, and is based on analogy between the human and the Trinity. For indication of the weight of tradition behind the doctrine, one that may well owe much to the *De Trinitate* of Saint Augustine, see Whitla, *The Central Truth*, 46–51, and also 32–4.
104   *glossa*   gloss (explanatory note) (Latin).
   Theotypas   fictional.
115   *James and Peter*   They were killed about 43 and about 67.
122–3   'His [the glorified Christ's] head and his hairs were white like wool, as white

as snow; and his eyes were as a flame of fire; And his feet like unto fine brass, . . . And he had in his right hand seven stars: and out of his mouth went a sharp two edged sword' (Revelation i 14–6).

125 Revelation i 17.

131–2 'That which was from the beginning, which we have heard, which we have seen with our eyes, which we have looked upon, and our hands have handled, of the Word of life' (1 John i 1); 'In the beginning was the Word, and the Word was with God, and the Word was God' (John i 1).

134 *love's way: to rise, it stoops* The thought is frequent in Browning's verse. Compare, for instance, 'Saul', 252: 'that stoop of the soul which in bending upraises it too'.

140 *Patmos isle* in the Aegean; Revelation i 9.

141 *Revelation* i 11.

149 *pen a letter* the Epistles of Saint John.

158 *Antichrist already in the world* 'this is that spirit of antichrist, whereof ye have heard that it should come; and even now already is it in the world' (1 John iv 3).

163 *call down fire* 'James and John . . . said, Lord, wilt thou that we command fire to come down from heaven, and consume them' (Luke ix 54).

165 Christ gave the Seventy 'power to tread on serpents and scorpions' (Luke x 19).

177 *Where is the promise of His coming?* 'Where is the promise of his coming?' (2 Peter iii 4).

186 'the whole world lieth in wickedness' (1 John v 19).

194 *unborn people* including the Higher Critics.

211 *first*] once *MS*.

212,13] Closed with and cast and conquered, crucified *MS.*, *1864–1864* (*2 edn*).

231 *insubordinate* an unusual use of the word, not exactly covered by any definition in *OED*, to apply to objects rather than people.

234 *succinct* compact.

241 *dispart, dispread* dissolve, spread apart.

254 *emprise* enterprise.

264 *extends*] hath waxed *MS*.

267 'time that takes survey of all the world, / Must have a stop' (*1 Henry IV* V. 4.83–4).

271 *proof* test.

279 *Prometheus* The Titan stole fire from Zeus and gave it to men.

283 *sophist* fallacious arguer.

284 *myth*] tale *MS*.

Aeschylus Of the Greek dramatist's trilogy dealing with Prometheus, only *Prometheus Bound* survives. A fragment attributed to one of the lost plays does, however, have satyrs dancing round a fire (285–6).

303 The Transfiguration is described in Luke ix 29–35.

305 *trod the sea* Matthew xiv 25–33.

brought the dead to life the raising of Lazarus (John xi 1–45).

306 *wring this from*] do this with *MS*.

310 *I forsook and fled* 'And they all forsook him, and fled' (Mark xiv 50). (The disciples' abandoning of Christ in Gethsemane.) In John xix, 26–35, John is at the Crucifixion, however; Browning follows Mark, and, perhaps significantly, Renan. Renan makes much of John's 'lie' about being at the Crucifixion; for Browning, the point is really irrelevant.

322 *whispering*] saying *MS*.

328 *glozing* comment.

329 *Ebion . . . Cerinthus*   The former, if he existed at all, founded a sect that believed Jesus man, not God. Cerinthus is said to have lived in Ephesus at the same time as John; one story has it that he taught Ebion. Cerinthus did not believe in the divinity (or, really, in the humanity) of Christ. Both figures serve as surrogates for the Higher Critics.

330   *our*]   us *MS.*, *1864–1864 (2 edn)*.

361   *Idly*]   Barely *MS.*

  Ephesus   the ancient city, in the south-west of what is now Turkey.

370–421   John presents the Higher Criticism.

378   *Our mind receives but what it holds*   The thought is a commonplace, but the phrasing may owe a debt to Coleridge: 'we receive but what we give' ('Dejection: An Ode', 47).

390   *Certes*   certainly (archaism).

419   *So law in turn discards power*]   Power shall in turn discard Power *MS.*

439   *virtues*   efficacious qualities.

442   *boast*   claim.

448   *wheelwork*   piece of clockwork (an obvious anachronism).

452   *might be*]   is a *MS.*

460   *blind man shall receive his sight*   Jesus 'said unto them, Go and shew John again those things which ye do hear and see: The blind receive their sight . . .' (Matthew xi 4–5).

472   *void*   unnecessary.

474–81   the essence of Browning's reply to the Higher Critics.

530   *heathen bard's*   that of Aeschylus in the 'famous play', *Prometheus Bound*.

532   *ephemerals*   mortals.

565   *Atlas*   the Titan who carried the world on his shoulders.

566   *Given to the nobler midge*]   I give such to the midge *MS.*, *1864–8*.

592   *wait*   wait on, attend.

603   *mind*]   soul *MS.*

623   *jet*   spurt.

625   *pattern on the Mount*   the Ten Commandments received by Moses on Mount Sinai.

627   *copies*   the ideal maxims that Moses strove to present.

629   *type*   archetype.

634   *burthen*   probably, here, 'theme'. The Biblical usage, however, often means 'oracle', 'utterance'.

652   *fight the beasts*   The primary reference involves the Christian being thrown to the lions; but the phrasing recalls Saint Paul's 'I have fought with beasts at Ephesus' (1 Corinthians xv 32).

657   'Then went this saying abroad among the brethren, that that disciple should not die: yet Jesus said not unto him, He shall not die; but, If I will that he tarry till I come, what is that to thee?' (John xxi 23).

664   *breast to breast with God*   John xiii 23, 25.

665   *Cerinthus*   As in 329, Cerinthus stands as surrogate for the Higher Critics.

CALIBAN UPON SETEBOS

First published in *Dramatis Personae* on 28 May 1864. The poem was extensively revised in proof (Browning had special and natural problems with the poem's pronouns), but after *1864* revisions were minor, there being only two verbal changes. The date of composition is unknown, but it is generally felt that the poem was to some extent triggered by Darwin's *Origin of Species* (November 1859), and C. R. Tracy, '*Caliban upon Setebos*', *SP* XXXV, 1938, 487-99, argued for the winter of 1859-60, seeing the influence of Theodore Parker, whom the Brownings met in December 1859. Parker, a Unitarian, was an amateur biologist, and (as Tracy's article shows clearly) a man fascinated by the kind of questions that Browning's poem raises; in the month the Brownings met him, he was writing 'A Bumblebee's Thoughts on the Plan and Purpose of the Universe', and in his *Discourse of Matters Pertaining to Religion*, he wrote: 'A man rude in spirit must have a rude conception of God. He thinks the deity like himself. If a buffalo had a religion, his conception of deity would probably be a buffalo.' (The relevance of such remarks to Browning's poem is obvious.) Browning was also interested in the furore that followed the appearance of Darwin's book, and the topical appeal of an example of the 'missing link' is clear.

Browning's hero is the man-monster of *The Tempest* turned theologian – at the end of the play Caliban resolves to 'seek for grace' (V. 1.296), and the resolve may have sparked Browning's imagination; the original Caliban's character, situation and pronouncements lie behind almost everything in Browning's characterization. Setebos was the god of Caliban's dam, Sycorax (I. 2.373); the Quiet may well, as Tracy suggests, derive in part from the Unitarian conception of God. The 'Natural Theology' of the title is theology based on natural evidence (without revelation); the *Bridgewater Treatises* (*On the Power, Wisdom, and Goodness of God, as manifested in the Creation*) (1833-40) had greatly influenced the public imagination.

Browning valued the poem highly, it is a popular favourite, and it has excited much excellent discussion. One topic has been the poem's use of the third person (Caliban's first word – 'Will' – means 'he will', which means 'I will'), and the shifts from third to first person (see E. K. Brown, 'The First Person in "Caliban upon Setebos"', *MLN* LXVI, 1951, 392-5); the prevailing view is that Browning had Caliban normally use the third person essentially to stress his primitiveness. (The pronouns often confuse readers, as they did Browning himself: the Quiet is neuter [*it*], Setebos is third person with a capital [*He*]; Caliban – though he sometimes uses the first person – is generally third person without the capital [*he*], and frequently without the pronoun at all ['*Thinketh*'].) The main topic of discussion has been, however, Browning's intention in the poem. Is the poem satirical, and, if so, of what?: Calvinism?, the Higher Criticism with its thesis that God is created in the image of man?, natural theology (Browning often stresses the need of revelation fully to show God's nature)?, anthropomorphism (as suggested by the motto from Psalm i 21)? Others feel that the poem is not so much satirical as sympathetic to a Caliban groping his way towards some kind of adequate theology. The poem's obvious and basic source is *The Tempest*, and Browning was proud of his re-creation, but P. Honan has shown the debt the poem also owes to Belial's speech in 'the great consult' of *Paradise Lost* (II, 119-225) in 'Belial upon Setebos', *Tennessee Studies in Literature* IX, 1964, 87-98.

Besides the essays on the poem mentioned above, see Drew, *Poetry of Browning*, 150-54; J. Howard, 'Caliban's Mind', *VP* I, 1963, 249-57 (reprinted in Drew, *Robert Browning*, 223-33); L. Perrine, 'Browning's *Caliban upon Setebos*: A Reply', *VP* II, 1964, 124-7; Poston, *Loss and Gain*, 25-8; M. Timko, 'Browning upon Butler; or, Natural Theology in the English Isle', *Criticism* VII, 1965, 141-50.

Motto], Clearly a late addition to the *MS*. In *1868* it was inadvertently omitted.

5 *eft-things* newts or similar creatures.

7 *pompion* pumpkin.

16 *dam* Sycorax in *The Tempest* (I. 2.373); there her god is Setebos.

20 *Prosper and Miranda*   the protagonist of *The Tempest* (and Caliban's master) and his daughter. Prospero naps in the afternoon in Shakespeare's play.

23 *rank*   rebellious (an obsolete meaning).

27 *not the stars*   The stars are the realm of the Quiet, we learn later.

47 *auk*   a kind of sea-bird.

50 *pie*   perhaps the magpie; perhaps the pied woodpecker.

51 *oakwarts*   oak galls (Caliban's word is not in *OED*).

67 *skills*   avails

68 *I*   Caliban's first shift to the first person.

71 *bladdery*   bubbly.

72 *maggots*   fancies (Caliban has difficulty with abstractions).

79 *hoopoe*   a crested colourful bird.

83 *grigs*   grasshoppers or crickets.
  grigs] flies *MS*.

91 *cry,*] prayer *MS*.

92 *mankin three sound legs for one*] manikin three legs for his one *MS., 1864–1864 (2 edn)*; manikin three legs for one *1868*.

94 *lessoned*   having been taught a lesson.

97 *Making and marring*   'a fool finds mirth, / Makes a thing and then mars it' ('Childe Roland', 147–8).

103 A clear hit at doctrines of predestination: God, in the Westminster Confession of Faith, 'extendeth or witholdeth mercy as He pleaseth, for the glory of His sovereign power over His Creatures, to pass by, and to ordain them to dishonour and wrath for their sin, to the praise of His glorious grace'.

132 *something quiet*] some live Quiet *MS*.

137 *Quiet*] Other *MS*.

148 *hips*   fruit of the wild rose.

156 *oncelot*   ocelot or jaguar (Browning's variant is not in *OED*).

157 *ounce*   lynx or snow-leopard or cheetah.

161 *Ariel*   Prospero's airy servant in *The Tempest*.

175 *my*] the *MS*.

176 *my*] soft *MS*.

177 *orc*   probably, here, sea-monster.

190]   Wanting for little, hungering, aching not, *MS*.

205 *wattles*   twigs.

211 *ball*   meteor (fire-ball).

214–15 *newt . . . inside a stone*   The Victorians were fascinated by fossils, and rather given to melancholy rumination about them.

217 *me*] you *MS*.

227 *my*] his *MS*.

228 *I threat*] he threats *MS*.

229 *urchin*   hedgehog.

231 *my*] his *MS*.

232 *my*] his *MS*.

249 *nowhere*] never *MS*.

254 *we die*] it stop *MS*.

258 *films*   wings.
  pink] brown *MS*.

260 *painful*   taking pains.

268 *housed*] caved *MS*.

269 *me here*] him now *MS*.

274 *my*] his *MS*.
275 *myself*] himself *MS*.
276–8 Caliban's poetic powers match those he shows in *The Tempest*.
280 *rub*] die *MS*.
283 Decrepit will doze, doze, or wholly die. *MS*.
284 *What, what?*] There, see! *MS*.
  curtain thundercloud.
288 *pillared dust, death's house o' the move* a whirlwind that has picked up dust.

CONFESSIONS

First published in *Dramatis Personae* on 28 May 1864. Browning's few revisions in proof were minor; after *1864* there were no verbal changes. The poem was probably written in Italy in 1859 or early 1860: in a letter of 22 February 1860 Mrs Browning wrote 'it's mad, and bad, and sad', apparently having in mind line 35 of the poem.

MAY AND DEATH

First published in *The Keepsake* for 1857; Browning submitted the poem on 1 August of that year. With a few revisions it was reprinted in *Dramatis Personae*; after *1864* the text was unchanged. The 'Charles' of the poem was James Silverthorne, Browning's cousin and the son of the lady who paid for the publication of *Pauline*. He was a childhood friend and a witness at Browning's wedding. He died in May 1852 and the poem was probably written at some time in the following twelve months.

8 *Moon-births*] Moon's birth *1857*.
9 *be*] prove *1857*.
13 *plant* peachwort, the spotted persicaria. The plant, legend has it, grew beneath the Cross, and got its spotted leaves from Christ's blood.
18 *miss*] lose *1857*.

DEAF AND DUMB

First published when included with 'Dramatis Personae' in *1868*, and unchanged save for one punctuation mark in *1888*. The poem was written for the display of a sculptural group of Arthur and Constance, deaf and dumb children of Sir Thomas Fairbairn. The group, *Brother and Sister, or Deaf and Dumb*, was displayed at the International Exhibition of 1862 (a photograph of it appears in *BNL* 6, Spring 1971, 35); Browning gave the poem to the sculptor, Thomas Woolner, on 24 April 1862.

5 *vexed Love wreak* agitated Love express.
6 *insuppressive* insuppressible.

PROSPICE

First published in the *Atlantic Monthly* XVIII, June 1864, 694, a few days before its publication in *Dramatis Personae* on 28 May 1864. There were a few punctuation changes in proof; after *1864* the only verbal change was in the previously unrhymed line 25. The poem was probably written soon after Mrs Browning's death in June 1861; about the same time, Browning wrote in his wife's Testament, 'Thus I believe, thus I affirm, thus I am certain it is, that from this life I shall pass to another, there, where that lady lives of whom my soul was enamoured' (Dante, *Convivio* II, 9). For Browning it is an uncharacteristically personal poem. The title means 'Look forward' (Latin).

25   *out of pain*]   then a joy *MS., 1864–1864* (*2 edn*).

EURYDICE TO ORPHEUS

First published in the form of prose in the catalogue of the Royal Academy Exhibition of 1864 (page 13) where it served to describe Frederic Leighton's picture *Orpheus and Eurydice*. There it was signed and referred to as 'A fragment'. Called 'Orpheus and Eurydice', the poem was first published as verse in the *Selections* of 1865; and in *1868*, with its final title, it was included with 'Dramatis Personae'. All printings were verbally identical. DeVane (*Handbook*, 316) reports a manuscript with the date 5 April 1864; the manuscript in the Berg Collection of the New York Public Library is undated. Browning addressed his dead wife in 'Prospice', and it has been suggested that here to some extent he has her address him.

The musician Orpheus sought his dead wife Eurydice in the underworld, where his playing impressed Pluto so much that he allowed Eurydice to follow her husband back to earth, on condition that Orpheus not look back. But Orpheus looked back, and his wife disappeared.

Frederic Leighton and the Brownings had become friends in Italy; he had sketched Browning and designed Mrs Browning's tomb in Florence. The brother of Browning's friend and biographer, Mrs Orr, he remained a close friend of Browning. He was a painter of great importance in his day, later President of the Royal Academy, knighted, and elevated to the peerage.

YOUTH AND ART

First published in *Dramatis Personae* on 28 May 1864. It was slightly revised in proof; after *1864* it was virtually unchanged. The poem was probably written in Florence about 1860.

8   *Gibson*   John Gibson (1790–1866), the most celebrated English sculptor of his day, had his studio in Rome. Browning knew him well.

12   *Grisi*   Giulia Grisi (1811–69), the great Italian operatic soprano.

31   *shook*   trilled.

     E in alt   high E.

32   *chromatic scale*   scale which proceeds by semitones.

57   *Prince*   probably Albert, the Prince Consort. He died in 1861.

58   *bals-paré*   full-dress balls.

60   *R.A.*   member of the Royal Academy.

A FACE

First published in *Dramatis Personae* on 28 May 1864. There are minor differences between the original manuscript and the printers' manuscript of *Dramatis Personae*; after that, there were no verbal changes. The original manuscript, now in the Armstrong Browning Library of Baylor University, entitled 'Written on Emily in her Album, from which it is torn', is signed, and dated London, 11 October 1852.

The face is that of the first wife of Coventry Patmore, and the heroine of some of his poems; she died in 1862. Millais painted her in 1851; Woolner made a medallion of her about the same time.

3 *Tuscan's early art* The medieval art of Tuscany is highly gilded.
6–7 Mrs Patmore's beauty was in fact said to have been lost when she laughed.
8 *Yon*] Some *1852 MS.*
9 *buds*] studs *1852 MS.*
14 *Correggio* the Italian artist (*c.* 1489–1534).
17 *massed there*] mustered *1852 MS.*
22 *the*] a *1852 MS.*

A LIKENESS

First published in *Dramatis Personae* on 28 May 1864. A line was added in proof, and other changes made. After *1864* there were no verbal changes. Topical references and other factors suggest strongly that the poem was written in the latter half of 1858 or in 1859.

6 *daub* inferior painting.
16 *tandem-lasher* whip used in a two-wheeled vehicle.
18 *Tipton Slasher* the nickname of William Perry, from Tipton in Staffordshire, who became English boxing champion in 1850. He lost the title in 1857 to Tom Sayers.
19 *cards where pistol-balls mark ace* cards given a single mark by a bullet.
21 *Chablais* in the French Alps.
22 *Rarey drumming on Cruiser* Browning ordered J. S. Rarey's book on horse-taming when it was published (1858). Rarey is depicted whipping his horse 'Cruiser'.
23 *Sayers, our champion* Tom Sayers, English boxing champion, 1857–60.
30 *proboscis* The word is, except for humorous purposes as here, normally used of an elephant's trunk.
31 *Vichy* spa in central France.
34 *mezzotint* an engraved print.
42 *imbroglio* confused pile.
47] *not in MS.*
50 *National Portrait Gallery* the famous gallery in London.
54 *Marc Antonios* Marcantonio Raimondi was the leading Italian engraver of the early sixteenth century.
55 *Festina lentè* 'Make haste slowly' (Latin).
61 *Volpato* Giovanni Volpato was an eighteenth-century Italian engraver.
65 *occupy*] wile away *MS.*

MR SLUDGE, 'THE MEDIUM'

First published in *Dramatis Personae* on 28 May 1864. The manuscript is unlike that of other poems in the volume in appearing to be a rough draft rather than a fair copy, and, to an extent unequalled by other of Browning's printers' manuscripts, is heavily revised. A number of single lines were added, and many other revisions made in proof. After *1864* there were a few minor verbal revisions and a number in punctuation.

Though the condition of the manuscript suggests strongly that Browning revised the poem heavily shortly before *Dramatis Personae* went to press, the poem (or a substantial part of it) was in all probability drafted in 1859–60. Mrs Browning's reference to her husband's 'working at a long poem' of which she had not seen a line (18 May 1860), is generally taken to apply to 'Mr Sludge', especially since the poem's topical allusions are mainly to events of 1859–60. Given Mrs Browning's beliefs in spiritualism, Browning is unlikely to have worked on the poem for a year or so following her death.

The model for Sludge was Daniel Dunglas Home (1833–86) as the popular American medium himself readily recognized (see his *Incidents in My Life*, Second Series, New York, 1872 – Browning complained of Home's 'vomit of lies' here, and referred to Home as a 'dung-ball'). Browning had first met him at a séance in Ealing (see Betty Miller, 'The Séance at Ealing: A Study in Memory and Imagination', *Cornhill Magazine* CLXIX, 1957, 317–24) on 23 July 1855 (later in the year Home conducted séances in Florence and other Italian cities). Mrs Browning was initially impressed, and distressed at her husband's response to Home whom he always regarded as a fraud; in 1902 their son claimed that his mother had later much modified her opinion.

For general background, see K. H. Porter, *Through a Glass Darkly : Spiritualism in the Browning Circle*, University of Kansas Press, 1958. M. Millhauser believes that Robert Chambers, author of *Vestiges of Creation* (1844) and a disciple of Home, was in Browning's mind as he wrote his poem: see 'Robert Browning, Robert Chambers, and Mr. Home, the Medium', *VNL* 39, 1971, 15–19. Spiritualism was widely practised in the 1850s and 1860s and was a most controversial subject. Further information is available in the First Series of Home's book (1863) – which Browning denied reading – and in W. L. Phelps, 'Robert Browning on Spiritualism', *Yale Review* XXIII (1933), 125–38.

'Mr Sludge' is the only poem of Browning's clearly set in the United States, which Browning never visited though he had many American friends. Apart from Caliban, Sludge is Browning's only American hero, and he is the only one to speak what Browning meant to be American speech (J. V. Fleming reports that Browning's Americanisms are accurate in 'Browning's Yankee Medium', *American Speech* XXXIX, 1964, 26–32).

Among other treatments of what was Bernard Shaw's favourite Browning poem are: I. Armstrong, 'Browning's *Mr Sludge*, "The Medium"', *VP* II, 1964, 1–9 (reprinted in Drew, *Robert Browning*, 212–22); Drew, *The Poetry of Browning*, 143–8; D. F. Goslee, 'Mr Sludge the Medium – Mr Browning the Possessed', *SBHC* III, no. 2, 1975, 40–58; R. Kelly, 'Daniel Home, Mr. Sludge and a Forgotten Browning Letter', *SBHC* I, no. 2, 1973, 44–9; Poston, *Loss and Gain*, 28–41; Raymond, *The Infinite Moment*, 141–7; A Shapiro, ' "Participate in Sludgehood": Browning's "Mr. Sludge", the Critics, and the Problem of Morality', *Papers on Language and Literature* V, 1969, 145–55.

9 *Catawba* a light sparkling American wine.

16 *rowdy* ruffian (an American word; *OED*'s first recorded usage is in 1819).

35 *Franklin* Among other things, Benjamin Franklin was the first Postmaster of the US. In spiritualist circles, he was head of the 'College of Spirits' in the other world.

37 *Tom Paine* the great American political theorist (1737–1809).

54 *post* send quickly.

Greeley's newspaper the New York *Tribune*, edited by Horace Greeley (1811–72).

65 *Vs* V-notes: five-dollar notes or bills.

67 *this table* that used at the séance.

81 *nothing lasts, as Bacon came and said* Sludge may be thinking of Francis Bacon's essay *Of the Vicissitude of Things*, but it is more probable that he is attributing a platitude to an authority designed to impress his auditor.

112 *trucked* exchanged.

trucked] gave *cancelled MS. reading.*

117 *With cow-hide* that is, with a whip.

130 *grand*] fine *MS.*

134 *vulgarest* Sludge shares Browning's fondness for unusual superlatives.

credulity] incredulity *MS., 1864-8.*

136 *Johnson* Samuel Johnson (1709-84): 'All argument is against it; but all belief is for it.'

Wesley Samuel Wesley, father of the founder of Methodism, coped with a poltergeist in the winter of 1716-17.

137 *Mother Goose* The nursery rhymes adapted from the French were first published in English in Boston (1719).

140 *conceit* fancy.

158 a slight misquotation of *Hamlet* I. 5.166.

168 *Porson* Richard Porson, Cambridge Greek scholar, 1759-1808.

182 *glass ball* of the kind used by a crystal gazer.

183 *spirit-writing* the automatic writing 'dictated' or 'controlled' by a spirit.

218 *the stranger in your gates* the outsider, or partial convert – 'thy stranger that is within thy gates' (Deuteronomy v 14).

220] *an addition to the MS.*

guest without the wedding-garb stranger (Matthew xxii 11-14).

221 *doubting Thomas* sceptic – after the apostle who doubted Christ's resurrection (John xx 24-9).

229] *later addition to the MS.*

233 *Mexican War* the war between the United States and Mexico (1846-8).

237 *clubbing* gathering together.

246-7 *gulling you | To the top o' your bent* 'They fool me to the top of my bent' (*Hamlet* III. 2.401).

265 *canvas-backs* kind of North American duck.

269 *dizened* bedizened, gaily dressed.

280 *Pennsylvanian "mediums"* It was said that Pentecostal fire had descended upon parts of Pennsylvania, and that in one church, members of the congregation began to speak in foreign languages.

286 *Horseshoe* the Horseshoe (or Canadian) Falls at Niagara.

307 *lovers, friends and countrymen* In *Julius Caesar* (III. 2.13 and III. 2.78), the speeches of Brutus and Antony begin 'Romans, countrymen, and lovers', and 'Friends, Romans, countrymen'.

309 *Francis Verulam* Francis Bacon was made Baron Verulam in 1618. He did not live in York, or die in Wales, or live into the period of Cromwell's rule.

312 *when Cromwell reigned* Oliver Cromwell was Lord Protector (1653-8); he ruled, but did not 'reign'.

328 *kibes* chilblains, heels.

330 *Barnum* Phineas Taylor Barnum (1810-91) was the American showman, and a contemporary of Browning.

343 *Thirty-third Sonata* Beethoven wrote thirty-two piano sonatas.

344 *hopper* the receptacle receiving grain etc. at a mill.

345 *Shakers* American religious sect.

  G, with a natural F an impossibility – the scale of G demands F sharp.

346 *Stars and Stripes* Sludge perhaps means *The Star-Spangled Banner.*

  set to consecutive fourths Such an arrangement would be highly discordant.

353 *gamboge* a yellow gum-resin used as a pigment.

361 *posed* puzzled.

368] *not in MS.*

387 *cockered* pampered.

393 *kennel* gutter.

432 *souchong* a Chinese tea.

  smack taste.

433 *caddy . . . dram-bottle* tea-caddy . . . liquor-bottle.

434 *cruel* The adverbial usage is obsolete or dialectal.

461 *Very like a whale* Sludge quotes the agreeable Polonius (*Hamlet* III. 2.400).

480 *Saul and Jonathan* King Saul of Israel threw a javelin at his son Jonathan because of Jonathan's friendship for David (1 Samuel xx 33).

481 *Pompey and Caesar* Julius Caesar beat his son-in-law, Pompey the Great, at the Battle of Pharsalia.

500 *blow of blacks* blast of smuts.

516ᴧ17] And once begin the traffic, never fear *cancelled MS. reading.*

523 *fall West* move to the west – that is, to the United States.

526 *Broadway* a main street in New York City.

528 *lapstone* stone held in the lap to hammer leather on.

546 *rotten* *OED* does not record the word as a noun.

576 *prairie-dog* North American burrowing rodent.

577 *beck*] nod *MS., 1864–8.*

591 *Asaph* choirmaster (or eponym of a chorus of singers) of David's time, when crotchets and quavers did not exist.

595 *pothooks* hooked strokes in writing.

629] *not in MS.*

645 *Friends of a feather* alluding to the proverb, 'Birds of a feather flock together'.

649 *propose* bid.

654 *strut and fret his hour* 'A poor player / That struts and frets his hour upon the stage' (*Macbeth* V. 5.25–6).

655 *spawl* spit coarsely.

  target shield.

656] *not in MS.*

659 *tom-fool* buffoon in a play.

665] A capital point! Doing these pretty tricks *MS.*

667 *Swedenborg* The Swedish mystic (1688–1772) believed he had directly experienced divine revelation.

677 *snow gains*] it gains *MS., 1864–8.*

678 *Rahab* the prostitute who hid Joshua's spies. She and her household were spared when Jericho was destroyed (Joshua ii, and vi 17–23).

683 *live coal from the altar* 'Then flew one of the seraphims unto me, having a live coal in his hand, which he had taken with the tongs from off the altar' (Isaiah vi 6).

691–3 *Nelson . . . signal he was bothered with* At the Battle of Copenhagen, Nelson, ordered to withdraw, is reputed to have held his telescope to his blind eye and thus failed to see the signal.

693 *bothered with*] beaten *MS.*; bothered *1864–8.*

712 *scruff*] scuff *1864–8.*

724 *rare* splendid.

742 *Mars' Hill* the Areopagus at Athens, where Saint Paul told the Athenians they were 'too superstitious' (Acts xvii 22–34).

745 *new thing* 'For all the Athenians and strangers which were there spent their time in nothing else, but either to tell, or to hear some new thing' (Acts xvii 21).

747 *dung-heaps* Browning referred to Home as 'this dung-ball'.

772 *umber and bistre* brown pigments.

775 *fribble* trifler.

777 *faculty* intelligence.

784 *greenhorn* raw, inexperienced youth.

788 *Pasiphae* The lusty wife of Theseus fell in love with a bull.

790 *for their pains, like me*] all, as I hate you *MS.*

791–2 *thanklessness / Toward a deserving public*] having sinned / Against a respectable public *MS.*

802 *sympathetic ink* invisible ink.

803 *odic lights* The lights at séances were said to be emanations of Od (a word coined by Reichenbach in 1850), a spiritual force pervading Nature. In *Aurora Leigh* VII, 295–6, Mrs Browning had referred to 'That od-force of German Reichenbach / Which still from female finger-tips burns blue'.

  phosphor-match The white phosphorus of the match would glow in the dark.

805–6 *set / The crooked straight* 'the crooked shall be made straight' (Isaiah xl 4, Luke iii 5); 'That which is crooked cannot be made straight' (Ecclesiastes i 15) – similar biblical phrases abound.

807 *knocked*] thrown *MS., 1864–8.*

824 *home*] world *MS., 1864–8.*

832 *plate . . . delf* gold- or silver-plate . . . a kind of earthenware.

846 *Samuel's ghost appeared to Saul* 1 Samuel xxviii 14.

852 *Such things may be* 'Can such things be' (*Macbeth* III. 4.10).

884 *my life*] the world *MS.*

887 Sludge confuses Christmas Eve and New Year's Eve.

901] *not in MS.*

910 *raree-show* a show or spectacle – originally a peep-show carried in a box.

916 *weather-glass* barometer.

921 *Charles's Wain* the constellation of the Great Bear.

  twelve] nine *MS.*

929 *powder-plots* The Gunpowder Plot (1605) to blow up Parliament was discovered in time.

940 *Boston city*] all New York *MS.*

947 *special thanksgiving* Thanksgiving Day is an annual holiday in the US.

963 *dime* ten-cent coin.

968] *not in MS.*

972–4 *If the further bird . . . blue does* The thought, like much else in the poem, recalls 'Caliban upon Setebos'.

975] When you grew angry, took me by surprise *MS.*

1003 *sprang*] knew *MS.*; sprung *1864–8.*

1005] *not in MS.*

1027] *not in MS.*

1035 *canthus*] corner *MS.*; canthus *1864–8.*

  canthus corner of the eye.

1046 *dew-point* temperature at which dew forms.

1050 *cent. per cent.* one hundred per cent.

1055]   *not in MS.*

1060   *motes*   normally used of specks of dust; Sludge means 'small insects' (mites).

1066]   Multiply, and prove irresistible! *MS.*

1069   *offices*   acts of kindness.

1074   *Great and Terrible Name*   'Let them praise thy great and terrible name; for it is holy' (Psalm xcix 3).

1077   *Magnum et terribile*   'Great and Terrible' (Latin).

1086–8   *the Jews . . . Nor speak aloud*   Some Jews do not use the name of the Lord, which was originally deliberately ineffable (JHWH).

1101   *vulgar*]   proper *MS.*

1117   *The Name*]   'Nomen' *MS.*

    stomach-cyst   a minute organism: paramecium?

1124–6   Sludge describes a Leyden jar, an electrical condenser.

1140   *Bridgewater book*   The *Bridgewater Treatises* (*On the Power, Wisdom, and Goodness of God, as manifested in the Creation*) were published between 1833 and 1840.

1152   *crotchets*   fancies.

1157–8   *the son and heir* | *O'the kingdom*   'of such [little children] is the kingdom of heaven' (Matthew xix 14).

1159]   *not in MS.*

1167   *does its duty*]   to instruct me *MS.*

1170   *boblink*   bobolink, a North American bird.

1180   *Washington's oracle*   If Sludge has anything particular in mind, it has not been identified.

1186   *heir*   to the kingdom of line 1158.

1225   '*Time' with the foil in carte*   make a well-timed parry in fencing.

    jump their own height]   I'd like to know *MS.*

1226   *skate a five*   make the figure five on the ice.

1227   *Make the red hazard*   pocket the red ball in billiards.

1227–30]   Make the red hazard with the cue, do sums

                    Of fifty figures in their brain, swim, row,

                    Pull themselves up, overhead, with the left arm,

                    Trip on a tightrope stretched across the Falls *MS.*

(Blondin crossed a tightrope over Niagara Falls several times in 1859.)

1236   *heart . . . grey*]   time . . . out *MS.*

1253   *it lightens*   There is lightning.

1256   *when*   while.

1263   *stouter*   braver.

1268   *Jenny Lind*   the Swedish soprano (1820–87).

1269   *Emerson*   Ralph Waldo Emerson (1803–82), philosopher and writer.

    Benicia Boy   John C. Heenan, born in Benicia, California, American prizefighter, drew in 1860 with the English champion, Tom Sayers (referred to in 'A Likeness', 23).

1272]   These same tricks that emasculate the soul, *MS.*

1299   *Beacon Street*   a main street in Boston.

    Beacon Street]   The broad way *MS.*

1305–6   *lump . . . leaven it*   'a little leaven leaveneth the whole lump' (1 Corinthians v 6).

1325   *Quick*   alive.

1330–31   *Herodotus . . . Latin*   The Greek historian of the fifth century B.C. wrote in Greek.

1333 *Egyptian* Sludge's error for Babylonian. In I, 199, Herodotus tells of the rite by which every Babylonian female gave herself once in her life to any man at the temple of Aphrodite.

1338 *a many* an obsolete form of expression (compare 'a few').

1365 *topping* very high.

1374 *puffs* of wind.

1381 *cresset* vessel holding combustibles for a torch.

1392 *harlequin's pasteboard sceptre* In commedia dell'arte and pantomime, Harlequin often uses a kind of magic wand.

1409 *Mary Queen of Scots* Mary Stuart (1542–87), executed by Elizabeth I.

1411 *piques* stimulates.

1432 *Eutopia* In this spelling, the Greek means the 'ideal place' (Utopia means 'no place').

Here's true] This is *MS.*; Here is *1864–8*.

1433 *world well won* The subtitle of Dryden's play *All for Love* (1678) is *The World Well Lost*.

1436 *poet* Homer.

1439 *Lowell* J. R. Lowell (1819–91), writer and professor of belles-lettres at Harvard.

Lowell] Homer *MS.*

applause] and say *MS.*, *1864–8*.

1440 *Longfellow* poet and Harvard professor (1807–82).

1441 *Hawthorne* Browning knew the American novelist (1804–64) in Florence.

1451 *Old Country War* the American War of Independence from the 'Old Country', England.

1452 *Jerome Napoleon* Jérôme Bonaparte, youngest brother of Napoleon (1784–1860), had been briefly married to an American.

1454 *life in stones* alluding to fossil evidence for evolution.

1455 *Fire into fog* In theories of the nebular origin of the universe, the first state is imagined as a 'universal fire-mist' (Chambers's phrase in *Vestiges of the Natural History of Creation*, 1844). Millhauser (17) suggests that Browning may be alluding to Chambers in the preceding lines.

1457 Theseus escaped the Cretan labyrinth by following a thread laid by Ariadne.

1466 *Thebes* the Egyptian city fabled for its wealth.

1472 *Lady Jane Grey* Queen of England (1553) for nine days until Mary Tudor took over and executed her.

1479 *arnica* a tincture for wounds and bruises.

1484 *He's*] An *MS.*, *1864–88* (change made for second impression of *1888*).

1485–6 *And I've lost you, lost myself, | Lost all-l-l-l- ...*] *not in MS.*

1488 *prompts, and what's*] *1864, 1888*; is, and what *MS.*; must be, what *1868*.

1500 *R-r-r*] Aie *MS.*

1513ₐ14] Sure to succeed, the niggers say – who knows? *cancelled MS. reading.*

1523 *herring-pond* the Atlantic Ocean (not a Sludgism).

APPARENT FAILURE

First published in *Dramatis Personae* on 28 May 1864. There are no significant differences between manuscript and *1864*, and between *1864* and later printings. The poem was in all probability written in the summer of 1863 when Browning was staying in Brittany. The poem was a favourite of Tennyson's. And the building was not demolished. Browning had visited it in 1857, and seen the three bodies of the poem. On the poem, see J. Lucas, in *BSN* VI, No. 1, 1976, 17–23.

1–3 *Seven years since ... Prince* In June 1856 Browning witnessed the baptism of the only son of Napoleon III.
6 *Seine* the river on which Paris stands.
7 *Congress* The Imperial Congress met in Paris early in 1856 to end the Crimean War.
  Gortschakoff Prince Alexander Gortschakoff represented the Russians at the Congress of Paris.
8 *Cavour's appeal* Piedmont had aided the British and French in the Crimean War; and Count Cavour (1810–61), Prime Minister of Sardinia, had appealed for recognition of Piedmont as an independent state.
  Buol Count Karl Ferdinand Buol-Schauenstein (1797–1865) represented the Austrians at the Congress of Paris.
10 *Doric* an architectural style, simple and strong.
12 *Petrarch's Vaucluse* The fourteenth-century Italian poet lived for a while in Fontaine-de-Vaucluse in south-east France.
  Sorgue The fountain, celebrated by Petrarch, is the source of the Sorgue river.
39 *Tuileries* the palace of Napoleon III and earlier emperors.
43 *leveller* egalitarian.
  Empire Napoleon III had become Emperor of the former Republic in 1852.
46–7 *red ... / Or black* alluding to the gambling game, *rouge et noir*.

EPILOGUE

First published in *Dramatis Personae* on 28 May 1864. Changes between manuscript and *1864*, and between *1864* and later printings, are few and insignificant, except for the identification of the first and second speakers as David and Renan, made in the second edition of *Dramatis Personae* (the unidentified third speaker is obviously Browning himself). The poem was probably written very late in 1863 or early in 1864, after Browning had finished Renan's life of Jesus.

  In a number of respects (form, mood, imagery) the second part recalls 'Pictor Ignotus'. The poem's importance as a statement of Browning's religious position is universally recognized. See W. Kirkconnell, 'The *Epilogue* to *Dramatis Personae*', *MLN* XLI, 1926, 213–19 (reprinted in Drew, *Robert Browning*, 234–41).

1 *first of the Feast of Feasts* that of the dedication of Solomon's temple (1 Kings viii, and 2 Chronicles v).
3 *Levites* The priests' assistants in the Temple were traditionally chosen from the tribe of Levi.
13–21 'and when they lifted up their voice with the trumpets and cymbals and instruments of musick, and praised the Lord, saying, For he is good; for his mercy endureth for ever: that then the house was filled with a cloud, even the house of the Lord' (2 Chronicles v 13).
24 *that star* the one that 'stood' over the manger at the birth of Christ (Matthew ii 9).
29 *gyre on gyre* spiral on spiral.
96 *where's the need of Temple* Browning became less and less a church-goer in the latter half of his life.

99 *That*] And *MS*.
That one Face 'That Face, is the face of Christ. That is how I feel him' (Browning to Mrs Orr as quoted in *Contemporary Review* LX, 1891, 880).
101 *Become*] And be *MS*.

Balaustion's Adventure

Published by Smith, Elder on 8 August 1871. A second edition appeared in January 1872, a third in 1883. The manuscript is in the Library of Balliol College. Browning made some fairly minor revisions for *1871* in proof; there were no revisions for *1872* or *1883*, and few for *1888*. In the dedication to the young Countess Cowper who 'imposed' the task of writing the poem upon him, Browning refers to it as 'the most delightful of May-month amusements'. It was written hurriedly in May 1871; the manuscript is very clean, and appears to be the first and last draft of the poem.

The bulk of the poem is Balaustion's account of the performance of the earliest extant Euripides play, the *Alcestis* of 438 B.C. Mrs Browning had admired the Greek playwright, and the motto for *Balaustion's Adventure* comes from her *Wine of Cyprus* (1844). The 1850s and 1860s had seen a revival of interest in Greek drama, one manifestation of which was William Morris's handling of the Alcestis story in the first volume (1868) of *The Earthly Paradise*, a handling that includes one of the 'improvements' Balaustion suggests for the Greek play. The Victorians generally ranked Euripides below Aeschylus and Sophocles – indeed they not infrequently denounced him; but he was Browning's own favourite among the Greeks.

Browning called his later translations of the *Agamemnon* of Aeschylus and of the *Heracles* of Euripides (in *Aristophanes' Apology*), 'transcripts', but the 'transcript' of *Alcestis* in *Balaustion's Adventure* is a modernized adaptation, not a translation, and its general bent is somewhat different from that of its original. Balaustion of course comments on the production she saw in her home town; moreover, some speeches are shortened or deleted, the Chorus's role is reduced, Heracles is somewhat spiritualized, Admetus is less sympathetic (some of the more notable of Browning's excisions are lines expressing sympathy for Admetus) and his character and development perhaps somewhat richer than in Euripides' play (see F. M. Tisdel, '*Balaustion's Adventure* as an Interpretation of the *Alcestis* of Euripides', *PMLA* XXXII, 1917, 519–46). Browning probably saw personal significance in the play: Balaustion (whose name means 'Wild-pomegranate-flower') reminds one of other Browning heroines including his wife, and the portraits of Alcestis and Admetus, it is generally felt, are affected by points of resemblance to Mrs Browning and the poet himself – Admetus' insistence, for example, on not remarrying may derive from Browning's feelings about his recent relationship with Lady Ashburton. (The poem's biographical significance is treated most fully in J. H. Friend, 'Euripides Browningized: The Meaning of *Balaustion's Adventure*', *VP* II, 1964, 179–86.) The source for the poem's frame is Plutarch's *Life of Nicias*, which includes an account of the suffering of the Athenians captured in the expedition against Syracuse in 413 B.C. Some Athenians, Plutarch says, were, however, 'saved for the sake of Euripides', some even being freed for recounting stories from his plays. And, Plutarch adds, 'one need not wonder at the story that the Caunians, when a vessel of theirs would have put in at the harbour of Syracuse to escape pursuit by pirates, were not admitted at first, but kept outside, until on being asked if they knew any songs of Euripides, they declared that they did indeed, and were for this reason suffered to bring their vessel safely in'.

The 2,500 copies of the first edition quickly sold out; readers admired in particular the character of the heroine, who reappears in *Aristophanes' Apology*. On the poem see Irvine and Honan, *The Book, the Ring, and the Poet*, 457–60, and C. de L. Ryals, '*Balaustion's Adventure*: Browning's Greek Parable', *PMLA* LXXXVIII, 1973, 1040–48.

2   *Kameiros*   town on the west coast of the island of Rhodes.

4–5   *Petalé . . . Chrusion*   girl friends of Balaustion (the names come from Alciphron).

7   *Nikias*   Nicias (470–413 B.C.) was the last Athenian commander in the expedition against Sicily and its chief city of Syracuse during the Peloponnesian War. He had opposed the expedition, commanded it irresolutely, and was executed when captured.

14   *the League*   the Peloponnesian League led by Sparta, opposed to Athens and the Delian League in the Peloponnesian War, and ultimately victorious in 404 B.C. Rhodes joined it in 412 B.C.

17   *Knidos*   town in south-west Asia Minor.

20   *first*]   long *MS.*

21   *Ilissian*   The Ilissus river flows to the east and south of Athens.

27–41   *Rather go die . . . Follow me*   'I would not exchange for . . . all the envied valuables of his courts, our yearly Choës, the Lenaea in the theatre, a banquet such as we had yesterday, the exercises in the Lyceum and the Sacred Academy – no, I swear it by Bacchus and his ivy-wreaths, with which I would rather be crowned . . . than with all the diadems of Ptolemy. For where in Egypt shall I see a democracy enjoying liberty? the legislators in the sacred villages crowned with ivy? the roped enclosure? the election of magistrates? the feast of Pots? the Ceramicus? the marketplace? the law-courts? the dread goddesses? the mysteries? the Stenia? neighbouring Salamis, Psytallia, Marathon, all Greece in Athens, all Ionia, all the Cyclades?' (Alciphron 2, 3). Alciphron was a second-century Greek author of letters in the Lucianic mode between imaginary characters. Exact dates unknown. The above is the present editor's translation. Cf. the version in the Loeb Classical Library edition of the *Letters of Alciphron, Aelian and Philostratus* (1949).

28–9   *gate/Of Diomedes or the Hippadai*   the Diomeian and Hippades gates of ancient Athens (Browning errs in associating the former with Diomedes). The gates are mentioned together in Alciphron 3, 51.

32   *Lakonia*   the area in the south-east Peloponnesus of which Sparta was the capital.

33   *Choës and Chutroi*   'the Jugs' and 'the Pots': names of the second and third days of the Athenian late-winter festival, the Anthesteria.

34   *Agora, Dikasteria, Poikilé*   respectively, the market-place and centre of public life of Athens, the judicial panels, the covered and decorated colonnade on the north side of the Agora.

35   *Pnux, Keramikos; Salamis*   respectively, the meeting-place in Athens of the general assembly of freemen, a district in Athens famous for its potteries, the island off the west coast of Attica where the Athenians beat the Persians in the naval battle of 480 B.C.

36   *Psuttalia, Marathon*   an islet near Salamis and site of the Greek land victory after the naval battle, and the plain twenty-two miles from Athens where the Athenians and Plataeans beat the Persians in 490 B.C.

37   *Dionusiac theatre*   the Athenian Theatre just south of the Acropolis, where the plays of Aeschylus, Sophocles, Euripides and Aristophanes were first presented.

43 *Kaunos* city in south-west Asia Minor, north of Rhodes.

48 *cheek* The word is used of various parts of a ship; here, probably, the wood at the bows used to secure the beak-head.

50 *Point Malea* the extreme south-east point of the Greek mainland, notorious for storms.

52 *so broke*] and so *MS, 1871*.

54 *Cos* The island, about sixty miles north-west of Rhodes, was a member of the Delian League.

62 *keles* transliteration of the Greek word (it is not in *OED*) for a light vessel.

  one-benched one-banked (that is, with all oars on one level).

63 *Lokrian* Two districts were known as Locris. Presumably here the reference is to the inhabitants of the wilder of the two, western Locris, north of the Gulf of Corinth.

  Thessaly the area of eastern Greece lying south of Macedonia.

75 *genius* the tutelary god or attendant spirit of classical belief.

76–80 *song of ours . . . all be lost* Balaustion translates the song in *The Persians* (lines 402–5) of Aeschylus (who fought at Salamis).

82 *Churned the black water white* 'Churning the blackness hoary' (*The Ring and the Book* X, 1108).

85 *stadia* The Greek *stadium* was 600 Greek feet (about 607 English feet).

87 *Ortugia* island at the mouth of the port of Syracuse.

106–7 *captives . . . corn* According to Thucydides, the enslaved prisoners of Athens' Sicilian expedition got a daily ration of about half a pint of water and a pint of corn. Branded with the sign of the horse, they slaved in the stone-quarries of Syracuse.

123 *ossifrage* osprey.

134 *born upon the battle-day* Euripides spent much of his life on Salamis, but only tradition has it that he was born on the day of the battle. His birthdate is now generally set four years before it. He was about forty years younger than Aeschylus.

135 *salpinx* ancient Greek trumpet.

140 *Gulippos* the Spartan victor over the Athenians in Sicily in 413 B.C.

141 *Demosthenes* The Athenian leader, sent with reinforcements for Nicias, was also executed in 413 B.C.

145 *Region of the Steed* The quotation is from Sophocles, *Oedipus at Colonus*, 668; the play was not produced until 401 B.C. See *Aristophanes' Apology*, lines 3500–3512, where the same Chorus, the one reputedly spoken by Sophocles when charged with senility, is referred to, and the story given.

159 *Decadence* The charge of decadence was often laid against Euripides in his own lifetime and in the Victorian age.

163 *born latest* Dionysus (Bacchus) is only a minor deity in Homer. Only with Hesiod in the eighth century B.C. did he become an Olympian.

167 *rhesis* set speech or discourse. The usage here is the first recorded by *OED*.

169 *monostich* one-line epigram; Browning refers to the 'thrust and parry' of stichomythia (brisk dialogue in single lines) common in Greek plays.

171–80 *Any such happy man . . . sacrifice* Browning follows Plutarch's *Life of Nicias*.

183 *Euoi* (usually rendered 'Evoe') Bacchanalian exclamation.

184 *Oöp* exclamation of surprise.

  owl-shield The owl was the emblem of Athens (and of Pallas Athena).

185 *Sacred Anchor* proverbial Greek expression for 'last hope'.

187 *Babai* exclamation of surprise.

187–8   *what a word … teeth's enclosure*   translating a favourite epic periphrasis of Homer's (see *Odyssey* I, 64, for instance).

189   *Thrace*   area to the north-east of Greece.

210   *Rosy Isle*   Rhodes (the name means 'Rosy Isle').

214   *strophe, with the turn-again*   The Greek *strophe* means 'turning', the expression 'turn-again' translates the Greek *antistrophe*. The Choruses of Greek plays generally included strophes followed by antistrophes, the latter repeating metrical patterns established in the former.

215   *verse that ends all, proverb-like*   Greek plays generally end with a Choric platitude.

222   *Glaukinos' archonship*   Glaucinus was the archon eponymus (the chief magistrate who gave his name to the year) in 438 B.C. when *Alcestis* was first performed.

225   *Lenean feast*   a Dionysian festival held in Athens in late January.

226   *the perfect piece*   The same phrase is used of *Herakles* (*Aristophanes' Apology*, 3534).

230   *Temple*   Of the two famous temples in Syracuse, neither was sacred to Heracles; but Plutarch refers to a temple of Heracles and to honours done him by the Syracusans.

256   *Talent*   a valuable gift; the silver would have been worth a considerable sum in today's money.

258   *a second time*   The first time is in *Alcestis*.

265   *one man*   His name in *Aristophanes' Apology* is Euthukles.

271   *Peiraieus*   the port of Athens.

272   *Anthesterion-month*   February–March.

283   *boast the bay*   claim the poetic laurels.

284   *Agathon … Iophon*   Athenian tragic poet (*c.* 448–400 B.C.); and the son of Sophocles, also a tragic poet.

285   *Kephisophon*   slave of Euripides, said (by Aristophanes!) to have collaborated in his plays, and to have made love to his wife.

293   *Sokrates*   The great philosopher (469–399 B.C.) was a friend of Euripides.

306   *brisk little somebody*   The diminutive Alfred Austin, whom Browning was to attack in *Pacchiarotto* (1876), had criticized Browning violently in 1869 and 1871.

310   *mask of the actor*   Actors in Greek plays were masked.

318   *power that makes*   The concept of the poet as 'maker' is Greek and occurs frequently in Browning. In 1869, Austin had insisted that poets and poems are born, not made.

338   *Baccheion*   the temple of Dionysus.

360   *Pherai*   city in Thessaly.

362   *Apollon*   Apollo speaks the prologue to *Alcestis*.

372   *forgers of the thunderbolt*   the Cyclopes.

374   *I surmise*   Balaustion's surmise is correct. The prologue of *Alcestis* does not give Zeus' motive for killing Asclepius.

383   *Moirai*   the three Fates.

386   *Hades*   the underworld.

412   *heapy*   full or consisting of heaps.

430   *domes*   mansions (poeticism).

438   *Pelias*   the father of Alcestis, son of Poseidon and Tyro.

443   *rapid interchange*   the 'rhetorical tennis' of stichomythia.

476–7   *Eurustheus … steeds*   Eurystheus, King of Argos, laid on Heracles the Twelve Labours, one of which was to fetch away the man-eating horses of the Thracian Diomedes.

489–90 *rites/O' the sword* cutting the hair of the dead.

499–501 *As in came stealing … friends to those unhappy here* The Chorus of *Alcestis* is made up of old men of Pherae.

516 *Paian* 'Healer' (Apollo).

539 *Lukia or the sand-waste, Ammon's seat* Lycia was in south-west Asia Minor; Ammon was an Egyptian god, identified by the Greeks with Zeus, whose main temple was in the Libyan desert.

541 *instant* close at hand.

544 *Phoibos' son* Asclepius, Greek god of medicine.

580 *Mistress* Hestia, goddess of hearth and home.

642 *peplos* Greek woman's outer garment.

685 *pharos* transliteration of Greek word for 'cloak' (the only usage in this sense recorded in *OED*).

728 *Iolkos* town in Thessaly, home of the father of Alcestis.

733 *Charon* ferryman of the dead over the river Styx.

741 *Hades* god of the Underworld.

865 *Orpheus* son of Apollo and greatest of musicians whose powers nearly allowed him to bring his wife Eurydice back from Hades.

866 *Koré* 'Maid', an Attic name for Persephone, queen of Hades.

868 *Plouton's dog* Pluto is a euphemistic name for Hades, the god of the Underworld. The dog is the monstrous Cerberus, which guarded the entrance to Hades.

888 *what would seem so pertinent* Balaustion's rebuke of Admetus is probably more modern than Greek. Most authorities agree that *Alcestis* does not suggest that Admetus is to be criticized for the bargain he made.

938 *she passed away* the only 'natural' death on stage in extant Greek drama.

980 *one-frontleted* *OED* records 'frontlet' only as a noun.

996 *Acherontian lake* Acheron was one of the rivers of Hades.

1000 *seven-stringed mountain-shell* The traditional Greek lyre had seven strings; the 'mountain-shell' is that of a tortoise, used as a sounding-board.

1003 *Karneian month* August–September.

1006 *Athenai* Athens.

1010 *Kokutos' stream* Cocytus was a tributary of Acheron in Hades.

1038 *Disposure* arrangement (rare).

1047 *Herakles* Heracles, son of Zeus and Alcmene, strongest of the demigods and greatest of Greek heroes, engaged in innumerable adventures and labours.

1089 *Tirunthian* The city of Tiryns was in the territory of Eurystheus.

1097 *Bistones* Diomedes was king of the Bistones in Thrace.

1115 *Ares, king o' the targe* Diomedes, owner of the man-eating horses, was son of Ares (Mars), god of war.

1122 *Lukaon* not, despite annotators, the king of Arcadia, but apparently a son of Ares and Pyrene who challenged Heracles to single combat.

1123 *Kuknos* Cycnus, son of Ares and Pelopia, was killed by Heracles.

1143 *Perseus* He was the maternal great-grandfather of Heracles.

1197–1216] In the manuscript a few passages and lines are interpolated in the copy. This is the longest such passage.

1207 *snake* the Hydra of Lerna, killed by Heracles as his second Labour.

1233 *Argos* the principal town of Argolis, south of Corinth.

1261 *lyric Puthian* Apollo, so-called because he had slain the Python. He was a master of the lyre.

1268 *Othrus* Othrys, a wild area in Thessaly, home of wild beasts and centaurs.

1277 *Boibian lake* Lake Boebeis is near Mount Ossa in Thessaly.

1279 *sun's steeds*   the horses of the chariot of Helios, which drew the sun across the sky.

1281 *Molossoi*   The Molossi were a people of Epirus in north-west Greece.

1282 *Pelion*   mountain in Thessaly.

1334 *help, by*]   by *MS*.

1352 *peak and pine*   'dwindle, peak and pine' (*Macbeth* I. 3. 23).

1468-9 *Ludian . . . Phrugian*   Lydia and Phrygia were areas in Asia Minor.

1501 *spark*   lover.

1512 *hydra*   here (see 1456), water-snake.

1559 *Akastos*   Acastus was the brother of Alcestis.

1563 *childlessly*   not in *OED*; apparently a Browning coinage.

1597 *Hermes*   The messenger of the gods guided the dead to Hades.

1601 *Bride of Hades*   Persephone.

1697 *Turannos*   tyrannus; 'tyrant' in the Greek sense of 'supreme ruler'.

1717-18 *Ai, ai,/Pheu, pheu, e, papai*   'Woe, woe, alas, alas, o strange!'

1735 *pest o' the marish*   The Lernaean Hydra lived in a swamp.

1736 *steeds*]   *MS, this edition; stud 1871-88.*

1777 *humours*   moods.

1801 *Kupris*   Cypris, the Cyprian: Aphrodite.

1858 *Larissa*   the chief city of Thessaly.

1880 *God surmount the man*]   man surmount himself *MS*.

1881 *hand*]   soul *MS*.

1883-4 *Elektruon, Tiruns' child,/Alkmené*   Alcmene, mother of Heracles, was the daughter of Electryon, king of Tiryns.

1897 *boltered*   clotted.

1969 *his*   the choric speaker's, not Admetus'.

2023 *loved the cool*]   were alive *MS*.

2064-5 *Thrakian tablets . . . down upon*   Orpheus, greatest of musicians, is thought to have come from Thrace, where the Orphic literature and mysteries were inscribed on tablets.

2065-6 *remedy/Which Phoibos gave*   Apollo was also god of medicine.
  Asklepiadai   the sons and descendants of Asclepius.

2073 *endure*]   sustain *MS*.

2076 *Chaluboi*]   Thaluboi *MS*. The Chalybes were an iron-working people of Asia Minor south of the Black Sea.

2316 *Gorgon*   female monster whose look turned men to stone.

2377 *Sthenelos*   son of Perseus and Andromeda, father of Eurystheus.

2383 *tetrarchy*   four quarters (of Thessaly).

2390 *friendly moralists*   the Chorus. The same (or virtually the same) lines end four other plays of Euripides.

2398-9 *my poet failed . . . Sophokles got the prize*   Sophocles won the prize in 438 B.C.; Euripides won second prize.

2408 *crater*   large wine-bowl.

2412 *The Human . . . tears*   See motto. Balaustion quotes Mrs Browning's *Wine of Cyprus*.

2430 *Mainad*   priestess of Dionysus.

2469]   *not in MS*.

2475 *soul*]   word *MS*.

2490-92 *minor . . . triumph*   A minor chord can be changed into a major chord by altering one note in it.

2494 *glory*   Apollo.

2521] *not in MS.*

2525 *death*] love *MS.*

2551 *oh wife* The passage beginning with these words strikes most readers as having biographical relevance.

2568 *Never be*] Shut eyes to *MS.*

2574 *Emprise* enterprise.

2599-2601 *Admetos . . . yoked to* At the demand of Pelias and with the help of Apollo, Admetus came to woo Alcestis in a chariot drawn by lions and boars.

2624 *lost maidenhood that lingered*] much maidenhood that remained *MS.*

2624-6 *lost maidenhood . . . Hades' throne* Persephone (Koré) was carried off by Hades while gathering flowers in Enna in Sicily.

2626 *Sudden was startled*] Plucked of a sudden *MS.*

2656] *not in MS.*

2663 *critic-friend of Syracuse* glancing reference to August Wilhelm von Schlegel (1767-1845), whose *Dramatic Art and Literature*, a new edition of which appeared in 1871, was extremely hostile to Euripides. Browning attacked his views in *Aristophanes' Apology.*

2665] *not in MS.*

2668 *poetess* Elizabeth Barrett Browning, whose *Wine of Cyprus* is again quoted in line 2671 (see motto and 2412).

2672 *Kaunian painter* Browning's friend, Sir Frederic Leighton, painted in 1871 his picture of *Hercules Wrestling with Death for the Body of Alcestis*. The painting is described in the following lines.

2682 *hoary impotence*] impotence of grief *MS.*

2697 *our Poikilé* that is, London's National Gallery.

Prince Hohenstiel-Schwangau, Saviour of Society

First published by Smith, Elder in mid-December 1871. No separate second edition was required (the first was still being advertised twenty years later). For *1888* Browning added one passage of nine lines (2135-43), but otherwise revision was slight (the statement in DeVane, *Handbook,* 358, that the whole poem was repunctuated is at best misleading). The manuscript is in the Library of Balliol College; it is clearly the working draft of the poem, and changes within it are extensive: as often elsewhere, Browning had trouble with tense and pronouns, and scores of lines are added here and there. Differences between MS and *1871* are also extensive, but individual revisions are seldom of much significance.

On Napoleon III, as on spiritualism, Browning and his wife did not agree, and it seems puzzling that in 1859-60 he should have undertaken poems on both topics. He and his wife had planned to publish jointly on 'the Italian question', and Browning had perhaps written a good deal (*Prince Hohenstiel-Schwangau* is usually identified as the long poem on which Mrs Browning reported his working early in 1860), but in March 1860 Mrs Browning wrote (*Letters* II, 368-9) that her husband had destroyed his poem as one that no longer 'suited the moment' after the armistice at Villafranca in July 1859 between France and Austria – her ode, 'Napoleon III in Italy', eulogistic as always of the Emperor, appeared in *Poems Before Congress* (1860). All this does not quite square with DeVane's statement (*Handbook,* 359) that Villafranca gave 'the first impetus' to the writing of *Prince Hohenstiel-Schwangau,* or with Browning's own comments about the poem's origins. In the manuscript, Browning notes: 'A few lines of the rough sketch written at Rome, 1860' (DeVane, *Handbook,* 358, misleadingly substitutes 'draft' for 'sketch'). It seems likely that the 'sketch' was what the word implies: Browning writes (1 January 1872): 'I really wrote – that is, conceived the poem, twelve years ago in the Via del Tritone – in a little handbreadth of prose' (Hood, *Letters*, 152) – using 'wrote' for 'conceived' is, incidentally, characteristic of Browning and other nineteenth-century writers, something that needs to be kept in mind with his statement of 25 January 1871: 'I wrote, myself, a monologue in his [Napoleon's] name twelve years ago.' At any rate, Browning's poem dealing with Napoleon III was in some sense begun in Rome in 1859 or 1860, and was concluded after Napoleon's exile to England after the catastrophic Franco-Prussian War of 1870–71. In the manuscript, Browning notes that he 'resumed' the poem in mid-August 1871 and completed it a few weeks later on 7 October. How much, if anything, he had by him in verse to 'resume' is uncertain, but, at most, a very few hundred lines are probably in question, since Browning refers (1 October 1871) to '1,800 absolutely new lines'. The comparatively clean condition of the manuscript for the first few hundred lines may suggest that they are a fair copy of earlier lines; on the other hand the manuscript shows that by 1 October 1871 he had written a total of, at most, 1,908 lines. The probable conclusion is that no verse lines survived – if indeed there ever were any – from 1860, and that the present poem is, conception and prose sketch apart, entirely a product of 1871.

In another sense, however, the poem is a product of many years. The Brownings were steeped in Napoleon III – doubtless a good deal more than Browning would have wished – and the poem's essential sources lie in newspapers, and in discussions about the Emperor, perhaps the chief political figure of his age. In addition, Browning had almost certainly read some of Napoleon's works, particularly his *Napoleonic Ideas* (1839), and books and articles dealing with him; he read Robert Buchanan's poem *Napoleon Fallen* very shortly after its publication (January 1871).

In March 1871 the former Emperor arrived to live again as an exile in England. Palmerston described him as having a mind 'like a rabbit warren'; the modern historian J. M. Thompson has called him 'the Hamlet of French History'. He remains a riddle – as he was to his contemporaries. He was thus the kind of figure to appeal to Browning as a subject – had he not existed it would have been necessary for Browning to invent him. Despite his measure of pity for the exile, Browning generally regarded the man with extreme distaste, but his statements (1 January 1872): 'I put forward what excuses I thought the man was likely to make for himself,' and, still more, 'It is just what I imagine the man might, if he pleased, say for himself,' are surely accurate; and contemporary reviewers of the poem found themselves at odds over the attitude that the poem conveyed towards the Emperor. The Sphinx remains inscrutable in Browning's poem as he was in life.

The title, deriving from a Bavarian castle, Hohen-Schwangau, was suggested by W. C. Cartwright. The subtitle translates a standard Bonapartist epithet for the man.

For a Browning poem, sales were initially good (1,400 copies in five days), but soon tailed off. The poem, which Browning called 'a sample of my very best work', is probably the least-read of all his works, and among critics only G. K. Chesterton seems really to have admired it. The few criticisms that have been offered of the poem tend to include noteworthy gaffes, and K. L. Knickerbocker has pointed out that most critics commenting on the poem have, demonstrably, not read it. Two essays by critics who have read it are P. Drew's in his *Poetry of Browning*, 291–303, and C. de L. Ryals, '*Prince Hohenstiel-Schwangau*: Browning's "Ghostly Dialogue"', in *Nineteenth Century Literary Perspectives*, ed. C. de L. Ryals, Duke University Press, 1974, 115–28. See also a related essay by Flavia Alaya, 'The Ring, the Rescue, and the Risorgimento: Reunifying the Brownings' Italy', *BIS* VI, 1978, 1–41. The most helpful secondary reading is, however, material about Napoleon III (even an encyclopedia article) since, to an extent unusual even in Browning, the poem has not its meaning alone; it virtually demands what the contemporary reader would have had: some acquaintance with the career of Napoleon III, and some personal feeling about him.

Motto From the *Heracles* of Euripides, 1275–6, 1279–80. The translation is Browning's; for his later version of the lines see *Aristophanes' Apology*, 4906–11. The labour of Heracles alluded to in the third line is that of bringing the monstrous dog Cerberus from Hades to earth; the ills of the fourth line are his murders in madness of his wife and children. By the 'one more labour' that 'crowned the edifice' for Napoleon III, Browning almost certainly meant the Franco-Prussian War of 1870–71 (the pun on 'crowned' is presumably intended); Liberty 'crowned the edifice' is a famous phrase from an early speech of the Emperor.

6–8 *Oedipus . . . Sphinx* The Sphinx was the mysterious monster that held Thebes in its control, and killed when its riddle was unanswered. When Oedipus solved the riddle, the Sphinx was killed. The epithet was often applied to the enigmatic Napoleon.

8 *Leicester Square* in central London. In 1871 Napoleon was living in exile at Chislehurst (where he died just over a year after Browning's poem was published), but he had spent periods of exile in England, 1838–40 and 1847–8. The Square at the time was badly run-down, and there had been considerable discussion as to whether it should be renovated. The Italian-owned Sablonnier Hotel on the Square had a largely foreign clientele and may have been in Browning's mind as the location of the dream. It was pulled down in 1870.

11 *jealous for* vigilant in guarding.

rede interpretation (*OED*'s only example of the word in this sense).

12 *Jealous* zealous.

14 *Home* D. D. Home, spiritualist, model for Mr Sludge.

stilts and tongs part of Home's 'medium-ware' for his frauds.

18 *Corinth* Early Corinth was famed for its wealth and luxury.

19 *dull Thebes* Thebes, and Boeotians generally, were reputed stupid, and the city, the place associated with the Sphinx, was regarded as unexciting.

21 *man of sixty* Napoleon III was sixty in 1868. If Browning had a definite date in mind for the reverie, the line, like 474, suggests 1868 (or early 1869). But line 137 may hint at a date of 1860, and line 511 seems to demand it. The inconsistencies may be the result of (a) fusing lines written in 1860 and 1871; (b) and/or carelessness; (c) deliberately confusing the issue in a way appropriate for reverie; (d) making the Prince's age and the date of his taking power different from those of Napoleon III. But 1860 (not 1868, the hitherto unanimous assumption of the few scholars who have raised the question) seems right, because: (a) line 511 is definite; (b) it involves no *internal* inconsistency; (c) the Prince – with the possible exception of the twist at the end of the poem – never alludes to any historical event after 1860. It should be noted that his ramblings tend, if measured against historical facts, to be vague (a 'ghostly dialogue' he calls it) rather than specific, and very selective (there is, for instance, no reference to the Crimean War).

48 *Euclid* the Greek mathematician of the early third century B.C., and source of future mathematical speculation (the Prince has just drawn his straight line between two points).

49   *square the circle*   do the impossible.

59   *quadrature*   act of squaring.

74   *somebody in Thrace*   Democritus, the Greek philosopher, born about 460 B.C. in Thrace, and best known for his atomic theories.

133   *Residenz*   German form of 'Residency': the Prince's Palace (Napoleon's was the Tuileries).

135   *Galvanically*   as if electrically stimulated.

137   *last July*   The phrase may support a date of 1860 for the reverie; on 11 July 1859 Napoleon met the Austrian Emperor at Villafranca. No similar significance is possible for July 1867.

186   *Pradier Magdalen*   statue of Mary Magdalen by James Pradier (1790–1852).

188   *aigrette*   decorative spray for the head.

196   *grim guardian of this Square*   an equestrian statue of George I. He had every right to look grim; neglected, vandalized, and ridiculed in *Punch*, he was sold in 1872 for sixteen pounds. See line 308.

197   *quarter-day*   one of the four days in the year when rents and other charges were due.

280   *stabilify*   make stable (described as 'very rare' by *OED*, which cites only this example).

302   *redescribe*   again mark out the form.

308   *plaster-monarch on his steed*   See line 196.

309   *ell*   old measure of length, forty-five inches.

333   *immobility*]   the stability *MS*.

342–63]   A leaf with these lines is inserted in the manuscript.

355   *economy*   way of ordering affairs.

384   *dabster*   all-round expert ('applied depreciatively' – *OED*, citing this use).

393   *round to square*   See line 49.

423   *I find advance i' the main*   'Ever since the world has existed, there has been progress' (*Napoleonic Ideas,* 29). Parallels between Napoleon III's brief book and the poem are numerous.

429   *smoothed*]   good *MS*.

430]   *not in MS*.

439   *Fourier*   French Utopian social philosopher (1772–1837).

   Comte   French philosopher, founder of the Positivist school, social reformer (1798–1857). He lost his professorship when Napoleon became Emperor.

450   *toe*]   foot *MS*.

   kibe   chilblain (usually on the heel – hence, presumably, the change above).

474   *twenty years*   Napoleon became President in 1848. See note on line 21.

504]   What is! – all capabilities for good – *MS*.

511   *'sixty*   1860. See note on line 21.

515–16   *life a burden . . . insignificant*   all clichés; probably no specific reference is intended.

517   *O littleness of man*   In his *Song of Ocean* Victor Hugo (in exile 1851–70) wrote of Napoleon the Little; the name stuck and became the title of a Hugo book, and the phrase here may just allude to it. But the primary reference here and in the following lines is to Byron's *Childe Harold's Pilgrimage* IV, clxxix–clxxxiii, a passage that annoyed Browning (see *Sordello* VI, 1–7; and *Fifine at the Fair,* 1105–28).

517–18]   'O littleness of man!' and then, for fear
          The Powers should punish his egregious lie, *MS*.

522   *emblem of immensity*   'symbols of immensity' (*Sordello* VI, 3); 'image of eternity' (the sea) (*Childe Harold's Pilgrimage* IV, clxxxiii). But the phrases are Romantic commonplaces, as Browning stresses here.

539 *having*] *MS.*, this edition; leaving *1871–88*.

Bond Street fashionable street in London.

544 *hitch into a stanza* 'Whoe'er offends, at some unlucky time /Slides into verse, and hitches into rhyme, /Sacred to Ridicule his whole life long' (Pope, *Horatian Satires* II, i, 78–80). Compare *The Ring and the Book* VIII, 149.

550 *lordly* punning on *Lord* Byron.

568–9 *a little lower than /The angels . . . glory-crowned* 'Thou madest him [man] lower than the angels: to crown him with glory and worship' (Psalm viii, 5).

581 *earth's best geometer* Plato. Plutarch (*Symposiacs* viii, 2) quotes Plato as saying, 'God always plays the Geometer.' See 'Easter Day', 92

613 *twangs the never-failing taunt*] is the never-failing cry *MS.*

638 *friends*] fools *MS.*

677 *behemoth* the great beast of Job xl 15.

680] I say, the fane from whence we see defile *MS.*

684 *enter, and concede*] why, suppose, inside *MS*

716–18 *Hercules . . . day* Hercules, engaged on one of his Labours to get the apples of the Hesperides, temporarily bore the earth on his shoulders while Atlas went to fetch apples.

721 *Oeta* mountain in southern Thessaly; site of the funeral pyre of Hercules.

767 *emprise* enterprise.

782 *Proudhon* French social theorist of an anarchistic bent (1809–65), twice imprisoned under Napoleon III.

787 *Great Nation* France: *'La Grande Nation'* was a standard phrase much used by Napoleon III.

819 *once upon a time* In 1830–31 Napoleon worked for Italian liberty.

839 *Imparting*] Tossing its *MS.* (The *MS.* reading seems preferable, and to emend is tempting, especially since the *MS.* phrase is difficult to read, and one suspects a compositor's guess produced 'Imparting'.)

853 *Rafael* the great Italian painter (1483–1520).

861–5] *a marginal addition to the MS.*

862–5 *Peter's Dome . . . hearts* In the Prince's image, the Basilica of Saint Peter (the 'scorpion-body') has for its nippers the two semi-circular colonnades of the Square (see 'Christmas-Eve', 536–8).

892 *cool Cayenne* The capital of French Guiana is anything but cool. Nearby was the convict settlement of Devil's Island.

898 *nor lives by bread alone* 'Man shall not live by bread alone' (Matthew iv 4; Luke iv 4).

919 *the bodily want serve first, said I* In his *Extinction of Poverty* (1844), Napoleon III stressed the point in theory. His practice was different.

934–5 *Barabbas deputy/In lieu of his concurrent* Pilate released Barabbas rather than Jesus as the mob, persuaded by the chief priests and elders, wished (Matthew xxvii 15–21).

935 *concurrent* rival claimant (described by *OED* in this sense as rare except as a Gallicism).

936] *not in MS.*

953 *fining* refining (compare line 1321).

987 *jelly-lump* the protoplasm.

998 *Practise as exile* Napoleon III spent most of his first forty years in exile, and six of the years in France were spent in prison.

1010 *You shuffle through your part* 'When my part in the farce is shuffled through' (*Paracelsus* III, 592).

1020 *repine if*] content that *MS*.

1029–35 *the Persian ... apparel* The story is told in Herodotus vii, 31.

1098] Unaltered in the main, – enough for me *MS*.

1108–11 *Kant ... Pure Reason* The philosophy of the German philosopher (1724–1804) is of a highly metaphysical kind. The keystone of his work is *The Critique of Pure Reason*.

1145 *Terni* the city in central Italy near the famous waterfall.

1157 *time is short and art is long* 'Art is long and time is fleeting' (Longfellow, *Psalm of Life*). 'The life so short, the craft so long to learn' (Chaucer's translation of an epigram of Hippocrates).

1161] Observe the marvel that will come of that, *MS*.

1187 *Laocoön* the celebrated ancient sculpture in the Vatican of Laocoön and his two sons struggling with serpents.

1197 sheer] mere *MS*.

1223 *Thiers-and-Victor-Hugo exercise* Adolphe Thiers (1797–1877), historian and statesman, was appointed President of France in August 1871 (while Browning was writing *Prince Hohenstiel-Schwangau*). He had just previously negotiated the preliminary treaty of Versailles with Prussia, and ordered the Commune of Paris put down. In 1851 he had opposed Napoleon III and had had to go into exile. Hugo (1802–85), bitter foe of Napoleon, had lived twenty years in exile, before returning after the War to public acclaim and political power.

1230 *Thiers-Hugo to the*] historian to his *MS*.

1234 *chose the Assembly* Napoleon III returned to France after the February Revolution of 1848, and was elected to the Assembly.

1235 *President* Napoleon III was elected President in December 1848.

1238 *proper term of years was out* Napoleon's term expired in 1852, and constitutionally he could not be re-elected. On 2 December 1851 there was a *coup d'état*. The Assembly was dissolved, universal suffrage was restored, and a plebiscite gave Napoleon dictatorial powers. In November 1852 he became Emperor of the French.

1243 *promise*] purpose *MS., 1871*.

1287 *chose truth* feared God *MS*.

1304 *anticize* sport grotesquely (a nonce-word? Described by *OED* as very rare, with only this example).

1363 *unstridulosity* absence of harsh noise. A nonce-word: *OED* records (without defining) the usage here. 'Stridulosity' does not exist.

1371–2 *Dock ... /The electoral body short* In 1850 the Assembly restricted suffrage, and allowed an 'angry' Napoleon to pose as the defender of Liberty against the autocratic Assembly. Universal suffrage was restored after the *coup d'état*, but once Napoleon had dictatorial power the vote was again restricted.

1417 *There was uprising* The army quickly and ruthlessly controlled uprisings.

1450 *Sagacity* Sagacity speaks for worldly wisdom and opportunism, and is opposed by 'Head-servant', the idealistic Prince. On 18 October 1862 Browning wrote of Napoleon's 'wise principle' of entrusting his work 'to a man of opposite feeling'; the thought may have suggested the opposition of Sagacity and Head-servant.

1511–13 *God who comes/Before and after ... helps nor hinders* 'Sure he that made us with such large discourse, /Looking before and after, gave us not /That capability and god-like reason /To fust in us unused' (*Hamlet* IV.4.37–40).

1534–8 *Rome ... success* In 1849 Napoleon, former fighter for Italian freedom, sent a French army to destroy the newly proclaimed republic in Rome under Mazzini and to restore Pius IX to Rome (where the Pope continued to need French support against his opposition).

1544] *not in MS.*

1558 *Capitol where Brennus broke his pate* About 390, Brennus, the Gaulish general, overran Italy and took Rome, but not its Capitol. His failure here marked the turning-point of the conflict. Napoleon alluded to him in his *Napoleonic Ideas*, and Browning, in *Sordello* III, 588-92.

1560] *not in MS.*

1561] Not for a moment one mean motive stayed *MS.*

1584] *not in MS.*

1597 *the war came* the war for the liberation of Italy.

1599 *the old day* the period of the French Revolution.

1614-17]. Till the world rise and put a nuisance down. *MS.* (In a letter of 19 October 1870, Browning refers to 'the extinguishment of this inveterate nuisance' [Napoleon III] – *Dearest Isa*, 348.)

1616 *the world spoke plain at last* after the defeat of Napoleon Bonaparte.

1622 *pet]* old *MS.*

1672 *boulevard-building . . . theatre* In the early 1850s Napoleon began the programme of building a freshly planned Paris. If a specific theatre is referred to, it is probably the Opéra, work on which began in 1863.

1684 *Wisdom]* Nature *MS.*

1696 *Terror* perhaps suggestive of the Reign of Terror (1793-4) during the French Revolution.

   vantage-coign 'coign of vantage' (*Macbeth* I.6.8).

1721 *barbican* outer fortification.

1733 *dagger o' lath* just 'wooden sword' here, without allusion to the weapon worn by the Vice in the old Morality plays.

1809 *paints a landscape]* tints a Venus *MS.*

1839 *sen'night* week (archaism).

1856-9 *beat the sword . . . fig-tree* 'they shall beat their swords into ploughshares, and their spears into pruning hooks: nation shall not lift up sword against nation, neither shall they learn war any more. /But they shall sit every man under his vine and under his fig tree' (Micah iv 3-4); see also Isaiah ii 4.

1867 *admeasurement* measuring to determine dimensions.

1875 *twenty years* See line 917.

1880 *Come with me and deliver Italy* France and Sardinia went to war with Austria in 1859. Napoleon's bark proved worse than his bite.

1884 *old bad day* Perhaps the Prince refers to the French intervention of 1849.

1892-3 *patch of province . . . honorarium-fee* See 1902-3. 'It [Napoleon's war on Austria] was a great action; but he has taken eighteenpence for it, which is a pity' (Mrs Browning, *Letters* II, 385, quoting her husband on Napoleon's taking Savoy).

1898 *pitch* highest point; here, probably, the point to which a falcon soars before swooping on its prey.

1902-3 *Savoy / And Nice* France annexed the provinces in 1860.

1904-5 *Metternich . . . stay where he resides* the Austrian statesman (1773-1859), chief arbiter of Europe, foe of liberalism. Given the date of his death, the place where he resides may be Hell. (Just possibly, however, the reference may be to 'young' Metternich, the Austrian ambassador to Paris at the time.)

1907-8] I' the other road!
                    So Italy was free. *MS.*

1908   With this line Browning originally had the poem end. In the manuscript his indication of the place and date (30 September 1871) is deleted, and the ink changes with line 1909. The statement 'Italy was free' is ironic in the light of Napoleon's betrayal of the Italian cause by his quickly patched-up armistice with Austria of Villafranca (where Sardinia was not even represented), the peace which very briefly shook even Mrs Browning's faith in Napoleon. In fact Sardinia gained only Lombardy (Napoleon of course got his 'honorarium-fee' the next year) – though other states in 1860 also joined with Sardinia. And in May 1860 Garibaldi and his Thousand landed in Sicily. The Kingdom of Italy was proclaimed in March 1861 (*after* the Prince of Browning's poem delivers his monologue?). Venetia joined Italy only in 1866, and Rome and the Papal States only four years later when Napoleon's protection of Papal power was no longer possible with the Franco-Prussian War.

1913–19   *ball o' the world . . . foot o' the mountain*   with a glance at the fable of Sisyphus.

1922   *fittest man to rule*   A plebiscite made Napoleon Emperor in November 1852, but the statement is ironic: Napoleon's election was in large measure owing to his name.

1934   *pick o' the world*   Eugénie de Montijo (1826–1920), daughter of the conde de Teba and a Scottish noblewoman, was Napoleon's pick.

1941   *Your right to constitute what king you will*   'I never, when liking Napoleon most, sympathized a bit with his dynastic ambition for his son' (Browning, in a letter of 19 July 1870, in *Dearest Isa*, 340). Napoleon's son was born in 1856; Napoleon spoke of 'a new dynasty sprung from the ranks of the people', and 'an heir destined to perpetuate a national system'.

1951   *scarecrows*]   bugbears *MS*.

1953–83   Behind the paragraph seems to lie a measure of self-defensiveness. There were considerable doubts as to whether Napoleon III was his father's son, doubts reflected in the opening sentence of Hugo's *Napoleon the Little*: 'Charles Louis Napoleon Bonaparte . . . is the son of Hortense de Beauharnais, married by the Emperor to Louis Napoleon, King of Holland.'

1975   *Salvatore*   Salvator Rosa (1615–73), Italian painter.

1984   *Rome*   Napoleon spent several months in Rome in his younger days.

1985]   *not in MS*.

1986   *little wayside temple*   The temple, which Browning had visited, had no connection with the tradition of lines 2001–7; and Browning asked Mrs Orr to correct him in her *Handbook* (170n.), which was first published in 1885. Her correction was, however, made unnecessary in *1888*, since there (but not in *1871*) the Prince himself explains the confusion as dream-induced (lines 2136–43).

1987   *mild river that makes oxen white*   The Clitumnus river in Umbria was noted for the sacrificial cattle on its banks (Vergil, *Georgics* II, 146).

1988   *un-mouse-colours*   *color sorcino*, mouse colour, is a reddish colour.

1990   *shrine*   Shrines to Clitumnus and other deities adorned the river's source.

1994   *Land of the Ox*   'Italia' probably derives from the Italic 'Vitelia': 'Calf-land'.

2002–7   *Each priest . . . name*   The priest ('Rex Nemoriensis') of Diana in the Temple near Lake Nemi was a runaway slave who killed his predecessor after issuing a formal challenge in a prescribed manner.

2017–22]   *a later addition to the MS*.

2044]   *not in MS*.

2066   *legitimate blockhead*   Louis XVI had subnormal intelligence.

2073   *pendule*   clock (the first French word in the poem).

2073] *not in MS.*

2078] *not in MS.*

2080–81 *A nod/Out-Homering Homer* 'I feel aggrieved whenever good Homer nods' (Horace, *Ars Poetica*, 359); 'Nor is it Homer nods, but we who dream' (Pope, *Essay on Criticism* I, 177).

2120 *prince o' the power o' the air* the Devil (Ephesians ii 2).

2133 *words deflect* a characteristic Browning theme.

2135–43] *not in MS., 1871.*

2136–43 *'Clitumnus' did I say . . . awake.* See lines 1986–2007 and notes on them.

2141 *Nemi* Lake Nemi is in the Alban Mountains near Aricia, a few miles from Rome. Here there was a temple to Diana Nemoriensis, to which the 'Tradition' of lines 2002–7 (see note) did apply.

2150–55 *My Cousin-Duke . . . stays* If Browning meant the Duke to suggest a particular person, the identity, as well as the point of the letter, may well be of considerable importance. Suggestions include (a) Prince Napoleon, son of Bonaparte's brother, who had married the daughter of Victor Emmanuel in 1859 (Florentine edition); (b) 'No doubt Browning had Bismarck in mind' (Drew, *Poetry of Browning*, 268); (c) 'presumably William I or Bismarck' (Drew, *Poetry of Browning*, 298). The letter, it is assumed, is one having something to do with provoking the Franco-Prussian War, and the date of the poem is 1868. But a date of 1868 (or 1860 or early 1869) is not a likely one for Browning to choose for a letter contributing very directly to the Franco-Prussian War. The present editor's guess is that if Browning had in mind anything very specific, he thought of the reverie as set in 1860, of Prince Napoleon as the 'Cousin-Duke', and of the letter as one offering further French involvement in the fight for Italian freedom, one in which Prince Napoleon was actively engaged. In August 1860 emissaries from Cavour told Napoleon III of Cavour's plans to preserve 'the national and monarchical character of the Italian movement', but Napoleon gave only spiritual support, and, in fact, opposed Garibaldi and Sardinia with French troops in Rome and Latium. In a letter of 19 October 1870 (*Dearest Isa*, 348), Browning wrote: 'had he [Napoleon III] kept his word to Italy . . . he would have had an Italian army to help him two months ago.' In Browning's view, it is clear, Napoleon III's failure to support Italy lost France the Franco-Prussian War. At any rate the conclusion projects the capricious casualness of the Prince's dealings. Perhaps in the very lack of specificity, and in the whimper rather than the bang, lies the point of the lines.

Index of Titles

Abt Vogler   777
After   651
Andrea del Sarto   643
Another Way of Love   734
Any Wife to Any Husband   561
Apparent Failure   860
Artemis Prologizes   365

BALAUSTION'S ADVENTURE   867
Before   650
Bishop Blougram's Apology   617
Bishop Orders His Tomb at Saint Praxed's Church, The   413
Boot and Saddle   348
Boy and the Angel, The   448
By the Fire-Side   552

Caliban upon Setebos   805
Cavalier Tunes   347
'Childe Roland to the Dark Tower Came'   585
Christmas-Eve   463
CHRISTMAS-EVE AND EASTER-DAY   461
Cleon   712
Confessional, The   422
Confessions   812
Count Gismond   351
Cristina   376

Deaf and Dumb   814
Death in the Desert, A   787
'De Gustibus –'   701
Dîs Aliter Visum; or, Le Byron de Nos Jours   768
DRAMATIC LYRICS   345
DRAMATIC ROMANCES AND LYRICS   393
DRAMATIS PERSONAE   745

Earth's Immortalities   447
Easter-Day   496
Englishman in Italy, The   403
Epilogue [to *Dramatis Personae*]   862
Epistle Containing the Strange Medical Experience of Karshish, the Arab
   Physician, An   565
Eurydice to Orpheus   816
Evelyn Hope   534

Face, A   819
Fame   447
Flight of the Duchess, The   424
Flower's Name, The   416
Fra Lippo Lippi   540

Garden Fancies   416
Give a Rouse   348
Glove, The   455
Gold Hair   759
Grammarian's Funeral, A   730
Guardian-Angel, The   710

Heretic's Tragedy, The   724
Holy-Cross Day   705
Home-Thoughts, from Abroad   412
Home-Thoughts, from the Sea   412
How It Strikes a Contemporary   605
'How They Brought the Good News from Ghent to Aix'   395

In a Balcony   665
In a Gondola   358
In a Year   653
Incident of the French Camp   355
Instans Tyrannus   580
In Three Days   652
Italian in England, The   399

James Lee's Wife   747
Johannes Agricola in Meditation   378

Laboratory, The   420
Last Ride Together, The   608
Life in a Love   604
Light Woman, A   593
Likeness, A   819
Lost Leader, The   410
Lost Mistress, The   411
Love   447
Love Among the Ruins   527
Love in a Life   603
Lovers' Quarrel, A   529

Marching Along   347
Master Hugues of Saxe-Gotha   612
May and Death   814
Meeting at Night   451
Memorabilia   643
MEN AND WOMEN   525
Mesmerism   573
Misconceptions   737

Mr Sludge, 'The Medium' 821
My Last Duchess 349
My Star 580

Nationality in Drinks 452

Old Pictures in Florence 656
One Way of Love 734
One Word More 737

PARACELSUS 35
Parting at Morning 452
Patriot, The 611
PAULINE 5
Pictor Ignotus 397
Pied Piper of Hamelin, The 383
PIPPA PASSES 297
Popularity 722
Porphyria's Lover 380
Pretty Woman, A 582
PRINCE HOHENSTIEL-SCHWANGAU, SAVIOUR OF SOCIETY 943
Prospice 815
Protus 704

Rabbi Ben Ezra 781
Respectability 592
Rudel to the Lady of Tripoli 375

Saul 689
Serenade at the Villa 578
Sibrandus Schafnaburgensis 417
Soliloquy of the Spanish Cloister 356
Song ('Nay but you, who do not love her') 448
SORDELLO 149
Statue and the Bust, The 595

Through the Metidja to Abd-el-Kadr 381
Time's Revenges 453
Toccata of Galuppi's, A 550
Too Late 773
'Transcendentalism: A Poem in Twelve Books' 735
Twins, The 721
Two in the Campagna 728

Up at a Villa – Down in the City 536

Waring 368
Woman's Last Word, A 539
Women and Roses 702
Worst of It, The 764

Youth and Art 816

Index of First Lines

About that strangest, saddest, sweetest song   869
Ah, did you once see Shelley plain   643
Ah, Love, but a day   747
A king lived long ago   331
All I believed is true   573
All June I bound the rose in sheaves   734
All service ranks the same with God   343
All's over then: does truth sound bitter   411
All that I know   580
Among these latter busts we count by scores   704
As I ride, as I ride   381
'As like as a Hand to another Hand!'   755

Beautiful Evelyn Hope is dead!   534
Boot, saddle, to horse, and away!   348
But do not let us quarrel any more   643
But give them me, the mouth, the eyes, the brow!   816

Christ God, who savest man, save most   351
Cleon the poet (from the sprinkled isles   712
Come close to me, dear friends; still closer; thus!   37

Day!   299
Dear and great Angel, wouldst thou only leave   710
Dear, had the world in its caprice   592

Escape me?   604

Fear death? – to feel the fog in my throat   815
Fee, faw, fum! bubble and squeak!   706
Flower o' the broom   541
Fortù, Fortù, my beloved one   403

Give her but a least excuse to love me!   325
Grand rough old Martin Luther   721
Grow old along with me!   781
Gr-r-r – there go, my heart's abhorrence!   356

Had I but plenty of money, money enough and to spare   536
Hamelin Town's in Brunswick   383
Heap cassia, sandal-buds and stripes   105
'Heigho!' yawned one day King Francis   455
Here's the garden she walked across   416

Here's to Nelson's memory! 453
Here was I with my arm and heart 773
Hist, but a word, fair and soft! 612
How very hard it is to be 496
How well I know what I mean to do 552

I am a goddess of the ambrosial courts 365
I am a painter who cannot paint 321
I am poor brother Lippo, by your leave! 540
I could have painted pictures like that youth's 397
I dream of a red-rose tree 702
If one could have that little head of hers 819
I hear a voice, perchance I heard 64
I know a Mount, the gracious Sun perceives 375
I leaned on the turf 751
I only knew one poet in my life 605
I said – Then, dearest, since 'tis so 608
Is all our fire of shipwreck wood 747
I send my heart up to thee, all my heart 358
I sprang to the stirrup, and Joris, and he 395
It is a lie – their Priests, their Pope 422
It once might have been, once only 816
It was roses, roses, all the way 611
I've a Friend, over the sea 453
I will be quiet and talk with you 749
I wish that when you died last May 814
I wonder do you feel today 728

June was not over 734
Just for a handful of silver he left us 410

Karshish, the picker-up of learning's crumbs 565
Kentish Sir Byng stood for his King 347
King Charles, and who'll do him right now? 348

Let's contend no more, Love 539
Let them fight it out, friend! things have gone too far 650
Let the watching lids wink! 304
Let us begin and carry up this corpse 730

Morning, evening, noon and night 448
My first thought was, he lied in every word 585
My heart sank with our Claret-flask 452
My love, this is the bitterest, that thou 561

Nay but you, who do not love her 448
Never any more 653
Nobly, nobly Cape Saint Vincent to the North-west died away 412
No, for I'll save it! Seven years since 860
No more wine? then we'll push back chairs, and talk 617
Now! 665

Now, don't, sir! Don't expose me! Just this once!   821
Now that I, tying thy glass mask tightly   420

Of the million or two, more or less   580
Oh Galuppi, Baldassaro, this is very sad to find!   550
Oh, good gigantic smile o' the brown old earth   755
Oh, the beautiful girl, too white   759
Oh, to be in England   412
Oh, what a dawn of day!   529
Only the prism's obstruction shows aright   814
On the first of the Feast of Feasts   862
Out of the little chapel I burst   463
Overhead the tree-tops meet   340
Over the sea our galleys went   112

Pauline, mine own, bend o'er me – thy soft breast   7
Plague take all your pedants, say I!   417

Room after room   603
Round the cape of a sudden came the sea   452

Said Abner, 'At last thou art come! Ere I tell, ere thou speak   689
See, as the prettiest graves will do in time   447
She should never have looked at me   376
So far as our story approaches the end   593
So, I shall see her in three days   652
Some people hang portraits up   819
So, the year's done with!   447
Stand still, true poet that you are!   722
Still ailing, Wind? Wilt be appeased or no?   752
Stop, let me have the truth of that!   768
Stop playing, poet! May a brother speak?   735
[Supposed of Pamphylax the Antiochene   787

Take the cloak from his face, and at first   651
That fawn-skin-dappled hair of hers   582
That second time they hunted me   399
That's my last Duchess painted on the wall   349
That was I, you heard last night   578
The bee with his comb   341
The grey sea and the long black land   451
The Lord, we look to once for all   724
The morn when first it thunders in March   656
The rain set early in tonight   380
There is nothing to remember in me   757
There's a palace in Florence, the world knows well   595
There's heaven above, and night by night   378
There they are, my fifty men and women   737
The swallow has set her six young on the rail   748
The year's at the spring   311

This is a spray the Bird clung to   737
Thus the Mayne glideth   129

Up jumped Tokay on our table   452

Vanity, saith the preacher, vanity!   413

What is he buzzing in my ears?   812
What's become of Waring   368
Where the quiet-coloured end of evening smiles   527
Who will, may hear Sordello's story told   151
['Will sprawl, now that the heat of day is best   805
Would it were I had been false, not you!   764
Would that the structure brave, the manifold music I build   777

You have seen better days, dear? So have I   945
You know, we French stormed Ratisbon   355
You'll love me yet! – and I can tarry   335
You're my friend   424
Your ghost will walk, you lover of trees   701